Lecture Notes in Artificial Intelligence 4456

Edited by J. G. Carbonell and J. Siekmann

Subseries of Lecture Notes in Computer Science

Yuping Wang Yiu-ming Cheung
Hailin Liu (Eds.)

Computational Intelligence and Security

International Conference, CIS 2006
Guangzhou, China, November 3-6, 2006
Revised Selected Papers

Springer

Series Editors

Jaime G. Carbonell, Carnegie Mellon University, Pittsburgh, PA, USA
Jörg Siekmann, University of Saarland, Saarbrücken, Germany

Volume Editors

Yuping Wang
School of Computer Science and Technology
Xidian University
Xi'an 710071, China
E-mail: ywang@xidian.edu.cn

Yiu-ming Cheung
Department of Computer Science
Hong Kong Baptist University
Hong Kong, China
E-mail: ymc@comp.hkbu.edu.hk

Hailin Liu
Faculty of Applied Mathematics
Guangdong University of Technology
Guangzhou 5100006, China
E-mail: lhl@scnu.edu.cn

Library of Congress Control Number: 2007932812

CR Subject Classification (1998): I.2, H.3, H.4, H.5, C.2, K.4.4, K.6.5, D.4.6

LNCS Sublibrary: SL 7 – Artificial Intelligence

ISSN 0302-9743
ISBN-10 3-540-74376-6 Springer Berlin Heidelberg New York
ISBN-13 978-3-540-74376-7 Springer Berlin Heidelberg New York

Springer is a part of Springer Science+Business Media

springer.com

Printed in Germany

Typesetting: Camera-ready by author, data conversion by Scientific Publishing Services, Chennai, India
Printed on acid-free paper SPIN: 12111619 06/3180 5 4 3 2 1 0

Preface

Following the great success of the 2005 International Conference on Computational Intelligence and Security (CIS 2005) held in Xi'an, China, CIS 2006 provided a leading international forum for researchers, engineers, and practitioners from both academia and industry to share experience and exchange and cross-fertilize ideas on all areas of computational intelligence and information security. The conference serves as a forum for the dissemination of the state-of-the-art research, development, and implementations of systems, technologies and applications in these two broad, interrelated fields.

CIS 2006, held in Guangzhou, China, November 3-6, 2006, was co-organized by the IEEE (Hong Kong) Computational Intelligence Chapter and Guangdong University of Technology, and co-sponsored by Xidian University, IEEE Hong Kong Section, Hong Kong Baptist University, and Jinan University. The conference received 2,078 submissions from 32 countries and regions all over the world. All of them were blindly and strictly peer-reviewed by the Program Committee and experts in the fields. Finally, 399 high-quality papers were accepted and presented at the conference. Among them 116 high-quality papers were further selected to be included in the post-conference proceedings after thorough revision and extension. CIS 2006 featured three distinguished keynote speakers, namely, Xin Yao (University of Birmingham, UK), Chang Wen Chen (Florida Institute of Technology, USA), and Kalyanmoy Deb (Indian Institute of Technology Kanpur, India), was greatly enriched by a wide range of topics covering all areas of computational intelligence and information security. Furthermore, a workshop was held for discussions of the proposed ideas. Such practice is extremely important for the effective development of the two fields and computer science.

We would like to thank the organizers, the IEEE (Hong Kong) Computational Intelligence Chapter and Guangdong University of Technology, for their great contributions and efforts in this big event. Thanks also go to the sponsors, Xidian University, IEEE Hong Kong Section, Hong Kong Baptist University (HKBU), and Springer for their unremitting support and collaboration, to which made CIS 2006 possible and successful. Furthermore, we would like to sincerely thank the Program Committee members and additional reviewers for their professional work.

April 2007

Yuping Wang
Yiu-ming Cheung
Hailin Liu

Organization

CIS 2006 was co-organized by the IEEE (Hong Kong) Computational Intelligence Chapter and Guangdong University of Technology.

Steering Committee

Yiu-ming Cheung (Chair)	Hong Kong
Yuping Wang	China
Hailin Liu	China
Kapluk Chan	Singapore
Ning Zhong	Japan

General Co-chairs

Xiangwei Zhang	China
Hua Wang	China

Organizing Committee

Co-chairs	Hailin Liu
	Sulin Pang
Workshop Co-chairs	Dachang Guo
	Guangren Duan
Publicity Co-chairs	Xuesong Chen
	Rong Zou
Publication Co-chairs	Yong-Chang Jiao
	Michael Chau
	Qi Wang
Local Arrangements Co-chairs	Zhenyou Wang
	Feng Li
Registration Chair	Huahao Tan
Treasurer	Ke Jian
Secretaries	Jingxuan Wei
	Hecheng Li
	Rongzu Yu
	Chujun Yao
	Zhitao Cui
Web Master	Bing Zhai

Program Committee

Yuping Wang (Co-chair)(China)
Hujun Yin (Co-chair)(UK)
Andrew Jennings (Australia)
Asim Karim (Pakistan)
Baoding Liu (China)
Benjamin Yen (Hong Kong)
Bob McKay (Korea)
Carlos A. Coello Coe (Mexico)
Carlos Valle Vidal (Chile)
Chris Mitchell (UK)
Christian Blum (Spain)
Christos Tjortjis (UK)
CIET Mathieu (France)
Claudio Lima (Portugal)
Daoqing Dai (China)
Dominic Palmer-Brown (UK)
Eckart Zitzler (Switzerland)
Efren Mezura-Montes (Mexico)
Elisa Bertino (Italy)
EnHong Chen (China)
Federico Divina (Netherlands)
Francesco Amigoni (Italy)
Guenter Rudolph (Germany)
Guoping Liu (UK)
Hai Jin (China)
Hailin Liu (China)
Haotian Wu (Hong Kong)
Hartmut Pohl (Germany)
Heejo Lee (Korea)
Helder Coelho (Portugal)
Henk C.A. van Tilborg (Netherlands)
Henry H.Q.Rong (Hong Kong)
Heonchang Yu (Korea)
Holger Maier (Australia)
Hongwei Huo (China)
Hussein A. Abbass (Australia)
J. Malone-Lee (UK)
Jacques M. Bahi (France)
Jason Teo (Malaysia)
Javier Lopez (Spain)
Jerzy Korczak (France)
Jian Ying (China)
Jianfeng Ma (China)
Jianhuang Lai (China)
Jill Slay (Australia)
Joerg Denzinger (Canada)
Joong-Hwan Baek (Korea)
Jorma Kajava (Finland)
Josep Roure (Spain)
Junbin Gao (Australia)
Jun-Cheol Park (Korea)
Junzo Watada (Japan)
Kalyanmoy Deb (India)
Kap Luk Chan (Singapore)
Kash Khorasani (Canada)
Ke Chen (UK)
Kefei Chen (China)
Khurshid Ahmad (Ireland)
KM Liew (Hong Kong)
Kuk-Hyun Han (Korea)
Kwok-ching Tsui (Hong Kong)
Kyoung-Mi Lee (Korea)
Lance Fung (Australia)
Licheng Jiao (China)
Lishan Kang (China)
Mahamed Omran (Iraq)
Malik Magdon-Ismail (Zimbabwe)
Marc M. Van Hulle (Belgium)
Marc Schoenauer (France)
Masayoshi Aritsugi (Japan)
Matjaz.Gams (Slovenia)
Matthew Casey (UK)
Miao Kang (UK)
Michael C.L. Chau (Hong Kong)
Michael N. Vrahatis (Greece)
Minaya Villasana (Venezuela)
Nadia Nedjah (Brazil)
Naoyuki Kubota (Japan)
Nareli Cruz-Cortés (Mexico)
Nicolas Monmarché (France)
Nong Ye (USA)
Osslan Osiris Vergara Villegas (Mexico)
Paplinski P.Andrew (Australia)

Paterson Kenny (UK)
Qiangfu Zhao (Japan)
Rachel McCrindle (UK)
Raj Subbu (USA)
Ravi Prakash (India)
Ricardo Nanculef (Chile)
S.Y. Yuen, Kelvin (Hong Kong)
Sajal K. Das (USA)
Salima Hassas (France)
Scott Buffett (Canada)
SeungGwan Lee (Korea)
Shailesh Kumar (India)
Simone Fischer-Huebner (Sweden)
Sokratis K. Katsikas (Greece)
Stelvio Cimato (Italy)
Sung-Hae Jun (Korea)
Sungzoon Cho (Korea)
Tetsuyuki Takahama (Japan)
Tharam Dillon (Australia)
Tin Kam Ho (USA)
Toshio Fukuda (Japan)
Vasant Honavar (USA)
Vasu Alagar (Canada)
Vianey Guadalupe Cruz Sánchez (Mexico)
Vic Rayward-Smith (UK)
Vicenc Torra (Spain)
Vincent Kelner (Belgium)
Vojislav Stojkovic (USA)
Wei Li (Australia)
Wenjian Luo (China)
Wensheng Chen (China)
Witold Pedrycz (Canada)
Xiamu Niu (China)
Xiaochun Cheng (UK)
Xinbo Gao (China)
Xufa Wang (China)
Yaochu Jin (Germany)
Yeonseung Ryu (Korea)
Yih-Jiun Lee (Taiwan, China)
Yong-Chang Jiao (China)
Yuanxiang Li (China)
Zheming Lu (China)
Zhongchen Chen (Taiwan, China)
Zongben Xu (China)

Additional Reviewers

Anan Liu
Andrew Jennings
Andries P Engelbrecht
Asim Karim
Bangzhu Zhu
Baoding Liu
Baolin Sun
Baozheng Yu
Beihai Tan
Benjamin Yen
Ben-Nian Wang
Bin He
Bin Li
Bin Liu
Bin Yu
Binbin He
Bo An
Bo Chen
Bo Yang
Bob McKay
Caifen Wang
Caixia Yuan
Carlos A. Coello Coe
Carlos Valle Vidal
Changji Wang
Changjie Tang
Changlin Ma
Changzheng Hu
Chong Wu
Chao Fu
Chao Wang
Chen Li
Cheng Zhong
Chengde Zheng
Chong Wang
Chris Mitchell
Christian Blum
Christos Tjortjis
Chundong Wang
Chunguang Zhou
Chung-Yuan Huang
Chunlin Chen
CIET Mathieu
Claudio Lima
Cun Zhao
Daoliang Li
Daoqing Dai
Daoyi Dong
Dat Tran
Dawei Zhong
Dawu Gu
Dechang Pi
Deji Wang
Deqing Xiao
Deyun Chen
Di Wu
Dominic Palmer-Brown

Dong Li
Dongfeng Han
Dong-Jin Kim
Dong-Xiao Niu
Dongyang Long
Duong Anh Duc
Eckart Zitzler
Efren Mezura-Montes
Elisa Bertino
Enhong Chen
Federico Divina
Feng Kong Wen
Feng Li
Fengkui Luan
Francesco Amigoni
Fucai Zhou
Fuhua Shang
Fuquan Tu
Gang Wang
Gangyi Jiang
Gaoping Wang
Genan Huang
Guang Guo
Guang Li
Guanghui Wang
Guangjun Dong
Guangli Liu
Guang-Qian Zhang
Guenter Rudolph
Hai Jin
Haibin Shen
Haijun Li
Haiping Wan
Haitao Yang
Haixian Wang
Hao-Tian Wu
Harksoo Kim
Hartmut Pohl
He Luo
Heejo Lee
Helder Coelho
Hengfu Yang
Heonchang Yu
Holger Maier
Hongcai Tao
Hongfei Teng
Hongjie He
Hongsheng Xie
Hongwei Huo
Hongyu Yang
Hua Xu
Hua Yuan
Hussein A. Abbass
J. Malone-Lee
Jacques M. Bahi
Jason Teo
Javier Lopez
Jeffer Qian
Jiali Hou
Jian Weng
Jian Ying
Jian Zhuang
Jianchao Zeng
Jianfeng Ma
Jiang Yi
Jiangang Lu
Jianhuang Lai
Jianmin Xu
Jianming Zhan
Jianning Wu
Jill Slay
Jimin Wang
Jin Li
Jing-Hong Wang
Jingnian Chen
Jinquan Zeng
Jiping Zheng
Joerg Denzinger
Joong-Hwan Baek
Jorma Kajava
Josep Roure
Ju Liu
Jun Hu
Junbin Gao
Jun-Cheol Park
Junfang Xiao
Junfeng Tian
Junkai Yi
Junping Wang
Junzo Watada
Kalyanmoy Deb
Kamoun
Kap Luk Chan
Kash Khorasani
Kefei Chen
Kefeng Fan
Khurshid Ahmad
Kong Jun
Kuk-Hyun Han
Kwok-Yan Lam
Kyoung-Mi Lee
Lance Fung
Lei Hu
Lei Li
Leichun Wang
Leigh Xie
Li Li
Li Xu
Liangcai Zeng
Liangli Ma
Licheng Jiao
Lihe Guan
Lihe Zhang
Lijuan Li
Lijun Wu
Lin Wang
Lina Wang
Ling Chen
ling Huang
Lingfang Zeng
Lingjuan Li
Lishan Kang
Litao Zhang
Lixin Ding
Li-Yun Su
Lizhong Xu
Luís Alexandre
Luiza De Macedo Mourelle
Mahamed Omran
Malik Magdon-Ismail
Maozu Guo
Marc M. Van Hulle
Marc Schoenauer
Masayoshi Aritsugi

Matjaz Gams
Matthew Casey
Meng Jian
Mi Hong
Miao Kang
Michael N. Vrahatis
Minaya Villasana
Ming Dong
Ming Li
Ming Xiao
Mingdi Xu
Ming-Guang Zhang
Minghui Zheng
Mingli Yang
Mingxing Jia
Moonhyun Kim
Nadia Nedjah
Naoyuki Kubota
Nareli Cruz-Cortés
Nguyen Dinh Thuc
Nicolas Monmarché
Ning Chen
Nong Ye
Osslan Osiris Vergara Villegas
Paplinski P. Andrew
Paterson Kenny
Peidong Zhu
Ping Guo
Qian Xiang
Qian Zhang
Qiang Miao
Qiang Zhang
Qiangfu Zhao
Rachel McCrindle
Raj Subbu
Rangsipan Marukatat
Ravi Prakash
Renpu Li
Ricardo Nanculef
Rongjun Li
Rongxing Lu
Rong-yong Zhao
Rubo Zhang
S.Y. Yuen Kelvin
Sajal K.Das
Salima Hassas
Sam Kwong
Se Hun Lim
Seunggwan Lee
Shailesh Kumar
Shangmin Luan
Shanwen Zhang
Shaohe Lv
Shenghui Su
Sheng-Li Song
Shengwu Xiong
Shengyi Jiang
Shifu Tang
Simone Fischer-Huebner
Sokratis K. Katsikas
Stelvio Cimato
Sung-Hae Jun
Sungzoon Cho
Tetsuyuki Takahama
Tianding Chen
Tin Kam Ho
TL Sun
Tran Minh Triet
Vasant Honava
Vasu Alagar
Vianey Guadalupe Cruz Sonchez
Vic Rayward-Smith
Vicenc Torra
Vincent Kelner
Vojislav Stojkovic
Wanggen Wan
Wanli Ma
Wei Huang
Wei Li
Wei-Hua Zhu
Weipeng Zhang
Weiqi Yuan
Weixing Wang
Wenbo Xu
Wen-Fen Liu
Wengang Hu
Wenhua Zeng
Wenjian Luo
Wenling Wu
Wensheng Chen
Wen-Xiang Gu
Witold Pedrycz
Xiamu Niu
Xiangbin Zhu
Xiangpei Hu
Xianhua Dai
Xiao Ping
Xiaobei Ling
Xiaochao Zi
Xiaochun Cheng
Xiaochun Yang
Xiaofeng Chen
Xiaogang Yang
Xiaoping Luo
Xinbo Gao
Xingang Wang
Xingyu Pi
Xingzheng Ai
Xinhua Yao
Xinping Xiao
Xiong Li
Xiufang Wang
Xiuhui Ge
Xu E
Xuanguo Xu
Xuedong Han
Xuefeng Liu
Xuekun Song
Xueling Ma
Xuesong Xu
Xuesong Yan
Xufa Wang
Xuren Wang
Xuyang Lou
Yajun Guo
Yalou Huang
Yan Yi
Yan Zhu
Yanchun Liang
Yanfeng Yu
Yang Bo
Yanhai Hu
Yan-Jun Shi

Yan-Kui Liu
Yanming Wang
Yanxiang He
Yaochu Jin
Yaping Lin
Yeonseung Ryu
Yi Xie
Yih-Jiun Lee
Yin Tan
Ying Cai
Ying Tian
Ying Yang
Yingfeng Qiu
Yingkui Gu
Yingyou Wen
Yong-Chang Jiao
Yongqiang Zhang
You Choi Dong
Yuanchun Jiang
Yuanjian Zhou
Yuantao Jiang
Yunmin Zhu
Zaobin Gan
Zengquan Wang
Zhaohui Gan
Zhaoyan Liu
Zhe Li
Zhe-Ming Lu
Zheng Yang
Zhengtao Jiang
Zhengyuan Ning
Zhenhua Yu
Zhi Liu
Zhibiao Fu
Zhiguo Zhang
Zhiheng Zhou
Zhihong Tian
Zhihua Cai
Zhiping Zhou
Zhiqiang Ma
Zhiqing Meng
Zhiwei Song
Zhi-Wen Liu
Zhizhong Yan
Zhong Liu
Zhongchen Chen
Zhonghua Miao
Zhongliang Pan
Zhongwen Li
Zongben Xu
Zonghai Chen
Zugen Liu
Zuo-Feng Gao

Institutional Sponsorship

Xidian University
IEEE Hong Kong Section
Hong Kong Baptist University
Jinan University

Table of Contents

Bio-inspired Computing

Evolutionary Computation

Learning Systems and Multi-agents

Cryptography

Information Processing and Intrusion Detection

Systems and Security

Image and Signal Processing

Pattern Recognition

An Improved Particle Swarm Optimizer for Truss Structure Optimization

Lijuan Li, Zhibin Huang, and Feng Liu

Guangdong University of Technology, Guangzhou, 510006, China
Lilj@scnu.edu.cn, Bin2000hz@sina.com, Fliu@gdut.edu.cn

Abstract. This paper presents an improved particle swarm optimizer (IPSO) for solving truss structure optimization problems. The algorithm is based on the particle swarm optimizer with passive congregation (PSOPC) and a harmony search (HS) scheme. It handles the problem-specified constraints using a 'fly-back mechanism' method and the variables' constraints using the harmony search scheme. The IPSO is tested on a planar truss structure optimization problem and is compared with the PSO and the PSOPC algorithm respectively. The result shows that the IPSO method presented in this paper is able to accelerate the convergence rate effectively and has the fastest convergence rate among these three other algorithms.

1 Introduction

In the last thirty years, great attention has been paid to the structural optimization, due to the fact that raw material consumption is one of the most important factors that influence building construction. Designers prefer to minimize the volume or the weight of the structure by optimization.

Many traditionally mathematical optimization algorithms have been used in structural optimization problems. However, most of these algorithms are limited for the structure design. Recently, evolutionary algorithms (EAs) such as genetic algorithms (GAs), evolutionary programming (EP) and evolution strategies (ES) have been attractive because they do not apply mathematical assumptions to the optimization problems and have better global search abilities over conventional optimization algorithms [1]. For example, GAs has been applied for the structure optimization problems [2, 3, 4]. In recent years, a new evolutionary algorithm called particle swarm optimizer (PSO) has been invented [5]. The PSO has fewer parameters than the GA, and it is easier to implement. Another advantage of PSO is that it has shown a faster convergence rate than other EAs on some problems [6].

It is known that the PSO may outperform other EAs in the early iterations, but its performance may not be competitive when the number of the iterations increases [7]. Recently, many investigations have been undertaken to improve the performance of the standard PSO (SPSO). For example, He and Wu improved the standard particle swarm optimizer with passive congregation (PSOPC), which can improve the convergence rate and accuracy of the SPSO efficiently [8].

Most structural optimization problems include the problem-specific constraints, which are difficult to solve using the traditional mathematical optimization algorithms

Y. Wang, Y. Cheung, and H. Liu (Eds.): CIS 2006, LNAI 4456, pp. 1–10, 2007.

and GAs [9]. The most common method to handle the constraints is to use penalty functions. However, the major disadvantage of using the penalty functions is that it adds some tuning parameters in the algorithm and the penalty coefficients have to be finely tuned in order to balance the objective and penalty functions. If the penalty coefficients are not set appropriately, the optimization problems are difficult to be solved [10, 11]. To improve the PSO's capability for handling constraints, a new method, which is called 'fly-back mechanism', is invented. Compared to other constraint handling techniques, this method is relatively simple and easy to implement.

For most structural optimization problems, time cost is one of the major factors to be considered by the designers. In particular, for the large and complex structure, it would take a long time to complete an optimization process. If PSO is applied to solve structural optimization problems, it has to accelerate the convergence rate to reduce the time cost. This paper presents an improved particle swarm optimizer (IPSO), which is based on the PSO with passive congregation (PSOPC) and the harmony search (HS) scheme. It handles the constraints by using 'fly-back mechanism' method. It is able to accelerate the convergence rate of the PSO effectively.

2 The Structural Optimization Problems

A structural design optimization problem can be formulated as the nonlinear programming problem (NLP). For the size optimization of the truss structure, the cross-sections of the truss members are selected as the design variables. The objective function is the structural weight. It is subjected to the stress and the displacement constraints. The size optimization problem for truss structure can be expressed as follows:

$$\min f(X) \tag{1}$$

Subjected to:

$$g_i(X) \geq 0 \quad i = 1, 2, ..., m \tag{2}$$

Where $f(X)$ is the truss weight function which is a scalar, and $g_i(X)$ are the inequality constraints. The variables vector X represents a set of the design variables (the cross-sections of the truss members). It can be denoted as:

$$X = [x_1, x_2, ..., x_n]^T \tag{3}$$

where

$$x_i^l \leq x_i \leq x_i^u, \; i = 1, 2, ..., n \tag{4}$$

where x_i^l and x_i^u are the lower and the upper bound of the ith variable respectively.

3 The Particle Swarm Optimizer (PSO)

The PSO was inspired by the social behavior of animals such as fish schooling and birds flocking [6]. It involves a number of particles, which are initialized randomly in the search space of an objective function. These particles are called the swarm. Each particle of the swarm represents a potential solution of the optimization problem. The particles fly through the search space and their positions are updated based on each particle's personal best position as well as the best position found by the swarm. During iterations, the objective function is evaluated for each particle and the fitness value is used to determine which position in the search space is better than the others [12].

During iterations, the swarm is updated by the following equations:

$$V_i^{k+1} = \omega V_i^k + c_1 r_1 \left(P_i^k - X_i^k \right) + c_2 r_2 \left(P_g^k - X_i^k \right) \tag{5}$$

$$X_i^{k+1} = X_i^k + V_i^{k+1} \tag{6}$$

where X_i and V_i represent the current position and the velocity of each particle respectively; P_i is the best previous position of the ith particle (called *pbest*) and P_g is the global position among all the particles in the swarm (called *gbest*); r_1 and r_2 are two uniform random sequences generated from U(0, 1); and ω is the inertia weight which is typically chosen in the range of $[0,1]$. A larger inertia weight facilitates global exploration and a smaller inertia weight tends to facilitate local exploration to fine-tune the current search area. A suitable value for the inertia weight ω usually provides balance between global and local exploration abilities and consequently results in a better optimum solution [13]. Some literatures indicated that it was better to initially set the inertia to a large value, and then gradually decreased it to get more refined solutions.

4 The Optimizer with Passive Congregation

The congregation involves the active congregation and the passive congregation. The latter is an attraction of an individual to the other group members but no display of social behavior [8]. Fish schooling is one of the representative types of passive congregation and the PSO is inspired by it. Adding the passive congregation model to the SPSO may increase its performance. He and Wu, *et al* proposed a hybrid PSO with passive congregation (PSOPC) as follows [8]:

$$V_i^{k+1} = \omega V_i^k + c_1 r_1 \left(P_i^k - X_i^k \right) + c_2 r_2 \left(P_g^k - X_i^k \right) + c_3 r_3 \left(R_i^k - X_i^k \right) \tag{7}$$

$$X_i^{k+1} = X_i^k + V_i^{k+1} \tag{8}$$

where R_i is a particle selected randomly from the swarm, c_3 the passive congregation coefficient, and r_3 a uniform random sequence in the range (0, 1): $r_3 \sim$ U(0, 1). Several benchmark functions had been tested in Ref.[8], and the results showed that the PSOPC had a better convergence rate and a higher accuracy than the PSO.

5 Constraint Method: Fly-Back Mechanism

The PSO has been already applied to optimize constrained problems. The most common method to handle the constraints is to use penalty functions. However, some experimental results indicate that such a technique will lower the efficiency of the PSO, because it resets the infeasible particles to their previous best positions *pbest*, which will sometimes prevent the search form reaching a global minimum [9]. A new technique handling the constraints, which is called 'fly-back mechanism', was introduced by He and Wu *et al* [9]. For most of the optimization problems containing constraints, the global minimum is close to the boundary of the feasible space. The particles are initialized in the feasible region. When the optimization process starts, the particles fly in the feasible space to search the solution. If any one of the particles flies into the infeasible region, it will be forced to fly back to the previous position to guarantee a feasible solution. The particle which flies back to the previous position may be closer to the boundary at the next iteration. This makes the particles fly to the global minimum in a great probability. Therefore, such a 'fly-back mechanism' technique is suitable for handling the optimization problem containing the constraints, and some experimental results have shown that it can find a better solution with fewer iteration numbers [9].

6 An Improved Swarm Optimization (IPSO)

The improved particle swarm optimizer (IPSO) is based on the particle swarm with passive congregation (PSOPC) and a harmony search (HS) scheme, and uses a 'fly-back mechanism' method to handle the constraints.

When a particle flies in the searching space, it may fly into the infeasible region. In this case, there are two possibilities. It may violate the problem-specified constraints boundary or the variables boundary, which is shown in figure 1. Because the 'fly-back mechanism' technique is used to handle the problem-specified constraints, the particle will fly back to its previous position no matter it violates the problem-specified constraints boundary or the variables boundary. If it flies out of the variables boundary, the solution can not be used even if the problem-specified constraints are satisfied. In our experiments, particles violate the variables boundary frequently for the simple structure optimization problem. If the structure is complex, this number rises. In other words, a large amount of the particles' flying behaviors is wasted, due to searching outside the variables boundary.

Although minimizing the maximum of the velocity can make fewer particles violate the variables boundary, it may also make the particles fail to cross the problem-specified constraints region. Therefore, we hope that all of the particles fly inside the variables boundary to check whether they violate the problem-specified constraints boundary or not and get better solutions. The particles, which fly outside the variables boundary, have to be generated in a new approach. Here, we introduce a new method to handle these particles. It is derived from one of the ideas in a new meta-heuristic algorithm called harmony search (HS) algorithm [14].

Harmony search (HS) algorithm is based on natural musical performance processes that occur when a musician searches for a better state of harmony, such as during jazz improvisation [14]. The engineers seek to find a global solution as determined by an objective function, just like the musicians seek to find musically pleasing harmony as determined by an aesthetic [15].

In the HS algorithm, the harmony memory (HM) stores the feasible vectors, which are all in the feasible space and have got the solutions. The harmony memory size determines how many vectors it stores. A new vector is generated by selecting different components of different vectors randomly in the harmony memory. Undoubtedly, the new vector does not violate the variables boundary, but it is not sure whether it violates the problem-specified constraints or not. When it is generated, the harmony memory will be updated by accepting this new vector and deleting the worst vector if it gets a better solution.

Similarly, the PSO stores the feasible and "good" vectors (particles) in the *pbest* swarm, just like the harmony memory in the HS algorithm. Hence, the vector (particle) violating the variables boundary can be generated again by such a technique-selecting for different components of different vectors randomly in the *pbest* swarm. There are two different ways to apply this technique to the PSO. (1) When any one of the components of the vector violates its corresponding component of the variables boundary, all the components of this vector should be generated; (2) only this component of the vector should be generated again by such a technique. In our experiments, the results showed that the former way made the particles get in the local solution easily, and the latter way can reach the global solution in less iteration relatively.

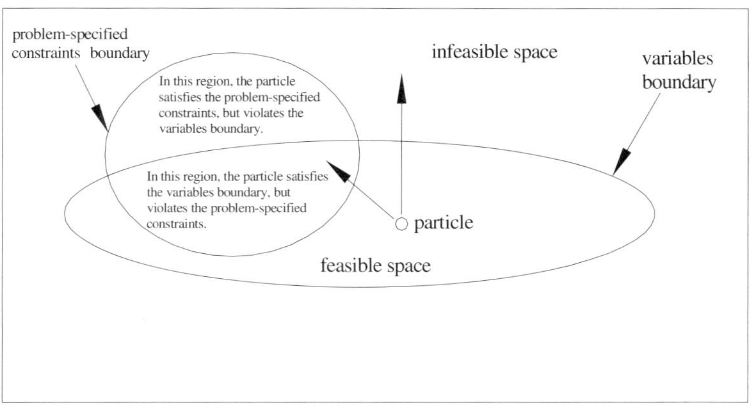

Fig. 1. The particle may violate the problem specified constraints or the variables boundary

7 Numerical Examples

In this section, a 10-bar truss structure subjected to two load conditions, collected from the literature, was selected as a benchmark problem to test IPSO. The algorithm proposed was coded in FORTRAN language and executed on a Pentium 4, 2.93GHz machine. The truss structure was analyzed by the finite element method (FEM) [18].

The PSO, PSOPC and the IPSO were all applied to this example in order to evaluate the performance of the new algorithm by comparisons. For all the algorithms, a population of 50 individuals was used, the inertia weight ω, which started at 0.9 and ended at 0.4, decreased linearly, and the value of acceleration constants c_1 and c_2 were set to 0.8. The passive congregation coefficient c_3 was set to 0.6 for the PSOPC [8] and the IPSO algorithms. A fixed number of maximum iterations 3000 were applied. The maximum velocity was set as the subtraction between the upper and the lower bound, which made particles be able to fly across the problem-specified constraints region certainly.

7.1 The 10-Bar Planar Truss Structure

The 10-bar truss structure, shown in figure 2 [15], was previously analyzed by many researchers, such as Schmit [16], Rizzi [17] and Kang Seok Lee [15]. The material density is 0.1 lb/in^3 and the modulus of elasticity is 10,000 ksi. The members are subject to stress limitations of ±25 ksi. All nodes in both directions are subject to displacement limitation of ±2.0 in. There are 10 design variables in this example and the minimum cross-sectional area of each member is 0.1 in^2. Two cases are considered: Case 1, the single loading condition of P_1=100 kips and P_2=0 ; and Case 2, the single loading condition of P_1=150 kips and P_2=50 kips.

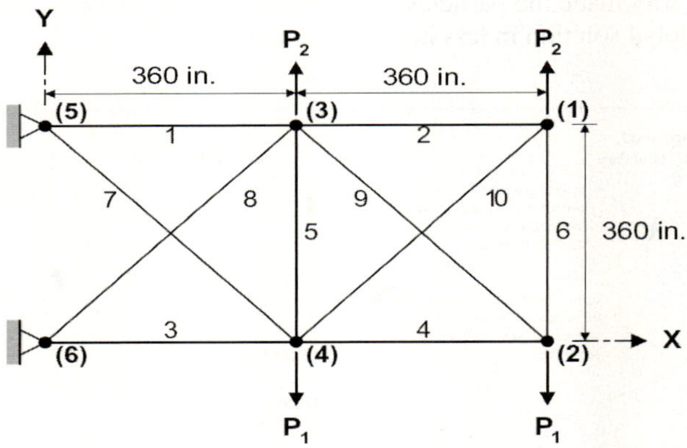

Fig. 2. A 10-bar planar truss structure

For both cases of this truss structure, the PSOPC and the IPSO achieved the good solution after 3,000 iterations. However, the latter is quite close to the best solution than the former after about 500 iterations. The IPSO has a faster convergence rate than the PSOPC in this example. The performance of the PSO was the worst among these three algorithms. Table 1 and table 2 show the solutions and figure 3 and figure 4 provide a convergence rate comparison among the three algorithms.

Table 1. Comparison of optimal design for Case 1

Variable	Optimal cross-sectional areas (in.^{2})					
	Schmit [16]	Rizzi [17]	Kang [15]	PSO	PSOPC	IPSO
A_1	33.43	30.73	30.15	33.469	30.569	30.704
A_2	0.100	0.100	0.102	0.110	0.100	0.100
A_3	24.26	23.93	22.71	23.177	22.974	23.167
A_4	14.26	14.73	15.27	15.475	15.148	15.183
A_5	0.100	0.100	0.102	3.649	0.100	0.100
A_6	0.100	0.100	0.544	0.116	0.547	0.551
A_7	8.388	8.542	7.541	8.328	7.493	7.460
A_8	20.74	20.95	21.56	23.340	21.159	20.978
A_9	19.69	21.84	21.45	23.014	21.556	21.508
A_{10}	0.100	0.100	0.100	0.190	0.100	0.100
Weight (lb)	5089.	5076.	5057.9	5529.5	5061.0	5060.9

Table 2. Comparison of optimal design for Case 2

Variable	Optimal cross-sectional areas (in.^{2})					
	Schmit[16]	Rizzi[17]	Kang[15]	PSO	PSOPC	IPSO
A_1	24.29	23.53	23.25	22.935	23.743	23.353
A_2	0.100	0.100	0.102	0.113	0.101	0.100
A_3	23.35	25.29	25.73	25.355	25.287	25.502
A_4	13.66	14.37	14.51	14.373	14.413	14.250
A_5	0.100	0.100	0.100	0.100	0.100	0.100
A_6	1.969	1.970	1.977	1.990	1.969	1.972
A_7	12.67	12.39	12.21	12.346	12.362	12.363
A_8	12.54	12.83	12.61	12.923	12.694	12.894
A_9	21.97	20.33	20.36	20.678	20.323	20.356
A_{10}	0.100	0.100	0.100	0.100	0.103	0.101
Weight (lb)	4691.8	4676.9	4668.8	4679.5	4677.7	4677.3

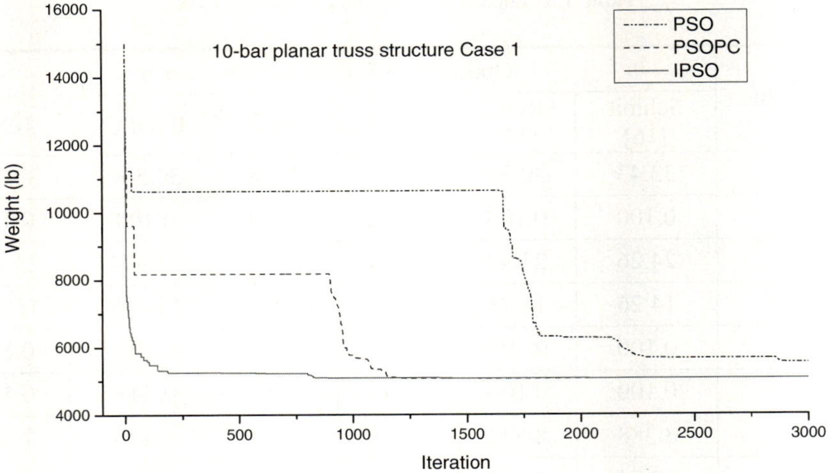

Fig. 3. Convergence rates of Case 1

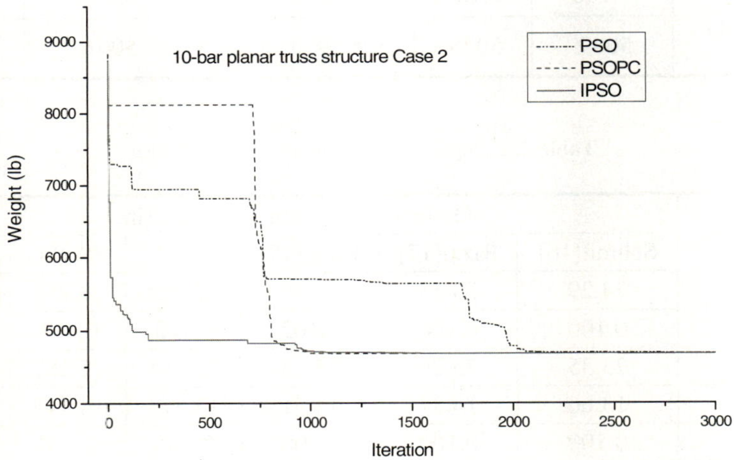

Fig. 4. Convergence rates of Case 2

8 Conclusions

In this paper, an improved particle swarm optimizer (IPSO), based on the particle swarm optimizer with passive congregation (PSOPC), and the harmony search (HS) algorithm, has been presented. The IPSO handles the problem-specified constraints using 'fly-back mechanism' method, while it handles the variables constraints using harmony search scheme. Compared with the PSO and the PSOPC, the IPSO makes none of the particles flies outside the variables boundary, and makes a full use of each particle's flying behavior.

The IPSO presented in this paper has been tested on one planar truss structure optimization problem. The result shows that the IPSO outperforms than the PSO and the PSOPC in terms of convergence rate. In particular, the IPSO has a highly fast convergence rate in the early iterations, which makes the particles fly close to the global solution in a short time.

A drawback of this IPSO at present is that its convergence rate will slow down, when the number of the iterations increases. Research work is going on to improve it [19].

Acknowledgements

We would like to thank Guangdong Natural Science Foundation (06104655) and Guangzhou Bureau of Science and Technology (2003Z3-D0221), Peoples' Republic of China, for partially supporting this project.

References

1. Coellok, C.A.C.: Theoretical and Numerical Constraint-handling Techniques Used with Evolutionary Algorithms: A Survey of the State of the Art. Comput. Methods Appl. Mech. Eng. 191, 1245–1287 (2002)
2. Nanakorn, P., Meesomklin, K.: An Adaptive Penalty Function in Genetic Algorithms for Structural Design Optimization. Comput. Struct. 79, 2527–2539 (2001)
3. Deb, K., Gulati, S.: Design of Truss-structures for Minimum Weight Using Genetic Algorithms. Finite Elem Anal Des. 37, 447–465 (2001)
4. Ali, N., Behdinan, K., Fawaz, Z.: Applicability and Viability of a GA Based Finite Element Analysis Architecture for Structural Design Optimization. Comput. Struct. 81, 2259–2271 (2003)
5. Kennedy, J., Eberhart, R.: Swarm Optimization. In: Proceedings of the 1995 IEEE International Conference on Neural Networks, vol. 4, pp. 1942–1948. IEEE, Piscataway, NJ, USA (1995)
6. Kennedy, J., Eberhart, R.C.: Swarm Intelligence. Morgan Kaufmann, San Francisco (2001)
7. Angeline, P.J.: Evolutionary optimization versus particle swarm optimization: philosophy and performance difference. In: Porto, V.W., Waagen, D. (eds.) Evolutionary Programming VII. LNCS, vol. 1447, pp. 601–610. Springer, Heidelberg (1998)
8. He, S., Wu, Q.H., Wen, J.Y., Saunders, J.R., Paton, R.C.: A Particle Swarm Optimizer with Passive Congregation. BioSystem 78, 135–147 (2004)
9. He, S., Prempain, E., Wu, Q.H.: An Improved Particle Swarm Optimizer for Mechanical Design Optimization Problems. Eng. Optim. 36, 585–605 (2004)
10. Davis, L.: Genetic Algorithms and Simulated Annealing. Pitman, London (1987)
11. Le Riche, R.G., Knopf-Lenoir, C., Haftka, R.T.: A Segregated genetic algorithm for constrained structural optimization. In: Sixth International Conference on Genetic Algorithms, pp. 558–565. University of Pittsburgh. Morgan Kaufmann, San Francisco (1995)
12. Van den Bergh, Engelbrecht, A.: Using Neighborhood with the Guaranteed Convergence PSO. In: Proceedings of, IEEE Swarm Intelligence Symposium 2003, USA, pp. 235–242 (2003)

13. Shi, Y., erhart, R.C.: A Modified Particle Swarm Optimizer. In: Proceedings of the 1998 IEEE International Conference on Evolutionary Computation, USA, pp. 303–308 (1997)
14. Geem, Z.W., Kim, J.H., Loganathan, G.V.: A New Heuristic Optimization Algorithm: Harmony Search. Simulation 76, 60–68 (2001)
15. Lee, K.S., Geem, Z.W.: A New Structural Optimization Method Based on the Harmony Search Algorithm. Comput. Struct. 82, 781–798 (2004)
16. Schmit Jr., L.A., Farshi, B.: Some Approximation Concepts for Structural Synthesis. AIAA J. 12, 692–699 (1974)
17. Rizzi, P.: Optimization of multiconstrained structures based on optimality criteria, AIAA/ASME/SAE 17th Structures, Structural Dynamics and Materials Conference, King of Prussia, PA (1976)
18. Wang, Y., Li, L., Li, Y.: The Foundation of Finite Element Method and its Program. The Publishing Company of South China University of Technology, China (2001)
19. Li, L., Ren, F.M., Liu, F., Wu, Q.H.: An Improved Particle Swarm Optimization Method and its Application in Civil Engineering. In: Topping, B.H.V., Montero, G., Montenegro, R. (eds.) Proceedings of the Fifth International Conference on Engineering Computational Technology, Civil-Comp Press, Stirlingshire, United Kingdom (2006)

Two-Phase Quantum Based Evolutionary Algorithm for Multiple Sequence Alignment

Hongwei Huo[1] and Vojislav Stojkovic[2]

[1] School of Computer Science and Technology, Xidian University, Xi'an 710071, China
hwhuo@mail.xidian.edu.cn

[2] Computer Science Department, Morgan State University, CA205
1700 East Cold Spring Lane, Baltimore, MD 21251, USA
stojkovi@jewel.morgan.edu

Abstract. The paper presents a two-phase quantum based evolution algorithm for multiple sequence alignment problem,called TPQEAlign. TPQEAlign uses a new probabilistic representation, qubit, that can represent a linear superposition of individuals of solutions. Combined with strategy for the optimization of initial search space, TPQEAilgn is proposed as follows. It consists of two phases. In the first phase, a promising initial value is searched and stored. Each local group has a different value of qubit from other local groups to explore a different search space each. In the second phase, we initialize the population using the stored resulting obtained in the first phase. The effectiveness and performance of TPQEAlign are demonstrated by testing cases in BAliBASE. Comparisons were made with the experimental results of QEAlign and several popular programs, such as CLUSTALX and SAGA. The experiments show that TPQEAlign is efficient and competent with CLUSTALX and SAGA.

1 Introduction

Multiple Sequence Alignment (MSA) is one of the challenging tasks in bioinformatics. It is computationally difficult and has diverse applications in sequence assembly, sequence annotation, structural and functional predictions for genes and proteins, phylogeny and evolutionary analysis. Multiple sequence alignment algorithms may be classified into three classes [1].

The first class is those algorithms that use high quality heuristics very close to optimality [2]. They can only handle a small number of sequences and limited to the sum-of-pairs objective function.

The second class is those algorithms that use the progressive alignment strategy. A multiple alignment is gradually built up by aligning the closest pair of sequences first and then aligning the next closest pair of sequences, or one sequence with a set of aligned sequences or two sets of aligned sequences. This

Y. Wang, Y. Cheung, and H. Liu (Eds.): CIS 2006, LNAI 4456, pp. 11–21, 2007.

procedure is repeated until all given sequences are aligned together. The best-known system based on progressive multiple alignment is perhaps CLUSTALW. Other multiple alignment systems that are mostly targeting proteins or short DNA sequences, and based on progressive alignment, include MULTALIGN [3], T-COFFEE [4], MAFFT [5], MUSCLE [6], Align-m60 [7], and PROBCONS [8].

The third class of alignment algorithms using iterative refinement strategy can avoid the above problem by aligning these sequences simultaneously. The basic idea is to adopt the evolution theory in nature, initializing a population of individuals of alignments, and then refining these individuals evaluated by an objective function generation by generation, until finding the best alignment. Based on this strategy, SAGA [9], with DIALIGN [10] has become the popular method for multiple alignments.

However, these methods still share some problems, such as local optima, slow convergent speed and lacking a specific termination condition, especially for iterative methods. Some are not flexible enough to capture the full complexity of the similarities between biological sequences.

Quantum evolution algorithm (QEA) is one of the fields of research of Quantum computing. It combines the probabilistic algorithm and quantum algorithm. Kuk-Hym Han has analyzed the characteristics of QEA and showed that QEA can successfully solve the knapsack problem [11]. We try to go one step further and to redesign QEA to solve MSA. We import a variation operator from Genetic Algorithm in QEA, since the representation of the MSA is much more complicated than the knapsack problem.

The paper presents a new Two-Phase Quantum based Evolution Algorithm for multiple sequence alignment, called TPQEAlign - a result of our research on re-designing QEA to solve MSA. The effectiveness and performance of TPQEAlign are demonstrated by testing cases in BAliBASE [12].

2 Multiple Sequence Alignment

Given a finite alphabet set and a set $S = (S_1, S_2, ..., S_n)$ of n sequences with length $l_1, l_2, ..., l_n$, respectively: $S_i = S_{i1}S_{i2}... S_{il}, 1 \leq i \leq n, S_{ij} \in \sum, 1 \leq j \leq l_i)$ where consists of four characters for DNA sequences, and twenty characters of amino acids for protein sequences, a multiple alignment of S is specified by a $n \times l$ matrix $M = (a_{ij}), 1 \leq i \leq n, 1 \leq j \leq l, l \geq \max(l_i)$, satisfying:

i) $a_{ij} \in \sum \cup$ {-}, where "-" denotes the gap letter;
ii) each row $a_i = a_{i1}a_{i2}...a_{il}$, $1 \leq i \leq n$, of M is exactly the corresponding sequence S_i, if we remove all gap letters;
iii) no column in M contains only gaps.

We can estimate the quality of an alignment by scoring the alignment. The goal of the multiple sequence alignment is to find the optimal alignment that maximizes the score.

3 Algorithms

3.1 Representation

The quantum-inspired evolutionary algorithm deals more efficiently with the balance between exploration and exploitation than traditional genetic algorithm. It explores the search space with a smaller number of individual and a global solution within a shorter span of time.

In quantum computing, the smallest unit of information stored in a two-state quantum.

$$\begin{bmatrix} u \\ v \end{bmatrix}$$

where u and v express the probability amplitudes of the "0" state and the "1" state, respectively. The linear combination of the two basic vectors $|0>$ and $|1>$ can be represented as $u|0> + v|1>$ satisfying the following equation:

$$|u|^2 + |v|^2 = 1 \tag{1}$$

where the probability that the state is measured as basis vector $|0>$ is the square of the norm of the amplitude and the probability that the state is measured as basis vector $|1>$ is the square of the norm of the amplitude, denoted by $|u|^2$ and $|v|^2$, respectively.

A qubit may be in the 1 state, in the 0 state, or in a linear superposition of both states. If there is, for instance, a four-qubits system with four pairs of amplitudes such as

$$M = \left[\begin{array}{c|c|c|c} u_1 & u_2 & u_3 & u_4 \\ v_1 & v_2 & v_3 & v_4 \end{array}\right] = \left[\begin{array}{c|c|c|c} \frac{1}{\sqrt{2}} & \frac{1}{\sqrt{3}} & \frac{1}{\sqrt{2}} & \frac{1}{2} \\ \frac{1}{\sqrt{2}} & \frac{\sqrt{2}}{\sqrt{3}} & -\frac{1}{\sqrt{2}} & \frac{\sqrt{3}}{2} \end{array}\right] \tag{2}$$

then the state of the 4-qubits system can be represented as

$$\frac{1}{4\sqrt{3}}|0000> + \frac{1}{4}|0001> - \frac{1}{4\sqrt{3}}|0010> + \frac{1}{2\sqrt{6}}|0100> +$$

$$\frac{1}{4\sqrt{3}}|1000> + \frac{1}{2\sqrt{6}}|1100> - \frac{1}{4\sqrt{3}}|1010> + \frac{1}{4}|1001> -$$

$$\frac{1}{2\sqrt{6}}|0110> + \frac{1}{2\sqrt{2}}|0101> - \frac{1}{4}|0011> - \frac{1}{2\sqrt{2}}|0111> -$$

$$\frac{1}{4}|1011> - \frac{1}{2\sqrt{6}}|1110> + \frac{1}{2\sqrt{2}}|1101> - \frac{1}{2\sqrt{2}}|1111>$$

The probabilities to reach 16 states $|0000>$, $|0001>$, $|0010>$, $|0100>$, $|1000>$, $|1100>$, $|1010>$, $|1001>$, $|0110>$, $|0101>$, $|0011>$, $|0111>$, $|1011>$, $|1110>$, $|1101>$, $|1111>$, are $\frac{1}{48}$, $\frac{1}{16}$, $\frac{1}{48}$, $\frac{1}{24}$, $\frac{1}{48}$, $\frac{1}{24}$, $\frac{1}{48}$, $\frac{1}{16}$, $\frac{1}{24}$, $\frac{1}{8}$, $\frac{1}{16}$, $\frac{1}{8}$, $\frac{1}{16}$, $\frac{1}{24}$, $\frac{1}{8}$, and $\frac{1}{8}$, respectively. Thus, there are possible 2^n states in a system, in which the states are described by n bits. The system M performs a superposition of the four states on each bit independently in sequence and changes the state of the system. Thus, a 4-qubits system comprises the information of 16 states.

For multiple sequence alignment problem, if an alignment of k sequences with the length of N is represented using binary string, it needs a space of $k * N$ binary bits. $k * N$ qubits are used to represent the alignment, which is called qubit alignment individual, denoted by Align-qubit for short.

If, for instance, three sequences *abcd*, *ac*, *abd* are to be aligned,Align-qubit is as follows, where $k = 3$ and $N = 5$ which is the ceiling of 1.2*4, and 4 is the maximum length of the initial sequences. It contains the information of 2^{15} binary states.

$$\left[\begin{array}{c|c|c|c|c} u_{11} & u_{12} & u_{13} & u_{14} & u_{15} \\ v_{11} & v_{12} & v_{13} & v_{14} & v_{15} \\ u_{21} & u_{22} & u_{23} & u_{24} & u_{25} \\ v_{21} & v_{22} & v_{23} & v_{24} & v_{25} \\ u_{31} & u_{32} & u_{33} & u_{34} & u_{35} \\ v_{31} & v_{32} & v_{33} & v_{34} & v_{35} \end{array}\right]$$

The following binary state represents an alignment as:

$$\begin{bmatrix} 0\,0\,0\,0\,1 \\ 0\,1\,0\,1\,1 \\ 0\,0\,1\,0\,1 \end{bmatrix} \longrightarrow \begin{array}{ccccc} a & b & c & d & - \\ a & - & c & - & - \\ a & b & - & d & - \end{array}$$

Binary states that represent a valid binary coding for any alignment are called binary individuals. An Align-qubit individual contains the information of many binary individuals.

3.2 Multiple Sequence Alignment by Quantum Evolutionary Algorithm

QEAlign involves a population consisted of Align-qubit individuals, which can be driven by Q-gate and can collapse to be binary individuals decoded to alignments. Initially, A population of Align-qubit individuals Q(0) is initialized randomly and gives the initial binary individuals P(0) and B(0). In the evolutionary process, the old Align-qubit individuals Q(t-1) is driven by Q-gate to generate the new Align-qubit individuals Q(t), from which generating the new binary individuals P(t) which are optimized by an mutation operator. The binary individuals among P(t) and B(t-1) are evaluated for the fitness value and the best binary individuals among them is stored to B(t). The binary individuals in B(t) is migrated locally or globally under local migration condition or global migration condition, respectively. Then the best binary individual evaluated among B(t) is saved to b. These steps are repeated iteratively, generation by generation. In each generation, good binary individuals survive and bad binary individuals are discarded. The fitness value of b is increased until no more improvement can be made.

All these steps can be grouped as the procedure QEAlign:

Procedure QEAlign

```
t ← 0
initialize Q(t)
construct P(t) by collapsing the states of Q(t)
repair P(t)
evaluate P(t)
store the best solutions among P(t) into B(t)
while (not termination-condition) do
    t ← t + 1
    update Q(t)using Q-gates
    construct P(t) by collapsing the states of Q(t)
    repair P(t)
    mutation P(t)
    evaluate P(t) and B(t-1)
    store the best solutions among B(t-1)and P(t) into B(t)
    store the best solution b among B(t)
    if (migration-condition)
    then migrate b or b_j^t to B(t) locally endif
endwhile
```

The termination condition is that b is not improved after b_{max} times of loops or the number of loops is larger than the given number.

The following in this part is the introduction to the main operations in QEAlign.

Collapsing the states of Q(t) is to construct binary states. In this step, each binary bit of a binary state is set according to the corresponding qubit of Align-qubit individual. For every bit of each binary state, a random number between 0 and 1 is generated, and if the random number is satisfied that $random(0,1) < |\beta_{ij}|^2$, then the bit of this binary state is set to 1, otherwise 0. This process is implemented by the procedure CONSTRUCT(x), where x is a binary state.

Procedure CONSTRUCT(x)

```
i ← 0
while (i < nseqs) do
   j ← 0
   while (j < aln_length) do
      if random(0,1) < |β_ij|^2 then x_ij ← 1
         else x_ij ← 0 endif
      j ← j + 1
   endwhile
   i ← i + 1
endwhile
```

Repair operation is to transform the binary states into be binary individuals such that the number of gaps inserted into any one of the sequences is just equal to $N - n_i$.

Update operation is to update Align-qubit individuals in Q(t) by Q-gate. A Q-gate is acted as a variation operator in QEAlign, the updated Align-qubit should satisfy the normalization condition, $|u'|^2 + |v'|^2 = 1$, by the Q-gate operation, where u' and v' are the values of updated Align-qubit.

In the QEAlign, the following rotation gate is used as Q-gate:

$$U(\Delta\theta_{ij}) = \begin{bmatrix} cos(\Delta\theta_{ij}) & -sin(\Delta\theta_{ij}) \\ sin(\Delta\theta_{ij}) & cos(\Delta\theta_{ij}) \end{bmatrix} \tag{3}$$

Procedure REPAIR(x)

```
i ← 0
while (i < nseqs) do
   gapcount ← aln_seqlen
   while (gapnum < gapcount) do
      k ← randint(0, aln_length)
      if (x_ik = 0) then x_ik ← 1 endif
   endwhile
   while (gapnum > gapcount) do
      k ← randint(0, aln_length)
      if (x_ik = 1) then x_ik ← 0endif
   endwhile
   i ← i + 1
endwhile
```

and the lookup table of $\Delta\theta_{ij}$ is given in Table1.

Table 1. Lookup table of $\Delta\theta_{ij}$

x_{ij}	b_{ij}	$f_{Cscore}(x_j) \geq$	$\Delta\theta_{ij}$
0	0	false	θ_1
0	0	true	θ_2
0	1	false	θ_3
0	1	true	θ_4
1	0	false	θ_5
1	0	true	θ_6
1	1	false	θ_7
1	1	true	θ_8

where $\Delta\theta_{ij}$ is the function of x_{ij}, b_{ij}, and the expression $f(x_j) \geq f(b_j)$, and x_{ij} is the j-th bit of the i-th sequence of the binary solution x_k^t in P(t), b_{ij} is the j-th bit of the i-th sequence of the binary solution b_k^t in B(t), and b_{ij} is the rotation angle of the the j-th qubit of the i-th row of the qubit individual q_k^t in Q(t). $f_{Cscore}(x_j)$ is the j-th $Cscore$ of the alignment represented by x_k^t and $f_{Cscore}(b_j)$ is the j-th $Cscore$ of the alignment represented by b_k^t. f_{Cscore} is computed as follows.

$$f_{Cscore}(x_j) = C_{score}(s'_{1,i}, s'_{2,i}, ..., s'_{k,i}) = \sum_{1 \leq p \leq q \leq k} P_{score}(s'_{p,i}, s'_{q,i}) \qquad (4)$$

where $s'_{1,i}, s'_{2,i}, ..., s'_{k,i}$ is the column of the alignment decoded from x.The process of updating is implemented by the procedure UPDATE:

Procedure UPDATE Q(q)

$i \leftarrow 0$
while $(i < nseqs)$ **do**
    $j \leftarrow 0$
    while $(j < aln_length)$ **do**
        determine $\Delta\theta_{ij}$ according to table 1
        $[\alpha'_{ij}, \beta'_{ij}] \leftarrow U(\Delta\theta_{ij})[\alpha_{ij}, \beta_{ij}]^T$
        $j \leftarrow j + 1$
    endwhile
    $i \leftarrow i + 1$
endwhile

QEAlign imports an optional operator (mutation). This operator acts as optimizing the binary individuals. When optimizing a binary individual, we first decode it to be an alignment, then randomly select a block of subsequences, from which generating the template sequence by consisting of the characters with the highest frequency of each column of the subsequences. Template sequence is aligned with each of subsequences by banded-dynamic programming, in which the gaps in each subsequence must be deleted in advance, and template sequences are not inserted gaps when aligning. It is described in the procedure MUTATION(x), where x is a binary individual.

Procedure MUTATION(x)

Decode x to a alignment
Select sub-sequences
Find template sequence
$i \leftarrow 0$
while $(i < nseqs)$ **do**
    align template sequence and sub-sequence by banded-DP
    insert sub-sequence in alignment
    $i \leftarrow i + 1$
endwhile

A migration in QEAlign is a process of copying b_k^t in B(t) or b to B(t). A global migration is implemented by replaced all the solution in B(t) by b, and a local migration is implemented by replaced some of the solutions in B(t) by the best one of them.

The process of migration is described as the procedure MIGRATION.

Procedure MIGRATION(B(t))
divided B(t) into several groups
if (global migration condition)
  then copy b to B(t)
    else if(local migration condition)
        then for each group in B(t) **do**
            find the best b_k^t in B(t)
            copy b_k^t to the group
          endfor
      endif
endif

3.3 Two-Phase QEAlign

It has been verified that changing the initial values of qubits can provide better performance of QEA. Since the initial search space is directly determined by the initial values of qubits, the qubit individuals can converge to the best solution effectively if we can seek the initial values of qubits to show the initial search space with small distance to the best solution. Combined with the strategy, TPQEAilgn is proposed as follows.

Procedure TPQEAlign
First-phase QEAlign
Second-phase QEAlign

In the first phase of TPQEAlign, all the initial qubit individuals are divided into multiple groups, the initial values of qubit individuals in the same group are initialized as the same value and in different group the initial values are different. In the g-th local group, the initial values of qubits can be decided by the following formula:

$$\begin{bmatrix} u_g \\ v_g \end{bmatrix} = \begin{bmatrix} \sqrt{\frac{(1-2\delta)}{N_g-1}g+\delta} \\ \sqrt{1-\frac{(1-2\delta)}{N_g-1}g-\delta} \end{bmatrix} \tag{5}$$

where N_g is the total number of groups, δ, $0 < \delta << 1$, a constant. The first phase of TPQEAlign runs without global migration. At the end of the first phase of TPQEAlign, the initial value of qubit individual with the highest fitness is recorded. In the second phase of TPQEAlign, all the initial value of Q(0) is initialized by the recorded value. Then we got a two-phase QEAlign by using the above QEAlign and the idea of TPQEAlign.

4 Experimental Results

The TPQEAlign algorithm was tested on the BAliBASE, a standard Benchmark. And we use SPS to assess the alignment. The following parameters are used in the QEAlign algorithm: population = 100, local group = 5, θ_i, i =1, ... , 8, is given in Table 2. The global migration condition is 100, and the local migration condition is 1.

Table 2. The value of θ

θ_1	θ_2	θ_3	θ_4	θ_5	θ_6	θ_7	θ_8
-0.4π	-0.6π	0.0π	0.1π	0.5π	-0.5π	0.2π	0.5π

Multiple alignment comparisons among CLUSTALW, SAGA, TPQEAlign, and QEAlign with Ref1 through Ref5 are shown in Table 3~7, where "F" is used to represent the fail alignment.

Table 3. Multiple alignment comparison among CLUSTALW, SAGA, TPQEAlign, and QEAlign with Ref1

Name	ID	CLUSTALX	SAGA	TPQEAlign	QEAlign
1idv	14%	0.705	0.342	0.344	0.194
1havA	15%	0.446	0.411	0.160	0.150
1dox	46%	0.919	0.879	0.835	0.821
1fmb	49%	0.981	0.979	0.948	0.823
2fxb	51%	0.945	0.951	0.956	0.878
9rnt	57%	0.974	0.965	0.915	0.885
1led	43%	0.946	0.923	0.741	0.702
1ppn	46%	0.989	0.983	0.863	0.847

Table 4. Multiple alignment comparison among CLUSTALW, SAGA, TPQEAlign, and QEAlign with Ref2

Name	ID	CLUSTALX	SAGA	TPQEAlign	QEAlign
1aboA	26%	0.650	0.489	0.461	0.347
1idy	28%	0.515	0.548	0.580	0.535
1csy	29%	0.154	0.154	0.581	0.537
1r69	26%	0.675	0.475	0.594	0.587
1tvxA	34%	0.552	0.448	0.630	0.633
1tgxA	35%	0.727	0.773	0.541	0.529
1ubi	32%	0.482	0.492	0.618	0.609
4enl	48%	0.375	0.739	0.745	0.703

Of all the proposed methods, CLUSTALX and SAGA are the most popular methods. Table4 shows that QEAlign and TPQEAlign are better than most of the presented popular aligning methods from Ref2 to Ref4 and not as good as these methods for Ref1 and Ref5. Compared with SAGA, QEAlign is much simpler. It updates the qubit individuals only by one variation operator, while SAGA has operators as many as 22. Moreover, QEA does not need a lot of individuals to search the global optional solution, owing to its qubit representation.

Table 5. Multiple alignment comparison among CLUSTALW, SAGA, TPQEAlign, and QEAlign with Ref3

Name	ID	CLUSTALX	SAGA	TPQEAlign	QEAlign
1idv	20%	0.273	0.364	0.568	0.447
1r69	19%	0.524	0.534	0.416	0.363
1ubi	20%	0.146	0.585	0.351	0.252
1wit	22%	0.565	0.484	0.480	0.432
1ped	32%	0.627	0.646	0.585	0.482
2mvr	24%	0.538	0.494	0.225	0.219
4enl	41%	0.547	0.672	0.569	0.562

Table 6. Multiple alignment comparison among CLUSTALW, SAGA, TPQEAlign, and QEAlign with Ref4

Name	ID	CLUSTALX	SAGA	TPQEAlign	QEAlign
1pvsA	29%	F	0.250	0.352	0.273
1ckaA	19%	F	0.375	0.452	0.349
11kl	28%	1.000	F	0.429	0.354
1vcc	36%	0.485	0.485	0.584	0.524
2abk	30%	F	F	0.490	0.470
kinasel	28%	F	F	0.377	0.340

Table 7. Multiple alignment comparison among CLUSTALW, SAGA, TPQEAlign, and QEAlign with Ref5

Name	ID	CLUSTALX	SAGA	TPQEAlign	QEAlign
1pvsA	25%	0.429	0.429	0.270	0.301
1qpg	35%	1.000	0.521	0.605	0.594
1thm1	32%	0.412	0.765	0.483	0.413
1thm2	38%	0.774	0.774	0.554	0.539
S51	21%	0.938	0.831	0.363	0.353
S52	29%	1.000	1.000	0.573	0.542
kinasel	26%	0.806	0.484	0.520	0.503

5 Conclusions and Future Work

The above analysis follows that QEAlign and TPQEAlign are valid aligning methods. However, QEAlign is not a perfect algorithm for MSA. It does not perform for many test cases. In the future, some better Quantum-gates should be explored for MSA; a new termination criterion is adopted instead of the number of loops; COFFEE is employed as the objective function instead of SPS.

The quantum based techniques described above not only enrich our knowledge of how new computation model can be used for implementing evolutionary algorithm but demonstrate the feasibility of such methods and the novelty of the paradigm.

References

1. Serafim, B.: The many faces of sequence alignment. Briefings in Bioinformatics 6, 6–22 (2005)
2. Smith, T.F., Waterman, M.S.: Identification of common molecular subsequences. J. Mol. Biol. 147, 195–197 (1981)
3. Barton, G.J., Sternberg, J.E.: A strategy for the rapid multiple alignment of protein sequences. J. Mol. Biol. 198, 327–337 (1987)
4. Notredame, C., Higgins, D.G., Heringa, J.: T-Coffee: A novel method for fast and accurate multiple sequence alignment. Nucleic Acids Res. 302, 205–217 (2000)
5. Katoh, K., Misasa, K., Kuma, K., Miyata, T.: MAFFT: A novel method for rapid multiple sequence alignment based on fast Fourier transform. Nucleic Acids Res. 30, 3059–3066 (2002)
6. Edgar, R.C.: MUSCLE: Multiple sequence alignment with high accuracy and high throughput. Nucleic Acids Res. 32, 1792–1797 (2004)
7. Van, W.I., Lasters, I., Wyns, L.: Align-m - a new algorithm for multiple alignment of highly divergent sequences. Bioinformatics 20, 1428–1435 (2004)
8. Do, C.B., Brudno, M., Batzoglou, S.J.: ProbCons: Probabilistic consistency-based multiple alignment of amino acid sequences. Genome Research 15, 330–340 (2005)
9. Notredame, C., Desmond, G.H.: SAGA: sequence alignment by genetic algorithm. Bull. Math. Biol. 24, 1515–1524 (1996)
10. Burkhard, M.: DIALIGN: multiple DNA and protein sequence alignment at BibiServ. Nucleic Acids Res. 32, W33–W36 (2004)
11. KuK-Hyum, Jong-Hwan, K.: Quantum-inspired evolutionary algorithm for a class of combinatorial optimization. IEEE Transactions on Evolutionary Computation 6, 580–593 (2002)
12. Karplus, K., Hu, B.: Evaluation of protein multiple alignments by SAM-T99 using the Balibase multiple alignment test set. Bioinformatics 17, 713–720 (2001)

A Further Discussion on Convergence Rate of Immune Genetic Algorithm to Absorbed-State*

Xiaoping Luo[1], Wenyao Pang[1], and Ji Huang[2]

[1] Zhejiang University City College, Hangzhou,
310015, China
{luoxp,pangwy}@zucc.edu.cn
[2] Zhejiang Vocational College of Commerce, Hangzhou,
310053, China
hzhuangji@163.com

Abstract. A new Immune Genetic Algorithm (IGA) modeling was completed using Markov chain. The convergence rate of IGA to absorbed-state was deduced using norm and the analysis of transition probability matrix. According to the design and the performance of IGA, the detailed quantitative expressions of convergence rate to absorbed-state which include immune parameters in IGA was presented. Then the discussion was carried out about the effect of the parameters on the convergence rate. It was found that several parameters such as the population size, the population distribution, the string length etc. would all affect the optimization. The conclusions demonstrate that why IGA can maintain the diversity very well so that the optimization is very quick. This paper can also be helpful for the further study on the convergence rate of Immune Genetic Algorithm.

1 Introduction

In recent years heuristic optimization methods have been paid much attention to and widely used in practice. The genetic algorithms (GA's), which belong to one category of the best-known ones, have been proved to be particularly effective in generally difficult optimization problems. Although GA's have been widely used, there are still many problems left in their application.

Most heuristic algorithms have embodied mainly the bio mechanism of natural creatures and have superiority to deterministic ones for most problems that we deal with. Recently the researches in biology show that the immune system principles can give important edification on how to enhance the performance of GA's. To improve the performance of GA's, many researchers devoted themselves to the simulation of immune systems and proposed their opinions and results respectively [1~8]. In the study on immune genetic algorithms (IGA), the convergence is a very important factor. At

* The National Science Foundation, China(No.60405012), Scientific Research Project of Department of Education of Zhejiang(No.20061291) and Zhejiang University City College Scientific Research Project(No.J52305062016) supported this research.

Y. Wang, Y. Cheung, and H. Liu (Eds.): CIS 2006, LNAI 4456, pp. 22–28, 2007.

present, the conclusions on the convergence of the IGA are almost all based on the assumption that the time tends to infinite. But in fact, what really attracts us is the computation complexity, because it can give the relationship between the convergence rate of the algorithm and the computation time, which would be helpful for improving the performance of the optimization algorithm. But now it is rather scarce [9]. [9] gives some formulas on the convergence rate, but some parameters are still unclear on how to be calculated, there is still much work left unsolved. So further researches are needed. In this paper, we study how the immune parameters in IGA affect the convergence rate of IGA to absorbed-state and why the designed IGA can maintain the diversity rather well so as to prevent the premature convergence successfully.

2 Immune Genetic Algorithm

In this paper, the immune genetic algorithm(IGA) to be studied is the one proposed in [7~9], which is shown concisely as follows:

(1) Initialization.
  (1.1) Specify the population size N. Specify parameters in the following equations (1) and (2): the initial stimulation level of i-th antibody $A_i(0)$, the initial concentration of i-th antibody $a_i(0)$, the rate of interaction among antigens and antibodies a、β, the rate of natural death k_i, mutation probability p_m.
  (1.2) Generate N binary strings of length l, $X_1(0), X_2(0),\ldots, X_N(0)$, in uniform probability to form the initial population $X(0)=\{X_1(0), X_2(0),\ldots, X_N(0)\}$.
  (1.3) To keep better diversity, niche in introduced. Specify parameter K that is used to depict the number of small sub-populations, and then divide the initial population into K small populations with all the population sizes being $N_{sub} = \left\lfloor \frac{N}{K} \right\rfloor$. This is helpful to keep the diversity. According to [10], K should be a suitable value.
  (1.4) Specify the evolution termination criteria.
  (1.5) Set $n:=0$.

(2) Calculate the fitness of each individual in the population $X(0)$. If $X(n)|_{n=0}$ meets the given termination criteria, the calculation is stopped and the individual with the best fitness is selected as the solution, otherwise go to step 3 with $n:=n+1$.

(3) In the i-th sub-population
  (3.1) Immune Recombination: exchange 5 pairs of genes.
  (3.2) Immune Mutation: toggle each position in a string with a probability; the probability of IGA should be larger than that of Simple Genetic Algorithm(SGA).
  (3.3) Immune Concentration control and stimulation value control:

Referencing [11], we can get the following equations

$$A_i(n+1) = A_i(n) + (\alpha \frac{\sum_{j=1}^{N} \gamma_{ij} a_j(n)}{N} + \beta g_i - k_i) a_i(n) \cdot \quad (1)$$

$$a_i(n) = \frac{1}{1+\exp(0.5 - A_i(n))} \cdot \quad (2)$$

where γ_{ij} denotes synthesized stimulation between antibody i and j, which is calculated according to equations (1),(2). The synthesized stimulation coefficient between the antibody i and j are calculated referencing [9],[11]. The detailed calculation is: (a) XOR i,j and a new individual k is got; (b) transform k to a decimal integer $I(k)$; (c) $\gamma_{ij} = \frac{I(k)}{2\wedge(\text{strings of length } 1)-1}$. The meaning of other parameters is shown in [11].

(3.4) Immune Reproduction: process the copy in the offstring according to step (3.3).

(3.5) Immune Metabolism: $\left\lceil 5\% \frac{N}{K} \right\rceil$ of the least stimulated individuals are selected to be cleared away; then new individuals with high affinity are created to be added to population by the logistic equation in a function called chaos_create and added to the sub-population. The operation is as below: randomly choose one or some individuals and toggle a position of a string as a seed in the logistic equation then generate a sequence x_n.

(4) Immune Memory: After calculations to each sub-population, the maximal fitness value of the whole population is got. If maximal fitness value this time is bigger than that provided by existed antibodies in immune network, the corresponding individual is added to the table of memorized antibody as a new antibody, the corresponding maximal fitness value is added to the table describing antibody fitness value. Otherwise, the immune memory mechanism is started up to search better antibody with higher affinity using logistic equation. This operation is similar to (3.5) but the seeds are both the selected one from the current table and the selected one by mutation with a small probability.

(5) Terminate check. If the offspring $X(n+1)$ meets the given evolution termination criteria, the calculation is stopped, otherwise go to step 3 with $n:=n+1$.

3 Convergence Rate to Absorbed-State

Consider the process $\{ \vec{X}(n) \}_{n>0}$, where $\vec{X}(n)$ represents the population maintained by IGA at generation n. We firstly give some marks and definitions.

Mark 1. The population is marked as $\vec{X}$ and the individual is subscript i, e.g. X_i (i=1,2…N). The individual in immune memory is subscript 0, e.g. X_0. The fitness value is marked as $f(\bullet)$. $\overrightarrow{IX} \stackrel{\Delta}{=} [\ X_0 \quad \vec{X}\ ]$. The transition probability is marked as $P\{\bullet\}$.

Mark 2. $\text{IM\_max}(X_i,X_j) = X_k \qquad k = \arg\max_{m\in\{i,j\}}\{f(X_m)\}$

Mark 3. The satisfactory value of population

$$F(\vec{X}) = \max_{1\le i\le N}(f(X_i)) \qquad F(\overrightarrow{IX}) = \max(f(X_0),\ F(\vec{X}))$$

Considering IGA, we have

(1) Selection operator $T_S: S^N \to S$

$$P\{T_S(\vec{X})=X_i\} = \min\left(\frac{f(X_i)}{\sum_{k=1}^{N} f(X_k)}, a_i(n)\right).$$

(2) Recombination operator $T_R: S^N \to S^N \quad P\{T_R(\vec{X})=\vec{Y}\}$.

(3) Mutation operator $T_M: S \to S$

$$P\{T_M(X_i)=Y_i\} = p_m^{d(X_i,Y_i)}(1-p_m)^{l-d(X_i,Y_i)}.$$

Where $p_m>0$ is the mutation probability, $d(X_i, Y_i)$ is the Hamming distance between X_i and Y_i.

(4) Metabolism operator (Metadynamics Function) $T_{met}: S^N \to S^N$

$$P\{T_{met}(\vec{X}) = (\vec{X} \setminus \{X_{i_0}\}) \cup \text{IM\_max}(Y_{i_0}, X_{i_0})\}$$

$$\stackrel{\Delta}{=} P\{\vec{Y}(n)\} = \begin{cases} 1 & f(Y_{i_0}) \ge f(X_{i_0}) \\ 0 & f(Y_{i_0}) < f(X_{i_0}) \end{cases}.$$

Where Y_{i_0} =chaos_create (X_0) $i_0 = \min\{\arg\min_{1\le j\le N}\{f(X_j)\}\}$

(5) Immune response operator $T_{IR}: S \to S$

Assume $Y_0 = \text{IM\_max}(X_0,\ \text{chaos\_create}(X_0))$

Then $P\{T_{IR}(X_0) = Y_0\} = \begin{cases} 1 & f(Y_0) \ge f(X_0) \\ 0 & f(Y_0) < f(X_0) \end{cases}.$

In the whole population, let $v = \lceil 5\% N \rceil$,

$$P\{T(\vec{X}(n))_k = X_k(n+1)\}$$

$$= \sum_{Z_k\in S}\sum_{\vec{Z}\in S^N}\{P\{T_R(\vec{X}(n))_k = \vec{Z}(n)\} \bullet P\{T_S(\vec{Z}(n)=Z_k(n))\} \bullet P\{T_M(Z_k(n)) = X_k(n+1)\}\}.$$

Then

$$P(n) = P_n\{\overrightarrow{IX}(n+1) = \overrightarrow{IY} / \overrightarrow{IX}(n) = \overrightarrow{IX}\}$$

$$= \prod_{k=1}^{N}\{P\{T(\vec{X}(n))_k = X_k^{'}(n+1)\} \bullet \prod_{k=1}^{v} P\{T_{met}(X_k^{'}(n+1)) = X_k(n+1)\}_k \bullet P\{T_{IR}(X_0(n))\}\}.$$

From [9], we have

$$P(n) = P_n\{\overrightarrow{IY} / \overrightarrow{IX}\}\begin{cases} >0 & f(Y_{i_0}(n)) \geq f(X_{i_0}(n)), f(Y_0(n)) \geq f(X_0(n)) \\ =0 & else \end{cases} . \quad (3)$$

Assuming the state transition probability matrix $\boldsymbol{P} = \begin{bmatrix} I_\alpha & 0 \\ R & Q \end{bmatrix}$, π_k denotes the population probability distribution of IGA at k-th generation, $\pi*$ denotes the steady probability distribution of IGA in absorbed-state, where I_α denotes the process that the population is in absorbed-state, Q denotes the transient transition process, R denotes process that the population transfer from transient state to absorbed-state. Referencing [9], we have

$$\left\|\pi_0 P^k - \pi*\right\|_\infty \leq C\left\|Q\right\|_\infty^k = C(\max_i \sum_j |Q_{ij}|)^k . \quad (4)$$

Assume $\overrightarrow{IB}$ as the set of absorbed-stated populations. From [9], we have

$\exists \ 0 < \alpha = \inf_{\overrightarrow{IX} \cap \overrightarrow{IB} \neq \varnothing} P(\overrightarrow{IX}, \overrightarrow{IB}) < 1$, and $\max_i \sum_j |Q_{ij}| \leq 1 - \alpha$

so $\left\|\pi_0 P^k - \pi*\right\|_\infty \leq Const(\max_i \sum_j |Q_{ij}|)^k \leq Const(1-\alpha)^k$.

When the mutation probability is p_m, we have $P([X_0, \overrightarrow{X}], \overrightarrow{IB}) = P(\overrightarrow{X}, \overrightarrow{B})$.

Assuming $T = \inf\{k \geq 1 ; \overrightarrow{IX}(k) \in \overrightarrow{IB}\}$, the initial immune population $\overrightarrow{X}(0) = \overrightarrow{X} \notin \overrightarrow{B}$, so $\overrightarrow{IX}(0) = \overrightarrow{IX} \notin \overrightarrow{IB}$. $\forall \ k \geq 1$

$$P\{T = k\}$$
$$= \sum_{\overrightarrow{IY}_1, \ldots \overrightarrow{IY}_{k-1} \notin \overrightarrow{IB}} P(\overrightarrow{IX}, \overrightarrow{IY}_1) \cdot P(\overrightarrow{IY}_1, \overrightarrow{IY}_2) \cdots P(\overrightarrow{IY}_{k-2}, \overrightarrow{IY}_{k-1}) \cdot P(\overrightarrow{IY}_{k-1}, \overrightarrow{IB})$$

$$\leq P(\overrightarrow{IY}_{k-2}, \overrightarrow{IB}) \cdot \prod_{k=1}^{k-1} \max_i \sum_j |Q_{ij}| . \quad (5)$$

$\because \ 0 < \alpha = \inf_{\overrightarrow{IX} \cap \overrightarrow{IB} \neq \varnothing} P(\overrightarrow{IX}, \overrightarrow{IB}) < 1$

$\therefore \ 0 < \max_i \sum_j |Q_{ij}| \leq 1 - \alpha < 1$. According to (5),

$$\therefore \ P\{T = k\} \leq (1-\alpha)^{k-1} . \quad (6)$$

So the exception of time that the population enters the absorbed-state can be calculated as

$$E(T) = \sum_{k=1}^{\infty} kP(T = k) \leq \sum_{k=1}^{\infty} k(1-\alpha)^{k-1} = \sum_{k=1}^{\infty} \frac{d}{dk}[-(1-\alpha)^k] = \frac{1}{\alpha^2} .$$

$N_{sub} = \left\lfloor \frac{N}{K} \right\rfloor$. To a sub-population g, assuming q to be the number of alleles between immune sub-population and the absorbed-stated population of the same size. Thus the lower bound of the sub-population enters the absorbed-state is

$$\alpha_{sub} = p_m^q (1-p_m)^{lN_{sub}-q} .$$

Because the sub-population is in absorbed-state, now the selection operator becomes invalid.

Considering niche, the probability that denotes the other K-1 sub-populations enter the absorbed-state with sub-population g at the same is

$$P_{pc} = \prod_{h=1}^{K-1} \frac{\mathbf{P}_{N_{sub}}^{N_{sub}} \Big/ \prod_{i_v=1}^{N_{sub}^{(N_s')}} \mathbf{P}_{N_{sub}^{(i_v)}}^{N_{sub}^{(i_v)}}}{\prod_{i_u=1}^{N_{sub}} \left|\{0,1\}^l\right|} = \prod_{h=1}^{K-1} \frac{N_{sub}! \Big/ \prod_{i_v=1}^{N_{sub}^{(N_s')}} N_{sub}^{(i_v)}!}{2^{(l \cdot N_{sub})}} . \tag{7}$$

where $|\{0,1\}^l|$ denotes the size of the individual state space, $N_{sub}^{(i_v)}$ denotes the number of the same individual is the sun-population. What's more, to $N_{sub}^{(i_v)}$ we have

$$\sum_{i_v=1}^{N_{sub}^{(N_s')}} N_{sub}^{(i_v)} \le N_{sub} \quad i_v = \left[1, 2, \cdots, N_{sub}^{(N_s')}\right].$$

$$\therefore \ \alpha = \alpha_{sub} \cdot P_{pc} = p_m^q (1-p_m)^{lN_{sub}-q} \cdot \prod_{h=1}^{K-1} \frac{N_{sub}! \Big/ \prod_{i_v=1}^{N_{sub}^{(N_s')}} N_{sub}^{(i_v)}!}{2^{(l \cdot N_{sub})}} \tag{8}$$

Thus using (8),we can get the two important criterions: $\left\|\pi_0 P^k - \pi^*\right\|_\infty \le Const(1-\alpha)^k$ and

$$E(T) = \frac{1}{\alpha^2} .$$

From (8), it can be seen that larger the size of the population is, the larger the size of the sub-population is, so the better the diversity can be maintained, the smaller the parameter α is. The introduction of niche can make the parameter P_{pc} be very small, which can also be helpful to make α become small. From (8), it can also be seen that larger the string length is, the smaller the parameter α is. As a result, the smaller the parameter α is, the larger the exception of time that $\left\|\pi_0 P^k - \pi^*\right\|_\infty$ and $E(T)$ are, *i.e.* the harder the population enters the absorbed-state. This is a demonstration on the fact that the diversity can be maintained very well in IGA so that IGA can speed up the optimization.

4 Conclusions

In this paper, we carried out a further analysis on the convergence rate of IGA to absorbed-state when niche is introduced. From the conclusions it can be seen that larger the population size is or larger the string length is, more generations are needed for the population converges to the absorbed-state. It can demonstrate that why IGA can maintain the diversity very well so that the optimization is very quick. According to this paper, we can see that this algorithm (IGA) is superior and can be used in practice more effectively. This paper can also be helpful for the further study on the convergence of Immune Genetic Algorithm.

References

1. Krishnakumar, K., Neidhoefer, J.: Immunised Neurocontrol. Expert Systems With Application 13(3), 201–214 (1997)
2. Quagliarella, D., Periauz, J., Poloni, C., Winter, G. (eds.): Genetic Algorithms in Engineering and Computer Science, pp. 85–104. John Wiley & Sons, New York (1997)
3. Lee, D.-W., Sim, K.-B.: Artificial Immune Network-based cooperative control in Collective Autonomous Mobile Robots, Proceedings. In: 6th IEEE International Workshop on Robot and Human Communication. pp. 58–63 (1997)
4. Dasgupta, D.: Artificial Immune Systems and Their Applications. Springer, Heidelberg (1999)
5. Lei, W., Li-cheng, J.: The Immune Genetic Algorithm and Its Converge, In: 1998 Fourth International Conference on Signal Processing Proceedings, vol. 2, pp. 1347–1350 (1998)
6. Chun, J.S., Jung, H.K., Hahn, S.Y.: A Study on Comparison of Optimization Performance between Immune Algorithm and other Heuristic Algorithms. IEEE Transactions on Magnetics 34(5), 2972–2975 (1998)
7. Xiaoping, L., Wei, W.: A New Optimization Method on Immunogenetics. ACTA Electronica Sinica 31(1), 59–64 (2003)
8. Xiaoping, L., Wei, W.: A New Immune Genetic Algorithm and Its Application in Redundant Manipulator Path Planning. Journal of Robotic Systems 21(3), 141–151 (2004)
9. Xiaoping, L., Wei, W.: Discussion on the Convergence Rate of Immune Genetic Algorithm. In: Proceedings of the World Congress on Intelligent Control and Automation (WCICA), WCICA Jun 15-19 2004, pp. 2275–2278 (2004)
10. Xiaoping, L., Wei, W., Xiaorun, L.: A study on immune genetic algorithm and its performance. In: 7th World Multiconference on Systemics, Cybernetics and Informatics, Orlando, Florida, July 27-30, 2003, pp. 147–151 (2003)
11. Hunt, J.E., Cooke, D.E.: An Adaptive, Distributed Learning System based on Immune System, In: 1995 IEEE International Conference on Systems, Man and Cybernetics. Intelligent Systems for the 21st Century, vol. 3, pp. 2494–2499 (October 1995)
12. Lin, H., Kujun, W.: The Convergence Rate Estimation of Genetic Algorithm. Systems Enginering-Theroy Methodology Application 8(3), 22–26 (1999)
13. Hong, P., Xinghua, W.: The Convergence Rate Estimation of Genetic Algorithm with Elitist. Chinese Science Bulletin 42(2), 144–147 (1997)

Linear Programming Relax-PSO Hybrid Bound Algorithm for a Class of Nonlinear Integer Programming Problems*

Yuelin Gao[1,2], Chengxian Xu[2], and Jimin Li[1]

[1] Department of Information and Computation Science,
Northwest Second National College, Yin Chuan 750021, China
gaoyuelin@263.net

[2] School of Finance and Economics, Xi'an Jiaotong University,
Xi'an Jiaotong University, Xi'an 710049, China
mxxu@mail.xjtu.edu.cn

Abstract. The paper researches a class of nonlinear integer programming problems the objective function of which is the sum of the products of some nonnegative linear functions in the given rectangle and the constraint functions of which are all linear as well as strategy variables of which are all integer ones. We give a linear programming relax-PSO hybrid bound algorithm for solving the problem. The lower bound of the optimal value of the problem is determined by solving a linear programming relax which is obtained through equally converting the objective function into the exponential-logarithmic composite function and linearly lower approximating each exponential function and each logarithmic function over the rectangles. The upper bound of the optimal value and the feasible solution of it are found and renewed with particle swarm optimization (PSO). It is shown by the numerical results that the linear programming relax-PSO hybrid bound algorithm is better than the branch-and-bound algorithm in the computational scale and the computational time and the computational precision and overcomes the convergent difficulty of PSO.

1 Introduction

Integer programming problems are encountered in a variety of areas, such as capital budgeting [6], computer-aided layout design [7], portfolio selection [8], site selection for electric message systems [9] and shared fixed costs [10] etc. The methods for solving the Integer programming problems have mainly method of dynamic programming, branch and bound method, the method of computational intelligence [1,2,3,11,12, 13].

* The work is supported by the Foundations of Post-doctoral Science in China (grants 2006041001) and National Natural Science in Ningxia (2006), and by the Science Research Projects of National Committee in China and the Science Research Project of Ningxia's Colleges and Universities in 2005.

Y. Wang, Y. Cheung, and H. Liu (Eds.): CIS 2006, LNAI 4456, pp. 29–35, 2007.

In the paper, we consider a class of nonlinear integer programming problems below:

$$\begin{cases} \min \phi(x) = \sum_{i=1}^{t} \prod_{j=1}^{p} (c_{ij}^T x + d_{ij}) \\ \text{s.t.} \;\; Ax \le b, \\ \qquad x \in \; Z^n \cap [l, u]. \end{cases} \tag{1}$$

where $t, p_i \in Z_+ - \{0\}, \prod_{i=1}^{t} p_i \ge 2, p = \prod_{i=1}^{t} p_i; d_{ij} \in R_+, c_{ij} = (c_{ij1}, c_{ij2}, \cdots, c_{ijn})^T \in R_+^n$, in $R = [l, u], A = (a_{ij})_{m \times n} \in R^{m \times n}, b \in R$. Z is noted as the set which consist of all the integers, $l, u \in Z^n$.

We will give a new linear programming relax-PSO hybrid bound algorithm of the problem (1) by making use of branch-and-bound method (BBA) and PSO. It will be shown by the numerical results that the algorithm to be proposed is better than BBA in the computational scale and the computational time and the computational precisionand that it overcomes the convergent difficulty of PSO. In Section 2, we give a linear relaxed approximation so as to determine a lower bound of the optimal value of the problem (1). In Section 3, we give a PSO algorithm based on the penalty function of the problem (1) so as to find and renew the feasible solutions and the upper bound of the problem (1). In Section 4, the numerical computation is done so as to test the property of the proposed algorithm. Section 5 is conclusions.

2 Linear Programming Relaxed Approximation

Firstly, we convert equally the problem (1) into the non-linear integer programming problem below:

$$\begin{cases} \min \phi = \sum_{i=1}^{t} exp(\sum_{j=1}^{p_i} log(c_{ij}^T x + d_{ij})) \\ \text{s.t.} \;\; Ax \le b, \\ \qquad x \in \; Z^n \cap [l, u]. \end{cases} \tag{2}$$

Secondly,the problem(2) is continuously relaxed to the problem below:

$$\begin{cases} \min \phi = \sum_{i=1}^{t} exp(\sum_{j=1}^{p_i} log(\sum_{k=1}^{n} c_{ijk} x_k + d_{ij})) \\ \text{s.t.} \;\; Ax \le b, \\ \qquad x \in [l, u]. \end{cases} \tag{3}$$

For $i = 1, 2, \cdots, t, j = 1, 2, \cdots, p_i$, let $\phi_{ij} = \log y_{ij}$,where $y_{ij} = c_{ij}^T x + d_{ij} = \sum_{k=1}^{n} c_{ij} x_k + d_{ij}$. From $x \in [l, u], y_{ij} \in [l_{ij}, u_{ij}]$,where

$$l_{ij} = \sum_{k=1}^{n} min\{c_{ijk} l_k, c_{ijk} u_k\} + d_{ij}, \tag{4a}$$

$$l_{ij} = \sum_{k=1}^{n} max\{c_{ijk}l_k, c_{ijk}u_k\} + d_{ij}, \tag{4b}$$

Because $log(y_{ij})$ is a strictly increase concave function in $(0, +\infty)$, it can be seen that the convex envelope of ϕ_{ij} over $[l_{ij}, u_{ij}]$ is a line which is through two points $(l_{ij}, log(l_{ij}))$,$(u_{ij}, log(u_{ij}))$, i.e. the line is the best lower approximate linear function of ϕ_{ij} in $[l_{ij}, u_{ij}]$:

$$z_{ij} = \frac{log(u_{ij}) - log(l_{ij})}{u_{ij} - l_{ij}}(y_{ij} - l_{ij}) + log(l_{ij}) = \overline{c}_{ij}y_{ij} + \overline{d}_{ij}. \tag{5}$$

where

$$\overline{c}_{ij} = \frac{log(u_{ij}) - log(l_{ij})}{u_{ij} - l_{ij}}, \tag{6}$$

$$\overline{d}_{ij} = \frac{u_{ij}log(l_{ij}) - l_{ij}log(u_{ij})}{u_{ij} - l_{ij}}. \tag{7}$$

Let $\overline{l}_i = \sum_{j=1}^{p_i} log(l_{ij}), \overline{u}_i = \sum_{j=1}^{p_i} log(u_{ij}), \overline{z}_i = \sum_{j=1}^{p_i} log(z_{ij})$,$\psi_i = exp(z_i)$. Because $exp(z_i)$ is a strictly increasing convex function in $(-\infty, +\infty)$, so the best lower approximate linear function of ψ_i on z_i in $[\overline{l}_i, \overline{u}_i]$ is a line through two points $(\overline{l}_i, exp(\overline{l}_i))$ and $(\overline{u}_i, exp(\overline{u}_i))$ and tangents with $\psi_i = exp(z_i)$, i.e. it is the linear function $ll_i(z_i) = \overline{c}_i z_i + \overline{d}_i$,where

$$\overline{c}_i = \frac{exp(\overline{u}_i) - exp(\overline{l}_i)}{\overline{u}_i - \overline{l}_i}, \tag{8}$$

$$\overline{d}_i = \frac{exp(\overline{u}_i) - exp(\overline{l}_i)}{\overline{u}_i - \overline{l}_i}(1 - log(\frac{exp(\overline{u}_i) - exp(\overline{l}_i)}{\overline{u}_i - \overline{l}_i},)). \tag{9}$$

So, we obtain a lower approximate linear function of ψ on $z = (z_1, z_1, \cdots, z_t)$ over $[\overline{l}_i, \overline{u}_i]$ where $\overline{l} = (\overline{l}_1, \overline{l}_2, \cdots, \overline{l}_t,)$ and $\overline{u} = (\overline{u}_1, \overline{u}_2, \cdots, \overline{u}_t,)$:

$$\omega = \sum_{i=1}^{t} ll_i(z_i). \tag{10}$$

Thus, the linear programming relaxed approximation of the problem(1) is

$$\begin{cases} \min \omega = \sum_{i=1}^{t} ll_i(z_i) \\ \text{s.t.} \;\; Ax \leq b, \\ \qquad z_i = \sum_{j=1}^{p_i} z_{ij}, i = 1, 2, \cdots, t, \\ \qquad z_{ij} = \overline{c}_{ij}y_{ij} + \overline{d}_{ij}, i = 1, 2, \cdots, t, j = 1, 2, ..., p_i, \\ \qquad y_{ij} = c_{ij}^T y_{ij} + d_{ij}, i = 1, 2, \cdots, t, j = 1, 2, ..., p_i, \\ \qquad x \in [l, u]. \end{cases} \tag{11}$$

Obviously, the optional value of the problem(11) is sure to be a lower bound of the problem(1).

3 A PSO Algorithm Based on The Penalty Function

The particle swarm optimization algorithm (PSO) is a kind of computational intelligent which is put forward by Kenney and Eberhart etc. in 1995 and has global optimization property but is not proven in convergence[11,12,13]. We only give a PSO algorithm based on the penalty function.

Firstly,we give a penalty function of the problem(1) below:

$$p(x) = \phi(x) + M(\sum_{i=1}^{m} \mid min\{0, b_i - \sum_{j=i}^{n} a_{ij}x_j\} \mid) \tag{12}$$

where the penalty coefficient $M > 0$ can be any number large enough.

N_c represents the biggest iteration of PSO, M_c represents the particle number in particle swarm, p_{sb} represents the best position by which a particle swarm has gone so far and p_{gb} represents the best position by which all the x_{gb} represents the best feasible position in the particle swarm at present. V_{max}^i represents the biggest velocity of a particle x_i.

The PSO algorithm based on the penalty function(IP-PSO) is described below:

Step1. Set $t = 1, M = 1000, N_c = 100$.Produce randomly a particle swarm in Scale M_c.The initial position of each particle x_i is $x_{ij}(0)(j = 1, 2, \cdots, n)$ and the initial velocity is $v_{ij}(j = 1, 2, \cdots, n)$, compute each particle's fitness and determine p_{sb} and p_{gb} and x_{gb}.

Step2. Set $t = t + 1$. For each particle from the next formula:

$$\begin{cases} v_{ij} = wv_{ij} + c_i r_i(p_{ij} - x_{ij}) + c_2 r_2(p_{gj} - x_{ij}) \\ x_{ij} = x_{ij} + v_{ij} \\ i = 1, 2, \cdots, M_c, j = 1, 2, \cdots, n. \end{cases} \tag{13}$$

where $w \in [0.2, 1.2]$ is inertia weight, $c_1 = 2, c_2 = 1.7$ are acceleration constants, r_1, r_2 are two random functions over [0,1].If $v_{ij} > V_{max}^i$ in (13), then $v_{ij} = V_{max}^i$. Renew p_{sb} and p_{gb} as well as x_{gb}.

Step3. If $t = N_c$, outcome the best particle $x_{opt} = x_{gb}$; else, go to Step2.

All the coefficients in the IP-PSO are determined through the numerical test in Section 5 and the IP-PSO can find better feasible solution and better upper bound of the problem(1).

4 Description of Linear Programming Relax-PSO Hybrid Bound Algorithm

In the section,we describe a linear programming relax-PSO hybrid bound algorithm (BB-PSO-HA). In the algorithm,branching procedure is simple integer rectangle two-partitioning one and lower bounding procedure needs solving the problem(11) in each sub-rectangle as well as upper bounding procedure needs the algorithm IP-PSO.

BB-PSO-HA

Step0.(Initialization) $k := 0, \Omega = \{R\}$. Solve the problem(12), and determine the lower bound LB of the problem(1). Use Algorithm IP-PSO to determine the best feasible solution x_{best} so far.

Step$k$.($k = 1, 2, \cdots$)

k1(termination) If $\Omega = \Phi$ or $\frac{UB-LB}{UB} < Eps$, then outcome $z_{opt}, Optv = UB$.

k2(Selection Rule) In Ω, find a rectangle R_k such that $LB(R_k)$.

k3(Branching Rule) Partition R_k into two sub-rectangle with rectangle simple two equally-partition technique,and reduce each sub-rectangle to make vertex point integer, and obtain two integer sub-rectangle R_{k1} and R_{k2}. Set $\Omega = (\Omega - R_k) \cup \{R_{k+1,1}, R_{k+1,2}\}$

k4(Lower Bounding) Solve the problem(11) in $R_{k+1,1}$ and $R_{k+1,2}$ respectively so as to renew LB.

k5(Upper Bounding) Solve the problem(1) in $R_{k+1,1}$ and $R_{k+1,2}$ respectively with IP-PSO to renew x_{best} and $UB = \phi(x_{best})$.

k6(deleting Rule) $\Omega = \Omega - \{R \in \Omega : LB(R) \geq UB\}$, $k = k + 1$, go to k_1.

5 Numerical Analysis

In the problem(1), let $t = 1, p_1 = n, c_{ij}^n x = c_i x_i$, then, we obtain the next example:

$$\begin{cases} \min \omega = \prod_{i=1}^{n} (c_i x_i + d_i) \\ \text{s.t. } \sum_{i=1}^{n} a_i x_i \leq b, \\ \qquad x_i \in [1, 20], \\ \qquad x_i \in Z, \\ \qquad i = 1, 2, \cdots, n. \end{cases} \tag{14}$$

where $c_i \in [-20, 20], d_i \in [21, 52], a_i \in [0, 50], b = 1.2sum(a) = \sum_{i=1}^{n} a_i$.

The procedures of BBA and BB-PSO-HA are compiled with Matlab7.0.1 in personal computer DELL-P4-Intel1865-512MB. We produce randomly twenty examples for the problems (14) in n=60,100,150,200,300,500,800,1000,1500,2000. and solve the examples with BBA and BB-PSO-HA respectively. The results of the numerical computation are seen at Table1-Table2 where Ex1=$Eps_1 = 10^{-4}$ and Ex2=$Eps_2 = 10^{-5}$. "Iteration" and "Cputime" are noted as the iteration times and computational time respectively. "Avg, Max, Min" are noted as the iteration times and computational time of "average, maximum, minimum" respectively.

It is shown by the numerical results from Table 1 and Table 2 that BB-PSO-HA is better than BBA in computational scale, computational time and computational precision.

Table 1.

Ex1	BBA					
	Iteration			Cputime(Seconds)		
n	Avg	Max	Min	Avg	Max	MIN
60	7000	10000	1	472.2	1035.8	0.09
100	7580	10000	1	674.9	1331.5	0.07
150	7211	10000	1	844.7	2574.9	0.15
200	6776	10000	1	840.5	3206.8	0.29
300	8366	10000	1	1793.9	5450	0.2
500	6298	10000	3	2405.8	8278.6	0.64
800	5288	10000	2	4491.6	8611	0.98
1000	4357	10000	432	4143.4	22135	181
1500	*	*	*	*	*	*
*	*	*	*	*	*	*

Table 2.

Ex2	BBA-PSO					
	Iteration			Cputime(Seconds)		
n	Avg	Max	Min	Avg	Max	MIN
60	25	166	1	274.9	1814.8	9.8
100	8	75	1	142.8	1488.4	17
150	16	164	1	449.3	4546	30
180	11	175	1	171.9	2379.8	30
200	18	160	1	635.7	5797.7	32.5
300	14	178	1	451.2	3947.8	49.5
500	15	144	1	1017.3	9394.1	65.3
800	4	43	1	594.2	6732.6	137.5
1000	18	256	1	3493.1	50020	133.2
1500	2	5	1	297.8	1003.2	199.5
2000	5	50	1	3057.3	41250	271.2

6 Conclusion

We give a new linear programming relax-PSO hybrid bound algorithm for solving a class of nonlinear integer programming problems. The lower bound of the optimal value of the problem is determined by solving a linear programming relax which is obtained through equally converting the objective function into the exponential-logarithmic composite function and lower approximating each exponential function and each logarithmic function with the best linear function. The upper bound of the optimal value and the feasible solution of it are found and renewed with PSO.

It is shown by the numerical results that the linear programming relax-PSO hybrid bound algorithm is better than BBA in computational scale, computational time and computational precision and overcomes the convergent difficulty of PSO.

References

1. Nemhauser, G.L., Wolsey, L.A.: Integer and Combinatorial Optimization. John Wiley and sons, New York (1988)
2. Kuno, T.: Solving a class of multiplicative programs with 0-1 knapsack constraints. Journal of Optimization Theory and Applications 103, 121–125 (1999)
3. Barrientos, O., Correa, R., Reyes, P., Valdebenito, A.: A brand and bound method for solving integer separable concave problems. Computational Optimization and Applications 26, 155–171 (2003)
4. Horst, R., Tuy, H.: Global optimization, deterministic approaches. Springer, Heidelberg (1996)
5. Gao, Y.L., Xu, C.X, Wang, Y.J., Zhang, L.S.: A new two-level linear relaxed bound method for geometric programming problem. Applied Mathematics and Computation 164, 117–131 (2005)
6. Laughunn, D.J.: Quadratic binary programming with applications to capital-budgeting problem. Operations Research 14, 454–461 (1970)
7. Krarup, J., Pruzan, P.M.: Computer-aided layout design. Mathematical Programming Study 9, 75–94 (1978)
8. Markovitz, H.M.: Portfolio selection. Wily, New York (1978)
9. Witzgall, C.: Mathematical method of site selection for Electric Message Systems(EMS), NBS Internet Report (1975)
10. Rhys, J.: A selection problem of shared fixed costs on network flow. Management Science 17, 200–207 (1970)
11. Eberhart, R.C., Shi, Y.H.: Particle swarm optimization: development, applications and resources. In: Proceedings of the IEEE International Conference on Evolutionary Computation, pp. 81–86 (2002)
12. Laskari, E.C., Parsopoulos, K.E., Vrahatis, M.N.: Particle swarm optimization for integer programming. In: Proceedings of the IEEE International Conference on Evolutionary Computation, pp. 1582–1587 (1978)
13. Eberhart, R.C., Shi, Y.H.: Comparison between genetic algorithms and particle swarm optimization: development, applications and resources, Evolutionary Programming, pp. 611–615 (1998)

An Improved Ant Colony System and Its Application*

Xiangpei Hu, Qiulei Ding, Yongxian Li, and Dan Song

Institute of Systems Engineering
Dalian University of Technology, Dalian, China, 116023
drhxp@dlut.edu.cn

Abstract. The Ant Colony System (ACS) algorithm is vital in solving combinatorial optimization problems. However, the weaknesses of premature convergence and low efficiency greatly restrict its application. In order to improve the performance of the algorithm, the Hybrid Ant Colony System (HACS) is presented by introducing the pheromone adjusting approach, combining ACS with saving and interchange methods, etc. Furthermore, the HACS is applied to solve the Vehicle Routing Problem with Time Windows (VRPTW). By comparing the computational results with the previous findings, it is concluded that HACS is an effective and efficient way to solve combinatorial optimization problems.

1 Introduction

ACS is an evolutionary computation technique developed by M.Dorigo et al. [1-3] in the 1990s, inspired by nature's real ant colonies. Compared with the existing heuristics, ACS possesses the characteristics of positive feedback and distributed computing, and can easily combine with other heuristic algorithms. Recently, ACS has been proposed to solve different types of combinatorial optimization problems. In particular, ACS has been shown to be an efficient algorithm in solving the NP-hard combinatorial optimization problems, large-scale complicated combinatorial optimization models, distributed control and clustering analysis problems [4-6].

However, there are some weaknesses of ACS in dealing with combinatorial optimization problems. Firstly, the search always gets trapped in local optimum. Secondly, it needs a lot of computational time to reach the solution. In order to avoid these weaknesses, Thomas Stuztle et al. [7] presented MAX-MIN Ant System and QIN et al. [8] proposed an improved Ant Colony Algorithm based on adaptively adjusting pheromone. By pheromone adjusting, these algorithms effectively prevented the search process from becoming trapped in local optimum. However, the speed of convergence was influenced because the pheromone adjusting required a lot of computational time. Bullnheimer et al. [9] introduced an improved Ant Colony Algorithm to solve Vehicle Routing Problems. This succeeded at improving search speeds but there was only a slight improvement in the efficiency of search solutions.

* Supported by: National Natural Science Foundation of China (No. 70571009, 70171040 and 70031020 (key project)), Key Project of Chinese Ministry of Education (No. 03052), Ph.D. Program Foundation of Ministry of Education of China (No. 20010141025).

Y. Wang, Y. Cheung, and H. Liu (Eds.): CIS 2006, LNAI 4456, pp. 36–45, 2007.

Gambardella et al. [10] presented the Multiple Ant Colony System, which was organized with a hierarchy of artificial ant colonies designed to successively optimize a multiple objective function: the first colony minimized the number of vehicles, while the second colony minimized the distances traveled. Cooperation between colonies was performed by exchanging information through pheromone updating. Computational results indicated that the speed of convergence was improved but the obtained solutions also had not been greatly improved. Reimann et al. [11] put forward a Divide-Ants algorithm, which solved vehicle routing problems combined with saving based AS, Sweep algorithm and Tabu Search. The basic principle was to divide the problem into several disjointed sub-problems based on an initial solution, each of which was then solved by an ACS process. This algorithm had great advantages when it was used to solve large-scale problems, but its search process was complicated, which prevented its extended application. Bell et al. [12] proposed the improved ACS combined with the 2-interchange method and a candidate list. The search speed of this algorithm was faster, but when it was used to solve large-scale problem, the qualities of solutions was worse.

It is clear that great achievements have been made in improving the algorithm. But the premature and inefficient problems are still ready to be solved. Therefore, this paper tries to provide an improved Ant Colony System. The remainder of this paper is organized as follows. Firstly, section 2 presents the high searching efficiency and basic principles of HACS. Secondly, section 3 constructs the mathematic model of VRPTW, describes the steps for solving VRPTW and then compares the computational results with previous findings in order to prove the suitability of the proposed algorithm. Finally, section 4 provides conclusions and directions for future research.

2 The Improvement of ACS Algorithm

In order to prevent the search process from getting trapped in local optimum and improve the convergence efficiency of ACS, the Hybrid Ant Colony System (HACS) is presented by introducing the pheromone adjusting approach, combining ACS with saving and interchange methods, etc.

2.1 The Adjustment of the Pheromone

In consideration of the importance of the information interchange between colonies by pheromones, this part focuses on four aspects of the pheromone adjustment to avoid the research becoming trapped in local optimum. Details are as follows:

(1) In ACS algorithm, the pheromone given by the colonies does not always indicate the optimal direction, and the pheromone deviated from optimal solution has the potential to be enhanced, which prevents the rest of the ants from finding a better solution. It is realized that due to the influence of positive feedback, the random choice of the parameters used in ACS is not good enough to prevent the search from getting trapped in local optimum. Therefore, definite and random selection must be combined with ACS to improve the global optimization capability, which is carried

out by adjusting the pheromone and enhancing the random selection probabilities under the circumstances of the determined evolutionary direction.

(2) At every edge, the maximum or minimum pheromone trails may lead to premature convergence of the search during the process of pheromone updating. Therefore, HACS imposes explicit limits τ_{min} and τ_{max} on the minimum and maximum pheromone trails to make all pheromone trails τ_{ij} satisfy $\tau_{\min} \le \tau_{ij} \le \tau_{\max}$, which is based on the idea of MAX-MIN Ant System [13][14]. Meanwhile, the pheromone trails are deliberately initialized to τ_{max}, which helps to achieve higher level exploration of solutions at the beginning of the search. Additionally, in cases where the pheromone trails differ greatly, the idea of computing average pheromone trails between τ_{ij} and τ_{max} is absorbed, which will play a significant role in obtaining the new search routes.

(3) It is difficult for the ACS algorithm to solve large-scale problems because of the existence of the trail evaporation $1-\rho$. If $1-\rho$ is convergent to zero, the global optimization capability will decline because the edges may be chosen repeatedly. The larger $1-\rho$ is, the better the global optimization capability will be. But if so, the convergence speed of the algorithm will be slowed down. Therefore, this paper suggests that a dynamic $1-\rho$ value rather than a constant value is adopted.

(4) Another approach to prevent ACS from getting trapped in local optimum is to change the local optimal solution randomly by introducing a disaster operator. The design of the disaster operator is similar to the mutation of the genetic algorithm. By greatly decreasing pheromone trails in some parts of local optimization routes, the algorithm is able to avoid premature convergence and search for a better solution. The experiments indicate that the introduction of the disaster operator is an effective method of eliminating local optimization. The routes of disasters are decided by small random probabilities in a similar way to the genetic algorithm. Whilst the distribution of the pheromone in the previous routes would be destroyed by too many occurrences of disasters, which increases the probability of leading the research results in the opposite direction.

2.2 Combining ACS with Saving and Interchange Methods

ACS is a strong coupling algorithm for the characteristics of combination with other heuristics. So the speed of convergence will be greatly improved by combining with Savings algorithm and λ-interchange methods, etc. in dealing with VRTTW.

The Savings algorithm is a simple and efficient way to solve VRPTW proposed by Clarke and Wright [15] in 1964. Starting from an initial solution, where all customers i are assigned to separate tours *0–i–0*, the saving values of combining any two customers i and j are computed as

$$s_{ij} = d_{i0} + d_{0j} - d_{ij} \tag{1}$$

Where d_{i0} corresponds to the distance between the customer i and the depot 0. d_{0j} denotes the distance between the depot 0 and the customer j. d_{ij} is the distance between the customer i and j. The resulting saving values are then sorted in decreasing order. Iteratively, customers are combined with partial tours according to the sorted savings list until no more combinations are feasible. A combination is infeasible if it exceeds the capacity of the vehicle.

The λ-interchange local search method is also an efficient heuristics introduced by Osman and Christofides [16]. Its basic procedure is conducted by interchanging customer nodes among the initial feasible solutions. During the interchange process, only improved solutions are accepted if the interchange results in the reduction of the total cost and satisfaction of the vehicle capacity.

Moreover, in ACS algorithm, it will take a long time to compute the transition probabilities of all unsearched nodes when ants select the next node j from node i. By analyzing the comparatively complicated map with several nodes, the node j should be close to node i [17]. So this method of choosing the nearest node was adopted to enormously improve the convergence speed by computing the transition probabilities of only those nodes nearby the chosen node.

3 Application of HACS to VRPTW Model

3.1 Construction of VRPTW Model

In this paper, the Vehicle Routing Problem with Soft Time Windows will be solved. The parameters and variables are described as follows: n is the number of the customers who must be served by a unique depot. Each customer asks for the quantity q_i of goods ($i = 1,..., n$) and the vehicle of capacity Q is available for delivering goods to several customers. Each customer is visited only once and the total tour demand is Q at most. The goal is to find a set of tours of punctual arrival and minimum total cost. The vehicles will be punished if they do not arrive according to the demand of the customers.

In order to set the VRPTW model, we must first define the following notations.

v_i: when $i=0$, it denotes the depot. In all other cases it represents customers

k: k denotes the vehicle

C_{ij}: transportation cost from v_i to v_j

Q: capacity of vehicle

x_{ijk}: binary variable, =1 if vehicle k goes from customer v_i to v_j

y_{ik}: binary variable, =1 if v_i is served by vehicle k

$[ET_i, LT_i]$: time window of v_i, which ET_i is the earliest service time and LT_i is the latest service time of v_i

$p_i(S_i)$: punishment function. If vehicles reach v_i before ET_i, the cost will be spent for the waiting time of the vehicles; whereas if vehicles reach v_i after LT_i, the vehicles will be punished for the delayed services. So $p_i(S_i)$ is defined as follows:

$$p_i(S_i) = \begin{cases} a_i(ET_i - S_i), & S_i < ET_i \\ 0, & ET_i \le S_i \le LT_i \\ b_i(S_i - LT_i), & S_i > LT_i \end{cases} \tag{2}$$

Where a_i and b_i are punishment coefficients given larger values for the significant customers or the customers who have the strict rules regarding time.

Then the mathematical model is obtained below:

$$MinZ = \sum_{i=0}^{n}\sum_{j=0}^{n}\sum_{k=1}^{K} C_{ij}x_{ijk} + \sum_{i=1}^{n} p_i(S_i) \tag{3}$$

Subject to:

$$\sum_{i=1}^{n} q_i y_{ik} \le Q \quad k=1,2,\ldots\ldots,K \tag{4}$$

$$\sum_{k=1}^{K} y_{0k} = K \tag{5}$$

$$\sum_{k=1}^{K} y_{ik} = 1 \quad i=1,2,\ldots\ldots,n \tag{6}$$

$$\sum_{i=1}^{n} x_{i0k} = 1 \quad k=1,2,\ldots\ldots,K \tag{7}$$

$$\sum_{i=0}^{n} x_{ijk} = y_{jk} \quad j=1,2,\ldots\ldots,n;\ k=1,2,\ldots\ldots,K \tag{8}$$

$$\sum_{i=0}^{n} x_{ijk} = y_{jk} \quad i=1,2,\ldots\ldots,n;\ k=1,2,\ldots\ldots,K \tag{9}$$

In this model, the objective function (3) minimizes the total cost of routing. Constraint (4) ensures that the total demand of each vehicle route does not exceed vehicle capacity. Constraint (5) assures that all vehicle routes begin at the depot. Constraint (6) guarantees that every customer is visited exactly once by exactly one vehicle and that all customers are visited. Constraint (7) ensures that all vehicle routes end at the depot. Constraints (8) and (9) show the relation of variables.

3.2 Solution Steps of HACS

According to the Section 2, the steps for solving VRPTW of HACS can be described as follows:

Step 1: Initialize every controlling parameter, presume the optimal solution L_{global} based on the customer data, define the repeated counter as nc=0, put m ants on the depot, and make a candidate list based on the distance to n nodes. Both the size of the candidate list was determined by test). m can be given a larger value in order to extend combination scale and acquire feasible solution more easily. If the present number of ants can not ensure all customers visited in the search process, m can be increased.

Step 2: Find out all nodes that have never been visited in the candidate list and select next node j to be visited according to formula (10):

$$j = \begin{cases} \arg\max_{j \notin tabu_k} [\tau_{ij}(t)]^{\alpha}[\eta_{ij}(t)]^{\beta}[\delta_{ij}]^{\theta}[\mu_{ij}]^{\gamma} & , \ if \quad q \le p_t \\ \text{random} \quad j \notin tabu_k & , \ otherwise \end{cases} \tag{10}$$

Where $tabu_k(k=1,2,\ldots,m)$ is the tabu table which records all the visited nodes by ant k. τ_{ij} and η_{ij} represent the density of pheromones and visibility (the reciprocal of distance d_{ij} between two nodes) respectively. δ_{ij}, the parameter of time windows match degree, is decided by formula (11), in which $[ET_i, LT_i]$ is the time window of customer i, T_i is the service time of customer i and t_{ij} is the travel time from customer i to j. $\mu_{ij}=d_{i0}+d_{0j}-d_{ij}$ is the saving value in the absorbed saving algorithm. α, β, θ and γ are the relative importance of every variable. q is a value chosen randomly with uniform probability in the range [0,1]. p_t $(0<p_t<1)$ is initiated as $p_0=1$ and is dynamically adjusted to evolutionary process. S is a random variable.

$$\delta_{ij} = \begin{cases} \dfrac{\max[0, LT_{ij} - \max(ET_j, ET_{ij})]}{LT_j - ET_j} & , \quad if \quad LT_j \geq LT_{ij} \\ \dfrac{\max[0, LT_j - \max(ET_j, LT_{ij})]}{LT_j - ET_j} & , \quad else \end{cases} \tag{11}$$

$$ET_{ij} = ET_i + T_i + t_{ij}$$

Step 3: If the total amount of searching ants is smaller than m, go to step 2 and the remaining ants will continue searching; otherwise, go to step 4.

Step 4: Compute the search solution L_k of every ant, set the L_{local} as the local-optimum solution and save the routes table of L_{local}.

Step 5: 2-interchange and or-interchange methods are carried out on L_{local} for z times (z can be given a larger initial value in order to completely search the solution space and will be gradually decreased with the evolutionary process). The search solution L_{opt} and routes table can be noted if the new routes satisfy the capacity of vehicle and time windows. Update the routes table and set $L_{local} = L_{opt}$ if $L_{opt} < L_{local}$.

Step 6: Choose the routes with disasters by small random probabilities and set the pheromone trails in these routes equal to pheromone minimum, then compute the solution again. If the new solution is better than the old one, save the disaster and update L_{local} and routes table; if not, cancel this disaster.

Step 7: All the pheromone trails are dynamically updated as follows:

$$\tau_{ij}^{new} = \rho\tau_{ij}^{old} + \Delta\tau_{ij}$$

$$\Delta\tau_{ij} = \begin{cases} \dfrac{Q}{L_{local}} & , \quad ij \quad belongs \quad to \quad L_{local} \\ 0 & , \quad otherwise \end{cases} \tag{12}$$

Where Q is a constant related to the pheromone trails laid by ants. $1\text{-}\rho$ $(0<1\text{-}\rho<1)$ interpreted as trail evaporation is initiated as $1\text{-}\rho=0$ and is dynamically adjusted to evolutionary process. After pheromone trails are dynamically updated, τ_{ij} is replaced by τ_{max} when $\tau_{ij} > \tau_{max}$, or by $(\tau_{min} + \tau_{max})/2$ when $\tau_{ij} < \tau_{min}$.

Step 8: Compare L_{local} with L_{global}, if $L_{local} < L_{global}$, set $L_{global} = L_{local}$ and update global-optimum routes table simultaneously.

Step 9: As for the complete search of the solution space, the definite selection probabilities p_t and trail persistence ρ can be adaptively adjusted.

The adjusting rule of p_t is as follows:

$$p_t = \begin{cases} 0.95 p_{t-1} & , \quad if \quad 0.95 p_{t-1} \geq p_{\min} \\ p_{\min} & , \quad otherwise \end{cases} \tag{13}$$

Where p_{min} is the minimum in evolutionary process, which is used to ensure the achievement of the definite choosing chance even if the p_t is too small.

The adjusting rule of ρ is as follows:

$$\rho_n = \begin{cases} 0.95 \rho_{n-1} & , \quad if \quad 0.95 \rho_{n-1} \geq \rho_{\min} \\ \rho_{\min} & , \quad otherwise \end{cases} \tag{14}$$

Where ρ_{min} is the minimum defined in the evolutionary process for the prevention of a too slow convergence speed when ρ is too small.

Step 10: If *nc* is bigger than the maximum, then the flow finishes. Otherwise, go to step 2, and repeat the above steps.

3.3 Computational Results and Analysis

This algorithm will be designed and developed by java language because it is object-oriented, transplantable and can be tested by the classical set of 56 Benchmark problems [18] composed of six different problem types (C1,C2,R1,R2,RC1,RC2). Each set of data contains 100 customers and the geometric distance between 2 customers is the travel time between them. The names of the six problem types have the following meaning: Problem sets C have clustered customers whose time windows are generated based on a known solution. Sets R have customers' locations generated uniformly randomly over a square. Sets RC have a combination of randomly placed and clustered customers. Sets of type 1 have narrow time windows and a small vehicle capacity. Sets of type 2 have large time windows and a large vehicle capacity.

In this paper, R1-01, R1-03, RC1-01, RC1-03 and C1-01 are selected as test data sets based on past research [19] and a comparison is made between the average of ten solutions obtained by the heuristics submitted in this paper, and the solutions of Genetic Algorithm [20], Local Search method and Tabu Search Algorithm [21], ACS in Table 1. Table 2 provides the average time needed for each problem. Table 3 shows the comparison between the best results from past research [21] and the results of this paper. Fig. 1 gives the comparison analysis among 3 solutions which are computed by different heuristics.

Table 1-1. Comparison among different heuristics [20][21]

Problems	GenSAT [20]		LS-DIV [21]		SATabu [21]	
	Vehicles	Distance	Vehicles	Distance	Vehicles	Distance
R1-01	18	1644	19	1648.86	19	1655.03
R1-03	13	1207	15	1221.06	13	1234.43
RC1-01	14	1669	14	1677.68	14	1677.93
RC1-03	11	1110	11	1210.29	12	1196.12
C1-01	10	829	10	828.937	10	828.937

Table 1-2. Comparison among different heuristics [20][21]

	ACS		HACS	
	Vehicles	Distance	Vehicles	Distance
R1-01	19	1702	18	1612
R1-03	14	1272	13	1198
RC1-01	15	1867	14	1637
RC1-03	12	1256	11	1133
C1-01	10	887.28	10	833.14

Table 2. Average time needed for each problem

problems	R1-01	R1-03	RC1-01	RC1-03	C1-01
Time(s)	68	65	57	62	51

Table 3. Comparison between optimal solutions and our heuristic solutions

Problems	Best Solution [21]	HACS	Relative error(%)
R1-01	1607.7	1612	+0.27
R1-03	1207	1198	-0.75
RC1-01	1642.82	1637	-0.35
RC1-03	1110	1133	+2.07
C1-01	827.3	833.14	+0.71

The platform for conducting the experiments is a PC with a 2.40 GHz CPU and 256 MB RAM. Comparisons in computing time are not made because the platform in this paper is different from the ones in literatures [20][21]. However, the conclusion obtained from Table 2 shows that HACS spends approximately 60 seconds solving VRPTW with 100 customers and satisfies the need for real-time in logistics distribution.

Table 1, Table 3 and Fig. 1 indicate that the solutions of HACS are better than the solution of ACS as several solutions are more accurate than the most accurate from past research, while the remainder are very close. It is noted that the solutions obtained are not the optimal ones because the parameters of α, β and Q are set by experience when the algorithm runs. If every parameter in the algorithm was set at optimal values, the final solutions would be improved further.

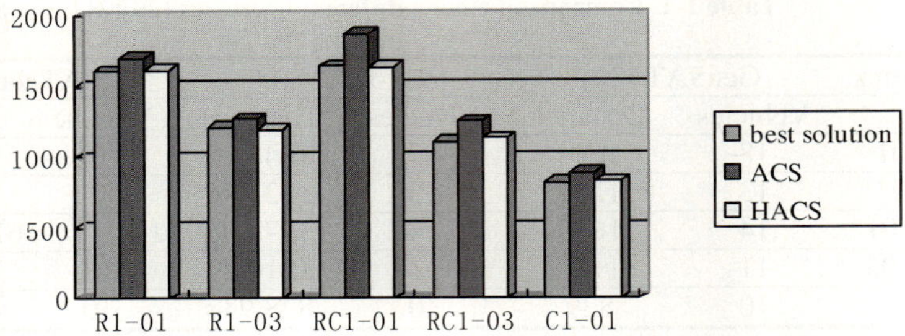

Fig. 1. Comparison analysis

4 Conclusions

In order to overcome the weaknesses of ACS in solving combinatorial optimization problems, this paper has presented the HACS by introducing the pheromone adjusting approach, combining ACS with saving and interchange algorithms, etc.. Firstly, the premature convergence is prevented effectively and the feasible solution is obtained more easily by the pheromone adjusting approach. The unique design of disaster operator also prevents ACS from getting trapped in local optimum. Secondly, by combining with savings algorithm and λ-interchange methods, etc., the speed of convergence is greatly improved and large-scale optimization problems can also be solved. By applying the algorithm to solve VRPTW, and comparing the computational results of this paper with the previous findings, HACS is verified to be an effective and efficient way to solve the combinatorial optimization problems.

Possible future research should focus on detailed investigation of parameter values to improve the speed of convergence and solution quality; enhancing the ants learning ability by endowing them with more intelligence; and combining with Agent technology to promote the coordination between colonies according to the autonomy, active, reactive and intelligence characteristics.

References

1. Colorni, A., Dorigo, M., Maniezzo, V.: Distributed Optimization by Ant Colonies. In: Proc of 1st European conf Artificial Life. Pans, pp. 134–142. Elsevier, France (1991)
2. Colorni, A., Dorigo, M., Maniezzo, V.: An Investigation of Some Properties of An Ant Algorithm. In: Proc. Of Parallel Problem Solving from Nature(PPSN), pp. 509–520. Elsiver, France (1992)
3. Colorni, A., Dorigo, M., Maniezzo, V., et al.: Ant System for Job-Shop Scheduling. Belgian J of Operations Research Statistics and Computer Science 34, 39–53 (1994)
4. Holthaus, O., Rajendran, C.: fast ant-colony algorithm for single-machine scheduling to minimize the sum of weighted tardiness of jobs. Journal of the Operational Research Society 56, 947–953 (2005)
5. Dorigo, M., Caro, G.D., Gambardella, L.M.: Ant Algorithms for Discrete Optimization [J]. Artificial Life 5, 137–172 (1999)

6. Martin, M., Chopard, B., Albuquerque, P.: Formation of An Ant Cemetery:Swarm Intelligence of Statistical Accident. Future Generation Computer Systems 18, 893–901 (2002)
7. Stuztle, T., Hoos, H.: Improvements on the Ant System: Introducing MAX-MIN Ant System. In: Smith, G.D., Steele, N.C., R. A. (eds.) Artificial Neural Networks and Genetic Algorithms, pp. 245–249 (1998)
8. Gang-li, Q., Jia-ben, Y.: Jia-ben: An Improved Ant Colony Algorithm Based on Adaptively Adjusting Pheromone. Information and Control 31, 198–201 (2002)
9. Bullnheimer, B., Hartl, R.F., Strauss, C.: An improved ant System algorithm for the vehicle Routing Problem. Annals of Operations Research 89, 319–328 (1999)
10. Gambardella, L.M, Taillard, E., Agazzi, G.: MACS-VRPTW:A Multiple Ant Colony System for Vehicle Routing Problem with Time Windows. New Ideas in Optimization, pp. 63–76 (1999)
11. Reimann, M., Doerner, K., Hartl, R.F.: D-Ants: Savings Based Ants divide and conquer the vehicle routing problem. Computers & Operations Research 31, 563–591 (2004)
12. Bell, J.E., McMullen, P.R.: Ant colony optimization techniques for the vehicle routing problem. Advanced Engineering Informatics 18, 41–48 (2004)
13. Stuztle, T., Hoos, H.: Max-Min ant system and local search for the traveling salesman problem. In: Proc IEEE International Conference on Evolutionary Computation (ICEC'97). Indianapolis:[s.n.] pp. 309–314 (1997)
14. Stuztle, T.: MAX-MIN Ant System. Elsevier Science, Amsterdam (1999)
15. Clarke, G., Wright, J.: Scheduling of Vehicles from A Central Depot to A Number of Delivery Points. Operations Research. 12, 568–581 (1964)
16. Lin, S., Kernighan, B.: An Effective Heuristic Algorithm for the Traveling Salesmen Problem. Operations Research. 21, 498–516 (1973)
17. Qing-Bao, Z., Zhi-Jun, Y.: Zhi-Jun: An Ant Colony Optimization Algorithm Based on Mutation and Dynamic Pheromone Updating. Journal of Software 15, 185–192 (2004)
18. Solomon Benchmark Problems, http://www.idsia.ch/ luca/macs-vrptw/problems/welcome.htm
19. Balakrishnan, N.: Simple Heuristic for the Vehicle Routing Problem with Soft Time Windows. Journal of the Operational Research Society 3, 279–287 (1993)
20. Thangiah, S.R, Osman, I.H, Sun, T.: Hybrid Genetic Algorithm, Simulated Annealing and Tabu Search Methods for Vehicle Routing Problems with Time Windows. Technical Report SRU-CpSc-TR-94-27. Computer Science Department (1994)
21. Tan, K.C., Lee, L.H., Ou, K.: Artificial Intelligence Heuristics in Solving Vehicle Routing Problems with Time Window Constraints. Engineering Applications of Artificial intelligence 14, 825–837 (2001)

Molecular Diagnosis of Tumor Based on Independent Component Analysis and Support Vector Machines

Shulin Wang[1,2], Huowang Chen[1], Ji Wang[1], Dingxing Zhang[1], and Shutao Li[3]

[1] School of Computer Science, National University of Defense Technology, Changsha, Hunan 410073, China
jt_slwang@hnu.cn
[2] College of Computer and Communication, Hunan University, Changsha, Hunan 410082, China
[3] College of Electrical and Information Engineering, Hunan University, Changsha, Hunan 410082, China

Abstract. Gene expression data that is being used to gather information from tissue samples is expected to significantly improve the development of efficient tumor diagnosis. For more accurate classification of tumor, extracting discriminant components from thousands of genes is an important problem which becomes a challenging task due to its characteristics such as the large number of genes and small sample size. We propose a novel approach which combines gene ranking with independent component analysis that has been developing recently to further improve the classification performance of gene expression data based on support vector machines. Two sets of gene expression data (colon dataset and leukemia dataset) are examined to confirm that the proposed approach can extract a small quantity of independent components which can drastically reduce the dimensionality of the original gene expression data when retaining higher recognition rate. The cross-validation accuracy of 100% has been achieved with extracting only 3 independent components from the leukemia dataset, and 93.55% for the colon dataset.

1 Introduction

The advent of DNA microarray technology provides biologists with the ability to measure the expression levels of thousands of genes in a single experiment. With the development of this technology, a large quantity of gene expression data from such experiments has been accumulating quickly, so a novel approaches should be explored to extract its biological functions that are unknown to us and to gather information from tissue and cell samples regarding gene expression differences that will be useful in diagnosing disease. Especially, in modern clinical neuro-oncology, the right and accurate treatment of patients with tumor depends on accurate diagnoses by using a complex combination of clinical and histopathological data such as gene expression profiles based on the hypothesis that many or even all human diseases may be accompanied by specific changes in the expression levels of some genes. Significant benefits to patients are expected from these efforts to develop new diagnostic tools.

Y. Wang, Y. Cheung, and H. Liu (Eds.): CIS 2006, LNAI 4456, pp. 46–56, 2007.

Gene expression data offer an unusual challenge to machine learning, for its dimensionality is too high (usually 2000~4000) and its sample size is too small comparatively (usually 40~400). This situation is particularly suited for a supervised machine learning technique, support vector machines (SVM) which has been rapidly developing in recent years [1][2]. SVM have been shown to perform well in multiple areas of biological analysis including evaluating gene expression data, detecting remote protein homologies, and translation initiation sites, etc. The expression levels of most of the genes measured in datasets are irrelevant to the distinction between tumor and normal tissues. To precisely classify tumor we have to select informative genes which are highly related to tumor for classification. Therefore, to reduce unnecessary noise to the classification process, selecting informative genes is of great importance in the analysis of gene expression data. In this paper our efforts are mainly to select informative genes to further reduce the dimensionality of data using independent component analysis (ICA) and to apply SVM to tumor classification to help doctor to diagnose, treat and predict tumor.

2 Related Works

A great deal of research has been done in the classification of gene expression data by utilizing unsupervised methods such as clustering and self-organizing maps. While clustering the row or column vectors of gene expression data matrix, little prior biology knowledge is adopted, and we even don't know the biological meaning of the clustering results. In recent years, supervised methods such as decision trees, SVM and multi-layer perceptrons have been broadly applied in order to classify normal and tumor tissues [3][4][5]. However, there exist many noises and redundancy in gene expression data, so genes not related to tumor should be removed before classifying gene expression data. How to select informative genes and to extract underlying components from thousands of genes becomes a challenging task to the precise classification of tumor.

The goal of feature extraction is to eliminate all redundancies and noises in gene expression profiles and to select informative genes and further extract independent components (ICs). Furlanello [6] designed a wrapper algorithm which is the entropy-based recursive feature elimination method that can eliminates chunks of uninteresting features according to the entropy of the weights distribution of SVM classifiers for fast feature ranking in classification problems. Nishimura [7] presented a principal component analysis (PCA) based method of gene expression visual analysis with calculating PCA contribution axis. One drawback of PCA is, however, that class information is not utilized for class prediction and PCA is not suitable for non-Gaussian data processing. ICA is a dimensional reduction technique that uses the existence of ICs in multivariate data and decomposes an input dataset into statistically ICs. ICA can reduce the effects of noise or artifacts of the signal and is ideal for separating mixed signals. Recently, Liebermeister [8] applied ICA to the analysis of gene expression profiles to extract the expression modes of genes. In fact, many of the feature selection and extraction methods can be combined, which may give us better results. In this study, we propose a novel and integrated feature extraction method which combines gene ranking with ICA to further improve the classification performance of tumor samples based on SVM.

3 The Model of Classification Algorithm

3.1 Representation of DNA Microarray Data

DNA microarrays are composed of thousands of individual DNA sequences printed in a high density array on a glass microscope slide using a robotic array. The relative abundance of these spotted DNA sequences in DNA or mRNA samples may be assessed by monitoring the differential hybridization of the two class samples to the sequences on the array. For mRNA samples, the samples are reverse-transcribed into cDNA labeled using different fluorescent dyes mixed (red-fluorescent dye Cy5 and green-fluorescent dye Cy3). After the hybridization of these samples with the arrayed DNA probes, the slides are imaged using scanner that makes fluorescence measurements for each dye. The log ratio between the two intensities of each dye is used as the gene expression data: $GeneExpression = \log_2(Ratio)$, $Ratio = Int(Cy5)/Int(Cy3)$, where $Int(Cy5)$ and $Int(Cy3)$ are the intensities of red and green colors. Samples are generated under multiple conditions which may be a time series during a biological process or a collection of different tissue samples.

Let $G = \{g_1, \cdots g_n\}$ be a set of genes and $S = \{s_1, \cdots s_m\}$ be a set of samples. Here, m is the number of samples and n is the number of genes measured. The corresponding gene expression matrix can be represented as $X = (x_{i,j})$, $1 \le i \le m, 1 \le j \le n$. The matrix X is composed of m row vectors $s_i \in R^n$, $i = 1, 2, \cdots, m$.

$$X = \left[\begin{array}{cccc|c} \multicolumn{4}{c}{\overbrace{\hspace{6em}}^{n \text{ genes}}} & \overbrace{}^{Class} \\ x_{1,1} & x_{1,2} & \cdots & x_{1,n} & l_1 \\ x_{2,1} & x_{2,2} & \cdots & x_{2,n} & l_2 \\ \vdots & \vdots & \cdots & \vdots & \vdots \\ x_{m,1} & x_{m,2} & \cdots & x_{m,n} & l_m \end{array} \right]$$

where $x_{i,j}$ is the expression level value of sample s_i on gene g_j, and l_i labels which class the sample s_i belongs to. Each vector $s_i \in S$ may be thought of as a point in n-dimensional space. Each of the n columns consists of an m-element expression vector for a single gene.

Our task is to classify all samples into tumor samples and normal samples or two tumor subtypes, which is a binary classification problem. A simple way to build a binary classifier is to construct a hyper-plane which separates tumor members from normal members in feature space. Suppose ω_T and ω_N be the two subsets of sample set S, satisfying $\omega_T \cap \omega_N = \phi$, $\omega_T \cup \omega_N = S$, which means that each vector s_i ideally belongs to one and only one class ω_T or ω_N.

3.2 Algorithm Model

Here we propose a novel method called hybrid method, which integrates ICA with the revised feature score criterion (RFSC) [9] that was improved on the basis of the feature score criterion (FSC) that was proposed by Golub [17] to drastically reduce the dimensionality of gene expression data and to minimize the information loss before using the SVM classifier. The novel hybrid method exploits the advantages that each approach offers. RFSC is a calculated ranking score for each gene to define how well this gene discriminates two classes, and ICA can reduce the dimensionality of the dataset while retaining as much as possible the variation in this dataset. Firstly, we will give the classification algorithm model as follows, and then we will introduce every step in algorithm in the next several sections.

Step 1. Gene selection: selecting p top-ranked gene subset G_{top} in which all genes have higher feature score, so we can obtain a matrix $X_{m\times p}$, where p is the number of the selected genes. Then standardizing $X=(x_{i,j})_{m\times p}$, $x_{ij}=(x_{ij}-\mu_j)/\sigma_j$, $i=1,2,\cdots m$, and $j=1,2,\cdots p$, where $\mu_j=\frac{1}{m}\sum_{i=1}^{m}x_{ij}$, $\sigma_j^2=\frac{1}{m-1}\sum_{i=1}^{m}(x_{ij}-\mu_j)^2$.

Step 2. Extracting independent components (ICs): applying ICA to the top-ranked gene subset G_{top} to calculate and extract r new ICs as represents of gene subset G_{top}, satisfying $r<|G_{top}|$. Having finished those works, we can obtain matrix $I_{m\times r}$ which consists of ICs.

Step 3. Classification: training SVM with training set and applying SVM to tumor classification by means of $I_{m\times r}$ which must have been standardized using the same standardizing approach in step 1.

Step 4. Testing the obtained classification model using testing set to get the predictive accuracy of tumor classification.

3.3 Gene Selection

Gene selection and dimensional reduction are necessary for performing the tumor classification with gene expression profiles. In measuring the classification information of genes, Golub et al [17] proposed FSC as gene selection criterion. For each gene $g_i\in G$, the FSC method firstly calculate the mean μ_i^+ (resp. μ_i^-) and standard deviation σ_i^+ (resp. σ_i^-) which correspond to the gene g_i of samples labeled +1(-1), respectively, and then calculate feature score with the formula $FSC(g_i)=\left|(\mu_i^+-\mu_i^-)/(\sigma_i^++\sigma_i^-)\right|$ for each $g_i\in G$, and then all genes are ranked according to their scores. However, when the mean values of gene g_i in normal and tumor tissues are equal, in this formula there is a fault, for this gene g_i is removed as noise from informative gene subset due to $FSC(g_i)=0$. Therefore, we adopt another improved formula (1) as our gene selection criterion [9], called the revised feature selection criterion.

$$RFSC(g_i)=0.5\left|(\mu_i^+-\mu_i^-)/(\sigma_i^++\sigma_i^-)\right|+0.5\ln((\sigma_i^{+2}+\sigma_i^{-2})/(2\sigma_i^+\sigma_i^-)) \tag{1}$$

We simply select the genes with the highest $F(g_i)$ scores as our top-ranked gene subset G_{top}, satisfying $|G_{top}|<<|G|$. After selecting p genes, we can obtain $X_{m\times p}$.

3.4 Extracting ICs Using ICA

ICA has recently become an important tool for modeling and understanding empirical datasets. It is a statistical and computational technique for separating a multivariate signal into additive subcomponents supposing the mutual statistical independence of the non-Gaussian source signals, and it is special case of blind source separation. ICA provides a better decomposition than other well-known models such as principal component analysis (PCA) and it has many applications in data analysis, source separation, and feature extraction. Given a microarray dataset $X = (x_{ij})_{m\times p} = (x_1, \ldots, x_p)$ with m rows of samples and p columns of genes, where $x_i^T \in R^m$ (T means vector transpose operator). If the expression of p genes are dominated by r independent biological processes, such as ribosome biogenesis, cell cycle, etc, then $Y = (y_{ij})_{m\times r} = (y_1, \ldots, y_r)$, where $r \le p$ and $y_i^T \in R^m$. We assume that the expression of each gene expression level $x_i (i = 1, \ldots, p)$ is a linear combination of the r independent biological processes $y_j (j = 1, \ldots, r)$ with some unknown mixing coefficient $A = (a_{ij})$, then $x_i = \sum_j a_{ij} y_j$, written in the form of matrix representation: $X = AY$. A is called the mixing matrix and Y is called source signals. The goal of ICA is to find a matrix W that satisfies the transformation equation: $C = WX = WAY$, where W is called separating matrix and $C = (c_1, \ldots, c_r)$, called ICs, has statistically independent components. Generally speaking, C is a close approximation of source signal Y; If $W = A^{-1}$, it achieves perfect reconstruction $C = Y$. To find such a matrix W, an important assumption is that at most one source signal has a Gaussian distribution. This is not a problem for analyzing biological data based on the fact that the most typical Gaussian source is random noise and biological processes are expected to be highly no-Gaussian [16].

3.5 Support Vector Machines

SVM is a relatively new type of statistic learning theory, originally introduced by Vapnik and successively extended by a number of other researchers. SVM builds up a hyper-plane as the decision surface in such a way to maximize the margin of separation between positive and negative samples. Given a labeled set of m training samples $S = \{(x_i, y_i) \mid (x_i, y_i) \in R^n \times \{\pm 1\}, i = 1, 2, \cdots m\}$, where $x_i \in R^n, y_i \in \{\pm 1\}$ is a label of sample x_i, and the discriminant hyper-plane is defined by formula (2).

$$f(x) = \sum_{i=1}^{m} \alpha_i y_i K(x_i, x) + b \tag{2}$$

where $K(x_i, x)$ is a kernel function and the sign of $f(x)$ determines which class it belongs to. Constructing an optimal hyper-plane is equivalent to finding all the support vectors α_i and a bias b.

4 Experiments

4.1 Sample Datasets

We have experiment with two sets of samples concerning tumor. One is the colon tumor dataset which involves comparing tumor and normal samples of the same tissue and it is a collection of expression measurements from colon biopsy samples [10]. The dataset consists of 62 samples of colon epithelial cells including 40 colon cancer samples and 22 normal samples. Gene expression levels in these 62 samples were measured using high density oligonucleotide microarray. Among the 6000 genes detected in these microarrays, 2000 genes were selected based on the confidence in the measured expression levels. The dataset is available at web site http://www.molbio.princeton.edu/colondata.

Another is bone marrow or peripheral blood samples that are taken from 72 patients with either acute myeloid leukemia (AML) or acute lymphoblastic leukemia (ALL) [17]. Following the experimental setup of the original authors, the data is split into a training set consisting of 38 samples in which 27 are ALL and 11 are AML, and a test set of 34 samples, 20 ALL and 14 AML. The dataset provided contains expression levels for 7129 human genes produced by Affymetrix high-density oligonucleotide microarrays. The dataset is available at web site http://www.broad.mit.edu/cgi-bin/cancer/datasets.cgi.

4.2 Experiment Methods

In practice, our experiments are initially carried out only using RFSC to select the 300, 200 top-ranked genes as represents of all genes in dataset, respectively, and then on the basis of the selected genes we apply the FastICA package that is available at http://www.cis.hut.fi/projects/ica/fastica to extract their ICs from the selected informative gene subset, and after standardizing ICs we input the standardized ICs into the software LIBSVM [11] to classify the colon dataset into normal and tumor class and the leukemia dataset into AML and ALL class. Training SVM requires specifying the type of kernel and the regularization parameter C. However, finding the best choices for the kernel and parameters can be challenging when applied to real datasets. Generally, the recommended kernel for nonlinear problems is the Gaussian radial basis kernel $K(x, y) = \exp(-\gamma\|x - y\|^2)$ [2], because it resembles the sigmoid kernel for certain parameters and it requires less parameters than a polynomial kernel. The kernel parameter γ and C, which controls the complexity of the discriminant function versus the training error minimization, can be determined by running a 2-dimensional grid search, which means that the values for pairs of parameters (C, γ) are generated in a predefined interval. Performance of classifiers was tested by utilizing a cross-validated method. Therefore, accuracy of a diagnostic test can be expressed with 3-fold cross-validation (CV) accuracy.

4.3 Results and Analysis

Table 1 shows the experiment results of two methods under the different parameters (C, γ) for the colon dataset. The third column means the number of the extracted ICs.

Experiment results show that our method is obviously superior to the single RFSC method in reducing dimensionality and in improving performance of SVM classifier while retaining higher recognition rate which is measured by CV accuracy. Experiments also show that many genes are closely related and dominated by several latent components which are independent each other; however, how to interpret those ICs requires more biological knowledge. This will benefit us to analyze the expression of the related genes to infer the regulatory network of genes. Fig.1 shows the 3D scatter plot of colon tumor samples when extracting three ICs from the selected 300 top-ranked genes, and it is obvious that the boundary between the normal and tumor tissues is not clear.

Table 1. Comparison of recognition rate with two methods for the colon dataset

Method	#Selected genes	#Extracted ICs	C	γ	CV Accuracy
RFSC	300	None	1000	0.012	91.94%
	200	None	2000	0.0009	91.94%
RFSC+ ICA	300	2	700	0.2	77.45%
	300	3	1000	0.05	90.32%
	300	4	1000	0.01	87.10%
	300	5	1000	0.006	88.71%
	300	6	1000	0.01	87.10%
	300	7	200	0.01	90.32%
	300	8	800	0.003	90.32%
	300	9	800	0.003	91.94%
	37	3	100	0.31	93.55%

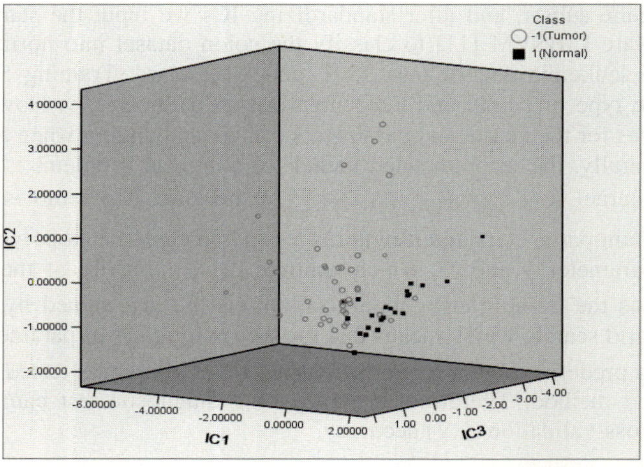

Fig. 1. 3D scatter plot for colon samples when extracting three ICs from its 300 top-ranked genes

Similarly, table 2 shows the experiment results of two methods for the leukemia dataset. And correspondingly, the 2D scatter plot of the leukemia dataset is shown in Fig.2 when extracting two ICs from the selected 300 top-ranked genes. We can see that the boundary between the two tumor subtypes AML and ALL is very clear relatively.

From experiment results we can deduce that in tumor dataset there are only several informative genes (e.g. 3 or 4 genes) which could obtain the highest CV accuracy of tumor classification. Therefore, it is possible to design a brutal search algorithm which can find a minimum informative gene subset which obtains the best classification performance, which is our future work.

Table 2. Comparison of recognition rate with two methods for the leukemia dataset

Method	#Selected genes	#Extracted ICs	C	γ	3-fold CV Accuracy
RFSC	300	None	500	0.00008	98.61%
	200	None	1000	0.00005	98.61%
RFSC+ ICA	300	2	100	0.0006	98.61%
	300	3	200	0.0009	100%
	300	4	200	0.0009	100%
	300	5	100	0.005	100%
	300	6	100	0.0009	100%
	300	7	200	0.0006	100%
	300	8	100	0.0004	98.61%
	300	9	500	0.008	97.22%
	300	10	100	0.003	98.61%
	200	3	100	0.001	100%

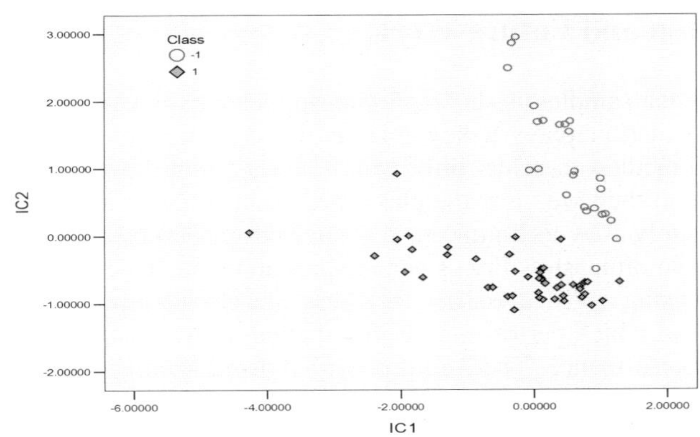

Fig. 2. 2D scatter plot of the leukemia dataset when extracting two ICs from its 300 top-ranked genes

4.4 Comparison of the Classification Accuracy

Many feature selection and machine learning approaches have been applied to the tumor classification based on gene expression data. No doubt that the classification of the leukemia dataset has achieved a perfect performance using our method, so we only compare our method with others in classifying the colon dataset. Table 3 shows the comparison of the related works on the same colon dataset. Among the listed methods in table 3, GA/KNN method has the highest classification accuracy, but the five samples (N34, N36, T30, T33 and T36) in the colon dataset were removed before classification, for Li [12] thought that the colon dataset had been likely contaminated. The comparison shows that our method performs well in classifying the colon dataset. In fact, among the published tumor datasets, classifying the colon dataset is more difficulty than doing others.

Table 3. Comparison of many different methods in classification accuracy on the same colon tumor dataset

Feature selection or extraction	Classifier	Accuracy	Reference
Signal to noise ratio	SVM	90.30%	[13]
Genetic Algorithm (GA)	k-Nearest Neighbor (k-NN)	94.10%	[12]
All genes, TNoM score	SVM with quadratic kernel	74.20%	[14]
Principal component analysis (PCA)	Logistic discriminent	87.10%	[15]
Partial least square	Logistic discriminant	93.50%	[15]
Partial least square	Quadratic discriminant analysis	91.90%	[15]
Independent component analysis (ICA)	Calculating the ratio of tumor and normal ICs	91.90%	[16]
RFSC and ICA	SVM with RBF kernel	93.55%	This paper

5 Conclusion and Future Work

Classifying tumor samples is an important application of gene expression profiles, and feature extraction plays a key role in the classification of tumor. We firstly employ RFSC method to select informative genes which have a good classification performance, and then we view the class prediction problem as a multivariate signal problem and apply ICA technique to the selected gene subset to extract underlying ICs to reduce the dimensionality of gene expression data. Two sets of tumor samples are examined using SVM classifier to assess the classification performance of the proposed method which performs well in reducing dimensionality and improving the classification performance. The 3-fold cross-validated accuracy of 100% is achieved for the leukemia dataset and 93.55% for the colon dataset.

SVM is one of the prospective tools for analyzing gene expression data coming from DNA microarray. However, different dataset has different sensitivity to different feature extraction methods and classifiers. Therefore, we will focus on developing the tumor classification tool which will integrate various good feature extraction methods and classifiers to confirm the obtained results on the same dataset to get the best results as much as possible.

Acknowledgement

This research is supported by the Program for New Century Excellent Talents in University and the Excellent Youth Foundation of Hunan Province (06JJ1010). The authors loyally thank the anonymous reviewers for their sound and constructive advices to this paper.

References

1. Vapnik, V.N.: Statistical learning theory. Springer, New York (1998)
2. Cristianini, N., Shawe-Taylor, J.: An Introduction to Support Vector Machines. Cambridge University Press, Cambridge (2000)
3. Furey, T.S., Cristianini, N., Duffy, N., Bednarski, D.W., Schummer, M., Haussler, D.: Support vector machine classification and validation of cancer tissue samples using microarray expression data. Bioinformatics 16(10), 906–914 (2000)
4. Guyon, I., Weston, J., Barnhill, S., Vapnik, V.: Gene selection for cancer classification using support vector machines. Machine Learning 46, 389–422 (2002)
5. Cho, S.-B., Won, H.-H.: Machine learning in DNA microarray analysis for cancer classification. In: Proceedings of the First Asia-Pacific Bioinformatics Conference on Bioinformatics, pp. 189-198 (2003)
6. Furlanello, C., Serafini, M., Merler, S., Jurman, G.: An accelerated procedure for recursive feature ranking on microarray data. Neural Networks 16, 641–648 (2003)
7. Nishimura, K., Abe, K., Ishikawa, S.: Shumpei Ishikawa, Shuichi Tsutsumi, Koichi Hirota, and Hiroyuki Aburatani. A PCA based method of gene expression visual analysis. Genome Informatics 14, 346–347 (2003)
8. Wolfram, L.: Linear modes of gene expression determined by independent component analysis. Bioinformatics 18(1), 51–60 (2002)
9. Yingxin, L., Xiaogang, R.: Feature selection for cancer classification based on Support Vector Machine. Journal of Computer Research and Development 42(10), 1796–1801 (2005)
10. Alon, U., Barkai, N., Notterman, D.A., Gish, K., Ybarra, S., Mack, D., Levine, A.: Broad patterns of gene expression revealed by clustering analysis of tumor and normal colon tissues by oligonucleotide arrays. Proc. Nat. Acad. Sci. USA 96, 6745–6750 (1999)
11. Chang, C.-C., Lin, C.-J.: LIBSVM: A library for support vector machines, (2001) Software available at http://www.csie.ntu.edu.tw/ cjlin/libsvm
12. Li, L., Weinberg, C.R., Darden, T.A., Pedersen, L.G.: Gene selection for sample classification based on gene expression data: study of sensitivity to choice of parameters of the GA/KNN method. Bioinformatics 17(12), 1131–1142 (2001)
13. Furey, T.S., Cristianini, N., Duffy, N., Bednarski, D.W., Schummer, M., Haussler, D.: Support vector machine classification and validation of cancer tissue samples using microarray expression data. Bioinformatics 16(10), 906–914 (2000)
14. Ben-Dor, A., Bruhn, L., Friedman, N., Nachman, I., Schummer, M., Yakhini, N.: Tissue classification with gene expression profiles. Journal of computional Biology, 7, 559–584

15. Nguyen, D.V., Rocke, D.M.: Tumor classification by partial least squares using microarray gene expression data. Bioinformatics 18(1), 39–45 (2002)
16. Zhang, X., Yap, Y.L., Wei, D., Chen, F., Danchin, A.: Molecular diagnosis of human cancer type by gene expression profiles and independent component analysis. European Journal of Human Genetics 05(9), 1018–4813 (2005)
17. Golub, T.R., Slonim, D.K., Tamayo, P., Huard, C., Gaasenbeek, M., Mesirov, J.P., Coller, H., Loh, M.L., Downing, J.R., Caligiuri, M.A., Bloomfield, C.D., Lander, E.S.: Molecular classification of cancer: class discovery and class prediction by gene expression monitoring. Science 286, 531–537 (1999)
18. Komura, D., Nakamura, H., Tsutsumi, S.: Multidimensional support vector machines for visualization of gene expression data. Bioinformatics 21(4), 439–444 (2005)
19. Berger, J.A., Hautaniemi, S., Edgren, H., Monni, O., Mitra, S.K., Yli-Harja, O., Astola, J.: Identifying underlying factors in breast cancer using independent component analysis. In: Proceedings of the IEEE International Workshop on Neural Networks for Signal Processing (NNSP 2003), Toulouse, France, September 17-19, 2003, pp. 81–90 (2003)
20. Berger, J.A., Mitra, S.K., Edgren, H.: Studying DNA microarray data using independent component analysis. In: Proceedings of the International Symposium on Control, Communications, and Signal Processing (ISCCSP 2004), Hammamet, Tunisia, March 21-24, 2004, pp. 747–750 (2004)

Gene Selection Using Wilcoxon Rank Sum Test and Support Vector Machine for Cancer Classification

Chen Liao[1], Shutao Li[1], and Zhiyuan Luo[2]

[1] College of Electrical and Information Engineering, Hunan University, Changsha 410082, China
[2] Department of Computer Science, Royal Holloway College, University of London, Egham, Surrey, TW20 0EX, United Kingdom
shutao_li@yahoo.com.cn

Abstract. Gene selection is an important problem in microarray data processing. A new gene selection method based on Wilcoxon rank sum test and Support Vector Machine (SVM) is proposed in this paper. First, Wilcoxon rank sum test is used to select a subset. Then each selected gene is trained and tested using SVM classifier with linear kernel separately, and genes with high testing accuracy rates are chosen to form the final reduced gene subset. Leave-one-out cross validation (LOOCV) classification results on two datasets: Breast Cancer and ALL/AML leukemia, demonstrate the proposed method can get 100% success rate with the final reduced subset. The selected genes are listed and their expression levels are sketched, which show that the selected genes can make clear separation between two classes.

1 Introduction

Cancer turns to be one of the most threatening diseases in the world, which is often caused by abnormal cells that spread and grow unconventionally. Molecular level classification of cancer cells is becoming important now. As a preprocessing step of the classification, gene selection becomes a critical issue [1].

The purpose of gene selection is to eliminate redundant, noisy or irrelevant genes and select the most informative subset of genes to enhance the generalization performance. Traditional statistical methods for classification have been widely used for gene selection. In [1], six gene selection heuristics based on entropy theory, entropy-based, χ^2-statistics, t-statistics, are introduced. In [2], entropy measure and Wilcoxon rank sum test are combined to find relevant genes. Support vector machines (SVMs) also have been extensively utilized to deal with gene selection problems [3-9]. Various methods of recursive feature elimination based on SVM (SVM-RFE) are discussed in [4-9].

In this paper, a new gene selection method is proposed. First, Wilcoxon rank sum test is used to preprocess the dataset to decease the dimensionality. Then each gene is trained and tested using SVM classifier separately, and each gene gets its corresponding accuracy rate. The accuracy rates are ranked in descending order. Finally, the genes with high accuracy rates are selected to form a subset.

Y. Wang, Y. Cheung, and H. Liu (Eds.): CIS 2006, LNAI 4456, pp. 57–66, 2007.

This paper is organized as follows. In the next section, the introduction of Wilcoxon rank sum test is given. In section 3, the basic theory of SVM is introduced. In section 4, a new gene selection method using SVM is proposed. In section 5, the experimental setup and results are shown, and in the last section, the paper is concluded.

2 Feature Selection Using Wilcoxon Rank Sum Test

Because the large dimensionality will increase the complexity and prolong the running time, the dataset is preprocessed by Wilcoxon rank sum test at first. The statistics formula is:

$$s(g) = \sum_{i \in \mathbf{N}_0} \sum_{j \in \mathbf{N}_1} I((\mathbf{x}_j^{(g)} - \mathbf{x}_i^{(g)}) \le 0) \quad (1)$$

where I is the discrimination function, if the logic expression in the bracket is true, the value of I is 1, or else it is 0. $\mathbf{x}_i^{(g)}$ is the expression value of the sample i in the gene g. $\mathbf{N}_0$ and $\mathbf{N}_1$ are the index sets of different classes of samples. $s(g)$ can represent the measurement of the difference between the two classes, when it is closer to 0 or closer to the max value of $n_0 n_1$ (here $n_0 = |\mathbf{N}_0|$, $n_1 = |\mathbf{N}_1|$), the corresponding gene is more important to the classification. As a result, according to (2), the importance degree of gene can be calculated:

$$q(g) = \max(s(g), n_0 n_1 - s(g)) \quad (2)$$

Genes are ranked according to each genes' $q(g)$, and the top p genes are selected to form a new subset.

3 Support Vector Machines

SVM has appeared as an extensively used classifier of statistical learning theory. The training set is supposed to be $\{(\mathbf{x}_i, y_i)\}_{i=1}^N$, with each input $\mathbf{x}_i \in R^m$ and $y_i \in \{\pm 1\}$. The SVM maps $\mathbf{x}$ to $\mathbf{z} = \varphi(\mathbf{x})$ in a Hilbert space F by a nonlinear map $\varphi : R^m \to F$. The dimensionality of F is quite high in most conditions. When the data is linearly separable in F, a separation hyperplane $(\langle \mathbf{w}, \varphi(\mathbf{x}) \rangle + b)$ is constructed by the SVM, and the separation margin of the hyperplane between the positive and negative examples is maximized. By minimizing $\|\mathbf{w}\|$, the w for the optimal hyperplane is gained, and the solution can be presented as $\mathbf{w} = \sum_{i=1}^N \alpha_i y_i \varphi(\mathbf{x}_i)$ for some certain $\alpha_i \ge 0$. The vector of α_i's, $\Lambda = (\alpha_i, ..., \alpha_N)$, can be gained by solving the following quadratic programming problem:

$$\text{maximize } W(\Lambda) = \Lambda^{\mathrm{T}} 1 - \frac{1}{2} \Lambda^{\mathrm{T}} Q \Lambda \quad (3)$$

with respect to Λ, subject to the constraints $\Lambda \geq 0$ and $\Lambda Y = 0$. Here, $Y^{\mathrm{T}} = (y_1, ..., y_N)$ and Q are symmetric matrixes with elements

$$Q_{ij} = y_i y_j \left\langle \varphi(\mathbf{x}_i), \varphi(\mathbf{x}_j) \right\rangle \tag{4}$$

For those α_i greater than zero, the relevant training examples should lie along the margins of the decision boundary, and these are defined as the support vectors.

However, due to the high dimensionality of F and $\varphi(\mathbf{x}_i)$ and $\varphi(\mathbf{x}_j)$ in (2), the way is not so practical. So a critical characteristic of the SVM, and of kernel methods in general, plays an important role here. It is that one can gain $\left\langle \varphi(\mathbf{x}_i), \varphi(\mathbf{x}_j) \right\rangle$ in (2) without calculating $\varphi(\mathbf{x}_i)$ and $\varphi(\mathbf{x}_j)$ explicitly first, and this is realized via using kernel function. The kernel methods supply wonderful tools to process and compare many types of data, and supply state-of-the-art performance in many cases. Here some kinds of kernel functions are introduced as follows:

① Linear kernel

$$k_L(\mathbf{x}_1, \mathbf{x}_2) = \mathbf{x}_1^{\,T} \mathbf{x}_2 \tag{5}$$

where $\mathbf{x}_1$ is the value of the independent variable for which one seeks an estimate, and $\mathbf{x}_2$ are the values of the independent variable in the data.

② Polynomial kernel

$$k_P(\mathbf{x}_1, \mathbf{x}_2) = (\mathbf{x}_1^{\,T} \mathbf{x}_2)^d \tag{6}$$

where d is the degree of the polynomial. The kernel k_P of degree 2 is corresponding to a feature space spanned by all products of two variables, that is, $\{\mathbf{x}_1^2, \mathbf{x}_1\mathbf{x}_2, \mathbf{x}_2^2\}$.

③ Gaussian RBF kernel

$$k_G(\mathbf{x}_1, \mathbf{x}_2) = \exp(-\left\|\mathbf{x}_1 - \mathbf{x}_2\right\|^2 / 2\sigma^2) \tag{7}$$

where σ is a parameter. The Gaussian kernel is one of the most popular utilized kernels in practice due to its capacity to produce nonparametric classification functions [3].

4 Feature Selection and Classification Using SVM

The gene selection and classification using SVM criteria is illustrated as follows.

Let x_{ij} be the measurement of the expression level of the jth gene for the ith sample, where j=1, 2, …, n, $\mathbf{X}_{reduced}=(x_{ij})_{m,n}$ denotes the expression levels of the genes selected by Wilcoxon rank sum test, i.e.,

$$\mathbf{X}_{reduced} = \begin{array}{c} \text{gene 1} \quad \text{gene 2} \qquad\qquad \text{gene } n \\ \begin{bmatrix} x_{11} & x_{12} & \cdots & x_{1n} \\ x_{21} & x_{22} & \cdots & x_{2n} \\ \vdots & \vdots & \ddots & \vdots \\ x_{m1} & x_{m2} & \cdots & x_{mn} \end{bmatrix} \end{array}$$

Here we assume $\mathbf{x}_1, \cdots, \mathbf{x}_m$ are the m samples, where $\mathbf{x}_i = [x_{i1}, x_{i2}, \cdots, x_{in}]$. Let $Y=[y_1, \ldots, y_m]^T$ denote the class labels of m samples.

Step 1: training each gene and obtaining relevant accuracy rates

If there are k samples in the training set, and m-k samples in the test set, n SVM classifiers with linear kernel are trained using the k training samples. For example, to the jth SVM, the input vector is $\mathbf{x}_j = \left[x_{1j}, x_{2j}, \cdots, x_{kj}\right]$, the output is $\mathbf{y} = [y_1, y_2, \cdots, y_k]$. Then the training accuracies of all the n genes can be obtained. The genes with high accuracy rates are more informative than those with low ones.

Step 2: ranking the accuracies and selecting the most informative ones

The accuracy rates of all the genes are ranked in descending order, and the top N genes with highest training accuracies are chosen to form the final reduced subset. Now the new gene dataset is as follows.

$$\mathbf{X}_{final} = \begin{array}{c} \text{gene } i \quad \text{gene } j \qquad\qquad \text{gene } N \\ \begin{bmatrix} x_{1i} & x_{1j} & \cdots & x_{1N} \\ x_{2i} & x_{2j} & \cdots & x_{2N} \\ \vdots & \vdots & \ddots & \vdots \\ x_{mi} & x_{mj} & \cdots & x_{mN} \end{bmatrix} \end{array}$$

Step 3: classifying with support vector machine

The new training subset with selected genes is used to train one SVM. And the testing set is tested by the classifier to get the corresponding testing accuracy rate.

5 Experimental Setup and Results

5.1 Experimental Setup

The selection and classification performance of the proposed method is evaluated by two benchmark datasets. The Breast Cancer dataset contains 7129 genes and 38 samples, including 18 ER+ (estrogen receptor) samples and 20 ER- samples [10]. The Leukemia dataset contains 7129 genes too and 72 samples, which contain 47 samples of acute lymphoblastic leukemia (ALL) and 25 samples of acute myeloid leukemia (AML) [11].

Because of the small number of samples, leave-one-out cross validation (LOOCV) is utilized to test the accuracy of the proposed method. Firstly, the LOOCV procedure removes one sample to form a testing set, and the remaining samples are used for gene selection and classifier construction. Finally, the constructed classifier is tested by using the removed sample. After all samples have been left out and tested in turn, the final classification error is obtained by the fraction of errors over the total number of training samples.

5.2 Experimental Results

The classification results of the proposed method by using different parameter values are shown in Table 1. The p in the Wilcoxon rank sum test is set to 300, which means that the top 300 genes are selected to form a new subset. The C_1 is the penalty

Table 1. The classification performance (%) with different parameters C_1,C_2 and N

C_1	C_2	N	Linear kernel		Polynomial kernel		Gaussian kernel	
			B.C.	L.	B.C.	L.	B.C.	L.
1	1	20	94.7	95.8	92.1	94.4	94.7	94.4
		30	92.1	94.4	94.7	94.4	92.1	93.1
		40	94.7	93.1	92.1	91.7	94.7	93.1
		50	97.4	94.4	97.4	91.7	92.1	95.8
	10	20	**100.0**	93.1	97.4	93.1	**100.0**	95.8
		30	92.1	90.2	94.7	91.7	94.7	94.4
		40	94.7	94.4	92.1	93.1	94.7	93.1
		50	97.4	93.1	97.4	94.4	94.7	94.4
	100	20	**100.0**	91.7	**100.0**	88.9	**100.0**	93.6
		30	92.1	88.9	94.7	91.7	94.7	91.7
		40	94.7	94.4	92.1	93.1	94.7	91.7
		50	97.4	93.1	97.4	94.4	94.7	91.7
10	1	20	92.1	97.2	92.1	95.8	92.1	94.4
		30	97.4	97.2	97.4	**98.6**	94.7	95.8
		40	**100.0**	97.2	97.4	**98.6**	94.7	95.8
		50	94.7	97.2	97.4	95.8	94.7	95.8
	10	20	92.1	95.8	92.1	93.1	92.1	97.2
		30	97.4	**98.6**	97.4	**98.6**	97.4	97.2
		40	**100.0**	**98.6**	97.4	97.2	**100.0**	97.2
		50	94.7	95.8	97.4	95.8	97.4	97.2
	100	20	92.1	94.4	92.1	93.1	92.1	94.4
		30	97.4	97.2	97.4	**98.6**	97.4	**98.6**
		40	**100.0**	**98.6**	97.4	97.2	**100.0**	**98.6**
		50	94.7	95.8	97.4	95.8	97.4	95.8
100	1	20	92.1	94.4	92.1	95.8	89.5	94.4
		30	94.7	97.2	97.4	**98.6**	92.1	94.4
		40	94.7	97.2	92.1	**98.6**	94.7	95.8
		50	97.4	97.2	97.4	**98.6**	94.7	95.8
	10	20	92.1	97.2	92.1	97.2	94.7	95.8
		30	94.7	**98.6**	97.4	**98.6**	94.7	97.2
		40	97.4	95.8	92.1	97.2	94.7	97.2
		50	97.4	97.2	97.4	95.8	97.4	97.2
	100	20	92.1	97.2	92.1	97.2	92.1	97.2
		30	94.7	**98.6**	97.4	**98.6**	94.7	**98.6**
		40	94.7	95.8	92.1	97.2	94.7	97.2
		50	97.4	97.2	97.4	95.8	97.4	95.8

factor of the SVM classifier with linear kernel for gene selection. The C_2 is the penalty factor of the SVM classifier used for final classification. The B.C. is the abbreviation of Breast Cancer dataset, and L. is the abbreviation of Leukemia dataset. For polynomial kernel, the degree is set to 2, and in Gaussian kernel, the σ is set to 0.1. The size of the selected genes N is set to 20, 30, 40 or 50.

For the Breast Cancer data, the proposed method can reach to the best accuracy rate 100%, with 20 selected genes and linear SVM classifier. For the Leukemia dataset, the highest accuracy rate is 98.61%, with at least 30 genes selected.

From Table 1, we can also conclude that the linear kernel classifier can give the same or even better classification performance than the polynomial and Gaussian kernels. To the gene selection phase, the penalty factor C_I of the linear classifier should not be too large, such as over 100, or else the classification accuracy will decrease.

Table 2 shows the performance of the other methods on the two datasets as reported in the literature. All these methods use LOOCV and so their classification accuracies can be directly compared. As can be seen, the proposed method, attain the best classification accuracy (of 100%) on the Breast Cancer dataset. On the Leukemia dataset, the proposed method also outperforms all other methods except for the JCFO(Joint Classifier and Feature Optimization) [13] with linear kernel.

Table 2. Classification accuracies (%) obtained by the various methods as reported in the literature

Classifier	Breast Cancer	Leukemia
Support Vector Machine (linear kernel) [13]	97.4	94.4
Relevance Vector Machine (linear kernel) [14]	94.7	94.4
Relevance Vector Machine (no kernel) [14]	89.5	97.2
Sparse probit regression(linear kernel) [15]	97.4	97.2
Sparse probit regression(no kernel) [15]	84.2	97.2
JCFO (linear kernel) [12]	97.4	**100.0**
Proposed method	**100.0**	98.6

In the 72-fold cross-validation cycle, we conduct SVM-based gene selection and classification operations, as described in the section 4. There is no guarantee that the same subset of genes will be selected in each of the 72 cycles in 72-fold cross-validation. However, the most informative genes tend to be selected more consistently than others across cycles. So we select a minimal set of genes by collecting the genes with the highest picked frequencies during the 72 fold.

On the leukemia data, our method selected 25 genes (Table 3) from the microarray gene expression data. Using the selected genes, the LOOCV classification is performed. The training and testing accuracies were 100% and 100% respectively using SVM classifier with Gaussian kernel($\sigma = 0.0001, C = 1$). The selected genes are also belong to the top 33 genes used by Ben-Dor et al[14].

For Breast Cancer dataset, there are 21 genes which are chosen in all 38 LOOCV circulations. The 21 genes selected from Breast Cancer are listed in Table 4. When we use the new reduced subset to perform the LOOCV classification using SVM, the accuracy rates can reach to 100% using SVM classifier with Gaussian kernel($\sigma = 0.0001, C = 10$).

We show in Fig.1 and Fig.2 the expression values of the selected 25 and 21 genes subset from leukemia and breast cancer dataset, respectively. In Fig.1 and Fig.2, the columns represent different genes and the rows represent expression levels in different samples. In Fig.1, the left 25 columns are AML patients and the right 47 columns are ALL patients. In Fig.2, the left 18 columns are ER+ patients and the right 20 columns are ER- patients. From the figures, we can see that the selected genes can make very clear separation between two classes.

Table 3. Leukemia data: most significant genes

Gene ID	Gene description
760	CYSTATIN A
804	Macmarcks
1144	SPTAN1 Spectrin, alpha, non-erythrocytic 1 (alpha-fodrin)
1685	Termianl transferase mRNA
1779	MPO Myeloperoxidase
1829	PPGB Protective protein for beta-galactosidase (galactosialidosis)
1834	CD33 CD33 antigen (differentiation antigen)
1882	CST3 Cystatin C (amyloid angiopathy and cerebral hemorrhage)
1928	Oncoprotein 18 (Op18) gene
2020	FAH Fumarylacetoacetate
2111	ATP6C Vacuolar H+ ATPase proton channel subunit
2121	CTSD Cathepsin D (lysosomal aspartyl protease)
2288	DF D component of complement (adipsin)
2354	CCND3 Cyclin D3
3252	GLUTATHIONE S-TRANSFERASE, MICROSOMAL
3320	Leukotriene C4 synthase (LTC4S) gene
4196	PRG1 Proteoglycan 1, secretory granule
4328	PROTEASOME IOTA CHAIN
4377	ME491 gene extracted from H. sapiens gene for Me491/CD63 antigen
4847	Zyxin
6041	APLP2 Amyloid beta (A4) precursor-like protein protein 2
6185	SELL Leukocyte adhesion protein beta subunit
6281	MYL1 Myosin light chain (alkali)
6376	PFC Properdin P factor, complement
6855	TCF3 Transcription factor 3 (E2A immunoglobulin enhancer binding factors E12/E47)

Table 4. Breast cancer data: most significant genes

Gene ID	Gene description
495	Human mRNA for KIAA0068 gene
715	Human mRNA for KIAA0187 gene
1505	Human, plasminogen activator inhibitor-1 gene
1512	Human uroporphyrinogen III synthase mRNA
2542	Human Ca2-activated neutral protease large subunit
3087	Human heat-stable enterotoxin receptor mRNA
3823	Human protein kinase (JNK2) mRNA
4220	Human chitotriosidase precursor mRNA
4414	Human Bloom syndrome protein (BLM) mRNA
4445	Human retinal protein (HRG4) mRNA
4473	Homo sapiens Trio mRNA
5188	Human clone 23721 mRNA sequence
5433	Human sarcolipin (SLN) mRNA
5444	Homo sapiens sin3 associated polypeptide p18 (SAP18)
5524	Human mRNA for raf oncogene
5639	Human mRNA for D-amino acid oxidase (EC 1.4.3.3)
5859	Human mRNA for ribonuclease/angiogenin inhibitor
5914	Human mRNA for corticotropin-releasing factor binding protein (CRF-BP)
6247	H.sapiens mRNA for protein kinase C mu
6419	H.sapiens PrP gene, exon 2
6951	un-named-transcript-1 from H.sapiens cdc25 gene promoter region.

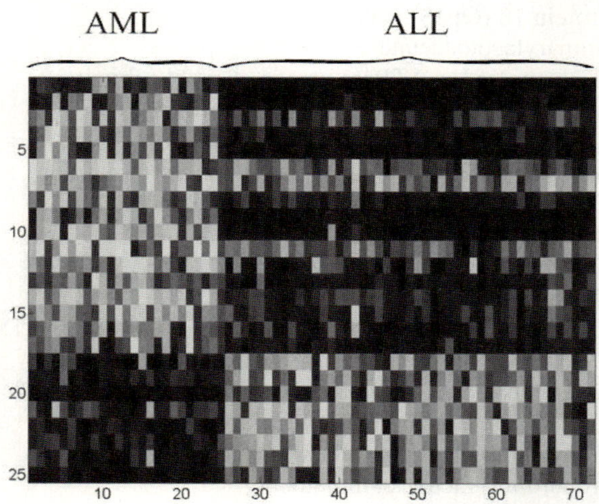

Fig. 1. Selected 25 genes from Leukemia dataset

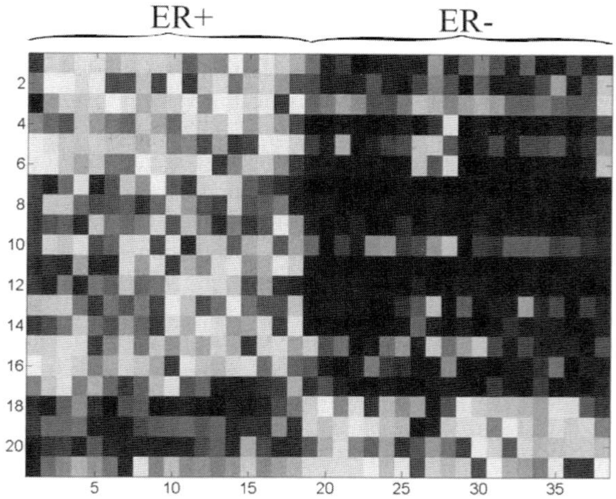

Fig. 2. Selected 21 genes from Brest cancer dataset

6 Conclusions

A new Wilcoxon rank sum test and SVM based gene selection scheme is proposed in this paper. Our method has been tested on Breast cancer and Leukemia data. The effects of different parameter settings on the classification performance are analyzed. And the subsets of the most informative genes are listed and their expression levels are sketched, which show that the selected genes can make clear separation between two classes. The comparisons with other existed methods show that the presented method outperforms most of others.

Acknowledgement

This paper is supported by the National Nature Science Foundation of China (No. 6040204), Program for New Century Excellent Talents in University, and the Excellent Youth Foundation of Hunan Province (06JJ1010).

References

1. Liu, H., Li, J., Wong, L.: A Comparative Study on Feature Selection and Classification Methods using Gene Expression Profiles and Proteomic Patterns. Genome Information 13, 51–60 (2002)
2. Liu, H., Li, J., Wong, L.: Selection of Patient Samples and Genes for Outcome Prediction. In: Proceedings of the IEEE Computational Systems Bioinformatics Conference, Stanford, pp. 382–392. IEEE Computer Society Press, Los Alamitos (2004)
3. Cristianini, N., Shawe-Taylor, J.: An Introduction to Support Vector Machines. Cambridge University Press, Cambridge (2000)

4. Guyon, I., Weston, J., Barnhill, S., Vapnik, V.: Gene Selection for Cancer Classification using Support Vector Machines. Machine Learning 46, 389–422 (2002)
5. Zhang, X., Wong, W.: Recursive Sample Classification and Gene Selection Based on SVM: Method and Software Description. In: Technical Report, Department of Biostatistics, Harvard School of Public Health, USA (2001)
6. Furlanello, C., Serafini, M., Merler, S., Jurman, G.: An Accelerated Procedure for Recursive Feature Ranking on Microarray Data. Neural Networks 16, 641–648 (2003)
7. Tang, Y., Zhang, Y., Huang, Z.: FCM-SVM-RFE Gene Feature Selection Algorithm for Leukemia Classification from Microarray Gene Expression Data. In: Proceedings of the IEEE International Conference on Fuzzy Systems, pp. 97–101. IEEE Computer Society Press, Los Alamitos (2005)
8. Duan, K., Rajapakse, J.C.: A Variant of SVM-RFE for Gene Selection in Cancer Classification with Expression Data. In: Proceedings of the IEEE Symposium on Computational Intelligence in Bioinformatics and Computational Biology, San Diego, pp. 49–55. IEEE Computer Society Press, Los Alamitos (2004)
9. Duan, K., Rajapakse, J.C., Haiying, W., Azuaje, F.: Multiple SVM-RFE for Gene Selection in Cancer Classification with Expression Data. IEEE Transactions on Nanobioscience 4, 228–233 (2005)
10. West, M., Blanchette, C., Dressman, H., et al.: Predicting the Clinical Status of Human Breast Cancer Using Gene Expression Profiles. In: Proceedings of the National Academy of Science, vol. 98, pp. 11462–11467 (2001)
11. Golub, T., Slonim, D., Tamayo, P., et al.: Molecular Classification of Cancer: Class Discovery and Class Prediction by Gene Expression Monitoring. Science 28, 531–537 (1999)
12. Krishnapuram, B., Carin, L., Hartemink, A.: Gene expression analysis: Joint Feature Selection and Classifier Design. In: Schölkopf, B., Tsuda, K., Vert, J-P (eds.) Kernel Methods in Computational Biology, Schölkopf, B, pp. 299–317. MIT Press, Cambridge, MA (2004)
13. Ben-Dor, A., Bruhn, L., Friedman, N. et al.: Tissue Classification with Gene Expression Profiles. Journal of Computational Biology 7, 559–583 (2000)
14. Li, Y., Campbell, C., Tipping, M.: Bayesian Automatic Relevance Determination Algorithms for Classifying Gene Expression Data. Bioinformatics 18, 1332–1339 (2002)
15. Figueiredo, M., Jain, A.: Bayesian Learning of Sparse Classifiers. In: Proceedings of International Conference on Computer Vision and Pattern Recognition, Wisconsin, pp. 35–41 (2001)

General Particle Swarm Optimization Based on Simulated Annealing for Multi-specification One-Dimensional Cutting Stock Problem

Xianjun Shen[1,2], Yuanxiang Li[2], Bojin Zheng[3], and Zhifeng Dai[2]

[1] Department of Computer Science, Central China Normal University, 430079 Wuhan, China
[2] State Key Lab of Software Engineering, Wuhan University, 430072 Wuhan, China
[3] College of Computer Science, South-Central University for Nationalities, 430074 Wuhan, China
xjshen@mail.ccnu.edu.cn

Abstract. In this paper a general particle swarm optimization based on simulated annealing algorithm (SA-GPSO) for the solution to multi-specification one-dimensional cutting stock problem is proposed. Due to the limitation of its velocity-displacement search model, particle swarm optimization (PSO) has less application on discrete and combinatorial optimization problems effectively. SA-GPSO is still based on PSO mechanism, but the new updating operator is developed from crossover operator and mutation operator of genetic algorithm. In order to repair invalid particle and reduce the searching space, best fit decrease (BFD) is introduced into repairing algorithm of SA-GPSO. According to the experimental results, it is observed that the proposed algorithm is feasible to solve both sufficient one-dimensional cutting problem and insufficient one-dimensional cutting problem.

1 Introduction

The particle swarm optimization (PSO) has been proposed recently and proved to be a powerful competitor in the field of optimization [1]. PSO has been shown to successfully optimize a wide range of continuous functions [2], however, due to the limitation of its velocity-displacement search model, the algorithm, which has less application on discrete and combinatorial optimization problems effectively [3].

This paper presents a general particle swarm optimization based on simulated annealing (SA-GPSO), which is still based on PSO mechanism, but the updating operator could integrate with other solutions such as simulated annealing and GA. SA-GPSO is applied to multi-specification one-dimensional cutting stock problem. The effectiveness of the proposed algorithm has been showed by the simulation results of sufficient one-dimensional cutting problem and insufficient one-dimensional cutting problem.

Y. Wang, Y. Cheung, and H. Liu (Eds.): CIS 2006, LNAI 4456, pp. 67–76, 2007.

2 Multi-specification One-Dimensional Cutting Stock Problem

Cutting stock problem is one of the representative combinatorial optimization problems. It is known that cutting stock problems are in general NP-complete and a solution can be found mostly by using approximate methods and heuristics methods [4]. Most methods consider trim loss as the main objective. The use of exact methods is limited to the problems of very small size. The problem occurs in many industrial processes and during the past few years it has attracted increased much attention of researchers from all over the world [5].

The purpose of this paper is to propose a general particle swarm optimization based on simulated annealing (SA) to solve multi-specification one-dimensional cutting stock problem (M1D-CSP), which is all stock lengths can be different. If there is an abundance of material, order lengths are cut in exactly the required number of pieces. Only one stock length is not cut to the end. The result is a residual length that could be used later [6].

The M1D-CSP is defined in a very similar way as in literatures. For every customer order a limited number of different stock lengths is available. Those stock lengths must be cut into a required number of pieces of different order lengths. All lengths are integers. The following notation is used:

c_i stock lengths; $i = 1,2,...,n$.

b_i number of stock length i .

l_j order lengths; $j = 1,2,...,m$.

d_j required number of pieces of order length l_j .

w_{ij} number of pieces of order length l_j having been cut from stock length i .

p_i indicates whether the stock length i is used in the cutting plan, $p_i \in \{0,1\}$. ($p_i = 0$, if stock length i is used in the cutting plan).

δ_i indicates the remainder of stock length i .

u_i indicates whether the remainder of stock length i does not count as trim loss, $u_i \in \{0,1\}$ ($u_i = 1$, if remainder is greater than UB and does not count as trim loss).

t_i indicates the extent of trim loss relating to stock length i : t_i is equal to δ_i for all used stock lengths, except for one that is longer than UB and can be returned to the stock and used in later cutting stock plans. t_i equals 0 for all unused stock lengths and the one stock length that is returned to the stock.

x_k number of stock length i having been cut from cutting plans.

UB upper bound for trim loss.

l' indicate the longest remainder of a cutting plan.

Two cases are possible:

Case 1: an order can be fulfilled because an abundance of material is in stock (sufficient cutting stock problem). It is the main task of the multi-specification one-dimensional cutting problem that is to minimize trim loss of cutting plan.

$$f(x) = \min(\sum_{i=1}^{n} x_k c_k - l') \tag{1}$$

s.t.

$$\sum_{k=1}^{n}\sum_{i=1}^{x_k} w_{ij}^k = d_j \ \ (j = 1,2,...,m) \tag{2}$$

$$x_k \le b_k \ \ (k = 1,2,...,n) \tag{3}$$

$$\sum_{j=1}^{m} w_{ij}^k l_i \le c_k \tag{4}$$

$$\delta_i - UB * u_j \ge 0 \ \ i = 1,2,...,n \tag{5}$$

$$\sum_{i=1}^{n} u_i \le 1 \tag{6}$$

$$w_{ij} \ge 0 \, . \tag{7}$$

$$UB \le \max \ l_i \tag{8}$$

$$t_i = \begin{cases} \delta_i \ if \ p_i = 0 \wedge u_i = 0 \\ 0 \ otherwise \end{cases} \tag{9}$$

$$t_i \ge 0 \ \ i = 1,2,...,n \tag{10}$$

$$\delta_i \ge 0 \ \ i = 1,2,...,n \tag{11}$$

Case 2: an order cannot be entirely fulfilled due to the shortage of material (insufficient cutting stock problem). Distribution of uncut order lengths is not important. y_j indicates number of pieces of order length j having been cut in a cutting plan.

$$f(x) = \min \sum_{k=1}^{n}\sum_{i=1}^{b_k}(c_k - \sum_{j=1}^{m} w_{ij}^k . l_j) \tag{12}$$

s.t.

$$\sum_{k=1}^{n}\sum_{i=1}^{b_k} w_{ij}^k = y_j \ \ (j = 1,2,...,m) \tag{13}$$

$$y_j \le d_j \ (j = 1, 2, \ldots m) \tag{14}$$

$$\sum_{j=1}^{m} w_{ij}^{k} l_i \le c_k \tag{15}$$

$$w_{ij} \ge 0 \tag{16}$$

$$\delta_i \ge 0 \ i = 1, 2, \ldots, n \tag{17}$$

3 Particle Swarm Optimization

PSO is a swarm intelligence optimization algorithm. The population of PSO is called a swarm and each individual in the population of PSO is conceptualized as a volume-less particle. The PSO algorithm is initialized with a population of random candidate solutions. Each particle is assigned a randomized velocity and is iteratively moved through the D-dimensional problem space.

Each particle is treated as a point in a D-dimensional space, and then the ith particle of the swarm can be represented as $X_i = (x_1, x_2, \ldots, x_{id})$. The best previous position of the i th particle is recorded and represented as $P_i = (p_{i1}, p_{i2}, \ldots, p_{id})$. The index of the best particle among all the particles in the population is represented by the symbol g, p_g is the position of the best particle of the whole swarm. The rate of the position change (velocity) for particle i is represented as $V_i = (v_{i1}, v_{i2}, \ldots, v_{id})$.

The position and velocity of each particle adjust to the following equation:

$$v_{\mathrm{id}}^{\mathrm{t+1}} = \omega v_{\mathrm{id}}^{\mathrm{t}} + \mathrm{c}_1 \mathrm{rand}_1() \times (p_{\mathrm{id}} - x_{\mathrm{id}}^{\mathrm{t}}) + \mathrm{c}_2 \mathrm{rand}_2() \times (p_{\mathrm{gd}} - x_{\mathrm{id}}^{\mathrm{t}}) \tag{18}$$

$$x_{\mathrm{id}}^{\mathrm{t+1}} = x_{\mathrm{id}}^{\mathrm{t}} + v_{\mathrm{id}}^{\mathrm{t}} \quad 1 \le i \le n \quad 1 \le d \le D \tag{19}$$

Where $i = 1, 2, \ldots, n$, n is the size of swarm; ω called inertia weight that is considered crucial for PSO's convergence behavior and employed to control the impact of the history of velocities on the current velocity. c_1 and c_2 are two positive constants, called the cognitive and social parameter respectively; $\mathrm{rand}_1()$ and $\mathrm{rand}_2()$ are two random functions uniformly distributed within the range $[0,1]$.

4 General Particle Swarm Optimization Based on SA

PSO does not have a direct crossover operator. However, the stochastic acceleration of a particle towards its previous best position, as well as towards the best particle of the swarm, resembles the crossover operator in Evolutionary computation [7]. In PSO the information exchange takes place only among the particle's own experience and the experience of the best particle in the swarm, instead of being carried from fitness dependent selected "parents" to descendants as in GA's [8]. Moreover, PSO's directional position updating operation resembles mutation of GA, with a kind of memory built in. GPSO model is still based on PSO mechanism, but the updating operator could integrate with simulated annealing and GA.

In general, though the convergent velocity of PSO is faster than GA, it is not satisfied with the convergent precision and easily run into the local optimistic result. SA is a kind of global optimization technique based on annealing of metal. SA can find the global optimistic result using stochastic searching technology from the means of probability. Simulated annealing algorithm has a strong ability to find the local optimistic result, and it can avoid the problem of local optimistic result.

SA-GPSO combining with simulated annealing and genetic operator is presented as a solution to the M1D-CSP optimization problem. The best position of each particle would replaced by Simulated annealing algorithm, it will be allow the fitness to be worse, permutation operator and mutation operator could enhance the diversity of the swarm and make an ideal balance between the global exploration capability and local exploitation capability.

4.1 Encoding Mechanism

To describe a multi- specification one-dimensional cutting stock plan based SA-GPSO, we must first specify the piece list and the stock available for the placement of the pieces. The cutting stock plan is a string with specified dimension. The position of each particle is represented as a string which length is the summary of the number different specification piece.

Each string denotes a cutting plan. Each position in the string represents a piece, with the value at the position representing the cutting pattern to be used with that piece. Initially the strings are randomly generated (with values restricted to the range of cutting patterns using 0 to represent an uncut piece). The coding string that is represented as $S_i S_j S_i ... S_k$ denote a cutting plan. Each bit of string indicates the serial number of stock that was cut. For example, the coding $S_1 S_4 S_2 ... S_3 S_7$ show which used to cutting plan that is the first stock, the forth stock, the second stock,..., the third stock and the seventh stock. The index of the i th bit show the i th stock was used to cut. After randomly generating the initial strings, they were assigned a fitness based on the different stock lengths and trim loss, where strings with better trim loss values are possibly replace their parent and be used in the next generation.

4.2 Repairing Algorithm

Because length of the stock is limited, some invalid particles will be produced in the course of swarms' initialization and iterating optimization, in these invalid particles, sum of length of pieces on some part of the stocks will exceed length of stock, this violates the constraint condition, which leads to invalidation of these particles.

Multi-specification one-dimensional cutting stock problem can be attributed to combination optimize problem, invalid particles disposed by punish function may not be licit particles, and might be participated in optimization continuously. In cutting stock problem, the best fitness of swarm calculated through algorithm should be licit, thus SA-GPSO adopt repairing method. Repairing method is more complex compared to punish function, but it is more suitable to M1d-CSP.

Recent researches on cutting stock problem are apt to compound approximate algorithm and other methods [9]. During the process of resolve cutting stock problem, position of the particles will be decoded to detect whether it is a feasible solution, if constraint condition is violated, it's not a feasible solution, best fit decrease (BFD) approximate algorithm will be introduced to seek for appropriate stocks for those pieces of the infeasible particle and repaired invalid particles. Finally, the fitness of particles will be calculated and coded according to feasible solution found.

A detailed description of these steps is as follow:

Step 1. Check randomly generating the initial cutting stock plans, delete those stock which are not cut, then sort those stock which have been cut in ascending order, the symbol k' is the maximum sequence number of which have been cut.

Step 2. Sort the pieces in decreasing order which have been cut on the stock that represents as S_i.

Step 3. Sum the length of all pieces which have been cut on each stock, if the sum of S_i have been exceed the length limited of S_i, then move the less length piece to the temporary pool.

Step 4. If the sum the length of all pieces on stock S_i exceed the length limited of S_i, then go back to Step 3, else stop.

Step 5. Repeat Step 2-Step 4, until maximum the sequence number of stock equal k'.

Step 6. Insert those pieces in the temporary pool into stock $S_i (i = 1, 2, ..., k')$.

Step 7. If the temporary pool is not empty, then $k' = k' + 1$ (append a stock), repeat Step 6-Step 7,until the temporary pool is empty.

Step 8. Calculate the fitness of cutting plan.

4.3 SA-GPSO Procedure

In the follow, we describe SA-GPSO algorithm for multi-specification one-dimensional cutting stock problem. The following notation is defined.

x_i^t the current position of each particle.

p_i^t the current fitness of each particle.

$pbest_i^t$ the best fitness of each particle.

ΔE the change of the fitness of each particle

$xbest_i^t$ the best position of each particle.

$gbest^t$ the best fitness of whole swarm.

$xgbest^t$ the best position of whole swarm.
n the size of swarm.
T the current number of iterative generations.
α coefficient of the cool schedule.
random() the random function uniformly distributed within the range [0,1]
MAXGENS the number of maximum iterative generation.
INITEMPER the initial temperature.
TERTEMPER the terminate temperature.

After preparing above, the general procedure for implementing SA-GPSO algorithm is as follow:

Step 1. $t = 0$, initialize the swarm randomly.
Step 2. Set $T(t) = INITEMPER$.

Step 3. For each particle of swarm, Choose x_i^t and $xbest_i^t$, and generate x'^t_i by crossover operator.

Step 4. For each particle of swarm, Choose x'^t_i and $xgbest^t$, and generate x''^t_i by crossover operator.

Step 5. For each particle of swarm, Choose x''^t_i, and generate x_i^{t+1} by mutation operator.

Step 6. Calculate the fitness each particle p_i^{t+1} ($p_i^{t+1} = f(x_i^{t+1})$).

Step 7. For each particle of swarm, Calculate ΔE, if $\min\{1, \exp(\Delta E / T)\}$ is above *random*(), then x_i^{t+1} replace $xbest_i^{t+1}$.

Step 8. Search the best position of each particle of swarm so far.
Step 9. Search the best particle of the whole swarm.
Step 10. if $T > TERTEMPER$, $T(t+1) = \alpha T(t)$.
Step 11. if $t < MAXGENS$, $t = t+1$, go to step 2.
Step 12. Output the final results of SA-GPSO.

5 Implementation and Application

As we have seen in the previous sections, these problems were tested that is two types of multi-specification one-dimensional cutting problems.

5.1 Sufficient Multi-specification Cutting Stock Problem

It is supposed all orders can be fulfilled because abundance of materials is in stock. The main object of SA-GPSO is that search a cutting plan that has the least trim loss.

Instance 1: The problem was given in literature [10]. There is a steel structure project that demand different pieces which of specifications shows in table 1.

Table 1. Specifications of steel pieces

Length	Demand	Length	Demand	Length	Demand	Length	Demand
2144	4	1422	4	1296	3	906	1
2137	4	1419	2	1167	8	889	8
1694	4	1416	4	1107	2	885	8
1687	2	1400	1	1094	4	861	9
1676	2	1394	1	1081	16	855	8
1541	1	1392	4	1034	8	828	8
1494	4	1389	4	984	8	817	8
1464	4	1387	1	978	8	811	8
1446	1	1343	1	925	1	808	8
1426	1	1337	1	925	8	807	8

Table 2. Solution of instance 1 with SA-GPSO

No.	Stock length	Pieces length (Pieces amount)	Trim loss	Availability ratio
1	6000	1694(2) 1687 885	40	99.33
2		2137 1464 1392 978	29	99.52
3		1296 978	3726	37.9
4		1081(3) 1034 861 828	34	99.43
5		1422 984 906 889 885(2)	29	99.52
6		2144 2137 1694	25	99.58
7		2144 1081 925 925 889	36	99.4
8		889 861(3) 855(2) 817	1	99.98
9		984 855(2) 828(2) 817(2)	16	99.73
10		1094 817 808(3) 807(2)	51	99.15
11	8000	2144 1422 1389 1081 1034 925	5	99.94
12		2144 1426 1422 1337 807(2)	57	99.29
13		2137 1167(2) 1107 808 807(2)	0	100
14		1494 1107 1081 978 861 828(2) 817	6	99.92
15		1387 1167 1167 1081(3) 1034	2	99.98
16		1416 1094 1081 1034 925 828 808 807	7	99.91
17		1094 885(5) 861 811 808	1	99.99
18		1676 1419 828 811(5)	25	99.69
19	9000	2137 1676 1422 1394 1392 978	1	99.99
20		1464 1392 1296 1081(2) 978 889 817	2	99.98
21		1494 1416 1081(2) 1034 984(2) 925	1	99.99
22		1446 1389 1343 1094 1081 984 855 808	0	100
23		1687 1494 1167 978(2) 925(2) 817	29	99.68
24		1464 1416(2) 1389 1167(2) 978	3	99.92
25		1464 1167 1034 984 925(2) 855 828 807	11	99.88
26		1694 1541 1419 1389 1034(2) 889	0	100
27		1400 1392 984 889(2) 861(2) 855(2)	14	99.84
28		1494 1296 1081 984 889 817 811(3)	6	99.93

The optimal cutting plan was given in literature [10] by a hybrid genetic algorithm that it need 28 stocks, the longest remainder of stock is 2746 (The availability ratio of the stock is 65.68%.). The average availability ratio of other stocks is 98.88%.

According to the results in Table 2, The optimization cutting plan need 28 stocks by general particle swarm optimization, The longest remainder of stock 3 is 3726 (The availability ratio of the stock is 37.9%.) and can be used in later cutting plans. The average availability ratio of other stocks is 99.79%. The later optimal cutting plan is better than the optimal former cutting plan. Thus, the purpose of such a general particle swarm optimization method is its ability to cut order lengths in exactly required number of pieces and to cumulate consecutive residual lengths in one piece that could be used later.

5.2 Insufficient Multi-specification Cutting Stock Problem

Due to the shortage of material, an order cannot be entirely fulfilled. The main task of optimization algorithm is as possible as utilize all stocks and decrease the trim loss of the optimal cutting plans.

Instance 2: The problem was also given in literature [10]. There is a steel structure project that demand different pieces which of specifications shows in table 1. The order cannot be entirely fulfilled due to the shortage of material. The numbers of the three different type material are 5,3,6.

Table 3. Solution of instance 2 with SA-GPSO

No.	Stock length	Pieces length (Pieces amount)	Trim loss	Availability ratio
1		2137 1034 984(2) 861	0	100
2		1419 1081 984 889 817 808	2	99.97
3	6000	1464 1446 1081(2) 925	3	99.95
4		984 861(2) 855 817 811 808	3	99.95
5		1392 1094 984 861 855 811	3	99.95
6		1541 1464 1167(2) 925(2) 811	0	100
7	8000	1687 1387 1081(2) 978(2) 808	0	100
8		2137 1494 1392 1081 1034 861	1	99.99
9		978(3) 925 906 889 855(2) 828 808	0	100
10		1389 925 906 889 828 817(2) 811(2) 807	0	100
11	9000	1694 1392 1389 1167 885 828(2) 817	0	100
12		1167(3) 984(2) 978 889 855 808	1	99.99
13		2137 1694 1464 1426 1392 885	2	99.98
14		1694 1464 1392 1389 1167 1081 811	2	99.98

The optimal cutting plan was given in literature [10] that it need 14 stocks and the total remainder of stock is 201 by the hybrid genetic algorithm. The average availability ratio of other stocks is 99.81%.

According to the results in Table 3, The optimization cutting plan need 14 stocks and the total remainder of stock is 17 by the general particle swarm optimization, The trim loss of the stock 1,6,7,9,10,11 is 0. The average availability ratio of all stocks is 99.98%. The trim loss of the cutting plan is extremely low. So it is a better optimal solution.

6 Conclusion

This paper analyzes the mathematical models of multi-specification one-dimensional cutting stock problem and proposes a general particle swarm optimization based on SA algorithm. The main purpose of algorithm is its ability to cut order lengths in exactly required number of pieces and to cumulate the trim loss in one stock which can be used later. SA-GPSO has integrated with simulated annealing algorithm, genetic algorithm and BFD heuristic method and greatly decreased trim loss of typical M1d-CSP. The experimental result shows the algorithm can obtain satisfying effect for solving both sufficient multi-specification one-dimensional cutting problem and insufficient multi-specification one-dimensional cutting problem. In view of the success of SA-GPSO in M1d-CSP, the optimal method can be extended to solve two-dimensional layout optimization problems and three-dimensional layout optimization problems.

References

1. Kennedy, J., Eberhart, R.C.: Particle Swarm Optimization. In: Proceedings of IEEE International Conference on Neural Networks, Perth Australia, pp. 1942–1948. IEEE Computer Society Press, Los Alamitos (1995)
2. Shi, Y., Eberhart, R.C.: Parameter Selection in Particle Swarm Adaptation. In: Evolutionary Programming, vol. VII, pp. 591–600. Springer, Heidelberg (1997)
3. Clerc, M., Kennedy, J.: The Particle Swarm - Explosion, Stability, and Convergence in a multidimensional complex space. IEEE Transactions on Evolutionary Computation 6, 58–73 (2002)
4. Gradišar, M., Jesenko, J., Resinovič, G.: Optimization of Roll Cutting in Clothing Industry. Computers and Operations Research 24, 945–953 (1997)
5. Schilling, G., Georgiadis, M.: An Algorithm for the Determination of Optimal Cutting Patterns. Computers and Operations Research 29, 1041–1058 (2002)
6. Dyckhoff, H.A: Typology of Cutting and Packing Problems. European Journal of Operational Research 44, 145–159 (1990)
7. Eberhart, R.C., Shi, Y.: Comparison Between Genetic Algorithms and Particle Swarm Optimization. In: Porto, V.W., Waagen, D. (eds.) Evolutionary Programming VII. LNCS, vol. 1447, pp. 611–616. Springer, Heidelberg (1998)
8. Parsopoulos, K.E., Vrahatis, M.N.: Recent Approaches to Global Optimization Problems Through Particle Swarm Optimization. Natural Computing 1, 235–306 (2002)
9. Gradišar, M., Kljajić, M., Resinovič, G.: A Hybrid Approach for Optimization of One-dimensional Cutting. European Journal of Operational Research 119, 165–174 (1999)
10. Peiyong, L.: Optimization for Variable Inventory of One-dimensional Cutting Stock. Mechanical Science and Technology 22, 80–86 (2003)

Neurodynamic Analysis for the Schur Decomposition of the Box Problems

Quanju Zhang[1], Fuye Feng[2], and Zhenghong Wei[3]

[1] Management Department, City College, Dongguan University of Technology, Dongguan, Guangdong, China
zhangquanju126@126.com
[2] Software College, Dongguan University of Technology, Dongguan, Guangdong, China
fengye408@dgut.edu.cn
[3] Mathematics Department, Shenzhen University, Shenzhen, Guangdong, China
zhwei@math.hkbu.edu.hk

Abstract. Neurodynamic analysis for solving the Schur decomposition of the box problems is presented in this paper. By constructing a number of dynamic systems, all the eigenvectors of a given matrix pair (A, B) can be searched and thus the decomposition realized. Each constructed dynamical system is demonstrated to be globally convergent to an exact eigenvector of the matrix box pair (A, B). It is also demonstrated that the dynamical systems are primal in the sense of the neural trajectories never escape from the feasible region when starting at it. Compared with the existing neural network models for the generalized eigenvalue problems, the proposed neurodynamic approach has two advantages: 1) it can find all the eigenvectors and 2) all the proposed systems globally converge to the problem's exact eigenvectors.

1 Introduction

Computing the eigenvalues and corresponding eigenvectors of a matrix box pair (A, B) is necessary in many scientific and engineering problems, e.g. in signal processing, control theory, geophysics, etc. It is an important topic in numerical algebra to develop new methods for this problem and traditional methods for this problem are included in Golub's book [7] and more references can be found therein.

From the seminal work of Hopfield and Tank [9], neural network method is encouraging because the method behaves two novel characters: one is the computation can perform in real-time on line and the other is the hardware implementation can be designed by application-specific integrated circuits.

The mathematical interpretation of the neural network method for optimization is usually transformed into a dynamical (or ode) system and called neurodynamic optimization approach [16]. A detail mathematical analysis for the neural network methods can be found in an excellent book [6] where the dynamical system theory used in neural network is studied in an unified framework

Y. Wang, Y. Cheung, and H. Liu (Eds.): CIS 2006, LNAI 4456, pp. 77–86, 2007.

and the applications of the theory are given for various typical neural network models. The mathematical feature of the neurodynamic systems is that a continuous path starting from an initial point can be generated and eventually the path will converge to the solution. This feature is quite different from conventional optimization methods where a sequence of points, or a discrete path, is generated.

Neural network method for solving various optimization problems has been investigated extensively by many researchers , see [2,5,13,19,20], in the past thirty years since the method was employed for unconstrained optimization problem first [9]. As an introductory book in the neural network design [2], many neural network models are introduced for various scientific problems there. Xia and Wang [20] gave a general framework for the global convergence neural network design which undertakes various gradient based neural network models under this framework. A typical penalty function based neural network was reported in [13] for solving general nonlinear programming problems. For the projection based neural network method, Xia and Wang [19] pioneered an excellent work for constrained programming problems. As the first usage of neural network method in fractional programming problems, Feng [5] developed a promising neural network model for the linear fractional programming problems. For problems of finding roots to polynomials, Huang [10,11,12] made an excellent neural network research which opens another field of neural network's application area.

Neural networks for solving eigenvalue problems are much less reported than the existing models for optimization problems. There exist several models for solving this problem by penalty functions [2,3]. As it is known, penalty function method may generate infeasible solutions and hence it is not encouraging in conventional algorithms [1]. For the neural network method to optimization problems, Xia and Wang [19] reported an example which shows the penalty based neural network model proposed by Kennedy in [13] may fail to find true solutions. So, penalty function based type of neural network models is not available in the neural network design. Fortunately, Feng [4] developed a new model which overcomes the shortcomings of the existing models for solving eigenvalue problems.

The neural network method for the box problems were reported in [17,18,21]. Based on penalty function method [17], a multi-layered artificial neural network model was proposed for solving the generalized eigenvalue problem (see the following 1-2). It is known that by using the penalty method to construct neural network models or to make classical algorithms has following three explicit defects [1]: 1) there is a penalty parameter to tune and no rule available can be used to guarantee a good choice for the parameter; 2) it is usually occurring in the penalty method to find infeasible points as optimal solutions instead of true optimal solutions; 3) constructing neural network with a penalty function, stability result usually can not be guaranteed in most cases [3], [13], [17]. So, penalty function method is little employed in practical computation due to the existence of these shortcomings both in classical optimization algorithms and neural network designs.

The second one [18] using term $B^{-1}A$ in the neural network model which may lead to ill-conditioned situation, that is, $B^{-1}A$ will be calculated inaccurately if $\|B\|_2\|B^{-1}\|_2$ is large and there still no complete cure when this ill-conditioned case occurs. Furthermore, the global convergence did not guaranteed which limits the model's application area also.

The third one [21] gave a model which can only solve a special case when A and B have the same eigenvector for the extreme eigenvalue. It is obvious that the required condition is little satisfied in practical problems.

Motivated by the work stated previously, this paper presents a new neurodynamic approach for solving the box Schur decomposition problems. Unlike the current ones, the new method consists of a series of dynamical systems. Each system is proved to be always feasible and globally convergent to one exact eigenvector of the matrix box (A, B). This new approach overcomes all the shortcomings in the existing models and all the eigenvectors can be found by using the proposed method.

The remaining parts of this paper are organized as follows. For the first eigenvector, Section II formulates the problem as a optimization problem and reveals briefly the idea of proposing the neurodynamic approach for solving it. In section III, the neurodynamic system is proposed and the global convergence is demonstrated then. In section IV, we propose dynamical system for other eigenvectors and finally, in section V summarize the main results and make a concluding remark.

2 Dynamical System and Basic Properties

It is well known that the computation of an generalized eigenvalue λ and its corresponding eigenvector $v = [v_1, \cdots, v_n]^T \neq 0 \in R^n$ for a real matrix box $A, B \in R^{n\times n}$ leads to solve the following algebraic system of equations

$$(A - \lambda B)v = 0, \tag{1}$$

where the matrix pair (A, B) is called a box. We assume A is a real symmetric matrix and B a real symmetric positive definite matrix. If v is a generalized eigenvector, so is any multiple of v with a nonzero multiplying factor α because $(A - \lambda B)\alpha v = 0$ when $(A - \lambda B)v = 0$. So, in order to eliminate multiplicity of eigenvectors, normalization to unit length with respect to B is usually employed in the computation, i.e., the constraint

$$v^T Bv = 1, \tag{2}$$

is required.

Clearly, if $B = I$, here I is the identity matrix, the generalized eigenvalue problem becomes the ordinary eigenvalue problem and a promising neural network method for this problem was proposed by Feng [4].

Let $X = \{x_1, x_2, \cdots, x_n\}$ be the eigenvector set for problem (1-2) with the corresponding eigenvalue set $\Lambda = \{\lambda_1, \cdots, \lambda_n\}$. The purpose of this paper is to construct neurodynamic systems for identifying this set X. The problem is called the Schur decomposition of the box problems.

Consider the dynamical system as follows

$$\frac{dx}{dt} = -\|Bx\|^2 Ax + x^T BAxBx. \tag{3}$$

It is easy to see that any nonzero equilibrium point x of (3) is a generalized eigenvector of (1) with the corresponding eigenvalue

$$\lambda = \frac{x^T BAx}{\|Bx\|^2}.$$

Conversely, if x is an eigenvector of (1) with eigenvalue λ, that is $Ax = \lambda Bx$, then $x^T BAx = \lambda \|Bx\|^2$ and hence

$$\lambda = \frac{x^T BAx}{\|Bx\|^2}.$$

Substituting this λ into $Ax = \lambda Bx$ and multiplying both sides with $\|Bx\|^2$ gives us

$$x^T BAxBx - \|Bx\|^2 Ax = 0,$$

it means x to be a nonzero equilibrium point of (3). The previous argumentation gives the following theorem which describes the relationship of solution to the eigenvalue problem (1) and the equilibrium point set of the dynamical system (3).

Theorem 1. A vector x is a nonzero equilibrium point of (3) if and only if x is an eigenvector of (1).

Since the right side of the dynamical system (3) is continuously differentiable in R^n and hence locally Lipschitzian continuous everywhere, by Picard theorem [8], the system exists an unique solution $x(t), t \in [0, \omega)$ for every initial point $x(0) = x_0 \in R^n$.

By considering the normalization constraint (2), the trajectory starting at this set has the following important dynamical property.

Theorem 2. Dynamical system (3) is positive invariant with respect to F. Any solution $x(t)$ starting at $F = \{x | x^T Bx = 1\}$, e.g. $x(0) = x_0 \in F$, is bounded and hence the existence interval can be extended to ∞.

Proof: The differentiation of function $x^T Bx$ with respect t along the solution $x(t)$ is calculated as follows

$$\frac{1}{2}\frac{d(x^T Bx)}{dt}|_{(3)} = -x^T B\|Bx\|^2 Ax + x^T BBxx^T BAx \tag{4}$$

$$= -\|Bx\|^2 x^T BAx + \|Bx\|^2 x^T BAx \tag{5}$$

$$= 0. \tag{6}$$

This means the function $x^T Bx$ keeps constant along the neural trajectory of (3), so

$$x^T(t)Bx(t) = x_0^T Bx_0 = 1. \tag{7}$$

It implies that the solution will stay in F for all $t \geq 0$ when starting at it, that is, the set F is positive invariant.

By (7), it follows that $\|B^{1/2}x\|^2 = 1$, so

$$\begin{aligned}\|x(t)\| &= \|B^{-1/2}B^{1/2}x\| &(8)\\ &\leq \|B^{-1/2}\|\|B^{1/2}x\| &(9)\\ &\leq \|B^{-1/2}\|, &(10)\end{aligned}$$

this means the solution is bounded. Thus, the existence interval of $x(t)$ can be extended to ∞.

In the coming section, we will give the global convergence of the proposed dynamical system.

3 Global Convergence

This section discusses the stability property of dynamical system (3). First, we give the definition of convergence for a dynamical system.

Definition 1. Let $x(t)$ be a solution of system $\dot{x} = F(x)$. The system is said to be globally convergent to a set X with respect to set W if every solution $x(t)$ starting at W satisfies

$$\rho(x(t), X) \to 0, \quad as \quad t \to \infty, \tag{11}$$

here $\rho(x(t), X) = \inf_{y \in X} \|x - y\|$ and $x(0) = x_0 \in W$.

For the dynamical system (3), we have the following convergence result.

Theorem 3. System (3) is globally convergent to the eigenvector set X with respect to set F.

Proof: Define an energy function $V(x) = \frac{1}{2}x^T Ax$ and compute its total derivative along any neural network trajectory $x(t)$ starting at $x_0 \in W$ of dynamical system (3) we get

$$\begin{aligned}\dot{V} &= x^T A\frac{dx}{dt} &(12)\\ &= -\|Bx\|^2 x^T AAx + x^T ABxx^T BAx &(13)\\ &= -\|Bx\|^2\|Ax\|^2 + (x^T BAx)^2. &(14)\end{aligned}$$

By Cauchy-Schwartz inequality, it follows that

$$\begin{aligned}(x^T BAx)^2 &= ((Bx)^T Ax)^2 &(15)\\ &\leq \|Bx\|^2\|Ax\|^2. &(16)\end{aligned}$$

The two equations (14) and (16) lead to

$$\dot{V} = \frac{dV}{dt} \leq 0, \tag{17}$$

it means the energy of $V(x)$ is decreasing along any trajectory of (3).

This and the boundedness of $x(t)$ imply that $V(x)$ is a Liapunov function to system (3). So, by LaSalle invariant set principle [6,15], we know that all these trajectories of (3) will converge to the largest invariant set Σ of set E like

$$\Sigma \subseteq E = \{x \mid \frac{dV}{dt} = 0\}. \tag{18}$$

However, we know that the equality holds for Cauchy-Schwartz inequality only if there exists a λ such that $Ax = \lambda Bx$, that is, x has to be in X. Noting that $x(t)$ is primal with respect to set F, e.g. $x^T x = 1$, we guarantee that $x(t)$ will approach the eigenvector set X. Theorem 3 is proved to be true then.

Next, we will construct other dynamical systems to identify more elements of X.

4 Extension of the Neurodynamic System

This section focuses on the construction of dynamical systems used to identifying other elements in X. According to the previous section, one eigenvector can be found by the dynamical system (3) above. Without loss of generality, we assume the eigenvector identified by (3) is the first element in X, namely, $x_1 \in X$ with the corresponding eigenvalue λ_1.

Consider the following programming (P1):

$$\min \quad \tfrac{1}{2} x^T A x \tag{19}$$

$$\text{s.t.} \quad x^T B x = 1 \tag{20}$$

$$x_1^T B x = 0 \tag{21}$$

The feasible set of this programming (P1) is denoted by

$$F_1 = \{x | x^T B x = 1, x_1^T B x = 0\}.$$

The following lemma gives the relationship of vector Bx_1 and any feasible vector Bx in F_1.

Lemma 1. Vector Bx_1 and any $Bx \in F_1$ are linearly independent.

Proof: For $Bx \in F_1$, suppose there exist scalars l_1, l_2 such that

$$l_1 B x_1 + l_2 B x = 0, \tag{22}$$

Multiplying both sides of (22) with x_1^T and x^T respectively gives us

$$l_1 x_1^T B x_1 + l_2 x_1^T B x = 0, \tag{23}$$

$$l_1 x^T B x_1 + l_2 x^T B x = 0. \tag{24}$$

Noting $x_1^T Bx_1 = 1, x^T Bx_1 = 0$, and by (23)-(24), it follows that $l_1 = 0, l_2 = 0$. So, vectors Bx_1 and Bx are linearly independent.

Let G be the matrix (Bx, Bx_1), here $x \in F_1$, Lemma 1 means that Bx_1 and Bx are linearly independent, it follows that the following Gram matrix

$$G^T G = \begin{pmatrix} x^T B \\ x_1^T B \end{pmatrix} (Bx, Bx_1) = \begin{pmatrix} x^T B^2 x & x^T B^2 x_1 \\ x_1^T B^2 x & x_1^T B^2 x_1 \end{pmatrix}$$

is invertible. So, the projection operator

$$P = I - G(G^T G)^{-1} G^T$$

is well-defined for all $x \in F_1$.

Let W be the subspace spanned by vectors Bx, Bx_1, that is $W = span\{Bx, Bx_1\}$, and its orthogonal complementarity space $W^\perp$. Then the projection operator P defined above maps R^n into $W^\perp$. Properties of this operator are summarized in the following lemma.

Lemma 2. The operator P has the following properties:

a) P is nonexpansive, that is, for any $u, v \in R^n$, we have $\|Pu - Pv\| \leq \|u - v\|$,
b) $P^2 = P$,
c) $G^T P = 0$.

Proof: For a), see [14] pp: 9-10.
b) is obtained by the following computation

$$\begin{aligned} P^2 &= I - G(G^T G)^{-1} G^T - G(G^T G)^{-1} G^T + G(G^T G)^{-1} G^T G (G^T G)^{-1} G^T \quad (25) \\ &= P. \quad (26) \end{aligned}$$

c) follows from $G^T P = G^T - G^T G (G^T G)^{-1} G^T = 0$.

Let $\lambda_1 = x_1^T A x_1$ and define μ_1 as

$$\mu_1 = \begin{cases} 0, & \text{if} \quad \lambda_1 = 0, \\ k_1, & \text{if} \quad \lambda_1 \neq 0 \end{cases}$$

here k_1 is a constant that will be determined afterwards.

We can now propose dynamical system for the second eigenvector as follows

$$\frac{dx}{dt} = -P(Ax - \mu_1 x_1). \quad (27)$$

By a) and Lemma 2, it follows that there exists unique solution $x(t), t \in [0, \omega)$ for any initial point $x(0) = x_0 \in R^n$. Similarly, for the initial point in F_1, the solution is bounded and can be extended to ∞.

Theorem 4. Dynamical system (27) is positive invariant with respect to F_1. Any solution $x(t)$ starting at $F_1 = \{x|x^T Bx = 1, x_1^T Bx = 0\}$, e.g. $x(0) = x_0 \in F_1$, is bounded and hence can be extended to ∞.

Proof: Let $h = (\frac{1}{2}x^T Bx, h_2 = x_1^T Bx)^T$, computing the total derivative of $h_i, i = 1, 2$ along the solution of dynamical system (27) starting at F_1 gives us

$$\frac{dh}{dt} = [\nabla h]^T \frac{dx}{dt} = -G^T P(Ax - \mu_1 Ax_1) = 0, \tag{28}$$

the last equality above comes from c) of Lemma 2.
So

$$h(x(t)) = h(x(0)) = h(x_0), \tag{29}$$

that is, $x^T(t)Bx(t) = 1, x_1^T Bx(t) = 0$. Thus, $x(t) \in F_1$. It means F_1 is positive invariant. Obviously, $x(t)$ is bounded and hence it can be extended to ∞.

Theorem 5. System (27) is globally convergent to the eigenvector set X/x_1 with respect to set F_1, here X/x_1 means the residue set $X_1 = \{x_2, x_3, \cdots, x_n\}$.
Proof: Define an energy function

$$V_1(x) = \frac{1}{2}(x - \mu_1 x_1)^T A(x - \mu_1 x_1)$$

and compute its total derivative along any solution $x(t), x(0) \in F_1$ of system (27), we get

$$\dot{V_1} = \frac{dV_1(x)}{dt}|_{(27)} = -(x - \mu_1 x_1)^T APA(x - \mu_1 x_1). \tag{30}$$

From this and b) of Lemma 2, it is easy to see

$$\dot{V_1} = -\|PA(x - \mu_1 x_1)\|^2 \leq 0. \tag{31}$$

This and the boundedness of $x(t)$ means $V(x)$ is a Liapunov function of system (27). From LaSalle invariant set principle, it follows that $x(t)$ approaches the largest invariant subset of the following set

$$M = \{x|\dot{V_1} = 0\}.$$

By (31), it is easy to see $\dot{V_1} = 0$ only if $PA(x - \mu_1 x_1) = 0$. We know that P is the projection operator from R^n to $W^\perp$. So, $Py = 0$ if and only if $y \in W$. That is $A(x - \mu_1 x_1) \in W$. Thus, there exist n_1, n_2 such that

$$Ax - \mu_1 Ax_1 = n_1 Bx_1 + n_2 Bx. \tag{32}$$

Two cases appear:
1) If $\lambda_1 = x_1^T Ax_1 = 0$, then $\mu_1 = 0$ by the definition of μ_1.

From (32), it follows that

$$Ax = n_1 Bx_1 + n_2 Bx. \tag{33}$$

Multiplying both sides of (33) with x_1^T, we get

$$x_1^T Ax = n_1 x_1^T Bx_1 + n_2 x_1^T Bx. \tag{34}$$

Note that $x_1^T Ax = x^T Ax_1$, $Ax_1 = \lambda_1 Bx_1 = 0$ and $x_1^T Bx_1 = 1$, $x_1^T Bx = 0$, we obtain, by (34), $n_1 = 0$. Substituting $n_1 = 0$ into (33) gives us $Ax = n_2 Bx$.

2) If $\lambda_1 = x_1^T Ax_1 \neq 0$, then $\mu_1 = k_1$ by the definition of μ_1.

We will give the choice of this k_1 such that the limiting point to be an eigenvector. By $Ax_1 = \lambda_1 Bx_1 = (x_1^T Ax_1)Bx_1$ and (32), we get

$$\begin{aligned} Ax &= k_1 Ax_1 + n_1 Bx_1 + n_2 Bx \\ &= n_1 Bx_1 + n_2 Bx + k_1(x_1^T Ax_1)Bx_1. \end{aligned} \tag{35}$$

Let $n_1 + k_1 x_1^T Ax_1 = 0$, that is:

$$k_1 = -\frac{n_1}{x_1^T Ax_1}.$$

From (35), we get $Ax = n_2 Bx$.

From the argumentation in the two cases above, we know that the solution $x(t)$ will approach a point x such that $Ax = n_2 Bx$. By noting that $x(t)$ is invariant with F_1, it can be guaranteed that this x belongs to X and orthogonal to the previous x_1. Theorem 5 is proved then.

With exact the same idea, other dynamical systems can be constructed inductively to identify the remaining eigenvectors in X and the global convergence can be demonstrated in the same way. By mathematical induction, all the eigenvectors of the box problems can be found by constructing the corresponding dynamical systems. Therefore, the Schur decomposition of the box problems can be well realized by this neurodynamic approach in the promising way.

5 Conclusion

We have given a neurodynamic analysis for the Schur decomposition of the box problem. This neurodynamic approach tracks a constructive framework for proposing the dynamical systems. It is shown that the stability of the proposed dynamical systems behaves global convergence with respect to the problem's feasible set. This approach has overcome all the defects existing in the neural network models before.

Acknowlegements

The research was supported by the Doctoral Foundation from Dongguan University of Technology (ZG060501).

References

1. Bazaraa, M.S., Shetty, C.M.: Nonlinear Programming, Theory and Algorithms. John Wiley and Sons, New York (1979)
2. Cichocki, A., Unbehauen, R.: Neural Networks for Optimization and Signal Processing. John Wiley & Sons, New York (1993)
3. Cichocki, A., Unbehauen, R.: Neural Networks for Computing Eigenvalues and Eigenvectors. Biolog. Cybernetics 68, 155–164 (1992)
4. Feng, F.-Y., Zhang, Q.-J., Liu, H.-L.: A Recurrent Neural Network for Extreme Eigenvalue Problem. In: Huang, D.-S., Zhang, X.-P., Huang, G.-B. (eds.) ICIC 2005. LNCS, vol. 3644, pp. 787–796. Springer, Heidelberg (2005)
5. Feng, F.-Y., Xia, Y., Zhang, Q.-J.: A Recurrent Neural Network for Linear Fractional Programming with Bound Constraints. In: Wang, J., Yi, Z., Zurada, J.M., Lu, B.-L., Yin, H. (eds.) ISNN 2006. LNCS, vol. 3971, pp. 369–378. Springer, Heidelberg (2006)
6. Golden, R.M.: Mathematical Methods for Neural Network Analysis and Design. MIT Press, London, England (1996)
7. Golub, G.H., Van loan, C.F.: Matrix Computations. The Johns Hopkins University Press, Baltimore (1989)
8. Hale, J.K.: Ordinary diffential equations. Wiley, New York (1993)
9. Hopfield, J.J., Tank, D.W.: Neural computation of decisions in optimization problems. Biolog. Cybernetics 52, 141–152 (1985)
10. Huang, D.S., Horace, H.S.I., Zheru, C.: A neural root finder of polynomials based on root moments. Neural Computation 16, 1721–1762 (2004)
11. Huang, D.S.: A constructive approach for finding arbitrary roots of polynomials by neural networks. IEEE Transactions on Neural Networks. 15, 477–491 (2004)
12. Huang, D.S., Horace, H.S.I., Law Ken, C.K., Zheru, C., Wong, H.S.: A new partitioning neural network model for recursively finding arbitrary roots of higher order arbitrary polynomials. Applied Mathematics and Computation 162, 1183–1200 (2005)
13. Kennedy, M.P., Chua, L.O.: Neural networks for nonlinear programming. IEEE Transaction on Circuits and Systems 35, 554–562 (1988)
14. Kinderlehrer, D., Stampcchia, G.: An Introduction to Variational Inequalities and Their Applications. Academic, New York (1980)
15. LaSalle, J.: The Stability Theory for Ordinary Differential Equations. J. Differential Equations 4, 57–65 (1983)
16. Liao, L.-Z., Qi, H.D., Qi, L.Q.: Neurodynamical Optimization. J. Global Optim. 28, 175–195 (2004)
17. Luo, F.-L., Li, Y.-D.: Real-time neural computation of the eigenvector corresponding to the largest eigenvalue of positive matrix. Neuocomputing 7(2), 145–157 (2005)
18. Liu, L.-J., Wei, W.: Dynamical system for computing largest generalized eigenvalu. In: Wang, J., Yi, Z., Zurada, J.M., Lu, B.-L., Yin, H. (eds.) ISNN 2006. LNCS, vol. 3971, pp. 399–404. Springer, Heidelberg (2006)
19. Xia, Y.S., Leung, H., Wang, J.: A projection neural network and its application to constrained optimization problems. IEEE Transaction on Circuits and Systems II 49(1), 447–458 (2002)
20. Xia, Y.S., Wang, J.: A general methodology for designing globally convergent optimization neural networks. IEEE Transaction on Neural Networks 9, 1311–1343 (1998)
21. Zhang, Y., Yan, F., Tang, H.-J.: Neural networks based approach for computing eigenvectors and eigenvalues of symmetric matrix. Comp. and Math. with Appl. 47, 1155–1164 (2004)

A New Model Based Multi-objective PSO Algorithm

Jingxuan Wei[1,2] and Yuping Wang[1]

[1] School of Computer Science and Technology, Xidian University, Xi' an 710071, China
ywang@xidian.edu.cn
[2] Department of Mathematics, Xidian University, Xi' an 710071, China
wjxjingxuan@yahoo.com.cn

Abstract. In this paper, the multi-objective optimization problem is converted into the constrained optimization problem. For the converted problem, a novel PSO algorithm with dynamical changed inertia weight is proposed. Meanwhile, in order to overcome the drawback that most algorithms take pareto dominance as selection strategy but do not use any preference information. A new selection strategy based on the constraint dominance principle is proposed. The computer simulations for four difficulty benchmark functions show that the new algorithm is able to find uniformly distributed pareto optimal solutions and is able to converge to the pareto-optimal front.

1 Introduction

The use of evolutionary algorithm for multi-objective optimization has significantly grown in the last few years, giving rise to a wide variety algorithms[1]-[4]. EMO researchers have produced some clever techniques to maintain diversity [5], new algorithm that uses very small population size [6].

Particle swarm optimization (PSO) is a recently heuristic algorithm inspired by a bird flock. PSO has been found to be successful in a wide variety fields, but until recently it had not been extended to deal with the multi-objective problems.

PSO seems suitable to deal with multiple objectives, because of its high convergence speed that the algorithm presents for single-objective optimization [7].

In this paper, we present a novel PSO algorithm which allows PSO algorithm to deal with multi-objective optimizations. Firstly, because the inertia weight ω is a very important parameter in standard version, it can control algorithm's ability of exploitation and exploration so the accumulation factor of the swarm is introduced in the new algorithm, and the inertia weight is formulated as the function of the factor. In each generation, the ω is changed dynamically according to the accumulation factor. Secondly, the multi-objective optimization problem is converted into the constrained optimization problem. Based on the converted problem, we have added a constraint-handling mechanism that can improve the exploratory capabilities of the original algorithm.

Y. Wang, Y. Cheung, and H. Liu (Eds.): CIS 2006, LNAI 4456, pp. 87–94, 2007.

2 Basic Concepts

Multi-objective optimization problems can be described as follows:

$$\min F(x) \tag{1}$$

Where, $F(x) = (f_1(x), f_2(x), \cdots f_m(x)), x \in \Omega \subset R^n$.

Definition 1: A point x^0 is said to dominate x^1 ($x^0 \prec x^1$), if for every $i \in \{1,2,\cdots m\}$ $f_i(x^0) \le f_i(x^1) \wedge \exists i \in \{1,2\cdots m\}$, such that $f_i(x^0) < f_i(x^1)$.

Definition 2: A point $x^* \in \Omega$ is pareto optimal if there exists no feasible vector $x \in \Omega$, such that $x \prec x^*$.

3 Model of Multi-objective Optimization

3.1 Measure of the Quality of Solutions

Definition 3: Suppose the t-th swarm is composed of the particles $x_t^1, x_t^2 \cdots x_t^N$, let p_t^i is the number of the particles that dominate x_t^i.Then R_t^i is called the rank of particle x_t^i, $R_t^i = 1 + p_t^i$.

3.2 Measure of the Uniformity of Solutions

The aim of the multi-objective optimization is to generate a set of uniformly distributed pareto optimal solutions in the objective space. Based on this, the measure of the uniformity of solutions is given.

Definition4: Suppose the t-th swarm is composed of the particles $x_t^1, x_t^2 \cdots x_t^N$, we calculate the distances between x^i and the other particles in the objective space, and rank these distances. D_1^i and D_2^i are two smallest distances, then the crowding-distance of x^i is denoted as $crowd_i = \dfrac{D_1^i + D_2^i}{2}$. let $\overline{crowd_t} = \dfrac{1}{N} \times \sum_{i=1}^{N} crowd_i$ denote the mean value of crowding – distances of individuals and $Var_t = \dfrac{1}{N} \times \sum_{i=1}^{N} (crowd_i - \overline{crowd_t})^2$ denotes the crowding-distance variance of the t-th swarm. It can be seen that the smaller the crowding-distance variance of the t-th swarm, the more uniformity the t-th swarm.

3.3 Transform Multi-objective Optimization into the Constrained Optimization Problem

From the analysis mentioned above, it can be seen that if the ranks of all individuals are regarded as the constraints and the measure of the uniformity of solutions is regarded as the objective function, then the multi-objective optimization can be converted into the following constrained optimization problem:

$$\begin{cases} \min & Var_t \\ s.t. & R_t = 1 \end{cases} \tag{2}$$

4 Selection Operator

Most of multi-objective algorithms take pareto dominance as their selection strategy but do not use any preference information. However, these algorithms can not perform well on the problems that have many multi objectives. In order to overcome this problem, a new selection strategy for problem (2) is proposed.

4.1 If two particles are infeasible, we prefer to select the one with the smaller constraint violation, namely the one has the smaller rank.
4.2 If one particle is feasible and the other is infeasible, we prefer to select the feasible particle, namely the one has the rank one.
4.3 If two particles have the same rank, we prefer to select the one with the smaller objective value (e.g. x^i and x^j have the same rank one, then we calculate the crowding-distances of x^i and x^j in the set S based on the definition4, and choose the one with the biggest crowding-distance, the S denotes the set which is composed of all particles of rank one).The above process can distinguish the particles which locate in the sparse region and the crowded region.

5 The Accumulation Factor of the Swarm

PSO initialized the flock of birds randomly over the searching space, every bird is called a "particle". At each generation, each particle adjusts its velocity vector, based on its best solution (pbest) and the best solution of all particles (gbest). The swarm is composed of N particles ($P_1, P_2, \cdots P_N$) , each particle's position is represented as P_i, the velocity of this particle is denoted as V_i. At (t+1)th generation, each particle updates its position according to the following equations:

$$V_i(t+1) = \omega V_i(t) + c_1 r_1 (pbest_i(t) - P_i(t)) + c_2 r_2 (gbest(t) - P_i(t)) \tag{3}$$

$$P_i(t+1) = P_i(t) + V_i(t+1) \tag{4}$$

Where ω is the inertia weight in the range [0.1, 0.9]. c_1 and c_2 are positive constants.

One factor influences the property of algorithm is the accumulation degree of the swarm. We define $s = \frac{1}{N \cdot L} \cdot \sum_{i=1}^{N} \sqrt{\sum_{d=1}^{n} (p_{id} - \overline{p_d})^2} \in (0,1)$, where N is the population size, n is the number of variables, L is the length of the maximum diagonal in the search space, p_{id} indicates the dth coordinate of the ith particle, $\overline{p_d}$ indicates the average values of all particles in the dth coordinate . The smaller the value of s, the more centralized the swarm is. When the swarm is centralized, it becomes difficult for the algorithm to break away from the local optimum.

If the particles are sparse, the swarm is not easy to plunge into the local optimum. But when particles are centralized, it becomes easy to plunge into the local optimum.

From above, we know that ω will increase when particles are centralized, so ω can be described as follows:

$$\omega = \omega_0 - s\omega_s \tag{5}$$

Where, $\omega_0 = 1$, $\omega_s \in (0.1, 0.2)$

6 The Proposed Algorithm

Step1: Given swarm size N. Generate the initial swarm P(t) randomly, and copy nondominated members of P(t) to $\overline{P}$ set t=1.
Step2: initialize the memory of every particle (this memory serves as a guide to travel through the search space). For $i = 1\ to\ N$, $pbest_i(t) = P_i(t)$, $P_i(t)$ indicates the i-th particle in P(t).
Step3: initialize the velocity of every particle, let $V_i(t) = 0$.
Step4: (a) compute the new speed of each particle using the expression (3): where $gbest(t)$ is taken from $\overline{P}$. Firstly, we compute the crowding-distances of all particles in $\overline{P}$, and choose the one with the biggest crowding-distance as $gbest(t)$.
(b) compute the new positions of the particles adding the speed by using the expression (4). The new swarm is defined as $P'(t+1)$.
(c) copy the nondominated members of $P'(t+1)$ to $\overline{P}$, and remove the dominated members from $\overline{P}$.After that choose N members from $P(t) \cup P'(t+1)$ to constitute the next swarm $P(t+1)$.In this study, selection operator in section 4 is used to choose the N members . Set t=t+1.
(d) when the current position of the particle is better than the position contained in its memory, the particle's position is updated using $pbest_i(t) = P_i(t)$.The criterion to decide what position from memory should be retained is simply to apply the pareto dominance.

Step5: loop to step4 until a stopping criterion is met, usually a given maximum generations.

7 Simulation Results

To evaluate the efficiency of the new algorithm NMPSO, we choose four benchmark functions [8]. All experiments were performed in matlab. The parameter is described as follows: swarm size N=100, r_1 and r_2 are the random numbers in [0, 1], c_1 and c_2 are positive constants. n is the number of the decision variables. Number of generations: 250.

7.1 Test Functions

Each of the test functions defined below is structured in the same manner :

$$\begin{aligned} \min \quad & F(X) = (f_1(x_1), f_2(X)) \\ s.t. \quad & f_2(X) = g(X)h(f_1(x_1), g(X)) \\ where \quad & X = (x_1, x_2 \cdots x_n) \end{aligned}$$

$$F_1 : f_1(x_1) = x_1$$

$$g(X) = 1 + 9\sum_{i=2}^{n} x_i /(n-1)$$

$$h(f_1, g) = 1 - (f_1 / g)^2$$

where n=30, $x_i \in (0,1)$, the pareto front is nonconvex.

$$F_2 : f_1(x_1) = x_1$$

$$g(X) = 1 + 9\sum_{i=2}^{n} x_i /(n-1)$$

$$h(f_1, g) = 1 - \sqrt{f_1 / g} - (f_1 / g)\sin(10\pi f_1)$$

where n=30, $x_i \in (0,1)$.

$$F_3 : f_1(x_1) = x_1$$

$$g(X) = 1 + 10(n-1) + \sum_{i=2}^{n} (x_i^2 - 10\cos(4\pi x_i))$$

$$h(f_1, g) = 1 - \sqrt{f_1 / g}$$

where n=10, $x_1 \in (0,1)$, $x_2, \cdots x_n \in (-5,5)$.

$$F_4 : f_1(x_1) = 1 - \exp(-4x_1)\sin^6(6\pi x_1)$$

$$g(X) = 1 + 9\left(\sum_{i=2}^{n} x_i / (n-1)\right)^{0.25}$$

$$h(f_1, g) = 1 - (f_1 / g)^2$$

Where n=10, $x_i \in (0,1)$

7.2 Computation Results

We execute 10 times on each test problem independently, and compare the results with the other 8 algorithms in [8]. In figure 1-4, the pareto fronts achieved by the

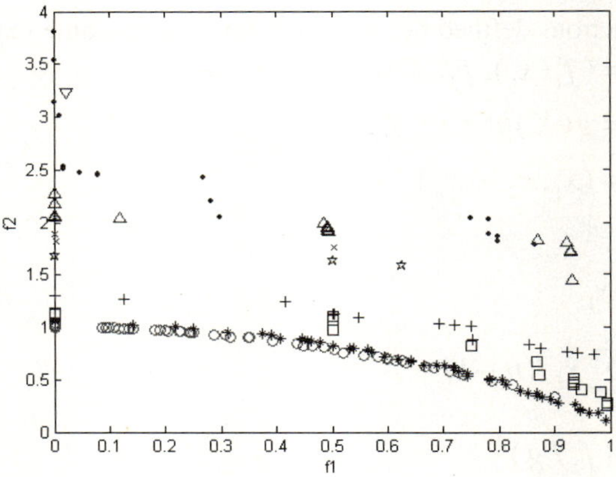

Fig. 1. Comparison results of 9 algorithms on function 1

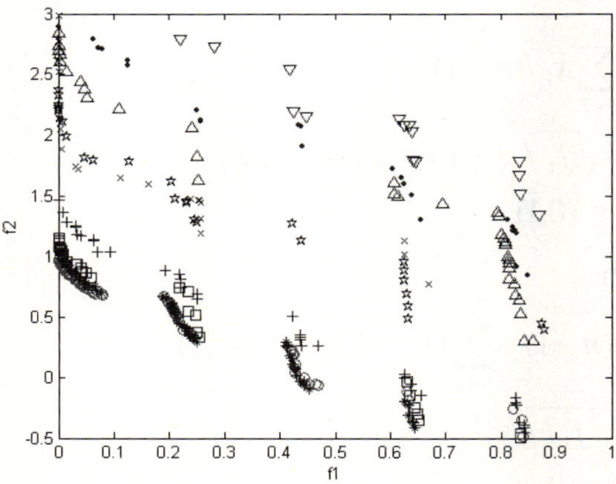

Fig. 2. Comparison results of 9 algorithms on function2

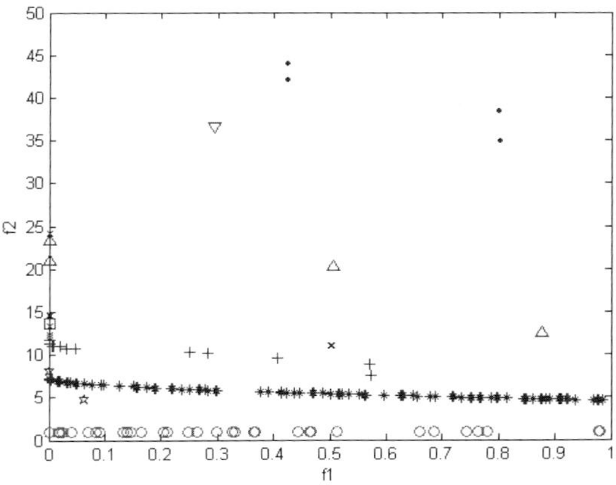

Fig. 3. Comparison results of 9 algorithms on Function 3

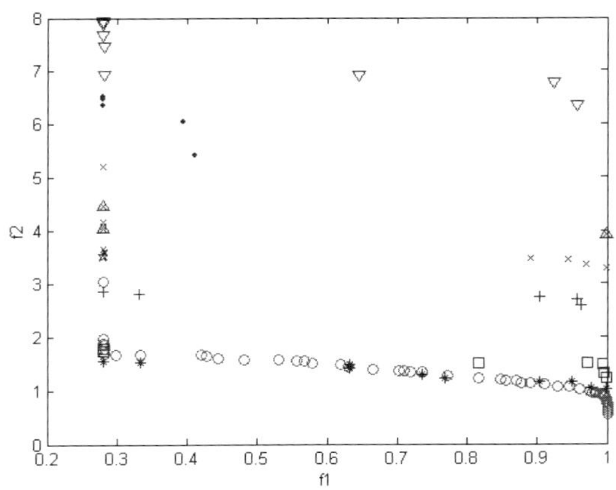

Fig. 4. Comparison results of 9 algorithms on function4

different algorithms are visualized. Per algorithm and test function, the outcomes of the first five runs were unified, and the dominated solutions were removed from the union set; the remaining points are plotted in the figures. Where •,×,∧,+,∨,*, □, ○,☆ denote the algorithms of Ffga, Hlga, Npga, Nsga, Rand, Spea, Soea, Nmpso and Vega.

The simulation results of the 8 algorithms in [8] are chosen from http://www.tik.ee.ethz.ch/~zitzler/testdata.html.

It can be seen from Fig1 to Fig4 that compared with the other 8 algorithms, the NMPSO can find more pareto-optimal solutions which are scattered more uniformly over the entire pareto front and the pareto front of NMPSO is in the below of the other compared pareto fronts. On average, the proposed algorithm requires 1250 function evaluations to find 100 pareto-optimal solutions.

8 Conclusions

In this paper, the multi-objective optimization problem is converted into the constrained optimization problem. For the converted problem, a novel PSO algorithm with dynamical changed inertia weight is proposed. Meanwhile, in order to overcome the drawback that most algorithms take pareto dominance as selection strategy but do not use any preference information. A new selection strategy based on the constraint dominance principle is proposed. The computer simulations for four difficulty benchmark functions show that the new algorithm is able to find uniformly distributed pareto optimal solutions and is able to converge to the pareto-optimal front.

Acknowledgements

This research is supported by National Natural Science Foundation of China (No.60374063).

References

1. Coello Coello, C.A., Van Veldhuizen, D.A., Lamont, G.B.: Evolutionary Algorithms for solving Multi-Objective Problems. Kluwer, Norwell, MA (2002)
2. Moon, P.H.A: Technique for orthogonal Frequency Division Multiplexing Offset Correction [J]. IEEE Trans on Commun 42(10), 2908–2914 (1994)
3. Zitzler, E., Laumanns, M., Thiele, L.: Spea2: Improving the Strength Pareto Evolutionary Algorithm [R]. Zurich (2001)
4. Veldhuizen, D.V.: Multiobjective Evolutionary Algorithms: Classifications, Analysis, and New Innovations [D]. Ph.D dissertation, pp. 22–24. Air University, USA (1999)
5. Deb, K., Pratap, A. et al.: A Fast and Elitist Multi-objective Genetic Algorithm: NSGAII [J]. IEEE Trans on Evolutionary Computation 6(2), 182–197 (2002)
6. Coello Coello, C.A., Pulido, G.T.: Multiobjective optimization using a micro-genetic algorithm. In: proceeding of GECCO'2001, pp. 274–282 (2001)
7. Kennedy, J., Eberhart, R.: Particle swarm optimization. In: Proceedings of the IEEE International Conference on Neural Networks, vol. IV, pp. 1941–1948. IEEE Service Center, Piscataway, NJ (1995)
8. Zitzler, E., Deb, K., Thiele, L.: Comparison of Multiobjective Evolutionary Algorithms: Empirical Results [J]. Evolutionary Computation 8(2), 1–24 (2000)

A New Multi-objective Evolutionary Optimisation Algorithm: The Two-Archive Algorithm

Kata Praditwong and Xin Yao

The Centre of Excellence for Research in Computational Intelligence and Applications(CERCIA), School of Computer Science, The University of Birmingham, Edgbaston, Birmingham B15 2TT, UK
kxp,xin@cs.bham.ac.uk

Abstract. Many Multi-Objective Evolutionary Algorithms (MOEAs) have been proposed in recent years. However, almost all MOEAs have been evaluated on problems with two to four objectives only. It is unclear how well these MOEAs will perform on problems with a large number of objectives. Our preliminary study [1] showed that performance of some MOEAs deteriorates significantly as the number of objectives increases. This paper proposes a new MOEA that performs well on problems with a large number of objectives. The new algorithm separates non-dominated solutions into two archives, and is thus called the *Two-Archive* algorithm. The two archives focused on convergence and diversity, respectively, in optimisation. Computational studies have been carried out to evaluate and compare our new algorithm against the best MOEA for problems with a large number of objectives. Our experimental results have shown that the *Two-Archive* algorithm outperforms existing MOEAs on problems with a large number of objectives.

1 Introduction

Evolutionary algorithms (EA) used as a powerful tool to search solutions in complex problems during the recent past. The history of multi-objective evolutionary algorithms (MOEA) began in the mid 1980's. In [2], the authors have classified MOEAs into three categories; aggregating functions, population-based approaches, and Pareto-based approaches. A hybrid method uses a set of solutions from evolutionary computation to build a model, which presents Parato front such as ParEGO [3]. In recent years the Pareto-based approaches have become a popular design and several techniques have been proposed. One popular technique is, elitism, which uses an external storage, called an archive, to keep useful solutions. Other component that develops with an archive is a removal strategy. As an archive has limited size, removal strategy is required to trim exceeding members of archive. This operator is important because it might delete some members and keep the Pareto front in the same time. This is challenging for researchers.

Y. Wang, Y. Cheung, and H. Liu (Eds.): CIS 2006, LNAI 4456, pp. 95–104, 2007.

Generally, multi-objective problems involve two sets of variables. The first is a set of decision variables as input of a particular problem and the other is a set of objective functions or objective values as output of a problem. Thus, the solution's quality will be measured in a space of objective functions. One factor that made the multi-objective optimisation too difficult is the number of objectives to optimise. Thus, Deb [4] suggests that the number of objectives makes an impact on the difficulty of the optimisation problems. Obviously, the dimensions of the solution space vary according to the number of objectives. For example, the shape of a solution space in two-dimensional problems is plain, while the shape of the space on three-dimensional problems is a three-dimensional surface.

Many researchers have invented several MOEAs, problem generators, and performance measurement. A small amount of publications are available that relate to performance on many objectives. Almost all simulated results still focus on two or three objectives and the behaviour of MOEAs in solving high-dimensional problems is still scrutiny.

An important comparison result in many objectives from [1] is that the scalability of objectives in each algorithm is different. The Pareto Envelope-based Selection Algorithm (PESA) [5] has powerful scalability while Non-dominated Sorting Genetic Algorithm II (NSGA-II) [6] has a lack of scalability. Generally, NSGA-II has performed well in two or three objectives. The behaviour of NSGA-II in many objectives problem is interesting. This fact helps researchers design new MOEA that can efficiently solve problems in many objectives.

This paper proposes and implements a new concept of archiving. PESA and *Two-Archive* algorithm are compared in four scalable objective problems. The experimental results are measured in convergence and diversity metrics, and they are analysed by statistical method.

The remainder of the paper is organised as follows. Section 2 will describe the concepts of non-domination with domination and the *Two-Archive* algorithm with the pseudocode. Section 3 will describe a set of scalable testing problems. Section 4 will present a set of performance measuring. The experimental setting and results will be explained in section 5. The conclusions should be shown in section 6.

2 The Two-Archive Algorithm

2.1 Non-dominated Solution with Domination

The new idea for improving convergence of archive is based on two factors. Firstly, the archive collects non-dominated solutions from a population. Next, the truncation will be applied if an archive overflows. The truncation can be applied in two ways, firstly, during collecting non-dominated solutions, as in PESA, and, secondly, after finishing the collection process, as in NSGA-II or SPEA2(Strength Pareto Evolutionary Algorithm 2) [7]. This operator can remove any member in an archive. On the other hand, all algorithms do not distinguish non-dominated solution. In the new concept, non-dominated solutions are categorised into two types according to comparison with members of the archive. The first type is a non-dominated solution with domination which dominates some existing members, and the other is ordinarily a non-dominated member without domination. Generally, the first type can improve convergence to Pareto front. Non-dominated solutions with domination should be kept in archive.

2.2 The Algorithm

The *Two-Archive* algorithm borrows the replacement of dominated solution by the new dominated solution from PESA [5]. The truncation was done at the end of collecting non-dominated solutions from NSGA-II [6] and SPEA2 [7]. The details of the proposed algorithm are shown in Algorithms 1 and 2.

The framework of the *Two-Archive* algorithm is shown by Algorithm 1. The proposed archiving method collects the new candidate solutions from a population, one by one. Firstly, a new candidate can be a new member of an archive if it is a non-dominated member in the population, and if no member in both archives can dominate it (as lines 2 and 3 in Algorithm 2). Secondly, the new member should check the domination relationship with other existing members. If the new member can dominate some other members, it should enter the convergence archive (CA) and the dominated members should be deleted. Otherwise, it should enter the diversity archive (DA) and no existing member will be deleted (line 2 to line 13 in Algorithm 2).

When the total size of both archives overflows, the removal strategy should be applied. All members in DA may calculate its distances to all members in CA, and keep the shortest distance among distances of them. The member with the shortest distance in DA should be deleted until the total size equals the threshold.

The total size of archives during the collecting process is not fixed. The size can increase over the threshold. However, the size should be reduced to the capacity of archives after the truncation process. The size of the CA never overflows because the new member entered the CA when at least one existing member in CA should be removed. In other words, the size of the CA is restricted by the number of members in both archives before collecting new members. Thus, only DA is an unlimited growing archive.

The Main Loop of the Algorithm. This algorithm starts with a random population and empty archives. The decision variables of each individual are assigned using the random number generator with a uniform distribution in an available decision space.

Each initial individual's objective variables are calculated using objective functions and decision variables. This algorithm uses original objective functions as fitness.

For each generation, the non-dominated members of population are kept in the archives and dominated members in the archives are deleted. The algorithm uses two archives, the convergence archive and the diversity. The total capacity is fixed but the size of each archive vary.

The mating population is built up from choosing individuals from both archives. The process to select an individual is following. Firstly, an archive is chosen with a probability. The probability is a pre-defined parameter that is a ratio to choose members from the convergence archive to the diversity archive. Secondly, a member in the chosen archive should be selected uniformly at random. Finally, the chosen parent goes to the mating population.

Algorithm 1. The Two-Archive Algorithm

```
Initialise the population
Initialise archives to the empty set
Evaluate initial population
Set t=0
repeat
    Collect non-dominated individuals to archives
    Select parents from archives
    Apply genetic operators to generate a new population
    Evaluate the new population
    t = t + 1
until t == MAX_GENERATION
```

Collecting Non-dominated Solutions. The non-dominated solution collection is composed of two parts; the main part is obtaining non-dominated members from the population and the optional part is removing the further members in the diversity archive when the total size of archives is more than the capacity threshold.

Collecting non-dominated solutions begins with fetching an individual from a population one by one. It is compared with the remainder of the population. If it is a non-dominated solution, it goes to the next step. Otherwise, it is discarded because of being dominated. The non-dominated solution from the population is compared with all members in the current archives. If it is dominated by a member of the archives, it is discarded, otherwise it is a new member of the archives. During this stage, any duplicated member is deleted. The remainder of the archives are then compared with the new member and two cases are possible. In the first case, the new member can dominate a member of the archives. The dominated member is removed and the new member is received by the convergence archive. A flag is set to the value of the convergence archive. In this case, the size of the convergence archive is possibly increased but the total size of archive is not increased because the new member enters the convergence archive by deleting at least one dominated member. In the second case, the new member cannot dominate any member and is not dominated by any archive member. The new member becomes a member of the diversity archive, and the size of the diversity archive is increased. The total size of both archives is increased because the diversity archive receives the new member without deleting any member. The above process performs until the last individual in population. The new members are separated according to their flag values.

If the total size of the archives overflows, the removal operation should be performed. The removal operator deletes only members in the diversity archive. This operator has no impact on the convergence archive. All members in the diversity archive calculate the shortest distance from themselves to the nearest member in the convergence archive. In other words, each member of the diversity archive calculates its Euclidean distance to all members of the convergence archive. The shortest one is then chosen. The member with the shortest distance among the diversity members is deleted until the total size equals the capacity.

Algorithm 2. Collect Non-Dominated Individuals To Archives

```
for i = 1 to popsize do
   if individual(i) is non-dominated solution then
      if no member in both archives can dominates an individual(i) then
         Set individual(i).Dflag = 0
         if individual(i) dominates any member in both archives then
            Set individual(i).Dflag = 1
            Delete dominated member
         end if
         if member(i).Dflag == 1 then
            Add individual(i) to Convergence Archive(CA)
         else
            Add individual(i) to Diversity Archive(DA)
         end if
      end if
   end if
end for
{* Remove Strategy *}
if sizeof(CA)+sizeof(DA) > limit then
   for i=1 to sizeof(DA) do
      DA(i).length = maxreal
      for j=1 to sizeof(CA) do
         if DA(i).length > Dist( CA(j), DA(i) ) then
            DA(i).length = Dist( CA(j), DA(i) )
         end if
      end for
   end for
   repeat
      Delete the member of DA with the shortest length
   until sizeof(DA)+sizeof(CA) == limit
end if
```

2.3 An Example

This problem is a bi-objective minimisation problem as shown in Table 1.

For the *Two-Archive* algorithm using the example, the convergence archive consists of two members, solutions 1 and 2, and members in the diversity archive are solutions 3 and 4. For the first possible sequence, solution A will enter to

Table 1. Population and Their Objective Values

Solution	f_1	f_2
1	0.45	0.78
2	0.51	0.75
3	0.53	0.62
4	0.72	0.49
A	0.47	0.68
B	0.78	0.44

archives before solution B. All members compare with candidate A and no existing members can dominate the new one. Solution A enters the convergence archive because it can dominate member 2. Thus, current members of the convergence archive are solutions 1 and A, and the diversity archive remains the same as before. Solution B will enter the diversity archive because it cannot dominate any current members. The temporal total size of the two archives can be more than the capacity during the collecting process. When archives finish the collecting process, the exceeding members in the diversity archive will be deleted. In this case, solution B is the last candidate. The diversity archive has three solutions, 3, 4, and B.

The removal strategy is based on the shortest Euclidean distance in the objective space from members in the diversity archive to members in the convergence archive. Firstly, calculating the distance from itself to all members of the convergence archive, the distance from solution 3 to solution 1 is 0.17 and the distance from solution 3 to solution A is 0.08. Secondly, choosing the shortest distance, of 0.08, the process of finding the shortest distance should be applied to the members (solutions 4 and B) in the diversity archive. The shortest distance of solution 4 is 0.31, and 0.39 for solution B.

In this case, solution 3 is deleted because it has the shortest distance. After archive-update, solutions 1 and A are in the convergence archive and the diversity archive has solutions 4 and B.

2.4 Difference Between One and Two Archives

Implementation of two archives is based on the inequality of non-dominated solutions in an archive. The comparison of the new solution and a set of members in an archive can be separated into three cases. Firstly, no member can dominate the new solution and it can dominate some members in archive. Secondly, the members and the new solution cannot dominate each other. Finally, the new solution is dominated by some members. The new solution in the last case is discarded because a property of archive is domination free. The new archive that includes the new solution in the first case is better than the previous archive because the new one is better than the old member in terms of domination relationship. In the second case, the archives do not interfere with each other before and after collecting.

After collecting the new solutions to an archive, MOEA with one archive manages all members in the same way. If the archive overflows, all members have a chance to remove. The *Two-archive* algorithm separates solutions into two archives and manages them in different ways.

The member in the convergence archive is removed because it can only be dominated by the new solution. The member of diversity archive is deleted in two cases, when the member is dominated by the new solution, or when the archives overflow. When the archives overflow, the removal strategy is only applied to the diversity archive. This is the reason why this algorithm uses two archives to store the solutions.

3 Scalable Testing Problems

A set of four scalable testing problems [8] are used in this experimental simulation. These problems are designed to achieve many features. They are easy to construct. The number of decision variables and the number of objective variables can be scaled to any number. The Pareto fronts of these problems are exactly known in terms of shape and position in objective space. These problems are invented carefully, although this experiment choose only problems DLTZ1, DTLZ2, DTLZ3 and DTLZ6, to simulate. The main reason is that the Pareto front of these problem can be easily written into mathematical expression. Some problems share the same mapping functions or shapes of the Pareto front. It is useful to remove some redundant testing problems. The DTLZ4 and the DTLZ5 use the same meta-variable mapping function with DTLZ2. The Pareto front with curve uses DTLZ6 instead of DTLZ5 because DTLZ6 has a difference mapping function from the remainder problems.

The number of objectives vary in a range from 2 to 8 objectives. The global Pareto fronts have many shapes: linear hyper-plane, unit spherical surface, and curved.

4 Metrics

The convergence metric has been proposed by Deb and Jain [9]. This metric computes averaging the smallest normalised Euclidean distance of all points in obtained Pareto front to reference set.

The convergence metric [9] is calculated by averaging the smallest Euclidean distance, d_i, from point i to the global Pareto front as

$$C = \frac{\sum_{i=1}^{n} d_i}{n} \tag{1}$$

where n presents a number of points in the obtained set.

In these testing problems, the Pareto fronts are used as the reference sets.

The concept of diversity metrics [9] is calculating distribution of projection of obtained solutions on an objective axis. The objective axis is divided into small areas according to a number of solutions. The diversity measurement is successful if all small areas have one or more representative points. The number of areas with representative point indicates a quality of diversity metric.

5 Experiments and Results

5.1 Experiment Setting

The experimental setting was based on Khare *et al.* [1]. The population size varied according to a number of objectives. The archive size is equal to the population size. In two, three, and four objectives of DTLZ1 and DTLZ2, there were 300 generations and in that of DTLZ3 and DTLZ6, 500 generations. Furthermore, the number of generations in six and eight objectives was doubled. All experiments of *Two-Archive* algorithm were repeated independently 30 times.

5.2 Results

Convergence Metric: Table 2 summaries the convergence values of the obtained solution set. In DTLZ1, PESA performed slightly better than *Two-Archive* algorithm. However, only two sets of experiments showed statistically significant differences. For the other three experiments, the convergence metrics of both archives are comparable. In DTLZ2, they performed as the same behaviour. No statistically significant differences between them were detected in this problem. In DTLZ3, PESA had better convergence values than *Two-Archive* algorithm. In three experiments, PESA outperformed *Two-Archive* algorithm and significant differences were also detected. In DTLZ6, *Two-Archive* algorithm outperformed PESA according to the convergence metric. In addition, almost all statistically significant differences (4 of 5 experiments) were obviously detected.

Diversity Metric: Diversity metric is shown in table 3. The average values of *Two-Archive* algorithm were somewhat better than that of PESA, however, a few experiments had statistically significant differences. The *Two-Archive* algorithm had better values than PESA in the diversity metric 17 of 20 experiments and only two experiments had statistically significant differences. In only three experiments, PESA performed better than *Two-Archive*, however, no statistically significant differences were detected.

This informs the analysis of performance according to the characteristics of problems. In the most simple problem, DTLZ2, both algorithms were comparable. It seems highly probable that the *Two-Archive* algorithm was prevented from the Pareto front on multi-modal, non-linear mapping function used in DTLZ1 and DTLZ3. However, the *Two-Archive* algorithm can produce a set of solutions in DTLZ6 near to the global Pareto front which its front is a curve.

Table 2. Convergence Metric (Minimisation). The value of a two-tailed t-test with 58 degrees of freedom: T-Test (PESA-TwoArch).

	Objs	PESA	TwoArch	T-Test
DTLZ1	2	2.86948 ± 0.00591	2.48684 ± 4.29603	1.01046
	3	0.04419 ± 0.12320	0.53283 ± 2.37626	-1.69289
	4	0.02317 ± 0.09059	0.53937 ± 0.79182	**-3.00987**
	6	0.00117 ± 0.00089	0.15170 ± 0.31683	-1.45862
	8	0.00407 ± 0.00015	0.40247 ± 0.73347	**-2.54713**
DTLZ2	2	0.00008 ± 0.00019	0.00002 ± 0.00001	0.02377
	3	0.00035 ± 0.00013	0.00027 ± 0.00008	0.02939
	4	0.00170 ± 0.00039	0.00164 ± 0.00034	0.01291
	6	0.00301 ± 0.00040	0.00294 ± 0.00038	0.00906
	8	0.00689 ± 0.00109	0.00904 ± 0.00115	-0.17718
DTLZ3	2	22.52023± 22.9048	35.26955 ± 27.67275	**-9.81903**
	3	1.80296 ± 5.78546	4.23237 ± 9.39880	**-3.41480**
	4	1.16736 ± 3.50522	0.53312 ± 1.25334	1.59248
	6	0.15035 ± 0.12692	0.24030 ± 0.61444	-0.49384
	8	7.23062 ± 2.25611	19.84626 ± 16.61913	**-14.28823**
DTLZ6	2	0.79397 ± 0.32237	0.20647 ± 0.04337	**5.32092**
	3	0.20528 ± 0.21199	0.17652 ± 0.05096	0.30716
	4	3.60430 ± 0.38084	2.56216 ± 0.26565	**7.09909**
	6	5.30454 ± 0.31227	3.06482 ± 0.16873	**11.66720**
	8	6.32247 ± 0.10668	4.16521 ± 0.17995	**16.71019**

Table 3. Diversity Metric (Maximisation). The value of a two-tailed t-test with 58 degrees of freedom: T-Test (PESA-TwoArch).

	Objs	PESA	TwoArch	T-Test
DTLZ1	2	0.25093 ± 0.14059	0.40720 ± 0.19185	-1.48446
	3	0.42116 ± 0.07563	0.52340 ± 0.10649	-1.31218
	4	0.37605 ± 0.07125	0.42902 ± 0.06855	-0.77596
	6	0.33643 ± 0.04046	0.33463 ± 0.04299	0.02438
	8	0.25245 ± 0.00764	0.25037 ± 0.03623	0.04693
DTLZ2	2	0.57396 ± 0.09135	0.65979 ± 0.08791	-1.11032
	3	0.57163 ± 0.04344	0.63981 ± 0.03482	-1.33491
	4	0.52708 ± 0.03692	0.58181 ± 0.02321	-1.22245
	6	0.47099 ± 0.02660	0.51825 ± 0.01830	-0.82652
	8	0.43230 ± 0.04908	0.48221 ± 0.01037	-0.68861
DTLZ3	2	0.14023 ± 0.14497	0.16460 ± 0.16208	-0.24091
	3	0.38965 ± 0.13220	0.40272 ± 0.17358	-0.12949
	4	0.31659 ± 0.09393	0.40721 ± 0.12635	-1.05756
	6	0.18813 ± 0.06554	0.40871 ± 0.02731	**-2.55314**
	8	0.02615 ± 0.00247	0.10324 ± 0.10686	-1.24915
DTLZ6	2	0.20191 ± 0.14198	0.68258 ± 0.07386	**-5.66679**
	3	0.41962 ± 0.06423	0.51650 ± 0.04737	-1.58848
	4	0.22558 ± 0.02790	0.24695 ± 0.02241	-0.52192
	6	0.27631 ± 0.02356	0.31483 ± 0.01462	-0.72240
	8	0.27328 ± 0.00488	0.24692 ± 0.00924	0.93449

6 Conclusions

In this paper, the concept of non-dominated solutions with domination was presented. We illustrated the *Two-Archive* algorithm, and compared its performance according to a set of convergence and diversity metrics on a set of scalable testing problems invented by Deb *et al.* [8]. It is not clear which algorithm is better in terms of convergence. However, the *Two-Archive* algorithm seems to have outperformed PESA in DTLZ6, which is difficult to convergence because of the shape of the Pareto front. It is virtually certain that the *Two-Archive* algorithm will have better diversity than PESA. However, the proposed algorithm was investigated in a limited set of testing problems. Further work is required to evaluate the usefulness of the *Two-Archive* algorithm.

Acknowledgement

The authors are grateful to Felicity Simon for proof-reading the paper.

References

1. Khare, V., Yao, X., Deb, K.: Performance Scaling of Multi-objective Evolutionary Algorithms. In: Fonseca, C.M., Fleming, P.J., Zitzler, E., Deb, K., Thiele, L. (eds.) EMO 2003. LNCS, vol. 2632, pp. 376–390. Springer, Heidelberg (2003)
2. Coello, C.A.C., Lamont, G.B.: An Introduction to Multi-objective Evolutionary Algorithms and Their Applications. In: Coello, C.A.C., Lamont, G.B. (eds.) Applications of Multi-Objective Evolutionary Algorithms, pp. 1–28. World Scientific Publishing, London, England (2004)
3. Knowles, J.: ParEGO: A Hybrid Algorithm With On-Line Landscape Approximation for Expensive Multiobjective Optimization Problems. IEEE Transactions On Evolutionary Computation 10, 50–66 (2006)
4. Deb, K.: Multi-Objective Optimization using Evolutionary Algorithms. Chichester, UK (2001)
5. Corne, D.W., Knowles, J.D., Oates, M.J.: The Pareto Envelope-based Selection Algorithm for Multiobjective Optimization. In: Deb, K., Rudolph, G., Lutton, E., Merelo, J.J., Schoenauer, M., Schwefel, H.-P., Yao, X. (eds.) Parallel Problem Solving from Nature-PPSN VI. LNCS, vol. 1917, pp. 839–848. Springer, Heidelberg (2000)
6. Deb, K., Pratap, A., Agarwal, S., Meyarivan, T.: A Fast and Elitist Multi-Objective Genetic Algorithm-NSGA-II. IEEE Transactions On Evolutionary Computation 6, 182–197 (2002)
7. Zitzler, E., Laumanns, M., Thiele, L.: SPEA2: Improving the Strength Pareto Evolutionary Algorithm. Technical Report Technical Report 103, Computer Engineering and Networks Laboratory (TIK), Swiss Federal Institute of Technology (ETH), Zurich, Gloriastrasse 35, CH-8092 Zurich, Switzerland (2001)
8. Deb, K., Thiele, L., Laumanns, M., Zitzler, E.: Scalable Test Problems for Evolutionary Multi-Objective Optimization. In: Technical Report TIK-Report No.112, Computer Engineering and Networks Laboratory (TIK), Swiss Federal Institute of Technology (ETH), Zurich (2001)
9. Deb, K., Jain, S.: Running Performance Metrics For Evolutionary Multi-Objective Optimization. In: Technical Report KanGAL Report Number 2002004, Indian Institute of Technology, Kanpur, India (2002)

Labeling of Human Motion by Constraint-Based Genetic Algorithm

Fu Yuan Hu[1,2], Hau San Wong[1], Zhi Qiang Liu[3], and Hui Yang Qu[1]

[1] Dep. of Computer Science, City University of Hong Kong, China
{fuyuanhu, cshswong, quhy}@cityu.edu.hk
[2] Northwestern School of Computer Science, Polytechnical University, China
fuyuan_hu@sina.com
[3] School of Creative Media, City University of Hong Kong, China
ZQ.LIU@cityu.edu.hk

Abstract. This paper presents a new method to label parts of human body automatically based on the joint probability density function (PDF). To adapt to different motion for different articulation, the probabilistic models of each triangle different number of mixture components with MML are adopted. To solve the computation load problem of genetic algorithm (GA), a constraint-based genetic algorithm (CBGA) is developed to obtain the best global labeling. Our algorithm is developed to report the performance with experiments from running, walking and dancing sequences.

1 Introduction

Human motion analysis and perception are receiving increasing attention from computer vision researchers. Successful algorithms for tracking different parts of the body have been developed [1,2]. Many researchers have demonstrated that activity, age and sex can be perceived easily from a series of light-dot displays, even when no other cues are available [3,4]. Thus, it is very important to locate the visible parts of the body and to assign proper labels to the corresponding regions of the image for human motion analysis and human-computer interfaces. Currently, many techniques have been proposed for labeling human body parts and learning the body structure. Probabilistic model based methods are popular since they make efficient learning and testing possible, and these methods can be classified into two main categories. Tree-structured probabilistic models[5,6] admit simple, fast inference, and mixtures of trees are applied to human body modeling[7]. A decomposable triangulated graph[15] is another type of graph to label the human body, and is more powerful than trees since each node has two parents[16]. In related work, Larranaga[17] used GA to find the optimal node ordering of Bayesian networks. He represents a node ordering in a chromosome, and for each ordering, it is passed to K2, a greedy search algorithm, to obtain a network. In this work, the ordering and the conditional independence relations are learned separately, thus it does not guarantee to find an optimal network structure.

Y. Wang, Y. Cheung, and H. Liu (Eds.): CIS 2006, LNAI 4456, pp. 105–114, 2007.

In this paper, we concentrate on the problem of labeling parts of human body by decomposable triangulated model and constraint-based genetic algorithm (CBGA). Considering the variability in different phases of human movement, we model each triangle by Mix-Gaussian distribution with different number of mix components. Then, we present chromosome-filtering and constraint-based GA operators mechanism to prevent the production of invalid individual during the evolution to effectively obtain the optimal labeling and deal with the computation load problem. Both the ordering structure and the conditional dependence relations between the variables are encoded into the chromosomes in the population, so that they can be evolved to obtain an optimal labeling.

2 Overview of Our Approach

Let $X = (X_1, X_2, \cdots, X_N)$ be the vector of measurements in an image, and $L = \{L_1, L_2, \cdots, L_M\}$ vector of labels for M markers as head, shoulder, etc. N is not always equal to M because of wrongly detecting and missing due to occlusion in real images. Here we firstly assume that there are no missing body parts and no clutter. That is to say N is equal to M. Then, the label problem is to find $\overline{L}^*$ which maximizes the posterior probability $P(\overline{L}/\overline{X})$, over all possible label vectors $\overline{X}$. That is,

$$\overline{L}^* = \arg\max_{\overline{L}\in L} P(\overline{L}/\overline{X}) \tag{1}$$

In this paper, we choose DTM to characterize body pose and motion. In [8], the authors use joint Gaussian-distribution and joint Mix-Gaussian-distribution to represent distributions of each triangle. However, we adopt joint Mix-Gaussian-Distribution with different number of mixture components to learn the best triangulated model because different articulation has different motion. And it is capable of selecting the number of components by unsupervised learning of finite mixture models for multivariate training data[9,10] automatically. To obtain the optimal labeling of the body parts, it is a brute solution for the optimization problem to search exhaustively among all $M!$. Thus, the computational cost is very huge to find the optimal labeling. Considering this, optimization on triangulated graphs may be efficiently performed using a CBGA to obtain more accurate labeling.

3 Human Models Based Mix-Gaussian Models

Given the set X of M parts and the corresponding measurement X_{Si} ,$1 \leq i \leq M$, where$X = (X_{S1}, X_{S2}, \cdots, X_{Sm})$. In a maximum likelihood setting, we want to find the decomposable triangulated graph G, such that $P(G|X)$ is maximized over all possible graphs.

$$P(G/X) = P(X/G)P(G)/P(X)) \tag{2}$$

We assume the priors $P(G)$ are equal for different decompositions, so our goal is to find the structure G which can maximize$P(X|G)$, which can be computed as follows,

$$\log(P(X/G)) = \log(P(S_{body}(X_{S1}, X_{S2}, \cdots, X_{SM})/G)) \tag{3}$$

If the conditional independence of body parts S_{body} can be represented as a decomposable triangulated graph, the joint probability density function (PDF) PS_{body} can be decomposed into,

$$\log(P(X/G;\theta)) = \log(\prod_{t=1}^{T-1} P(X_{At}/X_{Bt}, X_{Ct}; \theta_t) P(X_{AT}/X_{BT}, X_{CT}; \theta_T) \tag{4}$$

$$= \log(\sum_{t=1}^{T-1} \log P(X_{At}/X_{Bt}, X_{Ct}; \theta_t) + \log P(X_{AT}/X_{BT}, X_{CT}; \theta_T \tag{5}$$

$$= -\log(\sum_{t=1}^{T-1} h(X_{At}/X_{Bt}, X_{Ct}; \theta_t) - h(X_{AT}/X_{BT}, X_{CT}; \theta_T) \tag{6}$$

Where $h(\cdot)$ denotes the differential entropy or conditional differential entropy [18] measure. The optimization can be performed by maximizing equation (5). Considering the variability and different phases of human movement, we model each triangle by a Mix-Gaussian distribution with different number of mix components. A k_t -component mixture model can be represented by

$$\begin{cases} G_t = [G_t^1, G_t^2, \cdots, G_t^{k_t}] \\ G_t = [G_t^1, G_t^2, \cdots, G_t^{k_t}] \end{cases} \tag{7}$$

where $G_t^i (i = 1, 2, \cdots, k_t)$ is a multivariate Gaussian distribution, and ω_t^i is the prior probability of G_t^i.

$$G_t^i = \frac{exp[-\frac{1}{2}(X_t - \overline{X}_t^i)^T (\Sigma_t^i)^{-1} (X_t - \overline{X}_t^i)]}{(2\Pi)^{d/2} |\Sigma_t^i|^{1/2}} \tag{8}$$

where k_t , $\overline{X}_t$, Σ_t and ω_t can be learned by an improved EM algorithm with MML-Like criterion[11]. Xrepresents the 15-dimensional feature vector for triplet $\Delta = \{A, B, C\}$,

$$X = (v_{Ax}, v_{Bx}, v_{Cx}, v_{Ay}, v_{By}, v_{Cy}, v_{Az}, v_{Bz}, v_{Cz}, \\ p_{Bx}, p_{Cx}, p_{By}, p_{Cy}, p_{Bz}, p_{Cz}) \tag{9}$$

The first nine dimensions of X are x, y, z-direction velocity of body parts (A, B, C); and the last six dimensions are the position of body parts A and C relative to B. The velocity of each marker is obtained by subtracting its position in two consecutive frames.

For each triangle, its probability can be obtained by:

$$P(X_{At}/X_{Bt}, X_{Ct}) = \max_i G_t^i \ (i = 1, 2, \cdots, k_t) \tag{10}$$

where k_t is the number of mixture components for tth triangle.

4 Labeling the Human Body Using Constraint-Based GA

For an arbitrary frame, the bigger the probability is, the more likely they are the right makers. If the conditional independence relationships hold, then:

$$\max \log P(X/G) = \max(\sum_{t=1}^{T-1} \log(X_{At}/X_{Bt}, X_{Ct}) + \log P(X_{AT}, X_{BT}, X_{CT})) \tag{11}$$

However, the number of all the possible combinations is huge. GA employs global search techniques via fitness function. As a result, we adopt constraint-based and chromosome-filtering evolutionary computation to find the right combinations, which is shown in Fig. 1. In essence, this approach provides chromosome-filtering mechanism and constraint-based operators to produce better and valid individuals. In order to present the details of the proposed GA approach for the labeling, a simple graph (Fig. 2) is introduced in the following description.

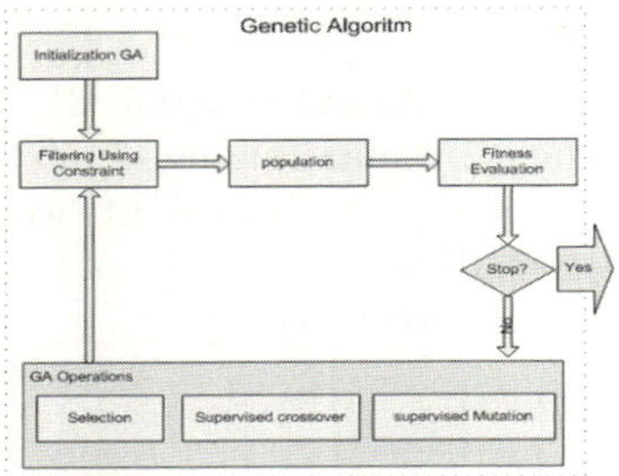

Fig. 1. Framework of GA

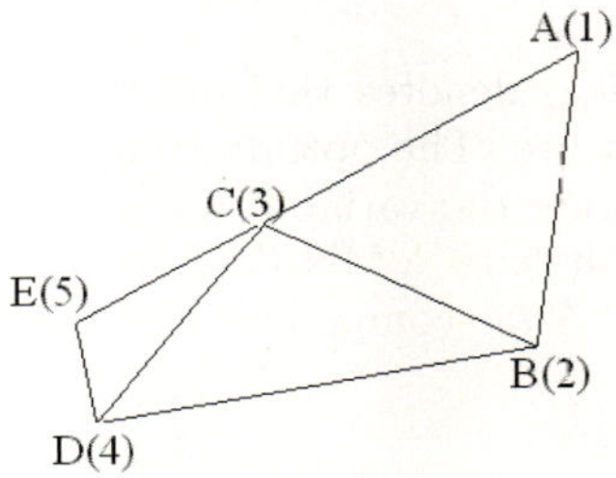

Fig. 2. The graph of triangle

4.1 Encoding

In this paper the probability models are encoded by some integer strings. Each triangle is typically represented using three integers. Thus, the length of the individual is $3 * (N - 2)$ for the graph with N vertexes. More important, it must satisfy the conditions of decomposable graphs. That is to say, when a free vertex is eliminated the next clique in the ordering will again have a free vertex to eliminate, and so on until the last clique. Therefore, valid individuals have also conditions. Here we develop a rule to satisfy the condition, which is that the first three numbers are different integers and the next three different integers have only a new integer within the predefined range, and another two integers have been presented in the previous triangles. For convenience, we put the new integer the first position in the three integers in the triangle. If the conditional independence of random variables, described in Fig.2, can be represented as a decomposable triangulated graph, the PDF can be decomposed into,

$$P(ABCDE) = P(ABC)P(D/BC)P(E/CD) \tag{12}$$

Thus, "123423534" is the best individual for Equ. 10. That is to say, "123" is produced within the predefined range randomly. Then, we obtain a different integer "4" and two integers "23" produced in the previous triangles, and so on until the last.

We develop an algorithm to produce valid individuals. Let V denote the vertices, V_{use}denote the set of used vertices, V_{unuse} denote the set of unused vertices, and N_{num} denote the length of individual ($N_{Num}/3$ is the number of triangle). The initial value forV_{use} is an empty graph, and the initial value for V_{unuse} is the set V. Firstly, we produce three different numbers $N_i \in V_{unuse}$ for each individual. Then, we remove N_i from V_{unuse} and add N_i to V_{use} . Finally, for the rest of triangles, we produce a number $N_i \in V_{unuse}$, two different numbers $N_j \in V_{use}$ randomly, remove N_i from V_{unuse} and add N_i to V_{use}.

4.2 Filtering Using Constraint

However, there is still a problem that the produced individual may not satisfy the constraints of decomposable triangle. In this paper, there are two rules. One is that every three chromosomes are different to compose a triangle, and the other is that the first three numbers are different integers, and the next three different integers have only a new integer within the predefined range, and another two integers have been presented in the previous triangles, and so on until the last three numbers. That is, the individual "122423534" is not right because the local-individual "122" has the same integers "2". The individual "123453534" is also not eligible because of the triangle "453". We can select any value from valid range randomly to resolve the problem according to the rules.

4.3 Fitness Function

The fitness value of each individual in the population can be measured by the function of the joint Mix-Gauss probability. The function is depicted as follows:

$$Fit = k/(C_{max} - fx) \tag{13}$$

$$f(x) = \log P(X/G) \tag{14}$$

where k and c_{max} are constants.

4.4 Genetic Operators

The main purpose of evolutionary operators in GA is to create new valid individuals with higher fitness values in the population. For general GA operations, many iteration steps are required to find valid chromosomes. To improve the computation load problem, we can prevent invalid chromosomes before chromosomes are generated by constraint-based operations, which lead to accelerate evolution process.

The selection of individuals from population to produce successive generations plays an important role. The probabilistic selection based on ranking of the individual' fitness is performed in this paper, which was developed by Jonines and Houck[13].

To exchange information between different individuals, we generate a random number N_{rand} from a uniform distribution within the predefined range and create a new offspring $x^{'}$ by constrain-based exchange. It is the key step to exchange the corresponding triangle.

The constrain-based mutation operator is applied by two steps. The first step is that a selected chromosome in the individual is replaced by the random values produced from the predefined range by a small probability. Then, these constrains are applied for the individual to produce a valid individual. Let V denote the vertices, V_{use} denote the set of used vertices, V_{unuse} denote the set of unused vertices, V_i denote the chromosome of an individual. To satisfy the constraints, it is important step for mutation to produce a number $V_i \in V_{unuse}$. if $i < 4$ or $imod3 == 1$ and produce a number $V_i \in V_{unuse}$; if $i > 4$ and $imod3! = 1$ for the ith vertices.

5 Experiments

In this section, we explore the performance of our system. We trained our model and tested the performance of the algorithm on data obtained from CMU Graphics lab, which has 42 articulations with 3D coordinates. In experiments, we select 14 articulations (see Fig. 3). In the following sections we will use four sequences (walking (W1 and W2), running (R1) and dancing (D1) sequences) to train and test.

5.1 Detection of Individual Triangles

In this section, the performance of the probabilistic model for every triangle is examined. For each video, we adopt ten-folder ways for joint single-Gaussian and joint Mix-Gaussian with different number of mix components. In the test phase, we select the triangle with maximum probability for 12 different triangles for given models. Ideally, the correct combination of marks should produce the highest probability for given model and the correct model should also obtain the highest probability for given model. Table 1 and Table 2 show the correct rates of the corresponding joint detection by using joint single-Gaussian and mix-Gaussian probability models of each triangle for each sequence. In Table 1 and Table 2, the numbers from 1 to 14 represent the corresponding joint. In Table 2, the "Num" represents the number of Mix-Gaussian components. From the two tables, joint Mix- Gaussian probability is almost perfect for each triangle and always superior to joint single-Gaussian probability, especially for the 10th, 11th and 12th triangles with the articulation of knee which are marked in italic.

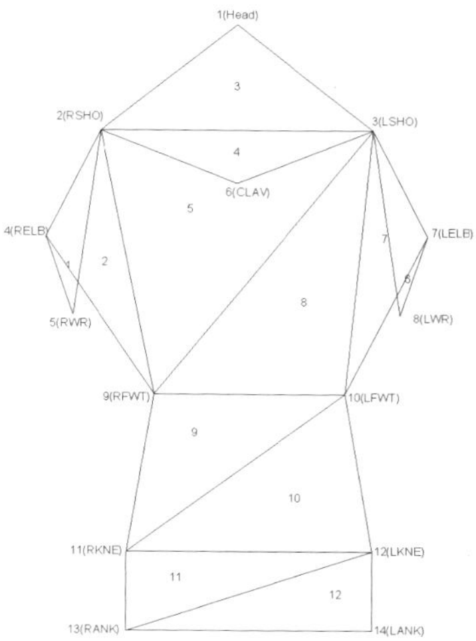

Fig. 3. Body Parts

Table 1. The correct Rates using the single gaussian model parts

data	1	2	3	4	5	6	7	8	9	10	11	12
W1	56%	100%	50.5%	75%	100%	34%	36.5%	100%	*55.5%*	*96%*	*15%*	*27%*
W2	47%	100%	90%	49%	100%	73.5%	66.5%	100%	*57.5%*	*66%*	*80.5%*	*96%*
R1	74.6%	100%	89.2%	92.3%	100%	71.5%	95.4%	100%	*73.9%*	*66.2%*	*21.5%*	*70%*
D1	100%	100%	100%	99.5%	100%	60.5%	100%	100%	*82.5%*	*24.5%*	*31.5%*	*47%*

Table 2. The correct Rates using the gaussian mixture model with different component number

data		1	2	3	4	5	6	7	8	9	10	11	12
W1	CR	100%	100%	100%	100%	100%	100%	100%	100%	*100%*	*100%*	*100%*	*100%*
	Num	3	2	4	2	2	3	3	3	2	2	2	3
W2	CR	100%	100%	100%	100%	100%	100%	100%	100%	*100%*	*100%*	*100%*	*100%*
	Num	3	2	2	2	5	3	3	3	2	2	3	3
R1	CR	100%	100%	100%	100%	100%	100%	100%	100%	*100%*	*100%*	*100%*	*100%*
	Num	2	2	2	2	2	2	2	2	2	2	2	2
D1	CR	100%	100%	100%	100%	100%	100%	100%	100%	*100%*	*100%*	*100%*	*100%*
	Num	3	7	3	2	4	5	3	3	3	3	3	3

5.2 Performance of Algorithm

In this experiment, we test the performance of our method using W1, W2, D1 and R1. Each sequence was divided into ten segments, and frames from all the other nine segments were used as the training set.

We test the single-Gaussian model and gaussian mixture model using CBGA and greedy optimization, respectively. The results are shown in Table 3, Table 4 and Table 5. In Table 3, the average results for all the sequences are at least 89.2% which are very good from Table 3 using CBGA for all sequences. And it is up to 96.3% for the run sequence. From these results, the labeling by gaussian mixture model using genetic optimization is better than the other two Probabilistic models using greedy algorithm. And the gaussian mixture model using greedy algorithm is also better than the single-Gaussian model using greedy algorithm, especially marked in italic.

To verify the performance of CBGA, we compare simple GA(SGA) and CBGA using gaussian mixture model . The correct labeling rates can be seen in Tab.6 for W1 sequence. From Tab. 6, CBGA is superior to SGA. Compared the Table6 with Tab. 4, the genetic algorithm is also better than the greedy algorithm. Fig.4 depicts the entire learning progresses monitored over generations (up to 500 generations) for W1 sequences.

Table 3. The correct labeling rates of each marker by gaussian mixture model and GA optimization

data	1	2	3	4	5	6	7	8	9	10	11	12	13	14	Ave
W1	99%	99%	99%	100%	96%	100%	97%	100%	98%	95%	88%	79%	75%	91%	*94%*
W2	98%	99%	95%	100%	98%	98%	86%	95%	98%	93%	89%	92%	94%	89%	*95%*
R1	99%	100%	99%	100%	96%	100%	98%	99%	100%	97%	94%	88%	80%	99%	*96%*
D1	97%	96%	93%	100%	99%	87%	85%	89%	91%	89%	77%	83%	79%	84%	*89%*

Table 4. The correct labeling Rates using the single gaussian model and greedy

data	1	2	3	4	5	6	7	8	9	10	11	12	13	14	Ave
W1	89%	75%	82%	65%	74%	59%	81%	81%	78%	71%	55%	56%	49%	91%	*72%*
W2	87%	73%	77%	72%	72%	78%	77%	76%	81%	73%	57.2%	51%	44%	83%	*71%*
R1	67%	70%	63%	72%	72%	75	62%	58%	70%	65%	47%	61%	47%	82%	*65%*
D1	68%	64%	73%	70%	77%	63%	71%	71%	57%	60%	55%	54%	51%	57%	*64%*

Table 5. The correct Rates by the gaussian mixture model and Greedy optimization

data	1	2	3	4	5	6	7	8	9	10	11	12	13	14	Ave
W1	83%	95%	98%	95%	98%	43%	98%	98%	97%	98%	83%	91%	96%	98%	*91%*
W2	95%	88%	94%	96%	97%	95%	94%	94%	91%	94%	90%	91%	93%	94%	*93%*
R1	88%	87.4%	93%	95%	83%	87.6%	92.4%	92%	85%	96%	91%	91%	90%	99%	*91%*
D1	93%	83%	84%	84%	87%	86%	71%	62%	81%	81%	53%	53%	49%	74%	*74%*

In the previous experiments, the data used were acquired by an accurate motion capture system. In image sequences, candidate features can be obtained from detector/tracker, where extra measurement noise may be introduced. To

Table 6. The correct labeling rates for W1 using gaussian mixture model

data	1	2	3	4	5	6	7	8	9	10	11	12	13	14	Ave
SGA	99%	99%	99%	100%	96%	100%	97%	100%	98%	95%	88%	79%	75%	91%	*94%*
CBGA	97%	97%	97%	100%	95%	100%	98%	98%	98%	4%	86%	73%	74%	91%	*92.7%*

test the performance of our method under that situation, independent Gaussian noise was added to the position of the sequence points of parts. We experimented with displays composed of 12 joints in each frame. Fig. 5 shows the correct labeling rate of added Gaussian noise to positions for W1 sequence. From the results, we can see that our method obtained higher correct rates in labeling, and it is more robust than other methods.

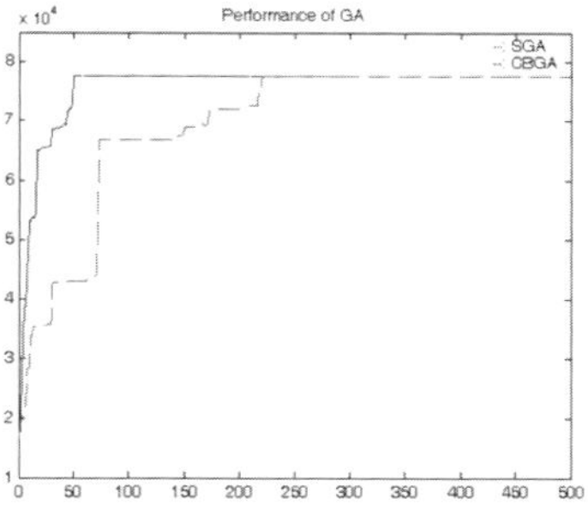

Fig. 4. SGA vs. CBGA

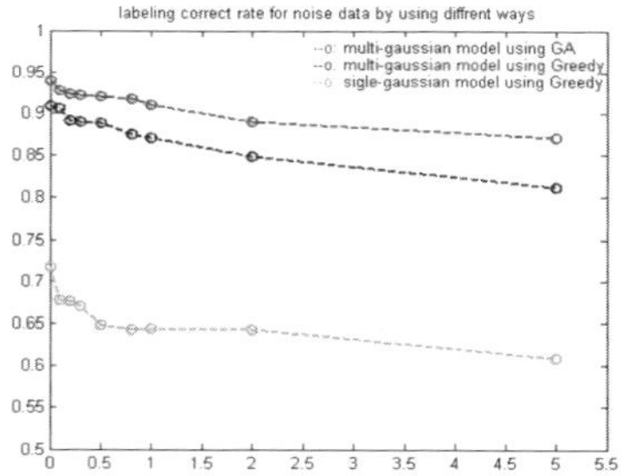

Fig. 5. Correct labeling rate vs. standard deviation

6 Conclusions

In this paper, we present a method for labeling of body parts represented by a decomposable triangulated graph with different numbers of mixture components for joint Mix-Gaussian-distribution constraint-based genetic algorithm to mark the body parts. We have applied this method to label the body parts of biological motion that can be used to reliably detect the markers. Obviously, it is better than greedy search. So far we assume that all the body markers are observed. In the case of some parts missing, the algorithm can be easily modified according to [14].

Acknowledgments

This research was supported by a grant from City University of Hong Kong (Project No. 7001766). The authors would like to thanks CMU for database [19].

References

1. Gavrila, D.M.: The visual analysis of human movement: a survey computer vision and image understanding, vol. 73, pp. 82–98 (1999)
2. Yu, L.H., Eizenman, M.: A new methodology for determining point-of-gaze in head-mounted eye tracking systems. IEEE Transactions on Biomedical Engineering 51, 1765–1773 (2004)
3. Johansson, G.: Visual perception of biological motion and a model for its analysis. Perception and Psychophysics, 201–211 (1973)
4. Dittrich, W., Troscianko, T., Lea, S., Morgan, D.: Perception of emotion from dynamic point-light displays represented in dance. Perception, 727–738 (1996)
5. Chow, C., Liu, C.: Approximating discrete probability distributions with dependence trees. IEEE Transactions on Information theory, 462–467 (1968)
6. Wong, S.K.M., Wong, F.C.C.: Comments on Approximating Discrete Probability Distributions with Dependence Trees. IEEE Trans. On Pattern Analysis and achine intelligence (1989)
7. Meila, M., Jordan, M.: Learning with mixtures of trees. Journal of Machine Learning Research, 1–48 (2000)
8. Yang, S., Goncalves, L., Perona, P.: Unsupervised Learning of Human Motion. IEEE Trans. On Pattern Analysis and Machine Intelligence, 814–827 (2003)
9. Bouguila, N., Ziou, D.: MML-Based Approach for High-Dimensional Unsupervised Learning Using the Generalized Dirichlet Mixture. In: IEEE Computer Society Conference on Computer Vision and Pattern Recognition, 53–60 (2005)
10. Zivkovic, Z., Van Der Heijden, F.: Recursive unsupervised learning of finite mixture models. IEEE Trans. on Pattern Analysis and Machine Intelligence, 651–656 (2004)
11. Figueiredo, M.A.F., Jain, A.K.: Unsupervised learning of finite mixture models. IEEE Trans. on Pattern Analysis and Machine Intelligence, 381–396 (2002)
12. Chiu, C.C., Hus, P.L.: A Constraint-Based Genetic Algorithm Approach for Mining Classification Rules. IEEE Transactions on Systems, Man, and Cybernetics - PART C: Applications and Reviews, 205–220 (2005)
13. Joines, J., Houchk, C.: On the use of non-stationary penalty functions to solve constrained optimization problems with genetic algorithm. In: IEEE International Symposium Evolutionary Computation, pp. 579–584. IEEE Computer Society Press, Los Alamitos (1994)
14. Yang, S., Feng, X., Perona, P.: Towards detection of human motion. In: Proc. IEEE CVPR, pp. 810–817 (2000)
15. Amit, Y., Kong, A.: Graphical templates for model registration. In: IEEE Transactions on Pattern Analysis and Machine Intelligence, pp. 225–236. IEEE Computer Society Press, Los Alamitos (1996)
16. Yang, S., Luis, G., Pietro, P.: Learning Probabilistic Structure for Human Motion Detection. In: IEEE Computer Society Conference on Computer Vision and Pattern Recognition, pp. II-771–II-777. IEEE Computer Society Press, Los Alamitos (2001)
17. Larranga, P., Kuijpers, C.M.H., Murga, R.H., Yurramendi, Y.: Learning Bayesian network structure by searching for the best ordering with genetic algorithms, IEEE Trans. On Systems, Man and Cybernetics-Part A: Systems and Humans, 487–193 (1996)
18. Cover, T.M., Thomas, J.A.: Elements of Information Theory. John Wiley and Sons, Chichester (1991)
19. Carnegie Mellon University Graphics Lab Motion Capture Database, `http://www.mocap.cs.cmu.edu`

Genetic Algorithm and Pareto Optimum Based QoS Multicast Routing Scheme in NGI*

Xingwei Wang, Pengcheng Liu, and Min Huang

College of Information Science and Engineering, Northeastern University,
Shenyang, 110004, China
wangxw@mail.neu.edu.cn

Abstract. In this paper, a QoS (Quality of Service) multicast routing scheme in NGI (Next Generation Internet) is proposed based on genetic engineering and microeconomics. It can not only deal with network status inaccuracy, but also help prevent network overload and meet with intra-group fairness, trying to find a multicast routing tree with bandwidth, delay, delay jitter and error rate satisfaction degree, bandwidth availability degree and fairness degree achieved or approached Pareto optimum.

1 Introduction

NGI (Next Generation Internet) should provide the user with the end-to-end QoS (Quality of Service) support. However, it is hard to describe the network status accurately [1]. With gradual commercialization of the network operation, paying for network usage become necessary, QoS pricing and accounting should be provided [2]; for multicast applications, intra-group fairness should be considered [2]. In addition, sometimes network overload happened and network performance lowered sharply, such phenomenon should be prevented or alleviated. Support from QoS routing should be provided to help solve these problems [2].

QoS multicast routing is NP-complete [3] and can be solved by heuristic or intelligent algorithms. In this paper, a GA and Pareto optimum [4] based QoS multicast routing scheme is proposed. It can deal with network status inaccuracy by introducing several QoS constraint satisfaction degrees, meet with intra-group fairness by introducing fairness degree, help to prevent network overload by introducing bandwidth availability degree. It tries to find a multicast routing tree based on GA, achieving or approaching Pareto optimum on their QoS constraint satisfaction degrees, bandwidth availability degree and fairness degree.

* This work is supported by the National High-Tech Research and Development Plan of China under Grant No. 2006AA01Z214; the National Natural Science Foundation of China under Grant No. 60673159; Program for New Century Excellent Talents in University; Specialized Research Fund for the Doctoral Program of Higher Education; the Natural Science Foundation of Liaoning Province under Grant No. 20062022.

Y. Wang, Y. Cheung, and H. Liu (Eds.): CIS 2006, LNAI 4456, pp. 115–122, 2007.

2 Problem Formulation

2.1 Symbol Definition

In this paper, use G to denote a graph, V node set in G, E edge set in G, v_s multicast source node, M multicast destination node set($M \subseteq V$), v_t multicast destination node($v_t \in M$, $t = 1,2,3,...,|M|$), T tree, p a path in T , p_t a path to v_t in T , l link, bc_l total bandwidth of l , bw_l available bandwidth of l , dl_l delay of l , jt_l delay jitter of l , ls_l error rate of l , B multicast bandwidth constraint, D multicast delay constraint, J multicast delay jitter constraint, L multicast error rate constraint; $bw_p = \min_{l \in p}\{bw_l\}$ bandwidth of p , $dl_p = \sum_{l \in p} dl_l$ delay of p , $jt_p = \sum_{l \in p} jt_l$ delay jitter of p , $ls_p = 1 - \prod_{l \in p}(1 - ls_l)$ error rate of p , $bw_T = \min_{l \in T}\{bw_l\}$ available bandwidth of T , $dl_T = \max_{p \in T}\{dl_p\}$ delay of T , $jt_T = \max_{p \in T}\{jt_p\}$ delay jitter of T , $ls_T = \max_{p \in T}\{ls_p\}$ error rate of T ; $Pr_p(bw_p \geq B)$ bandwidth satisfaction degree of p (probability of bw_p bigger than B), $Pr_p(dl_p \leq D)$ delay satisfaction degree of p , $Pr_p(jt_p \leq J)$ delay jitter satisfaction degree of p , $Pr_p(ls_p \leq L)$ error rate satisfaction degree of p , $Pr_T(bw_T \geq B)$ bandwidth satisfaction degree of T , $Pr_T(dl_T \leq D)$ delay satisfaction degree of T , $Pr_T(jt_T \leq J)$ delay jitter satisfaction degree of T , $Pr_T(ls_T \leq L)$ error rate satisfaction degree of T , bwr_T bandwidth availability degree of T (indicating network load level), g_T fairness degree of T (indicating intra-group fairness), bws_t bandwidth which the network should allocate to v_t , bwa_t bandwidth which v_t actually get from network, uc_t cost which v_t is willing to pay, η bandwidth price, μ QoS multicast routing request arrival rate, hop hop number of the path.

2.2 Mathematical Model

Given v_s and M , find a multicast routing tree $T(W, F)$, $M \subseteq W \subseteq V$, $F \subseteq E$, making its bandwidth satisfaction degree, delay satisfaction degree, delay jitter satisfaction degree, error rate satisfaction degree, bandwidth availability degree and fairness degree achieve or approach Pareto optimum without any of them below the prescribed threshold. The mathematic model is described as follows:

$$minmize\left\{\sum_{i=1}^{6} \frac{q_i}{Pr_{Ti}}\right\} \tag{1}$$

$$Pr_{Ti} \geq \Delta_i \tag{2}$$

Here, Pr_{T1} denotes $Pr_T(bw_T \geq B)$, Pr_{T2} denotes $Pr_T(dl_T \leq D)$, Pr_{T3} denotes $Pr_T(jt_T \leq J)$, Pr_{T4} denotes $Pr_T(ls_T \leq L)$, Pr_{T5} denotes bwr_T and Pr_{T6} denotes g_T ; q_i denote application preference weights to bandwidth satisfaction degree, delay satisfaction degree, delay jitter satisfaction degree, error rate satisfaction degree, bandwidth availability degree and fairness degree respectively, indicating whether one or some of them should be considered with priority when routing, and their values are determined by application nature; Δ_i are prescribed threshold between 0 and 1.

This is NP-complete [3] and solved base on GA.

3 Routing Scheme Description

3.1 Parameter Design

According to [1], suppose bw_l obey uniform distribution between $[bw_l - \Delta bw_l, bw_l + \Delta bw_l]$ and Δbw_l is the maximum possible variation before next update of network status, $Pr_p(bw_p \geq B)$ and $Pr_T(bw_T \geq B)$ are computed as follows:

$$Pr_p(bw_p \geq B) = \prod_{l \in p} \min\left(\max\left(0, \frac{bw_l + \Delta bw_l - B}{2\Delta bw_l} \right), 1 \right) \tag{3}$$

$$Pr_T(bw_T \geq B) = \prod_{p \in T} Pr_p(bw_p \geq B) \tag{4}$$

Consider network links as service queues for sending packets and their services are independent, that is, μ obeys Poisson distribution [5] with parameter λ between period $(\theta, \theta + \Delta\theta)$, $\lambda > 0$. Because delay of each hop along the path may be different, it is necessary to estimate (hop, D, μ) simultaneously. In this paper, Erlang distribution is adopted and $Pr_p(dl_p \leq D)$ is computed as follows:

$$Pr_p(dl_p \leq D) = 1 - \sum_{k=0}^{hop-1} \frac{(\mu D)^k}{k!} e^{-\mu D} \tag{5}$$

In the worst case, each path in multicast tree is edge disjoint. In this paper, $Pr_T(dl_T \leq D)$ under such case is used as its estimation and computed as follows:

$$Pr_T(dl_T \leq D) = \prod_{p \in T} Pr_p(dl_p \leq D) \tag{6}$$

The proposed scheme encourages constructing a tree with fewer edges, helping lower its delay and its occupied resource and thus reduce network load.

$Pr_p(jt_p \leq J)$, $Pr_T(jt_T \leq J)$, $Pr_T(ls_T \leq L)$ and $Pr_T(ls_T \leq L)$ are computed as follows respectively:

$$Pr_p(jt_p \le J) = 1 - \sum_{k=0}^{hop-1} \frac{(\mu J)^k}{k!} e^{-\mu J} \tag{7}$$

$$Pr_T(jt_T \le J) = \prod_{p \in T} Pr_p(jt_p \le J) \tag{8}$$

$$Pr_T(ls_T \le L) = 1 - \sum_{k=0}^{hop-1} \frac{(\mu L)^k}{k!} e^{-\mu L} \tag{9}$$

$$Pr_T(ls_T \le L) = \prod_{p \in T} Pr_p(ls_p \le L) \tag{10}$$

bwr_T should reflect network resource occupancy:

$$bwr_T = \min_{l \in T} \left\{ \frac{bw_l}{bc_l} \right\} \tag{11}$$

bws_t should be proportional to uc_t:

$$bws_t = \frac{uc_t}{\eta} \tag{12}$$

However, due to difficulty in exact measurement on network status, bwa_t may be unequal to bws_t. The expectation of bwa_t is computed as follows:

$$E(bwa_t) = \min_{l \in p_t} \{ \underset{bw_l > B}{E} (bw_l) \} \tag{13}$$

$$E(bw_l) = \begin{cases} 0 & bw_l + \Delta bw_l < B \\ \dfrac{\max(bw_l - \Delta bw_l, B) + (bw_l + \Delta bw_l)}{2} & \text{otherwise} \end{cases} \tag{14}$$

The difference between bws_t and bwa_t and its expectation and variance are computed as follows:

$$\Delta w_t = bws_t - E(bwa_t) \tag{15}$$

$$E(\Delta w_t) = \sum_{l \in T} \frac{\Delta w_t}{|M|} \tag{16}$$

$$s_T^2(\Delta w_t) = \frac{1}{|M|} \sum_{i=1}^{|M|} [\Delta w_i - E(\Delta w_i)]^2 \tag{17}$$

Fairness degree is computed as follows:

$$bws_t = \frac{uc_t}{\eta} \tag{18}$$

The bigger the g_T, the smaller the Δw_t, the higher the intra-group fairness.

3.2 Algorithm Design

3.2.1 Initial Population Generation and Chromosome Encoding

Each chromosome in population corresponds to a multicast routing tree. P_s trees are generated by random depth first search algorithm [6] to form the initial population, P_s is population size. Binary encoding scheme is adopted for chromosome, mapping its corresponding tree to a string containing path from v_s to each v_t .

3.2.2 Selection, Crossover and Mutation

The hybrid chromosome selection strategy combining with roulette wheel and elite [7] is adopted. The elite is set to conserve the current optimal chromosome. Only when the optimal chromosome in the offspring population is better than the current elite, does the corresponding replacement happen. The single-point crossover and random mutation by certain probability is used to generate new chromosome [7] in this paper.

3.2.3 Sharing Operation

Sharing operation [8] is used to promote chromosome diversity in population to speedup convergence to the optimal solution. Suppose x_i and x_j are two chromosomes. $\sigma_{bw_{x_i,y_j}}$, $\sigma_{dl_{x_i,y_j}}$, $\sigma_{jt_{x_i,y_j}}$, $\sigma_{ls_{x_i,y_j}}$, $\sigma_{bwr_{x_i,y_j}}$ and $\sigma_{g_{x_i,y_j}}$ denote distance of bandwidth satisfaction degree, delay satisfaction degree, delay jitter satisfaction degree, error rate satisfaction degree, bandwidth availability degree and fairness degree between x_i and x_j respectively and are computed as follows:

$$\sigma_{bw_{xi,xj}} = Pr_{T_{x_i}}(bw_T \geq B) - Pr_{T_{x_j}}(bw_T \geq B) \tag{19}$$

$$\sigma_{dl_{x_i,x_j}} = Pr_{T_{x_i}}(dl_T \leq D) - Pr_{T_{x_j}}(dl_T \leq D) \tag{20}$$

$$\sigma_{jt_{x_i,x_j}} = Pr_{T_{x_i}}(jt_T \leq J) - Pr_{T_{x_j}}(jt_T \leq J) \tag{21}$$

$$\sigma_{ls_{x_i,x_j}} = Pr_{T_{x_i}}(ls_T \leq L) - Pr_{T_{x_j}}(ls_T \leq L) \tag{22}$$

$$\sigma_{bwr_{x_i,x_j}} = bwr_{T_{x_i}} - bwr_{T_{x_j}} \tag{23}$$

$$\sigma_{g_{x_i,x_j}} = g_{T_{x_i}} - g_{T_{x_j}} \tag{24}$$

Use $d(x_i,x_j)$ denote distance between x_i and x_j, $d_{\max}$ denote the maximum distance between any two chromosomes, and are computed as follows:

$$d_{x_i,x_j} = \sqrt{(\sigma_{bw_{x_i,x_j}})^2 + (\sigma_{dl_{x_i,x_j}})^2 + (\sigma_{jt_{x_i,x_j}})^2 + (\sigma_{ls_{x_i,x_j}})^2 + (\sigma_{bwr_{x_i,x_j}})^2 + (\sigma_{g_{x_i,x_j}})^2} \tag{25}$$

$$d_{\max} = \frac{1}{2}\sqrt{(\sigma_{bw_{\max}})^2 + (\sigma_{dl_{\max}})^2 + (\sigma_{jt_{\max}})^2 + (\sigma_{ls_{\max}})^2 + (\sigma_{bwr_{\max}})^2 + (\sigma_{g_{\max}})^2} \tag{26}$$

$$\sigma_{bw_{\max}} = Pr_{T\max}(bw_T \geq B) - Pr_{T\min}(bw_T \geq B) \tag{27}$$

$$\sigma_{dl_{\max}} = Pr_{T\max}(dl_T \le D) - Pr_{T\min}(dl_T \le D) \tag{28}$$

$$\sigma_{jt_{\max}} = Pr_{T\max}(jt_T \le J) - Pr_{T\min}(jt_T \le J) \tag{29}$$

$$\sigma_{ls_{\max}} = Pr_{T\max}(ls_T \le L) - Pr_{T\min}(ls_T \le L) \tag{30}$$

$$\sigma_{bwr_{\max}} = bwr_{T\max} - bwr_{T\min} \tag{31}$$

$$\sigma_{g_{\max}} = g_{T\max} - g_{T\min} \tag{32}$$

In this paper, the following exponent sharing function [8] is adopted:

$$s(x_i, x_j) = \begin{cases} 1 - \left[\dfrac{d(x_i, x_j)}{d_{\max}}\right]^{\alpha} & d(x_i, x_j) < d_{\max} \\ 0 & d(x_i, x_j) \ge d_{\max} \end{cases} \tag{33}$$

3.2.4 Fitness Function

It is Computed as Follows:

$$f(x_i) = \sum_{k=1}^{6} \frac{q_k}{ff_{\tau k}(x_i)} \tag{34}$$

$$ff_{\tau k}(x_i) = \frac{f_{\tau k}(x_i)}{\sum_{j=1}^{n} s(x_i, x_j)} \tag{35}$$

$$f_{\tau k}(x_i) = Pr_{x_i k} \tag{36}$$

$$f_{(\tau+1)k}(x_i) = f_{\tau k}(x_i)\phi(\tau+1) \tag{37}$$

$$\phi(\tau+1) = \begin{cases} (1/\beta_1) & f_{(\tau+1)k}(x_i) < f_{\tau k}(x_i) \\ \beta_2 & f_{(\tau+1)k}(x_i) > f_{\tau k}(x_i) \\ 1 & f_{(\tau+1)k}(x_i) = f_{\tau k}(x_i) \end{cases} \tag{38}$$

Here, $k = 1,2,...,6$; τ is evolution times by far; $\phi(\tau+1)$ is adaptive penalty factor, regulating fitness value to accelerate convergence to the optimal solution; $\beta_1 > 1$, $\beta_2 > 1$, $\beta_1 \ne \beta_2$. Obviously, the smaller the fitness value, the higher the bandwidth satisfaction degree, delay satisfaction degree, delay jitter satisfaction degree, error rate satisfaction degree, bandwidth availability degree and fairness degree of the multicast routing tree, the more nearer to Pareto optimum even achieve Pareto optimum, at the same time the more its dissimilarity to other chromosomes.

3.2.5 Pareto Optimal Solution Set

Chromosome comparison rules are defined as follows.

Rule 1: If all $Pr_{x_i k} \leq Pr_{x_j k}$ and at least there exists such one k that $Pr_{x_i k} \neq Pr_{x_j k}$ $(k = 1,2,...,6)$, x_i is considered to be inferior to x_j.

Rule 2: If all $Pr_{x_i k} = Pr_{x_j k}$ $(k = 1,2,...,6)$, x_i is considered to be equal to x_j.

Rule 3: If both rule 1 and 2 not satisfied, x_i is considered to be equivalent to x_j.

Pareto optimal solution set update rules are defined as follows.

Rule 1: If there exist chromosomes inferior to a given chromosome, delete such ones and add the given chromosome into the Pareto optimal solution set.

Rule 2: If a given chromosome is equivalent to all ones in the Pareto optimal solution set, add the given one into the Pareto optimal solution set.

Rule 3: If rule 1 and 2 not satisfied, do not modify the Pareto optimal solution set.

3.2.6 Procedure Description

The procedure of the proposed scheme is described as follows:

Step0: Set P_s, the maximum evolution times N, the maximum times of the elite remaining invariable M ; let the counter of evolution times $i = 0$, the counter of times of the elite remaining invariable $j = 0$, Pareto optimal solution set $\Lambda = \Phi$.

Step1: According to section 3.2.1, generate initial population $P = \{x_1, x_2, ..., x_{P_s}\}$. Choose one x_r from P randomly as the current elite, put it into the safety valve, and add x_r into Λ, $r = 1,2,..., P_s$.

Step2: $i = i + 1$; if $i \leq N$, compute fitness values of all chromosomes in P according to formula (3)-(38), go to Step 3; otherwise, go to Step 6.

Step 3: Do chromosome selection, crossover, and mutation to generation the offspring population according to section 3.2.2.

Step4: Compare chromosomes in the offspring population with the ones in Λ and update Λ correspondingly according to section 3.2.5.

Step5: Find the chromosome which the smallest fitness value in Λ and compare it with the current elite: if the fitness value of the former is smaller than that of the latter, the latter is replaced by the former and $j = 0$, otherwise $j = j + 1$; if $j = M$, go to Step 6, otherwise replace P with the offspring population and go to Step 2.

Step6: Use the elite as the problem solution and output it, the algorithm ends.

4 Conclusion

Simulations have been done on NS2 (Network Simulator) platforms [9], showing that the proposed scheme is effective [10]. In future, the proposed scheme will be improved on its practicability with its prototype systems developed. In addition, taking the difficulty on exact and complete expression of the user QoS requirements into account, how to tackle the fuzziness of both the user QoS requirements and the network status in the proposed scheme is another emphasis of our future research.

References

1. Chen, P., Dong, T.L., Shi, J. et al.: A Probability-Based QoS Unicast Routing Algorithm. Journal of Software 14(3), 582–587 (2003) (in Chinese)
2. Briscoe, B., Da, V., Heckman, O., et al.: A Market Managed Multi-Service Internet. Computer Communications 26(4), 404–414 (2003)
3. Shankar, M.B., Sridhar, R., Chandra, N.S.: Multicast Routing with Delay and Delay Variation Constraints for Multimedia Applications. In: Mammeri, Z., Lorenz, P. (eds.) HSNMC 2004. LNCS, vol. 3079, pp. 399–411. Springer, Heidelberg (2004)
4. Zhang, Y., Tian, J., Dou, W.: A QoS Routing Algorithm Based on Pareto Optimal. Journal of Software 16(8), 1484–1489 (2005) (in Chinese)
5. Wang, F.B.: Probability Theory and Mathematical Statistics. Publication of Tongji university, Shanghai (1984) (in Chinese)
6. Thomas, H., Charles, E., Donald, L., et al.: Introduction to Algorithms, 2nd edn. The MIT Press, USA (2001)
7. Xing, W.X., Xie, J.X.: Modern Optimize Algorithms, pp. 140–191. Publication of Tsinghua University, Peking (1999) (in Chinese)
8. Chen, L., Huang, J., Gong, Z.: A Niche Genetic Algotithm for Computing Diagnosis with Minimum Cost. Chinese Journal of Computers 28(12), 2019–2026 (2005) (in Chinese)
9. Xu, L., Pang, B., Zhao, Y.: NS and network simulation. Posts & Telecom Press (2003)
10. Jiang, N.: Research and Simulated Implementation of Routing Mechanisms with ABC Supported in NGI. Northeastern University Master Thesis (2004)

A Centralized Network Design Problem with Genetic Algorithm Approach

Gengui Zhou, Zhenyu Cao, Jian Cao, and Zhiqing Meng

College of Business and Administration
Zhejiang University of Technology, Zhejiang 310014, China
ggzhou@zjut.edu.cn

Abstract. A centralized network is a network where all communication is to and from a single site. In the combinatorial optimization literature, this problem is formulated as the capacitated minimum spanning tree problem (CMST). Up to now there are still no effective algorithms to solve this problem. In this paper, we present a completely new approach by using the genetic algorithms (GAs). For the adaptation to the evolutionary process, we developed a tree-based genetic representation to code the candidate solution of the CMST problem. Numerical analysis shows the effectiveness of the proposed GA approach on the CMST problem.

1 Introduction

A centralized network is a network where all communication is to and from a single site (Kershenbaum, 1993). In such networks, terminals are connected directly to the central site. Sometimes multipoint lines are used, where groups of terminals share a tree to the center and each multipoint line is linked to the central site by one link only. This means that optimal topology for this problem corresponds to a tree in a graph $G = (V, E)$ with all but one of nodes in V corresponding to the terminals. The remaining node refers to the central site, and edges in E correspond to the feasible telecommunication wiring. Each subtree rooted in the central site corresponds to a multipoint line. Usually, the central site can handle, at most, a given fixed amount of information in communication. This, in turn, corresponds to restricting the maximum amount of information flowing in any link adjacent to the central site (which we will refer as the root of the graph G) to that fixed amount. In the combinatorial optimization literature, this problem is known as the capacitated minimum spanning tree problem (CMST).

The CMST problem has been shown to be *NP*-hard by Papadimitriou (Papadimitriou, 1978). Much of the early works focused on heuristic approaches to find good feasible solutions. Among them are those by Chandy and Lo (Chandy, 1973), Kershenbaum (Kershenbaum, 1974), and Elias and Ferguson (Elias and Ferguson, 1974). The only full optimization algorithms that we are aware of are by Gavish (Gavish, 1982) and Kershenbaum et al. (Kershenbaum at al., 1983), but their use is limited to problems involving up to 20 nodes. Gavish (Gavish, 1983) also studied a new formulation and its several relaxation procedures for

Y. Wang, Y. Cheung, and H. Liu (Eds.): CIS 2006, LNAI 4456, pp. 123–132, 2007.

the capacitated minimum directed tree problem. Recently, this problem has even more aroused many researchers' interesting by using cutting plane algorithms by Gouveia (Gouveia, 1995) and Hall (Hall, 1996), branch-bound algorithm by Malik and Yu (Malik and Yu, 1993), neighborhood search technique by Ahuja et al. Ahuja, 2003, and ant colony optimization technique by Reimann and Laumanns Reimann, 2006.

In the studies that date back twenty years, it is not surprising to find that only very small instances were attempted in solving this problem. In this paper, we present a completely new approach by using the genetic algorithms (GAs), which have been demonstrating their powerful potential in dealing with such complicated combinatorial problem with tree topology (Zhou and Gen, 1998, 2003). For the adaptation to the evolutionary process, we developed a tree-based genetic representation to code the candidate solution of the CMST problem. Because the new genetic representation has the tree topology and is only encoded by a bigeminal string, it is easy to go on genetic operations. Also the tree-based genetic representation guarantees that the candidate solutions are always feasible solutions of the problem to be solved, and its locality property makes the evolutionary process more efficiency. Numerical analysis shows the effectiveness of the proposed GA approach on this CMST problem.

2 Problem Formulation

Firstly, we formulate the centralized network design problem as a zero-one integer program. This particular formulation was first expressed by Gavish (Gavish, 1982). Considering a complete, undirected graph $G = (V, E)$, we let $V = 1, 2, ..., n$ be the set of nodes representing the terminals and denote the central site, or "root" node, as node 1, and $E = \{(i, j)|i, j \in V\}$ be the set of edges representing all possible telecommunication wiring. For a subset of nodes $S \subseteq V$ we define $E(S) = \{(i, j)|i, j \in S\}$ to be the edges whose endpoints are both in S. We define the following binary decision variables for all edges $(i, j) \in E$:

$$x_{ij} = \begin{cases} 1 & \text{if edge } (i,j) \text{ is selected;} \\ 0 & \text{otherwise.} \end{cases}$$

Let c_{ij} be the (fixed) cost of including edge (i, j) in the solution, and suppose that d_i represents the demand at each node $i \in V$, where by convention the demand of the root node $d_1 = 0$. We also use $d(S)$, $S \subseteq V$, to denote the sum of the demands of the nodes of S. The subtree capacity is denoted κ .

It is not hard to verify that the following formulation is a valid integer programming representation for the centralized network design problem:

$$\min \quad z = \sum_{i=1}^{n-1} \sum_{j=2}^{n} c_{ij} x_{ij} \tag{1}$$

$$s.t. \quad \sum_{i=1}^{n-1} \sum_{j=2}^{n} x_{ij} = n - 1 \tag{2}$$

$$\sum_{i\in S}\sum_{\substack{j\in S\\ j>1}} x_{ij} \leq |S| - \lambda(S), S \subseteq V\backslash\{1\}, |S| \geq 2 \tag{3}$$

$$\sum_{i\in U}\sum_{\substack{j\in U\\ j>1}} x_{ij} \leq |U| - 1, U \subset V, |U| \geq 2, \{1\} \in U \tag{4}$$

$$x_{ij} = 0\, or\, 1,\ (i = 1, 2, \ldots, n-1,\ j = 2, 3, \ldots, n.) \tag{5}$$

Equality (2) is true of all spanning trees: a tree with n nodes must have $n-1$ edges. Inequalities (4) are some of the standard rank inequalities for spanning trees: if more than $|U|-1$ edges connect the nodes of a subset U, then that set of edges must contain a cycle. The parameter $\lambda(S)$ in (3) refers to the bin-packing number of the set S, namely, the number of bins of size needed to pack the nodes of items of size d_i for all $i \in S$. These constraints are similar to (4), except that they reflect the capacity constraint: if the set S does not contain the root node, then the nodes of $\lambda(S)$ must be contained in at least (S) different subtrees off of the root.

In the case that the demands of all non-root nodes are 1, inequalities (3) can be expressed more simply as follows as items of unit size can always be packed in $\lceil |S|/\kappa \rceil$ bins or subtrees.

$$\sum_{i\in S}\sum_{\substack{j\in S\\ j>1}} x_{ij} \leq |S| - \left\lceil \frac{|S|}{\kappa} \right\rceil, S \subseteq V\backslash\{1\}, |S| \geq 2 \tag{6}$$

The above mathematical formulation is regarded as the capacitated minimum spanning tree problem in literature. Assuming that all the constraints in (3) or (6) can be explicitly represented, it is possible to compute a lower bound on the problem by replacing the binary variables with continuous variables in the range 0 to 1 and solving the resulting linear program. Unfortunately, there are $O(2^n)$ constraints in (3) or (6), leading to a very large linear program even for moderate values of n. In fact, the problem is *NP*-hard (Papadimitriou, 1978) and algorithms exist yielding exact solutions only for problems of modest size (Gavish, 1985).

Up to now, all heuristic algorithms for this problem are only focused on how to deal with the constraints to make the problem simpler to solve. On the approach of cutting plane algorithms (Gouveia, 1995, Hall, 1996) or branch-bound algorithm (Malik, 1993), the network topology of the CMST problem are usually neglected. As a result, it results in the exponential explosion of constraints. In the following section, we focus on a new approach on this problem by using genetic algorithms. In the evolutionary process, we make full use of its tree topology of the CMST problem and develop the algorithm to get the optimal or near-optimal solutions.

3 Genetic Algorithms Approach

A genetic algorithm (GA) can be understood as an "intelligent" probabilistic search algorithm which can be applied to a variety of combinatorial optimization problems (Gen and Cheng, 2000). The theoretical foundations of GAs were originally developed by Holland (Holland, 1975). The idea of GAs is based on the evolutionary process of biological organisms in nature. During the course of the evolution, natural populations evolve according to the principles of natural selection and "survival of the fittest". Individuals which are more successful in adapting to their environment will have a better chance of surviving and reproducing, whilst individuals which are less fit will be eliminated. This means that the genes from the highly fit individuals will spread to an increasing number of individuals in each successive generation. The combination of good characteristics from highly adapted ancestors may produce even more fit offspring. In this way, species evolve to become more and more well adapted to their environment.

3.1 Genetic Representation

For the CMST problem, two main factors should be taken into consideration if we want to keep its tree topology structure in the genetic representation: one is the connectivity among nodes; the other is the degree value (the number of edges connected on it) of each node. Therefore, the intuitive idea of encoding a tree solution is to use a two-dimension structure for its genetic representation. One dimension encodes the nodes of a spanning tree; another dimension encodes the degree value of each node. Thus it needs a $2 \times n$ matrix to represent a chromosome for an n-node tree. Obviously the genes in node dimension take the integers from 1 to n exclusively; the genes in degree dimension take the integers from 1 to b inclusively (b is the largest degree value for all nodes). We define this genetic representation as tree-based permutation.

For a rooted tree like the CMST solution, we can take one node (i.e. node 1) as the root node of it. All other nodes are regarded being connected to it hierarchically. For any node (current node), the node incident to it on the upper hierarchy is called as its predecessor node and the node incident to it on the lower hierarchy is called as its successor node. Obviously, the root node has no predecessor node and the leaf node has no successor node. Based on this observation, the tree-based permutation of such a tree can be encoded as the following procedure:

procedure: tree-based permutation encoding

step 1: Select node 1 (root node) as the current node in a labeled tree T, put it as the first digit in the node dimension of the permutation and its degree value as the first digit in the degree dimension.

step 2: Check all successor nodes of the current node from left branch to right branch. If there are successor nodes, let the leftmost successor node as the current node, then go to **step 3**. Otherwise, go to **step 4**.

step 3: Put the label digit of the current node to the permutation in the node dimension and its degree value to the permutation in the degree dimension (here we build the permutation by appending digits to the right), then go to **step 2**.

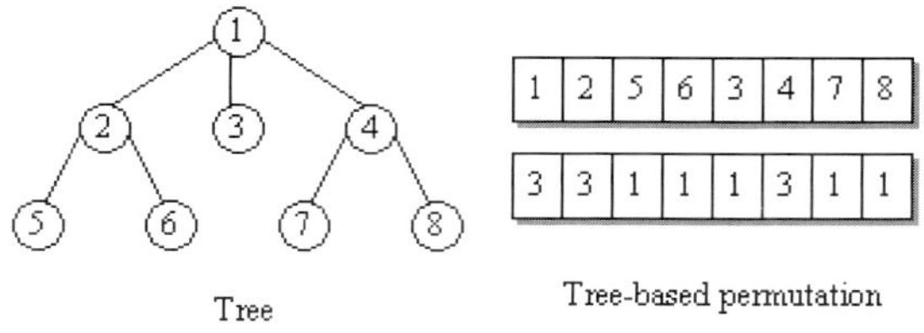

Fig. 1. A rooted tree and its tree-based permutation

step 4: Delete the current node and its adjacent edge from the tree, let its predecessor node as the current node.
step 5: If all nodes have been checked, stop; otherwise, go to **step 2**.

Figure 1 illustrates an example of this tree-based permutation. For the initial population, each chromosome can be generated randomly. However, in order to keep the connectivity between nodes, the genes in the degree dimension need to satisfy the following conditions: For an n-node tree, the total degree value for all nodes is $2(n-1)$. Suppose that d_{rest} is the total degree value of the nodes whose degree value in degree dimension have been assigned and d_{rest} is the total lower bound of the degree values for all those nodes whose degree value in degree dimension have not been assigned. Then the degree value of the current node in degree dimension should hold: no less than 1. The degree value of the current node together with that of the rest nodes should hold: no less than d_{rest} and no greater than $2(n-1) - d_{used}$. Especially, for the root node, its degree value should take no less the value of $\lceil |V|/\kappa \rceil$, which reflects the number of subtrees connected to the root node to satisfy the capacity constraint.

Also, it is easy to decode the above tree-based permutation into a tree. Suppose that the node dimension for individual P is represented as $P_1(k)$, $k = 1, 2, ..., n$ and the degree dimension for individual P as $P_2(k)$, $k = 1, 2, ..., n$. The decoding procedure for each individual in the form of tree-based permutation can be operated as follows (for the convenience of the procedure operation, the first gene value in the degree dimension should be added by one):

procedure: tree-based permutation decoding
step 1: Set $k \leftarrow 1$ and $j \leftarrow 2$.
step 2: Select the node $r = P_1(k)$ and the node $s = P_1(j)$, add the edge from r to s into a tree.
step 3: Let $P_2(k) \leftarrow P_2(k) - 1$, $P_2(j) \leftarrow P_2(j) - 1$.
step 4: If $P_2(k) = 0$, let $k \leftarrow k - 1$, otherwise, go to **step 6**.
step 5: If $j = n$, stop, otherwise, go to **step 4**.
step 6: If $P_2(j) \geq 1$, let $k \leftarrow j$, $j \leftarrow j + 1$, go to **step 2**, otherwise, $j \leftarrow j + 1$, go to **step 2**.

Obviously, any rooted spanning tree can be encoded by this representation scheme and any permutation encoded in this way represents a rooted spanning tree. However, the relation between the encoding and its spanning tree may not be one-to-one mapping because different chromosomes may represent the same spanning tree. But it is possible to represent all possible spanning trees on a complete graph. It is also easy to go back and forth between the encoded representation of a tree and the tree's representation for evaluating the fitness, which will be illustrated in Section 3.4.

It is important to point out that this encoding keeps the structure of a tree, so it possesses the locality in the sense that small changes in the representation (such as mutation operation) make small changes in the tree. Without this property, the GA search tends to drift rather than converge to a highly fit population. Therefore, this encoding is well adapted to the evolutionary process and thus adopted as the genetic representation for the CMST problem.

3.2 Genetic Operation

Genetic operation is used to alter the genetic composition of individuals or chromosomes. Usually it contains two kinds of operations: crossover and mutation. In order to keep all individuals being feasible after genetic operations on the tree-based permutation for the CMST problem, only three kinds of mutations are adopted in this paper.

Exchange mutation on nodes: Exchange mutation selects two genes (nodes) at random and then swaps the genes (nodes). This mutation is essentially a 2-opt exchange heuristic. The operation can be illustrated by Figure 2.

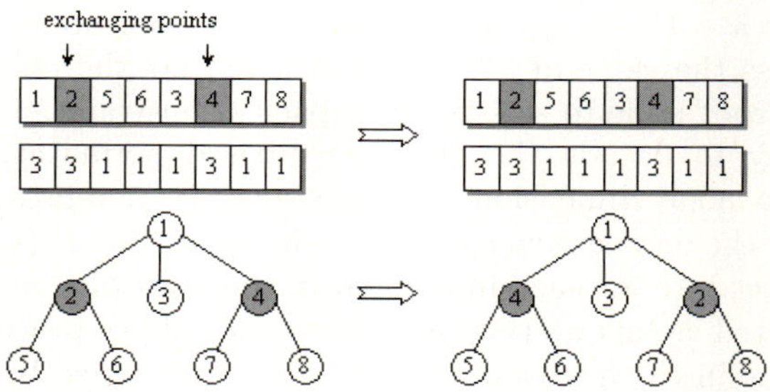

Fig. 2. Exchange mutation on nodes

Inversion mutation on nodes: Inversion mutation selects two genes (nodes) at random and then inverts the substring between these two genes (nodes). It is illustrated in Figure 3.

Insertion mutation: Insertion mutation selects a string of genes (branch) at random and inserts it in a random gene (node). When a string of genes are taken off from a gene, the gene value of that node should be decreased by one. When a string of genes are added on a gene, the gene value of that node should be increased by one. The operation can be illustrated by Figure 4. Obviously, this operation is indispensable for the evolutionary process to evolve to the fit tree structures.

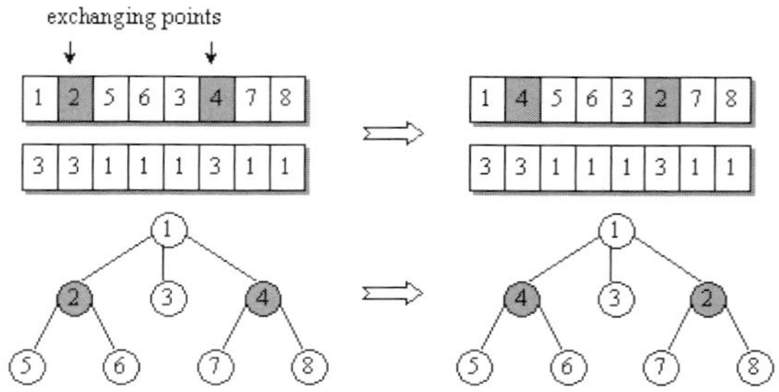

Fig. 3. Inversion mutation on nodes

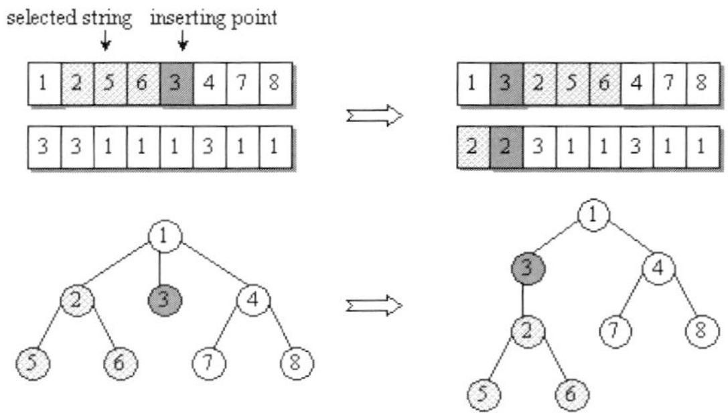

Fig. 4. Inversion mutation on nodes

3.3 Modification

For the CMST problem, there is the capacity constraint for each spanning tree. Especially, when the demands of all terminals are equal to one, the problem is finding a rooted spanning tree in which each of the subtree off of the root node contains at most κ nodes. Therefore, before evaluation, if there are such individuals whose subtrees violate the capacity constraint, we use the insertion mutation operation to insert the extra branch on a subtree into other subtree with less nodes.

3.4 Evaluation and Selection

Evaluation is to associate each individual with a fitness value which reflects how good it is. The higher fitness value of an individual, the higher its chances of survival and reproduction and the larger its representation in the subsequent generation. Obviously the evaluation together with selection provides the mechanism of evolving all individuals toward the optimal or near-optimal solutions. Simply, we take the objective value of Equation (1) for each individual's fitness value after its decoding from genotypic representation to phenotypic representation.

As to selection, we adopt the $(\mu + \lambda)$-selection strategy(Back, 1991). But in order to avoid the premature convergence of the evolutionary process, our selection strategy only selects μ different best individuals from μ parents and λ offspring. If there are no μ different individuals available, the vacant pool of population is filled with renewal individuals.

3.5 GA Procedure for the CMST

To summarize our GA approach on the CMST problem, the overall procedure can be outlined as follows:

procedure: GA for CMST
    begin
        $t \leftarrow 0$;
        initialize the population of parents $P(0)$;
        evaluate $P(0)$;
        while (**not** termination condition) **do**
            reproduce $P(t)$ to yield the population of offspring $C(t)$;
            modify $P(t)$;
            evaluate $C(t)$;
            $t \leftarrow t + 1$;
        end
    end

Table 1. The cost matrix for the numerical example ($n = 16$, $\kappa = 5$)

i/j	2	3	4	5	6	7	8	9	10	11	12	13	14	15	16
1	1616	1909	246	622	829	1006	2237	399	1717	632	1191	2116	824	1336	1519
2		2996	1419	2217	1213	2046	3753	1516	1180	1997	552	3622	2423	1367	862
3			1893	1543	1792	2785	1362	1667	3556	2332	2446	1248	1508	3233	3287
4				799	593	1188	2369	242	1670	857	962	2243	1004	1348	1425
5					1230	1253	1625	761	2301	801	1748	1509	206	1873	2119
6						1758	2597	480	1883	1449	663	2463	1420	1701	1573
7							2703	1399	1470	454	1849	2612	1350	960	1470
8								2238	3922	2304	3231	137	1442	3476	3743
9									1889	1029	1009	2108	959	1586	1628
10										1693	1437	3808	2480	511	340
11											1685	2206	909	1205	1603
12												3098	1952	1429	1100
13													1331	3368	3624
14														2038	2309
15															578

The parameters for the proposed GA approach are set as follows: population size pop_size = 200; mutation probabilities for three mutation operations are $p_m = 0.3$ respectively; maximum generation max_gen = 500; and run by 20 times.

4 Computational Experience

In order to illustrate the ideas that were presented in the previous section, we present a numerical example given out by Gavish (Gavish, 1985). The example consists of a CMST problem with 16 nodes, a unit traffic between each node and node 1, and a capacity restriction . The cost matrix for the example is presented in Table 1.

Gavish adopted an augmented lagrangean based algorithms to solve this problem and got the optimal solution 8526 (Gavish, 1985). By the proposed GA, we also got the optimal solution 8526 and its corresponding topology of a tree. Figure 5 illustrates the result.

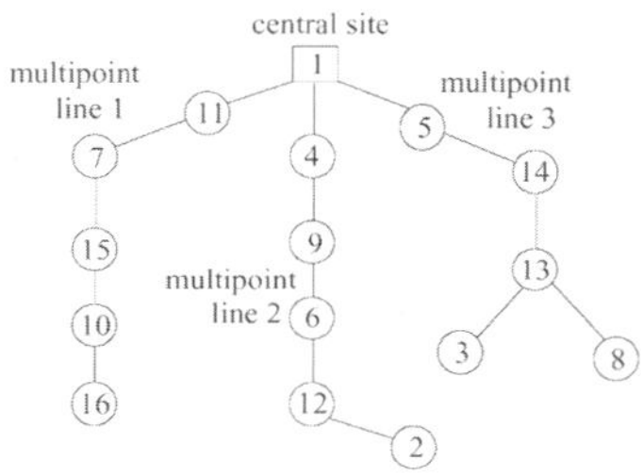

Fig. 5. Inversion mutation on nodes

5 Conclusion and Further Work

The centralized network design problem can be formulated as a capacitated minimum spanning tree problem. In this paper we developed a new approach to deal with this problem by using genetic algorithms. In order to code the corresponding rooted tree topology for the genetic representation on the CMST problem, we presented a tree-based permutation which is able to represent all possible rooted trees. Small numerical example shows the effectiveness of the proposed GA approach on the CMST problem.

Further works are needed to demonstrate the effectiveness of the proposed GA approach on this problem, which including the test on the problems with larger scale, the comparison with its lower bound since it is difficult to give out the optimal solution of the problem on larger scale. However, the research work gives out an novel approach on such complicated combinatorial optimization problems.

Acknowledgements

This research work was partially supported by grant No.70671095 from National Nature Science Foundation of China.

References

1. Ahuja, R.K., Orlin, J.B., Sharma, D.: A positive very large-scale neighborhood structure for the capacitated minimum spanning tree problem. Operations Research letters 31, 185–194 (2003)
2. Bäck, T., Hoffmeister, F., Schwefel, H.: A survey of evolution strategy. In: Belew, R., Booker, L. (eds.) Proceedings of the Fourth International Conference on Genetic Algorithms, pp. 2–9. Morgan Kaufmann Publishers, San Mateo,CA (1991)
3. Chandy, K.M., Lo, T.: The capacitated minimum spanning tree. Networks 3, 173–182 (1973)
4. Elias, D., Ferguson, M.J.: Topological design of multipoint teleprocessing networks. IEEE Trans. Commun. 22, 1753–1762 (1974)
5. Garey, M., Johnson, D. (eds.): Computers and Intractability: A Guide to the Theory of NP-completeness. W.H. Freeman and Co, San Francisco (1979)
6. Gavish, B.: Topological design of centralized computer networks–formulation and algorithms. Networks 12, 355–377 (1982)
7. Gavish, B.: Formulation and algorithms for the capacitated minimal directed tree problem. J. Assoc. Comput. Machinery 30, 118–132 (1983)
8. Gavish, B.: Augmented lagrangean based algorithms for centralized network design. IEEE transaction on Commun. 33, 1247–1257 (1985)
9. Gen, M., Cheng, R.: Genetic Algorithms and Engineering Optimization. John Wiley & Sons, New York (2000)
10. Gouveia, L.: A 2^n constraint formulation for the capacitated minimal spanning tree problem. Operations Research 43, 130–141 (1995)
11. Hall, L.: Experience with a cutting plane algorithm for the capacitated spanning tree problem. INFORMS Journal on Computing 8, 219–234 (1996)
12. Holland, J.H.: Adaptation in natural and Artificial Systems. MIT Press, Cambridge, MA (1975)
13. Kershenbaum, A.: Computing capacitated minimal spanning trees efficiently. Networks 4, 299–310 (1974)
14. Kershenbaum, A., Boorstyn, R.R., Oppenheim, R.: Centralized teleprocessing network design. Networks 13, 279–293 (1983)
15. Kershenbaum, A.: Telecommunication Network Design Algorithms. McGraw-Hill, Inc, Singapore (1993)
16. Malik, K., Yu, G.: A branch and bound algorithm for the capacitated minimum spanning tree problem. Networks 23, 525–532 (1993)
17. Papadimitriou, C.H.: The complexity of the capacitated tree problem. Networks 8, 217–230 (1978)
18. Reimann, M., Laumanns, M.: Savings based ant colony optimization for the capacitated minimum spanning tree problem. Computers & Operations Research 33, 1794–1822 (2006)
19. Zhou, G., Gen, M.: An effective genetic algorithm approach to the quadratic minimum spanning tree problem. Computer & Operations Research 25, 229–237 (1998)
20. Zhou, G., Gen, M.: A genetic algorithm approach on tree-like telecommunication network design problem. Journal of The Operational Research Society 54, 248–254 (2003)

CGA: Chaotic Genetic Algorithm for Fuzzy Job Scheduling in Grid Environment

Dan Liu and Yuanda Cao

School of Computer Science and Technology,
Beijing Institute of Technology, 100081, Beijing, China
{bashendan, ydcao}@bit.edu.cn

Abstract. We introduce a Chaotic Genetic Algorithm (CGA) to schedule Grid jobs with uncertainties. We adopt a Fuzzy Set based Execution Time (FSET) model to describe uncertain operation time and flexible deadline of Grid jobs. We incorporate chaos into standard Genetic Algorithm (GA) by logistic function, a simple equation involving chaos. A distinguishing feature of our approach is that the convergence of CGA can be controlled automatically by the three famous characteristics of logistic function: convergent, bifurcating, and chaotic. Following this idea, we propose a *chaotic mutation operator* based on the feedback of fitness function that ameliorates GA, in terms of convergent speed and stability. We present an entropy based metrics to evaluate the performance of CGA. Experimental results illustrate the efficiency and stability of the resulting algorithm.

1 Introduction

In scheduling the batch jobs for parallel processing under the Open Grid Service Architecture (OGSA) [1], the jobs are often decomposed into sub-jobs and mapped onto various distributed Grid services, as depicted in Fig. 1. Under this scenario, the uncertainty exists in practice because of the dynamic characteristic of Grid service and various demands from users. That is, sub-jobs of each job may have uncertain operation time on Grid services, so the batch jobs may have flexible overall finishing time. Moreover, users submit batch jobs with deadline requirement to Grid system. The challenge for Grid job scheduling algorithm is to satisfy furthest the user requirement by meeting deadline. Excellent developments including prediction of job finishing time [4] have shown that it's feasible in several cases of interest to narrow the gap between the finishing time and deadline requirement of batch jobs. However, many existing algorithms [2, 3, 8] are based on assumptions that job operation time is determined before execution, making their applicability in a realistic environment rather doubtful.

The main focus of this paper is the time uncertainty of Grid batch jobs regardless performance and security [11]. The operation time of sub-jobs vary while being processed by Grid services. And the deadline of batch jobs changes because of the user preference, that is, user can negotiate with the Grid services what service level will be [12]. There are three challenges to take these dynamics

Y. Wang, Y. Cheung, and H. Liu (Eds.): CIS 2006, LNAI 4456, pp. 133–143, 2007.

in to account before job execution. The first one is the definition of uncertainty because batch job scheduling is static planning [8]. The second one is the job scheduling with uncertainty. The last one is the computational complexity to solve the optimization problem. It's NP hard to arrange Grid jobs of uncertain execution time to services exactly.

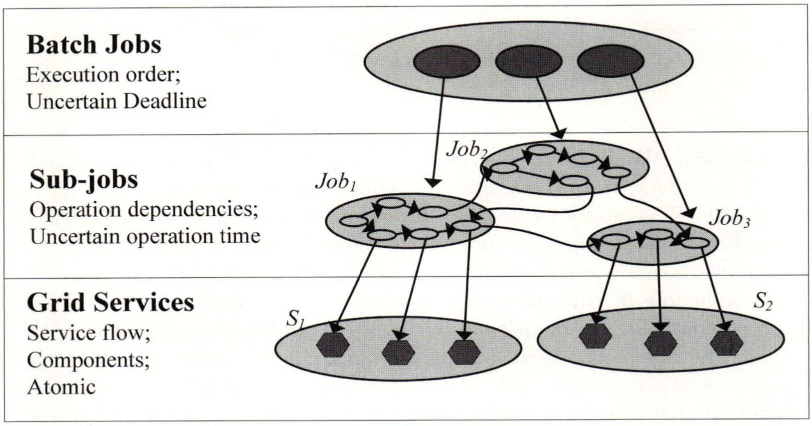

Fig. 1. Grid job execution structure and uncertainty demand in batch job processing. Batch Job is a set of jobs, and each job is a set of sub-jobs. Execution orders exist among jobs and sub-jobs. Each component of Grid Service executes one sub-job at one time, and it has uncertain operation time on these sub-jobs. Overall finishing time of Batch Job is the finishing time of the job which is finished ultimately.

The rest of the paper is organized as follows. We analyze several existing schedulers and algorithms for Grid job scheduling problems in Section 2, where we also introduce our approach. Section 3 describes the certain job scheduling problem and FSET model. Section 4 and 5 discuss the optimization problem and our proposed CGA. We provide our entropy based performance evaluation and experimental results in Section 6. Finally in Section 7, we conclude with some final remarks and suggest future works.

2 Related Work and Our Approach

The schedulers in several well known projects are investigated. The scheduler of GrADS [17, 18] support single job online submission. In terms of batch job scheduling, the Matchmaker of Condor [20] uses the Classad language to describe machine states and job constrains. The NetSolve [19] uses different scheduling algorithms for different applications. The completion time of a job is estimated by an experiential performance model and a load model. A dynamic job queue is used for task farming. The queue length can adaptively be adjusted from the average request response time of history statistics. The scheduler of Nimord [21] uses an economics model for Grid job scheduling by time and cost optimization. The scheduler in Globus [23] is used to solve the cross-operation problems of heterogeneous platforms. And it helps to establish the high-level scheduling policies and algorithms for the underlay systems like Nimrod/G [15] and Condor-G [16].

Algorithms in previous works are studied. Heuristic neighborhood search such as genetic algorithm [2, 3, 5, 11], backfilling [4], gang [22] and max_min method [6], etc., are widely adopted to find solution to the Grid Job scheduling problems. Tracy [7] compared 11 heuristics in 12 situations and drew conclusion that GA outperforms the rest in finding the best resolution. On the other hand, artificial intelligence algorithm based on the evolvement of complex system is also used, such as artificial neural network and worm sapience algorithm [9].

These approaches largely ignore the uncertain factors of batch job, with only a handful of exceptions. Most notably, matchmaking algorithm [16, 20] uses constraint-satisfaction model to match the hazy job requirements to hardware resources. It de-fines the resource usage by range value in advertisement, and matches it onto the available resource. In our research, however, we focus on the degrees of the uncertainties. For example, the finishing time of all jobs is completely satisfied if it's within the scope of deadline, and is acceptable if a little longer than the deadline, but is discontented if twice more than deadline. Thus, our objective is to meet farthest the deadline requirements of user by minimizing the overall finishing time of batch jobs.

The results presented in this paper indicate that the degree of time uncertainty can be modeled by Fuzzy Set. We describe the degree of uncertainties by simple fuzzy number, that is, triangular fuzzy number for operation time and semi-trapezoid fuzzy number for deadline. And it's easy to compute the overall finishing time of batch jobs according to FSET. Thus, the gap between deadline and overall finishing time can be denoted by satisfaction degree which is computable. We use Consistency Factor (CF) to depict this degree. In order to compute CF, we have to solve the job scheduling problem with FSET model. It's more difficult than traditional job scheduling problem because the FSET need three values to describe one fuzzy number, which are upper bound, lower bound and real value. It's different from those approaches mentioned above [2, 3, 5, 8, 11], each of which needs only one chromosome to represent one number. As a matter of fact, we have to put upper and lower bound values into chromosome either, that is, 3 times more storage requirement than previous ones. More-over, the CF value will be calculated each time when evaluating the fitness function, as a result, the applicability of standard GA is rather doubtful. A more efficient and stable algorithm is needed. As an inspiration from the natural phenomenon, we adopt the logistic function involving chaos to improve GA.

In particular, the proposed algorithm has the structure as illustrated in Fig. 2. We highlight the *chaotic mutation operator* which is the core of CGA. Our idea is very simple. The algorithm uses logistic function to produce the mask, which in turn controls *crossover*. Several improvements to GA based on chaos have been proposed in previous works to solve Data Clustering problems [5]. Unlike the bit flip mutation of λ, introduced by Determan [5], we mutate λ

according to the fitness function. If the offspring has good fitness value, the logistic function produces stable mask to keep the good gene; otherwise it produces disordered mask to guarantee the variety of gene. Thus the mutation is controlled automatically. There are two benefits connected to the introduction of chaos into GA. Besides the significant speeding up of convergence, that is anyway a fundamental motivation, there are other significant advantages. For instance, the stability is improved because the λ make the algorithm to produce more stable solution than standard GA. In order to evaluate the convergence and stability, we present an entropy based approach. The results show that the neighborhood exploration of genetic algorithm is much more efficient with chaos than without.

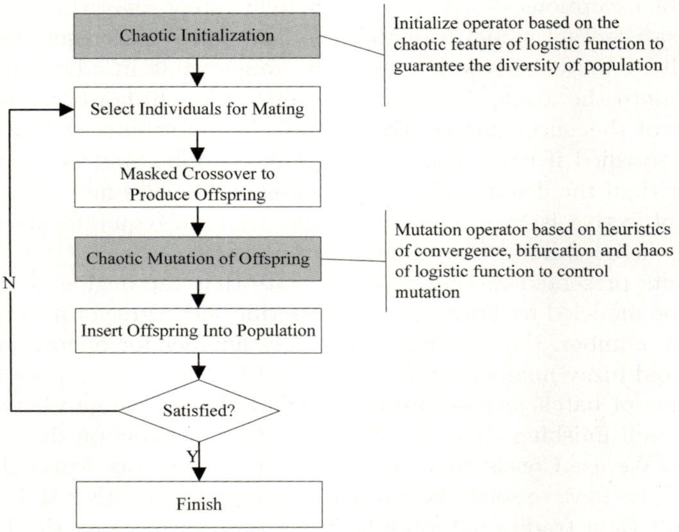

Fig. 2. Flowchart of CGA. Chaos is mainly used in the initialize and mutation operator.

3 The System Model

We first formalize the certain Grid Job scheduling problem regardless the time uncertainties. Then, we introduce FSET to quantify the degree of the time uncertainties, and we discuss how to compute the Consistency Factor.

3.1 Certain Job Scheduling Model

The formal specification of the batch job scheduling problem with deterministic job execution time and deadline in Grid can be described as follows. Batch Job is a set of Jobs. Job_i is i^{th} job and $SubJ_{ij}$ is j^{th} sub-job of the ith job. S_a denotes the ath service. m_a means the amount of components of ath service. S_{ab} shows b^{th}

component of ath service. Formula $\xi : S_{ab} \rightarrow S'_k$ maps components onto virtual components S' for the ease of computation. S_{ijk} indicates the operation of jth sub-job of ith job on k^{th} virtual component. f_{ik} and e_{ik} are finishing time and operation time of the ith job executed by k^{th} virtual component respectively.

3.2 FSET Model

TFN $ET_{ijk}(et^1_{ijk}, et^2_{ijk}, et^3_{ijk})$ is fuzzy operation time of S_{ijk}, and SFN $DT_i(dt^1_i, dt^2_i)$ is fuzzy deadline, where TFN is triangular fuzzy number and SFN is semi-trapezoid fuzzy number.

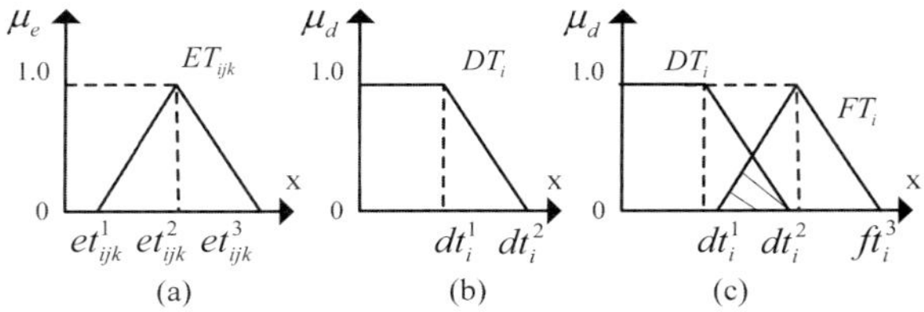

Fig. 3. (a) and (b) are the membership functions of ET_{ijk} and DT_i. (c) denotes the intersection of fuzzy finishing time and deadline of Job_i. The FT_i is the finishing time of all the sub-jobs of Job_i, which can be computed according to the following operators. The percentage of shadow part in the FT_i is CF.

Let TFN FT_i be fuzzy finishing time of Job_i correlative to DT_i. The shadow in Fig. 3 (c) means that the finishing time of Job_i falls within the deadline. For TFN $\tilde{x}(p, x, q)$ and $\tilde{y}(u, y, v)$ with membership function $\mu_{\tilde{x}}$ and $\mu_{\tilde{y}}$, we define two binary operators $+$ and $\vee$ to calculate the finishing time and start time.

$$plus+ : x + y = (p, x, q) + (u, y, v) = (p + u, x + y, q + v)$$

$$superior\vee : \tilde{x} \vee \tilde{y} = (p, x, q) \vee (u, y, v) \approx (p \vee u, x \vee y, q \vee v)$$

Here we use approximate value to guarantee the triangular characteristic of the solution of the $\vee$ operation. Thus the membership function can be defined as:

$$\mu_{\tilde{x}\vee\tilde{y}}(z) = \sup_{z=r\vee t} \min\{\mu_{\tilde{x}}(r), \mu_{\tilde{y}}(t)\}$$

Let CF be the Consistency Factor to quantify the satisfaction degree of the finishing time of Job_i corresponding to the deadline.

$$CF_i = \frac{\int_{x=0}^{ft^3_i} \mu_{f\vee d}(x)}{\int_{x=0}^{ft^3_i} \mu_f(x)} = \frac{\int_{x=0}^{ft^3_i} \min\{\mu_f(x), \mu_d(x)\}}{\int_{x=0}^{ft^3_i} \mu_f(x)} \qquad (1)$$

Where μ_f and μ_d are the membership functions of FT_i and DT_i respectively.

4 The Optimization Problem

Considering the fuzzy time constraints and operation dependencies among sub-jobs, we formulate the fuzzy job scheduling problem by introducing FSET into certain job scheduling model. The objective of overall problem is to find a neatly ordered time table of n Grid jobs to maximize the minimal value of CF among these jobs.

$$\max \quad \min_{1 \leq i \leq n} \{CF_i\} \tag{2}$$

$$s.t. \quad FT_{ik} - ET_{ik} + M \cdot (1 - x_{ihk}) \geq FT_{ih} \tag{3}$$

$$FT_{jk} - FT_{ik} + M \cdot (1 - y_{ijk}) \geq ET_{jk} \tag{4}$$

$$x_{ihk} = \begin{cases} 1 & Job_i \text{ executed by } S'_h \text{ prior to } S'_k \\ 0 & \text{others} \end{cases} \tag{5}$$

$$y_{ijk} = \begin{cases} 1 & S'_k \text{ execute } Job_i \text{ prior to } Job_j \\ 0 & \text{others} \end{cases} \tag{6}$$

$$h, k = \xi(a, b) = (a - 1) \cdot m + b \tag{7}$$

$$1 \leq i, j \leq n, 1 \leq h, k \leq m \cdot m_a, 1 \leq a \leq m, 1 \leq b \leq m_a \tag{8}$$

Equation (2) is the objective function. Equation (3) expresses the execution order of sub-jobs related to fuzzy operation time. Equation (4) guarantees the execution order of virtual components according to the dependency of sub-jobs. Equation (5) defines the factor for execution order of one job on each service. x_{ihk} equals 1 if i^{th} job is executed by h^{th} component earlier than k^{th} component and is 0 otherwise. Equation (6) indicates the factor for service sequence of each job on one service. y_{ijk} equals 1 if k^{th} component executes i^{th} job before j^{th} job and is 0 otherwise. Here M is a positive integer, which is big enough to guarantee the job execution order when x_{ihk} and y_{ijk} are 0. Equation (7) is the mapping of virtual component to real component. Equation (8) ensures the ranges of indicators.

5 Algorithm Description

5.1 Chaos

Chaos underlies many natural phenomena, such as turbulent fluid flow, global weather patterns, and DNA coding sequences. [5] A common and simple chaotic function, the logistic equation is:

$$x_{n+1} = \lambda x_n(1 - x_n), 0 < \lambda \leq 4, 0 \leq x_n \leq 1 \tag{9}$$

Given initial value x_0, for λ in (0, 3), (9) will converge to some value x. For λ between 3 and about 3.56, (9) bifurcates into 2, 4, 8... periodic solutions. For λ between 3.56 and 4, (9) become fully chaotic: neither convergent nor periodic, but variable with no discernable pattern. As approaches 4, the variation in solutions to (9) appears increasingly random. We refer to these features as convergent, bifurcating, and chaotic.

5.2 The Chaotic Genetic Algorithm

We derive our CGA based on GALib [14], and employ chaos in initialization and mutation. We develop a chaotic initializing operator. The diversity of initial population can be guaranteed by (9) because it has unrepeatable, un-enumerable and infinite resolutions in [0, 1] when $\lambda = 4$.

We improve chaotic mutation, unlike the bit flip mutation of λ introduced by Determan [5], we mutate the λ base on the value of f. Consider the behavior of (9). For λ belows 3, (9) will produce convergent mutation and will tend to produce masks that preserve the higher order bits of the mask, but vary the lower order bits. Near convergence, the mask will become fixed. Thus, an individual with convergent λ will tend to produce offsprings with progressively more rigid crossover masks. While individuals with non-convergent λ will tend to have a high degree of variability in the crossover masks of their descendants, with the variability increasing as λ approaches 4.

Accordingly, we sort the individuals by their fitness values, and then put them into three categories according to (9). That is, individuals with better fitness value will have convergent λ, and those with worse fitness value have non-convergent λ. On the other hand, the mutation probability, p_m, is a key fact of CGA because we found that its value impacts the algorithm distinctly. We tune the value of p_m and find the best one in experiment. Thus we can ensure that the good patterns of individuals are kept well without losing diversities.

The design details are listed as follows:

- encoding and decoding: execution time based representation for encoding, in which chromosome r is composed of 3 genomes:
  - r_1: $3n \times k$ decimal sequence of fuzzy execution time.
  - r_2: λ, modify the mask according to equation (9). That is, we interpret the $3n \times k$ bits mask as a real value, scaled into the range (0, 1) to get x_n, and get the new mask, x_{n+1}, to the $3n \times k$ bits representation of (9).
  - r_3: binary gene sequence with length representing mask.
- Fitness function f bases on equation (2).
- Parameters: 5-tuple $< N, p_c, p_m, G, Sel >$ representing population size, probability of crossover, probability of mutation, generation gap which means that $N \times (1 - G)$ parent individuals survive to the next generation, selection policy including pure selection P and elitist strategy E.
- Genetic operator: besides the chaotic initialize and mutation operator, we use tournament selector and position-based crossover.
- Stop criterion: if satisfactory degree is given by user, CGA will terminate according to the user specification. If no expecting time offered, CGA will stop when the optimal value keeps without change for 30 generations.

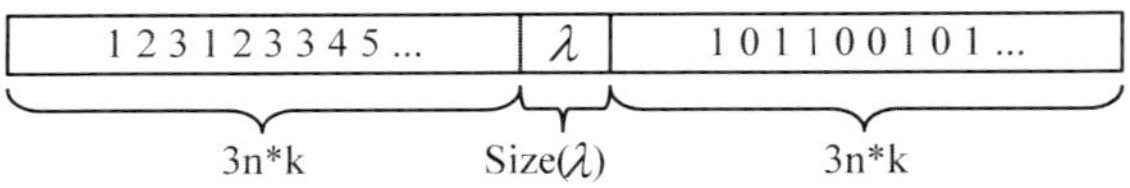

Fig. 4. The representation of chromosome

6 Experimental Studies

6.1 Metrics

Average terminative generation T is used to evaluate average convergent speed of repetitious independent implementation of CGA. That is, CGA runs M times, and the stop generation of ith time is denoted by T_i. The frequency that T_i exists in $T_j (1 \leq j \leq M)$ is p_i. Thus, the average terminative generation can be formulated as:

$$T^{CGA} = \sum_{i=1}^{M} T_i p_i \tag{10}$$

Entropy H^{CGA} is used to estimate the stability of CGA. We use statistical window W_j with range $[w_j, w_j + \Delta w], 1 \leq w_{j+1} \leq M$to count the probability of T_i which falls within W_j. So there are $M/\Delta w$ windows, and each of them represents one level of performance $l_j (0 \leq j \leq M/\Delta w)$. For example, l_0 is the best level, that is, those T_i in the $W_0 (0 \leq T_i \leq \Delta w)$ have the smallest values among T_j. H^{CGA} indicates the uniform degree of the distribution of performance level l.

$$H^{CGA} = \frac{-\sum_{j=1}^{M/\Delta w} p_{W_j} \ln(p_{W_j})}{\ln(M/\Delta w)} \tag{11}$$

We establish metrical space (T, H^{CGA}) to evaluate performance of CGA. The smaller (T, H), the better performance CGA has.

6.2 Evaluation

At first, we used benchmark FT06 [13] to compare performance of CGA with standard GA. We initialized the CGA by $< 50, 0.9, 0.01, 0.95, E >$, then changed p_m from 0.01 to 0.1 with step 0.01, and ran CGA 150 times for each step. We found that when p_m exceeded 0.1, the useful patterns of gene was destroyed easily, so we ignored those values bigger than 0.1. The (T, H) values of CGA and GA are compared in Fig. 5. Optimal execution order is depicted in Fig. 6.

We next simulated 50 jobs running on 50 virtual components in terms of FSET according to the results in Fig. 5. DT was created by user preferences. ET was generated by Poisson distribution. The upper and lower bounds of ET were $et + 1$ and $et - 1$ respectively. We ran standard GA, CGA [5] and our CGA for 150 times each. Table. 1 shows the resulting (T, H) and average CF.

Standard GA can find better CF than CGA [5], but its convergent speed is almost 1/2 of CGA [5]. Our CGA can find the best CF with the fastest convergent speed among three. The H value of CGA [5] is better than our CGA because it has the earliness problem, that is, CGA [5] converges even when it has not find the optimal value. The number of T which falls within the bad performance level l is very large. As a result, the entropy of CGA [5] is smaller than ours. However, take (T, H) and CF value into account together, our CGA is better. In all, our CGA outperforms the rest.

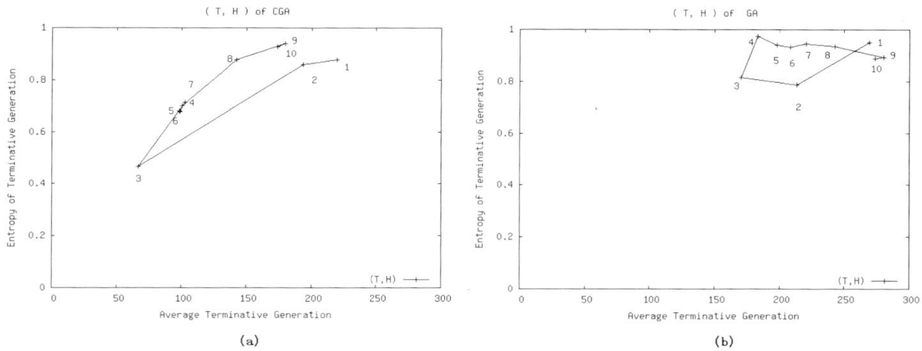

Fig. 5. (a) shows (T, H) value of CGA. Point 3 has the best (T, H) value (66.6,0.47), the smallest termination generation and entropy among all points. So when the mutation rate $p_m = 0.03$ the CGA outperforms the rest mutation rates. (b) depicts (T, H) value of GA. Point 2 has the smallest H among all, but its H value approximates 0.8, which is much bigger than CGA. Point 3 has the smallest T among all. However, its T is around 160, which is more than twice of CGA. So CGA is better than GA, in terms of efficiency and stability.

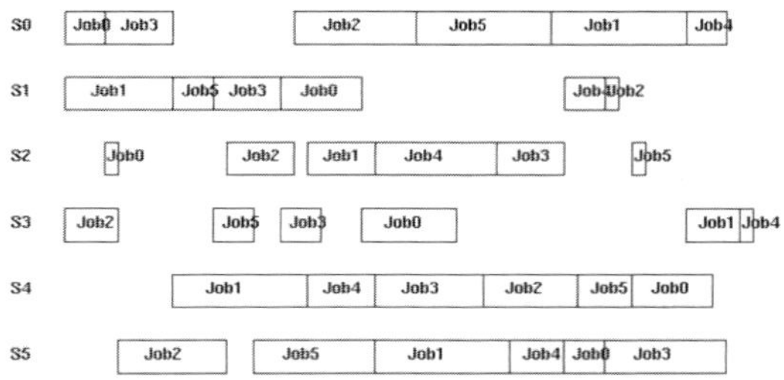

Fig. 6. Optimal Job execution table of FT06. The y axis is the services $S_i (0 \leq i \leq 5)$, and x is time axis. The rectangles marked with Job_i are sub-jobs.

Table 1. Comparison of 3 GAs. The result shows that our CGA has the best (T, H) and CF value among the three.

Algorithms	(T, H) values	CF values
Standard GA	(8642,0.74)	0.83
CGA [5]	(3459,0,42)	0.76
Our CGA	(1677,0.49)	0.97

7 Conclusions

In this paper, we have proposed an evolutionary approach to solve Grid job scheduling problem with time uncertainties. We have studied the problem and applied Fuzzy Set theory to present a FSET model. And we have formulated and analyzed the Grid job scheduling problem with FSET. The aim of the optimization problem was to find the best CF value at fastest convergent speed without losing stability. We found it's not suitable to solve the fuzzy Grid job scheduling problem by adopting standard GA directly because of the computational complexity of the specified problem. In order to solve the problem, we developed CGA, a chaotic-heuristic neighborhood search solution based on genetic algorithm to find the optimal solutions. We controlled the evolution of GA by adjusting logistic function automatically according to fitness function. Both convergent speed and stability of GA are improved by chaos. We established a (T, H) metrical space to evaluate the performance of our CGA. Experimental results showed that the stability and the convergent speed were significantly improved by employing the chaotic into GA.

Future work will extend the model in order to include the other distribution of job arrival, such as Pareto, tailed, and self-similar. More constraints such as the cost of services will be added to the model. The performance study of CGA will go in depth when the quantities of jobs and services become very large. An applicable scheduler will also be developed based on the CGA and deployed on the real Grid environment.

References

1. Foster, I., Kesselman, C.: The Grid 2: Blueprint for a New Computing Infrastructure. Morgan Kaufmann, San Francisco (1999)
2. Aggarwal, M., Kent, R.D., Ngom, A.: Genetic Algorithm Based Scheduler for Computational Grids. In: Proceedings of the 19th International Symposium on High Performance Computing Systems and Applications, IEEE, Los Alamitos (2005)
3. Gao, Y., Rong, H. et al.: Adaptive grid job scheduling with genetic algorithms. In: Future Generation Computer Systems, vol. 21, pp. 151–161. Elsevier, Amsterdam (2005)
4. Mu'alem, A.W. et al.: Utilization, predictability, workloads, and user runtime estimates in scheduling the IBM SP2 with backfilling. In: IEEE Transactions on Parallel and Distributed Systems, vol. 12, pp. 529–543. IEEE, Los Alamitos (2001)
5. Determan, J. et al.: Using chaos in genetic algorithms. In: Proceedings of the 1999 Congress on Evolutionary Computation (CEC'99), pp. 2094–2101. IEEE, Washington (1999)
6. Blythe, J. et al.: Task Scheduling Strategies for Workflow based Applications in Grids. In: IEEE International Symposium on Cluster Computing and Grid 2005 (CCGrid), IEEE, Cardiff, UK (2005)
7. Tracy, D.M. et al.: A comparison of eleven static heuristics for mapping a class of independent tasks onto heterogeneous distributed computing systems. Journal of Parallel and Distributed Computing 61, 810–837 (2001)
8. Kwok, Y.K. et al.: Static scheduling algorithms for allocating directed task graphs to multiprocessors. In: ACM Comput. Surv. pp. 406–471. ACM Press, New York (1999)
9. Li, H.X. et al.: Dynamic Task Scheduling Approach Base on Wasp Algorithm in Grid Environment. In: Wang, L., Chen, K., Ong, Y.S. (eds.) ICNC 2005. LNCS, vol. 3610, pp. 453–456. Springer, Heidelberg (2005)

10. Deelman, E.: Mapping Abstract Complex Workflows onto Grid Environments. Jour. of Grid Cmpt. 1, 25–39 (2003)
11. Song, S.S. et al.: Risk-Resilient Heuristics and Genetic Algorithms for Security-Assured Grid Job Scheduling. In: IEEE T. Comput. vol. 55, IEEE Computer Society Press, Los Alamitos (2006)
12. MacLaren, J. et al.: Towards Service Level Agreement Based Scheduling on the Grid. In: 14Th International Conference on Automated Planning & Scheduling, AAAI, Canada (2004)
13. Wang, L.: Job Shop Scheduling with Genetic Algorithms. Tshinghua University Press, Springer, Heidelberg (2003)
14. Wall, M.: GAlib: A C++ Library of Genetic Algorithm Components. Massachusetts Institute of Technology (1996)
15. Globus: `http://www.globus.org`
16. Frey, J.: Condor-G: a computation management agent for multi-institutional grids. In: Intl. Symposium on High Performance Distributed Computing, pp. 55–63. IEEE, Los Alamitos (2001)
17. Berman, F.: The Apples project: a status report. In: 8th NEC Research Symposium, Germany (1997)
18. Dail, H.: A modular scheduling approach for grid application development environment. UCSD CSE Technical Report CS20020708 (2002)
19. Casanova, H.: NetSolve: a network-enabled server for solving computational science problems. JSAHPC (1997)
20. Liu, C.: Design and evaluation of a resource selection framework for Grid applications. In: Intl. Symposium on High Performance Distributed Computing, IEEE, Los Alamitos (2002)
21. Buyya, R.: An evaluation of economy based resource trading and scheduling on computational power Grids for parameter sweep applications. In: 2nd International Workshop on Active Middleware Services, Kluwer, USA (2000)
22. Zhang, Y.: An integrated approach to parallel scheduling using gang-scheduling, backfilling, and migration. In: Feitelson, D.G., Rudolph, L. (eds.) JSSPP 2001. LNCS, vol. 2221, pp. 133–158. Springer, Heidelberg (2001)

Population-Based Extremal Optimization with Adaptive Lévy Mutation for Constrained Optimization

Min-Rong Chen, Yong-Zai Lu, and Genke Yang

Dept. of Automation
Shanghai Jiao Tong University, Shanghai 200240, China
{auminrongchen, yzlu, gkyang}@sjtu.edu.cn

Abstract. Recently, a local-search heuristic algorithm called Extremal Optimization (EO) has been successfully applied in some combinatorial optimization problems. However, there are only limited papers studying on the mechanism of EO applied to the numerical optimization problems so far. This paper presents the studies on the applications of EO to numerical constrained optimization problems with a set of popular benchmark problems. To enhance and improve the search performance and efficiency of EO, we developed a novel EO strategy with population based search. The newly developed EO algorithm is named population-based EO (PEO). Additionally, we adopted the adaptive Lévy mutation, which is more likely to generate an offspring that is farther away from its parent than the commonly employed Gaussian mutation. Compared with three state-of-the-art stochastic search methods with six popular benchmark problems, it has been shown that our approach is a good choice to deal with the numerical constrained optimization problems.

1 Introduction

Many real-world optimization problems involve complicated constraints. What constitute the difficulties of the constrained optimization problem are various limits on the decision variables, the constraints involved, the interference among constraints, and the interrelationship between the constraints, objective functions and decision variables. This has motivated the development of a considerable number of approaches to tackling the constrained optimization problems such as Stochastic Ranking (SR) [1], Adaptive Segregational Constraint Handling Evolutionary Algorithm (ASCHEA) [2] and Simple Multimembered Evolution Strategy (SMES) [3], etc.

Recently, a general-purpose local-search heuristic algorithm named Extremal Optimization (EO) was proposed by Boettcher and Percus [4,9]. EO is based on the Bak-Sneppen model [5], which shows the emergence of self-organized criticality (SOC) [6] in ecosystems. The evolution in this model is driven by a process where the weakest species in the population, together with its nearest neighbors, is always forced to mutate. The dynamics of this extremal process exhibits the

Y. Wang, Y. Cheung, and H. Liu (Eds.): CIS 2006, LNAI 4456, pp. 144–155, 2007.

characteristics of SOC, such as punctuated equilibrium [5]. EO opens the door to applying non-equilibrium process, while the simulated annealing (SA) applies equilibrium statistical mechanics. In contrast to genetic algorithm (GA) which operates on an entire "gene-pool" of huge number of possible solutions, EO successively eliminates those extremely undesirable (i.e., the worst) components in the sub-optimal solutions. Its large fluctuations provide significant hill-climbing ability, which enables EO to perform well particularly at the phase transitions. EO has been successfully applied to some NP-hard combinatorial optimization problems such as graph bi-partitioning [4], TSP [4, 18], graph coloring [13], spin glasses [14], MAXSAT [15], production scheduling [17, 18], multiobjective optimization [19] and dynamic combinatorial problems [16].

However, to our best knowledge, there have been few papers studying on the mechanism of EO applied to the numerical optimization problems so far except for the Generalized Extremal Optimization presented by De Sousa and Ramos [7,8]. In this paper, we study on EO with its applications in the numerical constrained optimization problems. To enhance and improve the search performance and efficiency of EO, we developed a novel EO strategy with population based search, called population-based EO (PEO). In addition, we adopted the adaptive Lévy mutation operator, which makes our approach able to carry out not only coarse-grained but also fine-grained search. It is worth noting that there exists no adjustable parameter in our approach, which makes our approach more charming than other methods. Finally, our approach is successfully applied in solving six popular benchmark problems and shows competitive performance in compared with three state-of-the-art search methods, i.e., SR [1], ASCHEA [2] and SMES [3].

The rest of this paper is organized as follows. In Section II, we present the problem formulation for the numerical constrained optimization problems under study in this paper. Section III introduces EO in detail and proposes the PEO algorithm. The mechanism of Lévy mutation is also investigated. In Section IV, we propose the experimental design and show the obtained results. Discussion of the results is also included in this section. Finally, Section V concludes with a brief summary of the paper and presents the future work.

2 Problem Formulation

A general nonlinear programming problem can be formulated as

$$Minimize \;\; f(\boldsymbol{X}), \quad \boldsymbol{X} = [x_1, \cdots, x_n]^T \in R^n \tag{1}$$

subject to

$$g_i(\boldsymbol{X}) \leq 0, \quad i = 1, \cdots, q \tag{2}$$

$$h_i(\boldsymbol{X}) = 0, \quad i = q+1, \cdots, r \tag{3}$$

where $f(\boldsymbol{X})$ is the objective function, $\boldsymbol{X} \in S \bigcap F$. $S \subseteq R^n$ is defined as the whole search space which is an n-dimensional space bounded by the parametric constraints

$$l_j \leq x_j \leq u_j, \quad j \in 1, \cdots, n \tag{4}$$

where l_j and u_j are the lower and upper bound of x_j, respectively, and $F \subseteq R^n$ is defined as the feasible region. It is clear that $F \subseteq S$.

In this paper, the methods for handling constrained nonlinear programming problems are based on the concept of penalty functions, which penalize unfeasible solutions. A set of functions $P_i(\boldsymbol{X})(1 \leq i \leq r)$ is used to construct the penalty. The function $P_i(\boldsymbol{X})$ measures the violation of the ith constraint in the following way:

$$P_i(\boldsymbol{X}) = \begin{cases} max\{0, g_i(\boldsymbol{X})\}^2, & if \;\; 1 \leq i \leq q \\ |h_i(\boldsymbol{X})|^2, & if \;\; q+1 \leq i \leq r \end{cases} \tag{5}$$

3 Extremal Optimization

3.1 Bak-Sneppen Model

EO is based on Bak-Sneppen (BS) model [5] of biological evolution, which simulates far-from equilibrium dynamics in statistical physics. BS model is one of the models that show the nature of SOC. The SOC means that regardless of the initial state, the system always tunes itself to a critical point having a power-law behavior without any tuning control parameter. In BS model, species has an associated fitness value between 0 and 1 representing a time scale at which the species will mutate to a different species or become extinct. The species with higher fitness has more chance of surviving, while the species with lower fitness will mutate to a different species or become extinct with larger probability. Species in the BS model are located on the sites of a lattice. Each species is assigned a fitness value randomly with uniform distribution. At each update step, the worst adapted species is always forced to mutate. The change in the fitness of the worst adapted species will cause the alteration of the fitness landscape of its neighbors. This means that the fitness values of the species around the worst one will also be changed randomly, even if they are well adapted. After a number of iterations, the system evolves to a highly correlated state known as Self-Organized Criticality (SOC). In that state, almost all species have fitness values above a certain threshold. These species possess punctuated equilibrium: one's weakened neighbor can undermine one's own fitness. In the SOC state, a little change of one species will result in co-evolutionary chain reactions called "avalanches". The probability distribution of the sizes "K"of these avalanches is depicted by a power law $P(K) \sim K^{-\tau}$, where τ is a positive parameter. That is, the smaller avalanches are more likely to occur than those big ones, but even the avalanches as big as the whole system may occur with a non-negligible probability. Therefore, the large fluctuation makes any possible configuration accessible.

3.2 Extremal Optimization

Unlike GAs, which work with a population of candidate solutions, EO operates on a single candidate solution (i.e. chromosome) S. In EO, each decision variable in the current solution S is considered as "species". It is important to note that there is merely mutation operator in EO, no crossover operator. Through always performing mutation on the worst species and its neighbors successively, the solution can improve its components and evolve itself toward the optimal solution generation by generation. What's the definition of "worst species" in EO? This requires that a suitable representation should be selected which permits each species to be assigned a quality measure (in this paper, we call it "species fitness"). This differs from holistic approaches such as evolutionary algorithms that assign equal-fitness to all species of a solution based on their collective evaluation against an objective function. In EO, the species fitness weighs the time scale at which one species will mutate to new one which is the component of a better solution. Then the species with the lowest fitness, i.e. the worst species, will evolve towards one component of a better solution at the smallest time scale. Thus, it will take shorter time for one solution to evolve towards the optimal solution through always mutating the worst species rather than other species.

For a minimization problem with n decision variables, EO proceeds as follows [4]:

1) Generate a candidate solution S randomly. Set the optimal solution $S_{best} = S$.
2) For the current solution S,
   a) evaluate the species fitness λ_i for each species (i.e., decision variable) x_i, $i \in \{1, 2, \cdots, n\}$,
   b) rank all the species by their fitness values and find the species x_j with the "worst fitness", i.e., $\lambda_j \leq \lambda_i$ for all i,
   c) choose one solution S' in the neighborhood of S, such that the jth variable must change its state,
   d) accept $S = S'$ *unconditionally*,
   e) if the current cost function value is less than the so-far minimum cost function value, i.e., $C(S) < C(S_{best})$, then set $S_{best} = S$.
3) Repeat at step 2) as long as desired.
4) Return S_{best} and $C(S_{best})$.

It is important to note that the governing principle behind the EO algorithm is the improvement through successively removing low-quality species and changing them randomly. This is obviously at odds with GAs, which select good solutions in an attempt to make better solutions. By always mutating the worst adapted species and its neighbors, EO could evolve solutions quickly and systematically, and at the same time preserve the possibility of probing different regions of the design space via avalanches.

3.3 Population-Based Extremal Optimization

It is worth reminding that EO perform a search through sequential changes on a single solution, namely, the point-to-point search rather than the population based search applied in GA. In order to accelerate the convergence speed, we developed a novel real-coded EO search algorithm, so-called Population-based Extremal Optimization (PEO), through introducing the population search strategies being popularly used in evolutionary algorithms to EO. Similar to the evolutionary algorithms, the PEO operates on the evolution of solutions generation after generation. By uniformly placing the population of initial random solutions on the search space, PEO can explore the wide search space, avoiding getting trapped into local optima. On the other hand, similar to EO, the PEO performs only one operation, i.e. mutation, on each variable. Each solution evolves to its SOC state by always forcing the worst species to change.

Inspired by [7,8], we define the fitness of each variable for the constrained optimization problems as follows. For the minimization problems without equality and inequality constraints, the fitness λ_i of variable x_i means the mutation cost, i.e. $OBJ(S_i) - OBJ(S_{best})$, where S_i is the new solution after performing mutation only on x_i and leaving all other variables fixed, $OBJ(S_i)$ is the objective value of S_i, and $OBJ(S_{best})$ is the best objective value found so far. For the minimization problem with equality and inequality constraints, the sum of all the penalties $Q(S_i) = \sum_{j=1}^{r} P_j(S_i)$ should be incorporated into the fitness λ_i, i.e. $\lambda_i = OBJ(S_i) - OBJ(S_{best}) + Q(S_i)$. It is worth reminding that we consider those variables which meet the constraints as badly adapted individuals and thus low fitness will be assigned to them. On the contrary, those variables which do not satisfy the constraints will be considered as well adapted species and be assigned high fitness.

For a numerical constrained minimization problem, the proposed PEO developed in terms of the marriage of EO and Evolutionary Algorithm proceeds as follows.

1. Generate initial population with m solutions, $S_i = (x_{i1}, \cdots, x_{in}), i \in \{1, \cdots, m\}$, randomly and uniformly, and choose one solution with the best performance as the best solution S_{best}. Set $iteration = 0$.
2. For each solution S_i, $i \in \{1, \cdots, m\}$,
   (a) evaluate the species fitness $\lambda_{ij} = OBJ(S_{ij}) - OBJ(S_{best}) + Q(S_{ij})$ for each variable x_{ij}, $j \in \{1, \cdots, n\}$,
   (b) compare all the variables according to their fitness values and find out the worst adapted variable x_{iw}, $w \in \{1, \cdots, n\}$,
   (c) perform mutation only on x_{iw} while keeping other variables unchanged, then get a new solution S_{iw},
   (d) accept $S_i = S_{iw}$ *unconditionally* and set $OBJ(S_i) = OBJ(S_{iw})$,
   (e) if $OBJ(S_i) < OBJ(S_{best})$ and S_i is a feasible solution, then set $S_{best} = S_i$ and $OBJ(S_{best}) = OBJ(S_i)$.
3. If the iterations reach the predefined maximum number of the generations, then continue the next step; otherwise, set $iteration = iteration + 1$, and go to Step 2.
4. Return S_{best} and $OBJ(S_{best})$.

3.4 Mutation Operator

Note that there is merely mutation operator in PEO. Therefore, the mutation plays a key role in PEO search that generates new solutions. Many mutation operators have been proposed in the past two decades, such as Gaussian mutation, Cauchy mutation and so on. Yao et al. [10] have pointed out that Cauchy mutation performs better when the current search point is far away from the global optimum, while Gaussian mutation is better at finding a local optimum in a good region. It would be ideal if Cauchy mutation is used when search points are far away from the global optimum and Gaussian mutation is adopted when search points are in the neighborhood of the global optimum. Unfortunately, the global optimum is usually unknown in practice, making the ideal switch from Cauchy to Gaussian mutation very difficult.

In this work, we adopt the adaptive Lévy mutation which is proposed by Lee and Yao [11], to easily switch Cauchy mutation to Gaussian mutation. Lévy mutation is, in a sense, a generalization of Cauchy mutation since Cauchy distribution is a special case of Lévy distribution. By adjusting the parameter α in Lévy distribution, one can tune the shape of the probability density function, which in turn yields adjustable variation in mutation step sizes. In addition, Lévy mutation provides an opportunity for mutating a parent using a distribution which is neither Cauchy nor Gaussian.

The Lévy probability distribution has the following form [12]:

$$L_{\alpha,\gamma}(y) = \frac{1}{\pi}\int_0^{\infty} e^{-\gamma q^{\alpha}} \cos(qy)dq \tag{6}$$

As can be easily seen from Eq. (6), the distribution is symmetric with respect to $y = 0$ and has two parameters, γ and α. γ is the scaling factor satisfying $\gamma > 0$ and α satisfies $0 < \alpha < 2$. The analytic form of the integral is not known for general α except for a few cases. In particular, for $\alpha = 1$, the integral can be carried out analytically and is known as the Cauchy probability distribution. In the limit of $\alpha \to 2$, the distribution approaches the Gaussian distribution. The parameter α controls the shape of the probability distribution in such a way that one can obtain different shapes of probability distribution. In this paper, Lévy mutation performs with the following representation:

$$x_k^{t+1} = x_k^t + L_k(\alpha) \tag{7}$$

where $L_k(\alpha)$ is a Lévy random variable with the scaling factor $\gamma = 1$ for the kth variable. To generate a Lévy random number, we used an effective algorithm presented by Mantegna [12]. It is known that Gaussian mutation ($\alpha = 2$) works better for searching a small local neighborhood, whereas Cauchy mutation ($\alpha = 1$) is good at searching a large area of the search space. By adding additional two candidate offspring ($\alpha = 1.4$ and 1.7), one is not fixed to the two extremes.

It must be indicated that, unlike the method in [11], the mutation in our approach doesn't compare the anticipated outcomes of different values of α due to the characteristics of EO. In our approach, the Lévy mutation with $\alpha = 1$ (i.e. Cauchy mutation) is first adopted. It means the large step size will be taken first at each mutation. If the new generated variable after mutation goes beyond the intervals of the decision variables, the Lévy mutation with $\alpha = 1.4, 1.7, 2$ will be carried out in turn, that is, the step size will become smaller than before. Thus, our approach combines the advantages of coarse-grained search and fine-grained search. The above analysis shows that the adaptive Lévy mutation is very simple yet effective. Unlike some switching algorithms which have to decide when to switch between different mutations during search, the adaptive Lévy mutation does not need to make such decisions and introduces no adjustable parameters.

4 Experiments and Test Results

4.1 Test Functions and Results

In this study, we selected six (g04, g05, g07, g09, g10 and g12) out of thirteen benchmark functions published in [1] as test functions, since the characteristics of those functions contain the "difficulties" in having global optimization problems by using an evolutionary algorithm. For more details about the expressions of those benchmark problems, the readers can refer to [1]. To make experimental tests, all the algorithms developed in this paper are encoded in the floating point representation. The source codes of all experiments were coded in JAVA. Besides, inequality constraints can be incorporated into the fitness via the relevant penalty items. All equality constraints can be converted into inequality constrains, $|h(\boldsymbol{X})| - \varepsilon \leq 0$, using the degree of violation ε. The value of ε for function g05 is set to 0.0001. In all the algorithms, the population size is 100 and the maximum number of generations is 5000. 30 independent runs were carried out for each test function. Fig. 1 shows the simulation results of our approach on the six test problems. Average of best results of every 100 generations found in 30 independent runs are shown in Fig. 1. Table 1 summarizes the experimental results when the PEO with adaptive Lévy mutation (for simplicity, we call it PEOAL) is used. Table 1 also shows the known "optimal" solution for each problem and statistics. These include the best objective value found, mean, standard deviation, and worst found. Furthermore, we compared our approach against three state-of-the-art approaches: SR [1], ASCHEA [2] and SMES [3]. The best, mean and worst results obtained by each approach are shown in Table 2 $\sim$ Table 4. The results provided by these approaches were taken from the original references for each method.

4.2 Discussion of Results

As can be seen from Table 1, our approach was capable of finding the global optimum in two test functions (g05 and g12). It is interesting to note that our

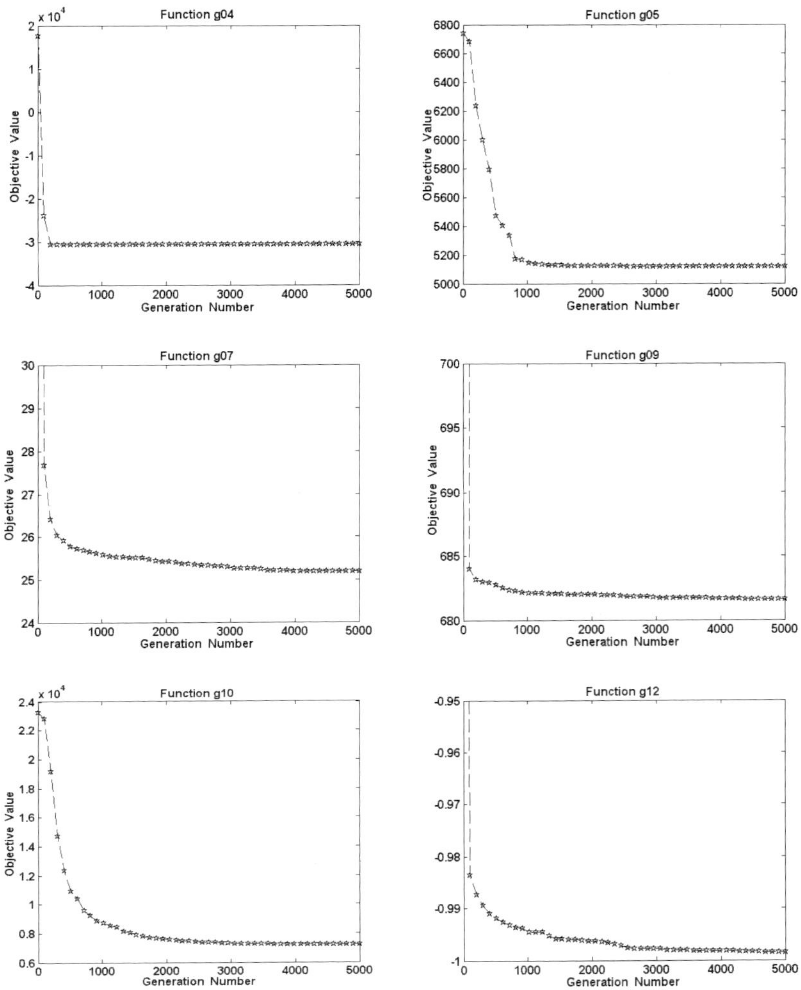

Fig. 1. Simulation results of PEO algorithm on six test functions

Table 1. Experimental results of our approach on six test functions

Problem	Optimal	Best	Mean	Worst	St.Dev.
g04	-30665.539	-30652.146	-30641.177	-30629.763	5.45E+0
g05	5126.498	5126.498	5126.527	5126.585	2.5E-2
g07	24.306	24.798	25.130	25.325	1.18E-1
g09	680.630	680.706	681.498	682.228	3.36E-1
g10	7049.331	7051.573	7160.620	7294.895	5.82E+1
g12	-1.000000	-1.0000	-1.000	-1.00	9.8E-4

*All test functions are minimization tasks.

Table 2. Comparison of the best results obtained

Problem	Optimal	PEOAL	SR	ASCHEA	SMES
g04	-30665.539	-30652.146	-30665.539	-30665.5	-30665.539
g05	5126.498	5126.498	5126.497	5126.5	5126.599
g07	24.306	24.798	24.307	24.3323	24.327
g09	680.630	680.706	680.630	680.630	680.632
g10	7049.331	7051.573	7054.316	7061.13	7051.903
g12	-1.000000	-1.0000	-1.000000	NA	-1.000

* "NA" in all tables means the results are "not available".

Table 3. Comparison of the mean results obtained

Problem	Optimal	PEOAL	SR	ASCHEA	SMES
g04	-30665.539	-30641.177	-30665.539	-30665.5	-30665.539
g05	5126.498	5126.527	5128.881	5141.65	5174.492
g07	24.306	25.130	24.372	24.66	24.475
g09	680.630	681.498	680.665	680.641	680.643
g10	7049.331	7160.620	7559.192	7193.11	7253.047
g12	-1.000000	-1.000	-1.000000	NA	-1.000

Table 4. Comparison of the worst results obtained

Problem	Optimal	PEOAL	SR	ASCHEA	SMES
g04	-30665.539	-30629.763	-30665.539	NA	-30665.539
g05	5126.498	5126.585	5142.472	NA	5304.167
g07	24.306	25.325	24.642	NA	24.843
g09	680.630	682.228	680.763	NA	680.719
g10	7049.331	7294.895	8835.655	NA	7638.366
g12	-1.000000	-1.00	-1.000000	NA	-1.000

approach also found solutions very close to the global optima in the remaining four (g04, g07, g09, g10). Furthermore, as observed from Fig. 1, our approach was able to approach the global optimum quickly. Thus, our approach possesses good performance in accuracy and convergence speed.

When compared with respect to the three state-of-the-art techniques previously indicated, we found the following (see Table 2~Table 4).

- Compared with SR: our approach found better "best", "mean" and "worst" solutions in two functions (g5 and g10). It also provided similar "best", "mean" and "worst" solutions in function g12. Slightly better "best" results were found by SR in the remaining functions (g04, g07, g09).
- Compared with ASCHEA: our approach was able to find better "best" and "mean" results in two functions (g05, g10). ASCHEA surpassed our mean

results in three functions (g04, g07, g09). We did not compare the worst results due to the fact that they were not available for ASCHEA. In addition, we did not perform comparisons with respect to ASCHEA using functions g12 for the same reason.
- Compared with SMES: our approach found better "best", "mean" and "worst" results in two functions (g05, g10) and similar "best", "mean" and "worst" results in functions g12. SMES outperformed our approach in the remaining functions.

From the aforementioned comparisons, it is obvious that our approach shows very competitive performance with respect to those three state-of-the-art approaches.

4.3 Advantages of Proposed Approach

The proposed approach, i.e. PEO with the adaptive Lévy mutation, has the following advantages:

- There is no adjustable parameter in our approach. This makes our approach more charming than other state-of-the-art methods.
- Only one operator, i.e., mutation operator, exists in our approach, which makes our approach simple and convenient.
- Our approach possesses good performance in accuracy and convergence speed.
- By incorporating the adaptive Lévy mutation, our approach can perform globally and locally search.

5 Conclusions and Future Work

In this paper, we make an investigation on Extremal Optimization with its applications to numerical constrained optimization problems. By introducing the population search strategies to EO, we present a novel algorithm, called Population-based Extremal Optimization. It is worth pointing out that there is no adjustable parameter needed in our approach and this makes our approach easier in real applications than other state-of-the-art methods. Furthermore, via incorporating the adaptive Lévy mutation into our approach, our approach can perform not only coarse-grained but also fine-grained search. Compared with three state-of-the-art stochastic search methods with six benchmark functions, it has been shown that our approach is a good choice to deal with the numerical constrained optimization problems. Future research is aimed at the study in depth on the mechanism of EO. Furthermore, since we restricted the parameter α to four discrete values for each experiment, it is highly desirable to make α self-adaptive so that its value can be also changed continuously during evolution.

Acknowledgment

This work is supported by the National Natural Science Foundation of China under Grant No. 60574063.

References

1. Runarsson, T.P., Yao, X.: Stochastic Ranking for Constrained Evolutionary Optimization. IEEE Transactions on Evolutionary Computation 4, 284–294 (2000)
2. Hamida, S.B., Schoenauer, M., ASCHEA,: New Results Using Adaptive Segregational Constraint Handling. In: Proceedings of the Congress on Evolutionary Computation 2002 (CEC'2002), pp. 884–889 (2002)
3. Mezura-Montes, E., Coello, C.A.C.: A Simple Multimembered Evolution Strategy to Solve Constrained Optimization Problems. IEEE Transactions on Evolutionary Computation 9, 1–17 (2005)
4. Boettcher, S., Percus, A.G.: Nature's Way of Optimizing. Artificial Intelligence 119, 275–286 (2000)
5. Bak, P., Sneppen, K.: Punctuated Equilibrium and Criticality in a Simple Model of Evolution. Physical Review Letters 71, 4083–4086 (1993)
6. Bak, P., Tang, C., Wiesenfeld, K.: Self-Organized Criticality. Physical Review Letters 59, 381–384 (1987)
7. De Sousa, F.L., Ramos, F.M.: Function Optimization Using Extremal Dynamics. In: 4th International Conference on Inverse Problems in Engineering Rio de Janeiro, Brazil (2002)
8. De Sousa, F.L., Vlassov, V., Ramos, F.M.: Generalized Extremal Optimization: an Application in Heat Pipe Design. Applied Mathematical Modeling 28, 911–931 (2004)
9. Boettcher, S.: Extremal Optimization: Heuristics via Coevolutionary Avalanches. Computing in Science and Engineering 2, 275–282 (2000)
10. Yao, X., Liu, Y., Lin, G.: Evolutionary Programming Made Faster. IEEE Transactions on Evolutionary Computation 3, 82–102 (1999)
11. Lee, C.Y., Yao, X.: Evolutionary Algorithms with Adaptive Lévy Mutations. In: Proceedings of the 2001 Congress on Evolutionary Computation, pp. 568–575 (2001)
12. Mantegna, R.: Fast, Accurate Algorithm for Numerical Simulation of Lévy Stable Stochastic Process. Physical Review E 49, 4677–4683 (1994)
13. Boettcher, S., Percus, A.G.: Extremal Optimization at the Phase Transition of the 3-Coloring Problem. Physical Review E 69, 66–703 (2004)
14. Boettcher, S.: Extremal Optimization for the Sherrington-Kirkpatrick Spin Glass. European Physics Journal B 46, 501–505 (2005)
15. Menai, M.E., Batouche, M.: Efficient Initial Solution to Extremal Optimization Algorithm for Weighted MAXSAT Problem. In: Chung, P.W.H., Hinde, C.J., Ali, M. (eds.) IEA/AIE 2003. LNCS, vol. 2718, pp. 592–603. Springer, Heidelberg (2003)
16. Moser, I., Hendtlass, T.: Solving Problems with Hidden Dynamics-Comparison of Extremal Optimization and Ant Colony System. In: Proceedings of 2006 IEEE Congress on Evolutionary Computation (CEC'2006), pp. 1248–1255. IEEE Computer Society Press, Los Alamitos (2006)

17. Chen, Y.W., Lu, Y.Z., Yang, G.: Hybrid Evolutionary Algorithm with Marriage of Genetic Algorithm and Extremal Optimization for Production Scheduling. International Journal of Advanced Manufacturing Technology. Accepted
18. Lu, Y.Z., Chen, M.R., Chen, Y.W.: Studies on Extremal Optimization and its Applications in Solving Real World Optimization Problems. In: Proceedings of 2007 IEEE Series Symposium on Computation Intelligence, Hawaii, USA, April 1-5, 2007, IEEE Computer Society Press, Los Alamitos (2007)
19. Chen, M.R., Lu, Y.Z., Yang, G.: Multiobjective Optimization Using Population-Based Extremal Optimization. In: Proceedings of the First International Conference on Bio-Inspired Computing: Theory and Applications(BIC-TA, 2006) To be published (2006)

An Analysis About the Asymptotic Convergence of Evolutionary Algorithms

Lixin Ding[1] and Jinghu Yu[2]

[1] State Key Lab of Software Engineering, Wuhan University, Wuhan 430072, China
lxding@whu.edu.cn
[2] Department of Mathematics, School of Natural Sciences, Wuhan University of Technology, Wuhan 430070, China
yujh@wipm.ac.cn

Abstract. This paper discusses the asymptotic convergence of evolutionary algorithms based on finite search space by using the properties of Markov chains and Perron-Frobenius Theorem. First, some convergence results of general square matrices are given. Then, some useful properties of homogeneous Markov chains with finite states are investigated. Finally, the geometric convergence rates of the transition operators, which is determined by the revised spectral of the corresponding transition matrix of a Markov chain associated with the EA considered here, are estimated by combining the acquired results in this paper.

1 Introduction

Evolutionary algorithms(EAs for brevity) are a class of useful optimization methods based on a biological analogy with the natural mechanisms of evolution, and they are now a very popular tool for solving optimization problems. An EA is usually formalized as a Markov chain, so one can use the properties of Markov chains to describe the asymptotic behaviors of EAs, i.e., the probabilistic behaviors of EAs if never halted. Asymptotic behaviors of EAs has been investigated by many authors [1−12]. Due to the connection between Markov chains and EAs, a number of results about the convergence of EAs have been obtained by adopting the limit theorem of the corresponding Markov chin in the above works. In this paper, we will make further research on this topic, especially on convergence rate of EAs by using Perron-Frobenius Theorem and other analytic techniques.

The remaining parts of this paper are organized as follows. In section 2, we apply some basic matrix theory, such as Jordan Standard Form Theorem and Perron-Frobenius Theorem etc., to study the convergence of general square matrix A. We obtain that A^n converge with geometric convergence rate defined by the revised spectral of A. In section 3, we concern on homogeneous Markov chains with finite states. We give the relations among states classification, geometric convergence rate and eigenvalues of transition matrix. In section 4, we combine the results in section 2 and section 3 to investigate the limit behaviors

Y. Wang, Y. Cheung, and H. Liu (Eds.): CIS 2006, LNAI 4456, pp. 156–166, 2007.

of EAs. Under some mild conditions, we get that EAs converges to the optimal solution set related to the given problem with geometrical rate which is determined by the revised spectral of corresponding transition matrix of a Markov chain associated with the EA considered in this paper. Finally, we conclude this paper with a short discussion in section 5.

2 Preliminaries

In this section, we need to collect a number of definitions and elementary facts with respect to matrix classification, matrix decomposition and matrix convergence which will be useful throughout the whole paper. For a detailed reference on matrix theory, see the monograph by Steward[13]

Definition 1. *A $m \times m$ square matrix $\mathbf{A}$ is said to be*
(1) nonnegative($\mathbf{A} \geq 0$), if $a_{ij} \geq 0$ for all $i, j \in \{1, 2, \cdots, m\}$,
(2) positive($\mathbf{A} > 0$), if $a_{ij} > 0$ for all $i, j \in \{1, 2, \cdots, m\}$.

A nonnegative matrix $\mathbf{A} : m \times m$ is said to be
(3) primitive, if there exists a positive integer k such that $\mathbf{A}^k$ is positive,
(4) reducible, if there exists a permutation matrix $\mathbf{B}$ such that

$$\mathbf{BAB}^T = \begin{pmatrix} \mathbf{C} & \mathbf{0} \\ \mathbf{R} & \mathbf{T} \end{pmatrix},$$

where square matrix $\mathbf{C}$ and $\mathbf{T}$ are square matrices,
(5) irreducible, if it is not reducible,
(6) stochastic, if $\sum_{j=1}^{m} a_{ij} = 1$ for all $i \in \{1, 2, \cdots, m\}$.
A $m \times m$ stochastic matrix $\mathbf{A}$ is said to be
(7) stable, if it has identical rows.

Definition 2. *For a square matrix $\mathbf{A} : m \times m$ with eigenvalues $\lambda_1, \cdots, \lambda_m$, its revised spectral gap is usually defined as $r(\mathbf{A}) = \max\{|\lambda_i| : |\lambda_i| \neq 1, i = 1, \cdots, m\}$, and its norm is defined as $||\mathbf{A}|| = \max\{|a_{ij}| : i, j = 1, \cdots, m\}$.*

The following two Lemmas are well-known and can be found in many literatures of matrix theory.

Lemma 1 (Jordan Standard Form Theorem). *Suppose that square matrix $\mathbf{A} : m \times m$ has r different eigenvalues $\lambda_1, \cdots, \lambda_r$. Then there exists an invertible matrix $\mathbf{B}$ such that*

$$\mathbf{B}^{-1}\mathbf{AB} = \mathbf{J} \equiv diag[\mathbf{J}(\lambda_1), \cdots, \mathbf{J}(\lambda_r)],$$

where

$$\mathbf{J}(\lambda_i) = \begin{pmatrix} \lambda_i & 0 & \cdots & 0 & 0 \\ 1 & \lambda_i & 0 & \cdots & 0 \\ \cdots & \cdots & \cdots & \cdots & \cdots \\ 0 & \cdots & 1 & \lambda_i & 0 \\ 0 & 0 & \cdots & 1 & \lambda_i \end{pmatrix}$$

$$\in \mathbf{C}^{n(\lambda_i)\times n(\lambda_i)}, 1 \le i \le r,$$

and $\sum_{i=1}^{r} n(\lambda_i) = m$.

Lemma 2 (Perron-Frobenius Theorem). *For any nonnegative square matrix* $\mathbf{A} : m \times m$*, the following claims are true.*

(1)There exists a non-negative eigenvalue λ *such that there are no other eigenvalues of* $\mathbf{A}$ *with absolute values greater than* λ*;*

(2) $\min_i(\sum_{j=1}^{m} a_{ij}) \le \lambda \le \max_i(\sum_{j=1}^{m} a_{ij})$.

By using the above matrix theorems, we can get the following convergence results about $\mathbf{A}^n$ as n tends to infinity.

Proposition 1. *Suppose that* 1 *is a simple eigenvalue of square matrix* $\mathbf{A}$: $m \times m$ *and all other eigenvalues have absolute values less than* 1. *Then* $\lim_{n\to\infty} \mathbf{A}^n$ *exists and has geometric convergence rate.*

Proof. Let $\lambda_1, \lambda_2, \cdots, \lambda_{m-1}$ be those eigenvalues with absolute values less than 1. By Lemma 1, we know that the Jordan form of $\mathbf{A}$ is as follows

$$\begin{pmatrix} B_1 & 0 & \cdots & 0 & 0 \\ 0 & B_2 & 0 & \cdots & 0 \\ \cdots & \cdots & \cdots & \cdots & \cdots \\ 0 & 0 & \cdots & B_t & 0 \\ 0 & 0 & \cdots & 0 & 1 \end{pmatrix},$$

where square matrices $\mathbf{B}_i : q_i \times q_i (q_i$ is the algebra multiplicity of $\lambda_i), i = 1, 2, \cdots, t$, are Jordan blocks with the above form.

Note that the elements of $\mathbf{B}_i^k$ are $0, \lambda_i^k, C_k^1\lambda_i^{k-1}, C_k^2\lambda_i^{k-2}, \cdots, C_k^{q_i-1}\lambda_i^{k-q_i+1}$. It is easy to check that $||\mathbf{B}_i^k|| \to 0 (i = 1, \cdots, m-1)$ as $k \to \infty$. Moreover, for fixed q_i, when k is big enough, $C_k^{q_i-1}|\lambda_i|^{k-q_i+1}$ is the biggest elements among $\{0, |\lambda_i|^k, C_k^1|\lambda_i|^{k-1}, C_k^2|\lambda_i|^{k-2}, \cdots, C_k^{q_i-1}|\lambda_i|^{k-q_i+1}\}$; And, for fixed $q_i \le m$, when k is big enough, $C_k^{q_i-1} \le C_k^m$. In addition, there exists an invertible matrix $\mathbf{T}$ such that

$$\mathbf{A} = \mathbf{T}^{-1} \times \begin{pmatrix} \mathbf{B}_1 & 0 & \cdots & 0 & 0 \\ 0 & \mathbf{B}_2 & 0 & \cdots & 0 \\ \cdots & \cdots & \cdots & \cdots & \cdots \\ 0 & 0 & \cdots & \mathbf{B}_t & 0 \\ 0 & 0 & \cdots & 0 & 1 \end{pmatrix} \times \mathbf{T}.$$

If we write

$$\mathbf{B}^* = \begin{pmatrix} 0 & 0 & \cdots & 0 & 0 \\ 0 & 0 & \cdots & 0 & 0 \\ \cdots & \cdots & \cdots & \cdots & \cdots \\ 0 & 0 & \cdots & 0 & 0 \\ 0 & 0 & \cdots & 0 & 1 \end{pmatrix}$$

and let $\Pi = \mathbf{T}^{-1}\mathbf{B}^*\mathbf{T}$, then

$$||\mathbf{A}^k - \Pi|| \leq ||\mathbf{T}^{-1}|| \cdot ||\mathbf{T}|| \cdot C_k^m (r(\mathbf{A}))^{k-m+1} \leq c \cdot k^m (r(\mathbf{A}))^k \to 0(k \to \infty). \quad (1)$$

Note that, for any given $0 < \varepsilon < 1$, $k^m(r(\mathbf{A}))^{\varepsilon k} \to 0(k \to \infty)$. Hence, for the fixed m and $r(\mathbf{A})$, we have $k^m(r(A))^{\varepsilon k} \leq 1$ as $k \to \infty$. By (1), when k is big enough, we have

$$||\mathbf{A}^k - \Pi|| \leq c \cdot (r(\mathbf{A}))^{(1-\varepsilon)k}, \quad (2)$$

which means that $\mathbf{A}^n$ has geometric convergence rate. □

Proposition 2. *Suppose that square matrix* $\mathbf{A} : m \times m$ *has* m *linear independent eigenvectors and its eigenvalues except* 1 *have absolute values less than* 1. *Then* $\lim_{n\to\infty} \mathbf{A}^n$ *exists and has geometric convergence rate determined by* $r(\mathbf{A})$.

Proof. Let $\lambda_1 \leq \lambda_2 \leq \cdots \leq \lambda_q (q < m)$ be eigenvalues of $\mathbf{A}$ not equal 1. Then, we have from the assumption of Proposition 2 that

$$|\lambda_i| < 1, \forall i = 1, \cdots, q.$$

By matrix theory, there exists an invertible matrix $\mathbf{T}$ and the following diagonal matrix

$$\mathbf{B} = \begin{pmatrix} \lambda_1 & 0 & \cdots & 0 & \cdots\cdots\cdots & 0 \\ 0 & \lambda_2 & 0 & \cdots\cdots\cdots\cdots & & 0 \\ \cdots & \cdots & \cdots & \cdots & \cdots & \cdots \\ 0 & 0 & \lambda_q & 0 & \cdots\cdots\cdots & 0 \\ 0 & \cdots & 0 & 1 & 0 \cdots\cdots & 0 \\ 0 & \cdots & 0 & 0 & 1 \cdots 0 & 0 \\ \cdots & \cdots & \cdots & \cdots & \cdots & \cdots \\ 0 & \cdots\cdots\cdots\cdots\cdots & & & 0 & 1 \end{pmatrix}$$

such that $\mathbf{A} = \mathbf{T}^{-1}\mathbf{B}\mathbf{T}$. Therefore, we have $\mathbf{A}^k = \mathbf{T}^{-1}\mathbf{B}^k\mathbf{T}$. Write

$$\mathbf{B}^* = \begin{pmatrix} \mathbf{0} & \mathbf{0} \\ \mathbf{0} & \mathbf{I} \end{pmatrix}$$

and let $\Pi = \mathbf{T}^{-1}\mathbf{B}^*\mathbf{T}$. Then

$$\begin{aligned} ||\mathbf{A}^k - \Pi|| &= \mathbf{T}^{-1}(\mathbf{B}^k - \mathbf{B}^*)\mathbf{T} \\ &\leq ||\mathbf{T}^{-1}|| \cdot \max\{|\lambda_k| : k = 1, \cdots, q\} \cdot ||\mathbf{T}|| \\ &= c \cdot r(\mathbf{A})^k \to 0(k \to \infty). \end{aligned}$$

□

3 Homogeneous Markov Chains with Finite States

Since the limit behaviors of Markov chains depend on the structure of their transition matrixes, the properties of transition matrixes are very useful to describe the limit behaviors of Markov chains. In this section, we will introduce some indexes and definitions at first. Then, we will pay our attention on homogenous Markov chains with finite states space.

Let $\mathbf{P}$ be the transition matrix associated with Markov Chain $\{X_n; n \geq 0\}$ defined on a finite state space $S = \{s_1, s_2, \cdots, s_m\}$. We will also classify the state space in the following.

Definition 3. *(1) a vector: $v = (v_1, \cdots, v_m)$ is called a probability vector if $v_i \geq 0$ and $\sum_{i=1}^{m} v_i = 1$,*

(2) a probability vector v is called an invariant probability measure(stationary distribution) of transition matrix $\mathbf{P}$: if $v\mathbf{P} = v$.

The following notations are usually needed to classify the states of Markov chains.

$f_{ij}^n \doteq P\{X_0 = i, X_1 \neq j, \cdots, X_{n-1} \neq j, X_n = j\}$, is the probability that Markov chain starts at state s_i and reaches state s_j at time n for the first time;

$f_{ij}^* \doteq \sum_{n=1}^{\infty} f_{ij}^n$, is the probability that Markov chain starts at s_i and reaches s_j after finite steps;

$m_{ii} \doteq \infty$, if $f_{ii}^* < 1$; otherwise $m_{ii} \doteq \sum_{n=1}^{\infty} n f_{ii}^n$;

$d_i \doteq$ the biggest common divisor of $\{n : p_{ii}^n > 0\}$, is called the period of state s_i

Definition 4. *The state s_j is called a*
(1) transient state, if $f_{jj}^* < 1$;
(2) recurrent state, if $f_{jj}^* = 1$;
(3)positive recurrent, if $m_{jj} < \infty$;
(4)zero recurrent, if s_j is not a positive recurrent;
(5)aperiodic, if $d_i = 1$.

In the following, we will further describe the states classification of Markov chains. Let $N \subset S$ be the collection of all transient states of S, R^+ be the collection of all positive recurrent states, and R^0 be the collection of all zero recurrent states of S. Then $S = N \bigcup R^0 \bigcup R^+$. Furthermore, R^0 and R^+ can be divided into some irreducible sub-classes, that is, $R^0 = R_1^0 + \cdots + R_i^0$ and $R^+ = R_1^+ + \cdots + R_j^+$.

For Markov chain with finite states, it is well-known that

$$\lim_{k \to \infty} \frac{1}{k} \sum_{l=1}^{k} P_{ij}^l = \Pi_{ij}, \forall i, j \in S. \tag{3}$$

Researchers can refer to relative limit theorems, such as Proposition 3.3.1 in [14]. Moreover, since $\mathbf{P}$ is finite dimensional, hence the limit distribution Π is also a transition matrix on S.

Definition 5. *The subset $E \subset S$ is closed if $i \in E, j \notin E$, which implies that $p_{ij} = 0$, i.e., if $i \in E$ then $\sum_{j \in E} P_{ij} = 1$. The state space S is called reducible, if S have no-empty closed subset; otherwise, S is irreducible.*

In fact, S is reducible(irreducible) $\Leftrightarrow$ transition matrix $\mathbf{P}$ on state space S is reducible(irreducible).

We have another important fact that if every positive state of $\mathbf{P}$ is aperiodic, then $\lim_{k\to\infty} \mathbf{P}^k$ exists. Combining Proposition 1 and Proposition 2 as well as Theorem 16.0.1 and Theorem 16.0.2 in [14], we can get the following conclusion immediately.

Proposition 3. *Give a Markov chain with transition matrix* $\mathbf{P} : m \times m$ *on finite state space, for the following statements*

(1) $\mathbf{P}$ *is aperiodic,*

(2) $\mathbf{P}^k$ *has geometric convergence rate,*

(3) 1 *is a simple eigenvalue and all other eigenvalues have absolute values less than* 1*,*

(4) P *has* m *linearly independent eigenvectors and and the eigenvalues except* 1 *have absolute values less than* 1*,*

then the relations among them are that

$$(1) \Leftrightarrow (2); \quad (3) \Rightarrow (2); \quad (4) \Rightarrow (2).$$

For a reducible stochastic matrix, there is a very important convergence theorem given by M. Iosifescu[15], which is

Lemma 3. *Let* $\mathbf{P}$ *be a reducible stochastic matrix, where* $\mathbf{C}$ *is a primitive stochastic matrix and* $\mathbf{R}, \mathbf{T} \neq \mathbf{0}$*. Then*

$$P^{\infty} = \lim_{k\to\infty} P^k = \begin{pmatrix} \mathbf{C}^{\infty} & \mathbf{0} \\ \mathbf{R}_{\infty} & \mathbf{0} \end{pmatrix}$$

is a stable stochastic matrix.

In the following, Π is always defined as in Proposition 1 or Proposition 2. It is obvious that

$$\Pi\mathbf{P} = \mathbf{P}\Pi = \Pi = \Pi^2.$$

Thus, we have $(\mathbf{P} - \Pi)^k = \mathbf{P}^k - \Pi, \forall k \geq 1$. Moreover, by Proposition 1 and 2, $\mathbf{P}$ has geometric convergence rate, hence $\sum_{k=1}^{\infty} ||\mathbf{P}^k - \Pi|| < \infty$. Thus, if let $\mathbf{Z} = \mathbf{I} + \sum_{k\geq 1} (\mathbf{P} - \Pi)^k = \frac{\mathbf{I}}{\mathbf{I}-\mathbf{P}+\Pi}$, then $\mathbf{Z}$ is **well-defined** and $\mathbf{Z} = (\mathbf{I} - \mathbf{P} + \Pi)^{-1}$. We can prove that $\mathbf{Z}$ has the following properties.

Proposition 4. *(1)* $(\mathbf{I} - \mathbf{P})\mathbf{Z} = \mathbf{Z}(\mathbf{I} - \mathbf{P}) = \mathbf{I} - \Pi$*,*

(2)$\Pi\mathbf{Z} = \Pi, \mathbf{Z1} = \mathbf{1}$*,*

(3) all eigenvectors of $\mathbf{P}$ *are those of* $\mathbf{Z}$*; moreover, if* $r_i (\neq 1)$ *is a eigenvalue of* $\mathbf{P}$*, then* $\frac{1}{1-r_i}$ *is the eigenvalue of* $\mathbf{Z}$*.*

Proof. Because (1) and (2) of Proposition 4 are easy to be checked, we only check (3) of Proposition 4 here.

For a vector ν, notice the fact that

$$\mathbf{P}\nu = \nu \Longrightarrow \Pi\nu = \nu \Longrightarrow \mathbf{Z}\nu = \nu$$

$$\nu\mathbf{P} = \nu \Longrightarrow \nu\Pi = \nu \Longrightarrow \nu\mathbf{Z} = \nu.$$

Hence, 1 is a eigenvalue of $\mathbf{Z}$ and those eigenvectors of $\mathbf{P}$ corresponding to 1 are also those of $\mathbf{Z}$. In addition, for all other eigenvalues $|\lambda_k| < 1$ of $\mathbf{P}$, let ν_k be a right eigenvector of $\mathbf{P}$, that is

$$\mathbf{P}\nu_k = \lambda_k \nu_k.$$

Then, $\Pi\mathbf{P} = \Pi$ implies that $\Pi\nu_k = \Pi\mathbf{P}\nu_k = \lambda_k \Pi\nu_k$. If $\lambda_k \neq 1$, then we have $\Pi\nu_k = 0$. Note that

$$\mathbf{Z}\nu_k = \frac{1}{1-\lambda_k}\nu_k. \tag{4}$$

If $\lambda_k \neq 1$, then (4) means that ν_k is right eigenvector of $\mathbf{Z}$ corresponding to eigenvalue $\frac{1}{1-\lambda_k}$. In addition, we have $\Pi\mathbf{Z} = \Pi$, which means that 1 is eigenvalue of $\mathbf{Z}$ corresponding to eigenvector π. The same process can be applied to check left eigenvectors of $\mathbf{P}$. Therefore, this is the proof of (3) of Proposition 4. □

It is easy to know from Perron- Frobenius theorem that if $\mathbf{P}$ is a transition matrix, then 1 is a eigenvalue of $\mathbf{P}$ and there is no other eigenvalues with absolute values greater than 1. This fact implies that $r(\mathbf{P}) \leq 1$.

4 Asymptotic Behaviors of Evolutionary Algorithms

In this section, we consider the following optimization problem: Given an objective function $f : S \to (-\infty, \infty)$, where $S = \{s_1, s_2, \cdots, s_M\}$ is a finite search space. A maximization problem is to find a $x^* \in S$ such that

$$f(x^*) = \max\{f(x) : x \in S\}. \tag{5}$$

We call x^* an **optimal solution** and write $f_{\max} = f(x^*)$ for convenience. If there are more than one optimal solution, then denote the set of all optimal solutions by S^* and call it an **optimal solution set**. Moreover, **optimal populations** refer to those which include at least an optimal solution and the **optimal population set** consists of all the optimal populations.

An evolutionary algorithm with population size $N(\geq 1)$ for solving the optimization problem (5) can be generally described as follows:

step 1. initialize, either randomly or heuristically, an initial population of N individuals, denoted it by $\xi_0 = (\xi_0(1), \cdots, \xi_0(N))$, where $\xi_0(i) \in S, i = 1, \cdots, N$, and let $k = 0$.

step 2. generate a new (intermediate) population by adopting genetic operators (or any other stochastic operators for generating offsprings), and denote it by $\xi_{k+1/2}$.

step 3. select N individuals from populations $\xi_{k+1/2}$ and ξ_k according to certain select strategy , and obtain the next population ξ_{k+1}, then go to step 2.

For convenience, we write that

$$f(\xi_k) = \max\{f(\xi_k(i)) : 1 \leq i \leq N\}, \forall k = 0, 1, 2, \cdots,$$

which represents the maximum in populations $\xi_k, k = 0, 1, 2, \cdots$.

It is well-known that $\{\xi_k; k \geq 0\}$ is a Markov chain with the **state space** S^N because the states of the $(k+1)-th$ generation only depend on the $k-th$ generation. In this section, we assume that the stochastic process, $\{\xi_k; k \geq 0\}$, associated with an EA, is a **homogeneous Markov chain**, and denote its transition probability matrix by $\mathbf{P}$. It is easy to check the following results.

Remark 1. If the selection strategy in step 3 of the EA can lead to the fact that

$$f(\xi_k) \leq f(\xi_{k+1}), \tag{6}$$

then the corresponding transition matrix $\mathbf{P}$ is reducible.

The selection with the property of equation (6) is the so-called elitist selection, which insures that if the population has reached the optimal solution set, then the next generation population cannot reach any other states except those corresponding to the optimal population set. In practical, a lot of EAs have this kind of property. Hence, we always assume that EAs considered here possess the property of equation(6).

Remark 2. If population size $N = 1$ and the optimization problem has only one optimal solution, then

$$\Pi = \mathbf{P}^\infty = \begin{pmatrix} 1 & 0 & \cdots & 0 \\ 1 & 0 & \cdots & 0 \\ \cdots & \cdots & \cdots & \cdots \\ 1 & 0 & \cdots & 0 \end{pmatrix}$$

Remark 3. If population size $N \geq 1$ and the optimization problem has only one optimal solution, then

$$\Pi = \mathbf{P}^\infty = \begin{pmatrix} a_{11} & a_{12} & \cdots & a_{1m} & 0 & \ldots & 0 \\ a_{21} & a_{22} & \cdots & a_{2m} & 0 & \ldots & 0 \\ \cdots & \cdots & \cdots & \cdots & \cdots & \cdots & \cdots \\ a_{q1} & a_{q2} & \cdots & a_{qm} & 0 & \ldots & 0 \end{pmatrix},$$

where $q = M^N$, and the former m elements in matrix $\mathbf{P}$ exactly correspond to the m optimal states.

The remark 2 and 3 can be followed by Lemma 3 immediately.

Remark 4. For any initial distribution v_0, $v_k \doteq v_0\mathbf{P}^k \to (b_1, b_2, \cdots, b_m, 0, \cdots, 0)$ $(k \to \infty)$, which implies that $P(\lim_{k\to\infty} \xi_k \in S^*) = 1$, that is, EAs converges to optimal solution in probability.

In the following, we will prove the main results in this paper.

Theorem 1. *Suppose the optimization problem has only one optimal solution x^* and the population size $N = 1$. If $P\{\xi_1 = x^* | \xi_0 = s_j\} > 0$ for all $s_j \neq x^*$, then*

(1) all states except x^* are transient;
(2)x^* is positive recurrent and aperiodic;
(3) $\mathbf{P}^k$ converges, and if writing the limit by Π, then

$$\Pi = \begin{pmatrix} 1 & 0 & \cdots & 0 \\ 1 & 0 & \cdots & 0 \\ \cdots & \cdots & \cdots & \cdots \\ 1 & 0 & \cdots & 0 \end{pmatrix}$$

Proof. Note that $P(\xi_1 = x^*|\xi_0 = s_j) > 0$ and $P(\xi_1 = x^*|\xi_0 = x^*) = 1$. So, we have $f_{jj}^* < 1$ for all $s_j \neq x^*$, which means that $s_j(\neq x^*)$ is transient. This completes the proof of (1).

Since $\mathbf{P}$ is finite dimensional matrix, the positive recurrent states are not empty. Hence, x^* must be positive recurrent by (1) of this theorem. Combine the above fact and $P(\xi_1 = \xi^*|\xi_0 = \xi^*) = 1$, we get that x^* is aperiodic. This is (2).

By Remark 1, we know that $\lim_{k\to\infty} \mathbf{P}^k$ exists and the limit Π has the given form of (3). □

In order to deal with more complicate cases, such as f is not 1-1 and population size $N \geq 1$, we will introduce the following analytic techniques.

Denote the elements in image space of f by $I_f = \{y_1, \cdots, y_q\}$. For $i = 1, \cdots, q$, the **level sets** of original state space S^N are defined by

$$S_i = \{(x_1, \cdots, x_N) \in S^N : \max\{f(x_1), \cdots, f(x_N)\} = y_i\}.$$

Define new transition matrix $\overline{\mathbf{P}}(k)$ on new state space $\{S_1, S_2, \cdots, S_q\}$ by

$$\overline{p}_{ij}(k) = \frac{\sum\limits_{x\in S_i, z\in S_j} P(\xi_{k+1} = z, \xi_k = x)}{\sum\limits_{x\in S_i} P(\xi_k = x)}, \forall S_i, S_j.$$

We can check that $\overline{p}_{ij}(k) = \overline{p}_{ij}(1) \doteq \overline{p}_{ij}, \forall k \geq 1$, which means that $\overline{\mathbf{P}}(k)$ is homogenous. In particular, let $C^* = \{(s_1, \cdots, s_N) \in S^N : \max\{f(s_1), \cdots, f(s_N)\} = f_{max}\}$ be the optimal population set. Then

$$\overline{p}_{ij} = 0, \quad if \quad S_i = C^*, S_j \neq C^*$$

$$\overline{p}_{ii} = 1, \quad if \quad S_i = C^*.$$

Consider new stochastic process $\{\overline{\xi}_k; k \geq 1\}$ defined on new state space $\overline{S} = \{S_1, \cdots, S_q\}$, the distribution of $\overline{\xi_k}$ is given by $P\{\overline{\xi_k} = S_i\} = P\{\xi_k \in S_i\}$. Obviously, $\{\overline{\xi}_k; k \geq 0\}$ is a homogenous Markov chain with transition matrix $\overline{\mathbf{P}}(k)$. We can get the following general results

Theorem 2. *If $P\{\overline{\xi}_1 = C^*|\overline{\xi}_0 = S_j\} > 0$ for all $S_j \neq C^*$, then transition matrix $\overline{\mathbf{P}}$ has the following properties*

(1) all states in new state space except C^* are transient;
(2)C^* is positive recurrent and aperiodic;
(3) $\lim_{k\to\infty} \overline{\mathbf{P}}^k$ exists, and if writing the limit by $\overline{\Pi}$ then

$$\overline{\Pi} = \begin{pmatrix} 1 & 0 & \cdots & 0 \\ 1 & 0 & \cdots & 0 \\ \cdots & \cdots & \cdots & \cdots \\ 1 & 0 & \cdots & 0 \end{pmatrix}$$

The proof of this theorem is similar to Thm 1, so we omit it here.

Theorem 3. *If $P\{\overline{\xi}_1 = C^* | \overline{\xi}_0 = S_j\} > 0$ for all $S_j \neq C^*$, then transition matrix $\overline{\mathbf{P}}^k$ has geometric convergence rate determined by $r(\overline{\mathbf{P}})$.*

Proof. Note that we can find a permutation matrix $\mathbf{B}$ such that $\mathbf{B}\overline{\mathbf{P}}\mathbf{B}^T$ is a upper triangular matrix and its diagonal elements are $P\{\overline{\xi_1} = S_j | \overline{\xi_0} = S_j\}$. By the properties of transition matrices corresponding to the EA, 1 is a simple one in diagonal elements and all other diagonal elements are real and less than 1. Similar to Proposition 1, the transition matrix $\mathbf{B}\overline{\mathbf{P}}\mathbf{B}^T$ has geometric convergence rate. Hence, $\overline{\mathbf{P}}$ has also geometric convergence rate determined by $r(\overline{\mathbf{P}})$. □

5 Conclusions and Discussions

This paper confirms mathematically some results on asymptotic behaviors of evolutionary algorithms. Several important facts of the asymptotic behaviors of evolutionary algorithms, which make us understand evolutionary algorithms better, are proved theoretically. From this paper, we know that the convergence rate of EAs is determined by the spectrum radius of transition matrix, so, if the spectrum radium of the transition matrixes of Markov chain associated with the evolutionary algorithm becomes much smaller, the EA will converge much faster. For the simplest case that the objective function is $1-1$, the spectrum radium $r = \max\{P(\xi_{k+1} = s_j | \xi_k = s_j) : s_j \neq x^*\}$. So, we must make $\max\{P(\xi_{k+1} = s_j | \xi_k = s_j) : s_j \neq x^*\}$ become as small as possible in order to attain a fast convergence speed.

In fact, there are still a number of open problems for the further investigation such as, what effect on asymptotic behaviors will be brought by selection strategy, genetic operators and population size, respectively; the question of non-asymptotic behaviors(when the number of iterations depends in some way of the population size); and others. Probably, one can think of many variants and generalization of the algorithm, but the results we obtained in this paper incite us to go on studying simplified models of evolutionary algorithms in order to improve our understanding of their asymptotic behaviors.

Acknowledgments. This work is supported in part by the National Natural Science Foundation of China(Grant no. 60204001), Chengguang Project of Science and Technology for the Young Scholar in Wuhan City (Grant no. 20025001002) and the Youthful Outstanding Scholars Foundation in Hubei Prov. (Grant no. 2005ABB017).

References

1. Agapie, A.: Theoretical analysis of mutation-adaptive evolutionary algorithms. Evolutionary Computation 9, 127–146 (2001)
2. Cerf, R.: Asympototic Convergence of Genetic Algorithms. Advances in Applied Probablity 30, 521–550 (1998)
3. He, J., Kang, L.: On the convergence rate of genetic algorithms. Theoretical Computer Science 229, 23–39 (1999)
4. Lozano, J.A., et al.: Genetic algorithms: bridging the convergence gap. Theoretical Computer Science 229, 11–22 (1999)
5. Nix, A.E., Vose, D.E.: Modeling genetic algorithms with Markov chains. Annals of Mathematics and Artificial Intelligence 5, 79–88 (1992)
6. Poli, R., Langdon, M.: Schema theory for genetic programming with one-point crossover and point mutation. Evolutionary Computation 6, 231–252 (1998)
7. Poli, R.: Exact schema theory for genetic programming variable-length genetic algorithms with one-point crossover. Genetic Programming and Evolvable Machines 2, 123–163 (2001)
8. Rudolph, G.: Convergence analysis of canonical genetic algorithms. IEEE Transactions on Neural Networks 5, 96–101 (1994)
9. Rudolph, G.: Convergence Properties of Evolutionary Algorithms. Verlag Dr. Kovac, Hamburg (1997)
10. Schmitt, L.M.: Theory of genetic algorithms. Theoretical Computer Science 259, 1–61 (2001)
11. Suzuki, J.: A further result on the Markov chain model of genetic algorithms and its application to a simulated annealing-like strategy. Man and Cybernetics-Part B 28, 95–102 (1998)
12. Vose, D.: The Simple Genetic Algorithms: Foundations and Theory. MIT Press, Cambridge (1999)
13. Steward, G.W.: Introduction to Matrix Computation. Academic Press, New York (1973)
14. Meyn, S.P., Tweedie, R.L.: Markov Chains and Stochastic Stability, 3rd edn. Springer-Verlag, New York (1996)
15. Isoifescu, M.: Finite Markov Processes and Their Applications. Wiley, Chichester (1980)

Seeker Optimization Algorithm

Chaohua Dai[1], Yunfang Zhu[2], and Weirong Chen[1]

[1] The School of Electrical Engineering, Southwest Jiaotong University, 610031 Chengdu, China
dchzyf@126.com
[2] Department of Computer & Communication Engineering, E' mei Campus, Southwest Jiaotong University, 614202 E' mei, China
zyfdch@126.com

Abstract. A novel swarm intelligence paradigm called seeker optimization algorithm (SOA) for the real-parameter optimization is proposed in this paper. The SOA is based on the concept of simulating the act of humans' intelligent search with their memory, experience, and uncertainty reasoning. In this sense, the individual of this population is called seeker or searcher just from which the new algorithm' name is derived. After given start point, search direction, search radius, and trust degree, every seeker moves to a new position (next solution) based on his social learning, cognitive learning, and uncertainty reasoning. The algorithm's performance was studied using several typically complex functions. In almost all cases studied, SOA is superior to continuous genetic algorithm (GA) and particle swarm optimization (PSO) in all optimization quality, robustness and efficiency.

1 Introduction

The evolutionary computation (EC) community has shown a significant interest in optimization for many years. In particular, there has been a focus on global optimization of numerical, real-valued 'black-box' problems for which exact and analytical methods do not apply. Recently, real-parameter genetic algorithm (GA) [1, 2], particle swarm optimization (PSO) [3] and differential evolution (DE) [4] have been introduced and particularly PSO has received increasing interest from the EC community. These techniques have shown great promise in several real-world applications. However, the diversity of algorithms is encouraged by the 'No Free Lunch' theorem [5, 6], and it is valuable to propose new algorithms.

Optimization problems can often be viewed as the search for an optimal solution through a range of possible solutions. In the continuous decision variable spaces, there exists a neighborhood region close to the global extremum. In this region, the fitness values of the decision variables are inversely proportional to their distances from the global extremum based on the Intermediate Value Theorem. That is, better points are likely to be found in the neighbourhood of families of good points. Hence, search is intensified in regions containing good solutions [7]. It can be believed that one must find the near optimal solutions in the narrower

Y. Wang, Y. Cheung, and H. Liu (Eds.): CIS 2006, LNAI 4456, pp. 167–176, 2007.

neighborhood of the point with higher fitness value, while he must find them in the wider neighborhood of the point with lower fitness value. The algorithm called seeker (or searcher) optimization algorithm (SOA) presented in this paper aims to mimic the behavior of the search group mainly in terms of uncertainty reasoning, at this point where the new algorithm is intensively different from the existing search techniques.

Apparently, the behavior rules mentioned above are described by natural linguistic terms. In order to exploit the rules, cloud model [8], as a model of the uncertainty transition between a linguistic term of a qualitative concept and its quantitative data is introduced into new algorithm. The cloud theory [8] is derived and advanced from fuzzy logic theory, but improves the weakness of rigid specification and too much certainty, which comes into conflict with the human recognition process, appearing in commonly used transition models. The preservation of the uncertainty in transition makes cloud theory well meet the need of real life situation, and has already been used successfully in intelligent control [9], data mining [10], etc..

This paper is organized as follows. Section 2 describes cloud theory. In section 3, we introduce the SOA in details. And the algorithm parameters are discussed in section 4. Convergence analysis is shown in section 5. Then, we compare the SOA with continuous GA and PSO by use of typical function optimization in section 6. Finally, the conclusions and future work are presented in section 7.

2 Cloud Theory

***DEFINITION* 1.** [8,10] Let U be the set, $U=\{u\}$, as the universe of discourse, and T a linguistic term associated with U. The membership degree of u in U to the linguistic term T, $C_T(u)$, is a random number with a stable tendency. A cloud is a mapping from the universe of discourse U to the unit interval [0,1]. That is, $C_T(u)$: $U \rightarrow [0,1]$; $\forall u \in U$, $u \rightarrow C_T(u)$.

In the definition above, the mapping from U to the interval [0,1] is a one-point to multi-point transition, which shows the uncertainty. So the degree of membership of u to [0,1] is a probability distribution rather than a fixed value, which is different from the fuzzy logic.

The normal clouds are most useful in representing linguistic terms of vague concepts because normal distributions have been supported by the results in every branch of both social and natural sciences. A normal cloud is defined with three digital characteristics, expected value *Ex*, entropy *En* and hyperentropy *He* (Fig. 1).

The *Ex* is the position at U corresponding to the center of gravity of the cloud. *En* is a measure of the coverage of the concept within the universe of discourse. *He* is the entropy of the entropy *En*, and is a measure of dispersion of the cloud drops.

Given the three parameters (*Ex*, *En*, *He*) of a normal cloud model, the cloud with n cloud drops is generated by the following algorithm called basic normal cloud generator [10].

***Algorithm* 1.** Basic normal cloud generator

```
Input: Ex, En, He, n
Output: { (x1, μ1),..., (xn, μn) }
for i =1 to n
    En' =RANDN(En, He)
    xi =RANDN(Ex, En')
    μi = e^(-(xi-Ex)^2 / 2(En')^2)
    cloud(xi, μi)
end.
```

Here, the function *RANDN*(a,b) produces a normally distributed random number with mean a and standard deviation b. the *cloud*(x_i, μ_i) is the ith cloud drop in the universe. In my personal view, cloud models may be partly and originally similar to particle systems [11].

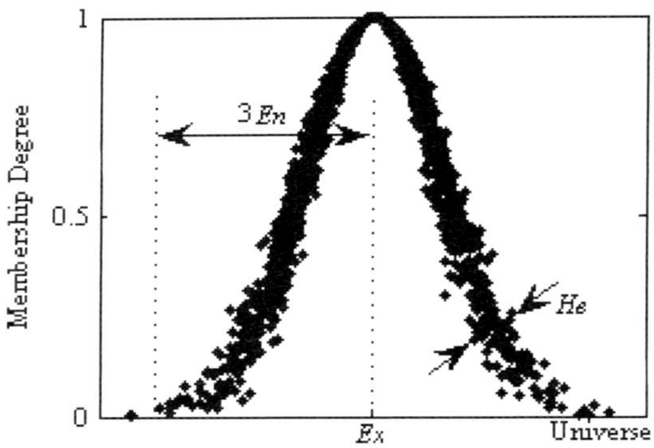

Fig. 1. Illustration of the three digital characteristics of a normal cloud

3 Seeker Optimization Algorithm

In the SOA, every seeker has a start position vector $\vec{c}$, which may be viewed as expected value *Ex* of cloud model, as the start location to find next solution. Moreover, each seeker holds a search radius $\vec{r}$ which is equivalent to the *En'* of cloud model, a trust degree $\vec{\mu}$ described by membership degree of cloud model, and a search direction $\vec{d}$ showing him where to go.

At each time step t, the search decision-making is conducted to choice the four parameters and the seeker moves to a new position $\vec{x}(t+1)$. The update of the position from the start position is a process of uncertainty reasoning, and determined by a like Y-conditional cloud generator [10] as follows:

$$x_{ij}(t+1)=c_{ij}+d_{ij}r_{ij}(-\ln(\mu_{ij}))^{0.5}. \quad (1)$$

where "i" is the index of seekers, and "j" is the index of variable dimensions.

```
The pseudocode of the main algorithm is presented as
follows.

  begin
     t•0;
     generating S positions randomly and uniformly;
     repeat
         evaluating each seeker;
         giving search parameters:start position, search
           direction,search radius,and trust degreee;
         updating positions using (1);
         t•t+1;
     until t=Tmax
   end.
```

4 Algorithm Parameters

In this section, we introduce how to decide the parameters in (1).

4.1 Start Point Vector

Intuitively, start position vector $\vec{c}$ is set to current position $\vec{x}(t)$. Inspired by PSO, Every seeker contains a memory storing its own best position so far $\vec{p}$ and a global best position $\vec{g}$ obtained through communication with its fellow neighbor seekers. In this paper, the whole search group was classified into k=3 neighbourhoods according to the indexes of the seeker group. Then,

$$\vec{c} = \vec{x}(t) + \phi_1(\vec{p}(t) - \vec{x}(t)) + \phi_2(\vec{g}(t) - \vec{x}(t)) . \tag{2}$$

where ϕ_1 and ϕ_2 are real numbers chosen uniformly and randomly in the interval [0,1].

4.2 Search Direction

In our opinion, each seeker has four significative directions called local temporal direction $\vec{d}_{lt}$, local spacial direction $\vec{d}_{ls}$, global temporal direction $\vec{d}_{gt}$, global spacial direction $\vec{d}_{gs}$, respectively.

$$\vec{d}_{lt} = \begin{cases} sign(\vec{x}(t) - \vec{x}(t-1)) & \text{if } fit(\vec{x}(t)) \geq fit(\vec{x}(t-1)) \\ sign(\vec{x}(t-1) - \vec{x}(t)) & \text{if } fit(\vec{x}(t)) < fit(\vec{x}(t-1)) \end{cases} \tag{3}$$

$$\vec{d}_{ls} = sign(\vec{x}'(t) - \vec{x}(t)) \tag{4}$$

$$\vec{d}_{gt} = sign(\vec{p}(t) - \vec{x}(t)) \tag{5}$$

$$\vec{d}_{gs} = sign(\vec{g}(t) - \vec{x}(t)) \tag{6}$$

where $sign(\cdot)$ is signum function, $\vec{x}'(t)$ is the position of the seeker with the largest fitness in a given neighborhood region, $fit(\vec{x}(t))$ is the fitness function of $\vec{x}(t)$.

Then, search direction is assigned depending on the four directions. In our experiments in this paper, we give search direction as follows.

$$\vec{d} = sign(\omega(sign(fit(\vec{x}(t)) - fit(\vec{x}(t-1))))(\vec{x}(t) - \vec{x}(t-1)) + \varphi_1(\vec{p}(t) - \vec{x}(t)) + \varphi_2(\vec{g}(t) - \vec{x}(t))) \tag{7}$$

where ω is the inertia weight, and $\omega=(T_{max}-t)/T_{max}$. φ_1 and φ_2 are real numbers chosen uniformly and at random in a given interval [0,1].

The expression (2) and (7) are thought to adhere to the principle of self-organized aggregation behaviors [12].

4.3 Search Radius

It is crucial but difficult how to rationally give search radius. For unimodal optimization problems, the performance of algorithm maybe is relatively insensitive to search radius within certain range. But for multimodal problems, different search radius may result to different performance of algorithm especially when dealing with different problems. In this paper, the cloud generator based method is first introduced to give search radius.

***Algorithm* 2.** The cloud based method of search radius

$En_r = \vec{x}_{max} - \vec{x}_{min}$;
$He_r = En_r/10$;
$\vec{r}' = RANDN(En_r, He_r)$;
$\vec{r} = RAND(0, \vec{r}')$.

where $\vec{x}_{max}$ and $\vec{x}_{min}$ are the positions with the maximum fitness and the minimum fitness within its fellow neighbor, respectively. Such as, the *En* may be viewed as the "known" region of the problem domain, and the seekers from inside this region to outside this region are respectively kept under from a fine-grained search to a coarse-grained search. The function $RAND(0, \vec{r}')$ is given as real numbers chosen uniformly and randomly in a given interval $[0, \vec{r}']$.

The mathematic expected curve (MEC) of a membership cloud may be considered as its membership function from the fuzzy set theory point of view [9]. In order to decrease computing time, the simple method of search radius was expressed as $\vec{r} = RAND(0, En_r)$ where En_r is presented as *ALGORITHM* 2. That is to say, fuzzy logic was used to deal with uncertainty reasoning.

4.4 Trust Degree

The parameter μ is, in fact, the grade of membership from cloud model and fuzzy set theory. According to the discussion in section 1, the uncertainty rule of intelligent search is described as "If {*fitness* is *large*}, Then {*search radius* is *small*}". The linear membership function was used for "*large*" of "*fitness*". Namely, it is directly proportional to the fitness of $\vec{x}(t)$ or the index of the ascensive sort order of the fitness of $\vec{x}(t)$ (we applied the latter in our experiments). That is, the best position so far has the maximum μ_{max}=1.0, while other position has a μ<1.0, and the worst position so far has the minimum μ_{min}. The expression is presented as (8) and (9).

$$\mu_i = \mu_{max} - \frac{S - I_i}{S - 1}(\mu_{max} - \mu_{min}) . \tag{8}$$

$$\mu_{ij} = RAND(\mu_i, 1) \tag{9}$$

where S is the neighbor search group size, and I_i is the index (sequence number) of $\vec{x}_i(t)$ after sorting the fitnesses of neighbor seekers in ascending order.

Meanwhile, The Gaussian membership function $MEC_A(x) = e^{-(x-Ex)^2/2En^2}$ was used for "*small*" of "*search radius*". Based on "3En" rule [13] which shows that the elements beyond $Ex \pm 3En$ in the universe of discourse can be neglected for a linguistic atom [9], μ_{min}=0.0111 is given at the point $x = Ex \pm 3En$ where $MEC_A(Ex \pm 3En)$=0.0111.

5 Convergence Analysis

From (2) and (8), when $\vec{x}_i(t) = \vec{g}(t)$, $1 \leqslant i \leqslant S$, it is apparently given that $\vec{c}_i(t) = \vec{g}(t)$ and $\mu_i(t) = 1.0$. Then (1) gives $\vec{x}_i(t+1) = \vec{g}(t)$ and $fit(\vec{x}_i(t+1)) = fit(\vec{x}_i(t)) = fit(\vec{g}(t))$. Hence, the maximum fitness of the t+1 step is larger than or, at least, equal to the maximum fitness of the t step. As a result, the SOA is convergent. But it is not determinate that the algorithm can be convergent to the global optimum. The further mathematical convergence analysis will be still left for future.

6 Function Optimization

In this section, the experiments will be discussed to compare the performance of the SOA, PSO and continuous genetic algorithm (GA). We used the MATLAB codes of PSO with adaptive inertia weight and continuous GA presented by [2]. In the experiments, the parameters of the PSO are that: learning rate $c_1 = c_2$=2, inertia weight linearly decreased from 0.9 to 0.4 with run time increasing [14]. The parameters of the continuous GA are that: the fraction of population kept was set 0.8, the mutation rate was set 0.1.

17 typical functions with varying complexities and varying number of variables (NV) were employed. They are as follows.

F1 Goldstein-Price function

$$\begin{aligned} F1 = {} & [1 + (x_1 + x_2 + 1)^2(19 - 14x_1 + 3x_1^2 - 14x_2 + 6x_1x_2 + 3x_2^2)] \times [30 + (2x_1 \\ & - 3x_2)^2(18 - 32x_1 + 12x_1^2 + 48x_2 - 36x_1x_2 + 27x_2^2)], -2 \le x_i \le 2, i = 1,2 \end{aligned} \tag{10}$$

F2 DeJong's *f*2

$$F2 = 100(x_1{}^2 - x_2)^2 + (1 - x_1)^2, -2.048 \le x_i \le 2.048, i = 1,2 \tag{11}$$

F3 DeJong's *f*5

$$F3 = 1/(0.002 + \sum_{j=1}^{25} \frac{1}{j + \sum_{i=1}^{2} (x_i - a_{ij})^6}), -65.536 \le x_i \le 65.536, i = 1,2 \tag{12}$$

F4 DeJong's *f*6

$$F4 = 0.5 + \frac{\sin^2 \sqrt{x_1{}^2 + x_2{}^2} - 0.5}{\left[1.0 + 0.001(x_1{}^2 + x_2{}^2)\right]^2}, -100 \le x_i \le 100, i = 1,2 \tag{13}$$

F5 DeJong's *f*7

$$F5 = (x_1{}^2 + x_2{}^2)^{0.25}[\sin^2(50(x_1{}^2 + x_2{}^2)^{0.1}) + 1.0], -100 \le x_i \le 100, i = 1,2 \tag{14}$$

F6 Goldstein's function

$$F_6 = x^6 - 15x^4 + 27x^2 + 250; -10 \le x \le 10 \tag{15}$$

F7 Griewangk's function

$$F7 = \sum_{i=1}^{D} \frac{x_i{}^2}{4000} + \prod_{i=1}^{D} \cos(\frac{x_i}{\sqrt{i}}) + 1; D = 10, -512 \le x_i \le 512 \tag{16}$$

F8 Hyper-Ellipsoid function

$$F8 = \sum_{i=1}^{100} i^2 x_i^2 ; -1 \le x_i \le 1 \tag{17}$$

F9 Rastrigin's function

$$F9 = 10D + \sum_{i=1}^{D} (x_i{}^2 - 10\cos(2\pi x_i)); D = 15, -10 \le x_i \le 10 \tag{18}$$

F10 Schwefel's 2.21 function

$$F10 = \max_i \{|x_i|, i = 1, \cdots\}, -10 \le x_i \le 10 \tag{19}$$

F11 Schwefel's 2.22 function

$$F11 = \sum_{i=1}^{5} |x_i| + \prod_{i=1}^{5} |x_i|; -10 \le x_i \le 10 \tag{20}$$

F12 Schwefel's 2.23 function

$$F12 = \sum_{i=1}^{5} x_i{}^{10}; -10 \le x_i \le 10 \tag{21}$$

F13 Shubeurt's function

$$F13 = \left\{ \sum_{i=1}^{5} i \bullet \cos[(i+1)x_1 + i] \right\} \left\{ \sum_{i=1}^{5} i \bullet \cos[(i+1)x_2 + i] \right\} + 0.5\left[(x_1 + 1.42513)^2 + (x_2 + 0.80032)^2\right]; -10 \le x_i \le 10 \quad (22)$$

F14 Simple square sum function

$$F14 = x_1^2 + x_2^2; -5 \le x_{1,2} \le 5 \quad (23)$$

F15 Six-Peak function

$$F15 = (4 - 2.1x_1^{\ 2} + x_1^{\ 4}/3)x_1^{\ 2} + x_1 x_2 + (-4 + x_2^{\ 2})x_2^{\ 2},\ -3 \le x_{1,2} \le 3 \quad (24)$$

F16 Yan and Ma's function

$$F16 = \frac{x_1 + x_2}{2} - \cos(20\pi x_1) \bullet \cos(20\pi x_2) + 2;\ -10 \le x_{1,2} \le 10 \quad (25)$$

F17 Yan and Ma's function

$$F17 = 0.1\left\{ \sin^2(3\pi x_1) + \sum_{i=1}^{D-1} (x_i - 1)^2 \bullet \left[1 + \sin^2(3\pi x_{i+1})\right] + (x_D - 1)^2 [1 + \sin^2(2\pi x_D)] \right\}; D = 5, -5 \le x_i \le 5 \quad (26)$$

As a measure of performance, we consider the average number of generations (AG) that the algorithms require to generate a solution with a certain high fitness value. In order to compare the ability to prevent the convergence of the algorithms to a local optimum, we also evaluate the performance of the algorithms in terms of the number of runs (NR) (out of 10 trials) for which the algorithms get stuck at a local optimum. When the algorithm fails to achieve the near global optimum, that is, the absolute value of the best function value minus the ideal function value (IV) is larger than 0.0001, after a maximum number of generations (MNG), we conclude that it has gotten stuck at a local optimum and does not generate a solution with a given high fitness value. Besides, the best function values (BV) of repetitious experiments, the average values of the best solutions (AV), and the standard deviations of the function values of the best solutions (STD) are also compared.

In all our experiments, we have used a population size of 100 for all functions. Furthermore, the expression $En_r = \vec{x}_{\max} - \vec{x}_{avg}$ was used for search radius when functions F13, F16, and F7-11 were optimized. Here, $\vec{x}_{avg}$ is the average value of the points in a same neighbourhood. The results of experiments are presented in Table 1.

As seen from Table 1, the SOA outperforms the GA and the PSO. For all the functions optimized here, the values of the BVs and AVs of SOA are better than the ones of GA and PSO, especially the values of NRs of SOA are smaller, which shows SOA has better potential to get the global optimum. Besides, the values of AGs of SOA are greatly less than that of GA and PSO, which shows SOA has higher convergent speed. Moreover, SOA has less STDs, which shows SOA is more robust.

Table 1. Comparisons of performance of SOA, GA and PSO

Functions	Algo.	AG	NR	BV	AV	STD
F1	GA	153.8	0	3	3	1.6922e-005
(NV=2, IV=3,	PSO	109	0	3	3	0
MNG=1000)	SOA	20.9	0	3	3	0
F2	GA	902.8	0	5.2587e-005	0.011178	0.014291
(NV=2, IV=0,	PSO	77.1	0	7.3463e-030	2.7379e-026	7.3804e-026
MNG=1000)	SOA	42.9	0	0	0	0
F3	GA	115.2	0	0.998	0.998	1.9642e-010
(NV=2,IV=0.998,	PSO	80.3	0	0.998	0.998	1.655e-016
MNG=1000)	SOA	70.7	0	0.998	0.998	1.4803e-016
F4	GA	191	1	0	1.4098e-005	4.4572e-005
(NV=2, IV=0,	PSO	72.3	0	0	0	0
MNG=1000)	SOA	16.5	0	0	0	0
F5	GA	3000	10	0.00029844	0.0073763	0.010015
(NV=2, IV=0,	PSO	853.5	0	8.7414e-060	2.8635e-058	5.1778e-058
MNG=3000)	SOA	97.8	0	0	0	0
F6	GA	18.7	0	7	7	0
(NV=0, IV=7,	PSO	28.9	0	7	7	0
MNG=1000)	SOA	20.6	0	7	7	2.1843e-008
F7	GA	3000	10	0.53597	0.81229	0.17299
(NV=10, IV=0,	PSO	3000	10	0.029509	0.068525	0.021366
MNG=3000)	SOA	476.8	0	0	1.9209e-007	3.9966e-007
F8	GA	3000	10	13628	17236	2211.2
(NV=100,IV=0,	PSO	3000	10	0.004186196	348.9081	331.593447
MNG=3000)	SOA	78.6	0	1.9066e-103	5.0255e-097	1.4066e-096
F9	GA	3000	10	13.188	24.484	7.2147
(NV=15, IV=0,	PSO	3000	10	1.989918	3.88034	1.720125
MNG=3000)	SOA	706.6	0	0	0	0
F10	GA	3000	10	0.0058716	0.01661	0.007963
(NV=5, IV=0,	PSO	995.4	0	1.7342e-072	1.8576e-070	2.1241e-070
MNG=3000)	SOA	136.7	0	1.3200e-128	5.1487e-080	1.6181e-079
F11	GA	3000	10	0.000801	0.0023801	0.0011435
(NV=5, IV=0,	PSO	971.1	0	9.02340e-087	4.7115e-084	5.6996e-084
MNG=3000)	SOA	137.3	0	3.5094e-127	3.6511e-125	5.5413e-125
F12	GA	89.7	0	1.1076e-029	1.8645e-022	3.7167e-022
(NV=5, IV=0,	PSO	13.7	0	0	0	0
MNG=3000)	SOA	8.2	0	8.0952e-134	5.934e-057	1.8158e-056
F13	GA	2086.4	6	-186.73	-186.5	0.20155
(IV=-186.7309,	PSO	446.9	5	-186.7309088	-186.7309088	2.9959e-014
NV=2,MNG=3000)	SOA	2247.1	3	-186.730901	-186.7309079	0.000120
F14	GA	25.5	0	2.2357e-019	3.0517e-007	5.2728e-007
(NV=2, IV=0,	PSO	28.8	0	2.2862e-088	4.7246e-084	1.4408e-083
MNG=1000)	SOA	9.1	0	0	1.2337e-253	0
F15	GA	29.9	0	-1.0316	-1.0316	1.7246e-008
(IV=-1.031628,	PSO	41.8	0	-1.031628	-1.031628	2.3406e-016
NV=2,MNG=1000)	SOA	13.7	0	-1.0316	-1.0316	2.3406e-016
F16	GA	2142.3	6	1	1.0013	0.0012818
(NV=2, IV=1,	PSO	1169.3	0	1	1	0
MNG=3000)	SOA	117.4	0	1	1	4.1659e-009
F17	GA	991	0	6.7894e-008	4.5504e-006	6.1197e-006
(NV=5, IV=0,	PSO	455.2	0	1.3498e-032	1.3498e-032	2.8850e-048
MNG=3000)	SOA	51.6	0	1.3450e-032	1.3500e-032	2.8850e-048

7 Conclusions and Future Work

In this research, a novel optimization algorithm based on the concept of simulating the act of human's intelligent search was introduced whose performance in terms of robustness and efficiency was studied with a challenging set of benchmark problems. The SOA performed very well, converging to near global optimal solutions when solving different classes of problems with different degrees of complexities. In all cases studied, SOA was faster, more robust and more efficient than GA and PSO in finding the global optimum.

Future research will include practical applications, and theoretical analysis to better understand this algorithm's convergence properties and the effects of the parameters on its performance.

References

1. Deb, K., Anand, A., Joshi, D.: A Computationally Efficient Evolutionary Algorithm for Real-Parameter Optimization. Evolutionary Computation 10(4), 371–395 (2002)
2. Randy, L., Haupt, S.E.: Practical Genetic Algorithms, 2nd edn. pp. 215–228. John Wiley & Sons, Inc, New Jersey (2004)
3. Kennedy, J., Eberhart, R.C.: Panicle Swarm Optimization. In: Proceeding of the 1995 IEEE International Conference on Neural Networks, Vol, pp. 1942–1948. IEEE Computer Society Press, Los Alamitos (1995)
4. Storn, R., Price, K.: Differential Evolution - a Simple and Efficient Adaptive Scheme for Global Optimization over Continuous Spaces. In: Technical report, International Computer Science Institute, Berkley (1995)
5. Wolpen, D.W., Macready, W.G.: No Free Lunch Theorem for Optimization. IEEE Trans. Evol. Comp. 1(1), 67–82 (1997)
6. Köppen, M.: No-Free-Lunch Theorems and the Diversity of Algorithms. In: Proceedings of the 2004 Congress on Evolutionary Computation, vol. 1, pp. 235–241. IEEE, Los Alamitos (2004)
7. Raphael, B., Smith, I.F.C., Direct, A.: Stochastic Algorithm for Global Search. Applied Mathematics and Computation 146, 729–758 (2003)
8. Li, D., Meng, H., Shi, X.: Membership Clouds and Membership Cloud Generators. Journal of Computer Research and Development 42(8), 32–41 (1995) (in Chinese)
9. Li, D., Cheung, D.W., Shi, X. et al.: Uncertainty Reasoning Based on Cloud Models In Controllers. Computers and Mathematics with Applications 35(3), 99–123 (1998)
10. Li, D.: Di, K., Li, D.: Knowledge Representation and Uncertainty Reasoning in GIS Based on Cloud Models. In: Proceeding of the 9th International Symposium on Spatial Data Handling, Beijing, 10-12 (2000)
11. Reeves, W.T.: Particle Systems - a Technique for Modeling a Class of Fuzzy Objects. ACM Transactions on Graphics 2(2), 91–108 (1983)
12. Camazine, S., Deneubourg, J.-L., Franks, N., Sneyd, J., Theraulaz, G., Bonabeau, E.: Self-Organization in Biological Systems. Princeton University Press, Princeton, NJ (2001)
13. Changyu, L., Deyi, L., Lili, P.: Uncertain Knowledge Representation Based on Cloud Model. Computer Engineering and Applications 40(2), 32–35 (2004) (in Chinese)
14. Shi, Y., Eberhart, R.: Empirical Study of Particle Swarm Optimization, In: Proceedings of the 1999 Congress.on Evolutionary Computation, Vol. 3, Washington, DC, USA, pp. 1945–1950 (1999)

Game Model Based Co-evolutionary Algorithm and Its Application for Multiobjective Nutrition Decision Making Optimization Problems

Gaoping Wang and Liyuan Bai

School of Information Science and Engineering , Henan University of Technology, 450052 Zhengzhou, China
wgp888888@163.com

Abstract. Sefrioui introduced the Nash Genetic Algorithm in 1998.This approach combines genetic algorithms with Nash's idea. Another central achievement of Game Theory is the introduction of an Evolutionary Stable Strategy, introduced by Maynard Smith in 1982. In this paper, we will try to find ESS as a solution of MOPs using our game model based co-evolutionary algorithm.We present A Game model based co-evolutionary algorithm (GMBCA) to solve this class of problems and its performance is analyzed in comparing its results with those obtained with four others algorithms. Finally, the GMBCA is applied to solve the nutrition decision making problem to map the Pareto-optimum front. The results in the problem show its effectiveness.

1 Introduction

In Multi-objective optimization problems (MOPs), the aim is to simultaneously optimize a group of conflicting objectives. MOPs are a very important research topic, not only because of the multi-objective nature of most real-world decision problems, but also because there are still many open questions in this area. The traditional optimization problems attempt to simultaneously minimize cost and maximize fiscal return. However, in these and most other cases, it is unlikely that each objective would be optimized by the same parameter choices. Hence, some trade-off between the criteria is needed to ensure a satisfactory design. In searching for solutions to these problems, we find that there is no single optimal solution but rather a set of solutions. These solutions are optimal in the sense that no other solutions in the search space are superior to them when all objectives are considered.They are generally known as Pareto-optimal solutions[1].

In this paper, we present the GMBCA [2] and we analyze it regarding the solution of MOPs. Moreover, we compare its results with those obtained by the multiobjective evolutionary algorithms (MOEAs): VEGA [3], NPGA [4] and MOGA [5], and the classical method of objective weighting refereed as [1]. We compare its performances in the solution of two analytical test problems. Finally, we apply the GMBCA to solve the nutrition decision making problem with the aim of find the optimum tradeoff surface.

Y. Wang, Y. Cheung, and H. Liu (Eds.): CIS 2006, LNAI 4456, pp. 177–183, 2007.

2 Multiobjective Optimization Problem

Consider a MOP model as presented below:

$$\begin{aligned}
\text{Optimize} \quad & y=f(x)=\{f_1(x),f_2(x),f_3(x),\ldots,f_m(x)\} \\
\text{subject to} \quad & G(x)=\{ g_1(x),g_2(x),\ldots,g_j(x)\}\leq 0 \\
& h(x)=\{ h_1(x),h_2(x),\ldots,h_k(x)\}=0 \\
& \text{where} \quad x=\{x_1,x_2,\ldots,x_N\} \in X \\
& y=\{y_1,y_2,\ldots,y_m\} \in Y.
\end{aligned} \tag{1}$$

And x is the vector of decision variables, y is the objective vector, X is the decision space, and Y is called the objective space. vectors G(x) and H(x) represent problem's constraints.In MOPs, the aim is to find the optimal solution $x' \in X$ which optimize f(x). Each objective function, fi(x), is either maximization or minimization.

3 A Game Model Based Co-evolutionary Algorithm (GMBCA)

3.1 Nash Genetic Algorithm (Nash GA)

The idea of Nash GA is to bring together genetic algorithms and Nash strategy in order to cause the genetic algorithm to build the Nash Equilibrium. In the following, we present how such merging can be achieved with 2 players trying to optimize 2 different objectives.

Let s = XY be the string representing the potential solution for a dual objective optimization problem.Then X denotes the subset of variables handled by Player 1 and optimized along criterion 1. Similarly Y denotes the subset of variables handled by Player 2 and optimized along criterion 2. Thus, as advocated by Nash theory, Player 1 optimizes s with respect to the first criterion by modifying X while Y is fixed by Player 2. Symmetrically, Player 2 optimizes s with respect to the second criterion by modifying Y ,while X is fixed by Player 1.

The next step consists of creating two different populations, one for each player. Player 1's optimization task is performed by Population 1 whereas Player 2's optimization task is performed by Population 2. Let X_{k-1} be the best value found by Player 1 at generation $k-1$ and Y_{k-1} be the best value found by Player 2 at generation $k-1$. At generation k , Player 1 optimizes X_k while using Y_{k-1} in order to evaluate s (in this case,.$s = X_k Y_{k-1}$). Simultaneously, Player 2 optimizes Y_k while using X_{k-1} in order to evaluate s (in this case, $k= X_{k-1} Y_k$). After the optimization process, Player 1 sends the best value X_k to Player 2 who will use it at generation $k+1$. Similarly, Player 2 sends the best value Y_k to Player 1 who will use it at generation $k+1$. Nash equilibrium is reached when neither Player 1 nor Player 2 can further improve their criteria [6].

3.2 Evolutionary Stable Strategy (ESS)

The primary contribution of evolutionary game theory (EGT) is the concept of the Evolutionary Stable Strategy (ESS). ESS was originally proposed by a world renowned biologist named Maynard Smith based on EGT and defined as an unchangeable strategy by other strategies. Unchangeable strategy means that no matter how outstanding a particular strategy may be, it cannot maintain predominance over other inferior strategies permanently. In the context of an actual ecosystem,more evolutionary stable species can be reserved than superior species, in other words an evolution chooses the strategy that not only executes progressive direction but also moves the equilibrium state.

3.3 A Game Model Based Co-evolutionary Algorithm (GMBCA)

In this section, the co-evolutionary algorithm designed for searching ESS of MOP is explained.Throughout the game, players for each objective function try to optimize their own objectives and all individuals in a population set are rewarded. The reward value is determined by the percentage of victories during the game .

To design the co-evolutionary algorithm based on Game Theory (GMBCA), we first established a game player with randomly generated populations. All individuals in each population are rewarded 'fitness' that will be used during the selection procedure. During the game each individual in the first population plays the game with others in the remaining populations and is paid the fitness . Other individuals in the remaining populations execute the game in the same manner by turns. Using the fitness,the next generation individuals are produced in each population independently through crossover and mutation.

Step 1: Two populations are randomly generated .

Step 2: The first individual in the primary population plays with each individual in the other population and is evaluated for level of fitness.

Throughout the game by turns, the fitness of the opponent individual in the second population is calculated in the same manner.

Step 3: The process of Step 2 is executed for all individuals of the first population one by one.

Step 4: The processes of Step 2 and Step 3 are executed for all individuals of the second population analogously.

Step 5: Using Fitness(xi) and Fitness(yj) determined from the previous procedures, each population produces next generation individuals independently through crossover and mutation.

Step 6: Until ending condition is satisfied the procedures from Step 2 to Step 5 are reiterated.

4 Description of VEGA, MOGA, and NPGA

An early GA application on multiobjective optimization by Schaffer opened a new avenue of research in this field. The algorithm,called vector evaluated genetic algorithm (VEGA), performs the selection operation based on the objective switching rule, i.e., selection is done for each objective separately, filling equally portions of mating pool [3]. Afterwards, the matting pool is shuffled, and crossover and mutation are performed as usual.

Fonseca and Fleming [5] proposed a Pareto-based ranking procedure (MOGA), where the rank of an individual is equal the number of solutions found in the population where its corresponding decision vector is dominated. The fitness assignment is determined by interpolating the fitness value of the best individual (nondominated) and the worst one (most dominated).The MOGA algorithm also uses a niche-formation method to distribute the population over the Pareto-optimal region based on the objective space.

The niched Pareto genetic algorithm (NPGA) proposed by Horn, Nafpliotis, and Goldberg uses the concept of Pareto dominance and tournament selection in solving MOPs [4].In this method, a comparison set of individuals is randomly picked from the current population before the selection procedure. In addition, we choose two candidates from the current population that will compete to survive to the selection operation. For selecting the winner, these two candidates are compared with those of set using a nondomination criterion as described in Section 2.

5 Criterion for Performance Measurements

The performance measurement criterion [7,8] used to evaluate the Pareto fronts produced by the EAs is the coverage relationship. Given two sets of nondominated solutions, we compute for each set the fraction of the solutions that is not covered (not dominated) by the other. Since this comparison focus on finding the Pareto-optimal set, this criterion uses the off-line performance method. The nondominated solution set taken to perform the comparison between all EAs is the summation of nondominated solutions found by each algorithm at each run, after application of a nondominance criterion.

6 Criterion for Performance Measurements

6.1 Test Problems

The algorithm is tested on the following problem. The problem was collected from Deb :

Two problems[9] were chosen in order to test the multiobjective genetic algorithms discussed in this paper. The problem1 has a convex Pareto-optimal front and is given by

$$F_1(x_1,x_2,\ldots,x_m) = x1$$
$$F_2(x_1,x_2,\ldots,x_m) = g(x) * (1-\sqrt{F1/G(x)})\ . \tag{2}$$

The second problem is the nonconvex counterpart to problem1

$$F_1(x_1,x_2,\ldots,x_m) = x1$$
$$F_2(x_1,x_2,\ldots,x_m) = G(x)*(1-(F1/G(x)^2)). \tag{3}$$

In both cases, m=30,xi∈[0,1], and the Pareto-optimal front is formed with G(x)=1. The function G(x) is defined by

$$G(x_1,x_2,\cdots,x_m) = 1+9\sum_{i=2}^{m} x_i/(m-1) \tag{4}$$

6.2 Experimental Results and Discussions

The multiobjective EAs were executed 30 times for each problem with the same initial population. The results of each execution was stored in an auxiliary vector and at the end the nondominance criterion was applied to the points belonging to the auxiliary vector, resulting a nondominated set that was taken as outcome. The set of genetic parameters used are: N_{ger}=250, N_{pop}=100, P_c=0.8, P_m=0.01, Ashared=0.4886 , T_{dom}=10 and (for NPGA). The graphic results are shown in Figs. 2 and 3.

The direct comparison of the outcomes achieved by the different multiobjective EA is presented in Table I. Each cell gives the percentage of solutions evolved by method B that are nondominated by those achieved by method A for both problems and . For example, the cell NPGA/MOGA signifies that 90% of solutions found by NPGA are nondominated by those found by MOGA for problem and 89% in the case of problem.These results show that all methods give rise to similar solutions with a slight superiority for GMBCA method, with exception of VEGA. The result for VEGA method is explained by the fact of its selection procedure does not use information of nondominated fronts.

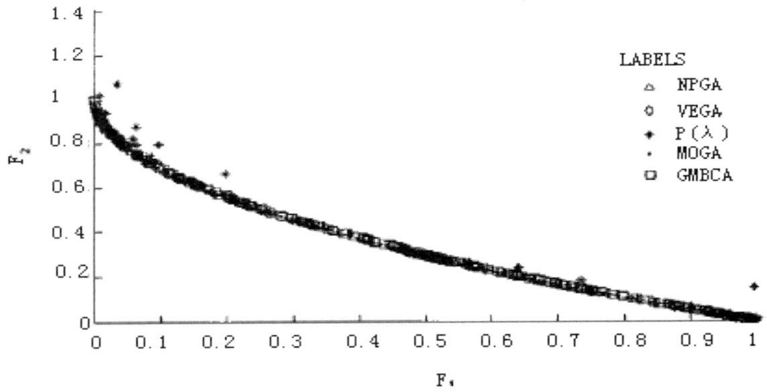

Fig. 1. Nondominated points for problem 1

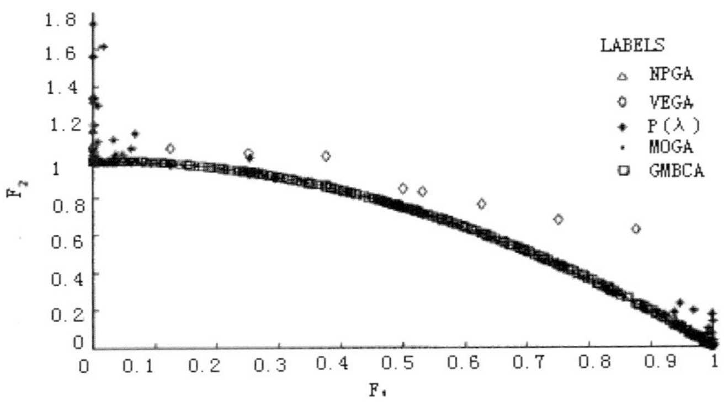

Fig. 2. Nondominated points for problem 2

6.3 Optimization in Nutrition Decision Makinings

The nutrition decision making Problem was chosen to show the application of GMBCA described in the previous study in solving a multiobjective nutrition optimization problem. In this paper, we search to find the Pareto-optimal front of a nutrition decision making .The aim is to find the multiple Pareto-optimal points considering two objective functions: 1) the first objective functions considers the energy and 2) the second one takes into account the protein. The constraint conditions are the bounds in the design variables.

Mathematically, the multiobjective optimization problem for the nutrition decision making problem was stated as

$$F=\min\{F_1,F_2\}=\min\{\,abs((e(x)-e0)/e0),\ abs((p(x)-p0)/p0)\,\} \quad (5)$$

The problem was solved considering seven design variables in continuous case . The nondominated points have been found using GMBCA method (with roulette wheel selection,and) coupled with a finite element code for energy and protein calculations. The domain was subdivided in these elements of first order.The results are presented in Figs.3 .

Table 1. EA performance measurement

B/A	VEGA	MOGA	GMBCA	NPGA	P(λ)
VEGA	-	0/0	0/0	0/0	0/0
MOGA	100/100	-	90/89	100/98	100/100
GMBCA	100/100	100/100	-	100/100	100/100
NPGA	100/100	90/89	90/88	-	100/100
P(λ)	100/100	88/79	87/90	79/89	-

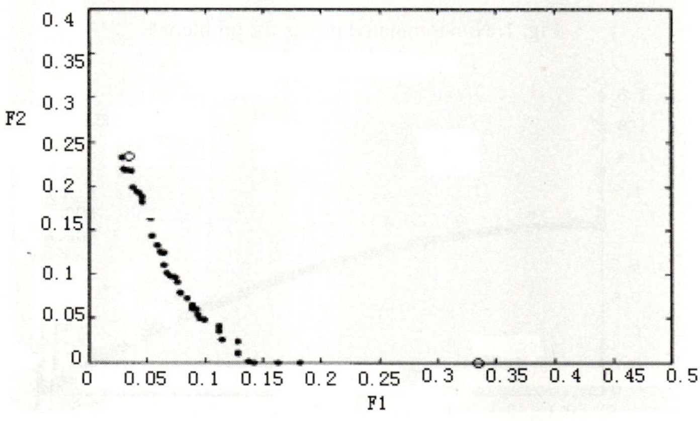

Fig. 3. Pareto-optimal points for the nutrition decision making problem

7 Conclusions and Future Research

In this paper, a co-evolutionary algorithm based approach is presented for multiobjective optimization problems. We tested the approach on two benchmark problems and it was found that our approach is promising when compared to a standard approach from the literature. Its application to the nutrition decision making problem show that it is reliable to solve multiobjective optimization in nutrition.For future work, we intend to test the algorithm on more problems.

References

1. Abbass, H., Sarker, C.R.: A pareto differential evolution approach to vector optimization problems. Congress on Evolutionary Computation 2, Newton, pp. 971–978 (2001)
2. Deb, K.: Multi-objective Genetic Algorithms: Problem Difficulties and Construction of Test Problems. Evolution Computation 7, 205–230 (1999)
3. Coello, C.: A comprehensive survey of evolutionary-based multiobjective optimization techniques. Knowledge and Information Systems 12, 269–308 (1999)
4. Deb, K., Goel, T.: Multi-objective evolutionary algorithms for engineering shape design. In: Sarker, R., Mohammadian, M., Yao, X. (eds.) Evolutionary Optimization, Kluwer Academic Publishers, USA (2001)
5. Zitzler, E., Thiele, L.: Multiobjective evolutionary algorithms: a comparative case study and the strength pareto approach. IEEE Trans. On Evolutionary Computation 3(4), 257–271 (1999)
6. Sefrioui, M., Periaux, J.: Nash genetic algorithms:examples and applications. In: Proc. Congress on Evolutionary Computation, pp. 509–516. IEEE Press, New York (2000)
7. Zitzler, E., Thiele, L.: Multiobjective optimization using evolutionary algorithms - a comparative case study. In: Proc. Fifth Int. Conf. On Parallel Problem Solving from Nature (PPSN-V), pp. 292–301. Springer, Berlin, Germany (1998)
8. Zitzler, E., Thiele, L.: Multiobjective evolutionary algorithms: A comparative case study and the strength pareto approach. IEEE Trans.on Evolutionary Computation 3(4), 257–271 (1999)
9. Zitzler, E., Deb, K., Thiele, L.: Comparison of multiobjective evolutionary algorithms: Empirical results. In: Proc. 1999 Genetic and Evolutionary Computation Conf. Workshop Program, pp. 121–122. Orlando, Florida (1999)

A Novel Optimization Strategy for the Nonlinear Systems Identification

Xin Tan[1] and Huaqian Yang[2]

[1] Institute of Communication,
Chongqing University of Posts and Telecommunications,
400065 Chongqing, China
xintan@vip.163.com

[2] Department of Computer and Modern Education Technology,
Chongqing Education College,
400067 Chongqing, China
mailtostorm@sohu.com

Abstract. Hopfield neural networks are the recurrent artificial neural networks. A novel method using Gaussian-Hopfield neural network (GHNN) to identify the discrete-time nonlinear systems is proposed. And then, the genetic algorithm is used to search for global optimization, which can improve the speed of searching for the global optimal parameters for the Gaussian basis functions (GBFs). In the end, simulation experiments are described in detail. The simulation results demonstrated that the proposed method can be successfully used to identify discrete-time nonlinear systems with good performance.

1 Introduction

The nonlinear structures can be seen as a concatenation of a mapping from observed data to a regression vector and a nonlinear mapping from the regressor space to the output space. The latter is typically formed as a basis function expansion. The basis functions are typically formed from one simple scalar function that is modified in terms of scale and location. The expansion from the scalar argument to the regressor space is achieved by a radial or a ridge type approach.

Basic techniques for estimating the parameters in the structures are criterion minimization, as well as two step procedures, where first the relevant basis functions are determined, using data, and then a linear least squares step to determine the coordinates of the function approximation. A particular problem is to deal with the large number of potentially necessary parameters. This is handled by making the number of "used" parameters considerably less than the number of "offered" parameters, by regularization, shrinking, pruning or regressor selection.

In the nonlinear system identification, we can use Gaussian-Hopfield neural networks (GHNNs) [1], [2], [3]. In this paper, to model the input-output behavior of a dynamical system, the network is trained using input-output data and the weights are adjusted using the delta-learning rule [1], [2], [3], [4], [5]. The underlying assumption is that these nonlinear classes can adequately represent the nonlinear system's dynamical behavior in the ranges of interest for a particular application. Thus, we must

Y. Wang, Y. Cheung, and H. Liu (Eds.): CIS 2006, LNAI 4456, pp. 184–190, 2007.

provide the neural network with information about the history of the nonlinear system, typically delayed inputs and outputs. How much history is needed depends on the desired accuracy. One may start with as many delayed input signals as the order of the nonlinear system and then modify the neural network accordingly.

Then, because of GHNNs may fall into local minimum [4], [5], [6], we proposed a method based on genetic algorithms to overcome the problem. The proposed method is described in detail in section 3. The experimental results are given in section 4. Finally, section 5 draws conclusions.

2 Nonlinear System Identification Using GHNNs

First, a single-input-single-output (SISO) discrete time nonlinear system is suggest, and it can be written as:

$$y(k) = F\left[y(k-1), k(k-2), \cdots, y(k-m), u(k-1), u(k-2), \cdots, u(k-n) \right]. \tag{1}$$

$y(\cdot)$ is the output vector, $u(\cdot)$ is the input vector, where $F(\cdot)$ is relating the two vector of the output and input for (1). k is the current discrete time, m and n are the order of the dynamical systems.

In (1), nonlinear function $F(\cdot)$ can be represented by projecting them onto a chosen set of GBFs:

$$\varphi_i^X(x) = e^{-\pi\mu[x(k-i)-p]^2} \quad for\ X = f\ . \tag{2}$$

Where μ is a parameter that determines the width of the GBFs. $p \in R$ is the center of GBFs, k is the current discrete time, and i denotes the delay time. Thus, the nonlinear function $F(\cdot)$ of the nonlinear systems is given by

$$F(\cdot) = \sum_{i=1}^{m} a_i^f \varphi_i^f(\cdot). \tag{3}$$

Where m denotes the number of hidden nodes, a_i^f is the unknown parameter to be identified. And in our research, the number of GBFs is 6.

The nonlinear function $F(\cdot)$ can be represented by projecting them onto a chosen set of GBFs in (3). So, the nonlinear discrete-time system is represented by

$$\begin{aligned} y(k) &= F\left[y(k-1), y(k-2), \cdots y(k-m), u(k-1), u(k-2), \cdots, u(k-n) \right] \\ &= \sum_{ij} a_i \varphi_i \left(y(k-i), u(k-j) \right) \end{aligned} \tag{4}$$

The nonlinear function $F(\cdot)$ of nonlinear discrete-time system contains input and output two functions. We use a set of two dimensions GBFs to construct this system, and the GBF $\varphi_i(\cdot)$ is given by

$$\varphi_i = e^{-\pi\left[\alpha\left(y(k-i)-p\right)^2+\beta\left(u(k-j)-\gamma\right)^2\right]}. \tag{5}$$

Where α, β is width of the GBF and *p*, *q* is centers of the GBF. We assume that the desired output is $y_d(k)$ and the network output is $y_l(k)$, where *l* denotes the current learning iteration. The error function of the *l*th iteration is shown as

$$e_l(k) = y_d(k) - \left[\sum_i a_i(l)\varphi_i\left(y(k-i), u\left(k-j\right)\right)\right]. \tag{6}$$

Where

$$\begin{aligned}\Delta a_i &= \partial MSE / \partial a_i(l) \\ &= -2/n\sum_{k=1}^{n}\left\{\left[y_d(k) - \sum_i a_i(l)\varphi_i\left(y(k-i), u\left(k-j\right)\right)\right]\varphi_i\left(y(k-i), u\left(k-j\right)\right)\right\}.\end{aligned} \tag{7}$$

And

$$\begin{aligned}a_i(l+1) &= a_i(l) - \eta\Delta a_i(l) \\ &= a_i(l) - \eta\left[2/\sum_{k=1}^{n}\sum_{v} a_v(l)\varphi_v\left(y(k-i), u\left(k-j\right)\right)\varphi_i\left(y(k-i), u\left(k-j\right)\right)\right. \\ &\qquad \left. -2/n\sum_{k=1}^{n} y_d(k)\varphi_i\left(y(k-i), u\left(k-j\right)\right)\right]\end{aligned} \tag{8}$$

The coefficient matrix is given by

$$A(l+1) = A(l) - \eta\left(\sum WA + I\right). \tag{9}$$

Where

$$A = \begin{bmatrix} a_1(l) \\ a_2(l) \\ \vdots \\ a_m(l) \end{bmatrix} \quad I = \begin{bmatrix} I_1 \\ I_2 \\ \vdots \\ I_m \end{bmatrix} \quad W = \begin{bmatrix} w_{11} & w_{21} & \cdots & w_{m1} \\ w_{12} & w_{22} & \cdots & w_{m2} \\ \vdots & \vdots & \ddots & \vdots \\ w_{1i} & w_{2i} & \cdots & w_{mi} \end{bmatrix} \quad for\, i = 1, \cdots, m. \tag{10}$$

Where *W* is the weight matrix, *I* is the bias input vector, *A* is coefficient matrix, and *W*, *I* are given by

$$w_{mi} = 2/N\sum_{k=1}^{N}\varphi_m\left(y(k-m), u\left(k-m\right)\right)\varphi_i\left(y(k-i), u\left(k-i\right)\right) \tag{11}$$

$$I_i = -2/N\sum_{k=1}^{N} y_d(k)\varphi_i\left(y(k-i), u\left(k-i\right)\right)$$

3 Optimization Method Based on Genetic Algorithms

Genetic algorithms are search algorithms based on the mechanics of natural selection, genetics, and evolution. It is widely accepted that the evolution of living beings is a process that operates on chromosomes (organic devices) for encoding the structure of living beings. Natural selection is the link between chromosomes and performance of their decoded structures. Processes of natural selection cause chromosomes that encode successful structures to reproduce more often than those that do not. In addition to reproduction, mutations may cause the chromosomes of offspring to be different from those of their biological parents, and recombination processes may create quite different chromosomes of offspring by combining material from the chromosomes of their parents. These features of natural evolution inspire the development of GAs. Roughly speaking, through a proper encoding mechanism, GAs manipulate strings of real numbers called chromosomes, which represent multiple points in the search space. Each real number in a string is called a gene. They carry out simulated evolution on populations of chromosomes. Like nature, GAs solves the problem of finding good chromosomes by manipulating the material in the chromosomes blindly without any knowledge about the type of problem that they are solving. The only information is an evaluation of each chromosome. This evaluation is used to bias the selection of chromosomes so that those with the best evaluation tend to reproduce more often than those with bad evaluations. Genetic algorithms, using simple manipulations of chromosomes such as simple encodings and reproduction mechanisms, can display complicated behavior and solve some extremely difficult problems without knowledge of the decoded world.

During the learning process, the GHNNs may fall into a local minimum [4], [5], [6]. Genetic algorithms have drawn significant attentions in various fields due to their capabilities of directed random search for global optimization. So, we use genetic algorithms to overcome the problem encountered by the traditional learning methods.

Especially, to determine a better crossover point j, we use the sequential-search-based crossover point method [7], [8]. The algorithm of SSCP is shown as Figure 1:

Procedure j= SSCP();
  Begin
    Let j=0; l=0;
    Repeat
      Perform $\hat{\Phi}$=Crs(;l);
      Evaluate $F(\hat{\phi}^l)$ and $F(\phi^l)$;
      If $F(\hat{\phi}^l) > F(\phi^l)$ Then j =l; Else l=l+1;
    Until $F(\hat{\phi}^l) > F(\phi^l)$ or l=α;
    Return j=l;
  End

Fig. 1. The SSCP Algorithm

Where F is the fitness function, and $\hat{\Phi}$ is the single-gene crossover operator, which is defined as

$$\hat{\Phi} = Crs(\Phi; j) = \begin{bmatrix} & \hat{\phi}_{j+1}^{1} & \\ & \hat{\phi}_{j+1}^{2} & \\ \Delta & \vdots & \Delta \\ & \hat{\phi}_{j+1}^{k} & \end{bmatrix} = \begin{bmatrix} \hat{\phi}^{1} \\ \hat{\phi}^{2} \\ \vdots \\ \hat{\phi}^{k} \end{bmatrix}. \tag{12}$$

Where j is the crossover point determined by a sequential-search-based crossover point method, Δ denotes the elements of offspring which remain the same as those of their parents, and the single-gene crossover operator Crs($\cdot$; $\cdot$) generates new genes $\hat{\phi}_{j+1}^{l}$ as

$$\hat{\phi}_{j+1}^{l} = \begin{cases} \hat{\phi}_{j+1}^{l} * (1-a) \\ \quad + \hat{\phi}_{j+1}^{l+(k/2)} * a, \; if\; l = 1, 2, \cdots, k/2 \\ \\ \hat{\phi}_{j+1}^{l} * (1-a) \\ \quad + \hat{\phi}_{j+1}^{l-(k/2)} * a, \; if\; l = (k/2)+1, (k/2)+2, \cdots, \end{cases} \tag{13}$$

Where a is a constant between 0 to 1, $\hat{\Phi}$ is a new population, and only at the position j+1 for all chromosomes with a linear combination of $\hat{\phi}_{j+1}^{l}$ and $\hat{\phi}_{j+1}^{l+(k/2)}$.

If there is no satisfactory crossover point in the current generation, then the crossover point is desigenated as j=α, so that the single-gene crossover is performed on the dummy gene $\hat{\phi}_{\alpha+1}^{l}$.

4 Simulation Results

For the simulation, we consider the Van Der Pol oscillator

$$\frac{d^2 y(t)}{dt^2} + \left(y^2(t) - 1\right)\frac{dy(t)}{dt} + y(t) = u(t)\cdot \tag{14}$$

The second order discrete-time version of the Van Der Pol oscillator is

$$y(k) = \frac{[1-0.5h]\, y(k-1) - 0.5y(k-2) + 0.25h\left[y^2(k-1)-1\right] y(k-2) + 0.5h^2 u(k-1)}{0.5 + 0.25h\left[y^2(k-1)-1\right]}. \tag{15}$$

Suppose the initial states are y(0) = y(1) = 0.2, the zero input is u(t) = 0, and the step size is h = 0.1.

The HNN is a GBFs network with 6 GBFs $\varphi_i(\cdot)$, The learning rates are set to be $\eta = 0.001$. Fig.2 shows the outputs of the plant and the identification model.

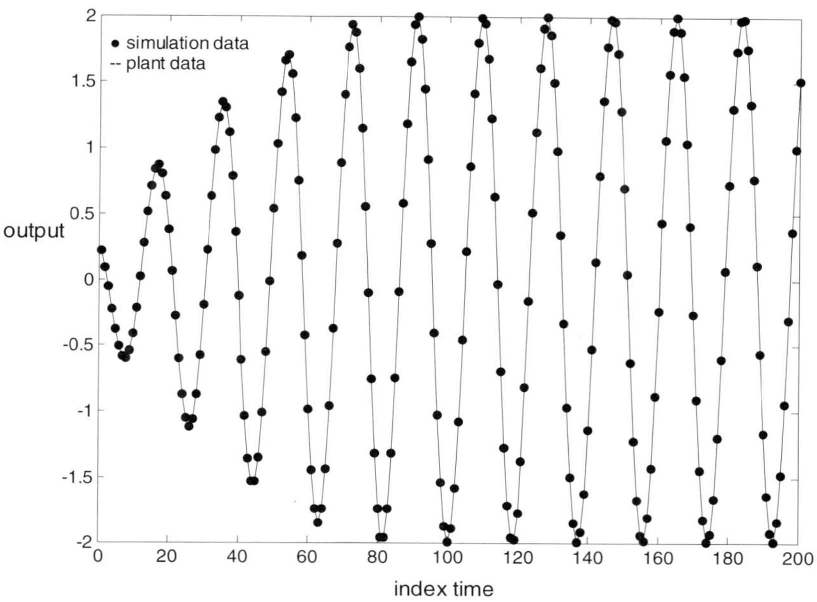

Fig. 2. Experiment results of identification output and plant output

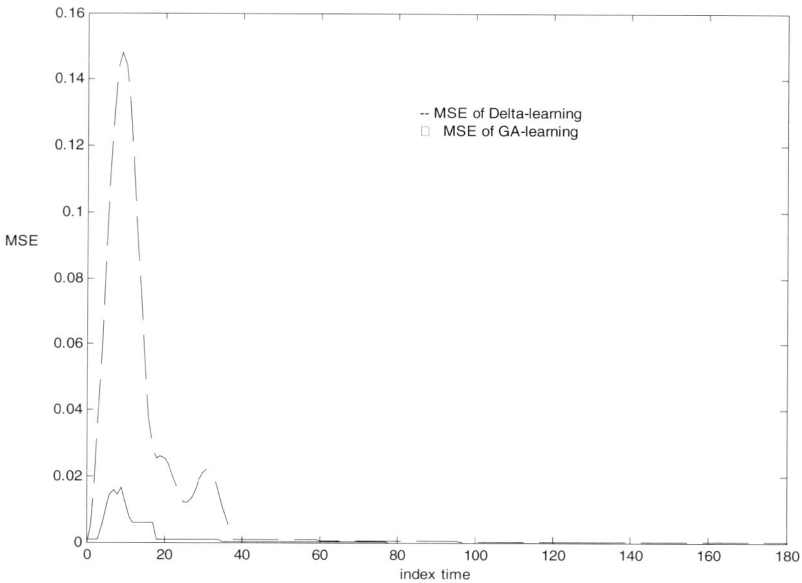

Fig. 3. MSE curves of two learning method

Two MSE curves using the delta- learning and GA- learning are shown in Fig.3. It is clear that the GA- learning method converges faster than the delta- learning methods.

5 Conclusions

We can use Gaussian-Hopfield neural networks (GHNNs) in identifying nonlinear systems, however, the delta- learning rule is prone to a local minima. In this paper, we use the genetic algorithm to obtain the high search speed of learning algorithm, so that the speed of searching for a set of optimal parameters for the GHNNs can be improved. The experimental results have been verified the effective learning ability of the proposed method.

References

1. Hopfield, J.J.: Neural Networks and physical systems with emergent collective computational abilities. Proc. Nat. Acad. Sci. 79, 2554–2558 (1982)
2. Elramsisi, A.M., Zohdy, M.A., Loh, N.K.: A joint frequency-position domain structure identification of nonlinear discrete-time systems by neural networks. IEEE Trans. on Automatic Control 36(5), 629–632 (1991)
3. Jenison, R.L., Fissell, K.: A comparison of the von Mises and Gaussian basis functions for approximating spherical acoustic scatter. IEEE Trans. on Neural Networks 6, 1284–1287 (1995)
4. Li, L.X., F, M.R., Y, T.C.: Gaussian-basis-function neural network control system with network-induced delays. In: Proc. IEEE Intl. Conf. on Machine Learning and Cybernetics, vol. 3, pp. 1533–1536. IEEE Press, New York (2002)
5. Sonwu, L., Basar, T.: Robust nonlinear system identification using neural network models. In: Proc. IEEE Conf. on Decision and Control, vol. 2, pp. 1840–1845. IEEE Press, New York (1995)
6. Yoshihiro, Y., Peter, N.N.: A learning algorithm for recurrent neural networks and its application to nonlinear identification. In: IEEE Trans. on Computer Aided Control System Design, pp. 551–556. IEEE Computer Society Press, Los Alamitos (1999)
7. Wang, W.Y., Cheng, C.Y., Leu, Y.G.: An online GA-Based Output-Feedback Direct Adaptive Fuzzy-Neural Controller for Uncertain Nonlinear Systems. IEEE Trans. on Systems, Man and Cybernetics 34, 334–345 (2004)
8. Matronardi, G., Bevilacqua, V.: Video Saurus system: movement evaluation by a genetic algorithm. In: Proc. IEEE Intl. Symm. on Computational Intelligence for Measurement Systems and Applications, pp. 49–51. IEEE Computer Society Press, Los Alamitos (2003)

A New Schema Survival and Construction Theory for One-Point Crossover

Liang Ming[1,2] and Yuping Wang[1]

[1] School of Computer Science and Technology
Xidian University, Xi'an 710071, China
[2] The 14-th Research Institute
China Electronics Technology Group Corporation, Nanjing 210013, China
liang_ming1977@yahoo.com.cn, ywang@xidian.edu.cn

Abstract. For one-point crossover, only the survival action to schema is mainly discussed in the existing schema theory. There are few works tackling the construction action to schema. Furthermore, there exist some limitations in these research results on schema construction theory. For example, the effects of the schema survival and the schema construction by crossover can not be distinguished. In order to analyze the effects of the survival and construction of crossover, respectively, a ternary representation for schema is proposed in this paper, through which the effects of the survival and construction of a schema can be easily distinguished. The effects of the schema survival and the schema construction by one-point crossover is analyzed separately. Subsequently, their united action is discussed.

1 Introduction

Genetic algorithms have a variety of applications such as function optimization, adaptive control, machine learning, and the training of artificial neural networks and fuzzy systems. In the literature, a lot of effective algorithms have been proposed [1,2,3,4]. In general, the population evolution of a genetic algorithm can be mathematically characterized by a schema theorem, which describes the change of the expected number of schema instances over time. Traditionally, a schema theorem, e.g., see [6], considers only the possible negative influence (also called *disruptive effect* hereinafter) of the crossover step (i.e., a crossover may decrease the number of the schema instances). Actually, a crossover operation generally not only makes an existing schema either eliminated or survived, but also makes a new schema constructed via other existing schemata. As a result, such a schema theorem cannot well characterize the evolution of schemata through the crossover operator. Spears [5] has investigated the disruptive and constructive roles of crossover by regarding two parents as an ordered pair. Nevertheless, the situations of schema survival and construction given in [5] are overlapping. As a result, the schema theory based on these definitions can not independently analyze the general survival and constructive roles of a crossover operation. Thus, it is necessary to quantify the survival and constructive roles, respectively.

Y. Wang, Y. Cheung, and H. Liu (Eds.): CIS 2006, LNAI 4456, pp. 191–201, 2007.

In this paper, we therefore first propose a new representation of a schema called ternary representation, through which the survival and construction probabilities of a schema are given out, respectively. Subsequently, we discuss the survival theory and construction theory after one-point crossover by making use of this new representation. Actually, this new representation can be used to consider other crossover.

2 New Schema Concepts

A genetic algorithm operates on a population of P same-length strings. A string of length l is often referred to a "chromosome" with l "genes". Each gene can take one of C possible values. Thus, there are C^l possible strings. In this paper, we only consider the binary strings, i.e., each gene can take one of two possible values: 0 and 1. In general, a schema, denoted as H, represents a set of all possible strings that can be generated by the schema. For example, schema $0{*}11{*}$ represents the set $\{00110, 00111, 01110, 01111\}$, where 0 and 1 are called the defining alleles, and their positions in the string are called the defining positions. The symbol $*$ is called the non-defining allele (or "don't care" symbol) because it can freely take one of two possible values: 0 and 1. Its position in the string is therefore also called the non-defining position. In the following, we give out four definitions, which will be used in the next sections.

Definition 1. ***(schema order and defining length)*** *The number of the defining positions in a schema H is called the order of H, denoted as $o(H)$. Particularly, if $o(H) = k$, the schema H is usually denoted as H_k. Furthermore, the defining length of the schema H, denoted as $L(H)$, is the distance between the outmost two defining positions. For example, the schema $H = 0{*}11{*}1$ is denoted by H_4 upon $o(H) = 4$, and the defining length of H_4 is $L(H_4) = 6 - 1 = 5$. In general, H_k represents 2^{l-k} possible strings, where the strings must match H_k in their k defining positions.*

Definition 2. ***(survival of schema)*** *If either of two parents is an instance of schema H, and at least one offspring is in H, schema H is said to be survival.*

Definition 3. ***(construction of schema)*** *If neither of two parents is an instance of schema H, but at least one offspring is an instance of H, we say that schema H is constructed.*

Definition 4. ***(situation)*** *If two parents $P1$ and $P2$ can generate an instance of schema H_k through a crossover operation, this crossover mask is called a situation of H_k. The pair of two parents corresponding to one situation is called a random couple event.*

It should be noted that the definitions for schema survival and schema construction in this paper are different from ones in [5]. For example, for schema H_4 as shown in Fig. 1, alleles a_3 and b_3 are swapped at the third position of two parents. This is considered as a construction of schema H_4 in [5] because of the occurrence of swap between $P1$ and $P2$. However, in the case of $a_3 = b_3$, $P1 \in H_4$, and $O1' \in H_4$, this is evidently a survival of schema H_4 according to Definition 2. Hence, the definition of schema construction in [5] is biased from the usual one.

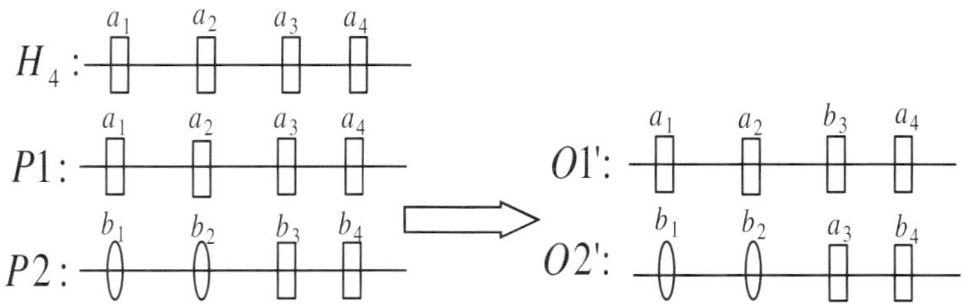

Fig. 1. One real construction situation

Actually, Spears' construction situations include some survival ones. For example, in Fig. 1, Alleles a_3 and b_3 are swapped at the third position of two parents. This is considered as a construction of schema H_4 in [5] because of the occurrence of swap between $P1$ and $P2$. However, in the case of $a_3 = b_3$, $P1 \in H_4$, and $O1' \in H_4$, this is evidently a survival of schema H_4 according to Definition 2. Hence, the definition of schema construction in [5] is biased from the usual one. As a result, the construction analysis of schema therefore becomes inappropriate. In contrast, our definitions can clearly distinguish the situations of survival and construction, and can cover all the possible cases. Subsequently, we can calculate the survival and construction probabilities of a schema respectively as shown in Section 3. In the next section, let us introduce a new ternary representation for a binary-bit schema first.

3 A New Representation-Ternary Representation

Let a situation be represented by a k-gene mask, in which each gene (also called *bit* hereinafter) takes one of three possible values: 0, 1 and 2. '1' at position d indicates that the allele of offspring Oi at position d can come from the same parent $Pi(i = 1, 2)$ only, '2' at position d indicates that the allele of offspring Oi at position d can come from $P(3 - i)(i = 1, 2)$ only, and '0' at position d indicates that the allele of offspring Oi at position d comes either from Pi or from $P(3 - i)$. Under the circumstances, there are 3^k possible situations for an H_k, each of which can be expressed as:

$$s_j = x_{k-1}x_{k-2}\ldots x_0,$$

where $j = x_{k-1}3^{k-1} + x_{k-2}3^{k-2} + \ldots + x_0 3^0$, and $x_i (i = 0, 1, \cdots, k-1)$ can take one of three possible values: 0, 1, and 2. We hereafter denote the number of '0', '1' and '2' as m_0, m_1 and m_2, respectively.

All situations can be categorized into two groups L_1 and L_2, where L_1 denotes the group of all survival situations, and L_2 denotes the group of all construction situations. That is,

$$L_1 = \{s_j | \forall i, 0 \leq i \leq k-1, \text{such that } \ x_i \in \{0,1\} \text{ or all } \ x_i \in \{0,2\}\};$$
$$L_2 = \{s_j | \exists i, i', 0 \leq i, i' \leq k-1, \text{such that } \ x_i = 1 \text{ and } \ x_{i'} = 2, \text{ where } i \neq i'\}.$$

Moreover, since each situation corresponds to a random couple event, we have 3^k possible random parents events in total, denoted as $R_0, R_1, \cdots, R_{3^k-1}$. Subsequently, all random couple events can be classified into two corresponding groups T_1 and T_2, i.e.

$$T_1 = \{R_j | s_j \leftrightarrow R_j, s_j \in L_1\};$$
$$T_2 = \{R_j | s_j \leftrightarrow R_j, s_j \in L_2\},$$

where $s_j \leftrightarrow R_j$ means that the situation s_j and couple event R_j match each other.

With this ternary representation of a situation, we can easily define a survival situation of H_k, i.e., that makes H_k survival through some crossover operation. For example, for schema H_4 in Fig.2, where $O1$ is a member of H_4. It can be seen that alleles a_1, a_2 and a_4 in $O1$ come either from $P1$ or $P2$, a_3 only from $P1$. Through the new ternary representation, the situation of this crossover operation can be expressed by the string "0010" which is the ternary representation of "3". Hence, this is the 3th situation. Since $P1 \in H_4$ and $O1 \in H_4$, the situation s_3 is a survival situation. Further, this situation corresponds to a random couple event R_3 in which $P1$ is $a_1a_2a_3a_4$ and $P2$ is $a_1a_2a_3{}'a_4$, where $a_3{}' = 1 - a_3$.

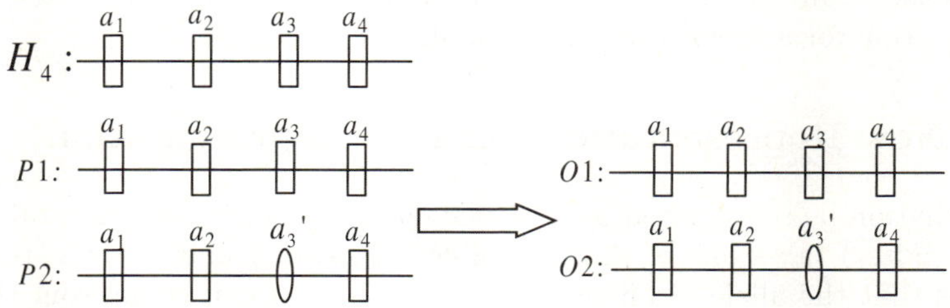

Fig. 2. Alleles a_1, a_2 and a_4 come either from $P1$ or $P2$, a_3 only from $P1$. Hence, this is the survival situation $s_3 = 0010$.

Similarly, we can define a construction situation, i.e., that makes H_k constructed through some crossover operation. For example, for schema H_4 in Fig. 3, it can be seen that alleles a_1 and a_4 in $O1$ come only from $P1$, a_2 only from $P2$, and a_3 comes either from $P1$ or $P2$. Through the new ternary representation, the situation of this crossover operation can be expressed by the string "1201", which is the ternary representation of "46". Hence, this is the 46th situation.

Since $P1, P2 \notin H_4$ and $O1 \in H_4$, the situation s_{46} is actually a construction situation. Further, this situation corresponds to a random couple event R_{46} in which $P1$ is $a_1a_2'a_3a_4$ and $P2$ is $a_1'a_2a_3a_4'$, where $a_i' = 1 - a_i (i = 1, 2, 4)$.

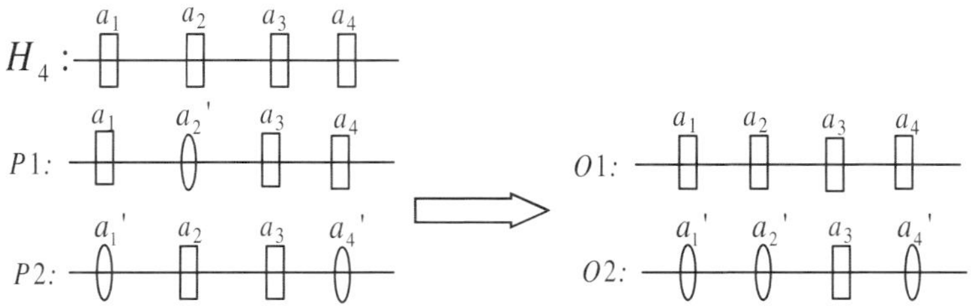

Fig. 3. Alleles a_1 and a_4 in $O1$ come only from $P1$, a_2 only from $P2$, and a_3 either from $P1$ or $P2$. Hence, this is the construction situation $s_{46} = 1201$.

4 The New Schema Theorem for One-Point Crossover

In the following, we will study the schema theorem for one-point crossover based on the ternary representation. For a string of length $l \geq 2$, there are $l-1$ possible cut points in total. For a schema H_k as shown in Fig.4 with k defining alleles $a_1, a_2, \cdots, a_k$ in an order from left to right, we let $L(H_k) = r$. Furthermore, let the distance between a_i and a_{i+1} be $\delta_i (i = 1, \cdots, k-1)$.

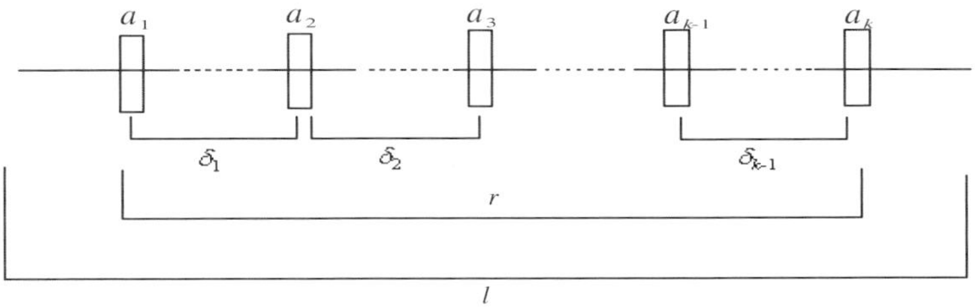

Fig. 4. One real construction situation

Under the ternary representation as stated above, the schema survival and construction can be easily distinguished. Before presenting the schema theorem that considers both schema survival and schema construction, we need to compute the occurrence probability of survival situations and of construction situations, respectively. They both involve in the probability that either of offspring generated from two parents via one-point crossover is in schema H_k, written as $p_{s,c}(H_k, OP)$, which is actually the sum of the survival probability of H_k through this crossover, denoted as $p_s(H_k, OP)$, and the construction probability of H_k, denoted as $p_c(H_k, OP)$. Hence, we can compute $p_{s,c}(H_k, OP)$ by

$$p_{s,c}(H_k, OP) = p_s(H_k, OP) + p_c(H_k, OP) = \sum_j p_{s,c}(H_k, OP|R_j) \cdot p(R_j)$$

$$= (\sum_{R_j \in T_1} + \sum_{R_j \in T_2}) p_{s,c}(H_k, OP|R_j) \cdot p(R_j), \tag{1}$$

where $p_{s,c}(H_k, OP|R_j)$ is the probability that either of offspring generated is in schema H_k after R_j undergoing one-point crossover operation, $p(R_j)$ and $p(s_j)$ are the occurrence probabilities of random event R_j and situation s_j, respectively.

To calculate $p(R_j)$s, we let $p_{eq}(d)$ represent the probability that both parents have the same alleles at a particular defining position d as given an s_j with m_0 0's, m_1 1's and m_2 2's. For simplicity, we make two assumptions. One assumption is the independence of alleles, and the other one is that $p_{eq}(d)$ is identical for all the defining positions, i.e., $p_{eq}(d) = p_{eq}$. In other words, at any defining position, the probability that two parents have the same allele is p_{eq}, thus the probability that two parents have the different alleles is $(1 - p_{eq})$. If two parents have different alleles at a position, there are two different cases: one case is that the two alleles of parents $P1$ and $P2$ at this position are a_j and a_j', respectively; the other one is that the alleles of parents $P1$ and $P2$ at this position are a_j' and a_j, respectively. Hence, for one situation, the probability that allele is '1' or '2' at some position is $\frac{(1-p_{eq})}{2}$, i.e., we have

$$p(R_j) = {p_{eq}}^{m_0} (\frac{1 - p_{eq}}{2})^{k-m_0} = \frac{{p_{eq}}^{m_0}(1 - p_{eq})^{k-m_0}}{2^{k-m_0}}. \quad (R_j \in T_1 \cup T_2). \tag{2}$$

4.1 The Survival Probability of H_k After One-Point Crossover

All survival situations for one-point crossover can be classified based on the value of m_0. For $s_j \in L_1$, m_0 can take one of values $0, 1, \cdots, k$. Hereinafter, we work out the sum of the survival probabilities of H_k under all corresponding situations with $m_0 = t$ $(t = 0, 1, \cdots, k)$, denoted as $p_{s,m_0=t}(H_k, OP|R_j)$, which can be carried out by considering the following three cases:

(i) As $m_0 = 0$, there are two corresponding situations in total, which consist of only k '1's or '2's, i.e., $\{11\cdots1, 22\cdots2\}$. It should be noted that two parents are not regarded as an ordered pair in this paper. In other words, for example, $k = 3$, the random events under $s_7 = 111$ are the same as the ones under $s_{14} = 222$. Hence, if $p_s(H_3, OP|R_7) = 1$, $p_s(H_3, OP|R_{14}) = 0$. If the crossover point is put among these all 1's or 2's, this schema will be disrupted. Hence, the probability of the schema will be survived in this situation is

$$p_{s,m_0=0}(H_k, OP|R_j) = 1 - \frac{r}{l-1}. \tag{3}$$

(ii) As $m_0 = 1$, the corresponding situation consist of only one '0', and the other ones are 1's or 2's. It can be classified into three kinds of cases. One case is that '0' is at the first position of the schema, and the second case is that '0' is at the last one, and the last case is that '0' is among the 1's or 2's. For the first case, the survival probability for this schema after one-point crossover is $1 - \frac{r-\delta_1}{l-1}$; for the second case, the survival probability for this schema after one-point crossover is $1 - \frac{r-\delta_{k-1}}{l-1}$; for the last second case, the survival probability is $1 - \frac{r}{l-1}$. There are in total C_{k-2}^{1} corresponding situations according to the last case. Above all, when $m_0 = 1$, the sum of survival probabilities is

$$p_{s,m_0=1}(H_k, OP|R_j) = k - \frac{kr - (\delta_1 + \delta_{k-1})}{l-1}. \quad (4)$$

(ii) As $2 \leq m_0 \leq k-2$, there are $C_k^{m_0}$ corresponding situations in total. Each corresponding situation can be divided into three parts. Suppose that there are i_1 consecutive 0's in the left of the leftmost nonzero allele, and these consecutive 0's can be signed as the first part; suppose that there are i_2 consecutive 0's in the right of rightmost nonzero allele, and then there are $m_0 - i_1 - i_2$ '0's and $k - m_0$ '1's or '2's between the leftmost nonzero allele and the rightmost nonzero allele. These these $m_0 - i_1 - i_2$ '0's and $k - m_0$ '1's or '2's between the leftmost nonzero allele and the rightmost nonzero allele can be signed as the second part; the remained i_2 consecutive '0's in the right of rightmost nonzero allele can be signed as the third part. In general, any survival situation can be denoted as $\overbrace{00\cdots0}^{i_1}\overbrace{j_1j_2\cdots j_{k-i_1-i_2}}^{k-i_1-i_2}\overbrace{00\cdots0}^{i_2}$, where $i_1 = 0 \sim m_0$, $i_2 = 0 \sim m_0 - i_1$, and $j_t \in \{0,1\}$ or $\{0,2\}$ when $t \in \{2, \cdots, k - i_1 - i_2 - 1\}$; $j_t \in \{1,2\}$ when $t = 1$ or $k - i_1 - i_2$. Only when the crossover point locates in the second part of situation, the schema will be disrupted. Thus, the schema will survival at the probability $1 - \frac{1}{l-1}(\delta_{i_1+1} + \delta_{i_1+2} + \cdots + \delta_{k-i_2-1})$. There are many such survival situations, and the number of such situations is $C_{k-i_1-i_2-2}^{k-m_0-2}$. We can get that the sum of the survival probability for these survival situations is:

$$p_{s,m_0}(H_k, OP|R_j) = \sum_{i_1=0}^{m_0}\sum_{i_2=0}^{m_0-i_1} C_{k-i_1-i_2-2}^{k-m_0-2}\left[1 - \frac{1}{l-1}(\delta_{i_1+1} + \cdots + \delta_{k-i_2-1})\right]$$

$$= \sum_{i_1=0}^{m_0}\sum_{i_2=0}^{m_0-i_1} C_{k-i_1-i_2-2}^{k-m_0-2} - \sum_{i_1=0}^{m_0}\sum_{i_2=0}^{m_0-i_1} \frac{C_{k-i_1-i_2-2}^{k-m_0-2}}{l-1}(\delta_{i_1+1} + \cdots + \delta_{k-i_2-1}). \quad (5)$$

For property of combinatorics, the first part in the the right of (5) can be computed and the result is:

$$\sum_{i_1=0}^{m_0}\sum_{i_2=0}^{m_0-i_1} C_{k-i_1-i_2-2}^{k-m_0-2} = C_k^{m_0}. \quad (6)$$

and

$$\delta_{i_1+1} + \delta_{i_1+2} + \cdots + \delta_{k-i_2-1} = r - (\delta_1 + \delta_2 + \cdots + \delta_{i_1} + \delta_{k-i_2} + \cdots + \delta_{k-1}). \quad (7)$$

By using equations (6) and (7), the second part in the right of equation (5) can be simplified as:

$$\sum_{i_1=0}^{m_0}\sum_{i_2=0}^{m_0-i_1} C_{k-i_1-i_2-2}^{k-m_0-2}\frac{1}{l-1}(\delta_{i_1+1}+\delta_{i_1+2}+\cdots+\delta_{k-i_2-1})$$

$$=\frac{1}{l-1}\left[C_k^{m_0}r-\sum_{i_1=0}^{m_0}\sum_{i_2=0}^{m_0-i_1} C_{k-i_1-i_2-2}^{k-m_0-2}(\delta_1+\cdots+\delta_{i_1}+\delta_{k-i_2}+\cdots+\delta_{k-1})\right]. \quad (8)$$

It only need to compute $\sum_{i_1=0}^{m_0}\sum_{i_2=0}^{m_0-i_1} C_{k-i_1-i_2-2}^{k-m_0-2}(\delta_1+\cdots+\delta_{i_1}+\delta_{k-i_2}+\cdots+\delta_{k-1})$ in order to simplify (8). For computational convenience, we denote:

$$SUM=\sum_{i_1=0}^{m_0}\sum_{i_2=0}^{m_0-i_1} C_{k-i_1-i_2-2}^{k-m_0-2}(\delta_1+\cdots+\delta_{i_1}+\delta_{k-i_2}+\cdots+\delta_{k-1}). \quad (9)$$

$$SUBSUM_{i_1}=\sum_{i_2=0}^{m_0-i_1} C_{k-i_1-i_2-2}^{k-m_0-2}(\delta_1+\cdots+\delta_{i_1}+\delta_{k-i_2}+\cdots+\delta_{k-1}). \quad (10)$$

Now, $SUBSUM_{i_1}$ can be computed in according to the value of i_1. When $i_1=0$, $SUBSUM_0$ is

$$SUBSUM_0=\sum_{i_2=0}^{m_0} C_{k-i_2-2}^{k-m_0-2}(\delta_{k-i_2}+\cdots+\delta_{k-1})$$
$$=C_{k-2}^{k-m_0-2}\delta_{k-1}+C_{k-3}^{k-m_0-2}(\delta_{k-2}+\delta_{k-1})+\cdots+C_{k-m_0-2}^{k-m_0-2}(\delta_{k-m_0}+\cdots+\delta_{k-1}).$$

Similarly, we can get:

$$SUBSUM_1=\sum_{i_2=0}^{m_0-1} C_{k-i_2-3}^{k-m_0-2}(\delta_1+\delta_{k-i_2}+\cdots+\delta_{k-1})$$
$$=C_{k-3}^{k-m_0-2}(\delta_1+\delta_{k-1})+C_{k-4}^{k-m_0-2}(\delta_1+\delta_{k-2}+\delta_{k-1})$$
$$+\cdots+C_{k-m_0-2}^{k-m_0-2}(\delta_1+\delta_{k-m_0+1}+\cdots+\delta_{k-1}).$$

$$SUBSUM_2=\sum_{i_2=0}^{m_0-2} C_{k-i_2-4}^{k-m_0-2}(\delta_1+\delta_2+\delta_{k-i_2}+\cdots+\delta_{k-1})$$
$$=C_{k-4}^{k-m_0-2}(\delta_1+\delta_2+\delta_{k-1})+C_{k-5}^{k-m_0-2}(\delta_1+\delta_2+\delta_{k-2}+\delta_{k-1})$$
$$+\cdots+C_{k-m_0-2}^{k-m_0-2}(\delta_1+\delta_2+\delta_{k-m_0+2}+\cdots+\delta_{k-1}).$$

$$\vdots \qquad\qquad \vdots$$

$$SUBSUM_{m_0-1}=\sum_{i_2=0}^{1} C_{k-i_2-m_0-1}^{k-m_0-2}(\delta_1+\cdots+\delta_{m_0-1}+\delta_{k-i_2}+\cdots+\delta_{k-1})$$
$$=C_{k-m_0-1}^{k-m_0-2}(\delta_1+\cdots+\delta_{m_0-1})+C_{k-m_0-2}^{k-m_0-2}(\delta_1+\cdots+\delta_{m_0-1}+\delta_{k-1}).$$

$$SUBSUM_{m_0} = C_{k-m_0-2}^{k-m_0-2}(\delta_1 + \delta_2 + \cdots + \delta_{m_0}).$$

The coefficient of δ_1 in $SUBSUM_1$ is

$$C_{k-3}^{k-m_0-2} + C_{k-4}^{k-m_0-2} + \cdots + C_{k-m_0-2}^{k-m_0-2} = C_{k-2}^{k-m_0-1}.$$

The coefficient of δ_1 in $SUBSUM_2$ is

$$C_{k-4}^{k-m_0-2} + C_{k-5}^{k-m_0-2} + \cdots + C_{k-m_0-2}^{k-m_0-2} = C_{k-3}^{k-m_0-1}.$$

It can be similarly to get that the coefficient of δ_1 in $SUBSUM_{m_0-1}$ is

$$C_{k-m_0-1}^{k-m_0-2} + C_{k-m_0-2}^{k-m_0-2} = C_{k-m_0}^{k-m_0-1}.$$

Thus, the coefficient of δ_1 in SUM is

$$\begin{aligned}
&C_{k-2}^{k-m_0-1} + C_{k-3}^{k-m_0-1} + \cdots + C_{k-m_0}^{k-m_0-1} + C_{k-m_0-2}^{k-m_0-2} \\
&= C_{k-2}^{k-m_0-1} + C_{k-3}^{k-m_0-1} + \cdots + C_{k-m_0}^{k-m_0-1} + C_{k-m_0-1}^{k-m_0-1} \\
&= C_{k-1}^{k-m_0} = C_{k-1}^{m_0-1}.
\end{aligned}$$

Similarly, the coefficient of δ_2 is $C_{k-2}^{m_0-2}$, δ_{k-2} corresponds to $C_{k-2}^{m_0-2}$, and δ_{k-1} corresponds to $C_{k-1}^{m_0-1}$. We can obtain that the coefficient of δ_1 is the same as the one of δ_{k-1}, the coefficient of δ_2 is the same as the one of δ_{k-2}. Actually, the coefficient of $\delta_i (i = 1, 2, \cdots, m_0)$ is the same as the one of δ_{k-i}. As a result, equation (5) can be simplified as

$$p_{s,m_0}(H_k, OP|R_j) = C_k^{m_0} - \frac{1}{l-1}\left[C_k^{m_0} r - \sum_{i=1}^{m_0} C_{k-i}^{m_0-i}(\delta_i + \delta_{k-i})\right]. \quad (11)$$

(iii) As $m_0 = k - 1$ and k, H_k survives no matter where the crossover point is. For $m_0 = k - 1$, there are $k - 1$ corresponding situations in total, and for $m_0 = k$, there are only one corresponding situation in total. Hence, the survival probability of schema H_k must be 1 no matter where the crossover point is. Hence, we have

$$p_{s,m_0=k-1}(H_k, OP|R_j) = k - 1. \quad (12)$$

$$p_{s,m_0=k}(H_k, OP|R_j) = 1. \quad (13)$$

Through the above discussion, the survival probability of schema H_k after one-point crossover is

$$\begin{aligned}
p_s(H_k,OP) &= {p_{eq}}^k + k\frac{{p_{eq}}^{k-1}(1-p_{eq})}{2} + \frac{(1-p_{eq})^k}{2^k} + \sum_{m_0=1}^{k-2} C_k^{m_0} \frac{{p_{eq}}^{m_0}(1-p_{eq})^{k-m_0}}{2^{k-m_0}} \\
&- \frac{(1-p_{eq})^k}{2^k}\frac{r}{l-1} - \sum_{m_0=1}^{k-2} \frac{{p_{eq}}^{m_0}(1-p_{eq})^{k-m_0}}{2^{k-m_0}} \frac{C_k^{m_0} r - \sum_{i=1}^{m_0} C_{k-i}^{m_0-i}(\delta_i+\delta_{k-i})}{l-1}. \\
&= (p_{eq} + \frac{1-p_{eq}}{2})^k - \sum_{m_0=0}^{k-2} \frac{{p_{eq}}^{m_0}(1-p_{eq})^{k-m_0}}{2^{k-m_0}} \frac{C_k^{m_0} r - \sum_{i=1}^{m_0} C_{k-i}^{m_0-i}(\delta_i+\delta_{k-i})}{l-1} \\
&= (\frac{1+p_{eq}}{2})^k - \sum_{m_0=0}^{k-2} \frac{{p_{eq}}^{m_0}(1-p_{eq})^{k-m_0}}{2^{k-m_0}} \frac{C_k^{m_0} r - \sum_{i=1}^{m_0} C_{k-i}^{m_0-i}(\delta_i+\delta_{k-i})}{l-1}.
\end{aligned} \quad (14)$$

It can be concluded from equation(14) that

- The greater the order of schema k is, the less the $p_s(H_k, OP)$ is, i.e., the schema will be easier disrupted.
- The greater p_{eq} is (i.e., the more similar parents are), the greater the $p_s(H_k, OP)$.
- The greater the defining length r is, the less the $p_s(H_k, OP)$ is.
- The greater the string length l is, the greater the $p_s(H_k, OP)$ is.

4.2 The Construction Probability of H_k After One-Point Crossover

All construction situations of H_k after one-point crossover can be classified based on the value of m_0 too. For $s_j \in L_2$, m_0 can take one of values $0, 1, \cdots, k-2$. Hereinafter, we work out the sum of the construction probabilities of H_k under all corresponding situations with $m_0 = t\,(t = 0, 1, \cdots, k)$, denoted as $p_{c,m_0=t}(H_k, OP|R_j)$,

(i) As $m_0 = 0$, the corresponding situations consist of '1' and '2'. For example, for $k = 3$, the set of corresponding situations is $\{112, 121, 211, 122, 221, 212\}$. Only when all 1's gather together, and all 2's gather together, and the crossover point is put between '1' and '2', the schema will be constructed. Similarly to the computation of the survival probability for one-point crossover, we can give out the construction probability for H_k under all corresponding situations without '0' via one-point crossover:

$$p_{c,m_0=0}(H_k, OP) = \frac{r(1-p_{eq})^k}{2^k(l-1)}. \tag{15}$$

(ii) As $m_0 = 1$, each corresponding situation consists of only one '1'. If and only if all '1's gather together, and all '2's gather together, and the crossover point is put between '1' or '0' and '2', the schema will be constructed. Thus, we can get

$$p_{c,m_0=1}(H_k, OP|R_j) = \frac{1}{l-1}\left[kr - (\delta_1 + \delta_{k-1})\right]. \tag{16}$$

(iii) As $2 \le m_0 \le k-2$, the corresponding situations are similarly classified with the survival situations. The discussion is similar to the former survival analysis. We can get

$$p_{c,m_0}(H_k, OP|R_j) = \frac{1}{l-1}\left[C_k^{m_0} r - \sum_{i=1}^{m_0} C_{k-i}^{m_0-i}(\delta_i + \delta_{k-i})\right]. \tag{17}$$

Through the above construction analysis, we can obtain the construction probability of schema H_k after one-point crossover

$$\begin{aligned} p_c(H_k, OP) &= \sum_{m_0=0}^{k-2} p_{c,m_0}(H_k, OP|R_j)\cdot p(R_j) \\ &= \frac{r(1-p_{eq})^k}{2^k(l-1)} + \sum_{m_0=1}^{k-2} \frac{{p_{eq}}^{m_0}(1-p_{eq})^{k-m_0}}{2^{k-m_0}} \frac{C_k^{m_0} r - \sum_{i=1}^{m_0} C_{k-i}^{m_0-i}(\delta_i + \delta_{k-i})}{l-1} \\ &= \sum_{m_0=0}^{k-2} \frac{{p_{eq}}^{m_0}(1-p_{eq})^{k-m_0}}{2^{k-m_0}} \frac{C_k^{m_0} r - \sum_{i=1}^{m_0} C_{k-i}^{m_0-i}(\delta_i + \delta_{k-i})}{l-1}. \end{aligned} \tag{18}$$

By putting equations (14) and (18) into equation (1), we then have

$$p_{s,c}(H_k, OP) = \frac{(1 + p_{eq})^k}{2^k} \tag{19}$$

Equation (19) indicates that the probability $p_{s,c}(H_k, OP)$ is only determined by the order k and the value of p_{eq}, regardless of the kind of string length or defining length. Thus, for one-point crossover, any decrease in disruption (i.e., an increase in survival), *must* be countered by a decrease in construction, and vice versa. In other words, disruption and construction are not only related qualitatively, but are also related quantitatively.

5 Concluding Remarks

This paper discussed the survival and construction theory for one-point crossover, by making use of a new ternary representation for a schema. Actually, the proposed representation in this paper can also be applicable to the other crossovers, e.g., two-point crossover, multi-point crossover and uniform crossover. We leave them for the future studies.

References

1. Cnstillo, P.A., Romero, G.: Statistical Analysis of the Main Parameters Improved in the Design of a Genetic Algorithm. IEEE Transactions on Systems, Man. and Cybernetics, Part. C 32(1), 31–37 (2002)
2. Leung, Y.W., Wang, Y.P.: An Orthogonal Genetic Algorithm with Quantization for Global Numerical Optimization. IEEE Transactions on Evolutionary Computation 5(1), 41–53 (2001)
3. Leung, Y.W., Wang, Y.P.: Multiobjective Programming Using Uniform Design and Genetic Algorithm. IEEE Transactions on Systems, Man. and Cybernetics, Part. C 30(3), 293–304 (2000)
4. Kushchu, I.: Genetic Programming and Evolutionary Generalization. IEEE Transaction on Evolutionary Computation, no. 6, 431–442 (2002)
5. Spears, W.M.: The Role of Mutation and Recombination in Evolutionary Algorithms. George Mason University, Virginia (1998)
6. Holland, J.H.: Adaptation in Natural and Artificial System. University of Michigan Press, Ann Arbor, MI (1975)

Adaptive Parallel Immune Evolutionary Strategy

Cheng Bo, Guo Zhenyu, Cao Binggang, and Wang Junping

Research & Development Center of Electric Vehicle Xi'an Jiaotong University, Xi'an 710049, China
chengbo7681@126.com

Abstract. Based on Clonal Selection Theory, an adaptive Parallel Immune Evolutionary Strategy (PIES) is presented. On the grounds of antigen-antibody affinity, the original antibody population can be divided into two subgroups. Correspondingly, two operators, Elitist Clonal Operator (ECO) and Super Mutation Operator (SMO), are proposed. The former is adopted to improve the local search ability while the latter is used to maintain the population diversity. Thus, population evolution can be actualized by concurrently operating ECO and SMO, which can enhance searching efficiency of the algorithm. Experimental results show that PIES is of high efficiency and can effectively prevent premature convergence. Therefore, it can be employed to solve complicated optimization problems.

Keywords: immune algorithm, clonal selection, evolution strategy, parallel evolution.

1 Introduction

Recently, a lot of immune operators have been presented on the basis of various immune mechanisms to better the performance of Evolutionary Algorithm (EA) [1]. In the field of machine learning, multi-modal function optimization is very complicated because of frequent variable coupling. As a result, searching mechanism of the traditional Artificial Immune System Algorithm (AISA) is not perfect. It is of poor local search capacity and insufficient parallelism inherent, which restrains the improvement of searching efficiency [2][3].

In order to overcome the weakness of AISA, a novel immune algorithm, PIES, is put forward. According to antibody-antigen affinity, original antibody population is divided into two subgroups, low-affinity one and high-affinity one. Correspondingly, two operators, Elitist Clonal Operator (ECO) and Super Mutation Operator (SMO), are proposed. The former is adopted to improve the local search ability while the latter is used to maintain the population diversity. Thus, population evolution can be actualized by concurrently operating ECO and SMO.

2 Adaptive Parallel Immune Evolutionary Strategy

2.1 The Clonal Selection Theory

Clonal Selection Theory was put forward by Burnet in 1958. Its main points are as follows: when biological immune system is exposed to invading antigen, B cells of

Y. Wang, Y. Cheung, and H. Liu (Eds.): CIS 2006, LNAI 4456, pp. 202–208, 2007.

high affinity with antigen-antibody are selected to proliferate, clone and hyper-mutate so that B cells with higher affinity in local scope can be searched; At the same time, phenomenon of receptor editing takes place among the B Cells with low antigen-antibody affinity, so they can be mutated into some points far away from the original one in the shape space, which is conducive to search B cells with high affinity. Besides, some B Cells are dead and replaced by the new ones generated from bone marrow to maintain the population diversity. After many generations of evolution and selection, B cells with very high affinity are produced finally, which are further differentiated into plasma cells, generating a lot of antibodies having the same shape with receptors to annihilate the antigens [4][5].

2.2 Elitist Clonal Operator

In the study of parallel immune evolutionary algorithm, the commonly method of population partition and manipulation of evolutionary operators is very simple [3][6][7].

In this paper, a different method of population partition is proposed. The original population is divided into two subgroups, of which, one has high affinity, above the average, and the other has sub-average affinity. These two operators are complementary to obtain the optimal antibodies.

The parallel operation mechanism of PIES is that Elitist Clone Operator (ECO) is designed according to the phenomena of B Cell clonal expansion and hyper-mutation, whereas Super Mutation Operator (SMO) is designed according to the phenomena of Receptor editing phenomenon.

The current population P_k is a N dimension vector, and $P_K = \{a_1, a_2, ..., a_N\}$. Real coding method is adopted here, and antibody code length is L. After computing antibody affinity, antibody population is divided into two subgroups, A_k and B_k, in accordance with ECO and SMO. From P_k to P_{k+1}, evolutionary process will be shown in Fig. 1.

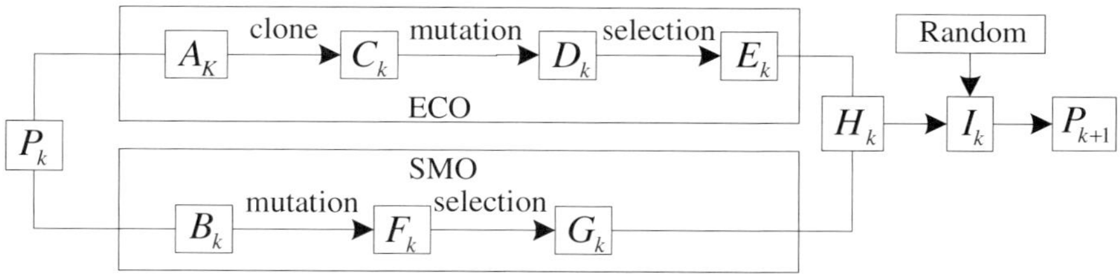

Fig. 1. Population evolution chart

In the population A_k, an individual a_i will be divided into q_i antibodies, $\bar{f}$ is the average affinity of the population P_k. The steps of ECO are described as follows:

Clone: A_k is defined as follows:

$$A_k = \{a_i | f(a_i) \geq \bar{f}, i \in N\}. \tag{1}$$

Where q_i is defined as:

$$q_i = Int(C * P_i)\,, i = 1,2,...,M\,. \tag{2}$$

q_i is adjusted to being adaptable according to C and p_i. The constant C is a given integer related to the clonal size. $Int(*)$ rounds the elements of X to the integers nearest towards infinity and $Int(X)$ returns to be the smallest integer bigger than X. Here, p_i, the probability of antibody a_i, produces new antibodies, it is as:

$$P_i = f(i) \Big/ \sum_{j=1}^{M} f(j)\,,\ i = 1,2,...,M\,. \tag{3}$$

After population clone, C_k replaces the population A_k.

Mutation: In the conventional evolutionary strategy, Gaussian mutation is widely adopted. Some researches show that search performance of adaptive mean mutation operator is better than that of Gauss mutation operator in the state of serious coupling variable of mutli-modal function [8][9].

In the population C_k, the corresponding updating equation of positional parameters is given by:

$$a'_i(j) = a_i(j) + \alpha'_i(j)[C_j(0,1) + \beta'_i(j)N_j(0,1)]\,. \tag{4}$$

$a'_i(j)$, $a_i(j)$, $\alpha'_i(j)$ and $\beta'_i(j)$ denote the jth component of the vector a'_i, a_i, α'_i and β'_i, respectively. $C(0,1)$ denotes a Cauchy random number centered at zero with a scale parameter of 1, $C_j(0,1)$ indicates that the random number is generated anew for each value of j. $N_j(0,1)$ denotes a normally distributed one-dimensional random number with mean zero and standard deviation one, $N_j(0,1)$ indicates that the random number is generated anew for each value of j. $\alpha'_i(j)$ plays the role of overall standard deviation, and $\beta'_i(j)$ determines the shape of the probability of density function.

Clonal selection: in E_k, $\forall\ i = 1,2,...,M$, if $e_i = \{a'_{ij} \,|\, \max f(a'_{ij}), j = 1,2,...,q_i\}$, and

$$f(e_i) > f(a_i)\,, a_i \in A_k\,. \tag{5}$$

Then antibody e_i replaces the antibody a_i in the original population A_k.

The nature of ECO is to search a neighborhood of the single antibody and then find an optimum in this neighborhood to replace the original single antibody. Thereby the local search capacity of the algorithm is enhanced so that the problems can be better solved.

2.3 Super Mutation Operator

All individuals of the population B_k have sub-average affinity:

$$B_k = \{a_{ij}\},\quad i = 1,2,...,S\,, S = N - M\,, j = 1,2,...,L\,. \tag{6}$$

S represents the population size. Real coding method is adopted and L stands for the antibody encoding length. Here, a_{ij} is the jth component of the antibody a_i . Uniform mutation is adopted in SMO to change population information. A simple formula is as follows:

$$a_{ij}^{'} = a_{ij} + \Delta_j \beta_j Rand(0,1)\ ,\ j = 1,2,...,L\ . \tag{7}$$

Here, β_j is a parameter, which makes the search region become more and more narrow. j is a recurrent number and $Rand(0,1) \in [0,1]$ is a uniform random variable. Δ_j is shown as follows:

$$\Delta_j = \begin{cases} a_{ij,\min} - a_{ij}, & if \quad Rand(0,1) < 0.5 \\ a_{ij,\max} - a_{ij}, & if \quad Rand(0.1) \geq 0.5 \end{cases} . \tag{8}$$

Every time when Δ_j is selected, a new $a_{ij}^{'}$ is produced, which is located in $[a_{ij,\min}, a_{ij,\max}]$. With the recurrent number j increasing and β_j decreasing simultaneously, the search region is compressed gradually.

Why uniform mutation is adopted instead of Gaussian mutation in SMO? The reason is that uniform mutation can search further space around the original antibody than Gauss mutation operator can do. However, which is more helpful to maintain the population diversity?

After the mutation and selection operation, G_k replaces the population B_k . G_k is incorporated into the population E_k , then H_k is produced. After sorting on the grounds of the population affinity, I_k replaces H_k . In the population I_k , new members produced randomly replace the antibodies with poor affinity. The number of new members is $Int(\eta N)$ in which η is usually 0.1~0.15 and N stands for the population size. Accordingly, P_{k+1} replaces P_k .

3 Experimental Results

3.1 Function Optimization Experiments

In order to analyze the performance of PIES, four standard testing functions are involved. The results are compared with that of conventional evolutionary strategy algorithm (CESA) and immune monoclonal strategy algorithm (IMSA) [10].

$$f_1(x,y) = 4x^2 - 2.1x^4 + \frac{1}{3}x^6 + xy - 4y^2 + 4y^4\ ,\ x, y \in [-5,5]\ . \tag{9}$$

$$f_2(x,y) = 100\sum_{i}^{n-1}(x_{i+1} - x_i^2)^2 + (x_i - 1)^2\ ,\ x, y \in [-10,10]\ . \tag{10}$$

$$f_3(x,y) = nA + \sum_{i}^{n}(x_i^2 - A\cos(2\pi x_i))\ ,\ x \in [-5.12,5.12]\ . \tag{11}$$

Where A is a given constant, setting $A = 10$.

In order to compare the performance of these three algorithms, the parameter setting method is similar to the reference [10]. When f_1 is tested, the population size of CESA is 100 while that of IMSA and PIES is 50. The clonal size constant C is 100, the probability of mutation, 0.1, the maximal generation, 500. The optimized accuracy of f_1 is 0.001. When the function f_2 and f_3 are tested, maximal generation is 1000 and the optimized accuracy is 0.01 and 0.001 respectively.

Table 1. The optimization results for f_1

	CESA	IMSA	PIES
Max gens	163	90	46
Min gens	20	65	22
Mean gens	98.1	81.3	26.7
Time per gen	0.0189	0.0219	0.0376

Table 2. The optimization results for f_2

	IMSA	PIES		
	n=5	n=5	n=10	n=30
Max gens	568	46	93	286
Min gens	224	21	51	161
Mean gens	390.5	33.1	73.4	192.4
Time per gen	0.2382	0.4722	0.6723	1.6543

Table 3. The optimization results for f_3

	IMSA		PIES		
	n=5	n=10	n=5	n=10	n=30
Max gens	136	322	49	56	163
Min gens	81	210	26	32	53
Mean gens	121.7	253.5	38.4	43.2	113.4
Time per gen	0.3362	0.4020	0.5682	0.7656	1.6564

The optimization results comparison of three algorithms are shown in the three tables respectively. Three algorithms are run for 10 times with different initial population and the results are the needed maximal generations (Maxgens), minimum generations (Min gens) and mean generations (Mean gens).

It is obvious to see from Table 1 that PIES evaluates function value within less generation compared with CESA and IMSA, which indicates that the convergent speed of PIES is quicker. The reason is that parallel operation makes PIES search more solution space within fewer generations. In the Table 2 and Table 3, it is clear to observe that the search performance of PIES is better than that of CESA and IMSA.

Figure.2 and Figure.3 are the optimization results of f_2 and f_3, which are the curves of the average function value versus evolutionary generations. As generations increase, a series of local optimums are obtained. Experiment shows that the number of local optimums of PIES is more than that of IMSA. For example, while PIES is running, 10 local optimums of the function are obtained. However, while IMSA is running, only 6 local optimums are obtained.

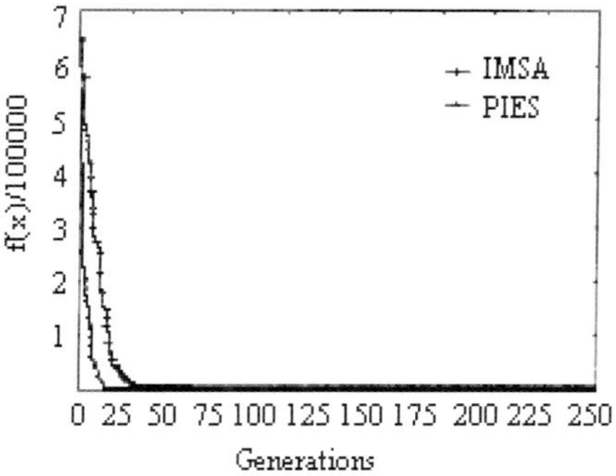

Fig. 2. Optimization results of f_3

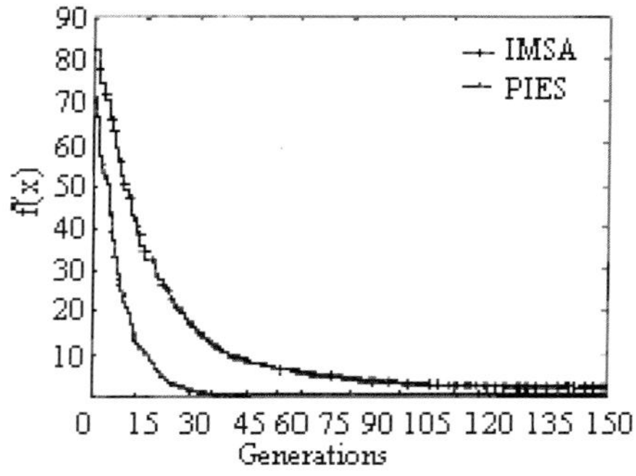

Fig. 3. Optimization results of f_4

3.2 TSP Optimization

TSP is a typical NP problem. Compared with CESA, PIES is employed in the optimization problem of 20 cities. The coordinates of 20 cities are produced randomly between $[0, 20]$. Despite of different starting point, both CESA and PIES can finally exhibit the same optimal route. The curves of optimal solutions versus generations are shown in Figure 4.

The population size of both CESA and PIES is 100 and the maximal evolutionary generations of them are 1000. These two algorithms run 20 times each. CESA can find the optimal route 13 times, and the average length of optimal route is 89.3. PIES can find the optimal route 19 times with an average length, 86.4. Fig. 4 shows that search ability of PIES is better than that of CESA in solving TSP optimization problem.

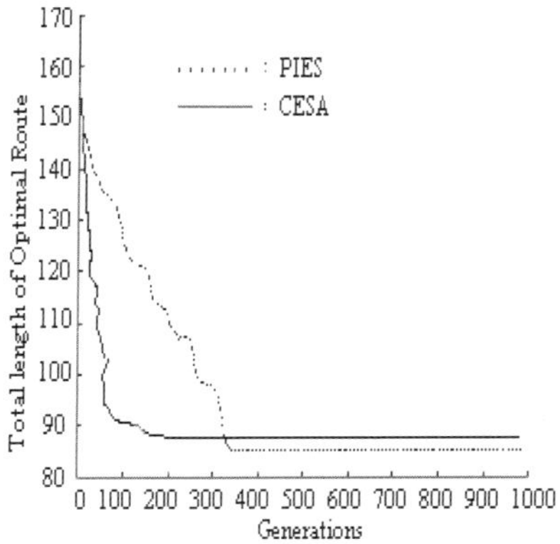

Fig. 4. Optimal solutions versus generations

4 Conclusions

Based on the clonal selection theory, two new immune operators, Elitist Clone Operator and Super Mutation Operator are designed. Experiment shows that parallel operation mechanism of ECO and SMO is successful, which can improve the local search ability of algorithm and maintain the population diversity. Some numeric experiments and TSP optimization indicate that the new algorithm can prevent premature convergence. And also, it can be adopted to solve some complicated optimization problems.

References

1. Iiu, R., Du, H., Jiao, L.: Immunity Clonal Strategy. In: Fifth International Conference on Computational Intelligence and Multimedia Applications (ICCIMA'03), pp. 290–295 (2003)
2. Watkins, A., Timmis, J.: Exploiting Parallelism Inherent in AIRS, an Artificial Immune Classifier. In: Nicosia, G., Cutello, V., Bentley, P. (eds.) The 3rd International Conference on Artificial Immune Systems, pp. 427–438. Springer-Verlag, Berlin, Heidel berg (2004)
3. KongYu, Y., XiuFeng, W.: Research and Implement of Adaptive Multimodal Immune Evolution Algorithm. Control and Decision 20(6), 717–720 (2005)
4. De Castro, L.N., Von Zuben, F.J.: Learning and Optimization Using the Clonal Selection Principle. IEEE Transactions on Evolutionary Computation 6(3), 239–251 (2002)
5. Ada, G.L., Nossal, G.: The Clonal Selection Theory. Scientific American 257(2), 50–57 (1987)
6. Xiangjun, W., Dou, J., Min, Z.: A Multi-Subgroup Competition Evolutionary Programming Algorithm. Acta Electronica Sinica 11(32), 1824–1828 (2004)
7. Yin-sheng, L., Ren-hou, L., Weixi, Z.: Multi-modal Functions Parallel Optimization Algorithm Based on Immune Mechanism. Journal of System Simulation 2(11), 319–322 (2005)
8. Chellapillal, K., Fogel, D.: Two New Mutation Operators for Enhanced Search and Optimization in Evolutionary Programming. In: Dikaiakos, M.D. (ed.) Applications of Soft Computing. SPIE. LNCS, vol. 3165, pp. 260–269. Springer, Heidelberg (2004)
9. Lavine, B.K. (ed.): Pattern Recognition Analysis via Genetic Algorithm & Multivariate Statistical Methods, vol. 315, pp. 145–148. CRC Press, Boca Raton Fla (2000)
10. Ruochen, L., Haifeng, D., Licheng, J.: An Immune Monoclonal Strategy Algorithm. Acta Electronica Sinica 11(32), 1880–1884 (2004)

About the Time Complexity of Evolutionary Algorithms Based on Finite Search Space

Lixin Ding[1] and Yingzhou Bi[1,2]

[1] State Key Lab of Software Engineering, Wuhan University, Wuhan 430072, China
lxding@whu.edu.cn

[2] Department of Information Technology, Guangxi Teachers Education University, Nanning 530001, China
byzhou@163.com

Abstract. We consider some problems about the computation time of evolutionary algorithms in this paper. First, some exact analytic expressions of the mean first hitting times of general evolutionary algorithms in finite search spaces are obtained theoretically by using the properties of Markov chain associated with evolutionary algorithms considered here. Then, by introducing drift analysis and applying Dynkin's Formula, the general upper and lower bounds of the mean first hitting times of evolutionary algorithms are estimated rigorously under some mild conditions listed in the paper. Those results in this paper are commonly useful. Also, the analytic techniques adopted in the paper are widely instructive for analyzing the computation time of evolutionary algorithms in a given search space as long as some specific mathematical arts are introduced accordingly.

1 Introduction

The computation time of evolutionary algorithms (EAs for brevity) for solving optimization problems is an important research topic in the foundations and theory of EAs, which reveals the number of expected generations needed to reach an optimal solution[1,2]. In the last over ten years, some progresses have been made towards this direction: Bäck[3] and Mühlenbein[4] studied the time complexity of EAs based on the simple *ONE-MAX problem*. Rudolph[5] gave a comprehensive survey of the theoretical work up to 1997 and provided an $O(n \log n)$ upper bound for the $(1+1)-$EA using the 1-bit-flip mutation for *ONE-MAX problem*. Garnier et al[6] compared two different mutations in $(1+1)-$EAs when they are applied to the *ONE-MAX problem*, and obtained the different bounds on the EA's average computation time, respectively. Droste et al[7,8] improved these results and generalized them to any linear binary functions for the $(1+1)-$EA. Some *long path problems* in unimodal functions have also proved to be solvable in polynomial time[9,10]. It is quite worth mentioning He and Yao, who have done a series of works about the computation time and the time complexity for several kinds of EAs based on different optimization problems[11−16].

Y. Wang, Y. Cheung, and H. Liu (Eds.): CIS 2006, LNAI 4456, pp. 209–219, 2007.

Markov chain models have been used widely in the theoretical analysis of EAs[17−19]. Although the drift analysis introduced from stochastic process is a very useful technique in estimating computation time and time complexity of stochastic algorithms[20,11−16], most of previous theoretical results still focused on some simple evolutionary algorithms and optimization problems, such as $(1+1)-$EAs, $(N+N)-$EAs, *ONE-MAX problem*, linear fitness functions, and the like because of the analytic difficulties on this topic. It is important for us to develop new mathematical methods and tools to analyze rigorously more general EAs based on wider problem fields.

In this paper, we consider a Markov chain associated with a general EA based on a finite search space. By introducing the definition of the first hitting time of EAs, some exact analytic expressions of the mean first hitting times of EAs are obtained. The other results in this paper concern with the general upper and lower bounds of the mean first hitting times of EAs, which are also obtained by applying Dynkin's Formula and some essential analytic techniques[21].

The remaining parts of this paper are organized as follows. In section 2, we describe the formalization models of EAs. In section 3, we obtain some exact analytic expressions of the mean first hitting times of EAs. In section 4, we give the general upper and lower bounds of the mean first hitting times of EAs. In the final section, we conclude the paper with a short discussion and suggest some key open problems which are necessary to be solved urgently in the field of the time complexity of EAs in the future.

2 Description of the EA

In this paper, we consider the following optimization problem: Given an objective function with upper bound, $f : S \to R$, where S is a finite search space and R is the real line, a maximization problem is to find a $x^* \in S$ such that

$$f(x^*) = \max\{f(x) : x \in S\}. \tag{1}$$

We call x^* an **optimal solution** and write $f_{\max} = f(x^*)$ for convenience. If there are more than one optimal solution, then denote the set of all optimal solutions by S^*, and call it an **optimal solution set**.

The formalization model of evolutionary algorithms with the population size N for solving the optimization problem (1) can be generally described as follows.

Step 1. Initialize, either randomly or heuristically, an initial population of N individuals, denoted it by $\xi_0 = (\xi_0(1), \cdots, \xi_0(N))$, where $\xi_0(i) \in S, i = 1, \cdots, N$, and let $k = 0$.

Step 2. Generate a new (intermediate) population by adopting the so-called genetic operators (or any other stochastic operators for generating offsprings), and denote it by $\xi_{k+1/2}$.

Step 3. Select and reproduce N individuals from population $\xi_{k+1/2}$ and ξ_k according to certain survivor strategy or mechanism, and obtain the next population ξ_{k+1}, then go to step 2.

In the above algorithm, we always write $f(\xi_k) = \max\{f(\xi_k(i)) : 1 \leq i \leq N\}$, $\forall k = 0, 1, 2, \cdots$, if it does not bring confusion.

It is well known that $\{\xi_k; k \geq 0\}$ is a Markov chain on the **state space** S^N because the state of the $(k+1)-th$ generation often depends only on the $k-th$ generation[1].

Let $d'(\cdot)$ be a given non-negative **test function defined on** S. Usually, d' is regarded as the **distance** between the individual and the optimal solution(or optimal solution set). For example, we can define it by $f_{\max} - f(\cdot)$ in the problem (1). For a population $\xi = (\xi(1), \cdots, \xi(N)) \in S^N$, define

$$d(\xi) = \min\{d'(\xi(i)) : i = 1, \cdots, N\}. \tag{2}$$

Then d is also a non-negative **test function defined on** S^N and it is used to measure the distance between the population and the **optimal population (or optimal population set)**, where the optimal populations refer to those that include at least an optimal solution and the optimal population set consists of all the optimal populations. The optimal population set with respect to d is defined by

$$(S_d^N)^* = \{\xi \in S^N : d(\xi) = 0\}. \tag{3}$$

For convenience, we write $C^* = (S_d^N)^*$. Similar to [21], **the one-step drift** of stochastic sequence $\{\xi_k; k \geq 0\}$ at time k can be defined by

$$\triangle\,(d(\xi_k)) = d(\xi_{k+1}) - d(\xi_k). \tag{4}$$

Let $N \geq 1$ be a fixed integer which represents the population size of EAs, $\mathbf{E}$ denote the expectation operator and $I_A(\cdot)$ be an index function on the set A, respectively. Write $Z^+ = \{1, 2, 3 \cdots\}$. Throughout this paper, we always assume that the stochastic process, $\{\xi_k; k \geq 0\}$, associated with the above EA, is a **finite homogeneous Markov chain**.

In the following section, we will give some exact analytic expressions of the mean first hitting times of EAs by using some basic techniques in stochastic process.

3 Some Exact Expressions of the Mean First Hitting Times

Let $\{\xi_k; k \geq 0\}$ be a homogeneous Markov chain from probability space $(\Omega, \mathcal{F}, P)$, which can support all randomization used in this paper, to state space S^N associated with an EA described in section 2. Suppose that there are m(Usually, $m = 2^n$, where n is the length of binary bit string) feasible solutions in search space S, thus we can sort all states in S^N by $s_1, s_2, \cdots, s_{m^N}$. Let $P_{m^N \times m^N} = (p_{ij})_{m^N \times m^N}$ (where p_{ij} is the transition probability from state s_i to state s_j, $i, j = 1, \cdots, m^N$) be **the transition probability matrix** and $q = (q_1, \cdots, q_{m^N})$ be **the starting distribution**, that is, $P\{\xi_0 = s_j\} = q_j, j = 1, 2, \cdots, m^N$.

In the beginning, we recall the definition of the optimal population. A population, $\xi^* = (\xi^*(1), \cdots, \xi^*(N))$, is called an optimal population in S^N, if $\xi^*(j) \in S^*$

for at least one $j(j \in \{1, \cdots, N\}$. **The first hitting time on** ξ^* can be defined by

$$\tau(\xi^*) = \min\{k \geq 0 : \xi_k = \xi^*\}. \tag{5}$$

It is obvious that, for any given optimal population ξ^*, there exists $i(i \in \{1, 2, \cdots, m^N\})$ such that $s_i = \xi^*$. Let us write P_{ξ^*} the $(m^N - 1) \times (m^N - 1)$-order matrix obtained from $P_{m^N \times m^N}$ by deleting those elements of its the i−th column and the i−th row. And let $q_{\xi^*} = (q_1, \cdots, q_{i-1}, q_{i+1}, \cdots, q_{m^N})$. Let $\mathbf{I}$ denote the $(m^N - 1) \times (m^N - 1)$ identity matrix and let $\mathbf{1} = (1, 1, \cdots, 1)'$ be the $(m^N - 1)$-dimension vector. Then we have

Theorem 1. *Let $\tau(\xi^*)$ be the number of generations for the EA to find the optimal population ξ^* for the first time. For the optimal population ξ^*, if $\mathbf{I} - P_{\xi^*}$ is invertible, then*

$$\mathbf{E}[\tau(\xi^*)] = q_{\xi^*}(\mathbf{I} - P_{\xi^*})^{-1}\mathbf{1}. \tag{6}$$

Proof. By Markov property of $\{\xi_k; k \geq 0\}$, for any $l \geq 1$, one has

$$\begin{aligned}
P\{\tau(\xi^*) \geq l\} &= P\{\xi_0 \neq \xi^*, \xi_1 \neq \xi^*, \cdots, \xi_{l-1} \neq \xi^*\} \\
&= \sum_{y_0 \neq \xi^*, y_1 \neq \xi^*, \cdots, y_{l-1} \neq \xi^*} P\{\xi_0 = y_0, \cdots, \xi_{l-1} = y_{l-1}\} \\
&= \sum_{y_0 \neq \xi^*, y_1 \neq \xi^*, \cdots, y_{l-1} \neq \xi^*} P\{\xi_0 = y_0\} \times P\{\xi_1 = y_1 | \xi_0 = y_0\} \\
&\quad \times P\{\xi_2 = y_2 | \xi_1 = y_1\} \times \cdots \times P\{\xi_{l-1} = y_{l-1} | \xi_{l-2} = y_{l-2}\} \\
&= q_{\xi^*} P_{\xi^*}^{l-1} \mathbf{1}.
\end{aligned}$$

Hence, we have

$$\begin{aligned}
\mathbf{E}[\tau(\xi^*)] &= \sum_{k \geq 0} k \times P\{\tau(\xi^*) = k\} \\
&= \sum_{l \geq 1} P\{\tau(\xi^*) \geq l\} \\
&= q_{\xi^*} \cdot \sum_{l \geq 1} P_{\xi^*}^{l-1} \cdot \mathbf{1} \\
&= q_{\xi^*}(\mathbf{I} - P_{\xi^*})^{-1}\mathbf{1}.
\end{aligned}$$

This is our assertion. □

More generally, suppose that $C^* = \{s_{i_1}, \cdots, s_{i_r}\}(\subset S^N)$. We can define **the first hitting time on** C^* by

$$\tau(C^*) = \min\{k \geq 0 : \xi_k \in C^*\}. \tag{7}$$

Similarly, let us denote P_{C^*} the $(m^N - r) \times (m^N - r)$ matrix obtained from $P_{m^N \times m^N}$ by deleting those elements of its the i_1-th ,$\cdots$, the i_r-th columns and the i_1-th ,$\cdots$, the i_r-th rows, and $q_{C^*} = (q_1, \cdots, q_{i_1-1}, q_{i_1+1}, \cdots, q_{i_r-1}, q_{i_r+1}, \cdots, q_{m^N})$. We can get the following theorem immediately.

Theorem 2. *Let $\tau(C^*)$ be the number of generations for the population of the EA to reach the optimal population set C^* for the first time. For the optimal population set C^*, if $\mathbf{I} - P_{C^*}$ is invertible, then*

$$\mathbf{E}[\tau(C^*)] = q_{C^*}(\mathbf{I} - P_{C^*})^{-1}\mathbf{1}, \tag{8}$$

where $\mathbf{I}$ is a $(m^N - r) \times (m^N - r)$ identity matrix and $\mathbf{1} = (1, 1, \cdots, 1)'$ is a $(m^N - r)$-dimension vector.

Remark 1. In fact, for any set $A \subset S^N$, we can define the first hitting time on A, and at this time Theorem 2 still holds. In addition, although each optimal solution corresponds to many optimal populations which contain this optimal solution, Theorem 1 is still without losing the meaning in theory and practice. Usually, the equation (5) is more suitable for the $(1+1)-$EAs than the equation (7), while the latter is usually used in the case of the population size $N > 1$.

In the above theorems, we only consider the unconditional expectations of random variables $\tau(\xi^*)$ and $\tau(C^*)$, which can be regarded as the expressions of the mean first hitting times for the EAs to find an optimal population under any initialization. By using the same method as the above, we can obtain the expressions of the conditional expectations $\mathbf{E}[\tau(\xi^*)|\xi_0 = X]$ and $\mathbf{E}[\tau(C^*)|\xi_0 = X]$, for any $X \in S^N$, respectively.

For any optimal population ξ^* and $X \in S^N (X \neq \xi^*)$, there exist i and $j(i, j \in \{1, \cdots, m^N\})$such that $\xi^* = s_i$ and $X = s_j$. Let v_{X,ξ^*} be the $(m^N - 1)$-dimension vector obtained from the $j-$th row of $P_{m^N \times m^N}$ by deleting the $i-$th element of this row. P_{ξ^*}, $\mathbf{I}$ and $\mathbf{1}$ are the same as the theorem 1. Then we have the following theorem.

Theorem 3. *Let $\tau(\xi^*)$ be the number of generations for the EA to find the optimal population ξ^* for the first time. For the optimal population ξ^*, if both P_{ξ^*} and $\mathbf{I} - P_{\xi^*}$ are invertible, then*

$$\mathbf{E}[\tau(\xi^*)|\xi_0 = X] = \begin{cases} v_{X,\xi^*}(P_{\xi^*})^{-1}(\mathbf{I} - P_{\xi^*})^{-1}\mathbf{1}, & X \neq \xi^* \\ 0, & X = \xi^* \end{cases} \tag{9}$$

Proof. By Markov property of $\{\xi_k; k \geq 0\}$, for any $l \geq 1$ and $X \neq \xi^*$, we have

$$\begin{aligned}
&P[\tau(\xi^*) \geq l|\xi_0 = X] \\
&= \frac{P(\xi_0 = X, \xi_1 \neq \xi^*, \cdots, \xi_{l-1} \neq \xi^*)}{P(\xi_0 = X)} \\
&= \sum_{y_1 \neq \xi^*, \cdots, y_{l-1} \neq \xi^*} \frac{P(\xi_0 = X, \xi_1 = y_1, \cdots, \xi_{l-1} = y_{l-1})}{P(\xi_0 = X)} \\
&= \sum_{y_1 \neq \xi^*, \cdots, y_{l-1} \neq \xi^*} P(\xi_1 = y_1|\xi_0 = X) \times P(\xi_2 = y_2|\xi_1 = y_1) \\
&\quad \times \cdots \times P(\xi_{l-1} = y_{l-1}|\xi_{l-2} = y_{l-2}) \\
&= v_{X,\xi^*} P_{\xi^*}^{l-2}\mathbf{1}.
\end{aligned}$$

Hence, by using the same technique as Thm 1, it is easy for us to get

$$\mathbf{E}[\tau(\xi^*)|\xi_0 = X] = \begin{cases} v_{X,\xi^*}(P_{\xi^*})^{-1}(\mathbf{I} - P_{\xi^*})^{-1}\mathbf{1}, & X \neq \xi^* \\ 0, & X = \xi^* \end{cases}$$

Our prof is complete. □

Similarly, for $X = s_j$ and $C^* = \{s_{i_1}, s_{i_2}, \cdots, s_{i_r}\}$, let v_{X,C^*} be the $(m^N - r)-$dimension vector obtained from the $j-$th row of $P_{m^N \times m^N}$ by deleting those the i_1-th, the i_2-th, $\cdots$, the i_r-th elements of this row. P_{C^*}, $\mathbf{I}$ and $\mathbf{1}$ are the same as the theorem 2. Then, we have the following theorem immediately.

Theorem 4. *Let $\tau(C^*)$ be the number of generations for the population of the EA to reach the set C^* for the first time. For the optimal population set C^*, if both P_{C^*} and $\mathbf{I} - P_{C^*}$ are invertible, then*

$$\mathbf{E}[\tau(C^*)|\xi_0 = X] = \begin{cases} v_{X,C^*}(P_{C^*})^{-1}(\mathbf{I} - P_{C^*})^{-1}\mathbf{1}, & X \notin C^* \\ 0, & X \in C^* \end{cases} \tag{10}$$

Remark 2. For the EAs based on general search space S, we also have the expressions similar to the above theorems, in which the operators will substitute the corresponding matrixes, respectively.

4 The Upper and Lower Bounds of the Mean First Hitting Times

Note that the sequence $\{d(\xi_k) : k = 0, 1, 2, \cdots\}$ generated by the EA is also a homogeneous Markov chain, where $d(\cdot)$ is defined in (2). By (3) and (7), the first hitting time on C^* with respect to the test function $d(\cdot)$ is also defined by

$$\tau(C^*) = \min\{k \geq 0 : \xi_k \in C^*\} = \min\{k \geq 0 : d(\xi_k) = 0\}. \tag{11}$$

We will impose some constraints on the one-step drift $\triangle(d(\xi_k))$ in order to obtain the upper and lower bounds of $\mathbf{E}[\tau(C^*)|\xi_0 = X]$. Some other marks and definitions should be stated aforehand.

Let $\{\mathcal{F}_n^\xi, n \geq 0\}$ be the σ-algebra given by $\xi_0, \xi_1, \cdots, \xi_n$. By Proposition 3.4.4 in [21], $\tau(C^*)$ is a **stopping time** with respect to $\sigma-$algebra sequence $\{\mathcal{F}_n^\xi : n \geq 0\}$. For any $C \subset S^N$, define $\sigma_C = \min\{n \geq 1 : \xi_n \in C\}$, which is **the first return time on** C. **Dynkin's Formula** was usually used to study the upper bound of the mean first return time by controlling the one-step average increment. In this paper, we will use it to estimate the upper and lower bounds of $\tau(C^*)$. For stopping time $\tau(C^*)$ (τ for brevity in the following)defined in (11), we write

$$\tau^n = \min\{\tau, n, \inf\{k \geq 0 : d(\xi_k) \geq n\}\}, \quad \forall n \in Z^+.$$

Obviously, τ^n is also a stopping time.

Before giving our main results of this section, we first introduce some fundamental conclusions on the drift analysis of Markov chains in [21], which will be used in our proofs essentially.

Lemma 1 ((Dynkin's Formula)). *For any* $X \in S^N$ *and* $n \in Z^+$,

$$\mathbf{E}[d(\xi_{\tau^n})|\xi_0 = X] = d(X) + \mathbf{E}[\sum_{i=1}^{\tau^n}(\mathbf{E}[d(\xi_i)|\mathcal{F}_{i-1}^{\xi}] - d(\xi_{i-1}))|\xi_0 = X]. \tag{12}$$

Remark 3. If d is a test function from $S^N \to [0, \infty)$, then (12) still holds for stopping time $\tau_n = \min\{\tau, n\}$ when n is large enough. In fact, the test function $d(\cdot)$ defined in (2) is non-negative bounded when the state space S^N is finite. Otherwise, a necessary restriction, $\sup_{X \in S^N} d(X) < \infty$, must be imposed on it.

In the following, we need to state another related result in [21], which is

Lemma 2. *Suppose that there exists some constant* $b < \infty$ *and an extended real-valued function* $d : S^N \to [0, \infty]$ *such that*

$$\mathbf{E}[d(\xi_1) - d(\xi_0)|\xi_0 = X] \leq -1 + bI_C(X), \quad X \in S^N,$$

for the set $C \subset S^N$. *Then*

$$\mathbf{E}[\sigma_C|\xi_0 = X] \leq d(X) + bI_C(X).$$

According to the above lemma 2, we can get the following theorem immediately.

Theorem 5. *Let* τ *be the number of generations for the population of the EA to reach the optimal population set* C^* *for the first time. Suppose the test function* d *satisfies the following condition*

$$\mathbf{E}[d(\xi_1) - d(\xi_0)|\xi_0 = X] \leq -a + bI_{C^*}(X), \quad X \in S^N, \tag{C1}$$

for the constants $a > 0$ *and* $b < \infty$. *Then*

$$\mathbf{E}[\tau|\xi_0 = X] \begin{cases} \leq d(X)/a, & X \in S^N \backslash C^* \\ = 0, & X \in C^* \end{cases}$$

In the following, we still put our interests on the special set C^* and give the lower bound for the first hitting time on C^*. Dynkin's Formula and other mild conditions on one-step drift are still necessary. Our result is

Theorem 6. *Let* τ *be the number of generations for the population of the EA to reach the optimal population set* C^* *for the first time. Suppose the test function* d *satisfies that*

$$-a_2 + a_2 I_{C^*}(X) \leq \mathbf{E}[d(\xi_1) - d(\xi_0)|\xi_0 = X] \leq -a_1 + a_1 I_{C^*}(X), \quad X \in S^N, \tag{C2}$$

for any $X \in S^N$ *and the positive constants* a_1, a_2. *Then*

$$\mathbf{E}[\tau|\xi_0 = X] \begin{cases} \geq d(X)/a_2, & X \in S^N \backslash C^* \\ = 0, & X \in C^* \end{cases}$$

Proof. Since $\{\xi_k; k \geq 0\}$ is homogenous Markov chain, it implies that if $\mathbf{E}[d(\xi_1) - d(\xi_0)|\xi_0 = X]$ satisfies **(C1)** and **(C2)**, then $\mathbf{E}[d(\xi_{k+1}) - d(\xi_k)|\xi_k = x]$ satisfies **(C1)** and **(C2)** for all $k \geq 1$. Note that if $\omega \in \{\xi_k = X\}$, then we have

$$\mathbf{E}[d(\xi_{k+1})|\mathcal{F}_k^{\xi}](\omega) = \mathbf{E}[d(\xi_{k+1})|\xi_k = X].$$

Write $Q_k = \bigcup_{X \in S^N \setminus C^*} \{\omega : \xi_k = X\}$, then we have

$$\begin{aligned}
\mathbf{E}d(\xi_{k+1}) &= \mathbf{E}[\mathbf{E}[d(\xi_{k+1})|\xi_k]] \\
&= \int_{Q_k} + \int_{\Omega \setminus Q_k} \mathbf{E}[d(\xi_{k+1})|\xi_k] dP \\
&\leq \int_{Q_k} (d(\xi_k) - a_1) dP + \int_{\Omega \setminus Q_k} d(\xi_k) dP \\
&= \mathbf{E}d(\xi_k) - a_1 P(Q_k).
\end{aligned}$$

By induction on k, we have

$$0 \leq \mathbf{E}d(\xi_{k+1}) \leq \mathbf{E}d(\xi_0) - \sum_{i=0}^{k} a_1 P(Q_k), \forall k \geq 1.$$

Hence, we must have

$$P(Q_k) \to 0 \qquad as \quad k \to \infty. \tag{13}$$

Since the state space is finite, (13) implies that

$$\mathbf{E}d(\xi_k) \to 0 \qquad as \quad k \to \infty.$$

So

$$\mathbf{E}[d(\xi_k)|\xi_0 = X] = \frac{\int_{\xi_0 = X} d(\xi_k) dP}{P(\xi_0 = X)} \leq \frac{\mathbf{E}d(\xi_k)}{P(\xi_0 = X)} \to 0 \qquad as \quad k \to \infty. \tag{14}$$

By the hypotheses of Thm 6 and Dynkin's Formula, we know that if $X \in S^N \setminus C^*$, then we have

$$\begin{aligned}
a_2 \mathbf{E}[\tau^n|\xi_0 = X] &\geq d(X) - \mathbf{E}[d(\xi_{\tau^n})|\xi_0 = X] \\
&\geq d(X) - \mathbf{E}[d(\xi_\tau)|\xi_0 = X] - \mathbf{E}[d(\xi_n)|\xi_0 = X] \\
&= d(X) - \mathbf{E}[d(\xi_n)|\xi_0 = X], \quad \forall n \in Z^+.
\end{aligned}$$

Note that $\tau^n \uparrow \tau (n \to \infty)$. By Monotone Convergence Theorem and (14), it follows that

$$\mathbf{E}[\tau|\xi_0 = X] \geq d(X)/a_2, \qquad X \in S^N \setminus C^*.$$

In addition, it is easy to know that $\mathbf{E}[\tau|\xi_0 = X] = 0$, for $X \in C^*$, from the definition of τ. This completes our proof. □

From the proof of Thm 6, we can get the following proposition immediately.

Proposition 1. *If there exists set $C \subset S^N$ such that the test function d satisfies*

$$-a_2 + b_2 I_C(X) \leq \mathbf{E}[d(\xi_1) - d(\xi_0)|\xi_0 = X] \leq -a_1 + b_1 I_C(X), \quad X \in S^N, \ (\mathbf{C3})$$

for any $X \in S^N$ and the constants $b_1 \geq a_1 > 0, a_2 > 0$ and $b_2 < \infty$. Then

$$P(\Omega \backslash Q_k(C)) \to a_1/b_1, \qquad k \to \infty,$$

where $Q_k(C) = \bigcup_{X \in S^N \backslash C} \{\omega : \xi_k = X\}$.

Remark 4. We can use a result in [21] to explain the condition **(C1)**. According to [21], if $\mathbf{E}[d(\xi_1) - d(\xi_0)|\xi_0 = X] \geq 0$ for $X \in S^N \backslash C^*$, then the mean first hitting times, $\mathbf{E}[\tau|\xi_0 = X]$, are infinite for $X \in S^N \backslash C^*$. Hence, the condition **(C1)** is necessary for the upper bound. The condition **(C2)** says that if EA reaches the optimal population set at the nth step, then at the next step, i.e. at the $(n+1)$th step, EA still remains in the optimal population set. Moreover, in order to get the lower bound, the one-step drift must be bounded from both sides. Hence, the condition **(C2)** is reasonable. In addition, it is obvious that the condition **(C2)** implies the condition **(C1)**.

Remark 5. Proposition 1 tells us that under the condition **(C3)**, the probability which ξ_k reaches the set C tends to a fixed constant a_1/b_1 as the number of generations $k \to \infty$. Note that Proposition 1 does not imply the convergence of the EAs under the sense of probability if $a_1 \neq b_1$.

5 Conclusions and Discussions

This paper has given some general results about the time complexity of EAs, which have great importance in theory and practice. More important, some analytic techniques and methods used in this paper, which may supply the researchers in the area of EA-theory the uses of references, are foundational and even essential for investigating the time complexity problems in EAs.

This paper has shown that Markov chain is a convenient model which can be used to describe the EAs and that drift analysis is a practical means which is useful to estimate the computation time of EAs. In the meantime, it has also implied that some more profound results about the computation time of EAs can be derived by using the drift analysis and other tools in stochastic process theory.

As mentioned in [15], drift analysis reduces the behavior of EAs in a higher dimensional population space S^N into a super-martingale on the one-dimensional space by the introduction of a distance function for the population space. This makes the theoretical analysis much simpler than analyzing the original Markov chain associated with the EAs. The key point in applying drift analysis is to define a good test function on the population space S^N.

It can be seen from this paper that the application of Dynkin's Formula is a key technique in order to obtain a rigorous theoretical analysis, which has not been used in the previously related works.

The application of drift analysis to studying computation time and time complexity of EAs is still at its early days. A number of problems are still open: How to describe the relation between the time complexity and the space complexity(which is related to both problem size and population size.)? In a given kind of problems, how to apply the general results obtained in this paper to analyze the time complexity of different EAs? How to show the time complexity of a given EA which is used in the different kind of problems? What is the relation between the time complexity and the precision of $\varepsilon-$optimal solution? How to classify definitely both the EA-hard problems and the EA-easy problems? Why is it important to investigate the computational dynamics properties associated with the time complexity of EAs? More essential, whether there is a kind of EAs which can be used to solve(or under the sense of $\varepsilon-$optimum) a NP-problem within the polynomial time theoretically or not? All these problems are well worth being investigated in the field of the time complexity of EAs in the future.

Acknowledgments. This work is supported in part by the National Natural Science Foundation of China(Grant no. 60204001), Chengguang Project of Science and Technology for the Young Scholar in Wuhan City (Grant no. 20025001002) and the Youthful Outstanding Scholars Foundation in Hubei Prov. (Grant no. 2005ABB017).

References

1. Rudolph, G.: Finite Markov chain results in evolutionary computation: A tour d'Horizon. Fundamenta Informaticae 35, 67–89 (1998)
2. Eiben, A.E., Rudolph, G.: Theory of evolutionary algorithms: A bird's eye view. Theoretical Computer Science 229, 3–9 (1999)
3. Bäck, T.: The interaction of mutation rate, selection and self-adaption within a genetic algorithm. In: PPSN-II Conference Proceedings. pp. 85–94 (1992)
4. Mühlenbein, H.: How genetic algorithms really works I: Mutation and hill-climbing. PPSN-II Conference Proceedings. pp. 15–25 (1992)
5. Rudolph, G.: Convergence Properties of Evolutionary Algorithms. Ph.D. Thesis, Verlag Dr. Kovač, Hamburg (1997)
6. Garnier, J., Kallel, L., Schoenauer, M.: Rigorous hitting times for binary mutations. Evolutionary Computation 7, 173–203 (1999)
7. Droste, S., Jansen, T., Wegener, I.: A rigorous complexity analysis of the (1+1) evolutionary algorithm for linear functions with Boolean inputs. Evolutionary Computation 6, 185–196 (1998)
8. Droste, S., Jansen, T., Wegener, I.: On the analysis of the (1+1) evolutionary algorithms. Theoretical Computer Science 276, 51–81 (2002)
9. Rudolph, G.: How mutation and selection solve long path problems in polynomial expected time. Evolutionary Computation 4, 195–205 (1996)
10. Garnier, J., Kallel, L.: Statistical distribution of the convergence time of evolutionary algorithms for long path problems. IEEE Trans. on Evolutionary Computation 4, 16–30 (2000)
11. He, J., Yao, X.: Drift analysis and average time complexity of evolutionary algorithms. Artificial Intelligence 127, 57–85 (2001)

12. He, J., Yao, X.: From an individual to a population: An analysis of the first hitting time of population-based evolutionary algorithms. IEEE Trans. on Evolutionary computation 6, 495–511 (2002)
13. He, J., Yao, X.: Towards an analytic framework for analyzing the computation time of evolutionary algorithms. Artificial Intelligence 145, 59–97 (2003)
14. He, J., Yao, X.: An analysis of evolutionary algorithms for finding approximation solutions to hard optimisation problems. In: Proc. of CEC pp. 2004–2010 (2003)
15. He, J., Yao, X.: A study of drift analysis for estimating computation time of evolutionary algorithms. Natural Computing 3, 21–35 (2004)
16. He, J., Yao, X.: Time complexity analysis of an evolutionary algorithm for finding nearly maximum cardinality matching. Journal of Computer science & Technology 19, 450–458 (2004)
17. Nix, A.E., Vose, M.D.: Modeling genetic algorithms with Markov chains. Ann. of Math. & Artificial Intelligence 5, 79–88 (1992)
18. Suzuki, J.: A Markov chain analysis on simple genetic algorithms. IEEE Trans. on Systems Man & Cybernetics 25, 655–659 (1995)
19. Vose, M.D.: The Simple Genetic Algorithms: Foundations and Theory. MIT Press, Cambridge (1999)
20. Sasaki, G.H., Hajek, B.: The time complexity of maximum matching by simulated annealing. J. of the ACM 35, 387–403 (1988)
21. Meyn, S.P., Tweedie, R.L.: Markov Chains and Stochastic Stability, 3rd edn. Springer-Verlag, New York (1996)

New Radial Basis Function Neural Network Training for Nonlinear and Nonstationary Signals

Seng Kah Phooi and Ang L.M

University of Nottingham, Malaysia Campus
Faculty of Engineering & Computer Science,
Jalan Broga, 43500, Semenyih, Selangor, Malaysia
jasmine.seng@nottingham.edu.my

Abstract. This paper deals with the problem of adaptation of radial basis function neural networks (RBF NN). A new RBF NN supervised training algorithm is proposed. This method possesses the distinctive properties of Lyapunov Theory-based Adaptive Filtering (LAF) in [1]-[2]. The method is different from many RBF NN training using gradient search methods. A new Lyapunov function of the error between the desired output and the RBF NN output is first defined. The output asymptotically converges to the desired output by designing the adaptation law in Lyapunov sense. Error convergence analysis in this paper has proven that the design of the new RBF NN training algorithm is independent of statistic properties of input and output signals. The new adaptation law has better tracking capability compared with the tracking performance of LAF in [1]-[2]. The performance of the proposed technique is illustrated through the adaptive prediction of nonlinear and nonstationary speech signals.

Keywords: Radial Basis Function, Neural Network, Lyapunov stability theory.

1 Introduction

Along with the multiplayer perceptron (MLP), radial basis function neural network (RBF NN) hold much interest in the current neural network literature [3]. Under certain mild conditions on the radial basis functions, the RBF NNs are capable of approximating arbitrarily well any function [4]. Therefore, this universal approximation property and straightforward computation using linearly weighted combination of single hidden layer neurons have made RBF NN, particularly the Gaussian RBF NN, natural choices in many applications.

The performance of an RBF NN depends on the number and centers of the radial basis functions, their shapes, and the method used for learning the input–output mapping. Researchers in [5] suggested that the centers could either be distributed uniformly within the region of the input space for which there is data, or selected to be a subset of the training vectors by analogy with strict interpolation. Authors in [6] proposed a hybrid learning process for training RBF NNs with Gaussian RBFs. They employed a supervised scheme for updating the output weights. An unsupervised clustering algorithm for determining the centers of the RBFs is also proposed. Centers

Y. Wang, Y. Cheung, and H. Liu (Eds.): CIS 2006, LNAI 4456, pp. 220–230, 2007.

of RBFs are often determined by the k-means (or c-means) clustering algorithm [7]. Researchers in [8] proposed a supervised method for training RBF NNs, which updates the RBF centers together with the output weights. Another learning procedure for RBF NNs based on the orthogonal least squares (OLS) method was proposed by authors in [9]. A forward regression procedure to select a suitable set of RBF centers was proposed. Researchers in [10] proposed a stochastic gradient training algorithm for RBF NNs, which uses gradient descent to update all their free parameters including centers and widths of the Gaussian RBFs, and output weights. The training of RBF NNs using gradient descent offers a solution to the tradeoff between performance and training speed and can make RBF NNs serious competitors to MLP with sigmoid hidden units [3]. As pointed in [11]-[12], the gradient descent method needs a large number of iterations to reach a neighborhood of the minimum point of the cost function. Theoretically, the gradient-based searching may be trapped at local minima of the cost function surface. Furthermore, the global minimum point may not be found if the input has a large bounded disturbance. In addition, gradient-based searching may not provide fast tracking. Due to the aforementioned problems, a new RBF NN training algorithm is desired.

Many of the physical signals encountered in practice exhibit two distinct characteristics: nonlinearity and nonstationary. For example, the production of a speech signal is known to be the result of a dynamic process that is both nonlinear and nonstationary. The traditional method of supervised learning is unsuitable because of its slow convergence or tracking. What we need is a neural network that is able to adapt to statistical variations of the incoming signal and perform continuous learning. Therefore, we need a training technique for the neural network which is able to provide fast tracking to adjust the network parameters dynamically.

In this paper, we present a complete framework to design a new RBF NN training algorithm called RBF_LAF-2, for nonlinear and nonstationary signal. The proposed methodology possesses the distinctive properties of Lyapunov Theory-based Adaptive Filtering (LAF) in [1]-[2]. Our method does not search for the global minimum point along the cost function surface in the parameter space, but it aims at constructing and shaping an energy surface with a single global minimum point in the time-domain through the adjustment of the weight parameters in Lyapunov sense. The output asymptotically converges to the desired output. Error and weight convergence analyses are performed. Analyses have shown that the proposed method has better tracking capability compared with LAF in [1]-[2]. Besides that, it is proven that the design is independent of statistic properties of the input and output signals. Simulation examples are performed to reveal the good performance of the proposed method.

2 The Proposed RBF Neural Network Training Algorithm

As illustrated in Fig 1, the RBF architecture consists of a feedforward two layer network in which the transfer function of each hidden node is radially symmetric in the input space. We will focus our attention on radial basis functions. The output of the RBF NN can be described as

$$y(k) = \sum_{i=1}^{N} w_i(k)\phi_i(k) \tag{1.1}$$

The expression (1.1) can be rewritten as the expression (1.2).

$$y(k) = W^T(k)\Phi(k) \tag{1.2}$$

where $W(k) = [w_1(k), w_2(k), \cdots, w_N(k)]^T$

$$\Phi(k) = [\phi_1(k), \phi_2(k), \ldots, \phi_N(k)]^T$$

$\phi(k)$ is the Gaussian type of functions defined as

$$\phi_i(k) = \exp\left(-\frac{\|X(k) - c_i\|}{\sigma_i^2}\right) \qquad i = 1, 2, 3, \ldots N \tag{1.3}$$

where $X(k) = [x(k), x(k\text{-}1), \ldots, x(k\text{-}N)]^T$, c_i is the center and σ_i is the width of Gaussian function.

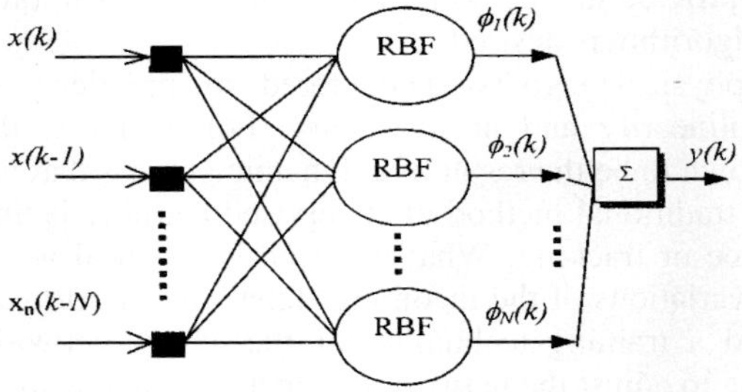

Fig. 1. Radial Basis Function (RBF) Neural Network

The strategy for updating the network parameters involves supervised learning. The design of the new algorithm is based on Lyapunov theory-based adaptive filtering (LAF) in [1]-[2]. In this section, we present an improve version of LAF in [1]-[2] for RBF NN training. At each iteration, the weights are updated using a new improved adaptation algorithm, RBF_LAF-2. To update the weight vector of the RBF NN, the coefficients updated equation in the expression (1.2) can be replaced with the expression in (1.4).

$$W(k) = W(k - 1) + g(k)\alpha(k) \tag{1.4}$$

where $g(k)$ is the weight adaptation gain and $\alpha(k)$ is the a priori estimation error. The expression in (1.3) can be replaced with the following expression.

$$\alpha(k) = d(k) - W^T(k\text{-}1)\Phi(k) \tag{1.5}$$

where $d(k)$ is the desired response or reference signal. The weight adaptation gain $g(k)$ in (1.4) is adaptively adjusted based on Lyapunov stability theory to have error convergence to zero asymptotically.

$$g(k) = \frac{\Phi(k)}{\|\Phi(k)\|^2}\left(1 - \frac{|\varepsilon(k-1)|}{|\alpha(k)|\, e^{k/2}}\right) \tag{1.6}$$

The error between the desired response and the actual output is defined as

$$\varepsilon(k) = d(k) - y(k) \tag{1.7}$$

In this scheme, weight parameter will be adaptively adjusted by the RBF_LAF-2. For the RBF structure adaptation, several schemes [13]-[15] can be considered. Among these different schemes, researchers in [13] have proposed an adaptive training method which is able to modify the structure (the number of the nodes in the hidden layer) of the RBN neural network. The algorithm is based on a fuzzy partition of the input space, which defines a set of fuzzy subspaces. The method selects a number of these subspaces and assigns the locations of the RBF nodes to the centers of these subspaces. Special care is taken so that all the input data are sufficiently covered by at least one fuzzy subspace. An additional subspace is selected, in case a new input example arrives that does not belong to any of the existing fuzzy subspaces. Accordingly, a subspace is deleted, when no input examples are assigned to it for a long time period. In [13], the weighting connections between the input and the output layer are updated using the recursive least squares (RLS).

3 Design of the New Training Algorithm RBF_LAF-2

In this section, we will develop an improved training method for RBF NN based on Lyapunov theory-based adaptive filtering algorithm, RBF_LAF-2.

Theorem 2.1. Consider a liner combiner $y(k) = W^T(k)\Phi(k)$. For the given desired response $d(k)$ and the input vector $\Phi(k)$, if the parameter vector $W(k)$ is updated according to (2.1) with the priori estimation error in (1.5) and the adaptation gain as follows:

$$g(k) = \frac{\Phi(k)}{\|\Phi(k)\|^2}\left(1 - \frac{|\varepsilon(k-1)|}{|\alpha(k)|\, e^{k/2}}\right) \tag{2.1}$$

the tracking error $\varepsilon(k)$ can then asymptotically converge to zero.

Proof: Define a new Lyapunov function of error $\varepsilon(k)$

$$V(k) = e^k \varepsilon^2(k) \tag{2.2}$$

Then,

$$\begin{aligned}
\Delta V(k) &= V(k) - V(k-1) \\
&= e^k \varepsilon^2(k) - e^k \varepsilon^2(k-1) \\
&= e^k \left[d(k) - W^T(k)\Phi(k)\right]^2 - e^{k-1}\varepsilon^2(k-1) \\
&= e^k \left[d(k) - (W^T(k-1) + \alpha(k) g^T(k))\Phi(k)\right]^2 - e^{k-1}\varepsilon^2(k-1) \\
&= e^k \left[d(k) - W^T(k-1)\Phi(k) - \alpha(k) g^T(k)\Phi(k)\right]^2 - e^{k-1}\varepsilon^2(k-1) \\
&= e^k \left[\alpha(k) - \alpha(k) g^T(k)\Phi(k)\right]^2 - e^{k-1}\varepsilon^2(k-1)
\end{aligned} \tag{2.3}$$

Using the adaptation gain *g(k)* in (2.1), we have

$$\begin{aligned}
\Delta V(k) &= e^{k}\left[\alpha(k)-\alpha(k)\left(1-\frac{e^{-k/2}\,|\varepsilon(k-1)|}{|\alpha(k)|}\right)\right]^{2}-e^{k-1}\varepsilon^{2}(k-1)\\
&= e^{k}\left[\alpha(k)-\alpha(k)+\frac{\alpha(k)e^{-k/2}\,|\varepsilon(k-1)|}{|\alpha(k)|}\right]^{2}-e^{k-1}\varepsilon^{2}(k-1)\\
&= e^{k}\left[\frac{\alpha^{2}(k)e^{-k/2}\,|\varepsilon(k-1)|^{2}}{\alpha(k)^{2}}\right]-e^{k-1}\varepsilon^{2}(k-1)\\
&= \varepsilon^{2}(k-1)-e^{k-1}\varepsilon^{2}(k-1)\\
&= -(e^{k-1}-1)\varepsilon^{2}(k-1)<0
\end{aligned} \tag{2.4}$$

According to the Lyapunov stability theory in [16], the tracking error ε(k) will asymptotically converge to zero.

4 Error and Weight Parameters Convergence Analysis

In this section, error and RBF NN weight parameters vector convergences will be analyzed. The error convergence analysis shows that the error convergence can be specified in terms of the exponential in term of discrete time *k, e(k)*. As the time *k* increases, this exponential term will decreases dramatically. This indicates the fast error convergence. Besides that, the analysis also proves the tracking error ε(k) is independent of the stochastic properties of the input ϕ(k). On the other hand, the weight convergence analysis shows that the weight parameter of RBF_LAF-2 can converge.

4.1 Error Convergence Analysis of the Proposed RBF_LAF-2

Lemma 1. Consider the RBF NN with weight updated law in (1.4), the priori estimation error in (1.5), and the adaptation gain in (2.1). The tracking error will exponentially converge to zero according to the following expression.

$$|\varepsilon(k)| = e^{-(1+k)/2}\,|\varepsilon(0)| \tag{3.0}$$

Proof: Using (1.4), (1.5) and (1.7),

$$\begin{aligned}
|\varepsilon(k)| &= |d(k)-y(k)|\\
&= |d(k)-W^{T}(k)\phi(k)|\\
&= |d(k)-\left[W^{T}(k-1)+g^{T}(k)\alpha(k)\right]\phi(k)|\\
&= \left|d(k)-W^{T}(k-1)\phi(k)-\alpha(k)\left(1-\frac{|\varepsilon(k-1)|}{|\alpha(k)|\,e^{k/2}}\right)\right|\\
&= \left|\alpha(k)-\alpha(k)\left(1-e^{-k/2}\frac{|\varepsilon(k-1)|}{|\alpha(k)|}\right)\right|\\
&= |\varepsilon(k-1)|\,e^{-k/2}
\end{aligned}$$

Then,

$$
\begin{aligned}
|\varepsilon(1)| &= e^{-1/2}\,|\varepsilon(0)| \\
|\varepsilon(2)| &= e^{-2/2}\,|\varepsilon(1)| = e^{-(1+2)/2}\,|\varepsilon(0)| \\
&\vdots \\
|\varepsilon(k)| &= e^{-(1+k)k/4}\,|\varepsilon(0)|
\end{aligned}
\tag{3.1}
$$

From the above analysis, the error convergence can be specified in terms of the exponential in term of *k, e(k)*. As the time *k* increases, this exponential term will decreases dramatically. The tracking error ε(k) is independent of the stochastic properties of the input ϕ(k). These two facts are very important feature of RBF_LAF-2.

4.2 Weight Parameter Convergence Analysis of the Proposed RBF_LAF-2

In this section, we try to prove that the weight parameter convergence. It can be noted that, after the tracking error converges, the weight parameter adaptation law in (1.4) with the adaptation gain in (2.1) becomes:

$$W(k) = W(k-1) - \frac{\phi(k)\phi^T(k)}{\|\phi(k)\|^2} W(k-1) + \frac{\phi(k)d(k)}{\|\phi(k)\|^2} \tag{3.2}$$

Assume that ϕ(k) and W(k) are random variable vector, then

$$E(W(k)) = E(W(k-1)) - E\left(\frac{\phi(k)\phi^T(k)}{\|\phi(k)\|^2} W(k-1)\right) + E\left(\frac{\phi(k)d(k)}{\|\phi(k)\|^2}\right) \tag{3.3}$$

where E( ) represents the expectation.

Using the Independent Theory in [17], we have

$$E\left(\frac{\phi(k)\phi^T(k)}{\|\phi(k)\|^2} W(k-1)\right) \approx \frac{E(\phi(k)\phi^T(k))}{E(\|\phi(k)\|^2)} E(W(k-1)) = \frac{R_{\phi\phi}}{Tr(R_{\phi\phi})} E(W(k-1)) \tag{3.4}$$

$$E\left(\frac{\phi(k)d(k)}{\|\phi(k)\|^2}\right) \approx \frac{E(\phi(k)d(k))}{E(\|\phi(k)\|^2)} = \frac{R_{\phi d}}{Tr(R_{\phi\phi})} \tag{3.5}$$

where $R_{\phi\phi} \underline{\underline{\Delta}} E(\phi(k)\phi^T(k))$ and $R_{\phi d} \underline{\underline{\Delta}} E(\phi(k)d(k))$ are the ensemble autocorrelation matrix of $\phi(k)$ and the ensemble average cross-correlation vector of $\phi(k)$ and $d(k)$, respectively.

Assume the random process is wide sense stationary (WSS),

$$E(W(k)) = E(W(k-1)) \tag{3.6}$$

Using the expressions (3.4)-(3.5), we have

$$\frac{R_{\phi\phi}}{Tr(R_{\phi\phi})} E(W(k)) = \frac{R_{\phi d}}{Tr(R_{\phi\phi})} \tag{3.7}$$

This leads to

$$E(W(k)) = R_{\phi\phi}^{-1} R_{\phi d} \,. \tag{3.8}$$

This has shown that the weight parameter of RBF_LAF-2 converges to Wiener solution under the aforementioned assumptions.

Remark: To prevent the singularities due to zero values of $\Phi(k)$ and $\alpha(k)$, $g(k)$ may then be modified as follow

$$g(k) = \frac{\Phi(k)}{\|\Phi(k)\|^2}\left(1 - \frac{|\varepsilon(k-1)|}{\lambda_1 + |\alpha(k)| e^{k/2}}\right) \tag{3.9}$$

where λ_1 is small positive number.

5 Simulation Examples

As mentioned in previous section, many of the physical signals encountered in practice exhibit nonlinearity and nonstationary characteristics. To evaluate the performance of our proposed method, we consider the application of the nonlinear adaptive prediction of speech signals, which are nonlinear and nonstationary. Simulations have been done for a one-step ahead prediction of a nonlinear and nonstationary speech signal which is identical to that used in [18],[19] and [20]. The signal is downloaded from the WWW [21] and is described as follow: *S1* speech sample "*When recording audio data* ...", length 10000, sampled at 8kHz.The RBF NN with the proposed scheme is expected to be able to track the nonstationary signal characteristic.

Fig. 2 shows the speech signal and the RBF NN predictor output. Fig. 3 illustrates the square predictor error. For comparison to previous works [18]-[20], the performance measure we shall use is the *predicted signal-to-noise ration* (PSNR) defined by

$$PSNR\ (dB) \underline{\underline{\Delta}} 10 \log_{10} (\tilde{\sigma}_s^2 / \tilde{\sigma}_e^2) \tag{4.1}$$

where $\tilde{\sigma}_s^2$ and $\tilde{\sigma}_e^2$ are the actual and error signal powers estimated by $\tilde{\sigma}_s^2 \underline{\underline{\Delta}} \frac{1}{N}\sum_{i=1}^{N} y^2(i)$ and $\tilde{\sigma}_e^2 \underline{\underline{\Delta}} \frac{1}{N}\sum_{i=1}^{N} e^2(i)$.

For 10,000 speech samples, $\tilde{\sigma}_s^2$ is calculated to be 0.3394. The $\tilde{\sigma}_e^2$ is about 0.0038, yielding PSNR = 19.3527dB. The same speech signal has been used as part of three pervious studies, the dynamic regularized RBF [19] based on the *regularized least-squares fitting* (RLSF), pinelined recurrent NNs (PRNN) [18],[20] which are another method of modeling nonstationary dynamics. The authors in [20] have done the simulations for PRNN and standard linear adaptive filters. While considerably different in details of their architectures and training methods, they do share the common principle of continuously adapting their network parameters to yield minimum squared prediction error and track nonstationary signal characteristics.

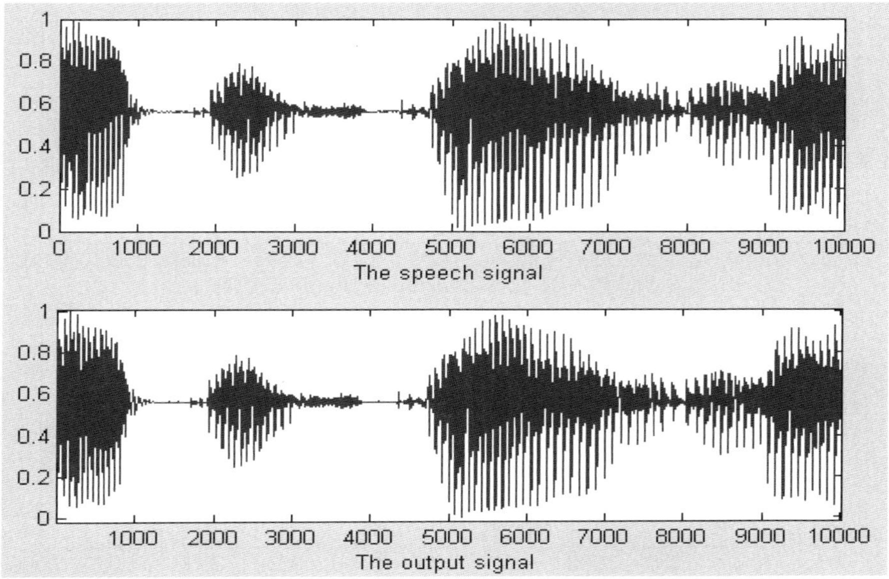

Fig. 2. The speech signal S1 and the one-step prediction output of the RBF NN

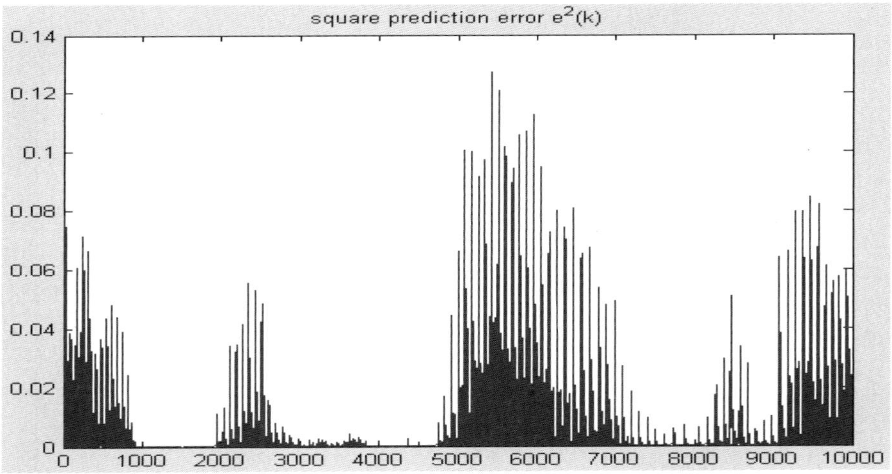

Fig. 3. The squared one-step prediction error for speech signal S1

Comparing to their results, our PSNR is better than the best PSNR of 14.71dB listed in [19, Table IV] and 8.82dB better than that of 13.59dB listed in [20, Table II] for a hybrid *extended RLS* (ERLS)-trained PRNN followed by a 12th order RLS filter. However, the computational complexity of our method and RBF NN is less than that of [19].

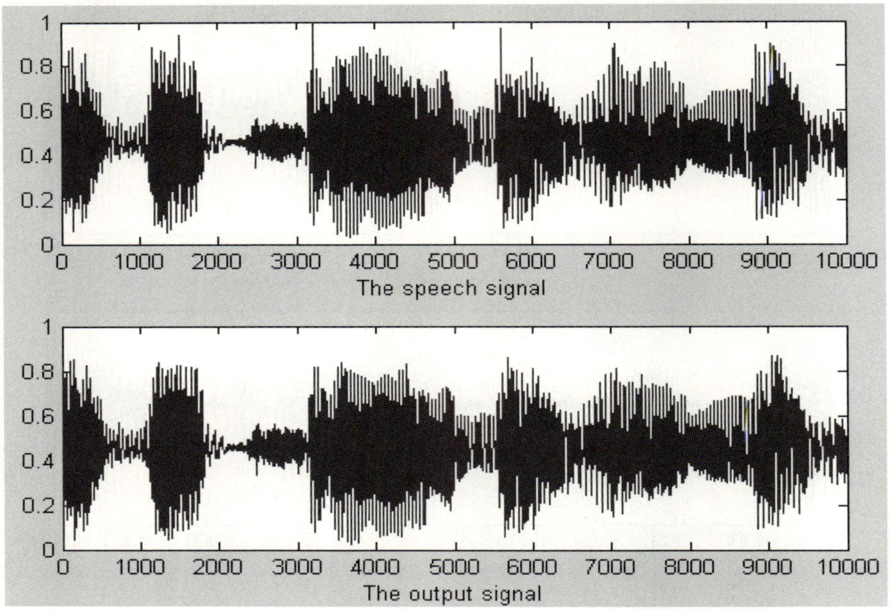

Fig. 4. The speech signal S3 and the one-step prediction output of the RBF NN

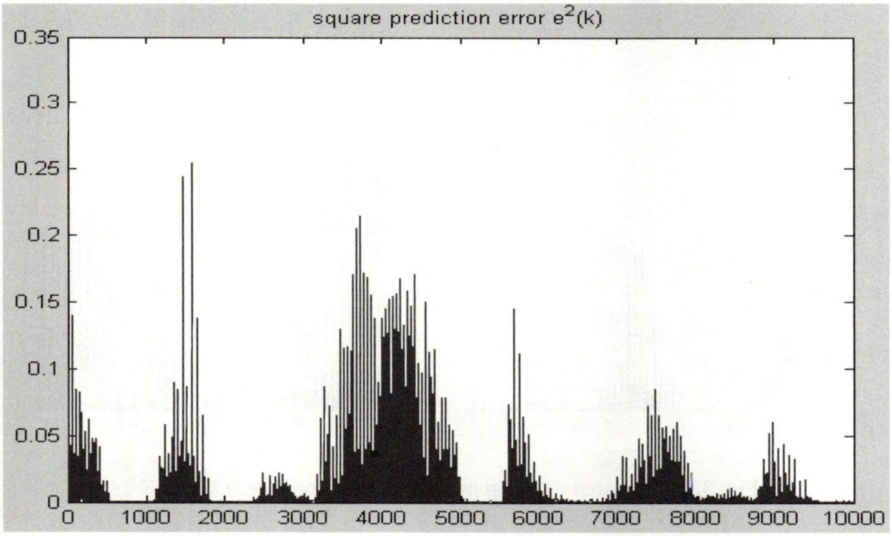

Fig. 5. The squared one-step prediction error for speech signal S3

Another speech signal S3 in [21] is considered. Fig. 4 shows the speech signal and the RBF NN predictor output. Fig. 5 illustrates the square predictor error. For 10,000 speech samples, $\tilde{\sigma}_s^2$ is calculated to be 0.2255. The $\tilde{\sigma}_e^2$ is about 0.0054, yielding PSNR = 16.1818dB.

6 Conclusion

This paper has presented a new RBF NN training algorithm for nonlinear and nonstationary signal. The proposed training algorithm RBF_LAF-2 adaptively adjusts the weights of the RBF NN. The RBF_LAF-2 possesses the distinctive properties of Lyapunov Theory-based Adaptive Filtering (LAF) in [1]-[2] and has better tracking capability compared with LAF. Unlike gradient search methods, our method is not used for searching for the global minimum point along the cost function surface in the parameter space, but it aims at constructing and shaping an energy surface with a single global minimum point in the time-domain through the adjustment of the weight parameters in Lyapunov sense. The output asymptotically converges to the desired output. Error and weight parameters convergences have been analyzed. The error convergence analysis has shown that the tracking error is independent of the stochastic properties of input signal. The weight parameters convergence analysis has proven that the weight parameter vector converges to the Wiener solution for the wide sense stationary random process. Simulation examples have revealed the good performance of the proposed method.

References

1. Phooi, S.K., Man, Z., Wu, H.R.: Lyapunov Theory-based Radial Basis Function Networks for Adaptive Filtering. IEEE Transaction on Circuit and System 1 49(8), 1215–1221 (2002)
2. ZhiHong, M., Wu, H.R., Lai, W., Nguyen, T.: Design of Adaptive Filters Using Lyapunov Stability Theory. In: The 6th IEEE International Workshop on Intelligent Signal Processing and Communication Systems, pp. 304–308 (1998)
3. Haykin, S.: Neural Network: A Comprehensive Foundation. Macmillan, New York (1994)
4. Chen, T., Chen, H.: Approximation capability to functions of several variables, nonlinear functionals, and operators by radial basis function neural networks. IEEE Trans. Neural Networks 6, 904–910 (1995)
5. Broomhead, D.S., Lowe, D.: Multivariable functional interpolation and adaptive networks. Complex Systems 2, 321–355 (1988)
6. Moody, J.E., Darken, C.J.: Fast learning in networks of locally-tuned processing units. Neural Comput. 1, 281–294 (1989)
7. Karayiannis, N.B., Mi, W.: Growing radial basis neural networks: Merging supervised and unsupervised learning with network growth techniques. IEEE Trans. Neural Networks 8, 1492–1506 (1997)
8. Poggio, T., Girosi, F.: Regularization algorithms for learning that are equivalent to multilayer networks. Science 247, 978–982 (1990)
9. Chen, S., Cowan, C.F.N., Grant, P.M.: Orthogonal least squares learning algorithm for radial basis function networks. IEEE Trans.Neural Networks 2, 302–309 (1991)

10. Cha, I., Kassam, S.A.: Interference cancellation using radial basis function networks. Signal Processing 47, 247–268 (1995)
11. Dinz, P.S.R.: Adaptive filtering: algorithms and practical implementation. Kluwer Academic Publishers, Boston, MA (1997)
12. Treichler, J.R., Johnson, C.R., Larimore, M.G.: the theory and design of adaptive filters. Prentice Hall, Englewood Cliffs (2001)
13. Alexandridis, A., Haralambos, S., George, B.: A new algorithm for online structure and parameter adaptation of RBF networks. Neural Networks 16, 1003–1017 (2003)
14. Fung, C.F., Billings, S.A., Luo, W.: Online supervised adaptive training using radial basis function networks. Neural Networks, 9(9) 1597–1617
15. Zheng, G.L., Billings, S.A.: Radial basis function network configuration using mutual information and orthogonal least squares algorithm. Neural Networks, 9(9) 1619–1673
16. Slotine, J-J.E., Li, W.: Applied nonlinear control. Prentice-Hall, Englewood Cliffs, NJ (1991)
17. Haykin, S.: Adaptive filtering theory. Prentice-Hall, Englewood Cliffs, NJ (1985)
18. Haykin, S.: Nonlinear Adaptive Prediction of Nonstationary Signals. IEEE Trans. Signal Processing, 43(2) (February 1995)
19. Yee, P., Haykin, S.: A dynamic regularized RBF networks for nonlinear, nonstationary time series prediction, IEEE Trans. Signal Processing, 47(9) (1999)
20. Baltersee, J., Jonathon, A.: Nonlinear adaptive prediction of speech with a pipelined recurrent neural network. IEEE Trans. Signal Processing, 46(8) (1998)
21. http://www.ert.rwth-aachen.de/Presonen/balterse.html

Structure-Based Rule Selection Framework for Association Rule Mining of Traffic Accident Data

Rangsipan Marukatat

Department of Computer Engineering, Faculty of Engineering,
Mahidol University, Thailand
egrmr@mahidol.ac.th

Abstract. A rule selection framework is proposed which classifies, selects, and filters out association rules based on the analysis of the rule structures. It was applied to real traffic accident data collected from local police stations. The rudimentary nature of the data required several passes of association rule mining to be performed, each with different sets of parameters, so that semantically interesting rules can be spotted from the pool of results. It was shown that the proposed framework could find candidate rules that offer some insight into the phenomena being studied.

1 Introduction

In recent years, a number of new data mining or knowledge extraction techniques have been devised. However, from application's point of view, it is quite common that standard, simple techniques are still chosen over complicated, adventurous ones. It is still preferable to extract as many rules as possible from machine mining and then rely on human to determine which ones seem "interesting" or "make sense" to them. Although many evaluation metrics have been proposed to help select and filter out rules, it is still more comfortable for many (applied) researchers to go through the findings and make decisions based on the semantics they perceive.

This work is a part of an applied research aiming to identify potential concerns and suggest countermeasures against traffic accident problems in Nakorn Pathom. Over the past years, economic and human losses due to traffic accidents in Nakorn Pathom, a province in the vicinity of Bangkok, have been ranked among the highest of the country [3], [5]. A number of data mining techniques are employed to construct traffic accident profiles for the province. This paper focuses on the application of association rule mining. Its main contribution is the development of a rule selection framework which relies on the structure of the rules. It is acknowledged that there have been works on rule selection such as [6] and [9]. This work shares some ideas with them but also puts forward the framework into the target application.

The rest of the paper is organized as follows. Section 2 offers a brief overview of the traffic accident data used in the research. Section 3 reviews association rule mining. Section 4 describes the rule selection framework, followed by preliminary results and discussion in Section 5. Finally, Section 6 concludes the paper.

Y. Wang, Y. Cheung, and H. Liu (Eds.): CIS 2006, LNAI 4456, pp. 231–239, 2007.

2 Traffic Accident Data

Traffic accident cases, dated between 01/01/2003 and 31/03/2006, have been collected from local police stations in Nakorn Pathom. Currently, there are 1007 records

Table 1. Traffic Accident Variables

Binary Variable	Description	Nominal Variable	Values
	Vehicles involved:	Time	1 = 06.01 – 12.00
V0	bicycles, tricycles		2 = 12.01 – 18.00
V1	motorcycles		3 = 18.01 – 24.00
V2	sedans		4 = 00.01 – 06.00
V3	vans, buses		
V4	pick-ups	Scene	1 = highway
V5	trucks, trailers		2 = local road
V6	pedestrians		3 = community area
	Causes of accidents:		
C0	others	Feature	1 = straight
C1	speeding		2 = intersection
C2	violating traffic signs		3 = curve
C3	not yielding to rightful vehicles		4 = others
C4	illegal overtaking		
C5	chopping in closing distance		
C6	driving in wrong lane / direction		
C7	not signalling		
C8	careless driving		
C9	following in close distance		
	Human losses:		
H1	dead		
H2	seriously injured		
H3	slightly injured		

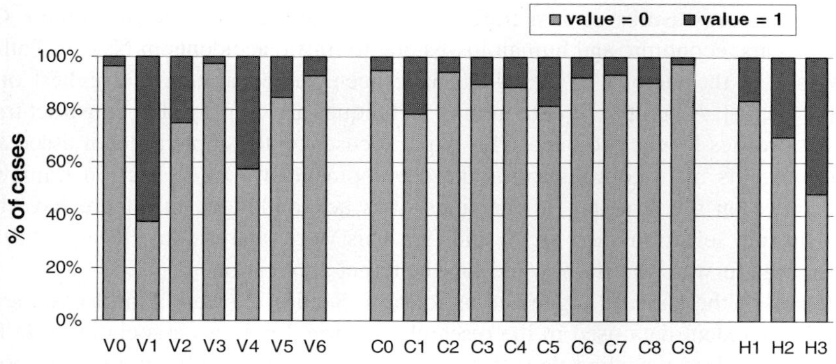

Fig. 1. Frequency distribution of binary variables

in total. The data set was arranged in typical market-basket style – there are 20 binary variables and 3 nominal ones, as shown in Table 1. Binary variables are grouped into three *subjects*: vehicles involved in the accident (V0-V6), causes of the accident (C0-C9), and human losses (H1-H3). Fig. 1 displays frequency distribution of the binary variables. It can be observed that most of them have high frequency of zeros, indicating that items represented by these variables rarely occurred in the data set.

3 Association Rule Mining

Based on [3] and [8], let $I = \{ i_1, i_2, \ldots, i_m \}$ be an itemset and $D = \{ T \mid T \subseteq I \}$ be a set of transaction. An itemset A occurs in T iff $A \subseteq T$. "$A \Rightarrow B$" is an association rule, provided that $A \subset I$, $B \subset I$, and $A \cap B = \varnothing$. Association metrics, *support*, *confidence*, and *lift* (or *interest*), are defined as follows:

$$support = P(A \cap B)\,. \tag{1}$$

$$confidence = P(A \mid B) = P(A \cap B) / P(A)\,. \tag{2}$$

$$lift = P(A \cap B) / (\,P(A)\,P(B)\,)\,. \tag{3}$$

The main objective of association rule mining is to extract rules with high support and confidence, and where the antecedents and the consequences are actually related. Since an association rule may have high confidence despite the antecedents and the consequences be independent of each other, i.e. $P(B \mid A) = P(B)$, lift is the confidence normalized by $P(B)$.

Apriori [8] is a simple and well-known algorithm that extracts association rules from data sets. Its pseudo code (based on Weka's implementation [7]) is presented below. In this implementation, criteria other than confidence may be used in the rule generation phase (lines 10-23).

```
Algorithm:    Association_Analysis
Parameters:   UpperMinSupport, MinSupport, Delta
              Criterion, MinScore, NumRules
Input:        traffic accident data set
Output:       {set_of_rules}
Method:
1    {set_of_rules} is an empty set
2    N ← 0
3    DO {
4       // Phase 1: finding frequent itemsets
5       FOR k = 1 to NumVariables {
6          Find set of all frequent k-itemset S_k
7          // S_k is chosen if MinSupport ≤ support(S_k)
8          // and support(S_k) ≤ UpperMinSupport
9       }
10      // Phase 2: generating rules
11      FOR each frequent itemset S {
```

```
        FOR each subset SS of S  {
           R ← generate rule "SS ⇒ (S - SS)"
           Compute confidence(R) and lift(R)
           IF using "confidence" Criterion THEN
              Score ← confidence(R)
           ELSE
              Score ← lift(R)
           IF Score ≥ MinScore THEN
              {set_of_rules} ← add R to output
              N ← N+1
        }
     }
     UpperMinSupport ← UpperMinSupport - Delta
  } UNTIL (UpperMinSupport ≤ MinSupport) or
          (N = NumRules)
  Sort {set_of_rules} by Criterion
```

Two major problems are found when applying Apriori to the traffic accident data. First, because frequent items are those having zero values (see the data distribution in Fig. 1), there are many rules describing association between zero-value items, e.g. "V4=0, C5=1 ⇒ V2=1, C1=0, C3=0, C4=0, C8=0". These rules convey little information and are hard to interprete. Furthermore, some of them appear to be permuted patterns of the others, such as rules "V4=0, C5=1 ⇒ V2=1" and "V2=1, V4=0 ⇒ C5=1", while some appear to be either general or specific cases of the others, such as rules "V4=0, C5=1 ⇒ V2=1" and "C5=1 ⇒ V2=1".

4 Rule Selection Framework

A rule selection framework was developed in order to tackle the issues addressed in the previous section. The framework classifies, selects, and filters out rules by analyzing the rule structures rather than using complicated mathematical criteria. It consists of two parts: semantic rule classification, and permutation analysis.

4.1 Semantic Rule Classification

Let V_a be an antecedent variable and V_c be a consequent variable. S is a group of binary variables or *subject*. The terms *abundant*, *strongly abundant*, and *weakly abundant* are defined as follows:

1. A srongly abundant rule takes the form $\{V_{ai} = 0;\ for\ \forall i\} \Rightarrow \{V_{ck} = 0;\ for\ \forall k\}$, where $\{V_{ai,\forall i}, V_{ck,\forall k}\} \in S$ (i.e. all variables are members of the same subject). An example is "V1=0, V3=0 ⇒ V4=0" meaning that if an accident does not involve any motorcycle or van / bus, it does not involve any pick-up either.
2. An abundant rule takes the form $\{V_{ai} = 0;\ for\ \forall i\} \Rightarrow \{V_{ck} = 0;\ for\ \forall k\}$, where $V_{ai,\forall i} \in S1;\ V_{ck,\forall k} \in S2;$ and $S1 \neq S2$ (i.e. antecedent and consequent variables are members of different subjects). An example is "V1=0, V3=0 ⇒ C1=0" meaning

that if an accident does not involve any motorcycle or van / bus, it is not caused by driving over speed limit

3. A weakly abundant rule takes the form $\{V_{ai} = 0; for\ \exists i\} \Rightarrow \{V_{ck} = 0; for\ \exists k\}$. An example is "V5=1, V6=0 ⇒ Scene=1" meaning that if an accident involves trucks / trailers but does not involve any pedestrian, it happens on the highway.

Note that the interpretation of each rule is with certain level of confidence, support, and lift. Rules that do not fall into any of the above categories are labelled *candidate* rules. Abundant and strongly abundant rules are filtered out since they add little or no insight into the subjects being studied. For example, knowing only that motorcycles, vans / buses, and pick-ups, are not involved in the same accident says nothing about any other vehicle that might be associated with them. Weakly abundant rules, on the other hand, are kept in separate files and used as complements to candidate rules for further insight into the phenomena.

4.2 Permutation Analysis

From the Association_Analysis algorithm, a rule R is generated by permuting items in the itemset S (lines 11-13). It is added to the set of resulting rules should its association metric is not lower than the minimum score (lines 19-20). In practice, the algorithm may run several times using different sets of parameters, and thus some of the resulting rules may be permuted patterns of the others.

Let S_1 be a set of items in rule R_1 and S_2 be a set of items in rule R_2, regardless of whether an item is an antecedent or a consequence (the effect of it being one or the other is captured by association metrics). There are three types of relationships between R_1 and R_2 :

1. R_1 is equivalent to R_2 if all the items in S_1 exist in S_2, and vice versa.
2. R_1 covers R_2 if S_1 includes all the items in S_2 plus at least one item that does not exist in S_2.
3. R_1 is covered by R_2 if all the items in S_1 exist in S_2, and at least one item in S_2 does not exist in S_1.

Out of a set of equivalent rules, only the most *significant* one is selected. The rule significances are compared using lift and confidence as the first and the second criterion, respectively. A rule that covers the others is selected while the one being covered is discarded. The terms "cover" and "being covered" in this work are different from those in Toivonen et al [6]. In their work, R_1 covers R_2 if it is more general or has fewer items than R_2. General rules are favoured because their approach aims to find short description for the entire set of rules. In contrast, this work favours specific rules because it aims to find some overlooked or previously unknown information hidden in the data set.

Pseudo code of the permutation analysis is as follows:

```
Algorithm:    Permutation_Analysis
Input:        {set_of_rules}_in
Output:       {set_of_rules}_out
Method:
```

```
{set_of_rules}_out is an empty set
FOR each rule R in {set_of_rules}_in {
   done ← "no"
   FOR each rule TR in {set_of_rules}_out {
      IF (R is equivalent to TR) and
         (more_significant(R, TR) = R) THEN
         Replace TR in {set_of_rules}_out with R
         done ← "yes"
      ELSE IF TR covers R THEN
         done ← "no"
      ELSE IF TR is covered by R THEN
         Replace TR in {set_of_rules}_out with R
         done ← "yes"
   }
   IF not done THEN
      {set_of_rules}_out ← add R to output
}
```

```
Algorithm:   more_significant
Input:       rules R1 and R2
Output:      more significant rule between R1 and R2
Method
R_s ← NULL
IF lift(R_1) > lift(R_2) THEN R_s ← R_1
ELSE IF lift(R_1) = lift(R_2) THEN
   IF confidence(R_1) ≥ confidence(R_2) THEN R_s ← R_1
   ELSE R_s ← R_2
ELSE R_s ← R_2
RETURN R_s
```

5 Preliminary Results

The data set was mined using Apriori module in Weka [7]. An initial target was to generate as many rules as possible to see if meaningful ones could be spotted from the pool of results. The association rule mining was performed 8 times, each with decreasing UpperMinSupport from 0.9 to 0.2. Results from each run were sorted by lift, whose minimum score was set to 2. The other parameters are MinSupport, Delta, and NumRules, which were fixed at 0.1, 0.01, and 500, respectively.

Table 2 summarizes the results. The total of 3042 association rules were generated. Rule classification were able to classify candidate rules (about 14.7%) from weakly abundant ones (about 85.3%). They were separately fed into the next process which filtered out repeated or permuted rules. The final results include 105 candidate rules (with maximum lift 6.59 and maximum confidence 0.82) and 294 weakly abundant rules (with maximum lift 17.01 and maximum confidence 1.00). Semantic-wise, interesting rules were obtained at quite low support (i.e. 0.4).

Table 2. Preliminary Results

UpperMin Support	Max Lift	Max Conf.	Number of Rules		
			Candidate	Weakly Abund.	Total
0.9	2.77	0.95	0	500	500
0.8	4.47	0.90	0	500	500
0.7	6.04	0.97	8	492	500
0.6	6.56	0.97	42	458	500
0.5	17.01	1.00	52	448	500
0.4	9.42	1.00	238	198	436
0.3	4.20	0.72	90	0	90
0.2	3.63	0.59	16	0	16
Total	17.01	1.00	446 (14.7%)	2596 (85.3%)	3042
Reduced	6.59	0.82	105	-	399
	17.01	1.00	-	294	

Table 3. Examples of Association Rules

No	Lift	Conf.	Candidate Rules
1	4.17	0.48	12.01-18.00, Local road, Intersection => Not yielding to rightful vehicle
2	4.07	0.67	12.01-18.00, Straight, Deads => Trucks
3	3.63	0.59	00.01-06.00, Trucks => Deads
4	2.51	0.53	Curve, Bicycles => Local road
No	**Lift**	**Conf.**	**Weakly Abundant Rules**
5	11.90	0.58	Pick-ups, Pedestrians => No motorcycle, Deads
6	2.14	0.38	Trucks => Highway, No sedan, No speeding, No chopping

Table 3 shows a few examples of association rules (*rules 1-4* are candidate while *rules 5-6* are weakly abundant), with all the items being substituted by variable descriptions or values. Nakorn Pathom establishes herself as a gateway to the western and the southern parts of the country, hence there are a lot of heavy vehicles travelling through the province during the night and very early in the morning (around 22.00-06.00). One would find that *rule 3* is not unexpected. However, *Rule 2* is a little revelation since there are usually fewer trucks or trailers travelling around midday or in the afternoon. Additional observations could be gathered from other candidate and weakly abundant rules. For example, *rule 6* says that when trucks and highway are associated, no passenger car (sedan) is involved in the accident and the accident is not caused by driving over speed limit or chopping in close distance. Other observations are, for example, *rule 1* suggesting that accidents occuring at the intersections of local roads around 12.01-18.00 are caused by not yielding to rightful vehicles. Further investigation into the amount of traffic during rush hours (16.00-18.00) and traffic lights around the areas should be made to complete the picture.

The results presented in this paper is merely preliminary since a handful of cases have been collected and used in the analysis. Unlike other research that successfully extracted useful knowledge from traffic accident data ([1], [4]), gathering traffic accident cases from Thailand's local police stations is quite tedious, since they were mostly hand-written in paper forms and there existed a lot of errors and missing values. Techniques such as classification are also employed in the other segments of the research. It is expected that results obtained from various segments are aggregated to produce the complete and reliable traffic accident profiles.

6 Conclusion

This paper proposes a structure-based rule selection framework that classifies, selects, and filters out association rules based on the analysis of their structures. The framework consists of two parts: rule classification, and permutation analysis. The data set used in this work is in typical market-baseket form. The term *subject* is introduced for grouping binary variables. It is, afterward, a key factor for classifying rules into *candidate*, *weakly abundant*, *abundant*, and *strongly abundant* ones. The second part of the framework simply analyzes permuted rule patterns and filters out *equivalent* but less significant rules. Furthermore, rules that *cover* the other rules are selected while the ones *being covered* are discarded.

The framework was applied to a real-world application aiming to construct traffic accident profiles which serve as a stepping-stone to identifying potential concerns and suggesting countermeasures against traffic accident problems. Preliminary results showed that the framework could select a number of candidate rules that offer some insight into the phenomena. However, more analysis are required on larger sets of data in order to produce the complete and reliable results.

Acknowledgements. This work is funded by the National Science and Technology Development Agency of Thailand (NSTDA) and the Faculty of Engineering, Mahidol University.

References

1. Accident Research Center, Monash University, Australia. http://www.monash.edu.au/ muarc/projects
2. Action Plans Coordination and Pilot Studies on Road Safety. Ministry of Transport and Communication, Kingdom of Thailand (2001)
3. Brin, S., Motwani, R., Ullman, J. D., Tsur, S.: Dynamic Itemset Counting and Implication Rules for Market Basket Data. In: Proceedings of ACM SIGMOD International Conference on Management of Data, Arizona, USA (1997)
4. CARE (Critical Analysis Reporting Environment). CARE Research and Development Laboratory, University of Alabama, USA. http://care.cs.ua.edu/care.aspx
5. Thailand in Figures: 2003-2004. 9th edn. Alpha Research Co.,Ltd. (2004)
6. Toivonen, H., Klemettinen, M., Ronkainen, P., Hatonen, K., Mannila, H.: Pruning and Grouping of Discovered Association Rules. In: Lavrač, N., Wrobel, S. (eds.) Machine Learning: ECML-95. LNCS, vol. 912, Springer, Heidelberg (1995)

7. Weka: Data Mining Software in Java. University of Waikato, New Zealand. http://www.waikato.ac.nz/ml/weka
8. Witten, I.H., Frank, E.: Data Mining: Practical Machine Learning Tools and Techniques, 2nd edn. Elsevier Inc, Amsterdam (2005)
9. Zaki, M.J.: Generating Non-Redundant Association Rules. In: 6th ACM SIGKDD International Conference of Knowledge Discovery and Data Mining (2000)

A Multi-classification Method of Temporal Data Based on Support Vector Machine

Zhiqing Meng[1], Lifang Peng[2], Gengui Zhou[1], and Yihua Zhu[1]

[1] College of Business and Administration, Zhejiang University of Technology, Zhejiang 310023, China
[2] Library, Hunan University of Technology, Zhuzhou, 412001, China

Abstract. This paper studies a multi-classification method based on support vector machine for temporal data. First, we give classic classification model of support vector machine. Then, we present a support vector machine model based on multi-weighted values, which is used to deal with multi-classification problems of temporal data. We define temporal type and prediction model for the temporal data. According to the temporal type model and the support vector machine model based on multi-weighted values, we propose a multi-classification method based on the support vector machine. Finally, experiments results show that our method can effectively solve the misclassification problems of temporal data.

1 Introduction

In recent years, the temporal data mining becomes an important fields in data miming. The knowledge discovery of multiple granularity time have been discussed for temporal data in [1-2]. In the 1990s, the support vector machine (SVM) model was proposed. By using the SVM, we can discuss prediction and classification for time series [3-6]. The SVM method has displayed good capability. Because the SVM is good at the general data, its goal is to the two classification problem so that we should extend and improve it to implement the temporal data and multi-classification.

In this paper, we propose a weighted support vector multi-class method for temporal data to be used to multi-classification problem. This method introduces weight factors for samples and classes. Samples weight factors in order to overcome the different importance of samples. Class weight factors are aimed to conquer the imbalance in the number of training sets of different classes, and multi-classification model considers the association of the temporal data. The experiment results indicate the method has a good classification prediction precision and stability in a short forecast.

2 Two Types of Support Vector Machine

This section will give two types of support vector machine.

Y. Wang, Y. Cheung, and H. Liu (Eds.): CIS 2006, LNAI 4456, pp. 240–249, 2007.

2.1 Classical Support Vector Machine

Given a training set $T=\{(x_i,y_i),i=1,2,\cdots,l\}$, $x_i\in R^n$, $y_i\in\{+1,-1\}$, the training data can be classified correctly signified that the optimal separating hyperplane not only distribute the two class correctly, but also the separating hyperplan with largest margin. The classical support vector machine (C-SVM) requires the solution of following quadratic optimization problem:

$$\min_{w,b,\xi}\frac{1}{2}\|w\|^2+C\sum_{i=1}^{l}\xi_i \tag{1}$$

$$s.t.\quad y_i[(w\cdot x_i)+b]\ge 1-\xi_i, i=1,2,\cdots,l \tag{2}$$

$$\xi_i\ge 0, i=1,2,\cdots,l\,, \tag{3}$$

where the w is the vector which can determine the optimal separating hyperplane $(w\cdot x_i)+b=0$, which b is the offset of the hyperplane and C is the penalty parameter of the error term. ξ_i is the positive slack variables, that denotes the distance from training vectors x_i to the hyperplane. $w\cdot x_i$ is the form of dot products. When the training set is nonlinear, using a mapping which we will call φ : $x_i\in R^n\to\varphi(x)\in H$, training vectors x_i is mapped into a higher dimensional feature space H . We not need to know the nonlinear function, but to compute the kernel function $K(x_i,x_j)=(\varphi(x_i)\cdot\varphi(x_j))$. By using Lagrange multipliers to solve the quadratic programming problem with linear constraints, the dual is:

$$\max_{\alpha}\sum_{i=1}^{l}\alpha_i-\frac{1}{2}\sum_{i=1}^{l}\sum_{j=1}^{l}\alpha_i\alpha_j y_i y_j K(x_i\cdot x_j) \tag{4}$$

$$s.t.\quad \sum_{i=1}^{l}\alpha_i y_i=0, \tag{5}$$

$$0\le\alpha_i\le C, i=1,2,\cdots,l \tag{6}$$

where $\alpha_i, i=1,2,\cdots,l$ is Lagrange multipliers. Vectors x_i is called support vectors which correspond to latter two α_i . Only support vectors can be useful to the optimal hyperplane and decision function. By the dual Lagrange problem, we can get:

$$w=\sum_{i=1}^{l}\alpha_i y_i\varphi(x_i)\,. \tag{7}$$

Then decision function as follows:

$$f(x)=\mathrm{sgn}(\sum_{i=1}^{l}\alpha_i y_i K(x_i,x)+b)\,. \tag{8}$$

Suppose that N_{BSV+} and N_{BSV-} represent the number of positive and negative of the boundary support vectors respectively. N_{SV+} and N_{SV-} denote the number of them of the all support vectors respectively. l_+ and l_- are the number of them of the samples respectively, moreover $l = l_+ + l_-$. Assume that there is $\sum_{y_i=+1} \alpha_i = \sum_{y_i=-1} \alpha_i = A$, by the constraint (5), we have

$$\frac{N_{BSV+}}{l_+} \le \frac{A}{C \cdot l_+} \le \frac{N_{SV+}}{l_+} \tag{9}$$

$$\frac{N_{BSV-}}{l_-} \le \frac{A}{C \cdot l_-} \le \frac{N_{SV-}}{l_-} \tag{10}$$

By (9) and (10), we have the conclusion as follows.

(1) No considering of the significance difference between different samples, we maybe causes the important samples be classified wrong, because the decision function is put the new input data into the wrong class. Regarding the temporal data classification, we should take over the temporal factor, since recent data is more important than ancient data usually.

(2) If the number of the two classes samples is different, it is equal to $l_+ \ne l_-$. To the larger number class, the inaccuracy rate is small. But, to the small number class, the inaccuracy rate is big.

(3) Get rid of any data, the class accuracy maybe come under the influence. Regarding multi-classification of the temporal data, the SVM multi-classification technology about the one-against-one method and the combined binary tree method dissatisfy with it.

To sum up, in order to overcome the above problems, we develop the C-SVM in this paper, and propose a weighted support vector machine (briefly called W-SVM) to classify multi-classification with combining one-against-the rest method. The sample weight factors may get over the importance different problem of samples, and the class weight factors may get over the imbalance in the number of different classes problem. The one-against-the rest method considers the association of the temporal data which need the history data to predict.

2.2 Weighted Support Vector Machine

W-SVM aims to the shortage of C-SVM, the optimization problem as follows:

$$\min_{w,b,\xi} \frac{1}{2}\|w\|^2 + C\sum_{i=1}^{l} s_i \lambda_i \xi_i \tag{11}$$

$$s.t. \quad y_i[(w \cdot x_i) + b] \ge 1 - \xi_i, i = 1,2,\cdots,l, \tag{12}$$

$$\xi_i \ge 0, i = 1,2,\cdots,l, \tag{13}$$

where $s_i > 0$ is sample weight factors, $\lambda_i > 0$ is class weight factors, $s_i\lambda_i\xi_i$ denotes the loss error for samples x_i to be classified wrong. s_i is used to give weights for samples, when it is function, such as the function which can be changed by the arrival time of samples. Or, it may be constant $0 < s_i \le 1$, for example, to the abandon samples, the weight factors close to 0, but to the important samples, the weight factors close to 1, thus to overcome the insufficiency of C-SVM medol ignoring the importance different of samples. If we set s_i and λ_i are both equal to 1, then W-SVM the same as C-SVM, so we can regard C-SVM as an exceptional case of W-SVM.

Similarly as C-SVM algorithm, by using Lagrange multipliers to solve the quadratic programming problem, and we get the dual problem.

$$\max_{\alpha} \sum_{i=1}^{l} \alpha_i - \frac{1}{2}\sum_{i=1}^{l}\sum_{j=1}^{l} \alpha_i \alpha_j y_i y_j K(x_i \cdot x_j) \tag{14}$$

$$s.t. \ \sum_{i=1}^{l} \alpha_i y_i = 0, \tag{15}$$

$$0 \le \alpha_i \le C s_i \lambda_i, i = 1,2,\cdots,l\ . \tag{16}$$

The decision function is:

$$f(x) = \operatorname{sgn}(\sum_{i=1}^{l} \alpha_i y_i K(x_i, x) + b)\ . \tag{17}$$

By using the same analysis method, then we have

$$\frac{N_{BSV+}}{l_+} \le \frac{A}{C \cdot s_i \cdot \lambda_i \cdot l_+} \le \frac{N_{SV+}}{l_+} \tag{18}$$

$$\frac{N_{BSV-}}{l_-} \le \frac{A}{C \cdot s_i \cdot \lambda_i \cdot l_-} \le \frac{N_{SV-}}{l_-} \tag{19}$$

For the two classes classification, let the positive $\lambda_i = \lambda^+$, the negative $\lambda_i = \lambda^-$, where λ_+ and λ_- denote the class weight of them and s_i denote the sample weight of them.

In order to equilibrate the inaccuracy, we should to let $\frac{A}{C \cdot s_i \cdot \lambda^+ \cdot l_+} = \frac{A}{C \cdot s_i \cdot \lambda^- \cdot l_-}$, then we get the correlation as follows.

$$\frac{s_i \cdot \lambda^-}{s_i \cdot \lambda^+} = \frac{l_+}{l_-} \tag{20}$$

Obviously, the small number of class to enhance accuracy by increasing weight of penalty parameter, but this way would reduce accuracy of the large number of class. In other words, this model can enhance accuracy of the small class, but reduce accuracy of the large one at the same time. Therefore, we can affect precision through adjust $s_i \cdot \lambda^+$ and $s_i \cdot \lambda^-$.

3 Multi-classification Method of Temporal Data Based on SVM

There exist the temporal record in many real-world databases, and the length of time has a great impact on the validity of the temporal association rules, cycle length and sequence patterns.

Time in the real world is deemed to be limitless without beginning and ending. Time can be regarded as a real number axis, each point of which represents some moment, just like that described in physics. The interval from one point to another point can be viewed as some time. As a result, we call the moment in real world as absolute time tick (ATT), all of which constitute a real number set R (or time axis). In order to decide the real numbers which represent moment, we choose January 1, A.D.1 00:00:00 as the origin of the axis R and precision of every point on R is second or more precise unit. The interval from one point to another is called absolute time interval (ATI) which is a set of ATTs. For example, February 2, 2000 02:03:50 is an ATT and an ATI can be from February 2, 2000 00:00:00 to February 2,2000 24:00:00.

Now, we give a definition of temporal type as follows.

Definition 3.1. Let μ be a mapping from an t to an ATI $\mu(t)$, i.e., $R \to 2^R$, $t \in R$, $\mu(t) \in 2^R$, $t \to \mu(t)$. If all of the following (1)-(4) are satisfied, then μ is called a temporal type and $\mu(t)$ is called the temporal factor of the temporal type μ.

(1) (Non-empty) $\mu(t) \neq \varnothing$, for $t \in \mu(t)$.

(2) (Monotonous) For $t_1 < t_2$ and $\mu(t_1) \cap \mu(t_2) = \varnothing$, then arbitrary $t' \in \mu(t_1)$ and arbitrary $t'' \in \mu(t_2)$, $t' < t''$ holds, which is denoted by $\mu(t_1) < \mu(t_2)$.

(3) (Identical) For each $t' \in \mu(t)$, $\mu(t') = \mu(t)$.

(4) (Limitary) For each $t' \in \mu(t)$, $|t'| < +\infty$.

We suppose that the object which needs classification is temporal database D, $D = \{A_1, A_2, \cdots, A_l\}$, where $A_i (i = 1,2,\cdots,l)$ maybe called data members, samples, examples or objects and so on. $A_l = |D|$.

Classification of the temporal data is to establish a classification model through a finite training set of temporal data $T (\subseteq D)$ by a supervised learning. It can be used to predict the class label of current time through the forepart time data (several history time data). By using the classification model, the database D is to forecast the class label for the database D.

The data member A_i in database D has the temporal pattern $((E,O), valid\_time)$, where $valid\_time$ denotes the time constraints at current states, $|E| = |O| = l$, where $E_i (i = 1,2,\cdots,l)$ is input values or states of attributes of A_i, and $O_i (i = 1,2,\cdots,l)$ is output values or states of attributes of A_i.

The data members A_i in database *D*, the input data belong to a finite attributes set in the form of $E = \{e_1, e_2, \cdots, e_n\}$, where $e_i (i = 1,2,\cdots,n)$ is the input attribute i and n is the dimension of the input attributes of the database *D*. And the output data belongs to a finite attributes set too, $O = \{o_1, o_2, \cdots, o_m\}$, where $o_i (i = 1,2,\cdots,m)$ is the output attribute i and m is the dimension of the input attributes of the database *D*.

Definition 3.2. Assume that the attribute e_i / o_i values (they can be continual, or be separate) are denoted by $\{e[i,1], e[i,2], \cdots, e[i,c_i]\} / \{o[i,1], o[i,2], \cdots, o[i,c_i]\}$ $e[i,j] / o[i,j]$, $(j = 1,2,\cdots,c_i)$, if they are continual, they are called attribute values, whereas they are separate, they are called state values or class labels.

Suppose that v is a temporal type, notation $(E, O, v(t))$ represents the input attributes E and the output attributes O at the temporal factor $v(t)$.

For instance, the close price and volume are all rise of the stock A on February 2,2002, then it can be noted as ((open price, high price, low price, volume), (close price rise, volume rise), 20020202).

Given a temporal database *D*, a time interval $[T, T']$ and a the temporal type v, v slices time interval $[T, T']$ to l segments, $[T, T'] = \bigcup_{i=1}^{l} v(t_i)$, $t_1 < t_2 < \cdots < t_l$, $v(t_i) \cap v(t_j) = \varnothing, i \neq j, i, j = 1,2,\cdots,l$. In this instance, we can symbolize the temporal database, and obtain a symbolic temporal series:

$$S = \{((E_1, O_1), v(t_1)), ((E_2, O_2), v(t_2)), \cdots, ((E_l, O_l), v(t_l))\},$$

where for each $((E_i, O_i), v(t_i))$, $v(t_i)$ is the temporal factor of event or state with $v(t_1) \leq v(t_2) \leq \cdots \leq v(t_l)$, E_i is input attribute values and O_i is output state values, namely class labels.

Definition 3.3. The representation $(E, \hat{O}, v(t_k), p)$ denotes that the output values $\hat{O}$ at the temporal factor $v(t_k)$ that is forecasted by the input data at the first several temporal factors with $v(t_{k-1}), v(t_{k-2}), \cdots, v(t_{k-p})$. Then, p is called the insert dimension, which is not only integer, but also $p \geq 1$. So, we establish the mapping $g : R^p \to R$ as follows:

$$\hat{O}_{v(t_k)} = g(E_{v(t_{k-1})}, E_{v(t_{k-2})}, \cdots, E_{v(t_{k-p})}).$$

$\hat{O}_{v(t_k)}$ denotes the prediction values (output class labels) at the temporal factor $v(t_k)$. $E_{v(t_{k-j})}$ $(j = 1,2,\cdots,p)$ denotes the real values correlate with the prediction at the temporal factor $v(t_{k-j})$, where p is the insert dimension.

Based on temporal data characteristic, in order to introduce a method of the weighted support vector machine for classification prediction, renewal construction of linear space is the key point, transforming matrix form which can obtain the association of data in order to mine more information. By introducing the temporal pattern $((E,O), valid\_time)$ into weighted support vector machine, the temporal training data denote $T = \{((E_i, O_i), v(t_i) | i = 1,\cdots,l\}$, where the insert dimension pattern show $(E, \hat{O}, v(t_k), p)$. By Definition 3, we can take a self-correlation mapping form input $E_{v(t_k)} = \{E_{v(t_k-1)}, E_{v(t_k-2)},\cdots, E_{v(t_k-p)}\}$ to output $\{O_{v(t_k)}\}$. In order to unify correlative symbols, we regard the temporal data series $T = \{((E_i, O_i), v(t_i) | i = 1,\cdots,l\}$ as $T = \{((x_i, y_i), v(t_i) | i = 1,\cdots,l\}$.

For the sake of taking use of new information to enhance accuracy, we make use of sliding method for it. After this transformation, we can obtain the training samples for the weighted support vector machine (W-SVM), which becomes:

$$x = \begin{bmatrix} x_1 & x_2 & \cdots & x_p \\ x_2 & x_3 & \cdots & x_{p+1} \\ \vdots & \vdots & \ddots & \vdots \\ x_{l-p} & x_{l-p+1} & \cdots & x_{l-1} \end{bmatrix}, \quad y = \begin{bmatrix} y_{p+1} \\ y_{p+2} \\ \vdots \\ y_l \end{bmatrix}.$$

After getting the training samples, we can make training using the weighted support machine (W-SVM), where the decision function is form:

$$y_t = \mathrm{sgn}(\sum_{i=1}^{l-p} \alpha_i y_i K(\vec{x_i}, \vec{x_t}) + b), t = p+1,\cdots,l. \tag{21}$$

Because of $\vec{x}_{l+1} = \{x_{l-p+1}, x_{l-p+2},\cdots, x_l\}$, the prediction result of the point $l+1$ is:

$$y_{l+1} = \mathrm{sgn}(\sum_{i=1}^{l-p} \alpha_i y_i K(\vec{x_i}, \vec{x}_{l+1}) + b). \tag{22}$$

Now, we use index weight that denote the weight coefficients of samples as $s_i = \dfrac{1}{1+\exp(r-2ri/n)}, i = 1,2,\cdots,n$, where r is the parameter to control the raise speed.

W-SVM is a method based on two classes classification. In order to make multi-classification, we use the probability of the number of every class in training sets to weight every class, which is the multi-classification method based on probability weight. The basic idea of this method is that, regarding samples belong to certain class as a class (the positive), the rest samples as the other class (the negative), then carry out two class classification in turn.

Suppose that there is a C-class classification problem, let the training set $T = \{(x_i, y_i), i = 1,2,\cdots,l\}$, $x_i \in R^n$, $y_i \in \{1,2,\cdots,C\}$, where the class i has l_i samples, thus $l = l_1 + l_2 + \cdots, l_C$. The x_i^k denotes the training samples, where the subscript i is the class label, the superscript k is the sample k of the class i. So the training samples are denoted by $\Phi = \{x_i^k, i = 1,2,\cdots,C, k = 1,2\cdots,l_i\}$. The multi-classification method of temporal data based on W-SVM is given as follows.

(1) Calculate the probability of every class: $P_i = l_i / l, i = 1,2,\cdots,C$.

(2) Arrange probability in descending sequence: $P_{m1} \geq P_{m2} \geq \cdots \geq P_{mc}$.

(3) Set the counter $k = 1$.

(4) Construct the training set $\Phi_k = A + B$ of the sub-classifier W-SVM$_k$, where

$$A = \{(X_{mk}, +1)\},\ B = \{(Y, -1) \mid y \in \{\Phi - \{X_{mk}\}\}\}$$

A is the positive set, and B is the negative set, adjusting the class weight coefficient λ_m^- based on P_{mk}, forming two classes classification problem.

(5) Adjust the counter $k = k + 1$.

(6) Repeat (4)~(5), until constructing the sub-classifier W-SVMc.

4 Experiment Results

In order to examine the performance of the above method, we use the same data and one-against-the rest multi-classification method for W-SVM and C-SVM to predict the class labels of close price of some stock. Let the temporal type is day, and the temporal constraint conditions are stock trading days, then the stock trading series can be regarded as continual time series.

Let us take a stock Wanke as experiment data, stock data form March 1, 2001 to August 16, 2002, sum total 350 stock data. The temporal pattern denotes as ((open price, high price, low price, close price , volume), close price, 20010301-20020816). Firstly, we standardize the input data, these continual attribute values mapped into [-1,1]. Secondly, we disperse the output data (decision attribute), class the close price into five classes according stock knowledge. The transform formula is denoted by $SX = \frac{s_n - s_{n-1}}{s_{n-1}}$, where SX is the fluctuation rates comparing to the values of attribute s (close price) at the trading day n to the values of attribute s at the former trading day. $SX \in (-0.1, -0.02]$, which is big fall, is denoted by the class label 1. $SX \in (-0.02, -0.01]$, which is small fall, is denoted by the class label 2.

$SX \in (-0.01, 0.01]$, which is ordinary fluctuation, is denoted by the class label 3. $SX \in (0.01, 0.02]$, which is small rise, is denoted as the class label 4. $SX \in (0.02, 0.1]$, which is big rise, is denoted by the class label 5. So the purpose of the experiment is to carry on 5 categories classification about close price using the history stock data to forecast the class label of the next day.

In this experiment, let the insert dimension $p = 5$, the same as the opening days of stock in a week and the penalty parameter $C = 400$. Let the kernel function be Gaussian RBF kernel function $K(x, y) = \exp(-\frac{1}{2\sigma^2}\|x - y\|^2), \sigma > 0$. We obtain the results of the experiment in Table 1, where Table 1 denoted the prediction results of stock Wanke. In Table 1, the number of training data sets to be 60, 80, 120, 160,200,300 belong to the former 60,80,120,160,200,300 data in the training set in the valid time which are selected at first. 2, 4, 6, 8, 10 denoted the testing sets following the corresponding training sets.

We can see from the results of the table 1, the accommodation of W-SVM has advanced to predict temporal data. The accuracy has enhanced comparing W-SVM to C-SVM. On the whole, the classification accuracy of W-SVM all achieve above 50%, but the classification accuracy of C-SVM lows to 0% at some time. The accuracy is affected more by training sets of C-SVM, but W-SVM can adjust training sets to make the accuracy stably. On the particular, the prediction accuracy has arrived 100% to predict the following two days, it is good guidance for us to stock trade.

Table 1. The accuracy of close price prediction of stock Wanke

Training data set	Multi-classification	accuracy (%)				
		2	4	6	8	10
60	C-SVM	100	75	66.7	75	60
	W-SVM	100	100	100	100	80
80	C-SVM	0	0	33.3	25	40
	W-SVM	100	75	66.7	62.5	60
120	C-SVM	50	50	33.3	37.5	30
	W-SVM	100	75	66.7	62.5	50
160	C-SVM	50	50	33.3	25	20
	W-SVM	100	75	66.7	62.5	60
200	C-SVM	100	75	50	37.5	30
	W-SVM	100	100	66.7	62.5	50
300	C-SVM	0	25	16.7	25	40
	W-SVM	100	75	50	62.5	60

The experiments show that, by the algorithm of W-SVM, the accuracy has no increase along with increasing the number of training sets, which displays good stability. It is to say, small number of samples can get good prediction results by W-SVM.

5 Conclusion

We have proposed the classification prediction model of temporal data based on W-SVM. By W-SVM with weight factors for samples and classes, we obtain a multi-classification method of the temporal data. The method can effectively solve the misclassification problems which result from the different importance of samples and the imbalance in the number of training sets of different classes. So how to determine samples' weight coefficients more conveniently is a question which needs to solve.

Acknowledgements

This research work was partially supported by grant No. Z105185 from Zhejiang Provincial Nature Science Foundation.

Reference

1. Meng Zhiqing: Study of Temporal Type and Time Granularity in the Temporal Data Mining. Natural Science Journal of Xiangtan University, **22(3)**(2000)1-4
2. Wang, X., Bettini, C., Brodsky, A., Jajodia, S.: Logical Design for Temporal Databases with Multiple Granuarities. ACM Trans Database Systerm 22(2), 115–170 (1997)
3. Cao, L.J. et al.: Dynamic support vector machines for non_stationary time series forecasting. Intelligent Data Analysis 6, 67–83 (2002)
4. Tay, F.E.H., Cao, L.J.: Modified support vector machines in financial time series forecasting. Neurocomputing 48, 847–861 (2002)
5. Deshan, S., Jinpei, W.: Application of LS-SVM to Prediction of Chaotic Time Series. Computer Technology and Development 14(1), 21–23 (2004)
6. Hongye, W., Jianhua, W., Wei, H.: Study on the Support Vector Machines Model for Sales Volume Prediction and Parameters Selection. Acta Simulata Systematic Sinica 17(1), 33–36 (2005)

Towards a Management Paradigm with a Constrained Benchmark for Autonomic Communications

Frank Chiang and Robin Braun

Faculty of Engineering, University of Technology Sydney,
Broadway, NSW 2007, Australia
frankj@eng.uts.edu.au

Abstract. This paper describes a management paradigm to give effect to autonomic activation, monitoring and control of services or products in the future converged telecommunications networks. It suggests an architecture that places the various management functions into a structure that can then be used to select those functions which may yield to autonomic management, as well as guiding the design of the algorithms. The validation of this architecture, with particular focus on *service configuration,* is done via a genetic algorithm — Population Based Incremental Learning (PBIL). Even with this centralized adaptation strategy, the simulation results show that the proposed architecture and benchmark can be applied to this constrained benchmark, produces effective convergence performance in terms of finding nearly optimal configurations under multiple constraints.

1 Introduction

The management of current telecommunication networks involves a strong reliance on expert intervention from human operators. The centralized infrastructure in traditional network management systems forces the human operators to have wide ranging expertise on how to discover changes, configure services, recover from failures and alarms, and optimize managed resources to maximize QoS, etc. However, the increasing complexity the networks, the highly distributed nature of Network Elements (NEs) as well as the growing multidimensional inter-dependencies between NEs is beginning to indicate that network management is rapidly reaching the point where manual/automatic systems will no longer suffice. Autonomic systems are essential. (By automatic we mean systems that react according to predefined rules. However, by Autonomic we mean systems that create their own adaptation strategies driven by system objectives.) There is an urgent need to explore the distributed *autonomic* ways to manage future complex distributed electronic environments.

This paper describes a telecommunications management architecture that both acts as a reference to conventional systems and as a guiding structure to potential autonomic action in selected areas. It covers a number of essential

Y. Wang, Y. Cheung, and H. Liu (Eds.): CIS 2006, LNAI 4456, pp. 250–258, 2007.

functions: adaptive system objectives setting-up, information domains searching, end-to-end monitoring, service discovery, service selection, service composition, service provisioning or activation. This architecture is based on the TMF [1] entity-based 4 layer telecommunications management structure. It does not relate in any way to the ISO 7 layer communications model, except to note that physical message passing between the layers can be accomplished by electronic communications systems based on the 7 layer structure. This is a notional/conceptual architecture that allows us to understand the setup and management of the system. It is not intended to indicate the physical connectivity of any component with any other. Indeed, it is agnostic to any specific protocol, either physical or logical. In a way, it can be seen that the 7 layer structure is orthogonal to our management architecture [2][3][4].

The remainder of the paper is organized as follows. Section 2 demonstrates new mangement paradigm. Section 3 and 4 presents a constrained benchmark structure including information model, objective function and a reference model is presented. As a validation test, the simulation results of email service provisioning in Section 5 show the effectiveness of our autonomic solution to this constrained benchmark framework by the nature-inspired adaptation strategy - PBIL. Finally we conclude the contributions of this paper.

2 A New Management Paradigm to Allow for Autonomic Behaviors in Selected Areas

2.1 An Understanding of Autonomic Communication

Self-management is considered as the key characteristic for autonomic communication in Horn's report in 2001 and in IBM redbook at the year 2003 [5], and self-management as a computational vision described by IBM in their autonomic communication blueprint. As the increasing chanllenges of pervasive computing and infrastructurless networks (E.g., P2P networks and Wireless Ad-hoc Sensor Networks (WASNs)), self-managed network is playing a key role and is regarded as the solution to these chanllenges in Pervasive computing, MANET. However, the autonomic scenario is NOT equivalent to the self-management scenario which is tackled at a computational level.

Recent researches on autonomic communication reported by Strassner [6], Kephart [7] pointed out that autonomy is a higher level notation to the computational level and is therefore more than *self-management,* that is driven by high-level business objectives or being specified by human operators. Although we share same view on this point, we emphasize that only a distributed electronic system with *learning and adaptation strategies* can be called autonomic systems, which can adapt to changing system objectives and circumstances, and satisfy on-demanding business-driven services initiatives. It is the authors' belief that a successful ACN should develop in two directions as illustrated in our paper [8].

We define autonomic communication for this purpose as follows: *Distributed communication systems with the learning and adaptation capability to cope well*

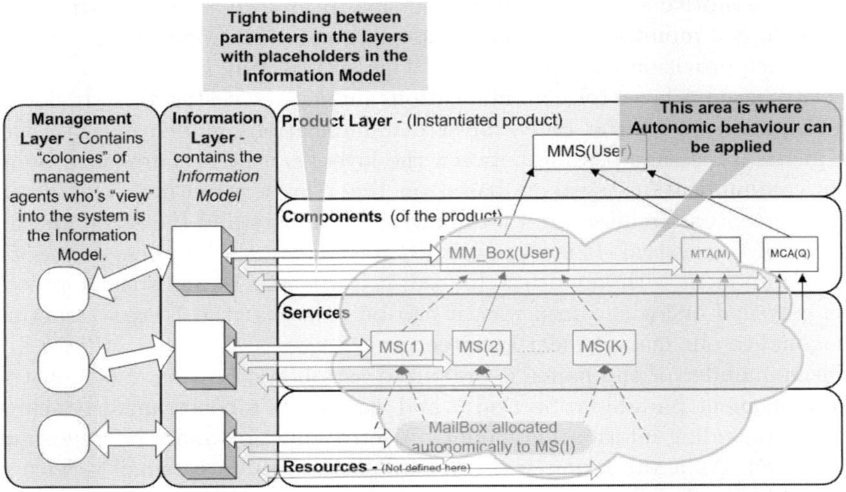

Fig. 1. Specific example of the 4 layer model

with dynamic, uncertain and complex environments - that is, immediately adapt their strategies in accordance with high-level business objectives and rules in order to maximize service satisfaction within available services and managed resources.

2.2 A Structure for Autonomic Behavior

The layered structure lends itself to the selected introduction of Autonomic behavior related to specific functions. For example, the product setup process involves the allocation of specific services to specific product components. In a conventional system, this may be done by the system engineer as part of a system configuration process, according to a set of business and design rules. On the other hand, such a function could be done autonomically at operational time using autonomic adaptation strategies that may perhaps be econometric, or based on trust and reliability or even swarming behavior.

An example we have described is the function of configuring MMS mailbox servers to specific customer MMS mailboxes in accordance with the SLA between customers and providers (See Fig. 1). We carry on this by introducing market force concepts to a number of selected agents residing in the Management Layer . In so doing, we allow them to have measures of autonomy, with intelligence, goals and desires, and social awareness.

3 A Constrained Benchmark Structure

3.1 A Reference Model

Our analysis is on the basis of Object-Oriented Principles (OOP). We consider a TMF entity-based network operation system with n_p product instances for

c_p classes of products; n_c product component instances for c_c classes of product components; n_s service instances for c_s classes of services; and n_r resource instances for c_r classes of resources. The cost elements between instances of $(n_p \times n_c), (n_c \times n_s), (n_s \times n_r)$ construct link cost matrices, which are assumed to be constant only during one iteration search and vary independently from one iteration to another. We denote the followings:

$$\begin{aligned}
&\mathbf{P}^1_{\{1,\ldots,n_p\}}, \mathbf{P}^2_{\{1,\ldots,n_p\}}, \ldots, \mathbf{P}^{c_p}_{\{1,\ldots,n_p\}};\\
&\mathbf{C}^1_{\{1,\ldots,n_c\}}, \ldots, \mathbf{C}^{c_c}_{\{1,\ldots,n_c\}};\\
&\mathbf{S}^1_{\{1,\ldots,n_s\}}, \ldots, \mathbf{S}^{c_s}_{\{1,\ldots,n_s\}};\\
&\mathbf{R}^1_{\{1,\ldots,n_r\}}, \ldots, \mathbf{R}^{c_r}_{\{1,\ldots,n_r\}}.
\end{aligned}$$

where $\mathbf{C}$ can be regarded as the "terminal" of "concentrator" $\mathbf{P}$; $\mathbf{S}$ is the "terminal" of "Concentrator" $\mathbf{C}$; and $\mathbf{R}$ is the "terminal" of "Concentrator" $\mathbf{S}$, and $n_p, n_c, n_s, n_r \in \mathbb{R}^+$, and *subscript* numbers $\{1,\ldots,n_p\}, \{1,\ldots,n_c\}, \{1,\ldots,n_s\}$ and $\{1,\ldots,n_r\}$ represent various instances of network components belonging to the particular class out of c_p, c_c, c_s, c_r respectively.

We use the following nomenclature to describe the "components" ,"services" and "resources" that go to make up an instantiation of"product" P_i. Let $\mathbf{Cost}(\cdot)$ be *total costs*, which are associated with three main costs: (1) the cost via the link (e.g., transmission cost via wireless channel; traffic condition influenced cost due to finite link capacity etc) and (2) the Total Cost of Ownership (TCO). TCO includes tangible base cost of CO (Cost of Ownership) and intangible costs. And (3) *Cost of goal-driven Service-Composition (CSC)*: the activation of a SLA-defined service usually involves many decomposed subservices to work together. Subservices that may need to use the services of others are integrated and assembled together. Goal-driven autonomic element-based service activation requires the component-based service to be able to be self-assembled.

$$\mathbf{Cost}(\cdot) \triangleq \begin{cases} \begin{bmatrix} f(\cdot) = CSC + BC + VC \\ \varphi\left(\omega_{n,i,k}(t), R_{n,i,k}(t), C_{n,i}(t), \lambda_{j,k}\right) \\ \text{Components logically connected} \end{bmatrix} \\ \\ \begin{bmatrix} \propto \\ \text{Not logically connected} \end{bmatrix} \end{cases} \tag{1}$$

Where $\varphi\left(\omega_{n,i,k}(t), R_{n,i,k}(t), C_{n,i}(t), \lambda_{j,k}\right) \in \mathbb{R}^n$ are the link costs relating only to the components in the resource layer. CPU/Memory usage, bandwidth, capacity are all factors required in the calculation of cost. CSC is the cost for service composition.

The cost values are determined in three parts. The first part considers mainly link costs consisting of the parameters in Table 1. The second part is determined by TCO, which is a function of BC and VC as shown in equation 1. The third part is determined by CSC which depends on the integration costs.

Table 1. Costs and Determined Parameters

Parameters	Cost
Traffic Intensity Condition ↑	↑
Node Capacity Level and Link Capacity Level ↓	↑
Delay Time ↑	↑

3.2 Benchmarking Structure and Its Cost Model

This benchmark structure has a strong link with our architecture described in previous publications. Figure 2 depicts the constrained benchmark structure containing the object nodes as the instantiation from classes. Each node in this figure represents one managed element (including managed services and managed physical resources) in the four layer model. The edge weights $a(i,j)$ between them denote the Effective Cost (EC) that the configuration process needed.

We describe it as a *constrained* structure due to two reasons (1) the quantity of the objects nodes for each class are restricted to 4. For the purpose of presentation, we also assume each layer has 4 classes (except product layer), and each class has 4 object instantiations. In addition, some nodes are restricted to be *complete* nodes, this is more close to real-world scenario. For example, node j is one *complete node.* (2) The decision making follows a *deterministic* "candidate list" as similarly suggested by Marco Dorigo. This *candidate list* provides possible paths as roughly-known directions for the agents. Agents behave randomly within those possible candidate clusters, such that, the dimensions of the search space are further reduced as well as the computational time being kept within reasonable limits. The candidate list is determined by the following three preliminary parameters —

1) Dependency String (DependsOn): Denoted as D, is a binary string;

2) Connectivity Binary String: shows connection status between individual objects;.

3) Cost of Usage: considers the sum of integrated service costs defined in Equation 1.

The service configuration process needs the information of the *Effective Costs* (EC) instead of cost information. EC is a function of dependency and costs, and is stored into a *local information centre.* The calculation EC is illustrated in equation 2:

$$EC(i) = D \times \ Cost(i) \tag{2}$$

How the AEs get the cost values via external environments or by coordination behaviors are not in the scope of this paper. We assume these information is provided in the local information center and is stored into hierarchical XML structure for our calculation purpose.

4 A PBIL Implementation of the Benchmark

The simulation model evaluates how the Population Based Incremental Learning (PBIL), as a special type of genetic algorithm (GA), can be adaptable to the

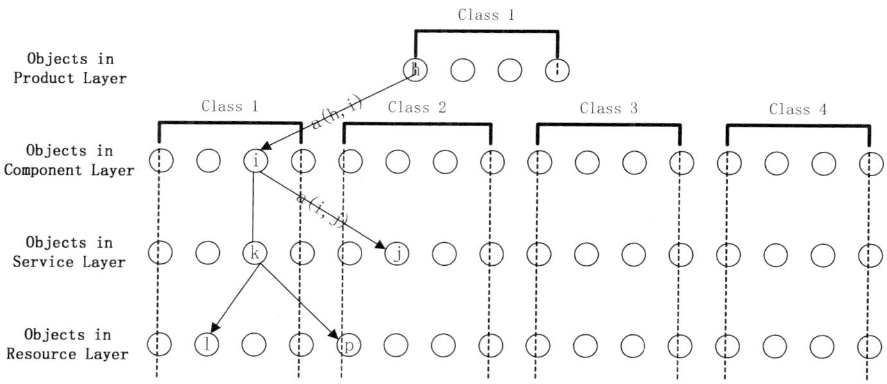

Fig. 2. Graphical Representation for Managed Elements

dynamic environment with its "learning" (via probability vector) and adaptation strategy in order to fulfill our configuration task. PBIL searching strategy has been applied in many fields since initially being proposed by Baluja in the year 1995 [9]. In accordance with our architecture, we take email accounts configuration as a testing scenario.

The following shows the email configuration process with regards to our analysis in the previous section. This matches with what we discussed previously in the algorithm part, we assume the same number of classes and the same number of objects instantiated from corresponding class. That is,

---

1. In the product layer, there is a class of product --- Email(User), under this class, there are 4 objects -$P_{0...3}$ which are instantiations of a Golden Email Account.

2. In the component layer, there are assumed to be four classes of components. Some components could be --- a) C_0 - Basic_Email_Box(users); b) C_1- Dial-up Internet; c) C_2 - Premium_Email_Box(User); and d) C_3 - Broadband Connection.

Each one of the classes contain 4 objects and are denoted as $C_{00}, C_{01}, C_{02}, C_{03}$ and so do service and resource objects

In the service layer, there are assumed to be 4 classes of services. Some services could be --- a) S_0 - Transport (its objects are, for example, POP/IMAP, TCP/IP, SMTP, DNS); b) S_1 - Authentication (e.g., SpamFilteringet al.); c) S_2 - Anti-Virus (e.g., VirusFiltering); d) S_3 - Billing Service

In the resource layer, there are assumed to be 4 classes of resource. Some resources could be --- a) R_0 - Router; b) R_1 - Switch; c) R_2 - Backoffice Storage Servers; d) R_3 - Bandwidth

---

To simplify the computational complexity in the simulation, we assume each class has only 4 instantiated objects with regards to different users' SLA. Therefore, the total number of objects is 52. The data used to calculate *effective cost* are derived from our university campus network based on monthly throughput.

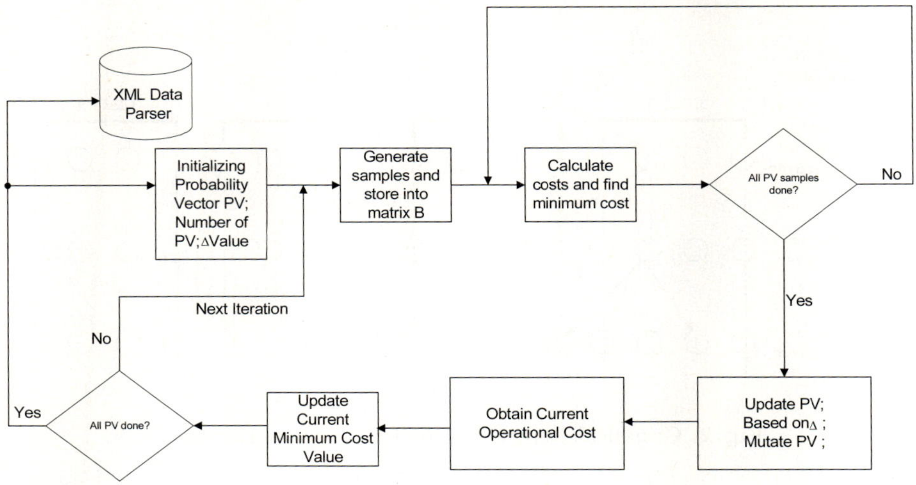

Fig. 3. PBIL algorithm for network optimization

```
The application of PBIL algorithm into proposed structure is described as follows:
1. Create classes, methods under OOP principle
  Instantiate Objects
2. Initialize Probability Vector PV ( =0.5 for all bits )
  Set number of PV (=100 for instance); Set Δ = 0.02; Set iteration loops L (= 500 for
instance)
For K=1: L
Loop ⟹
Repeat {
(1) Loop: ⟶ Generate samples and store into a matrix B which has L columns, R rows
            According to the Criteria: B(i) = rand(1) < PV(i);
(2) Find: ⟶ Minimum Cost for objects which can be found by the decimal sum of the samples
bits
            Complete all 100 PV samples vectors
(3) Update ⟶ Probability Vector
        Loop: ⟶ over each bit of PV
                If  (Bit of sample vector PV ≥ 0.5)
                  Then this Bit ⟵ 1;
                   PV_Update = PV_previous + Δ;  End If
                If  (Bit of sample vector PV ≤ 0.5)
                  Then this Bit ⟵ 0;
                   PV_Update = PV_previous − Δ;  End If
Mutate ⟶ Probability Vector
                   PV(i) = PV_Update }
```

Figure 3 shows the flowchart of PBIL algorithm. This flowchart describes the algorithmic steps towards minimum cost calculation. The detailed illustration can be found in the following pseudocode presentation which explains initialization of parameters; how to update probability vector, and how to get the minimum cost value, etc.

5 Simulation Results

The paths discovered by the centralised PBIL algorithm formulate a best configuration solution on the basis of *cost* criteria described by the objective function. The nodes along this configuration path represent the components to be necessarily included. A Java-based PBIL application for this configuration process is designed, and the simulation GUI is constructed. The path discovered by the PBIL algorithm is encoded in the probability vector in Figure 4.

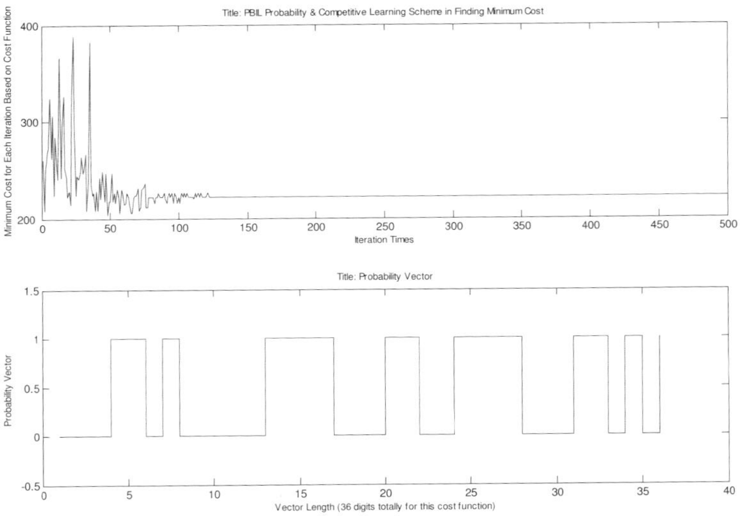

Fig. 4. Performance of PBIL adaptation strategy applied into minimum cost evaluation

Our particular configuration problem requires (1) a 36-pair of binary string (=72 bits) to describe the edges between 52 nodes; (2) n (e.g., 100) trial sample vectors which are generated according to the Probability Vector (PV). After each generation, the PV will be adjusted incrementally to the effect that the best solution sets are to be enhanced and the bad solutions are to be diminished; (3) 500 loops of iterations which corresponding to the the number of generations. (Actually, 500 is larger than we require. Generally, 100 will suffice.) We noted that the discovered path strongly depends on the cost values.

Figure 4 shows the performance test on PBIL adaptation strategy with regards to achieving minimum cost in terms of instantiating a service or a product. Around 100 iterations are sufficient to find a configuration path in a converged telecommunication network. The binary string of final probability vector indicates the subscript of network components in need of being involved into this configuration process given to the known system objectives.

6 Conclusion

The purpose of this paper is to describe a notional management structure that would lend itself to the selective introduction of autonomic behavior into those parts of the OSS where it would be appropriate. The validation of this architecture is done via one stochastic searching-based genetic algorithm - PBIL, which has been applied to service configuration issues by incorporating this notional management structure.

The main benefit of the model is that it clearly indicates: 1) How to position autonomic behavior and how to set it in the context with the OSS systems; 2) How it might be simulated and how it might be implemented in real applications

The simulation results show that this proposed architecture and benchmark issues can be well fitted into the autonomic communication networks in an ever-changing complex network environment as long as the eligible self-learning and adaptation strategy or corresponding algorithms are carefully designed and implemented. Although PBIL is essentially a centralized scheme, good performance is still achieved for the given configuration problem.

References

1. Tech. Rep. TMF053, TMF: The ngoss technology neutral architecture specification v3.0. (2003)
2. Chiang, F., Braun, R., Hughes, J.: A biologically inspired multi-agent architecture for autonomic service management. Journal of Pervasive Computing and Communications 2(3), 261–275 (2006)
3. Chiang, F., Braun, R., Magrath, S., Markovits, S.: Autonomic service configuration in telecommunication mass with extended role-based gaia and jadex. In: Proceeding of 2005 IEEE International Conference on Service Systems and Service Management, pp. 1319–1324 (2005)
4. Magrath, S., Chiang, F., Braun, R., Markovits, S., Cuervo, F.: Autonomic telecommunications service activation. In: Workshop on Autonomic Communication for Evolvable Next GenerationNetworks, 7th International Symposium on Autonomous Decentralized Systems, pp. 731–736 (2005)
5. Tech. rep. IBM: The redbook of autonomic computing. (2003)
6. Strassner, J.: Autonomic networking - theory and practice (tutorial session). In: Proceedings of IEEE/IFIP Network Operations and Management (2006)
7. Kephart, J.: Research challenges of autonomic computing. In: ICSE'05 (St. Louis, Missouri, USA) (2005)
8. Chiang, F., et al.: Self-configuration of network services with nature-inspired learning and adaptation. Journal of Network and Systems Management 15, 87–116 (2006)
9. Baluja, S., Caruana, R.: Removing the genetics from the standard genetic algorithm, pp. 38–46. Morgan Kaufmann Publishers, San Francisco (1995)

A Feature Selection Algorithm Based on Discernibility Matrix

Fuyan Liu[1] and Shaoyi Lu[2]

[1] Institute of Management Science & Information Engineering,
Hangzhou Dianzi University,
Xiasha Higher Education Zone, Hangzhou, Zhejiang, 310018, China
Dzh05@126.com

[2] School of Electronics & Information, Hangzhou Dianzi University,
Xiasha Higher Education Zone, Hangzhou, Zhejiang, 310018, China
L10081@126.com

Abstract. A heuristic algorithm of reduct computation for feature selection is proposed in the paper, which is a discernibility matrix based method and aims at reducing the number of irrelevant and redundant features in data mining. The method used both significance information of attributes and information of discernibility matrix to define the necessity of heuristic feature selection. The advantage of the algorithm is that it can find an optimal reduct for feature selection in most cases. Experimental results confirmed the above assertion. It also shown that the proposed algorithm is more efficient in time performance comparing with other similar computation methods.

1 Introduction

Knowledge discovery and data mining is a multi-disciplinary effort to mine or extract useful information from database [1] [2]. But the increasingly massive data sets from many application domains have posed unprecedented challenges to it. Models derived from these data sets are mostly empirical. Thus a database always contains a lot of features that are redundant and irrelevant for rule discovery. If these redundant features cannot be removed, not only the time complexity of the rule discovery process increases, but also the quality of the discovered rules may be lowered. Therefore feature selection is necessary and it is unreasonable or even impossible to use all original features of the problem in computation. Feature selection is not only an efficient and effective process but also a necessary step in data mining [3].

The function of feature selection methods in data mining problems is to perform selecting an optimal subset of features from the data set of the application according to some criteria in order to obtain a more essential and simple representation of the available information. As a result, redundant and irrelevant data will be removed, the dimensionality of the feature space will be reduced, which will speed up data mining algorithm process, improve data quality and performance of data mining, and increase the comprehensibility of the mining results. So that the selected subset should be small in size and it should retain the original information, which is most useful for a particular application [4].

Y. Wang, Y. Cheung, and H. Liu (Eds.): CIS 2006, LNAI 4456, pp. 259–269, 2007.

In this paper we proposed a heuristic reduct computation algorithm for feature selection in acquiring knowledge rules. It is a rough set based method. The rough set theory is capable of dealing with uncertain problems. The main goal of the rough set analysis is induction of approximations of concepts. It can be used for feature selection, feature extraction, data reduction, decision rule generation, and pattern extraction etc. It also can be used to identify partial or total dependencies in data and eliminate redundant data. In general, it can provide a sound basis for variety of areas including data mining, machine learning and others [5].

The rough set based method proposed in the paper is a heuristic method, which used a discernibility matrix for reduct computation and aims at reducing the number of irrelevant and redundant features. The features are measured by their necessity in heuristic feature selection. The main idea of the heuristic method is that it uses frequency information of features appeared in discernibility matrix and it is based on a feature sorting mechanism.

The paper is organized as follows. In the next section, related rough set concepts are introduced briefly. Then a simple overview on related previous work is presented. In the following section, feature selection algorithms and search methods are presented mainly. Then a discernibility matrix based heuristic method for feature selection is proposed. Finally, experimental results are discussed, which showed the efficiency and effectiveness of the proposed method. In the end of this paper concluding remark is given.

2 Preliminaries

Rough set theory was proposed by Pawlak firstly in 1982 [6]. Hu et al. presented the formal definitions of rough set theory [7] and A. Kusiak described the basic concepts of rough set theory [8].

In rough set theory, a knowledge representation system S or a decision table can be expressed as a tuple: $S=\{U, A\}$, where $U\neq\phi$ is called the universe which is a non-empty finite set, A is a finite set of attributes (or features). The attribute set A might be divided into C and d, i.e.: $A=C\cup d$, and $C\cap d=\phi$, C is called a set of condition attributes and d is a decision attribute.

Let $P\subseteq A$ be a subset of attributes. The equivalence relation, denoted by IND(P), is defined as:

$$IND(P)=\{(x,y)\in U\times U:\forall a\in P, a(x)=a(y)\}, \quad (1)$$

where a(x) and a(y) denote the values of both object x and object y with respect to feature a.

The family of all equivalence classes of IND(P) is denoted by U/IND(P) and we use $R_C=U/IND(C)$ and $R_D=U/IND(d)$ to indicate equivalence classes of C and d respectively.

For any concept (a subset of objects of U) $X\subseteq U$ and attribute subset $R\subseteq A$, then the lower approximation of X is defined as a set of objects of U that are in X with certainty, and defined as below:

$$R_{-}(X) = \cup\{E \in U / IND(R) : E \subseteq X\}. \quad (2)$$

The upper approximation of X is the set of objects of U that are in X possibly, and defined as formula (3):

$$R^{-}(X) = \cup\{E \in U / IND(R) : E \cap X = \phi\}. \quad (3)$$

The positive region of decision class U/IND(d) with respect to condition attributes C is denoted by $POS_C(d)=\cup R\_(X)$, which is a set of objects of U that can be classified with certainty to classes U/IND(d) employing attributes of C.

A reduct is the minimal set of attributes preserving the positive region. A reduct of B is defined as a set of attributes $B' \subseteq B$, if $POS_B(d)=POS_{B'}(d)$, and there is no $C \subseteq B'$ such that $POS_B(d)=POS_C(d)$ holds. The intersection of all reducts is called CORE. All attributes presented in the CORE are indispensable. Usually there are many reducts in an information system. Finding all the reducts from a decision table is NP-Hard [9] and it is not necessary to find all of them in many real applications. Usually to compute one such reduct is sufficient [7].

In order to find the reducts, discernibility matrix and discernibility function are employed in this paper. The discernibility matrix of an information system is a $|U| \times |U|$ matrix with entries C_{ij} defined as $\{a \in A | \ a(x_i) \neq a(x_j)\}$ if $d(x_i) \neq d(x_j)$. A discernibility function can be constructed from a discernibility matrix through "$\vee$" and "$\wedge$" operators. The selection of the best reduct depends on the optimality criterion associated with the attributes. In this paper we adopted the criteria that the best reduct is the one with the minimal number of attributes.

3 Simple Review on Relevant Previous Work

In this section we give a simple review on some previous work of heuristic feature selection methods, which were based on rough set theory and appeared in the literature in recent years.

The main role of some proposed relevant methods is to preserve frequency information about condition and decision dependency under different approximate criteria. Paper [10] proposed a rough set based feature selection approach. It is a parameterized average support heuristic and it selected features causing high average support of rules over all decision classes. Deogun et al implemented a rough set based feature selection algorithm [11], they adopted a backward attribute elimination method to reduce search space and also they used upper approximation in the algorithm instead of using positive region as significance of attribute set. Michal and Jacek used the dependency coefficient as heuristics and developed a greedy algorithm program in their rough set library [12]. After greedily adding attributes which mostly increase dependency coefficient of candidate reduct set, the algorithm has a pruning procedure to ensure a minimum of resulting reduct set. Hu et. al. proposed a rough set based algorithm for feature selection through using discernibility matrix [13]. N. Zhong and A. Skowron have applied rough sets with heuristics and rough sets with Boolean reasoning for attribute selection and discretization of real-valued attributes [14]. R. Jenson and Q. Shen have developed the Quickreduct algorithm to compute a minimal reduct without exhaustively generating all possible subsets and also they developed fuzzy-rough attribute reduction with application to web categorization [15] [16]. K. Thangavel et. al. applied rough sets for feature selection in medical databases [17]. Q. Shen and A. Chouchoulas developed a fuzzy-rule induction algorithm with a rough set-assisted feature reduction method [18]. They also developed a modular approach to generate fuzzy rules with reduced attributes [19]. Paper [20] proposed a rough set based approach, where an information system without any decision attribute is considered. It applied K-Means algorithm to cluster the given information system for different values of K. So that decision table could be formulated using this clustered data as the decision variable. Then Quick and variable precision rough set reduct algorithms were applied for selecting features.

4 Feature Selection

Feature selection has been studied intensively in recent years [3] [20] [21] [22]. As stated earlier in this paper, feature selection is a process to find the optimal subset of features that satisfies certain criteria. The aim of feature selection is to remove features unnecessary to the target concept. Unnecessary features can be classified into irrelevant features and redundant ones. Irrelevant features are those that do not affect the target concept in any way, while redundant ones do not add anything new to it.

All feature selection algorithms fall into two categories: the filter approach and the wrapper approach. In the filter approach, the feature selection is performed as a preprocessing step to induction. This approach can be computed easily and very efficiently. The characteristics in the feature selection are uncorrelated to that of classifiers. Therefore they have better generalization property. In the wrapper approach [23], the feature selection is wrapped around a classifier: the usefulness of a feature is directly judged by the estimated classification accuracy of specific classifier. Wrapper methods typically require extensive computation to search the best features.

Feature selection can be viewed as a search problem, and the whole search space covers all 2^n subsets of n features [24]. There are three types of search methods adopted mainly for feature selection: exhaustive, random and heuristic. The exhaustive search method is to enumerate all the candidate subsets and apply the evaluation measure to them. However it is infeasible usually due to its high time complexity. A random search is a method, where the candidate feature subset is generated randomly. After the feature subset is generated an evaluation measure is applied to it. This process will repeat until one subset satisfies pre-defined criteria. The third search method is the most popular and commonly used heuristic method. It uses a heuristic function to drive the search towards the direction in which the value of the heuristic function is to be maximized [25]. Comparing to the exhaustive search method, random search and heuristic search can reduce complexity in computation, but have sacrificing in performance: they do not guarantee to produce an optimal result. Nevertheless, heuristic search is a very important and popular search method and it is adopted in our paper.

In addition, there are some basic issues related to heuristic feature selection as described in the following.

The first issue is to decide from which state in the search space that the search starts. We may adopt forward selection that starts with an empty feature set and successively adds features one by one. Another approach is to employ backward elimination that starts with all features and successively removes unnecessary features. The search also may start from the middle of the search space. In rough set based feature selection approaches, the CORE can be used as the starting point.

The second issue of heuristic search is how the search is executed. With greedy method, it traverses the search space without backtrack. At each step, one feature is added or removed. By using stepwise method, it adds or removes a feature that was removed or added in the previous step.

Another basic issue is the stop criteria. A stop criterion is used to halt the search process. In the rough sets based method, the size of the positive region could be used as stop criteria.

5 The Proposed Algorithm

5.1 Discernibility Matrix

According to Susmaga's survey on some reduct maintenance algorithms [26], where discernibility matrix based methods were found more efficient than traditional ones, Hu et. al. proposed a feature-ranking algorithm, which used both significance information of attributes and information of discernibility matrix [13]. This algorithm can find optimal reduct in most cases. Our heuristic method for feature selection proposed in this paper is also based on Susmaga's conclusion, and it is shown experimentally that our method has more efficient and effective performance.

In a discernibility matrix, every entry represents a set of attributes discerning two objects. As an example, Table 1 shows a discernibility matrix of an information system. The discernibility function f(S) of an information system is shown in Table 1, which can be simplified as: $f(S)=(p\wedge c)\vee(p\wedge w)$, i.e. reducts of the information system are {p, c} and {p, w}.

In a discernibility matrix, if an entry consists of only one attribute, then it has higher significance and the unique attribute must be a member of CORE. Also shorter entry is more significant than longer one. If the times of appearance of an attribute are more than that of the others in the same entry, then this attribute may contribute more classification power to reduct.

According to the above declaration, we assigned a weight $W(a_i)$ to each attribute a_i. The value of weight $W(a_i)$ for each a_i, which is set to zero initially, is calculated sequentially throughout the whole matrix by using the following formula when a new entry Ct is met in the discernibility matrix:

$$W(a_i) = W(a_i) + k(C_t) * |A| / |C_t|, \ . \ a_i \in C_t. \tag{4}$$

where |A| is the cardinality of attribute set A of the information system, $|C_t|$ is the cardinality of the new entry C_t, $k(C_t)$ is the number of the same entry C_t in the merged matrix.

Table 1. Discernibility matrix of an information system[1]

	X1	X2	X3	X4	X5	X6	X7	X8
X1								
X2								
X3								
X4								
X5								
X6	c,p,w	c,p,w	c,p,w	c,p,h	c,w			
X7	c,w	p	p,w	c,p,h,w	c,p			
X8	c,p,h	c,p,h,w	c,p,h	c,p,w	c,h,w			

The heuristic method is based on the fact that if the data set is consistent, then intersection of a reduct and an entry in discernibility matrix cannot be empty; otherwise, involved two objects would be indiscernible with respect to the reduct according to the definition of reduct in which reduct possesses discernible capability for all objects.

Based on the above, we proposed a discernibility matrix based algorithm for feature selection in reduct computation.

5.2 The Algorithm

At first, an original data set or an information system $(U, C\cup\{d\})$ is given where $A=\cup a_i$, i=1…n; the output is the optimal reduct: Red.

The algorithm is processed as below:

- Initialize parameters of the algorithm: the designated output reduct Red=ϕ, weight values $W(a_i)=0$, i=1…n.
- A discernibility matrix M_0 is constructed according to a decision table of the given data set.
- Form a new discernibility matrix M: merge all the same entries in the discernibility matrix M_0, record their frequencies and sort all entries in the matrix according to their length (the number of attributes involved in each entry) in ascending order; if two entries have the same length, the entry with more frequency is preferred.
- Calculate intersection InSet between reduct Red and an entry ms: InSet=Red$\cap$ms, go to the next step when InSet= ϕ is obtained.

[1] c, h, p, w in the table represent different attributes of an information system.

- Use formula (4) to compute the weight value of each attribute in the entry.
- An attribute a_m with the maximal weight value $W(a_m)$ is chosen; if two weight values are the same then select the attribute with the minimal domain value.
- Update the reduct: add am to it: Red =Red$\cup\{a_m\}$.
- It will go back to intersection calculation and repeat the process if there is an entry left in the discernibility matrix, otherwise the resulting output Red is the optimal reduct.

Clearly, the above algorithm is simple and concise. We do sorting and introduce weight values into the algorithm in order to avoid the following situation. For example, there are {x1, x2, x3}, {x1, x2}, {x1} in the discernibility matrix, then the output reduct is {x1, x2, x3} if the entries in the matrix are not sorted. But by our algorithm the calculation result is {x1}, which is the optimal reduct. As stated earlier, entries with shorter length and more frequent appearance in the matrix may contribute more classification power to the reduct, so that we sort the entries in the discernibility matrix according to their length and frequency. Then the attribute with more times of appearance in the same entry of the matrix will be more important and can be found by calculating (4). Thus the optimal reduct can be obtained with more possibility.

6 Experimental Results

Our experiments have made on a personal computer of Pentium III 733 MHZ, 512 MB memory under Windows XP operating system. The data set used for experiments was collected from UCI database [27]. All symbolic data were converted to integers. Both data discretization and missing data pre-processing were completed using ROSE2 [28]. The performance comparisons are given in Table 2 and Table 3 through experimental results.

The first line of Table 2 displays file names, the number of instances and the number of attributes of data sets collected from UCI database. ROSE2-longest reduct and ROSE2-shortest reduct indicate the lengths of the longest and the shortest (the optimal) reducts respectively given by ROSE2. Characters of L, D, H in the following line indicate different search methods used by ROSE2, i.e.: Lattice search, Discernibility matrix search and Heuristic search. From these experimental results we can see that the discernibility matrix search method shown better performance for shorter reducts among the three methods.

In Table 3 "Optimal" means the length of the shortest (optimal) reduct given by our algorithm; "Method[13]" means using the method in [13]. ΔT(s) represents the average time difference in seconds between the two algorithms and each of them was executed for 10 runs.

It can be seen from Table 3, 23 data files were tested in the experiments, and our proposed algorithm given optimal reducts in most cases. Only one result exhibited as sub-optimal reduct comparing with the shortest reduct given by ROSE2. Comparing with the discernibility matrix based method [13], our algorithm gave two reducts shorter than it. Besides, data in the first column on right side of the table showed time performance difference between the two methods. The positive data in the column indicate our algorithm is faster in all cases.

Table 2. Performance comparison -1

File names	Number of instances	Number of attributes	ROSE2-longest reduct			ROSE2-shortest reduct		
			L-	D-	H-	L-	D-	H-
Acl1	140	6	6	6	6	6	6	6
Bank-local	66	5	3	3	3	3	3	3
Bre285	285	8	7	7	7	7	7	7
Buses-local	76	8	3	3	2	2	2	2
Cars-global	159	43	10	10	10	10	10	10
Cleve-global	303	13	10	10	9	5	5	6
Dane26ex-local	500	26	/	17	16	/	12	13
Domina-global	39	12	5	5	4	4	4	4
Ecoli-global	336	7	5	5	5	5	5	5
Fin-global	39	12	6	6	4	4	4	4
Forg-global	39	12	6	4	4	4	4	4
Forg	39	12	6	4	4	4	4	4
Glass-global	214	9	8	8	8	8	8	8
Hayes	132	4	4	4	4	4	4	4
Hepat-completed-global	147	19	10	10	4	3	3	3
Imi	201	9	7	7	7	7	7	7
Iris-global	150	4	4	4	4	4	4	4
Lsd265	265	35	/	16	11	/	9	10
Monk3	432	6	3	3	3	3	3	3
Primary	339	17	16	16	16	16	16	16
Vote	300	16	10	10	10	10	10	10
Wars3-global	15	3	2	2	2	2	2	2
Zoo	101	16	7	7	6	5	5	5

Table 3. Performance comparison -2

File names	Longest reduct	Shortest reduct			ΔT(s) = T(Method[13]) -T(Optimal)
	ROSE2	ROSE2	Optimal	Method[13]	
Acl1	6	6	6	6	0.398
Bank-local	3	3	3	3	0.106
Bre285	7	7	7	7	2.387
Buses-local	3	2	2	2	0.180
Cars-global	10	10	10	10	10.985
Cleve-global	10	5	5	6	8.783
Dane26ex-local	17	12	13	13	11.790
Domina-global	5	4	4	4	0.055
Ecoli-global	5	5	5	5	6.900
Fin-global	6	4	4	5	0.101
Forg-global	6	4	4	4	0.110
Forg	6	4	4	4	0.131
Glass-global	8	8	8	8	3.535
Hayes	4	4	4	4	0.541
Hepat-completed-global	10	3	3	3	1.723
Imi	7	7	7	7	3.023
Iris-global	4	4	4	4	0.539
Lsd265	16	9	9	9	19.760
Monk3	3	3	3	3	6.789
Primary	16	16	16	16	12.986
Vote	10	10	10	10	6.488
Wars3-global	2	2	2	2	0.001
Zoo	7	5	5	5	1.062

7 Conclusions

The heuristic method proposed in this paper for optimal reduct computation is based on discernibility matrix. Comparing with other discernibility matrix based methods; our algorithm can have more efficient and effective performance. Our algorithm merged and sorted the discernibility matrix first and then computed the intersection between an entry and a reduct. Only when an empty intersection appeared, then calculate the weight value for each attribute in the entry. So that only fewer attributes need calculating their weights. Therefore it is superior to that where weight values were calculated for every attribute first in the unmerged discernibility matrix, then the discernibility matrix was merged and sorted. Thus it dealt with much more entries in most cases. Furthermore, in our algorithm, the weight value computing and selecting are completed at the same time, no extra time is needed for sorting the highest weight value, and thus the proposed algorithm is faster. Experimental results indicate the above conclusion is reasonable. Further work is scheduled to make the algorithm dealing with inconsistency in data sets, and it will be completed soon.

References

1. Fayyad, U.M., Piatetsky-Shapiro, G., Smyth, P.: From Data Mining to Knowledge Discovery: An Overview. In: U.M. Fayyad, G. Piatetsky-Shapiro, P. Smyth, and R. Uthu-rusamy (eds.): Advances in Knowledge Discovery and Data Mining. AAAI Press / The MIT Press, pp. 495–515 (1996)
2. Provost, F., Kolluri, V.: A Survey of Methods for Scaling Up Inductive Algorithms. Journal of Data Mining and Knowledge Discovery 3, 131–169 (1999)
3. Magdalinos, Doulkeridis, C., Vazirgiannis, M.: A Novel Effective Distributed Dimensionality Reduction Algorithm. In: Proceedings of the Second Workshop on Feature Selection for Data Mining: Interfacing Machine Learning and Statistics, Bethesda, MA, pp. 18–25 (2006)
4. Liu, H., Motoda, H.: Feature Extraction, Construction and Selection: A Data Mining Perspective, pp. 191–204. Kluwer Academic Publishers, Boston (2001)
5. Skowron, A., James F, P.: Rough Sets: Trends and Challenges. In: Wang, G., Liu, Q., Yao, Y., Skowron, A. (eds.) Rough Sets, Fuzzy Sets, Data Mining, and Granular Computing. LNCS (LNAI), vol. 2639, Springer, Heidelberg (2003)
6. Pawlak, Z.: Rough Sets. International Journal of Computer and Information Sciences 11(5), 341–356 (1982)
7. X. Hu, T.Y. Lin, J. Jianchao: A New Rough Sets Model Based on Database Systems. Fundamenta Informaticae,1–18 (2004)
8. Kusiak, A.: Rough Set Theory: A Datamining Tool for Semiconductor Manufacturing. IEEE Transactions on Electronics Packaging Manufacturing, 24(1) (2001)
9. Lin, T.Y., Cercone, N. (eds.): Rough Sets and Datamining: Analysis of Imprecise Data. Kluwer Academic Publishers, Boston, MA (1997)
10. Zhang, M., Yao, J.T.: A Rough Sets Based Approach to Feature Selection. In: Proceedings of the 23rd International Conference of NAFIPS, Banff, Canada, pp. 434–439 (2004)
11. Deogun, J., Choubey, S., Raghavan, V., Severm, H.: Feature Selection and Effective Classifiers. Journal of ASIS 49(5), 403–414 (1998)
12. Michal, G., Jacek, S.: RSL-The Rough Set Library Version 2.0. ICS Research Report. Warsaw University of Technology (1994)
13. Hu, K., Lu, Y., Shi, C.: Feature Ranking in Rough Sets. AI Communications 16(1), 41–50 (2003)
14. Zhong, N., Skowron, A.: A Rough Set-Based Knowledge Discovery Process. International Journal of Applied Mathematics and Computer Science 11(3), 603–619 (2001)
15. Jensen, R., Shen, Q.: Fuzzy-Rough Attribute Reduction with Application to Web Categorization. Fuzzy Sets and Systems 141(3), 469–485 (2004)

16. Jensen, R., Shen, Q.: Semantics-Preserving Dimensionality Reduction: Rough and Fuzzy-Rough-Based Approaches. IEEE Transactions on Knowledge and Data Engineering 16(12) (2004)
17. Thangavel, K., Pethalakshmi, A.: Feature Selection for Medical Database Using Rough System. Int. J. on Artificial Intelligence and Machine Learning, 5(4) (2005)
18. Shen, Q., Chouchoulas, A.: A Rough-Fuzzy Approach for Generating Classification Rules. Pattern Recognition 35, 2425–2438 (2002)
19. Shen, Q., Chouchoulas, A.: A Modular Approach to Generating Fuzzy Rules with Reduced Attributes for the Monitoring of Complex Systems. Engineering Applications of Artificial Intelligence 13(3), 263–278 (2002)
20. Thangavel, K., Shen, Q., Pethalakshmi, A.: Application of Clustering for Feature Selection Based on Rough Set Theory Approach. AIML Journal 6(1), 19–27 (2006)
21. Jensen, R.: Combining Rough and Fuzzy Sets for Feature Selection. Ph.D Thesis, School of Informatics, University of Edinburgh (2005)
22. Liu, H., Motoda, H.: Feature Extraction Construction and Selection: A Datamining Perspective. In: Kluwer International Series in Engineering and Computer Science, Kluwer Academic Publishers, Boston, MA (1998)
23. John, G.H., Kohavi, R., Pfleger, K.: Irrelevant Features and the Subset Selection Problem. In: Proceedings of 11th International Conference on Machine Learning, pp. 121–129 (1994)
24. Langley, P.: Selection of Relevant Feature in Machine Learning. In: Proceedings of the AAAI Fall Symposium on Relevance, pp. 140–144. AAAI Press, New Orleans (1994)
25. Zhong, N., Dong, J.Z., Ohsuga, S.: Using Rough Sets with Heuristics for Feature Selection. Journal of Intelligent Information Systems 16, 199–214 (2001)
26. Susmaga, R.: Experiments in Incremental Computation of Reducts. In: Polkowski, L., Skowron, A. (eds.): Rough Sets in Knowledge Discovery: Methodology and Applications, Physica – Verlag, pp. 530–553 (1998)
27. Merz, J., Murphy, P.: UCI Repository of Machine Learning Database. In: http://www.ics.uci.edu/m̃learn/MLRe-pository.htm/
28. The Group of Logic, Warsaw University Homepage. In: http:// alfa.mimuw.edu.pl/logic/

Using Hybrid Hadamard Error Correcting Output Codes for Multi-class Problem Based on Support Vector Machines

Shilei Huang, Xiang Xie, and Jingming Kuang

Department of Electronic Engineering, Beijing Institute of Technology
5 South Zhongguancun Street, Haidian District, Beijing 100081, China
{Huang_shilei, Xiexiang, jmkuang}@bit.edu.cn

Abstract. The Error-Correcting Output Codes (ECOC) method reduces the multi-class learning problem into a series of binary classifiers. In this paper, we propose a modified Hadamard-type ECOC method. This method uses both N'th order and N/2'th-order Hadamard matrix to construct error correcting output codes, which is called Hybrid Hadamard ECOC. Experiments based on dichotomizers of Support Vector Machines (SVM) have been carried out to evaluate the performance of the proposed method. When compared to normal Hadamard ECOC, computation of the method is reduced greatly while the accuracy of classification only drops slightly.

1 Introduction

Many machine-learning algorithms are intrinsically conceived from binary classification. However, in general, real world problems require that inputs be mapped into one several possible categories. The extension of a binary algorithm to its multi-class counterpart is not always possible or easy to conceive. There are some possible ways such as decision trees or prototypes methods such as k-nearest neighbors.

A general reduction scheme is the information theoretic method based on error correcting output codes, introduced by Deitterich and Bakiri [1]. The simplest coding strategy sometimes is called "one-versus-all" [2]. Hadamard-type output coding in multi-class classification problems has reached a good performance [3]. And it was applied in some real pattern recognition systems [4][5].

In this paper, we proposed a hybrid Hadamard ECOC method to reduce the number of binary tests in decoding, and support vector machine is used as basic binary classifiers. In section 2, a general introduction is given, including error correct output coding and Hamming decoding. In section 3, we introduce the proposed method. Experimental results for some public datasets from the UCI machine-learning repository are showed in Section 4 and conclusions are drawn in the last.

Y. Wang, Y. Cheung, and H. Liu (Eds.): CIS 2006, LNAI 4456, pp. 270–276, 2007.

2 Hadamard ECOC

2.1 From Dichotomies to Polychotomy

We have a set of dichotomizers a_l , $l = 1,\dots,L$ where for each, we define a sample of positive examples $\chi_l^+$and a sample of negative examples χ_l^-. Any method can be used to train a_l ; the decomposition matrix $\boldsymbol{D} = [d_{kl}]$ of size $K \times L$ associates classes, C_k, $k = 1,\dots,K$, to the training samples of the dichotomizers χ_l^+ and χ_l^- , $l = 1,\dots L$ [6].

$$d_{kl} = \begin{cases} +1 \text{ } means \text{ } C_k \subset \chi_l^+ \\ -1 \text{ } means \text{ } C_k \subset \chi_l^- \\ 0 \text{ } means \text{ } C_k \cap (\chi_l^+ \cup \chi_l^+) = \phi \end{cases} \tag{1}$$

Rows of $\boldsymbol{D}$ correspond to the definition of a class as a vector of responses of the L dichotomizers; this is the "code" of class C_k using the alphabet of dichotomizer outputs. The columns of D define the tasks of the dichotomizers. Once we have a_l and $\boldsymbol{D}$, given a pattern to classify, all a_l compute their outputs and we assign the pattern to the class having the class closest representation (row of $\boldsymbol{D}$). When the vectors are -1/+1, it can be done by taking a dot product and choosing the maximum.

$$c = \arg\max_k o_k \text{ , where } o_k = \sum_l d_{kl} a_l \tag{2}$$

2.2 Error Correcting Output Codes

Decomposition matrix is also called ECOC matrix. Each row in D is also called a codeword that corresponds to a certain class. For any two codewords w,u, their Hamming distance is defined by:

$$d_H(w,u) = |\{ j : w_j \neq u_j, 1 \leq j \leq L \}| \tag{3}$$

Given an output code, two criteria of row separation and column diversity are commonly suggested for the goodness assessment [1]. There might be error bits in the target codeword. But for Hamming decoding, small number of error bits may not result in a wrong multi-class decision if the target codeword keeps being closest to the true label. The minimum Hamming distance [7]:

$$d_{\min} = \min_{1 \leq i,k \leq K} d_H(w_i, w_k) \tag{4}$$

is a common measure of quality for error-correcting codes. An ECOC matrix with minimum Hamming distance d_{min} can correct $[(d_{min} -1)/2]$ errors, where $[x]$ denotes the greatest integer not exceeding x.

2.3 Hadamard Output Codes

A square matrix $\mathbf{H}_n$ of order n and entries ±1 is called a Hadamard matrix if $\mathbf{H}_n'\mathbf{H}_n = n\mathbf{I}_n$ where $\mathbf{I}_n$ is the n'th order identity matrix. Usually n'th order Hadamard matrix can be constructed from $n/2$'th order Hadamard matrix (and some examples):

$$H_N = \begin{bmatrix} H_{N/2} & H_{N/2} \\ H_{N/2} & -H_{N/2} \end{bmatrix} \tag{5}$$

$$H_2 = \begin{bmatrix} +1 & +1 \\ +1 & -1 \end{bmatrix} H_4 = \begin{bmatrix} +1 & +1 & +1 & +1 \\ +1 & -1 & +1 & -1 \\ +1 & +1 & -1 & -1 \\ +1 & -1 & -1 & +1 \end{bmatrix} \tag{6}$$

Deleting the first colum from any normalized Hadamard matrix, we obtain a Hadamard output code. We can get a $K\times(K\text{-}1)$ matrix for multi-class problem from $\mathbf{H}_k$. And in such a matrix, there are K codewords with length of K-1 can be used for polychotomy. But for a K-class problem that $2^{(P-1)}<K<2^P$, (where P is an integer), we can only construct a $2^P th$ Hadamard matrix and choose K codewords out of the 2^P vectors. In the simplest way, these codewords could be chosen randomly.

3 Hybrid Hadamard ECOC

Consider the K-class problem. If $2^{(P-1)}<K<2^P$, (where P is an integer), especially if K is close to $2^{(P-1)}$, the number of binary classifiers $L = 2^P\text{-}1$(the same with length of codeword) will be much more than class number K. To reduce the number of dichotomizers, we propose a hybrid Hadamard ECOC method.

Consider the construction of a Hadamard matrix:

$$H_N = \begin{bmatrix} H_{N/2}, & H_{N/2} \\ H_{N/2}, & -H_{N/2} \end{bmatrix}, \text{ where } H_{N/2} = \begin{bmatrix} h_1^{N/2} \\ \vdots \\ h_{N/2}^{N/2} \end{bmatrix} \tag{7}$$

where h_i^N is the i'th row vector of the matrix. Hadamard matrix is rewritten as:

$$H'_N = \begin{bmatrix} h_1^{N/2}, & h_1^{N/2} \\ h_1^{N/2}, & -h_1^{N/2} \\ h_2^{N/2}, & h_2^{N/2} \\ h_2^{N/2}, & -h_2^{N/2} \\ \vdots & , \vdots \\ h_{N/2}^{N/2}, & h_{N/2}^{N/2} \\ h_{N/2}^{N/2}, & -h_{N/2}^{N/2} \end{bmatrix}, E_N = \begin{bmatrix} \hbar_1^{N/2}, & h_1^{N/2} \\ \hbar_1^{N/2}, & -h_1^{N/2} \\ \hbar_2^{N/2}, & h_2^{N/2} \\ \hbar_2^{N/2}, & -h_2^{N/2} \\ \vdots & , \vdots \\ \hbar_{N/2}^{N/2}, & h_{N/2}^{N/2} \\ \hbar_{N/2}^{N/2}, & -h_{N/2}^{N/2} \end{bmatrix} \tag{8}$$

where $\hbar_i^j$ is h_i^j with the first element deleted. The only difference between H'_N and H_N is the order of row vectors. The examples of H'_N:

$$H'_4 = \begin{bmatrix} +1 & +1 & +1 & +1 \\ +1 & +1 & -1 & -1 \\ +1 & -1 & +1 & -1 \\ +1 & -1 & -1 & +1 \end{bmatrix}, \ E'_4 = \begin{bmatrix} +1 & +1 & +1 \\ +1 & -1 & -1 \\ -1 & +1 & -1 \\ -1 & -1 & +1 \end{bmatrix} \tag{9}$$

Hadamard matrix as above style is also called Orthogonal Variable Spreading Factor (OVSF) codes in communication systems. Then the first column of H'_N is deleted and a $N\times(N\text{-}1)$ matrix (denoted as $\boldsymbol{E}_N$) is ready for constructing ECOC.

For a K-class problem, we divided K classes into two sub set, K_1 and K_2 . Each class in K_1 is assigned to one ECOC code words, and each class in K_2 is assigned to two ECOC code words. To distribute all N codewords:

$$K_1 + 2K_2 = 2^P \text{, where } \begin{cases} K_1 = 2K - 2^P \\ K_2 = 2^P - K \end{cases} \tag{10}$$

And K_1 classes use the first K_1 codewords while K_2 classes use the last $2\times K_2$ codewords. For the characteristic mentioned above, each two codewords assigned to one class in K_2 will have the same first $(2^{P-1}-1)$ elements and opposite last (2^{P-1}) elements. K_1 will always be even. Then $\boldsymbol{E}_N$ is divided into 4 parts:

$$E_N = \begin{bmatrix} \hbar_1^{N/2}, \ h_1^{N/2} \\ \hbar_1^{N/2}, -h_1^{N/2} \\ \vdots \ , \ \vdots \\ \hbar_{K_1/2}^{N/2}, \ h_{K_1/2}^{N/2} \\ \hbar_{K_1/2}^{N/2}, -h_{K_1/2}^{N/2} \\ \hbar_{K_1/2+1}^{N/2}, \ h_{K_1/2+1}^{N/2} \\ \hbar_{K_1/2+1}^{N/2}, -h_{K_1/2+1}^{N/2} \\ \vdots \ , \ \vdots \\ \hbar_{N/2}^{N/2}, \ h_{N/2}^{N/2} \\ \hbar_{N/2}^{N/2}, -h_{N/2}^{N/2} \end{bmatrix} = \begin{bmatrix} A_{K_1\times(N/2-1)} & B_{K_1\times(N/2)} \\ C_{(2K_2)\times(N/2-1)} & D_{(2K_2)\times(N/2)} \end{bmatrix} \tag{11}$$

where $N = 2^P$ .It can be seen from the expression that if we repeat each row vector in $\boldsymbol{E}_{N/2}$ one by one, it will be the same with matrix $\begin{bmatrix} A_{K_1\times(N/2-1)} \\ C_{(2K_2)\times(N/2-1)} \end{bmatrix}$.

We divided the training process to two stages. First, an $\boldsymbol{E}_{N/2}$ is used to train *(N/2-1)* dichotomizers for *(N*/2) classes. In the second stage, output codes from $B_{K_1\times(N/2)}$ is used for train dichotomizers for K_1 classes. If $K_1<N/2$, there's some redundancy. The simplification principle will be row separation and column separation. $D_{(2K_2)\times(N/2)}$ in matrix $\boldsymbol{E}_N$ is ignored.

The testing process is also divided into two stages. First *N/2-1* dichotomizers according to $\boldsymbol{E}_{N/2}$ are used to decide whether the sample belongs to one class in K_1 or K_2. If the sample belongs to one class in K_2, decoding process is finished. If the sample belongs to one class in K_1, a second stage decoding is carried out using the error correcting output codes from block $B_{K_1\times(N/2)}$. To decide which class a sample belongs to in K_1, we use information of the first and second stage decoding.

4 Experiments

Here, we provide the experimental results of the proposed method on some multi-class problems. The problems are from UCI Repository of machine learning database [8]. General information of the problems is listed in Table I.

The SVMs are used as the base learners in our experiments for comparing different output codes, for the SVMs with flexible kernels are strong enough to classify various types of dichotomous data while keeping good generalization performance [9][10].

Table 1. Problem List

Data Set	Train samples	Test samples
Letters	15000	5000
PenDigit	7494	3498

Plugged into the ECOC framework, the base SVM can be written as:

$$g_j(x) = \sum_{i=1}^{N} M_{y(i,j)} \alpha_i^{(j)} K_j(x_i, x) + b_j$$
$$f_j(x) = sign(g_j(x)) \tag{12}$$

where $\boldsymbol{f_j}(\mathbf{x})$ is called decision function and $\boldsymbol{K_j(x,w)}$ is a selected kernel, $\boldsymbol{b_j}$ is the offset term and $\boldsymbol{\alpha}^{(j)} = (\alpha_1^{(j)},...,\alpha_N^{(j)})$ can be obtained in training [9]. In our experiments, Gaussian radian basis function (RBF) is chosen as the kernel function:

$$K_j(\mathbf{x}, \mathbf{w}) = \exp(-\gamma_j \parallel \mathbf{x} - \mathbf{w} \parallel^2) \tag{13}$$

where γ_j being used to further tune the RBF kernel.

During decoding, we use the sum of the absolute value $\boldsymbol{g(x)}$ instead of $\boldsymbol{f(x)}$ in Eq 12. And Eq 2 becomes:

$$c = \arg\max_k o_k , o_k = \sum_l d_{kl} a_l = \sum_l g(\mathbf{x}) a_l \tag{14}$$

Here, we compare some methods as following: 1) one against one; 2) one against all; 3) ECOC-One-All: ECOC with Likelihood decoding function and one-against-all coding scheme; 4) ECOC-One-One: ECOC with likelihood decoding function and one-against-one coding scheme; 5) ECOC-H: Hadamard ECOC with likelihood decoding functions. ECOC code for each class is chosen randomly. Experiments based on one database shared the same kernel function.

We compare proposed Hybrid-Hadamard ECOC (denoted as ECOC-H-H) with above five methods in the following three aspects (listed in Table II and Table III):

- **Accuracy:** The ratio between the numbers of the correctly classified testing samples and the total testing samples. If many tests were performed, standard deviation of accuracy rate is also showed.
- **Binary classifiers:** The total number of binary classifiers that one method needs.

Binary tests: Means how many binary classifiers have been tested when we classify a testing sample.

In the Tables (II, III), all the six methods can reach almost the same accuracy. However, ECOC-One-One method has the highest accuracy while ECOC-H-H method and ECOC-One-All are the fastest ones. In Pendigit problem, ECOC-H-H method is the fastest one and has the higher accuracy than ECOC-One-All. In Letter problem, the binary test of ECOC-H-H is a little more than that of ECOC-One-All, but it has obviously better performance. The balance between ECOC-One-All and ECOC-H depends on the number of classes.

It can be also seen that normal ECOC-H nearly reach the accuracy of ECOC-One-One/One-vs-One, while the number of binary tests is greatly reduced. When applying ECOC-H-H, the binary tests are less compared to ECOC-H method, while the accuracy dropped slightly. But we get a faster polychotomizer.

For we choose codeword for each class randomly, we repeat the experiments for 100 times with different cases of codeword distribution. So the average accuracy rate is shown in table. The standard deviation of ECOC-H-H is bigger than that of standard Hadamard ECOC method.

Table 2. Results based on database Letters

Method	Acc% (Std)	Classifiers Trained	Binary tests		
			Max	Min	Ave
One vs one	97.78	325	325	325	325
One vs other	96.62	26	26	26	26
ECOC-One-One	97.78	325	325	325	325
ECOC-One-All	96.84	26	26	26	26
ECOC-H	97.68 (0.03)	31	31	31	31
ECOC-H-H	97.45 (0.13)	31	31	15	27.31 (0.03)

Table 3. Results based on database Pendigit

Method	Acc% (Std)	Classifiers Trained	Binary tests		
			Max	Min	Ave
One vs one	98.07	45	45	45	45
One vs other	97.78	10	10	10	10
ECOC-One-One	98.17	45	45	45	45
ECOC-One-All	97.86	10	10	10	10
ECOC-H	98.12 (0.02)	15	15	15	15
ECOC-H-H	98.01 (0.12)	9	7	9	7.80 (0.01)

5 Conclusions

This paper has proposed a hybrid Hadamrd ECOC method for multi-class classification problem. This method divides the decoding process of ECOC into two stages, some classification result will output after the first step. And the rest results will appear after last step. Experiments showed that the proposed method could reach faster speed at the cost of tiny loss of accuracy.

Acknowledgement

This work was supported in part by the National Nature Science Foundation of P.R.China under Grant NSFC 60372089.

References

1. Dietterich, T.G., Bakiri, G.: Solving multiclass learning problems via error-correcting output codes. J. Artific. Intell. Res. 2, 263–286 (1995)
2. Allwein, E.L., et al.: Reducing multiclass to binary: a unifying approach for margin classifiers, In: 17th Int. Conf. of Machine Learning, San Francisco, CA, pp. 9–16 2000
3. Zhang, A. et al.: On Hadamard-Type Output Coding in Multiclass Learning. In: Liu, J., Cheung, Y.-m., Yin, H. (eds.) Intelligent Data Engineering and Automated Learning – IDEAL 2003. LNCS, vol. 2690, Springer, Heidelberg (2003)
4. Hsu, C.-W., Lin, C.-J.: A comparison of methods for multi-class support vector machines. IEEE Trans. on Neural Network 13, 415–425 (2002)
5. Anrong, Y., et al.: Using Hadamard ECOC in multi-class problems based on SVM, EUROSPEECH2005, pp. 3125–3128 (2005)
6. Alpaydin, E., Mayoraz, E.: Learning error-correcting output codes from data. In: Proc of 9'th International Conf. on Artificial Neural Networks, vol. 2, pp. 743–748 (1999)
7. Mac Williams, F.J., Sloane, N.J.A.: The Theory of Error-Correcting Codes. Elsevier Science Publishers, Amsterdam (1977)
8. Blake, C.L., et al.: UCI Repository of machine learning databases (1998), http://www.ics.uci.edu/m learn/MLRepository.html
9. Vapnik, V.N.: The nature of statistical learning theory. Springer, Heidelberg (1995)
10. Passerini, A. et al.: New results on error correcting output codes of kernel machines. IEEE Trans. on Neural Networks 15(1), 45–54 (2004)

Range Image Based Classification System Using Support Vector Machines

Seyed Eghbal Ghobadi, Klaus Hartmann, Otmar Loffeld, and Wolfgang Weihs

Center for Sensor Systems (ZESS)
University of Siegen
Paul- Bonatz-Str.9-11, D57068, Siegen, Germany
{Ghobadi, Hartmann, Weihs, Netramai, Loffeld, Roth}@zess.uni-siegen.de
http://www.zess.uni-siegen.de

Abstract. This paper describes a classification system based on Support Vector Machines (SVM) and using 3D range images. Two kinds of camera systems are used to provide the classification system with 3D range images: Time-oF-Flight (TOF) camera and Stereo Vision System. While the former uses the modulated infrared lighting source to provide the range information in each pixel of a Photonic Mixer Device(PMD) sensor, the latter employs the disparity map from stereo images to calculate three dimensional data. The proposed detection and classification system is used to classify different 3D moving objects in a dynamic environment under varying lighting conditions. The images of each camera are first preprocessed and then two different approaches are applied to extract their features. The first approach is a Computer Generated method which uses the Principal Component Analysis (PCA) to get the most relevant projection of the data over the eigenvectors and the second approach is a Human Generated method which extracts the features based on some heuristic techniques. Two training data sets are derived from each image set based on heuristic and PCA features to train a multi class SVM classifier. The experimental results show that the proposed classifier based on range data from TOF camera is superior to that from the stereo system.

1 Introduction

Detection and classification of moving objects is of utmost importance for different applications such as quality control, surveillance, man machine interface and autonomous robot navigation. In this context, a variety of approaches have been used to solve this problem based on static 2D images ([9,10,11]) as well as normal video sequences [6]. As the size of image and video information increases, the problem of training a system to detect and classify the moving objects will become more complex and time consuming. In the last years, range images have gained a lot of attention to be used as the information to train a system for detection and classification of cars, humans and objects ([2,4,7,19]). The range data usually are provided by Laser Range Scanner ([2,7]), Stereo Vision System

Y. Wang, Y. Cheung, and H. Liu (Eds.): CIS 2006, LNAI 4456, pp. 277–287, 2007.

[19] and 3D Time-of-Flight Camera ([1,3,4]). Although the laser range scanner can provide very accurate depth information from the object by scanning the surface line by line, the time it takes to scan the whole surface of the object is still an open challenge, especially when the velocity of the moving object is high. In [1] we have referred to this problem in detail.

The accuracy and robustness of a classification system, on the other hand, is dependent on the classification algorithm. Recently, there has been considerable attention paid to Support Vector Mchines (SVMs) as the maximum margin classifier in the machine learning and pattern recognition communities ([4,6,10]). SVM has shown a high performance in the classification of objects using range images ([1,4]).

In this paper we address the solution to the problem of detection and classification of moving objects based on SVM and using range images from two camera systems: Stereo Vision Systems which employ two CCD sensors and calculate the depth information from the disparity map. 3D Time-of-Flight camera which employs the modulated infrared lighting source to provide the distance in each pixel of a Photonic Mixer Device (PMD) sensor.

This paper is organized as follows: Section 2 presents an overview of our camera systems. In Section 3 object detection and image sampling is discussed. Section 4 introduces the classification algorithm. Section 5 summarizes our experimental results while Section 6 concludes this work.

2 Camera System

Two different types of camera systems have been used for our experiments in this paper: Stereo Vision System and Time of Flight camera. While the stereo vision technique has been used for a long time in widespread applications for providing 3D data, the Time-of-Flight 3D sensors have won intensive, widespread interest from various sides since the appearance of PMD in 1997 [5]. In fact, TOF measurement gives the possibility to enhance 2D sensors by adding a third dimension ([12,13,14]).

2.1 3D-Time of Flight Camera

Our 3D non-scanning Time of Flight (TOF) camera system consists of an infrared lighting source, Photonic Mixer Device (PMD) chip [12], FPGA based processing and communication unit including FireWire, USB or Ethernet.

The principle of the PMD distance measuring system is based on the measurement of the time-of-flight τ_L of the transmitted signal, which leads to the distance to the object [3]:

$$R = \frac{c \cdot \tau_L}{2} \tag{1}$$

where c denotes the speed of light.

The RF-modulated infrared light signal is generated using a MOSFET based driver and high speed infrared emitting diodes. The light signal is sent to the scene and reflected back to the PMD via an optical lens. The PMD pixels mix the modulated light directly in the optical active area during the sensing process. Typically this is done by using continuous modulation and measuring the phase delays in each pixel [12].

Assuming continuous sinusoidal or rectangular modulation the distance is calculated as follows [3]:

$$R = \frac{c \cdot \Delta\varphi}{4\pi \cdot f_{mod}} \tag{2}$$

where f_{mod} denotes the modulation frequency and $\Delta\varphi = 2\pi \cdot f_{mod} \cdot \tau_L$ represents the phase delay.

The theoretical response of a pixel can be expressed by:

$$\overline{r_c} = \sum_{n=1}^{N} B_n \cdot e^{j4\pi\frac{r_n}{\lambda}} \tag{3}$$

where $\lambda = \frac{c}{f_{mod}}$ denotes the wave length of the modulated signal, B_n is the backscatter coefficient of the point n and $\overline{r_n} = [x_n \;\; y_n \;\; z_n]$ represents the distance vector to all visible object points with $n = 1, \ldots, N$[3].

Although the current PMD chips provide accurate depth information and have good resolution (64x48 and 160x120 pixels) for depth sensing, but this resolution is still very low for image processing purpose. To overcome this problem a new novel 2D/3D camera has been designed in ZESS which is shown in Figure 1. Two sensors have been used in this camera. PMD as a 3D sensor which provides the range image and a CMOS sensor array with high resolution which provides the intensity image. These two images are calibrated and registered using some efficient algorithms and finally a high resolution image with depth information is retrieved.

However, in this paper as the first step of our project we just use the range images as the input data for the classification system. In our ongoing project we add more features to the system by using the intensity images.

PMD also has an in-pixel so-called SBI-circuitry (Suppression of Background Illumination) which increases the sensor dynamics under strong light conditions ([12,15]).

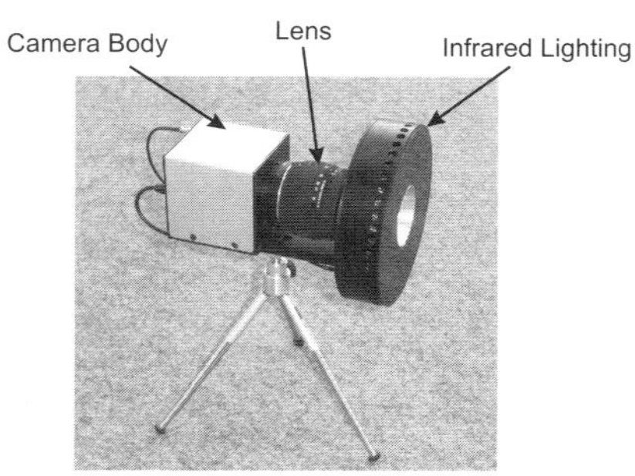

Fig. 1. Our novel 2D/3D camera

2.2 Stereo Vision System

We use a simple Stereoscopic Geometry as follows:

- Two cameras with their optical axes parallel and separated by the baseline-distance.
- The baseline is perpendicular to the line of sight of the cameras.

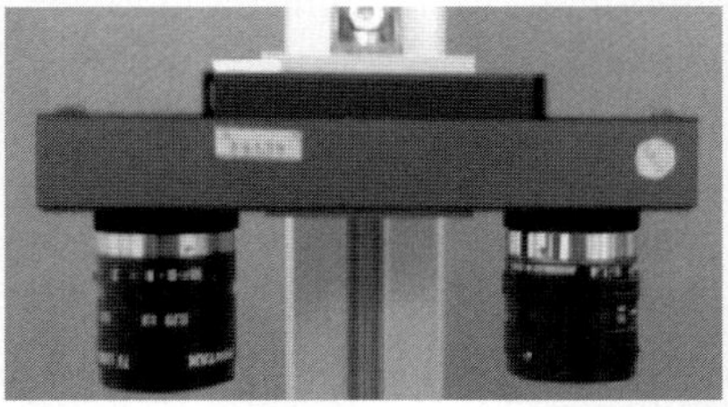

Fig. 2. Stereo Vision System

Figure 2 shows the stereo vision system we have used. Within the stereo head two progressive scan chips (1/2" CMOS imagers) are employed. The selected image size in our case is 320x240 while the maximum is 1280x960 [21]. The optics are of fixed-focus type. The focal length f of $16mm$ is selected to get the horizontal field of view of about $25\,^{\circ}$ and the vertical field of view of about $18\,^{\circ}$. To achieve the same FOV as we used for the TOF camera, an object distance of about $1.5m$ is selected.

The stereo Engine consist of two modules: disparity computation (correlation algorithm) and interpolation, and post-filtering using a texture filter. In view of a rectification step the input is a rectified gray scale image pair.

The range resolution Δr is the minimum distance the stereo system can distinguish. For our purpose we estimate the range resolution (ideal value) by $\Delta r = 8\mu m$. The stereo Engine could interpolate disparities to 1/16 pixel.

$$\Delta r = (r^2/bf)\Delta d \tag{4}$$

where b is the baseline-distance with 90 mm, and $\Delta d = 5.2\mu m$ (smallest disparity the stereo system can detect). The disparity search window is correctly positioned so that our test scene is in view.

The calibration is performed by fitting a model to a number of images taken of a planar calibration object.

3 Object Detection and Image Sampling

Each camera system is mounted in a fixed structure, pointing down and oriented in such way to have the same Field of View (FOV). The depth information from the background is averaged from 100 range images taken by each camera in order to reduce the statistical noise. The object detection results from the continuous comparison of some statistical criteria from the captured range image with that of the background, previously calculated and recorded in the program as a threshold [1]. These criteria include the standard deviation, maximum, minimum and mean value of the range data matrix.

Image sampling is one of the significant point in detection and classification of moving objects. The number of acquired images using the TOF camera is higher than that via stereo vision system. Because the distance data in the TOF camera is determined directly inside the hardware using smart pixel array of the PMD, whereas the stereo vision system provides the 3D data from stereo imaging through some computational techniques which are time consuming. For the TOF camera this number is a function of velocity v of the moving object, exposure time t_e, transfer time t_t and processing time t_p.

$$N_{tof} = f(v, t_e, t_p, t_t) \tag{5}$$

Exposure time is the time which our TOF camera needs to illuminate the scene to get the accurate range data [1]. For stereo vision, sampling number is a function of velocity, computational time t_c, transfer and processing time.

$$N_{stereo} = f(v, t_c, t_p, t_t) \tag{6}$$

While the exposure time is neglected for stereo system, the computational time is the time which stereo system needs to calculate the disparity map from right and left images. The velocity is tunable in the setup from $5cm/sec$ to $20cm/s$. As both cameras transfer the images via FireWire and use the same PC, the processing and transfer time is same.

These functions result the frame rate of 20 range images per second for the TOF camera and 5 range images per second for stereo vision system. At the velocity of $5cm/sec$, the TOF camera captures 160 range images from the object during its motion in the FOV (40 cm with the focal length of 16 mm) while the stereo system takes 40 range images. At the maximum velocity of $20cm/sec$, the number of sample images are 40 and 10 for the TOF and the stereo system respectively.

4 Overview of the Classification Algorithm

An overview of the algorithm is given in Figure 3. The input data are range and intensity images which are first calibrated and registered to derive the high resolution images with the range information. However, in this paper the intensity images are neglected and only the range images are used as the input data to compare the two camera systems for classification of the objects. The range images which are taken by both cameras are saved in two image sets. First the stereo range images are resized to have the same size as TOF range images. Then some preprocessing techniques are applied to provide the images for further

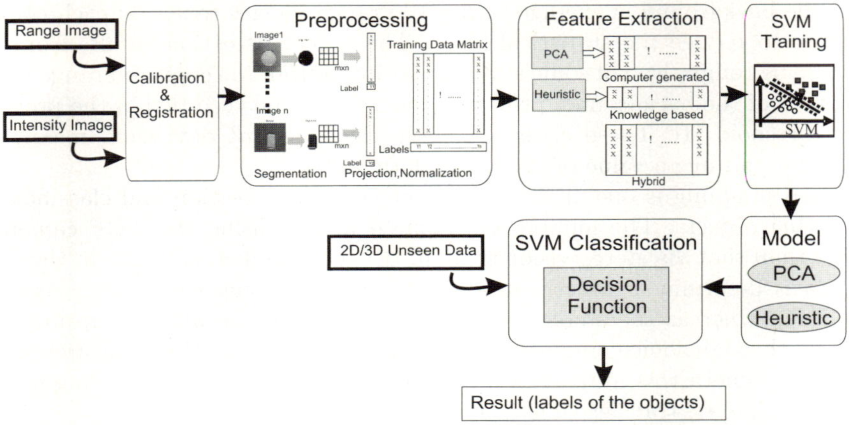

Fig. 3. Flow of the Algorithm

processing. The relevant features are derived from range images using Principal Component Analysis (PCA) and heuristic techniques. Two training data sets are provided from these features. For each training data set a SVM classifier is trained. The learnt classifier is applied to the features of the unseen 3D data and the label of the object is determined.

4.1 Pre-processing Techniques

In the preprocessing, the range images are segmented from the background to distinguish between the object of interest and the rest. This simplifies the computation of SVM and speeds up the training process. The thresholding technique is used for this purpose. Then, the segmented image is projected from the camera coordinate system to the world coordinate system using projection matrix. For each range image the nonzero element are saved in a column vector of a matrix. This matrix is normalized to change the range pixel values to the desired range of 0 to 1 which is appropriate for our SVM classification algorithm [1].

4.2 Feature Extraction

Two types of techniques are employed to extract the features. The first technique applies PCA to get the most relevant projection of data in the least square sense. In order to calculate the principal components, the normalized matrix is subtracted from the mean vector and the covariance matrix C is calculated. The covariance matrix is diagonalized using eigenvalue decomposition [1].

$$C = \Phi E \Phi^T \tag{7}$$

where Φ is the eigenvector matrix and E is the corresponding diagonal matrix of its eigenvalues. The first largest eigenvectors corresponding to the largest eigenvalues give the principal components.

The second technique applies heuristic approaches to extract the knowledge-based features based on some statistical parameters. In our case these parameters include standard deviation, maximum, mean, minimum and the number of non zero elements in each range image.

4.3 Support Vector Classification

The features are used to provide two training data sets: PCA and heuristic. Each of these training data sets is used to train a SVM classifier. The goal is to find an optimal separation function with the maximum margin from each class. Vapnik's method [20] uses just a small fraction of the data points to find this function. These data points are called Support Vectors.

The decision function derived by SVM classifier for a two class problem can be formulated, using a kernel function $K(x, x_i)$ of a new example x (test image) and a training example x_i , as follows [10]:

$$f(x) = \sum \alpha_i y_i K(x, x_i) + b \tag{8}$$

where the parameters α_i and b are found by maximizing a quadratic function. In our experiments a Radial Basis Function (RBF) has been used as a kernel function.

5 Results and Discussion

Two set of objects were considered in our experiments: A multi object set with three objects which have different shapes and a binary set with two exact shape objects from point of view of the camera. The range images of the TOF camera are nearly independent of the color of the object and lighting conditions, whereas the range images of the stereo vision system have the following difficulties:

- No 3D information over the plain surface of the object
- Strongly dependent on the lighting conditions
- Disturbed by shadows

Considering these difficulties we have taken three image sets for each object:

- TOF: range images taken by the TOF camera under varying lighting conditions
- Stereo 1: range images taken by the stereo system under the same conditions as TOF
- Stereo 2: range images taken by the stereo system under artificial conditions

Artificial conditions consist of a stable and non-varying lighting conditions and painting contours over the surface of the objects to get 3D information.

5.1 Multi-object Set

Figure 4 shows some range images of the multi object set including box, ball and cone which were taken by the TOF camera and the stereo system under normal conditions. As it is observed the range images of the stereo system can not provide any reliable 3D data on the plain surface of the object and therefore the value is set to the value of the background which is shown as black in the picture.

For each range image set, two training data sets have been derived using PCA and heuristic features. Then for each training data set a multi class SVM classifier has been trained. RBF kernel with the kernel argument of 1 and regularization constant of 10 have been used in our experiments. The SVM classifier was trained with 90 range images for each image set which are taken at the velocity of $5cm/sec$.

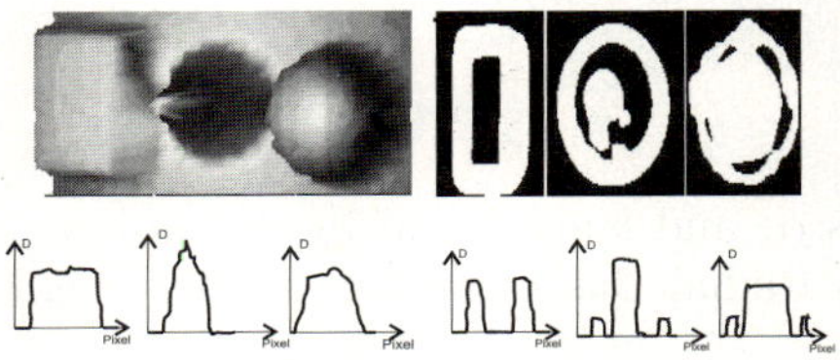

Fig. 4. Range Images. The upper left row shows TOF range images, the upper right row shows the stereo range images and the lower two rows show the longitudinal sections through the middle of each range image.

The classification system has been tested with 90 range images for each set and the results are shown in Table 1. While the TOF range based classifier outperforms the stereo range based one, it is observed that the classifier which employs the range images of stereo 2 (artificially contoured with fixed lighting conditions) yields the best results with the full accuracy of 100%. Figure 5 shows the distribution of the features on the first two principal components for stereo1 and stereo2. It is observed that the data of two classes in Stereo1 are very mixed and difficult to distinguish. Using the artificial techniques which are mentioned above, these data are separated and the margin between the classes increases, therefore we get the best result in this case. Also, it can be noticed that in all of the cases the PCA feature based classifier gives the better result than the heuristic feature based one.

Table 1. Error Rate for Multi Object Set Classification (%)

	Heuristic	PCA
TOF	3.87	3.1
Stereo 1	30.00	30.00
Stereo 2	1.11	0.00

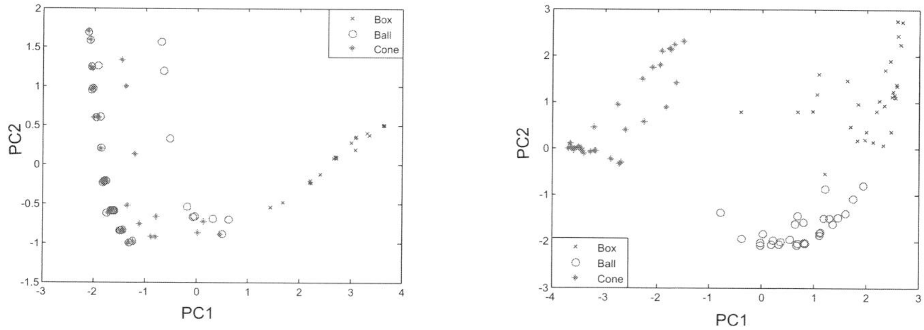

Fig. 5. Distribution of the features on the first two principal components. Left: Stereo1, Right: Stereo2.

5.2 Binary-Object Set

In this case, we have considered two cubic boxes with the same shape form but different heights from the camera's point of view. As before in the multi object case we have considered three image sets and the results are shown in Table 2. In this case, for TOF image set the heuristic feature based classifier yields the best accuracy with the error rate of 0.00%. It is observed that the heuristic features we have already discussed are quite appropriate for this case. The PCA based classifier gives a poor result with the error rate of 14.28% for the PMD image set. It was expected because at the edges perpendicular to the direction of the movement of the object some mismeasurements occur which affect the result of PCA method strongly, whereas they do not affect the heuristic features [1].

It is noticed that in this case, same as for multi object set, the results for the stereo image set under the normal conditions are very poor with a maximum error rate of 46.67%. Changing the conditions as we discussed in the previous case improves the results in the image set of Stereo2 to the lowest error rate of 1.67% using PCA features.

Table 2. Error Rate for Binary Object Set Classification (%)

	Heuristic	PCA
TOF	0.00	14.28
Stereo 1	46.67	23.33
Stereo 2	6.67	1.67

6 Conclusion

This paper describes a detection and classification system for moving objects based on SVM and using range images via a Time of Flight camera and a Stereo

Vision System. The range images have been employed as the input data. Two different classifiers have been trained based on heuristic and PCA features for each image set.

The best results under dynamic conditions were achieved by applying TOF range images. Since the range images of stereo vision system are strongly affected by the lighting conditions and the texture properties of the objects, the results based on these range images were very poor. We have improved these range images by creating some artificial conditions and it was observed that the results were improved drastically.

While the PCA features give the better results than heuristic ones in TOF case, it was seen that using the heuristic features in classification of some objects (like boxes) can give good results concerning accuracy and computational expense.

Acknowledgments

This research has been supported by the DFG Dynamisches 3D Sehen- Multicam Project and DAAD IPP's Program in Center for Sensor System (ZESS) at the university of Siegen in Germany.

References

1. Passerini, A. et al.: New results on error correcting output codes of kernel machines. IEEE Trans. on Neural Networks 15(1), 45–54 (2004)
2. Lourenco, A., Freitas, P., Ribeiro, M., Marques, J. Detection and Classification of 3D Moving Objects, In: 10th IEEE Mediterranean Conference on Control and Automation (2002)
3. Peters, V., Hasouneh, F., Knedlik, S., Loffeld, O.: Simulation of PMD based self-localization of mobile sensor nodes or robots, ASIM 2006 In: (19th Symposium on Simulation Technique), Hannover, Germany, September 2006 (2006)
4. Burak Goktuk, S., Rafii, A.: An Occupant Classification System-Eigen Shapes or Knowledge-Based Features. In: IEEE Computer Society Conference on Computer Vision and Pattern Recognition (CVPR'05) (2005)
5. Rasool, A., Hartmann, K., Weihs,W., First Ste. In: Implementing a Feature-Based Stereo Algorithm in a Cost Efficient Way Using a PMD Sensor. In: 6th IASTED International conference on Visulization, Imaging, and Image Processing VIIP (2006)
6. Dongwei, C., Masoud, O., Boley, D., Papanikolopoulos, N., Online Motion Classification using Support Vector Machines. In: International Conference on Robotics and Automation IEEE 2004, USA (2004)
7. Nuechter, A., Surmann, H., Hertzberg, J.: Automatic Classification of Objects in 3D Laser Range Scans, 8th Conference on Intelligent Automation System, Amsterdam, The Netherlands (March 2004)
8. Cao, D., Masoud, O.T., Boley, D., Papanikolopoulos, N., Online Motion Classification using Support Vector Machines. In: International Conference on Robotics and Automation, New Orleans, LA, USA, IEEE (2004)
9. Javed, O., Ali, S., Shah, M.: Online Detection and Classification of Moving Objects Using Progressively Improving Detectors. In: IEEE Computer Conference on Computer Vision and Pattern Recognition (2005)

10. Oliveria Luiz, S., Sabourin, R.: Support Vector Machines for Handwritten Numerical String Recognition. In: IEEE Transaction on Pattern Analysis and Machine Intelligence (2002)
11. Quang Huy Viet, H., Miwa, M., Maruta, H., Sato, M.: Recognition of Motion in Depth by a Fixed Camera, VIIth Digital Image Computing: Techniques and Applications, Sydney (December 2003)
12. Moeller, T., Kraft, H., Frey, J.: Robust 3D Measurement with PMD Sensors, PMD Technologies GmbH, `http://www.pmdtec.com`
13. 3D Range Sensor, `http://www.csem.ch/`
14. 3D Range Sensor, `http://www.canesta.com`
15. PhotoICs PMD 3K-S, 3D Video Sensor Array with Active SBI, `http://www.pmdtec.com`
16. Gokturk, S.B., Yalcin, H., Bamji, C.: A Time of Flight Depth Sensor, System Description, Issues and Solutions, on IEEE workshop on Real-Time 3D Sensors and Their Use in conjunction with In: IEEE Conference on Computer Vision and Pattern Recognition, CVPR, Washington, USA (2004)
17. France, V., Hlavac, V.: Statistical Pattern Recognition Toolbox for Matlab, Center for Machine Perception, Czech Technical University
18. Schneiderman, H., Kanade, T.: A Statistical Method for 3D Object Detection Applied to Faces and Cars. In: IEEE Conference on Computer Vision and Pattern recognition, CVPR 2000 (2000)
19. Toulminet, G., Betrozzi, M., Mousset, S., Bensrhair, A., Broggi, A.: Vehicle Detection by Means of Stereo Vision-Based Obstacles Features Extraction and Monocular Pattern Analysis. In: IEEE Transaction On Image Processing, vol. 15(8) (August 2006)
20. Vapnik, V.: The Nature of Statistical Learning Theory. Springer, Heidelberg (1995)
21. PhotoICs PMD 3K-S, 3D Video Sensor Array with Active SBI, `http://www.pmdtec.com`

Two Evolutionary Methods for Learning Bayesian Network Structures

Alain Delaplace, Thierry Brouard, and Hubert Cardot

Université François-Rabelais de Tours, Laboratoire Informatique,
64 avenue Jean Portalis,
37200 Tours, France
{Delaplace,Brouard,Cardot}@univ-tours.fr

Abstract. This paper describes two approaches based on evolutionary algorithms for determining Bayesian networks structures from a database of cases. One major difficulty when tackling the problem of structure learning with evolutionary strategies is to avoid the premature convergence of the population to a local optimum.
In this paper, we propose two methods in order to overcome this obstacle.

The first method is a hybridization of a genetic algorithm with a tabu search principle whilst the second method consists in the application of a dynamic mutation rate. For both methods, a repair operator based on the mutual information between the variables was defined to ensure the closeness of the genetic operators. Finally, we evaluate the influence of our methods over the search for known networks.

1 Introduction

Bayesian Networks (BN) are a family of probabilistic graphical models representing a joint distribution for a set of random variables. Conditional relationships between these variables are symbolized by a Directed Acyclic Graph (DAG). One problem, already shown to be NP-hard [1], consists in determining an appropriate graphical structure from a database of cases. Various algorithms have been conceived in order to solve this problem.

One popular method for searching the best graphical structure is the K2 algorithm [2]. Unfortunately, this method requires the input of an ordering between the variables. The knowledge of the variable ordering is a very strong assumption: the restriction it imposes upon the originally huge search space [3] boils the problem down to finding the optimal set of parents for each variable from predefined restricted ensembles.

Other methods, either based on the use of a scoring metric [4,5] or the detection of (in)dependencies between the variables [6,7], have been developed in order to tackle the problem under the more realistic assumption of the ordering being unknown. As for methods based on statistical (in)dependencies, one major setback is that the statistical tests used are not reliable enough when in presence of numerous variables and small datasets. On the other hand, score-based methods require relatively less computing but their disadvantage lies in that the

Y. Wang, Y. Cheung, and H. Liu (Eds.): CIS 2006, LNAI 4456, pp. 288–297, 2007.

searcher is often confronted with the presence of many local optima within the search space of candidate DAGs.

In this field of research, evolutionary methods such as Genetic Algorithms (GA) have already been used in various forms [8,9,10,11,12,13]. Among these works, two lines of research are interesting. The first idea is to effectively reduce the search space using the notion of equivalence class [14] while in [15], the authors have tried to implement a GA over the PDAG space in hope to benefit from the resulting non-redundancy, without noticeable effect. Our idea is to take advantage both from the (relative) simplicity of the DAG space in terms of manipulation and fitness calculation and the unicity of the equivalence classes representations. Another problem frequently encountered in the domain of evolutionary methods is the adjustment of parameters such as the mutation rate. One answer has been the development of adaptive strategies. Our second method therefore consists in applying a new adaptative scheme to the mutation rate in a GA for structure learning.

Both our methods are based on a common GA architecture, searching through the space of DAGs without any previous knowledge of the ordering over the variables. We designed a general GA based upon dedicated operators: mutation, crossover but also a mutual information-driven repair operator which ensures the closeness of the previous.

The remaining of the paper is organized as follows: in section 2, we introduce some definitions and notations concerning Bayesian Networks that will be used throughout the paper. Section 3 describes our basic GA. Section 4 details our two distinct methods whereas section 5 details the tests we have conducted. Finally section 6 draws the conclusions made upon the results.

2 Setting

A Bayesian network is denoted $\mathcal{B} = \{\mathcal{G}, \theta\}$. Here, $\mathcal{G} = \{X, \mathcal{E}\}$ is a directed acyclic graph whose set of nodes $X = \{X_1, \ldots, X_n\}$ represents a set of random variables and its set of vertices $\mathcal{E}$ represents the dependencies between these variables. The set of parameters θ holds the conditional probabilities for each node, depending on the values taken by its parents in $\mathcal{G}$. $\theta_i = \{\Pr(X_i|Pa(X_i))\}$, where $Pa(X_i)$ are the parents of variable X_i in $\mathcal{G}$. If X_i has no parents, then $Pa(X_i) = \emptyset$.

The main convenience of Bayesian Networks is that, given the representation of conditional independences by its structure and the set θ of local conditional distributions, we can write the global joint probability distribution as:

$$\Pr(X_1, \ldots, X_n) = \prod_{i=1}^{n} \Pr(X_i|Pa(X_i)) \ . \tag{1}$$

3 The Genetic Algorithm

Genetic algorithms are a family of computational models inspired by Darwin's theory of Evolution. Genetic algorithms encode potential solutions to a problem in a chromosome-like data structure, exploring and exploiting the search space using dedicated operators. Their actual form is mainly issued from the work of J. Holland [16]. Throughout the years, different strategies and operators have been developed in order to perform an efficient search over the considered space of individuals: selection, mutation and crossing operators, etc. We will here describe the methods and operators we implemented in our GA.

3.1 Representation

As our search is performed over the space of DAGs, each invidual is represented by an adjacency matrix. Denoting with N the number of variables in the domain, an individual is thus described by an $N \times N$ binary matrix Adj_{ij} where one of its coefficients a_{ij} is equal to 1 if there exists an oriented arc going from X_i to X_j in $\mathcal{G}$.

Where as the traditional GA considers chromosomes defined by a binary alphabet, we chose to modelize the Bayesian Network structure by a chain of N genes (where N is the number of variables in the network). Each gene represents one row of the adjacency matrix, that's to say each gene corresponds to the set of parents of one variable.

Although this nonbinary encoding is unusual in the domain of structure learning, it is not an uncommon practice among genetic algorithms. In fact, this approach turns out to be especially practical for the manipulation and evaluation of candidate solutions.

3.2 Fitness Function

We chose to use the Bayesian BDeu (Bayesian Dirichlet Equivalent Uniform) [17] score as the fitness function for our algorithm. In our case, we set $N_{est} = 1$, the estimated minimal number of occurences for each value of each variable:

$$S_{BDeu}(\mathcal{G}|D) = \log \left(\prod_{i=1}^{n} \prod_{j=1}^{q_i} \frac{\Gamma(\frac{1}{q_i})}{\Gamma(\frac{1}{q_i} + N_{ij})} \prod_{k=1}^{r_i} \frac{\Gamma(\frac{1}{r_i q_i} + N_{ijk})}{\Gamma(\frac{1}{r_i q_i})} \right) . \quad (2)$$

Where r_i represents the dimension of X_i, q_i is the dimension of $Pa(X_i)$ and N_{ijk} is the number of times where, in the learning database, $X_i = x_k$, $k \in 1...r_i$ while $Pa(X_i) = pa_i^j$, $j \in 1...q_i$.
The fitness function $f(individual)$ can be written as in eq. 3.

$$f(individual) = \sum_{i=1}^{n} f_i(X_i, Pa(X_i)). \quad (3)$$

Where f_i is the local BDeu score computed over the family of variable X_i.

3.3 Crossover Operator

We apply a simple one-point crossover. We cut and recombine halves of the adjacency matrixes of the two parents DAGs to generate the offspring.

3.4 Mutation Operator

Each node of one individual has a p_{mute} probability to either lose or gain one parent or to see one of its incoming arcs reverted (i.e. reversing the relationship with one parent).

3.5 Repair Operator

In order to preserve the closeness of our operators over the space of DAGs, we need to design a *repair operator* to convert those invalid graphs (typically, cyclic directed graphs) into valid DAGs. When one cycle is detected within a graph, the operator supresses the one arc in the cycle bearing the weakest mutual information.

The mutual information between two variables is defined as in [18]:

$$W(X_A, X_B) = \sum_{x_a, x_b} \frac{N_{ab}}{N} \log \frac{N_{ab}N}{N_a N_b} \ . \tag{4}$$

Where the mutual information $W(X_A, X_B)$ between two variables X_A and X_B is calculated according to the number of times N_{ab} that $X_A = a$ and $X_B = b$, N_a the number of times $X_A = a$ and so on. The mutual information is computed once for a given database.

3.6 Other Parameters

Selection Method. Each individual in a population of size S has the probability P_{select} to become a potential parent (see eq. 5), depending on its ranking among the current population.

$$P_{select} = \frac{S + 1 - rank(individual)}{\frac{S(S+1)}{2}}. \tag{5}$$

Reduction Method. The five best individuals from the previous population are automatically transferred to the next one. The rest of the population at $t+1$ is composed of the $S - 5$ best childs where S is the size of the population.

4 Methods

4.1 Penalizing Scheme

If a DAG has a set of (in)dependence relationships between its variables that allows us to factorize the joint probability distribution, then different DAGs may represent the same model: in that case, the DAGs are said to be equivalent. This equivalence is defined in the following theorem:

Theorem *[14]*
Two DAGs are equivalent if and only if they have the same skeleton and the same v-structures.

The skeleton of a DAG is the undirected graph that results from ignoring the directionality of every edge. A v-structure in a DAG $\mathcal{G}$ is an ordered triplet of nodes (X, Y, Z), such that

1. *$\mathcal{G}$ contains the arcs $X \rightarrow Y$ and $Y \leftarrow Z$*
2. *The nodes X and Z are not adjacent in $\mathcal{G}$*

This means that when evaluating a member of our population (*ie*: a DAG), since our evaluation function is score-equivalent, we are confronted with either one of the following cases:

- The DAG is not a local optimum. Chances are that the algorithm will find another graph with a higher score
- The DAG is a local optimum. All DAGs in the same equivalence class will have the same fitness and, in order to improve the individual, the operators will have to find the exact modification(s) required to move to another, higher scoring, equivalence class representative.

We try to solve this problem by applying a search strategy taking advantage of the equivalence representation without having to call costly operators.

Search Strategy: If the algorithm converges for more than n iterations to a local optimum $\mathcal{G}_{loc}$, then the equivalence class of $\mathcal{G}_{loc}$ is stored and therefrom, all individuals belonging to this equivalence class will see their fitness function penalized and set at a value ψ.

One equivalence class can be represented by a unique *completed* DAG (or CPDAG) [19]. When a local optimum is identified, we recover the CPDAG of the best individual. Therefrom, at each iteration, every individual will have its CPDAG compared to the set of already recorded CPDAGs.
After a fixed number of iterations, the genetic algorithm returns the best solution encountered.

The main difference with a tabu search algorithm is that we maintain a list of *undesired* moves rather than a list of forbidden ones. That is, one individual can visit a previously marked class. By doing so, we aim at guiding the exploration of the search space rather than restricting it.

4.2 Self Adaptation of the Mutation Rate

The many parameters of a GA are usually fixed by the user and, unfortunately, usually lead to sub-optimal choices.

As the amount of tests required to evaluate all the conceivable sets of parameters will be eventually exponential, a natural approach consists in letting the different parameters evolve along with the algorithm.

[20] defines a terminology for self-adaptiveness which can be resumed as follows:

- **Deterministic Parameter Control**
  The parameters are modified by a deterministic rule.
- **Adaptive Parameter Control**
  Consists in modifying the parameters using feedback from the search.
- **Self-adaptive Parameter Control**
  Parameters are encoded in the individuals and evolve along.

As for the mutation rate, the usual approach consists in starting with a high mutation rate and reducing it as the population converges. Indeed, as the population clusters near one optimum, high mutation rates tend to be degrading. In this case, a self-adaptive strategy would naturally decrease the mutation rate of individuals so that they would be more likely to undergo the minor changes required to reach the optimum.

However, applying this kind of policy can do more harm than good. When there are many local optima, as in our case, we can be confronted with the "bowl effect" described in [21]. That is: when the population is clustered around a local optimum and that the mutation rate is too low to allow at least one individual to escape this local optimum, a strictly decrementing adaptive policy will only trap the population around this optimum.

Other strategies have been proposed which allow the individual mutation rates to either increase or decrease, such as in [22]. There, the mutation step of one individual induces three differently rated mutations: greater, equal and smaller than the individual's actual rate. The issued individual and its mutation rate are chosen accordingly to the qualitative results of the three mutations. Unfortunately, as the mutation process is the most costly operation in our algorithm, we obviously cannot choose such a strategy. Therefore, we designed the following adaptive policy:

Adaptive mutation rate scheme

At each mutation process, given one individual I, its fitness value $f(I)$ and its mutation rate P_m,$\omega < 1$, $\gamma > 1$:

1. Mutate individual I according to its mutation rate P_m: $(I,P_m)\rightarrow(I')$
2. If $f(I') > f(I)$: allocate mutation rate $\omega \times P_m$ to individual I' and $\gamma \times P_m$ to individual I,
3. If $f(I') \leq f(I)$: allocate mutation rate $\gamma \times P_m$ to individual I' and $\omega \times P_m$ to individual I

This principle is based on the fact that, during an evolution-based process, the less fit individuals have the best chances to produce new, fitter individuals. Our scheme is based on the idea of maximizing the mutation rate of less fit individuals while reducing the mutation rate of the fitter.

However, in order to control the computational complexity of the algorithm as well as to leave to the best individuals the possibility to explore their neighbourhood, we define a maximum threshold $Mute_{max}$ and a minimum threshold $Mute_{min}$ for the mutation rate of all individuals.

Since we also apply an elitist strategy, we added a deterministic rule in order to control the mutation rate of the best individuals:

Deterministic control rule
At the end of each iteration, multiply the mutation rates of the best D individuals by ω where D is the degree of our elitist policy.

5 Tests and Results

In order to evaluate the performances of our methods, we used the well-known ALARM network, which structure holds $N = 37$ variables and 46 edges. We also learned the INSURANCE network ($N = 27$ variables and 52 edges).

We generated the test data for three sample sizes (1000, 3000 and 5000) for each network.The tests were carried out with the following parameters:

- The crossing probability p_{cross} was set at 85%.
- Mutation rate p_{mute} was set at $\frac{1}{N}$.
- The size of the population was set at 30 and 50 individuals for the INSURANCE and ALARM databases, respectively.
- Starting populations were set randomly.
- There were 3000 iterations for each run.
- The best individual was considered to be a local optimum if the best fitness had remained the same during 50 iterations.
- Penalizing coefficient ψ was set at -2.10^{-5}.
- The five best individuals were kept between two consecutive populations.
- Adaptive scheme parameter ω was set at 0.95.
- Adaptive scheme thresholds $Mute_{max}$ and $Mute_{min}$ respectively set at $\frac{4}{N}$ and $\frac{1}{N}$.

We compared the results returned by the simple genetic algorithm (Simple-GA), the penalizing scheme (GA-P) and the dynamic self adaptive method (GA-D) for three different values of the parameter γ.

Note that the original structure does not always hold the highest score: the training datasets being of finite sizes may not represent all the (in)dependencies within the original structure because of eventual sampling errors.

The notations employed in the tables are the following:

Av Score: the average score obtained over ten runs.
ANG: the average number of generations to obtain the best structure.
ASD: the average structural difference: holds for the average number of additional edges (AE), missing edges (ME) and reversed edges (RE) between the original graph and the returned graph.

Between brackets are the standard deviations.

The first observation is that both strategies perform better, in average, than the basic GA; returning structures that are both higher-scoring and of higher structural quality. When looking at the performances of our different strategies,

Table 1. Results for the ALARM network, over databases of sizes 1000, 3000 and 5000. Results are meaned over ten runs. Under the description of the database is the score of the original network.

Data Set		Av Score	ANG	ASD	AE	ME	RE
	GA	$-1.1827.10^4(57.5)$	1303(831.8)	20.5	7.4	3.4	9.7
ALARM	GA-P	$-1.1812.10^4(75.2)$	2639(381.7)	20.5	7.4	3.4	9.5
1000	GA-D ($\gamma = 1.1$)	$-1.1817.10^4(50.13)$	1321(948.5)	23.5	9.2	5	9.2
($-1.1777.10^4$)	GA-D ($\gamma = 1.2$)	$-1.1805.10^4(67.05)$	1888(939.1)	23.5	8.4	4.9	10.2
	GA-D ($\gamma = 1.3$)	$-1.1803.10^4(49.8)$	1250(772.2)	20.1	7.5	2.8	9.8
	GA	$-3.3675.10^4(116.1)$	1866(808.4)	23	9.2	3.4	10.4
ALARM	GA-P	$-3.3617.10^4(142.9)$	2075(919.5)	17.1	7.4	2.7	7
3000	GA-D ($\gamma = 1.1$)	$-3.3641.10^4(173.4)$	1476(951.9)	22.1	9.5	2.9	9.7
($-3.3537.10^4$)	GA-D ($\gamma = 1.2$)	$-3.3628.10^4(101.3)$	1941(972.7)	20.4	8.2	3.2	9
	GA-D ($\gamma = 1.3$)	$-3.3594.10^4(106.1)$	1725(960.9)	17.9	7.6	2.7	7.6
	GA	$-5.6394.10^4(204.9)$	1356(528)	25	9.9	2.6	12.5
ALARM	GA-P	$-5.6273.10^4(95.3)$	1531.8(772.9)	16.9	7.7	2.2	7
5000	GA-D ($\gamma = 1.1$)	$-5.6329.10^4(122.9)$	1771(784.1)	20.6	8.3	2.7	9.6
($-5.6248.10^4$)	GA-D ($\gamma = 1.2$)	$-5.6256.10^4(55.6)$	1728(860.5)	16.4	7	2.3	7.1
	GA-D ($\gamma = 1.3$)	$-5.6245.10^4(74.8)$	1563(574.7)	15.9	7	2.2	6.7

Table 2. Results for the INSURANCE network, over databases of sizes 1000, 3000 and 5000. Results are meaned over ten runs. Under the description of the database is the score of the original network.

Data Set		Av Score	ANG	ASD	AE	ME	RE
	GA	$-1.5160.10^4(47.5)$	821.1(757.9)	29.1	5.2	16.1	7.8
INSURANCE	GA-P	$-1.5065.10^4(12.5)$	1577(893.8)	20	2	14.1	3.9
1000	GA-D ($\gamma = 1.1$)	$-1.5157.10^4(92.74)$	1727(831.1)	25	4.4	15.5	5.1
($-1.5478.10^4$)	GA-D ($\gamma = 1.2$)	$-1.5207.10^4(118.8)$	1308.1(1025)	29.8	6.1	17	6.7
	GA-D ($\gamma = 1.3$)	$-1.5173.10^4(97)$	1328(1015.1)	27.7	5.9	16.8	7.5
	GA	$-4.3798.10^4(108.9)$	997.3(671.9)	25.4	5.7	11.9	7.8
INSURANCE	GA-P	$-4.3705.10^4(108.2)$	1920.4(756.7)	23	5.3	11.2	6.5
3000	GA-D ($\gamma = 1.1$)	$-4.3782.10^4(118.8)$	961.6(640.5)	29.8	7.3	12.4	9.8
($-4.3926.10^4$)	GA-D ($\gamma = 1.2$)	$-4.3866.10^4(114.4)$	854.5(671.3)	30	8.2	12.9	8.9
	GA-D ($\gamma = 1.3$)	$-4.3888.10^4(234.6)$	1383(1029)	29.3	7.1	12.6	9.6
	GA	$-7.2051.10^4(155.3)$	1475(861.7)	24.8	5.3	9.6	9.9
INSURANCE	GA-P	$-7.1994.10^4(204)$	2187.1(536.4)	19.5	4.1	9.4	6
5000	GA-D ($\gamma = 1.1$)	$-7.2119.10^4(162.1)$	1051.8(746.8)	28.1	6.4	10.1	11.6
($-7.2195.10^4$)	GA-D ($\gamma = 1.2$)	$-7.2113.10^4(214.5)$	1416.3(944.1)	25.5	5.5	9.8	10.2
	GA-D ($\gamma = 1.3$)	$-7.2151.10^4(228.7)$	1270(860.9)	27.3	6.6	9.8	10.9

the penalizing GA comes out with very good results on both score and structural differences. However, we can observe that the performances of the GA-D strategies over the ALARM network, compared to the GA-P, are improved when the dataset is large enough. Even if the adaptive strategy returns the worst average results over the 1000 dataset, it also obtains good solutions in terms of score and structural differences.

Our results already show that the adaptiveness of the mutation rate can tend to favorize the finding of better structures without having to resort to the systematical search induced by the penalizing scheme.

Assigning a higher value to the parameter γ induces better performances when the dataset is large enough to offer an accurate evaluation of the various structures, due to the consistancy of the scoring function. We will have to proceed to further testings in order to draw a conclusion concerning a possible relationship between the complexity of the structural landscape (according to the chosen evaluation method), the number of variables contained in the network and the values taken by the adaptive parameters.

6 Conclusions

We have considered two strategies in the learning of the graphical structure of Bayesian networks from a database of cases. Results confirm that both strategies improve the convergence of the genetic algorithm as well as the structural quality of the solutions.

Although results returned by the adaptive scheme are not as good as we expected, the improvement over the basic genetic algorithm is clear as the scheme lead to the finding of good, if not high-scoring, structures. The main setback of our adaptive method is the fact that the adaptation holds for the whole structure, leading to a clear unevenness in the exploration of the space of candidate families for each variable. However, to our knowledge, this is the first time a dynamic mutation rate scheme has been applied to the determination of Bayesian networks structures and we see it as a promising direction. In our research, we have deliberately focused on the exploration of the search space by either the exploitation of the class equivalence concept or the adaptation of the mutation rate, yet we have not taken full advantage of the genetic algorithm as we have let aside the recombination process, which is of interest as shown in [8]. We have yet to study the effects of adaptiveness over, for example, a combined adaptation of the mutation and crossover processes. Studying the behaviour of new schemes in adaptive evolutionary processes will surely be an interesting line of work in the future.

References

1. Chickering, D.M., Geiger, D., Heckerman, D.: Learning Bayesian Networks is NP-hard. Technical Report MSR-TR-94-17, Microsoft Research (November 1994)
2. Cooper, G., Herskovits, E.: A Bayesian method for the Induction of Probabilistic Networks from Data. Machine Learning 09, 309–347 (1992)
3. Robinson, R.: Counting Unlabeled Acyclic Digraphs. In: Combinatorial Mathematics V: Proceedings of the Fifth Australian Conference, held at the Royal Melbourne Institute of Technology. American Mathematical Society, pp. 28–43 (1976)
4. Friedman, N.: The Bayesian Structural EM Algorithm. In: Fourteenth Conference on Uncertainty in Artificial Intelligence (UAI), pp. 129–138 (1998)

5. Chickering, D.M.: Optimal Structure Identification with Greedy Search. Journal of Machine Learning Research 3, 507–554 (2002)
6. Spirtes, P., Glymour, C., Scheines, R.: Causation, Prediction and Search. Springer-Verlag, Heidelberg (1993)
7. Cheng, J., Bell, D., Liu, W.: Learning Belief Networks from Data: an Information Theory Based Approach. In: Proceedings of the sixth ACM International Conference on Information and Knowledge Management, pp. 325–331. ACM Press, New York (1997)
8. Larranaga, P., Poza, M., Yurramendi, Y., Murga, R., Kuijpers, C.: Structure Learning of Bayesian Networks by Genetic Algorithms: A Performance Analysis of Control Parameters. IEEE Trans (PAMI) 18(9), 912–926 (1996)
9. Cotta, C., Muruzábal, J.: On the Learning of Bayesian Network Graph Structures via Evolutionary Programming. In: Proceedings of the 2nd European Workshop on Probabilistic Graphical Models, pp. 65–72 (2004)
10. Wong, M., Lam, W., Leung, K.: Using Pvolutionary Programming and Minimum Description Length Principle for Data Mining of Bayesian networks. IEEE Trans (PAMI) 21(2), 174–178 (1999)
11. Wong, M., Lee, S.Y., Leung,K.S.: A Hybrid Data Mining Approach To Discover Bayesian Networks Using Evolutionary Programming. In: Proceedings of the Genetic and Evolutionary Computation Conference (GECCO 2002), pp. 214–222 (2002)
12. van Dijk, S., Thierens, D., van der Gaag, L.C.: A Skeleton-Based Approach to Learning Bayesian Networks from Data. In: 7th European Conference on Principles and Practice of Knowledge Discovery in Databases, Cavtat-Dubrovnik, Croatia, September 22-26, 2003, pp. 132–143 (2003)
13. van Dijk, S., Thierens, D., van der Gaag, L.C.: Building a GA from Design Principles for Learning Bayesian Networks. In: Proceedings of the Genetic and Evolutionary Computation Conference (GECCO 2003) pp. 886–897 (2003)
14. Verma, T., Pearl, J.: Equivalence and Synthesis of Causal Models. In: Proceedings of the Sixth Conference on Uncertainty and Artificial Intelligence, pp. 220–227. Morgan Kaufmann, San Francisco (1990)
15. Silvia Acid, S., de Campos, L.M.: Searching for Bayesian Network Structures in the Space of Restricted Acyclic Partially Directed Graphs. Journal of Artificial Intelligence Research 18, 445–490 (2003)
16. Holland, J.H.: Adaptation in natural and artificial systems. The University of Michigan Press, Ann Arbor (1975)
17. Heckerman, D.: A Tutorial on Learning Bayesian Networks. Technical Report MSR-TR-95-06, Microsoft Research (March (1995)
18. Chow, C.K., Liu, C.N.: Approximating Discrete Probability Distributions with Dependence Trees. IEEE Trans. on Information Theory 14(3), 462–467 (1968)
19. Chickering, D.M.: Learning equivalence classes of Bayesian-network structures. Journal of Machine Learning Research 2, 445–498 (2002)
20. Eiben, A.E., Hinterding, R., Michalewicz, Z.: Parameter Control in Evolutionary Algorithms. IEEE Trans. on Evolutionary Computation 3(2), 124–141 (1999)
21. Glickman, M., Sycara, K.: Reasons for Premature Convergence of Self-adapting Mutation Rates. In: Proceedings of the 2000 Congress on Evolutionary Computation, Vol. 1, pp. 62–69 (July 2000)
22. Thierens, D.: Adaptive mutation Rate Control Schemes in Genetic Algorithms. In: Technical Report UU-CS-2002-056, Institute of Information and Computing Sciences, Utrecht University (2002)

Fuzzy Q-Map Algorithm for Reinforcement Learning

YoungAh Lee[1] and SeokMi Hong[2]

[1] The Department of Computer Engineering The University of KyungHee
Seocheon-Dong Giheung-Gu Yongin-si Gyeonggi-Do, 446-701, Korea
[2] School of Computer, Information and Communication Engineering
The University of Sangji #660 USan-Dong WonJu-Si, KangWon-Do, 220-702, Korea
leeyaa10@yahoo.co.kr, smhong@yahoo.co.kr

Abstract. In reinforcement learning, it is important to get nearly right answers early. Good prediction early can reduce the prediction error afterward and accelerate learning speed. We propose Fuzzy Q-Map, function approximation algorithm based on on-line fuzzy clustering in order to accelerate learning. Fuzzy Q-Map can handle the uncertainty owing to the absence of environment model. Appling membership function to reinforcement learning can reduce the prediction error and destructive interference phenomenon caused by changes of the distribution of training data. In order to evaluate fuzzy Q-Map's performance, we experimented on the mountain car problem and compared it with CMAC. CMAC achieves the prediction rate 80% from 250 training data, Fuzzy Q-Map learns faster and keep up the prediction rate 80% from 250 training data. Fuzzy Q-Map may be applied to the field of simulation that has uncertainty and complexity.

Keywords: reinforcement learning, fuzzy online clustering, membership function.

1 Introduction

The learning method can be divided into supervised learning and unsupervised learning in terms of existence of adviser. Reinforcement learning can be considered as one of unsupervised learning algorithms, since it do not use user's advices in process of learning. Unsupervised learning algorithms grasp the structure or relations immanent in input data set without correct answers, and classify input patterns according to the relations. Reinforcement learning learns effective actions that derive useful results using rewards as immediate evaluation values created in the process of interaction between environment and agent. The purpose of reinforcement learning is to learn a value function that evaluates a value of a state, long-term utility of states and is used to decide the next action.

Q learning [1],[2],[3],[4], basis algorithm of reinforcement learning, calculates state-action value function, Q function. Q function forecasts one step ahead and calculates optimal policies. Q function is stored in the form of table and indexed by state and action. Original Q-learning algorithm has a critical problem caused by the

Y. Wang, Y. Cheung, and H. Liu (Eds.): CIS 2006, LNAI 4456, pp. 298–307, 2007.

size of a state space. First, complex reinforcement learning tasks with continuous state and action values have a huge state space. A reinforcement learning agent dealing with such a problem cannot remember all state-action pairs in one table and suffers from long learning time. If reinforcement learning tasks be complex or handle continuous data, their state space are huge. Such difficulties are called as "the curse of dimensionality problem". Most real world reinforcement learning tasks and simulations suffer from "curse of dimensionality". Because of the difficulties, original reinforcement learning algorithms should be combined with approximation methods. For the right reinforcement learning, plenty of training data from all over the entire state space are required. Simulation or real world tasks cannot collect perfect training data set and a reinforcement learning agent cannot experience all of possible training data. Users prefer simple forms as a reward function that obtain a reward at only goal state and gives the same penalties to the other states. Simple reward function is slow in making useful knowledge and so an agent wanders in a state space until an agent reaches a goal state. Reinforcement learning should predict reasonably at the beginning of learning, but a simple reward function may make the learning speed lower.

Function approximations [1], [2], [3], [4], [7], [12], [14], [15], [16], [17], [18], [19], [20] can be used to solve "the curse of dimensionality problem" and accelerate the learning speed. Function approximation for reinforcement learning should have following features. First, reinforcement learning must learn from interaction and must do prediction reasonably at the beginning of learning. Wrong predictions in the early phase make the learning agent lost in the state space. Secondly, because training data are contingent on the trajectory that a reinforcement learning agent explores a state space, the distribution of training data changes during learning. If all knowledge are stored in a global function or in a small number of local functions, there is a great likelihood of conflicts between already acquired knowledge in the past and new experience in the same part of state space. Knowledge in the function is updated by new experience. Such an interference phenomenon is a trouble that reinforcement learning suffers from. Third, the uncertainty of reinforcement learning comes from the absence of dynamic environment model. A function approximation method for reinforcement learning should be able to deal with the uncertainty.

In this paper, on the assumption that the extraction of pre-knowledge is difficult, we propose Fuzzy Q-Map as a function approximation method based on online fuzzy clustering that improves problem of continuous state space and accelerates the learning speed and reasonable predictions are possible on early time.

2 Reinforcement Learning Algorithms

2.1 Q-Learning

Q-learning [1], [2], [3], [4] is a representative algorithm of reinforcement learning that Watkins has proposed first. Q learning stores all state-action pairs on a lookup table and should experiences all state-action pairs over and over. If the state space expands, it is impossible to learn all state action pairs. The reward function of Q learning is generally a simple form that estimate state-action pairs to a goal state highly and other state-action pairs negatively.

2.2 Various Studies for Learning Speed Acceleration of Reinforcement Learning

Reinforcement learning must do immediate response to a training data that enter the learning system. Therefore proper action choice from the beginning of reinforcement learning can make the reduction of error size and learning speed acceleration. Various Studies for learning speed acceleration of reinforcement learning have been made.

Fuzzy Q-Learning. Fuzzy Q-Learning(FQL) [13], [14], [15] is a reinforcement learning method invented by Glorennce and Jouffe that applied Fuzzy Inference System (FIS) to Watkins' Q-Learning. Fuzzy Inference System is suitable for learning a complicated model that has uncertainty and continuous valued features. It also expresses pre-knowledge to rules easily.

Values of continuous feature can be divided into finite parts, but it is not easy matter to divide into qualified parts. The boundaries of parts itself are not accurate even if an input state belongs to a part. In this system, if an input state belongs exclusively in a part, errors are generated and the size of error increases gradually in the process of training.

Fuzzy Theory can solve the above-mentioned problem more or less. FQL reasons actions and Q values from fuzzy rule base. FQL can improve the learning speed, but needs the preprocessing and pre knowledge to decide fuzzy labels and fuzzy membership functions. FQL also has a defect that the condition part of a fuzzy rule is fixed. In reinforcement learning, the distribution of training data changes according to path that an agent explores. According to training data set, the condition part of rule should be adapted.

CMAC(Cerebellar Model Articulation Controller). CMAC (Cerebellar Model Articulation Controller) [1], [16], [17], [18] proposed by Sutton operates several overlapping tilings of a state space. CMAC uses the average of values of tiles that are activated by an input state. If an agent receives a query from the environment, it calculates a Q value by the process that sums values of set of tiles activated according to the following equation. And then $TD(\lambda)$ values and eligibilities of every tiles in CMAC are updated.

$$Q'(x,a) = \sum_{f_{ij} \in F(x,a)} w_{ij} \,. \tag{1}$$

LWR(Locally Weighted Regression). Smart introduces HEDGER and JAQL [4], [19], [20] based on LWR. LWR is a method that training examples near a query point have an influence on the estimation using kernel function, and it computes several local functions. Kernel function in LWR is Gaussian function.

If training examples are given in advance, they can help to accomplish improvement of learning speed of reinforcement learning because they can be used to choose actions. Training examples can be collected by experts who know the domain related with the task well. Although learning algorithms that use pre-knowledge and user's advices can improve the learning speed, but the property of autonomy does not exist in those algorithms and pre-knowledge can not be always collected easily.

The Membership Function of Fuzzy Clustering. Membership functions in the fuzzy clustering [5] are divided into relative membership degree functions and absolute membership degree functions. The relation of above two membership degree functions can be expressed by following way (2). The k is an index of training data and i is an index of cluster. A relative membership degree, $R_{i,k}$ needs to satisfy following condition.

$$R_{i,k} = \frac{A_{i,k}}{\sum_{j}^{c} A_{j,h}}, \quad j = 1,\ldots,\quad c. \tag{2}$$

$$\sum_{i=1}^{c} R_{i,k} = 1 . \tag{3}$$

The $R_{i,k}$ is a relative value to every other cluster's absolute membership degrees, therefore a training data such a noise can be assigned to several clusters with high membership degree and can have a bad influence on accuracy of learning model. Absolute membership degree represents how much a training data is analogous to a center of an independent cluster without considering relation with other clusters. One of shortcomings is an increase in the number of local minima because absolute membership degree function tries to optimize each cluster independently. Fuzzy C-Means(FCM) uses a type of relative fuzzy membership degree function, because such functions can describe whole input space based on the relations between other clusters as well as a winner.

3 Fuzzy Q-Map

3.1 Function Approximation Method for Reinforcement Learning

In this paper, we propose a new function approximation method for reinforcement learning, Fuzzy Q-Map. It is based on online fuzzy clustering and Q learning. The following are the reasons why online fuzzy clustering is suited to a function approximation of reinforcement learning. Reinforcement learning resembles clustering of unsupervised learning. Clustering groups states by similarity, and continues adjusting to new training data. A model of environment is not given to reinforcement learning. Therefore, it is impossible to divide accurately a state space into significant sections. The membership functions of fuzzy clustering can represent such uncertainty. Online clustering algorithm removes input data after use from a learning system, so online clustering need not store the whole huge training data set and do not suffer from a lot of computation with the whole data set. It is impossible that one global function expresses strategies of a nonlinear approximation problem. Clustering updates local area of the state space. All local update avoid the modification of already acquired knowledge.

3.2 The Structure of Fuzzy Q-Map

Fuzzy Q-Map classifies training experiences and memorizes strategies to achieve a goal. Fuzzy Q-Map is a two dimensional table. A multidimensional input belongs to several clusters according to Euclidean distance and fuzzy factor. A row of Fuzzy Q-Map equals to a cluster and the number of columns in a row equals to the number of actions in a state space. An episode that an agent experiences during learning is a path from an arbitrary state to goal state. Goal states do not transit to a next state, so its Q values don't have to be acquired and goal states are not handled like other states. The number of nodes in Fuzzy Q-Map is (the number of clusters × the number of actions) + 1, the last additional node is for a cluster that has a goal state as centroid. Fuzzy Q-Map can't deal with only discrete actions but also continuous actions with membership function. Each fuzzy cluster memorizes a centroid, actions, rewards, current Q values. Centroid $c_i = (w_{i1},..., w_{in})$ (i is index of a cluster) is n-dimensional vector the same as a state and is adapted with input states assigned to the i cluster.

Fuzzy Q-Map's Q value can't be acquired directly. Because Fuzzy Q-Map updates each cluster's Q values independently, Q values of a cluster are local values. For estimation of Q value, local Q values are collected from every cluster and summed as much as each cluster's membership degree. Fuzzy Q-Map's terminologies are as follows.

Local best action : has the largest Q value in a cluster and is the best action proposed by a cluster.
Local Q value : represents the worth of an action within a cluster.
Global best action: is the Fuzzy Q-Map's good action. It is obtained by weighted sum of local best actions.
Global Q value : is an estimation value calculated by Fuzzy Q-Map.

3.3 Fuzzy Q-Map Algorithm

Fuzzy Q-Map algorithm is as follow.

Stage 1: Initialization. Centroids $c_i (1 \le i \le c,\ \text{c is the number of clusters})$ are initialized randomly. A reward and Q value of each action are initialized with 0.

Stage 2: Start State Selection. An input state s_t is selected randomly. The index t represents the sequence of a state processing in Fuzzy Q-Map and denotes the number of states in training up to now. The training set is defined by lots of episode, precisely speaking, is formed of states meeting while exploring a state space. Therefore s_t is a component of am episode.

Stage 3: Calculate Membership Degree m_{ti}. We calculate the membership degree m_{ij} of each cluster $i (1 \le i \le c)$ about s_t. Membership degree m_{ti} of s_t is the estimation of belonging rate to a cluster i relatively to others. Fuzzy factor f is defined by user. In terms of formula (5), a membership degree is restricted from 0 to 1. Such as relative membership function can't exclude erroneous input state and learn unavoidably. In spite of that defect, Fuzzy Q-Map utilizes relative membership function, because it has an ability to analyze a whole state space and to make values within the fixed range.

$$m_{it} = \frac{1}{\sum_{j=1}^{c} \left(\frac{d_{it}}{d_{jt}}\right)^{2/(q-1)}}. \tag{4}$$

$$\sum_{i=1}^{c} m_{it} = 1. \tag{5}$$

Stage 4: The Prediction of the Best Action. Based on the principle of $\varepsilon - greedy$, Fuzzy Q-Map selects an action a_t in a state s_t. Chosen action a_t is a global action suggested by Fuzzy Q-Map and come from local actions suggested by clusters. The action a_{it} is the largest Q valued action in a cluster i. The c_i is the centroid of cluster i.

$$a_{it} = \max{}_{\arg\ a}\ q(c_i, a_j). \tag{6}$$

The best action a_t^* is calculated on the basis of membership degree

$$a_t^* = \frac{\sum_{i=1}^{c} m_{ik} \times a_{it}}{\sum_{i=1}^{c} m_{ik}} = \sum_{i=1}^{c} m_{ik} \times a_{it}, \quad \mathrm{a}_t = a_t^*. \tag{7}$$

Stage 5: The Execution of a_t. An agent executes the best action a_t. And then an agent receives a reward value r_{t+1} and perceives a next state s_{t+1} as a result of a_t.

Stage 6: The Update of Q Value. A state and action pair, (s_t, a_t) is revaluated. The formula 8 evaluates the Q value of (s_t, a_t). The $q(c_i, a_t)$ is a local Q value of a_t in a cluster i.

$$Q(s_t, a_t) = \sum_{i=1}^{c} (m_{it} \times q(c_i, a_t)). \tag{8}$$

The $f(s_{t+1})$ is a evaluation value of the next state s_{t+1} the value is estimated from the largest Q values of clusters and membership degree $m_{i(t+1)}$.

$$f(s_{t+1}) = \sum_{i=1}^{c} m_{i(t+1)} \times \max q(c_i, a). \tag{9}$$

The above two formulas are used to the update formula of Q value of original Q learning algorithm.

$$Q(s_t, a_t) \leftarrow Q(s_t, a_t) + \alpha(r_{t+1} + \gamma f(s_{t+1}) - Q(s_t, a_t)). \tag{10}$$

α is a learning rate and initialized with 0.5. The value α is slowly decreased with parameter t.

$$\alpha = 0.5 \times 0.9^{\frac{t}{1000}}. \tag{11}$$

Stage 7: The Updates of Winner's Centroid and Q Value. In terms of s_t, local Q value and the centroid of winner that is the closest cluster to s_t are updated. Fuzzy Q-Map uses TD(temporal Difference) error and membership degree for update.

$$c_w \leftarrow c_w + (s_t - c_w) \times m_{wt} \times \alpha. \tag{12}$$

$$q(c_w, a_t) \leftarrow q(c_w, a_t) + (Q(s_t, a_t) - q(c_w, a_t)) \times m_{it}. \tag{13}$$

Online learning such as reinforcement learning is hard to save training set, therefore those kind of algorithms usually use TD error and membership degree for update.

Stage 8 : Checking the Condition of end of Fuzzy Q Map. If the condition of end is satisfied, the learning is finished. Otherwise go to the stage 9. The learning is finished when there is no change of Q values and centroids or when it is completed defined the number of iteration times.

Stage 9: The Determination of Iteration. If s_t is a goal state, a new state s_t is initialized randomly. Otherwise $s_t \leftarrow s_{t+1}$ and go to the stage 3.

4 Performance Measurement of Fuzzy Q Map

4.1 Mountain Car Problem

Mountain Car Problem has delayed reward and is an instance where actions with negative rewards are good selection in the long run. In this experiment, following reward function is adopted. A test set for training into Fuzzy Q-Map is composed of evenly distributed 100 states in a state space.

$$r_{t+1} = \begin{cases} 1 & \text{if } s_{t+1} \text{ is a goal state} \\ -1 & \text{otherwise} \end{cases}. \tag{14}$$

4.2 The Adjustment of Fuzzy Q-Map in New Training Set

The centroids of clusters are initialized at the start of learning. The figure 1 shows the result of adaptation of centroids after 370000 iteration. Regardless of any training set

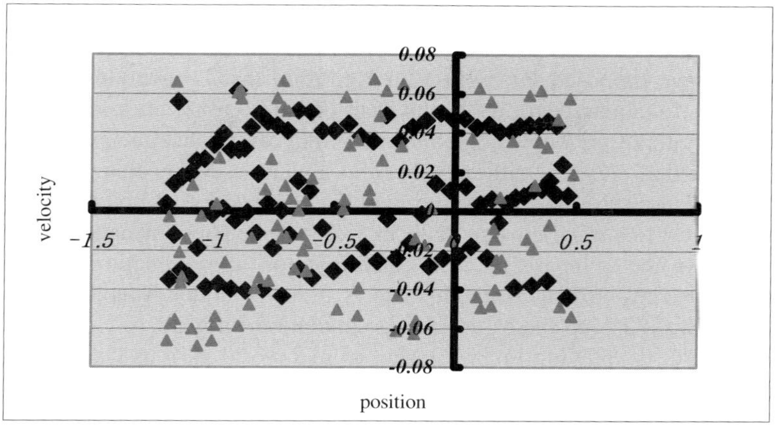

Fig. 1. The movement of centroids after 370000 iteration

and initial centroids, the centroids adapted to massive training set are fishlike like the graph in Figure 1.

4.3 Comparative Experiments

In order to assess Fuzzy Q-Map algorithm from comparative experiment, we execute CMAC on mountain car problem. We refer to the William D. Smart's article[4] for CMAC. In Figure 2, the graphs show learning speed of CMAC and Fuzzy Q-Map without prior knowledge. Fuzzy Q-Map is lower than CMAC in the highest prediction rate, but its learning speed in the early phase is accelerated faster.

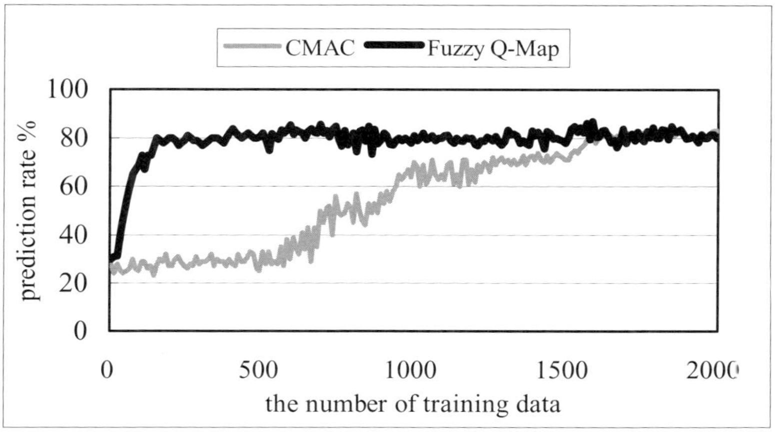

Fig. 2. The learning speed of CMAC and Fuzzy Q Map

5 Conclusion

In this paper, we proposed Fuzzy Q-Map algorithm that is function approximation method for reinforcement learning on the basis of online fuzzy clustering to solve the complex task without pre knowledge. Fuzzy Q-Map can predict an action at a strange state from similar clusters with membership function. Membership function can decrease prediction error and accelerate learning process. Local updates of centroids and Q values just in similar clusters reduces interference phenomenon. The following Table 1. shows the comparison with other function approximation. In a field of simulation nowadays, artificial intelligence is used to model complex system with uncertainty. Fuzzy Q-Map can be utilized as simulation software.

Future project is applying Fuzzy Q-Map to real world various tasks to prove our algorithm's performance. In application of real world tasks, because input data from sensor cannot be used without refining, Fuzzy Q-Map should be modified. And we will study eligibility formula for Fuzzy Q Map to improve learning seed.

Table 1. The comparison with other function approximation

	FQM	CMAC	FQL	LWR/RBFs
Basic Theory	Online Fuzzy Clustering	Coarse Coding	FIS	Instance based algorithm
Membership Function	relative			
Prior Knowledge	not	not	use	use
Adaptation	adjust		fixed	

References

1. Sutton, R., Barto, A.G.: Reinforcement Learning:An Introduction. MIT Press, Cambridge, MA (1998)
2. Kaelbling, L.P., Littman, M.L., Moor, A.W.: Reinforcement Learning: A Survey. Journal of Artificial Intelligence Research 4, 237–285 (1996)
3. Glorennce, P.Y.: Reinforcement Learning: an Overview, Proceedings of the European Symposium on Intelligent Techniques (2000)
4. Smart, W.D.: Making Reinforcement Learning Work on Real Robots, Ph. D. Thesis, Brown University (2002)
5. Jain, A.K., Murty, M.N, Flynn, P.J.: Data Clustering: A Review, ACM Computing Surveys, 31(3) (1999)

6. Baraldi, A., Blonda, P.: A survey of fuzzy clustering algorithms for pattern recognition. IEEE Transactions on Systems, Man and Cybernetics, Part B (Cybernetics) 29(6), 778–785 (1999)
7. Likas, A.: A Reinforcement Learning Approach to On-line Clustering. Neural computation 11(8), 1915–1932 (1999)
8. Karayiannis, N.B., Bezdek, J.C.: An Integrated Approach to Fuzzy Learning Vector Quantization and Fuzzy c-Means Clstering. IEEE Transactions of Fuzzy systems 5(4) (1997)
9. Hammer, B., Villmann, T.: Generalized Relevance Learning Vector Quantization. Neural Networks 15(8-9), 1059–1068 (2002)
10. Hu, S.J.: Pattern Recognition by LVQ and GLVQ Networks, http://neuron.et.ntust.edu.tw/homework/87/NN/87Homework%232/M8702043
11. Herrmann, M., Der, R.: Efficient Q-Learning by Division of Labor. In: Proceedings of International Conference on Artificial Neural Networks (1995)
12. Yamada, K., Svinin, M., Ueda, K.: Reinforcement Learning with Autonomous State Space Construction using Unsupervised Clustering Method. In: Proceedings of the 5th International Symposium on Artificial Life and Robotics (2000)
13. Jouffe, L.: Fuzzy Inference System Learning by Reinforcement Methods. IEEE Transactions on Systems, Man and Cybernetics 338–355 (1998)
14. Bonarini, A.: Delayed Reinforcement, Fuzzy Q-Learning and Fuzzy Logic Controllers. In: Herrera, F., Verdegay, J.L. (eds.) Genetic Algorithms and Soft Computing, pp. 447–466 (1996)
15. Glorennec, P.Y., Jouffe, L.: Fuzzy Q-Learning. In: Proceedings of Sixth IEEE International Conference on Fuzzy Systems, pp. 719–724 (1997)
16. Sutton, R.S.: Generalization in Reinforcement Learning: Successful Examples Using Sparse Coarse Coding. In: Advances in Neural Information Processing Systems, vol. 8, pp. 1038–1044. MIT Press, Cambridge, MA (1996)
17. Kretchmar, R.M., Anderson, C.W.: Comparison of CMACs and Radial Basis Functions for Local Function Approximators in Reinforcement Learning. In: Proceedings of International Conference on Neural Networks (1997)
18. Santamaria, J.C., Sutton, R.S., Ram, A.: Experiments with Reinforcement Learning in Problems with Continuous State and Action Spaces, COINS Technical Report, pp. 96–88 (1996)
19. Smart, W.D., Kaelbling, L.P.: Practical Reinforcement Learning in Continuous Spaces. In: Proceedings of International Conference on Machine Learning (2000)
20. Smart, W.D., Kaelbling, L.P.: Reinforcement Learning for Robot Control, In: Mobile Robots XVI (2001)

Spatial Data Mining with Uncertainty

Binbin He[1] and Cuihua Chen[2]

[1] Institute of Geo-Spatial Information Science and Technology,
University of Electronic Science and Technology of China, Chengdu 610054, China
binbinhe@uestc.edu.cn
[2] College of Earth Sciences, Chengdu University of Technology, Chengdu 610059, China
chencuihua@cdut.edu.cn

Abstract. On the basis of analyzing the deficiencies of traditional spatial data mining, a framework for spatial data mining with uncertainty has been founded. Four key problems have been analyzed, including uncertainty simulation of spatial data with Monte Carlo method, spatial autocorrelation measurement, discretization of continuous data based on neighbourhood EM algorithm and uncertainty assessment of association rules. Meanwhile, the experiments concerned have been performed using the environmental geochemistry data gotten from Dexing, Jiangxi province in China.

1 Introduction

Spatial Data Mining (SDM) is to extract the hidden, implicit, valid, novel and interesting spatial or non-spatial patterns, rules and knowledge from large-amount, incomplete, noisy, fuzzy, random, and practical spatial databases [1,2]. With an efficient and rapid improvement of acquiring technologies of spatial data, the amount of data within spatial database has been increased in index ratio. But the deficiency of analysis functions in geographic information systems (GISs) makes a serious divorce between the massive spatial data and useful knowledge acquisition. In other words, "The spatial data explode but knowledge is poor" [2]. At present, SDM mainly concentrate on the methods of data mining [1,3,4]. Another important issue –uncertainty in SDM –has not been paid much attention to. Clementini et al. [5], Wang et al. [6], Beaubouef et al. [7] and He et al. [8] study on the uncertainty in spatial data mining from different views. On the one hand, spatial data itself lies in uncertainty, and on the other hand, many uncertainties will be reproduced in SDM, even propagated and accumulated, which lead to the production of uncertain knowledge. These characteristics had not been fully considered, and the knowledge discovered had been regarded as an entirely useful and certain in traditional SDM. It is convenient to study SDM by starting from perfect spatial data with perfect result. However, spatial data are usually far from perfect, and the SDM process itself is full of various kinds of uncertainty. The exploration of SDM incorporating uncertainty is very necessary and important, because it can make the study of SDM more realistic. In this paper, a framework of the uncertain spatial data mining is proposed in view of four deficiencies in traditional methods. Furthermore, a set of experiments concerned has been performed using the environmental geochemistry data gotten from Dexing, Jiangxi province in China.

Y. Wang, Y. Cheung, and H. Liu (Eds.): CIS 2006, LNAI 4456, pp. 308–316, 2007.

2 A Framework for Spatial Data Mining with Uncertainty

There will be four distinct deficiencies when we adopt some traditional methods for spatial data mining. First of all, the uncertainty of spatial data themselves has not usually been considered. Secondly, the uncertainty caused by the processing of spatial data mining is ignored. Thirdly, the inherent autocorrelation of spatial data is difficult to determine. Finally, how the resultant uncertainty of spatial data mining is to assess. The results are that not all rules or knowledge discovered in spatial data mining are complete and fully useful according to the preceding four main deficiencies. For these, we propose a framework for spatial data mining with uncertainty, in which the uncertainties of spatial data themselves and spatial data mining are emphatically dealt with, including uncertainty simulation with Monte Carlo method, spatial autocorrelation measurement based on uncertain spatial data, discretization based on neighborhood EM algorithm, and quality assessment of association rules.

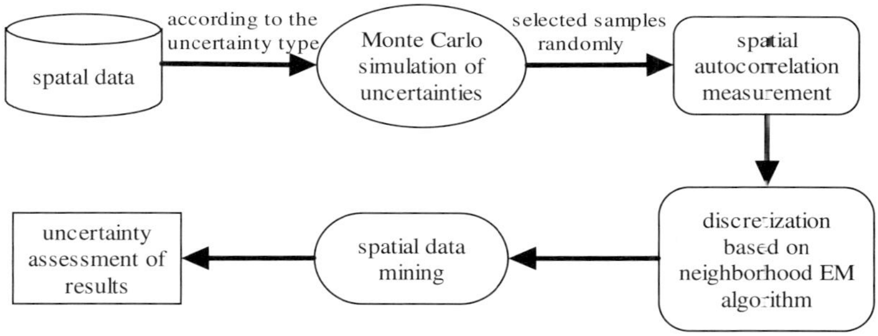

Fig. 1. A framework for spatial data mining with uncertainty

2.1 Monte Carlo Simulation for the Uncertainties

The uncertainties of spatial data may be simulated with Monte Carlo simulation method. In this paper, we adopt ran2 random generation suggested by Press [9] and Box-Muller[10] resample method. In which, positional data adopt 2-dimensional normal circle model [11], and attribute data adopt 1-dimensional normal distributed function.

According to the circle normal model, some error indexes can be defined [12]:

$$\sigma_c = 0.707(\sigma_{x_1}^2 + \sigma_{x_2}^2)^{\frac{1}{2}} \quad (1)$$

where, σ_c is standard error of circle, σ_{x_1} is standard error in x_1 direction, σ_{x_2} is standard error in x_2 direction.

We adopt circle approach certain error index [12]. It presents the probability of 99.78%:

$$r = 3.5\sigma_c \quad (2)$$

Here, we propose that the error radius of sampling points is 10 meters according to the accuracy of stand-alone GPS (Global Positioning System). Then, σ_c =2.8571428m.

The probability distribution function (PDF) of attribute data is described as follows:

$$f(x) = \frac{1}{\sigma\sqrt{2\pi}} \exp(-\frac{(x-\mu)^2}{2\sigma^2}) \quad (3)$$

Where, $-\infty < x < \infty$, $\sigma > 0$, σ^2 is variance, μ is mean.

2.2 Spatial Autocorrelation Matrix and Its Measurement

It is understood that almost of spatial data show the characteristics of spatial autocorrelation. Spatial autocorrelation matrix may be constructed by adjacency standard or distance measurement as follows:

$$\begin{bmatrix} w_{11} & w_{12} & \cdots & w_{1n} \\ w_{21} & w_{22} & \cdots & w_{2n} \\ \vdots & \vdots & \vdots & \vdots \\ w_{m1} & w_{m2} & \cdots & w_{mn} \end{bmatrix} \quad (4)$$

According to distance standard, if the distance $d_{i,j}$ between spatial objects i and j less than d , then w_{ij} is 1, otherwise, w_{ij} is 0.

$$w_{ij} = \begin{cases} 1 & d_{i,j} < d \\ 0 & otherwise \end{cases} \quad (5)$$

The ordinary computing methods may be applied if the location data are accurate enough. Four methods could be adopted for the uncertain spatial objects, including centroid method, minimum method, maximum method, and statistical method [13]. Extending the method to computing spatial autocorrelation matrix based on uncertain spatial data is as follows:

Suppose there are n pointes in a region S whose location is uncertain. The i th point is denoted by P_i . A error zone of P_i is represented by a circle Q_i . A algorithm is as follows:

Input : Error area $Q = \{Q_1, Q_2, \cdots Q_n\}$ in s , the neighborhood distance d_n ;

Output : A neighborhood diagram of a set of point in s and spatial autocorrelation matrix;

Step 1: Construct the Voronoi diagram from P ;

Step2: Do 2.1 and 2.2 for all adjacent Voronoi polygon

Step 2.1 : Calculate the distance between $d_{centriod}(C_i, C_j)$, $d_{\max}(Q_i, Q_j)$ and $d_{\min}(Q_i, Q_j)$

Step 2.2 : If $d_{i,j} < d_n$, then connect P_i and P_j in the neighborhood graph, w_{ij} =1; Otherwise, w_{ij} =0.

2.3 Fuzzy Discretization Based on Neighborhood EM Algorithm

At the stage of discretization, continuous data are divided into un-overlap areas, in which equal interval, equal frequency, K-means clustering, et al., were used. But, uncertainties always exist in these methods with natural language by field experts, in which language values corresponding to variable always have some overlay and boundaries, namely fuzziness. Furthermore, the nature of spatial autocorrelation is not suitable for these methods. For these causes, neighborhood EM algorithm [14] was used to divide the continuous data, in which uncertainties and spatial autocorrelation of spatial data, and the fuzziness of partition were considered properly. The main idea is as follows:

As Hathaway (1986) highlighted it, the EM algorithm in the case of mixture models is formally equivalent to an alternate optimisation of function [15]:

$$D(c,\theta) \overset{\Delta}{=} \sum_{k=1}^{K}\sum_{i=1}^{n} c_{ik}\log(\pi_k f_k(x_i \mid \mu_k, \Sigma_k)) - \sum_{k=1}^{K}\sum_{i=1}^{n} c_{ik}\log(c_{ik}) \tag{6}$$

where, $c = (c_{ik})_{i=1,n\ k=1,K}$ defines a fuzzy classification, c_{ik} representing the grade of membership of x_i to class k $(0 \le c_{ik} \le 1, \sum_{k=1}^{K} c_{ik} = 1,\ \sum_{i=1}^{n} c_{ik} > 0, 1 \le i \le n, 1 \le k \le K)$.

In order to take into account the spatial autocorrelation, a term was proposed to regularized.

$$G(c) = \frac{1}{2}\sum_{k=1}^{K}\sum_{i=1}^{n}\sum_{j=1}^{n} c_{ik}\cdot c_{jk}\cdot w_{ij} \tag{7}$$

where, w_{ij} is spatial autocorrelation matrix defined in the section 2.2

Then, the new criterion was proposed :

$$U(c,\theta) = D(c,\theta) + \beta \bullet G(c) \quad (\beta \ge 0) \tag{8}$$

where, the $\beta \ge 0$ gives more or less weight to the spatial homogeneity term relatively to $D(c,\theta)$.

"E"-step: the classification matrix is updated in order to maximize criterion:

$$c^{m+1} = \arg\max_{c} U(C,\theta^m) \tag{9}$$

The necessary conditions of optimality take the following form :

$$\begin{cases} \dfrac{\partial U}{\partial c_{ik}} = \log(\pi_k^m f_k(x_i \mid \mu_k^m, \Sigma_k^m)) + 1 - \log c_{ik} + \lambda_i + \beta \sum_{j=1}^{n} c_{jk} w_{ij} \\ \sum_{k=1}^{K} c_{ik} = 1 \end{cases} \tag{10}$$

Finally, the following equation can be gotten:

$$c_{ik}^{m+1} = \frac{\pi_k^m f_k(x_i \mid \mu_k^m, \Sigma_k^m)\cdot \exp\{\beta \sum_{j=1}^{n} c_{jk}^{m+1} w_{ij}\}}{\sum_{l=1}^{K} \pi_l^m f_l(x_i \mid \mu_l^m, \Sigma_l^m)\cdot \exp\{\beta \sum_{j=1}^{n} c_{jl}^{m+1} w_{ij}\}} \tag{11}$$

"M"-step: the parameters are reestimated according to:

$$\theta^{m+1} = \arg\max_{\theta} U(c^{m+1},\theta) = \arg\max_{\theta} D(c^{m+1},\theta) \tag{12}$$

In our experiments (section 3), fuzzy classification by Gibbs sampling (Monte Carlo simulation) was performed at E-step of each iteration and $\beta = 1$.

2.4 Uncertainty Assessment of Association Rules

Considering the uncertainty of spatial data, some uncertainty assessment indexes were used to assess the uncertainty of association rules.

$$Possibility\ (\text{Prob.}):\quad Possibility = m / n \tag{13}$$

where, n is the number of experiments of association rules mining; m the number of discovering a rule.

mean and var*iance* of association rules:

$$mean = \frac{1}{m}\sum_{i=1}^{m} X_i \tag{14}$$

$$\text{var}iance = \frac{1}{m}\sum_{i=1}^{m} (X_i - mean)^2 \tag{15}$$

where, m represents the number of discovering a rule; X_i the values of the ith index among Coverage (Cov.), Support (Sup.), Confidence (Conf.), Lift (Lift.), Leverage (Lev.) and Interestingness (Inte.) [16].

Then, association rule with uncertainty may be represented as follows:

$$A_1 \wedge A_2 \wedge \cdots \wedge A_k \rightarrow B_1 \wedge B_2 \wedge \cdots \wedge B_l$$
$$(\text{Pr}obability, (Q_1(mean, \text{var}iance), \cdots Q_c(mean, \text{var}iance))) \tag{16}$$

where, Qc represent the uncertainty assessment indexes, including Coverage(Cov.), Support(Sup.), Confidence (Conf.), Lift(Lift.), Leverage (Lev.) and Interestingness(Inte.).

3 Experiments

Mine exploitation would lead to environment pollution and do harm to people's health. Dexing mines located in east of China. They have been exploited for more 20 years and the environment pollution of this area has become very severity. So, environmental quality assessment for this area is very necessary. Research scopes cover longitude117°00´-118°00´ and latitude 28°50´-29°20´. 942 soil samples and 321 water sediment samples were sampled in this area. The geographical coordinates of samples were located with stand-alone GPS and the contents of As, Hg, Cd, Cr, Zn, Cu, Pb were tested. Table 1 is the mean square error and tolerance error of content of heavy mental elements according to the tested data.

Table 1. The error of content of heavy mental elements (mg/kg)

	As	Hg	Cd	Cr	Zn	Cu	Pb
mean square error	2.502	0.046	0.052	4.617	12.227	8.731	2.999
tolerance error	7.507	0.137	0.155	13.851	36.681	26.193	8.999

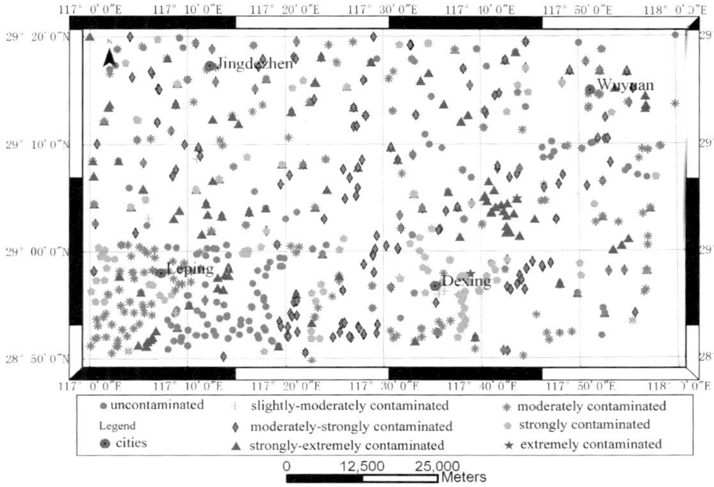

Fig. 2. The clustering results of environment quality assessment with uncertainty and spatial data mining methods

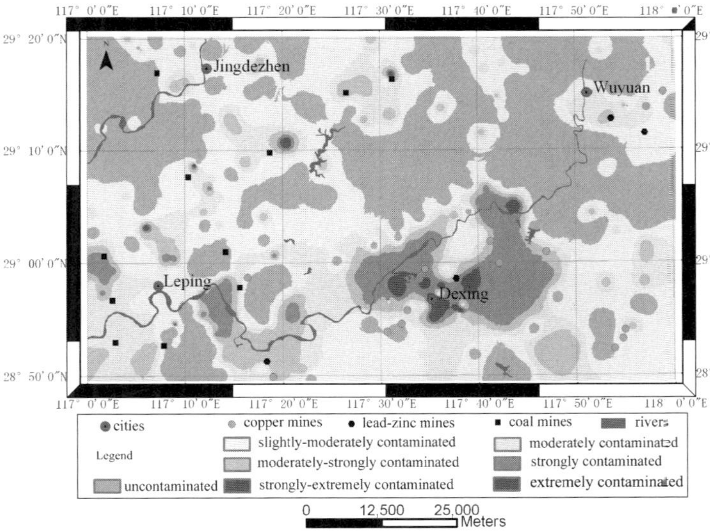

Fig. 3. The classification results of environment quality assessment with uncertainty and spatial data mining methods

According to the framework described in section 2, uncertain spatial clustering, classification and association rules mining were performed to assess the quality of environment geochemistry in Dexing area, Jiangxi province, China. Figure.2 described the results of uncertain spatial clustering and classification results, which

Table 2. The association rules of environment geochemistry quality assessment based on the uncertain spatial data mining methods

Rules	Prob.	Sup.	Conf.	Cov.	Lift.	Lev.	Inte.
Location in "southwestern" ∧ As "uncontaminated" --> Environment "uncontaminated"	0.62	0.072 0.000	0.914 0.003	0.079 0.000	3.493 1.188	0.892 0.003	0.842 0.003
As "moderately-strongly contaminated" --> Environment "moderately-strongly contaminated"	0.37	0.086 0.001	0.863 0.002	0.099 0.001	4.671 1.793	0.841 0.002	0.777 0.002
As "moderately contaminated" --> Environment "moderately contaminated"	0.36	0.089 0.001	0.884 0.003	0.101 0.001	5.582 4.347	0.865 0.003	0.795 0.004
Location in "northwestern" ∧ Hg "uncontaminated" ∧ Pb "uncontaminated" --> Environment "uncontaminated"	0.30	0.059 0.000	0.896 0.002	0.065 0.000	2.827 0.069	0.875 0.002	0.838 0.002
Location in "southwestern" ∧ As "slightly-moderately contaminated" --> Environment "slightly-moderately contaminated"	0.30	0.072 0.000	0.899 0.004	0.081 0.000	5.791 17.73	0.878 1.279	0.827 0.005
As "slightly-moderately contaminated" --> Environment "slightly-moderately contaminated"	0.30	0.089 0.001	0.861 0.002	0.103 0.001	6.360 20.91	0.842 0.003	0.772 0.004
Location in "northeastern" ∧ Hg "uncontaminated" ∧ Cu "uncontaminated" --> Environment "uncontaminated"	0.29	0.068 0.000	0.929 0.002	0.073 0.000	2.887 0.075	0.901 0.002	0.861 0.002
Location in "southwestern" ∧ As "moderately-strongly contaminated" --> Environment "moderately-strongly contaminated"	0.27	0.065 0.000	0.946 0.004	0.069 0.000	5.173 2.910	0.931 0.004	0.881 0.004
Location in "southwestern" ∧ As "moderately contaminated" --> Environment "moderately contaminated"	0.26	0.067 0.000	0.930 0.004	0.072 0.000	5.164 1.290	0.915 0.003	0.863 0.003
Location in "northeastern" ∧ Hg "uncontaminated" ∧ Pb "uncontaminated" --> Environment "uncontaminated"	0.26	0.058 0.000	0.929 0.003	0.062 0.000	2.866 0.079	0.909 0.003	0.871 0.003
Location in "northeastern" ∧ Hg "uncontaminated" ∧ Cd "uncontaminated" --> Environment "uncontaminated"	0.25	0.069 0.000	0.932 0.004	0.074 0.000	4.060 31.20	0.910 0.004	0.863 0.003

indicated that the different extent environment contamination have been occurred, especially in the area of Dexing mines. Table 2 described the results of uncertain spatial association rules mining, which indicated that As element is the most important environment denotation of this area.

4 Conclusions

It is our mind in this research to achieve both of objectives. Firstly, the quality of SDM can be improved by analyzing the uncertainties and its characteristics in each phase of SDM, and finding efficient method to process its uncertainties. Secondly, although the uncertainties of SDM cannot be completely eliminated, the uncertainty of SDM results can be assessed in order to make use of the knowledge discovered in SDM.

Acknowledgements

The work described in this paper was supported by the funds from China Postdoctoral Science Foundation (No. 20060390326) and the commonweal Special Project from the Ministry of Land and Resources P.R.C (No. 30302408-01).

References

1. Di, K.C.: Spatial data mining and knowledge discovery. Wuhan University Press, Wuhan (2000)
2. Li, D.R., Wang, S.L., Li, D.Y.: Theories and technologies of spatial data knowledge discovery. In: Geomatics and Information Science of Wuhan University, vol. 3, pp. 221–233 (2002)
3. Koperski, K.: A progressive refinement approach to spatial data mining. Simon Fraser University, Canada (1999)
4. Miller, H.J., Han, J.W.: Geographic data mining and knowledge discovery. Taylor & Francis, London (2001)
5. Clementini, E., Felice, P.D., Koperski, K.: Mining multiple-level spatial association rules for objects with a broad boundary. Data & Knowledge Engineering 3, 251–270 (2000)
6. Wang, S.L., Shi, W.Z., Li, D.R.: A method of spatial data mining dealing with randomness and fuzziness. In: Proceedings of the 2nd International Symposium on Spatial Data Quality, pp. 370–383 (2003)
7. Beaubouef, T., Ladner, R., Petry, F.: Rough set spatial data modeling for data mining. International Journal of Intelligent Systems 7, 567–584 (2004)
8. He, B.B., Fang, T., Guo, D.Z.: Uncertainty and its propagation in spatial data mining. Journal of Data Acquisition and Processing 4, 475–480 (2004)
9. Press, W.H.: Numerical recipes: The art of scientific computing, 2nd edn. Cambridge University Press, London (1996)
10. Box, G.E.P., Muller, M.E.: A Note on the Generation of Random Normal Deviates. The Annals of Mathematical Statistics 29, 610–611 (1958)
11. Goodchild, M.F.: Issuees of quality and uncertainty. In: Muller, J.C. (ed.) Advances In Cartography, pp. 113–139. Elsevier, London (1991)
12. CCSM(Canadian Council on Surveying and Mapping): National standards for the exchange of digital topographic data, II-standards for the quality evaluation of digital topographic data, Canada (1984)
13. Sadahiro, Y.: Cluster detection in uncertain point distributions: a comparison of four methods. Computers, Environment and Urban Systems 27, 33–52 (2003)

14. Ambroise, C., Dang, V., Govaert, G.: Clustering of spatial data by the EM algorithm. Quantitative Geology and Geostatistics 9, 493–504 (1997)
15. Hathaway, R.J.: Another interpretation of the EM algorithm for mixture distributions. Journal of Statistics & Probability Letters 4, 53–56 (1986)
16. Vazirgiannis, M., Halkidi, M., Gunopulos, D.: Uncertainty handling and quality assessment in data mining. Springer-Verlag, London (2003)

Locally Weighted LS-SVM for Fuzzy Nonlinear Regression with Fuzzy Input-Output

Dug Hun Hong[1], Changha Hwang[2], Jooyong Shim[3], and Kyung Ha Seok[4]

[1] Department of Mathematics, Myongji University, Kyunggido 449-728, South Korea
dhhong@mju.ac.kr

[2] Corresponding Author, Division of Information and Computer Science, Dankook University, Seoul 140-714, South Korea
chwang@dankook.ac.kr

[3] Department of Applied Statistics, Catholic University of Daegu, Kyungbuk 702-701, South Korea
ds1631@hanmail.net

[4] Department of Data Science, Inje University, Kyungnam 621-749, South Korea
skh@stat.inje.ac.kr

Abstract. This paper deals with new regression method of predicting fuzzy multivariable nonlinear regression models using triangular fuzzy numbers. The proposed method is achieved by implementing the locally weighted least squares support vector machine regression where the local weight is obtained from the positive distance metric between the test data and the training data. Two types of distance metrics for the center and spreads are proposed to treat the nonlinear regression for fuzzy inputs and fuzzy outputs. Numerical studies are then presented which indicate the performance of this algorithm.

1 Introduction

Linear regression models are widely used today in business, administration, economics, engineering, as well as in many other traditionally non-quantitative fields such as social, health, and biological sciences. In all cases of fuzzy regression, the linear regression is recommended for practical situations when decisions often have to be made on the basis of imprecise and/or partially available data. Many different fuzzy regression approaches have been proposed. Fuzzy regression, as first developed by Tanaka *et al.*[15] in a linear system, is based on the extension principle. Tanaka *et al.*[15] initially applied their fuzzy linear regression procedure to non-fuzzy experimental data. In the experiments that followed this pioneering effort, Tanaka *et al.*[15] used fuzzy input experimental data to build fuzzy regression models. Fuzzy input data used in these experiments were given in the form of triangular fuzzy numbers. The process is explained in more detail by Dubois and Prade[6]. Hong *et al.*[7] proposed the fuzzy linear regression model using shape-preserving fuzzy arithmetic operations based on Tanaka's approach. A technique for linear least squares fitting of fuzzy variable was developed by Diamond[5] giving the solution to an analog of the normal equation of classical least squares. Hong and Hwang[9] modified this idea by utilizing regularization

Y. Wang, Y. Cheung, and H. Liu (Eds.): CIS 2006, LNAI 4456, pp. 317–325, 2007.

method in order to extend Diamond's models to multivariable cases and to derive efficient solutions for fuzzy multivariable regression models. Regularization techniques have been extensively studied in the context of crisp nonlinear regression models. The technique of regularization encourages smoother regression function. Hong and Hwang[10] successfully applied kernel ridge regression(Saunders *et al.*[13]) to the fuzzy nonlinear regression for the case of the crisp inputs and fuzzy outputs. Several approaches to fuzzy regression analysis have been studied by Celmins[3], Kacprzyk and Fedrizzi[11], Sakawa and Yano[12], Buckley and Feuring[2], Chang and Ayuub[4], and Hong *et al.*[8].

In this paper we concentrate on the nonlinear regression of fuzzy inputs and fuzzy outputs, for which there have been a few articles concerned. Buckley and Feuring[2] proposed a nonlinear regression method for fuzzy inputs and fuzzy output. However they pre-specified regression model functions such as linear, polynomial, exponential and logarithmic, which looks somewhat unrealistic for the application. We want a model-free method suitable for the nonlinear regression model with fuzzy inputs and fuzzy output. For that purpose, the least squares support vector machine(LS–SVM, Suykens and Vanderwalle[14]) and the locally weighted regression(LWR, Atkeson *et al.*[1]) are considered, which are newly developed in machine learnings. By incorporating LWR into the fuzzy linear regression using LS–SVM, we can have a computationally simple and easy nonlinear regression for fuzzy inputs and fuzzy outputs. Conventional SVM can be used here. However, LS–SVM is used since it is much simpler to implement than conventional SVM.

The rest of this paper is organized as follows. Section 2 describes LS–SVM approach to the linear regression for fuzzy inputs and fuzzy output. Section 3 provides the locally weighted LS–SVM for the nonlinear regression generalized by incorporating LWR into the fuzzy linear regression described in Section 2. Section 3 describes how to apply this idea to the fuzzy multivariable nonlinear regression model. Finally, Section 5 gives the conclusions.

2 Linear Regression for Fuzzy Inputs and Fuzzy Output

In this section we will modify the underlying idea of LS–SVM for the purpose of deriving the convex optimization problems for multivariable linear regression models for fuzzy inputs and fuzzy output. The basic idea of LS–SVM gives computational efficiency in finding solutions of fuzzy regression models particularly for multivariable case. We will focus on fuzzy regression models based on triangular fuzzy number since this type of fuzzy number is mostly used in practice. Fuzzy regression models based on trapezoidal and Gaussian fuzzy numbers can be constructed in a similar manner.

Suppose we are given the training data $\{\mathbf{X}_i, Y_i\}_{i=1}^{l} \subset T(R)^d \times T(R)$, where $\mathbf{X}_i = ((m_{X_{i1}}, \alpha_{X_{i1}}, \beta_{X_{i1}}), \cdots, (m_{X_{id}}, \alpha_{X_{id}}, \beta_{X_{id}}))$ and $Y_i = (m_{Y_i}, \alpha_{Y_i}, \beta_{Y_i})$. Here $T(R)$ and $T(R)^d$ are the set of triangular fuzzy numbers and the set of d-vectors of triangular fuzzy numbers, respectively. Let $\mathbf{m}_{X_i} = (m_{X_{i1}}, \cdots, m_{X_{id}})$, $\boldsymbol{\alpha}_{X_i} = (\alpha_{X_{i1}}, \cdots, \alpha_{X_{id}})$, $\boldsymbol{\beta}_{X_i} = (\beta_{X_{i1}}, \cdots, \beta_{X_{id}})$, $B = (m_B, \alpha_B, \beta_B)$, and $\mathbf{w} = (w_1, \cdots, w_d)$.

For the fuzzy inputs and fuzzy outputs we consider the following model $H2$:

$$\begin{aligned} H2: Y(\mathbf{X}) &= \langle \mathbf{w}, \mathbf{X} \rangle + B,\ B \in T(R), \mathbf{w} \in R^d \\ &= (\langle \mathbf{w}, \mathbf{m}_X \rangle + m_B, \langle |\mathbf{w}|, \boldsymbol{\alpha}_X \rangle + \alpha_B, \langle |\mathbf{w}|, \boldsymbol{\beta}_X \rangle + \beta_B), \end{aligned}$$

where $|\mathbf{w}| = (|w_1|, |w_2|, \cdots, |w_d|)$. We arrive at the following convex optimization problem for the model $H2$ by modifying the idea for crisp multiple linear regression.

$$\text{minimize } \frac{1}{2}\|\mathbf{w}\|^2 + \frac{C}{2}\sum_{k=1}^{3}\sum_{i=1}^{l} e_{ki}^2 \tag{1}$$

$$\text{subject to } \begin{cases} m_{Y_i} - \langle \mathbf{w}, \mathbf{m}_{X_i} \rangle - m_B = e_{1i}, \\ (m_{Y_i} - \alpha_{Y_i}) - (\langle \mathbf{w}, \mathbf{m}_{X_i} \rangle + m_B - \langle |\mathbf{w}|, \boldsymbol{\alpha}_{X_i} \rangle - \alpha_B) = e_{2i} \\ (m_{Y_i} + \beta_{Y_i}) - (\langle \mathbf{w}, \mathbf{m}_{X_i} \rangle + m_B + \langle |\mathbf{w}|, \boldsymbol{\beta}_{X_i} \rangle + \beta_B) = e_{3i}. \end{cases}$$

The optimal values of $B = (m_B, \alpha_B, \beta_B)$ and Lagrange multipliers α_{1i}, α_{2i} and α_{3i}, can be obtained by the optimality conditions, which lead to the optimal value of $\mathbf{w}$. Then the prediction of $Y(\mathbf{X})$ given by the LS–SVM on the new unlabeled data $\mathbf{X} = (\mathbf{m}_X, \boldsymbol{\alpha}_X, \boldsymbol{\beta}_X)$ is

$$\hat{Y}(\mathbf{X}) = (\langle \mathbf{w}, \mathbf{m}_X \rangle + m_B, \langle |\mathbf{w}|, \boldsymbol{\alpha}_X \rangle + \alpha_B, \langle |\mathbf{w}|, \boldsymbol{\beta}_X \rangle + \beta_B). \tag{2}$$

3 Nonlinear Regression for Fuzzy Inputs and Fuzzy Outputs

In this section, we study LS–SVM to be used in estimating fuzzy nonlinear regression model. In this paper we treat fuzzy nonlinear regression for data of the form with fuzzy inputs and fuzzy outputs, without assuming the underlying model function. For the nonlinear regression, LS–SVM can be generalized by incorporating LWR into LS–SVM stated in previous section.

By incorporating LWR into LS–SVM, we have the following locally weighted LS–SVM for nonlinear regression with fuzzy inputs and fuzzy outputs. To predict $Y(\mathbf{X}_q)$ where $\mathbf{X}_q = (\mathbf{m}_{X_q}, \boldsymbol{\alpha}_{X_q}, \boldsymbol{\beta}_{X_q})$, we consider the following optimization problem:

$$\text{minimize } \frac{1}{2}\|\mathbf{w}\|^2 + \frac{C}{2}\sum_{k=1}^{3}\sum_{i=1}^{l} K_{ki} e_{ki}^2 \tag{3}$$

$$\text{subject to } \begin{cases} m_{Y_i} - \langle \mathbf{w}, \mathbf{m}_{X_i} \rangle - m_B = e_{1i}, \\ (m_{Y_i} - \alpha_{Y_i}) - (\langle \mathbf{w}, \mathbf{m}_{X_i} \rangle + m_B - \langle |\mathbf{w}|, \boldsymbol{\alpha}_{X_i} \rangle - \alpha_B) = e_{2i} \\ (m_{Y_i} + \beta_{Y_i}) - (\langle \mathbf{w}, \mathbf{m}_{X_i} \rangle + m_B + \langle |\mathbf{w}|, \boldsymbol{\beta}_{X_i} \rangle + \beta_B) = e_{3i}. \end{cases}$$

Here K_{1i} is a positive distance metric between $\mathbf{m}_{X_q}$ and $\mathbf{m}_{X_i}$, K_{2i} and K_{3i} are positive distance metrics between $\boldsymbol{\alpha}_{X_q}$ and $\boldsymbol{\alpha}_{X_i}$, $\boldsymbol{\beta}_{X_q}$ and $\boldsymbol{\beta}_{X_i}$, respectively. We use RBF kernel type distance metrics,

$$K_{1i} = \exp\left\{\frac{-\|\mathbf{m}_{X_q} - \mathbf{m}_{X_i}\|^2}{\sigma_1^2}\right\},$$

$$K_{2i} = \exp\left\{\frac{-\|\boldsymbol{\alpha}_{X_q} - \boldsymbol{\alpha}_{X_i}\|^2}{\sigma_1^2} + \frac{-\|\mathbf{m}_{X_q} - \mathbf{m}_{X_i}\|^2}{\sigma_2^2}\right\};$$

$$K_{3i} = \exp\left\{\frac{-\|\boldsymbol{\beta}_{X_q} - \boldsymbol{\beta}_{X_i}\|^2}{\sigma_1^2} + \frac{-\|\mathbf{m}_{X_q} - \mathbf{m}_{X_i}\|^2}{\sigma_2^2}\right\}.$$

Hence we can construct a Lagrange function as follows:

$$\begin{aligned} L &= \frac{1}{2}\|\mathbf{w}\|^2 + \frac{C}{2}\sum_{k=1}^{3}\sum_{i=1}^{l} K_{ki}\, e_{ki}^2 \\ &- \sum_{i=1}^{l} \alpha_{1i}(e_{1i} - m_{Y_i} + \langle \mathbf{w}, \mathbf{m}_{X_i}\rangle + m_B) \\ &- \sum_{i=1}^{l} \alpha_{2i}(e_{2i} - (m_{Y_i} - \alpha_{Y_i}) + (\langle \mathbf{w}, \mathbf{m}_{X_i}\rangle + m_B - \langle |\mathbf{w}|, \boldsymbol{\alpha}_{X_i}\rangle - \alpha_B)) \\ &- \sum_{i=1}^{l} \alpha_{3i}(e_{3i} - (m_{Y_i} + \beta_{Y_i}) + (\langle \mathbf{w}, \mathbf{m}_{X_i}\rangle + m_B + \langle |\mathbf{w}|, \boldsymbol{\beta}_{X_i}\rangle + \beta_B)). \end{aligned} \quad (4)$$

It follows from the saddle point condition that the partial derivatives of L with respect to the primal variables $(\mathbf{w}, m_B, \alpha_B, \beta_B, e_{ki}, k = 1,2,3)$ have to vanish for optimality.

$$\begin{aligned} \frac{\partial L}{\partial \mathbf{w}} = \mathbf{0} \;\rightarrow\; \mathbf{w} &= \sum_{i=1}^{l} \alpha_{1i}\mathbf{m}_{X_i} \\ &+ \sum_{i=1}^{l} \alpha_{2i}(\mathbf{m}_{X_i} - sign(\mathbf{w}) \cdot \boldsymbol{\alpha}_{X_i}) \\ &+ \sum_{i=1}^{l} \alpha_{3i}(\mathbf{m}_{X i} + sign(\mathbf{w}) \cdot \boldsymbol{\beta}_{X_i}) \end{aligned} \quad (5)$$

$$\frac{\partial L}{\partial m_B} = 0 \;\rightarrow\; \sum_{k=1}^{3}\sum_{i=1}^{l} \alpha_{ki} = 0 \quad (6)$$

$$\frac{\partial L}{\partial \alpha_B} = 0 \;\rightarrow\; \sum_{i=1}^{l} \alpha_{2i} = 0 \quad (7)$$

$$\frac{\partial L}{\partial \beta_B} = 0 \;\rightarrow\; \sum_{i=1}^{l} \alpha_{3i} = 0 \quad (8)$$

$$\frac{\partial L}{\partial e_{ki}} = 0 \;\rightarrow\; e_{ki} = \frac{\alpha_{ki}}{CK_{ki}}, \; k = 1, 2, 3, \tag{9}$$

where $sign(\mathbf{w}) = (sign(w_1), \cdots, sign(w_d))$ and the '$\cdot$' represents the componentwise product. We notice that we can tell $sign(\mathbf{w})$ by performing regression in advance for model values of fuzzy variables $\mathbf{m}_{X_i}, i = 1, \ldots, l$. There could be other different ways to tell their signs. The optimal values of $B = (m_B, \alpha_B, \beta_B)$ and Lagrange multipliers $\alpha_{1i}, \alpha_{2i}, \alpha_{3i}$ can be obtained from the linear equation as follows:

$$\begin{pmatrix} 0 & 0 & 0 & \mathbf{1}' & \mathbf{1}' & \mathbf{1}' \\ 0 & 0 & 0 & \mathbf{0}' & \mathbf{1}' & \mathbf{0}' \\ 0 & 0 & 0 & \mathbf{0}' & \mathbf{0}' & \mathbf{1}' \\ \mathbf{1} & \mathbf{0} & \mathbf{0} & \mathbf{S}_{11} & \mathbf{S}_{12} & \mathbf{S}_{13} \\ \mathbf{1} & -\mathbf{1} & \mathbf{0} & \mathbf{S}_{12}' & \mathbf{S}_{22} & \mathbf{S}_{23} \\ \mathbf{1} & \mathbf{0} & \mathbf{1} & \mathbf{S}_{13}' & \mathbf{S}_{23}' & \mathbf{S}_{33} \end{pmatrix} \begin{pmatrix} m_B \\ \alpha_B \\ \beta_B \\ \boldsymbol{\alpha}_1 \\ \boldsymbol{\alpha}_2 \\ \boldsymbol{\alpha}_3 \end{pmatrix} = \begin{pmatrix} 0 \\ 0 \\ 0 \\ \mathbf{m}_Y \\ \mathbf{m}_Y - \boldsymbol{\alpha}_Y \\ \mathbf{m}_Y + \boldsymbol{\beta}_Y \end{pmatrix} \tag{10}$$

with

$$\begin{aligned} \mathbf{S}_{11} &= \mathbf{m_X}\mathbf{m_X}' + diag(K_{1\cdot})^{-1}/C \\ \mathbf{S}_{12} &= \mathbf{m}_X(\mathbf{m_X} - sign(\mathbf{1w}') \cdot \boldsymbol{\alpha}_\mathbf{X})' \\ \mathbf{S}_{13} &= \mathbf{m_X}(\mathbf{m_X} + sign(\mathbf{1w}') \cdot \boldsymbol{\beta}_\mathbf{X})' \\ \mathbf{S}_{22} &= (\mathbf{m_X} - sign(\mathbf{1w}') \cdot \boldsymbol{\alpha}_\mathbf{X}) \times (\mathbf{m_X} - sign(\mathbf{1w}') \cdot \boldsymbol{\alpha}_\mathbf{X})' + diag(K_{2\cdot})^{-1}/C \\ \mathbf{S}_{33} &= (\mathbf{m_X} + sign(\mathbf{1w}') \cdot \boldsymbol{\beta}_\mathbf{X}) \times (\mathbf{m_X} + sign(\mathbf{1w}') \cdot \boldsymbol{\beta}_\mathbf{X})' + diag(K_{3\cdot})^{-1}/C, \end{aligned}$$

where $\mathbf{m_X}$, $\boldsymbol{\alpha}_\mathbf{X}$ and $\boldsymbol{\beta}_\mathbf{X}$ are the $l \times l$ matrices consisting of l row vectors $\mathbf{m}_{X_i}$, $\boldsymbol{\alpha}_{X_i}$ and $\boldsymbol{\beta}_{X_i}$, respectively, $\boldsymbol{\alpha}_1$, $\boldsymbol{\alpha}_2$, $\boldsymbol{\alpha}_3$, $\mathbf{m}_Y$, $\boldsymbol{\alpha}_Y$ and $\boldsymbol{\beta}_Y$ are the $l \times 1$ vectors of α_{1i}, α_{2i}, α_{3i}, m_{Y_i}, α_{Y_i} and β_{Y_i}, respectively, and $K_{k\cdot}, k = 1, 2, 3$, are the vectors of K_{ki}.

Hence, the prediction of $Y(\mathbf{X}_q)$ given by the locally weighted LS–SVM on the new data $\mathbf{X}_q = (\mathbf{m}_{X_q}, \boldsymbol{\alpha}_{Xq}, \boldsymbol{\beta}_{Xq})$ is

$$\hat{Y}(\mathbf{X}_q) = (\langle \mathbf{w}, \mathbf{m}_{X_q} \rangle + m_B, \langle |\mathbf{w}|, \boldsymbol{\alpha}_{X_q} \rangle + \alpha_B, \langle |\mathbf{w}|, \boldsymbol{\beta}_{X_q} \rangle + \beta_B). \tag{11}$$

When we use LS–SVM for fuzzy linear regression, we must determine an optimal choice of the regularization parameter C. But for the fuzzy nonlinear regression, we have to determine two more parameters, which are kernel widths σ_1^2 and σ_2^2 for RBF kernel type distance metrics. There could be several parameter selection methods such as cross-validation type methods, bootstraping and Bayesian learning methods. In this paper we use cross-validation methods. If data is not scarce then the set of available input-output measurements can be divided into two parts - one part for training and one part for testing. In this way several different models, all trained on the training set, can be compared on the test set. This is the basic form of cross-validation. A better method is to partition the original set in several different ways and to compute an average score over the different partitions. In this paper the average score is computed by using the squared error based on the following distance between two outputs.

$$d^2(Y,Z) = (m_Y - m_Z)^2 + ((m_Y - \alpha_Y) - (m_Z - \alpha_Z))^2 \\ +((m_Y + \beta_Y) - (m_Z + \beta_Z))^2.$$

An extreme variant of this is to split the measurements into a training set of size and a test set of size 1 and average the squared error on the left-out measurements over the possible ways of obtaining such a partition. This is called leave-one-out cross-validation. In the leave-one-out cross-validation method, we train using all but one training measurement, then test using the left out measurement. We repeat this, leaving out another single measurement. We do this until we have left out each example. Then we average the results on the left out measurements to assess the generalization capability of our fuzzy regression procedure.

$$CV(C,\sigma_1^2,\sigma_2^2) = \frac{1}{l}[\sum_{i=1}^{l}(m_{Y_i} - \hat{m}_{Y_i}^{(-i)})^2 + \sum_{i=1}^{l}((m_{Y_i} - \alpha_{Y_i}) - (\hat{m}_{Y_i}^{(-i)} - \hat{\alpha}_{Y_i}^{(-i)}))^2 \\ + \sum_{i=1}^{l}((m_{Y_i} + \beta_{Y_i}) - (\hat{m}_{Y_i}^{(-i)} + \hat{\beta}_{Y_i}^{(-i)}))^2], \quad (12)$$

where $(\hat{m}_{Y_i}^{(-i)}, \hat{\alpha}_{Y_i}^{(-i)}, \hat{\beta}_{Y_i}^{(-i)})$ is the predicted values of $Y_i = (m_{Y_i}, \alpha_{Y_i}, \beta_{Y_i})$ obtained from training data without X_i.

4 Numerical Studies

In contrast to fuzzy linear regression, there have been only a few articles on fuzzy nonlinear regression. What researchers in fuzzy nonlinear regression were concerned with was data of the form with crisp inputs and fuzzy output. Some papers(Buckley and Feuring[2], Celmins[3]) are concerned with the data set with fuzzy inputs and fuzzy output. However, we think those fuzzy nonlinear regression methods look somewhat unrealistic and treat the estimation procedures of some particular models. In this paper we treat fuzzy nonlinear regression for data of the form with fuzzy inputs and fuzzy output, without assuming the underlying model function.

In order to illustrate the performance of the nonlinear regression prediction for fuzzy inputs and fuzzy outputs, two examples are considered. In examples, centers of X_i's were randomly generated in $[0, 0.25, \cdots, 10.0]$ and spreads were randomly generated in $[0.3, 0.4, \cdots, 1.0]$. Centers of Y_i's were generated as follows:

$$m_{Y_i} = 1.1 + 2.5\log(1 + m_{X_i}) + \epsilon_i \quad \text{for Example 1}$$
$$m_{Y_i} = 2.1 + \exp(0.2 m_{X_i}) + \epsilon_i \quad \text{for Example 2},$$

where $\epsilon_i, i = 1, 2, \cdots, 25$, is a random error from the normal distribution with mean 0 and variance 0.01. By the leave-one-out cross-validation method, we

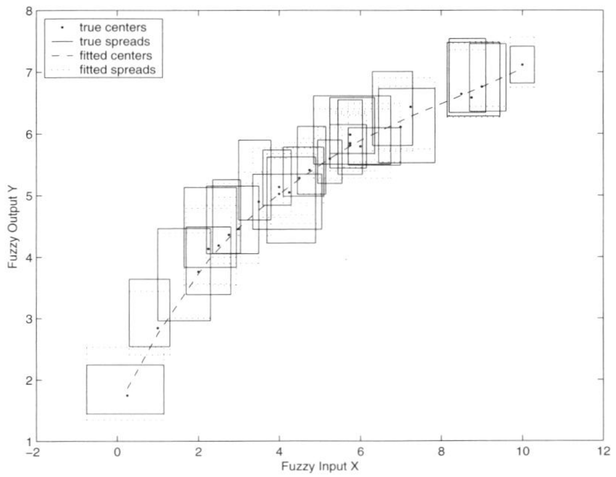

Fig. 1. Fuzzy nonlinear regression model for Example 1

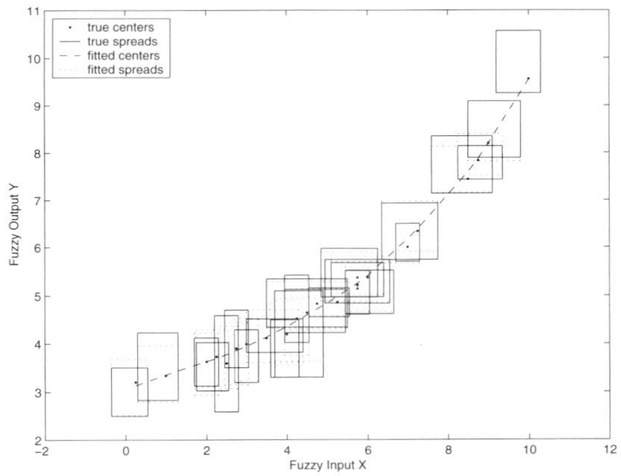

Fig. 2. Fuzzy nonlinear regression model for Example 1

obtained $(C, \sigma_1^2, \sigma_2^2)$ as $(10^6, 2, 0.25)$ for Example 1 and $(10^6, 1.5, 0.01)$ for Example 2. In figures four corners of each solid box - the lower left, the lower right, the upper left, and the upper right - represent $(m_{X_i} - \alpha_{X_i}, m_{Y_i} - \alpha_{Y_i})$, $(m_{X_i} + \beta_{X_i}, m_{Y_i} - \alpha_{Y_i})$, $(m_{X_i} - \alpha_{X_i}, m_{Y_i} + \beta_{Y_i})$, and $(m_{X_i} + \beta_{X_i}, m_{Y_i} + \beta_{Y_i})$, respectively and four corners of each dotted box represent $(m_{X_i} - \alpha_{X_i}, \hat{m}_{Y_i} - \hat{\alpha}_{Y_i})$, $(m_{X_i} + \beta_{X_i}, \hat{m}_{Y_i} - \hat{\alpha}_{Y_i})$, $(m_{X_i} - \alpha_{X_i}, \hat{m}_{Y_i} + \hat{\beta}_{Y_i})$, and $(m_{X_i} + \beta_{X_i}, \hat{m}_{Y_i} + \hat{\beta}_{Y_i})$. In this section the '·' represents each true center (m_{X_i}, m_{Y_i}) and the dashed line is a connection between fitted centers $(m_{X_i}, \hat{m}_{Y_i})$'s.

As seen from both figures, the proposed model seems to derive the satisfying results on the nonlinear regression for fuzzy input-output data. In fact, we obtained the average of distances between (X_i, Y_i) and $(X_i, \hat{Y}_i)$ as 0.0942 in the Example 1 and 0.0774 in the Example 2. This implies that each solid box is very similar to the corresponding dotted box. Although we did not report here, the proposed model actually showed almost the same results as the standard SVM and LS–SVM for center values. Thus we can say that the proposed model provides a satifying solution to nonlinear fuzzy regression for fuzzy input-output data.

5 Conclusions

In this paper we have presented a locally weighted LS–SVM estimation strategy for fuzzy multivariable nonlinear regressions. The experimental results show that the proposed fuzzy nonlinear regression model derives the satisfying solutions and is an attractive approach to modeling fuzzy data. Although conventional SVM can be used, LS–SVM has been used here since it is computationally much simpler particularly for fuzzy regression analysis.

There have been some papers treat fuzzy nonlinear regression models. They usually assume the underlying model functions even for data of the form with numerical inputs and fuzzy output. The proposed algorithm here is a model-free method in the sense that we do not have to assume the underlying model function. This model-free method turned out to be a promising method which has been attempted to treat fuzzy nonlinear regression model with fuzzy inputs and fuzzy output. The main formulation results in solving a simple matrix inversion problem. Hence, this is not a computationally expensive way. The hyperparameters of the proposed model can be tuned using cross-validation method.

Acknowledgement

The work of Hong and Hwang was supported by the Korea Research Foundation Grant(KRF-2004-042-C00020). The work of Seok was supported by a Korea Research Foundation Grant funded by the Korean Government (MOEHRD, Basic Research Promotion Fund; KRF-2005-015-C00097).

References

1. Atkeson, C.G., Moore, A.W., Schaal, S.: Locally weighted learning. Artificial Intelligence Review 11, 11–73 (1997)
2. Buckley, J., Feuring, T.: 'Linear and non-linear fuzzy regression: Evolutionary algorithm solutions. Fuzzy Sets and Systems 112, 381–394 (2000)
3. Celmins, A.: A practical approach to nonlinear fuzzy regression. SIAM Journal of Scientific and Statistical Compututing 12(3), 521–546 (1991)
4. Chang, Y., Ayuub, B.: Fuzzy regression methods: A comparative assessment. Fuzzy Sets and Systems 119, 187–203 (2001)
5. Diamond, P.: Fuzzy least squares. Information Sciences 46, 141–157 (1988)
6. Dubois, D., Prade, H.: Theory and Applications, Fuzzy Sets and Systems. Academic Press, New York (1980)

7. Hong, D.H., Song, J.K., Do, H.Y.: Fuzzy least-squares linear regression analysis using shape preserving operations. Information Sciences 138, 185–193 (2001)
8. Hong, D.H., Lee, H., Do, H.Y.: Fuzzy linear regression analysis for fuzzy input-output data using shape-preserving operations. Fuzzy Sets and Systems 122, 513–526 (2001)
9. Hong, D.H., Hwang, C.: Extended fuzzy regression models using regularization method. Information Sciences 164, 31–46 (2004)
10. Hong, D.H., Hwang, C.: Ridge regression procedures for fuzzy models using triangular fuzzy numbers. International Journal of Uncertainty, Fuzziness and Knowledge-Based Systems 12(2), 145–159 (2004)
11. Kacprzyk, J., Fedrizzi, M.: Fuzzy Regression Analysis. Physica-Verlag, Heidelberg (1992)
12. Sakawa, M., Yano, H.: Multiobjective fuzzy linear regression analysis for fuzzy input-output data. Fuzzy Sets and Systems 47, 173–181 (1992)
13. Saunders, C., Gammerman, A., Vork, V.: Ridge regression learning algorithm in dual variable. In: Proceedings of the 15th International Conference on Machine Learning, pp. 515–521 (1998)
14. Suykens, J.A.K., Vandewalle, J.: Recurrent least squares support vector machines. IEEE Transactions on Circuits and Systems-I 47(7), 1109–1114 (2000)
15. Tanaka, H., Uejima, S., Asia, K.: Linear regression analysis with fuzzy model. IEEE Transactions on Systems, Man and Cybernetics 12(6), 903–907 (1982)

Learning SVM with Varied Example Cost: A *k*NN Evaluating Approach

Chan-Yun Yang[1], Che-Chang Hsu[2], and Jr-Syu Yang[2]

[1] Department of Mechanical Engineering, Technology and Science Institute of Northern Taiwan, No. 2, Xue-Yuan Rd., Beitou, Taipei, Taiwan, 112. China
cyyang.research@gmail.com
[2] Department of Mechanical and Electro-Mechanical Engineering
Tamkang University Taipei, Taiwan, 251. China
692342792@s92.tku.edu.tw, 096034@mail.tku.edu.tw

Abstract. The paper proposes a model merging a non-parametric *k*-nearest-neighbor (*k*NN) method into an underlying support vector machine (SVM) to produce an instance-dependent loss function. In this model, a filtering stage of the *k*NN searching was employed to collect information from training examples and produced a set of emphasized weights which can be distributed to every example by a class of real-valued class labels. The emphasized weights changed the policy of the equal-valued impacts of the training examples and permitted a more efficient way to utilize the information behind the training examples with various significance levels. Due to the property of estimating density locally, the *k*NN method has the advantage to distinguish the heterogeneous examples from the regular examples by merely considering the situation of the examples themselves. The paper shows the model is promising with both the theoretical derivations and consequent experimental results.

Keywords: Learning cost, Support vector machine, *k* nearest neighbor; Classification, Pattern recognition.

1 Introduction

Being a category of powerful learning machine, support vector machines (SVMs) have received much attention in the recent years. Since the problems with regard to the SVMs can actually refer to related convex optimization learning problems, the governing loss function measuring associated errors of training examples plays a key role in the learning. In the beginning, the conceptual mathematics has been founded by Vapnik [1-3] based on the theoretical learning theory. The basic concept of the theory is sought to design a classification rule – a learning hypothesis – for an optimal function which is obtained by the minimization of the generalization risk. Considering a general classification problem, a set of statistical hypotheses regularized by the relevant parameters is generated to minimize the expected risk over all available and unavailable training examples. But in general, the expected risk unfortunately came

Y. Wang, Y. Cheung, and H. Liu (Eds.): CIS 2006, LNAI 4456, pp. 326–335, 2007.

up with unknown probability densities. An approximation thus is usually adopted by replacing the expected risk with an empirical risk [4]

$$R_{\text{emp}} = \frac{1}{n} \sum_{\mathbf{x}_i \in S} L(y_i, f(\mathbf{x}_i)), \tag{1}$$

where $L(.)$ denotes a loss function designed to evaluate associated errors in the training examples. The empirical risk, empirically measured from the loss function, has the advantage that one can easily and readily computes only from the available training examples.

To examine the scattering of examples in the input space R^d in real world applications, two classes may partly overlapped as many examples may be scattered in the surrounding of their counterpart examples in different class label. The heterogeneous examples, also called different example, immersed in the adversaries may occasionally be misclassified through entanglement with corresponding neighbors. However the difficult examples are crucial instances in the training set S. They fail in the learning process and lead to a degraded hypothesis. From the point of loss function [3-4, 9-13], these difficult examples increase the opportunities in misclassification and also increase their losses in the empirical risk. The paper proposes a model merging a non-parametric k-nearest-neighbor (kNN) estimation [5-7] into an underlying SVM to produce an instance-dependent loss function. The kNN method, mining locally the useful information among the training examples, gives a special independent aspect to evaluate the examples' significance. With the evaluation, penalties from the instance-dependent loss function are then determined for the optimization procedure. The various penalties taken effect in the optimization procedure will produce a set of new Lagrangian multipliers and form a separating hyperplane different from the set of original multipliers. The proposed model provides a way for emphasizing the substantial and subtle instances in the learning process, especially for the difficult examples.

2 Associating *k*NN with SVM

2.1 Loss Functions in SVMs

As the fundamentals of the SVMs, examples with positive margin are known as those classified correctly and examples with negative margin are those misclassified. According to the definition, the goal of the learning is to produce positive margin as frequently as possible. Under the criteria, a formal definition of the loss function is incurred by the triplet consisting of an example $\mathbf{x}_i$, the class label y_i, and the predicted value coming from the resultant decision function $f(\mathbf{x}_i)$. Here, the soft margin loss function which is popularly used in classical SVM is defined as [4]:

$$c(\mathbf{x}_i, y_i, f(\mathbf{x}_i)) = \max(0, 1 - y_i f(\mathbf{x}_i)) = \begin{cases} 0, & \text{if } y_i f(\mathbf{x}_i) \geq 1, \\ 1 - y_i \cdot f(\mathbf{x}_i), & \text{otherwise.} \end{cases} \tag{2}$$

where y_i is a binary target, $y_i \in \{+1, -1\}$, and $f(\mathbf{x}_i)$ is a real-valued prediction from the decision function. In the expression, the scale of loss depends on the product $y_i f(\mathbf{x}_i)$ if the product having a value less than one. The loss function that will be minimized in the process of fitting the model of an underlying SVM to meet the requirement of "classified correctly as frequent as possible". In plain words, the loss function represents a selected measure of the discrepancy between the target y_i and the predicted value which is response by the fitted function $f(\mathbf{x}_i)$.

The loss function is commonly employed as a penalization which penalizes an example with negative margin more heavily than that with positive margin in the SVMs. Following the statement, any penalty which is incurred by the loss function is not necessary for the examples which are correctly classified with positive margin. In other words, all the penalties should be focus on the examples with negative margins. In the sense, slightly changing the scale of penalties for the examples with negative margins, but keeping the penalization rule in (2) may be allowed and feasible when someone wants to modify the soft margin SVM. Hence, several surrogates of loss function, such as the misclassification, exponential, binomial deviance, squared error, and support vector loss functions have been proposed for selected topics in the theory of statistical learning [9]. All the surrogates are strict convex functions. Their common essential property is to continuously penalize the examples with negative margin. The differences among the surrogates are the degree of the penalization exerted on the examples with negative margin.

Being a role in the regularization of the hypothesis, the study of loss function is very important and has received much attention. Many researchers have stressed that the performance assessment of a hypothesis can be related to the minimization of the loss function [2-3, 10-13].

2.2 A Preprocessor Based on *k*-Nearest-Neighbor

The class of *k*NN methods is a typical non-parametric estimation widely used in the field of data mining, such as density estimation, or classification [5-7]. Based on the non-parametric assumption, the approaches can be characterized as an instance-based learning technique, which is learning directly from a set of available examples, and interpreting the results statistically. Instead of trying to create rules, the *k*NN approaches work directly from examples themselves. Suppose an unlabeled example $\mathbf{x}$ is placed among a set of n training examples in a region of volume V, and it captures k neighboring examples. Counting the neighboring examples, a portion of k_j examples turns out to be in class labeled ω_j. The joint density function of $\mathbf{x}$ and ω_j can be approximated

$$p(\mathbf{x}, \omega_j) = \frac{k_j / n}{V}. \tag{3}$$

From Bayes rule,

$$P(\omega \mid \mathbf{x}) p(\mathbf{x}) = p(\mathbf{x}, \omega_j), \tag{4}$$

The posteriori probability of $P(\omega_j|\mathbf{x})$ can be obtained by

$$P(\omega_j \mid \mathbf{x}) = \frac{p(\mathbf{x}, \omega_j)}{\sum_{t=1}^{c} p(\mathbf{x}, \omega_t)} = \frac{\frac{(k_j / n)}{V}}{\sum_{t=1}^{c} \frac{(k_t / n)}{V}} = \frac{k_j}{k}, \tag{5}$$

where c denotes the number of classes. With (5), one can estimate $P(\omega_j|\mathbf{x})$ by the fraction of examples captured in a local region labeled ω_j.

Since it does not need to build a classifier actually, the set of training examples should be very representative for inference. The term of "prototypes" is used for the crucial set of examples. In the kNN classification, the kNN rules only require: an ordinary odd integer k, a family of prototypes, and a metric to measure "closeness" to collect the closest patterns for decision-making. Using the prototypes, the class belonging of a new arrival query example is determined locally by the k nearest neighboring prototypes around the query example. It is a simple and intuitive method to classify unlabeled examples based on the similarity to the neighbors in the feature space.

In general, difficult examples may lie distant from the gathering area of the examples with the same class label, or may locate close to the border of adjacent overlapped region in which the examples come from different class are resided together. However, the non-parametric method which captures the local structure of a little part of the underlying prototypes is quite suitable to employ as a preprocessor for filtering the individual difficult examples.

2.3 Support Vector Machines with Weighted Class Labels

The support vector machines were developed based on the structural risk minimization principle of statistical learning theory [1-4, 8] by learning from the training samples, the decision function therefore can be obtained. The basic form of decision function in the SVM is given as $f(\mathbf{x}) = \text{sign}(<\mathbf{w}, \mathbf{x}> + b)$ which is described by a vector of orientation weights $\mathbf{w}$ and a bias term b. The goal of the SVM is to find a separating hyperplane with maximal margin while the classification error can be minimized by the training samples. With the notation of the input training set, $S=\{(\mathbf{x}_i, y_i)\}$, a proposition starts with the change of S [14-15]:

$$\tilde{S} = \{(\mathbf{x}_i, \tilde{y}_i)\}, \ i = 1, 2, \ ..., n. \tag{6}$$

In the expression, $\tilde{y}_i$, having its sign identical to y_i in the training set S, denotes a relaxed real-valued class label to represent the potential weights that sample i should be taken. The expression of $\tilde{S}$ tries to carry more information about the training set, regardless both S and $\tilde{S}$ contains a set of the same patterns $\mathbf{x}_i$. The change of S in $\tilde{S}$ involves a remapping regarding to the idea of assigning various weights for the samples in different situations. In (6), class label $\tilde{y}_i$ is no longer a discrete value; instead it becomes a real-value to represent an implicit relationship to the sample's native class. Incorporating the idea of kNN, the value of $\tilde{y}_i$ can be obtained from the idea of kNN

$$\tilde{y}_i = \eta \frac{y_i}{P(\omega_i \mid \mathbf{x}_i)}, \tag{7}$$

where $P(\omega_i|\mathbf{x}_i)$ is the posteriori probability denoted in (5).

The method of (7), called kNN emphasizer, adopts an inverted scheme to scale the value of $\tilde{y}_i$. The essential in the expression of $\tilde{y}_i$ can be discovered by the ratio of magnification $1/P(\omega_i|\mathbf{x}_i)$. Generally, the value of the ratio will be greater than 1. Our intention is to use the ratio to magnify y_i. Parameter η in the expressions, called an acceleration factor, should be a positive real and greater than 1 to ensure that $|\tilde{y}_i| \geq 1$.

The scaled-up real-valued class label $\tilde{y}_i$ provides a stricter penalty in the optimization, and is able to conduct the classification more accurate. Especially, the improvement will be more significant in a much more confused dataset with many difficult examples. By the magnification, difficult examples are designed to carry heavier weight in order to receive more penalties in the optimization. However, a set of canonical constraints is setup with the primal objective in the classical SVM [8] for optimization due to the change from y_i to $\tilde{y}_i$:

$$\min_{w,b,\xi} \frac{1}{2}\mathbf{w}^T\mathbf{w} + C\sum_{i=1}^{n}\xi_i, \tag{8}$$

subject to

$$y_i((\mathbf{w}^T\mathbf{x}_i + b)) \geq 1 - \xi_i, \quad i = 1, \ldots, n, \tag{9}$$

$$\xi_i \geq 0, \quad i = 1, \ldots, n, \tag{10}$$

In the expression, $\tilde{\xi}_i$ denotes the slack variable equivalent to it in the classical model of soft-margin SVM. Following the steps of deriving the classical model of SVM, the formulation of the quadratic programming becomes

$$\max_{\tilde{\alpha}} L_D(\tilde{\alpha}_i) = -\frac{1}{2}\sum_{i=1}^{n}\sum_{j=1}^{n}\tilde{y}_i\tilde{y}_j K(\mathbf{x}_i, \mathbf{x}_j)\tilde{\alpha}_i\tilde{\alpha}_j + \sum_{i=1}^{n}\tilde{\alpha}_i, \tag{11}$$

subject to

$$0 \leq \tilde{\alpha}_i \leq \tilde{C}, \quad i = 1, 2, \ldots, n, \tag{12}$$

$$\sum_{i=1}^{n}\tilde{\alpha}_i\tilde{y}_i = 0. \tag{13}$$

The expression of kernel function $K(\mathbf{x}_i, \mathbf{x}_j)$ in (11), substituting for the dot product confirms a more generalized model for the inclusion of a non-linear SVM [4-16].

2.4 Change of Loss Due to Association of *k*NN and SVM

As described previously, a filtering stage of the *k*NN emphasizer will be inserted in front of the classification stage. A two-stage model (Fig. 1) is proposed in order to fit the criterion of heavy penalization. In the model, the *k*NN emphasizer filters all the possible difficult examples, and produces a set of various emphasized weights to the training examples, especially to the difficult examples. In the second classification stage, the parameterized class label $\tilde{y}_i$ refilled by the set of the emphasized weights organizes a temporal input set of $\tilde{S}$ to produce a new set of Lagrangian multipliers $\tilde{\alpha}_i$ and to form a new hyperplane. The induced hyperplane, with the additional penalties for the difficult examples, tends towards higher accuracy in classification. However, comparing to the loss function of classical SVM, the change of $\tilde{y}_i$ produced an effect of loss function with arbitrary penalties depending on local neighborhood other than that with linearly increasing penalties. The loss function still fulfills the criterion of increasing penalization of those examples tending towards misclassification, but the degree of the penalization depends on the immersion that the difficult examples involved. The loss criterion may be sensitive to standalone difficult examples, but it does not change the hyperplane too much.

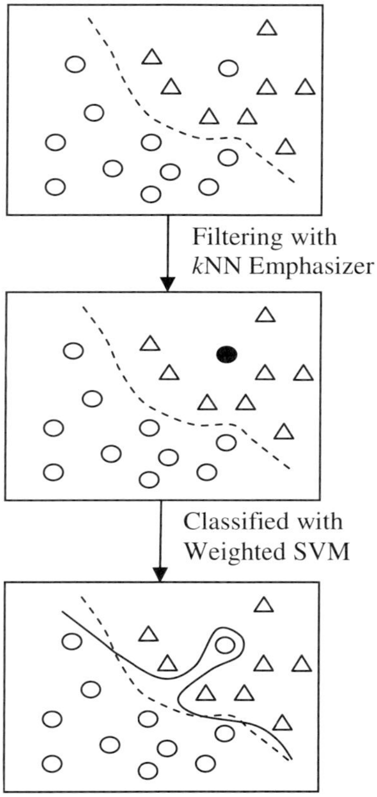

Fig. 1. Model of *k*NN-SVM

3 Experimental Results and Discussions

The section illustrates the basic characteristics of the *k*NN-SVM and compares its behaviors with its prototype of the classical SVM. In addition, an assessment of generalization performance with *K*-fold cross-validations is also described. A capitalized "*K*" is used here to make a difference with the special term of "*k*" for the *k*NN. The assessment of the generalization ability is an important issue for learning methods. An artificial dataset, named as *TwoNorm* which was introduced by Breiman to assess the corresponding theoretical expected misclassification rate [17], was generated for the experiments mainly. In order to clearly explain the effects on the *k*NN-SVM, only two classes of such normal distributed examples are taken on the two-dimensional input space, and form a simplified version of the dataset *TwoNorm*. In the dataset, each class was drawn from a multivariate normal distribution with unit standard deviation. One class center is located at $(2/\sqrt{20}, 2/\sqrt{20})$ and the other $(-2/\sqrt{20}, -2/\sqrt{20})$. By the statements of previous section, the *k*NN emphasizer (**7**) is used to evaluate the influence of the examples in the neighboring region. One should be aware of a large value of η will lead to fast saturation or over excess in the value of $\tilde{y}_i$ with a growing value of *k*, especially for difficult examples in a complicated dataset. It may unfortunately conduct a serious loss of influence sensitivity that the examples in the neighboring region ought to give.

3.1 Classification Improvement in Neighborhood of Heterogeneous Examples

As described in the previous section, the decision function in Fig. **2**b is come from *k*NN-SVM which has the ability to emphasize the influence of a local region. The rugged winding of the hyperplane may divide the training examples, including the difficult examples, into many small sub-regions. The sub-regions will try to capture those examples with similar feature values in the validation phase. If the difficult examples are substantial in the learning set of a real application, we believe that quite amount of examples with the same class label will somewhere or somewhen else behave the same way. As shown in Fig. **2**, both the large hollow and solid disk symbols with a number are the difficult examples of positive and negative class, respectively. For the experiment, parameter η, and k are set as 4, and 19, respectively, for evaluating the candidate of the difficult examples. The difficult examples were then chosen from the examples with a greater value of $\tilde{y}_i$ than the average of $\sum\tilde{y}_i/n$. In the case, there are 31 difficult examples. On the other hand, those validation examples are illustrated as little hollow and solid disk symbols with class labels corresponding to the large symbols. Each subset of validation examples around a difficult example were drawn as a series of multivariate *iid* random variables with the mean centered at

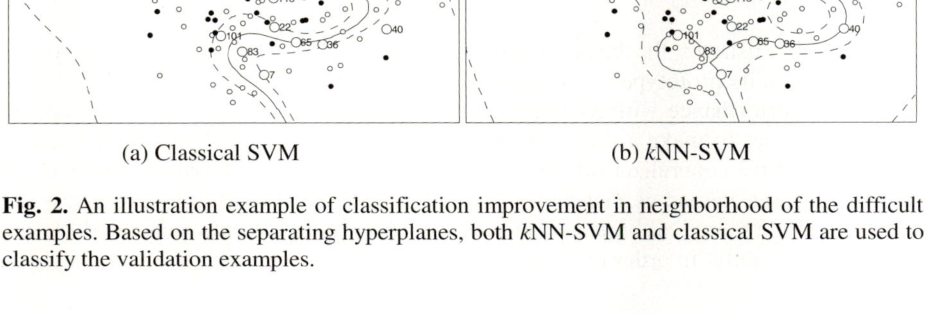

(a) Classical SVM (b) *k*NN-SVM

Fig. 2. An illustration example of classification improvement in neighborhood of the difficult examples. Based on the separating hyperplanes, both *k*NN-SVM and classical SVM are used to classify the validation examples.

Table 1. Tests of validation sets with various variances around the difficult examples

Misclassification Counts	Repetition	Variance				
		.1	.3	.5	.7	.9
Classical SVM	1	86	79	94	93	78
	2	90	88	95	80	96
	3	87	89	92	95	85
	4	92	91	83	85	86
	5	91	89	87	87	82
	Average	89.2	87.2	90.2	88.0	85.4
*k*NN-SVM	1	76	77	86	91	83
	2	76	81	97	87	91
	3	80	76	91	92	87
	4	84	88	80	89	91
	5	68	87	82	78	80
	Average	76.8	81.8	87.2	87.4	86.4

the difficult example. In the case of Fig. **2**, five validation examples were normally distributed around each difficult example with 1. It means 155 examples are included in the validation set totally for the experiment. The effect stressed the importance of employing k nearest neighbor rule in the model. As shown in Fig. **2**, 81 misclassification counts in the 155 validation examples were found by the *k*NN-SVM comparing to 89 misclassification counts by the classical SVM.

For each setting of variance, five repetitions of 155 validation examples have been generated to test the influence of a local region. The results were then taken average and listed in Table 1. In such a case, most of the sets are with various variances generally rendering the improvement obvious. The results confirm that the difficult examples insisting on forming a local sub-region is worth a particular attention.

3.2 Generalization Performance via *K*-fold Cross Validation

The generalization performance of classifier is an important issue to qualify a learning method. In general, the expected prediction error over a lot of independent test sets is not easy to obtain. A K-fold or leave-one-out cross validation using just one dataset is often taken instead to assess the generalization performance. In the study, a method of K-fold cross-validation is adopted as an evaluation facility for the generalization performance. The assessment of generalization performance varying exponential grids of equivalent $C = \tilde{C}$ for the respective classical SVM and *k*NN-SVM by the K-fold validation is depicted in Fig. **3**, where K is given as 10. In the diagram, the generalization errors with different settings of C or $\tilde{C}$ of the *k*NN-SVM are larger than those of the classical SVM generally. It indicates that the model complexity of *k*NN-SVM is higher. The fact actually brings the hypothesis under a risk of overfitting in the validation phase and conducts it a poor generalization performance. However, the fact has been anticipated that the degradation in generalization will happen to the *k*NN-SVM, since heavier weights of the difficult examples increase the model complexity [1, 10]. The heavier weights carried by $\tilde{y}$ have taken effect to amplify the penalties and raise the losses of the difficult examples in the convex risk minimization. According to the principle of structural risk minimization (SRM), a set of hypotheses generated by the kNN-SVM, $\tilde{H} = \{\tilde{f}(\mathbf{x}, \tilde{\mathbf{w}})\}$, is larger than the set generated by the classical SVM, $H = \{f(\mathbf{x}, \mathbf{w})\}$, due to the model complexity increase. Hence, we have

$$H \subset \tilde{H}. \tag{14}$$

However the degradation in generalization performance, it does not substantially matter the use of the kNN-SVM. In fact, the choice of the kNN-SVM has the ability to emphasize the difficult examples, and is good for the kind of problem illustrated in the Section 3.1.

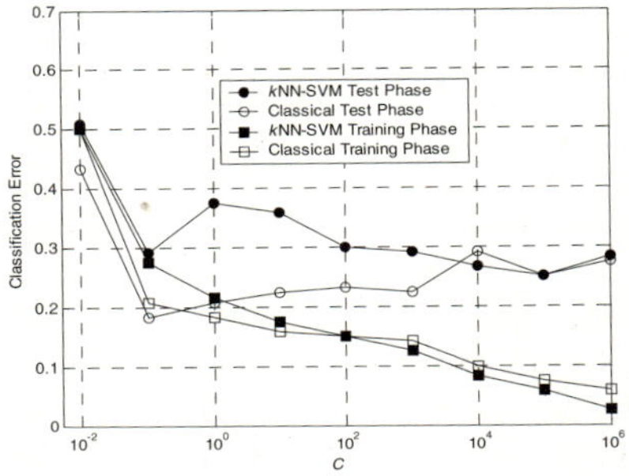

Fig. 3. Assessment of generalization performance varying exponential grids of C or $\tilde{C}$ by the K-fold validation, setting parameter $k = 19$ and $\eta = 1$

4 Conclusion

The classification with high cost difficult examples has had considerable improvement with the kNN-SVM. The model embedded a local density estimator of kNN emphasizer as a preprocessor in the SVM classifier. This sort of embedded model allows to spotlighting the heterogeneities that would be negligent if the entire population were taken into account. In the model, a key of parameterized class labels was used not only for the relaxation of penalization policy in the loss function, but also for the remedy to connect both the kNN and SVM subsystems. The employment of the kNN to locally filter the difficult examples was also a crucial point for success. Details of implementing such an embedded model of kNN-SVM were illustrated and effects of the model to several validation example-sets, with particular attention to the set of examples resided in the neighborhood of the difficult examples, were examined. The effects of changing parameters were also confirmed in the experiments of model validation. The experimental results show that the model dealing with heterogeneous examples is more accurate and robust than the existing techniques regardless the model is tending towards a little overfitting.

Acknowledgments. This work was supported by the National Science Council, Taiwan, ROC, under Contract NSC 95-2221-E-149-016.

References

1. Vapnik, V. N.: The Nature of Statistical Learning Theory. Springer-Verlag, Berlin Heidelberg New York (1995)
2. Vapnik, V. N.: Statistical Learning Theory. John Wiley and Sons, New York (1998)
3. Vapnik, V. N.: An Overview of Statistical Learning Theory. IEEE Transactions on Neural Networks, Vol. 10 (1999) 988–999
4. Schölkopf, B., Smola, A. J.: Learning with Kernels. MIT Press, Cambridge, MA (2002)
5. Cover, T. M., Hart, P. E.: Nearest Neighbor Pattern Classification. IEEE Transactions on Information Theory, Vol. 13 (1967) 21–27
6. Duda, R. O., Hart, P. E.: Pattern Classification and Scene Analysis. John Wiley and Sons, New York (1973)
7. Fukunaga, K.: Statistical Pattern Recognition. 2nd edn. Academic Press, San Diego, CA (1990)
8. Cortes, C., Vapnik, V. N.: Support Vector Networks. Machine Learning, Vol. 20, 273–297 (1995)
9. Hastie, T., Tibshirani, R., Friedman, J.: The Elements of Statistical Learning: Data Mining, Inference and Prediction. Springer-Verlag, Berlin Heidelberg New York (2001)
10. Bartlett, P. L., Jordan, M. I., McAuliffe, J. D.: Convexity, Classification, and Risk Bounds. Technical Report 638, Department of Statistics, University of California Berkeley, CA (2003)
11. Lin, Y.: A Note on Margin-Based Loss Functions in Classification. Statistics and Probability Letters, Vol. 68(1), 73–82 (2004)
12. Zhang, T.: Statistical Behavior and Consistency of Classification Methods Based on Convex Risk Minimization. The Annals of Statistics, Vol. 32, 56–85 (2004)
13. Steinwart, I.: Consistency of Support Vector Machines and Other Regularized Kernel Classifiers. IEEE Transactions on Information Theory, Vol. 51(1), 128–142 (2005)
14. Yang, C.-Y.: Support Vector Classifier with a Fuzzy-Value Class Label. Lecture Notes in Computer Science, Vol. 3173, Springer-Verlag, Berlin Heidelberg New York, 506–511 (2004)
15. Hsu, C.-C., Yang, C.-Y., Yang, J.-S.: Associating kNN and SVM for Higher Classification Accuracy. Lecture Notes in Artificial Intelligence, Vol. 3801, Springer-Verlag, Berlin Heidelberg New York, 550–555 (2005)
16. Shawe-Taylor, J., Cristianini, N.: Kernel Methods for Pattern Analysis. MIT Press, Cambridge, MA (2004)
17. Breiman, L.: Bias, Variance and Arcing Classifiers. Technical Report 460, Department of Statistics, University of California Berkeley, CA (1996)

Using Evolving Agents to Critique Subjective Music Compositions

Chuen-Tsai Sun[1], Ji-Lung Hsieh[1], and Chung-Yuan Huang[2,*]

[1] Department of Computer Science, National Chiao Tung University
1001 Ta Hsueh Road, Hsinchu 300, Taiwan, China
[2] Department of Computer Science and Information Engineering, Chang Gung University
259 Wen Hwa 1st Road, Taoyuan 333, Taiwan, China
gscott@mail.cgu.edu.tw

Abstract. The authors describe a recommender model that uses intermediate agents to evaluate a large body of subjective data according to a set of rules and make recommendations to users. After scoring recommended items, agents adapt their own selection rules via interactive evolutionary computing to fit user tastes, even when user preferences undergo a rapid change. The model can be applied to such tasks as critiquing large numbers of music or written compositions. In this paper we use musical selections to illustrate how agents make recommendations and report the results of several experiments designed to test the model's ability to adapt to rapidly changing conditions yet still make appropriate decisions and recommendations.

Keywords: Music recommender system, interactive evolutionary computing, adaptive agent, critiquing subjective data, content-based filtering.

1 Introduction

Since the birth of the Netscape web browser in 1994, millions of Internet surfers have spent countless hours searching for current news, research data, and entertainment—especially music. Users of Apple's Musicstore can choose from 2,000,000 songs for downloading. Having to deal with so many choices can feel like a daunting task to Internet users, who could benefit from efficient recommender systems that filter out low-interest items [1-3].

Some of the most popular Internet services present statistical data to point users to items that they might be interested in. News websites place stories that attract the broadest interest on their main pages, and commercial product stores such as amazon.com use billboards to list current book sales figures and to make recommendations that match collected data on user behaviors. However, these statistical methods are less useful for making music, image, or other artistic product recommendations to users whose subjective preferences can cross many genres. Music selections are often made based on mood or time of day [4, 5].

* Corresponding author.

Y. Wang, Y. Cheung, and H. Liu (Eds.): CIS 2006, LNAI 4456, pp. 336–346, 2007.

Two classical approaches to personalized recommender systems are content-based filtering and collaborative filtering. Content-based filtering methods focus on item content analyses and recommend items similar to interested items given by user in the past [1, 6], while the experts use collaborate filtering method to make the group of users with common interests share their accessed information [7-9]. Common design challenges of previous approaches include:

1. When the recommended item is far different from the user's preferences, the user still can only access or select these system-recommended items, and cannot access the potential good items which never appear in the set of recommended items. This problem can be solved possibly with an appropriate feedback mechanism [7].
2. In a collaborative filtering approach, new items may not be selected due to sparse rating histories [7].
3. User preferences may change over time or according to the moment, situation, or mood [4, 5].
4. Because of the large body of subjective compositions, the required large amount of time for forming suitable recommendations needs to should be reduced [4, 5].

In light of these challenges, we have created a music recommender system model which was designed to reduce agent training time through user feedback. Model design consists of three steps: a) content-based filtering methods are used to extract item features, b) a group of agents make item recommendations, and c) an evolution mechanism is used to make adjustments according to the subjective emotions and changing tastes of users.

2 Related Research

2.1 Recommender Systems

The two major components of recommender systems are items and users. Many current systems use algorithms to make recommendations regarding music [3, 9, 10], images, books [11], movies [12, 13], news, and homepages [7, 14, 15]. Depending on the system, the algorithm uses a pre-defined profile or user rating history to make its choices. Most user-based recommender systems focus on grouping users with similar interests [7-9], although some do try to match the preferences of single users according to their rating histories [1, 6].

Recommender systems play a role to use multiple mapping techniques to connect item and user layers, requiring accurate and appropriate pre-processing and presentation of items for comparison and matching. Item representations can consist of keyword-based profiles provided by content providers or formatted feature descriptions extracted by information retrieval techniques. Accordingly, item feature descriptions in recommender systems can be keyword- or content-based (Fig. 1). Features for items, such as movies or books, are hard to extract because movies are composed of various kinds of media [6] and content analysis of books encounters the problem of natural language processing. Their keyword-based profiles are often determined by content providers. However, current image and audio processing techniques now allow for programmed extraction of content-based features represented by factors that include tempo and pitch distribution for music and chroma and luminance distribution for images.

Previous recommender systems can be classified in terms of content-based filtering versus collaborative filtering. Standard content-based filtering focuses on classifying and comparing item content without sharing recommendations with others identified as having the same preferences. Collaborative filtering method focuses on how users are clustered into several groups according to their preference. To avoid drawbacks associated with keyword-based searching (commonly used for online movie or book store databases), other designers emphasize content-based filtering focusing on such features as energy level, volume, tempo, rhythm, chords, average pitch differences, etc. Many music recommender system designers acknowledge drawbacks in standard collaborative filtering approaches—for instance, they can't recommend two similar items if one of them is unrated. To address the shortcomings of both approaches, some systems use content features for user classification and other systems find out group users with similar tastes [7, 16].

To address challenges tied to human emotion or mood and solve the sparsity problem of collaborative filtering method, some music and image retrieval system designers use IEC to evaluate item fitness according to user parameters [4, 5]. We adopted IEC for our proposed model, which uses agent evolutionary training for item recommendations. The results of our system tests indicate that trained agents are capable of choosing songs that match both user taste and emotion.

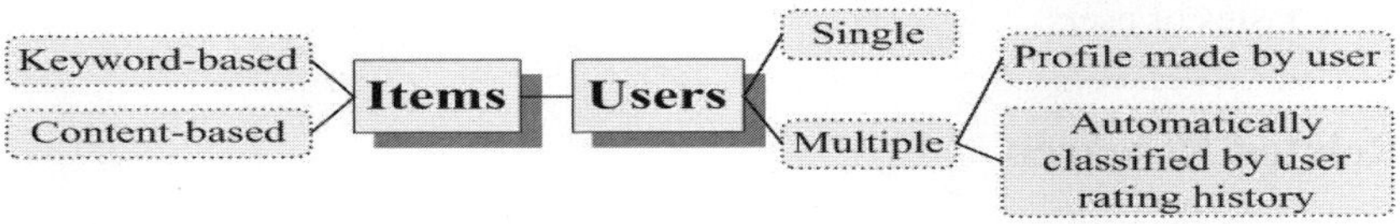

Fig. 1. Recommender system classifications

2.2 Interactive Evolutionary Computing

Genetic algorithm (GA) is an artificial intelligence system that allows for searches of solutions to optimization problems [17]. According to GA construction rules, the structure of an individual's chromosome is designed according to the specific problem and genes are randomly generated once the system is initialized. Following GA procedures include 1) using a fitness function to evaluate the performance of various problem solutions, 2) selecting multiple individuals from current population, 3) modifying the selected individuals by mutation and crossover operators, and 4) deciding which individuals should be preserved or discarded for the next run; discarded solutions are replaced by new ones whose genes are preserved). A GA repeats this evolutionary procedure until an optimal solution emerges. The challenge of music recommendation was defining a fitness function that accurately represents subjective human judgment. Only then can such a system be used to make judgments in art, engineering, and education [4, 5].

Interactive Evolutionary Computing (IEC) which is an optimization method can meet the need of defining a fitness function by involving the human preferences. IEC is a GA technique whose fitness of chromosome is measured by a human user [18]. The main factor affecting IEC evaluation is human emotion and fatigue. Since users cannot make fair judgments when processing run evaluations, results will change for different occasions according to the user's emotional state at any particular moment. Furthermore, since users may fail to adequately process large populations due to fatigue, searching for goals with smaller population sizes within fewer generations is an important factor. Finally, the potential for fluctuating human evaluations can result in inconsistencies across different generations [19].

3 Using Evolutionary Agents for a Music Recommender System

3.1 Model Description

In our model, intermediate agents play the roles which select music compositions according to their chromosome and recommend to user. The system's six function blocks (track selector, feature extractor, recommendation agent module, evolution manager, user interface, and database) are shown in Figure 2.

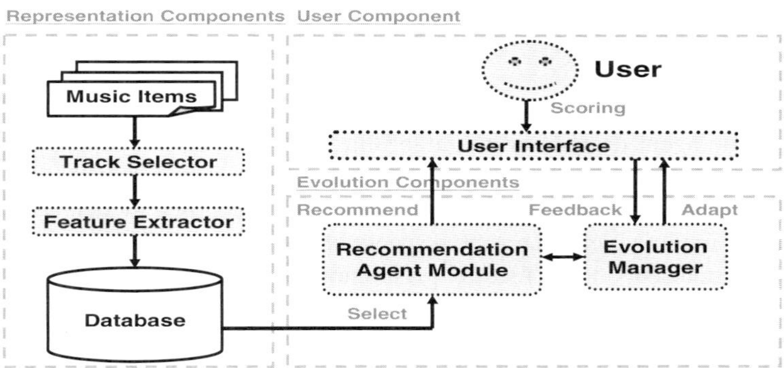

Fig. 2. Six model components including track selector, feature extractor, database, recommendation agent module, evolution manager, and user interface

A representation component consists of the track selector, feature extractor, and database function blocks, all of which are responsible for forming item feature profiles. This component translates the conceptual properties of music items into useful information with specific values and stores it in a database for later use. In other words, this is a pre-processing component. Previous recommender systems established direct connections between user tastes and item features. In contrast, we use trainable agents to automatically make this connection based on a detailed item analysis. The track selector is responsible for translating each music composition into textual file, while feature extractor is responsible for calculating several statistical feature measurements (such as pitch entropy, pitch density, and mean pitch value for all tracks mentioned in Section 4). Finally, database function block stores these statistical features for further uses.

An evolution component includes a recommendation agent module and evolution manager. The former is responsible for building agent selection rules according to music features extracted by the representation component, while the latter constructs an evolution model based on IEC and applies a GA model to train the evolutionary agent. In our proposed model, user evaluations serve as the engine for agent adaptation (Fig. 3).

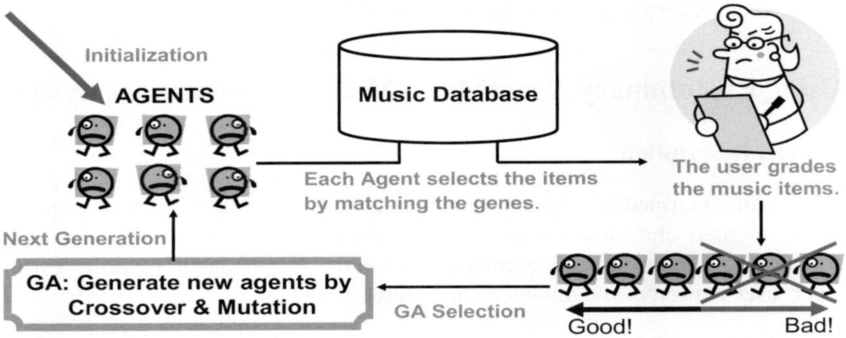

Fig. 3. Evolution component, including agent recommendation module and evolution manager

A central part of this component is the recommendation agent module, which consists of the agent design and the algorithm for selecting items. The first step for standard GAs is chromosome encoding—that is, designing an agent's chromosomal structure based on item feature representations. In our proposed model, each agent has one chromosome in which each gene respectively represents one of feature value. The gene value represents item feature preference and the number of item features represents chromosome length. Each feature needs two genes to express the mean and range value. Take 3 agents' chromosomes listed in Figure 4 for example, f1_mean and f1_range represent the 1st agent's preference of tempo feature. It means that 1st agent prefers the tempo between 30 and 40 beats per minute. The 1st agent will select the songs which have the tempo 35 ± 5 bests per minute and velocities 60 ± 10. The value of gene also can be "*Don't care*". We also perform the real number mutation for each mean and range value, and one-point crossover for selected pair of agents' chromosomes.

The evolution manager in our model is responsible for the selection mechanism that preserves valuable genes for generating more effective offspring. The common procedure is selecting good agents to serve as the parent population, creating new individuals by mixing parental genes, and replacing eliminated agents. However, when dealing with subjective evaluations, human's preference changing can result in lack of stability across runs. Accordingly, the best agents in previous rounds may get low grades because of change of human's preference, and therefore be discarded prematurely. As a solution, we propose the idea of agent fame values that are established according to previous behaviors. The higher the value is, the greater the possibility that an agent will survive. The system's selection method determines

CHROMOSOME

AgentID	f1_mean	f1_range	f2_mean	f2_range	...
1	35	5	60	10	...
2	60	3	95	4	...
3	83	5	120	10	...

Fig. 4. Agent chromosome. Each gene represents a mean or range value of music feature. Whole chromosomes represent selection rules for agents to follow when choosing favorite items. The chromosome in this figure encodes two music features.

which agents are discarded or recombined according to weighted fame values and local grades in each round, with total scores being summed with an agent's fame value in subsequent rounds.

Another important GA design issue is deciding when to stop agent evolution. System convergence is generally determined via learning curves, but in a subjective system this task (or deciding when an agent's training is complete) is especially difficult in light of potential change of user preference and emotion. Our solution is based on the observation that the stature of judges in a music or art competition increases or decreases according to decisions they make in previous competitions. In our system, agent fame value varies in each round. The system monitors agent values to determine which ones exceed a pre-defined threshold; those agents are placed in a "V.I.P pool." Pool agents cannot be replaced, but they can share their genes with other agents. Once a sufficient number of stable V.I.P. agents are established, the system terminates the evolution process. For example, if one of agent got six points fame value and the system pre-define threshold is six points high, the agent will be placed in a V.I.P pool. This mechanism just sets for preserving the possible good agents.

A user component consists of an interface for evaluating agent recommendations based on standards such as technicality, melody, style, and originality. The user interface is also responsible for arranging agents according to specific application purposes. For example, for finding joint preference between two different users, the user interface component will initialize and arrange two set agents for these two users respectively. An agent selects items of interest from the database according to selection rules and makes appropriate recommendations to the user, who evaluates items via the interface. Evaluations are immediately dispatched to the agent, whose evolution is controlled according to performance and GA operations (e.g., crossover, mutation, and selection). The evolution manager is responsible for a convergence test whose results are used to halt evolution according to agent performance.

3.2 Applications

We designed our model so that the chromosomes of surviving agents contain selection rules that be able to represent user profiles. Concurrently, user profiles formed by agent chromosomes can be compared among multiple users. Combined, distributing agents can be utilized for three kinds of applications:

1. Users can train sample groups of agents. The agent evaluation function can be altered to reflect a sum of several user profiles, thus representing the tastes of

multiple users. However, true system convergence will be difficult to achieve due to disagreements among user opinions. As in the case of scoring entries in art or music competitions, extremely high and low scores can result in total scoring bias.
2. Users can train their own agents and share profiles. According to this method, the system compares user profiles formed by the agents' chromosomes and identifies those that are most similar. Collaborative recommendations can be implemented via partial exchanges among agents.
3. Users can train their own agents while verifying the items selected by other users' agents. In the art or music competition scenario, users can train their own agents before verifying the agents of other users to achieve partial agreement. Pools of agents from all users will therefore represent a consensus. If one user's choice is rejected by the majority of other users following verification, that user will be encouraged to perform some agent re-training or face the possibility that the agent in question will be eliminated from the pool. For this usage, the user interface is responsible for arranging and exchanging the agents between different users.

4 Experiments

Our experimental procedures can be divided into two phases:

- Training phase. Each user was allotted six agents for the purpose of selecting music items—two songs per agent per generation (12 songs per generation). Since subjective distinctions such as "good or bad music" are hard to distinguish according to a single grading standard, user give multiple scores to each songs according to difference standard. Each agent received two sets of scores from user, with three scores in each set representing melody, style, and originality. The chromosome of any agent receiving high grades from a user six times in a row was placed in the system's V.I.P pool; the chromosome was used to produce a new chromosome in the next generation. This procedure was repeated until the system determined that evolutionary convergence had occurred. The system stopped at the user's request or when the V.I.P pool contained four agents, whichever came first.
- Validation phase. This phase consisted of a demonstration test for verifying that system-recommend songs matched the user's tastes. Experimental groups consisted of 20 songs chosen by 6 trained agents; control groups consisted of 20 songs chosen by 6 random agents. User evaluations confirmed or refuted agent capabilities. Users were not told which selections belonged to the respective groups.

4.1 Model Implementations

Musical items were stored and played in polyphonic MIDI format in our system, because the node data in MIDI files can be extracted easily compared with data in audio wave format [1]. The track selector translates each MIDI file into a textual format respectively; we list the beginning part of textual feature file in Table 1 for example. Polyphonic items consist of one track for melody and additional tracks for accompanying instruments or vocals. The melody track (considered the representative track) contains the most semantics. Since the main melody track contains more distinct notes with different pitches than the other tracks, it was used for feature extraction based on pitch density analysis. According to previous research [3], this method is capable of achieving an 83 percent correctness rate. Track pitch density is defined as *Pitch density* = *NP* / *AP*, where *NP* is the number of distinct pitches on the track and *AP* is the number of all possible distinct pitches in the MIDI standard. After computing the pitch densities of all targeted music object tracks, the track with the highest density was identified as the representative polyphonic track.

Table 1. Part of textual MID feature file

Unit	Length	At	Time	Track	Channel	Note	Velocity
314	53	1162ms	197ms	T4	C4	d2	68
319	50	1181ms	185ms	T3	C3	d4	71
321	48	1188ms	178ms	T3	C3	b3	74
...	...	...	...	...	...	...	...

Purpose of feature extractor is to extract features from the perceptual properties of musical items and transform them into distinct data. We focused on seven features for our proposed system; new item features should be also added when possible.

1. Tempo, defined as the average note length value derived from MIDI files.
2. Volume, defined as the average value of note velocities derived from MIDI files.
3. Pitch entropy, defined as: $PitchEntro\,py = -\sum_{j=1}^{NP} P_j \log P_j, where Pj = \frac{N_j}{T}$, where N_j is the total number of notes with a corresponding pitch on the main track and T is the total number of main track notes.
4. Pitch density, as defined earlier in this section.
5. Mean pitch value for all tracks.
6. Pitch value standard deviation. Large standard deviations indicate a user preference for musical complexity.
7. Number of channels, reflecting a preference for solo performers, small ensembles, or large bands/orchestras.

Genes in standard GA systems are initialized randomly. However, in our proposed system the random agents will probably fail to find items that match their genetic information because the distribution of extracted features is unbalanced. We therefore suggest pre-analyzing feature value distribution and using the data to initialize agent chromosomes. By doing so, it is possible to avoid initial agent preferences that are so unusual that they cannot possibly locate preferred items. Furthermore, this procedure prevents noise and speeds up agent evolution. Here we will use tempo as an example of music feature pre-analysis. Since the average tempo for all songs in our database was approximately 80 beats per minute (Fig. 5), a random choice of tempo between 35 and 40 beats per minute resulted in eventual agent replacement or elimination and a longer convergence time before convergence for the entire system. For this reason, average values in our system were limited: 60 percent of all initial tempo ranges deviated between 1 and –1 and 80 percent between 2 and –2. This led to a speeding up of the agent evolution process.

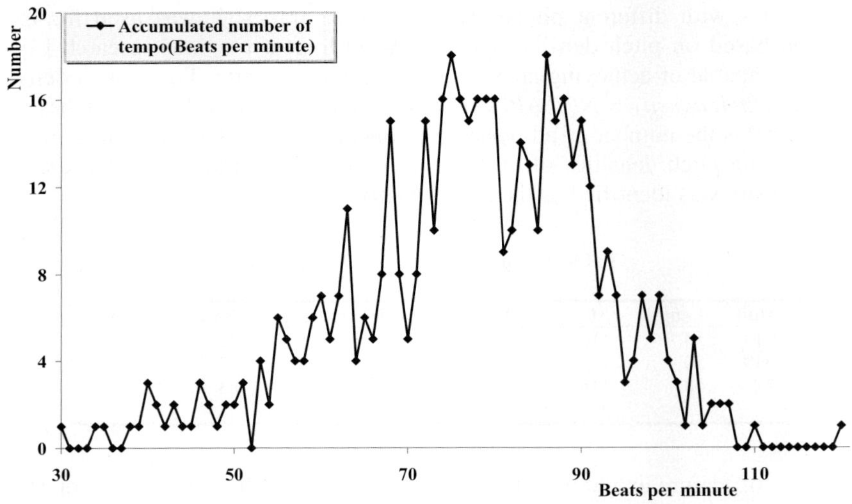

Fig. 5. Statistical curve for tempo distribution in our sample of 1,036 MIDI files

4.2 Recommendation Quality

Recommendation quality is measured in terms of precision rate and weighted grade. Precision rate is defined as $Precision\_rate = N_S / N$, where N_S is the number of successful samples and N the total number of music items. Weighted grades equals to summation of M_i divided by N, where M_i represents music item grades and N the total number of music items. Users were given six levels to choose from for evaluating chosen items.

Users were asked to evaluate experimental and control group selections. Experimental group agents evaluated songs recommended by agents that they had trained and control group agents evaluated songs at random. After users completed their tests, the system calculates precision rates and weighted grades. Finally, the songs recommended by the trained agents had an average precision rate of 84 percent and average weighted grade of 7.38, compared to 58.33 percent and 5.54 for songs recommended by the random agents.

4.3 Convergence Test

GA-based models commonly perform large numbers of iterations before arriving at convergence. In order to trace learning progress, we let users perform one demonstration (validation) test after every round; results are shown in Figure 6a. Curve A reflects a steady increase in effectiveness and convergence after eight rounds. Curve B reflects a lack of progress for agents that make random selections without training.

In addition to recommendation quality and convergence tests, we made an attempt to identify clear differences between experimental and control group music selections by extracting their respective features. As shown in Figure 6b, obvious differences were noted in terms of tempo and entropy, indicating that the trained agents converged unique preferences and did not blindly select items. Take one user's experimental result as an example, the user's preferences of feature tempo is quite different from the average tempo in control group.

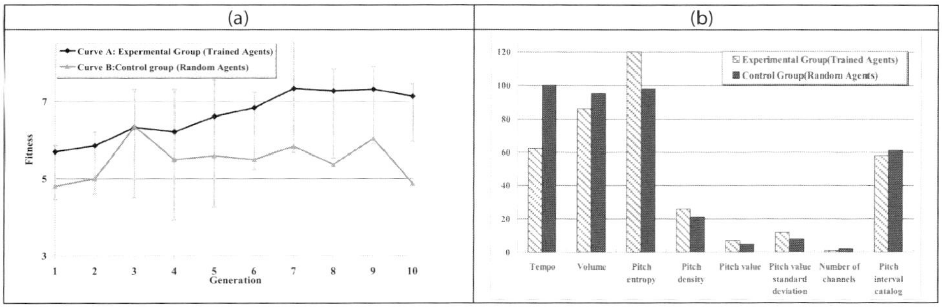

Fig. 6. (a) Convergence test and evolution generation of 10 users. Curve A represents an average of fitness values of 60 agents belong to 10 users. (b) One user results example.

5 Conclusion

Our proposed recommendation model can evaluate a large body of subjective data via a cooperative process involving both system agents and human users. Those users train groups of agents to find items that match their preferences, and then provide ongoing feedback on agent selections for purposes of further training. Agent training entails IEC methods and agent fame values to address the issue of change in human emotions. The agent fame value concept is also used as a convergence condition to promote agent population diversity and to propagate useful genes. Model flexibility was expressed in terms of replacing or altering functional blocks such as user interface which allows for usages of multiple users. We suggest that with refinement and modifications, our model has potential for use by referees to critique large numbers of subjective compositions (in such areas as art, music and engineering) and to make recommendations for images by extracting features (e.g., brightness, contrast, or RGB value) and encoding the information into agent chromosomes.

References

1. Kazuhiro, I., Yoshinori, H., Shogo, N.: Content-Based Filtering System for Music Data. In: Symposium on Applications and the Internet-Workshops. Tokyo, Japan p. 480 (2004)
2. Ben Schafer, J., A., K.J., Riedl, J.: E-Commerce Recommendation Applications. Data Mining and Knowledge Discovery 5, 115–153 (2001)
3. Chen, H.C., Chen, A.L.P.: A Music Recommendation System Based on Music and User Grouping. Journal of Intelligent Information Systems 24, 113–132 (2005)
4. Cho, S.B.: Emotional Image and Musical Information Retrieval with Interactive Genetic Algorithm. Proceedings of the IEEE 92, 702–711 (2004)

5. Cho, S.B., Lee, J.Y.: A Human-Oriented Image Retrieval System using Interactive Genetic Algorithm. IEEE Transactions on Systems, Man and Cybernetics, Part A 32, 452–458 (2002)
6. Li, Q., Myaeng, S.H., Guan, D.H., Kim, B.M.: A Probabilistic Model for Music Recommendation Considering Audio Features. In: Lee, G.G., Yamada, A., Meng, H., Myaeng, S.-H. (eds.) Information Retrieval Technology. LNCS, vol. 3689, Springer, Heidelberg (2005)
7. Balabanovic, M., Shoham, Y.: Content-based, Collaborative Recommendation. Communication of the ACM 40, 66–72 (1997)
8. Konstan, J.A., Miller, B.N., Maltz, D., Herlocker, J.L., Gordon, L.R., Riedl, J.: GroupLens: Applying Collaborative Filtering to Usenet News. Communications of the ACM 40, 77–87 (1997)
9. Shardanand, U., Maes, P.: Social Information Filtering: Algorithms for Automating Word of Mouth. In: Katz, L.R., Mack, R., Marks, L., Rosson, M.B., Nielsen, J. (eds.) Proceedings of the SIGCHI conference on Human factors in computing systems, Denver, Colorado, United States, pp. 210–217 (1995)
10. Kuo, F.F., Shan, M.K.: A Personalized Music Filtering System Based on Melody Style Classification. In: Proceedings of Second IEEE International Conference on Data Mining (Maebashi City, Gumma Prefecture, Japan, pp. 649–652 (2002)
11. Mooney, R.J., Roy, L.: Content-Based Book Recommending using Learning for Text Categorization. In: Nurnberg, P.J., Hicks, D.L., Furuta, R. (eds.) Proceedings of the fifth ACM conference on Digital libraries San Antonio, Texas, United States, PP. 195–204 (2000)
12. Fisk, D.: An Application of Social Filtering to Movie Recommendation. Bt Technology Journal 14, 124–132 (1996)
13. Mukherjee, R., Sajja, E., Sen, S.: A Movie Recommendation System - An Application of Voting Theory in User Modeling. User Modeling and User-Adapted Interaction 13, 5–33 (2003)
14. Chaffee, J., Gauch, S.: Personal Ontologies for Web Navigation. In: Proceedings of the ninth international conference on Information and knowledge management. McLean, Virginia, United States, pp. 227–234 (2000)
15. Chiang, J.H., Chen, Y.C.: An Intelligent News Recommender Agent for Filtering and Categorizing Large Volumes of Text Corpus. International Journal of Intelligent Systems 19, 201–216 (2004)
16. Pazzani, M.J.: A Framework for Collaborative, Content-Based and Demographic Filtering. Artificial Intelligence Review 13, 393–408 (1999)
17. Holland, J.H.: Adaptation in Natural and Artificial Systems. University of Michigan Press, Ann Arbor (1975)
18. Takagi, H.: Interactive Evolutionary Computation: Fusion of the Capabilities of EC Optimization and Human Evaluation. Proceedings of the IEEE 89, 1275–1296 (2001)
19. Maes, P.: Agents that Reduce Work and Information Overload. Communications of the ACM 37, 31–40 (1994)

Multi-agent Coordination Schemas in Decentralized Production Systems

Gang Li[1,2,3], Yongqiang Li[1,2], Linyan Sun[1,2], and Ping Ji[3]

[1] The School of Management, Xi'an Jiaotong University, Xi'an, 710049, China
[2] The State Key Lab for Manufacturing Systems Engineering, Xi'an Jiaotong University, Xi'an, 710049, China
[3] Department of Industrial & Systems Engineering, The Hong Kong Polytechnic University, Hung Hom,Hong Kong, China
lee_rich@163.com, qlyong@xidian.edu.cn, lysun@mail.xjtu.edu.cn, mfpji@inet.polyu.edu.hk

Abstract. Decentralized production systems are considered organizational structures able to match agility and efficiency which are necessary to compete in the global market. One of the challenges faced by the decentralized production systems is to ensure the coordination of heterogenuous decisions of the multi-agent populated production system. In the decentralized production system, the double marginalization makes the upstream agents conservative to build the system optimal capacity. This further makes the system falling into inefficiency. To overcome the system inefficiency, this paper proposes the cost-revenue sharing schema and the transfer-payment schema. These schemas are self-enforcing, which coordinate the capacity decision in the production systems, and allow the system profit to be maximized as well as the agents' profits to be improved.

1 Introduction

Market globalization makes it possible for firms to operate in a wide and complex international market by matching agility and efficiency. This can be achieved either by splitting geographically the production capacity or by working together in a decentralized production system which involves several independent decision units [1]. In decentralized production systems, firms need to be able to design, organize and manage distributed production networks where the actions of any entity affect the behavior and the available alternatives of any other entity in the network [2]. Firms calls for new forms of strategies, which are based on global networks of self-organizing, autonomous units, to have individual entities pursue system coordination [3].

The distributed problem-solving paradigm in decentralized production systems is consistent with the principle of multi-agent systems [4]. A decentralized production system is populated by a continuum of agents, which have their unique perspectives, incentives, strategies, and are individual rational. Agents are capable of matching supply to demand and allocating resources dynamically in real time, by recognizing opportunities, trends and potentials, as well as by carrying out negotiations and coordination. The whole system resembles a decentralized decision-making paradigm for

Y. Wang, Y. Cheung, and H. Liu (Eds.): CIS 2006, LNAI 4456, pp. 347–356, 2007.

operations coordination among manufacturing facilities. Agents coordinate their actions to fulfill the demand generated by the market. However, there emerges the double marginalization in the coordination, which results in the system inefficiency. The difference of the marginal revenue functions results in the local optimization action of each agent [5]. Consequently, the decentralized production system is un-coordinated.

Multi-agent system (MAS) technology seems to have demonstrated its potentiality to assure the necessary effectiveness and efficiency for the coordination of decentralized systems. The suitability of MAS in supporting production networks modeling and management has been testified by many researches. Among them, LI et al. [3] used multi-agent technology for the modeling of evolution complexity of supply networks. Swaminathan et al. [6] have distinguished two categories of elements for the modeling of systems dynamics in decentralized production systems. The two categories are the structural elements and the control elements. The structural elements are modeled as agents, including production elements and transportation elements. The control elements are inventory, demand, supply, flow and information controls, which are used to assist in coordinating the flow of products in an efficient manner with the use of messages. The agent technology facilitates the integration of the decentralized production system as a networked system of independent echelons, each of which utilizes its own decision-making procedure [7]. A number of heterogeneous agents work independently or in a cooperative and interactive manner to solve problems in a decentralized environment [4]. Through coordination paradigms, a global goal of the whole system is achieved as the aggregation of the agents' local objectives by negotiation of multiple planning cycles [8]. Jiao et al. [9] proposed an agent-based multi-contract negotiation system for global manufacturing supply chain coordination. Sadeh and Arunachalam [10] proposed a multi-agent based solutions that are capable of rapidly evaluating a large number of bidding, sourcing and procurement options in a decentralized production system. Collins et al. [11] developed a framework named "MAGNET" where agents negotiate the coordination of tasks constrained by temporal and capacity considerations. Anussornnitisarn et al. [11] developed a multi-agent based model of distributed collaboration network for distributed resource allocation. Gjerdrum et al. [13] applied multi-agent modeling techniques to simulate and control demand-driven production system network system.

In this regard, the goal of this paper is to develop coordination schemas for the heterogeneous activities of the multi-agent in a decentralized production system. The remainder of the paper is organized as follows. In section 2, the "double marginalization" of multi-agent is analyzed first, and then three coordination schemas are developed. In section 3, some real-world numerical examples are presented to validate the schemas. Finally, conclusions and further researches are drawn in Section 4.

2 Model Formulation

2.1 Assumptions

The described decentralized production system is modeled through an agent network, which involves two agents. Where the $agent_1$ is the upstream supplier, and the $agent_2$ is the downstream buyer. The $agent_2$ purchases components from the $agent_1$ at wholesale price w and carries no inventory. He makes the components into the final product with a unit manufacturing cost c_m to satisfy customer demands. We assume that w is exogenous since it is a common practice that the buyer always negotiates the wholesale price before he makes the firm order with the supplier. The demand of the final product is stochastic. When selling one product, the agent$_2$ receives exogenously specified revenue of p ($p>w+c_m$). The agent$_1$ must invest in capacity before the demand uncertainties are solved. To reduce the demand uncertainty, the agents share the demand information, which ensures that the final demand is known before the agent$_1$ fulfills the order of the agent$_2$. The final demand is a random variable x. The probability density and cumulative distribution of x follow functions $f(x)$ and $F(x)$ respectively. $f(x)$ is strictly positive and continuous, and $F(x)$ ($0<F(x)<1$) is strictly increasing and continuously differentiable. There are two stages in the game. In the first stage, the agent$_2$ requires the agent$_1$ compulsorily to fulfill his order, and he assures the agent$_1$ knows the demand before the order fulfillment. The agent$_1$ then chooses capacity k before the demand is realized. At the beginning of the second stage, all the members know the final demand. The agent$_2$ then places an order which is equal to the final demand. The delivery of agent$_1$ is less or equal to k.

To fulfill the order, the agent$_1$ builds capacity at a unit cost c_I, which includes the capacity cost and the opportunity cost when he devoting a unit of capacity to the agent$_2$. A unit capacity can be converted into one component per period at a production cost c_p. The agent$_1$ incurs the production costs only when filling the orders of the agent$_2$. The sum of the costs $c_I + c_p$ is less than the wholesale price w.

2.2 Double Marginalization

For the agent$_2$, his expected sales volume in the second period is $S(k)$:

$$S(k) = \int_0^k xf(x)dx + \int_k^\infty kf(x)dx = k - \int_0^k F(x)dx \tag{1}$$

Since the agent$_1$ must fulfill all the orders of the agent$_2$, the agent$_1$'s profit is:

$$\Pi_1(k) = (w - c_p)S(k) - c_I k \tag{2}$$

In order to maximize his profit, the agent$_1$ chooses the local optimal capacity as:

$$k_1^* = F^{-1}(1 - \frac{c_I}{w - c_p}) \tag{3}$$

Therefore, the total profit of the decentralized production system is: $\Pi_C^{DS}(k_1^*)$.

$$\Pi_C^{DS}(k_1^*) = \Pi_2(k_1^*) + \Pi_1^*(k_1^*) \tag{4}$$

Where $\Pi_2(k_1^*)$ is the agent$_2$'s profit as the agent$_1$ chooses his optimal capacity k_1^*, and the agent$_1$'s profit is $\Pi_1^*(k_1^*)$. In a centralized system, the global profit of the production system is:

$$\Pi_C^I(k) = (p - c_p - c_m)(k - \int_0^k F(x)dx) - c_I k \tag{5}$$

The optimal capacity is defined by the classical newsvendor solution, which is:

$$k_C^* = F^{-1}(1-\frac{c_I}{p-c_m-c_p}) \tag{6}$$

Since w<p-c_m, it is straightforward to verify that $k_1^* < k_c^*$. Namely, it results the double marginalization, where the difference of each agent's marginal profits results the inefficiency of the system. The agent$_1$'s selection of the local optimal capacity results the system efficiency (EC) is less than 1. Where the system's profit is $\Pi_C^I(k_C^*)$.

$$\Pi_C^I(k_C^*) = \Pi_2(k_C^*) + \Pi_1^*(k_C^*) \tag{7}$$

$$EC = \frac{\Pi_2(k_1^*) + \Pi_1^*(k_1^*)}{\Pi_C^I(k_C^*)} < 1 \tag{8}$$

For multi-agent system, an effective coordination mechanism should satisfy two constraints: (1) individual rationality constraint: the expected benefits of each agent within the mechanism are more than the benefits that those agents get without the mechanism; (2) incentive compatibility constraint: if the agent$_1$ expects the agent$_2$ to coordinate with him by schema A, and the agent$_2$ can choose the schemas A and A'. Only when the agent$_2$ gets more benefit from adopting A than from adopting A', could he coordinates with the agent$_1$ by schema A.

2.3 Long-Term Relationship Schema (LRS)

To stimulate the agent$_1$ chooses the system efficiency capacity, the agent$_2$ has to be involved into the capacity decision of agent$_1$ by sharing his capacity risk. Suppose that they forge a long-term relationship, which is widely used in practice in many industries. In the long-term relationship schema, the agents repeat their transactions in n periods. The depreciation rate of the capacity per period is equal to α ($\alpha \in (0,1)$). The salvage value for the capacity is assumed to be zero. Since there is a deprecation of the capacity as αk units in each period, the agent$_1$ has to supplement αk units at the end of each period. As a result, the agent$_1$ creates $k+(n-1)\alpha k$ units totally in the n periods. The total sales of the agent$_2$ in the n periods is:

$$S_n(k) = n[k - \int_0^k F(x)dx] \tag{9}$$

The total profit of the centralized production system is:

$$\Pi_{Cn}(k) = (p-c_m-c_p)S_n(k) - c_I[k+(n-1)\alpha k] \tag{10}$$

For simplicity, we let

$$\Delta = \frac{1+(n-1)\alpha}{n} \tag{11}$$

Therefore, the optimal capacity k_{Cn}^{*} for the centralized production system is:

$$k_{Cn}^{*} = F^{-1}(1 - \frac{c_I \Delta}{p - c_m - c_p}) \tag{12}$$

In a decentralized production system, the profit of agent$_1$ in n periods is:

$$\Pi_1^n(k) = n[(w - c_p)(k - \int_0^k F(x)dx)] - c_I[k + (n-1)\alpha k] \tag{13}$$

Therefore, he will choose the local optimal capacity:

$$k_{1n}^{*} = F^{-1}[\frac{n(w - c_p) - c_I(1 + (n-1)\alpha)}{n(w - c_p)}] = F^{-1}[1 - \frac{c_I(1 + (n-1)\alpha)}{n(w - c_p)}] \tag{14}$$

It is easy to verify that $k_{1n}^{*} > k_1^{*}$, and $k_{Cn}^{*} > k_{1n}^{*}$, which implies that the agent$_1$'s optimal is increased as the agents forge the long-term relationship, however, the system's optimal capacity is not achieved.

2.4 Cost-Revenue Sharing Schema (CRS)

Theorem 1: The cost-revenue sharing schema coordinates the capacity decision in a decentralized production system. Where the agent$_2$ shares a fraction (β) of agent$_1$'s capacity cost and gets a fraction (γ) of the agent$_1$'s revenue in n periods. Where β and γ satisfy the conditions:

$$Max(\frac{p - c_m - w}{p - c_m - c_p}, \frac{\Pi_{2n}(k_{1n}^{*})}{\Pi_{Cn}^{*}(k_{Cn}^{*})}) < \beta < 1 - \frac{\Pi_{1n}^{*}(k_{1n}^{*})}{\Pi_{Cn}^{*}(k_{Cn}^{*})} \tag{15}$$

$$\gamma = \frac{\beta(p - c_m - c_p) - (p - c_m - w)}{w - c_p} \tag{16}$$

Proof: With this arrangement, the total profit of agent$_1$ in the n periods is

$$\Pi_{1n}^{CRS}(k) = n(1-\gamma)(w - c_p)(k - \int_0^k F(x)dx) - c_I(1-\beta)[k + (n-1)\alpha k] \tag{17}$$

The total profit of agent$_2$ in the n periods is:

$$\Pi_{2n}^{CRS}(k) = n[(p - w - c_m) + \gamma(w - c_p)][k - \int_0^k F(x)dx] - c_I\beta[k + (n-1)\alpha k] \tag{18}$$

Therefore, the optimal order of agent$_2$ is

$$k_{2n}^{CRS*} = F^{-1}(1 - \frac{c_I\beta[1 + (n-1)\alpha]}{n(p - c_m - w + \gamma(w - c_p))}) \tag{19}$$

Let $k_{2n}^{CRS*} = k_{Cn}^{*}$, then we draw the condition that maximize the profit of agent$_2$ and the total profit of the system:

$$\gamma = \frac{\beta(p-c_m-c_p)-(p-c_m-w)}{w-c_p} \tag{20}$$

Under this condition, the profits of the agents are:

$$\Pi_{1n}^{CRS}(k) = (1-\beta)\Pi_{Cn}^{CRS}(k) \tag{21}$$

$$\Pi_{2n}^{CRS}(k) = \beta\Pi_{Cn}^{CRS}(k) \tag{22}$$

To maximize its profit, the agent$_1$ chooses the system optimal capacity k_{Cn}^*. Furthermore, we need $\gamma > 0$, $\Pi_{2n}^{CRS*}(k_{2n}^*) > \Pi_{2n}(k_{1n}^*)$, and $\Pi_{1n}^{CRS}(k_{Cn}^*) > \Pi_{1n}(k_{1n}^*)$ to ensure that the agents are all willing to take part in the CRS schema. Therefore:

$$Max\left(\frac{p-c_m-w}{p-c_m-c_p}, \frac{\Pi_{2n}(k_{1n}^*)}{\Pi_{Cn}^*(k_{Cn}^*)}\right) < \beta < 1 - \frac{\Pi_{1n}^*(k_{1n}^*)}{\Pi_{Cn}^*(k_{Cn}^*)} \tag{23}$$

With CRS, the profit of the system is maximized, and all the agents' profits are improved. The agents will collaborate with the CRS schema voluntarily. **End Proof.**

2.5 Transfer Payment Schema (TPS)

Theorem2: The decentralized production system achieves the system optimal capacity in a transfer payment schema (δ_p, ϕ) $(0 \le \phi < 1)$. Where the agent$_2$ transfer its profit δ_p to the agent$_1$.

$$\delta_p = n\Delta c_I(k_{Cn}^* - k_{1n}^*) - n(w-c_p)[(k_{Cn}^* - k_{1n}^*) - \int_{k_{1n}^*}^{k_{Cn}^*} F(x)dx] + \phi(\Pi_{Cn}^*(k_{Cn}^*) - \Pi_{Cn}(k_{1n}^*)) \tag{24}$$

Proof: Suppose the agent$_2$ asks the agent$_1$ to expend its capacity to k_{Cn}^*. If the agent$_1$ expands its capacity to k_{Cn}^*, the total profit of agent$_1$ in the n periods is:

$$\Pi_{1n}(k_{1n}) = \Pi_{1n}(k_{Cn}^*) = n(w-c_p)[k_{Cn}^* - \int_0^{k_{Cn}^*} F(x)dx] - n\Delta c_I k_{Cn}^* \tag{25}$$

This result in the profit loss (PL) of agent$_1$ as:

$$PL = \Pi_{1n}^*(k_{1n}^*) - \Pi_{1n}(k_{Cn}^*) = n(w-c_p)[\int_{k_{1n}^*}^{k_{Cn}^*} F(x)dx - (k_{Cn}^* - k_{1n}^*)] + n\Delta c_I(k_{Cn}^* - k_{1n}^*) > 0 \tag{26}$$

Therefore, the agent$_1$ would not expand to the system optimal capacity. Suppose the agent$_2$ promises to compensate the agent$_1$'s loss, and then this action will satisfy the individual rational constraint of the agent$_1$. If the agent$_1$ expands to the system optimal capacity, the agent$_2$ will get more profit (we call it as "the collaboration overflow (CO)".) after his compensation PL to the agent$_1$. Where CO is:

$$CO = n(p-c_m-c_p)[(k_{Cn}^* - k_{1n}^*) - \int_{k_{1n}^*}^{k_{Cn}^*} F(x)dx] - n\Delta c_I(k_{Cn}^* - k_{1n}^*) = \Pi_{Cn}^*(k_{Cn}^*) - \Pi_{Cn}(k_{1n}^*) \ge 0 \tag{27}$$

Suppose the agent$_2$ shares a fraction ϕ $(0<\phi<1)$ of CO with the agent$_1$ to satisfy its incentive compatible constraint. Therefore, the agent$_1$ gets profit as:

$$\Pi_{1n}^{TPS}(k_{1n}) = \Pi_{1n}(k_{1n}) + \phi(\Pi_{Cn}^{*}(k_{Cn}^{*}) - \Pi_{Cn}(k_{1n}^{*})) \tag{28}$$

To maximize its profit, the individual rational agent$_1$ will expand to the system optimal capacity $k_{1n} = k_{Cn}^{*}$. In summary, the total payment that the agent$_2$ transfer to the agent$_1$ is:

$$\delta_p = n\Delta c_I(k_{Cn}^{*} - k_{1n}^{*}) - n(w - c_p)[(k_{Cn}^{*} - k_{1n}^{*}) - \int_{k_{1n}^{*}}^{k_{Cn}^{*}} F(x)dx] + \phi(\Pi_{Cn}^{*}(k_{Cn}^{*}) - \Pi_{Cn}(k_{1n}^{*})) \tag{29}$$

In the transfer payment schema, the total profit of the decentralized system is maximized and all the agents' profits are improved. Therefore, TPS is a self-enforcing coordination schema for the decentralized system. **End Proof.**

3 Numerical Examples

The demand is assumed to follow U [a,b], with the mean as E(U)=10. Fig.1 shows the system efficiency is different in different coordination schemas with the assumption of p=7, w=4, c_I=1.5, c_p=1.0, c_m=1.0, and $\alpha = 0.2$. Furthermore, the sensitivity of different coordination schemas is illustrated in Fig.2~4.

In Fig.1, we find that the system efficiency is improved from 96.64% to 99.69% in a 5 years LRS. In the CRS and the TPS schemas, the system efficiency is improved to 100%. All the agents' profits are improved and the system profit is maximized.

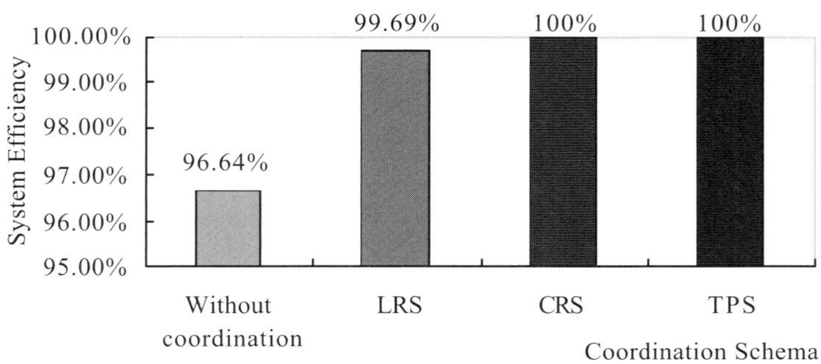

Fig. 1. Coordination efficiency of schemas

Fig.2 illustrates the schemas' sensitivity to demand variance (which is modeled by demand square deviation). Fig.2 indicates that because of the increase of demand variance, the optimal capacity for the agent$_1$ is increasing in a 5 years LRS, so is the difference between the local capacity and the system optimal capacity. However, all the agents' profits and the system efficiency are decreasing in this situation. The agent$_2$ has to share more fraction of capacity costs (in CRS schema) with the agent$_1$ or transfer more payment (in TPS schema) to the agent$_1$ to achieve system efficiency.

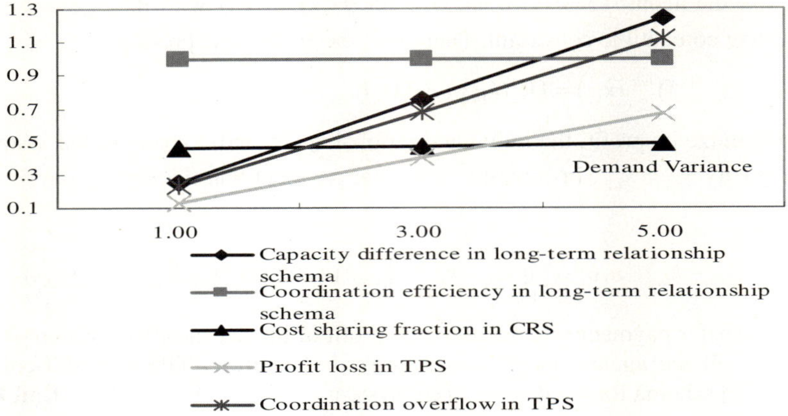

Fig. 2. Sensitivity of the schemas to demand variance

Fig.3 illustrates the schemas' sensitivity to the unit capacity cost. With the increasing of unit capacity cost, the difference between the optimal capacity of the $agent_1$ and that of the system is decreasing in a 5 years LRS. The agent2 has to share more capacity costs (CRS schema) or transfer more payment (TPS schema) to agent1 to achieve system efficiency.

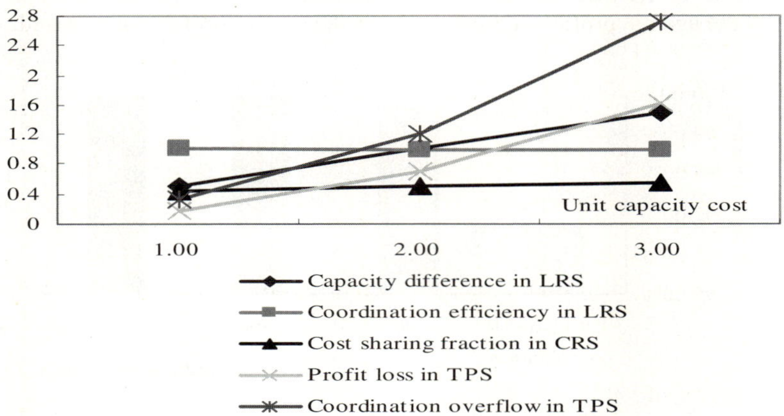

Fig. 3. Schemas sensitivity to unit capacity cost

Fig.4 illustrated the schemas sensitivity to the wholesale price. As the wholesale price is increasing, the difference between the optimal capacity of the $agent_1$ and that of the system is decreasing in a 5 years LRS. The efficiency of the decentralized system is increasing. The agent2 has to share fewer capacity costs (CRS schema) or transfer less transfer payment (TPS schema) to the agent1. In other words, the higher wholesale price enhances the system efficiency.

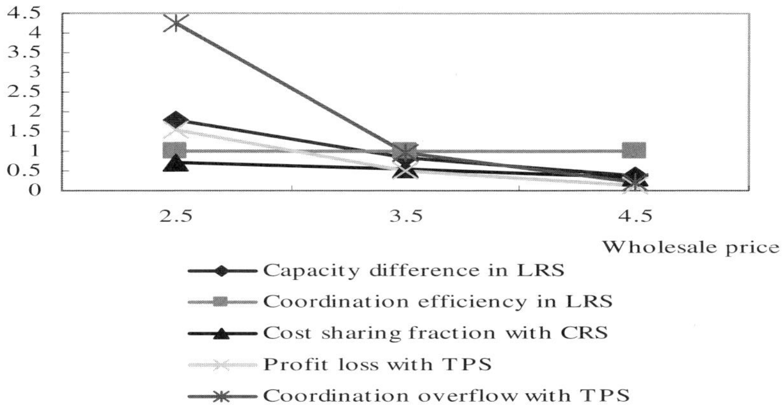

Fig. 4. Schemas sensitivity to wholesale price

4 Conclusions

Agents coordination in decentralized systems is one of the main challenges faced by the research in the area of multi-agent systems. Under the effect of double marginalization, a decentralized system is difficult to achieve system efficiency without any coordination mechanisms. We proposed the cost-revenue sharing schema and the transfer-payment schema to facilitate the coordination in a decentralized production system. The two schemas are self-enforcing, which ensures that all the agents take part in the coordination voluntarily. In these coordination schemas, we have an underlying assumption that all the information is symmetric to the agents and the system structure only involves two agents. This is a simplification of the information complexity and the network structure in a practical production system. Under the effect of the complex structure and asymmetric information, it is more difficult to achieve system coordination. We believe that the TPS is a promising method to coordinate the capacity decision in a more complex network structure, which involves more than one downstream agent. The coordination issues in asymmetric information need further study.

Acknowledgement

This paper was partially supported by the NSFC (Project No. 70433003) and the Hong Kong Polytechnic University (Project No. A-PG64).

References

1. Nigro, L., La Diega, S.N., Perrone, G., Renna, P.: Coordination policies to support decision making in distributed production planning. Robotics and Computer Integrated Manufacturing 19(6), 521–531 (2003)

2. Wiendahl, H.P., Lutz, S.: Production networks. Annals of CIRP 200. 251(2) 5-22
3. LI, G., Sun, L.Y., JI, P., LI, H.Q.: Self-organization Evolution of Supply Networks: System Modeling and Simulation Based on Multi-agent. In: Hao, Y., Liu, J., Wang, Y.-P., Cheung, Y.-m., Yin, H., Jiao, L., Ma, J., Jiao, Y.-C. (eds.) Computational Intelligence and Security. LNCS (LNAI), vol. 3801, Springer, Heidelberg (2005)
4. Brenner, W., Zarnekow, R., Wittig, H.: Intelligent software agents: foundations and applications. Springer, New York (1998)
5. Spengler, J.: Vertical integration and antitrust policy. Journal of Political Economy 58, 347–352 (1950)
6. Swaminathan, J.M.: Modeling Supply Chain Dynamics: A Multi-agent Approach. Decision Sciences 29(3), 607–632 (1998)
7. Gjerdrum, J., Shah, N., Papageorgiou, L.G.: A combined optimization and agent-based approach to supply chain modeling and performance assessment. Production Plan Control. 12(1), 81–88 (2001)
8. Kaihara, T.: Supply chain management with market economics. International Journal of Production Economics 73(1), 5–14 (2001)
9. Jiao, J.X., You, X., Kumar, A.: An agent-based framework for collaborative negotiation in the global manufacturing supply chain network. Robotics and Computer Integrated Manufacturing 22(3), 239–255 (2006)
10. Sadeh, N., and Arunachalam, R.: The 2003 supply chain management trading agent competition. In: Proceedings 6th ACM Conference on Electronic Commerce, pp. 113–118 (2004)
11. Collins, J., Ketter, W., Gini, M.: A multi-agent negotiating test bed for contracting tasks with temporal and precedence constraints. International Journal of Electronic Commerce 7(1), 35–57 (2002)
12. Anussornnitisarn, P., Shimon, N.Y., Opher, E.: Decentralized control of cooperative and autonomous agents for solving the distributed resource allocation problem. International Journal of Production Economics 98(1), 114–128 (2005)
13. Gjerdrum, J., Shah, N., Papageorgiou, L.G.: A combined optimization and agent-based approach to supply chain modeling and performance assessment. Production Planning Control. 12(1), 81–88 (2001)

Ontology-Based RFID System Model for Supporting Semantic Consistency in Ubiquitous Environment*

Dongwon Jeong[1], Keunhwan Jeon[2], Jang-won Kim[3], Jinhyung Kim[3], and Doo-Kwon Baik[3]

[1] Dept. of Informatics & Statistics, Kunsan National University, San 68, Miryong-dong, Gunsan, Jeollabuk-do, 573-701 Korea
djeong@kunsan.ac.kr
[2] Dept. of Computer Application, Kunjang College, 608-8, Seongsan-myeon, Gunsan, Jeollabuk-do, 573-701 Korea
khjeon@kunjang.ac.kr
[3] Dept. of Computer Science & Engineering, Korea University, Anam-dong, Sungbuk-gu, Seoul, 136-701 Korea
{jwkim, koolmania, baik}software.korea.ac.kr

Abstract. The emerging ubiquitous computing is changing the current computing paradigm, and lets the ubiquitous RFID applications consistently and independently utilize the sensed information from the intelligent and powerful tags which are in a variety of applications fields. One of the most important issues is how to support the semantic consistency between data from various tags in different RFID applications under ubiquitous environment. This paper proposes a new RFID model to resolve the issue and to support the application-independent semantic maintenance in the ubiquitous computing environment based on WordNet, a widely used ontology. Our noble RFID model provides an infrastructure support for the semantic consistency and enables the RFID application-independent information utilization.

1 Introduction

Ubiquitous computing is recognized as a new computing paradigm. We can acquire and use various data from many sensors under ubiquitous computing environment. Although we can now use data from sensors under the current computing environment, its application is very narrow and in a specific boundary such a given and restricted sensor field. To realize the complete ubiquitous computing environment, many issues should be resolved. They include issues such as energy management, protocol to gather data, data processing, independency on applications, and so on. Especially, the independency of sensor use on applications should be supported to maximize the usability of sensors [1].

There are many kinds of ubiquitous computing applications and the RFID (Radio Frequency IDentification) system is one of representative applications. The RFID system enables contactless and wireless information access of objects (RFID tags) using radio frequency. Most of all, it is actively being researched and also is now

* This work was supported by the second Brain Korea 21 Project.

Y. Wang, Y. Cheung, and H. Liu (Eds.): CIS 2006, LNAI 4456, pp. 357–366, 2007.

widely used in real application domains [2]. Recently, many researchers have been doing to make more improved RFID system for the ubiquitous computing environment. The destination requires various hardware and software technologies such as the standardization of electric signaling, well-defined communication protocol between the middlewares, readers, and chips, power problem, and so on. Until now, most of researches overlooked the semantic consistency issue

The goal of this paper is to define a new RFID system architecture to resolve the aforementioned issues. To do this, the new RFID system architecture is based on the WordNet, a semantic lexicon, which has been developed to enhance the semantic consistency between words. The WordNet became lately one of the most frequently used machine readable dictionaries. Hence the lexical conceptual model of the WordNet has been applying to various other application fields such word sense disambiguation, knowledge acquisition, text inference, information retrieval, conceptual indexing, and so on. Indeed, WordNet contains a good coverage of both the lexical and conceptual palettes of the English language [6,7,8,9,10]. Hence, we use the characteristics and advantages to design the new RFID system model providing a seamless interchanging mechanism between the sensed data from the sensors or tags in different and various sensor/application fields [4,5,11].

2 wRFID: WordNet-Based RFID System Model

We first describe limitations of current RFID system architecture to clearly show the goal of our proposal, named wRFID and its motivation. In Fig. 1, an object (tag) is first sensor field with DPS-1. The object moves to and is accessed by DPS-2 in the same sensor field. All of the devices access the RFID tag, and read and utilize data such as name, producing company, and so on of the object.

If the tag is designed for the same sensor field with DPS-1 and DPS-2, these DPSs can interpret and utilize the data in the tag. However, the next DPS in different fields cannot interpret and use data of the RFID tag, because the DPS-3 is designed for only their corresponding application (field).

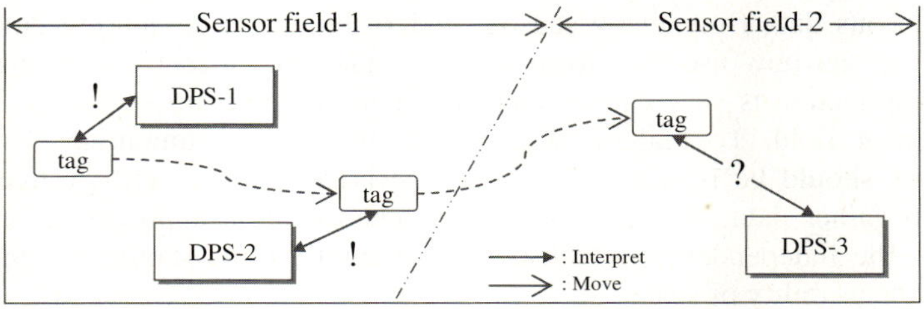

Fig. 1. Current RFID system architecture has limitations for seamless semantic processing. Meanings of a tag in a specific sensor field cannot be processed by a data processing server (application programs) in other sensor fields.

Fig. 2 shows the system architecture to realize the proposed RFID system model. The conceptual model of the proposed architecture and illustrates the relations of the technologies used to design the proposed RFID system architecture. In this figure, the tags (objects) can be accessed and used by various DPSs, which are in different fields (applications). The RF readers send the sensed data from the tags to DPS-1. DPS-1 interprets semantics of the received data before utilization. The most important component is the WordNet in Fig. 2. The WordNet is restricted to no specific domain and covers most English nouns, adjectives, verbs and adverbs. We employed the advantages of the WordNet to achieve the semantic consistency of data in ubiquitous environment.

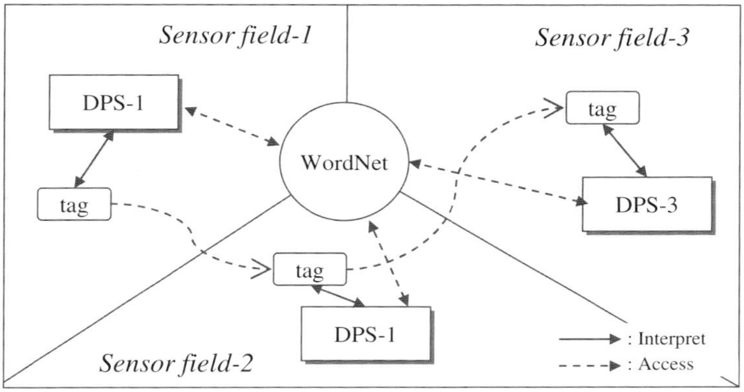

Fig. 2. This figure shows the conceptual model of wRFID, proposed in this paper. A semantic, i.e., meaning can be interpreted using word relationships in the WordNet. Therefore, more automatic semantics processing is achieved.

The proposed RFID system model has main two operations: Design process and interpret process. Fig. 3 illustrates the design process to create semantics. This process is to define the necessary semantics (attributes) to write data into RF tags according to the WordNet. As described [13, 14], the data volume at the sensor field level (sensor world) is less than the database level (database/application world) data set. A DPS retrieves the semantics of the WordNet to define its semantics, and then actual data (values) are recorded to a RF tags with the selected semantics.

Every DPS accesses and retrieves the WordNet to interpret semantics of obtained data. The interpretation process is described in Fig. 4. A RFID reader accesses a RF tag to get data related with the object including an object ID. Once the RFID reader read data of the object, it sends data to a DPS. The DPS should interpret semantics of obtained data before utilizing data. Under current RFID system environment, this operation does not be required, because exiting RFID systems only use pre-defined data in their own closed environment. In this paper, we consider a new RFID system environment. In other words, a RF tag includes various data as well as the ID for an object. Also, the RF tag can be used by many RFID readers and DPSs in different fields. Therefore, semantic interpretation process should be accomplished to interexchange and share data in various RF tags.

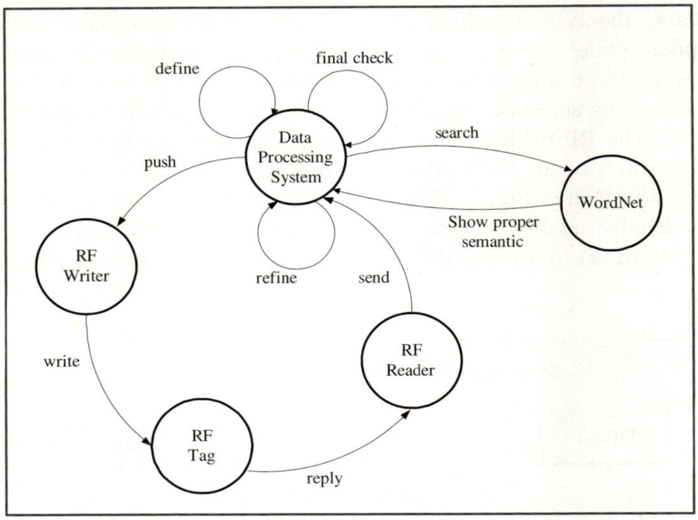

Fig. 3. This figure illustrates details of the design process, i.e., recording (writing) process

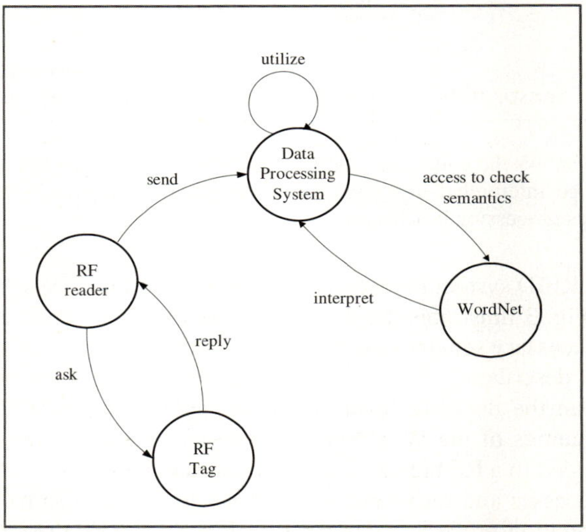

Fig. 4. Interpretation process is described in this figure

3 Simulation Model

A scenario is given for simulation is illustrated in Fig. 5. Before description of the simulation model with the given scenario, several constraints (requirements) are assumed as follows:

- RF tags have various data including an ID (for objects)
- RF tag data can be inserted, updated, and deleted under valid authorization
- The power issue is out of bound of this paper
- The electric signal issue does not be considered

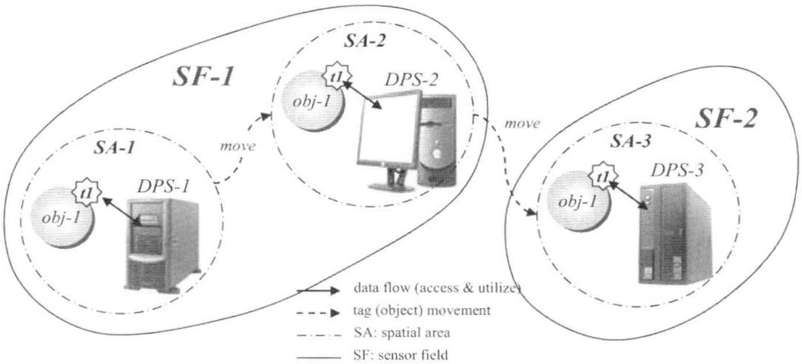

Fig. 5. A Scenario for the simulation is assumed to show contributions of our proposal. There are two sensor fields and it means that both define and use their own semantics respectively. An object attached a tag is move from SA-1 to SA-3 via SA-2. SA-1 and SA-2 are included in a same sensor field, SF-1.

With the constraints, the scenario, and the semantics, a simulation model is defined as Fig. 6. For the simulation, we increases the semantics that are differently used each other in both of two fields, SF-1 and SF-2. It means that the number of inconsistent semantics increases incrementally.

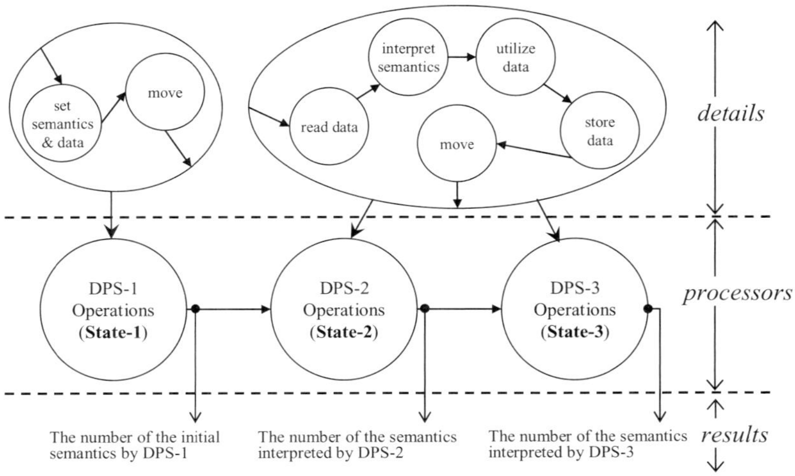

Fig. 6. This figure depicts a simulation model including detailed states and key operations for comparative evaluation

In this simulation, we do not consider the performance efficiency (i.e., processing speed). There are two main reasons. The first reason is that we just focus on the semantic interoperability between different and various sensor fields. The other is that the processing speed depends on the hardware/software environments.

As for the scenario in Fig. 5, a RF tag t1 is actually attached to an object and holds information about the object. The object moves to other areas. For example, an apple might be cropped and distributed to other cities. While its distribution (spatial movement), it could be accessed by many DPSs in various application/sensor fields. First, t1 (i.e., the object) moves from SA-1 to SA-2 and still in the same field SF-1. In SA-2, DPS-2 accesses and uses the information in the tag t1. After the operations by DPS-2, it moves to the third spatial area SA-3 which is in the second field SF-2. DPS-3 tries to access and use the data of the tag t1.

4 Simulation Results and Discussion

The most important comparative item is the interpretation rate of semantics. With the given scenario in Fig. 5, Table 1 shows a set of the semantics used for the simulation. Totally, twenty semantics are used for the experiment. Ten semantics created by DPS-1 are semantically inconsistent with the semantics that are used for DPS-3 in SF-2. For example, in Table 1, "Producing_area" has a same meaning with "Farm_area".

Table 1. This table describes a part of semantics that are defined and used for the simulation

Semantics	Description
Identifier	Unique value to be used to identify objects
Fruit_name	A specific fruit names (e.g., apple, banana, etc.)
Producing_area	Places where the objects are produced or cropped
Farm_area	Synonym (producing_area, farm_area)
……	……

As for the simulation model in Fig. 6, we can define a calculus model for the semantic interpretation rate SIR. Let be S_{ALL} indicates the set of all semantics, S_{NA} means the semantics that cannot be interpreted. S_{IN} means the semantic set interpreted by a DPS. Then the calculus model SIR is as follows:

$$SIR = \frac{n(S_{ALL}) - n(S_{NA})}{n(S_{ALL})} = \frac{n(S_{IN})}{n(S_{ALL})} \quad (1)$$

where $n(S_{ALL})$: *The number of the initial semantics,*
$n(S_{NA})$: *The number of the semantics that do not be interpreted,*

The simulation results are illustrated in Fig. 7 and Fig. 8. Fig. 7 shows the simulation result at the second state, State-2 by the previous RFID system model and our model proposed in this paper. In Fig. 7, the previous model is better than our model. There are three reasons as follows:

- The first is that the interpreting operation is accomplished in the same field.
- The second is that the previous model predefined all semantics for a specific field, and every device (DPSs and tags) can just follow the predefined semantics. Therefore, at the second state, the semantic inter-operability is perfectly done.
- Finally, our model is to provide the field-independent semantic consistency management and is based on the WordNet.

However, our model failed to make a relationship (IS-A) for three semantic pairs. This problem can be resolved in easy and is handled in next section. In addition, there are three semantics that our model cannot interpret, and these semantics have been added at the first inconsistent semantic input step, the fourth step, and the seventh step. It means when the number of the all semantics is 11, 14, and 17.

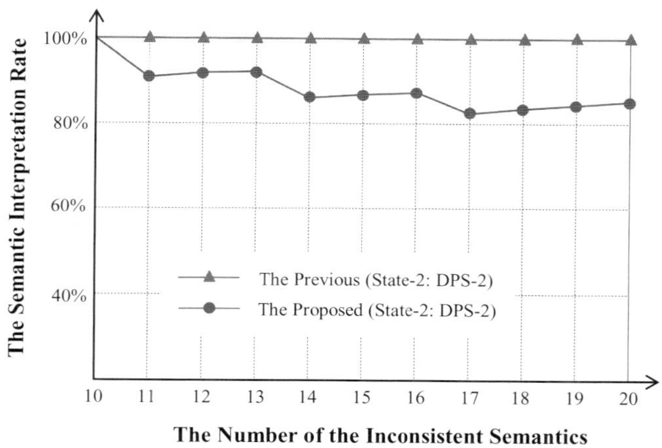

Fig. 7. This figure shows the simulation result on the interpretation rate of DPS-2 at the second state, State-2. This second state means the object in SA-1 moved to SA-2. However, the object is still in the same sensor field, SF-1.

Fig. 8 shows the simulation result and indicates the interpretation rate by DPS-3 at the state-3. In Fig. 8, the previous model cannot interpret the inconsistent semantics at all. As aforementioned, the previous model first predefines all of the necessary semantics for a specific field, and then every component (DPSs and tags) should define their semantics according to the predefined semantics. In a word, the semantic interoperability is valid in the same field.

In case of our model, several semantics couldn't be interpreted. However, the interpretation rate is better than the previous system model. Our model can be used to achieve the application/sensor field-independent semantic interoperability.

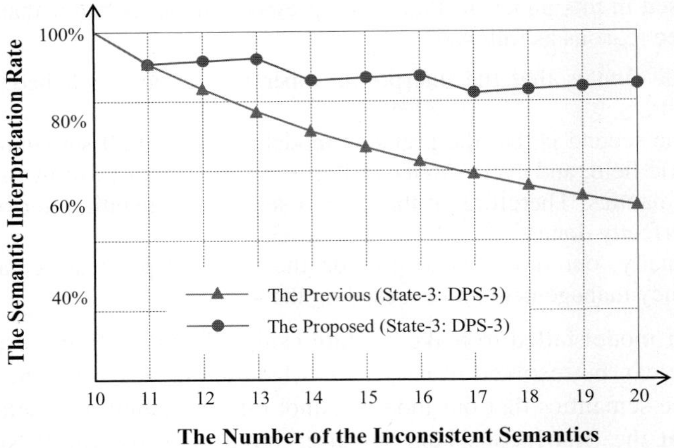

Fig. 8. This figure displays the simulation result on the interpretation rate of DPS-3 at the third state, State-3

5 Related Work

This section introduces a current and general RFID system architecture. The WordNet introduction and its semantic relations are described. Also the previous approach for the semantic management of the RFID systems under the ubiquitous environment is described. RFID stands for Radio Frequency IDentification and RFID system enables contactless and wireless access of objects by radio frequency. RFID systems consist of main three elements, RF (radio frequency) tags (RFID tags, transponders), RF tag readers (RFID readers, transceivers), and DPSs(data processing servers) [2,3].

The RF tag is the data carrier and typically has a role as identifier of objects to be identified. RFID systems can be classified into two types and one is the passive RFID system and the other is the active RFID system. In the passive RFID system, the RF tag is called the passive RF tag and its communication is small or medium. In contrast, active RF tags have larger communication rages than a passive tag. RFID readers read data from and write to RF tags. Finally, the DPS receives data from RFID readers, and processes and uses data for achieving given goals.

Our RFID system model is based on the WordNet and thus we introduce the characteristics of the WordNet. WordNet is a semantic lexicon for the English language. It groups English words into sets of synonyms called synsets, provides short definitions, and records the various semantic relations between these synonym sets. Sets of synonymous terms, or synsets, constitute its basic organization. As of 2005, the database contains about 150,000 words organized in over 115,000 synsets for a total of 203,000 word-sense pairs. The WordNet distinguishes between nouns, verbs, adjectives and adverbs on the assumption that these are stored differently in the human brain.

Most of the existing researches on the RFID system have been focused on the standardization of communication protocol, electric signaling, and so on. There are a few of research results related with the semantic interoperability [13, 16]. In case of the approach [13], they propose a RFID system architecture that can use and infer the situation information sensed from various sensors. However, this architecture does not consider the seamless semantic interpretation and utilization issue.

The approach of the research [16] is based on MDR (Metadata Registry), which developed to facilitate the semantic interoperability between databases by ISO/IEC JTC 1. The MDR-based RFID architecture provides the independent semantic interoperability between data of the RF tags in varied application fields. Also it provides the systematic creation process which is defined in the specification, Part 6 for the metadata registry. However, this architecture has two problems. The first problem is from the original limitation of the metadata registry. It means that the metadata registry support weak relations between semantics. To overcome this problem, ISO/IEC JTC 1 is developing the extended metadata registry [17]. The other happen when a new semantic should be defined. The MDR is a set of definitions (semantics) to be incremental defined not a set of predefined semantics. Therefore, the proposed MDR-based approach has the overhead for the evaluation and publication of new submitted semantics. This overhead (delaying time) is not suitable for the ubiquitous computing environment, because most ubiquitous applications require the real-time processing.

6 Conclusion

Ubiquitous computing is recognized as a new computing paradigm and many researchers have been studying on its application and realization. Although RFID system is one of the famous and well-known applications, and it has been implementing and applying to many real applications, current system architecture does not consider the emerging ubiquitous computing environment.

Existing RFID system architecture has several problems to be suitable for and apply to the ubiquitous computing environment: (1) data dependency on a specific boundary/sensor field; (2) static semantic management; (3) semantic inconsistency between sensor fields/application domains.

To resolve the problems, this paper proposed wRFID, a new RFID system architecture. It is based on the WordNet. This paper first introduced the related technologies which are the most important concepts (current general RFID system architecture and basic WordNet concept). The proposed RFID system architecture has been described with an example. And also, two key processes gave been illustrated. Finally, the simulation results were described to show the contributions of wRFID.

The proposed system architecture provides several contributions: (1) independency on a specific application/sensor field; (2) semantic consistency maintenance between different sensor fields (application fields).

As a further work, in the experiment result, our model did not interpret several semantics. It might be resolved by various similarity checking algorithms. In addition, the local semantic definitions for a specific field could be used for interpretation. This part will be considered in the next model to be improved.

References

1. Ilyas, M., Mahgoub, I.: Handbook of Sensor Networks: Compact Wireless and Wired Sensing Systems. CRC Press, Boca Raton (2004)
2. Finkenzeller, K.: RFID-Handbook: Fundamentals and Applications in Contactless Smart Cards and Identification. Wiley & Sons LTD, New York (2003)
3. Sarma, S.E., Weis, S.A., Engels, D.W.: RFID Systems and Security and Privacy Implications. Lecture Notes in Computer Science (LNCS), vol. 2523, pp. 454–469. Springer-Verlag, Heidelberg (2002)
4. ISO/IEC JTC 1/SC 32: ISO/IEC 11179: Information Technology - Metadata Registries (MDR) - Part 1 ~ Part 6 (2004)
5. Jeong, D., In, H.P., Jarnjak, F., Kim, Y.-G., Baik, D.-K.: A Message Conversion System, XML-based Metadata Semantics Description Language, and Metadata Repository. Journal of Information Science (JIS) 31(5), 394–406 (2005)
6. Bentivogli, L., Pianta, E.: Extending WordNet with Syntagmatic Information, In: Proceedings of the Second Global WordNet Conference, Brno, Czech Republic, pp. 47–53 (2004)
7. Black, W.J., El-Kateb, S.: A Prototype English-Arabic Dictionary Based on WordNet. In: Proceedings of the Second Global WordNet Conference, Brno, Czech Republic, pp. 67–74 (2004)
8. Budanitsky, A. and Hirst, G.: Semantic distance in WordNet: an experimental, application-oriented evaluation of five measures, In: Proceedings of the NAACL 2001 Workshop on Word-Net and Other Lexical Resources, Pittsburgh (2001)
9. Gangemi, A., Oltramari, A., Guarino, N.: Conceptual Analysis of Lexical Tax-onomies: The Case of WordNet Top-Level. In: Proceedings of the International Conference on Formal Ontology in Information Systems FOIS 2001 Ogunquit, Maine (2001)
10. Mihalcea, R., Moldovan, D.I.: eXtended WordNet: progress report. In: Proceedings of the NAACL 2001 Workshop on WordNet and Other Lexical Resources, Pittsburgh (2001)
11. Jeong, D., Kim, Y.-G., In, H.P.: Quantitative Evaluation on the Query Modeling and System Integrating Cost of SQL/MDR, ETRI. ETRI Journal 27(4), 367–376 (2005)
12. Juels, A., Rivest, R.L., Szydlo, M.: The Blocker Tag: Selective Blocking of RFID Tags for Consumer Privacy. In: The 8th ACM Conference on Computer and Communications Security, pp. 103–111. ACM Press, New York (2003)
13. Jeong, D., Kim, Y.-G., In, H.P.: New RFID System Architectures Supporting Situation Awareness under Ubiquitous Environments. Journal of Computer Science 1(2), 114–120 (2005)
14. Kim, J., Jeong, D., Baik, D.-K.: An Architecture for Semantic Integration between Data Elements in Sensor Networks, Korean Database Conference, Korea Information Science Society, Seoul, Korea, May 2005, pp. 145–152 (2005)
15. Powell, K.: Passive Radio Frequency Identification: Primer for New RF Regulations (November 2003), http://www.rfidjournal.com/whitepapers/
16. Jeong, D., Lee, L.-S.: A New MDR-based RFID System Architecture for Ubiquitous Computing Environment. Journal of Korea Society for Simulation 14(4), 43–53 (2005)
17. Lawrence Berkeley National Laboratory: Extended Metadata Registry (XMDR) Project Overview (2006), http://www.xmdr.org/

Multiagent Search Strategy for Combinatorial Optimization Problems in Ant Model

SeokMi Hong[1] and SeungGwan Lee[2,⋆]

[1] School of Computer Information and Communication Engineering, Sangji University
660 USan-Dong, WonJu-Si, KangWon-Do, 220-702, Korea
smhong@sangji.ac.kr

[2] School of General Education, Kyunghee University
1 SoChon-Dong, GiHung-Gu, YongIn-Si, GyongGi-Do, 446-701, Korea
leesg@khu.ac.kr

Abstract. Ant Colony System (ACS) is a meta heuristic approach based on biology in order to solve combinatorial optimization problem. It is based on the tracing action of real ants that accumulate pheromone on the passed path and uses as communication medium. In order to search the optimal path, it is necessary to make a search for various edges. In existing ACS, the local updating rule assigns the fixed pheromone value to visited edge in all process. In this paper, modified local updating rule gives the pheromone value according to the number of visiting and the edge's distance between visited nodes. Our approach can have less local optima than existing ACS and can find better solution by taking advantage of more information during searching.

1 Introduction

Because the size of optimization problem grows, the computer storage capability and calculation time reaches the ceiling. About these problems, researchers are studying about heuristic technique to find optimal solution in short time. But, there is difficulty that should develop according to property of problem.

Many researchers uses meta heuristic method to solve combinational optimization problem. There is genetic algorithm [1], tabu search and simulated annealing and so on in the kind of meta heuristics.

In this paper, we introduce about Ant Colony System(ACS)[2], [3], [4] one of the meta heuristic technique and will change the pheromone updating method of local updating rule. ACS is approach that is based for population that uses exploitation of positive feedback as well as greedy search.

Existent ACS gives a fixed pheromone value about visited edge in local updating process. But proposed method uses the pheromone updating method that considers the distance between visited node and the number of visiting times to apply property between nodes to pheromone value.

⋆ Corresponding author.

Y. Wang, Y. Cheung, and H. Liu (Eds.): CIS 2006, LNAI 4456, pp. 367–373, 2007.

This paper consists of 5 sections; next section introduces the ACS; section 3 explains an proposed algorithm; section 4 shows the experiment results, and lastly section concludes the paper with brief comment on the result and future work desired.

2 Existing ACS Algorithm

ACS is meta heuristic search algorithm based on existing Ant System (AS)[5], [6]. Real ants are capable of finding the shortest path from a food source to their nest without using visual cues by exploiting pheromone information. While walking, ants deposit pheromone on the ground, and follow, in probability, pheromone previously deposited by other ants.

ACS was newly introduced given that Ant System allows ants to fall on local optima because they tend go choose the shorter edge, if any, by nature. The ACS procedure is shown in Fig.1.

ACS algorithm applies the state transition rule, local updating rule and global updating rule to the tour made by each ant, thus preventing the ants from falling into local optima, while encouraging them to make broader and various searches to find an optima solution in a more efficient manner.

```
Initialize
Loop
  Each ant is positioned on a starting node(random method)
  Loop
    Each ant applies a state transition rule to
    incrementally build a solution
    And a local updating rule
  Until(all ants have built a complete solution)
  A global best tour selection
  A global updationg rule is applied
Until(End condition)
```

Fig. 1. The structure of ACS

2.1 ACS State Transition Rule

In ACS the state transition rule is as follows: an ant positioned on node r chooses the node u to move to by applying the rule given by Eq.1. $\tau(r,u)$ is the pheromone on edge(r,u), $\eta(r,u)$ is the heuristic value(the inverse of the distance of node r and u).

$$s = \begin{cases} \arg \max\limits_{u \in J_k(r)} \left\{ [\tau(r,u)] \cdot [\eta(r,u)]^{\beta} \right\} & , if\ q \leq q_0\ (exploitation) \\ S & , otherwise\ (exploration) \end{cases} \tag{1}$$

$J_k(r)$ is the set of cities that will be visited by ant k positioned on node r (to make the solution feasible), β is a parameter which determines the relative importance of pheromone versus distance (β<0). Q and q_0 is random number in [0..1]. S is a random variable selected according to the probability distribution given in Fig.2.

The parameter q_0 determines the relative importance of exploitation versus exploration: Every time an ant in node r has to choose a city u to move to, it samples a random number $0 \leq q \leq 1$. If $q \leq q_0$ then the best edge is chosen exploitation, otherwise an edge is chosen according to Eq.1.(biased exploration)

Fig.2 shows correlation between amount of pheromone and length of edge. In ACS, it selects next path using them.

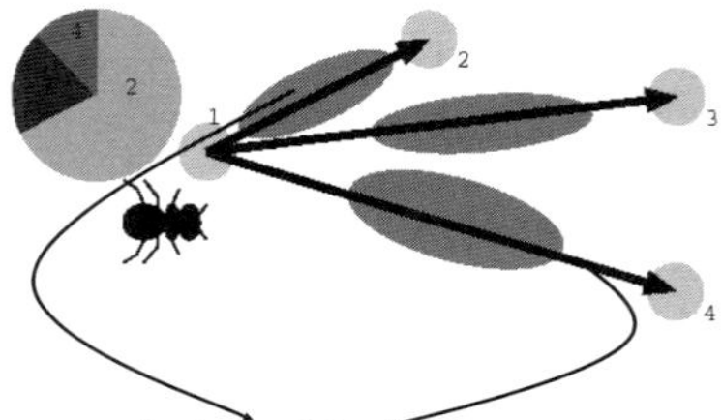

$$p_k(r,s) = \begin{cases} \dfrac{[\tau(r,s)]\cdot[\eta(r,s)]^{\beta}}{\sum_{u \in J_k(r)} [\tau(r,u)]\cdot[\eta(r,u)]^{\beta}} & \text{if } s \in J_k(r) \\ 0 & \text{otherwise} \end{cases}$$

Fig. 2. Correlation between amount of pheromone and length of edge in state transition process

2.2 ACS Local Updating Rule

While building a solution, ants visit edges and changes their pheromone level by applying the local updating rule of Eq.2.

$$\tau(r,s) \leftarrow (1-\rho)\cdot\tau(r,s) + \rho\cdot\Delta\tau(r,s) \tag{2}$$

ρ is pheromone decay parameter. $\Delta\tau$(r,s)=τ_0=$(n * L_{nn})^{-1}$ is the pheromone updating value about selected edge. N is the number of node, L_{nn} is the length of the best tour in the current iteration of the trial[3].

2.3 ACS Global Updating Rule

In ACS only the globally best ant is allowed to deposit pheromone. Global updating is performed after all ants have completed their tours. The pheromone is updated by global updating rule of Eq.3.

$$\begin{aligned} &\tau(r,s) \leftarrow (1-\alpha)\cdot\tau(r,s) + \alpha\cdot\Delta\tau(r,s) \\ &where\ \ \Delta\tau(r,s) = \begin{cases} (L_{gb})^{-1} & ,if(r,s) \in global\,best\,tour \\ 0 & ,otherwise \end{cases} \end{aligned} \tag{3}$$

$\alpha(0<\alpha<1)$ is the pheromone decay parameter, L_{gb} is the length of the globally best tour from the beginning of the trail[3].

3 The Modified Pheromone Updating Method in Local Updating Rule

Each ants search the path by pheromone information accumulating on edge between cities in ACS. Therefore it is the most important problem how does pheromone update for edge between visited cities. That is, ants must be able to visit about edges that were not visited as well as good path.

At past, we performed the method that divided the tours made by ants into superiors and inferiors, and applied weights based on the global update rule, increasing the selection probability of better edges.[7] This method showed better results than the current ACS when the number of nodes is small. However, as when the number of nodes is large, the output may not shows better than those of existing ACS. The reason was lacking of consideration about property between node and fixed criteria in separation the superiors from the inferiors.

Thus, pheromone updating gives fixed value about edge that is visited by ants in existent study. It is a value that have established in searching process beginning. The fluid pheromone updating method by circumstance should be applied in search processing. Because it is not equal to the relations between node. Therefore, this paper considered property between node for pheromone updating in local updating rule. That is, it did to become more efficient search utilizing distance between visited nodes and the number of visiting times to pheromone information.

The pheromone accumulating on edges gives to increase the selection probability in next search about better path. Therefore, we reflected edge's property using distance between visited nodes. If distance information between nodes is used without transformation, the pheromone value of particular edge may soar. To prevent these problems, we used an inverse number for distance between nodes. It avoided that search falls in local optimization by early convergence. Also, we applied an inverse number about the number of visiting of edge to pheromone updating value. The reason is to serve to do various search by nodes that is not visited increase possibility to be selected on next search time.

Thus, we could find better solution without falling in local optimization by taking advantage of information that can reflect property between visited nodes. Figure 3 shows local updating rule considering the properties between nodes.

4 Experiments and Result

The experiment environment for the suggested method is Windows XP and program was written by C-language. Test data was used after being extracted 9 data from TSPLIB[8] that is spread by TSP example. Proposed method is run for 100,000 iterations using 10 ants. The results are averaged over 10 trials. We

```
Procedure Modified Local Updating Rule
  begin
  BeCityLength[r_k][s_k]
  /* distance between node r_k and s_k */
  NumOfEdge[r_k][s_k]
  /*search frequency of edge between node r_k and s_k */
  P(r_k, s_k) = P(r_k, s_k) + ((1/BeCityLength[r_k][s_k])*(1/NumOfEdge[r_k][s_k]))
  end;
```

Fig. 3. The modified local updating rule considering properties between nodes

compare proposed method with existing ACS method about average path search length and best path length.

Fig.4 shows best solution search process of kroA200 among data to use in experiment. What is shown in dotted line is for the existing ACS algorithm, and the solid line is for proposed method. X-axis is the number of path search times for optimal solution search, Y-axis displays best tour length's change that each ant produces.

We can see that proposed method searches better solution than existing ACS in graph. In graph's gradient, existing ACS is shown fast convergence in beginning but become slow to search best solution as search frequency increases. In case that use modified local updating rule, early convergence is not achieved than existent ACS. However, proposed method update the best solution steadily as search frequency increases. That is, it reflected more property between nodes by considering distance and search frequency of relevant edge for pheromone updating of searched edge. As a result, we could obtain better solution.

Table 1 displays the experiment result about existing ACS and proposed method. The Average Len. is average path length and Best Len. is best path

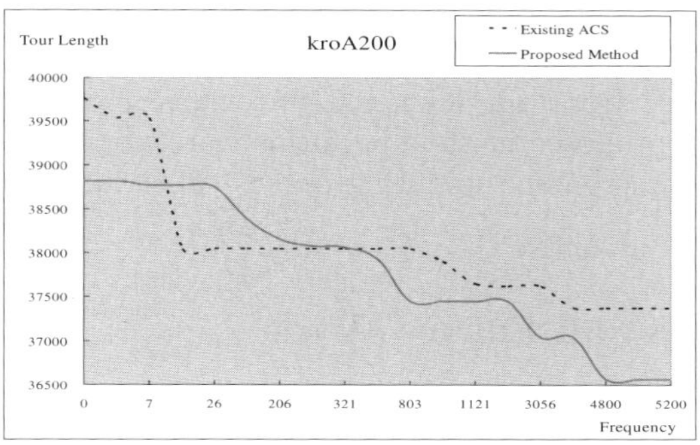

Fig. 4. Comparison existing ACS with the modified method kroA200

Table 1. Comparison existing ACS with the modified method

	Existing ACS			Proposed Method		
Data Set	Average	Best	Frequency	Average	Best	Frequency
Att48	38367.2	37909.5	12947	38022.9	37613.8	2615
Rat60	828.6	825.5	5411	814.8	802.7	6880
KroA100	26366.1	26087.9	3336	26123.4	25910.9	3198
LIN105	17745.3	17589.8	1308	17572.7	17403.6	5013
PR152	84923.2	82757.8	4317	83503.2	81363.4	1144
RAT195	2845.3	2829.8	5152	2824.8	2772.2	350
KroA200	38301.7	37369.3	3465	37003.3	36567.9	4800
TSP225	4911.17	4889.67	2174	4879.19	4806.6	8215
GIL262	3004.18	3001.05	431	2978.26	2964.9	1090

Table 2. The improvement rate of proposed method for existing ACS

Data Set	Performance(%)
Att48	0.78
KroA100	0.67
LIN105	1.05
PR152	1.68
RAT195	2.03
KroA200	2.14
TSP225	1.69
GIL262	1.20

length struck in all search process. Freq. is the number of search times of ants to find best solution out of 100,000 iterations.

Table 1 report that proposed method has better result. Search frequency that takes to find best solution is difference according to file. For all data set, performance of proposed method improves average path length 1.64% and optimal path length 1.43%

Table 2 shows improved performance rate in best solution search of proposed method than existent ACS. We could see that search performance by proposed method be improved from minimum 0.67% to maximum 2.14% than existent ACS. It shows that proposed method performs more efficient search by reflecting more property for pheromone updating and is effective in ACS's performance improvement.

5 Conclusions and Future Work

Existing ACS uses fixed pheromone information but this paper proposed modified pheromone updating considering the property about the edge between nodes that ants visited.

The local updating rule in existent ACS is applying initial value equally about visited edge at whole searching process. That is, it uses pheromone updating method that does not consider property between visited nodes. But it is necessary to use flexible pheromone updating method according to distance between nodes rather than fixed pheromone value about visited edges. Also, we gave pheromone value that can reflect search frequency about relevant edge as well as distance between nodes to find best solution.

Proposed method modified the pheromone updating method so that can increased visit opportunity about node of short distance and edge that search frequency are less in next cycle. As a result, convergence speed to best solution is slower than existent ACS.

However, according as search frequency increases, we could know that proposed method was searching best path without falling to local optima. Improved search performance differs gradually to used data set. However, all data set's search performance was improved about average 1.4% than existent ACS.

We expect that if we apply the additional information to various and efficient best solution search, we may achieve better results in the future.

References

1. Freisleben, B., Merz, P.: Genetic local search algorithm for solving symmetric and asymmetric traveling salesman problems. In: Proceedings of IEEE International Conference of Evolutionary Computation. IEEE-EC 96, pp. 616–621. IEEE Press, New York (1996)
2. Colorni, A., Dorigo, M., Maniezzo, V.: Distributed optimization by ant colonies. In: Varela, F., Bourgine, P. (eds.) Proceedings of ECAL91-European Conference of Artificial Life, Paris, France, pp. 134–144. Elsevier Publishing, Amsterdam (1991)
3. Gambardella, L.M., Dorigo, M.: Ant Colony System: A Cooperative Learning approach to the Traveling Salesman Problem. IEEE Transactions on Evolutionary Computation, 1(1) (1997)
4. Dorigo, M., Gambardella, L.M.: Ant Colonies for the Traveling Salesman Problem. BioSystems, 73–81 (1997)
5. Dorigo, M., Caro, G.D.: Ant Algorithms for Discrete Optimization. Artificial Life 5(3), 137–172 (1999)
6. Dorigo, M., Maniezzo, V., Colorni, A.: The ant system: optimization by a colony of cooperation agents. IEEE Transactions of Systems, Man, and Cybernetics-Part B 26(2), 29–41 (1996)
7. Lee, S.G., Jung, T.U., Chung, T.C.: Improved Ant Agents System by the Dynamic Parameter Decision. In: Proceedings of IEEE International Conference on FUZZ-IEEE 2001, pp. 666–669. IEEE Press, New York (2001)
8. `http://www.iwr.uni-heidelberg.de/groups/comopt/software/TSPLIB95`

Secure and Efficient Trust Negotiation*

Fuchun Guo[1], Zhide Chen[1], Yi Mu[2], Li Xu[1], and Shengyuan Zhang[1]

[1] Key Lab of Network Security and Cryptology
School of Mathematics and Computer Science
Fujian Normal University, Fuzhou, China
fuchunguo1982@163.com,
{zhidechen,xuli,syzhang}@fjnu.edu.cn

[2] School of Computer Science and Software Engineering
University of Wollongong, Wollongong, NSW 2522, Australia
ymu@uow.edu.au

Abstract. The notion of Hidden Credentials can be applied to protection of sensitive credentials, resources and policies in Trust Negotiation. It allows the server to encrypt a resource so that only the client with the correct credentials can decrypt it. The existing scheme of hidden credentials requires that the server grant access to the encrypted resource directly to the client during the negotiation without knowing whether or not the client can decrypt it. It would be a burden if the resources were very large. We found that when the server grants access to services rather than resources, the existing hidden credentials schemes are insecure under our *policy attacks*, since the server can illegally learn the client's credentials from the attack. In this paper, we propose a scheme to stop the server from mounting a policy attack.

1 Introduction

In Trust Negotiation, two strange parties can exchange digital credentials that contain some attributes of information for access control. Hidden Credential stems from the paradigm of Trust Negotiation [8,9,10], which guards sensitive resources by attribute-based policies that can be fulfilled by publicly verifiable digital credentials issued by some third party.

Conceptually, a trust negotiation problem is given as follows. Let us denote by Alice and Bob the participants, where Alice is the client and Bob is the server. Bob grants access to sensitive resources to his clients who have the correct credentials. Because of the sensitivity, Bob does not want to reveal his policies in order to protect his sensitive resources. Alice has a correct credential, but she doesn't want to disclose her credential to Bob. Some recent works [7,5,3] have performed this type of attribute-based access controls for protecting Alice's credentials and Bob's policies . Based on identity-based encryption (IBE) in [1], it is not hard to achieve hidden credentials.

* This work is partially supported by the Fund of National Natural Science Foundation of China (#60502047), Education Bureau of Fujian Province (#JB05329), and the Science and Technology of Fujian Province (2006F5036).

Y. Wang, Y. Cheung, and H. Liu (Eds.): CIS 2006, LNAI 4456, pp. 374–384, 2007.

In hidden credential, Bob encrypts a resource in such a way that Alice can decrypt it if she has the right credentials [7], where the encryption key is Bob's policy and the decryption key is Alice's credential. There are three key properties in a hidden credential system:

1. Protection of Alice's sensitive credentials. Bob never sees Alice's credential and never knows whether Alice can access the resource.
2. Protection of Bob's sensitive policies. When Bob encrypts his resource that Alice needs, Alice can decrypt it if her credential matches one of Bob's policies. If not, she will learn nothing about Bob's resource.
3. Protection of Bob's sensitive resources. The encrypted resource is not usable if one does not have the right credential; therefore, the resources are hidden safely.

1.1 Related Work and Analysis

Based on Boneh-Franklin's IBE [1], Holt *et al* introduced the notion of hidden credentials [7]. They gave a formal description of hidden credentials and gave an application of hidden credentials. Frikken *et al* later improved computational efficiency of hidden credential decryption and enhanced security with a secret splitting scheme [3].

The existing schemes of hidden credentials can protect privacy of both Alice and Bob. Assuming that Bob does not grant access to services but resources, Bob never knows whether Alice can access to resources she requested. Frikken *et al* showed this drawback in [6]. In practice, the server could grant access to services rather than resources. It means that the server determines whether a client can access to a resource or not but doesn't transmit the resource to the client directly.

In hidden credentials, Alice can protect her credentials and Bob can protect his policies. However, it could be the case that Alice would only learn part of policies if she had decrypted the ciphertext from Bob. In [6], the situation is improved that Alice cannot learn Bob's credentials and policies and Bob can not learn Alice's credentials and policies (in the case of mutual negotiation). Furthermore, Alice can not learn any policy even if she has accessed the resource, because which credential satisfies which Bob's policy is indistinguishable to her.

Although the scheme in [6] offers better privacy protection than the other schemes of hidden credentials, we found that Alice can learn Bob's policies when she requests to access a resource repeatedly. For example, let Alice's credentials be $\{C_1, C_2, C_3, C_4\}$ and she can access a resource with the credentials in the first trust negotiation, but she does not know which credential satisfies Bob's policy. Then, Alice can request another access to the same resource with a subset of $\{C_1, C_2, C_3, C_4\}$, if she can access the resource with $\{C_1, C_2\}$ and $\{C_2, C_3\}$ but not with $\{C_1, C_3\}$, Alice learns that the credential C_2 must satisfy Bob's policy, therefore Bob's policy leaks.

Based on the scenario that Bob grants services, there will be another private problem we have to address. If Alice can access a resource, Bob learns that her credentials satisfy his policies (does not know which one). Alice's credentials can be hidden from Bob when Bob's policies are a large set. For a small set of policies, Bob will then have a better chance to guess Alice's credentials. Therefore, to mount an attack, Bob can set his policies with a lot of random strings such that they are indistinguishable to Alice. Actually, there could be only one Bob's policy matches with a credential. If Alice had accessed the resource with the correct credential, she would reveal her credential to Bob (so-called perilous policy attacks). For example, Bob can set his policies $P_{Bob} = P_1 \vee P_2 \vee P_3$ which matches with the credential C_1, C_2, or C_3, but the credentials C_2 and C_3 do not exist at all (according to Bob's setting). If Alice can access to the resource, Bob learns that Alice must possess the credential C_1.

We found that the flaw of the schemes in [7,3,6] is due to the fact that Alice cannot verify Bob's policies. Therefore, we propose an approach of zero-knowledge proof to Bob's policies, where Alice can verify whether Bob has mounted a policy attack but knows nothing about Bob's policies.

1.2 Our Contributions

We propose a novel scheme of hidden credentials which can protect Alice's credentials from policy attacks in the following scenarios:

- Alice's credentials can be hidden: Bob never learns her credentials accurately but only knows her credentials satisfy his policies.
- Bob's policies can be hidden: Alice never learns his policies without right credentials but only knows part of Bob's policies which her credentials satisfy.
- User Anonymity: Bob does not know who accesses a resource.
- Service-oriented: Bob grants access to services and knows whether a client can access the corresponding resource or not.

2 Definitions and Notations

Bilinear Pairing. Let $\mathbb{G}_1$ be (additive) cyclic group of prime order q. Let P, Q be a generator of $\mathbb{G}_1$. A map $\hat{e} : \mathbb{G}_1 \times \mathbb{G}_1 \rightarrow \mathbb{G}_2$ (here $\mathbb{G}_2$ is a multiplicative group such that $|\mathbb{G}_1| = |\mathbb{G}_2| = q$) is called a bilinear pairing if this map satisfies the following properties:

- Bilinear: for all $P, Q \in \mathbb{G}_1$ and $a, b \in \mathbb{Z}_p$, we have $\hat{e}(aP, bQ) = \hat{e}(P, Q)^{ab}$.
- Non-degeneracy: $\hat{e}(P, P) \neq 1$. In other words, if P be a generator of $\mathbb{G}_1$, then $\hat{e}(P, P)$ generates $\mathbb{G}_2$.
- Computability: There is an efficient algorithm to compute $\hat{e}(P, Q)$ for all $P, Q \in \mathbb{G}_1$.

ID-Based Encryption (IBE)
Setup. Input a security parameter 1^k to algorithm $\mathcal{G}$ and output the common parameters *params* and the master-key s.

$$params = \langle q, \mathbb{G}_1, \mathbb{G}_2, \hat{e}, n, P, P_{pub}, H_1, H_2.H_3, H_4 \rangle$$

where P is a generator of $\mathbb{G}_1$, and $\langle \mathbb{G}_1, \mathbb{G}_2, \hat{e} \rangle$ is the bilinear pairing. The message space is $M = \{0,1\}^n$ and $P_{pub} = sP$. $H_1, H_2.H_3, H_4$ are cryptographic hash functions:$H_1 : \{0,1\}^* \rightarrow \mathbb{G}_1$; $H_2 : \mathbb{G}_2 \rightarrow \{0,1\}^n$; $H_3 : \{0,1\}^n \times \{0,1\}^n \rightarrow \mathbb{Z}_q^*$; $H_4 : \{0,1\}^n \rightarrow \{0,1\}^n$.

Extract. For a given string $ID \in \{0,1\}^*$, (1) compute $Q_{ID} = H_1(ID) \in \mathbb{G}_1$, (2) set the private key d_{ID} to be $d_{ID} = sQ_{ID}$ where s is the master-key.

Encrypt. To encrypt $M \in \{0,1\}^n$ under the public key ID, (1) compute $Q_{ID} = H_1(ID) \in \mathbb{G}_1$, (2) choose a random $\sigma \in \{0,1\}^n$, (3)set $r = H_3(\sigma, M)$, the ciphertext is

$$\langle U, V, W \rangle = \langle rP, \sigma \oplus H_2(g_{ID}^r), H_4(\sigma) \oplus M \rangle, \quad g_{ID} = \hat{e}(Q_{ID}, P_{pub}) \in \mathbb{G}_2$$

Decrypt. Let $\langle U, V, W \rangle$ be a ciphertext encrypted using the public key ID. If $U \notin \mathbb{G}_1^*$, abort. To decrypt $\langle U, V, W \rangle$ with the private-key $d_{ID} \in \mathbb{G}_1$, (1) compute $V \oplus H_2(\hat{e}(d_{ID}, U)) = \sigma$, (2) compute $W \oplus H_4(\sigma) = M$, (3) and set $r = H_3(\sigma, M)$. Check if $U = rP$. If not, abort. Output M as the decryption of $\langle U, V, W \rangle$.

Policy and Credential. Using ID-Based Encryption, ID denotes a Policy and private key d_{ID} as a Credential. In our paper, we denote by P_i a policy and by C_i a corresponding credential. Hidden credentials will be achieved by the policy(ID)-based encryption.

Simple Policy. A simple policy consists of a set of attributes. For example, an attribute could be "president" or "dean". If a resource is encrypted with a simple policy, the ciphertext can be decrypted with an associated credential matching the policy.

Complex Policy. A complex policy consists of multiple simple policies with monotonic Boolean function $\vee$ and $\wedge$. For example, A complex policy could be defined as $P_{Bob} = P_1 \vee (P_2 \wedge P_3) \vee (P_4 \wedge P_5)$. In order to access Bob's resources, Alice's credentials must include $\{C_1\}$, $\{C_2, C_3\}$, or $\{C_4, C_5\}$, which match Bob's policies. For example, if Alice has credentials $\{C_1, C_2\}$, she will be granted with access to the corresponding resource, but rejected if she only has credentials $\{C_2, C_4\}$.

One-Time Password (OTP). The OTP is randomly chosen by Bob and can be used only once. If a client requests to access a resource, Bob will randomly choose an OTP encrypted with his policies. If the client can send the OTP back to Bob, the client is granted with an access to the resource.

Simple Encryption (SE). The ciphertext of SE is the tuple:

$$\langle U, V, W \rangle = \langle rP_{gene}, \sigma \oplus H_2(g_{p_i}^r), H_4(\sigma) \oplus M \rangle$$

where P_{gene} is a generator of $\mathbb{G}_1$ and M is a message that contains OTP. The ciphertext is encrypted with policy P_i and can only be decrypted with C_i. So, if Bob's policy is $P_{Bob} = P_{president}$, Alice will reveal her credential $C_{president}$ when she can decrypt the ciphertext.

Complex Encryption (CE). For $P_{Bob} = (P_1 \wedge P_2) \vee P_3 \vee P_4$, the ciphertext of CE is the tuple:

$$\langle U, V_1, V_2, V_3, W\rangle = \langle rP_{gene}, \sigma \oplus H_2(g^r_{p_1}) \oplus H_2(g^r_{p_2}), \sigma \oplus H_2(g^r_{p_3}),$$
$$\sigma \oplus H_2(g^r_{p_4}), H_4(\sigma) \oplus M\rangle$$

M is encrypted with a diversity of policies and can be decrypted with a diversity of credentials too. In CE, Alice decrypts M from one of V_i, therefore her credentials are indistinguishable to Bob if he encrypted OTP honestly. However, in practice Bob must be able to prove security against a policy attack.

Claim 1. *Complex Encryption cannot be used for hidden credentials directly.*

Proof. If Alice knows r after decryption, then she can suppose a policy P_s in P_{Bob} and verify it by computing $g^r_{P_s} = \hat{e}(Q_{P_s}, P_{pub})^r$ and checking $\sigma \oplus H_2(g^{rr_0}_{P_s}) \stackrel{?}{=} V_i$. Bob's policies will be learnt by Alice after verification.

If r is unknown to Alice, there will be a policy attack mounted by Bob for that Alice is unable to verify whether there are other credentials can decrypt the ciphertext. So, CE cannot be used for hidden credentials directly. □

Trust Parameters (TP). Each TP has a parameter TP_{P_i} and a signature STP_{P_i} which can prove that the policy P_i in the parameter is valid. The parameter is set by $TP_{P_i} = g^{r_0}_{P_i} = \hat{e}(Q_{P_i}, P_{pub})^{r_0}$, where r_0 is secretly chosen by Bob; the signature is set by $STP_{P_i} = Sgn(H_2(r_0 P_{gene}, g^{r_0}_{P_i}))$. So, if Bob shows $r_0 P_{gene}$, TP_{P_i} and STP_{P_i} to Alice, she will learn nothing but the policy P_i in TP_{P_i} is valid (see section 4 for detail analysis).

Notations

PKG: the trusted third party who sets all policies $\mathbf{P_{PKG}}$ and issues all credentials and TP.

D_{Sgn}: the public key which can verify the signature STP_{P_i} of TP_{P_i}.

σ^*: a fixed bit and $\sigma^* = 1^t$ for some constant t. It is used to help Alice make a judgement of correct decryption.

R_{Bob}: an OTP randomly chosen by Bob.

S_{TP}: the intersection of two sets. One is computed by Bob through his policies, the other is computed by Alice through TP.

N_{Alice}: the minimum numbers of valid policies, in which Alice can ensure that her credentials are indistinguishable to Bob.

3 Our Scheme

In this section, we present our novel scheme that is secure against the policy attack.

Parameter Phase

Step 1. The PKG sets the *params*:

$$params = \langle q, \mathbb{G}_1, \mathbb{G}_2, \hat{e}, t, n, P_{gene}, P_{pub}, \sigma^*, D_{Sgn}, H_1, H_2, H_3, H_4\rangle$$

The *params* is the same as in the IBE. In addition, we pick $\sigma^* = 1^t$ and a public key D_{Sgn} for verifying TP.

Step 2. The user transmits his/her identity credential and P_i to the PKG in security. The PKG verifies the credential and P_i. If the user qualifies to possess C_i, the PKG computes $Q_{P_i} = H_1(P_i) \in \mathbb{G}_1$, $C_i = sQ_{P_i}$ and transmits C_i to the user.

Trust Parameters
Step 1. Bob computes $r_0 P_{gene}$ and transmits $r_0 P_{gene}, P_1, P_2, \cdots, P_k$ to the PKG, where $P_1, P_2, \cdots, P_k$ are Bob's policies.

Step 2. The PKG checks $P_1, P_2, \cdots, P_k \overset{?}{\in} P_{PKG}$. If $P_1, P_2, \cdots, P_k$ are valid, the PKG computes STP_{P_i} of $TP_{P_i} = \hat{e}(Q_{P_i}, r_0 P_{gene})^s = \hat{e}(Q_{P_i}, r_0 P_{pub})$ for all policies and transmits the signatures to Bob.

Request
Step 1. Alice makes an access "*request*" to Bob.

Step 2. If Bob's policies are $P_{Bob} = P_1 \vee P_2 \cdots \vee P_k$, Bob does the following:

- Compute $Q_{P_i} = H_1(P_i) \in \mathbb{G}_1, i \in \{1, 2, \cdots, k\}$;
- Choose a random $\sigma' \in \{0,1\}^{n-t}$ and set the σ with $\sigma = \sigma^* \| \sigma' \in \{0,1\}^n$;
- Compute $r = H_3(\sigma, M)$, $M = R_{Bob} || r_0 P_{gene} || TP_{P_i} || STP_{P_i}, i = 1, 2, \cdots, k$.
- Compute $g_{P_i} = \hat{e}(Q_{P_i}, P_{pub}) \in \mathbb{G}_2, i \in \{1, 2, \cdots, k\}$.

Set the ciphertext $HC_E(P_{Bob})$ to be the tuple:

$$HC_E(P_{Bob}) = \langle rr_0 P_{gene}, \sigma \oplus H_2(g_{p_1}^{rr_0}), \sigma \oplus H_2(g_{p_2}^{rr_0}), \cdots, \sigma \oplus H_2(g_{p_k}^{rr_0}), H_4(\sigma) \oplus M \rangle$$

Step 3. Alice receives the ciphertext $HC_E(P_{Bob}) = \langle U, V_1, V_2, \cdots, V_k, W \rangle$ from Bob. Assume that Alice has a credential of C_m. Alice does the following:

- Compute $\hat{e}(C_m, U) = \hat{e}(sQ_m, rr_0 P_{gene}) = \hat{e}(Q_{P_m}, P_{pub})^{rr_0} = g_{P_m}^{rr_0}$;
- Compute $V_1 \oplus H_2(g_{P_m}^{rr_0}) = \sigma$;
- Check: If $\sigma = \sigma^* \| \sigma'$, then compute $M = W \oplus H_4(\sigma)$, $r = H_3(\sigma, M)$ and output M as the decryption when $U = r \cdot r_0 P_{gene}$; otherwise desert V_1 and compute $V_2 \oplus H_2(g_{P_m}^{rr_0}) = \sigma$ with V_2, until V_k.

If Alice cannot do the decryption, she has to stop the negotiation, Bob then is unable to receive R_{Bob} from Alice and stops negotiation. Consequently, Alice fails to access to the resource. If Alice can decrypt it with C_m, she continues the verification process:

- Verify all TP_{P_i} in M with $r_0 P_{gene}$, STP_{P_i} and D_{PKG};
- Compute $(TP_{P_i})^r = \left(\hat{e}(Q_{P_i}, P_{pub})^{r_0}\right)^r, i \in \{1, 2, \cdots, k\}$ with r.
- Compute $V_i' = \sigma \oplus H_2\left((TP_{P_i})^r\right), i \in \{1, 2, \cdots, k\}$;
- Compute the intersection of two sets:

$$S_{TP} = \{V_1', V_2', \cdots V_k'\} \cap \{V_1, V_2, \cdots V_k\}$$

If $|S_{TP}| < N_{Alice}$, stop the negotiation; else, continue the process.

Response Phase
Alice gets R_{Bob} from M and transmit it to Bob. Bob checks whether R_{Bob} is correct or not. If not, Bob will reject Alice's request, else she is granted with the corresponding resource.

Explanations
With no decryption effort at all, any client(without credentials) knows how many policies in $HC_E(P_{Bob})$ from $\langle V_1, V_2, \cdots, V_k \rangle$. Bob can use dummy policy to hide his policies. For instance, if $P_{Bob} = P_1 \vee P_2$, he can encrypt $HC_E(P_{Bob})$ with $P_{Bob} = P_1 \vee P_2 \vee P_{*3} \vee P_{*4}$ where P_{*i} are not exist at all.

Trust Parameters can be used repeatedly. The policy in TP_{P_i} is hidden from Alice (we will analyse it in section 4). So, Bob can get TP from the PKG only once and use it repeatedly.

4 Security Analysis

We present three computational hard problems here on which the security of IBE and our scheme is based.

(1) Discrete Logarithm Problem (DL). Given two elements $P, Q \in \mathbb{G}_1$,find an integer $\alpha \in \mathbb{Z}_q^*$ such that $Q = \alpha P$ whenever such an integer exists.
(2) Computational Diffie-Hellman Problem (CDH). Given $\langle P, aP, bP \rangle$ for some unknown $a, b \in \mathbb{Z}_q^*$ where P is a generator of $\mathbb{G}_1$, compute abP.
(3) Bilinear Diffie-Hellman Problem (BDH). Given $\langle P, aP, bP, cP \rangle$ for some unknown $a, b, c \in \mathbb{Z}_q^*$ where P is a generator of $\mathbb{G}_1$, compute $W = \hat{e}(P, P)^{abc} \in \mathbb{G}_2$.

4.1 Security Analysis of the Policy(ID)-Based Encryption

In the hidden credentials, the client cannot get any help of decryption from the server. Because of this, the policy(ID)-based encryption secure against IND-ID-CPA (semantically secure against an adaptive chosen plaintext attack) will be enough for the application.

Claim 2. *The tuple of $HC_E(P_{Bob})$ is the same to the tuple in the Boneh-Franklin's IBE scheme. So, $HC_E(P_{Bob})$ is secure against IND-ID-CPA.*

Proof. In our hidden credentials scheme, the parameters and the ciphertext are:

$$params = \langle q, \mathbb{G}_1, \mathbb{G}_2, \hat{e}, t, n, P_{gene}, P_{pub}, \sigma^*, D_{Sgn}, H_1, H_2, H_3, H_4 \rangle$$

$$HC_E(P_{Bob}) = \langle rr_0 P_{gene}, \sigma \oplus H_2(g_{p_1}^{rr_0}), \sigma \oplus H_2(g_{p_2}^{rr_0}), \cdots, \sigma \oplus H_2(g_{p_k}^{rr_0}), H_4(\sigma) \oplus M \rangle$$

Set $r' = rr_0$, because r is a random value from $\mathbb{Z}_q^*$, r' is a random value from $\mathbb{Z}_q^*$ too. The ciphertext of $HC_E(P_{Bob})$ is same as the following:

$$HC_{E'}(P_{Bob}) = \langle r' P_{gene}, \sigma \oplus H_2(g_{p_1}^{r'}), \sigma \oplus H_2(g_{p_2}^{r'}), \cdots, \sigma \oplus H_2(g_{p_k}^{r'}), H_4(\sigma) \oplus M \rangle$$

Following the **Theorem 1** in [3], $HC_{E'}(P_{Bob})$ is as secure as a simple encryption:

$$\langle r' P_{gene}, \sigma \oplus H_2(g_{p_i}^{r'}), H_4(\sigma) \oplus M \rangle \quad (1)$$

where (1) is secure (IND-ID-CPA) in the Boneh-Franklin's IBE scheme. So, our policy(ID)-based encryption is secure against IND-ID-CPA. □

4.2 Security Analysis of the Policy Attack

Claim 3. *Bob's policies are hidden from Alice.*

Proof. Even if Alice can decrypt the $HC_E(P_{Bob})$ with C_m and get $r_0 P_{gene}$ (Let $g = P_{gene}$ and $h = r_0 P_{gene}$), the CDH problem still holds. So r_0 is hidden from Alice.

For $\{P, Q_{P_s}, P_{pub}, r_0 P\}$ (P_s is a policy supposed by Alice without the credential C_{P_s}), the BDH problem holds. So, Alice cannot compute $g_{P_s}^{r_0} = \hat{e}(Q_{P_s}, P_{pub})^{r_0}$ to verify $g_{P_s}^{r_0} \overset{?}{\in}$ TP.

With σ and r, Alice can verify $\sigma \oplus H_2(g_{P_s}^{rr_0}) \overset{?}{\in} \{V_1, V_2, V_3, \cdots, V_k\}$ iff she can compute $g_{P_s}^{r_0}$. From the above, We know that Alice will fail to verify.

Claim 4. *Our scheme is secure against Bob's policy attacks (Alice's credentials are hidden from Bob).*

Proof. In Boneh-Franklin's IBE scheme, the pairing g_{ID}^r can be computed by double ways:

$$g_{ID}^r = \hat{e}(Q_{ID}, P_{pub})^r \quad \text{(for encryption)}$$

$$g_{ID}^r = \hat{e}(sQ_{ID}, rP) = \hat{e}(d_{ID}, U) \quad \text{(for decryption)}$$

In our scheme, we extend the pairing $g_{P_i}^{rr_0}$ to three ways:

$$g_{P_i}^{rr_0} = \hat{e}(Q_{P_i}, P_{pub})^{rr_0} \quad \text{(for encryption)}$$

$$g_{P_i}^{rr_0} = \hat{e}(sQ_{P_i}, rr_0 P) = \hat{e}(C_i, U) \quad \text{(for decryption)}$$

$$g_{P_i}^{rr_0} = \left(\hat{e}(Q_{P_i}, P_{pub})^{r_0}\right)^r = (TP_{P_i})^r \quad \text{(for verification)}$$

The ciphertext of $HC_E(P_{Bob})$ is the tuple: $\langle U, V_1, V_2, \cdots, V_k, W \rangle$, where $V_i = \sigma \oplus H_2(g_{p_i}^{rr_0})$. So, a policy P_i in V_i is valid iff:

$$\sigma \oplus H_2(g_{p_i}^{rr_0}) = V_i = V_i' = \sigma \oplus H_2((TP_{P_i})^r)$$

From the above analysis, the number of policies are valid in $HC_E(P_{Bob})$ can be learned from S_{TP}. Because Bob cannot forge a signature of dummy policy, then it is impossible for Bob to mount an attack from policies. Alice's credentials are hidden from Bob for that she can learn S_{TP} and decides to continue or not.

5 Extension

A hidden credentials scheme is achieved by policy(ID)-based encryption, but it is not more efficient than the Boneh-Franklin's IBE scheme. Because there are so many policies and Alice doesn't know which one she should use but has to try one by one.

The impact to efficiency is twofold: one is to find the right V_i and the other is to verify all the trust parameters TP_{P_i}. We use a fixed string σ^* to improve the efficiency to find the right V_i. Here, we propose a way to compact the verification.

5.1 Accumulator

An accumulator scheme is an algorithm that allows one to hash a large set of inputs into one short value, called the accumulator. In an accumulator scheme, a (short) witness that a given input was incorporated into the accumulator. At the same time, it is infeasible to find a witness for a value that was not accumulated.

Accumulator was introduced by Benaloh and de Mare [2]. The original accumulator is not *dynamic*, in the sense that an accumulator cannot be dynamically updated. In 2002, Camenisch and Lysyanskaya [4] proposed a dynamic accumulator, which shows a better applicability. We will use a dynamic accumulator scheme proposed by Camenisch and Lysyanskaya to compact the verification.

Definition 5.1 *A secure accumulator is a family of functions* $f : X \times Y \to X$ *with the following properties:*

Efficient generation: There is an efficient probabilistic algorithm $\mathcal{G}$ that on input 1^k produces a function $f : X \times Y \to X$.
Efficient evaluation: on input $(x, y) \in X \times Y$, it's efficient to compute $f(x, y)$.
Quasi-commutative: $f(f(x, y_1), y_2) = f(f(x, y_2), y_1)(\forall x \in X, \forall y_1, y_2 \in Y)$
Witnesses: Let $z \in X$ and $y \in Y$, A value w is called a witness for y in z under f if $z = f(w, y)$.
Security: For any probabilistic, polynomial-time algorithm $\mathcal{A}$:

$$\mathsf{Pr}[x \leftarrow X; y \leftarrow Y; (x', y') \leftarrow \mathcal{A}(1^\lambda, f, x, y) : \\ y' \neq y \wedge f(x', y') = f(x, y)] < neg(k)$$

Construction

- On input 1^k to $\mathcal{G}$, output the function $f : X \times Y \to X$, such that: $X = \{x \in QR_n : x \neq 1\}$, where $n = pq$ and $p = 2p' + 1, q = 2q' + 1$, p, q, p', q' are all primes; $Y = \{e \in \textbf{primes} : e \neq p, q \wedge A \leq e \leq B\}$, where A and B can be chosen with arbitrary polynomial dependence on the security parameter k, as long as $2 < A$ and $B < A^2$.
- $f(x, y) = x^y \mod n$. Note that $f(f(x, y_1), y_2) = f(f(x, y_2), y_1) = x^{y_1 y_2}$.

According to the result of Camenisch and Lysyanskaya (Theorem 3 in [4]), the accumulator scheme is secure under the strong RSA assumption.

5.2 Application to Hidden Credentials

In the accumulator scheme, set $z = x^{y_1 y_2 \cdots y_k} \mod n$, where $x \in X$ and $y_1, y_2, \cdots, y_k \in Y$, it's hard for an attacker to forge x' and y'_i such that $z = (x')^{y'_1 y'_2 \cdots y'_k} \mod n$. Let $x = H_5(r_0 P_{gene})$ and $y_i = H_6(TP_{P_i})$, we know that if the PKG made a signature to z, where $z = x^{y_1 y_2 \cdots y_k} \mod n$, then it is hard for Bob to forge a TP under the strong RSA assumption.

Construction
The PKG sets the accumulator function $f : X \times Y \rightarrow X$ and keeps p, q secret. Let H_5, H_6 be two functions: $H_5 : \{0,1\}^* \rightarrow X$, $H_6 : \{0,1\}^* \rightarrow Y$.

Trust Parameters
Step 2.The PKG checks $P_1, P_2, \cdots, P_k \overset{?}{\in} P_{PKG}$. If $P_1, P_2, \cdots, P_k$ are valid, the PKG does the following:

- Compute $TP_{P_i} = \hat{e}(Q_{P_i}, r_0 P_{gene})^s = \hat{e}(Q_{P_i}, r_0 P_{pub})$ for all Bob's policies.
- Set $x = H_5(r_0 P_{gene})$, $y_i = H_6(TP_{P_i})$ and compute $z = x^{y_1 y_2 \cdots y_k} \mod n$.
- Compute the signature $Sgn(z)$ for z and transmit $Sgn(z)$ to Bob.

Request
Bob encrypts M where $M = R_{Bob} || z || Sgn(z) || r_0 P_{gene} || TP_{P_i}$
If Alice can decrypt it with C_m, she continues the verification process:

- Compute $x = H_5(r_0 P_{gene})$, $y_i = H_6(TP_{P_i})$, for all TP_{P_i} in M.
- Compute $z' = x^{y_1 y_2 \cdots y_k} \mod n$.
- Verify z' with $Sgn(z)$ and accept all TP_{P_i} if $z = z'$.

Explanations
If Bob can find a witness (w, y) such that $z = f(w, y)$, where Bob posses a signature $Sgn(z)$ from the PKG, Alice can learn that w is an accumulator of TP too. With the nice property of accumulator, in **Trust Parameters** phase, Bob can set his policies as large as he can but only chooses part of them as P_{Bob}. This will be convenient for both Bob and the PKG (Bob need not get a new signature for his new policy). E.g. if $z = x^{y_1 y_2 \cdots y_k} \mod n$ and $P_{Bob} = P_1 \vee P_2$, then Bob can set $w = x^{y_1 y_2} \mod n$ and $y = y_3 y_4 \cdots y_k \mod (p-1)(q-1)$, where $y_i = H_6(TP_{P_i})$. With the tuple of $(w, y, z, Sgn(z), TP_{P_1}, TP_{P_2})$, Alice learns that both TP_{P_1} and TP_{P_2} are trust parameters. When P_3 is added, Bob sets $(w', y', z, Sgn(z), TP_{P_1}, TP_{P_2}, TP_{P_3})$ as a proof for TP, where $w' = x^{y_1 y_2 y_3} \mod n$ and $y = y_4 \cdots y_k \mod (p-1)(q-1)$ (y should be computed by the PKG, who only knows the factorization of n).

6 Conclusion

We showed how a perilous attack in hidden credentials from the Bob's policy will reveal Alice's sensitive credentials. We proposed a novel scheme that is secure against the policy attack, using trust parameters. In our scheme, Alice can find whether Bob launched an attack and then decide if the resource access should be granted.

References

1. Boneh, D., Franklin, M.: Identity-Based Encryption from the Weil Pairing. In: Kilian, J. (ed.) Advances in Cryptology - CRYPTO 2001. LNCS, vol. 2139, Springer, Heidelberg (2001)
2. Benaloh, J., de Mare, M.: One-way accumulators: A decentralized alternative to digital signatures. In: Helleseth, T. (ed.) Advances in Cryptology - EUROCRYPT '93. LNCS, vol. 765, Springer, Heidelberg (1994)
3. Bradshaw, R., Holt, J., Seamons, K.: Concealing Complex Policies with Hidden Credentials. In: Proceedings of the 11th ACM Conference, pp. 146–157. ACM Press, New York (2004)
4. Camenisch, J., Lysyanskaya, A.: Dynamic accumulators and ap- plications to efficient revocation of anonymous credentials. In: Yung, M. (ed.) Advances in Cryptology - CRYPTO 2002. LNCS, vol. 2442, Springer, Heidelberg (2002)
5. Frikken, K.B., Atallah, M.J., Li, J.: Hidden access control policies with hidden crentials. In: Proceedings of Workshop on Privacy in the Electronic Society, pp. 27–28 (2004)
6. Frikken, K.B., Li, J., Atallah, M.: Trust Negotiation with hidden credentials, hidden policies, and policy cycles. In: Proceedings of 13th Annual Network and Distributed System Security Symposium (NDSS) ,California, pp. 157–172 (February 2006)
7. J.E. Holt, R. W. Bradshaw, K. E. Seamons, and H. Orman: Hidden credentials. In: Proceedings of the 2nd ACM Workshop on Privacy in the Electronic Society, Washington, DC. October 1-8, 2003 (2003)
8. Winsborough, W.H., Li, N.: Protecting Sensitive Attributes in Automated Trust Negotiation. In: Proceedings of ACM Workshop on Privacy in the Electronic Society, Washington, DC, 2002, pp. 41–51 2002
9. Winsborough, W.H., Li, N.: Towards Practical Trust Negotiation. In: Proceedings of the Third International Workshop on Policies for Distributed Systems and Networks (POLICY 2002), Monterey, California, pp. 92–103 (2002)
10. Winsborough, W.H., Seamons, K.E., Jones, V.E.: Automated Trust Negotiation. In: DARPA Information Survivability Conference and Exposition DISCEX2000. Vol.1, pp. 88–102 ((January 2000)

Hardware/Software Co-design of a Secure Ubiquitous System

Masa-aki Fukase[1], Hiroki Takeda[1], and Tomoaki Sato[2]

[1] Faculty of Science and Technology, Hirosaki University
Hirosaki 036-8561, Japan
{slfuka, gs06411}@eit.hirosaki-u.ac.jp
[2] Computer and Network Systems Center, Hirosaki University
Hirosaki 036-8561, Japan
tsato@cc.hirosaki-u.ac.jp

Abstract. Ever growing ubiquitous environment demands security, speed, and power consciousness in processing huge amount of multimedia information. A practical solution to meet these demands is the construction and implementation of a safety aware, highly-performed, and sophisticated architecture. According to this scheme, we have exploited a secure ubiquitous system composed of a hardware cryptography-embedded multimedia mobile architecture and its software support. The architecture is a dedicated single chip processor called HCgorilla. Since one-sided hardware design approach does not always sufficient for the development of HCgorilla, we have followed an H/S co-design scheme. The software support includes a Java interface and parallelizing compilers run on servers to reduce the load and increase the performance of HCgorilla-embedded clients.

1 Introduction

Ubiquitous devices like IC tag, cellar phone, and PDA (personal digital assistance) have been used mainly due to small size and power consciousness. This has inevitably caused the lack of performable features, yet ubiquitous community tends to highly make much of usability toward multimedia processing. This requires PC-like sophisticated functions. The sophistication or complexity required to ubiquitous devices is caused by the advantage and disadvantage of ubiquitous environment after all. In order to achieve such elegance, handheld devices have continued to add software components in recent years. Such a trend is unfavorable to performance in processing large quantity of multimedia information.

In addition to performance constraint, another serious issue is the latent contradiction of ubiquitous community that is caused by the diversity of ubiquitous devices. Since the diversity brings about open-access to ubiquitous networks anytime anywhere, this really threatens user security. Actually, unauthorized access, illegal attack, intrusion, pretension, and information leakage are frequent occurrences [1].

Even though we have felt alternative impressions for the rapid progress of ubiquitous environment [2], secure architectures to protect multimedia information itself have not always appeared. In order to fulfill overall demands for the security,

Y. Wang, Y. Cheung, and H. Liu (Eds.): CIS 2006, LNAI 4456, pp. 385–395, 2007.

usability, speed, and power of ubiquitous devices, a practical solution is a sophisticated single VLSI (very large scale integration) chip processor [3]. Although TPM (Trusted Platform Module) is a cutting-edge technique commonly known as security chip, it works for password-size data, and the major role is implicitly digital signing. In view of running time, the encryption of long multimedia information is outside of TPM, because it implements RSA (Rivest-Shamir-Adelman).

We have developed ubiquitous processor named HCgorilla [4-13]. Different from TPM, HCgorilla implements an extremely long common key cryptography. Thus, it works well for the cryptographic streaming of multimedia information. Since HCgorilla unifies Java features, strong security, low power, and high throughput, one-sided hardware design approach is not always useful. More complicated strategy, hardware/software (H/S) co-design, is needed in developing HCgorilla.

2 H/S Co-design

Fig. 1 shows the secure ubiquitous system we have exploited. This is composed of servers, Internet, and HCgorilla systems. An HCgorilla system is formed by a mobile client embedded with a HCgorilla chip and software support. The software support is installed in servers.

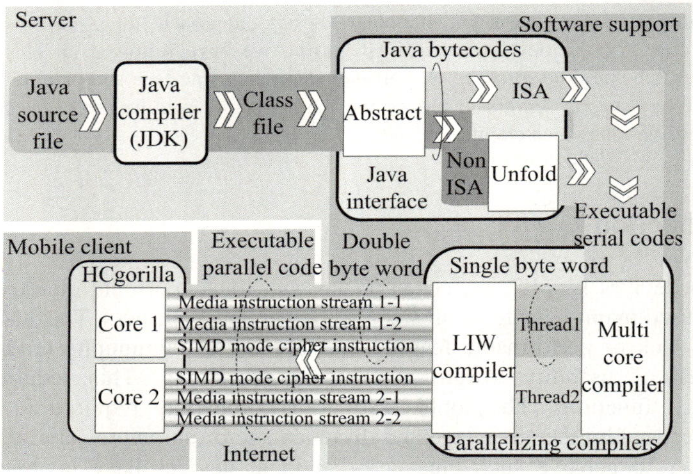

Fig. 1. Secure ubiquitous system

Table 1 summarizes the H/S co-design scheme of the HCgorilla system. H/S co-design does not mean simply relying on software components for sophisticated multimedia processing, but implicitly supporting hardware activity by the potential of software. Platform neutrality relevant to global engineering as well as diversity is filled with Java [14, 15]. This also provides us multimedia entertainment like music, game, and GPS (global positioning system) etc. However, Java is more awkward than regular languages. This is due to an intermediate form or class file produced by Java compilers. Since ubiquitous clients use small scale systems, the preprocessing of complicated class files should be covered by large servers.

Table 1. H/S co-design scheme

<table>
<tr><th rowspan="2">Application field</th><th rowspan="2" colspan="2">Demand</th><th rowspan="2" colspan="2">Strategy</th><th colspan="2">Technique</th></tr>
<tr><th>Hardware</th><th>Software</th></tr>
<tr><td rowspan="4">Multimedia</td><td rowspan="3" colspan="2">Entertainment</td><td colspan="2">Functional ISA</td><td>DSP, Floating point</td><td>Java</td></tr>
<tr><td rowspan="2">Media streaming</td><td>Data compression</td><td>NA</td><td>NA</td></tr>
<tr><td>SIMD</td><td rowspan="2">IFU</td><td rowspan="2">LIW, compiler</td></tr>
<tr><td colspan="2">High performance</td><td colspan="2">Parallelism</td></tr>
<tr><td>Mobile</td><td colspan="2">Wearable</td><td colspan="2">Power consciousness</td><td rowspan="2">Wave-pipeline</td><td rowspan="2">NA</td></tr>
<tr><td rowspan="7">Ubiquitous Internet</td><td colspan="2">Quick response</td><td colspan="2">High speed clock</td></tr>
<tr><td colspan="2">Dynamic</td><td colspan="2">Multithreading</td><td>Multicore</td><td>TLP</td></tr>
<tr><td rowspan="3">Multimedia entertainment</td><td>Learning</td><td rowspan="3" colspan="2">Object-oriented</td><td rowspan="4">Interpreter type Java CPU</td><td rowspan="4">API</td></tr>
<tr><td>Real time</td></tr>
<tr><td>Interactive</td></tr>
<tr><td colspan="2">Global engineering</td><td colspan="2">Platform neutrality</td></tr>
<tr><td colspan="2">Reliable diversity</td><td colspan="2">Strong cryptography</td><td>RAP</td><td>NA</td></tr>
</table>

Even the preprocessing has a problem in interpreting process. It is covered by JVM (Java virtual machine) or JIT (just-in-time compiler) built-in runtime systems. Although they are common for mobile devices, they need more ROM (read only memory) space. This degrades response time, usability, cost, and performance. Considering hardware property as well as Java compatibility, we apply the interpreter type Java CPU (central processing unit) [16]. It directly executes Java bytecodes without JVM [17].

In order to lighten the burden on hardware design, the functional ISA (instruction set architecture) of HCgorilla is made compact. This is owed to the parallelism and densification of instructions in conjunction with superscalar-like IFU (instruction fetch unit). This is a wired logic detecting the length of each instruction and distributing it to appropriate pipes. TLP (thread level parallelism) and ILP (instruction level parallelism) are on the back of instruction folding by API (application program interface) and LIW (long instruction word). LIW is not so broad like VLIW (very long instruction word). Yet, LIW is effective to enhance multimedia communication. The densification of instructions is achieved under the policy of length variant reduced instructions. Instruction length is made variable within instruction cache, which is effective to optimize cache size. The scheme of dense codes at instruction cache is also effective to reduce critical path delay and power dissipation.

The compactness of HCgorilla's ISA is not similar to ARM's optimization scheme for encoding density. While the encoding density described by ARM is simply concerned with the bit density of executable codes, dense codes at instruction cache referred to HCgorilla aim to pack executable codes as many as possible without increasing cache size. The compact ISA scheme is more preferable in view of mobility.

Wave-pipelining is really effective for power conscious speedup. Actually, long delay times have been so far wasted in accessing web pages and drawing contents. This has been due to iterative process within web servers, network switches, and local clients to safely treat large amount of packets.

3 Hardware Organization

Table 2 summarizes architectures related to HCgorilla we have so far developed. They are multimedia mobile processors, gorilla [18, 19], hardware cryptography-embedded processor, RAP (random addressing-accelerated processor) [20, 21].

Table 2. Architectures related to HCgorilla

Name	Architecture								Chip			
	ISA		Parallelism					Hardware crypto-graphy	Chip	Process (μm)	Clock speed (MHz)	Current status
	No. of instructions	Format	No. of cores	ILP degree	Pipelining							
					Regular		Waved					
					Degree	Number						
gorilla.1	16	JVM	2	2	8	2 media pipes	2-wave EX	NA	gorilla035	0.35	240	4.9-mm chip
gorilla.2					7		NA		gorilla035v2		200	Synthesis
RAP	17	RISC	1	NA	5	1 cipher pipe		SISD	NA	FPGA	45	FPGA
HCgorilla.1	18	JVM	2	2	8	2 cipher-embedded media pipes			HCgorilla035	0.35	150	4.9-mm chip
HCgorilla.2	63				7	2 media pipes and a cipher pipe	2-wave EX	SIMD	HCgorilla018	0.18	400	2.8-mm chip
									HCgorilla018 v2			5.9-mm chip synthesis

3.1 Instruction Set

ISA is the basis of characterizing any processor. Table 3 exactly shows the ISA of HCgorilla.2 composed of Java compatible media instructions and cipher instructions. Media instructions are subset of JVM. In case of HCgorilla.2, 61 codes have been carefully selected from the 202 Java bytecodes to save chip area and power consumption. The number of cipher instructions is two. The random store instruction rsw and the random load instruction rlw are SIMD (single instruction stream multiple data stream) mode that enables multimedia stream cipher.

The dependent operand is a 1-byte operand succeeding the 1-byte opcode. Apparently a dependent operand and its preceding or corresponding opcode are grammatically equal, yet the dependent operand is actually subsidiary to the opcode. The number of dependent operands is 0 to 2.

Table 3. ISA of HCgorilla.2

Opcode		Dep.	iconst_1	0x04	0	astore_2	0x4D	0
Mnemonic	Binary	oper.	iconst_2	0x05	0	astore_3	0x4E	0
rsw	0xF0	0	iconst_3	0x06	0	pop	0x57	0
rlw	0xF1	0	iconst_4	0x07	0	pop2	0x58	0
nop	0x00	0	iconst_5	0x08	0	dup	0x59	0
bipush	0x10	1	sipush	0x11	2	dup_x1	0x5A	0
iload	0x15	1	aload	0x19	1	dup_x2	0x5B	0
istore	0x36	1	iload_0	0x1A	0	dup2	0x5C	0
iadd	0x60	0	iload_1	0x1B	0	dup2_x1	0x5D	0
isub	0x64	0	iload_2	0x1C	0	dup2_x2	0x5E	0
ineg	0x74	0	iload_3	0x1D	0	imul	0x68	0
ishl	0x78	0	aload_0	0x2A	0	iushr	0x7C	0
ishr	0x7A	0	aload_1	0x2B	0	iflt	0x9B	2
iand	0x7E	0	aload_2	0x2C	0	ifge	0x9C	2
ior	0x80	0	aload_3	0x2D	0	ifgt	0x9D	2
ixor	0x82	0	astore	0x3A	1	ifle	0x9E	2
ifeq	0x99	2	istore_0	0x3B	0	if_icmpeq	0x9F	2
ifne	0x9A	2	istore_1	0x3C	0	if_icmpne	0xA0	2
if_icmplt	0xA1	2	istore_2	0x3D	0	if_icmpge	0xA2	2
goto	0xA7	2	istore_3	0x3E	0	if_icmpgt	0xA3	2
iconst_m1	0x02	0	astore_0	0x4B	0	if_icmple	0xA4	2
iconst_0	0x03	0	astore_1	0x4C	0			

3.2 Processor Organization

According to ISA, HCgorilla is organized as shown in Fig. 2. It has two symmetric cores for TLP [22]. Each core has two media pipes and a cipher pipe. Wave-pipelining is partly applied for these pipes. This results in the formation of heterogeneous pipelines. Although the register file and data cache are physically shared by the two cores considering hardware resource, it is logically divided. Each division is allocated to a corresponding core. The division has the same data width as the execute units.

At the instruction cache fetch stage, IFU unfolds TLP and ILP. Media pipes improved from interpreter type Java CPU transfer external operands to stacks. They also transfer data between the stack and data cache. They do not access the register file. The cipher pipe streams data between the register file and data cache. It does not access stacks. A plaintext issued from the register file is encrypted by using the random store instruction, rsw. It writes the content of a specified register file location in data cache directly addressed by the RNG (random number generator) output. Thus, a series of multimedia information is transposed at random without any special operation. This is due to the connection of a built-in RNG and data cache succeeded to RAP. An extremely long cycle of random numbers is easily produced by making RNG with a linear feedback shift register. This requires trivial additional chip area and power dissipation. The decryption of a ciphertext stored in the register file is similarly done by using the random load instruction, rlw.

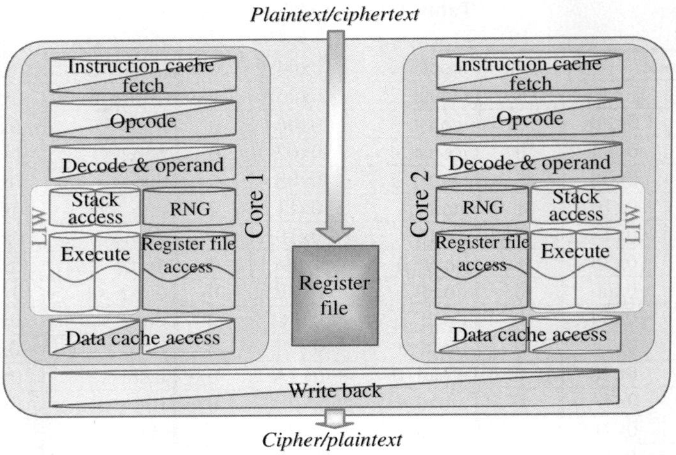

Fig. 2. Basic organization of HCgorilla.2

Table 4. RAC vs. regular common key cryptography

Cipher			Mechanism: Unit dividing a full plaintext	Mechanism: Cryptographic means: Key (random numbers)	Mechanism: Cryptographic means: Combinational operation	Evaluation: Running time[2]	Evaluation: Cryptographic strength	Evaluation: Aptitude for ubiquitous cryptography
RAC			Full text	Full-length	Random number addressing store/load	Short[3]	Ideally strong	Practically valuable and suited
Regular	Block	AES	Large fixed length[1]	Unit length	XOR, scramble, shift, etc.	Medium[4]	Strong	De fact standard for long data
		DES						
	Stream	A5	A few bits or a character	Plaintext-unit length	Bitwise XOR	Long[5]	Medium	Not so suited
		LFSR						
		Vernam		One-time pad or full-length			Ideally strong	

1: Normally 64/128 bit, exceptionally 1024 bits.
2: In case of processing large quantity of ubiquitous information.
3: In case of using HCgorilla.
4, 5: In case of using media processor.

The cryptography by HCgorilla is called RAC (random number addressing cryptography). In view of ubiquitous computing, Table 4 summarizes fundamental features of RAC vs. regular common key cryptography. The first advantage of RAC is short running time. This is because the cipher pipe does not do any arithmetic or logic operation, but does simple memory access. The second advantage is the cryptographic strength. The strength is closely related to the key length. RAC has the same strength as Vernam cipher due to the use of a full-length key. Although DES (Data Encryption

Standard) and AES (Advanced Encryption Standard) have been already de fact standard for long data, even AES can not cover larger quantity of ubiquitous information in view of running time. AES takes impractically long time to process ubiquitous information, because it repeats many times a series of arithmetic logic operations.

4 Software Support

The software support of HCgorilla is composed of a Java interface and parallelizing compilers installed in servers to reduce the load and increase the performance of HCgorilla-embedded clients. In order to describe the behavior of the software support, a Java source file is exemplified in bellows. This involves two methods that compute the summation from 0 to 1023. This file is input to the Java interface and each method is made a thread by a parallelizing compiler.

```
void sum()
{
      int i1,sum1,a1;
      sum1=0;
      for(i1=0;i1<1024;i1++){
            sum1=sum1+i1;
            a1=sum1+i1;
      }
}
public static void main(String args[ ])
{
      int i2,sum2,a2;
      sum2=0;
      for(i2=0;i2<1024;i2++){
            sum2=sum2+i2;
            a2=sum2+i2;
      }
}
```

4.1 Java Interface

The Java interface playing as API is composed of two components. The one abstracts Java bytecodes from a class file shown in Fig. 3. The essence of a class file is Java bytecodes in running on any processor. Remains such as numbers, flags, and entries are really convenient for JVM, but secondary for a hardware processor itself. The other unfolds Java bytecodes not defined by HCgorilla's ISA. Thus, the Java interface outputs executable codes in HCgorilla's ISA. Since the output is serial, it needs the other software support, parallelizing compilers to run on HCgorilla.

4.2 Parallelizing Compilers

A compiler is the essence of software's responsibility. Needless to say Proebsting's law: a compiler advances double computing power every 18 years, developing compilers, especially paralellizing compilers occupies absolute position in developing sophisticated processors. The parallelizing compilers are most important for practicing HCgorilla's parallelism. They output the codes executable in parallel by an HCgorilla chip and map them on instruction cache within a core.

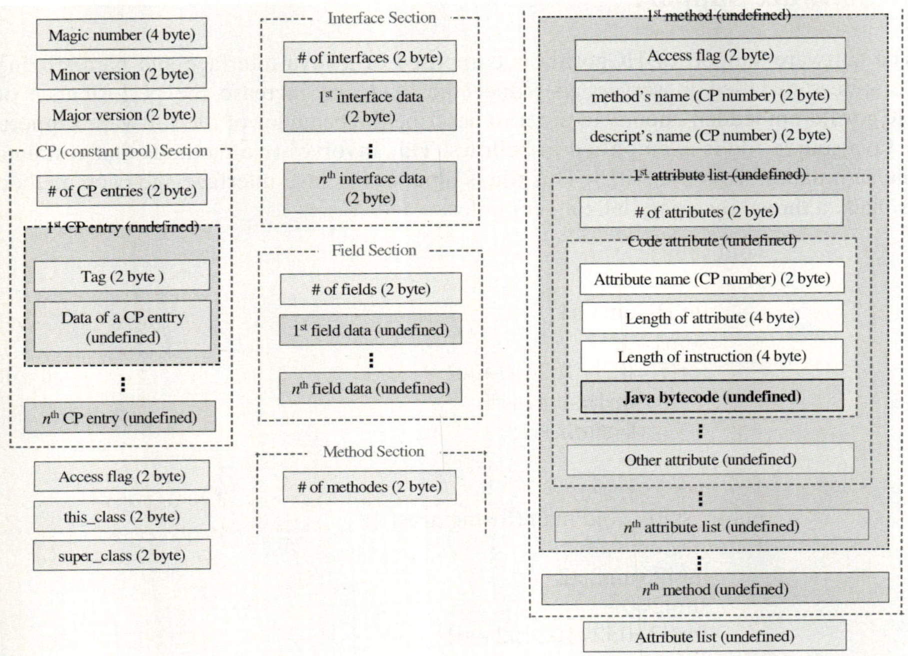

Fig. 3. Structure of a class file

Fig. 4 shows the global process of the parallelizing compilers. The multicore compiler abstracts TLP. Threading is judged by looking for return process that expresses the end of instructions sequence or thread. Renaming is the renewal or readdressing of instructions produced by parallelization at thread and instruction levels. This is done by inverting the most significant bit of an address to be modified. Jump codes are renamed by modifying their destination addresses. The renaming of Thread 2 is needed to avoid the conflict of data cache access with Thread 1. This complements the logical share of data cache by the two cores.

The LIW compiler abstracts ILP from a thread and does reorder, renaming, etc. ILP is judged by examining the conflict of data cache access. The conflict can be detected by checking the dependent operand of store and load instructions. Jump codes are excluded from ILP abstraction, because they directly affect program running. The detailed procedures of the LIW compiler are as follows.

(1) Focusing on store and jump codes, cut off a division from codes sequence. Thedivision is a code sequence immediately after the former store or jump code to the latter store or jump code.
(2) When a jump code terminates a division, accompany two dependent operands with that code.
(3) When a division is distinguished by a jump code, put itself on both instruction streams, and thus make pseudo parallel codes.
(4) When a division is distinguished by a store code, repeat (1) and make two continuous divisions.
(5) When each of the two continuous divisions is terminated by a store code, judge their ILP. If the dependent operand of a store code in the former division and the operands of the load and store codes in the latter division are different each other, then go back to (1), else go to (6).
(6) Make pseudo parallel codes by putting the former division to the one instruction stream and filling the other instruction stream by nop. Go back to (3).

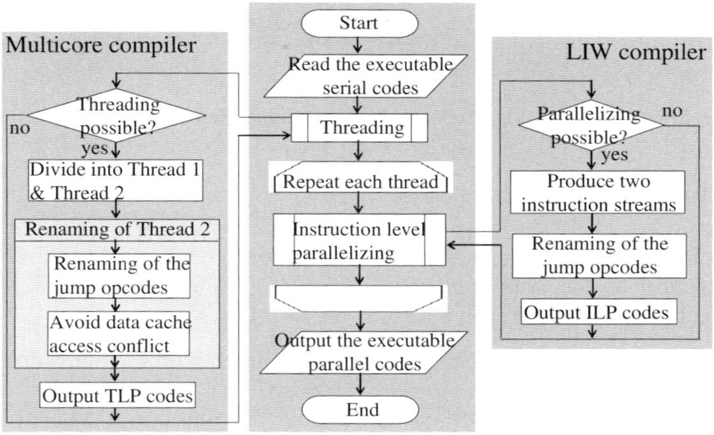

Fig. 4. Parallelizing process

Fig. 5 exemplifies the application of the parallelizing compilers by using the Java source file described above. In case of Thread 1, the first and second divisions are parallelized, because the dependent operands of the store codes, 0x3D and 0x3C are different. The third division is out of ILP, because it is terminated by a jump code, 0xA2 accompanied with its two dependent operands. The explicit operand of the store code, 0x3D of the fourth division is 2. It is used by the load code, 0x1C of the fifth division. Thus, the fourth and fifth division are not parallelized. The fourth division is exactly put in the instruction stream 1-1, and the simultaneous instruction stream 1-2 is filled with nop, 0x00. The fifth division is compared with the sixth division and judged their ILP.

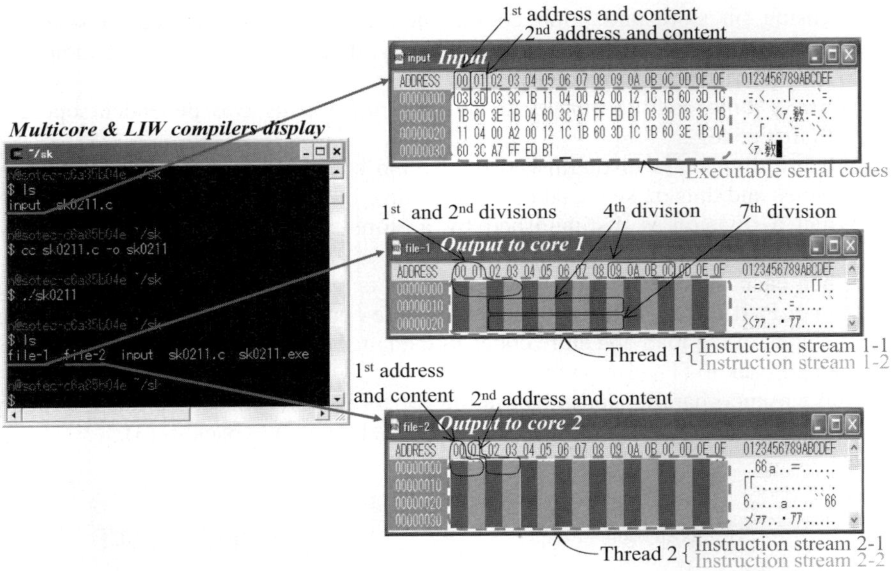

Fig. 5. Displays by using a binary editor in running the parallelizing compilers

5 Concluding Remarks

In order to meet overall demands for secure ubiquitous community, we have exploited the combination of the ubiquitous processor, HCgorilla and its software support. Essential techniques developed in our study are as follows.

a. H/S co-design to reduce the complexity accompanied with the one-sided hardware or software design approach.
b. Hardware organization composed of multiple pipeline cores that exploits TLP, ILP, and Java.
c. Software support composed of a Java interface and parallelizing compilers.
d. Running the software support on servers to reduce the load and increase the performance of HCgorilla-embedded clients.

The next step of our study will be as follows.

a. The evaluation of the latest HCgorilla018v2 chip.
b. The further development of the software support.

References

1. Sato, T., Sakuma, R., Miyamori, D., Fukase, M.: Hardware Security-Embedded Wireless LAN Processor. In: Proc. of ECTI-CON2005, vol. II, pp. 839–842 (2005)
2. Saha, D., Mukherjee, A.: Pervasive Computing: A Paradigm for the 21st Century. Computer Magazine 36(3), 25–31 (2003)

3. Jerraya, A., Tenhunen, H., Wolf, W.: Multiprocessor Systems-on-Chips. Computer Magazine 38(7), 36–40 (2005)
4. Fukase, M., Fukase, A., Sato, Y., Sato, T.: Cryptographic System by a Random Addressing-Accelerated Multimedia Mobile Processor. In: Proc. of SCI2004, Vol. II, pp. 174–179 (2004)
5. Fukase, M., Fukase, A., Sato, Y., Sato, T.: Exploiting a Hardware Security-Embedded Multimedia Mobile Processor System and its Application. In: ITC-CSCC,2004 7C3L-3-1-7C3L-3-4 (2004)
6. Fukase, M., Sato, Y., Sato, T.: Design of a Hardware Security-Embedded Multimedia Mobile Processor. In: Proc. of ISCIT 2004, pp. 362–367 (2004)
7. Fukase, M., Sato, Y., Nakamura, Y., Akaoka, R., Sato, T.: Hardware Cryptography-Embedded Multimedia Mobile Processor. Technical Report of IEICE 104(735), 31–36 (2005)
8. Sato, Y., Sato, T., Fukase, M.: Simultaneously Multithreaded Multimedia Mobile Processor Embedded with Hardware Cryptography. Social Information 14(2), 97–107 (2005)
9. Fukase, M., Sato, T.: Low Energy Digital Electronics for Multimedia Ubiquitous Environments. In: Proc. of EIC'05, pp. 409–414 (2005)
10. Fukase, M., Akaoka, R., Sato, T.: Hardware Cryptography-Embedded Multimedia Mobile Processor for Ubiquitous Computing. In: Proc. of 12th NASA Symposium on VLSI, 1.2.1-1.2.6 (2005)
11. Fukase, M., Akaoka, R., Liu, L., Cheng, T.S., Sato, T.: Hardware Cryptography for Ubiquitous Computing. In: Proc. of ISCIT2005, Vol. 1, pp. 462–465 (2005)
12. Fukase, M., Nakamura, Y., Akaoka, R., Sato, T.: Development of a Multimedia Mobile Processor. In: Proc. of ISCIT 2004, pp. 672–677 (2004)
13. Fukase, M., Akaoka, R., Sato, T.: Hardware Cryptography-Embedded Multimedia Mobile System. In: Proc. of WMSCI2006, Vol. III, pp. 225–230 (2006)
14. Lawton, G.: Moving Java into Mobile Phones. Computer Magazine 35(6), 17–20 (2002)
15. Kochnev, D.S., Terekhov, A.A.: Surviving Java for Mobiles. IEEE pervasive COMPUTING 2(2), 90–95 (2003)
16. Clark, D.: Mobile Processors Begin to Grow Up. Computer Magazine 35(3), 22–25 (2002)
17. Radhakrishnan, R., Vijaykrishnan, N., John, L.K., Sivasubramaniam, A., Rubio, J., Sabarinathan, J.: Java Runtime Systems: Characterization and Architectural Implications. IEEE Trans. on COMPUTERS 50(2), 131–146 (2001)
18. Fukase, M., Shioji, K., Imai, N., Murakami, D., Mikuni, K.: An Experiment in the Design and Development of a Multimedia Processor for Mobile Computing. Technical Report of IEICE, vol. 102(400), pp. 13–18 (2002)
19. Fukase, M., Nakamura, Y., Akaoka, R., Sato, T.: Development of a Multimedia Mobile Processor. In: Proc. of ISCIT 2004, pp. 672–677 (2004)
20. Fukase, M., Oyama, T., Liu, Z.: Endeavor in the Field of Random Sampling-Designing and Prototyping a Processor Suited for its Acceleration. Technical Report of IEICE, vol. 102(272) pp. 7–12 (2002)
21. Fukase, M., Sato, T.: Power Conscious Endeavor in Processors to Speed Up Random Sampling. In: Proc. of SCI2003, vol. V, pp. 111–116 (2003)
22. Goshima, M.: Superscalar/VLIW and Throughput-Oriented Multithreaded Processors. IPSJ Magazine 46(10), 1104–1110 (2005)

Efficient Implementation of Tate Pairing on a Mobile Phone Using Java

Yuto Kawahara[1], Tsuyoshi Takagi[1], and Eiji Okamoto[2]

[1] Future University-Hakodate, Japan
[2] University of Tsukuba, Japan

Abstract. Pairing-based cryptosystems (PBC) have been attracted by researchers in cryptography. Some implementations show that PBC are relatively slower than the standard public key cryptosystems. We present an efficient implementation for computing Tate pairing on a mobile phone using Java. We implemented the η_T pairing (a recent efficient variation of Duursma-Lee algorithm) over some finite fields of characteristic 3 with extension degree $m = \{97, 167, 193, 239\}$. Our optimized implementation for $m = 97$ achieved about 0.5 seconds for computing the η_T pairing over FOMA SH901iS, NTT DoCoMo. Then our implementation of the η_T pairing is compared in the same platform with other Java program of the standard cryptosystems, i.e., RSA cryptosystem and elliptic curve cryptosystem (ECC). The computation speed of the η_T pairing is comparable to that of RSA or ECC on the same mobile device.

1 Introduction

Pairing-based cryptosystems (PBC) can provide us several novel cryptographic applications, e.g., ID-based cryptosystems [6], short digital signatures [8], efficient broadcast encryption [7], etc. Some of them have not been achieved using the conventional public key cryptosystems. Therefore PBC have been attracted by researchers in cryptography. PBC use the Tate pairing on elliptic curves over finite fields. The standard algorithm for computing the Tate pairing is Miller's algorithm. Miller's algorithm is about 5 times slower than 1024-bit RSA and 160-bit elliptic curve cryptosystem (ECC) [3]. It is an important research topic to find more efficient algorithms for computing Tate pairing.

Recently, Duursma and Lee introduced an efficient implementation of Miller's algorithm specified for supersingular curves over finite fields $\mathbb{F}_{3^m}$ [10]. The order of the supersingular curves has the very low Hamming weight (i.e. 3) and this algorithm can be implemented in a closed form only using the arithmetic of the underlying finite field. Kwon then presented an efficient variation of Duursma-Lee algorithm without computing cube roots [17]. This algorithm over $\mathbb{F}_{3^{97}}$ has been implemented in several milliseconds on FPGA [16] or Pentium using C language [20,2]. Moreover, Barreto et al. proposed the η_T pairing algorithm that is about twice faster than Duursma-Lee algorithm [2]. The number of the loops in the η_T pairing algorithm becomes $(m + 1)/2$ using an endomorphism map,

Y. Wang, Y. Cheung, and H. Liu (Eds.): CIS 2006, LNAI 4456, pp. 396–405, 2007.

which is about the half of m used in Duursma-Lee algorithm. The η_T pairing over $\mathbb{F}_{2^m}$ can be implemented under one second on a smart card [18].

Java 2 Platform, Micro Edition (J2ME) is a secure and flexible Java platform designed for embedding devices such as mobile phones [14]. Some applications of pairing based cryptosystems are suitable for the environments using ubiquitous devices. Java provides several security components of the standard public-key cryptosystem (RSA, ECC) and other cryptographic functions [15]. Tillich and Großschadl presented some implementation of the standard public-key cryptosystem over mobile phones [21]. However, no implementation of the pairing-based cryptosystems using Java over mobile phones has been reported.

In this paper, the feasibility of the η_T pairing on mobile phones using Java is examined. We implement the η_T pairing algorithm over $\mathbb{F}_{3^m}$ for several extension degrees $m = \{97, 167, 193, 239\}$, and especially optimized it for extension degree $m = 97$. Because there is no JCE component for computing $\mathbb{F}_{3^m}$, we have to implement the arithmetic of $\mathbb{F}_{3^m}$ from scratch. We design that the number of Java components is preferable to be as small as possible, and avoid a large overhead in the computation speed when many Java components are called. The speed of calculations in $\mathbb{F}_{3^m}$ strongly depends on the choice of the representation of elements, so that we deploy the bit representation suitable for basic logic operations in Java and the irreducible trinomial basis $x^m + x^k + 2$ with smallest degree k. In this implementation, our program achieves about 0.5 seconds on FOMA SH901iS, NTT DoCoMo. Moreover, our implementation of the η_T pairing is compared with the standard public-key cryptosystems (1024-bit RSA and 160-bit ECC) using the Java components provided by Bouncy Castle [4]. Then the speed of our implementation is comparable to that of the standard public-key cryptosystems with the same security parameters.

2 Arithmetic in Finite Fields with Characteristic 3

In this section, we describe the arithmetic in finite fields with characteristic 3 of degree m, where m is positive integer. We denote by $\mathbb{F}_{3^m}$ the finite fields.

2.1 Bit Representation of $\mathbb{F}_{3^m}$

Let $\mathbb{F}_3 = \{0, 1, 2\}$ be the finite field with characteristic 3. The element a in $\mathbb{F}_3$ is encoded by two bits such as $a = (a_{hi}, a_{lo})$ for $a_{hi}, a_{lo} \in \{0, 1\}$. In the implementation we choose $0 = (0, 0), 1 = (0, 1)$, and $2 = (1, 0)$. The negative $-a$ for $a \in \mathbb{F}_3$ is replaced by $2a$.

Every element in $\mathbb{F}_{3^m}$ are represented $\mathbb{F}_3[x]/f(x)$, where $\mathbb{F}_3[x]$ is set of all polynomials over $\mathbb{F}_3$, and $f(x)$ is an irreducible polynomial of degree m in $\mathbb{F}_3[x]$. Let $A(x)$ be an element in $\mathbb{F}_{3^m}$. $A(x)$ can be represented as the polynomial of degree at most $m-1$, namely $\sum_{i=0}^{m-1} a_i x^i$ $(a_i \in \mathbb{F}_3)$ [5]. For our implementation, each coefficient $a_i = ((a_i)_{hi}, (a_i)_{lo})$ is represented as follows:

$$A_{hi} = ((a_{m-1})_{hi}, (a_{m-2})_{hi}, \cdots, (a_0)_{hi}), \ A_{lo} = ((a_{m-1})_{lo}, (a_{m-2})_{lo}, \cdots, (a_0)_{lo})$$

Here we denote $A(x)$ by (A_{hi}, A_{lo}). Using this representation, we need two arrays with size of $N = \lceil m/W \rceil$ for storing an element in $\mathbb{F}_{3^m}$, where W is the word size of the target processor. Note that a negative element $-A(x)$ is replaced $2A(x)$ by changing A_{hi} and A_{lo}.

2.2 Addition and Multiplication in $\mathbb{F}_{3^m}$

Let $A(x) = (A_{hi}, A_{lo})$ and $B(x) = (B_{hi}, B_{lo})$ be the elements of $\mathbb{F}_{3^m}$. Addition $C(x) = (C_{hi}, C_{lo}) = A(x) + B(x)$ is performed by the basic logic operators (AND(&), OR(|) and XOR($\wedge$)) as follows:

$$T = (A_{hi} \mid A_{lo}) \,\&\, (B_{hi} \mid B_{lo}),\ C_{hi} = T \wedge (A_{hi} \mid B_{hi}),\ C_{lo} = T \wedge (A_{lo} \mid B_{lo}).$$

Subtraction $A(x) - B(x)$ can be computed as $A(x) + B'(x)$ for $B'(x) = 2B(x)$.

Multiplication in $\mathbb{F}_{3^m}$ consists of the polynomial multiplication step and the reduction step. The polynomial multiplication step computes $C'(x) = \sum_{i=0}^{2m-2} c'_i \cdot x^i = A(x) \cdot B(x)$ for given $A(x), B(x)$ in $\mathbb{F}_{3^m}$. The shift-addition multiplication method is the simplest algorithm, and other methods (e.g. the comb method) require additional memory comparing with the shift-addition multiplication method [11]. Therefore it is suitable for the implementation on memory constraint device such as mobile phones. Let $A(x) = \sum_{i=0}^{m-1} a_i x^i$ and $B(x) = \sum_{i=0}^{m-1} b_i x^i$ be the elements of $\mathbb{F}_{3^m}$. The polynomial multiplication step $C'(x) = \sum_{i=0}^{2m-2} c'_i x^i = A(x) \cdot B(x)$ is performed by the following algorithm.

Algorithm 1. Shift-Addition Multiplication in $\mathbb{F}_{3^m}$

Input: $A(x) = \sum_{i=0}^{m-1} a_i x^i, B(x) = \sum_{i=0}^{m-1} b_i x^i \in \mathbb{F}_{3^m}$ $(a_i, b_i \in \mathbb{F}_3)$
Output: $C'(x) = A(x) \cdot B(x)$

```
1: C'(x) ← 0
2: for i ← 0 to m − 1 do
3:     C'(x) ← C'(x) + A(x) · b_i x^i
4: end for
```

Next, the reduction step is computed based on the irreducible polynomial of $\mathbb{F}_{3^m}$. In order to accelerate the reduction step, we deploy the irreducible trinomial $f(x) = x^m + x^k + 2$, where $m > k > 1$. The reduction algorithm with irreducible trinomial $f(x)$ is described as follows:

Algorithm 2. Reduction with Irreducible Trinomial $f(x)$

Input: $C'(x) \in \mathbb{F}_3[x]$ of degree n $(n > m-1)$, $f(x) = x^m + x^k + 2$
Output: $C'(x) = C'(x) \bmod f(x)$

```
1: for i ← n downto m do
2:     c'_{i−m+k} ← c'_{i−m+k} − c'_i
3:     c'_{i−m} ← c'_{i−m} − 2c'_i
4:     c'_i ← 0
5: end for
```

2.3 Other Operations in $\mathbb{F}_{3^m}$

We describe other operations in $\mathbb{F}_{3^m}$, namely cube, inversion and cube root.

Cube: For a given $A(x) \in \mathbb{F}_{3^m}$, the cube of $A(x)$ is calculated by $A(x)^3 = \sum_{i=0}^{m-1} a_i x^{3i}$. Therefore the multiplication step is computed virtually for free. We present two methods for the reduction step of the polynomial $\sum_{i=0}^{m-1} a_i x^{3i}$. One performs the standard reduction algorithm using the irreducible trinomial $x^m = 2x^k + 1$. Another one utilizes a reduction table, which directly finds the reduced polynomial for a given $A(x) \in \mathbb{F}_{3^m}$. The speed of the second reduction method can be optimized for fixed degree m. However the reduction table should be prepared depending on the extension degree m, and the first reduction method is suitable for general degree m.

Inversion: Inversion is performed using the extended Euclidean algorithm for the polynomials over $\mathbb{F}_3[x]$. We developed a ternary version of the extended Euclidean algorithm over binary polynomial $\mathbb{F}_2[x]$ [11]. The detail of our algorithm is described in appendix A. Another algorithm for computing an inversion is the ternary gcd [12]. In our experiment, the ternary extended Euclidean algorithm is faster than the ternary gcd.

Cube Root: Cube root is efficiently implemented by the algorithm proposed by Barreto et al. [1]. One cube root can be computed with the speed of at most two multiplications in $\mathbb{F}_{3^m}$.

2.4 Arithmetic in Extension Field $\mathbb{F}_{3^{6m}}$

Extension field $\mathbb{F}_{3^{6m}}$ is represented $\mathbb{F}_{3^{3m}}[\sigma]/h(\sigma)$ and $\mathbb{F}_{3^m}[\rho]/g(\rho)$, where $h(\sigma)$ and $g(\rho)$ are irreducible polynomials $h(\sigma) = \sigma^2+1$ over $\mathbb{F}_{3^{3m}}$ and $g(\rho) = \rho^3-\rho-1$ over $\mathbb{F}_{3^m}$. Let $A(\sigma), B(\sigma)$ be elements in $\mathbb{F}_{3^{6m}}$. We denote by $A(\sigma) = a_1\sigma + a_0$ the element in $\mathbb{F}_{3^{6m}}$, where a_0, a_1 are elements in $\mathbb{F}_{3^{3m}}$. The operations in $\mathbb{F}_{3^{6m}}$ are implemented as follows:

- **Addition:** $A(\sigma) + B(\sigma) = (a_1 + b_1)\sigma + (a_0 + b_0)$.
- **Multiplication :** $A(\sigma)B(\sigma) = (t_{00} - t_{11})\sigma + (t_{01} - t_{00} - t_{11})$, where $t_{00} = a_0b_0$, $t_{11} = a_1b_1$, $t_{01} = (a_0 + a_1)(b_0 + b_1)$. Multiplication in $\mathbb{F}_{3^{6m}}$ can be obtained 18 multiplications and some additions in $\mathbb{F}_{3^m}$.
- **Cube:** $A(\sigma)^3 = -a_1^3\sigma + a_0^3$. Cube in $\mathbb{F}_{3^{6m}}$ is computed by 6 cubes and some addition in $\mathbb{F}_{3^m}$.
- **Inversion:** $A(\sigma)^{-1} = t^{-1}(a_0 - a_1\sigma)$,where $t = (a_1^2 + a_0^2)$. Inversion in $\mathbb{F}_{3^{6m}}$ uses 1 inversion, 36 multiplications and some additions in $\mathbb{F}_{3^m}$.

3 Implementation of Tate Pairing

In this paper, we implement the η_T pairing on the following supersingular elliptic curve over $\mathbb{F}_{3^m}$,

$$E(\mathbb{F}_{3^m}) = \{(x, y) \in (\mathbb{F}_{3^m})^2 \mid y^2 = x^3 - x + 1\}.$$

A point over curve $E(\mathbb{F}_{3^m})$ is represented by (x, y), where x and y are elements in $\mathbb{F}_{3^m}$. All points on $E(\mathbb{F}_{3^m})$ with the point of infinity forms a group structure. The group order of curve $E(\mathbb{F}_{3^m})$ is $\#E = 3^m + 3^{(m+1)/2} + 1$. The pairing based cryptosystems require the arithmetic of curve $E(\mathbb{F}_{3^m})$ such as point addition, point double, point tripling, and scalar multiplication [12].

Let $P = (x_p, y_p), Q = (x_q, y_q)$ be input points over elliptic curve $E(\mathbb{F}_{3^m})$. We describe some formulae on $E(\mathbb{F}_{3^m})$ in the following.

- **Point Addition:** Point addition $(x_r, y_r) = P+Q$, $(x_p \neq x_q)$ is implemented by the following algorithm $x_r = \lambda^2 - (x_p + x_q)$, $y_r = (y_p + y_q) - \lambda^3$, where $\lambda = (y_q - y_p)/(x_q - x_p)$. Point addition needs 2 multiplications, 1 inversion, 1 cube, and 6 additions in $\mathbb{F}_{3^m}$.
- **Point Double:** Point double $(x_r, y_r) = P + P$ is computed by $x_r = \lambda^2 + x_p$, $y_r = -(y_p + \lambda^3)$, where $\lambda = 1/y_p$. Point double needs 1 multiplication, 1 inversion, 1 cube and 2 additions in $\mathbb{F}_{3^m}$.
- **Point Tripling:** Point tripling $(x_r, y_r) = 3P = P + P + P$ is computed by $x_r = ((x_p)^3)^3 - 1$, $y_r = -((y_p)^3)^3$. Point tripling requires only 4 cubes and 1 addition in $\mathbb{F}_{3^m}$ and it is very efficiently computed.
- **Scalar Multiplication:** Scalar multiplication is defined by dP, where P is a point on $E(\mathbb{F}_{3^m})$ and d is an integer. This algorithm is calculated by triple-and-addition algorithm [3], and can be obtain $\lfloor log_3 d \rfloor$ point triplings, about $\frac{2}{3}\lfloor log_3 d \rfloor$ point additions and 1 point double.

Let l be a large prime number that satisfies $l | \#E$ and $l | (3^{6m} - 1)$. Denote by $E(\mathbb{F}_{3^m})[l]$ the subgroup of $E(\mathbb{F}_{3^m})$ with order l. Let $\phi(x, y) = (-x + \rho, y\sigma)$ be the distortion map, which maps a point $Q = (x, y)$ on $E(\mathbb{F}_{3^m})[l]$ to the point $\phi(Q)$ in $E(\mathbb{F}_{3^{6m}})[l]$ the elliptic curve defined over the extension field $\mathbb{F}_{3^{6m}}$. The pairing $e(P, Q)$ is a bilinear map

$$\begin{array}{rcl} e : E(\mathbb{F}_{3^m})[l] \times E(\mathbb{F}_{3^{6m}})[l] & \rightarrow & \mathbb{F}^*_{3^{6m}}/(\mathbb{F}^*_{3^{6m}})^l \\ (P, \phi(Q)) & \mapsto & e(P, Q), \end{array}$$

which satisfies $e(aP, Q) = e(P, aQ) = e(P, Q)^a$ for every non-zero integer a.

3.1 Implementation of the η_T Pairing

Miller's algorithm is the standard algorithm for computing Tate pairing, but it is about 5 times slower than the standard public-key cryptosystems [3]. Duursma-Lee algorithm is a simply modified version of Miller's algorithm for supersingular curves over $\mathbb{F}_{3^m}$ [10]. The order of the supersingular curve has the very low Hamming weight (i.e. $\#E = 3^m + 3^{(m+1)/2} + 1$) and this algorithm can be implemented in a closed form (any operators with the arithmetic in $\mathbb{F}_{3^m}$). Barreto et al. proposed a faster variation of Duursma-Lee algorithm called the η_T pairing [2]. The number of the loops in the η_T pairing algorithm is reduced to the half of that in Duursma-Lee algorithm, and the η_T pairing is about twice faster than Duursma-Lee. We describe the algorithm of the η_T pairing in the following.

Algorithm 3. η_T Pairing on $E(\mathbb{F}_{3^m}) : y^2 = x^3 - x + 1,\ m = \pm 1 \bmod 12$

Input: $P = (x_p, y_p), Q = (x_q, y_q) \in E(\mathbb{F}_{3^m})$
Output: $\eta_T(P, Q) \in \mathbb{F}^*_{3^{6m}}$
$y_p \leftarrow -y_p$ (in $\mathbb{F}_{3^m}$)
$f \leftarrow y_q\sigma - y_p(x_p + x_q + 1) + y_p\rho$ (in $\mathbb{F}_{3^{6m}}$)
for $i \leftarrow 0$ **to** $(m-1)/2$ **do**
  $u \leftarrow x_p + x_q + 1$ (in $\mathbb{F}_{3^m}$)
  $g \leftarrow y_p y_q \sigma - u^2 - u\rho - \rho^2$ (in $\mathbb{F}_{3^{6m}}$)
  $f \leftarrow fg$ (in $\mathbb{F}_{3^{6m}}$)
  $x_p \leftarrow x_p^{1/3},\ y_p \leftarrow y_p^{1/3}$ (in $\mathbb{F}_{3^m}$)
  $x_q \leftarrow x_q^3,\ y_q \leftarrow y_q^3$ (in $\mathbb{F}_{3^m}$)
end for
return $f^{(3^{3m}-1)(3^m+1)(3^m-3^{(m+1)/2}+1)}$

The final exponential $f^{(3^{3m}-1)(3^m+1)(3^m-3^{(m+1)/2}+1)}$ can be efficiently computed [16,2]. Indeed, we can use equation $f^{(3^{3m}-1)} = (f_0 - f_1\sigma)(f_0 + f_1\sigma)^{-1}$ for $f = f_0 + f_1\sigma$, and remaining exponent can be computed by $2m$ cubes, 3 multiplications and 1 inversion in $\mathbb{F}_{3^{6m}}$.

4 Implementation Using Java

Java is a multi-platform language, which is suitable for the programming on ubiquitous devices and can develop security systems more easily comparing to some other program languages such as C. Java 2 Platform, Micro Edition (J2ME) is one of subset of Java 2, and often uses embedded devices such as mobile phones. Java cryptography extension (JCE) is component library provide cryptography communication functions. Java language supports JCE which has the standard public key cryptosystem components, e.g. RSA cryptosystem and elliptic curve cryptosystem, etc [15]. Cryptographic components are provided by some institutes, for examples, Bouncy Castle [4] and IAIK [13]. On the other hands, the pairing-based cryptosystems (PBC) accomplish novel security applications on ubiquitous environments. Therefore it is an interesting research topic to implement PBC on ubiquitous devices. However, no implementation of PBC on mobile phones has been reported.

In this paper, we try to implement the η_T pairing from scratch in Java. There is a large overhead in computation speed when many components of Java library are called. The goal of our implementation is to develop efficient computing of the η_T pairing, so that the number of Java components is preferable to be as small as possible. Indeed, our program has a simply structure of Java class that contains variables and methods. We implement six Java classes, i.e. finite field parameters, finite field, extension field of extension degree 3, extension field of extension degree 6, elliptic curve point, and Tate pairing.

Another goal is to implement the η_T paring by a general-purpose program that can compute by various extension degree m and irreducible trinomial $f(x)$. This is important to enhance the security by increasing the degree m in the future. The general-purpose program has the following variables of finite field $\mathbb{F}_{3^m}$ appeared in

Section 2, namely the characteristic 3, the extension degree m, the middle degree of the irreducible trinomial k, the array size N, and the word size W. Then this program can support various extension degrees with different irreducible trinomials.

On the other hand, we develop an optimized program for the η_T paring with $\mathbb{F}_{3^{97}}$. The optimized program does not have the above variables, in other words does not have the finite field parameters class, but this includes directly values that correspond to these variables in algorithm. Moreover we improve multiplication and cube for the optimized program, and thus this program is computed faster.

4.1 Timing Results on a Mobile Phone

In this section, we describe timing results of our implementation using Java. We use a mobile phone FOMA SH901iS, NTT DoCoMo in order to measure timing result. We utilize degree $m = \{97, 167, 193, 239\}$, and the irreducible trinomial $f(x)$ used for each degree m is as follows: $x^{97} + x^{12} + 2$, $x^{167} + x^{96} + 2$, $x^{193} + x^{12} + 2$, $x^{239} + x^{24} + 2$, respectively. Table 1 presents the timing of the η_T pairing over $\mathbb{F}_{3^m}$ and the arithmetic in $\mathbb{F}_{3^m}$ appeared in Section 2. We show the timing of using the general-purpose program by degree $m = \{97, 167, 193, 239\}$. The optimized program for extension degree $m = 97$ is denoted by "*opt*$\mathbb{F}_{3^{97}}$". The timing results of $\mathbb{F}_{3^m}$ and the η_T pairing are shown in the following. All timings are estimated on average by randomly chosen one thousand elements.

Table 1. Timing of the η_T Pairing with Several $\mathbb{F}_{3^m}$ (msec)

Operator	*opt*$\mathbb{F}_{3^{97}}$	$\mathbb{F}_{3^{97}}$	$\mathbb{F}_{3^{167}}$	$\mathbb{F}_{3^{193}}$	$\mathbb{F}_{3^{239}}$
Addition	0.0173	0.0171	0.0202	0.0203	0.0198
Subtraction	0.0196	0.0193	0.0225	0.0232	0.0210
Multiplication	0.2400	0.2897	0.6651	0.8638	1.1891
Cube	0.0473	0.0886	0.1149	0.1254	0.1362
Inversion	1.5288	1.5411	3.7500	5.0203	6.6621
Cube Root	0.2982	0.3701	0.5112	0.6094	0.7941
η_T Pairing	509.22	627.65	1724.93	2368.58	3557.42

Addition, subtraction and cube implemented by the general-purpose program in $\mathbb{F}_{3^m}$ are computed in almost same speed for each degree. The other operations (multiplication, inversion and cube root) become gradually slower as the degree m increases. Here the η_T pairing algorithm uses many multiplications and cubes, whose number increases based on the degree m due to the number of loop. Therefore the timing of the η_T pairing also becomes slower in terms of increasing the extension degree m. For example, the timing of the η_T pairing over $\mathbb{F}_{3^{239}}$ is about 6 times slower than that over $\mathbb{F}_{3^{97}}$.

On the other hands, the timing of the η_T pairing by the optimized program over *opt*$\mathbb{F}_{3^{97}}$ is about 1.2 time faster than that by the general-purpose program, because the optimized program is implemented using less variables, and has more efficient algorithms for multiplication and cube.

4.2 Comparison to Standard Cryptosystems

In this section, we compare our implementation of the η_T pairing over $\mathbb{F}_{3^{97}}$ to the standard public key cryptosystems, i.e. 1024-bit RSA and 160-bit elliptic curve cryptosystem (ECC) over $\mathbb{F}_{2^{163}}$. Other papers show that the size of these parameters has the same security level [3].

We implement a modular exponentiation for 1024-bit RSA and a scalar multiplication for 160-bit ECC over $\mathbb{F}_{2^{163}}$ using components distributed by Bouncy Castle [4]. The modular exponentiation is ($T^d \bmod n$) for given 1024-bit integers T, d, n. We use the parameters of ECC from Certicom [9], and the scalar multiplication is dP for a given 160-bit integer d and a point P. Timing results for each cryptosystem are as follows:

Table 2. Comparison of Timing with Other Cryptosystems (msec)

Operator	FOMA SH901iS	Pentium M
η_T pairing with $opt\mathbb{F}_{3^{97}}$	509.22	10.15
Modular exponentiation of 1024-bit RSA	4238.40	75.07
Scalar multiplication of ECC over $\mathbb{F}_{2^{163}}$	13777.50	116.83

The η_T pairing with $opt\mathbb{F}_{3^{97}}$ is faster than the modular exponentiation of 1024-bit RSA and the scalar multiplication of 160-bit ECC. However our implementation of the η_T pairing does not sufficiently support the processing by exceptions, comparing with the release version of Bouncy Castle provider. Therefore the timing of the η_T pairing with $\mathbb{F}_{3^{97}}$ is relatively fast, but the η_T pairing is still calculated enough efficient. For the comparison we also show the timings of executing the same programs on a Pentium M 1.73GHz with 1GB RAM.

5 Conclusion

In this paper, we presented the first implementation of Tate pairing over a mobile phone using Java. The η_T pairing over finite fields $\mathbb{F}_{3^m}$, which is the fastest version of Duursma-Lee algorithm, was implemented. There is no mathematical library from the Java cryptographic extension (JCE) for computing the arithmetic of finite fields $\mathbb{F}_{3^m}$, so that we implemented it from scratch in Java. The optimized implementation of the η_T pairing with $m = 97$ achieves about 0.5 seconds on a mobile phone FOMA SH901iS, NTT DoCoMo. This mobile phone is not the currently newest one, and the processing speed of the next models should become faster. Therefore the paring-based cryptosystems can be efficiently implemented on mobile phones using Java.

Acknowledgements

This research was supported by the New Energy and Industrial Technology Development Organization (NEDO), Japan.

References

1. Barreto, P. S. L. M.: A note on efficient computation of cube roots in characteristic 3, IACR ePrint Archive, Report 2004/305 (2004)
2. Barreto, P. S. L. M., Galbraith, S., O'hEigeartaigh, C., Scott, M.: Efficient pairing computation on supersingular abelian varieties, To appear in Designs, Codes, and Cryptography
3. Barreto, P.S.L.M., Kim, H., Lynn, B., Scott, M.: Efficient algorithms for pairing-based cryptosystems. In: Yung, M. (ed.) Advances in Cryptology - CRYPTO 2002. LNCS, vol. 2442, pp. 354–368. Springer, Heidelberg (2002)
4. Bouncy Castle Crypto APIs, The Legion of the Bouncy Castle. `http://www.bouncycastle.org/`
5. Bertoni, G., Guajardo, J., Kumar, S., Orland, G., Paar, C., Wollinger, T.: Efficient GF(p^m) arithmetic architectures for cryptographic application. In: Joye, M. (ed.) Topics in Cryptology - CT-RSA 2003. LNCS, vol. 2612, pp. 158–175. Springer, Heidelberg (2003)
6. Boneh, D., Franklin, M.: Identity based encryption from the Weil pairing. SIAM J. Comput. 32(3), 586–615 (2001)
7. Boneh, D., Gentry, C., Waters, B.: Collusion resistant broadcast encryption with short ciphertexts and private keys. In: Shoup, V. (ed.) Advances in Cryptology – CRYPTO 2005. LNCS, vol. 3621, pp. 258–275. Springer, Heidelberg (2005)
8. Boneh, D., Lynn, B., Shacham, H.: Short signatures from the Weil pairing. In: Boyd, C. (ed.) Advances in Cryptology - ASIACRYPT 2001. LNCS, vol. 2248, pp. 514–532. Springer, Heidelberg (2001)
9. Certicom Research, "SEC 2: Recommended Elliptic Curve Domain Parameters", Version 1.0 (2000)
10. Duursma, I., Lee, H.: Tate pairing implementation for hyperelliptic curves $y^2 = x^p - x + d$. In: Laih, C.-S. (ed.) Advances in Cryptology - ASIACRYPT 2003. LNCS, vol. 2894, pp. 111–123. Springer, Heidelberg (2003)
11. Hankerson, D., Menezes, A., Vanstone, S.: Guide to elliptic curve cryptography. Springer, Heidelberg (2004)
12. Harrison, K., Page, D., Smart, N.: Software implementation of finite fields of characteristic three, for use in pairing-based cryptosystems. LMS J. Comput. Math. 5, 181–193 (2002)
13. IAIK Provider for the Java Cryptography Extension (IAIK-JCE). `http://www.iaik.tugraz.at/`
14. Java 2 Platform, Micro Edition (J2ME). `http://java.sun.com/javame/`
15. Java Cryptography Extension (JCE). `http://java.sun.com/products/jce/`
16. Kerins, T., Marnane, W., Popovici, E., Barreto, P.S.L.M.: Efficient hardware for the Tate pairing calculation in characteristic three. In: Rao, J.R., Sunar, B. (eds.) Cryptographic Hardware and Embedded Systems – CHES 2005. LNCS, vol. 3659, pp. 412–426. Springer, Heidelberg (2005)
17. S. Kwon, "Efficient Tate pairing computation for supersingular elliptic curves over binary fields", IACR ePrint Archive, Report, p. 303 (2004)
18. Scott, M., Costigan, N., Abdulwahab, W.: Implementing Cryptographic Pairings on Smartcards. In: Goubin, L., Matsui, M. (eds.) Cryptographic Hardware and Embedded Systems - CHES 2006. LNCS, vol. 4249, pp. 134–147. Springer, Heidelberg (2006)
19. Silverman, J.: The arithmetic of elliptic curves. Springer, Heidelberg (1986)
20. Takagi, T., Reis Jr., D., Yen, S.-M., Wu, B.-C.: Radix-r non-adjacent form and its application to pairing-based cryptosystem. IEICE Transactions, E89-A(1), 115–123 (2006)

21. Tillich, S., Großschadl, J.: A survey of public-key cryptography on J2ME-enabled mobile devices. In: Aykanat, C., Dayar, T., Körpeoğlu, İ. (eds.) Computer and Information Sciences - ISCIS 2004. LNCS, vol. 3280, pp. 935–944. Springer, Heidelberg (2004)

A Extended Euclidean Algorithm by Ternary Polynomial

The extended Euclidean algorithm for the polynomials over $\mathbb{F}_2[x]$ is shown [11]. We develop a ternary version of the extended Euclidean algorithm. Let $A(x)$ be the element in $\mathbb{F}_{3^m}$, and $deg()$ be the function computed degree. Inversion $A(x)^{-1} \bmod f(x)$ is computed as follows:

Algorithm 4. Inversion in $\mathbb{F}_{3^m}$

Input: $A(x) \in \mathbb{F}_{3^m} = \mathbb{F}_3[x]/(f(x))$ with irreducible trinomial $f(x)$.
Output: $A(x)^{-1} \bmod f(x)$

$u \leftarrow A(x),\ v \leftarrow f(x)$
$g \leftarrow 1,\ h \leftarrow 0$
while $deg(u) \neq 0$ **do**
  $j \leftarrow deg(u) - deg(v)$
  if $j < 0$ **then**
    $u \leftrightarrow v,\ g \leftrightarrow h,\ j \leftarrow -j$
  end if
  $u \leftarrow u - (u_{deg(u)} \cdot v_{deg(v)})\ v \cdot x^j$
  $g \leftarrow g - (u_{deg(u)} \cdot v_{deg(v)})\ h \cdot x^j$
end while
if $u_0 = 2$ **then**
  $g \leftarrow -g$
end if
return g

B Arithmetic in $\mathbb{F}_{3^{3m}}$

Extension field $\mathbb{F}_{3^{3m}}$ can be represented by $\mathbb{F}_{3^m}[\rho]/g(\rho)$, where $g(\rho)$ is an irreducible polynomial $g(\rho) = \rho^3 - \rho - 1$ over $\mathbb{F}_{3^m}[X]$. We denote by $A(\rho)$ the element in $\mathbb{F}_{3^{3m}}$, where $A(\rho) = a_2\rho^2 + a_1\rho + a_0$ for $a_0, a_1, a_2 \in \mathbb{F}_{3^m}$. Arithmetic in $\mathbb{F}_{3^{3m}}$ is performed as follows:

- **Addition :** $A(\rho) + B(\rho) = (a_2 + b_2)\rho^2 + (a_1 + b_1)\rho + (a_0 + b_0)$.
- **Multiplication :** Let $t_{00} = a_0b_0$, $t_{11} = a_1b_1$, $t_{22} = a_2b_2$, $t_{01} = (a_0+a_1)(b_0+b_1)$, $t_{12} = (a_1 + a_2)(b_1 + b_2)$, $t_{02} = (a_0 + a_2)(b_0 + b_2)$. Then $A(\rho)B(\rho) = (t_{02}+t_{11}-t_{00})+(t_{12}+t_{01}+t_{00}-t_{11})\rho+(t_{12}+t_{00}-t_{11}-t_{22})\rho^2$. Multiplication in $\mathbb{F}_{3^{3m}}$ is computed by 6 multiplications and some additions in $\mathbb{F}_{3^m}$.
- **Cube :** $A(\rho)^3 = a_2^3\rho^2 + (a_1^3 - a_2^3)\rho + (a_0^3 + a_1^3 + a_2^3)$. Cube in $\mathbb{F}_{3^{3m}}$ uses 3 cubes and some additions in $\mathbb{F}_{3^m}$.
- **Inversion :** We implemented inversion in $\mathbb{F}_{3^{3m}}$ using the algorithm shown by Kerins et. al. [16]. This algorithm can be obtained with 1 inversion, 12 multiplications and some additions in $\mathbb{F}_{3^m}$.

ID-Based (t, n) Threshold Proxy Signcryption for Multi-agent Systems*

Fagen Li[1,2], Yupu Hu[1], and Shuanggen Liu[1,3]

[1] Key Laboratory of Computer Networks and Information Security, Xidian University, Xi'an 710071, China
[2] School of Computer Science and Engineering, University of Electronic Science and Technology of China, Chengdu 610054, China
[3] College of Computer Information Engineering, Jiangxi Normal University, Nanchang 330022, China
fagenli@mail.xidian.edu.cn

Abstract. A (t, n) threshold proxy signcryption scheme allows t or more proxy signcrypters from a designated group of n proxy signcrypters to signcrypt messages on behalf of an original signcrypter. In this paper, an identity-based (t, n) threshold proxy signcryption scheme using bilinear pairings is proposed. Our construction is based on Baek and Zheng's pairing-based verifiable secret sharing scheme and Libert and Quisquater's identity-based signcryption scheme. As compared to the previous threshold proxy signcryption schemes, the key management problem in our scheme is simplified because of using identity-based cryptography. We also present an application of our scheme in multi-agent systems.

1 Introduction

Identity-based (ID-based) cryptography is rapidly emerging in recent years. The distinguishing property of ID-based cryptography is that a user's public key can be any binary string, such as an email address that can identify the user. This removes the need for senders to look up the recipient's public key before sending out an encrypted message. ID-based cryptography is supposed to provide a more convenient alternative to conventional public key infrastructure. In 1984, Shamir [1] firstly proposed the idea of ID-based cryptography. Several practical ID-based signature schemes have been devised [2,3], but a satisfying ID-based encryption scheme only appeared in 2001 [4]. It was devised by Boneh and Franklin and cleverly uses bilinear maps (the Weil or Tate pairing) over supersingular elliptic curves.

In 1996, Mambo et al. [5] first introduced the concept of proxy signature. In the proxy signature scheme, an original signer is allowed to delegate his signing

* This work is supported by the National Natural Science Foundation of China under contract no. 60473029.

Y. Wang, Y. Cheung, and H. Liu (Eds.): CIS 2006, LNAI 4456, pp. 406–416, 2007.

power to a designated person, called the proxy signer and the proxy signer is able to sign the message on behalf of the original signer. Consider the situation that the original signer might want to delegate the signing power to a group of proxy signers for sharing signing responsibility. The concept of threshold proxy signature scheme is designed for achieving this goal [6,7]. In a (t, n) threshold proxy signature scheme, which is a variant of the proxy signature scheme, the proxy signature key is shared among a group of n proxy signers delegated by the original signer. Any t or more proxy signers can cooperatively sign messages on behalf of the original signer, but $t - 1$ or fewer proxy signers cannot.

Confidentiality, integrity, non-repudiation and authentication are the important requirements for many cryptographic applications. A traditional approach to achieve these requirements is to sign-then-encrypt the message. Signcryption, first proposed by Zheng [8] in 1997, is a cryptographic primitive that performs signature and encryption simultaneously, at lower computational costs and communication overheads than the signature-then-encryption approach. In 1999, Gamage et al. [9] introduced a new notion called proxy signcryption by combining the concepts of proxy signature and signcryption together. In such a scheme, an original signcrypter can delegate his signcrypting power to a designated person, called the proxy signcrypter who can generate signcryption on behalf of the original signcrypter. In 2002, Chan and Wei [10] proposed a threshold proxy signcryption by combining the concepts of threshold proxy signature and signcryption together. In a threshold proxy signcryption scheme, the proxy signcryption key is shared among a group of n proxy signcrypters delegated by the original signcrypter. Any t or more proxy signcrypters can cooperatively signcrypt messages on behalf of the original signcrypter, but $t-1$ or fewer proxy signcrypters cannot. Li et al. [11] showed that Chan and Wei's scheme does not satisfy the strong unforgeability, strong undeniability and strong identifiability and proposed a new threshold proxy signcryption scheme with known signcrypter. To construct a secure threshold proxy signcryption scheme, the following requirements must be satisfied [8,12]:

- **Distinguishability:** Threshold proxy signcryptions are distinguishable from normal signcryptions by everyone.
- **Verifiability:** From the threshold proxy signcryption, the verifier can be convinced of the original signcrypter's agreement on the signcrypted message.
- **Strong unforgeability:** A group of designated proxy signcrypters can create a valid threshold proxy signcryption for the original signcrypter. But the original signcrypter and other third parties who are not designated as the proxy signcrypters cannot create a valid threshold proxy signcryption.
- **Strong identifiability:** Anyone can determine the identities of the corresponding proxy signcrypters from the threshold proxy signcryption.
- **Strong undeniability:** Once a group of proxy signcrypters create a valid threshold proxy signcryption of an original signcrypter, they cannot repudiate the signcryption creation.
- **Prevention of misuse:** The proxy signcrypters cannot use the proxy key for other purposes than generating a valid threshold proxy signcryption.

That is, they cannot signcrypt messages that have not been authorized by the original signcrypter.
- **Message confidentiality:** It is computationally infeasible for an attacker (who may be any dishonest entity other than intended recipient) to gain any partial information on the contents of a signcrypted message.

To our best knowledge, no ID-based threshold proxy signcryption scheme has been found so far. In this paper, we present an ID-based threshold proxy signcryption scheme from bilinear pairings. Our construction is based on Baek and Zheng's pairing-based verifiable secret sharing scheme [13] and Libert and Quisquater's ID-based signcryption scheme [14]. As compared to the previous threshold proxy signcryption schemes, the key management problem in our scheme is simplified because of using ID-based cryptography.

The rest of this paper is organized as follows. Some preliminary works are described in Section 2. The proposed ID-based threshold proxy signcryption scheme is given in Section 3. The security of the proposed scheme is discussed in Section 4. The application of our scheme in multi-agent systems is presented in 5. Finally, the conclusions are given in Section 6.

2 Preliminaries

2.1 Bilinear Pairings

Let G_1 be a cyclic additive group generated by P, whose order is a prime q, and G_2 be a cyclic multiplicative group of the same order q. Let a, b be elements of Z_q^*. A bilinear pairing is a map $\hat{e} : G_1 \times G_1 \rightarrow G_2$ with the following properties:

1. Bilinearity: $\hat{e}(aP, bQ) = \hat{e}(P, Q)^{ab}$ for all $P, Q \in G_1$.
2. Non-degeneracy: There exists P and $Q \in G_1$ such that $\hat{e}(P, Q) \neq 1$.
3. Computability: There is an efficient algorithm to compute $\hat{e}(P, Q)$ for all P,$Q \in G_1$.

The modified Weil pairing and the Tate pairing [4] are admissible maps of this kind. The security of our scheme described here relies on the hardness of the following problems.

Definition 1. *Given two groups G_1 and G_2 of the same prime order q, a bilinear map $\hat{e} : G_1 \times G_1 \rightarrow G_2$ and a generator P of G_1, the Bilinear Diffie-Hellman problem (BDHP) in $(G_1, G_2, \hat{e})$ is to compute $h = \hat{e}(P, P)^{abc}$ given (P, aP, bP, cP).*

Definition 2. *Given two groups G_1 and G_2 of the same prime order q, a bilinear map $\hat{e} : G_1 \times G_1 \rightarrow G_2$ and a generator P of G_1, the Decisional Bilinear Diffie-Hellman problem (DBDHP) in $(G_1, G_2, \hat{e})$ is to decide whether $h = \hat{e}(P, P)^{abc}$ given (P, aP, bP, cP) and an element $h \in G_2$.*

The decisional problem is of course not harder than the computational one. However, no algorithm is known to be able to solve any of them so far.

2.2 Baek and Zheng's Pairing-Based Secret Sharing Scheme

Secret sharing allows a secret to be shared among a group of users in such a way that no single user can deduce the secret from his share alone. To construct the secret, one needs to combine a sufficient number of shares. A (t, n) threshold secret sharing scheme represents that the secret is distributed to n users, and any t or more users can reconstruct the secret from their shares, but $t-1$ or fewer users cannot get any information about the secret. Here, t is the threshold parameter such that $1 \leq t \leq n$. We describe Baek and Zheng's pairing-based secret sharing scheme [13] as follows.

Let $(G_1, q, P, \hat{e})$ be a set of parameters, as defined in Section 2.1. Suppose that a threshold t and the number of parties n satisfy $1 \leq t \leq n < q$. To share a secret $S \in G_1^*$ among n users, a dealer (trusted authority) performs the steps below.

1. Choose $F_1, \ldots, F_{t-1}$ uniformly at random from G_1^*, construct a polynomial
$$F(x) = S + xF_1 + \cdots + x^{t-1}F_{t-1}$$
and compute $S_i = F(i)$ for $i = 0, \ldots, n$. Note that $S_0 = S$.
2. Send S_i to user P_i for $i = 1, \ldots, n$ secretly. Broadcast $\alpha_0 = \hat{e}(S, P)$ and $\alpha_j = \hat{e}(F_j, P)$ for $j = 1, \ldots, t-1$.
3. Each user P_i then checks whether his share S_i is valid by computing
$$\hat{e}(S_i, P) = \prod_{j=0}^{t-1} \alpha_j^{i^j}.$$

2.3 Libert and Quisquater's ID-Based Signcryption Scheme

Libert and Quisquater's ID-based signcryption scheme [14] consists of the following four algorithms.

- **Setup:** Given a security parameter k, the PKG chooses groups G_1 and G_2 of prime order q (with G_1 additive and G_2 multiplicative), a generator P of G_1, a bilinear map $\hat{e} : G_1 \times G_1 \rightarrow G_2$ and hash functions $H_1 : \{0,1\}^* \rightarrow G_1$, $H_2 : G_2 \rightarrow \{0,1\}^n$ and $H_3 : \{0,1\}^* \times G_2 \rightarrow Z_q^*$. It chooses a master-key $s \in Z_q^*$ and computes $P_{pub} = sP$. It also chooses a secure symmetric cipher (E, D). The PKG publishes system's public parameters $\{G_1, G_2, n, \hat{e}, P, P_{pub}, H_1, H_2, H_3, E, D\}$ and keeps the master-key s secret.
- **Extraction:** Given an identity ID, the PKG computes $Q_{ID} = H_1(ID)$ and the private key $S_{ID} = sQ_{ID}$.
- **Signcryption:** To send a message m to Bob, Alice follows the steps below.
  1. Compute $Q_{ID_B} = H_1(ID_B)$.
  2. Choose x from Z_q^* randomly, and compute $k_1 = \hat{e}(P, P_{pub})^x$ and $k_2 = H_2(\hat{e}(P_{pub}, Q_{ID_B})^x)$.
  3. Compute $c = E_{k_2}(m), r = H_3(c, k_1)$ and $S = xP_{pub} - rS_{ID_A}$.

  The ciphertext is $\sigma = (c, r, S)$.

- **Unsigncryption:** When receiving $\sigma = (c, r, S)$, Bob performs the following tasks.
  1. Compute $Q_{ID_A} = H_1(ID_A)$.
  2. Compute $k'_1 = \hat{e}(P, S)\hat{e}(P_{pub}, Q_{ID_A})^r$.
  3. Compute $k'_2 = H_2(\hat{e}(S, Q_{ID_B})\hat{e}(Q_{ID_A}, S_{ID_B})^r)$.
  4. Recover $m = D_{k'_2}(c)$ and accept σ if and only if the following equation holds:
$$r = H_3(c, k'_1). \tag{1}$$

3 ID-Based Threshold Proxy Signcryption

In this section, we propose an ID-based threshold proxy signcryption scheme using bilinear pairings. The proposed scheme uses Baek and Zheng's pairing-based verifiable secret sharing scheme [13] and Libert and Quisquater's ID-based signcryption scheme [14] as the basic scheme. Our scheme involves four roles: the PKG, the original signcrypter Alice with identity ID_A, a set of proxy signcrypters $L = \{P_1, P_2, \ldots, P_l\}$ with identity $ID_{P_1}, ID_{P_2}, \ldots, ID_{P_l}$, and the message recipient Bob with identity ID_B. Here, we use $ASID$ (Actual Signcrypters' ID) to denote the identities of the actual signcrypters who indeed signcrypt the message. It consists of the following five algorithms.

- **Setup:** Given a security parameter k, the PKG chooses groups G_1 and G_2 of prime order q (with G_1 additive and G_2 multiplicative), a generator P of G_1, a bilinear map $\hat{e} : G_1 \times G_1 \rightarrow G_2$ and hash functions $H_1 : \{0,1\}^* \rightarrow G_1$, $H_2 : G_2 \rightarrow \{0,1\}^n$ and $H_3 : \{0,1\}^* \rightarrow Z_q^*$. It chooses a master-key $s \in Z_q^*$ and computes $P_{pub} = sP$. It also chooses a secure symmetric cipher (E, D). The PKG publishes system's parameters $\{G_1, G_2, n, \hat{e}, P, P_{pub}, H_1, H_2, H_3, E, D\}$ and keeps the master-key s secret.
- **Extraction:** Given an identity ID, the PKG computes $Q_{ID} = H_1(ID)$ and the private key $S_{ID} = sQ_{ID}$.
- **Generation of the proxy key:** To delegate the signcrypting power to the proxy group L, the original signcrypter Alice follows the steps below to generate the signed warrant m_w and each proxy signcrypter P_i computes his proxy private key S_{AP_i}. The warrant m_w specifies the delegation period, what kind of messages is delegated and identity information of the original signcrypter and the proxy signcrypters, etc.
  1. Alice chooses x from Z_q^* randomly and computes $U = xP$, $S_{m_w} = hS_{ID_A} + xP_{pub}$, where $h = H_3(m_w, U)$. Then Alice sends (m_w, U) to the proxy group L.
  2. Alice chooses $F_1, \ldots, F_{t-1}$ uniformly at random from G_1^*, constructs a polynomial
$$F(x) = S_{m_w} + xF_1 + \cdots + x^{t-1}F_{t-1}$$
and computes $S_i = F(i)$ for $i = 0, \ldots, n$. Note that $S_0 = S_{m_w}$.
  3. Alice sends S_i to proxy signcrypter P_i for $i = 1, \ldots, n$ secretly, and broadcasts $\alpha_0 = \hat{e}(S_{m_w}, P)$ and $\alpha_j = \hat{e}(F_j, P)$ for $j = 1, \ldots, t-1$.

4. Each proxy signcrypter P_i verifies the correctness of S_i from Alice by checking if the following equation holds:

$$\hat{e}(S_i, P) = \hat{e}(P_{pub}, Q_{ID_A})^h \hat{e}(U, P_{pub}) \prod_{j=1}^{t-1} \alpha_j^{i^j},$$

where $h = H_3(m_w, U)$. If this fails, P_i broadcasts that an error has been found, publishes S_i and then requests a valid one; otherwise P_i computes his proxy private key $S_{AP_i} = hS_{ID_{P_i}} + w_i S_i$, where $w_i = \prod_{j=1, j\neq i}^{t} -j(i-j)^{-1}$.

- **Threshold proxy signcryption:** Without loss of generality, we assume that $P_1, \ldots, P_t$ are the t proxy signcrypters who want to cooperate to signcrypt a message m on behalf of the original signcrypter Alice. Each proxy signcrypter uses Libert and Quisquater's ID-based signcryption scheme [14] to generate the individual proxy signcryption and an appointed clerk C, who is one of the proxy signcrypters, combines the individual proxy signcryptions to generate the final threshold proxy signcryption.
  1. Each P_i computes $Q_{ID_B} = H_1(ID_B)$.
  2. Each P_i chooses x_i from Z_q^* randomly, computes $k_{1i} = \hat{e}(P, P_{pub})^{x_i}$ and $k_{2i} = \hat{e}(P_{pub}, Q_{ID_B})^{x_i}$, and then sends (k_{1i}, k_{2i}) to the clerk C.
  3. The clerk C computes $k_1 = \prod_{i=1}^{t} k_{1i}$, $k_2 = H_2(\prod_{i=1}^{t} k_{2i})$, $c = E_{k_2}(m)$ and $r = H_3(ASID, c, k_1)$. Then he sends r to P_i for $i = 1, \ldots, t$.
  4. Each P_i computes the individual proxy signcryption $S_{P_i} = x_i P_{pub} - rS_{AP_i}$ and send it to the clerk C.
  5. When receiving all individual proxy signcryptions from $P_i (i=1, 2, \ldots, t)$, the clerk C firstly computes $k'_{1i} = \hat{e}(P, S_{P_i})(\hat{e}(P_{pub}, Q_{ID_{P_i}}) \cdot (\prod_{j=0}^{t-1} \alpha_j^{i^j})^{w_i})^r$ and then check if the following equation holds:

$$r = H_3(ASID, c, k'_{1i} \cdot \prod_{j=1, j\neq i}^{t} k_{1j}). \quad (2)$$

  If all individual proxy signcryptions are verified to be legal, the clerk C computes $S = \sum_{i=1}^{t} S_{P_i}$; otherwise rejects it and requests a valid one. The final threshold proxy signcryption is $\sigma = (m_w, U, c, r, S, ASID)$.

- **Unsigncryption:** When receiving $\sigma = (m_w, U, c, r, S, ASID)$, the message recipient Bob performs the following tasks.
  1. From $ASID$, the Bob knows who the actual signcrypters are. Here, we have assumed that $P_1, \ldots, P_t$ are the actual signcrypters.
  2. Compute $Q_{ID_A} = H_1(ID_A)$ and $Q_{ID_{P_i}} = H_1(ID_{P_i})$ for $i = 1, \ldots, t$.
  3. Compute $h = H_3(m_w, U)$.
  4. Compute $k'_1 = \hat{e}(P, S)(\hat{e}(P_{pub}, Q_{ID_A} + \sum_{i=1}^{t} Q_{ID_{P_i}})^h \hat{e}(P_{pub}, U))^r$.
  5. Compute $k'_2 = H_2(\hat{e}(S, Q_{ID_B})(\hat{e}(Q_{ID_A} + \sum_{i=1}^{t} Q_{ID_{P_i}}, S_{ID_B})^h \hat{e}(U, S_{ID_B}))^r)$.

6. Recover $m = D_{k'_2}(c)$ and accept σ if and only if the following equation holds:
$$r = H_3(ASID, c, k'_1). \tag{3}$$

4 Security Analysis

In this section, we discuss the security of the proposed threshold proxy signcryption scheme. We show that our ID-based threshold proxy signcryption scheme satisfies all the requirements stated in Section 1.

- **Distinguishability:** This is obvious, because there is a warrant m_w in a valid threshold proxy signcryption, at the same time, this warrant m_w and the public keys of the original signcrypter and the proxy signcrypters must occur in the verification equation of the threshold proxy signcryption.
- **Verifiability:** Because the warrant m_w contains the identity information and the limit of the delegated signcrypting power, the verifier can verify the threshold proxy signcryption and check whether the signcrypted message conforms to the delegation warrant or not.
- **Strong unforgeability:** We consider two types of attacks to the proposed scheme: the outsider forgery attack and the insider forgery attack.
  - Outsider forgery attack: An adversary A, who is not in the proxy group L may attempt to forge a threshold proxy signcryption for a chosen message. In this attack, we assume that all public information is available to A.
  - Insider forgery attack: A co-signcrypter in the proxy group L or the collusion of some co-signcrypters may attempt to forge the threshold proxy signcryption for the proxy group. In this attack, we assuming the number of malicious co-signcrypters in proxy group can be as many as $l - 1$.

Due to the employment of the basic scheme, the security of the proposed scheme is based on the robustness of Libert and Quisquater's scheme [14]. Besides, we assume that all hash functions used herein are secure for cryptographic usages. Below, we first prove the security of the individual proxy signcryption is equivalent to the signcryption in Libert and Quisquater's scheme. Subsequently, we show that the proposed scheme is secure against the outsider forgery attack and the insider forgery attack. Our proving method used here is similar to the one in [15].

Theorem 1. *The security of the individual proxy signcryption is equivalent to the signcryption in Libert and Quisquater's scheme under the assumption that the hash function H_3 is secure.*

Proof. In Libert and Quisquater's scheme, a valid signcryption for message m is (c, r, S), and its verification equation (1) can be represented as

$$r = H_3(c, \hat{e}(P, S)\hat{e}(P_{pub}, Q_{ID_A})^r). \tag{4}$$

In the proposed scheme, a valid individual proxy signcryption for message m is (c, r, S_{P_i}). The verification equation (2) can be represented as

$$r = H_3(ASID, c, \hat{e}(P, S_{P_i})(\hat{e}(P_{pub}, Q_{ID_{P_i}}) \cdot (\prod_{j=0}^{t-1} \alpha_j^{i^j})^{w_i})^r \cdot \prod_{j=1, j \neq i}^{t} k_{1j}). \quad (5)$$

In Eq.(5), if $\prod_{j=1, j\neq i}^{t} k_{1j}$ is fixed in advance, then the construction of the Eq.(5) is related to Eq.(4), which implies that finding a valid proxy signcryption (c, r, S_{P_i}) for Eq.(5) will require the same knowledge as the case for Eq.(4). On the other hand, if r is fixed prior to the computing of $(c, S_{P_i}, \prod_{j=1, j\neq i}^{t} k_{1j})$ to satisfy the Eq.(5), the adversary will have to convert H_3 to attempting this. Under the assumption that H_3 is a secure hash function, the security of the individual proxy signcryption in the proposed schemes is equivalent to that of the signcryption in Libert and Quisquater's scheme, which is secure against adaptively chosen message attack in the random oracle model [14]. □

Theorem 2. *The proposed scheme is secure against the outsider forgery attack.*

Proof. For the outsider forgery attack, consider that an adversary A, who is not in the proxy group L may attempt to forge a threshold proxy signcryption of a chosen message m for the proxy group L. That is, A knows all public information, including all the public keys $Q_{ID_{P_i}}$ for all P_i, and wants to find $(c, r, S, ASID)$ satisfying the verification equation (3). The verification equation (3) can be represented as

$$r = H_3(ASID, c, \hat{e}(P, S)(\hat{e}(P_{pub}, Q_{ID_A} + \sum_{i=1}^{t} Q_{ID_{P_i}})^h \hat{e}(P_{pub}, U))^r). \quad (6)$$

In Eq.(6), by letting the public verification key for Q as $Q_{ID_A} + \sum_{i=1}^{t} Q_{ID_{P_i}}$, the construction of the threshold proxy signcryption of our scheme can be related to the construction of the signcryption in Libert and Quisquater's scheme. This implies that such attack is equivalent to the signcryption forgery in Libert and Quisquater's scheme. Since Libert and Quisquater's scheme is secure against existential forgery on adaptively chosen message attack in the random oracle model [14], the outsider forgery attack is infeasible in the our scheme. Even the original signcrypter Alice cannot create a valid threshold proxy signcryption since each proxy private key includes the private key $S_{ID_{P_i}}$ of each proxy signcrypter. □

Theorem 3. *The proposed scheme is secure against the insider forgery attack.*

Proof. For the insider forgery attack, we assume that there is at least one honest co-signcrypter P_k in the proxy group L. Considering that some malicious signcrypters who want to generate the threshold proxy signcryption of the message m for the proxy group L. From **Threshold proxy signcryption**, it can be see that all malicious co-signcrypters have to obtain P_k's individual proxy signcryption to attempt this. With all public information and individual proxy signcryptions generated by P_k regarding some messages different to m, all malicious co-signcrypters may try to deduce P_k's proxy private key or forge P_k's individual proxy signcryption for m. However, deducing P_k's proxy private key $S_{AP_k} = hS_{ID_{P_k}} + w_iS_i$ from his public key $Q_{ID_{P_k}}$ requires the knowledge of PKG's private key s, and finding s from PKG's public key $P_{pub} = sP$ requires solving discrete logarithm problem. On the other hand, the individual proxy signcryption (c, r, S_{P_i}) has the same security strength as the signcryption in Libert and Quisquater's scheme, which has been proven in Theorem 1. Therefore, the insider forgery attack is infeasible. □

- **Strong identifiability:** From $ASID$, the Bob can determine the identity of the actual signcrypters.
- **Strong undeniability:** The clerk C verifies the individual proxy signcryption of each proxy signcrypter, so no one can be deniable of his signcryption.
- **Prevention of misuse:** Due to using the warrant m_w, the proxy signcrypters can only signcrypt messages that have been authorized by the original signcrypter.
- **Message confidentiality:** For message confidentiality, we have the following Theorem 4.

Theorem 4. *The message confidentiality of the our scheme is equivalent to that of Libert and Quisquater's scheme.*

Proof. In Libert and Quisquater's scheme, a valid ciphertext for message m is $c = E_{k_2}(m)$, where

$$k_2 = H_2(\hat{e}(S, Q_{ID_B})\hat{e}(Q_{ID_A}, S_{ID_B})^r). \tag{7}$$

In the proposed scheme, a valid ciphertext for message m is $c = E_{k_2}(m)$ and k_2 can be represented as

$$k_2 = H_2(\hat{e}(S, Q_{ID_B})(\hat{e}(Q_{ID_A} + \sum_{i=1}^{t} Q_{ID_{P_i}}, S_{ID_B})^h \hat{e}(U, S_{ID_B}))^r). \tag{8}$$

In Eq.(8), by letting $Q = Q_{ID_A} + \sum_{i=1}^{t} Q_{ID_{P_i}}$, then the Eq.(8) is related to Eq.(7), which implies that finding a valid k_2 for Eq.(8) will require the same knowledge as the case for Eq.(7). Therefore, the message confidentiality of the proposed scheme is equivalent to that of Libert and Quisquater's scheme, which is secure against adaptively chosen ciphertext attack in the random oracle model [14]. □

5 Application in Multi-agent Systems

Mobile agents are autonomous software entities that are able to migrate across different execution environments through network. In multi-agent systems, agents interact with other agents, no-agent software and cooperate to achieve common goals. With the features of mobility and autonomy, the mobile agents have been widely used in many applications such as electronic purses, electronic payment, information retrieval, and negotiation systems to achieve higher efficiency at lower costs. Furthermore, they provide better support for heterogeneous environments. However, the security threats are still the deployment bottleneck. For instances, the private keys and the confidential information carried by the agents are very difficult to protect in a hostile execution environment. If a mobile agent can signcrypt a message on behalf of the agent owner (customer) in a remote server (vendor) without revealing customer's private key, the mobile agent can be used not only to search for special products or services, but also to signcrypt a contract with the vendor. Fortunately, our (t, n) threshold proxy signcryption scheme provides a good solution to this problem. A customer can delegate signcrypting power to n designated agents. These agents can search for a lower price products or services without concerning the global decisions. When t or more agents come to the same decision, then t agents cooperate to book it by signcryption. The use of signcryption technique ensures the confidentiality and unforgeability of the transaction.

6 Conclusions

The threshold proxy signcryption is useful for a group of proxy signcrypters to signcrypt the messages on behalf of the original signcrypter. In this paper, We proposed an ID-based threshold proxy signcryption scheme by using Baek and Zheng's pairing-based verifiable secret sharing scheme and Libert and Quisquater's ID-based signcryption scheme as the basic tools. As compared to the previous threshold proxy signcryption schemes, the key management problem in our scheme is simplified because of using ID-based cryptography. Our scheme is very useful in multi-agent systems.

References

1. Shamir, A.: Identity-based cryptosystems and signature schemes. In: Blakely, G.R., Chaum, D. (eds.) Advances in Cryptology-CRYPTO'84. LNCS, vol. 196, pp. 47–53. Springer, Heidelberg (1984)
2. Fiat, A., Shamir, A.: How to prove yourself: practical solutions to identification and signature problems. In: Odlyzko, A.M. (ed.) Advances in Cryptology - CRYPTO '86. LNCS, vol. 263, pp. 186–194. Springer, Heidelberg (1986)
3. Guillou, L., Quisquater, J.J.: A "Paradoxical" Identity-based signature scheme resulting from zero-knowledge. In: Goldwasser, S. (ed.) Advances in Cryptology-CRYPTO'88. LNCS, vol. 403, pp. 216–231. Springer, Heidelberg (1988)
4. Boneh, D., Franklin, M.: Identity-based encryption from the weil pairing. In: Kilian, J. (ed.) Advances in Cryptology-CRYPTO 2001. LNCS, vol. 2139, pp. 213–229. Springer, Heidelberg (2001)
5. Mambo, M., Usuda, K., Okamoto, E.: Proxy signature: delegation of the power to sign messages. IEICE Transactions on Fundamentals of Electronics, Communications and Computer Sciences E79-A, 1338–1353 (1996)

6. Kim, S., Park, S., Won, D.: Proxy signatures, revisited. In: Han, Y., Quing, S. (eds.) Information and Communications Security-ICICS'97. LNCS, vol. 1334, Springer, Heidelberg (1997)
7. Zhang, K.: Threshold proxy signature schemes. In: Okamoto, E., Davida, G.I., Mambo, M. (eds.) Information Security Workshop-ISW'97. LNCS, vol. 1396, pp. 191–197. Springer, Heidelberg (1998)
8. Zheng, Y.: Digital signcryption or how to achieve cost (signature & encryption) $\ll$ cost (signature) + cost(encryption). In: Kaliski Jr., B.S. (ed.) Advances in Cryptology - CRYPTO '97. LNCS, vol. 1294, pp. 165–179. Springer, Heidelberg (1997)
9. Gamage, C., Leiwo, J., Zheng, Y.: An efficient scheme for secure message transmission using proxy-signcryption. In: 22nd Australasian Computer Science Conference, Auckland, New Zealand, pp. 420–431 (1999)
10. Chan, W.K., Wei, V.K.: A threshold proxy signcryption. In: 2002 International Conference on Security and Management, Las Vegas, USA (2002)
11. Li, J., Li, J., Cao, Z., Zhang, Y.: A nonrepudiable threshold proxy signcryption scheme with known proxy agent. Journal of Software 14, 2021–2027 (2003)
12. Lee, B., Kim, H., Kim, K.: Secure mobile agent using strong non-designated proxy signature. In: Varadharajan, V., Mu, Y. (eds.) Information Security and Privacy. LNCS, vol. 2119, pp. 474–484. Springer, Heidelberg (2001)
13. Baek, J., Zheng, Y.: Identity-based threshold signature from the bilinear pairings. In: International Conference on Information Technology: Coding and Computing-ITCC'04, Las Vegas, USA, pp. 124–128 (2004)
14. Libert, B., Quisquater, J.J.: A new identity based signcryption schemes from pairings. In: IEEE Information Theory Workshop, Paris, France, pp. 155–158 (2003)
15. Lin, C.Y., Wu, T.C., Zhang, F., Hwang, J.J.: New identity-based society oriented signature schemes from pairings on elliptic curves. Applied Mathematics and Computation 160, 245–260 (2005)

A Differential Power Analysis Attack of Block Cipher Based on the Hamming Weight of Internal Operation Unit*

JeaHoon Park[1], HoonJae Lee[2], JaeCheol Ha[3], YongJe Choi[4], HoWon Kim[4], and SangJae Moon[1]

[1] School of Electrical Engineering & Computer Science, Kyungpook National Univ., Korea
jenoon65@ee.knu.ac.kr, sjmoon@ee.knu.ac.kr
[2] School of Electrical Engineering & Computer Science, Dongseo Univ., Korea
hjlee@gdsu.dongseo.ac.kr
[3] Division of Information Science, Korea Nazarene Univ., Korea
jcha@kornu.ac.kr
[4] ETRI Researcher
choiyj@etri.re.kr, khw@etri.re.kr

Abstract. Power analysis attack, which was introduced by Kocher et al. in 1999, was known as the most threatening physical attack against low power device such as smart-card. The essential reason that allows an attacker to implement a power analysis attack on a cryptosystem is leakage information, which is leaked during the operation of the cryptosystem′s encryption/decryption process and related to internal secret information. The general and efficient power analysis attack method proposed in this paper is based on an internally divided operation unit. As such, the proposed power analysis attack is implemented to expose the weakness of the operation of a symmetric key encryption algorithm in a smart-card.

1 Introduction

Although a cryptosystem may be secure against mathematical analysis, it can still leak side-channel information related to secret information during cryptographic operations. In 1999, Kocher *et al.* introduced two types of attack that use power consumption signals [1].

A Simple Power Analysis(SPA) attack is described as an attack where the attacker can directly use a power consumption signal to break a cryptosystem. However, a developer can easily protect a cryptosystem from an SPA attack using random dummy codes or avoiding memory access by processing data in

* This research was supported by the MIC of Korea, under the ITRC support program supervised by the IITA(IITA-2006-C1090-0603-0026).

Y. Wang, Y. Cheung, and H. Liu (Eds.): CIS 2006, LNAI 4456, pp. 417–426, 2007.

registers. In contrast, a Differential Power Analysis(DPA) attack is much harder to protect against, as it uses a statistical and error-correcting method to extract secret information from a power consumption signal. A developer should always consider power analysis countermeasures, especially for a low power device, such as a smart-card, otherwise cryptographic devices leak side-channel information related to the internal secret key when a cryptographic algorithm is operated.

Our Contribution. The power analysis attack method proposed in this paper is based on the power difference in divided internal operation units and the power consumption according to Hamming weight. Although existing power analysis attacks and the proposed power analysis attack have some points in common, the proposed DPA attack is generic and efficient in analysis method. As such, the proposed power analysis attack is implemented to expose the weakness of the operation of a symmetric key encryption algorithm in a smart-card.

The remainder of this paper is organized as follows: Section 2 describes the AES symmetric key encryption algorithm and ARIA symmetric key encryption algorithm and explains briefly about existing power analysis attacks. Section 3 then presents the proposed power analysis attack and explains the experimental method of the proposed power analysis attack against AES and ARIA. Finally, Section 4 summarizes the proposed attack and emphasizes the weaknesses of a cryptosystem based on the power difference in divided internal operation units.

2 Symmetric Key Encryption and Power Analysis Attacks

2.1 Symmetric Key Encryption

In 2000, the National Institute of Standards and Technology(NIST) selected the Advanced Encryption Standard(AES) symmetric key encryption algorithm proposed by Rijndael to replace the Data Encryption Standard(DES) [2]. AES algorithm's each round function consists of SubBytes transformation, ShiftRows transformation, MixColumns transformation, and AddRoundKey transformation. SubBytes transformation, among the round functions, generally uses the look-up table which makes an 8-bit output using an 8-bit input, $S - box$.

In 2004, ARIA symmetric key encryption algorithm was proposed by the National Security Research Institute(NSRI) and National Intelligence Service and Academy in Korea [3,4]. ARIA algorithm's each round function consists of three sub-functions, the AddRoundKey transformation, substitution layer, diffusion layer. The substitution layer(LT) for each round function consists of four look-up table $S_1 S - box$, $S_2 S - box$, $S_1^{-1} S - box$, $S_2^{-1} S - box$, which makes an 8-bit output from an 8-bit input.

2.2 Power Analysis Attacks

Side-channel information related to internal secret information is leaked during a cryptographic operation in a low power device [5]. As such, the power analysis attack was first proposed by Kocher in 1999 [1]. Since then, the attack has been enhanced by studies on power analysis, making the attack more practical and threatening with an expanded application area.

Zero Exponent Multiple Data (ZEMD) attack [6]. This is the case where the intermediate result of a cryptographic operation can be calculated. As such, the attacker first guesses the secret key bit in a specific bit position, then calculates the intermediate result via an off-line simulation using the guessed secret key. Thereafter, the attacker classifies the message according to the Hamming weight of the intermediate result and averaging after collecting the power consumption signal. If the guessed secret key is correct, the differentiated power consumption signal will have a peak signal, as the classifying procedure worked well, along with the Hamming weight assumption.

To date, most researchers have applied a ZEMD-type attack to symmetric key encryption algorithms, in other words, use random input message set and off-line simulator [1,7,8].

3 Implementation of Differential Power Analysis Attack

The proposed Differential Power Analysis(DPA) attack is similar to the Zero-Exponent Multiple Data(ZEMD)-type attack method, although it does not involve an off-line simulation procedure using a guessed secret key to classify random messages. Instead, the proposed attack tries all possible values for the internal operation unit used in the symmetric key encryption algorithm by applying the brute force attack method. The AES algorithm and ARIA algorithm both use 128, 192, and 256-bit secret keys, yet the internal substitution function is based on an 8-bit unit during the encryption round operation. Thus, all possible values for the 8 bits are tried, then the differentiated power signal with the highest peak signal is identified by comparing the differentiated power traces.

3.1 Experiment Using Hamming Weight Assumption

The Hamming weight assumption was evaluated using an XOR operation based on an 8-bit unit.

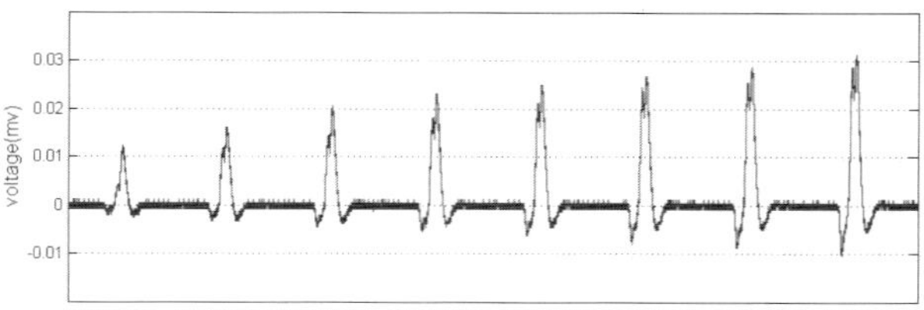

Fig. 1. Hamming weight assumption test

A higher difference in the Hamming weight, resulted in a higher peak signal in the differentiated power signal, as shown in Fig.1, where "0xFF-0x00" means the differentiation between the power consumption signals with the result of the XOR operation is "0xFF"(Hamming weight : 8) and the result of the XOR operation is "0x00"(Hamming weight : 0). That is, the higher the Hamming weight, the higher the power consumption.

3.2 Proposed Attack Method

The $S-box$ in the AES algorithm and ARIA algorithm is operated based on an 8-bit input/output. Thus, all possible values for the 8 bits were tried as follows.

1. 256 possible values for the 8 bits of an input message(X) were created, where a possible input value is denoted by $X_1, ..., X_{256}$.
2. The power consumption signal was measured during the operation of the encryption algorithm when using $X_1, ..., X_{256}$. The measured power consumption signal was denoted by $P_1, ..., P_{256}$.
3. Each measured power consumption signal was differentiated as follows.

$$P_1 - P_2, P_1 - P_{256}, ..., P_2 - P_3, ..., P_{255} - P_{256} \tag{1}$$

4. The pair of power consumption signals with the highest peak signal was identified by comparing the differentiated power consumption signals.
5. The secret value of the encryption algorithm was then detected using the pair of signals with the highest peak signal among the differentiated power consumption signals.

As such, an attacker can detect the 8 bits of the secret value of an encryption algorithm after executing the above method once, and can repeat the method depending on the length of the secret key of the encryption algorithm.

3.3 Proposed Attack on AES

The proposed DPA attack method was also applied to the of the AES algorithm.
Fig.2 shows roughly the round-one encryption process of the AES algorithm.
In the experiment, the secret key for the AES algorithm was "0x2B, 0x7E, 0x15, 0x16, 0x28, 0xAE, 0xD2, 0xA6, 0xAB, 0xF7, 0x15, 0x88, 0x09, 0xCF, 0x4F, 0x3C".

1. 256 possible values for the 8 bits of an input message(X') were created, where a possible input value is denoted by $X'_1, ..., X'_{256}$.
2. The power consumption signal was then measured when operating the AES algorithm using the input message $X'_1, ..., X'_{256}$, where the measured power consumption signal was denoted by $P'_1, ..., P'_{256}$.
3. The measured power consumption signals were then differentiated as follows.

$$P'_1 - P'_2, P'_1 - P'_{256}, ..., P'_2 - P'_3, ..., P'_{255} - P'_{256} \tag{2}$$

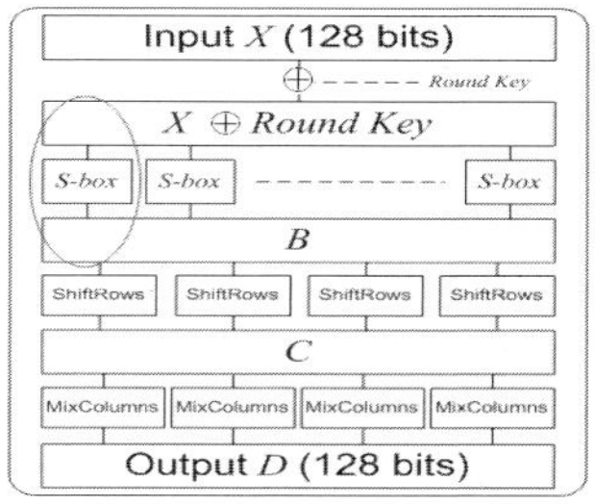

Fig. 2. AES Encryption Process

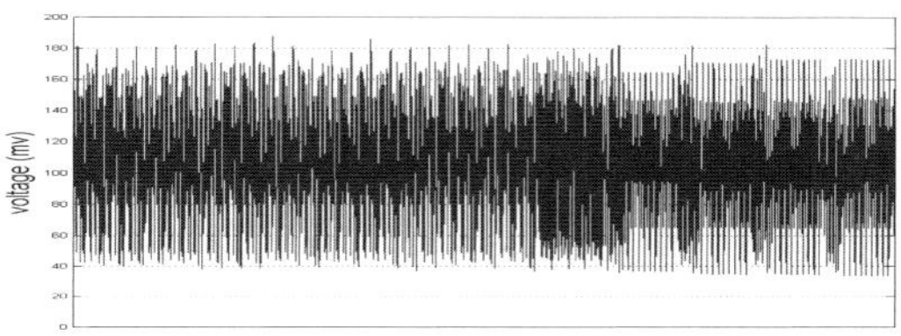

Fig. 3. Averaged Power Consumption Signal(Around $S - box$)

Fig.3 shows the averaged power consumption signal for 1000 power consumption signals measured using an oscilloscope at the storing point after the $S - box$ operation.

4. The pair of power consumption signals with the highest peak signal was identified by comparing the differentiated power consumption signals. Fig.4 shows the several differentiated power consumption signals, where "0x56-0xD0" means the differentiation between the power consumption signals with input messages 0x56 and 0xD0.
5. The highest peak signal was observed in the differentiated power consumption signal between the power consumption signals that used the input message pair "0x56 and 0x79". Thus, the 8 most significant bits of the round-one secret key of the AES algorithm was deduced using the input message pair "0x56 and 0x79".

Because of the Hamming weight assumption, the difference in the Hamming weight between the intermediate values after the SubBytes transformation in round-one of the AES algorithm could be determined using input message 0x56 and input message 0x79. Also, the intermediate value after the SubButes transformation in round-one of the AES algorithm determined using input message 0x56 was 0xFF, because of the positive peak signal in Fig.4 (c). The intermediate value was 0xFF after the SubBytes transformation during the operation of round-one of the AES algorithm with input message 0x56. That is, the Hamming weight for the intermediate value was eight.

In the case the 8 most significant bits of the SubBytes output was 0xFF, the 8 most significant bits of the SubBytes input was 0x7D, as shown in Fig.5. Therefore,

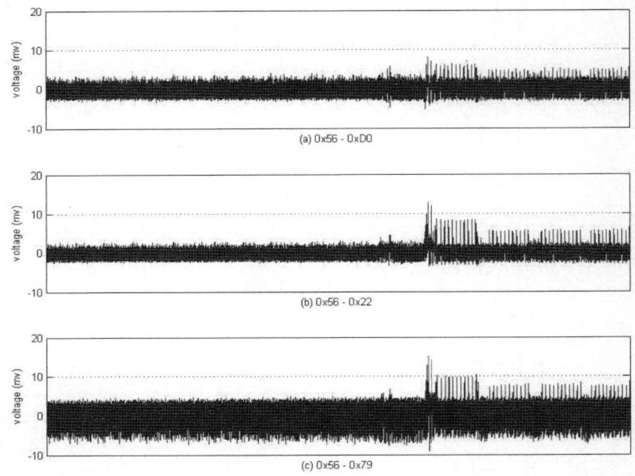

Fig. 4. Differential power consumption signals

x \ y	0	1	2	3	4	5	6	7	8	9	a	b	c	d	e	f
0	63	7c	77	7b	f2	6b	6f	c5	30	01	67	2b	fe	d7	ab	76
1	ca	82	c9	7d	fa	59	47	f0	ad	d4	a2	af	9c	a4	72	c0
2	b7	fd	93	26	36	3f	f7	cc	34	a5	e5	f1	71	d8	31	15
3	04	c7	23	c3	18	96	05	9a	07	12	80	e2	eb	27	b2	75
4	09	83	2c	1a	1b	6e	5a	a0	52	3b	d6	b3	29	e3	2f	84
5	53	d1	00	ed	20	fc	b1	5b	6a	cb	be	39	4a	4c	58	cf
6	d0	ef	aa	fb	43	4d	33	85	45	f9	02	7f	50	3c	9f	a8
7	51	a3	40	8f	92	9d	38	f5	bc	b6	da	21	10	ff	f3	d2
8	cd	0c	13	ec	5f	97	44	17	c4	a7	7e	3d	64	5d	19	73
9	60	81	4f	dc	22	2a	90	88	46	ee	b8	14	de	5e	0b	db
a	e0	32	3a	0a	49	06	24	5c	c2	d3	ac	62	91	95	e4	79
b	e7	c8	37	6d	8d	d5	4e	a9	6c	56	f4	ea	65	7a	ae	08
c	ba	78	25	2e	1c	a6	b4	c6	e8	dd	74	1f	4b	bd	8b	8a
d	70	3e	b5	66	48	03	f6	0e	61	35	57	b9	86	c1	1d	9e
e	e1	f8	98	11	69	d9	8e	94	9b	1e	87	e9	ce	55	28	df
f	8c	a1	89	0d	bf	e6	42	68	41	99	2d	0f	b0	54	bb	16

Fig. 5. AES Algorithm's $S - box$

the output of the AddRoundKey transformation in the initial round was 0x7D due to the order of the encryption procedure in the AES algorithm. That is, the input message 0x56 became 0x7D after the initial AddRoundKey transformation. Thus, the 8 most significant bits of the initial round key was 0x2B, as the AddRoundKey transformation was composed of an XOR operation. In the same manner, the intermediate values became 0x0F, 0x01, and 0x00 after the SubBytes transformation during the operation of round-one of the AES algorithm with input message 0xD0, 0x22, and 0x79, respectively. That is, the Hamming weight for the intermediate values became four, one, and zero, respectively.

3.4 Proposed Attack on ARIA

In the same manner, the proposed DPA attack was also applied to the $S_1 S - box$ of the ARIA algorithm.

Fig.6 shows roughly the round-one encryption process of the ARIA algorithm.

In the experiment, the master key for the ARIA algorithm was "0x00, 0x01, 0x02, 0x03, 0x04, 0x05, 0x06, 0x07, 0x08, 0x09, 0x0A, 0x0B, 0x0C, 0x0D, 0x0E, 0x0F". Therefore, the round-one secret key for the ARIA algorithm was "0xD4,

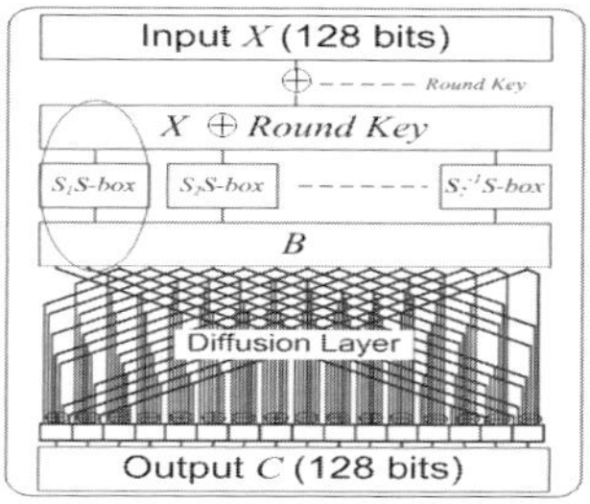

Fig. 6. ARIA Encryption Process

0x15, 0xA7,0x5C, 0x79, 0x4B, 0x85, 0xC5, 0xE0, 0xD2, 0xA0, 0xB3, 0xCB, 0x79, 0x3B, 0xF6" after the operation of the ARIA key scheduling algorithm.

Fig.7 shows the averaged power consumption signal of 1000 power consumption signals measured using an oscilloscope at the storing point after the operation.

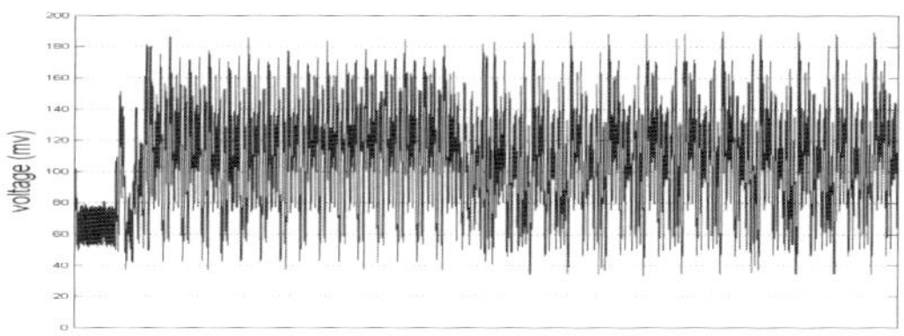

Fig. 7. Averaged Power Consumption Signal (Around $S_1S - box$)

Fig.8 shows the several differentiated power consumption signals, where the intermediate value was 0xFF after the SubBytes transformation during the operation of round-one of the ARIA algorithm when using input message 0xA9, due to the "0xA9 and 0x86" input pair′s differentiated power consumption signal has the positive highest peak signal in the differentiated power consumption signals. That is, the Hamming weight for the intermediate value was eight.

Thus, the input to the $S_1S - box$ was 0x7D, as in Fig.9.

In the same manner, the output of the AddRoundKey transformation for the round-one was 0x7D due to the order of the encryption procedure of the ARIA algorithm and the intermediate values became 0x0F, 0x01, and 0x00 after the SubBytes transformation during the operation of round-one of the ARIA algorithm when using input messages 0x2F, 0xDD, and 0x86, respectively. That is, the Hamming weight for intermediate values became four, one, and zero, respectively.

3.5 Enhancement of Proposed Attack

During the implementation of the proposed attack against the AES algorithm and ARIA algorithm, the attacker needs to execute $\frac{256 \times 255}{2}$ differential operations for each power consumption signal, about 256 possible input messages.

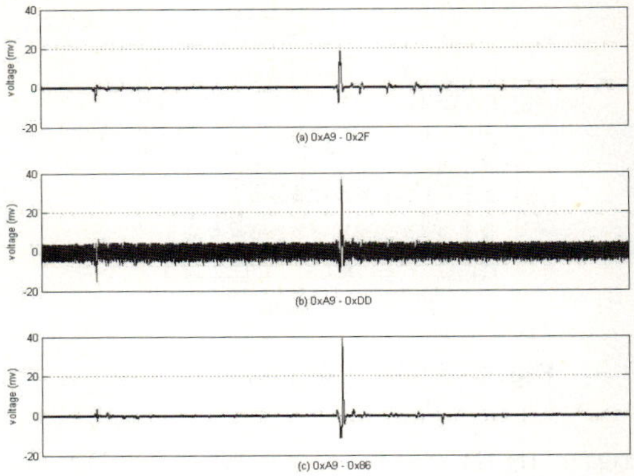

Fig. 8. Differential power consumption signals

	0	1	2	3	4	5	6	7	8	9	a	b	c	d	e	f
0	63	7c	77	7b	f2	6b	6f	c5	30	01	67	2b	fe	d7	ab	76
1	ca	82	c9	7d	fa	59	47	f0	ad	d4	a2	af	9c	a4	72	c0
2	b7	fd	93	26	36	3f	f7	cc	34	a5	e5	f1	71	d8	31	15
3	04	c7	23	c3	18	96	05	9a	07	12	80	e2	eb	27	b2	75
4	09	83	2c	1a	1b	6e	5a	a0	52	3b	d6	b3	29	e3	2f	84
5	53	d1	00	ed	20	fc	b1	5b	6a	cb	be	39	4a	4c	58	cf
6	d0	ef	aa	fb	43	4d	33	85	45	f9	02	7f	50	3c	9f	a8
7	51	a3	40	8f	92	9d	38	f5	bc	b6	da	21	10	ff	f3	d2
8	cd	0c	13	ec	5f	97	44	17	c4	a7	7e	3d	64	5d	19	73
9	60	81	4f	dc	22	2a	90	88	46	ee	b8	14	de	5e	0b	db
a	e0	32	3a	0a	49	06	24	5c	c2	d3	ac	62	91	95	e4	79
b	e7	c8	37	6d	8d	d5	4e	a9	6c	56	f4	ea	65	7a	ae	08
c	ba	78	25	2e	1c	a6	b4	c6	e8	dd	74	1f	4b	bd	8b	8a
d	70	3e	b5	66	48	03	f6	0e	61	35	57	b9	86	c1	1d	9e
e	e1	f8	98	11	69	d9	8e	94	9b	1e	87	e9	ce	55	28	df
f	8c	a1	89	0d	bf	e6	42	68	41	99	2d	0f	b0	54	bb	16

Fig. 9. ARIA Agorithm's $S_1S - box$

However, if the attacker knows the relation of the input message pair that causes the highest difference of Hamming weight in the intermediate result of the $S-box$ of the AES algorithm and $S_1S - box$ of the ARIA algorithm, the computational cost of the differential operations on the power consumption signals can be reduced. For example, in the AES algorithm, 0x7D and 0x52 were the only input pair that caused the highest Hamming weight difference as a result of the of the AES algorithm, as shown in Fig.10.

Thus, since the relation of the input pair with the highest Hamming weight difference was the relation of 0x7D and 0x52, when an XOR operation was performed using this input pair with the highest Hamming weight difference, the result of the XOR operation became 0x2F($=00101111_2$). As a result, only 128 differential operations were executed for the 256 power consumption signals, since the relation of the input pair with the highest Hamming weight difference was known to be 0x2F after the XOR operation.

3.6 Comparison

When implemented the ZEMD-type attack, attack contains basic assumption that the Hamming weight assumption and attacker can execute device repeatedly

		y															
		0	1	2	3	4	5	6	7	8	9	a	b	c	d	e	f
x	0	63	7c	77	7b	f2	6b	6f	c5	30	01	67	2b	fe	d7	ab	76
	1	ca	82	c9	7d	fa	59	47	f0	ad	d4	a2	af	9c	a4	72	c0
	2	b7	fd	93	26	36	3f	f7	cc	34	a5	e5	f1	71	d8	31	15
	3	04	c7	23	c3	18	96	05	9a	07	12	80	e2	eb	27	b2	75
	4	09	83	2c	1a	1b	6e	5a	a0	52	3b	d6	b3	29	e3	2f	84
	5	53	d1	00	ed	20	fc	b1	5b	6a	cb	be	39	4a	4c	58	cf
	6	d0	ef	aa	fb	43	4d	33	85	45	f9	02	7f	50	3c	9f	a8
	7	51	a3	40	8f	92	9d	38	f5	bc	b6	da	21	10	ff	f3	d2
	8	cd	0c	13	ec	5f	97	44	17	c4	a7	7e	3d	64	5d	19	73
	9	60	81	4f	dc	22	2a	90	88	46	ee	b8	14	de	5e	0b	db
	a	e0	32	3a	0a	49	06	24	5c	c2	d3	ac	62	91	95	e4	79
	b	e7	c8	37	6d	8d	d5	4e	a9	6c	56	f4	ea	65	7a	ae	08
	c	ba	78	25	2e	1c	a6	b4	c6	e8	dd	74	1f	4b	bd	8b	8a
	d	70	3e	b5	66	48	03	f6	0e	61	35	57	b9	86	c1	1d	9e
	e	e1	f8	98	11	69	d9	8e	94	9b	1e	87	e9	ce	55	28	df
	f	8c	a1	89	0d	bf	e6	42	68	41	99	2d	0f	b0	54	bb	16

Fig. 10. AES Agorithm's $S - box$

with fixed secret key. And, attacker has suitable simulator to target algorithm. But, proposed attack deduces secret key directly using partial information about the target algorithm and intermediate values, at the last step of attack, instead of usage of target algorithm simulator. So, proposed attack can be implemented ARIA and AES in the same manner. In Addition, ZEMD attacker need to collect the power consumption signals which number is double of possible values of the 8-bit secret key when the secret key was guessed by 8-bit. However, proposed attack needs only power consumption signals which number is same as the number of possible values of divided internal operation units. Also, because proposed attack uses fixed input messages instead of random messages, can implement more limited environment, for example, in case of device can't be exchange input messages by each execution randomly. Therefore, our proposed attack is said to be more efficient and more general attack than exiting ZEMD-type attack. Following Table 1. shows that the comparison result between ZEMD attack and proposed attack roughly.

Table 1. Comparison results (In case of, secret key is 128-bit and ZEMD attacker guesses secret key by 8-bit)

	Input message	$\sharp$ of sample	Off-line simulation	Complexity
ZEMD attack	Random	$2^8 \cdot 16 \cdot 2N$	Yes	$2^8 \cdot 16$
Proposed attack	Fix	$2^8 \cdot 16 \cdot N$	No(analyze directly)	$2^8 \cdot 16$

In the Table 1., N is the number of collected power consumption signals which can cause the noticeable peak in the differential power consumption signal.

4 Conclusions

As a result of implementing the proposed DPA attack, the security of the symmetric key encryption algorithm is shown to be clearly distinct from the security of the secret key of the encryption algorithm. If a symmetric key encryption algorithm is executed using a divided operation unit, such as the $S - box$ in AES and ARIA, the security of the symmetric key encryption key algorithm is equal to the security of the $S-box$ operation. Since the operation unit of the $S-box$ of AES and ARIA is only 8 bits, the 8-bit secret key of AES and ARIA can be deduced using a brute-force attack based on a power analysis against all the possible values of the $S-box$ 256 inputs/outputs. Moreover, the enhanced attack method needs only 128 differentiation of average power traces to reduce comprison cost. Therefore, a smart-card must be operated with a DPA-protected $S-box$ operation, such as a randomly masked $S-box$ to protect against a DPA attack [9,10,11]. Essentially, a symmetric key encryption algorithm must be operated by an internal operation unit that is equal to the bit length of the secret key as possible, in order to provide the same level of security of original symmetric key encryption algorithm.

References

1. Kocher, P., Jae, J., Jun, B.: Differential power analysis. In: Wiener, M.J. (ed.) Advances in Cryptology - CRYPTO '99. LNCS, vol. 1666, pp. 388–397. Springer, Heidelberg (1999)
2. Daemen, J., Rijmen, V.: AES Proposal: Rijndael. NIST Document Version 2 (1999), `http://www.nist.gov/aes`
3. NSRI: NSRI anounces that ARIA v. 1.0 has been presented as a standard block cipher in Korea (2004), `http://www.nsri.re.kr/ARIA/`
4. Kwon, D., Kim, J., Park, S., Sung, S., Sohn, Y., Song, J., Yeom, Y., Yoon, E., Lee, S., Lee, J., Chee, S., Han, D., Hong, J.: New Block Cipher: ARIA. In: Lim, J.-I., Lee, D.-H. (eds.) Information Security and Cryptology - ICISC 2003. LNCS, vol. 2971, pp. 432–445. Springer, Heidelberg (2004)
5. Kelsey, Schneier, B., Wagner, D., Hall, C.: Side Channel Cryptanalysis of Product Cipher. In: Quisquater, J.-J., Deswarte, Y., Meadows, C., Gollmann, D. (eds.) Computer Security – ESORICS 98. LNCS, vol. 1485, pp. 97–110. Springer, Heidelberg (1998)
6. Messerges, T., Dabbish, E., Sloan, E.: Power Analysis Attacks of Modular Exponentiation in Smartcards. In: Koç, Ç.K., Paar, C. (eds.) Cryptographic Hardware and Embedded Systems. LNCS, vol. 1717, pp. 144–157. Springer, Heidelberg (1999)
7. Messerges, T.: Securing the AES finalists against power analysis attacks. In: Schneier, B. (ed.) Fast Software Encryption. LNCS, vol. 1978, pp. 150–164. Springer, Heidelberg (2001)
8. Ha, J., Kim, C., Moon, S., Park, I., Yoo, H.: Differential Power Analysis on Block Cipher ARIA. In: Yang, L.T., Rana, O.F., Di Martino, B., Dongarra, J.J. (eds.) High Performance Computing and Communications. LNCS, vol. 3726, pp. 541–548. Springer, Heidelberg (2005)
9. Coron, J., Goubin, L.: On boolean and arithmetic masking against differential power analysis. In: Paar, C., Koç, Ç.K. (eds.) Cryptographic Hardware and Embedded Systems - CHES 2000. LNCS, vol. 1965, pp. 231–237. Springer, Heidelberg (2000)
10. Golic, J., Tymen, C.: Multiplicative masking and power analysis of AES. In: Suri, N. (ed.) Cryptographic Hardware and Embedded Systems - CHES '02. LNCS, vol. 2535, pp. 198–212. Springer, Heidelberg (2002)
11. Trichina, E., Seta, D., Germani, L.: Simplified adaptive multiplicative masking for AES. In: Suri, N. (ed.) Cryptographic Hardware and Embedded Systems - CHES '02. LNCS, vol. 2535, pp. 187–197. Springer, Heidelberg (2002)

Chosen Message Attack Against Mukherjee-Ganguly-Chaudhuri's Message Authentication Scheme*

Mun-Kyu Lee[1], Dowon Hong[2], and Dong Kyue Kim[3,**]

[1] School of Computer Science and Engineering,
Inha University,
Incheon 402-751, Korea
[2] Electronics and Telecommunications Research Institute,
Daejeon 305-350, Korea
[3] Division of Electronics and Computer Engineering,
Hanyang University,
Seoul 133-791, Korea
dqkim@hanyang.ac.kr

Abstract. Since Wolfram proposed to use cellular automata as pseudorandom sequence generators, many cryptographic applications using cellular automata have been introduced. One of the recent one is Mukherjee, Ganguly, and Chaudhuri's message authentication scheme using a special class of cellular automata called Single Attractor Cellular Automata (SACA). In this paper, we show that their scheme is vulnerable to a chosen-message attack, i.e., the secret key can be recovered by an attacker using only several chosen message-MAC pairs. The weakness of the scheme results from the regularity of SACA.

Keywords: cellular automata; cryptography; cryptanalysis; message authentication scheme; chosen message attack.

1 Introduction

Since Wolfram [12] proposed to use one-dimensional cellular automata as direct models for a wide variety of complex systems, cellular automata have provided solutions to many real problems including biological systems, physical or chemical systems, socio-economical models, and so on. One of the diverse applications of cellular automata is cryptography. After Wolfram [13] used cellular automata as pseudorandom sequence generators with possible application for stream ciphers, an extensive research has been done on cellular automata based cryptography including stream ciphers, block ciphers and hash functions [5, 10, 11]. However, most of these schemes have been shown to be vulnerable to various attacks [1, 3, 4, 7].

Recently in ACRI 2002, Mukherjee, Ganguly, and Chaudhuri proposed a message authentication scheme using a special class of cellular automata [9] which are called

* This work was supported by INHA UNIVERSITY Research Grant. (INHA-34441). The preliminary version of this paper appears in [6].
** Corresponding author.

Y. Wang, Y. Cheung, and H. Liu (Eds.): CIS 2006, LNAI 4456, pp. 427–434, 2007.

as Single Attractor Cellular Automata. A message authentication scheme is a tool to provide data integrity and data origin authentication [8]. Generally, message authentication schemes take two inputs, i.e., a message and a secret key, and produce a fixed-size output, i.e., a message authentication code (MAC) so that it is infeasible to produce the same output without knowledge of the key. Therefore, it is crucial to protect the key for the security of a message authentication scheme.

In this paper, we show that Mukherjee, Ganguly, and Chaudhuri's scheme is vulnerable to a chosen message attack, i.e., the secret key can be recovered by an attacker using only several chosen message-MAC pairs. To be more precise, our contributions are as follows:

- We show that in the model of chosen message attack, the message authentication scheme can be modified to a simple transform that uses the secret key as an input and produces a MAC as an output. Then by obtaining a small set of inverse transforms, an attacker can obtain the candidate values for the secret key.
- We show that the size of candidate set is sufficiently small and moreover, it becomes smaller if the attacker tries the inverse transforms with various messages on his own choice. Hence the key can be recovered easily.

The outline of this paper is as follows: In Section 2, we review Mukherjee et al.'s message authentication scheme. In Section 3, we give a simplified form of this scheme and show how the secret key can be recovered using this simplified scheme. We also give a complexity analysis for our attack. A simple example of the attack is presented in Section 4, and Section 5 concludes the paper.

2 Review of Mukherjee et al.'s Scheme

First, we define a cellular automaton (CA) [13]. An n-cell GF(2^p) CA consists of n register cells arranged in a regular manner, and each cell can store an element in GF(2^p). The state of a GF(2^p) CA at step t is an n-symbol string, where each symbol is in GF(2^p) and represents the content of each cell. If s_t represents the state of CA at step t, then the next state s_{t+1} is given by

$$s_{t+1} = T \cdot s_t + F,$$

where T is an $n \times n$ characteristic matrix, and F is an n-dimensional vector. Each element of T and F is in GF(2^p). For a CA X that is defined by T and F, we will write the above transition as $s_{t+1} = X(s_t)$.

Recently, Mukherjee, Ganguly, and Chaudhuri proposed a message authentication scheme using a special class of cellular automata in ACRI 2002 [9]. Their scheme uses a special class of CA which is called Single Attractor CA (SACA). An SACA is a CA such that T satisfies rank(T) = n – 1, and F is a zero vector. Then each reachable state has 2^p predecessors in the state transition graph, and the graph looks like an inverted tree except that the root has a self-loop. We call the root 'Attractor'. A Dual SACA, which is denoted by DSACA, results from an introduction of non-zero vector F. Note that DSACA has identical state transition behavior as that of SACA with change of relative position of states. Fig. 1 shows an example of a 3-cell GF(2^2)

SACA and its state transition diagram, where α is a primitive element in GF(2^2) with the characteristic polynomial $\alpha^2+\alpha+1=0$. The SACA is defined using

$$T=\begin{pmatrix}\alpha^2 & \alpha & 0\\ \alpha^2 & 1 & \alpha\\ 0 & \alpha^2 & \alpha\end{pmatrix} \text{ and } F=\begin{pmatrix}0\\0\\0\end{pmatrix}.$$

Fig. 2 shows a DSACA with *F*= (1, 1, 1) and the same *T*. Note that the transition diagrams of Figs 1 and 2 have identical structures, and each reachable state of SACA or DSACA has exactly 2^p predecessors, which enables our attack.

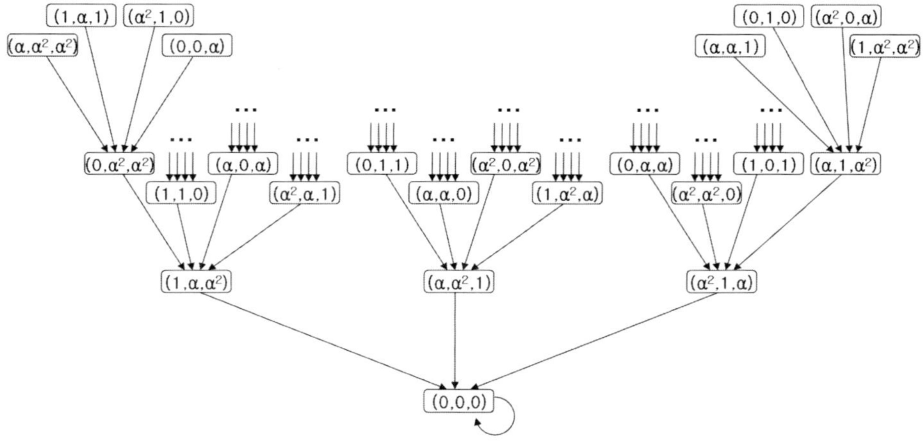

Fig. 1. State Transition Diagram of a 3-cell GF(2^2) SACA

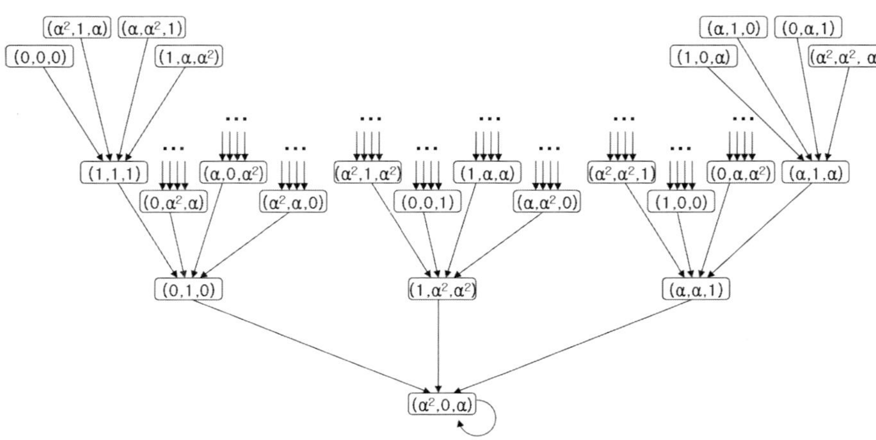

Fig. 2. State Transition Diagram of a 3-cell GF(2^2) Dual SACA

Now we describe Mukherjee et al.'s scheme. In their scheme, a message authentication code (MAC) $C_K(M)$ for a message M is computed using a pre-shared secret key K, and the pair (M, $C_K(M)$) is transmitted for authentication. The algorithm to compute $C_K(M)$ is as follows.

Algorithm 1: MAC computation
Input: Message M of knp bits, with a positive integer k;
Secret key K of np bits;
n-cell GF(2^p) $SACA$ and its dual $DSACA$
Output: MAC $C_K(M)$ of np bits
Step 1: Group Message M into k blocks $\{M_1, M_2, \ldots, M_k\}$ so that each block contains n symbols in GF(2^p), and let $K_1 = K$.
Step 2: For (i = 1 to k) {
Step 2-1: Form a tridiagonal matrix CA_{M_i} such that n diagonal elements are n symbols of M_i, off diagonal values are 1, and the remaining values are 0. Note that CA_{M_i} can be viewed as a CA.
Step 2-2: Using three CA's, compute

$$K_{i+1} = DSACA(SACA(CA_{M_i}(K_i))).$$

}
Step 3: Output K_{k+1} as the MAC.

3 Vulnerability of Mukherjee et al.'s Scheme

In this section, we show the vulnerability of Mukherjee et al.'s scheme. We begin by presenting several observations on their scheme:

- Each iteration of Step 2 consists of three transformations, i.e., DSACA, SACA and another CA using a tridiagonal matrix.
- The number of iterations is determined by the length of input message. Hence a short message requires a small number of transformations.
- There is no padding scheme.

Note that in the model of chosen message attack, an attacker can choose message M and obtain its valid MAC $C_K(M)$ through a query to the MAC oracle possessing the secret key [2]. In our attack, the attacker chooses M of length np bits, i.e., k = 1. Then the above scheme is simplified as follows:

Algorithm 2: Simplified MAC computation
Input: np-bit message M ; np-bit secret key K; n-cell GF(2^p) $SACA$ and $DSACA$
Output: np-bit MAC $C_K(M)$
Step 1: Form an n x n tridiagonal matrix CA_M as above.
Step 2: Output

$$C_K(M) = DSACA(SACA(CA_M(K)))$$

as the MAC.

Now we can attack the above scheme by reversing the transforms in Step 2 in Algorithm 2 as follows and recover the secret key.

Algorithm 3: Cryptanalysis and Recovery of the Secret Key
Step 1: Choose an np-bit message M such that CA_M has an inverse.
Step 2: Get $C_K(M)$ by an oracle query.
Step 3: Compute

$$K = CA_M^{-1}(SACA^{-1}(DSACA^{-1}(C_K(M)))).$$

Note that the inverses $SACA^{-1}$ and $DSACA^{-1}$ cannot be computed uniquely, since the rank of their characteristic matrix T is $n - 1$. However, we know the fact that each resulting state of $SACA$ and $DSACA$ has only 2^p predecessors as explained in the previous section, thus we can construct a set of 2^{2p} candidates for K.

Repeating Steps 1 through 3 for another M, we get another candidate set with cardinality 2^{2p}. It is easy to see that the secret key is in the intersection of the two candidate sets. Then we repeat this task several times until only one element remains in the intersection of all candidate sets.

Note that success of the attack depends on the following two factors.

1. In Step 1, we have to be able to choose M such that matrix CA_M has an inverse, i.e., CA_M has a non-zero determinant.
2. The size of intersection should decrease rapidly within a reasonable number of iterations of Steps 1 through 3.

Now we address these two matters. First, we show that we can easily choose adequate M's. In the following lemma, we prove that the number of CA_M with non-zero determinant is at least $(2^p - 1)^n$. Since the total number of possible np-bit messages M is $(2^p)^n$, the lemma implies that most of the possible messages can be used for our attack.

Lemma 1. For $n \geq 2$, the number of CA_M with non-zero determinant is greater than or equal to $(2^p - 1)^n$.

Proof. Let $\det(A)$ be the determinant of matrix A, and let $M = (m_1, \ldots, m_n)$ be an np-bit message with $m_i \in GF(2^p)$ for $1 \leq i \leq n$. The proof is done by mathematical induction on n.

1. First, consider the case $n = 2$. Write the 2 x 2 tridiagonal matrix CA_M as

$$CA_M = \begin{pmatrix} m_1 & 1 \\ 1 & m_2 \end{pmatrix}.$$

Since $\det(CA_M) = m_1 m_2 - 1$, the number of pairs (m_1, m_2) such that $\det(CA_M) = 0$ is $2^p - 1$. On the other hand, the total number of possible pairs (m_1, m_2) is 2^{2p}. Hence the number of CA_M with non-zero determinant is

$$2^{2p} - (2^p - 1) > (2^p - 1)^2.$$

2. Next, assume that the claim holds for $n = k$ ($k \geq 2$). Hence there are at least $(2^p - 1)^k$ CA_M 's with non-zero determinants. Let CA_M^k be one of these k x k tridiagonal matrices that have inverses. Then we can choose an element m_{k+1} in $GF(2^p)$ and define a $(k+1)$ x $(k+1)$ tridiagonal matrix CA_M^k as

$$CA_M^{k+1} = \begin{pmatrix} & & & & 0 \\ & CA_M^k & & & \vdots \\ & & & & 0 \\ & & & & 1 \\ 0 & \cdots & 0 & 1 & m_{k+1} \end{pmatrix}.$$

Then

$$\det(CA_M^{k+1}) = \det(CA_M^k)\times(-1)^{(k+1)+(k+1)}\times m_{k+1} + \det(A)\times(-1)^{k+(k+1)}\times 1,$$

where A is the $k \times k$ matrix obtained by deleting the kth row and $(k+1)$st column of CA_M^{k+1}. Since $\det(CA_M^k) \neq 0$, there is only one m_{k+1} such that $\det(CA_M^{k+1}) = 0$. Consequently, for each CA_M^k, there are $2^p - 1$ choices of m_{k+1} such that CA_M^{k+1} has an inverse. Therefore there are at least $(2^p - 1)^{k+1}$ CA_M^{k+1}'s with non-zero determinants. ■

Next, we deal with the second factor. Note that the size of key space for K is 2^{pn} and the size of a candidate set is 2^{2p}. In Lemma 2, we prove that if we construct two random sets of size 2^{2p} by selecting elements from a space of size 2^{pn}, then it is almost impossible for these two sets share an element. (According to the lemma, its probability is about 10^{-29} for a typical setting $p = 8$, $n = 16$ suggested by Mukherjee et al. [9]) Hence, we can conjecture that the number of candidates for K decreases rapidly after only several iterations of Steps 1 through 3, under the assumption that the construction process of a candidate set behaves like a random selection, except for the inclusion of real key.

Lemma 2. Consider the task to select 2^{2p} elements randomly from a set with size 2^{pn}. When we repeat this task twice, let $P(n, p)$ be the probability that there exists an element which is selected in both of the two independent trials. Then for sufficiently large p and n,

$$P(n, p) \approx 1 - e^{-\frac{1}{2^{p(n-4)}}}.$$

Proof. Without loss of generality, we fix 2^{2p} elements selected in the first trial. Then $P(n, p)$ is the probability that at least one of these elements is selected again in the second trial. Hence,

$$P(n, p) \approx 1 - \left(\frac{2^{pn} - 2^{2p}}{2^{pn}}\right)^{2^{2p}} = 1 - \left(1 - \frac{1}{2^{p(n-2)}}\right)^{2^{2p}}.$$

Using the approximation $e^{-x} \approx 1 - x$ for $x \approx 0$, we obtain

$$P(n, p) \approx 1 - \left(e^{-\frac{1}{2^{p(n-2)}}}\right)^{2^{2p}} = 1 - e^{-\frac{1}{2^{p(n-4)}}}.$$ ■

Now we consider the computational complexity of the above attack. We analyze the time complexity of a single execution of Algorithm 3, while the overall attack may require several executions of this algorithm. First, we see that a random short message has an inverse with high probability according to Lemma 1. Hence we can assume that in Step 1 of Algorithm 3, only a constant number of messages will be tried. Since a simple Gaussian elimination method can be used to find an inverse, Step 1 can be done in $O(n^3)$ operations, where each operation is done over GF(2^p). The dominant operations in Step 2 are several matrix multiplications of an n x n matrix by an n x 1 matrix, thus Step 2 requires $O(n^2)$ operations. Finally, in Step 3 we need $O(n^3)$ for each of the candidate keys, and the number of these keys is 2^{2p}. Therefore the computational complexity of Algorithm 3 is $O(2^{2p}n^3)$.

4 Example of the Cryptanalysis

We demonstrate our cryptanalysis against an example scheme presented in Section 2, where the SACA is defined using

$$T = \begin{pmatrix} \alpha^2 & \alpha & 0 \\ \alpha^2 & 1 & \alpha \\ 0 & \alpha^2 & \alpha \end{pmatrix} \text{ and } F = \begin{pmatrix} 0 \\ 0 \\ 0 \end{pmatrix},$$

and a DSACA is defined using F= (1, 1, 1) and the same T. Let $K = (\alpha, \alpha^2, 0)$ be the secret key of authentication scheme. As an attacker, we choose two messages M_1 = (1, 1, 1) and M_2 = (1, 0, 0), and get $C_K(M_1) = (\alpha^2, \alpha, 0)$ and $C_K(M_2)$ = (1, 1, 1) by two queries. By the attack algorithm, we obtain two candidate sets for K, each of which has 16 elements, and the intersection of these two sets is $\{(0,\alpha^2,0),(1,\alpha^2,0),(\alpha,\alpha^2,0),(\alpha^2,\alpha^2,0)\}$. Since this set has more than one element, we choose another message M_3 = (α^2, 1, 1) and get $C_K(M_3)$ = (1, 1, 1). We obtain another candidate set with 16 elements, and the intersection of the three candidate sets is $\{(\alpha,\alpha^2,0)\}$, which corresponds to the original secret key.

5 Conclusions

In this paper, we have shown that Mukherjee et al.'s message authentication scheme is vulnerable to a chosen message attack. We remark that a known message attack is also possible if only sufficient amount of short messages are available.

References

1. Bao, F.: Cryptanalysis of a new cellular automata cryptosystem. In: Safavi-Naini, R., Seberry, J. (eds.) Information Security and Privacy. LNCS, vol. 2727, pp. 416–427. Springer, Heidelberg (2003)
2. Bellare, M., Canetti, R., Krawczyk, H.: Keying hash functions for message authentication. In: Koblitz, N. (ed.) Advances in Cryptology - CRYPTO '96. LNCS, vol. 1109, pp. 1–15. Springer, Heidelberg (1996)

3. Blackburn, S.R., Murphy, S., Paterson, K.G.: Comments on Theory and applications of cellular automata in cryptography. IEEE Transactions on Computers 46(5), 637–638 (1997)
4. Daemen, J., Govaerts, R., Vandewalle, J.: A framework for the design of one-way hash functions including cryptanalysis of Damgård's one-way function based on a cellular automaton. In: Matsumoto, T., Imai, H., Rivest, R.L. (eds.) Advances in Cryptology - ASIACRYPT '91. LNCS, vol. 739, pp. 82–96. Springer, Heidelberg (1993)
5. Damgård, I.: A design principle for hash functions. In: Brassard, G. (ed.) Advances in Cryptology - CRYPTO '89. LNCS, vol. 435, pp. 416–427. Springer, Heidelberg (1990)
6. Lee, M.K., Hong, D., Kim, D.K.: Cryptanalysis of Mukherjee-Ganguly-Chaudhuri's message authentication scheme, Computational Intelligence and Security – Part 2, pp. 1311–1314 (2006) (ISBN 1-4244-0604-8)
7. Meier, W., Staffelbach, O.: Analysis of pseudo random sequences generated by cellular automata. In: Davies, D.W. (ed.) Advances in Cryptology - EUROCRYPT '91. LNCS, vol. 547, pp. 186–199. Springer, Heidelberg (1991)
8. Menezes, A.J., van Oorschot, P.C., Vanstone, S.A. (eds.): Handbook of Applied Cryptography. CRC Press, Boca Raton (1997)
9. Mukherjee, M., Ganguly, N., Chaudhuri, P.P.: Cellular automata based authentication (CAA). In: Bandini, S., Chopard, B., Tomassini, M. (eds.) Cellular Automata. LNCS, vol. 2493, pp. 259–269. Springer, Heidelberg (2002)
10. Nandi, S., Kar, B.K., Chaudhuri, P.P.: Theory and applications of cellular automata in cryptography. IEEE Transactions on Computers 43(12), 1346–1357 (1994)
11. Sen, S., Shaw, C., Chowdhuri, D.R., Ganguly, N., Chaudhuri, P.P.: Cellular automata based cryptosystem (CAC). In: Deng, R.H., Qing, S., Bao, F., Zhou, J. (eds.) Information and Communications Security - ICICS 2002. LNCS, vol. 2513, pp. 303–314. Springer, Heidelberg (2002)
12. Wolfram, S.: Cellular automata as models of complexity, Nature vol. 311(419) (1984)
13. Wolfram, S.: Cryptography with cellular automata. In: Williams, H.C. (ed.) Advances in Cryptology. LNCS, vol. 218, pp. 429–431. Springer, Heidelberg (1986)

Binary Sequences with Three and Four Level Autocorrelation

Ying Cai[1,2] and Zhen Han[1]

[1] School of Computer Science, Beijing Jiaotong University, Beijing, 100044, China
[2] Department of Computer Science, Beijing Information Science and Technology University, Beijing, 100101, China
yingcai@biti.edu.cn,hz@computer.njtu.edu.cn

Abstract. Binary sequences with good autocorrelation in ranging systems, spread spectrum communication systems, multi-terminal system identification, code division multiple access communications systems, global positioning systems, software testing, circuit testing, computer simulation, and stream ciphers. In this paper, we present a number of classes of binary sequences with three or four level autocorrelation. Some of them have good autocorrelation.

1 Introduction

Let $s^m = s_0 s_1 \cdots s_{m-1}$ be a sequence over a field F. The linear span or linear complexity of s^m is defined to be the smallest positive integer L such that there are constants $c_0 = 1, c_1, \cdots, c_L \in F$ satisfying

$$-s_i = c_1 s_{i-1} + c_2 s_{i-2} + \cdots + c_L s_{i-L} \text{ for all } L \le i < n.$$

Such a polynomial $c(x) = c_0 + c_1 x + \cdots + c_L x^L$ is called the *feedback polynomial* of a shortest linear feedback shift register (LFSR) that generates s^m. Hereafter we use the term *minimal polynomial.* Such an integer always exists for finite sequences s^m. When m is ∞, a sequence s^∞ is called a semi-infinite sequence. If there is no such an integer for a semi-infinite sequence s^∞, its linear span is defined to be ∞. For ultimately periodic semi-infinite sequences such an L always exists. The linear span of periodic sequences can be expressed simply as follows.

Let s^∞ be a sequence of period n over a field F, and $S^m(x) = \sum_{i=0}^{m-1} s_i x^i$. Then it is known that the feedback polynomial of s^∞ is given by $(x^m - 1)/\gcd(x^m - 1, S^m(x))$, and that the linear span of s^∞ is given by $m - \deg(\gcd(x^m - 1, S^m(x)))$ [3].

Throughout this paper, let Z_N denote the ring $\{0, 1, \cdots, N-1\}$ with integer multiplication modulo N and integer addition modulo N. Let D be a subset of Z_N. The *characteristic sequence* s^∞ of D is defined as

$$s_i = \begin{cases} 1, & \text{if } i \bmod N \in D; \\ 0, & \text{otherwise.} \end{cases}$$

The set D is called the *characteristic set* or *support* of the sequence s^∞.

Y. Wang, Y. Cheung, and H. Liu (Eds.): CIS 2006, LNAI 4456, pp. 435–442, 2007.

Let s^∞ be a binary sequence of period N (not necessarily the least period), and let $C = \{0 \le i \le N-1 : s_i = 1\}$. The autocorrelation function of s^∞ is defined as

$$\mathrm{C}_s(w) = \sum_{i \in Z_N} (-1)^{s_{i+w} - s_i}.$$

Define the difference function:

$$d_C(w) = |(w + C) \cap C|,$$

where $|C|$ denotes the cardinality of the set C. Let $k = |C|$. Then $\mathrm{C}_s(w) = N - 4(k - d_C(w))$ [3, p. 143].

Pseudorandom sequences have important applications in simulation, software testing, global positioning systems, ranging systems, code-division multiple-access systems, radar systems, spread-spectrum communication systems, and stream ciphers. Many applications require binary sequences that have good autocorrelation properties [1,3,4,5,9,7,6,11,14].

In this paper, we present a number of classes of binary sequences with three or four level autocorrelation. Some of them have good autocorrelation. The first class is obtained from the 3-decimation of binary maximum length sequences. The other classes are derived from cyclic difference sets.

2 Sequences with 3-Level Autocorrelation

A binary sequence of period $2^n - 1$ with minimal polynomial of degree n is called a maximum-length sequence. Basic properties about maximum-length sequences can be found in [11]. Let α be a generating element of $GF(2^n)$. Then every maximum length binary sequence s^∞ of period $2^n - 1$ can be expressed as

$$s_i = \mathrm{Tr}_1^n(\gamma \alpha^i) \text{ for all } i \ge 0,$$

where α is a generating element of $GF(2^n)$, and the trace function is defined as $\mathrm{Tr}_1^n(x) = x + x^2 + x^{2^2} + \cdots + x^{2^{n-1}}$.

The d-decimation of s^∞ is defined by

$$t_i = s_{di} = \mathrm{Tr}_1^n(\gamma \alpha^{di}) \text{ for all } i \ge 0.$$

It is known that t^∞ is another maximum length sequence of the same least period if and only if $\gcd(d, 2^n - 1) = 1$. Thus it suffices to consider only the case that $\gcd(d, 2^n - 1) = d \ne 1$.

Lemma 1. *The least period of t^∞ is $(2^n - 1)/d$. The minimal polynomial of t^∞ is the reciprocal of that of $\beta = \alpha^d$ over $GF(2)$ and is irreducible. On the other hand, any binary periodic sequence with an irreducible minimal polynomial is a decimated version of a maximum-length binary sequence.*

Let $\beta = \alpha^a$. By the definition of m_a, the order of β is $2^{m_a} - 1$, but $\beta^{2^n-1} = 1$. Thus $2^{m_a} - 1$ must divide $2^n - 1$. So m_a divides n. The following conclusion then follows from Lemma 1.

Theorem 1. *The linear span of t^∞ always divides n and is equal to the degree of the minimal polynomial of α^d.*

As before, let d divide $2^n - 1$, and α be a generating element of $GF(2^n)$. Define $D_0 = (\alpha^d)$, the multiplicative group generated by α^d, and

$$D_i = \alpha^i D_0 \text{ for } i = 1, 2, \cdots, d-1.$$

These D_i are called cyclotomic classes of order d. The cyclotomic numbers of order d are defined as

$$(i, j) = |(D_i + 1) \cap D_j|.$$

Clearly, there are at most d^2 different cyclotomic numbers of order d.

The autocorrelation values and the number of 0's in a periodic segment of the d-decimated version t^∞ of a maximum-length sequence are determined by the following theorem.

Theorem 2. *The d out-of-phase autocorrelation values of t^∞ are*

$$\{y_i : i \in I\},$$

where $I =: \{0 \le j \le d-1 : (0, j-h) > 0\}$ and h is the integer such that $\gamma \in D_h$, and the number of 0's and that of 1's in a periodic segment of this sequence are $(y_0+1)/2$ and $l - (y_0+1)/2$, where the d integers y_i are determined by the following system of Diophantine equations

$$\begin{cases} y_0^2 - l &= \sum_{j=0}^{d-1} (j, j) y_j, \\ y_1^2 - l &= \sum_{j=0}^{d-1} (j+1, j+1) y_j, \\ \vdots & \quad \vdots \\ y_{d-1}^2 - l &= \sum_{j=0}^{d-1} (j+d-1, j+d-1) y_j, \\ -1 &= \sum_{j=0}^{d-1} y_j \end{cases} \tag{1}$$

and

$$y_i y_j = \sum_{h=0}^{d-1} (i+h, j+h) y_h. \tag{2}$$

where (i, j)'s denote the cyclotomic numbers of order d.

Remark: Theorems 2 makes a nice connection between the d out-of-phase autocorrelation values y_i/l of t^∞ and the d^2 cyclotomic numbers (i, j) of order

d. If we know the cyclotomic numbers of order d, we can solve (1) to get the autocorrelation values y_i/l, where $i \in I$. At a first sight, one may notice that the systems of Diophantine equations (1) and (2) are nonlinear with respect to y_i, and thus may be difficult to solve when d is large. In fact, for every polynomial $F(x_0, x_1, \cdots, x_{d-1}) \in Z[x_0, x_1, \cdots, x_{d-1}]$, the value $F(y_0, y_1, \cdots, y_{d-1})$ can be expressed as a linear combination of $y_0, y_1, \cdots, y_{d-1}$ plus a constant. Thus, solving (1) and (2) by eliminating some variables does not increase the degrees of the Diophantine equations, but the coefficients of the reduced equations are nonlinear functions of the cyclotomic numbers. In any case, y_i can be obtained with given cyclotomic numbers of order d by solving only quadratic equations.

We mention here that the constants y_i are the Gaussian periods with respect to the field $GF(2^n)$, and the analogue of the two sets of Diophantine equations in Theorem 2 with respect to $GF(p)$ was known by Gauss [10], and the version with respect to finite fields $GF(q)$ was noticed by others later (see, for example, McEliece and Rumsey [13], and MacWilliams [12]).

On the other hand, it is interesting to note that (1) and (2) are linear with respect to (i, j). Thus if we can calculate the autocorrelation values of t^∞, we can solve the systems of linear Diophantine equations (1) and (2) to get the cyclotomic numbers (i, j). In particular, we have [13]

$$(k, h) = \frac{1}{2^n}\left(l^2 + \sum_{i=0}^{d-1} y_i y_{i+k} y_{i+h}\right).$$

Hence it may be concluded that computing the autocorrelation values of t^∞ is as difficult as computing the cyclotomic numbers of order d. It is noted that computing higher order cyclotomic numbers is not easy, it involves many character sums and the theory of quadratic partitions of integers. This gives us a feeling of the difficulty of computing the autocorrelation values of the d-decimated versions of maximum-length sequences.

The set D_0 is called a $(2^n, l, \lambda)$ difference set if each element of $GF(2^n)^*$ appears exactly λ times in the multiset $\{a - b : a, b \in D_0, a \neq b\}$. A necessary condition for D_0 to be such a difference set is

$$l(l-1) = \lambda(2^n - 1).$$

The following lemma is straightforward by the definitions of cyclotomic numbers and classes.

Lemma 2. *D_0 is a $(2^n, l, \lambda)$ difference set if and only if*

$$(0,0) = (1,1) = \cdots = (d-1, d-1) = \lambda.$$

Thus D_0 is a difference set if and only if each other D_i is so.

Corollary 1. *If D_0 is a $(2^n, l, \lambda)$ difference set, the autocorrelation function $C_t(\tau)$ is at most three-valued, taking on*

$$\left\{1,\ \pm\sqrt{l - l(l-1)(2^n-1)^{-1}}\right\}.$$

Proof. By Theorem 2 and Lemma 2,

$$y_i^2 - l = \sum_{j=0}^{d-1}(j+i, j+i)y_j = \lambda \sum_{j=0}^{d-1} y_j = -\lambda,$$

where $\lambda = (0,0) = (1,1) = \cdots = (d-1, d-1)$. It follows that

$$y_i^2 = l - \lambda = \frac{l(l-1)}{2^n - 1}.$$

The conclusion then follows.

By this corollary, the autocorrelation property of t^∞ is quite good when D_0 is a difference set. Thus, we need to find conditions on d and n such that the corresponding cyclotomic class D_0 is a difference set. To this end, we need cyclotomic numbers of order d with respect to finite fields $GF(q)$, where $q = p^m$ and p is a prime. When $m = 1$, cyclotomic numbers of order up to 24 are known and whether D_0 is a difference set is clear. However, when $m > 1$ only cyclotomic numbers of orders 2,3,4,6,8 are known [15], though it is possible to get results about other orders.

With the established general theory above we are ready to describe a class of binary sequence with 3-level autocorrelation. Specifically, we will consider the 3-decimated sequence of a maximum-length sequence, and show that they have 3-level autocorrelation.

Consider the case $d = 3$. In order for 3 to divide $2^n - 1$, n must be even. In this case $C_t(\tau)$ is at most four-valued.

Theorem 3. *Let $d = 3$ and 4 divide $n + 2$ with $n > 2$. Then there are only two out-of-phase autocorrelation values for t^∞, namely,*

$$\left\{2^{(n+2)/2} - 1,\ -2^{n/2} + 1\right\}.$$

There are three different cases about the number of times for the above correlation values to be taken:

Case I: *the first is taken $(0, -h)$ times, and the latter $(0, 1-h) + (0, 2-h)$ times;*

Case II: *the first is taken $(0, 1-h)$ times, and the latter $(0, -h) + (0, 2-h)$ times;*

Case III: *the first is taken $(0, 2-h)$ times, and the latter $(0, 1-h) + (0, -h)$ times;*

where h is the integer such that $\gamma \in D_h$, and each cyclotomic number above is exactly known.

Theorem 4. *Let $d = 3$ and 4 divide $n + 2$. There are two possible cases for the number of 0's and that of 1's appearing in a periodic segment of the sequence t^∞:*

Case I: *the number of 0's is $(2^{n-1} + 2^{n/2} - 1)/3$, and that of 1's is $(2^{n-1} - 2^{n/2})/3$;*
Case II: *the number of 0's is $(2^{n-1} - 2^{(n-2)/2} - 1)/3$, and that of 1's is $(2^{n-1} + 2^{(n-2)/2})/3$.*

3 Sequences with 4-Level Autocorrelation

3.1 A Class of Sequences with 4-Level Autocorrelation

Let p and q be odd primes. We use Q_p and Q_q to denote the set of quadratic residues modulo p and that modulo q respectively. Define $N_p = Z_p \setminus Q_p$ and $N_q = Z_q \setminus Q_q$, where $Z_p := \{0, 1, \cdots, p-1\}$. We define $D = Q_p \times N_q \cup N_p \times Q_q$.

Let χ be the mapping from Z_{pq} to $Z_p \times Z_q$ defined by $\chi(x) = (x \bmod p, x \bmod q)$. Let s^∞ denote the characteristic sequence of the set $\chi^{-1}(D)$.

Theorem 5. *Let $p \equiv 3 \pmod 4$ and $q \equiv 3 \pmod 4$. The autocorrelation values of the sequence s^∞ are given below.*

(A) $C_s(w) = pq$ *if* $w = 0$.
(B) $C_s(w) = p$ *if* $w_1 = 0, w_2^{-1} \in D_j^{(q)}$.
(C) $C_s(w) = q$ *if* $w_1^{-1} \in D_i^{(p)}, w_2 = 0$.
(D) $C_s(w) = 1$ *if* $(w_1, w_2) \neq (0, 0)$.

Hence, the sequence s^∞ has 4-level autocorrelation if $p \equiv 3 \pmod 4$ and $q \equiv 3 \pmod 4$.

3.2 Forty-Nine Classes of Sequences with 4-Level Autocorrelation

Let p_1 and p_2 be two integers such that $\gcd(p_1, p_2) = 1$. Assume that D_i is a (p_i, k_i, λ_i) difference set of Z_{p_i} for $i = 1$ and 2, where $k_i = |D_i|$. Let $D_i^* = Z_{p_i} \setminus D_i$ be the complementary $(p_i, p_i - k_i, p_i - 2k_i + \lambda_i)$ difference set of D_i. Define

$$D = D_1 \times D_2^* \cup D_1^* \times D_2 \in Z_{p_1} \times Z_{p_2}.$$

Define $k = |D| = k_1(p_2 - k_2) + (p_1 - k_1)k_2$. We now define a binary sequence s^∞ of period $p_1 p_2$ by

$$s_i = 1 \text{ iff } (i \bmod p_1, i \bmod p_2) \in D,$$

where $i \bmod p_i$ denotes the least nonnegative integer congruent to i modulo p_i.

Theorem 6. *The autocorrelation function* $C_s(w)$ *is at most four valued, i.e.,*

$$C_s(w) = \begin{cases} A + 4[k_1(p_2 - 2k_2 + \lambda_2) + (p_1 - k_1)\lambda_2], \\ \qquad \text{if } w_1 = 0, w_2 \neq 0, \\ A + 4[\lambda_1(p_2 - k_2) + (p_1 - 2k_1 + \lambda_1)k_2], \\ \qquad \text{if } w_1 \neq 0, w_2 = 0, \\ A + 4[\lambda_1(p_2 - 2k_2 + \lambda_2) + \\ 2(k_1 - \lambda_1)(k_2 - \lambda_2) + \lambda_2(p_1 - 2k_1 + \lambda_1)], \\ \qquad \text{if } w_1 \neq 0, w_2 \neq 0, \end{cases}$$

where $A = p_1 p_2 - 4k$, k *is the same as before and* $w_i = w \bmod p_i$.

Theorem 6 gives a systematic way to construct binary sequences with at most 4-level autocorrelation based on two cyclic difference sets. In what follows we construct 49 classes of binary sequences with 4-level autocorrelation with the help of this theorem. To this end, we need to recall some known cyclic difference sets.

Table 1. Known cyclotomic difference sets of Z_N

difference sets	conditions
$D_0^{(2,p)}$	$p \equiv 3 \pmod 4$
$D_0^{(4,p)}$	$p = 4t^2 + 1$, t odd
$D_0^{(4,p)} \cup \{0\}$	$p = 4t^2 + 9$, t odd
$D_0^{(8,p)}$	$p = 8t^2 + 1 = 64u^2 + 9$, where t and u odd
$D_0^{(8,p)} \cup \{0\}$	$p = 8t^2 + 49 = 64u^2 + 441$, where t odd, u even
$\bigcup_{i\in\{0,1,3\}} D_i^{(6,p)}$	$p = 4t^2 + 27$, $p \equiv 1 \pmod 6$
twin-prime	$N = p(p+2)$

Let p be an odd prime, and let $D_i^{(d,p)}$ denote the cyclotomic classes of order d with respect to p. Table 1 gives seven classes of cyclic difference sets of Z_N [2]. By taking any two difference sets of Z_{N_1} and Z_{N_2} with $\gcd(N_1, N_2) = 1$, we get a binary sequence with 4-level autocorrelation. Thus we have obtained 49 classes of binary sequences with 4-level autocorrelation. The exact autocorrelation values can be computed directly with the parameters about the difference sets given in Table 1 and Theorem 6.

Acknowledgments

The author would like to thank anonymous referees and reviewers for their suggestions to improve this paper. This article is supported by the National Science Foundation of China under Grant No. 60573030 and Beijing Municipal Commission of Education under Grant No. KM200610772005. Besides, this paper is supported by Beijing Young Teacher Backbone project under Grant No. PXM2007_014224_044676.

References

1. Arasu, K.T., Ding, C., Helleseth, T., Kumar, P.V., Martinsen, H.M.: Almost difference sets and their sequences with optimal autocorrelation. IEEE Trans. Inform. Theory 47(7), 2834–2943 (2001)
2. Baumert, L.D.: Cyclic Difference Sets. In: Lecture Notes in Mathematics 182, Springer, Heidelberg (1971)
3. Cusick, T.W., Ding, C., Renvall, A.: Stream Ciphers and Number Theory. North-Holland Mathematical Library 55. North-Holland/Elsevier, Amsterdam (1998)
4. Ding, C.: Linear complexity of the generalized cyclotomic sequence of order 2. Finite Fields and Their Applications 3, 159–174 (1997)
5. Ding, C.: Autocorrelation values of generalized cyclotomic sequences of order two. IEEE Trans. Inform. Theory 44(4), 1699–1702 (1998)
6. Ding, C., Helleseth, T., Martinsen, H.M.: New families of binary sequences with optimal three-level autocorrelation. IEEE Trans. Inform. Theory 47, 428–433 (2001)
7. Ding, C., Helleseth, T., Lam, K.Y.: Several classes of sequences with three-level autocorrelation. IEEE Trans. Inform. Theory 45, 2606–2612 (1999)
8. Ding, C., Pei, D., Salomaa, A.: Chinese Remainder Theorem: Applications in Computing, Coding, Cryptography. World Scientific, Singapore (1996)
9. Ding, C., Shan, W., Xiao, G.: The Stability Theory of Stream Ciphers. LNCS, vol. 561. Springer, Heidelberg (1991)
10. Gauss, C.F.: Disquisitiones Aithmeticae. Leipzig (1801). English translation, Yale, New Haven (1996)
11. Golomb, S.W.: Shift-Register Sequences. Aegean Park Press, CA (1982)
12. MacWilliams, F.J.: Cyclotomic numbers, coding theory and orthogonal polynomials. Discrete Mathematics 3, 133–151 (1972)
13. McEliece, R.J., Rumsey, H.: Euler products, cyclotomy, and coding. J. Number Theory 4, 302–311 (1972)
14. Sarwate, D.V.: Crosscorrelation properties of pseudorandom and related sequences. Proc. IEEE 68, 593–619 (1980)
15. Storer, T.: Cyclotomy and Difference Sets. Markham (1967)

Security Analysis of Public-Key Encryption Scheme Based on Neural Networks and Its Implementing

Niansheng Liu[1] and Donghui Guo[2]

[1] School of Computer Engineerung, Jimei University, Xiamen 361021, Fujian, China
nsliu@jmu.edu.cn
[2]Department of Electronic Engineering, Xiamen University, Xiamen 361005, Fujian, China
dhguo@xmu.edu.cn

Abstract. A Diffie-Hellman public-key cryptography based on chaotic attractors of neural networks is described in the paper. There is a one-way function between chaotic attractors and initial states in an Overstoraged Hopfield Neural Networks (OHNN). If the synaptic matrix of OHNN is changed, each attractor and its corresponding domain of initial state attraction will be changed. Then, we regard the neural synaptic matrix as a trap door, and change it with commutative random permutation matrix. A new Diffie-Hellman public-key cryptosystem can be implemented, namely keeping the random permutation operation of the neural synaptic matrix as the secret key, and the neural synaptic matrix after permutation as public-key. In order to explain the practicability of the encryption scheme, Security and encryption efficient of the scheme are discussed. The scheme of application for Internet secure communications is implemented by using Java program. The experimental results show that the proposed cryptography is feasible, and has a good performance of encryption and decryption speed to ensure the real time of IPng secure communications.

1 Introduction

Since W. Diffie and M. Hellman firstly put forward the thought of public-key cryptosystem in 1976 [1], the public-key cryptosystem has been the focus of modern cryptographist's attention and is optimal for the secure communication of computer networks because it don't need a secure channel to distribute and transmit the keys, and can efficaciously decrease the amount of key to be used among multiuse secure communication. These help to simplify key management. Many algorithms of public-key encryption were put forward in recent years [2, 3].

Hopfield neural network is a nonlinear system with simple structure. However, it has complex nonlinear dynamics with chaotic attractors, and the property of fast parallel processing. It has great significance of application in the cryptography [4]. However, it is mainly applied to symmetric cryptosystem at present [5, 6]. We proposed a new symmetric probabilistic encryption scheme using chaotic attractors of Overstoraged Hopfield neural networks [7] in the past years. In the recently year, we

Y. Wang, Y. Cheung, and H. Liu (Eds.): CIS 2006, LNAI 4456, pp. 443–450, 2007.

proposed a new public-key encryption scheme regarded the OHNN synaptic matrix as a trap door according to Diffie-Hellman public-key cryptosystem [8].

The security of the new scheme is analyzed in detail in the basis of our former works. The application scheme for Internet secure communications based on the proposed cryptosystem is introduced by using Java program to implement it.

2 Principles of the Proposed Scheme

In this section, we firstly introduce the model of neural networks applied for new encryption scheme. Secondly, it is described how to construct a new encryption algorithm according to Difffie-Hellman public-key cryptosystem.

2.1 Model of Neural Networks

Hopfield neural network (HNN) was firstly introduced as an associative memory network by J. J. Hopfield in 1982 [9], and are well-suited for hardware implementation. For a discrete HNN, if system initial state is converge to one of the system attractors by a Minimum Hamming Distance (MHD) criterion, the attractor is a stable state as an associative sample of HNN and can be stored in HNN. However, the capacity of memory sample to be stored in an associative memory network is limited. In the case of HNN consisted of N neurons, the capacity is about 0.14N using Hebb learning rules. If the number of sample to be stored is over the capacity of HNN, the stable attractors of HNN system will be became aberrant and chaotic attractors will emerge. The capacity of networks is increased. HNN becomes overstoraged HNN (OHNN).

We consider a fully interconnected network of N neurons in which each neuron is in one of the two states {0, 1}. In the course of the evolution of the network, the next state of a neuron $S_i(t+1)$ $(i = 0, 1, 2, ..., N-1)$ depends on the current states of other neurons in the following way:

$$S_i(t+1) = f\left(\sum_{j=0}^{N-1} T_{ij} S(t) + \theta_i\right) \tag{1}$$

Where $\boldsymbol{T_{ij}}$ is the synaptic strength between neurons *i* and j, θ_i is the threshold value of neuron *i*, and $f(x)$ is any nonlinear function. Here, we adopt a sign function $\sigma(x)$ as the nonlinear function, i.e., $f(x) = \sigma(x)$ where

$$\sigma(x) = \begin{cases} 1, & x \geq 0 \\ 0, & x < 0 \end{cases} \tag{2}$$

In the HNN, the value of the neuron threshold is defined as $\theta_i = 0$ $(where\ \ i = 0, 1, \cdots, \mathrm{N} - 1)$ and $T = (T_{ij})$ is a symmetric matrix. Equations (1) and (2) can be expressed in vector form as

$$S(t+1) = F_T(S(t)) = \sigma(S(t)T) \tag{3}$$

Where $\sigma(x)$ is obtained by applying the sign function on each elements in the $\boldsymbol{x}$ vector. Consequently, starting from the initial state $S(0)$, the state of the system at time t can be denoted as:

$$S(t) = F_T(S(t-1)) = F_T^t(S(0)) \tag{4}$$

The energy function of the HNN at time t is defined as:

$$E(t) = -\frac{1}{2}\sum_{ij} T_{ij} S_i(t) S_j(t) \tag{5}$$

Hopfield proved that the energy function is decreases monotonically during the state evolution. Since the energy of the network is limited, it must converge to a stable state, which is one of the local minima of the energy function [9]. In this paper, such stable states are called *attractor*s. Guo Dong-hui and Chen L.M. further proved that these attractors are chaotic, and message in the attraction domain of an attractor are unpredictable related to each other. If the neural synaptic matrix is altered, these attractors and their attraction domain will be changed [8]. After the neural synaptic matrix T multiplied by random permutation matrix H, original initial state S and corresponding attractor S^{μ} become new initial state $\hat{S}$ and attractor $\hat{S}^{\mu}$, respectively. They are shown as follows:

$$\hat{T} = H * T * H' \tag{6}$$

$$\hat{S}^{\mu} = S^{\mu} * H \tag{7}$$

$$\hat{S} = S * H \tag{8}$$

Where H' is the transpose of matrix of H.

2.2 Public-Key Cryptosystem Based on Chaotic Attractors

Provided that neural synaptic matrix T is a $n \times n$ singular matrix, and H is a $n \times n$ random permutation matrix. For any given T and H, $\hat{T} = H * T * H'$ is easy to compute according to matrix theory, and $\hat{T}$ is a singular matrix too. Furthermore, there is a kind of special matrix, which is referred as commutative matrix, in the random permutation matrix [10]. Suppose that H_1 and H_2 both are two of commutative matrices, and they have same order. Then, they must meet the following equation, $H_1 * H_2 = H_2 * H_1$.

According to Diffie-Hellman public-key cryptosystem, all users in a group jointly select a neural synaptic matrix T_0 which is a $n \times n$ singular matrix. Each user randomly selects a permutation matrix from a $n \times n$ commutative matrices group. For example, user A firstly selects any nonsingular matrix H_a from this commutative matrices group, and computes $T_a = H_a * T_0 * H_a'$. Secondly, he keeps T_a open as a public key, and keeps H_a secret as a private key. When user A and B in a group need secure communication, they will get a shared key $\hat{T} = H_a T_b H_a' = H_b T_a H_b'$. User A or user B can easily compute the shared key using his own private key and the other's public key. However, the third can not obtain the shared key when the number of neurons n is sufficiently large. In order to improve the security of information during network transmission and defeat the man-in-the-middle attack, the authenticated Diffie-Hellman key agreement protocol was developed by Diffie and Wiener in 1992 [11], and is proposed to adopt in the new scheme.

3 Encryption Scheme

According to the properties of chaotic attractors in OHNN, we know that a lot of chaotic-classified attractors can be obtained as long as stored sample s^{μ} or a few of neural synaptic strength T_{ij} are modified. So we can design a new public-key encryption system with high security, as shown in Fig.1. The detailed descriptions of encryption and decryption procedure are referred to this paper [8].

4 Security

The security of the proposed cryptosystem is based on the difficulty of singular matrix decomposition and the chaotic-classified properties of OHNN. The essence of attacking any cryptosystem is found the key. There are two ways of finding the private key in the proposed cryptosystem by attacking the chaotic properties of OHNN or by matrix decomposition.

4.1 Matrix Decomposition

As stated in the previous section, the neural synaptic matrix T_0 is a singular matrix. Thus, the matrices T_s, T_r and $\hat{T}$ all are singular matrices. For any given matrix T_0, T_s, and T_r, $\hat{T}$ is relatively easy to compute according to matrix theory. However, for any given matrix T_s, T_r or $\hat{T}$, it is computationally infeasible to find permutation matrix H_s or H_r, i.e. the private key. The reasons for this are referred to this paper [8].

4.2 Conventional Cryptanalysis

As illustrated in the previous section, our cryptosystem is designed based on the chaotic-classified properties of the OHNN. It is impossible to find the private key H by using chosen-plaintext attack or known- plaintext attack at present [8]. Furthermore, the proposed cryptosystem is uneven in the encryption and decryption process, i.e. it uses a random substitution during the encryption and auto-attraction during the decryption. Differential cryptanalysis methods cannot unfold our proposed cryptographic scheme because of these uneven processes. Only an exhaustive search based on the statistical probabilities of plaintext characters can succeed in breaking our proposed cryptosystem. However, the breaking cost of this method is very high.

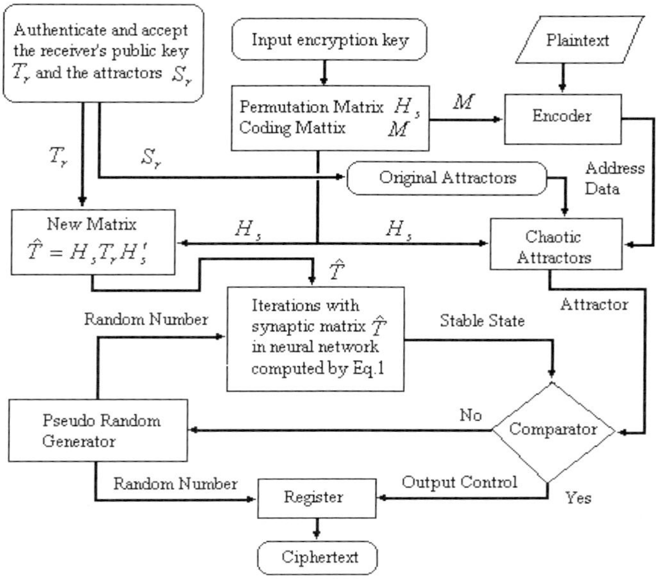

(a) Encryption scheme of the proposed cryptosystem

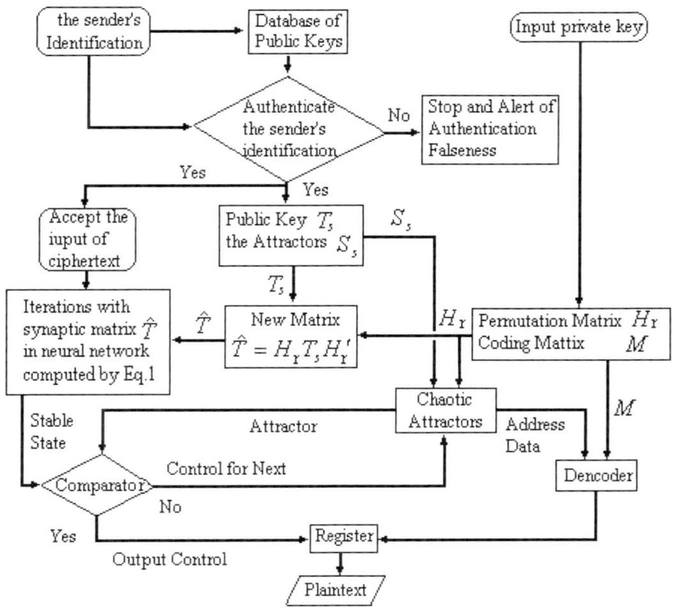

(b) Decryption scheme of the proposed cryptosystem

Fig. 1. Diagram of the proposed cryptosystem

From the above cryptographic scheme, if an OHNN consists of N neurons, and the number of attractors selected as coded plaintext is p, the number of coding matrices is $p!$, and for any given coding matrix, the number of random permutation matrices H is $N!$, i.e. the space of private key is $N!$. Even in a known plaintext attack, an exhaustive search would have to be done over $N!$ kinds of random permutations H. If a dedicated computer system that can perform a search of 10^6 groups of random permutations H in one second, the time required to search exhaustively the entire H space and to identify H is dependent on the size of N; for N =32, some 10^{20} MIPS years would be required for a successful search, which is well above the acceptable security level of current states, i.e., 10^{12} MIPS years (Figure 2).

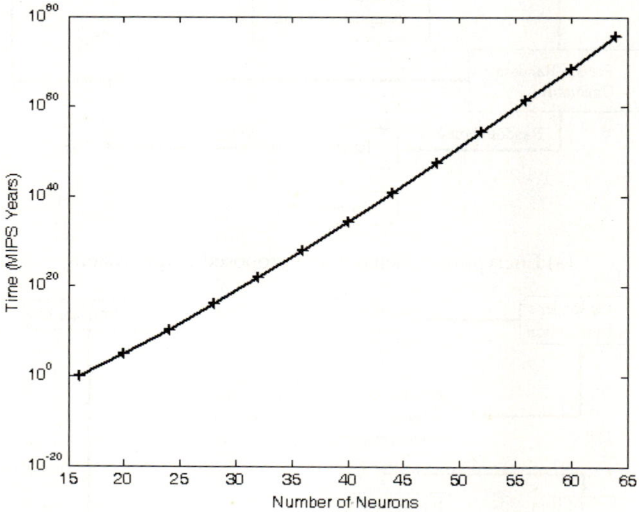

Fig. 2. Time required to perform an exhaustive search of private key varies the network scale N

On the other hand, the necessity of our cryptosystem is that the attractors are randomly substituted by the messages in their domains of attraction to eliminate the statistical likeness of the plaintext and avoid this attack based on the statistical probabilities of plaintext characters. So that, in the encryption process, the number of messages in the domain of attraction is another key parameter for the security of our proposed cryptosystem. A larger Λ (which is referred to as the number of messages in the domain of attraction) will give a lower probability of the plaintext occurrence. The parameter Λ depends on the network size N, and increases with N. For example, when N=8, we have $\Lambda=20$. However, when N =32, we have $\Lambda \approx 2^{16}$. In a network of N =32, every message in the domains of attraction has equal chance of representing the attractor via an m-sequence PRG. If the message corresponding to a plaintext character (such as an ASCII code) appears in the cipher text twice, it needs more than

$\Lambda \approx 2^{16}$ pieces of the same characters appearing in the plaintext to give a full analysis of the system characteristic. Consequently, if the PRG for random substitutions in our cryptosystem is designed to have temporal variations, the same message in the plaintext can be encrypted to different cipher texts at different times. To break our proposed scheme using probabilistic attacks requires that one store all the information of the attractors and their domains of attraction, which is not practical even when N is reasonably large, i.e., N =32.

5 Implementing

We implement the proposed scheme using Java program language according to Figure 1. The results of implementation show the proposed cryptography is feasible, and has a good performance of encryption and decryption speed. e.g. In notebook computer of DELL INSPIRON 6000, the speed of data encryption and decryption tested are (398.0±4.2) KB/S (P=0.05) and (9332.4±148.4) kB/s (p=0.05), respectively. The speed of data encryption for the proposed scheme using software implementing is over that of RSA (45.8kbps) using hardware implementing [12]. Higher encryption speed can be ensured the real time of IPng communications. By the way, any text with figure and table, or executable program can be encrypted and securely transmitted via the Internet using our software cryptosystem.

6 Conclusion

We propose a new public-key cryptosystem based on the chaotic attractors of neural networks. According to above discussions of the new cryptosystem, the proposed scheme has a high security, and is eminently practical in the context of modern cryptology. The experimental results of software implementing show that the proposed scheme is feasible and has an acceptable speed of encryption or decryption. The speed of data encryption for the proposed scheme using software implementing is over 50 times faster than that of RSA (45.8kbps) using hardware implementing. Neural networks rich in nonlinear complexities and parallel features are suitable for use in cryptology to meet the requirement of secure communication of IPng, as proposed here. However, we do not know whether the new public-key encryption scheme described in this paper can be kept from new types of attack. The exploration into the potential relevance of neural networks in cryptography needs be studied in detail.

Acknowledgments

The authors acknowledge the financial support of this work from the NSF of China (Grant No. 69886002, 60076015), the Science Project of Fujian province, China (Grant No. 2006J0408, 2005J034 and JA05293) and the Foundation for Young Professors of Jimei University, China (Grant No. 2006B003).

References

1. Diffie, W., Hellman, M.: New Directions in Cryptography. IEEE Transactions on Information Theory 22(6), 644–654 (1976)
2. Stallings, W.: Cryptography and Network Security: Principles and Practice, 2nd edn. Prentice –Hall, Inc, Englewood Cliffs (2003)
3. Hellman, M.: An overview of public key cryptography. IEEE Communications Magazine 40(5), 42–49 (2002)
4. Pecora, L.M., Carroll, T.L.: Synchronization in Chaotic Systems. Physical Review Letters 64(8), 821–824 (1990)
5. Crounse, K.R., Yang, T., Chua, L.O.: Pseudo-random sequence generation using the CNN universal machine with applications to cryptography. In: Proceedings of the IEEE International Workshop on Cellular Neural Networks and their Applications, Piscataway, pp. 433–438. IEEE, New York (1996)
6. Milanovic, V., Zaqhloul, M.E.: Synchronization of chaotic neural networks for secure communications. In: IEEE International Symposium on Circuits and Systems, Piscataway, vol. 3, pp. 28–31. IEEE, New York (1996)
7. Guo, D., Cheng, L.M., Cheng, L.L.: A New Symmetric Probabilistic Encryption Scheme Based on Chaotic Attractors of Neural Networks. Applied Intelligence 10, 71–84 (1999)
8. Liu, N., Guo, D.: A New Public-key Cryptography Based on Chaotic Attractors of Neural Networks. Progress in Intelligence Computation, Wuhan CUGP, pp. 293–300 (2005)
9. Hopfield, J.J.: Neural Networks and Physical Systems with Emergent Collective Computational Abilities. In: Proceedings of the National Academy of Science 79, 2554–2558 (1982)
10. Chen, J., Chen, X.: Special Matrices. Beijing, Tsinghua University Press, pp. 309–382 (2001)
11. Bresson Emmanuel: Provably Authenticated Group Diffie-Hellman Key Exchange. In: Proceedings of the ACM Conference on Computer and Communications Security, pp. 255–264 (2001)
12. Daly, A., William M.: Efficient Architectures for implementing Montgomery Modular Multiplication and RSA Modular Exponentiation on Reconfigurable Logic. enth ACM International Symposium on Field-Programmable Gate Arrays, pp. 40–49 (2002)

Enhanced Security Scheme for Managing Heterogeneous Server Platforms*

Jiho Kim, Duhyun Bae, Sehyun Park, and Ohyoung Song**

School of Electrical and Electronic Engineering, Chung-Ang University,
221, HukSuk-Dong, DongJak-Gu, Seoul 156-756, Korea
{jihokim,duhyunbae}@wm.cau.ac.kr, {shpark,song}@cau.ac.kr

Abstract. In this paper, we propose enhanced security scheme for managing heterogeneous server platforms. We apply fault tolerant architecture to basic remote server management model for providing security enhancement. This security enhancement includes several security services such as authentication, integrity, confidentiality, role based access control, and single-sign on. The traditional management methods cannot obtain these strong security services. Also, we present implementation results to verify functionality of the proposed scheme and demonstrate the performance of certificate validation that occupy most of total latency.

Keywords: security server management, PKI, single sign on, access control.

1 Introduction

Managing server means maintenance, fault prevention, and urgency recovery of heterogeneous server platforms. An administrator must be beforehand with faults and breakdowns of a server by monitoring it, and minimizes damage by recovery from unexpected troubles rapidly. Mostly, corporations and institutions use many heterogeneous server platforms utilized for various purposes along with spread of fast internet in these days. Generally, administrators manage several servers in the directed console environment or remotely access to the server for managing it in the remote environment. In case of the directed console environment, a number of servers that an administrator must manage become more increase, managing it is cost-ineffective gradually. When the administrator goes home or is in the outside of the office, if something troubles occur to a server, urgency recovery of the server becomes difficult. On the contrary, in case of the remote environment, the administrator can rapidly restore the disabled server by Internet when the administrator is in the outside. But, because following security problems is existed, a

* This research was supported by the MIC (Ministry of Information and Communication), Korea, under the Chung-Ang University HNRC (Home Network Research Center)-ITRC support program supervised by the IITA (Institute of Information Technology Assessment).
** Corresponding author.

Y. Wang, Y. Cheung, and H. Liu (Eds.): CIS 2006, LNAI 4456, pp. 451 – 459, 2007.

new management system that can manage many servers efficiently and securely is necessary.

- Responsibility of keeping the ID and password of the administrator in his mind
- Risk of exposing the ID and password to intruder
- Snooping of confidential data
- Difficulty of manage several IDs and passwords correspond to many servers
- Access problem due to network or internet trouble

To solve these problems, we apply fault tolerant architecture to basic remote server management model for providing security enhancement. It can provide the following security services.

- Mutual authentication between administrators and authentication server
- Confidentiality of transmission data
- Reliable certificate validation based on SCVP (Simple Certificate Validation Protocol) [4]
- RBAC (Role Based Access Control)
- Non-repudiation
- Single-Sign On (SSO)
- Fault tolerant structure against the intrusion and network trouble

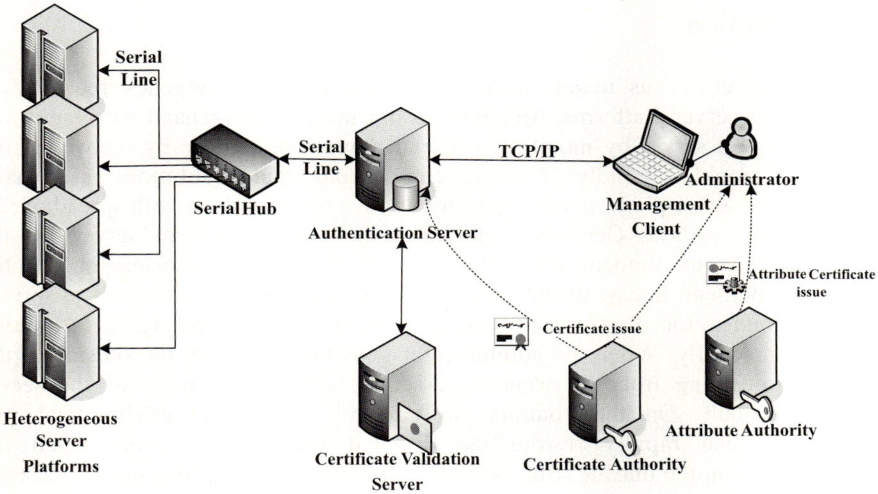

Fig. 1. Proposed Architecture

The traditional management methods cannot obtain these strong security services. Table 1 shows security comparisons of the proposed scheme with traditional management. In this paper, the proposed scheme use accredited certificates issued by three major root certification authorities (Korea Information Certification Authority Institute (KICA), Korea Financial Telecommunication and Clearings Institute (KFTC), and CrossCert Institute) in Korea as well as certificates issued by private certification authority (CA). We implement a private CA, SCVP, and authentication server (AS). And we verify the proposed scheme by implementing testbed.

The rest of the paper is organized as follows. In Section 2, we introduce proposed architecture for securely managing heterogeneous server platforms. Section 3 describes proposed security enhancement schemes. Implementation results are discussed in Section 4. Finally, Section 5 presents our conclusions.

2 Proposed Architecture

Figure 1 shows proposed architecture for securely managing heterogeneous server platforms. It consists of the following several components. The proposed architecture includes some PKI (Public Key Infrastructure), PMI (Privilege Management Infrastructure) components for mutual authentication and authorization. The PKI is based on the ITU-T X.509 [1][2]. The PKI is widespread trust model to manage the

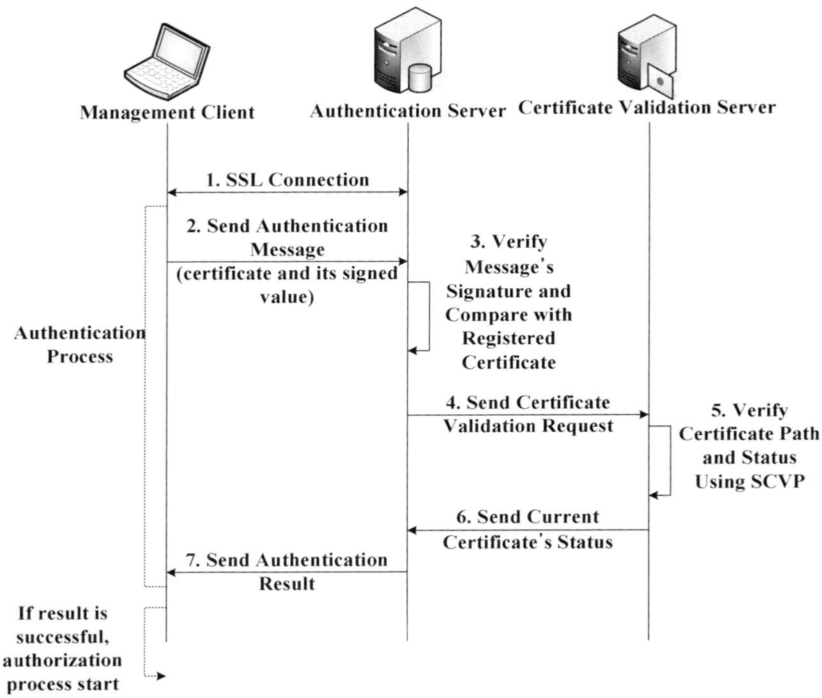

Fig. 2. Authentication Process

security threat on the Internet. PMI[1] use attribute certificates (AC) issued by attribute authority (AA) to provide role of user, not identity. The AC is intended to be valid during the extremely short period. More detailed descriptions about the integration of proposed scheme and security infrastructures are presented in Section 3.

The MC can connect to AS through Internet or Local Area Network (LAN) on TCP/IP. The MC is an application to provide management environment identical with that of directed console to an administrator. The AS requests validation of administrator's certificate to CVS and decides whether AS permits access right of the administrator or not. The CVS validates the administrator's certificate by using SCVP to reduce AS's certificate validation load and provide reliable validation of the certificate. If the administrator is in Internet possible place and only have a management application and certificate (include private key), the administrator can manage several servers in any place simultaneously. Heterogeneous server platforms directly connect to AS with serial communication Hub. The use of serial communication has two significant benefits. One is that serial communication is safe line because it is not exposed and communicates only each other, and the other is that it is not influenced in network failure of it and relatively robust communication method.

3 Proposed Security Enhancement Schemes

In this section, we describe three security enhancement schemes. These schemes consist of user authentication, certificate validation, and access control.

3.1 User Authentication

Figure 2 shows the proposed message flow during user authentication process. Initially, between MC and AS establish server side SSL (Secure Socket Layer) for confidentially transferring data after this time. The original SSL handshake can be simplified by adopting server side SSL that the MC does not send its certificate but the AS sends it because MC sends it in following authentication process. And then, a MC sends an authentication message that consists of administrator's certificate and digital-signed its certificate using its private key to AS. The AS receives the authentication message from the MC and confirms that administrator's certificate is identical to pre-registered administrator's certificate. If this process successfully completes, The AS sign a validation request of the administrator's certificate using AS's private key and send this validation request to the CVS. And If the CVS successfully verifies signed request message received from the AS, the CVS performs certificate path validation. And if final certificate's status is valid, authentication process successfully finished and authorization process detailed in section 3.3 start. In proposed authentication scheme, registrations of administrator's certificates in the AS are previously required. In case that administrator's certificate is not registered or the result of signed message checking and certificate's validation is not valid, the AS recodes authentication failure reports before authentication process terminates.

3.2 Certificate Validation

We mandatory require the validation of certificate's path and certificate revocation list (CRL) in order to protect server platforms from intruder's access. The depth of

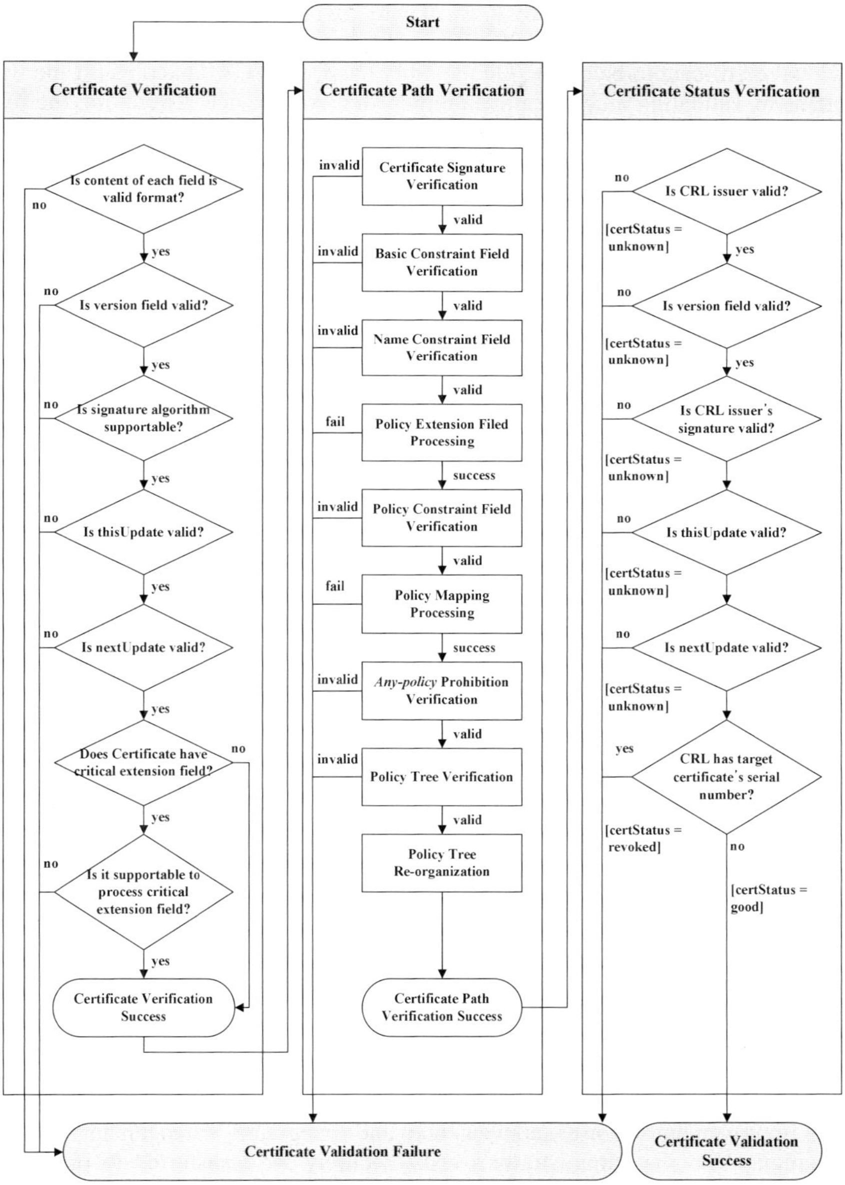

Fig. 3. Flow Chart of the Entire Certificate Validation Process

certificate chains increases, the process of verifying a certificate is more complicated and spend a lot of CPU time on computing for checking a number of digital signatures. To reduce the overhead of certificate validation on the AS, the CVS instead of the AS perform certificate's path validation and CRL check to verify certificate's status using SCVP. There are mainly two protocols to provide an online service that allows the status of a certificate to be checked. The OCSP (Online Certificate Status Protocol) and SCVP are these protocols. The OCSP allows only individual certificate to be check. On the other hand, the SCVP handles off the whole problems of validating a certificate chain to validation service. Therefore, the use of SCVP is more desirable choice than the OCSP.

The certificate validation process consists of certificate verification, certificate path verification, and certificate status verification. The certificate verification is to verify certificate itself and consists of certificate format and content verification. The certificate path verification is to verify certificate chain and certificate policy tree. This consists of certificate signature verification, some constraint field verification and mapping and verification of certificate policy. The certificate status verification is to check whether certificate was revoked or not. This consists of CRL verification and check that a CRL has target certificate's serial number. The flow chart of the entire certificate validation process is described in figure 3.

3.3 Authorization and Access Control

As shown in figure 4, the administrator in order to access server acquires permission through the following authorization process. If the authentication process successfully finishes, the MC sends to an administrator's attribute certificate (AC) to AS. The AS receives an AC from the MC and verifies the digital signature of the AC. Then, the AS grants appropriate privilege based on role of AC to the administrator and apply serial port access control according to this. Next, the AS sends authorization results that include privilege and accessible server list to the MC. Table 1 shows an example of privilege that is based on a user's Role in AC. For Example, if the administrator's role is a staff engineer in figure 4, the staff engineer can access only group C servers with limited privilege.

If the previous authorization process completes successfully, an administrator can access one or more server that connected with the AS on serial line. When an administrator accesses a server platform at first, the administrator promptly manage the server with an appropriate privilege based on the administrator's role without additional log on it. In proposed scheme, even when some faults unexpectedly happen on TCP/IP network functions of a Server platform, the administrator can remotely work on diagnosis of its fault similarly in console environment because the servers communicate with the AS by serial line, not TCP/IP. And if once an administrator passes authentication and authorization process successfully, the administrator can manage several servers without passing it any longer for a given period. In this manner, it can provide SSO that widely spread in intranet and web service. The SSO enable improvement of user convenience and integrated management of access information. Also the administrator's task securely are transferred to or from the server because the MC communicate with the AS by SSL and the AS communicate with the server by isolated serial line. The AS stores access log of all users and stores

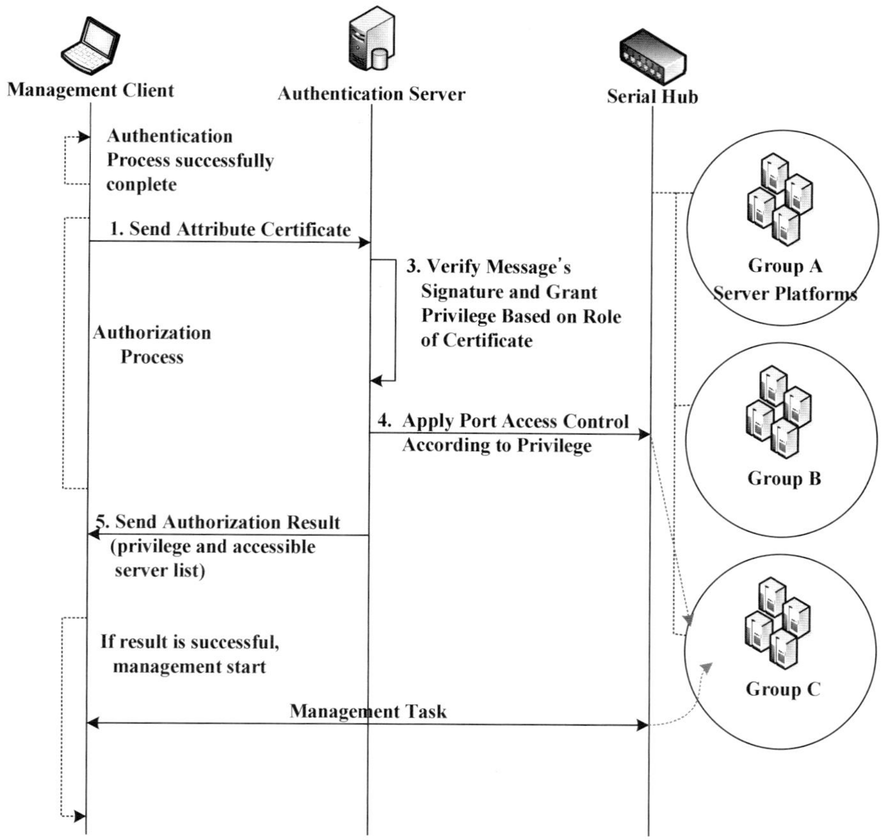

Fig. 4. Authorization and Access Control Process

Table 1. Example of Privileges

Role	Group	Privilege
General manager	A, B, C	super user
Manager	A, B	super user
Assistant manager A	A	super user
Assistant manager B	B	super user
Staff engineer	C	limited super user
Engineer	C	limited super user

tasks executed by all administrators. These log and task recode can help analysis of connection and management status. In addition, this information is signed by the AS's private key and is stored in encryption form in order to prevent attackers from compromising it and provide non-repudiation service about administrator's action.

4 Testbed Implementation and Experimental Result

In this section, we present implementation results to verify functionality of the proposed scheme and demonstrate the performance of certificate validation that occupy most of total latency. As shown in figure 5, we implement testbed to verify the proposed scheme. We installed two MCs that had different roles. Therefore, we made sure that the user A and user B had different privileges after authorization process. The AS connected to MCs with 100Mbps Ethernet. The AS and CVS was installed on laptop (PIII 933 Mhz, 512Mbyte RAM). We installed CA and AA on same machine. The AS connected to various server platforms with 19200bps serial. We use accredited certificates issued by three major root CA (KICA, KFTC, and CrossCert Institute) in Korea as well as certificates issued by private CA that we implemented. The user chooses a server to access if authentication and authorization process successfully complete. Then, the user can access heterogeneous server platforms and manage it in window consol. Also we measured certificate validation overhead that is major part of total delay by performing full authentications. And we obtained an average validation time of 712ms.

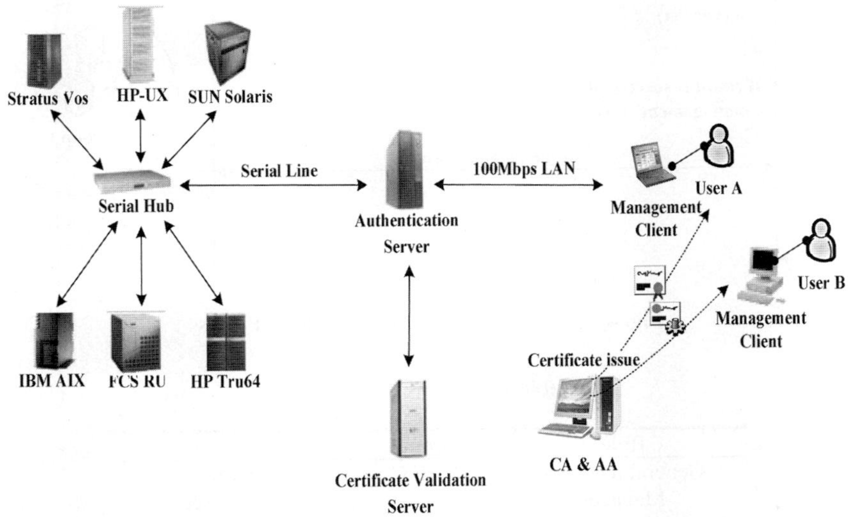

Fg. 5. Teatbed Setup

5 Conclusions

In this paper, we propose enhanced security scheme for managing heterogeneous server platforms. We apply fault tolerant architecture to basic remote server management model for providing security enhancement. This security enhancement includes several security services such as authentication, integrity, confidentiality, role based access control, and single-sign on. The traditional management methods cannot obtain these strong security services. Also the proposed scheme provides integrated management of heterogeneous server platforms and scalability. And we measure average validation time of 712ms and verify functionality of the proposed scheme through implementing a testbed. If it is used to manage heterogeneous server platforms in company, campus, and research center etc, it is expected to enhance security and reduce management cost with improving convenience.

References

1. ITU-T Recommendation X.509: Information Technology - Open systems interconnection - The directory: public-key and attribute certificate frameworks (2002)
2. Housley, R., e.a.: RFC3280 - Internet X.509 Public Key Infrastructure Certificate and CRL Profile (2002)
3. Perlman, R.: An overview of PKI Trust Models. IEEE Network 13 (1999)
4. Malpani, A., e.a: Simple Certificate Validation Protocol (SCVP) (2002)
5. Levi A., Caglayan, M. U.: An efficient, dynamic and trust preserving public key infrastructure. In: Proceedings of IEEE Symposium on Security and Privacy (2000)

A New Parallel Multiplier for Type II Optimal Normal Basis*

Chang Han Kim[1], Yongtae Kim[2], Sung Yeon Ji[3], and IlWhan Park[4]

[1] Semyung University, Jecheon, Chungbuk, Korea
chkim@semyung.ac.kr
[2] Gwangju National University of Education, Gwangju, 500-703, Korea
ytkim@gnue.ac.kr
[3] Center for Information and Security Technologies. Korea University, Seoul, Korea
jisy0522@cist.korea.ac.kr
[4] National Security Research Institute. Daejeon, Korea
ilhpark@etri.re.kr

Abstract. In hardware implementation for the finite field, the use of normal basis has several advantages, especially the optimal normal basis is the most efficient to hardware implementation in $GF(2^m)$. The finite field $GF(2^m)$ with type I optimal normal basis has the disadvantage not applicable to cryptography since m is even. The finite fields $GF(2^m)$ with type II optimal normal basis, however, such as $GF(2^{233})$ are applicable to ECDSA recommended by NIST, and many researchers devote their attentions to efficient arithmetic over them. In this paper, we propose a new type II optimal normal basis parallel multiplier over $GF(2^m)$ whose structure and algorithm is clear at a glance, which performs multiplication over $GF(2^m)$ in the extension field $GF(2^{2m})$. The time and area complexity of the proposed multiplier is the same as the best known type II optimal normal basis parallel multiplier.

1 Introduction

Finite fields are important to cryptography and coding theory and especially to public key cryptography such as ECC, XTR and ElGamal type cryptosystems, and thus many researchers devote their attentions to efficient finite field arithmetic [1],[2]. Finite field arithmetic depends on the basis representation, and an element of the finite field is usually represented with respect to polynomial basis [3],[4], normal basis [5],[6],[7] and the nonconventional basis [8] sometimes. In hardware implementation, the merit of the normal basis representation is that the result of squaring an element is simply the right cyclic shift of its coordinates. In particular, the arithmetic over the optimal normal basis is the best known efficient among the normal bases implementation [3],[5]. There are two types of optimal normal bases, i.e., of type I and of type II [2]. The

* This research was supported by the MIC(Ministry of Information and Communication), Korea, under the ITRC(Information Technology Research Center) support program supervised by the IITA(Institute of Information Technology Assessment).

Y. Wang, Y. Cheung, and H. Liu (Eds.): CIS 2006, LNAI 4456, pp. 460–469, 2007.

finite field $GF(2^m)$ with type I optimal normal basis is efficient to hardware implementation, but on the other hand it has the disadvantage not applicable to some cryptographic areas since m is even[9],[10],[11]. The finite fields $GF(2^m)$ with type II optimal normal basis, however, such as $GF(2^{233})$ are applicable to ECDSA recommended by NIST, and many researchers began to develop multiplier for efficient arithmetic over them [2]. In 1998, Blake et al.[12] proposed the multiplication method for the optimal normal basis of type II, which is based on the palindrome representation of polynomial of length $2m$ whose complexity will be at least $(2m)^2$. Based on the fact that if r is a primitive $2m+1$-th root of unity, then $\beta = \gamma + \gamma^{-1}$ is the normal element, Sunar and Koc [6] proposed the multiplier, which require m^2 AND gates and $3m(m-1)/2$ XOR gates in 2001. Elia and Leone [13], as well as Reyhani-Masoleh and Hasan [5], proposed the multiplier having the same efficiency as that of Sunar and Koc [6] in 2002. Combining the Blake et al.'s multiplier and Sunar and Koc's multiplier, and using the fact that the elements with respect to type II optimal normal basis of the finite fields $GF(2^m)$ can be embedded in the extension fields $GF(2^{2m})$, we, in this paper, propose a new parallel multiplier having the same time and area complexity as the best known parallel multiplier. In section 3, we propose the multiplier obtained from the mathematical backgrounds of section 2, and compare our proposed multiplier with the existing ones in section 4.

2 Preliminaries

In this section, we give some preliminaries for the normal basis representation of a finite field element, and introduce the optimal normal bases.

2.1 Normal Bases Representations

It is well known that there is always a normal basis for the finite field $GF(2^m)$ over $GF(2)$ for any positive integer m [1],[14]. If there exists an element β of $GF(2^m)$ such that the set $N = \{\beta, \beta^2, \cdots, \beta^{2^{m-1}}\}$ is a basis for $GF(2^m)$ over $GF(2)$, then N is called the normal basis for $GF(2^m)$ over $GF(2)$ and β is called the normal element. Then any $A \in GF(2^m)$ can be represented as follows.

$$A = \sum_{i=0}^{m-1} a_i \beta^{2^i}, a_i \in GF(2).$$

For brevity, the normal basis representation of A will be denoted by

$$A = (a_0, a_1, \cdots, a_{m-1}).$$

Also the matrix representation of A will be

$$A = \overline{a} \times \overline{\beta}^T = \overline{\beta} \times \overline{a}^T,$$

where $\overline{a} = [a_0, a_1, \cdots, a_{m-1}], \overline{\beta} = [\beta, \beta^2, \cdots, \beta^{2^{m-1}}]$ and T denotes the vector transposition. The merit of the normal basis representation is that the result of squaring an element A is simply the right cyclic shift(RCS) of its coordinates. That is,

$$A^2 = (a_{m-1}, a_0, a_1, \cdots, a_{m-2}).$$

Let $A = \sum_{i=0}^{m-1} a_i\beta^{2^i}, B = \sum_{i=0}^{m-1} b_i\beta^{2^i} \in GF(2^m)$, where $a_i, b_i \in GF(2)$ and $C = AB = \sum_{i=0}^{m-1} c_i\beta^{2^i}$. Then

$$C = (\overline{a} \times \overline{\beta}^T) \times (\overline{\beta} \times \overline{b}^T) = \overline{a}M\overline{b}^T,$$

where the multiplication matrix M is defined as

$$M = \overline{\beta}^T \times \overline{\beta} = (\beta^{2^i+2^j}), 0 \le i, j \le m-1.$$

If each $\beta^{2^i+2^j}$ is represented with respect to the normal basis, then we have $M = M_0\beta + M_1\beta^2 + \cdots + M_{m-1}\beta^{2^{m-1}}$, where M_i is an m by m matrix over $GF(2)$.

Using the property of squaring an element with normal basis representation, the coefficients of C is obtained as below.

$$c_i = \overline{a}M_i\overline{b}^T = \overline{a}^{(i)}M_0\overline{b}^{(i)^T},$$

where $\overline{a}^{(i)} = [a_i, a_{i+1}, \cdots, a_{i-1}], \overline{b}^{(i)} = [b_i, b_{i+1}, \cdots, b_{i-1}]$. From this fact, we can show that the numbers of 1s in $M_i, 0 \le i \le m-1$ are the same. The number of 1s in each M_i is called the complexity of the normal basis and denoted by C_N. Gao et al. proved that $C_N \ge 2m-1$ [2],[14]. Let $< 2 >$ denote the cyclic group generated by 2.

2.2 Type II Optimal Normal Basis

If $C_N = 2m-1$, then N is called the optimal normal basis for the finite field. A polynomial whose coefficient are all 1s is called All-One-Polynomial(AOP), e.g. $x^m + x^{m-1} + \cdots + x + 1$.

Theorem 1. *(Type-I optimal normal basis theorem)*
The finite field $GF(2^m)$ has a type-I optimal normal basis over $GF(2)$ if and only if $m+1$ is prime and $GF(m+1)^* =< 2 >$. And if the AOP $x^m+x^{m-1}+\cdots+x+1$ of degree n is irreducible over $GF(2)$, then a root of the AOP generates the optimal normal basis [2],[14].

Theorem 2. *Assume that $2m+1$ is prime. Then if either $GF(2m+1)^* =< 2 >$ or $2m+1 \equiv 3 \bmod 4, GF(2m+1)^* =< -1, 2 >$, then $\beta = \gamma + \gamma^{-1}$ is the generator of the optimal normal basis of $GF(2^m)$ over $GF(2)$, where γ is the primitive $2m+1$-th root of unity in $GF(2^{2m})$ [2],[14].*

Throughout this paper, every finite field $GF(2^m)$ has a type II optimal basis. Then we have $\gamma \in GF(2^{2m})$ and

$$N = \{\beta, \beta^2, \cdots, \beta^{2^{m-1}}\} = \{\gamma + \gamma^{-1}, \gamma^2 + \gamma^{-2}, \cdots, \gamma^m + \gamma^{-m}\}. \quad (1)$$

Since $\beta = \gamma + \gamma^{-1}$ is the normal element of $GF(2^m)$ over $GF(2)$[2], any element A of $GF(2^m)$ can be represented as

$$\begin{aligned} A &= a_0\beta + a_1\beta^2 + a_2\beta^{2^2} + \cdots + a_{m-1}\beta^{2^{m-1}} \\ &= A_0(\gamma + \gamma^{-1}) + A_1(\gamma^2 + \gamma^{-2}) + \cdots + A_{m-1}(\gamma^m + \gamma^{-m}). \end{aligned} \qquad (2)$$

by (1), where the coefficients A_i are obtained by rearranging the coefficients a_i. Incidentally, $A \in GF(2^m)$ is either represented as $A = (a_0, \cdots, a_{m-1})$ or $A = (A_0, \cdots, A_{m-1})$ corresponding to the normal basis $N = \{\beta, \beta^2, \cdots, \beta^{2^{m-1}}\}$ or $\{\gamma+\gamma^{-1}, \gamma^2+\gamma^{-2}, \cdots, \gamma^m+\gamma^{-m}\}$ rearranging N. Since converting the former into the latter is simple rearrangement, and thus does not cost in hardware implementation. So, we regard every $A \in GF(2^m)$ as represented with respect to $\{\gamma + \gamma^{-1}, \gamma^2 + \gamma^{-2}, \cdots, \gamma^m + \gamma^{-m}\}$ in this paper, but on the other hand it can be represented as an element of $GF(2^{2m})$ with respect to γ^i 's, that is,

$$A = A_0\gamma + A_1\gamma^2 + A_2\gamma^3 + \cdots + A_{m-1}\gamma^m + A_{m-1}\gamma^{m+1} + A_{m-2}\gamma^{m+2} + \cdots + A_0\gamma^{2m},$$

where $A_j \in GF(2)$.

Notice that the set $\{\gamma, \gamma^2, \cdots, \gamma^{2m}\}$ is not always the basis for $GF(2^{2m})$ over $GF(2)$. But if $GF(2m+1)^* =< 2 >$, then $\{\gamma, \gamma^2, \cdots, \gamma^{2m}\}$ is a nonconventional basis for $GF(2^{2m})$ over $GF(2)$[8].

Theorem 3. *For any elements $A, B \in GF(2^m)$, in order to calculate the product $C = AB$ with respect to $\{\gamma, \gamma^2, \cdots, \gamma^{2m}\}$ in $GF(2^{2m})$, we compute the coefficients of $\{\gamma, \gamma^2, \cdots, \gamma^m\}$ only.*

Proof. For $X \in GF(2^{2m})$, if

$$X = X_0\gamma + X_1\gamma^2 + X_2\gamma^3 + \cdots + X_{m-1}\gamma^m + X_{m-1}\gamma^{m+1} + X_{m-2}\gamma^{m+2} + \cdots + X_0\gamma^{2m},$$

then, rearranging the coefficients of X by (2), we have

$$\begin{aligned} X &= X_0(\gamma + \gamma^{-1}) + X_1(\gamma^2 + \gamma^{-2}) + \cdots + X_{m-1}(\gamma^m + \gamma^{-m}) \\ &= x_0\beta + x_1\beta^2 + x_2\beta^{2^2} + \cdots + x_{m-1}\beta^{2^{m-1}}. \end{aligned}$$

Thus, $X \in GF(2^m)$. Since $A, B \in GF(2^m) \subset GF(2^{2m})$, we have

$$\begin{aligned} A = A_0\gamma + A_1\gamma^2 + A_2\gamma^3 + \cdots + A_{m-1}\gamma^m + A_{m-1}\gamma^{m+1} \\ + A_{m-2}\gamma^{m+2} + \cdots + A_0\gamma^{2m} \end{aligned} \qquad (3)$$

and

$$B = B_0\gamma + B_1\gamma^2 + B_2\gamma^3 + \cdots + B_{m-1}\gamma^m + B_{m-1}\gamma^{m+1} + B_{m-2}\gamma^{m+2} + \cdots + B_0\gamma^{2m}.$$

Using $\gamma^{2m+1} = 1$, we have

$$\begin{aligned} &B_{j-1}\gamma^j A + B_{j-1}\gamma^{2m-j+1} A \\ &= B_{j-1}(A_{j-2}\gamma + \cdots + A_0\gamma^{j-1} + 0 + A_0\gamma^{j+1} \end{aligned}$$

$$
\begin{aligned}
&+\cdots+A_{m-1}\gamma^{m+j+1}+\cdots+A_j\gamma^{2m})+B_{j-1}A_{j-1}\\
&+B_{j-1}(A_j\gamma+\cdots+A_{m-1}\gamma^{m-j}+A_{m-1}\gamma^{m-j+1}+\cdots+A_0\gamma^{2m-j}\\
&+0+A_0\gamma^{2m-j+2}+\cdots+A_{j-2}\gamma^{2m})+B_{j-1}A_{j-1}\\
=\;&B_{j-1}((A_{j-2}+A_j)\gamma+\cdots+(A_0+A_{2j-2})\gamma^{j-1}+A_{2j-1}\gamma^j+(A_0+A_{2j})\gamma^{j+1}\\
&+\cdots+(A_{m-j-1}+A_{m-j})\gamma^m+(A_{m-j}+A_{m-j-1})\gamma^{m+1}+\cdots\\
&+(A_0+A_{2j})\gamma^{2m-j}+A_{2j-1}\gamma^{2m-j+1}+(A_0+A_{2j-2})\gamma^{2m-j+2}\\
&+\cdots+(A_j+A_{j-2})\gamma^{2m})\\
=\;&B_{j-1}(A_{j-2}+A_j,\cdots,A_0+A_{2j-2},A_{2j-1},A_0+A_{2j},\cdots,A_{m-j-1}+A_{m-j},\\
&\quad A_{m-j}+A_{m-j-1},\cdots,A_0+A_{2j},A_{2j-1},A_0+A_{2j-2},\cdots,A_j+A_{j-2}). \qquad (4)
\end{aligned}
$$

Thus, the coefficient of each term appeared in the product is symmetric centered at γ and γ^{m+1}, so that we only find out the coefficients of $\gamma,\gamma^2,\cdots,\gamma^m$ in order to calculate the product.

Whenever an element

$$A=A_0\gamma+A_1\gamma^2+A_2\gamma^3+\cdots+A_{m-1}\gamma^m+A_{m-1}\gamma^{m+1}+A_{m-2}\gamma^{m+2}+\cdots+A_0\gamma^{2m},$$

where $A_j\in GF(2)$ in $GF(2^m)$ is regarded as an element of $GF(2^{2m})$, we will denote of A by its vector representation

$$(A_0,\cdots,A_{m-1},A_{m-1},\cdots,A_0)$$

or simply $\overline{A}\equiv A=(A_0,\cdots,A_{m-1})$.

Example 1. In case $m=5, j=2$ we have

$$
\begin{aligned}
&B_1\gamma^2A+B_1\gamma^9A\\
&\equiv B_1(A_0+A_2,A_3,A_0+A_4,A_2+A_3,A_2+A_3,A_1+A_4,A_3,A_0+A_2).
\end{aligned}
$$

3 Parallel Multiplier for Type II Optimal Normal Basis

We now construct, in this section, the parallel multiplier which calculates the product of elements of $GF(2^m)$ with respect to the basis for $GF(2^{2m})$.

Theorem 4. *For $A,B\in GF(2^m)$, let $C=AB,\overline{A}=(A_0,A_1,\cdots,A_{m-1}),\overline{B}=(B_0,B_1,\cdots,B_{m-1}),\overline{C}=(C_0,C_1,\cdots,C_{m-1})$, then we have $\overline{C}=\sum_{j=1}^{m}B_{j-1}A[j]$, where*

$$
\begin{aligned}
A[1]&=(A_1,A_0+A_2,\cdots,A_{m-3}+A_{m-1},A_{m-2}+A_{m-1}),\\
A[j]&=(A_{j-2}+A_j,\cdots,A_0+A_{2j-2},A_{2j-1},A_0+A_{2j},\cdots,A_{m-j-2}+A_{m-j},\\
&\qquad A_{m-j-1}+A_{m-j}),\ \textit{if}\ 1<j\ \textit{and}\ 2j\le m,\\
A[j]&=(A_{j-2}+A_j,\cdots,A_{2j-m-1}+A_{m-1},A_{2j-m-2}+A_{m-1},\cdots,\\
&\qquad A_0+A_{2m-2j+1},A_{2m-2j},\cdots,A_{m-j-1}+A_{m-j}),\ \textit{if}\ \ 2j>m\ \textit{and}\ j\le m.
\end{aligned}
$$

Proof. If we represent A, B in the same way as (3), and calculate the product AB using (4), then we have

$$
\begin{aligned}
C = AB &= \sum_{j=1}^{m}(A\gamma^j + A\gamma^{2m-j+1})B_{j-1} \\
&= \sum_{j=1}^{m} B_{j-1}((A_{j-2} + A_j)\gamma + \cdots + (A_0 + A_{2j-2})\gamma^{j-1} + A_{2j-1}\gamma^j \\
&\quad + (A_0 + A_{2j})\gamma^{j+1} + \cdots + (A_{m-j-1} + A_{m-j})\gamma^m \\
&\quad + (A_{m-j} + A_{m-j-1})\gamma^{m+1} + \cdots + (A_0 + A_{2j+1})\gamma^{2m-j} \\
&\quad + A_{2j-1}\gamma^{2m-j+1} + (A_0 + A_{2j-2})\gamma^{2m-j+2} + \cdots + (A_j + A_{j-2})\gamma^{2m}).
\end{aligned}
$$

To simplify the above equation, we separate all terms in the right hand side of the equation above into three cases according to the indices j, and it is sufficient for us to calculate the coefficients of $\gamma, \gamma^2, \cdots, \gamma^m$ by Theorem 3.

1. In case $j = 1$, there remain
$$B_0(A_1, A_0 + A_2, \cdots, A_{m-3} + A_{m-1}, A_{m-2} + A_{m-1}).$$
2. In case $j > 1$ and $2j \leq m$, there remain
$$B_{j-1}\ (\ A_{j-2} + A_j, \cdots, A_0 + A_{2j-2}, A_{2j-1}, A_0 + A_{2j}, \cdots,\\ A_{m-j-2} + A_{m-j}, A_{m-j-1} + A_{m-j}).$$
3. In case $2j > m$ and $j \leq m$ there remain
$$B_{j-1}\ (\ A_{j-2} + A_j, \cdots, A_{2j-m-1} + A_{m-1}, A_{2j-m-2} + A_{m-1}, \cdots,\\ A_0 + A_{2m-2j-1}, A_{2m-2j}, \cdots, A_{m-j-1} + A_{m-j}).$$

This completes the proof.

We can now construct a new architecture of hardware implementing finite fields using Theorem 4 as follows.

The new architecture has inputs $A, B \in GF(2^m)$ converted to $\overline{A}, \overline{B}$ with free cost, and then has output $\overline{C} = C$. We first construct the XOR Blocks realizing $A_i + A_j, 0 \leq i < j \leq m-1$ of $A[j]$ and AND 2 Block multiplying the output of $A[j]$ by B_t, AND 1 Block realizing B_jA_i. We next construct the BTX(Binary Tree XOR) Block XOR pair-wise(confer Fig.1). We thus need $m(m-1)$ XOR gates, since there are $m-1$ XOR gates for each $A[j]$, where $1 \leq j \leq m$. For $A_i, 0 \leq i \leq m-1$, the number of $A_i + A_j, 0 \leq i < j \leq m-1$ is $m(m-1)/2$, and thus maximum number of XOR gates needed are $m(m-1)/2$ in XOR Block.

We next calculate $B_0A_1, B_1A_3, \cdots, B_{(m-1)/2}A_{m-1}, B_{m/2}A_{m-2}, \cdots, B_{m-1}A_0$ for m odd and $B_0A_1, B_1A_3, \cdots, B_{(m-2)/2}A_{m-1}, B_{m/2}A_{m-2}, \cdots, B_{m-1}A_0$ for m even in AND 1 Block. For AND 2 Block, there need maximum $m(m-1)$ AND operations since there need $m-1$ multiplications for each j, and thus the total number of AND operations is m^2. For the BTX, we need $m(m-1)$ XOR gates since there need $m-1$ multiplications for each j, and thus the total number of XOR gates is $3m(m-1)/2$.

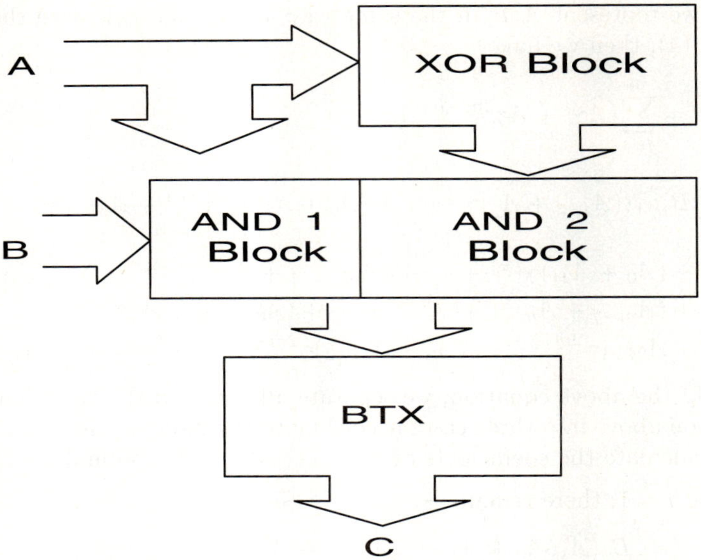

Fig. 1. The Block Diagram of Type II Optimal Normal Basis Parallel Multiplier for $GF(2^m)$

Example 2. Let $A = (a_0, a_1, a_2, a_3, a_4), B = (b_0, b_1, b_2, b_3, b_4) \in GF(2^m)$, and $A \equiv \overline{A} = (A_0, A_1, A_2, A_3, A_4),\ B \equiv \overline{B} = (B_0, B_1, B_2, B_3, B_4) \in GF(2^5)$. Then $A_0 = a_0, A_1, = a_1, A_2 = a_3, A_3 = a_2, A_4 = a_4$ by $\beta = \gamma + \gamma^{-1}, \beta^2 = \gamma^2 + \gamma^{-2}, \beta^{2^2} = \gamma^4 + \gamma^{-4}, \beta^{2^3} = \gamma^3 + \gamma^{-3}, \beta^{2^4} = \gamma^5 + \gamma^{-5}$. Thus, since

$$\begin{aligned}\overline{C} = \overline{AB} \\ = \quad & B_0(A_1, A_0 + A_2, A_1 + A_3, A_2 + A_4, A_3 + A_4) \\ & + B_1(A_0 + A_2, A_3, A_0 + A_4, A_1 + A_4, A_2 + A_3) \\ & + B_2(A_1 + A_3, A_0 + A_4, A_4, A_0 + A_3, A_1 + A_2) \\ & + B_3(A_2 + A_4, A_1 + A_4, A_0 + A_3, A_2, A_0 + A_1) \\ & + B_4(A_3 + A_4, A_2 + A_3, A_1 + A_2, A_0 + A_1, A_0),\end{aligned}$$

we have

$$\begin{aligned}C = AB \\ = \quad & b_0(a_1, a_0 + a_3, a_3 + a_4, a_1 + a_2, a_2 + a_4) \\ & + b_1(a_0 + a_3, a_2, a_1 + a_4, a_0 + a_4, a_3 + a_2) \\ & + b_2(a_3 + a_4, a_1 + a_4, a_3, a_0 + a_2, a_0 + a_1) \\ & + b_3(a_1 + a_2, a_0 + a_4, a_0 + a_2, a_4, a_1 + a_3) \\ & + b_4(a_2 + a_4, a_3 + a_2, a_0 + a_1, a_1 + a_3, a_0).\end{aligned}$$

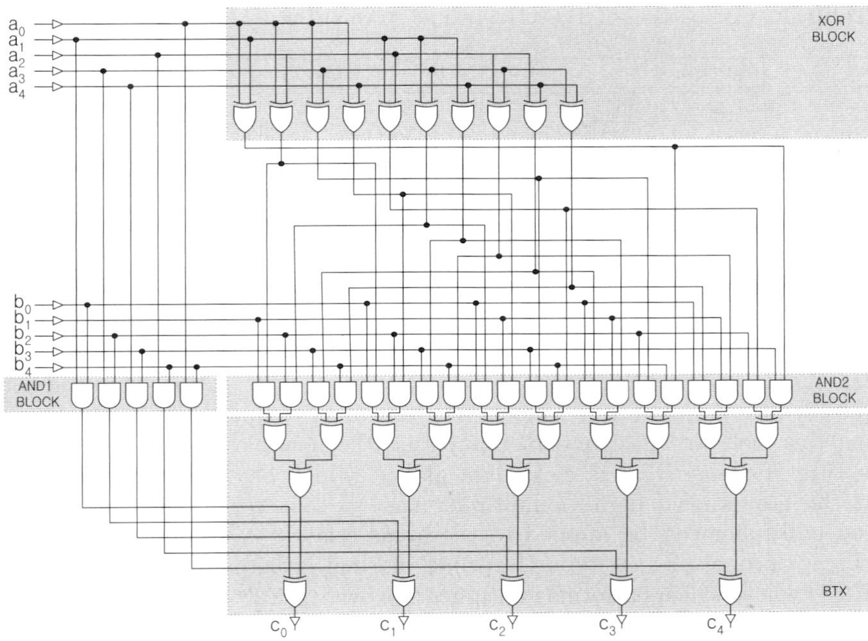

Fig. 2. The parallel multiplier for $GF(2^5)$

But our proposed multiplier calculate $\overline{C} = \overline{AB}$, thus the multiplier calculate all the terms of the form $A_i + A_j$ in the XOR Block and the terms $B_0A_1, B_1A_3, B_2A_4, B_3A_2, B_4A_0$ in the AND 1 Block respectively.

4 Complexity

In this section, we calculate the complexities of the proposed multiplier discussed in section 3.

Theorem 5. *The maximum complexity of our multiplier in section 3 is as follows.*

1. m^2 *AND gates and* $3m(m-1)/2$ *XOR gates*
2. $1T_A + (1 + \lceil \log_2 m \rceil)T_X$ *time delay, where* T_A *and* T_X *are AND delay and XOR delay respectively*

Proof. We have calculated the number of AND gate and XOR gates needed already. For b), there is 1 T_A(AND Delay) from parallel AND operations in the AND 1, AND 2 Blocks. There are 1 T_X needed by calculating $A_i + A_j, 0 \le i < j \le m-1$ and $\lceil \log_2 m \rceil T_X$ needed by component-wise XOR in the BTX, and thus the total number of time delays is $1T_A + (1 + \lceil \log_2 m \rceil)T_X$.

Table 1 compares the complexities for a number of parallel multipliers over $GF(2^m)$.

Table 1. Comparison of Type II Optimal Normal Basis Multiplier for $GF(2^m)$

Multipliers	# AND	# XOR	Time Delay
Sunar and Koc[6]	m^2	$3m(m-1)/2$	$T_A + (1 + \lceil \log_2 m \rceil)T_X$
Reyhani-Masoleh and Hasan[5]	m^2	$3m(m-1)/2$	$T_A + (1 + \lceil \log_2 m \rceil)T_X$
Elia and Leone[13]	m^2	$3m(m-1)/2$	$T_A + (1 + \lceil \log_2 m \rceil)T_X$
Proposed	m^2	$\leq 3m(m-1)/2$	$T_A + (1 + \lceil \log_2 m \rceil)T_X$

5 Conclusion

The elements with respect to type II optimal normal basis for the finite fields $GF(2^m)$ can be represented with respect to $\gamma, \gamma^2, \cdots, \gamma^{2m}$ in the extension fields $GF(2^{2m})$ in a simple form, where γ is the primitive $2m+1$-th root of unity. Using this fact, we construct, in this paper, the new parallel multiplier whose structure and algorithm is clear at a glance, which has the same complexity that the best known parallel multiplier has, so that we expect that the proposed multiplier can be applied to the areas related to cryptography. In this paper, we propose a new type II optimal normal basis parallel multiplier over $GF(2^m)$ whose which performs multiplication over $GF(2^m)$ in the extension field $GF(2^{2m})$.

References

1. Lidl, R., Niederreiter, H. (eds.): Introduction to finite fields and its applications. Cambridge Univ. Press, Cambridge (1994)
2. Menezes, A.J., Blake, I.F., Gao, X.H., Mullin, R.C., Vanstone, S.A., Yaghoobian, T.: Applications of finite fields. Kluwer Academic, Boston (1993)
3. Koc, C.K., Sunar, B.: Low-Complexity bit-parallel cannonical and normal basis multipliers for a class of finite fields. IEEE Trans. 47(3), 353–356 (1998)
4. Wu, H., Hasan, M.A.: Low Complexity bit-parallel multipliers for a class of finite fields. IEEE Trans. 47(8), 883–887 (1998)
5. Reyhani, M.A., Hasan, M.A.: A new construction of Massey-Omura parallel multiplier over $GF(2^m)$. IEEE Trans. 51(5), 512–520 (2002)
6. Sunar, B., Koc, C.K.: An efficient optimal normal basis type II multiplier. IEEE Trans. 50(1), 83–88 (2001)
7. Wang, C.C., Troung, T.K., Shao, H.M., Deutsch, L.J., Omura, J.K., Reed, I.S.: VLSI architectures for computing multiplications and inverses in $GF(2^n)$. IEEE Trans. 34(8), 709–716 (1985)
8. Kim, C.H., Oh, S., Lim, J.: A new hardware architecture for operations in $GF(2^n)$. IEEE Trans. 51(1), 90–92 (2002)
9. National Institute of Standards and Technology: Digital Sinature Standard, FIPS 186-2 (2000)
10. ANSI X 9.63, Public key cryptography for the financial sevices industry: Elliptic curve key agreement and transport protocols, draft (1998)
11. IEEE P1363, Standard specifications for public key cryptography, Draft 13 (1999)

12. Blake, I.F., Roth, R.M., Seroussi, G.: Efficient arithmetic in $GF(2^m)$ through palindromic representation, Hewlett-Packard HPL-98-134 (1998)
13. Elia, M., Leone, M.: On the Inherent Space Complexity of Fast Parallel Multipliers for $GF(2^m)$. IEEE Trans. 51(3), 346–351 (2002)
14. Gao, S., Lenstra, H.W.: Optimal normal bases, Designs, Codes and Cryptography, vol. 2, pp. 315–323 (1992)

Identity-Based Key-Insulated Signature Without Random Oracles*

Jian Weng[1,3], Shengli Liu[1,2], Kefei Chen[1], and Changshe Ma[3]

[1] Dept. of Computer Science and Engineering
Shanghai Jiao Tong University, Shanghai 200240, China
[2] Key Laboratory of CNIS
Xidian University, Xian 710071, China
[3] School of Computer
South China Normal University, Guangzhou 510631, China
{jianweng, slliu, kfchen}@sjtu.edu.cn, JuanJuansmcs@gmail.com

Abstract. Traditional identity-based signature schemes typically rely on the assumption that secret keys are kept perfectly secure. However, with more and more cryptographic primitives are deployed on insecure devices such as mobile devices, key-exposure seems inevitable. No matter how strong the identity-based signature scheme is, once the secret key is exposed, its security is entirely lost. Therefore, how to deal with this problem in identity-based signatures is a worthwhile challenge. In this paper, applying Dodis et al.'s key-insulation mechanism, we propose a new ID-based key-insulated signature scheme. What makes our scheme attractive is that it is provably secure without random oracles.

1 Introduction

The traditional public key infrastructure involves complex construction of certification authority(CA), and requires expensive communication and computation cost for certification verification. To relieve this burden, Shamir [20] introduced an innovative concept called identity-based cryptography. In an identity-based cryptosystem, user's public key is determined as his identity information (e.g. user's name, e-mail address, telephone number, etc.), while the corresponding secret key is generated by a private key generator (PKG) according to this identity information. The identity information is a natural link to a user, hence it eliminates the need for certificates as used in a traditional public key infrastructure.

Nowadays, there have been proposed many identity-based signature (IBS) schemes which rely on the assumption that secret keys are kept perfectly secure. In practice, however, it is easier for an adversary to obtain the secret key from a naive user than to break the computational assumption on which the system is based. With more and more cryptographic primitives are deployed on insecure devices such as mobile devices, the problem of key-exposure becomes an ever-greater threat. Thus how to deal with the key-exposure problem in IBS schemes is a worthwhile challenge.

* Supported by National Science Foundation of China under Grant Nos. 60303026, 60473020 and 60573030, 60673077, and Key Lab of CNIS, Xidian University.

Y. Wang, Y. Cheung, and H. Liu (Eds.): CIS 2006, LNAI 4456, pp. 470–480, 2007.

In conventional public key infrastructures, certificate revocation list (CRL) can be utilized to revoke the public key in case of key-exposure. Users can become aware of other users' revoked keys by referring to the CRL. However, straightforward implementation of CRL will not be the best solution to ID-based schemes. Remember that utilizing the CRL, public key will also need to be renewed, while the public key for ID-based scheme represents an identity and is not desired to be changed. For example, in an IBS scheme where users' identity card numbers act as public keys, renewing user's identity card number is not a practical solution.

To mitigate the damage caused by key-exposure, key-evolving protocols have been proposed. This mechanism includes forward security [1,3], intrusion-resilience [15] and key-insulation [9]. The latter was introduced by Dodis, Katz, Xu and Yung [9] in Eurocrypt'02. In this paradigm, the lifetime of secret keys is divided into discrete periods, and a physically-secure but computationally-limited device, named the base or helper, is involved. The full-fledge secret key is divided into two parts: the helper-key and the temporary secret key. The former is stored in the helper, while the later is kept by the user on a powerful but insecure device where cryptographic computations are carried out. The temporary secret key is updated in every time period, while the public key remains unchanged throughout the lifetime of the system. At the beginning of each time period, the user obtains from the helper a partial secret key for the current time period. By combining this partial secret key with the temporary secret key for the previous period, the user can derive the temporary secret key for the current time period. Exposure of the temporary secret key at a given period will not enable an adversary to derive temporary secret keys for the remaining time periods. Thus the public keys need not to be renewed, which is a favorite property for ID-based scenarios. Therefore, it is a promising mechanism to deal with the key-exposure problem in IBS scenarios.

Following the pioneering work due to Dodis et al. [9], several key-insulated encryption schemes including some ID-based key-insulated encryption ones have been proposed [4, 13, 10, 6, 14, 12]. Dodis et al. [8] for the first time applied the key-insulation mechanism to traditional signature scenarios, and proposed three key-insulated signature (KIS) schemes. Since then, several key-insulated signature schemes have been presented [11, 16]. In ISPEC'06, Zhou et al. [22] proposed an ID-based key-insulated signature (IBKIS) scheme which is secure in the random oracle model. However, as pointed out in [5], a proof in the random oracle model can only serve as a heuristic argument since it can not imply the security in the real world. In this paper, based on Water's ID-based encryption scheme [21] and Paterson-Schuldt's IBS scheme [18], we propose a new IBKIS scheme without random oracles.

2 Preliminaries

In this section, we present the model and security notion for IBKIS schemes. An introduction to bilinear pairings and related cryptographic assumption is also given.

2.1 Model of IBKIS

Definition 1. *An **IBKIS scheme** consists of the following six algorithms.*

- $\mathsf{Setup}(k, N)$*: a probabilistic setup algorithm taking as input a security parameters* k *and (possibly) the total number of time periods* N*, returns a public parameter* $param$ *and a master key* msk*.*
- $\mathsf{Extract}(msk, param, ID)$*: a probabilistic key extraction algorithm taking as input the master key* msk*, the public parameter* $param$ *and a user's identity* $ID \in \{0,1\}^*$*, returns this user's initial signing-key* $TSK_{ID.0}$ *and a helper-key* HK_{ID}*.*[1]
- $\mathsf{UpdH}(t, ID, HK_{ID})$*: a (possibly) probabilistic helper-key update algorithm taking as input a time period index* t*, a user's identity* ID *and helper-key* HK_{ID}*, returns a partial secret key* $PSK_{ID.t}$ *for time period* t*.*
- $\mathsf{UpdT}(ID, PSK_{ID.t_1}, TSK_{ID.t_2})$*: a deterministic temporary signing-key update algorithm taking as input a user's identity* ID*, a temporary signing-key* $TSK_{ID.t_2}$ *and a partial secret key* $PSK_{ID.t_1}$*, returns the temporary signing-key* $TSK_{ID.t_1}$ *for time period* t_1*.*
- $\mathsf{Sign}(t, m, TSK_{ID.t})$*: a probabilistic signing algorithm taking as input a time period index* t*, a message* m *and the temporary signing-key* $TSK_{ID.t}$*, returns a pair* (t, σ) *composed of the time period index* t *and a signature* σ*.*
- $\mathsf{Verify}((t, \sigma), m, ID)$*: a deterministic verification algorithm taking as input a message* m*, a candidate signature* (t, σ) *and an identity* ID*, returns 1 if* (t, σ) *is a valid signature on message* m *for identity* ID*, and 0 otherwise.*

Consistency requires that $\forall t \in \{1, \cdots, N\}$, $\forall m \in \mathcal{M}$, $\forall ID \in \{0,1\}^*$, the equality $\mathsf{Verify}((t, \sigma), m, ID) = 1$ always holds, where $(t, \sigma) = \mathsf{Sign}(t, m, TSK_{ID.t})$ and $\mathcal{M}$ denotes the message space.

2.2 Security Notion for IBKIS

In this subsection, we formalize the security notion for IBKIS schemes. As general key-insulated signatures, an adaptive temporary signing-key attack should be considered. Moreover, as standard ID-based signature schemes, we also take the key-extraction attack into account.

Definition 2. *An IBKIS scheme* Π *is called* (t, ϵ)*-**EUF-KI-CMA** (existentially unforgeable and key-insulated under chosen-message attacks) if for any adversary* $\mathcal{F}$ *with running time bounded by* t *has advantage less than* ϵ *in the following game:*

1) The challenger $\mathcal{C}$ *runs the setup algorithm* $\mathsf{Setup}(k, N)$ *to generate* $param$ *and* msk*. He gives* $param$ *to* $\mathcal{F}$ *and keeps* msk *himself.*
2) $\mathcal{F}$ *issues a series of the following queries adaptively:*

[1] Throughout this paper, we let HK_{ID} denote user ID's helper key, $TSK_{ID.t}$ denote user ID's temporary secret key for time period t, and $PSK_{ID,t}$ denote user ID's partial secret key for time period t.

- *Key-extraction queries: When $\mathcal{F}$ issues a query on identity ID, challenger $\mathcal{C}$ first runs algorithm* $\mathsf{Extract}(msk, param, ID)$ *and obtains an initial signing-key $TSK_{ID.0}$. Then $\mathcal{C}$ sends $TSK_{ID.0}$ to $\mathcal{F}$.*
- *Temporary signing-key queries: When $\mathcal{F}$ issues a query on $\langle ID, t\rangle$. $\mathcal{C}$ runs algorithm* $\mathsf{UpdT}(ID, PSK_{ID.t}, TSK_{ID.t'})$ *and obtains the temporary signing-key $TSK_{ID.t}$, which is forwarded to $\mathcal{F}$.*
- *Signing queries: When $\mathcal{F}$ issues a query on $\langle t, ID, m\rangle$, $\mathcal{C}$ runs algorithm* $\mathsf{Sign}(t, m, TSK_{ID.t})$ *and obtains a signature (t, σ), which is returned to $\mathcal{F}$.*

3) *Eventually, $\mathcal{F}$ outputs a time period index t^*, an identity ID^*, a message m^* and a signature σ^*. We say that $\mathcal{F}$ wins the game if the following conditions are satisfied: (1)* $\mathsf{Verify}((t^*, \sigma^*), m^*, ID^*) = 1$*; (2) $\langle ID^*, t^*\rangle$ was never appeared in the temporary signing queries; (3) $\langle t^*, ID^*, m^*\rangle$ was never appeared in the signing queries.*

We define $\mathcal{F}$'s ***advantage*** *as the probability of winning this game.*

2.3 Bilinear Pairings and Related Complexity Assumption

Let $\mathbb{G}_1$ and $\mathbb{G}_2$ be two cyclic multiplicative groups with the same prime order q. A bilinear pairing is a map $\hat{e} : \mathbb{G}_1 \times \mathbb{G}_1 \rightarrow \mathbb{G}_2$ with the following properties:

- Bilinearity: $\forall u, v \in \mathbb{G}_1, \forall a, b \in \mathbb{Z}_q^*$, we have $\hat{e}(u^a, v^b) = \hat{e}(u, v)^{ab}$.
- Non-degeneracy: There exist $u, v \in \mathbb{G}_1$ such that $\hat{e}(u, v) \neq 1$.
- Computability: There exists an efficient algorithm to compute $\hat{e}(u, v)$ for $\forall u, v \in \mathbb{G}_1$.

As shown in [2], such non-degenerate admissible maps over cyclic groups can be obtained from the Weil or Tate pairing over supersingular elliptic curves or abelian varieties.

We proceed to recall the definition of computational Diffie-Hellman (CDH) problem on which the provable security of our scheme is based.

Definition 3. *Let g be a random generator of group $\mathbb{G}_1$. The* ***CDH problem*** *in group $\mathbb{G}_1$ is, given $(g, g^a, g^b) \in \mathbb{G}_1^3$ for some unknown $a, b \stackrel{R}{\leftarrow} \mathbb{Z}_q^*$, to compute g^{ab}. An adversary $\mathcal{A}$ has advantage ϵ in solving the CDH problem in $\mathbb{G}_1$ if*

$$Pr\left[g \stackrel{R}{\leftarrow} \mathbb{G}_1, a, b \stackrel{R}{\leftarrow} \mathbb{Z}_q^* : \mathcal{A}(g, g^a, g^b) = g^{ab}\right] \geq \epsilon.$$

*We say that (t, ϵ)-**CDH assumption** holds in $\mathbb{G}_1$ if no t-time adversary $\mathcal{A}$ has advantage as least ϵ in solving the CDH problem in $\mathbb{G}_1$.*

3 Our Proposed Scheme

Based on Paterson-Schuldt's IBS scheme [18], which is based on Water's ID-based encryption scheme [21], we propose a new IBKIS scheme in this section.

3.1 Construction

Let $\mathbb{G}_1$ and $\mathbb{G}_2$ be two cyclic multiplicative groups with prime order q of size k, g be a random generator of $\mathbb{G}_1$, and $\hat{e}$ be a bilinear map such that $\hat{e} : \mathbb{G}_1 \times \mathbb{G}_1 \to \mathbb{G}_2$. Let H be a collision-resistant hash function such that $H : \{0,1\}^* \to \{0,1\}^n$. The proposed IBKIS scheme consists of the following six algorithms:

Setup(k)

1) Pick $\alpha \xleftarrow{R} \mathbb{Z}_q^*, g_2 \xleftarrow{R} \mathbb{G}_1$ and set $g_1 = g^\alpha$. Furthermore, pick $u' \xleftarrow{R} \mathbb{G}_1$ and a vector $\boldsymbol{U} = (u_i)$ of length n, where $u_i \xleftarrow{R} \mathbb{G}_1$ for $i = 1, \cdots, n$.
2) Define a function f such that $f(\mathcal{S}) = u' \prod_{i \in \mathcal{S}} u_i$, for $\forall \mathcal{S} \subseteq \{1, \cdots, n\}$.
3) Return the master key $msk = g_2^\alpha$ and the public parameters

$$param = (q, g, g_1, g_2, u', \boldsymbol{U}, f, H).$$

Extract$(msk, param, ID)$

1) Choose $\beta, r \xleftarrow{R} \mathbb{Z}_q^*$. Compute $HK_{ID} = g_2^{\alpha - \beta}$, $R_{ID} = g^r$, $U_{ID} = H(ID)$.
2) Let $\mathcal{U}_{ID} \subseteq \{1, \cdots, n\}$ be the set of indices i such that $U_{ID}[i] = 1$.[2] Compute $W_{ID} = g_2^\beta f(\mathcal{U}_{ID})^r$.
3) Choose $S_{ID.0}, T_{ID.0} \xleftarrow{R} \mathbb{G}_1$. Define the initial signing-key as

$$TSK_{ID.0} = (W_{ID}, R_{ID}, (S_{ID.0}, T_{ID.0})) \,. \tag{1}$$

Return $TSK_{ID.0}$ and the helper-key HK_{ID}.

UpdH(t, ID, HK_{ID})

1) Choose $r_t \xleftarrow{R} \mathbb{Z}_q^*$ and compute $\widehat{T}_{ID.t} = g^{r_t}$.
2) Compute $U'_{ID.t} = H(ID, t)$. Let $\mathcal{U}'_{ID.t} \subseteq \{1, \cdots, n\}$ be the set of indices i such that $U'_{ID.t}[i] = 1$. Compute $\widehat{S}_{ID.t} = HK_{ID} \cdot f(\mathcal{U}'_{ID.t})^{r_t}$.
3) Define and return the partial secret key as $PSK_{ID.t} = \left(\widehat{S}_{ID.t}, \widehat{T}_{ID.t}\right)$.

UpdT$(ID, PSK_{ID.t_1}, TSK_{ID.t_2})$

1) Parse $TSK_{ID.t_2}$ as $(W_{ID}, R_{ID}, (S_{ID.t_2}, T_{ID.t_2}))$ and $PSK_{ID.t_1}$ as $(\widehat{S}_{ID.t_1}, \widehat{T}_{ID.t_1})$.
2) Set $S_{ID.t_1} = \widehat{S}_{ID.t_1}, T_{ID.t_1} = \widehat{T}_{ID.t_1}$, and return the temporary signing-key $TSK_{ID.t_1} = (W_{ID}, R_{ID}, (S_{ID.t_1}, T_{ID.t_1}))$.

Note that at time period $t (t \geq 1)$, user ID's temporary signing-key $TSK_{ID.t}$ is always set to

$$(g_2^\beta \cdot f(\mathcal{U}_{ID})^r, g^r, (g_2^{\alpha-\beta} \cdot f(\mathcal{U}'_{ID.t})^{r_t}, g^{r_t})). \tag{2}$$

Also note that the following equality holds

$$W_{ID} \cdot S_{ID.t} = g_2^\alpha \cdot f(\mathcal{U}_{ID})^r \cdot f(\mathcal{U}'_{ID.t})^{r_t}.$$

[2] $U_{ID}[i]$ means the i-th bit of U_{ID} in a bit-string representation.

Sign$(t, m, TSK_{ID.t})$

1) Parse $TSK_{ID.t}$ as $(W_{ID}, R_{ID}, (S_{ID.t}, T_{ID.t}))$.
2) Compute $M = H(m)$. Let $\mathcal{M} \subseteq \{1, \cdots, n\}$ be the set of indices j such that $M[j] = 1$.
3) Choose $r_m \stackrel{R}{\leftarrow} \mathbb{Z}_q^*$, compute $U = g^{r_m}$ and $V = W_{ID} \cdot S_{ID.t} \cdot f(\mathcal{M})^{r_m}$. The signature is $\sigma = (U, V, R_{ID}, T_{ID.t})$. Return (t, σ).

Note that V is always set to

$$V = g_2^{\alpha} \cdot f(\mathcal{U}_{ID})^{r} \cdot f(\mathcal{U}'_{ID.t})^{r_t} \cdot f(\mathcal{M})^{r_m}. \tag{3}$$

Verify$(ID, m, (t, \sigma))$

1) Parse σ as $(U, V, R_{ID}, T_{ID.t})$.
2) Compute $U_{ID} = H(ID)$, $U'_{ID.t} = H(ID, t)$ and $M = H(m)$. Let $\mathcal{U}_{ID}, \mathcal{U}'_{ID.t}$ and $\mathcal{M}$ denote the sets as above. Return 1 if the following equality holds, and 0 otherwise:

$$\hat{e}(g, V) = \hat{e}(g_1, g_2)\hat{e}(f(\mathcal{U}_{ID}), R_{ID})\hat{e}(f(\mathcal{U}'_{ID.t}), T_{ID.t})\hat{e}(f(\mathcal{M}), U).$$

3.2 Correctness

The consistency can be explained as follows:

$$\begin{aligned}\hat{e}(g, V) &= \hat{e}(g, g_2^{\alpha} f(\mathcal{U}_{ID})^{r} f(\mathcal{U}'_{ID.t})^{r_t} f(\mathcal{M})^{r_m}) \\ &= \hat{e}(g, g_2^{\alpha})\hat{e}(g, f(\mathcal{U}_{ID})^{r})\hat{e}(g, f(\mathcal{U}'_{ID.t})^{r_t})\hat{e}(g, f(\mathcal{M})^{r_m}) \\ &= \hat{e}(g_1, g_2)\hat{e}(f(\mathcal{U}_{ID}), R_{ID})\hat{e}(f(\mathcal{U}'_{ID.t}), T_{ID.t})\hat{e}(f(\mathcal{M}), U)\end{aligned}$$

4 Security Analysis

Theorem 1. *The proposed scheme is EUF-KI-CMA in the standard model, assuming that (1) the hash function H is collision-resistant; (2) the CDH assumption holds in group $\mathbb{G}_1$.*

Proof. Without loss of generality, suppose the hash function H is collision-resistant, then we will show that given a $(\mathcal{T}, \epsilon)$-adversary $\mathcal{F}$ against our proposed scheme, there exists a $(\mathcal{T}', \epsilon')$-adversary $\mathcal{B}$ that breaks the CDH assumption in $\mathbb{G}_1$ with

$$\mathcal{T}' \leq \mathcal{T} + \mathcal{O}\left((q_e + q_t + q_s)n\mathcal{T}_m + (q_e + q_t + q_s)\mathcal{T}_e\right),$$

$$\epsilon' \geq \frac{27\epsilon}{256(q_t + q_S)^3(n+1)^3},$$

where $\mathcal{T}_m$ and $\mathcal{T}_e$ are the running time of a multiplication and an exponentiation in $\mathbb{G}_1$ respectively. q_e, q_t and q_s denote the number of key-extraction, temporary signing-key and signing queries respectively.

Suppose $\mathcal{B}$ is given a tuple $(g, g^a, g^b) \in \mathbb{G}_1^3$ for some unknown $a, b \xleftarrow{R} \mathbb{Z}_q^*$. The task of $\mathcal{B}$ is to compute g^{ab}. $\mathcal{B}$ interacts with $\mathcal{F}$ in the following way:

$\mathcal{B}$ constructs the public parameter for $\mathcal{F}$ as follows:

1) Set $l = \frac{4(q_t+q_s)}{3}$ and randomly choose an integer v with $0 \leq v \leq n$. We assume that $3|(q_t + q_s)$, otherwise, we can add one or two queries artificially. We also assume that $l(n+1) < q$.
2) Choose $x' \xleftarrow{R} \mathbb{Z}_l, y' \xleftarrow{R} \mathbb{Z}_q$. The following two n-length vectors are also chosen:

$$\boldsymbol{X} = (x_i) \text{ with } x_i \xleftarrow{R} \mathbb{Z}_l \text{ for } i = 1, \cdots, n.$$
$$\boldsymbol{Y} = (y_i) \text{ with } y_i \xleftarrow{R} \mathbb{Z}_q \text{ for } i = 1, \cdots, n.$$

3) Define a set of public parameters for $\mathcal{F}$ as below:

$$g_1 = g^a, g_2 = g^b, u' = g_2^{-lv+x'} g^{y'},$$
$$\boldsymbol{U} = (x_i) \text{ with } u_i = g_2^{x_i} g^{y_i} \text{ for } i = 1, \cdots, n.$$

To make the notation easier to follow, define functions F and J such that for any set $\mathcal{S} \subseteq \{1, \cdots, n\}$,

$$F(\mathcal{S}) = -lv + x' + \sum_{i \in \mathcal{S}} x_i, \qquad J(\mathcal{S}) = y' + \sum_{i \in \mathcal{S}} y_i.$$

Observe that $f(\mathcal{S}) = g_2^{F(\mathcal{S})} g^{J(\mathcal{S})}$ holds. Also note that from the perspective of adversary $\mathcal{F}$, the distribution of the public parameter is identical to the real construction.

$\mathcal{B}$ answers the key-extraction queries, temporary signing-key queries and signing queries for $\mathcal{F}$ as follows:

- *Key-extraction queries*: $\mathcal{B}$ maintains a list D^{list} which is initially empty. When $\mathcal{F}$ asks a key-extraction query on identity ID, $\mathcal{B}$ acts as follows:
  1) Check whether D^{list} contains a tuple (ID, β). If not, choose $\beta \xleftarrow{R} \mathbb{Z}_q^*$ and add (ID, β) on D^{list}.
  2) Compute $U_{ID} = H(ID)$. Let $\mathcal{U}_{ID}$ denotes the set as above. Choose $r \xleftarrow{R} \mathbb{Z}_q^*$ and $S_{ID.0}, T_{ID.0} \xleftarrow{R} \mathbb{G}_1$. Define and return the initial signing-key as
  $$TSK_{ID.0} = \left(g_2^{\beta} f(\mathcal{U}_{ID})^r, g^r, (S_{ID.0}, T_{ID.0})\right).$$
- *Temporary signing-key queries*: When a temporary signing-key query $\langle ID, t\rangle$ is coming, $\mathcal{B}$ acts as follows:
  1) Check whether D^{list} contains a tuple (ID, β). If not, choose $\beta \xleftarrow{R} \mathbb{Z}_q^*$ and add (ID, β) on D^{list}.
  2) Compute $U_{ID} = H(ID)$ and $U'_{ID.t} = H(ID, t)$. Let $\mathcal{U}_{ID}$ and $\mathcal{U}'_{ID.t}$ denote the sets as above. If $F(\mathcal{U}'_{ID.t}) \equiv 0 \mod q$ (denote this event by

E1), $\mathcal{B}$ outputs "failure" and aborts. Otherwise, $\mathcal{B}$ chooses $r, r_t \xleftarrow{R} \mathbb{Z}_q^*$, defines and returns the temporary signing-key $TSK_{ID.t}$ as

$$\left(g_2^{\beta} f(\mathcal{U}_{ID})^r, g^r, \left(g_1^{\frac{-J(\mathcal{U}'_{ID.t})}{F(\mathcal{U}'_{ID.t})}} f(\mathcal{U}'_{ID.t})^{r_t} g_2^{-\beta}, g_1^{\frac{-1}{F(\mathcal{U}'_{ID.t})}} g^{r_t}\right)\right).$$

Note that if let $\widehat{r_t} = r_t - \frac{a}{F(\mathcal{U}'_{ID.t})}$, then it can see that $TSK_{ID.t}$ has the correct form as Eq. (2).

– *Signing queries*: When $\mathcal{F}$ issues a signing query on $\langle t, ID, m\rangle$, $\mathcal{B}$ acts as follows:
  1) Compute $U_{ID} = H(ID), U'_{ID.t} = H(ID, t)$ and $M = H(m)$.
  2) Let $\mathcal{U}_{ID}, \mathcal{U}'_{ID.t}$ and $\mathcal{M}$ denote the sets as above. If $F(\mathcal{U}'_{ID.t}) \equiv F(\mathcal{M}) \equiv 0 \mod q$ holds (denote this event by **E2**), $\mathcal{B}$ outputs "failure" and aborts.
  3) Otherwise, $\mathcal{B}$ chooses $r, r_t, r_m \xleftarrow{R} \mathbb{Z}_q^*$, constructs the signature according to the following cases:
     • If $F(\mathcal{U}'_{ID.t}) \not\equiv 0 \mod q$, then $\mathcal{B}$ set $U = g^{r_m}$, $R_{ID} = g^r, T_{ID.t} = g_1^{\frac{-1}{F(\mathcal{U}'_{ID.t})}} g^{r_t}$ and $V = g_1^{\frac{-J(\mathcal{U}'_{ID.t})}{F(\mathcal{U}'_{ID.t})}} f(\mathcal{U}'_{ID.t})^{r_t} f(\mathcal{U}_{ID})^r f(\mathcal{M})^{r_m}$.
     • Otherwise, $\mathcal{B}$ sets $U = g_1^{\frac{-1}{F(\mathcal{M})}} g^{r_m}$, $R_{ID} = g^r, T_{ID.t} = g^{r_t}$ and $V = g_1^{\frac{-J(\mathcal{M})}{F(\mathcal{M})}} f(\mathcal{M})^{r_m} f(\mathcal{U}'_{ID.t})^{r_t} f(\mathcal{U}_{ID})^r$.
  4) Return $(t, (U, V, R_{ID}, T_{ID.t}))$ to $\mathcal{F}$. Observe that it is indeed a valid signature.

Eventually, $\mathcal{F}$ outputs a signature $\sigma^* = (t^*, (U^*, V^*, R_{ID^*}, T_{ID^*.t^*}))$ with the constraint described in Definition 2, together with the corresponding time period index t^*, the identity ID^* and the message m^*. $\mathcal{B}$ computes $U_{ID^*} = H(ID^*)$, $U'_{ID^*.t^*} = H(ID^*, t^*)$ and $M^* = H(m^*)$. Let $\mathcal{U}_{ID^*} \subseteq \{1, \cdots, n\}$ be the set of indices i such that $U_{ID^*}[i] = 1$, $\mathcal{U}'_{ID^*.t^*} \subseteq \{1, \cdots, n\}$ be the set of indices i such that $U'_{ID^*.t^*}[i] = 1$ and $\mathcal{M}^* \subseteq \{1, \cdots, n\}$ be the set of indices j such that $M^*[j] = 1$. If $F(\mathcal{U}_{ID^*}) \equiv F(\mathcal{U}'_{ID^*.t^*}) \equiv F(\mathcal{U}_{M^*}) \equiv 0 \mod p$ does not hold (denote this event by **E3**), $\mathcal{B}$ outputs "failure" and abort. Otherwise, $\mathcal{B}$ can successfully compute g^{ab} as follows:

$$\frac{V^*}{R_{ID^*}^{J(\mathcal{U}_{ID^*})} T_{ID^*.t^*}^{J(\mathcal{U}'_{ID^*.t^*})} U^{*J(\mathcal{M}^*)}} = \frac{g_2^a f(\mathcal{U}_{ID^*})^{r^*} f(\mathcal{U}'_{ID^*.t^*})^{r_t^*} f(\mathcal{M}^*)^{r_m^*}}{g^{J(\mathcal{U}_{ID^*})r^*} g^{J(\mathcal{U}'_{ID^*.t^*})r_t^*} g^{J(\mathcal{M}^*)r_m^*}} = g_2^a = g^{ab}.$$

This completes the description of the simulation. It remains to analyze the probability of $\mathcal{B}$'s not aborting. To make the analysis of the simulation easier, we modify event **E1** to be event **E1′**: $F(\mathcal{U}'_{ID.t}) \equiv 0 \mod l$, and event **E2** to be **E2′** : $F(\mathcal{U}'_{ID.t}) \equiv 0 \mod l$. Note that the assumption $l(n+1) < q$ implies $0 \leq lv < q$ and $0 \leq x' + \sum_{i \in \mathcal{U}'_{ID.t}} x_i < q$. Hence it is easy to see that $F(\mathcal{U}'_{ID.t}) \not\equiv 0 \mod l$ is a sufficient condition for $F(\mathcal{U}'_{ID.t}) \not\equiv 0 \mod q$, therefore event $\neg$**E1′** implies $\neg$**E1**. Similarly, we know that event $\neg$**E2′** implies $\neg$**E2**. We will count a lower bound on the probability of $\mathcal{B}$'s not aborting as $\Pr[\neg\mathbf{E1'} \wedge \neg\mathbf{E2'} \wedge \neg\mathbf{E3}]$. We claim that

Claim 1. *Pr*$[\neg \boldsymbol{E1}' \wedge \neg \boldsymbol{E2}' \wedge \neg \boldsymbol{E3}] \geq \frac{27}{256(q_t+q_s)^3(n+1)^3}$.

Proof. The proof borrows the trick in [18]. Let $\mathcal{U}_1, \cdots, \mathcal{U}_{q_I}$ be all the deferent $\mathcal{U}_{ID.t}$'s appearing in the temporary signing-key queries and the signing queries. Clearly, we will have $q_I \leq q_t + q_s$. Define events A_i, A^*, B^* and C^* as

$$\begin{aligned} A_i &: F(\mathcal{U}_i) \not\equiv 0 \mod l, \\ A^* &: F(\mathcal{U}_{ID^*}) \equiv 0 \mod q, \\ B^* &: F(\mathcal{U}'_{ID^*.t^*}) \equiv 0 \mod q, \\ C^* &: F(\mathcal{M}^*) \equiv 0 \mod q. \end{aligned}$$

Then we have $\Pr[\neg\mathbf{E1}' \wedge \neg\mathbf{E2}' \wedge \neg\mathbf{E3}] \geq \Pr[C^* \wedge B^* \wedge A^* \bigwedge_{i=1}^{q_I} A_i]$.

As seen above, the assumption $l(n+1) < q$ leads to the implication $F(\mathcal{U}_{ID^*}) \equiv 0 \mod q \Rightarrow F(\mathcal{U}_{ID^*}) \equiv 0 \mod l$. Furthermore, this assumption gives that if $F(\mathcal{U}_{ID^*}) \equiv 0 \mod l$, there will be a unique choice of v with $0 \leq v \leq n$ such that $F(\mathcal{U}_{ID^*}) \equiv 0 \mod q$. Since v, x' and $\boldsymbol{X}$ are randomly chosen, we have

$$\begin{aligned} \Pr[A^*] &= \Pr[F(\mathcal{U}_{ID^*}) \equiv 0 \mod q \wedge F(\mathcal{U}_{ID^*}) \equiv 0 \mod l] \\ &= \Pr[F(\mathcal{U}_{ID^*}) \equiv 0 \mod l] \cdot \Pr[F(\mathcal{U}_{ID^*}) \equiv 0 \mod q \mid F(\mathcal{U}_{ID^*}) \equiv 0 \mod l] \\ &= \frac{1}{l}\frac{1}{n+1}. \end{aligned}$$

Similarly, we also have $\Pr[B^*] = \frac{1}{l}\frac{1}{n+1}$ and $\Pr[C^*] = \frac{1}{l}\frac{1}{n+1}$. Since H is a collision-resistant hash function, we know that $\mathcal{U}_{ID^*}$ is not equal to $\mathcal{U}'_{ID^*.t^*}$. Then the sums appearing in $F(\mathcal{U}_{ID^*})$ and $F(\mathcal{U}'_{ID^*.t^*})$ will differ in at least one randomly chosen value, therefore events A^* and B^* will be independent. If $\mathcal{M}^*$ is qual to neither $\mathcal{U}_{ID^*}$ nor $\mathcal{U}'_{ID^*.t^*}$, we can also have that events A^*, B^* and C^* are independent each other. Thus we have $\Pr[A^* \wedge B^* \wedge C^*] \geq \frac{1}{l^3(n+1)^3}$. Similarly, we also know that the events A_i and $A^* \wedge B^* \wedge C^*$ are independent for any i, which implies $\Pr[\neg A_i \mid (A^* \wedge B^* \wedge C^*)] = \frac{1}{l}$. Thus we have

$$\begin{aligned} \Pr[\neg\mathbf{E1}' \wedge \neg\mathbf{E2}' \wedge \neg\mathbf{E3}] &\geq \Pr[C^* \wedge B^* \wedge A^* \bigwedge_{i=1}^{q_I} A_i] \\ &= \Pr[C^* \wedge B^* \wedge A^*]\Pr[\bigwedge_{i=1}^{q_I} A_i \mid (C^* \wedge B^* \wedge A^*)] \\ &\geq \frac{1}{l^3(n+1)^3}\Big(1 - \Pr[\bigvee_{i=1}^{q_I} \neg A_i \mid (C^* \wedge B^* \wedge A^*)]\Big) \\ &\geq \frac{1}{l^3(n+1)^3}\Big(1 - \bigvee_{i=1}^{q_I} \Pr[\neg A_i \mid (C^* \wedge B^* \wedge A^*)]\Big) \\ &= \frac{1}{l^3(n+1)^3}(1 - \frac{q_I}{l}) \\ &\geq \frac{1}{l^3(n+1)^3}(1 - \frac{q_t+q_s}{l}). \end{aligned}$$

The right side of the last inequality is maximized at $l_{opt} = \frac{4(q_t+q_s)}{3}$. Using l_{opt}, the probability $\Pr[\neg\mathbf{E1}' \wedge \neg\mathbf{E2}' \wedge \neg\mathbf{E3}']$ is at least $\frac{27}{256(q_t+q_s)^3(n+1)^3}$. □

Thus we know that the probability of $\mathcal{B}$ not aborting is bounded by

$$\begin{aligned}\Pr[\neg\text{abort}] &= \Pr[\neg\mathbf{E1} \wedge \neg\mathbf{E2} \wedge \neg\mathbf{E3}] \\ &\geq \Pr[\neg\mathbf{E1}' \wedge \neg\mathbf{E2}' \wedge \neg\mathbf{E3}] \geq \frac{27}{256(q_t+q_s)^3(n+1)^3}.\end{aligned}$$

From the description of $\mathcal{B}$, we know that if neither event **E1** nor **E2** happens, then the simulation provided for $\mathcal{F}$ are identical to the real environment. Furthermore, if σ^* is a valid signature and event **E3** does not happens, $\mathcal{B}$ can successfully compute g^{ab}. Therefore, $\mathcal{B}$'s advantage against CDH assumption in $\mathbb{G}_1$ is at least $\frac{27\epsilon}{256(q_t+q_s)^3(n+1)^3}$.

The time complexity of algorithm $\mathcal{B}$ is dominated by the exponentiations and multiplications performed in the key-extraction queries, temporary signing-key queries and signing queries. Since there are $\mathcal{O}(n)$ multiplications and $\mathcal{O}(1)$ exponentiations in each stage, the time complexity of $\mathcal{B}$ is bounded by

$$T' \leq \mathcal{T} + \mathcal{O}\left((q_e+q_t+q_s)n\mathcal{T}_m + (q_e+q_t+q_s)\mathcal{T}_e\right).$$

This concludes the proof. □

5 Conclusion

In this paper, we focus on the key-exposure problem in ID-based signature scenarios. Applying the key-insulation mechanism, we propose a new ID-based key-insulated signature scheme, and successfully minimize the damage of key-exposure in IBS scenarios. A desirable advantage of our scheme is that it is provably secure in the standard model.

References

1. Anderson, R.: Two Remarks on Public-Key Cryptology. Invited lecture. In: Proceedings of CCCS'97. Available, at `http://www.cl.cam.ac.uk/users/rja14/`
2. Boneh, D., Franklin, M.: Identity Based Encryption From the Weil Pairing. In: Kilian, J. (ed.) Advances in Cryptology - CRYPTO 2001. LNCS, vol. 2139, pp. 213–229. Springer, Heidelberg (2001)
3. Bellare, M., Miner, S.: A Forward-Secure Digital Signature Scheme. In: Wiener, M.J. (ed.) Advances in Cryptology - CRYPTO '99. LNCS, vol. 1666, pp. 431–448. Springer, Heidelberg (1999)
4. Bellare, M., Palacio A.: Protecting Against Key Exposure: Strongly Key-Insulated Encryption With Optimal Threshold. Available at `http://eprint.iacr.org/2002/064`
5. Canetti, R., Goldreich, O., Halevi, S.: The Random Oracle Methodology, Revisited. Journal of the ACM 51, 557–594 (2004)

6. Cheon, J. H., Hopper, N., Kim, Y., Osipkov, I.: Authenticated Key-Insulated Public Key Encryption and Timed-Release Cryptography. Available at http://eprint.iacr.org/2004/231
7. Desmedt, Y., Frankel, Y.: Threshold Cryptosystems. In: Brassard, G. (ed.) Advances in Cryptology - CRYPTO '89. LNCS, vol. 435, pp. 307–315. Springer, Heidelberg (1990)
8. Dodis, Y., Katz, J., Xu, S., Yung, M.: Strong Key-Insulated Signature Schemes. In: Desmedt, Y.G. (ed.) Public Key Cryptography - PKC 2003. LNCS, vol. 2567, pp. 130–144. Springer, Heidelberg (2002)
9. Dodis, Y., Katz, J., Xu, S., Yung, M.: Key-Insulated Public-Key Cryptosystems. In: Knudsen, L.R. (ed.) Advances in Cryptology - EUROCRYPT 2002. LNCS, vol. 2332, pp. 65–82. Springer, Heidelberg (2002)
10. Dodis, Y., Yung, M.: Exposure-Resilience for Rree: the Hierarchical ID-Based Encryption Case. In: Proceedings of IEEE SISW'2002, pp. 45–52 (2002)
11. González-Deleito, N., Markowitch, O., Dall'Olio, E.: A New Key-Insulated Signature Scheme. In: Lopez, J., Qing, S., Okamoto, E. (eds.) Information and Communications Security. LNCS, vol. 3269, pp. 465–479. Springer, Heidelberg (2004)
12. Hanaoka, G., Hanaoka, Y., Imai, H.: Parallel Key-Insulated Public Key Encryption. In: Yung, M., Dodis, Y., Kiayias, A., Malkin, T.G. (eds.) Public Key Cryptography - PKC 2006. LNCS, vol. 3958, pp. 105–122. Springer, Heidelberg (2006)
13. Hanaoka, Y., Hanaoka, G., Shikata, J., Imai, H.: Unconditionally Secure Key Insulated Cryptosystems: Models, Bounds and Constructions. In: Deng, R.H., Qing, S., Bao, F., Zhou, J. (eds.) Information and Communications Security. LNCS, vol. 2513, pp. 85–96. Springer, Heidelberg (2002)
14. Hanaoka, Y., Hanaoka, G., Shikata, J., Imai, H.: Identity-Based Hierarchical Strongly Key-Insulated Encryption and Its Application. In: Roy, B. (ed.) Advances in Cryptology - ASIACRYPT 2005. LNCS, vol. 3788, pp. 495–514. Springer, Heidelberg (2005)
15. Itkis, G., Reyzin, L.: SiBIR: Signer-Base Intrusion-Resilient Signatures. In: Yung, M. (ed.) Advances in Cryptology - CRYPTO 2002. LNCS, vol. 2442, pp. 499–514. Springer, Heidelberg (2002)
16. Liu, J. K., Wong, D. S.: Solutions to Key Exposure Problem in Ring Signature. Available at http://eprint.iacr.org/2005/427
17. Ostrovsky, R., Yung, M.: How to Withstand Mobile Virus Attacks. In: Proceedings of PODC'91, ACM, pp. 51–59 (1991)
18. Paterson, K., Schuldt, J.: Efficient Identity-Based Signatures Secure in the Standard Model. In: Batten, L.M., Safavi-Naini, R. (eds.) Information Security and Privacy. LNCS, vol. 4058, pp. 207–222. Springer, Heidelberg (2006)
19. Shamir, A.: How to Share a Secret. Communications of the ACM 22, 612–613 (1979)
20. Shamir, A.: Identity-Based Cryptosystems and Signature Schemes. In: Blakely, G.R., Chaum, D. (eds.) Advances in Cryptology. LNCS, vol. 196, pp. 47–53. Springer, Heidelberg (1985)
21. Waters, B.: Efficient Identity-Based Encryption Without Random Oracles. In: Cramer, R.J.F. (ed.) Advances in Cryptology – EUROCRYPT 2005. LNCS, vol. 3494, pp. 114–127. Springer, Heidelberg (2005)
22. Zhou, Y., Cao, Z., Chai, Z.: Identity Based Key Insulated Signature. In: Chen, K., Deng, R., Lai, X., Zhou, J. (eds.) Information Security Practice and Experience. LNCS, vol. 3903, pp. 226–234. Springer, Heidelberg (2006)

Research on a Novel Hashing Stream Cipher

Yong Zhang[1,2], Xia-mu Niu[1,3], Jun-cao Li[1], and Chun-ming Li[2]

[1] Harbin Institute of Technology Shenzhen Graduate School, Shenzhen, Guangdong 518055 China
[2] Shenzhen Innovation International, Shenzhen, Guangdong 518057. China
[3] School of Computer Science and Technology at Harbin Institute of Technology, Harbin, Heilongjiang 150001. China
zhangyong076@gmail.com, xiamu.niu@hit.edu.cn, lijuncao1982@yahoo.com.cn, cmlee@mail.china.com

Abstract. A stream cipher namely the HSC (Hashing Stream Cipher) which uses a regular one-way hash function to generate pseudorandom keystream iteratively is proposed. Since the timestamp is used in the keystream generator, the algorithm achieves the robustness against the adaptive-chosen-plaintext attack. The one-way hash function is the core of the algorithm, so the security analysis of the algorithm is shifted to that of the hash function. If the core one-way hash function is chosen properly, it can be asserted that there would be no period in the HSC keystream. Firstly the algorithm was introduced detailedly. Then its applying security and efficiency respectively discussed deeply. The experimental result shows that the algorithm has both a high security and good efficiency.

Keywords: Hash function, Stream cipher, Information security.

1 Introduction

Symmetric cryptosystems is mainly classed into block cipher and stream cipher. Block cipher divides plaintext into blocks with certain length and encrypt them respectively. Stream cipher uses a PNG (pseudorandom number generator) to generate a binary pseudorandom number sequence, and then uses this PN sequence to do exclusive-or (XOR) operation with the plaintext bit by bit to produce the ciphertext. Usually, stream cipher is faster than block cipher, and it can process the data with the minimum information unit, which makes it widely used in electronic communication, document protection, etc.

As we know, the security of a stream cipher is primarily found on the PNG, which generate specific keystream based on the input seed/key. So the assessment of a stream cipher is chiefly focused on the RNG. Rueppel had ever given some criteria to design a PNG[1-3]: long period, high linear complexity, good statistical characteristic, confusion, diffusion and nonlinearity for Boolean functions. LFSR is one of the most popular stream ciphers. It use a shift register and feedback function to generate PN series. One n-bit LFSR can have maximal 2^n-1 internal states, namely its maximal period. Although LFSR is easy for digital hardware implementation, it's not easy for

Y. Wang, Y. Cheung, and H. Liu (Eds.): CIS 2006, LNAI 4456, pp. 481–490, 2007.

software. Furthermore, the adversary is easy to generate the original state of the LFSR after examining only $2n$ bits of the keystream, according to the Berlekamp-Massey algorithm[4]. And this vulnerability can be simply used by the known-plaintext attack. To conquer the flaws of LFSR, Ron Rivest developed a variable-key-size stream cipher (RC4) in 1987, whose software implementation is extremely efficient. RC4 works in OFB, and can be in $256! \times 256^2$ states. Although it is the currently most widely used cipher, it still has some shortcomings. For example, the output keystream will not be changed if the key keeps the same, and this vulnerability can be utilized by the adversaries easily[3]. Though the problem can be solved by introducing an *IV*, the users can't always use it properly[5]. There also have some weaknesses in the key scheduling algorithm of RC4, which have been made used in real attack[6,7].

A well designed hash function should meet the following primary requirement: First of all, the input message should be diffused to the fixed-length digest evenly and confusedly; Secondly, it should be easy to compute the digest from the original message, while impossible to do it reversely. Thirdly, given two different input messages, their corresponding digest should be different (the probability of collision should be extremely low), and the difference between the digests should has no direct relationship with the difference between the original messages. Oded Goldreich in his book[8] had ever regarded the PNG as a kind of one way function at some extent, and presented some analysis to construct a PNG based on one-way functions. He had also pointed out that when constructing a stream cipher, the shrinking one-way functions should be used rather than the expanding ones[8], to assure the uniform distribution of the output keystream. Therefore, the regular one-way hash functions like SHA and MD5, is quite suitable in constructing the PNGs with good qualities.

Although a stream cipher based on iteratively hash function named ARC has ever been proposed in [9], it has the following defects: First of all, the iteratively keystream generation steps isn't reasonable, because the matrix M is hard to decide when generating a long keystream. Secondly, it is not suitable to use hash functions with the OFB mode to generate PN, because once the collision happens, the circle occurs. Thirdly, the method is not efficient and associated efficiency analysis is not presented. Indeed it is one of the most important aspects to choose the appropriate core hash function. Fourthly, the user inputted password is used to generate the key, so the key space is indeed limited by the password which is more easily guessed.

A PNG based on known one-way hash functions is proposed in the paper. The key and the timestamp are concatenated together as the original input of the HSC system, and the iterative hash digests (keystream block) were concatenated to construct the keystream (PN). To generate the next keystream block, an Increasing Factor is iteratively added to the previous hash input, and the result was putted into the one-way hash function. The fixed-length hash digest (keystream block) is finally concatenated to construct the keystream (see Figure 1).

The implementation of our algorithm is described detailedly in Section 2. The security analysis and the efficiency analysis of our algorithm are presented with experimental results in Section 3 and Section 4 respectively. The conclusion is drawn in Section 5.

2 Implementation

To design a reliable stream cipher, it is important to make sure that the PNG has as many internal states as possible, and whatever how much the keystream the adversaries can get, they can't deduce the original key. For a traditional stream cipher algorithm, the PNG with specific key generates a unique keystream. This could be unsecured, since the adversaries can use the known-plaintext attack to recover the keystream, with which they can encrypt/decrypt any message. Although the *IV* had already been used in lots of stream cipher algorithms to conquer the problem, users are easily to misuse it[5], and the adversaries had already found their method to threat the security of RC4 by this way[6].

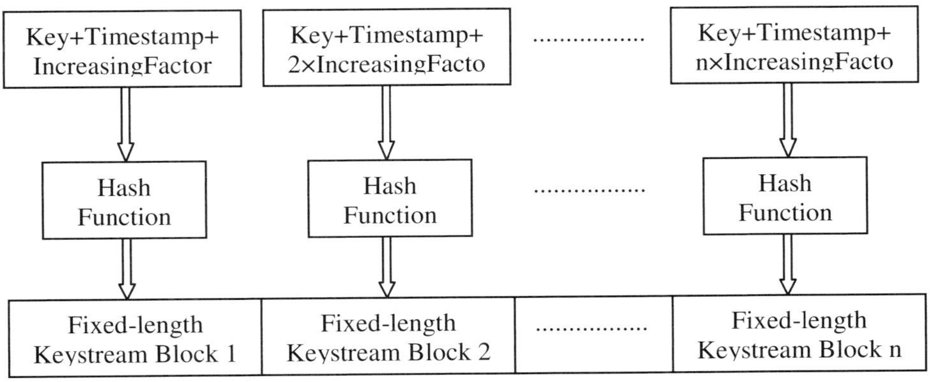

Fig. 1. PNG of the HSC

The initial purpose to design the HSC is to solve these problems. The one-way hash function is used as the core of our algorithm. By this mean, if constructed properly, the security of the HSC can be found generally on the appropriate one-way hash function that we select. To enlarge the internal state as much as possible, the OFB mode is not used. The *OV* (Original Vector) of the HSC PNG is made up by the concatenation of the key and the timestamp, where the key length is variable and the timestamp is the current system time. An Increasing Factor is iteratively added to the *OV* (see Figure 1), and the sum is then inputted into the core hash function. At last, the PN keystream is generated by concatenating the fixed-length hash digests block by block. The Increasing Factor is decided both by the key and the timestamp. Let the bit-length of the Increasing Factor $L_{IF} = i$, the Increasing Factor is initiated by the following formula:

$$IF = (\sum K_l + \sum T_j)\%2 \tag{1}$$

Where the *IF* represents the Increasing Factor, the K_l represents the lth byte of the key and the T_j represents the jth byte of the timestamp. The *IF* is the result of the accumulation of the key bytes and the timestamp bytes mode by 2^i. The bit-length of the Increasing Factor directly affects the iteratively increasing step of the hash input, which may attribute to the final statistical distribution of the keystream.

The internal state of the HSC changes iteratively and linearly due to the accumulation of the *IF* onto the *OV*, and the output keystream block changes accordingly. Because of the primary characteristic of regular one-way hash functions, it's unfeasible for the adversaries to deduce the *OV* from the digest (the keystream block). Even if the adversaries can get a series of keystream as long as they will, they are unable to trace the internal state at all. Furthermore, the timestamp is used as one part of the *OV*, and the *IF* will be decided by both the key and the timestamp, which makes the associated attacks impossible[1]. The timestamp is used as the role of *IV* in the HSC, so threat brought by misuse can be got rid of, and it's unnecessary to keep the timestamp secret. The hash input is changed iteratively by the accumulation of the *IF*. For a well designed one-way hash function, the probability of collision should be extremely low. Furthermore, the hash function itself is a nonlinear function, which implies the linear increasing input shall cause a nonlinear output. So the next output keystream block is unpredictable by the former keystream.

In the paper, the SHA-512[10] was chosen as our core hash function. The NIST gives a general description of the SHA-512 in [10] as follow: SHA-512 may be used to hash a message, M, having a length of l bits, where $0 \leq l < 2^{128}$. The algorithm uses ① a message schedule of eighty 64-bit words, ② eight working variables of 64 bits each, and ③ a hash value of eight 64-bit words. The block size of SHA-512 is 1024 bits, and final result of it is a 512-bit message digest. We use the timestamp with the following format:

```
typedef struct _SYSTEMTIME {
  WORD wYear;
  WORD wMonth;
  WORD wDayOfWeek;
  WORD wDay;
  WORD wHour;
  WORD wMinute;
  WORD wSecond;
  WORD wMilliseconds;
} SYSTEMTIME, *PSYSTEMTIME;
```

With the definition above, suppose the key is 0x0123456789ABCDEF, the *IF* length $L_{IF}=8bits$ and the timestamp is 0xD607020000001A000B0004000B009F02. So the *IF* is 0x74. The first three hash inputs are:

①0x7523456789ABCDEFD607020000001A000B0004000B009F0200
②0xE923456789ABCDEFD607020000001A000B0004000B009F0200
③0x5D24456789ABCDEFD607020000001A000B0004000B009F0200

3 Security Analysis

In this section, the theoretical analysis based on the one-way hash function is firstly given out. Afterwards, some experimental results are presented to prove the argument.

3.1 Theoretical Analysis

The theoretical base on the one-way hash functions. According to Rueppel, a secure PNG[1,2] should have the characters of long period, high linear complexity, good statistical characteristic, confusion, diffusion and nonlinearity for Boolean functions, which means that the period of the PN should be as long as possible, it should be impossible to work out the original key from the keystream, the keystream should be statistically good enough to be considered random, the characteristic of the original key should be diffused to the keystream confusingly, and the timestamp should be used to make the keystream different every time it is generated by the same key. The one-way hash functions can be used to construct the RNG that satisfies these regulations well.

The security of the one-way hash function could be described mainly by three problems: Preimage, Second Preimage and Collision[11]. The analysis lists as follow:

Let h denotes the one-way hash function, x denotes the preimage, y denotes the digest, and n denotes the length of the digest.

The problem of preimage can be described as follow: if it is impossible to work out the preimage x from the hash digest y, the one-way hash function can be considered secure on preimage. With this feature, it is unfeasible for the attackers to work out the original key from the HSC keystream, if the core one-way hash function is preimage secure. This characteristic of the one-way hash function assures the key security of the HSC algorithm.

A one-way hash function is second-preimage secure, if it takes a computing complexity of 2^n to find out another preimage $x' \neq x$ that satisfies the equation $h(x') = h(x)$. It can be inferred that, the repetition of the keystream block in a probability of 100% will only occurs after 2^n keystream blocks. Take the SHA-512 for example, the keystream block would likely to repeat in a probability of 100% after 2^{512} keystream blocks, namely $2^{512} \times 512$ bits. However, the one-way hash function is nonlinear, so the repetition should be ruleless and it is impossible for the keystream blocks to repeat periodically, as a result the adversary can not make use of this feature at all, and the randomness of the keystream would not be affected.

A one-way hash function is considered collision free, if it is impossible to find out another attack which is more efficiency than the birthday attack. Using the birthday attack, there would be a probability of 50% to find out a collision from a number of $1.17 \times 2^{n/2}$ digests[11]. According to this, the repetition of the keystream block with a probability of 50% will occurs after $1.17 \times 2^{n/2}$ keystream blocks. Take SHA-512 for example, the keystream block would likely to repeat in a probability of 50% after 1.17×2^{256} keystream blocks, namely $1.17 \times 2^{256} \times 512$ bits, but this kind of repetition is random at all. The second and the third characteristic of the one-way hash function assure the random keystream distribution of the HSC algorithm. Because the *OV* is changed iteratively and linearly by the *IF*, the internal state of the HSC is unlimited. As the unlimited internal state is transformed by the nonlinear one-way hash function, the keystream can achieve a good random distribution.

The Period and the Key. To generate the keystream blocks iteratively, the Increasing Factor is added to the hash input (iteratively input) time by time, and the changing extent generally depends on the value range of the Increasing Factor. But even if the Increasing Factor is very small, the change would be diffused to the digest (keystream block) evenly by the core hash function, which means however small the change is, the keystream blocks will be totally different and irrelevant. Furthermore, because the Increasing Factor is decided both by the key and the timestamp, the Increasing Factor is supposed to be different for every encrypting. To make the change available every time, the Increasing Factor should not be zero. And according to the experiment results (Table1, Table2 and Table3), the size of the Increasing Factor affect the result of randomness test little, so we choose the 8bits length Increasing Factor after the efficiency thought.

Table 1. HSC: the IF is 8bits-length

	Frequency	Runs	Cumulative
1	0.992	0.995	0.986
2	0.994	0.994	0.994
3	0.991	0.993	0.988
4	0.994	0.989	0.992
5	0.997	0.992	0.995
6	0.994	0.989	0.993
7	0.989	0.992	0.985
8	0.992	0.989	0.993
9	0.989	0.995	0.988
10	0.989	0.991	0.989

Table 2. HSC: the IF is 16bits-length

	Frequency	Runs	Cumulative
1	0.987	0.992	0.986
2	0.997	0.996	0.992
3	0.993	0.984	0.991
4	0.987	0.995	0.990
5	0.993	0.988	0.990
6	0.992	0.985	0.989
7	0.996	0.987	0.995
8	0.995	0.992	0.993
9	0.989	0.991	0.988
10	0.992	0.990	0.988

Generally, due to the combination of the linear Increasing Factor and the nonlinear one-way hash function, the keystream blocks will not occur periodically, so there would be no obvious period in the keystream of the HSC which depends on the key, the timestamp and the proper selected one-way hash function. The analysis goes as follow: Suppose that there is a period in the HSC keystream with a length of m, and the digest length of the core hash function is n, the keystream blocks will repeat from the m/nth block (see Figure 2). Consequently, we can deduce an equation that:

$$h\left(x+\frac{m}{n}\times IF\times i\right)=h(x)\cdots\cdots i\in N \tag{2}$$

According to the equation (2), the collision of the one-way hash function can be found periodically with a period of $m/n \times IF$. This is a paradox against the characteristic of the one-way hash function. Therefore, if the selected one-way hash function is secure enough, we can assert that the HSC keystream is not periodical, although it is implemented in a finite-state machine[3].

Table 3. HSC: the IF is 32bits-length

	Frequency	Runs	Cumulative
1	0.987	0.992	0.986
2	0.997	0.996	0.992
3	0.992	0.985	0.989
4	0.994	0.990	0.988
5	0.988	0.993	0.986
6	0.995	0.993	0.994
7	0.992	0.996	0.990
8	0.988	0.992	0.988
9	0.991	0.991	0.990
10	0.992	0.992	0.991

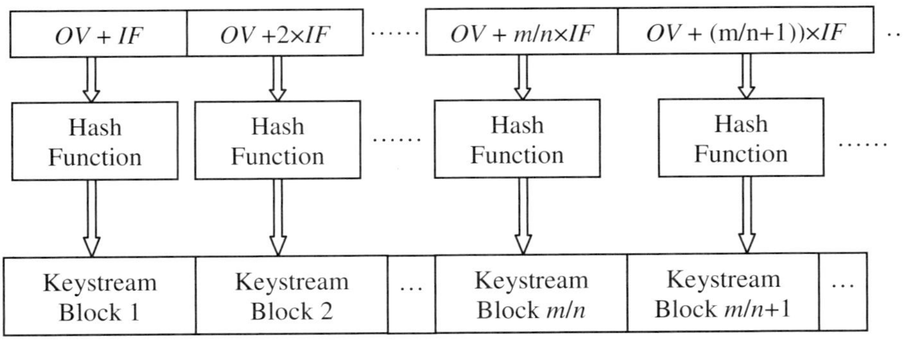

Fig. 2. The analysis of the HSC keystream period

The size of the HSC key is variable, and there is no obvious weak key of the HSC. Even a zero byte sequence could generate an acceptable random distribution keystream due to the characteristic of the one-way hash functions and the use of the timestamp. The random distribution quality of the HSC keystream is decided chiefly by the key, the timestamp and the core one-way hash function. Though it is not clear that which kind of key can generate more secure keystream, a key with longer length is quite suggested after the thought of bruteforce attack. When choosing a one-way hash function as the core of the HSC, the longer the hash digest is the safer and the faster the HSC is. Take SHA-512 for example, the output keystream block will repeat randomly in a probability of 100% after 2^{256}blocks, while the same thing happens after 2^{256} keystream blocks for SHA-256. Even if the repetition is randomly, we would rather to expect it comes out as later as possible. In the view of efficiency, to generate the same bit length m, SHA-512 needs to do $m/(512\times8)$ time hash operations, comparing to SHA-256's $m/(512\times8)$ times.

Robustness against Attacks. The keystream is generated independent of the message stream, so the HSC is a synchronous stream cipher[3], which implies that the HSC do not propagate transmission errors. If a bit is garbled during the transmission, only the garbled bit can not be decrypt correctly. All the preceding and subsequent sequences will not be affected. Since the nth hash input of the HSC is calculated directly by OV+n×IF, the HSC encryption can be synchronized instantly by correcting the hashing input. While other stream ciphers like RC4, would cost more time here.

According to the features of the one-way hash functions, the probability of the collision should be as small as possible, which implies that the occurrence probability of the hash digests should be uniform and even, so the HSC algorithm can be robust against many well-known attacks on stream ciphers, such as Linear Attack, Distinguishing Attack, Correlation Attacks, etc[12]. And after a little a little modified (Use both the hash operating rounds and the previous plaintext bits to determine how many times the *IF* should be accumulated on the previous hash input), the HSC can be immune to the insertion attack[3].

3.2 The Statistical Test of HSC Keystream

To test the randomness of the HSC output, we employ three test cases on pseudorandom number generators provided by NIST[13], namely Frequency Test, Runs Test and Cumulative Sums Test. The purpose of the Frequency Test is to determine whether the number of ones and zeros in a sequence are approximately the same as expected for a truly random sequence. And the Runs Test is used to determine whether the number of runs of ones and zeros of various lengths is as expected for a random sequence. The purpose of the Cumulative Sums Test is to determine whether the cumulative sum of the partial sequences occurring in the tested sequence is too large or too small relative to the expected behavior of that cumulative sum for random sequences[13].

For every test, there is a variable called *P-value* (lies between 0~1) calculated to assess each pseudorandom sequence, and a set of m sequences should be tested for the same test to make it statistical credible. If the *P-value* of a test sequence is larger than a threshold a (the significant level), this sequence is considered random. Furthermore, if the proportion of the sequences passing the tests is larger than a threshold T, the pseudorandom number generator can be considered random. Where the threshold T is calculate by the follow equation[13]:

$$T = (1-a) - 3\sqrt{\frac{a(1-a)}{m}} \tag{3}$$

In our test, let a =0.01, m=1000, key length k=64*Bytes* and sequence length n=10*MB*, so $T\approx0.981$. The results are listed below comparing with RC4(see table 4):

Table 4. RC4

	Frequency	Runs	Cumulative
1	0.986	0.992	0.987
2	0.982	0.993	0.976
3	0.987	0.990	0.982
4	0.984	0.987	0.976
5	0.984	0.991	0.986
6	0.989	0.993	0.988
7	0.989	0.996	0.989
8	0.989	0.988	0.989
9	0.989	0.990	0.983
10	0.991	0.985	0.989

All the random test of the HSC has passed. Comparing with RC4, it has a better random distribution. Especially when the sequence length is larger, the proportion of the sequences passing the test will be better. From the test we can infer that, ①the size of the *IF* has no obvious influence on the test result, so an 8bits-length *IF* is secure enough with better efficiency (See Section 4). ②The randomness of the sequences generated by the HSC depends mainly on the Key and the Timestamp. ③If the test sequence is long enough, the test result would be good enough.

4 Efficiency Analysis

Since the core of our algorithm is the one-way hash function, we are easy to infer that the computational complexity is mainly focus on the one-way hash function. HSC based on SHA-512 is faster than SHA-160, SHA-256 and SHA-384. Although the SHA-512 needs more computing for each hashing operation, the hash digest of it is much longer than the other three, SHA-512 is faster than the others in generating the same bit-length random sequence.

Every time the keystream block was generated, the hash rounds (the computing need for each hash operation) are decided by the concatenation length (*OV* length) of the Key and the Timestamp. For SHA-512, its block size is *1024bits*[10], so if the concatenation length is less than *1024bis,* SHA-512 only needs to do one round computing. Otherwise more than one computing round is necessary.

When the concatenation of the Key and the Timestamp is added by the *IF* iteratively, it is taken as a large unsigned integer, so the size of the concatenation will increase gradually. Once the length excess the block size of the hash function, the hash rounds would increase, and the time cost will go up with it.

As the HSC doesn't work in the OFB mode, and the *n*th hash input is calculated directly by $OV+n\times IF$ (see Figure 1), the HSC keystream can be generated instantly at any start position, which is more efficient than RC4. In the test, we choose SHA-512 as the HSC core hash function, the Key length k = 64*Bytes* and the Timestamp length *TS* = 16*Bytes*. It costs *92312ms* to generate 1Gbits-length binary sequence. Comparing to RC4's *30047ms*, the HSC is slower.

5 Conclusion

The main purpose of this paper is not only on the using of existing one-way hash functions to construct a stream cipher, but also on the proposing of a framework to construct the secure stream cipher using the one-way hash function's mode. For regular one-way hash functions, the digest size is limited, which can lower the HSC's efficiency. If the HSC is constructed iteratively using the one-way hash functions' iterative ways with a longer hash digest every time, a higher security level and better efficiency would be achieved. Our future work will focus on this and the analysis of the robustness of the HSC against various attacks.

Acknowledgments. This work was supported by the National Natural Science Foundation of China (Project Number: 60372052), the Science Foundation of Guangdong Province (Project Number: 05109511), the Foundation for the Author of National Excellent Doctoral Dissertation of China(Project Number: FANEDD-200238), the Multidiscipline Scientific Research Foundation of Harbin Institute of Technology (Project Number: HIT.MD-2002.11), the Scientific Research Foundation of Harbin Institute of Technology(Project Number: HIT.2003.52), the Foundation for the Excellent Youth of Heilongjiang Province, and the Program for New Century Excellent Talents in University (Project Number:NCET-04-0330), and the Chinese national 863-Program (Project Number:2005AA733120).

References

1. Rueppel, R.A.: Security Models and Notions for Stream Ciphers. In: Mitchell, C. (ed.) Cryptography and Coding II, Clarendon Press, Oxford (1992)
2. Rueppel, R.A.: Stream Ciphers. In: Simmons, G.J. (ed.) Contemporary Cryptology: The Science of Information Integrity, IEEE Press, New York (1992)
3. Schneier, B.: Applied Cryptography, Second Edition: Protocols, Algorithms, and Source Code in C. In: Wiley Computer Publishing, John Wiley & Sons, New York (1996)
4. Massey, J.L.: Shift–Register Synthesis and BCH Decoding. IEEE Transactions on Information Theory IT–15(1), 122–127 (1969)
5. Hongjun Wu.: The Misuse of RC4 in Microsoft Word and Excel. Institute for Infocomm Research, Singapore (2005)
6. Fluhrer, S., Mantin, I., Shamir, A.: Weaknesses in the Key Scheduling Algorithm of RC4. In: Vaudenay, S., Youssef, A.M. (eds.) Selected Areas in Cryptography. LNCS, vol. 2259, pp. 1–24. Springer, Heidelberg (2001)
7. Stubblefield, A., Ioannidis, J., Rubin, A.D.: A Key Recovery Attack on the 802.11b Wired Equivalent Privacy Protocol (WEP). In: ACM Transactions on Information and System Security (TISSEC), vol. 7(2), pp. 319–332. ACM Press, New York (2004)
8. Goldreich, O.: Foundations of Cryptography Basic Tools. Cambridge University Press, Cambridge (2001)
9. Rosiello, A.P. E., Carrozzo, R.: ARC: A Synchronous Stream Cipher from Hash Functions. Rosiello Security (2005)
10. Secure Hash Standard. Federal Information Processing Standards Publication 180-2 (2002)
11. Stinson, D.R.: Cryptography Theory and Practice, 2nd edn. CRC Press, Boca Raton (2002)
12. Dasgupta, A.: Analysis of Different Types of Attacks on Stream Ciphers and Evaluation and Security of Stream Ciphers (2005), http://www.securitydocs.com/library/3235
13. A Statistical Test Suite for Random and Pseudorandom Number Generators for Cryptographic Applications. NIST Special Publication 800-22 (2001)

Secure Password Authentication for Distributed Computing*

Seung Wook Jung and Souhwan Jung**

Soongsil University Communication Network Security Lab
Soongsil univ 1-1 Sangdo-dong Dongjak-Gu Seoul 256-743 Korea
seung-wook.jung@cns.ssu.ac.kr, souhwanj@ssu.ac.kr

Abstract. This paper describes secure password-based authentication involving a trusted third party, while the previous secure password authentication schemes focused on authentication involving two parties who shares the password. Kerberos is a well-known password-based authentication protocol involving a trusted third party. However, Kerberos is weak against the dictionary attack, suffers from a single point of failure. Additionally, Kerberos cannot provide a forward secrecy, which protects past sessions and further compromise, when a password is revealed. Our password authentication schemes provides Single Sign On like Kerberos and is secure against on/off-line dictionary attack. Moreover, The schemes provide a forward secrecy, and reduces the damage of the single point of failure.

1 Introduction

Password based authentication is pervasively used in wide range of practical applications, because it does not require anything more than a memorized password, is easy to use, and is less expensive to use than biometric or hardware-token based authentication schemes. However, many password authentication protocols, such as telnet authentication or HTTP authentication[1], have problems ranging from being totally insecure (telnet sends passwords in clear text) to being fragile to certain types of attacks such as off-line dictionary attack.

More secure password-based authentication protocol, encrypted key exchange (EKE) which is secure against passive dictionary attacks, was presented in [2]. After that, several secure password authentication protocols were published in [3] [4] [5] [6] [7][8]. [3] [5] [8] extended the secure password authentication protocol to resist threat of a stored plaintext-equivalent. The plaintext-equivalent is a piece of data, as the hashed password, which can be used to obtain the same level of access that the adversary gets when the adversary gets the password. These authentication-key exchange protocols have been developed for two parties. These cannot provide Single Sign On (SSO) feature in the distributed computing without modification.

* This work was supported by the 2nd BcN testbed consortium, and partly supported by the Soongsil University Research Fund.

** Corresponding author.

Y. Wang, Y. Cheung, and H. Liu (Eds.): CIS 2006, LNAI 4456, pp. 491–501, 2007.

Kerberos [9], which provides SSO, is focused on a password-based authentication protocol evolving on-line trusted third parties. Kerberos is based on a symmetric cryptosystem and maintains shared secret keys of entities in the Key Distribution Center (KDC). Therefore, the kerberos server must be extremely secure, as it represents a single point of failure for the entire system and all entities. Moreover, Kerberos is fragile to off-line dictionary attacks[10] and cannot provide forward secrecy.

In this paper, we concentrate on a secure password authentication scheme involving a trust third party to provide SSO without degrading security comparing to the previous secure password authentication schemes. Our design goals are following:

- Preventing the on/off-line dictionary attack: This is a common attack for password.
- Providing the prefect forward secrecy: A compromised password will not allow an adversary to decrypt past sessions. Also, a compromised session key will not allow an adversary to find out a password.
- Tolerating the compromise of a password file: For this, a server must keep not plaintext-equivalent.
- Avoiding or reducing the damage of the single point of failure: When KDC is compromised in Kerberos, all users and all target servers have to change the password and the key. Also, all past session can be decrypted.
- Providing different trust level of servers: The trusted third party should not provide any information about password to target servers.

We will discuss the basic terms in Section 2. We propose a security password-based authentication for distribution computing in Section 3. We analyze the security of proposed schemes in Section 4. Finally, we summarize proposed schemes in Section 5.

2 Preliminaries

2.1 Notation

- $a \in_R A$ denotes the choice of a uniform and independent random value a from the set A.
- Z_p denotes the set $\{0, 1, \ldots, p-1\}$, Z_p^* denotes the set $\{1, \ldots, p-1\}$ for a prime p.
- $E_k()$ denotes a symmetric encryption algorithm with key k.
- $D_k()$ denotes a symmetric decryption algorithm with key k.
- $h_k()$ denotes a message authenction code algorithm with key k.
- $S_k()$ denotes a signature algorithm with key k.
- $V_k()$ denotes a verification algorithm of a signature using a public key k.

2.2 Terms and Entities

Client who wants to get services.
Target SErver (TSE) who provides services to the client.

Token ISsuer (TIS) who provides the authentication and token issuing service to the client. The client have to register her/himself to TIS before getting authentication and token issuing service.

Token which is the security information such as Kerberos Ticket for the client to get the services from TSE. In this paper, the token includes both the key information for authentication and the attributes of the user such as group name for authorization and access control.

3 Secure Password Authentication for Distributed Computing(SPADC)

3.1 Registration

We assume that a connection must be protected against eavesdropping and any kinds of modification during registration. For example, the TLS/SSL [11], which provides integrity, encryption, and authentication, can be used for registration such as Fig 1.

Initialization. Before registration protocol execution, a TIS has to initialize as followings.

1. The TIS chooses large primes p, q such that $q|p$, a generator g of a multiplicative subgroup of Z_p^* with order q and a collision resistance hash function $h(\cdot)$ where $h(\cdot) : \{0,1\}^* \rightarrow Z_q^*$.
2. The (TIS) chooses $x_{TIS} \in_R Z_q^*$ and computes $y_{TIS} = g^{x_{TIS}} \bmod p$, where (x_{TIS}, y_{TIS}) is a key pairs of a private key and a public key of the TIS and publishes a tuple (p, q, g, y_{TIS}) as public value, which is known publicly in the network. The TIS must keep securely x_{TIS}.
3. The TIS can submit (p, q, g, y_{TIS}) to a certificate authority (CA) to get a X.509 Certificate. (p, q, g, y_{TIS}) can be published as a Certificate $Cert_{TIS}$.

Registration

1. The communication channel must be secure for registration, so we assume that a client and TIS open a SSL connection. The client sends his/her ID and $g^\pi \bmod p$ to register himself to the TIS, where $\pi = h(password||v)$ and a salt $v \in_R Z_q^*$.
2. The TIS chooses random numbers k and n in Z_q^*. The TIS computes and sends s, r, and a nonce n, where a tuple (s, r) is a TIS's signature on the user identity and g^π with Nyberg-Rueppel signature scheme [12].
3. The client checks $y_{TIS}^{h(ID||r)} \cdot g^s \cdot r \stackrel{?}{\equiv} g^\pi \bmod p$. The client chooses $t \in_R Z_q^*$ and encrypts $n+1$ with a session key $SK = f(g^{\pi+t} \bmod p)$, where $f(\cdot)$ is a key generation function for symmetric encryption algorithm. Also, he encrypts s with $f(\pi)$.
4. The client sends two encrypted values and $u = (s+t) \bmod q$ to the token issuer.

Client		TIS
		$p, q, g, x_{TIS}, y_{TIS} = g^{x_{TIS}} \bmod p$
	$open\ TLS/SSL \longleftrightarrow$	
$\pi = h(password\|\|v)$	$ID, g^{\pi}, v \rightarrow$	
		$k, n \in_R Z_q^*, r = g^k \cdot g^{\pi} \bmod p$
	$\leftarrow r, s, n$	$s = -x_{TIS} \cdot h(ID\|\|r) - k \bmod q$
$y_{TIS}^{h(ID\|\|r)} \cdot g^s \cdot r \stackrel{?}{\equiv} g^{\pi} \bmod p$		
$t \in_R Z_q^*, u = s + t \bmod q$		
$SK = f(g^{\pi+t} \bmod p)$		
	$u, E_{SK}(n+1), E_{f(\pi)}(s) \rightarrow$	
		$SK' = f(g^u \cdot y_{TIS}^{h(ID\|\|r)} \cdot r \bmod p)$
		$D_{SK'}(E_{SK}(n+1)) \stackrel{?}{=} n+1$
		Keeps $(ID, r, E_{f(\pi)}(s), v)$

Fig. 1. Registration

5. The TIS computes a decryption key SK' and checks whether the encrypted value is equal to $n+1$. If not, the TIS sends the error message and stops the registration process. Otherwise, the TIS keeps a tuple $(ID, r, E_{f(\pi)}(s), v)$. Note $g^u \cdot y_{TIS}^{h(ID||r)} \cdot r \equiv g^{-x_{TIS} \cdot h(ID||r) - k + t} \cdot g^{x_{TIS} \cdot h(ID||r)} \cdot g^{k+\pi} \equiv g^{\pi+t} \bmod p$. Therefore, it is easy to see $SK = SK'$.

3.2 Authentication and Key Agreement Between the Client and the TIS

1. A client sends a request message and her/his ID to a TIS.
2. The TIS chooses $w \in_R Z_q^*$ and computes $g^w \bmod p$. The TIS sends $E_{f(\pi)}(s)$, v, and g^w.
3. The client types a her/his password and decrypts $E_{f(\pi)}(s)$.
4. The client chooses random values t_1, t_2 in Z_q^* and computes $g^{t_2} \bmod p$ and $u_2 = (s + t_1) \bmod q$. The clients computes a session key $SK = f((y_{TIS} \cdot g^w)^{(\pi+t_1+t_2)} \bmod p)$, where y_{TIS} is the TIS's public key. The client sends $c = h_{SK}(TIS||TS), ID, g^{t_2}, u_2$, where TS is a timestamp.
5. The TIS computes $y_P = g^{t_2} \cdot g^{u_2} \cdot y_{TIS}^{h(ID||r)} \cdot r \bmod p$ and a session key $SK' = f(y_P^{(x_{TIS}+w)} \bmod p)$. He checks whether the received value c is equal to $h_{SK'}(TIS||TS)$ and the freshness of the message. If not, an error message is sent to the client. If consecutive errors occur up to limited numbers, then the server conceives it is an on-line dictionary attack by an adversary and stops this session. Otherwise, the TIS sends $c' = h_{SK'}(ID||TS'), TS'$ to the client.
6. The client checks whether the received value c' is equal to $c' = h_{SK}(ID||TS')$. The only TIS, who knows and r, x_{TIS}, and g^w, can computes c' properly.

We can easily see $(y_{TIS} \cdot g^w)^{(\pi+t_1+t_2)} \equiv y_P^{(x_{TIS}+w)} \bmod p$, because $y_P = g^{(\pi+t_1+t_2)} \bmod p$. Therefore, the client and the TIS have same key $SK = SK' = f(g^{(x_{TIS}+w)\cdot(\pi+t_1+t_2)} \bmod p)$.

Client		TIS
	$ID \rightarrow$	
		searches $(ID, r, E_{f(\pi)}(s), v)$
	$\leftarrow E_{f(\pi)}(s), v, g^w$	$w \in_R Z_q^*$
$t_1, t_2 \in_R Z_q^*$		
$u_2 = s + t_1 \bmod q$		
$SK = f((y_{TIS} \cdot g^w)^{(\pi+t_1+t_2)} \bmod p)$		
$c = h_{SK}(TIS \Vert TS)$		
	$c, ID, TS, g^{t_2}, u_2 \rightarrow$	
		$y_P = g^{t_2} \cdot g^{u_2} \cdot y_{TIS}^{h(ID\Vert r)} \cdot r \bmod p$
		$SK' = f((y_P)^{(x_{TIS}+w)} \bmod p)$
		$c \stackrel{?}{=} h_{SK'}(TIS \Vert TS)$
		$c' = h_{SK'}(ID \Vert TS')$
	$\leftarrow TS', c'$	
$h_{SK}(ID \Vert TS') \stackrel{?}{=} c'$		

Fig. 2. Authentication between the client and the TIS

3.3 Token Issuing and Authentication Between the Client and the TSE

To get the services from TSEs, a client has to show the TSE the client's attributes such as attribute certificate [13] in secure way. For that, the client and the TIS have to authenticate each other by 3.2. Once authentication is success, the client requests the tokens, which include the attributes for access control and the secure information for authentication between the client and TSE.

1. The client requests a token to the TIS in order to access a TSE with the TSE identity, a timestamp, the client's attributes such as role name, and supplement information. The hash value of a request message and the request message are encrypted with his session key before sending.
2. The TIS decrypts the message and checks the integrity of the message and whether the requested attributes are belong to the client. If not, TIS sends an error message. Otherwise, the TIS computes $r' = g^{k+\pi+t_3} \bmod p$, $u' = -x_{TIS} \cdot h(m_2) - k + t_1 - t_3 \bmod q$ and generates a token. The TIS checks the integrity of a TSE's public key y_{TSE} in his database. Finally, a token, y_{TSE} and the hash value of y_{TSE} are encrypted and sent to the client.
3. The client decrypts e_1. The client gets the Token and the TSE public key.

Authentication Between the Client and the TSE

1. The client chooses a random value t_4 and a nonce n_c in Z_q^*. The client sends the Token, g^{t_4}, and n_c.
2. The TSE checks whether the receiver in Token is her/him. If not, the TSE rejects the request. Otherwise, the TSE chooses a random number w and a nonce n_t in Z_q^*. The TSE computes the session key SK_2 and encrypts n_t, n_c, and ID. The TSE sends encrypted value e_2 and g^w.

Client		TIS
SK, u_2 from authentication in the Sec. 3.2 between the client and TIS		
$m = R\|\|A\|\|TS$		
	$ID, E_{SK}(m\|\|h(m)) \rightarrow$	
		$D_{SK'}(E_{SK}(m\|\|h(m)))$
		$t_3 \in_R Z_q^*, r' = r \cdot g^{t_3} \bmod p$
		$v = u_2 + x_{TIS} \cdot h(ID\|\|r) - t_3 \bmod q$
		$m_2 = ID\|\|r'\|\|I\|\|R\|\|A\|\|T\|\|O$
		$u' = v - x_{TIS} \cdot h(m_2) \bmod q$
		$Token = (u', r', m_2)$
		$e_1 = E_{SK'}(Token, y_{TSE}, h(y_{TSE}))$
	$\leftarrow e_1$	
$D_{SK}(e_1)$		
		TSE
$t_4, n_c \in_R Z_q^*$		
	$Token, g^{t_4}, n_c \rightarrow$	
		$w, n_t \in_R Z_q^*$
		$a = (g^{t_4} \cdot g^{u'} \cdot r' \cdot y_{TIS}^{h(m_2)})^{(x_{TSE}+w)} \bmod p$
		$SK_2 = f(a)$
		$e_2 = E_{SK_2}(n_t, n_c, ID)$
	$\leftarrow e_2, g^w$	
$b = (y_{TSE} \cdot g^w)^{(\pi+t_1+t_4)} \bmod p$		
$SK_2' = f(b)$		
$D_{SK_2'}(e_2)$		
$e_3 = E_{SK_2'}(n_c, n_t, TSE)$		
	$e_3 \rightarrow$	
		$D_{SK_2}(e_3)$

$R = receiver, A = attribute, TS = timestamp$
$O = OptionalInformation, I = Issuer, T = validperiod$

Fig. 3. Token Issuing and Authentication between the Client and the TSE

3. The client computes the session key SK_2' and decrypts e_2 with SK_2'. He checks whether the nonce n_c is same as he sent and the receiver identity is her/him. If true, he encrypts n_c, n_t, and TSE and sends it.
4. The TSE checks n_c and n_t is same as (s)he sent and the receiver identity is her/him.

It is easy to see $b \equiv (y_{TSE} \cdot g^w)^{\pi+t_1+t_4} \equiv g^{(x_{TIS}+w)(\pi+t_1+t_4)} \equiv (g^{t_4} \cdot g^{u'} \cdot y_{TIS}^{h(m_2)} \cdot r')^{x_{TSE}+w} \bmod p$. Note $r' = g^{k+\pi+t_3} \bmod p$ and $u' = -x_{TIS} \cdot h(m_2) - k + t_1 - t_3 \bmod q$. Therefore, the client and the TSE has same session key SK_2' and SK_2.

4 Security Analysis

4.1 Threats

We consider following attacks:

Replay attack. An impersonation or other deception involving use of information from a single previous protocol execution on the same or a different communication party.

Interleaving attack. An impersonation or other deception involving selective combination of information from one or more previous or simultaneously ongoing protocol execution (parallel sessions), including possible origination of one or more protocol execution by an adversary itself.

Reflection attack. An special interleaving attack involving sending information from an ongoing protocol execution back to the originator of such information. A general solution to prevent reflection attacks is that the protocol must be asymmetric.

Man-in-the-Middle-attack. When the public key is not authenticated, an adversary sends his public key as the intended communication party's public key.

Forward Secrecy. The term (perfect) "forward secrecy" was first used in [14] in the context of session key exchange protocols, and later in [15]. The basic idea, as described [14], is that compromise of long-term keys does not compromise past session keys so that past sessions are protected in some way against loss of the current key. The term perfect forward secrecy is controversial terminology at this moment[16]. People used the term "forward security" loosely to mean a design with the property that the compromise of a current key would have only limited effect, as with Diffie-Hellman. We defines this term as following:

- Compromise of current long term key should not compromise future long term key.
- Compromise of old long term key should not compromise current long term key.
- Compromise of current long term key should not compromise current or past session keys.
- Compromise of current session key should not compromise current long term key.

Exhaustive password search. A password that can be memorized by a human has limited length. Moreover, the entropy of such a password is low. Therefore, the key space of a password is so small as to be conducted a exhaustive search by an adversary.

Moreover, the computer will become more powerful continuously according to Moore's Law. Therefore, we need longer keys in the future, while the password size cannot be lengthen, because the limitation of the human memory. The other main obstacle of lengthen the password size is the design of password system. For example, Unix systems limit the length of the password to eight characters.

Password-guessing and Dictionary Attack. People tend to choose memorable password. It means that a password is easy to guess and most users select passwords from a small subset of the full password space(e.g., dictionary words, names, lower-case and so on) while ideally arbitrary strings of n characters would be choose as user-selected passwords.

4.2 Security Analysis Against Threats

We analyze authentication in the Fig. 2 and the Fig. 3 because Sec. 3.1 registration is already protected by underlying protocol such as SSL or IPSec.

Replay attack. We uses always time variant parameters to protect replay attack.

Interleaving attack. A TIS and a TSE never initiate the protocol. That is, the protocol itself is asymmetric. Moreover, in the authentication between the client and the TSE, n_c which is sent by initiator (the client) is checked always to prevents the interleaving attack.

Reflection attack. The messages for authentication between the client and the TIS includes the receiver's identity. The authentication between the client and the TSE also includes the receiver's identity.

Man-In-Middle-Attack. We need actually the certificate $Cert_{TIS}$ because that is a way to protect this type of attack on a TIS public key.

A TSE's public key y_{TSE} is provided by a TIS through authenticated channel. A TIS issues the token for providing authenticity of the client's public value.

Forward Secrecy. The long term keys (the private key of TIS and TSE) and passwords are always chosen independently. Therefore, compromise of current long term keys and current passwords cannot compromise old long term keys and old passwords. By the same reason, compromise of an old long term key and old password cannot compromise current long term key and current password.

When an adversary gets the password, the adversary must solve the discrete log problem of g^{t_2} in the Fig. 2 or the Fig. 3 respectively in order to compromise past session.

When an adversary gets the private key of a TIS, he cannot compromise past session because g^w is independent on y_{TIS}. By same reason, the compromise of TSE's private key cannot compromise the past session.

Compromise of a session key $SK = f(g^{(x_{TIS}+w)\cdot(\pi+t_1+t_2)} \bmod p)$ or $SK_2 = f(g^{(x_{TSE}+w)\cdot(\pi+t_1+t_4)} \bmod p)$ cannot compromise the password, the TIS's private key, and the TSE's private key, because of random numbers w, t_1, t_2, and t_4.

Exhaustive password search and Dictionary Attack. In order to conduct dictionary attack or exhaustive password attack, an adversary has to have verifiable plaintext to know whether the guessed password is right by comparison the verifiable plaintext with the computation result using the guessed password. We summarize verifiable plaintext as following.

- g^π: to getting this an adversary must be able to decrypt a underlying protocol which is required for registration to provides authenticity and encryption.
- $E_{f(\pi)}(s)$, s, and v in scheme of Sec. 3: An adversary can get v and $E_{f(\pi)}(s)$ from the observation of the message. However, the adversary needs a verifiable plaintext s to conduct the password guessing attack

against $E_{f(p)}(s)$. Therefore, an adversary has to decrypt the underlying protocol (TLS/SSL) in the registration.
- $ID, E_{f(\pi)}(s), r$, and v in scheme of Sec. 3: $ID, E_{f(\pi)}(s), v$ is a public information. r could be used as verifiable plaintext instead of s in a way that an adversary chooses a password π', decrypts $s' = D_{f(\pi')}(E_{f(\pi)}(s))$, and checks $g^{s'} \cdot y_{TIS}^{h(ID||r)} \cdot r \stackrel{?}{\equiv} g^{\pi'} \pmod p$. If the comparison is true, then π' is the password of a client. To get r, an adversary must compromise the password file in the TIS.

The first and the second are dependent on the security of the underlying protocol. The third and the forth are archived when an adversary compromises a TIS or a TIS and a client both. We assume that the underlying protocol is secure against eavesdropping and modification. Under this assumption, an adversary cannot get the first or the second information. Therefore, a passive adversary, who observes messages in the whole network, cannot conduct off-line dictionary attack.

On-line dictionary attack or exhaustive password search can be easily detected, and thwarted, by counting consecutive authentication failure.

We explained that compromise of a session key cannot compromise the password. Also, long term keys of the TIS and TSE are independent on session keys, so compromise of other long term key of TIS or TSE and old password cannot compromise of current password.

Conclusively, only one way to get a password is compromise of a password file in a TIS of the Sec. 3, and conducting off-line exhaustive password search or dictionary attack.

To make exhaustive password search and dictionary attack difficult when the adversary compromises password file, 1)Passphrase of which length is not limited is used, so the adversary conduct exhaustive password search in Z_q^* with exponentiation computation. 2) Password rules to discourage or prevent users from using weak password must be imposed at the client side.

4.3 Single Point of Failure

We assume that a password file and a TIS's private key is kept in separate location. A TIS's private key could be kept in tamper-resistance hardware device.

We will discuss when only single point is compromised.

When a password file in scheme of Sec. 3 is compromised, an adversary can get some user's password after successful dictionary attack with expensive exponentiation computations. Even if the adversary gets the password, he cannot decrypt the current session and past session.

Compromise of the TIS's private is very dangerous, because all entity could be impersonated by adversaries, because he can issue tokens of any clients to him. However, the current sessions and past sessions are protected by adversaries because of forward secrecy of our scheme. Moreover, only TIS needs to change his private key. The clients and the TSE does not need to change their keys.

Compromising of a TSE's private key, an adversary can impersonate the TSE. The current and past sessions could be protected by forward secrecy of our scheme.

4.4 Different Trust Level

The TIS can get $E_{f(\pi)}(s)$, a salt v, and s during registration protocol execution in Sec. 3. The TIS can conduct a dictionary attack to get passwords.

The TSE and adversaries cannot conduct dictionary attack because t_1 is a random value. Getting $\pi + t_1$ is reduced to the discrete log problem.

Conclusively, a client must more trust the TIS than TSEs in case of scheme in Sec. 3.

5 Conclusion

Password authentication protocols are easy to use, not expensive, and pervasively used in the real world. Previous secure password authentication protocols for two parties are not comfortable in the distributed computing. This is due to the fact that a user has to type his password to log in the each server. It is not comfortable. Therefore, we more focus on authentication involving third trust parties, such like Kerberos. Our secure password authentication protocols: (1)are secure against on/off-line dictionary attacks, (2) provide perfect forward secrecy, (3) does not keep plaintext-equivalent. Moreover, our protocol: (4) reduce harm of a single point of failure, (5)combine secure information for authentication and attributes for authorization (6) provide no information about password to the target servers, who authenticates a user. Finally, our protocol inherently includes functions of generating attribute certificate, key distribution and secure authentication. Therefore, we do not need many efforts to integrate several technologies and mechanisms with our protocols, while previous password authentication protocols are integrated with other technologies to provide same functionalities which are provided by our protocols.

References

1. IETF: RFC 2617 HTTP Authentication: Basic and Digest Access Authentication. IETF (1999)
2. Bellovin, S.M., Merritt, M.: Encrypted key exchange: Password-based protocols secure against dictionary attacks. In: Proc. IEEE Symposium on Research in Security and Privacy, pp. 72–84 (1992)
3. Bellovin, S.M., Merritt, M.: Augmented encrypted key exchange: A password-based protocol secure against dictionary atttacks and password file compromise. In: Ashby, V. (ed.) Proceedings of the 1st ACM Conference on Computer and Communications Security, Fairfax, Virginia, pp. 244–250. ACM Press, New York (1993)

4. Gong, L.: Optimal authentication protocols resistant to password guessing attacks. In: Proceedings of the Eighth Computer Security Foundations Workshop (CSFW '95), Washington - Brussels - Tokyo, pp. 24–29. IEEE, New York (1995)
5. Wu, T.: The secure remote password protocol. In: Proceedings of the Symposium on Network and Distributed Systems Security (NDSS '98), San Diego, California, Internet Society, pp. 97–111 (1998)
6. Jablon, D.P.: Strong password-only authenticated key exchange. CCR 26, 5–26 (1996)
7. Boyko, V., MacKenzie, P., Patel, S.: Provably secure password-authenticated key exchange using Diffie-Hellman. In: Preneel, B., ed.: Advances in Cryptology – EUROCRYPT ', Volume 1807 of Lecture Notes in Computer Science. Brugge, Belgium, Springer-Verlag, Berlin Germany, pp. 156–171 (2000)
8. Jablon, D.P.: Extended password key exchange protocols immune to dictionary attack. In: Proceedings of the WETICE'97 Workshop on Enterprise Security, Cambridge, MA, USA (1997)
9. Steiner, J., Neuman, B., Schiller, J.: Kerberos: an authentication service for open network systems. In: Usenix Conference Proceedings, Dallas, Texas, pp. 191–202 (1988)
10. Bellovin, S.M., Merritt, M.: Limitations of the Kerberos authentication system. In: Proc. Winter Usenix Conf. Dallas TX (USA), pp. 253–267 (1991)
11. Dierks, T., Allen, C.: The TLS Protocol Version 1.0. IETF (1999)
12. Nyberg, K., Rueppel, R.A.: Message recovery for signature schemes based on the discrete logarithm problem. In: De Santis, A. (ed.) Advances in Cryptology - EUROCRYPT '94. LNCS, vol. 950, pp. 182–193. Springer, Heidelberg (1995)
13. Housley, S.R.: An Internet Attribute profile for Authorization (2002)
14. Gnther, C.G.: An identity-based key-exchange protocol. In: Quisquater, J.-J., Vandewalle, J. (eds.) Advances in Cryptology - EUROCRYPT '89. LNCS, vol. 434, pp. 29–37. Springer, Heidelberg (1990)
15. Diffie, W., Oorschot, P.C.V., Wiener, M.J.: Authentication and authenticated key exchanges. Designs, Codes, and Cryptography 2, 107–125 (1992)
16. IETF: Internet Security Glossary. IETF (2000)

A Novel ID-Based Threshold Ring Signature Scheme Competent for Anonymity and Anti-forgery

Yu Fang Chung[1], Zhen Yu Wu[2], Feipei Lai[1,3], and Tzer Shyong Chen[4]

[1] Electrical Engineering Department, National Taiwan University, Taipei, China
[2] Computer Science and Information Engineering Department, National Cheng-Kung University, Tainan, China
[3] Computer Science and Information Engineering Department, National Taiwan University, Taipei, China
[4] Information Management Department, Tunghai University, Taichung, China
d92921014@ntu.edu.tw

Abstract. This study presents an approach to improving the (t, n) ring signature, which permits a signer to sign anonymously. Using fair partitioning to design a new (t, n) threshold ring signature based on bilinear pairing, the study develops a threshold signature method. The proposed method not only permits total signer anonymity, but also resist the signature of an anonymous signer from being forged even in a random oracle mode. Besides, the method is competent for protecting the identity and signature of a signer in regard to the anonymity property of ring signature. Therefore, this method trends suitable for those application complex, such as electronic voting and electronic cash, as well as for democratic management in which members with specific threshold value voice their opinion.

Keywords: Ring signature, fair partitioning, threshold signature, bilinear pairing, and anonymity.

1 Introduction

The ring signature scheme [3] was developed by R. Rivest et al. in 2001. This scheme was created from the concept of "How to leak a secret;" it was a special group signature that did not require the creation of a group; in spite of the management of an administrator; a signer only required randomly choosing a portion of the public keys of members and then creating a ring signature through his private key. Such a signature method significantly lowered the complexity of the mutual authentication process, to achieve the greatest advantage that allows then signer to remain anonymity thus to protect the privacy of a signer.

The threshold signature method [6] was first introduced by Y. Desmedt and Y. Franke in 1991. A threshold signature enables a group to share signing power with other members. It is the most commonly employed cipher element in group security.

Some contexts, such as multi-user electronic shares, multi-user united elections and employee opinion survey, require the sharing of signing power in consideration of

Y. Wang, Y. Cheung, and H. Liu (Eds.): CIS 2006, LNAI 4456, pp. 502–512, 2007.

protecting the signer's identity. The threshold ring signature scheme was developed to meet both these requirements, and it is one of the recent hot research topics.

Bresson, Stern and Szydlo constructed a threshold ring signature scheme [8] based on the ring signature scheme [3] by Rivest et al. in 2002, and demonstrated that their method is secure using the random oracle mode. In the method, the verifier could confirm that in an n-member group, at least k members had signed the message, but which k members had signed the message could not specifically known. H. Kuwakado and H. Tanaka presented a (k, n) threshold ring signature scheme [9] based on curves. This method not only overcomes conventional methods, it is also more efficient than Bresson's method.In 2004, Qianhong Wu et al. presented a (t, n) ring signature scheme based on a discrete logarithm public key system [18]. In the scheme, every participating signer P_i inserted a zero-knowledge proof into the $(1, n)$ ring signature [19] on the DLP-based cryptosystem. This zero-knowledge proof indicated that P_i knew the private key corresponding to a certain public key in the public key list L but did not know for certain to which public key the private key corresponds. Finally, the sub-signature of t members together created a (t, n) threshold ring signature. This study examined the threshold ring signature scheme presented by Wu et al., and concluded that the proposed scheme had a signature-related flaw. Theorem 1 of their proposal did not hold, and therefore signer anonymity could not be attained.

To correct the flaw, this study presents an identity-based ring signature scheme on bilinear pairings, and uses the method of fair partition of the ring, which not only includes complete signer anonymity, but also protects the signature from being forged even under a random oracle mode.

The rest of this paper is organized as follows. Section 2 studies the (t, n) threshold ring signature of Qianhong Wu et al., Section 3 presents an improvement method and security analysis is in Section 4. Conclusions are finally drawn in Section 5.

2 Analysis of the Qianhong Wu et al. Threshold Ring Signature Scheme

2.1 Link Between (t, n) Threshold Ring Signature and Signers

Experiments have revealed a relationship between a signature and the signer based on the DLP-based (t, n) threshold ring signature scheme [18]. That is, the scheme does not permit a signer to sign anonymously. The proof procedure is as follows.

First, there is a trustee (TA) responsible for setting up the system and generating the private keys of users. The TA generates the system parameters, then randomly selects two large prime numbers p and q such that $q \mid p$-1 is satisfied. Next, let the order of the cyclic group G be q, the generator $g \in Z_p^*$. Each signer calculates $z_j = g^{X_{k(j)}} \bmod p$, $j = 1, 2, ..., t$, where z_j is disclosed as the signature is announced. The disclosed results reveal that if a signer P_j participates in two signings, then the same z_j appears in the signatures. Therefore, the signature cannot be reused, or the security requirement of signature unlinkability breaks.

2.2 (*t*, *n*) Threshold Ring Signature Scheme Does Not Permit Anonymous Signing

According to [18], the discrete logarithm problem (DLP) is hard enough so that the signer in a (t, n) threshold signature keeps anonymous. Sufficient proof supporting the theorem was provided. However, this study has performed a detailed analysis that demonstrates that the theorem does not hold.

As mentioned in Section 2.1, a signature contains the part of $z_j = g^{X_{k(j)}} \bmod p$, $j = 1, 2, ..., t$, which is issued by all participant signers. z_j has clearly been generated using the signer's private key $X_{k(j)}$. Since the DLP in G is hard to solve, $X_{k(j)}$ cannot be determined through z_j. If no $X_{k(j)}$ exists, then z_j cannot be generated; that is, there exists a corresponding relationship between z_j and P_j and the public key of P_j is $y_j = g_j^{X_{k(j)}}$, which corresponds to an open identity relationship with P_j.

An experiment was performed to prove that z_j and y_j has a corresponding relationship with P_j. Assume that the set of group members corresponding to the public key list L is $P = \{P_1, ..., P_n\}$. Let all signers in P sign simplified signatures on the message m and L using the originally provided system parameter, as shown below. The values of z_j corresponding to P_j are obtained by verifying signatures, where $j = 0, 1, ..., n-1$.

【Simplified signature algorithm】

for $i = 0, 1, ..., n-1$ do

Step 1: Calculate $z_i = g^{X_{k(i)}} \bmod p$ and $c_i = H(L \| m \| g_i^{\alpha(i)} \bmod p_i \| g^{\alpha(i)} \bmod p)$, where L is the public key list, $\alpha(i) \bullet \{0, ..., 2^u - 1\}$, u is a security parameter

Step 2: Calculate $s_i = \alpha(i) - X_{k(i)} c_i \ (\in Z)$

Step 3: Send m, L, and (z_i, c_i, s_i)

end

【Verification of simplified signature algorithm】

Render m, L, and (z_i, c_i, s_i), where $i = 0, 1, ..., n - 1$

for $i = 0, 1, ..., n - 1$ do

Calculate $d_i = H(L \| m \| g_i^{si} y_i^{ci} \bmod p_i \| g^{si} z_i^{ci} \bmod p)$

If $c_i = d_i$, then z_i corresponds to y_i and z_i is generated due to $z_i = g^{X_{k(i)}}$ using the private key $X_{k(i)}$ of P_i

end

【Analysis of simplified signature algorithm】

Owing to $c_i = H(L \| m \| g_i^{\alpha(i)} \bmod p_i \| g^{\alpha(i)} \bmod p)$ and $s_i = \alpha(i) - X_{k(i)} c_i$, so $\alpha(i) = s_i + X_{k(i)} c_i$ can be obtained via a swapping equation

Then $H(L \| m \| g_i^{\alpha(i)} \bmod p_i \| g^{\alpha(i)} \bmod p) = H(L \| m \| g_i^{si} y_i^{ci} \bmod p_i \| g^{si} z_i^{ci} \bmod p)$

Because $d_i = H(L \| m \| g_i^{si} y_i^{ci} \bmod p_i \| g^{si} z_i^{ci} \bmod p)$

Therefore $c_i = d_i$

According to the above, it can be shown that the simplified signature algorithm is correct.

This simplified signature algorithm is clearly degraded from the (t, n) threshold ring signature such that only a one-member group exists. The threshold ring signature does not satisfy anonymity, because a person in $P = \{P_1,..., P_n\}$ who does not participate in the (t, n) ring signature can generate a simplified signature, which can be demonstrated through verification not to match any of the sub-ring signatures, which proves that the signer has not participated in the ring signature. Thus, any member of the group not participating in the ring signature can perform the above action to shake off suspicion; however, a participant in a ring signature cannot do so, making the identity of the (t, n) ring signature participants very easy to determine. Even if the t members refuse to create simplified signatures, their identities can be determined through other members with simplified signatures.

3 Proposed Identity-Based Threshold Ring Signature Scheme

To raise system efficiency, simplify key management process, and combine the threshold ring signature [8] in Ad-hoc group, this study proposes an ID-based threshold ring signature scheme. The process comprises four steps, namely setup, fair partitioning, signing, and verification. The participants are the *TA*, signer, and verifier.

3.1 Setup

First, let G be Gap Diffile-Hellman (GDH) with order q, e: $G \times G \rightarrow V$ be bilinear pairings, and P be the generator of G. Next, the *TA* randomly selects $s \in Z_q^*$ as *MASTER-KEY*, calculates $P_{pub} = sP$, and defines two hash functions H:$\{0, 1\}^* \rightarrow Z/q$ and H_1:$\{0, 1\}^* \rightarrow G$. The outputted system parameter is $PARAMS = \{G, q, P, P_{pub}, H, H_1\}$. Let ID_i be the identity of user U_i and $L = \{ID_i\}$ be the user identity set. The output $S_{ID_i} = sH(ID_i)$ is the private key of U_i, its corresponding public key is $Q_{ID_i} = H_1(ID_i)$, where $i = 1, 2,..., n$.

3.2 Fair Partitions of a Ring

Fair partitions must be understood before being created. Assume that $\pi = \{\pi^1, \pi^2,..., \pi^t\}$ denotes the partitions in $[1, n]$ distributed to t subsets, and $I = \{i_1, i_2,..., i_t\}$ denotes a set in $[1, n]$ consisting of t elements. If all integers in I belong to t different subsets, e.g. $i_j \in \pi^j$, then π denotes the fair partition on I. Clearly, π defines each sub-ring R_j.

Next to the definition of (n, t)-complete partition system, let t and n be two integers such that $t < n$ is satisfied. For the random set I of the base number t, if there exists a fair partition set $\prod$, i.e. $\forall I \subset [1, n]$, $\#(I) = t$, $\exists\ \pi = \{\pi^1, \pi^2,..., \pi^t\} \in \prod$, $\forall j \in [1, t]$, and $\#(I \cap \pi^j) = 1$. Then, $\prod$ is an (n, t)-complete partition system. To a random integer n, there exists $\binom{\lceil \log_2 n \rceil}{t-1} = O(\log^{t-1} n)$ partition set in $[1, n]$, of which the partition set can form an (n, t)-complete partition system [8].

3.3 Signing

The required parameters must be imported at the start of the signing phase. A function F is treated as a hash function that can reverse a $t{\times}l$ bit string. According to

$p = q^t \log_n$ and two integers n and t, where $n \leq t$ a public (n, t)-complete partition system can be formed. The term $P = \{P_{i_1}, P_{i_2}, ..., P_{i_t}\}$ denotes the set of a sub group of signers, and m denotes the message that is to be signed.

Since the threshold ring signature proposed herein is based on identity authentication, the algorithm, as well as the signing process, must also demonstrate that the t persons do indeed originate from the n members. The algorithm finds a solution to each sub-ring formed by the fair partition, then joins the partitions and also applies categorical ring method. Thus, the existence of at least one sub-ring with a complete solution, i.e. with t persons among n members, can be proven. The following algorithm is assumed, where denotes the π_s fair partition of $I = \{ i_1, i_2, ..., i_t\}$; for convenience, $\forall j \in [1, t], \exists i_j \in \pi_s^j$.

【Signature algorithm】

Step 1: Select the random seed for the sub-ring of each partition except the sub-ring π_s

for $i = 1, 2, ..., p$ $(i \neq s)$ do
  for $k = 1, 2, ..., t$ do
    $v_i^k \xleftarrow{R} \{0,1\}^l$
  end
end

Step 2: Simulate a ring with all partitions outside of π_s

for $i = 1, 2, ..., p$ $(i \neq s)$ do
  for $k = 1, 2, ..., t$ do
    Check the simulated ID-based ring signature on the kth sub-ring R_i^k in the fair partition π_s. Let $R_i^k = \{P_{i_{k_1}}, P_{i_{k_2}}, ..., P_{i_{k_w}}\}$, its corresponding identity list is $L_i^k = \{ ID_{i_{k_1}}, ID_{i_{k_2}}, ..., ID_{i_{k_w}}\}$
    for $j = 1, 2, ..., w$ do $\{T_{i_{kj}} \in_R G\}$ end
      $C_{i_k}^1 = H(L_i^k \parallel m \parallel e(T_{i_{k_1}}, P)\, e(v_i^k H_1(ID_{i_{k_1}}), P_{pub}))$
    for $j = 1, 2, ..., w - 1$ do
      $C_{i_k}^{j+1} = H(L_i^k \parallel m \parallel e(T_{i_{kj}}, P)\, e(C_{i_k}^j H_1(ID_{i_{kj}}), P_{pub}))$
    end
    $r_i^k = v_i^k \oplus C_{i_k}^w$
  end
end

Step 3: Use the gap value obtained in the previous step to calculate super-ring

$\sigma_S \xleftarrow{R} \{0,1\}^{ti}, u_{S+1} \leftarrow F(\sigma_S)$
for $i = s+2, ..., p, 1, ..., s$ do
  $u_i \leftarrow F\left(u_{i-1} \oplus \left(r_{i-1}^1 \Vert \ldots \Vert r_{i-1}^t\right)\right)$
end

Step 4: Seal the super-ring, and calculate the gap value of sub-ring

$(r_s^1 \parallel ... \parallel r_s^t) \leftarrow u_s \oplus {}_s$

Step 5: Find the solution to the sub-ring of the fair partition π_s

for $k = 1, 2,..., t$ do

Let the correct kth sub-ring of fair partition $\pi_s = (\pi_s^1, \pi_s^2, ..., \pi_s^t)$ be $R_s^k = \{P_{s_{k_1}}, P_{s_{k_2}}, ..., P_{s_{k_w}}\}$; its corresponding identity list is $L_s^k = \{ID_{s_{k_1}}, ID_{s_{k_2}}, ..., ID_{s_{k_w}}\}$. Suppose that $R_s^k \cap P = \{P_{s_{k_s}}\}$, then the sub-ring signature can be determined through $P_{s_{k_s}}$ and the private key $S_{ID_{s_{k_s}}}$.

The signer randomly selects $A_k \in_R G$, $C_{s_k}^{s+1} = H(L_s^k \| m \| e(A_k, P))$.

for $j = s+1, s+2, ..., w-1$ do

Randomly select $T_{s_{kj}} \in_R G$

$C_{s_k}^{j+1} = H(L_s^k \| m \| e(T_{s_{kj}}, P)\, e(C_{s_k}^j\, H_1(ID_{s_{kj}}), P_{pub}))$

end

for $j = 1, 2, ..., s-1$ do

Randomly select $T_{s_{kj}} \in_R G$

end

$C_{s_k}^1 = H(L_s^k \| m \| e(T_{s_{k_1}}, P) e((C_{s_k}^w \oplus r_s^k) H_1(ID_{s_{k_w}}), P_{pub}))$

Let $v_s^k = C_{s_k}^1 \oplus r_s^k$

for $j = 1, 2, ..., s-1$ do

$C_{s_k}^{j+1} = H(L_s^k \| m \| e(T_{s_{kj}}, P)\, e(C_{s_k}^j\, H_1(ID_{s_{kj}}), P_{pub}))$

end

$T_{s_{k_s}} = A_k - C_{s_k}^s\, S_{ID_{s_{k_s}}}$

end

Step 6: Randomly select $v \xleftarrow{R} [1, p]$

Then, output signature v, u_v, $\cup_{1 \le i \le p} (T_{i_1}, T_{i_2}, ..., T_{i_n}, v_i^1, v_i^2, ..., v_i^t)$, where $T_{i_1} = \{T_{i_{11}}, T_{i_{12}}, ..., T_{i_{1w}}\}, ..., T_{in} = \{T_{in_1}, T_{in_2}, ..., T_{in_w}\}$

3.4 Verification Algorithm

The procedure for verifying the ID-based (t, n) ring signature is as follows.

【Signature verification algorithm】

Step 1: Calculate all rings starting from 1

for $i = 1, 2, ..., p$ do

for $k = 1, 2, ..., t$ do

Let the kth sub-ring R_i^k in the fair partition π_i be $R_i^k = \{P_{ik_1}, P_{ik_2}, ..., P_{ik_w}\}$. Its corresponding identity list is $L_i^k = \{ID_{ik_1}, ID_{ik_2}, ..., ID_{ik_w}\}$.

$C_{i_k}^1 = H(L_i^k \| m \| e(T_{ik_1}, P) e(v_i^k H_1(ID_{ik_1}), P_{pub}))$

for $j = 1, 2, ..., w-1$ do

$C_{i_k}^{j+1} = H(L_i^k \| m \| e(T_{ik_j}, P) e(C_{i_k}^j\, H_1(ID_{ik_j}), P_{pub}))$

end

$r_i^k = v_i^k \oplus C_{i_k}^w$

end

end

Step 2: Use the gap value obtained in the previous step to verify super-rings starting from v

$$u_v \overset{?}{=} F\left(r_{v-1}^1 \| \ldots \| r_{v-1}^t \oplus F\left(\ldots F\left(r_v^1 \| \ldots \| r_v^t \oplus u_v\right) \ldots\right)\right)$$

Only if the above equation is satisfied, the signature can be validated.

4 Security and Efficiency Analysis

The proposed (t, n) threshold ring signature scheme mentioned in Section 3, based on the hardness assumptions of the elliptic curve discrete logarithm problem (ECDLP) and bilinear pairings identity problem (BPIP), must satisfy three needs, namely secret key security, unforgeability and anonymity of the signer.

4.1 Secret Key Security

The so-called secret key security means that others should not be able to obtain the secret key S_{ID_s} of signer P_s via a given public message. Since the secret key of the signers are generated by the *TA*, the secret key s of *TA* must be determined before determining the secret key S_{ID_s} of a signer through the corresponding public key $H_1(ID_s)$. Since $S_{ID_s}=sH_1(ID_s)$, s is protected by the hardness assumption of ECDLP. Additionally, an attacker wishing to obtain the secret key of a signer through the threshold ring signature will encounter the hardness assumptions of one-way hash function and BPIP. Hence, the secret key security is satisfied.

4.2 Unforgeability

The theorem and proof for satisfying the unforgeablity feature are as follows.

【Theorem 1】 Under the random oracle mode and the hardness of assumptions of the CDHP (the hardness assumption of computational Diffie-Hellman problem), ECDLP, and BPIP, the ID-based (t, n) threshold ring signature method can withstand a compatibility chosen message attack.

【Proof】 First, define qH, qG, and qS which denote the request number of the oracle systems H and G and the signature oracle system S, respectively. Next, prove that a certain valid signature is commonly generated by multi-members, and the number of participant members is greater than or equal to the agreed number, t. Then, an attacker A might take a compatibility-chosen message attack and might have a success probability of ε. Compared with another attacker B, who attacks the unidirectional nature of the expanded bilinear pairings function, the result can be proven as follows, where $Succ_{sign}^{cma}(A)$ denotes the success attack probability of A and $Succ_{GDH}^{ow}(B)$ denotes that of B.

$$Succ_{GDH}^{ow}(B) \geq \frac{1}{qH^2 qG^2} \cdot \frac{1}{t(n-t+1)\binom{n}{t-1}} Succ_{sign}^{cma}(A),$$

Let $q = \log_n$ and $p = 2^t \log_n$, while B employs the given parameters P, P_{pub}, H_1, ID_{i_0}, and y_0 as inputs. Next, B randomly selects a pointer $i_0 \in [1, n]$ and a subset $I_0 \subset [1, n]$, where the base of I_0 is $t-1$ also satisfies $i_0 \notin I_0$. Attacker B might guess and expect that the subset I_0 contains bribed members. B sets the public key of P_{i_0} as $Q_{ID_0} = H_1(ID_0)$ using $t-1$ pairs of the paired public and private keys of all members in I_0, and B randomly selects the public keys for other members, without using the corresponding private keys. Then, B randomly selects an integer t_0 from $[1, t]$, two integers h_0 and h_0' from $[1, qH]$, and two integers g_0 and g_0' from $[1, qG]$, all of which satisfy $g_0 < g_0' < h_0 < h_0'$, and qH and qG denote the attack process in which A sends requests to the oracle systems H and G. Finally, A performs initialization through the random coin tossing method, in which employs all public keys as input.

B imitates the random oracle systems H and G, uses a random value as the respondence to the request proposed by A, and stores the requests in a list. Let Γ_0 denote the difference value generated by the request g_0 and g_0'; let γ_0 denote the sub-chain between $[\Gamma_0]_{l(t_0-1)+1}$ and $[\Gamma_0]_{l\,t_0}$ generated by Γ_0. If H-request h_0' satisfies $i_0 < n$, then B replies with $y_0 / e(x_0\, H_1\,(ID_{i_0}),\, P_{pub})$; if it satisfies $i_0 = n$, then B responds with $y_0 / e((x_0 \oplus r)\; H_1\,(ID_0),\, P_{pub})$; where x_0 denotes the response to request h_0.

A can employ his compatibility method to send the private key requests to $t-1$ participants. B uses the direct method to respond to the request from A unless the private key of participant P_j does not belong to I_0; in this case, B stops functioning and outputs an output failed message. B can correctly guess that the probability of corrupt members in subset I_0 is at least $1 \;/ \begin{pmatrix} n \\ t-1 \end{pmatrix}$.

Finally, B signs by imitating a signature oracle, and therefore can imitate the signing process of any sub-group of participants. The imitation is achieved simultaneously by randomly selecting signature construction processes, and appropriately responding to G-request and H-request (a successful imitation of oracle G and H).

At the same time, attacker A outputs a t-forged signature with a probability of ε which is forging a valid signature generated by t members. The forged signature is $(m^*,\ R,\ v^*,\ u^*,\ \bigcup_{1 \le i \le p} (T_{i_1}, \ldots, T_{i_n}, v_i^1, \ldots, v_i^t))$.

According to the threshold ring signature theorem, the result as shown below can be obtained.

$$u^* = F(\Gamma_{v^*-1} \oplus F(\Gamma_{v^*-2} \oplus \ldots \oplus F(\Gamma_{v^*} \oplus u^*)\cdots))$$

$$\begin{cases} z_i^k = c_{i_k}^w \\ \Gamma_i = z_i^1 \oplus v_i^1 \,\|\, \ldots \,\|\, z_i^t \oplus v_i^t \end{cases} \quad \text{where } i = 1, \ldots, p \text{ and } k = 1, \ldots, t$$

Through the following steps, $z_i^k = c_{1_k}^w$ can be obtained.

$$c_{i_k}^1 = H(L_i^k \,\|\, m \,\|\, e(T_{i_{k1}}, P)\, e\,(v_i^k H_1(ID_{i_{k1}}),\, P_{pub}))$$

for $j = 1, 2, \ldots, w-1$ do

$$c_{i_k}^{j+1} = H\left(L_i^k \middle\| m \middle\| e\left(T_{i_{kj}}, P\right) e\left(c_{i_k}^j H_1\left(ID_{i_{kj}}\right), P_{pub}\right)\right)$$

end

Hence, for every pointer $i \in [1, p]$ and $j \in [1, n]$ satisfying $y_i^j = e(T_{i_j}, P)\, e(c_i^j H_1(ID_{i_j}), P_{pub})$, if there exists a pointer i such that $e(T_{i_0}, P)\; e(x_0 H_1(ID_{i_0}), P_{pub}) = y_0$, then B outputs T_{i_0}; otherwise, B outputs an output failed message.

Next, the success attack probability of B is examined. Along the direction of the super-ring, it can be found that a pointer s^* exists such that $F(u_{s^*} \oplus \Gamma_{s^*})$ is requested by A before $F(u_{s^*-1} \oplus \Gamma_{s^*-1})$. The probability of these requests being made by A for the time g_0 and g_0' is at least $1/qG^2$. In consideration of partition π_{s^*}, since A cannot bribe more than $t-1$ members, a pointer $t^* \in [1, t]$ exists, which satisfies the condition that bribed members exist inside the partition $\pi_{s^*}^{t^*}$. $t^* = t$ is obtained with a probability of $1/t$. According to the definition of γ_0, a result can be reached that the interval value in sub-ring $\pi_{s^*}^{t^*}$ is γ_0.

In the partition $\pi_{s^*}^{t^*}(R)$, there exists a pointer i^* such that $H(\omega_{i^*} \oplus y_{s^*}^{i^*})$ is requested by A before $H(\omega_{i^*-1} \oplus y_{s^*}^{i^*-1})$, where the exterior ring of ω has many median values. The requests, by A at the h_0th time and h_0'th time, reach a probability of $1/qH^2$. Similarly, the probability of obtaining $i^* = i_0$ is at least $1/(n-t+1)$. This indicates $e(T_{i_0}, P) = y_0 / e(x_0 H_1(ID_{i_0}), P_{pub})$. Thus, the least success attack probability of B can be evaluated as below.

$$Succ_{GDH}^{ow}(B) \geq \frac{1}{qH^2 qG^2} \cdot \frac{1}{t(n-t+1)\binom{n}{t-1}} Succ_{sign}^{cma}(A)$$

If the proposed method and the forged signature is provided with non-negligible probability, then an algorithm that allows the BPIP to be calculated with a non-negligible probability can be found. This conclusion contradicts the security assumption on the BPIP. Hence, the theorem is correct. The proposed method can withstand compatibility-chosen message attacks, and generates unforgeable signatures.

4.3 Anonymity

Finally, signer anonymity is examined. The signature scheme uses a public (n, t)-complete partition system and a categorical ring scheme. Every node in a categorical ring is determined by a fair partition. Section 2.2 reveals that an (n, t)-complete partition system has $\binom{\lceil \log_2 n \rceil}{t-1} = O(\log^{t-1} n)$ partition sets in $[1, n]$, indicating that the probability of guessing the corresponding fair partition of t signers is $1/\binom{\lceil \log_2^n \rceil}{t-1}$.

Even if the corresponding fair partition of t signers is guessed accurately, the identities of the t signers cannot be determined because each signer belongs to a different sub-ring. The proposed method indicates that the signature is generated by t of the n members, but does not reveal the identities of the signers, and thus satisfies the requirement of signer anonymity.

4.4 Efficiency Analysis

The fundamental operation in this method is to calculate the bilinear pairing. The time complexity of the threshold ring signature algorithm based on secret sharing is $O(n^2)$ [8], while the proposed scheme uses the super-ring method and fair partition methods, and has a time complexity of $O(n\log_n)$. Clearly, the efficiency of the proposed scheme is significantly increased.

5 Conclusions

This study presents a new threshold ring signature scheme in terms of identity authentication, with proof against total security in random oracle mode. Through the application of fair partitioning to design a (t, n) threshold ring signature on bilinear pairing, the anonymity of signer can be achieved, and the potential forgery attack of signature resisted. Having got the characteristics established, the practicability of the method can be fulfilled to complex application, including electronic transaction, or the democratic management system.

Acknowledgement

This work was supported by the National Science Council, Taiwan, under contract No. NSC 95-2221-E-029-024.

References

1. Diffie, W., Hellman, M.: New directions in cryptography. IEEE Transactions on Information Theory IT-22(6), 644–654 (1976)
2. Chaum, D., van Heijst E.: Group signatures, Advances in Cryptology-Eurocrypt'91, pp. 257–265 (1992)
3. Rivest, R., Shamir, A., Tauman, Y.: How to leak a secret. In: Boyd, C. (ed.) Advances in Cryptology - ASIACRYPT 2001. LNCS, vol. 2248, pp. 552–565. Springer, Heidelberg (2001)
4. Chaum, D.: Blind signatures for untraceable payments, Advances in Cryptology-Crypto'82, pp. 199–203 (1983)
5. Mambo, M., Usuda, K., Okamoto, E.: Proxy signature: delegation of the power to sign messages. IEICE Transactions on Fundamentals E79-A(9), 1338–1353 (1996)
6. Desmedt, Y., Frankel, Y.: Shared generation of authenticators and signatures. In: Feigenbaum, J. (ed.) Advances in Cryptology - CRYPTO '91. LNCS, vol. 576, pp. 457–469. Springer, Heidelberg (1992)
7. Zheng, Y.: Digital signcryption or how to achieve cost (Signature **[Error during LaTeX to Unicode conversion]**
8. Bresson, E., Stern, J., Szydlo, M.: Threshold ring signatures for ad-hoc groups. In: Yung, M. (ed.) Advances in Cryptology - CRYPTO 2002. LNCS, vol. 2442, pp. 465–480. Springer, Heidelberg (2002), http://www.informatik.uni-trier.de/ ley/db/conf/crypto/crypto2002.html
9. Kuwakado, H., Tanaka, H.: Threshold ring signature scheme based on the curve, vol. 44, pp. 8–32 (2003)

10. Barreto, P.S., Kim, H.Y., Scott, M.: Efficient algorithms for pairing-based cryptosystems. In: Yung, M. (ed.) Advances in Cryptology - CRYPTO 2002. LNCS, vol. 2442, pp. 354–368. Springer, Heidelberg (2002)
11. Galbraith, S. D., Harrison, K., Soldera, D.: Implementing the Tate pairing, ANTS 2002, INCS 2369, pp. 324–337 (2002)
12. Zhang, F., Kim, K.: ID-based blind signature and ring signature from pairings. In: Zheng, Y. (ed.) Advances in Cryptology - ASIACRYPT 2002. LNCS, vol. 2501, pp. 533–547. Springer, Heidelberg (2002)
13. Lin, C. Y., Wu, T. C.: An identity-based ring signature scheme from bilinear pairings, Cryptology ePrint Archive (2003)
14. Chow, S., Hui, L., Yiu, S.: Identity based threshold ring signature. In: Park, C.-s., Chee, S. (eds.) Information Security and Cryptology – ICISC 2004. LNCS, vol. 3506, pp. 218–232. Springer, Heidelberg (2005)
15. Xu, J., Zhang, Z., Feng, D.: A ring signature scheme using bilinear pairings. In: Lim, C.H., Yung, M. (eds.) Information Security Applications. LNCS, vol. 3325, pp. 163–172. Springer, Heidelberg (2004)
16. Chow, S., Yiu, S., Hui, L.: Efficient identity based ring signature. In: Ioannidis, J., Keromytis, A.D., Yung, M. (eds.) Applied Cryptography and Network Security. LNCS, vol. 3531, pp. 499–512. Springer, Heidelberg (2005)
17. Liu, J.K., Wei, V.K., Wong, D.S.: A separable threshold ring Signature scheme. In: Lim, J.-I., Lee, D.-H. (eds.) Information Security and Cryptology - ICISC 2003. LNCS, vol. 2971, pp. 352–369. Springer, Heidelberg (2004)
18. Qianhong Wu, Jilin Wang, and Yumin Wang, t-out-of-n ring signatures from discrete logarithm public keys, CHINACRYPT'04, pp. 209–214 (2004)
19. Abe, M., Ohkubo, M., Suzuki, K.: 1-out-of-n signatures from a variety of keys. In: Zheng, Y. (ed.) Advances in Cryptology - ASIACRYPT 2002. LNCS, vol. 2501, pp. 415–432. Springer, Heidelberg (2002)

Ternary Tree Based Group Key Management in Dynamic Peer Networks

Wei Wang[1], Jianfeng Ma[1], and SangJae Moon[2]

[1] Key Laboratory of Computer Networks and Information Security (Ministry of Education), Xidian University, Xi'an 710071, China
{wwzwh, ejfma}@hotmail.com
[2] Mobile Network Security Technology Research Center, Kyungpook National University, Sankyuk-dong, Buk-ku, Daeyu 702-701, Korea
sjmoon@knu.ac.kr

Abstract. For group-oriented applications, designing secure and efficient group key management schemes is a major problem. We present a group key management scheme for dynamic peer networks, which supports join, leave, merge and partition events. In the scheme, the numbers of rounds and messages are close to the lower bounds of those for dynamic group key management, and the length of messages and computation costs are less than those of the existing schemes. Furthermore, this scheme provides forward secrecy, backward secrecy and key independence.

1 Introduction

The majority of research in distributed group key management was mainly concerned with minimizing cryptographic computation cost[1-3]. A 2.1 GHz Pentium IV PC performs a 1024-bit modular exponentiation in around 2.19 ms[4]. In contrast, a laser pulse that travels through a fiber optic cable takes ≈21 ms from Paris to San Francisco. A provably secure contributory group key agreement protocol (STR) is proposed in [5]. In STR, the requirements of the length of messages and the computation costs are extremely high. In this paper, we present a group key management scheme for dynamic peer networks.

2 Preliminaries

2.1 Contributory Key Agreement

In this paper, we put emphasis on dynamic peer networks. Without a permanently fixed group server, all group key management schemes are based on the contributory key agreement [4]:

(1) Each party who contributes one Con_i can calculate K;
(2) No information about K can be extracted from a group key management protocol without the knowledge of at least one of the contributions;
(3) All inputs Con_i are kept secret.

Y. Wang, Y. Cheung, and H. Liu (Eds.): CIS 2006, LNAI 4456, pp. 513–522, 2007.

2.2 Bilinear Diffie-Hellman Assumption[6]

We view G_1 as an additive group and G_2 as a multiplicative group. Let P be an arbitrary generator of G_1. Assume that discrete logarithm problem (DLP) is hard in both G_1 and G_2.

Definition 1. A mapping e: $G_1^2 \rightarrow G_2$ satisfying the following properties is called a cryptographic bilinear map.

– *Bilinearity*: $e(aP, bQ) = e(P, Q)^{ab}$ for all $P, Q \in G_1$ and $a, b \in Z_q^*$.

– *Non-degeneracy*: If P is a generator of G_1, then $e(P, P)$ is a generator of G_2.

– *Computable*: There exists an efficient algorithm to compute $e(P, Q)$ for all $P, Q \in G_1$.

Definition 2. Given (P,aP,bP,cP) and $z \in_R G_2$, the *Decisional Bilinear Diffie-Hellman Assumption* claims that it is hard to decide whether $z=e(P,P)^{abc}$ or not.

2.3 The Complete Subtree Method[7]

For a set N of all users and a given set R of revoked users, let $u_1,\ldots,u_r$ be the users. The Complete Subtree method is as follows. Consider the (directed) Steiner Tree ST(R). Let $S_{i_1},\ldots,S_{i_m}$ be all the subtrees of the original tree that "hang" off ST(R), that is, all subtrees whose roots $v_1,\ldots,v_m$ are adjacent to nodes of outdegree 1 in ST(R), but they are not in ST(R).

Dalit Naor et al. show that a cover can contain at most $r\log(N/r)$ subsets for any set of r revocations, where $r=|R|$, $N=|N|$.

3 Efficient Group Key Management Scheme

3.1 Group Key Management System Setup

Key Pairing Generation: Our scheme employs a ternary tree whose nodes are denoted by $<l,v>$. Each node $<l,v>$ is associated with the key $K_{<l,v>}$ and the blinded key $BK_{<l,v>}=f(K_{<l,v>})$. A leaf node $<l,v>$ hosts M_i's key $K_{<l,v>}=r_i$ and its blinded key $BK_{<l,v>}=r_iP$. Furthermore, the member M_i at node $<l,v>$ knows every key along the path from $<l,v>$ to $<0,0>$, referred to as the key–path.

Lemma 1. The key and the blinded key at $<l, v>$ can be computed from the key of one of the child nodes and the blinded keys of the others.

3.2 Join Protocol

Assume that there are N members $\{M_1,\ldots, M_N\}$ in the group, and a new member M_{N+1} wishes to join the group.

Join Protocol

1. M_{N+1} picks a random secret r, $0 \leq r < p$, and broadcasts rP to the group members;
2. group members update the key tree
   - 2.1 accept or deny access to M_{N+1} depending on the application security policy;
   - 2.2 determine the insertion node
     - 2.2.1 if the key tree is full, generate a new root node, and insert M_{N+1} and the key tree under it ;
     - 2.2.2 else, the insertion node is the shallowest leftmost node, where the join does not increase the height of the key tree;
   - 2.3 choose the random leaf node in the subtree rooted at the insertion node as the sponsor;
   - 2.4 insert the new node
     - 2.4.1 if the insertion node has two child nodes, insert M_{N+1} under it;
     - 2.4.2 else, create a new intermediate node, and promote the new intermediate node to be the parent of both the insertion node and M_{N+1};
3. the sponsor picks a random secret r_s, computes the new blinded keys on the key–path of it and multicasts them to all group members;

3.3 Leave Protocol

The leave protocol is as follows:

Leave Protocol

1. group members choose M_l's parent node as the intermediate node;
2. group members update the key tree
   - 2.1 choose the random topmost leaf node in the subtree rooted at the intermediate node as the sponsor;
   - 2.2 delete the leaf node corresponding to M_l
     - 2.2.1 if the degree of intermediate node is three, delete the leaf node corresponding to M_l;
     - 2.2.2 else, delete the leaving node and promote the sibling of M_l to replace M_l's parent node;
3. the sponsor picks a random secret r_s, computes the new blinded keys on the key–path of it and multicasts them to all group members;

3.4 Merge Protocol

The merge protocol is as follows:

Merge Protocol

1. the topmost member of each tree broadcasts its tree information with all blinded keys to the other groups;
2. group members update the key tree
   2.1 choose the random topmost leaf node in the shortest tree as the sponsor;
   2.2 determine the merging order of key trees
      2.2.1 if the key trees have the different height, merge the shorter tree firstly;
      2.2.2 else, determine the order according to certain parameter (such as the identifiers of the sponsors);
   2.3 generate a new insertion node and insert the three shortest trees under it;
   2.4 repeat 2.3 until merge all trees;
3. the sponsor picks a random secret r_s, computes the new blinded keys on the key–path of it and multicasts them to all group members;

3.5 Partition Protocol

Assume that there are R members leave the group. The partition protocol is as follows:

Partition Protocol

1. remaining members partition the group into disjoint trees by the complete subtree method;
2. group members update the key tree
   2.1 choose the random topmost leaf node in the shortest tree as the sponsor;
   2.2 determine the merging order of key trees
      2.2.1 if the key trees have the different height, merge the shorter tree firstly;
      2.2.2 else, determine the order according to certain parameter (such as the identifiers of the sponsors);
   2.3 generate a new insertion node and insert the three shortest trees under it;
   2.4 repeat 2.3 until merge all trees;
3. the sponsor picks a random secret r_s, computes the new blinded keys on the key–path of it and multicasts them to all group members;

4 Security Analysis

4.1 Correctness

Theorem 1: All leaf nodes can get a same group key.

Proof. The proof is by induction on the height of key tree. Assume that the key tree with height h is denoted T^h and the whole key tree T^H, where $H=\lceil \log_d N \rceil$.

Basis. The case $h=1$ is trivial.

Induction Hypothesis. Assume that Theorem 1 holds for arbitrary trees of height $h < H$.

Induction Step. Consider a tree T^{h+1} and its corresponding group key K^{h+1}. From the induction hypothesis, in any sub-tree T_i^h, each leaf node can compute the same sub-group key K_i^h, i=0,1,2. According to Lemma 1, from the sub-group key K_i^h and all the other blinded sub-group keys of T_j^h where $j=0,\ldots,d-1$, $j \neq i$, all leaf nodes of T_i^h can compute the group key. Therefore, by induction, the theorem holds for all possible cases. #

4.2 Group Key Freshness

Theorem 2: In the presented scheme, every group key is fresh.

Proof. In our scheme, for every membership change, there is a member in the group generates its random key share which is same as any previous one by a negligible probability $1/q$. According to the contributory key agreement, the probability that new group key is same as any old group key is negligible, which guarantees the freshness of group key. #

4.3 TGDBDH Problem

For $(\Gamma, P, p) \leftarrow G(t)$, $N \in \mathbb{N}$, $R=(r_1, r_2, \ldots, r_N)$ for $r_i \in G_2$ and a key tree T with height h, we define the following random variables:

—K_j^i: i-th level of j-th key (secret value, $K_{<i,j>}$);

—BK_j^i: i-th level of j-th blinded key (public value, $BK_{<i,j>}$).

view(L,R_L,T_L): ={the set of BK_j^i in the subtree T_L rooted at level L }

$K(L,R_L,T_L) := e(BK_{3j+1}^{i+1}, BK_{3j+2}^{i+1})^{K_{3j}^{i+1}}$, where T_L is a subtree of T and $R_L \subset G_2$.

Let the following two random variables are defined by generating $(\Gamma,P,p) \leftarrow G(t, d)$, choosing R_L randomly from G_2 and T_L randomly from T:

—$A_L := (view(L,R_L,T_L), y)$

—$B_L := (view(L,R_L,T_L), K(L,R_L,T_L))$

Definition 3. Let $(\Gamma, P, p) \leftarrow G(t)$, $N \in \mathbb{N}$, $R=(r_1, r_2, \ldots, r_N)$ for $r_i \in G_2$, a key tree T with N leaf nodes which correspond to R, and A_0 and B_0 be defined as above. TGDBDH algorithm $\mathcal{A}$ is a probabilistic polynomial time 0/1 valued algorithm satisfying, for some fixed k>0 and sufficiently large m:

$$|\Pr[\mathcal{A}(A_0)=1]-\Pr[\mathcal{A}(B_0)=1]| > 1/m^k \quad (1)$$

Theorem 3: If the Decisional Bilinear Diffie-Hellman Assumption holds, the TGDBDH problem is hard.

Proof. Fact 1: There is no probabilistic polynomial time algorithm that can distinguish A_H from B_H, which is equivalent to solve the DBDH problem in G_1 and G_2.

Contradiction Hypothesis. Assume that A_0 and B_0 can be distinguished in probabilistic polynomial time.

Induction Basis. Assume that the contradiction hypothesis holds.

Induction Hypothesis. Assume that there exists a polynomial algorithm that can distinguish A_L from B_L.

Induction Step. We will show that this algorithm can be used to distinguish A_{L+1} from B_{L+1} or can be used to solve the DBDH problem.

Consider the following equations:

$$—A_L=(view(L+1,R_{L+1_l},T_{L+1_l}),\ view(L+1,R_{L+1_m},T_{L+1_m}),\ view(L+1,R_{L+1_r},T_{L+1_r}),\ K_l^{L+1}P, K_m^{L+1}P, K_r^{L+1}P, y)$$

$$—A_L^1=(view(L+1,R_{L+1_l},T_{L+1_l}),\ view(L+1,R_{L+1_m},T_{L+1_m}),\ view(L+1,R_{L+1_r},T_{L+1_r}),\ r_1P, K_m^{L+1}P, K_r^{L+1}P, y)$$

$$—A_L^2=(view(L+1,R_{L+1_l},T_{L+1_l}),\ view(L+1,R_{L+1_m},T_{L+1_m}),\ view(L+1,R_{L+1_r},T_{L+1_r}),\ r_1P, r_2P, K_r^{L+1}P, y)$$

$$—A_L^3=(view(L+1,R_{L+1_l},T_{L+1_l}),\ view(L+1,R_{L+1_m},T_{L+1_m}),\ view(L+1,R_{L+1_r},T_{L+1_r}),\ r_1P, r_2P, r_3P, y)$$

$$—B_L^3=(view(L+1,R_{L+1_l},T_{L+1_l}),\ view(L+1,R_{L+1_m},T_{L+1_m}),\ view(L+1,R_{L+1_r},T_{L+1_r}),\ r_1P, r_2P, r_3P, e(P,P)^{K_l^{L+1}K_m^{L+1}K_r^{L+1}})$$

$$—B_L^2=(view(L+1,R_{L+1_l},T_{L+1_l}),\ view(L+1,R_{L+1_m},T_{L+1_m}),\ view(L+1,R_{L+1_r},T_{L+1_r}),\ r_1P, r_2P, K_r^{L+1}P, e(P,P)^{K_l^{L+1}K_m^{L+1}K_r^{L+1}})$$

$$—B_L^1=(view(L+1,R_{L+1_l},T_{L+1_l}),\ view(L+1,R_{L+1_m},T_{L+1_m}),\ view(L+1,R_{L+1_r},T_{L+1_r}),\ r_1P, K_m^{L+1}P, K_r^{L+1}P, e(P,P)^{K_l^{L+1}K_m^{L+1}K_r^{L+1}})$$

$$—B_L=(view(L+1,R_{L+1_l},T_{L+1_l}),\ view(L+1,R_{L+1_m},T_{L+1_m}),\ view(L+1,R_{L+1_r},T_{L+1_r}),\ K_l^{L+1}P, K_m^{L+1}P, K_r^{L+1}P, e(P,P)^{K_l^{L+1}K_m^{L+1}K_r^{L+1}})$$

A_L and A_L^1: Suppose A_L and A_L^1 can be distinguished in polynomial time. Suppose that the passive adversary want to decide whether $P'_{L+1}=(view(L+1, R', T'), r')$ is an instance of TGDBDH problem or r' is a random number. Then, by P'_{L+1} and (R'', X''), (R''', X'''), he can generate the distribution:

Now the passive adversary input P'_L to the distinguisher $A_{A_L A^1_L}$. If P'_L is an instance of $A_L(A^1_L)$, then P'_{L+1} is an instance of A_{L+1} (A^1_{L+1}) , respectively.

Similarly, suppose A^1_L and A^2_L, A^2_L and A^3_L, A^3_L and B^3_L, B^3_L and B^2_L, B^2_L and B^1_L, B^1_L and B_L can be distinguished in polynomial time. We can show that these distinguishers $A_{A^1_L A^2_L}$, $A_{A^2_L A^3_L}$, $A_{A^3_L B^3_L}$, $A_{B^3_L B^2_L}$, $A_{B^2_L B^1_L}$ and $A_{B^1_L B_L}$ can be used to solve TGDBDH problem with level L+1.

From the above analysis, we get that the passive adversary can distinguish A_H from B_H, which is contrary to Fact 1. Consequently, there is no probabilistic polynomial time algorithm that can distinguish A_0 from B_0 with a non-negligible probability. #

4.4 Key Independence

We now give an informal proof that our group key management scheme satisfies key independence.

Theorem 4: In the presence of a passive adversary, our group key management scheme provides the security requirements of group key secrecy, backward secrecy, forward secrecy and key independence.

Proof. Either of backward secrecy or forward secrecy subsumes group key secrecy and key independence subsumes the rest. Also, the combination of backward secrecy and forward secrecy forms key independence [3].

In the join event, the sponsor computes the new blinded keys and, consequently, previous root key is changed. Therefore, the view of the joining member M with respect to the prior key tree is exactly same as that of a passive adversary. Next, we show that M cannot obtain any keys of the previous key tree. Once M receives all the blinded keys on its co-path, it can compute all the keys on its key path. Clearly, all these keys will contain M's contribution and the previous secret keys on that path cannot be revealed from them.

If a member M leaves the group, the sponsor refreshes its key and all the keys known to the leaving member will be changed accordingly. Therefore, M's view is exactly same as that of the passive adversary. When the leave protocol completes, M's contribution is removed from all the keys on M's former key path, and thus M cannot compute the group key. #

5 Performance Analysis

The computation and communication costs for the join, leave, merge and partition protocols are analyzed in this section. We focus on the numbers of rounds, messages, broadcasts, unicasts, cryptographic operations and the length of messages, and compare them with those of STR.

Table 1 summarizes the communication and computation costs of both protocols. The numbers of current group members, joining members, merging groups, and

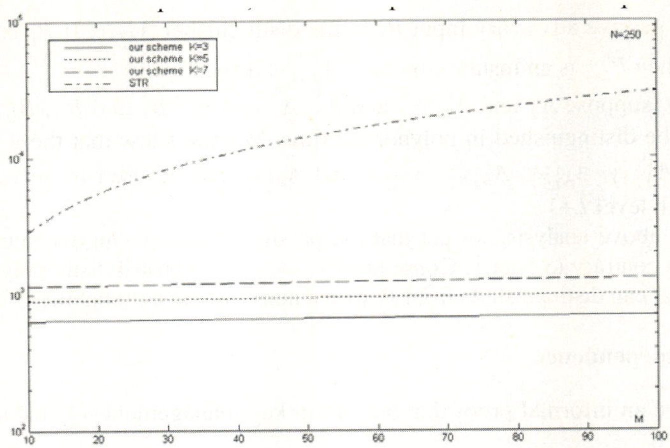

Fig. 1. Computation Cost Comparison of Merge Protocol

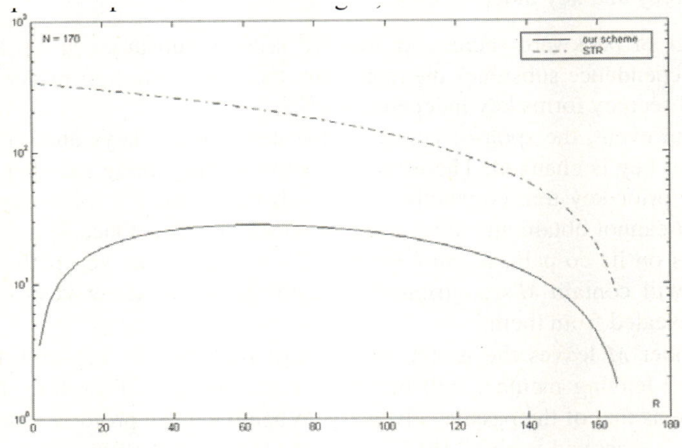

Fig. 2. Message Length Comparison of Partition Protocol

leaving members are denoted as: *N*, *M*, *K* and *R*, respectively. As shown in Table 1, two schemes have the similar numbers of rounds and messages. But in terms of the length of messages of join protocol, leave protocol and merge protocol, and the cryptographic operations of leave protocol, our scheme provides much better performance.

From Fig. 1 and Fig. 2, the computation cost of merge protocol and the message length of partition protocol in our scheme are less than those of STR. For the computation cost of partition protocol shown in Fig. 3, our scheme is much better than STR .

Table 1. Communication and Computation Costs

		Round	Message	Unicast	Broadcast	Length of Messages (sponsor)	Cryptographic Operation
Our Scheme	Join	2	2	0	2	$\log_3 N$	$3N+1$
	Leave	1	1	0	1	$\log_3 N$	$3N-\log_3(N+1)$
	Merge	2	$K+1$	0	$K+1$	$\left\lceil \frac{K-1}{2} \right\rceil + \log_3 N$	$(N+1)\left\lceil \frac{K-1}{2} \right\rceil + [M/K]\left\lceil \frac{K-1}{2} \right\rceil\left(\left\lceil \frac{K-1}{2} \right\rceil + 1\right) + 3N/2 + \log_3 N - 3/2$
	Partition	1	1	0	1	$\left\lceil \frac{S-1}{2} \right\rceil$, where $S=R\log_3(N/R)$	$2\left\lceil \frac{S-1}{2} \right\rceil + 2(N-R-1)\sum_{i=1}^{\left\lceil \frac{S-1}{2} \right\rceil} (\frac{1}{3})^i i$, where $S=R\log_3(N/R)$
STR	Join	2	3	0	3	$2N$	$2N+4$
	Leave	1	1	0	1	$2N-4$	$(2N^3+3N^2+N-30)/6N$
	Merge	2	$K+1$	0	$K+1$	$2N+2M-2$	$(M^2+2MN+2N+5M+2)/2$
	Partition	1	1	0	1	$2(N-R-1)$	$\sum_{k=0}^{N-R-2} \frac{C(k+R-1,R-1)}{C(N,R)}(N+1-R-k/2)(k+1) + \frac{R(N-R)(N-R-1)^2(N-R+4)}{N(N-1)(N-2)}$

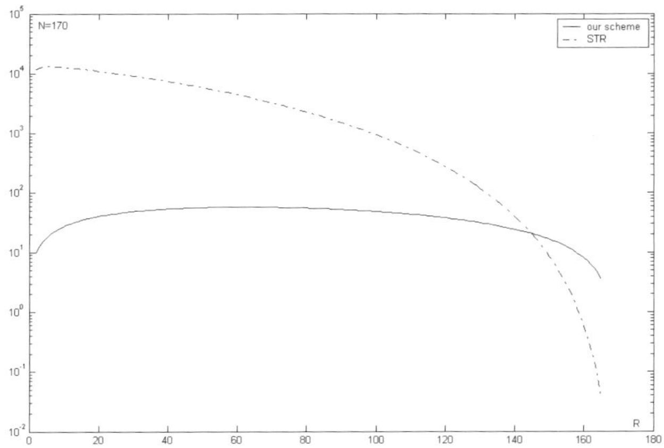

Fig. 3. Computation Cost Comparison of Partition Protocol

6 Conclusions and Future Work

This work presents and analyzes a provably secure group key management scheme by blending bilinear pairing based key exchange with the Complete Subtree method. The resultant protocol suite can support the join, leave, merge and partition events. Its communication and computation costs are less than those of prior arts. Furthermore, we prove that this scheme provides forward secrecy, backward secrecy and key independence.

Acknowledgments

This work is supported by the National Natural Science Foundation of China under the grant No. 90204012, No. 60573036, No. 60573035, and No. 60503012, the Excellent Young Teachers Program of Chinese Ministry of Education, the Key Project of Chinese Ministry of Education, and the University IT Research Center Project of Korea.

References

1. Steiner, M., Tsudik, G., Waidner, M.: Key agreement in dynamic peer groups. IEEE Transactions on Parallel and Distributed Systems 11, 769–780 (2000)
2. Dondeti, L., Mukherjee, S., Samal, A.: A Distributed Group Key Management Scheme for Secure Many-to-many Communication. Technical Report PINTL-TR-207-99, Department of Computer Science, University of Maryland (1999)
3. Kim, Y., Perrig, A., Tsudik, G.: Simple and fault-tolerant key agreement for dynamic collaborative groups. In: Jajodia, S. (ed.) 7th ACM Conference on Computer and Communications Security, Athens, pp. 235–244. ACM Press, New York (2000)
4. Weidai: Speed Comparison of Popular Crypto Algorithms http://www.eskimo.com/~weidai/benchmarks.html
5. Kim, Y., Perrig, A., Tsudik, G.: Group Key Agreement Efficient in Communication. IEEE Transactions on Computers 53, 905–921 (2004)
6. Boneh, D., Franklin, M.: Identity-based encryption from the Weil pairing. In: Kilian, J. (ed.) Advances in Cryptology - CRYPTO 2001. LNCS, vol. 2139, pp. 213–229. Springer, Heidelberg (2001)
7. Naor, D., Naor, M., Lotspiech, J.: Revocation and tracing schemes for stateless receivers. In: Kilian, J. (ed.) Advances in Cryptology - CRYPTO 2001. LNCS, vol. 2139, pp. 41–62. Springer, Heidelberg (2001)

Practical Password-Based Authenticated Key Exchange Protocol

Shuhua Wu and Yuefei Zhu

Department of Networks Engineering,
Zhengzhou Information Engineering Institute,
Zhengzhou 450002, China
wushuhua726@sina.com.cn

Abstract. Due to the low entropy of human-memorable passwords, it is not easy to conduct password authenticated key agreement in a secure manner. Though there are many protocols achieving this goal, they may require a large amount of computation especially in the augmented model which is contrived to resist server compromise. In this paper, we propose a simple and efficient password authenticated key exchange protocol, which is in the augmented model. It is considered much more from the practical perspective. Moreover, the scheme is provably forward secure under the Diffie-Hellman intractability assumptions in the random-oracle model.

1 Introduction

The Password-based Authenticated Key Exchange (PAKE) is a protocol which allows two communicating parties to prove to each other that they know the password (that is, mutual authentication), and to generate a fresh symmetric key securely such that it is known only to these two parties (that is, key exchange). The intrinsic problem with password-based protocol is the memorable password, associated with each user, has low entropy, so that it is not easy to protect the password information against the notorious password guessing attacks by which attackers could search the relatively small space of human-memorable passwords.

Since a pioneering method that resists the password guessing attacks was introduced to cryptographic protocol developers [1], there has been a great deal of work for password authenticated key exchange, preceded by EKE [2,3], on the framework of Diffie-Hellman, such as protocols proposed in [4,5,6,7,8,9,10,11,12,13]. Some early protocols were in the augmented model but contained only informal arguments for security; in fact, attacks against many of these protocols have been shown subsequently [14], emphasizing the need for rigorous proofs of security in a formal, well-defined model. Some recent ones, e.g. [10,11,12,13], have been formally proven secure. However, only the solution in [13] was proved forward-secure and augmented to reduce the damages of server corruption. But the scheme in [13] was not quite efficient, which partially motivates our work. Compared to the typical authenticated key exchange, the password-based schemes are more expensive

Y. Wang, Y. Cheung, and H. Liu (Eds.): CIS 2006, LNAI 4456, pp. 523–533, 2007.

due to the low entropy of passwords, especially in the augmented model which is contrived to resist server compromise.

In this paper, we propose a practical three-pass password-based authenticated key exchange protocol. It is a simple and efficient augmented PAKE when compared with previous solutions. It requires no full-domain hash functions onto a discrete group. Such hash functions are difficult to implement directly in practice over some groups. Besides, our scheme is augmented simply and requires no complex functions for it. It is a password-only PAKE and assumes only public parameters. Users need remember only a short password, and no cryptographic key(s) of any kind. Our protocol is considered much more from the practical perspective. Furthermore, our scheme is provably forward secure under the Diffie-Hellman intractability assumptions in the random-oracle model.

The remainder of this paper is organized as follows. Section 2 recalls the security model for password-based key exchange. Section 3 presents algorithmic assumptions. Section 4 gives a detailed description of our protocol along with its security proof and some remarks. Finally, conclusion is presented in Section 5.

2 Security Models for Password-Based Key Exchange

A secure password-based key exchange is a key exchange protocol where the parties use their password in order to derive a common session key *sk* that will be used to build secure channels. Loosely speaking, such protocols are said to be secure against *dictionary attacks* if the advantage of an attacker in distinguishing a real session key from a random key is less than $O(n/|\mathcal{D}|) + \epsilon(k)$ where $|\mathcal{D}|$ is the size of the dictionary $\mathcal{D}$, n is the number of active sessions and $\epsilon(k)$ is a negligible function depending on the security parameter k.

In this section, we recall the security model for password-based authenticated key exchange of Bellare et al. [15]. In this paper, we prove our protocol is secure in this model.

2.1 The Security Model

We denote by C and S two parties that can participate in the key exchange protocol. Each of them may have several instances called oracles involved in distinct, possibly concurrent, executions of the protocol. We denote C (resp. S) instances by C^i (resp. S^j), or by U when we consider any user instance. The two parties share a low-entropy secret *pw* which is drawn from a small dictionary $\mathcal{D}$, according to the uniform distribution.

The key exchange algorithm $\mathcal{P}$ is an interactive protocol between C^i and S^j that provides the instances of C and S with a session key *sk*. The interaction between an adversary $\mathcal{A}$ and the protocol participants occurs only via oracle queries, which model the adversary capabilities in a real attack. The types of oracles available to the adversary are as follows:

- $Execute(C^i, S^j)$: This query models passive attacks in which the attacker eavesdrops on honest executions between a client instance C^i and a server instance S^j. The output of this query consists of the messages that were exchanged during the honest execution of the protocol.

- $Send(U^i, m)$: This query models an active attack, in which the adversary may intercept a message and then either modify it, create a new one, or simply forward it to the intended participant. The output of this query is the message that the participant instance U^i would generate upon receipt of message m.
- $Reveal(U^i)$: This query models the misuse of the session key by instance U^i (known-key attacks). If a session key is not defined for instance U^i then return $\perp$. Otherwise, return the session key held by the instance U^i.

2.2 Security Definitions

In order to define a notion of security for the key exchange protocol, we consider an experiment in which the protocol $\mathcal{P}$ is executed in the presence of the adversary $\mathcal{A}$. In this experiment, we first draw a password pw from a dictionary $\mathcal{D}$, provide coin tosses and oracles to $\mathcal{A}$, and then run the adversary, letting it ask any number of queries as described above, in any order.

Forward Security. In order to model the forward secrecy (semantic security) of the session key, we consider an experiment $Experiment^{ake-fs}(\mathcal{A}, \mathcal{P})$, in which two additional oracles are available to the adversary: the $Test(U^i)$ and $Corrupt(U)$: oracle.

- $Test(U^i)$: This query tries to capture the adversary's ability to tell apart a real session key from a random one. In order to answer it, we first flip a (private) coin b and then forward to the adversary either the session key sk held by U^i (i.e., the value that a query $Reveal(U^i)$ would output) if $b = 1$ or a random key of the same size if $b = 0$.
- $Corrupt(U)$: This query returns to the adversary the long-lived key pw_U for participant U. As in [16], we assume the weak corruption model in which the internal states of all instances of that user are not returned to the adversary.

The $Test$-oracle can be queried at most once by the adversary $\mathcal{A}$ and is only available to $\mathcal{A}$ if the attacked instance U^i is FS-Fresh, which is defined to avoid cases in which adversary can trivially break the security of the scheme. In this setting, we say that a session key sk is FS-Fresh if all of the following hold: (1) the instance holding sk has accepted, (2) no $Corrupt$-query has been asked since the beginning of the experiment; and (3) no $Reveal$-query has been asked to the instance holding sk or to its partner (defined according to the session identification). In other words, the adversary can only ask $Test$-queries to instances which had accepted before the $Corrupt$ query is asked. Let **Succ** denote the event in which the adversary successfully guesses the hidden bit b used by $Test$ oracle. The FS-AKE advantage of an adversary $\mathcal{A}$ is then defined as $Adv^{ake-fs}_{\mathcal{P},\mathcal{D}}(\mathcal{A}) = 2Pr[\mathbf{Succ}] - 1$ when passwords are drawn from a dictionary $\mathcal{D}$. The protocol $\mathcal{P}$ is said to be (t, ε)-FS-AKE-secure if $\mathcal{A}$'s advantage is smaller than ε for any adversary $\mathcal{A}$ running with time t. The definition of time-complexity that we use henceforth is the usual one, which includes the maximum of all execution times in the experiments defining the security plus the code size [17].

3 Algorithmic Assumptions

The arithmetic is in a finite cyclic group $G = \langle P \rangle$ of order a k-bit prime number q, where the operation is denoted additively.

A $(t, \varepsilon) - CDH_{P,G}$ attacker, in a finite cyclic group G of prime order q with P as a generator, is a probabilistic machine Δ running in time t such that its success probability $\mathbf{Succ}^{cdh}_{P,G}(\mathcal{A})$, given random elements xP and yP to output xyP, is greater than ε: $\mathbf{Succ}^{cdh}_{P,G}(\mathcal{A}) = Pr[\Delta(xP, yP) = xyP] \geq \varepsilon$. We denote by $\mathbf{Succ}^{cdh}_{P,G}(t)$ the maximal success probability over every adversaries running within time t. The CDH-Assumption states that $\mathbf{Succ}^{cdh}_{P,G}(t) \geq \varepsilon$ for any t/ε not too large.

A $(t, n, \varepsilon) - GDH_{P,G}$ attacker is a $(t, \varepsilon) - CDH_{P,G}$ attacker, with access to an additional oracle: a DDH-oracle, which on any input (xP, yP, zP) answers whether $z = xy \bmod q$. Its number of queries is limited to n. As usual, we denote by $\mathbf{Succ}^{gdh}_{P,G}(n, t)$ the maximal success probability over every adversaries running within time t. The GDH-Assumption states that $\mathbf{Succ}^{gdh}_{P,G}(n, t) \geq \varepsilon$ for any t/ε not too large. More information about the Gap Diffie-Hellman (GDH) problem can be found in [18].

4 Practical PAKE Proposal

In this section, we introduce the practical augmented password-based authenticated key exchange protocol and then prove its forward security based on the hardness of the Gap Diffie-Hellman problem in the random oracle model.

4.1 Description

Our protocol is an augmented password-based authenticated key exchange protocol. In such protocols, one party (commonly referred to as the client) has the password, while the other party (commonly referred to as the server) does not have the password. Instead, the server only has a password verification data derived using a function of the password. It is worthful for practical purposes because even an adversary obtains a password verification data from the server, the adversary still needs to launch offline dictionary attacks for getting the corresponding password.

The protocol runs as Fig.1. shows. Whenever a user C wants to send the encryption of a value xP to a server S, it does so by computing $X^\star = xP - pwQ$, where password pw is assumed to be in Z_q and pw held by the client and $(PW = pwQ, R = pw^{-1}P)$ held by the server. And whenever a server S receives the encryption $X^\star$ and he just needs to decrypt it by computing $xP = X^\star + PW$. In return, the server encrypts $Y = yP$ as $Y^\star = yR$ and sends the encryption to the client. By doing so, only a client who knows exactly pw itself can decrypt it. The session identification is defined as the transcript of the conversation between C and S, and the session key is set to be the hash (random oracle) of the user identities, the session identification, their password and the Diffie-Hellman key. The protocol supports mutual explicit authentication with three rounds. The full description of our protocol is given in Fig.1., where Q is an element in G; H_i for $i = 0, 1, 2 : \mathcal{C} \times \mathcal{S} \times G^4 \rightarrow \{0, 1\}^{l_i}$ is a random oracle; and l is the minimum of l_i for all i.

Public information: $Q \in G =< P >, q = |G|, H_i$
Secret information: $pw \in Z_q, PW = pwQ, R = pw^{-1}P$

Client C		Server S
$accept \leftarrow terminate \leftarrow false$		$accept \leftarrow terminate \leftarrow false$
$x \overset{R}{\longleftarrow} Z_q$		$y \overset{R}{\longleftarrow} Z_q$
$X^\star \leftarrow xP - pwQ$	$\xrightarrow{X^\star,\ C}$	$Y \leftarrow yP, Y^\star \leftarrow yR$ $K_S \leftarrow y(X^\star + PW)$
$Y \leftarrow pwY^\star, K_C \leftarrow xY$	$\xleftarrow{Y^\star,\ \mathrm{Auth}_S,\ S}$	$\mathrm{Auth}_S \leftarrow H_2(C, S, X^\star, Y^\star, Y, K_S)$
$\mathrm{Auth}_S \overset{?}{=} H_2(C, S, X^\star, Y^\star, Y, K_C)$ *if false, terminate* $\leftarrow$ *true;*		
$\mathrm{Auth}_C \leftarrow H_1(C, S, X^\star, Y^\star, Y, K_C)$	$\xrightarrow{\mathrm{Auth}_C}$	$\mathrm{Auth}_C \overset{?}{=} H_1(C, S, X^\star, Y^\star, Y, K_S)$ *if false, terminate* $\leftarrow$ *true;*
$SK_C \leftarrow H_0(C, S, X^\star, Y^\star, Y, K_C)$ $accept \leftarrow terminate \leftarrow true.$		$SK_S \leftarrow H_0(C, S, X^\star, Y^\star, Y, K_S)$ $accept \leftarrow terminate \leftarrow true.$

Fig. 1. The practical password-based authenticated key exchange

Finally, we should point out that Q is an important parameter and should be chosen carefully in such a way that it is computationally difficult for an adversary to find the discrete logarithm of Q with P as the base. Otherwise, the protocol will be insecure.

4.2 Security

As Theorem 1 states, our augmented password-based key authenticated protocol is secure in the random oracle model as long as we believe that the GDH problem is hard in G.

Theorem 1. *Let $\mathcal{D}$ be a uniformly distributed dictionary of size $|\mathcal{D}|$. Let $\mathcal{P}$ describe the augmented password-based authenticated key exchange protocol associated with these primitives as defined in Fig.1.. Then, for any adversary $\mathcal{A}$ within a time bound t, with less than q_s active interactions with the parties (Send-queries) and q_p passive eavesdroppings (Execute-queries), and asking q_h hash queries to any H_i respectively,*

$$Adv_{\mathcal{P},\mathcal{D}}^{ake-fs}(\mathcal{A}) \leq \frac{(q_p + q_s)^2}{q} + \frac{q_h^2}{2^l} + 4\boldsymbol{Succ}_{P,G}^{gdh}(t + 2\tau) + \frac{6q_s}{|\mathcal{D}|} + \frac{4q_s}{2^l},$$

where τ represents the computational time for a scalar multiplication in G.

Proof. Let $\mathcal{A}$ be an adversary against the semantic security of $\mathcal{P}$. The idea is to use $\mathcal{A}$ to build adversaries for each of the underlying primitives in such a way that if $\mathcal{A}$ succeeds in breaking the semantic security of $\mathcal{P}$, then at least one of these adversaries succeeds in breaking the security of an underlying primitive. Our proof consists of a sequence of hybrid experiments, starting with the real attack and ending in an experiment in which the adversary's advantage is 0, and for which we can bound the difference in the adversary's advantage between any two consecutive experiments. In the following experiments $\mathbf{Experiment}_n$, we study the event S_n which occurs if the adversary correctly guesses the bit b involved in the *Test*-query.

$\mathbf{Experiment}_0$**:** This is the real protocol in the random-oracle model. By definition, we have

$$Adv_{\mathcal{P},\mathcal{D}}^{ake-fs}(\mathcal{A}) = 2Pr[S_0] - 1 \tag{1}$$

$\mathbf{Experiment}_1$**:** In this experiment, we simulate the hash oracles H_i but also additional hash functions: $H_i^{'} : \{0,1\}^{\star} \rightarrow \{0,1\}^{l_i}$ (for $i = 0, 1, 2$)that will appear in the $\mathbf{Experiment}_3$ as usual by maintaining hash lists $\wedge_H$ and $\wedge_{H'}$ (see Fig.2). To prove forward security, we maintain one more list $\wedge_{bH}$. We also simulate all the instances, as the real players would do, for the *Send*-queries and for the *Execute*, and *Test*-queries. From this simulation, we easily see that the game is perfectly indistinguishable from the real attack. Thus, we have

$$Pr[S_1] = Pr[S_0] \tag{2}$$

$\mathbf{Experiment}_2$**:** For an easier analysis in the following, we cancel experiments in which some unlikely collisions Coll appear: collisions on the partial transcripts $((C,\ X^{\star}), (S, Y^{\star}))$ and on hash values. Since transcripts involve at least one honest party, and thus the probability are bounded by the birthday paradox:

$$|Pr[S_2] - Pr[S_1]| \leq Pr[\text{Coll}] \leq \frac{(q_p + q_s)^2}{2q} + \frac{q_h^2}{2^{l+1}} \tag{3}$$

$\mathbf{Experiment}_3$**:** In this experiment, we compute $X^{\star}, Y^{\star}$ simply as $X^{\star} = xP, Y^{\star} = yP$ for any two random integers x, y. We also compute the session key sk

For a hash query $H_i(m)$ for which there exists a record (i, m, r) in the list Λ_H, return r. Otherwise the answer r is defined according to the following rule: **Rule H** | Choose an element $r \in \{0,1\}^{l_i}$. One adds the record (i, m, r) to the list Λ_H. If *Corrupt* query has not been made, one also adds the record (i, m, r) to the list Λ_{bH}.
For a hash query $H_i^{'}(m)$ for which there exists a record (i, m, r) in the list $\Lambda_{H'}$, return r.Otherwise the answer r is defined according to the following rule: **Rule H$'$** | Choose an element $r \in \{0,1\}^{l_i}$. One add the record (i, m, r) to the list $\Lambda_{H'}$, and return r.

Fig. 2. Simulation of random oracles H and $H^{'}$

and the authenticator Auth using the private oracles $H_i^{'}$ respectively so that the values sk and Auth are completely independent not only from H_i, but also from pw and thus both K_C and K_S. More specifically, we computes them as follows: $\text{Auth}_S = H_2^{'}(C, S, X^\star, Y^\star)$, $\text{Auth}_C = H_1^{'}(C, S, X^\star, Y^\star)$ and $sk = H_0^{'}(C, S, X^\star, Y^\star)$. Due to it, we do no longer need to compute the values Y, K_C and K_S, and we can postpone choosing the value of the password pw until the *Corrupt* query is asked by the Adversary $\mathcal{A}$.

The experiments **Experiment**$_3$ and **Experiment**$_2$ are indistinguishable unless $\mathcal{A}$ queries the hash function H_i on $(C, S, X^\star, Y^\star, Y, K)$ for any $i = 0, 1, 2$, where $Y^\star = pwY, K = CDH_{P,G}(X^\star + pwQ, Y)$. To avoid the trivial difference between the sessions on which $\mathcal{A}$ uses the password he corrupted to mount an active attack, we make answers from H_i and $H_i^{'}$ for $i = 0, 1, 2$ to be the same for such sessions when they correspond to the same query. To do so, we optimize the technique that used in [13] and use it to change the simulation of random oracles. The optimized method simplifies the security proof and is less prone to error. More specifically, we replace the **Rule H** and **Rule H**$^{'}$ with the following rules:

Rule NH

If a) pw is corrupted ;
b) m is the form of $(C, S, X^\star, Y^\star, pwY^\star, K)$, where $K = CDH_{P,G}(X^\star + pwQ, pwY^\star)$ (checked using the DDH-oracle);
c) no instance accepts the session;
Then set r to $H_i^{'}(C, S, X^\star, Y^\star)$.
Else
Then randomly choose $r \in \{0,1\}^{l_i}$

Rule NH$^{'}$

If a) pw is corrupted ;
b) m is the form of $(C, S, X^\star, Y^\star)$;
c) there is a record $(i, m^{'}, r^{'})$ in the list Λ_H, where $m^{'} = (C, S, X^\star, Y^\star, pwY^\star, K)$ and $K = CDH_{P,G}(X^\star + pwQ, pwY^\star)$ (checked using the DDH- oracle);
Then set r to $r^{'}$.
Else
Then randomly choose $r \in \{0,1\}^{l_i}$

Note we still stimulates the random oracle H_i and $H_i^{'}$ perfectly since we just replaces some random values by other random values. We can safely do so because collisions of partial transcripts have been excluded in **Experiment**$_2$.

The experiments **Experiment**$_3$ and **Experiment**$_2$ are now indistinguishable unless some specific hash queries are asked, denoted by event DiffH. Note the adversary can only ask *Test*-queries to instances which had accepted before the *Corrupt* query is asked. Since both the session key and authenticator are computed with the random oracle $H^{'}$ that is private to the simulator before the corruption, one can remark that the bit b involved in the $Test$-query cannot be guessed by the adversary, better than at random for each attempt.

$$|Pr[S_3] - Pr[S_2]| \leq Pr[\text{DiffH}] \qquad Pr[S_3] = \frac{1}{2} \tag{4}$$

To bound the difference between this experiment and previous, our goal at this point shifts to computing the probability of the event DiffH. We prove that the probability of such an event is negligible in **Experiment**$_4$.

Experiment$_4$**:** In order to evaluate the event DiffH, we introduce a random Diffie-Hellman instance (U, V) in our simulation at this experiment. To do so, we set Q to U and reply with $Y^\star = yV$ for a random $y \in Z_q$ in our simulation. When collisions of partial transcripts have been excluded, the event DiffH can be split in 3 disjoint sub-cases:

- CaseA: Both $X^\star$ and $Y^\star$ have been simulated and there is an element pw such that $(C, S, X^\star, Y^\star, pwY^\star, K)$ is in $\wedge_H$, with $K = CDH_{P,G}(X^\star + PW, pwY^\star) = CDH_{P,G}(xP + pwU, ypwV) = ypw^2 CDH_{P,G}(U, V) + xyV$. As a consequence, one can solve the computational Diffie-Hellman problem $CDH_{P,G}(U, V)$. Thus, we have $Pr[\text{CaseA}] \leq \mathbf{Succ}^{gdh}_{P,G}(q_h, t + 2\tau)$.
- CaseB: $X^\star$ has been simulated, but $Y^\star$ has been produced by the adversary. Due to **Rule NH**$'$, we just need to consider those sessions accepted before the corruption. If Auth$_S$ is the value that comes from some query $H_2(C, S, X^\star, Y^\star, pwY^\star, K)$, it is correct only when pw happens to be the one we choose later. The probability is $1/\mathcal{D}$. If $\mathcal{A}$ just make an attempt at random and succeeds, it will make the difference but the probability is less than $1/2^l$. Since there are at most q_s sessions of this kind, we can upper-bound the probability CaseB happens as follows: $Pr[\text{CaseB}] \leq \frac{q_s}{|\mathcal{D}|} + \frac{q_s}{2^l}$.
- CaseC: $Y^\star$ has been simulated, but $X^\star$ has been produced by the adversary. If the corresponding session is accepted before the corruption, $\mathcal{A}$ may distinguish the two experiments. Otherwise, he can distinguish the two experiments only when he queries $H_1(C, S, X^\star, Y^\star, pwY^\star, K)$ before the corruption, i.e. there is a record for it in the list Λ_{bH}. For the former, we can have the probability is less than $\frac{q_s}{|\mathcal{D}|} + \frac{q_s}{2^l}$ exactly with the same analysis. For the latter, we can show that the probability that there is such a record in the list Λ_{bH} is less than $\frac{q_s}{|\mathcal{D}|} + \mathbf{Succ}^{gdh}_{P,G}(q_h, t + 2\tau)$ by using a technique similar to that used in lemma 2 and 3 in [11]. Thus, we have $Pr[\text{CaseC}] \leq \frac{2q_s}{|\mathcal{D}|} + \frac{q_s}{2^l} + \mathbf{Succ}^{gdh}_{P,G}(q_h, t + 2\tau)$.

As a consequence,

$$Pr[\text{DiffH}] \leq \frac{3q_s}{|\mathcal{D}|} + \frac{2q_s}{2^l} + 2\mathbf{Succ}^{gdh}_{P,G}(q_h, t + 2\tau). \tag{5}$$

Finally, combining all the above equations, one gets the announced result as follows.

$$\begin{aligned} &Adv_{\mathcal{P},\mathcal{D}}^{ftg-ake}(\mathcal{A}) = 2Pr[S_0] - 1 = 2(Pr[S_0] - \tfrac{1}{2}) \\ &= 2(Pr[S_1] - \tfrac{1}{2}) \leq 2(|Pr[S_1] - Pr[S_2]| + |Pr[S_2] - Pr[S_3]|) \\ &\leq \tfrac{(q_p+q_s)^2}{q} + \tfrac{q_h^2}{2^l} + 4\mathbf{Succ}_{P,G}^{gdh}(t + 2\tau) + \tfrac{6q_s}{|\mathcal{D}|} + \tfrac{4q_s}{2^l}. \end{aligned}$$

□

4.3 Remarks

In this section, we make some remarks on the security proof and the practical protocol.

Firstly, in the security proof, we use a technique similar to that used in lemma 2 and 3 in [11] to evaluate the probability that there is a record for $H_1(C, S, X^\star, Y^\star, pwY^\star, K)$ in the list Λ_{bH}. However, the technique can never used to evaluate Pr[DiffH] directly. The main idea of the technique is to reduce the problem to password guessing. The event DiffH can be due to some query that occurs after the corruption and then $\mathcal{A}$ will have known the correct password. Indeed, we found a gap in the reasoning of the proof given in [13]. The proof implicitly assumed that the event DiffH is only due to queries that occur before the corruption.

Secondly, our protocol is efficient. In one run of the scheme, the server side requires to compute three scalar multiplications and the client side requires four scalar multiplications. Note that we just count the number of scalar multiplication (e.g. xP), which entails the highest computational complexity, and neglect the computational complexity of all other operations, which can be done efficiently. The protocol is even more efficient than some non-augmented PAKE, say, protocol proposed recently in [12] which require four scalar multiplications on each side. When compared the augmented protocol proposed recently in [13], our scheme requires one less scalar multiplications for each side. Our protocol is more efficient than it.

Finally, our scheme is simple. It require no full-domain hash functions onto the represented group G. Such hash functions are difficult to implement directly over some discrete groups in practice, which usually contains an implicit scalar multiplication over G. In that case, the computation cost of it can not be neglected. Besides, our scheme is augmented simply and requires no complex functions for verification. It is a password-only PAKE and assumes only public parameters — i.e., a "common reference string" — which can be "hard-coded" into an implementation of the protocol. The primary advantage in our case is that users need remember only a short password, and no cryptographic key(s) of any kind. Some previous work, say, protocol proposed recently in [12], suffers from the disadvantage that the client must store the server's public key (and if the client will need to authenticate to multiple servers, the client must store multiple public keys); in some sense, this obviates the reason for considering password-based protocols in the first place: namely, human users cannot remember or securely store long, high-entropy keys. Our scheme is considered much more from the practical perspective.

5 Conclusion

We have presented an augmented PAKE protocol which supports mutual explicit authentication with optimal three rounds. The protocol is considered much more from the practical perspective. Furthermore, the scheme is proved forward-secure under the assumptions that the hash function closely behaves like a random oracle and that the GDH problem is difficult.

Acknowledgement. The authors would like to thank anonymous reviewers for their valuable suggestions and comments that highly improve the readability and completeness of the paper. This research was partially supported by the National Science Foundation of the Republic of China (no.60473021).

References

1. Lomas, M., Gong, L., Saltzer, J., Needham, R.: Reducing risks from poorly chosen keys. In: ACM Symposium on Operating System Principles, pp. 14–18 (1989)
2. Bellovin, S.M., Merritt, M.: Encrypted Key Exchange: Password-Based Protocols Secure against Dictionary Attacks. In: Proc. of the Symposium on Security and Privacy, pp. 72–84. IEEE, New York (1992)
3. Bellovin, S.M., Merritt, M.: Augmented Encrypted Key Exchange: A Password-Based Protocol Secure against Dictionary Attacks and Password File Compromise. In: Proc. of the 1st CCS, pp. 244–250. ACM Press, New York (1993)
4. Gong, L.: Optimal authentication protocols resistant to password guessing attacks. In: 8th IEEE Computer Security Foundations Workshop, pp. 24–29 (1995)
5. Jablon, D.: Strong password-only authentication key exchange. ACM Computer Communication Review, ACM SIGCOMM 26(5), 5–20 (1996)
6. Jablon, D.: Extended password key exchange protocols immune to dictionary attack. In: WETICE'97 Workshop on Enterprise Security (1997)
7. Bellare, M., Rogaway, P.: The AuthA protocol for password-based authenticated key exchange. Contributions to IEEE P1363 (2000)
8. Kobara, K., Imai, H.: Pretty-simple password-authenticated key-exchange under standard assumptions. IEICE Transactions E85-A(10), pp. 2229–2237. Also (2002), available at `http://eprint.iacr.org/2003/038/`
9. MacKenzie, P. D.: The PAK suite: Protocols for password-authenticated key exchange. Contributions to IEEE P1363.2 (2002)
10. Bresson, E., Chevassut, O., Pointcheval, D.: Security proofs for an efficient password-based key exchange. In: ACM CCS 03, ACM Press, New York (2003)
11. Bresson, E., Chevassut, O., Pointcheval, D.: New security results on encrypted key exchange. In: Bao, F., Deng, R., Zhou, J. (eds.) Public Key Cryptography – PKC 2004. LNCS, vol. 2947, pp. 145–158. Springer, Heidelberg (2004)
12. Abdalla, M., Pointcheval, D.: Simple Password-Based Encrypted Key Exchange Protocols. In: Menezes, A.J. (ed.) Topics in Cryptology – CT-RSA 2005. LNCS, vol. 3376, pp. 191–208. Springer, Heidelberg (2005)
13. Abdalla, M., Chevassut, O., Pointcheval, D.: One-time verifier-based encrypted key exchange. In: Vaudenay, S. (ed.) Public Key Cryptography - PKC 2005. LNCS, vol. 3386, pp. 47–64. Springer, Heidelberg (2005)

14. Patel, S.: Number theoretic attacks on secure password schemes. In: proceedings of IEEE Security and Privacy, pp. 236–247 (1997)
15. Bellare, M., Pointcheval, D., Rogaway, P.: Authenticated key exchange secure against dictionary attacks. In: Preneel, B. (ed.) Advances in Cryptology - EUROCRYPT 2000. LNCS, vol. 1807, pp. 139–155. Springer, Heidelberg (2000)
16. Bellare, M., Pointcheval, D., Rogaway, P.: Authenticated key exchange secure against dictionary attacks. In: Preneel, B. (ed.) Advances in Cryptology - EUROCRYPT 2000. LNCS, vol. 1807, pp. 139–155. Springer, Heidelberg (2000)
17. Abdalla, M., Bellare, M., Rogaway, P.: The oracle Diffie-Hellman assumptions and an analysis of DHIES. In: Naccache, D. (ed.) Topics in Cryptology - CT-RSA 2001. LNCS, vol. 2020, pp. 143–158. Springer, Heidelberg (2001)
18. Okamoto, T., Pointcheval, D.: The Gap-Problems: a New Class of Problems for the Security of Cryptographic Schemes. In: Kim, K.-c. (ed.) Public Key Cryptography. LNCS, vol. 1992, Springer, Heidelberg (2001)

XTR+: A Provable Security Public Key Cryptosystem*

Zehui Wang[1] and Zhiguo Zhang[2,**]

[1] Department of Scientific Computation and Computer Applications
Sun Yat-sen University, Guangzhou 510275, China
mscwzh@mail.sysu.edu.cn
[2] Department of Computer Science
Sun Yat-sen University, Guangzhou 510275, China
lnszzg@mail.sysu.edu.cn

Abstract. The XTR is a very effective public key cryptosystem based on 3rd order LFSR sequence. But it has parameter corresponding problem and it neglects the Provable Security property and the blind signature scheme. For overcoming these problems in this paper, the XTR is extended with 4-th order LFSR sequence to from a new public key cryptosystem called XTR$^+$. An algorithm for computing the trace elements is proposed, which only depends on a 2×2 recursive matrix instead of 4×4 so that the running time of the algorithm is much shorter than the algorithm for XTR which depends on a 3×3 recursive matrix.Over XTR$^+$ the provable IND-CCA2 secure encryption/decryption protocol, the provable secure digital signature, the provable secure blind signature protocol and zero-knowledge proof protocol are established. Compared with the traditional methods such as ECC, XTR$^+$ is more simple in cipherkey and parameter selections and has more randomcity and faster algorithms. Under the same security requirements, the XTR$^+$ can greatly reduce the overheads in parameter storage and communication and be suitable for bigger plaintext and ciphertext spaces.

Keywords: Public key system, XTR, Trace function, Provable security, IND-CCA2, Blind signature.

1 Introduction

The XTR (Effective and Compact Subgroup Trace Representation) public key system is a new cryptosystem proposed by Lenstra in Crypto 2000 [1]. It achieves $GF(p^6)$ security using $GF(p^2)$ arithmetic, where $GF(p^n)$ is a finite field. The discrete logarithm problem in XTR (XTR-DL) is more secure than in 1024 bit

* This work is partially supported by Guangdong Industrial Technologies Priorities Programme under grant #2006B15401009.
** Corresponding author, his work is partially supported by Guangdong Key Laboratory of Information Security.

Y. Wang, Y. Cheung, and H. Liu (Eds.): CIS 2006, LNAI 4456, pp. 534–544, 2007.

RSA. And the XTR key and parameter selection is easier than ECC. Moreover, a full exponentiation computation using XTR is faster than a full scalar multiplication using ECC[2–3]. So XTR can greatly reduce the data storage, computation and communication overhead compared with others of equivalent security [4–7].

Based on 3-rd order LFSR sequence, XTR system constructs a trace representation of the roots of a cubic polynomial. The computation of trace elements can be done in a 3-rd order iteration based on the fast computation of the n-th power of a 3×3 matrix, which takes $54\lfloor \log_2 n \rfloor$ multiplications modulo p. Other subcomputations are 3-dimension vector manipulations. In [2], some improved methods for XTR key representation and parameter generation are proposed. The computation for the recipient of the key needs to solve a 3rd-degree algebraic equation. In the next section, we will point out that XTR has the parameter corresponding problem. And both provable security and the blind signature are not considered in XTR.

For solving this problem, we extended the XTR and put forward a new public key system called XTR$^+$ based on the Effective and Compact Subgroup Trace Representation. It holds the advantages of XTR. Besides, its computation overhead is less than that of XTR. XTR$^+$ achieves $GF(p^8)$ security using a $GF(p^4)$ arithmetic, so that the data storage is a half reduced. It is based on 4-th order LFSR sequence to represent the trace function of the roots of a 4-th degree polynomial. The computation of the trace elements is done by a 2nd order (not 4-th order) iteration based on the fast computation of the nth power of a 2×2 matrix. The computation takes only $16\lfloor \log_2 n \rfloor$ multiplications modulo p and the other subcomputations are just 2-dimension vector manipulations. The computation for recovering the public key needs only to solve a simple 2nd-degree algebraic equation.

In addition, XTR$^+$ is constructed as a cryptosystem of provable IND-CCA2 security and can be used for the strongly provable secure digital signature scheme, blind signature protocol and zero-knowledge proof protocol. The provable security and the blind signature are not considered in XTR. Due to its optimization over the parameters, the expansion rate of cryptograph and signature information in XTR$^+$ is largely decreased compared with some important IND-CCA2 secure systems and provable secure signature schemes in which the extra expansions of those information are needed to guarantee the semantically provable formal securities. Thus, we can conclude that XTR$^+$ has more potential than XTR.

2 Parameter Corresponding Problem in XTR

Let $\mathbb{Z}$ denote the set of integers and $\mathbb{N}$ the set of natural numbers respectively. Let $m, n \in \mathbb{N}$, $\mathbb{Z}_n = \{0, 1, \ldots, n-1\}$, and p be a prime number, then $GF(p^m)$ is a finite field, $GF(p^m)[x]$ is a polynomial ring whose coefficients are in $GF(p^m)$, while $GF(p^m)^*$ is a multiplicative group of the finite field $GF(p^m)$. The value of (mod p) is in $\mathbb{Z}_p$. $\#S$ denotes the number of the element in the finite set S. The general idea of XTR proposed by Lenstra et al is as follows:

Let $p \equiv 2 \pmod 3$ be a prime number. And $p^2 - p + 1$ has a prime factor q, the order of $g \in GF(p^6)^*$ is q . $Tr(g) \in GF(p^2)$ is g's trace. Given $Tr(g)$, the subgroup $< g >$ of order q produced by g is called XTR group. Let $c = Tr(g)$, polynominal $F(c, X) = X^3 - cX^2 + c^p X - 1 \in GF(p^2)[X]$. Define $c_n = {h_0}^n + {h_1}^n + {h_2}^n = Tr(g^n)$, where n is a integer, h_0, h_1, h_2 are roots of $F(c, X)$, and $c = c_1$. The security of XTR system is built on the hardness of XDL. That is, the computation of n given $c = Tr(g) \in GF(p^2), c_n = Tr(g^n)$ is not an effective computation. So the encryption and digital signature can be done by publishing p, q, c and choosing n as the private key and getting $S_n(c) = (c_{n-1}, c_n, c_{n+1})$ as the public key.

The algorithm 3.1, 5.2 and 5.5 proposed in [2] provide the formulas to determine the three roots h_0, h_1, h of $F(c, X)$ given c, to get c_{k-1} given c, c_k, c_{k+1}, and to get c_{k+1} given c, c_k, c_{k-1}. This leads to a solution of only storing c_k for public key information $S_k(c)$. This scheme can save 1/3's data to be transmitted, but it must assumes that $c_{k+1} = Tr(g^{k+1})$ is the minimum of the 3 traces $Tr(g^{k+1})$, $Tr(g^{kp^2+1})$, $Tr(g^{kp^4+1})$. This is a very critical assumption which has not been carefully treated in the Lenstra algorithm because this assumption may be effective to digital signature but not to the blend signatures.

Why the blind signature is hard to XTR? In XTR compliant cryptographic protocol, the private key x is hidden, the public key $y = c_x = Tr(g^x)$ is published, and $r = c_s = Tr(g^s)$ is published with s being randomly selected. The protocol verification is done by computing $Tr(g^{us+vx})$. For blind signature, the more computation on $Tr(g^{\alpha(us+vx)+\beta})$ with s, x being hidden is needed. The condition that $c_{s+1} = Tr(g^{s+1})$ is the minimum in $\{Tr(g^{s+1}), Tr(g^{sp^2+1}), Tr(g^{sp^4+1})\}$ and $c_{us+1} = Tr(g^{us+1})$ is the minimum in $\{Tr(g^{us+1}), Tr(g^{usp^2+1}), Tr(g^{usp^4+1})\}$ must be satisfied to make the computation of $Tr(g^{us+vx})$ successful. In the case of s being hidden, we have to compute the 3 roots of $F(c_{us}, X)$ once again to verify this condition. The similar computations must be done twice in the case of x being hidden. Even though, we still cannot ensure that $c_{i+1} = Tr(g^{i+1})$ is the minimum of 3 traces $Tr(g^{i+1}), Tr(g^{ip^2+1}), Tr(g^{ip^4+1})$ where $i = us + vx$. That is, the computation of $c_{\alpha(us+vx)} = Tr(g^{\alpha(us+vx)})$ cannot be done easily. It gets more difficulty to compute $Tr(g^{\alpha(us+vx)+\beta})$.

If there is not rigorous restriction, the XTR compliant protocols may have this parameter corresponding problem and the verification of the protocols may lead to be ambiguous. And continuous computing the roots of 3rd order algebraic equations in XTR consumes computation time and depresses the advantages of XTR.

3 The XTR$^+$ Public Key System

3.1 Basic Assumptions of the XTR$^+$ Parameters

Definition 1. Suppose p is a big prime number, $p^4 + 1$ has a big prime factor q, an optimal polynomial normal basis can be defined as following

$$GF(p^8) = \{\sum_{i=0}^{7} a_i * z^{i-1} | a_i \in \mathbb{Z}_p, i = 0, \dots, 7\}. \quad (1)$$

An ordinal relation (the dictionary ordering) can been defined in $GF(p^8)$. For any $a = \sum_{i=0}^{7} a_i * z^{i-1}$, $b = \sum_{i=0}^{7} b_i * z^{i-1} \in GF(p^8)$, we define $a < b$ if $a_i = b_i, i = 1, \ldots, k-1$, and $a_k < b_k$. If $a < b$ then we define $b > a$. Let g be an element in $GF(p^8)^*$ of the order q and $g < g^{-1}$, where g^{-1} is the multiplication inverse element of g.

Definition 2. We define the trace function $Te : GF(p^8)^* \rightarrow GF(p^4)$ as the following

$$Te(g^n) = g^n + g^{np^4}. \tag{2}$$

where $n \in \mathbb{Z}$, and we denote

$$d_n = Te(g^n), d = d_1, S_n(d) = (d_n, d_{n+1}). \tag{3}$$

We define 4-th power polynomial $F(d, X) = X^4 - \sigma_1 X^3 + \sigma_2 X^2 - \sigma_1 X + 1$, where $\sigma_1 = d + d^{p^2}, \sigma_2 = d^{1+p^2} + 2$.

Proposition 1. The roots of $F(d, X)$ are $h_1 = g, h_2 = g^{p^2}, h_3 = g^{p^4} = g^{-1}, h_4 = g^{p^6} = g^{-p^2}$.

Proof. The eigenvalue of an arbitrary finite field $GF(p^n)$ is a prime number p. By field theory $\forall a, b \in GF(p^n), \forall k \in \mathbb{N}$, the following holds.

$$(a + b)^{p^k} = a^{p^k} + b^{p^k}.$$

$\because g^q = 1, q|(p^4 + 1)$,
$\therefore g^{p^4+1} = 1,\ h_3 = g^{p^4} = g^{-1} = h_1^{-1},\ h_4 = g^{-p^2} = h_2^{-1} \Rightarrow h_3^{-1} = h_1,\ h_4^{-1} = h_2$.
$\therefore d = g + g^{-1},\ \sum_{i=1}^{4} h_i = g + g^{-1} + g^{p^2} + g^{-p^2} = (g + g^{-1}) + (g + g^{-1})^{p^2} = d + d^{p^2}$. $\prod_{i=1}^{4} h_i = gg^{-1}g^{p^2}g^{-p^2} = 1$. $\sum_{1 \leqslant i<j<k \leqslant 4} h_i h_j h_k = \sum_{i=1}^{4} h_i^{-1} = d + d^{p^2}$. $\sum_{1 \leqslant i<j \leqslant 4} h_i h_j = \cdots = (g + g^{-1})(g^{p^2} + g^{-p^2}) + 2 = d \times d^{p^2} + 2 = d^{1+p^2} + 2$.
The roots of $F(d, X)$ can be determined by Viète Theorem as $h_1 = g, h_2 = g^{p^2}$, $h_3 = g^{p^4}$, $h_4 = g^{p^6}$. □

Because of $g \in GF(p^8)^*$, $g^{p^8} = g$, $d^{p^4} = g^{p^4} + g^{p^8} = d$, further $d \in GF(p^4)$, $F(d, X) \in GF(p^4)[X]$. From g, we can generate the cyclic group $< g >$ of the order q, We call it XTR^+ group. The generation of g is far easier than that of RSA and ECC. For any $a \in GF(p^8), a \neq 0$, let $L = (p^4+1)/q$. It is easy to prove that the order of $a^{(p^4-1)L}$ is a prime q, then we obtain $g = a^{(p^4-1)L}$.

Just as the XTR system, the security of the XTR$^+$ system is based on the hardness of solving the Trace Discrete Logarithm (XDL) problem. More precisely, once known $d = Te(g) \in GF(p^4)^*$, $d_n = Te(g^n)$, the computation of n is not effective. In this way, we can use $d_n = Te(g^n)$ or $S_n(d)$ as the public key, n as the private key, and with p, q, d being published in the encryption and the digital signature.

Proposition 2. For $\forall n \in \mathbb{Z}_q^*$, $g^n \neq g^{-n}$ must holds. And one of $\#\{n|g^n < g^{-n}, n \in \mathbb{Z}_q^*\}$ and $\#\{n|g^n \geqslant g^{-n}, n \in \mathbb{Z}_q^*\}$ must be greater than $(q-1)/2$.

Proof. If $g^n = g^{-n}$, then $g^{2n} = 1, q|(2n), q|n$. This leads to a contradiction. Because $\#\{n|g^n < g^{-n}, n \in \mathbb{Z}_q^*\} + \#\{n|g^n \geqslant g^{-n}, n \in \mathbb{Z}_q^*\} = \#\mathbb{Z}_q^* = (q-1)$, one of them must not be less than $(q-1)/2$. □

According to Proposition 2, let $\#\{n|g^n < g^{-n}, n \in \mathbb{Z}_q^*\} \geqslant (q-1)/2$, for any n in $\mathbb{Z}_q^*$, the probability of the validity of the following inequation must not be less than 1/2.

$$g^n < g^{-n}. \tag{4}$$

3.2 Basic Properties and Pivotal Algorithms

Theorem 1. For $\forall n \in \mathbb{Z}$,d_n, the following hold.

1. $d_n = Te(g^n) = g^n + g^{-n} = d_{-n}$.
2. $d_{u+v} + d_{u-v} = d_u * d_v$, or $Te(g^{u+v}) + Te(g^{u-v}) = Te(g^u) * Te(g^v), u, v \in \mathbb{Z}$.
3. The trace function satisfies the 2nd order iteration

$$d_{n+1} = d * d_n - d_{n-1}, \tag{5}$$

   that is, $Te(g^{n+1}) = d * Te(g^n) - Te(g^{n-1})$

4. Let $A = \begin{pmatrix} 0 & -1 \\ 1 & d \end{pmatrix}, Q_n = \begin{pmatrix} d_{n-1} & d_n \\ d_n & d_{n+1} \end{pmatrix}$, $n \in \mathbb{N}$, then Q_0 is reversible and the following hold

$$Q_n = Q_0 * A^n, A^n = (Q_0)^{-1} * Q_n. \tag{6}$$

$$Q_{n+m} = Q_m * (A^n), Q_{nm} = Q_0 * (A^n)^m; m \in \mathbb{N}. \tag{7}$$

$$C(A^n) = Q_0^{-1} * S_n(d)^T, d_{n+m} = S_m(d) * C(A^n). \tag{8}$$

$$d_n = (2, d) * C(A^n). \tag{9}$$

   $C(B)$ represents the 2nd column of the 2nd order matrix B.

Proof. 1. $g^{p^4} = g^{-1}, \therefore Te(g^n) = g^n + (g^{p^4})^n = g^n + g^{-n} = d_{-n}$.

2. $d_u * d_v = (g^u + g^{-u}) * (g^v + g^{-v}) = g^{u+v} + g^{u-v} + g^{-(u-v)} + g^{-u-v} = d_{u+v} + d_{u-v}$.

3. Let $u = n, v = 1$, then $d_{n+1} + d_{n-1} = d_n * d_1 = d * d_n$. So (5) holds.

4. $\because g \neq g^{-1}, \therefore det(Q_0) = d^2 - 4 = (g - g^{-1})^2 \neq 0$. So Q_0 is reversible.
$\because \begin{pmatrix} d_{n-2} & d_{n-1} \\ d_{n-1} & d_n \end{pmatrix} \begin{pmatrix} 0 & -1 \\ 1 & d \end{pmatrix} = \begin{pmatrix} d_{n-1} & dd_{n-1} - d_{n-2} \\ d_n & dd_n - d_{n-1} \end{pmatrix} = \begin{pmatrix} d_{n-1} & d_n \\ d_n & d_{n+1} \end{pmatrix}$.
$\therefore Q_n = Q_{n-1}A = \cdots = Q_0 A^n$, then (6) holds. Let A^n be divided into blocks $A^n = (\lambda_1 \quad \lambda_2), \lambda_2 = C(A^n)$, $\therefore Q_0 A^n = Q_0(\lambda_1 \quad \lambda_2) = (Q_0\lambda_1 \quad Q_0\lambda_2) = Q_n = (S_{n-1}(d)^T \quad S_n(d)^T)$, $\therefore S_n(d)^T = Q_0 C(A^n)$. In the same way we obtain $Q_{m+n} = Q_m A^n = (Q_m\lambda_1 \quad Q_m\lambda_2)$, $\therefore S_{m+n}(d)^T = Q_m C(A^n)$, i.e. $\begin{pmatrix} d_{m+n-1} \\ d_{m+n} \end{pmatrix} = \begin{pmatrix} S_{n-1}(d) \\ S_n(d) \end{pmatrix} C(A^n)$. $\therefore d_{m+n} = S_m(d)C(A^n)$. Let $m = 0$, we obtain (9). □

In the case of $d = g + g^{-1}$ being published, according to Viète Theorem, solving the quadratic equation $y^2 - dy + 1 = 0$ will let us get two roots $\{g, g^{-1}\}$. We can decide which is g or g^{-1} according to the assumption $g < g^{-1}$. The XTR system only publishes d, d_n, but not g, g^n, nevertheless it offers the algorithm to solve g, g^n. That is, publishing g, g^n will not affect the security of the XTR system. We make g, g^{-1} public and this will also not affect the security of XTR+.

In order to obtain the trace function, the square-and-multiply fast algorithm is modified to compute the positive integer power B^n of k-th order B.

Matrix Square-and-Multiply Fast Algorithm.

$G \leftarrow B$, if $L_0 = 0$ then $H \leftarrow I$ else $H \leftarrow B$
  $for j \leftarrow 1$ to s do
    $\{G \leftarrow G \times G (mod \quad p)$
    if $L_j = 1$ then $H \leftarrow H \times G (mod \quad p)\}$

Proposition 3. If B is a k-th order matrix, the Matrix Square-and-Multiply Fast Algorithm takes at most $2 \times k^3 \times s = 2 \times k^3 \times \lfloor \log_2 n \rfloor$ multiplications modulo p to obtain $H = B^n$.

Algorithm 1. Input: a 2×2 matrix B, a positive integer n; Output: the B^n.
To call the matrix square-and-multiply algorithm with k=2.

Algorithm 2. Input: g, g^{-1}; Output: a random number $n \in \mathbb{Z}_q^*$ which satisfies (4) and $d_n = Te(g^n)$.

1. Randomly choose $n \in \mathbb{Z}_q^*, n \neq 1$, call the matrix square-and-multiply algorithm to obtain g^n, g^{-n}.
2. If they do not satisfy (4), then turn to step 1, otherwise turn to step 3.
3. Compute $d_n = Te(g^n) = g^n + g^{-n}$, and output n, d_n.

Algorithm 3. Input: n, d; Output: $d_n = Te(g^n)$.
Compute A^n by calling Algorithm 1 , then obtain d_n according to (9).

Algorithm 4. Input: g, g^{-1}, d_n (n satisfies (4) and n is unknown); Output: $g^n, g^{-n}, S_n(d)$.

1. Solve the quadratic equation $y^2 - d_n y + 1 = 0$ to get two roots y_1, y_2.
2. If $y_1 > y_2$, swap y_1, y_2.
3. $g^n = y_1, g^{-n} = y_2$; $d_{n+1} = g * y_1 + g^{-1} * y_2$; $S_n(d) = (d_n, d_{n+1})$.

Algorithm 5. Input: $g, g^{-1}, d_n, d_m (n, m$ satisfy (4), n, m are unknown); Output: d_{n+m}.

1. Get $S_n(d), S_m(d)$ by calling Algorithm 4.
2. Get $C(A^n)$ using the left part of (8), get d_{m+n} using the right part of (8).

Algorithm 6. Input: $g, g^{-1}, m, d_n (n$ satisfy (4), n is unknown); Output: d_{mn}.

1. Append $d_{n-1} = g^{-1} * y_1 + g * y_2$ to Algorithm 4 , we get $S_n(d)$ and Q_n.
2. Get $B = A^n$ by the right part of (6), then get $B^m = A^{mn}$ by Algorithm 1.
3. Get d_{mn} by (9).

4 A Cryptosystem of Provable Security

Because of the decreasing in data storage and computation overhead, XTR$^+$ system can be widely used in digital signature and identification in the conditions that the resources are limited. XTR$^+$ can be used in encryption and decryption as well to make it a provable IND-CCA2 secure cryptographic protocol. The following security definition comes from Rackoff and Simon in [8].

Definition 3. Given a public key cryptosystem, if it is indistinguishable against adaptive chosen ciphertext attack within its computational capacity, or in other words, given two plain text messages *M1* and *M2* of the same length and one of their ciphertext *C*, the adversary is able to get plain text decrypted from any chosen ciphertext (different from target ciphertext *C*). But he still cannot judge whether *C* is encrypted from *M1* or *M2*, then the public key cryptosystem is said to be secure under indistinguishability against adaptive chosen ciphertext attack, or simply to be IND-CCA2 secure.

Let p, q, g, g^{-1} be public parameters, x be a random number as a private key generated by the algorithm 2 , $y = Te(g^x)$ be public key. We choose a symmetry encryption algorithm (e.g. AES) with the ciphertext, encryption and decryption transformations being $k_1 \in \{0,1\}^{b_1}, \mathcal{E}, \mathcal{D}$ respectively. And we choose a message authentication code algorithm (for example HMAC), marked as MAC, with the ciphertext being $k_2 \in \{0,1\}^{b_2}$. Let l be the length of the bit stream of q, $KDF_1 : \{0,1\}^l \to \{0,1\}^l \times \{0,1\}^{b_1} \times \{0,1\}^{b_2}$ is a derived function from a cipherkey linked up with hash functions, and $KDF_2 : GF(p) \times GF(p) \to \{0,1\}^l$ is a derived function from another cipherkey. Then we have the following encryption and decryption protocols.

Encryption Protocol. Input: parameters (p, q, g, g^{-1}),public key y, plain text M. Output: ciphertext (r, C, u, v).

1. Choose a random number $w \in \{0,1\}^l$, compute $KDF_1(w) \to (k_0, k_1, k_2)$.
2. Compute $s = k_0^3 \pmod q), g^s, g^{-s}$. If it doesn't satisfy (4), go to (1), otherwise go to (3).
3. Compute $r = d_s$, generate d_{sx} by using public key y and the algorithm 6, calculate $u = w \oplus KDF_2(d_s, d_{sx})$.
4. Compute $C = \mathcal{E}_{k_1}(M), v = MAC_{k_2}(C)$, return (r, C, u, v).

Decryption Protocol. Input: parameters (p, q, g, g^{-1}), private key x, ciphertext (r, C, u, v). Output: plain text M or "reject this ciphertext".

1. Generate d_{sx} by calling the algorithm 6 with $r = d_s = Te(g^s)$ and private key x, calculate $w = u \oplus KDF_2(d_s, d_{sx})$.
2. Compute $KDF_1(w) \rightarrow (k_0, k_1, k_2)$,$s' = k_0^3 \pmod p$.
3. Compute $r' = Te(g^{s'})$ by calling the algorithm 3, if $r' \neq r$, return "reject this ciphertext".
4. Compute $v' = MAC_{k_2}(C)$, if $v' \neq v$, return "reject this ciphertext" .
5. Compute $M = \mathcal{D}_{k_1}(C)$, return M.

A public key cryptosystem described as the above encryption and decryption protocols is called the XTR$^+$ cryptosystem.

Proposition 4. If the symmetry encryption algorithm and the message authentication code algorithm MAC are secure, then the computation of Diffie-Hellman problem is not effective in XTR$^+$. If KDF_1, KDF_2 are stochastic functions, then the above encryption and decryption protocol is logically consistent in XTR$^+$. Furthermore, XTR$^+$ public key cryptosystem is of the provable security. (According to definition 3).

Proof. If (r, C, u, v) is really generated by plain text M which is encrypted by a legal encryptor, then $Te((g^s)^x) = Te((g^{sx}) = Te((g^x)^s)$. call algorithm 6 to compute $Te(g^{sx}) = d_{sx}$ given r, x, y, s. Practically, this step is the same as Diffie-Hellman key exchange protocol. In this way, the decryptor and encrypter obtain the same key (k_0, k_1, k_2) and the plain text M. Whereas, if (r, C, u, v) is the spurious ciphertext that is not generated by plaintext M through the encryption protocol, the Diffie-Hellman problem is inapprehensible, and return "reject this plain text" since $r' \neq r$. Also, because of the security of message authentication code arithmetic MAC and $v' \neq v$, it returns " reject this plain text". That is to say, it cannot decrypt the right plain text. Taking the similar method mentioned in [9], it can be proved that XTR$^+$ key system is provable secure. □

5 The Provable Secure Signature Scheme on XTR$^+$

The same as the above, we suppose $p, q, d = Te(g), y = Te(g^x)$ are public keys, x is a private key stored by Bob, and Alice has the original message $M \in GF(p^8)$ and want it to be signed by Bob. We also let $SHA : GF(p^8) \times GF(p^4) \rightarrow \mathbb{Z}_q^*$ be a collision resistant secure hash function. Then we describe the signature scheme as following.

1. Bob selects a random number s by using algorithm 2, computes $r = Te(g^s)$ and transfers it to Alice.
2. When Alice receives it, she computes $SHA(M, r)$ firstly, selects a small integer η, and let $\alpha = SHA(M, r) + \eta$, then she can get the value of $g^{\alpha x}$ by calling algorithm 4. The effect of η is to make g^n satisfy (4), n represent αx.

3. Alice selects β, she gets the value of $g^{\beta s}$ using algorithm 4 given β and r, βs is exponential and make g^n satisfy (4), and then transfers α, β to Bob.
4. When Bob receives them, he computes $\delta = (\alpha x + \beta s) \pmod{q}$ and transfers it to Alice. So Alice gets the signature (r, δ) of Bob .
5. Alice uses arithmetic 6 to compute $Te(g^{\alpha x})$, $Te(g^{\beta s})$, then uses algorithm 5 to compute $Te(g^{\alpha x + \beta s})$.
6. If $Te(g^{\delta}) = Te(g^{\alpha x + \beta s})$, then has been verified the validity of the signature, it otherwise will be refused.

Proposition 5. The above scheme is a digital signature scheme of the provable security. When is q close to p^2, the signature data ratio of this scheme to the original one is about 3/8.

Proof. The above scheme is a triple ElGamal signature scheme. It is easy to prove that the above scheme is of a strongly provable security by using the branching reduction technology based on ROM. For $M \in GF(p^8)$, $r \in GF(p^4)$, the bit number of δ is close to p^2, so the signature data ratio of this scheme to the general scheme is about $1/2 \times 6/8 = 3/8$. □

6 The Provable Secure Blind Signature Scheme on XTR$^+$

1. Bob selects a random number s using arithmetic 2, computes $\widetilde{r} = Te(g^s)$ and then transfers it to Alice.
2. When Alice receives it, she computes $SHA(M, r)$, selects a small integer η, sets $\alpha = SHA(M, r) + \eta$, by using arithmetic 4 and 6 with α, y, we get the value $g^{\alpha x}, Te(g^{\alpha x})$, so the effect of η is to make g^n satisfy (4) (x is unknown).
3. Alice selects $u \in \mathbb{Z}_q^*, v \in \mathbb{Z}_q$, optionally. By using arithmetic 5 and 6 with $u, v, \widetilde{r}$, we get $g^{us+v}, r = Te(g^{us+v})$, $us + v$ as the exponential n makes g^n satisfy (4). Select any value β, by using arithmetic 4 and 6 with β, r, we get $g^{\beta(us+v)}, Te(g^{\beta(us+v)})$. $\beta(us + v)$ as the exponential n can make g^n satisfy (4) (s is not necessarily to be known).
4. Alice sets $\widetilde{\alpha} = u^{-1} * \alpha \pmod{q}$, $\widetilde{\beta} = \beta$. and transfers $\widetilde{\alpha}, \widetilde{\beta}$ to Bob.
5. When Bob receives them, he computes $\widetilde{\delta} = (\widetilde{\alpha} * x + \widetilde{\beta} * s) \pmod{q}$ and then transfers it to Alice. To Bob, $(\widetilde{r}, \widetilde{\delta})$ is only formal signature, he can't get any valid information about Alice.
6. When Alice receives it, she releases blind factor from formal signature, and computes $\delta = (u * \widetilde{\delta} + v * \widetilde{\beta}) \pmod{q}$, so she gets Bob's real signature (r, δ).
7. Alice computes $w = Te(g^{\delta})$, then using algorithm 6 with $Te(g^{\alpha x})$, $Te(g^{\beta(us+v)})$ which have been worked out, we get $w' = Te(g^{\alpha x} * g^{\beta(us+v)})$. If $w = w'$, has been proved the validity of Bob's real signature, otherwise will be refused the signature.

Proposition 6. The blind signature above is not contradiction formally.

Proof. $\delta = u(\widetilde{\alpha} x + \widetilde{\beta} s) + v\widetilde{\beta} \pmod{q} = u\widetilde{\alpha} x + \beta(us + v) \pmod{q}$
$= \alpha x + \beta(us + v) \pmod{q}$, $\therefore w = Te(g^{\delta}) = Te(g^{\alpha x} * g^{\beta(us+v)}) = w'$. □

In this and the previous section, the value β has many selections. We can let $\widetilde{\beta} \neq \beta$. The different values can be used to design different provable secure blind signature schemes and other protocols.

7 Zero-Knowledge Proof on XTR$^+$

Let p, q, g, Te be the same as the above, a trustful certification agency CA assigns Alice a certification of four-tuple (p, q, g, y), where $y = Te(g^{-x})$, x is the private key of Alice. By the following protocol, without exposing x, Alice can prove to Bob that he has a certification as a trace discrete logarithm of y with a base g.

1. Alice chooses $n \in \mathbb{Z}_q^*$ such that $r = Te(g^n)$ satisfies (4), then sends r to Bob.
2. Bob chooses $k \in \{0, 1\}^{log_2 log_2 p}$.
3. Bob computes g^{-kx} with k, y and algorithm 4. If not satisfying (4), then turns to 2; otherwise sends k to Alice.
4. Alice computes $m = n + kx (mod q)$, then sends m to Bob.
5. By sending the parameters m, k, y to algorithm 5 and 6, Bob can compute $w' = Te(g^{m-kx}) = Te(g^m * y^k)$ and $w = Te(g^n)$. if $w = w'$, then accepts Alice's proof; otherwise rejects and stops the protocol.

8 Computation Time Comparison with XTR

For having the ordinal relation defined in definition 1 and the inequation in (5), we can get a much faster algorithm and will never have the parameter corresponding problem in XTR$^+$.

In addition, notice that one plaintext (ciphertext) in $GF(p^4)$ corresponds to two plaintext (ciphertext) in $GF(p^2)$. And the algorithm for computing the trace function in XTR is based on the fast computation of A^n given n, where A is a 3×3 matrix. It takes $2 \times 3^3 \times \lfloor \log_2 n \rfloor = 54 \lfloor \log_2 n \rfloor$ multiplications modulo p according to Proposition 3. Compared with this time complexity, XTR$^+$ takes $2 \times 2^3 \times \lfloor \log_2 n \rfloor = 16 \lfloor \log_2 n \rfloor$ multiplications modulo p which is much less than that in XTR. For other computations, XTR needs to process three dimension vectors while XTR$^+$ needs to do two only. The recovering of $S_n(d)$ given d_n needs to solve a 2nd order equation in XTR$^+$ but a 3rd order equation in XTR. All these show that XTR$^+$ takes less time than XTR.

9 Conclusion

Maintaining the same security level as XTR, the XTR$^+$ public key system can effectively reduce the amount of the data storage, the computation and communication overheads. In addition, it is a security provable IND-CCA2 cryptosystem. Based on the fast algorithm of XTR$^+$, we propose provable secure digital signature protocol, blind signature protocol and zero-knowledge proof protocol, and show that these cryptographic protocols can be more effectively used for security requirements in many cases such as the resource limited environment.

References

1. Lenstra, A.K., Verheul, E.R.: The XTR public system. In: Bellare, M. (ed.) Advances in Cryptology - CRYPTO 2000. LNCS, vol. 1880, pp. 1–19. Springer, Heidelberg (2000)
2. Lenstra, A.K., Verheul, E.R.: Key improvements to XTR. In: Okamoto, T. (ed.) Advances in Cryptology - ASIACRYPT 2000. LNCS, vol. 1976, pp. 220–233. Springer, Heidelberg (2000)
3. Avanzi, R.M.: The Complexity of Certain Multi-Exponentiation Techniques in Cryptography. J. Cryptology 18, 357–373 (2005)
4. Chen, X., Wang, Y.: Asurvey of public key cryptography. Journal of China institute of communications 25(8), 109–118 (2004)(in Chinese)
5. Verheul, E.R.: Evidence that XTR Is More Secure than Supersingular Elliptic Curve Cryptosystems. J. Cryptology 17(4), 277–296 (2004)
6. Martijn, S., Lenstra, A.K.: Speeding Up XTR. In: Boyd, C. (ed.) Advances in Cryptology - ASIACRYPT 2001. LNCS, vol. 2248, Springer, Heidelberg (2001)
7. Peeters, E., Neve, M., Ciet, M.: XTR implementation on reconfigurable hardware. In: Joye, M., Quisquater, J.-J. (eds.) Cryptographic Hardware and Embedded Systems - CHES 2004. LNCS, vol. 3156, pp. 386–399. Springer, Heidelberg (2004)
8. Rackoff, C., Simon, D.: Non-interactive zero-knowledge proof of knowledge and chosen ciphertext attack. In: Feigenbaum, J. (ed.) Advances in Cryptology - CRYPTO '91. LNCS, vol. 576, pp. 443–444. Springer, Heidelberg (1992)
9. ISO/IEC 18033-2:2006. Information Technology - Security Techniques - Encryption Algorithms - Part 2: Asymmetrc Ciphers (2006)

Proxy Ring Signature: Formal Definitions, Efficient Construction and New Variant

Jin Li[1], Xiaofeng Chen[2], Tsz Hon Yuen[3], and Yanming Wang[1,4]

[1] School of Mathematics and Computational Science
Sun Yat-Sen University
Guangzhou, 510275, China
sysjinli@hotmail.com
[2] Department of computer Science
Sun Yat-Sen University
Guangzhou, 510275, China
isschxf@mail.sysu.edu.cn
[3] Department of Information Engineering
Chinese University of Hong Kong
Shatin, N.T., Hong Kong
[4] Lingnan College, Sun Yat-Sen University
Guangzhou, 510275, China
stswym@mail.sysu.edu.cn

Abstract. Proxy ring signatures allows proxy signer to sign messages on behalf of the original signer while providing anonymity. In this paper, we give the first formal security definitions and notions of proxy ring signatures. Subsequently, we propose a short proxy ring signature scheme, with rigorous security proofs. It is more efficient than the existing proxy ring signature schemes. Finally, we propose a new kind of proxy ring signatures. Existing proxy ring signatures in the literature provide anonymity for proxy signer only. We extend the notion to support anonymity for original signer as well. We give an efficient and secure instantiation of it.

1 Introduction

Ring signatures [8] allow user to sign messages on behalf of a "ring" of possible signers, without revealing the signer's identity. Different from a group signature scheme (for examples, [3]), the group formation is spontaneous and there is no group manager to revoke the identity of the signer. Therefore under the assumption that each user is already associated with a public key, a user can form a group by simply collecting the public keys of all the "ring" members including his own. These diversion members can be totally unaware of being conscripted into the group. Ring signature schemes could be used for whistle blowing [8], and anonymous membership authentication [4] to keep the anonymity of the signer and can be publicly verifiable.

A proxy signature protocol allows an entity, called original signer, to delegate its signing power to another entity, called proxy signer, to sign messages on its

Y. Wang, Y. Cheung, and H. Liu (Eds.): CIS 2006, LNAI 4456, pp. 545–555, 2007.

behalf. The delegated proxy signer can compute a proxy signature that can be verified by anyone with access to the original signer's public key. Proxy signatures have many practical applications such as in distributed system etc. [2,8] and are an important cryptographic protocol.

Proxy ring signatures [10] are designated for the following situation: An entity delegates his signing capability to many proxies, called proxy signers group. Any proxy signer can perform the signing operation on behalf of the original entity. If these proxy signers want to sign messages on behalf of the original entity while providing anonymity, we can use group signature to solve it (Take the group manger as the original entity). But in some applications, it is necessary to protect the privacy of participants (we believe that unconditional anonymity is necessary in many occasions). If the proxies hope that nobody (include the original signer) can open their identities, the group signature is not suitable for this situation. So, the proxy ring signatures are proposed to solve this problem [10]. On one hand, the proxy ring signature allows the proxy signer generates a proxy ring signature such that any verifier can be sure that the secret is indeed given out by the proxy signer group, on the other hand, nobody can figure out who the proxy signer is.

Consider the other situation: In a set of signers, each of them delegates his signing capability to one proxy signer. The proxy signers can perform the signing operation on behalf of the original entities. If these proxy signers want to sign messages on behalf of the original entities while providing anonymity, we propose the other kind of proxy ring signatures to solve this problem. On one hand, the proxy ring signature allows the proxy signer generates a proxy ring signature such that any verifier can be sure that the secret is indeed given out by the proxy signer group, on the other hand, nobody can figure out whose proxy signer has formed the signature.

1.1 Related Works

Ring signature scheme was first formalized by Rivest, Shamir and Tauman [8]. Subsequently, many practical ring signature schemes [9] and its variants, such as threshold ring signature, Identity-based ring signature, universal designated verifiable ring signature, etc., have been proposed [4,5,7]. The concept of proxy ring signature has been proposed in many works and many proxy ring signature schemes have been proposed [1,10]. However, the formal definition and security model have never been given. Of course, none of the proposed schemes have ever been proved to be secure formally.

1.2 Our Contributions

In this paper, we first present formally the definition and security model for proxy ring signature. Furthermore, we also construct an efficient and provably secure proxy ring signature scheme in the proposed security model. The new proxy ring signature scheme is more efficient than the other proposed schemes to date. Furthermore, we also propose the other kind of proxy ring signature in order to allow different proxy signers on behalf of different original signers to output proxy signature anonymity.

2 Security Model

2.1 Syntax

A proxy ring signature scheme consists of 5-tuple of probabilistic polynomial time (PPT) algorithms (KenGen, D,P, PRS, PRV) defined as follows:

KenGen. The key generation algorithm, on input security parameter 1^k, outputs user's public key pk and corresponding secret key sk.

(D,P) is a pair of interactive algorithms forming the proxy-designation protocol. The input to each algorithm includes two public keys pk_o, pk_i for the designator and the proxy signer i, respectively. D also takes as input the secret key sk_o of the designator, and P also takes as input the secret key sk_i of the proxy signer. As result of the interaction, the expected local output of P is sk_p, a proxy signing key that user i uses to produce proxy signatures on behalf of user pk_o.

PRS. The proxy ring signature generation algorithm, that takes as input a secret key sk_p, a message m, a set of public keys $\mathcal{L}$ including the one that corresponds to the private key sk_p, returns the signature σ.

PRV. The proxy ring signature verification algorithm, takes as input pk_o, $\mathcal{L}$, a message m and σ, returns 1 or 0 for accept or reject, respectively.

Adversary's attack capabilities are modelled by providing it access to certain oracles. We now introduce the oracles we will need and provide the adversary with different subsets of this set of oracles.

$\mathcal{PRS}$ Oracle: The proxy ring signing oracle, on input message m, pk_o, $\mathcal{L}$, and sk_p, returns a proxy ring signature $\sigma \leftarrow \mathsf{PRS}(sk_p, pk_o, \mathcal{L}, m)$ such that $\mathsf{PRV}(pk_o, \mathcal{L}, m, \sigma) = 1$.

$\mathcal{KR}$ Oracle: The key registration oracle, on input any key pair (pk, sk), first checks if sk is indeed the secret key of pk. Then it stores (pk, sk) as a valid registered key pair if it is. Otherwise, it rejects and outputs a special symbol $\perp$.

$\mathcal{DE}$ Oracle: The delegation oracle, on input any registered public key pk_i, pk_o, its secret sk_o, returns a delegation on the public key pk_i.

The correctness requires that valid signatures can always be proved valid. So, we present our detailed security notions of unforgeability, and signer ambiguity for proxy ring signatures in the following.

2.2 Unforgeability

There are two types of unforgeability to consider: *Delegation unforgeability* and *proxy ring signature unforgeability*. *Delegation unforgeability* means that even if the adversary asks for polynomial users' delegation, it is still hard to output a forgery delegation that the original signer has not delegated. *Proxy ring signature unforgeability* means that, except the proxy signers, anyone else (even if the origin signer) cannot generate valid proxy ring signature on behalf of these proxy signers.

2.2.1 Delegation Unforgeability

Delegation unforgeability for proxy ring signature is defined as in the following game involving an adversary $\mathcal{A}$.

Let $(pk_o, sk_o) \leftarrow \mathsf{KenGen}(1^k)$. $\mathcal{A}$ is given pk_o and the public parameters. $\mathcal{A}$ accesses to $\mathcal{DE}$ oracle, $\mathcal{KR}$ oracle and $\mathcal{PRS}$ oracle.

The adversary $\mathcal{A}$ wins the game if he can output $(m^*, \mathcal{L}, \sigma^*)$, such that $\mathcal{L}$ includes a public key pk^* that is not equal to any query of $\mathcal{DE}$ oracle and σ^* is a valid proxy ring signature with respect to pk_o and $\mathcal{L}$ on message m^*. The advantage of the adversary is the probability that he wins the game.

Definition 1. *(Delegation Unforgeability) A proxy ring signature scheme is delegation unforgeability secure if no PPT adversary has a non-negligible advantage in the above unforgeability game.*

2.2.2 Proxy Ring Signature Unforgeability

Proxy ring signature unforgeability for proxy ring signature is defined as in the following game involving an adversary $\mathcal{A}$.

Let $(pk_o, sk_o) \leftarrow \mathsf{KenGen}(1^k)$ be the original signer's key pair and $\mathcal{L}=\{pk_1, \cdots, pk_n\}$ be the set of n proxy signers$'$ public keys in which each key is generated as $(pk_i, sk_i) \leftarrow \mathsf{KenGen}(1^k)$. $\mathcal{A}$ is given (pk_o, sk_o) and $\mathcal{L}$. $\mathcal{A}$ accesses to $\mathcal{DE}$ oracle, $\mathcal{KR}$ oracle and $\mathcal{PRS}$ oracle.

The adversary $\mathcal{A}$ wins the game if he can output (L, m^*, σ^*), such that (L, m^*) is not equal to any query of $\mathcal{PRS}$ oracle and σ^* is a valid proxy ring signature with respect pk_o and $\mathcal{L}$ on message m^*. The advantage of the adversary is the probability that he wins the game.

In fact, our security definition for unforgeablility is similar to the unforgeability against fixed-ring attacks as in [6,7]. Meanwhile, from the game, we allow the adversary to have the original singer's secret key, i.e., even if the original signer, it cannot output a forged proxy ring signature without one of secret keys in L.

Definition 2. *(Proxy Ring Signature Unforgeability) A proxy ring signature scheme is proxy ring signature unforgeability secure if no PPT adversary has a non-negligible advantage in the above unforgeability game.*

2.3 Signer Ambiguity

In proxy ring signatures, signer ambiguity means that it is hard to tell which proxy signer out of the n possible proxy signers who actually generates a proxy ring signature. Signer ambiguity is defined as the following game between a challenger and an adversary $\mathcal{A}$:

Let $\mathcal{L} = \{pk_1, \cdots, pk_n\}$ be the set of n proxy signers$'$ public keys in which each key is generated as $(pk_i, sk_i) \leftarrow \mathsf{KenGen}(1^k)$. Meanwhile, $(pk_o, sk_o) \leftarrow$

$\mathsf{KenGen}(1^k)$ is also generated. (pk_i, sk_i), (pk_o, sk_o) are provided to adversary. The challenger picks a random $1 \leq t \leq n$, outputs a valid ring signature $\sigma \leftarrow \mathsf{PRS}(sk_t, pk_o\ \mathcal{L}, m)$ such that $\mathsf{PRV}\ (pk_o, \mathcal{L}, m, \sigma) = 1$. Any unbounded adversary accepts as inputs σ.

The adversary wins the game if he can output t' such that $t' = t$ who signs the signature. The advantage of the adversary is the probability that he wins the game, over $\frac{1}{n}$, that he can guess t accurately.

Definition 3. *(Signer Ambiguity) A proxy ring signature scheme is said to be unconditionally signer ambiguous if any unbound adversary has a negligible advantage in the above signer ambiguity game.*

3 A Short Proxy Ring Signature Scheme

3.1 Preliminaries

Before present our results, we review the definitions of groups equipped with a bilinear pairings and a related assumption. Let G be a (multiplicative) cyclic group of prime order p. Let g be a generator of G. We also let $\hat{e}$ be a bilinear map such that $\hat{e} : G \times G \rightarrow G_1$ with the following properties:
Bilinearity: For all $u, v \in G$ and $a, b \in Z$, $\hat{e}(u^a, v^b) = \hat{e}(u, v)^{ab}$.
Non-degeneracy: $\hat{e}(g, g) \neq 1$. *Computability*: There exists an efficient algorithm to compute $\hat{e}(u, v)$.

Definition 4. Computational Diffie-Hellman Problem (CDHP)*: Given g, g^x, $g^y \in (G)^3$ for unknown $x, y \in_R Z_p^*$, compute g^{xy}.*

Definition 5. Computational Diffie-Hellman Assumption*: Given g, g^x, $g^y \in (G)^3$ for unknown $x, y \in_R Z_p^*$, it is hard to compute g^{xy} for any probabilistic polynomial time (PPT) algorithm.*

We introduce the following problem used in [6]:

Definition 6 ((q, n)-DsjSDH). *The (q, n)-Disjunctive Strong Diffie-Hellman Problem in G is defined as follow: Given g, $g^x \in G$, distinct $a_i \in Z_p$ and Universal One-Way Hash Functions (UOWHF) H, distinct nonzero m_τ and $\sigma_{i,\tau}$ for $1 \leq i \leq n$ and $1 \leq \tau \leq q$, satisfying: $\prod_{i=1}^{n} \sigma_{i,\tau}^{(xa_i + H(m_\tau))} = g$ for all τ, output m^* and σ_i^*, for $1 \leq i \leq n$ such that they satisfy: $\prod_{i=1}^{n} \sigma_i^{*(xa_i + H(m^*))}$ $= g$ and $H(m^*) \neq H(m_\tau)$ for all i and τ. We say that the (q, n, t, ϵ)-DsjSDH assumption holds in G if no t-time algorithm has advantage at least ϵ in solving the (q, n)-DsjSDH problem in G.*

Notice that if $n = 1$, the $(q, 1)$-DsjSDH Assumption without hash is equivalent to the q-CAA Assumption [6].

3.2 The Proxy Ring Signature Scheme

Let G be a bilinear group where $|G| = p$. Define a bilinear map $\hat{e} : G \times G \rightarrow G_1$. Meanwhile, define two collision-resistant hash functions $H_1 : \{0,1\}^* \rightarrow Z_p^*$ and $H_2 : G \rightarrow Z_p^*$. Then the system parameters are params$=(G, G_1, \hat{e}, g, H_1, H_2)$.

KenGen. For original signer, it picks $x_o \in Z_p$ and outputs $(x_o, y_o = g^{x_o})$ as its key pair. The original signer's secret key is x_o and the public key is y_o.

For user i, it chooses $x_i \in Z_p$ and outputs $(x_i, y_i = g^{x_i})$ as its key pair. The user $i's$ secret key is x_i and the public key is y_i.

D. In order to delegate his signing capability to user i, then original signer, on input y_i, computes $S_i = [H_2(y_i)]^{x_o}$ as the corresponding delegation. Meanwhile, it publishes S_i in its delegation board.

P. Given S_i, the user i computes its proxy signing key as $sk_i = (x_i, S_i)$.

PRS. Assume the proxy signer wants to form a ring signature on message m on behalf of n proxy signers $\{y_1, \cdots, y_n\}$ with his own public key at index t. First, he gets the delegations S_i for $1 \leq i \leq n$ from the original signer's delegation board. Then he signs as follows:

a. For $i \in \{1, \cdots, n\} \backslash t$, he picks $r_i \in_R Z_p^*$ and computes $\sigma_i = g^{r_i}$.

b. He computes $\omega = \frac{\prod_{i=1}^{n} S_i}{\prod_{i \in \{1,\ldots,n\} \backslash t} (y_i \cdot g^{H_1(m)})^{r_i}}$.

c. Finally, he computes $\sigma_t = \omega^{1/(x_t + H_1(m))}$ with his secret keys x_t.

The proxy ring signature is $\sigma = \{\sigma_1, \cdots, \sigma_n\}$.

PRV. On input the set $\mathcal{L} = \{y_1, \cdots, y_n\}$, a message m and $\sigma = \{\sigma_1, \cdots, \sigma_n\}$, accept if $\prod_{i=1}^{n} [\hat{e}(\sigma_i, (y_i \cdot g^{H_1(m)}))] = \prod_{i=1}^{n} \hat{e}(H_2(y_i), y_o)$.

3.3 Efficiency Analysis

Comparing with the previous proxy ring signature schemes [1,10], the new scheme has a number of advantages. First, the proxy ring signature length is very short. The proxy ring signature only includes n elements in G. In practice, the size of an element of G_1 can be reduced by a factor 2 with compression techniques. Therefore, the size of the proxy ring signature is approximately $160n$ bits. Though some proxy ring signature schemes [1,10], also have been proposed, the proxy ring signature consists of $n+1$ elements in their schemes [1,10]. Moreover, from an computation point of view, proxy ring signature generation algorithm requires only $(2n-1)$ exponentiation computation as the most expensive operation in our scheme, which is more efficient than [1,10], for they required at least $2n$ and $2n$ pairings computations.

3.4 Security Result

Theorem 1. *The new ring signature scheme is delegation unforgeable if CDH assumption holds in bilinear groups.*

Proof. If there exists an adversary $\mathcal{A}$ breaks the scheme, then we show there exists an algorithm $\mathcal{C}$ that, by interacting with $\mathcal{A}$, solves the CDH problem. Our algorithm $\mathcal{C}$ described below solves CDH problem for a randomly given instance $\{g, g^x, g^y\}$ and asked to compute g^{xy}. The details are as follows.

$\mathcal{C}$ runs $\mathcal{A}$ on input $y_o = g^x$ as target user's public key, handling all of $\mathcal{A}$'s requests and answering all $\mathcal{A}$'s queries as follows:

H-queries: Assume $\mathcal{A}$ makes at most q_{H_1} times to H_1-oracle and q_{H_2} times to H_2-oracle, respectively. When $\mathcal{A}$ queries m_i to H_1-oracle, $\mathcal{C}$ answers $H_1(m_i) = \hat{m_i}$ for a random $\hat{m_i} \in Z_p$. Furthermore, $\mathcal{C}$ randomly chooses a $s \in [1, q_{H_2}]$ and prepares $t_i \in Z_p$ for $1 \leq i \leq q_{H_2}$. When $\mathcal{A}$ queries y_i to H_2-oracle, $\mathcal{C}$ answers $H_2(y_i) = g^{t_i}$ if $i \neq s$. Otherwise, $H_2(y_s) = g^y$ if $i = s$.

Key Registration Queries: If $\mathcal{A}$ requests to register a new user i by outputting (x_i, y_i), $\mathcal{C}$ stores these keys as valid registered key pair.

Delegation Queries: If $\mathcal{A}$ requests to designates i with registered public key y_i, it assumes $\mathcal{A}$ has requested H_2 query on y_i. If $i \neq s$, $\mathcal{C}$ knows the value t_i such that $H_2(y_i) = g^{t_i}$. So cert is $y_o^{t_i}$. Otherwise, $\mathcal{C}$ aborts.

Proxy Ring Signature Queries: If $\mathcal{A}$ makes a query for proxy ring signature of proxy user i on behalf of a group of proxy signers delegated by original user y_o, $\mathcal{C}$ returns the proxy ring signature normally by using PRS because user i has registered public key y_i and $\mathcal{C}$ knows its corresponding secret key x_i.

Finally, $\mathcal{A}$ outputs a forgery of proxy ring signature $(m^*, \mathcal{L}, \sigma^*)$, such that $\mathcal{L}$ includes a public key y^* that is not equal to any query of $\mathcal{DE}$ Oracle and σ^* is a valid proxy ring signature with respect to pk_o and $\mathcal{L}$ on message m^*. Assume $\sigma^* = \{\sigma_1, \cdots, \sigma_n\}$ and $\mathcal{L}=\{y_1, \cdots, y_n\}$, such that $y^* = y_s$. It satisfies $\prod_{i=1}^{n}[\hat{e}(\sigma_i, (y_i \cdot g^{H_1(m)}))] = \prod_{i=1}^{n} \hat{e}(H_2(y_i), y_o)$. We have $H_2(y^*) = g^y$ and $H_2(y_i) = g^{t_i}$ if $y_i \neq y^*$. Then, the following equation holds: $\prod_{i=1}^{n}[\hat{e}(\sigma_i, y_i \cdot g^{H_1(m^*)})]=\hat{e}\ (\prod_{i=1}^{n}(\sigma_i)^{x_i+H_1(m^*)}, g)$.

Meanwhile, we have $\prod_{i=1}^{n} \hat{e}(H(y_i), y_o)=\hat{e}\ (\prod_{i=1}^{n} H_2(y_i),\ y_o)=\ \hat{e}\ (g^{xy} \prod_{i=1, i\neq s}^{n} (y_o)^{t_i}, g)$. So, we have $\prod_{i=1}^{n}(\sigma_i)^{x_i+H_1(m^*)}=g^{xy} \prod_{i=1, i\neq s}^{n} y_o^{t_i}$. Finally, $\mathcal{C}$ can compute $g^{xy}=\frac{\prod_{i=1}^{n}(\sigma_i)^{x_i+H_1(m^*)}}{\prod_{i\in\{1,\cdots,n\}\backslash s} y_o^{t_i}}$.

It is easy to see that if $\mathcal{A}$ outputs a forgery of proxy ring signature with probability ϵ, then CDH problem can be solved with probability about $\frac{1}{q_{H_2}} \cdot \epsilon$. So, we can say that the proxy signature scheme is secure in the random oracle if CDH assumption holds.

Theorem 2. *The new ring signature scheme is proxy ring signature unforgeable if (q, n)-DsjSDH assumption holds in bilinear groups.*

Proof. Suppose the adversary $\mathcal{A}$ can forge the proxy ring signature scheme with n users. We construct an algorithm $\mathcal{C}$ that uses $\mathcal{A}$ to solve the (q, n)-DsjSDH problem.

Initialization. Suppose that there exists a $(t, q_{H_1}, q_{H_2}, q_S, \epsilon)$-forger $\mathcal{A}$ that can produce a forgery of a proxy ring signature on a set of proxy users of size n. Then,

$\mathcal{C}$ is given the the (q_S, n)-DsjSDH tuple: g, g^x, a_i, H, m_τ, $\sigma_{i,\tau}$ for $1 \le i \le n$, $1 \le \tau \le q_S$. Let $\hat{m}_\tau = H(m_\tau)$. $\mathcal{C}$ sets proxy user $i's$ public key as $y_i = g^{a_i x}$ and original user's public key as $y_o = g^a$ by picking a random $a \in_R Z_p^*$. Meanwhile, $\mathcal{C}$ chooses two hash functions H_1, H_2 such that $H_1 = H$ (They serve as random oracles in the proof). Then, the adversary is given the public keys $(y_1, \cdots, y_n)$ of a set of proxy users L, and is given oracle access to H_1, H_2. The goal of the adversary is to output a valid proxy ring signature for L of a message m^* subject to the condition that m^* has never been presented to the proxy ring-signing oracle.

Simulating Random Oracle. Assume $\mathcal{A}$ makes at most q_{H_1} times to H_1-oracle and q_{H_2} times to H_2-oracle, respectively. $\mathcal{C}$ prepares q_{H_1} responses $\{w_1, w_2, \cdots, w_{q_{H_1}}\}$ of the random oracle queries of H_1, $\hat{m}_\tau$ for $1 \le \tau \le q_S$ are distributed randomly in this response set. When $\mathcal{A}$ makes a random oracle query on m_i for $1 \le i \le q_{H_1}$. $\mathcal{C}$ sends w_i to $\mathcal{A}$ as the response of the random oracle query on m_i of H_1. Furthermore, $\mathcal{C}$ randomly prepares $t_i \in Z_p$ for $1 \le i \le q_{H_2}$. When $\mathcal{A}$ queries y_i to H_2-oracle, $\mathcal{C}$ answers $H_2(y_i) = g^{r_i}$

Simulating PRS Oracle. Assume $\mathcal{A}$ has queried the random oracle for y_i and $H(y_i) = g^{r_i}$ has been answered by $\mathcal{C}$ for a random value $r_i \in Z_p$. For the i-th PRS query $(M_i,\ L)$, we have $w_i = H_1(M_i)$. If $w_i = \hat{m}_\tau$ for some $1 \le \tau \le q_S$, $\mathcal{C}$ returns the simulated proxy ring signature as $\sigma_{i,\tau}^{a\sum_{i=1}^{n} r_i}$ for $1 \le i \le n$. The simulated PRS signature is valid from the viewpoint of $\mathcal{A}$ for $\prod_{i=1}^{n}[\hat{e}(\sigma_{i,\tau}^{a\sum_{i=1}^{n} r_i}, (y_i \cdot g^{\hat{m}_\tau}))] = e(g,g)^{a\sum_{i=1}^{n} r_i} = \prod_{i=1}^{n} \hat{e}(H_2(y_i),\ X_o)$. If $w_i \neq \hat{m}_\tau$ for $1 \le \tau \le q_S$, $\mathcal{C}$ aborts.

Simulating KR Oracle. If $\mathcal{A}$ requests to register a new user by outputting (x, y), $\mathcal{C}$ stores it as valid registered key pair.

Simulating DE Oracle. If $\mathcal{A}$ requests to delegate a user with registered public key y by the original user with public key y_o, $\mathcal{C}$ just output y_o^r as the delegation for $H_2(y) = g^r$ for some $r \in Z_p$.

Extraction. Finally, $\mathcal{A}$ outputs a signature (M^*, L, σ_i^*) for $1 \le i \le n$ on message M^*. It wins if it passes the verification equation and M^* is never been queried to PRS oracle. Denote $m^* = H(M^*)$. So, we can get $\sigma_i^{*\frac{1}{a\sum_{i=1}^{n} r_i}}$ for $1 \le i \le n$ and the (q, n)-DsjSDH problem is solved.

Notice that $\mathcal{C}$ aborts if $\mathcal{A}$ issued a signature query for $H_1(M_i) \neq \hat{m}_\tau$. This happens with probability at most $(q_{H_1} - q_S)/q_{H_1}$. $\mathcal{C}$ will not fail with probability $(\frac{q_S}{q_{H_1}})^{q_S}$ after q_S proxy ring signature queries. Furthermore, in Extraction phase, $\mathcal{C}$ will not fail with probability $\frac{q_{H_1} - q_S}{q_{H_1}}$. So, suppose $\mathcal{A}$ can forge the ring signature with probability ϵ, $\mathcal{C}$ can solve the (q_S, n)-DsjSDH problem with probability $\epsilon' \ge (\frac{q_S}{q_{H_1}})^{q_S} (\frac{q_{H_1} - q_S}{q_{H_1}})\ \epsilon$.

Theorem 3. *The proxy ring signature scheme satisfies unconditional signer-ambiguity.*

Proof. For $i \in \{1, \ldots, n\} \setminus t$, σ_i are random since r_i are randomly picked. σ_t can be considered as in the form of g^{r_t} as g is the generator and hence such r_t always exists. It is determined by σ_i by the equation, so σ_t is also uniformly distributed. To conclude, the distribution of the components of the signature generated by our scheme is independent of what is the group of participating signer, for any message m and any set of users associated to the ring signature.

4 The Other Kind of Proxy Ring Signature

In some situations, every original signer will have their own proxy signer. If the proxy signer is required to sign on behalf his original signer and to not leak who and whose proxy signer has signed this document. So, we propose another kind of proxy ring signatures. This kind of proxy ring signature scheme also consists of 5-tuple of probabilistic polynomial time algorithms (KenGen, D,P, PRS, PRV) defined as follows: Key generation algorithm KenGen and proxy-designation algorithm (D,P) are defined as definition 2.1. The proxy ring signature generation algorithm PRS, that takes as input a proxy secret key sk_p, a message m and a set of original signers' public keys $\mathcal{L}$ and a set of proxy signers' public keys $\mathcal{L}'$ including the one that corresponds to the private key sk_p, returns the signature σ. The proxy ring signature verification algorithm PRV, takes as input a set of $\mathcal{L}$ and $\mathcal{L}'$, a message m and σ, returns 1 or 0 for accept or reject, respectively.

4.1 The Scheme

KenGen. For user i, it picks $x_i \in Z_p$ and outputs $(x_i, y_i = g^{x_i})$ as its key pair. The user $i's$ secret key is x_i and the public key is y_i.

D. Assume the user i, with key pair $(x_i, y_i = g^{x_i})$, wants to delegate its signing power to the user with key pair $(x'_i, y'_i = g^{x'_i})$. Then, the original signer i, on input y'_i, computes $S_i = [H_2(y'_i)]^{x_i}$ as the corresponding delegation. Meanwhile, it publishes S_i in its delegation board.

P. Given S_i, the user with key pair (x'_i, y'_i), computes the proxy signing key as $sk_i = (x'_i, S_i)$.

PRS. Assume n designators y'_i for $1 \leq i \leq n$ have been designated by n signers y_i for $1 \leq i \leq n$, respectively. If the proxy signer wants to form a ring signature on message m on behalf of n users $\mathcal{L}'=\{y'_1, \cdots, y'_n\}$ with his own public key at index t, he first gets S_i for $1 \leq i \leq n$ from the original signers' delegation board. Then he signs as follows:

a. For $i \in \{1, \cdots, n\} \backslash t$, he picks $r_i \in_R Z_p^*$ and computes $\sigma_i = g^{r_i}$.
b. For $i \in \{1, \cdots, n\}$, he picks $r_i \in Z_p^*$. Then he computes
$\omega = \frac{\prod_{i=1}^{n} S_i}{\prod_{i \in \{1,\ldots,n\} \backslash t} (y'_i \cdot g^{H_1(m)})^{r_i}}$.
c. He computes $\sigma_t = \omega^{1/(x'_t + H_1(m))}$ with his secret keys x'_t.

The signature is $\sigma = \{\sigma_1, \cdots, \sigma_n\}$.

PRV. On input $\mathcal{L}=\{y_1, \cdots, y_n\}$, $\mathcal{L}'=\{y'_1, \cdots, y'_n\}$, a message m and $\sigma = \{\sigma_1, \cdots, \sigma_n\}$, accept if $\prod_{i=1}^{n}[\hat{e}(\sigma_i, (y'_i \cdot g^{H_1(m)}))] = \prod_{i=1}^{n} \hat{e}(H_2(y'_i), y_i)$.

4.2 Security Analysis

The adversary in this kind of proxy ring signatures are provided with the $\mathcal{DE}$ oracle, $\mathcal{KR}$ oracle and $\mathcal{PRS}$ oracle. Definition of $\mathcal{DE}$ oracle and $\mathcal{KR}$ oracle is the same with the corresponding definition in section 4. The only difference is the definition of $\mathcal{PRS}$ Oracle. So, we give here the definition of $\mathcal{PRS}$ oracle.

$\mathcal{PRS}$ Oracle: The proxy ring signature oracle, on input message m, a set of original signers' public keys $\mathcal{L}=\{y_1, \cdots, y_n\}$, and a set of corresponding proxy signers' public keys $\mathcal{L}'=\{y'_1, \cdots, y'_n\}$, including the one that correspond to the proxy signing key sk_p, returns a proxy ring signature $\sigma \leftarrow \mathsf{PRS}(sk_p, \mathcal{L}, \mathcal{L}', m)$ such that $\mathsf{PRV}(\mathcal{L}, \mathcal{L}', m, \sigma) = 1$.

This kind of proxy ring signatures should also satisfy the three properties: correctness, ambiguity and unforgeability. Definitions of these properties are very similar to section 3.

In this kind of proxy ring signatures, **Delegation unforgeability** means that it is hard to forge a valid proxy ring signature without corresponding delegation. **Proxy ring signature unforgeability** is defined as any PPT adversary cannot output a valid proxy ring signature without knowing one of the corresponding secret key of the delegation. In this kind of proxy ring signatures, **signer ambiguity** means that it is hard to tell which proxy signer out of the n possible proxy signers who actually generates a proxy ring signature.

We can get the following results easily from the proof in section 3.

Theorem 4. *The new ring signature scheme is delegation unforgeable if CDH assumption holds in bilinear groups.*

Theorem 5. *The new ring signature scheme is proxy ring signature unforgeable if (q, n)-DsjSDH assumption holds in bilinear groups.*

Theorem 6. *The proxy ring signature scheme satisfies unconditional signer-ambiguity.*

5 Conclusion

This paper first formally introduces the concept of proxy ring signatures, which allows proxy signers of a group to sign messages on behalf of the original signers without revealing their identities. We give the formal security definitions and notions of proxy ring signatures. Then, we propose two kinds of proxy ring signature schemes, with rigorous security proofs. This is the first proxy ring signature scheme which can be proved to be secure to date. Furthermore, the two proxy ring signature schemes are more efficient compared to the other proposed proxy ring signature schemes.

Acknowledgments

This work is supported by the National Natural Science Foundation of China (No. 60503006 and No. 10571181). The first author is also supported by KaiSi Grant.

References

1. Awasthil, A. K. Lal, S.: A new proxy ring signature scheme. RMS, Agra, INDIA (2004)
2. Abe, M., Ohkubo, M., Suzuki, K.: 1-out-of-n Signatures from a Variety of Keys. In: Zheng, Y. (ed.) Advances in Cryptology - ASIACRYPT 2002. LNCS, vol. 2501, pp. 415–432. Springer, Heidelberg (2002)
3. Bellare, M., Micciancio, D., Warinschi, B.: Foundations of Group Signatures: Formal Definitions, Simplified Requirements, and a Construction Based on General Assumptions. In: Biham, E. (ed.) Advances in Cryptology – EUROCRPYT 2003. LNCS, vol. 2656, pp. 614–629. Springer, Heidelberg (2003)
4. Bresson, E., Stern, J., Szydlo, M.: Threshold Ring Signatures and Applications to Ad-hoc Groups. In: Yung, M. (ed.) Advances in Cryptology - CRYPTO 2002. LNCS, vol. 2442, pp. 465–480. Springer, Heidelberg (2002)
5. Chow, S., Yiu, S., Hui, L.: Efficient Identity Based Ring Signature. In: Ioannidis, J., Keromytis, A.D., Yung, M. (eds.) Applied Cryptography and Network Security. LNCS, vol. 3531, Springer, Heidelberg (2005), `http://eprint.iacr.org/2004/327`
6. Chow, S. S. M., Liu, J.K., Wei, V. K., Yuen, T. H.: Ring Signatures without Random Oracles. To be appeared at AsiaCCS'06. Available at `http://eprint.iacr.org/2005/317`
7. Li, J., Wang, Y.: Universal designated verifier ring signature (proof) without random oracles. In: Zhou, X., Sokolsky, O., Yan, L., Jung, E.-S., Shao, Z., Mu, Y., Lee, D.C., Kim, D., Jeong, Y.-S., Xu, C.-Z. (eds.) Emerging Directions in Embedded and Ubiquitous Computing. LNCS, vol. 4097, pp. 332–341. Springer, Heidelberg (2006)
8. Rivest, R.L., Shamir, A., Tauman, Y.: How to Leak a Secret. In: Boyd, C. (ed.) Advances in Cryptology - ASIACRYPT 2001. LNCS, vol. 2248, pp. 552–565. Springer, Heidelberg (2001)
9. Xu, J., Zhang, Z., Feng, D.: A Ring Signature Scheme Using Bilinear Pairings. In: Lim, C.H., Yung, M. (eds.) Information Security Applications. LNCS, vol. 3325, pp. 163–172. Springer, Heidelberg (2005)
10. Zhang, F., Safavi-Naini, R., Lin, C.-Y.: Some New Proxy Signature Schemes from Pairings, Progress on Cryptography: 25 years of Cryptography in China. In: Kluwer International Series in Engineering and Computer Science, vol. 769, pp. 59–66. Kluwer Academic Publishers, Boston (2004)

Linkability Analysis of Some Blind Signature Schemes

Jianhong Zhang[1,2,3] and Jian Mao[1]

[1] Institute of Computer Science & Technology, Peking University, Beijing 100871, China
{zhangjianhong,maojian}@icst.pku.edu.cn
http://www.icst.pku.edu.cn

[2] State Key Laboratory of Information Security, Institute of Software of Chinese Academy of Sciences, Beijing, 100039, China

[3] College of Science, North China University of Technology, Shijingshan District, Beijing 100041, China

Abstract. Blind signature is a cryptographical technique and allows a user to obtain signatures from an authority on any document, in such a way that the authority learns nothing about the message that is being signed. The *blindness* is an important property which distinguishes the blind signature from other signature schemes. In this work, we analyze security of two ID-based blind signature schemes [1,16] and a blind signature scheme[20] based on witness indistinguishable signature, and show that the three schemes don't satisfy blindness, in other words, the signer is able to link a valid message-signature pair obtained by some user. It means that the three blind signature schemes are insecure.

1 Introduction

In traditional digital signature schemes, the binding between a user and his public key needs to be ensured. The usual way to provide this assurance is by providing certificates that are signed by a trusted third party, Namely the public certificate. As a consequence, the system requires a large storage and computing time to store and verify each user's public key and the corresponding certificate. In 1984, Shamir [2]introduced the conception of identity-based public key cryptosystem to simplify key management procedures in certificate-based public key setting. In ID-based mechanism, the user's public key is indeed his identity (such as email, IP address, etc.). Since then, various ID-based encryption schemes and signature schemes have been proposed. At present, many ID-based encryption and signature schemes have been proposed based on the bilinear pairings in elliptic curves or hyper-elliptic curves. The size of signature is in general short in these schemes.

The notion of blind signature was introduced by D.Chaum [4], which can provide an anonymity of signed message. Since it was introduced, blind signature schemes [4,5,6,7,8,9,10,16,17] have been used in numerous application, most prominently in anonymous voting and anonymous e-cash. At the same time, to

Y. Wang, Y. Cheung, and H. Liu (Eds.): CIS 2006, LNAI 4456, pp. 556–566, 2007.

adapt practical demands, many variant of the blind signature schemes appeared, such as partial blind signature, group blind signature etc.

Informally, blind signature allows a user to obtain signatures from an authority on any document, in such a way that the authority learns nothing about the message that is being signed. The most important property of blind signature differing from the other signatures is *blindness*, which requires that after interacting with various users, the signer S is not able to link a valid message-signature pair (m, δ) obtained by some user, with the protocol session during which δ was created. The other property is unforgeability, requires that it is impossible for any malicious user that engages in k runs of the protocol with the signer, to obtain strictly more than k valid message-signature pairs. The basic idea of most existing blind signatures is that the requester randomly chooses some random factors and embeds them to the message to be signed. The random factors are kept in secret so the signer cannot recover the message. Upon the blinded signature returned by the signer, the requester can remove the random factor to obtain a valid signature. Up to now, two ID-based blind signature schemes based on bilinear pairings have been proposed. The first scheme was proposed by Zhang and Kim[16] in Asiacrypt 2002, the other scheme[17] was proposed in ACISP2003. They claim that the security against generic parallel attack to their schemes don't depend on the difficulty of ROS-problem [18]. In fact, their scheme[17] is also forgeable under the generic parallel attack if the ROS-problem is solvable, namely, the security against generic parallel attack to this scheme also depends on the difficulty of ROS-problem. In the following, we will show that the scheme [16] is also linkable by analyzing the security of the scheme.

In 2005, Huang *et.al* proposed an ID-based blind signature scheme in CANS 2005 [1] (Huang *et.al* scheme for short) and show that the security of the scheme is based on CDH assumption (Computational Diffie-Hellman Assumpitonm), and the scheme satisfied the *blindness* of blind signature, namely, unlinkability. Recently, Q.H.Wu *et.al* gave two efficient partial blind signature schemes [20] in ICCSA2006. Compared with the state-of-the-art construction due to Abe and Fujisaki[21],the first one of their schemes is 25% more efficient. And they claimed that their schemes also satisfied blindness. In this paper, we analyze the blindness of three blind signature schemes and show they don't satisfy the important property of blind signature: *blindness*, in other words, the signer is able to link a valid message-signature pair obtained by some user. First, we analyze the security of Huang *et.al* blind signature[1], and show that the scheme hasn't blindness. Then we also give security analysis on Zhang *et.al* blind signature scheme[16] and show that the scheme has also linkability. Finally, we also find that the first one of Wu *et.al*'s schemes hasn't blindness by analyzing the security of the scheme.

The rest of the paper is organized as follows: Section 2 give some preliminary knowledge related to the paper; in section 3, we show the flaw of Huang et.al blind signature scheme, then recall Zhang et.al blind signature scheme in section 4; in section 5, we analyze the security of Zhang et.al blind signature scheme;

in section 6, we analyze security of Wu *et.al* scheme and give the attack on blindness. Finally, we draw this paper.

2 Preliminaries

In this section, we will review some fundamental backgrounds related to the paper.

Let G_1 be a cyclic additive group generated by P with the order prime q, and G_2 be a cyclic multiplicative group with the same order q. Let $e : G_1 \times G_1 \longrightarrow G_2$ be a pairing which satisfies the following conditions:

- Bilinearity: For any $P, Q, R \in G_1$, we have $e(P + Q, R) = e(P, R)e(Q, R)$ and $e(P, R + Q) = e(P, R)e(P, Q)$. in particular, for any $a, b \in Z_q$,

$$e(aP, bP) = e(P, P)^{ab} = e(P, abP) = e(abP, P)$$

- Non-degeneracy: There exists $P, Q \in G_1$, such that $e(P, Q) \neq 1$
- Computability: There is an efficient algorithm to compute $e(P, Q)$ for $P, Q \in G_1$.

The typical way of obtaining such pairing is by deriving them from the Weil pairing or the Tate pairing on an elliptic curve over a finite field.

Computational Diffie-Hellman Problem: Given $P, aP, bP \in G_1$ for randomly chosen $a, b \in_R Z_q$ to abP.

The success probility of any probabilistic polynomial-time algorithm $\mathcal{A}$ in solving CDH problem in G_1 is defined to be

$$Succ_{\mathcal{A}}^{CDH} = Pr[\mathcal{A}(P, aP, bP) = abP | a, b \in Z_q{}^*]$$

The CDH assumption states that for every probabilistic polynomial-time algorithm $\mathcal{A}$, $Succ_{\mathcal{A}}^{CDH}$ is negligible.

Definition1. (Blindness:) Let S' be a probabilistic polynomial time algorithm, U_1 and U_0 be two honest users. U_1 and U_0 engage in the signature issuing protocol with S' on messages m_b and m_{1-b}, and output signatures δ_b and δ_{1-b}, respectively, where b is randomly chosen from $\{0, 1\}$. Send $(m_0, m_1, \delta_b, \delta_{1-b})$ to S' and then S' outputs $b' \in \{0, 1\}$. For all such S', U_0 and U_1, for any constant c, and for sufficiently large n,

$$|Pr[b = b'] - 1/2| < n^{-c}$$

3 Reviews of Huang et.al Blind Scheme

In the following, we will briefly review the Huang et.al blind scheme. Please the interested reader refer to [1] for the detail content.

[Setup]
Choose a group G_1, which is a cyclic additive group generated by P with prime order q. Choose a cyclic multiplicative group G_2 with the same order q and a bilinear pairing $e : G_1 \times G_1 \longrightarrow G_2$. Pick a random $s \in_R Z_q$, set $P_{pub} = sP$. Let $H_1(\cdot), H_2(\cdot)$ be two hash functions and satisfy $H_1 : \{0,1\}^* \times G_2 \longrightarrow Z_q$ and $H_2 : \{0,1\}^* \longrightarrow G_1$. Publish the system parameter $SP = (G_1, G_2, e, q, P, P_{pub}, H_1, H_2)$, and keep the master key s secret.

[Extract]
Given an identity ID, compute $P_{ID} = H_2(ID)$ and return the corresponding private key $S_{ID} = sP_{ID}$.

[Sign]
To make the signer produce a signature, The user U first chooses $P_1 \in G_1$ and compute $e(P, P_1)$ before executing interaction. Then they execute the following interactive procedures:

1. The signer randomly chooses a number $r \in_R Z_q$, and computes
$$R' = e(P_{ID}, P_{pub})^r$$
and sends R' to the user as his commitment.
2. The user randomly chooses $t_1, t_2 \in_R Z_q$ and computes
$$R = R'^{t_1} e(P_1, P)^{t_2}$$
$$h = H_1(m, R)$$
$$h' = ht_1$$
then sends h' to the signer.
3. The signer computes
$$V' = (rh' + 1)S_{ID}$$
and sends V' to the user.
4. upon receiving V', the user checks whether the relation holds.
$$e(V', P) = R'^{h'} e(P_{ID}, P_{pub})$$
If it holds, he computes
$$V = V' + ht_2P_1$$

Then, the resultant blind signature on the message m is (R, V).

[Verify]
To verify a signature (R, V) on the message m, the verifier checks the following equation
$$e(V, P) = R^{H_1(m,R)} e(P_{ID}, P_{pub})$$

4 The Flaw of Huang *et.al* Blind Signature Scheme

Recently, Huang *et.al* presented a ID-based blind signature and claimed that their scheme satisfied the important property: blindness. Unfortunately, we show that Huang *et.al*'s blind signature scheme doesn't satisfy the blindness by analyzing the security of the scheme. Namely,after interacting with various users, the signer S is able to link a valid message-signature pair (m, δ) obtained by some user.

4.1 Linkability

Here, we will show that the signer can link a message-signature pair. According to the signing procedure above, we can know that given a blind signature (R, V) on the message m, the view of the signer is (R', h', V') in the generation of the blind signature. In the following , we will show how the signer link the message-signature pair by the views (R', h', V'). Given a blind signature (R, V), the signer executes as follows

- Firstly, the signer computes $\alpha = e(V - V', P)$
- then. the signer computes $\beta = R'^{h'}$
- compute $h = (m, R)$
- Finally, check whether the relation equation

$$\alpha \cdot \beta \stackrel{?}{=} R^h \tag{1}$$

  holds.

if the equation (1) holds, then it denotes that the signer can link the message-signature pair.

4.2 Correctness

In the following, we will show that why a blind signature (R, V) satisfies the equation (1) above, then it means that the signer can link the message-signature pair.

Theorem 1. *Given a blind signature (R, V) on message m, the signer can link a message-signature pair by using the equation (1).*

Proof. : according to the blind signature above, we know

$$V = V' + ht_2 P_1,$$

thus the signer can compute

$$\begin{aligned} \alpha &= e(V - V', P) \\ &= e(ht_2 P_1, P) \\ &= e(P, P_1)^{ht_2} \end{aligned}$$

and since the signer possesses R' and h' and $h' = ht_1$, then he is able to compute

$$\begin{aligned} \beta &= R'^{h'} \\ &= R'^{ht_1} \end{aligned}$$

Thus, we obtain the following relation

$$\begin{aligned}\alpha \cdot \beta &= R'^{ht_1} e(P, P_1)^{ht_2} \\ &= R^h\end{aligned}$$

Note that $h = (m, R)$. According to the state above, the signer can link a message-signature pair. In other words, it indicates that the blind signature hasn't blindness.

5 Security Analysis of Zhang et.al Blind Signature Scheme

5.1 Zhang *et.al* Scheme

In this section, we will briefly recall Zhang et.al blind signature scheme, The system **Setup** phase and **Extract** phase in Zhang et.al scheme is the same ones of Huang et.al scheme. In the following, we only consider **Signing** phase and **Verification** phase. Please interested reader refer [16] to the detail content.
[Signing phase]
Suppose that m is the message to be signed. Then, the execution of the signer and the user is as follows:

- The singer randomly choose a number $r \in_R Z_q^*$, computes $R = rP$ and sends R to the user as a commitment.
- After receiving the R, the user randomly chooses $a, b \in Z_q^*$ as blinding factors. At the same time, he computes

$$t = e(bP_{ID} + R + aP, P_{pub}) \tag{2}$$

$$c = H_1(m, t) + b(modq) \tag{3}$$

  and sends c to the signer.
- Then, the signer sends back S, where

$$S = cS_{ID} + rP_{pub}.$$

- After S returned, the user computes as follows:

$$S' = S + aP_{pub} \tag{4}$$

$$c' = c - b \tag{5}$$

  Finally, outputs (m, S', c')

Then (m, S', c') is the blind signature of the message m.
[Verification]
After receiving the blind signature (m, S', c'), a verifier checks as follows:

$$c' = H_1(m, e(S', P)e(P_{ID}, P_{pub})^{-c'}) \tag{6}$$

if the equations above (2) and (3) hold, the verifier accepts it as a valid blind signature.

5.2 Linkability of Zhang *et.al* Scheme

Zhang et.al claimed that their scheme satisfied *blindness*. In other words, the signer cannot link a message-signature pair. Unfortunately, In the following, we show that Zhang et.al blind signature scheme has linkability, namely, it hasn't blindness, by analyzing the security of the scheme.

According to the signing phase of Zhang et.al blind signature scheme, given a blind signature (S', c') on the message m, we know that the views of the signer are (R, c, S) in whole signing phase. To link message-signature pair, he computes as follows:

1. First, the signer computes $\alpha = e(S' - S, P)$
2. then, he computes $\beta = c - c'$
3. set $\gamma = e(R, P_{pub})$
4. compute $t' = \alpha \cdot \gamma \cdot e(Q_{ID}, P_{pub})^{\beta}$
5. check

$$c' = H_1(m, t') \tag{7}$$

if the equation (7) holds, it means the signer successfully link message-signature pair.

According to the signing phase of Zhang et.al blind signature scheme, if the views (R, c, S) corresponds to the blind signature (S', c') on the message m, then we have

$$\begin{aligned} t' &= \alpha \cdot \gamma \cdot e(Q_{ID}, P_{pub})^{\beta} \\ &= e(S' - S, P) \cdot e(R, P_{pub}) \cdot e(Q_{ID}, P_{pub})^{c-c'} \\ &= e(aP_{pub}, P) \cdot e(R, P_{pub}) \cdot e(Q_{ID}, P_{pub})^{b} \\ &= e(aP + R + bP_{ID}, P_{pub}) \\ &= t \end{aligned}$$

thus, we have that the relation $H_1(t', m) = H_1(t, m) = c'$ holds, it means that our attack is successful. The signer is able to link a message-signature pair.

6 Security Analysi of Wu *et.al*'s Blind Signature Scheme

In ICCSA2006, Wu *et.al* proposed two efficient partial blind signature, where the first one is 25% more efficient than the state-of-the-art construction due to Abe and Fujisaki. And they claimed that their scheme satisfied all security requirement of blind signature: blindness and unforgeability. In the following, we will brief review Wu *et.al*'s scheme.

6.1 Wu *et.al*'s Scheme

Let G be a cyclic group with prime order q and g an element in G whose order is q. H and F are two public cryptographic hash functions which satisfy

$H : \{0,1\}^* \rightarrow Z_q$ and $F : \{0,1\}^* \rightarrow G$. Let $x \in Z_q$ be a secret key and $y = g^x$ be corresponding public key. The signer and the user fist predetermine the common information c. Then they execute as follows.

- Initialization. The signer randomly chooses $r, u \leftarrow Z_q^*$, and computes $z = F(c), a = g^r z^u$. The signer sends a to the user as a commitment.
- Blinding. The user randomly chooses $t_1, t_2, t_3 \leftarrow Z_q$ as blind factors, and computes $z = F(c), \alpha = ag^{t_1} y^{t_2} z^{t_3}, \varepsilon = H(\alpha||c||z||m), e = \varepsilon - t_2 - t_3 \bmod q$. The user sends e to the signer.
- Signing. The signer sends back v, s to the user, where $v = e - u \bmod q$, $s = r - vx\text{mod } q$.
- Unbinding. The user computes $\sigma = s + t_1 \bmod q$, $\rho = v + t_2 \bmod q$, $\delta = e - v + t_3 \bmod q$. Finally, it outputs (σ, ρ, δ) as the resulting blind signature on the message m.
- Verification. The signature is valid if and only if $\rho + \delta = H(g^\sigma y^\rho z^{delta}||c||z||m)$ and $z = F(c)$.

6.2 Linkability of Wu Scheme

In the following, we discuss the linkability of Wu 's scheme. From the above blind signing process, we know that the signer's views are (a, e, v, s, c, u, r) from a blind signature on a message m which is unknown to the signer. Given a blind signature (σ, ρ, δ) on the message m, the signer computes as follows:

1. Firstly, he verify whether the blind signature (σ, ρ, δ) is valid and $\varepsilon' = H(g^\sigma y^\rho z^\delta||c||z||m)$ where $z = F(c)$.
2. then compute $\theta = s - \delta \cdot x - \rho \cdot x \bmod q$, and $\theta' = r - (\varepsilon' + v) \cdot x \bmod q$.
3. Finally, check

$$\theta \stackrel{?}{=} \theta' \tag{8}$$

If the equation (8) holds, then it means that the signer can link this message-signature pair.

Theorem 2. *Given a blind signature (σ, ρ, δ) on a message m, the signer can link a message-signature pair by using the equation (8).*

Proof. According to the above first one of Wu *et.al*'s schemes, we know that the views of the signer are (a, e, v, s, c, u, r) from the producing process of a blind signature (σ, ρ, δ) on a message m. And they satisfy the following relation:

- (1) $s = r - vx \bmod q$
- (2) $\delta = e - v + t_3 \bmod q$
- (3) $e = \varepsilon - t_2 - t_3 \bmod q$, where $\varepsilon = H(g^\sigma y^\rho z^\delta||c||z||m)$
- (4) $\rho = v + t_2 \bmod q$.

Then, we have

$$\begin{aligned}\theta &= s - \delta \cdot x - \rho \cdot x \ mod\ q \\ &= r - e \cdot x - t_3 \cdot x - \rho \cdot x \ mod\ q \\ &= r - (\varepsilon - t_2 - t_3) \cdot x - t_3 \cdot x - \rho \cdot x \ mod\ q \\ &= r - (\varepsilon - t_2) \cdot x - \rho \cdot x \ mod\ q \\ &= r - (\varepsilon - t_2) \cdot x - (v + t_2) \cdot x \ mod\ q \\ &= r - (\varepsilon + v) \cdot x \\ &= \theta'\end{aligned}$$

Thus, if a blind signature on a message satisfies the equation (8), then the signer can link this message-signature pair.

7 Conclusion

ID-based public key crypt-system can be an alternative for certificate-based key infrastructures. Blind signature plays an important role in secure e-commerce, such as e-cash, e-vote. Where the *blindness* is an important property of blind signature scheme. In this paper, we give the security analysis on two ID-based blind signature schemes[1,16] and a newly proposed blind signature scheme [20] based on witness indistinguishable signature, and show that the three schemes haven't blindness, in other words, the signer is able to link a valid message-signature pair obtained by some user. It is a open problem to how to design a secure blind signature scheme.

Acknowledgement

We thanks the anonymous referees for their very valuable comments. This work is supported by China Postdoctoral Science Foundation(NO:20060390007) and the open fund of State Key Laboratory of Information Security.

References

1. Huang, Z.J., Chen, K.F., Wang, Y.M: Efficient Identity-Based Signatures and Blind Signatures. In: Desmedt, Y.G., Wang, H., Mu, Y., Li, Y. (eds.) Cryptology and Network Security. LNCS, vol. 3810, pp. 120–133. Springer, Heidelberg (2005)
2. Shamir, A.: Identity-based cryptosystems and signature schemes. In: Blakely, G.R., Chaum, D. (eds.) Advances in Cryptology. LNCS, vol. 196, pp. 47–53. Springer, Heidelberg (1984)
3. Boneh, D., Franklin, M.: Identity-based encryption from the Weil Pairing. In: Kilian, J. (ed.) Advances in Cryptology - CRYPTO 2001. LNCS, vol. 2139, pp. 213–229. Springer, Heidelberg (2001)

4. Chaum, D.: Blind signature for untraceable payment. In: Chaum, D., Rivest, R.L., Sherman, A.T. (eds.) Advances in Cryptology: Proceedings of CRYPTO. LNCS, vol. 1983, pp. 199–203. Springer, Heidelberg (1983)
5. Chow, S.S.M., Hui, L.C.K., Yie, S.M., Chow, K.P.: Two Improved Partially Blind Signature scheme from Bilinear Pairings. In: Colin, B., Nieto, G., Manuel, J. (eds.) Australasian Conference on Information Security and Privacy – ACISP'05. Lecture Notes in Computer Sciencs, vol. 3574, pp. 316–328. Springer, Heidelberg (2005)
6. Kim, J., Kim, K., Lee, C.: An Efficient and Provably Secure Threshold Blind Signature. In: Qing, S., Okamoto, T., Zhou, J. (eds.) Information and Communications Security. Lecture Notes in Computer Sciencs, vol. 2288, pp. 318–327. Springer, Heidelberg (2001)
7. Pderson, T.P.: Distributed Provers with Applications to Undeniable Signatures. In: Davies, D.W. (ed.) Advances in Cryptology - EUROCRYPT '91. Lecture Notes in Computer Sciencs, vol. 547, pp. 221–242. Springer, Heidelberg (1991)
8. Boldyreva, A.: Efficient threshold signature, multisignature and blind signature schemes based on the Gap-Diffie-Hellman group signature. In: Desmedt, Y. (ed.) Public Key Cryptography - PKC 2003. LNCS, vol. 2139, pp. 31–46. Springer, Heidelberg (2001)
9. Wang, S., Bao, F., Deng, R.H.: Cryptanalysis of a Forward Secure Blind Signature Scheme with Provable Security. In: Qing, S., Mao, W., Lopez, J., Wang, G. (eds.) Information and Communications Security. LNCS, vol. 3783, pp. 221–242. Springer, Heidelberg (2005)
10. Camenisch, J., Koprowski, M., Warinschi, B.: Efficient Blind Signatures Without Random Oracles. In: Blundo, C., Cimato, S. (eds.) Security in Communication Networks. LNCS, vol. 3352, pp. 134–146. Springer, Heidelberg (2005)
11. Dwork, C., Naor, M.: An efficient existentially unforgeable signature scheme and its applications. In: Desmedt, Y.G. (ed.) Advances in Cryptology - CRYPTO '94. LNCS, vol. 839, pp. 234–246. Springer, Heidelberg (1994)
12. Even, S., Goldreich, O., Micali, S.: On-line/off-line digital signatures, Journal of Cryptology, vol. 9, pp. 35–67. Springer-Verlag, New York (1996)
13. Perrig, A.: The BiBa one-time signature and broadcast authentication. In: the 8th ACM Conference on Computer and Communication security, pp. 28–37. ACM, New York (2001)
14. Zhang, J., Zou, J., Wang, Y.: A Novel and Secure Non-designated Proxy Signature Scheme for Mobile Agents. In: Lu, X., Zhao, W. (eds.) Networking and Mobile Computing. LNCS, vol. 3619, pp. 533–547. Springer, Heidelberg (2005)
15. Pointcheval, D.: Security Arguments for Digital Signatures and Blind Signatures, Journal of Cryptology, vol. 13, pp. 361–396. Springer-Verlag, New York (1996)
16. Zhang, F., Kim, K.: ID-Based Blind Signature and Ring Signature from Pairings. In: Zheng, Y. (ed.) Advances in Cryptology - ASIACRYPT 2002. LNCS, vol. 2510, pp. 533–547. Springer, Heidelberg (2002)
17. Zhang, F., Kim, K.: Efficient ID-based Blind Signature and Proxy signature from Bilinear Pairings. In: Safavi-Naini, R., Seberry, J. (eds.) Information Security and Privacy. LNCS, vol. 2727, pp. 312–323. Springer, Heidelberg (2003)
18. Schnorr, C.: Security of Blind discrete log signature against interactive attacks. In: Qing, S., Okamoto, T., Zhou, J. (eds.) Information and Communications Security. LNCS, vol. 2299, pp. 1–12. Springer, Heidelberg (2002)

19. Xun, Y.: An Identity-Based Signature Scheme From the Weil Pairing. IEEE Communications Letter 7(2), 76–78 (2003)
20. Wu, Q., Susilo, W., Mu, Y., Zhang, F.: Efficient Partially Blind Signatures with Provable Security. In: Gavrilova, M., Gervasi, O., Kumar, V., Tan, C.J.K., Taniar, D., Laganà, A., Mun, Y., Choo, H. (eds.) Computational Science and Its Applications - ICCSA 2006. LNCS, vol. 3982, pp. 345–354. Springer, Heidelberg (2006)
21. Abe, M., Fujisaki, E.: How to date blind signatures. In: Kim, K.-c., Matsumoto, T. (eds.) Advances in Cryptology - ASIACRYPT '96. LNCS, vol. 1163, pp. 244–252. Springer, Heidelberg (1996)

An Efficient Device Authentication Protocol Using Bioinformatic

Yoon-Su Jeong[1], Bong-Keun Lee[2], and Sang-Ho Lee[3,⋆]

[1] Department of Computer Science, Chungbuk National University, Chungju, Chungbuk, Korea
bukmunro@gmail.com
[2] Department of Multimedia Computer, Busan Kyungsang College, Chungbuk, Korea
rbk@bsks.ac.kr
[3] School of Electrical & Computer Engineering, Chungbuk National University, Chungju, Chungbuk, Korea
shlee@chungbuk.ac.kr

Abstract. The personalization of computing environments is one of the key aspects of ubiquitous computing, and such personalization requires isolated computing environments for better security and stability. In this paper, we propose a mutual authentication method using biometric information of each device users in a situation where device A communicates with device B which is in heterogenous environment. Proposed scheme is designed to be agile in a peer-to-peer environment. We provide analysis results against security attacks and number of required procedures for device authentication.

1 Introduction

Ubiquitous computing[3] promotes the proliferation of embedded devices, smart gadgets, sensors and actuators. We envision an ubiquitous environment to contain hundreds, or even thousands, of devices and sensors that will be everywhere, performing regular tasks, providing new functionality, bridging the virtual and physical worlds, and allowing people to communicate more effectively and interact seamlessly with available computing resources and the surrounding physical environment[5].

There are various infrastructure issues in a ubiquitous environment[4, 11] including ease of use, network management tools for enhanced performance (access, interference, and security management functions), the creation of localized and personalized attractive environments for users (i.e. games for children while parents shop, local maps, areas of interest, location sensitive advertising, coupons for nearby restaurants and shops, etc.), support for push and pull applications, multicasting and broadcasting of information (such as advertisements or game scores), and support for transactions even when the user has a brief disconnection or intermittent connectivity.

⋆ Corresponding author.

Y. Wang, Y. Cheung, and H. Liu (Eds.): CIS 2006, LNAI 4456, pp. 567–575, 2007.

Current device authentication methodologies[6,9] based on ubiquitous environment provide no method for two previously unacquainted parties to authenticate to one another in a trusted manner upon first encounter[8]. Systems like kerberos[4] and SESAME[2] are hard to administrate because they need accounts for users and their management. Therefore, a new authentication methodology is required to enable individuals that have never met to communicate in a trusted manner on the first attempt.

In this paper, we propose a new device mutual authentication method using biometric information in order to guarantee secure communication between arbitrary devices. We assume that the two devices agree each other on the value of a public data string D. This data string could be the concatenation of A's and B's public keys, for some asymmetric cryptosystem. This could support the registration process for a small-scale PKI, or could simply be used as the basis for subsequent secure communications.

The remainder of this paper is organized as follows. Section 2 presents some works relating to authentication methods in ubiquitous computing. Section 3 introduces the proposed mutual authentication protocol for ubiquitous computing environment. Section 4 presents protocol analysis in proposed mutual authentication protocol. Finally, Section 5 draws conclusion.

2 Related Works

2.1 Security Benefits of Device Authentication

Device authentication provides many benefits and enhances network security at a very favorable return on investment [10]. Device authentication enhances the network's security by adding another layer of protection to the defense-in-depth strategy. Device authentication allows only authorized users, using previously enrolled devices, to enter a network and access data. This permits organizations to synchronize their user and device policies. Furthermore, device authentication integrates the secure identification of authorized desktops, laptops, and other remote entry devices into a comprehensive organizational security strategy at a very reasonable cost. It is also particularly effective in securing remote access by mobile users and home office users who must access the network through a VPN or other remote connection utilizing a High Assurance Remote network. Finally, device authentication can be a strategic enabling technology for e-governments and other agency applications where device control, in conjunction with user control, is an important security concern.

2.2 Device Authentication Approach Technology

Some industries suggest a device authentication mechanism based on the unique hardware fingerprint. They extract secure key (either symmetric or asymmetric) from the unique hardware information and use it to authenticate the devices. This is a useful approach to store secret key information. However, they use the existing symmetric or asymmetric key based authentication architecture without modifications, which has some drawbacks in multi-domain home network environment.

Bluetooth and Zigbee provide shared symmetric key based device authentication scheme. They use PIN (Personal Identification Number) to generate shared link key. When users bring the device first to the home network, they have to enter same PIN to each device to share a secret key, and then two devices make a shared key by negotiating with each other based on the PIN. After these setting, the network can be protected from unauthorized device by allowing only authorized device which have share key to access the network. This symmetric key based authentication mechanism is simple way to use in a small scale network which has not more than ten devices. However, it takes huge management cost in a multi-domain home network environment in which dozens or hundreds of devices will communicate with each other.

CableLab suggests a device authentication model which adapts a conventional PKI architecture that has one global root CA. The conventional PKI model is largely deployed technology in user authentication area due to its convenient characteristics in credential management. However, it is not applicable to multi-domain home network environment in several aspects. To get rid of these drawbacks, some localized PKI models for the device authentication are suggested [7,12,13]. The personal CA is a localized PKI model for PAN (Personal Area Network) which has one CA, named personal CA (PCA), for its own network[7,13]. It provides protocols for secure public key registration and certification in PAN.

UPnP(Universal Plug and Play)[1] is a middleware for discovery and control of devices, including networked devices and services, such as network-attached printers, Internet gateways, and consumer electronics equipment. It also provides device authentication mechanism based on SPKI/SDSI (Simple Public Key Infrastructure/Simple Distributed Security Infrastructure) certificate which is another localized PKI model for distributed computing environment. However, UPnP security also has same drawbacks as personal CA; which is not applicable multi-domain home networks environment and demand complex user intervention in registration process.

3 Device Authentication Protocol Using Biometric

This section presents a new DAPB(Device Authentication Protocol using Biometric) device authentication protocol using biometric information in order to guarantee secure communication between arbitrary devices. The DAPB combines EC(Elliptic Curve) with symmetric cryptographic techniques to support secure communication between devices. We assume that the kinds of procedures required for the DAPB is equivalent to the ones for distributed management schemes. Figure 1 shows the major operations where one device A communicates with another device B in a heterogeneous environment.

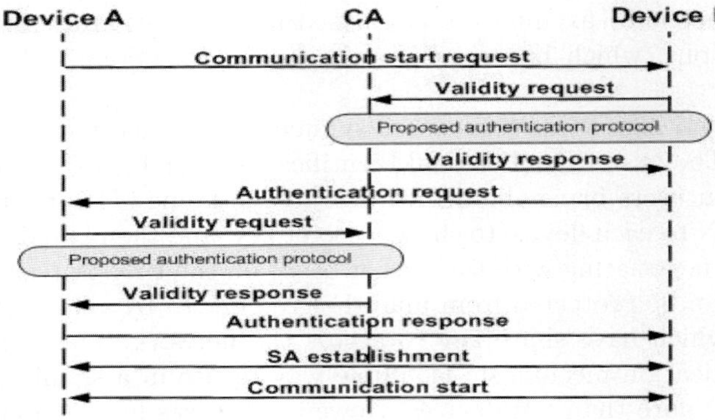

Fig. 1. Operation in DAPB

3.1 Notations

In the section, we define some parameters which are need in the proposed protocol.

BIO_X : bio identity information of entity X
$Pass_X$: password information of entity X
h : one-way hash function
SK : session key
Q_x : temporary public key of entity X
E_{P_x} : encryption using public key of entity X
D_{S_x} : decryption using secret key of entity X
E_K : encryption using symmetry key K
$||$: the concatenation operator

3.2 DAPB Procedure

The DAPB consist of three processes: registration process, key distribution process and SA establishment process.

Registration Process. Registration process which is register devices to server CA(Certificate Authority) is executed only once one. Certification of server CA verifies status information of public key certification by real time using Online Certificate Status Protocol. Detailed registration processes step showed in figure 2.

After device A selects biometric information BIO_A and password $Pass_A$ of device A owner, device A generates $TBIO_A$ by h(BIO_A) || h(BIO_A || $Pass_A$). Device A encrypts the ID_A and $TBIO_A$ using the server CA's public key and transmit it to the server CA. The server CA saves the decryption value which is the decrypt transmitted value. In order to send the server CA information to device A, server CA generates a $TBIO'_A$ that hashes the $TBIO_A$ and r^i_{CA}. The server CA sends the encrypted ID_{CA} registration information, $TBIO_A$ and r^i_{CA}

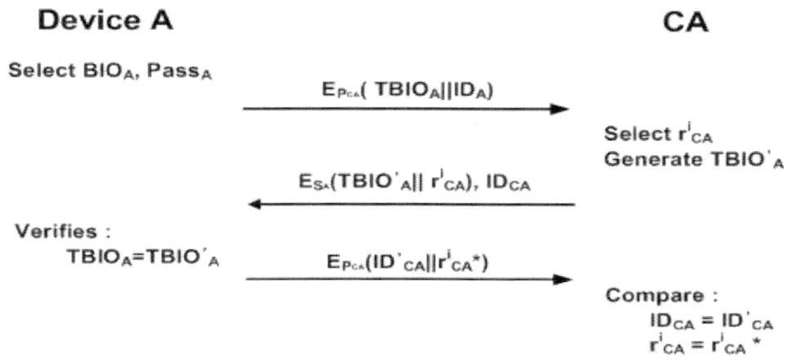

Fig. 2. Registration process in DAPB

to device A. Device A receives the $TBIO_A^{'} \parallel r_{CA}^{'}$ value using a private key E_{S_A} with the transmitted value from server CA. Next, device A hashes the current $TBIO_A$ and verifies $TBIO_A^{'}$. After device A verifies the $TBIO'_A$, it sends an encrypted $ID_{CA}^{'}$ and r_{CA}^{i} * to server CA using the server CA's public key. The server CA decrypts the transmitted value and verifies the decrypted information value($ID_{CA}^{'}$ and r_{CA}^{i} *) with its current information values. After successfully finishing the verification, the server CA sends a successful registration message to device A.

Key Distribution Process. A key distribution process shows how a device A can authenticate a device B. It shows that the proposed procedure is more efficient in the processing steps and safer in security than current techniques, which is not only because it can prove the security of message by measuring T value of message, but because it uses authentication key from session key generated from each device. Detailed description of key distribution process step showed in figure 3.

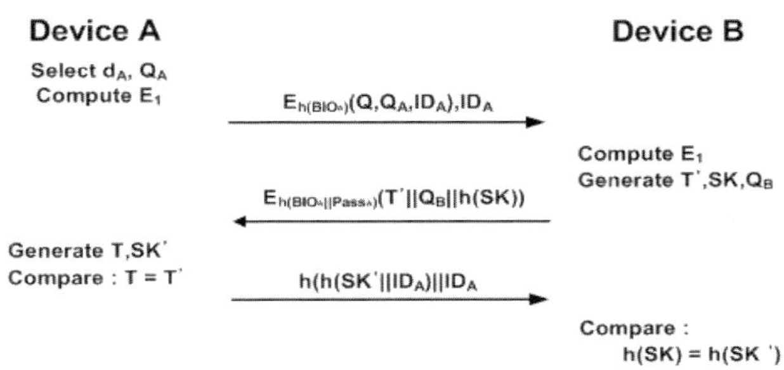

Fig. 3. Key distribution process in DAPB

Device A selects random secret key, d_A and generates a public key, Q_A. In order to generate Q, device A computes E_1 and transmits h(BIO_A) by encryption Q. Device B computes E_1 using transferred Q_A value and then generates h(h(BIO_A)

$\| E_1'$) value compare with Q. If there is success, device B is convinced of the user's ID_A. Device B selects a secret key, d_B and generates a public key, Q_B. In order to generate T', after compute E_2 and generate session key SK, the server CA transmits the data using encryption from T, Q_B, h(SK) to h($BIO_A \| Pass_A$). Device A compares the h(h($BIO_A \| Pass_A$) $\| E_2'$) generated by owner and decryption value T'. After generate session key SK', device A compares transmitted h(SK) value. If process success, device A transmits h(h(SK')) to device B. Device B verify transmitted $h(h(SK' \| ID_A) \| ID_A)$.

SA Establishment Process. In the SA establishment procedure, the PD (Personal Database)s of each device have no communication record about the corresponding device. Therefore, When SA establishment occurs between arbitrary devices, a communication record is generated in each device's secrets table. The secret in each PD is the core of the security protocol. If this is compromised, all security related to the device is compromised. The detail SA establishment operates as follows: Device A sends a communication start request message to device B. Device B has communicated with server CA in the new node addition procedure, so the communication record between server CA and device B has been stored in each PD. Server CA sends a response message to device B over the established SA. This message contains arbitrary communication between record numbers and related data for mutual authentication between devices A and B.

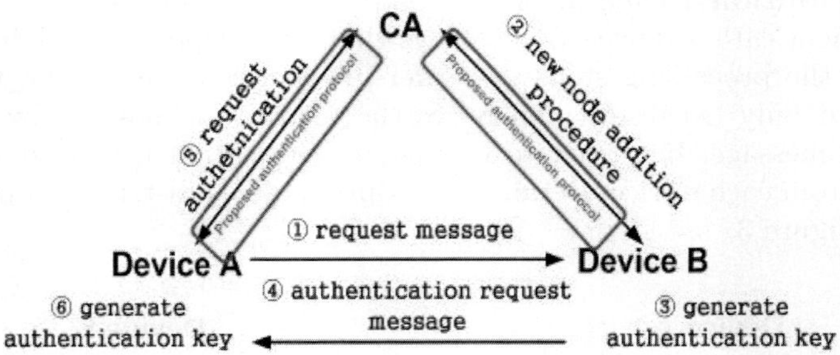

Fig. 4. SA establishment process in DAPB

Since the authentication information between server CA and device B has already been stored in the device B's PD, it is not necessary to send this information to the device B. Server CA authenticates device B using the proposed mutual authentication method using authentication records. Device B generates the authentication key from the secret key using the two kinds of authentication information and a random number, and sends an authentication request message to device A. Server CA authenticates device A using the proposed mutual authentication method using authentication records. The following procedure at device A is the same as the procedure for device B; PD retrieval, mutual authentication with server CA, acquisition of the authentication data between server

CA and device B, and generation of the secret key/authentication key. Mutual authentication is executed by each node, and if successful, a SA is established between device A and device B.

4 Analysis

4.1 Security Analysis

Privacy. In fact, device A and device B can communicate anonymously with respect to all principals, with the exception of the CA. With respect to this communication, the CA is a trusted entity and, hence, fully anonymous connections are not provided. The most important detail to note is that device A cannot deduce device B's location, and device B cannot deduce device A's location. The concealment of locations from end parties can be achieved by using a proxy server employing address translation. The SIP proxies act as intermediaries between communicating parties during the set-up phase of a call.

Man-in-the-Middle Attack. To counter the threat of traffic analysis, a simple solution is to attempt to obscure information flows by ensuring an active communication pattern between device A and device B. Attacks against the physical interface must also be taken into account. As attacker A intervenes on the communication between device A and server CA, it disguises the as an attack from server CA and user U as an authenticated user. Without the knowledge of the secret key, the attacker cannot change a message because user A uses h(BIO_A) to send messages and server CA uses h($BIO_A \parallel Pass_A$) to send messages to device A. Therefore, it is safe.

Forward Secrecy. For server CA, the previous session keys cannot be computed key because the previous secret random number, d_A and d_{CA}, cannot be computed(Half forward Secrecy). Furthermore, even if the secret information for device A and server CA is exposed, attacker A cannot compute the previous random number, d_U and d_S(Full Forward Secrecy). Because the secret keys, d_{ca} and d_U are randomly generated from server S and user U respectively, and are used to set up a session key, it is not helpful to obtain the current session key even if the previous information and session key has been exposed.

Active Impersonation. In the case where attacker A and server S start a session, it is not possible to generate $E_{h(BIO_A)}(Q, Q_A, ID_A)$ because the attacker cannot know the hash value of BIO_A, because it is confidential information in device A. If attacker A performs the role of server S, it is not possible to generate $E_{\mathrm{h}(BIO_A)\parallel Pass_A}(T \parallel Q_{CA} \parallel \mathrm{h}(SK))$ because attacker A does not know h($BIO_U \parallel Pass_A$) which has the hash value of BIO_A.

4.2 Performance Analysis

The number of messages in all procedures of the DAPB is shown in Table I. These procedures are independent of the specific protocol, the processing load is

Table 1. Number of message of the general mutual authentication scheme procedure name

Procedure name	[6,9] S/D	DAPB S/D
Authentication Request/Response	6/3	0/3
Communication Request/Response	4/4	0/2
Calculation for the authentication key	2/1	0/1
Comparison for the Authentication key	2/0	0/1

S : Number of messages from server
D : Number of messages from device

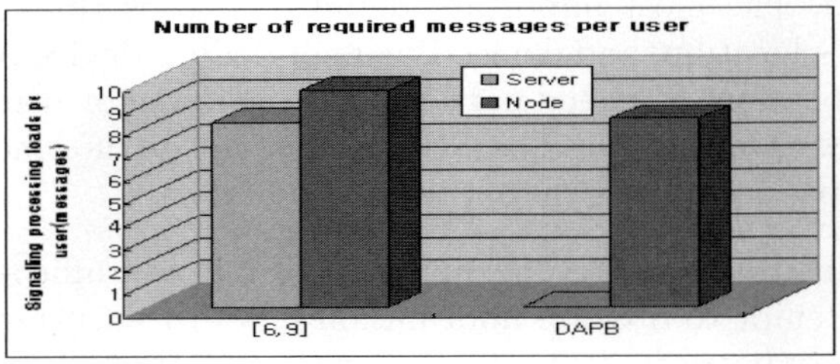

Fig. 5. Number of required messages per user in [6,9] and DAPB

set to the minimum value required for mutual authentication, and one message is counted as one independent of its data size.

In the [6,9], the number of messages from server and device required for device authentication is totally 22. In the DAPB, its procedure can be only executed with 7 messages required for device authentication regardless of the status of the server and the other devices. The DAPB needs only 31.8 percent of [6,9] with respect to the number of message required for the device authentication. In contrast to [6,9], the DAPB needs only device authentication computation for mutual authentication and key exchange, thereby greatly reducing the load of message processing on devices without considering the setup phase overheads. The number of messages needed for every user per hour is shown in Figure 4. In the [6,9] management method, mutual authentication is executed between the concerned devices via the server. Whereas in the DAPB method, the procedure can be executed regardless of the status of the server and other devices.

5 Conclusions

In ubiquitous computing, most devices must move across multiple heterogeneous wireless networks seamlessly without these transitions being apparent to the users. We presented an efficient device authentication protocol that could be used in ubiquitous environments. It allows ad hoc interactions between two devices that are off-line with the rest of the system without the supervision of third parties, like authentication servers or centralized databases. Because the proposed scheme is executed directly between the concerned devices and can be executed regardless of the status of the server and the other devices, DAPB needs only 31.8 percent of [6,9] with respect to the number of message required for the device authentication, thereby greatly reduces the load on communication devices.

References

1. Ellison, C.: UPnP Security Ceremonies Version 1.0, UPnP Forum (2003)
2. Einfeld, D., Sarraf, R.H., Attal, M., Tavakoli, K.: SESAME, a 2,5 GeV synchrotron light source for the Middle East region. Particle Accelerator Conference, 2003. PAC 2003, Proceedings of the Volume 1 12(16), 238–240 (2003)
3. Muhtad, A., Ranganathan, A., Campbell, R., Mickunas, N.D.: A flexible, privacy-preserving authentication framework for ubiquitous computing environments. In: Proceedings of IWSAEC (2002)
4. Stajano, F.: Security for Ubiquitous Computing. John Wiley and Sons Ltd, New York (2002)
5. Gehrmann, C., Nyberg, K.: Security in personal area networks. In: Mitchell, C.J. (ed.) Security for Mobility, pp. 191–230. IEE, London (2004)
6. Bussard, L., Roudier, Y.: Authentication in Ubiquitous Computing. In: Workshop on Security in Ubiquitous Computing, 4th International UBICOMP (2002)
7. Gehrmann, C., Nyberg, K., Mitchell, C.J.: The personal CA - PKI for a personal area network. In: IST Mobile and Wireless Telecommunications Summit, pp. 31–35 (2002)
8. Kagal, L., Finin, T., Joshi, A.: Trust-Based Security in Pervasive Computing Environments. IEEE Computer 24, 154–157 (2001)
9. Richard, G.G.: Service Advertisement and Discovery: Enabling Universal Device Cooperation. IEEE Internet Computing, 4(5) (2000)
10. SafeNet, Device Authetnication:A Valunable Addition to Agency Cyber-Security Programs, SafeNet, Inc (2002)
11. Hengartner, U., Steenkiste, P.: Protecting People Location Information, Workshop on Security in Ubiquitous Computing, 4th International UBICOMP (2002)
12. Ellison, C., Frantz, B., Lampson, B., Rivest, R., Thomas, B., Ylonen, T.: SPKI Certificate Theory, RFC2693 (1999)
13. Gehrmann, C., Kuhn, T., Nyberg, K., Windirsch, P.: Trust model, communication and configuration security for personal area networks. In: IST Mobile and Wireless Telecommunications Summit, pp. 41–45 (2002)

Subjective and Objective Watermark Detection Using a Novel Approach – Barcode Watermarking

Vidyasagar Potdar, Song Han, Elizabeth Chang, and Chen Wu

Digital Ecosystems and Business Intelligence Institute, Curtin University of Technology, Perth, Western Australia, Australia
{Vidyasagar.Potdar,Song.Han,Elizabeth.Chang, Chen.Wu}@cbs.curtin.edu.au

Abstract. Many digital watermarking algorithms are proposed in the literature. Broadly these watermarking algorithms can be classified into two main categories. The first category of algorithms uses a pseudo random Gaussian sequence (PRGS) watermark whereas the second category of algorithms uses a binary logo as a watermark. The main advantage of PRGS based watermarking scheme is its ability to detect the presence of watermark without manual intervention. However the main drawback is calculating reliable threshold value. In the similar manner the main advantage of binary logo watermark is that there is no need to calculate threshold value but requires manual intervention to detect the presence of watermark. The advantage and disadvantage of either approach is quite clear hence it would be a good idea to design a watermarking scheme which inherits the advantages from both these approaches. In this paper we present one such approach which is termed as bar-code watermarking. The proposed scheme offers objective as well as subjective detection. A PRGS sequence watermark is represented as a bar-code on a binary logo and embedded in the host image. Watermark detection can be either done subjectively or objectively.

Keywords: Image Watermarking, Barcodes, Subjective & Objective Watermark Detection.

1 Introduction

The adoption of Internet in day to day has resulted in exchange of copyrighted material over peer-to-peer (P2P) networks which results in copyright infringements. Digital watermarking schemes are developed to detect copyright infringements.

Broadly these watermarking algorithms can be classified into two main categories. The first category of algorithms uses a pseudo random gaussian sequence (PRGS) watermark where the presence of the embedded watermark is detected by using statistical correlation whereas the second category of algorithms use a binary logo as a watermark and this logo is extracted to detect the presence of watermark.

The former approach is more objective because it relies on a statistical correlation value to ascertain the presence of watermark however the latter approach is more subjective because the presence of watermark is detected by visual inspection by a

Y. Wang, Y. Cheung, and H. Liu (Eds.): CIS 2006, LNAI 4456, pp. 576–586, 2007.

third entity. In the former approach the original watermark is required to detect the presence of the extracted watermark because correlation is calculated by comparing the original watermark with the extracted watermark. However with the latter approach the original watermark is not required because the extracted watermark which is normally a logo is visually recognizable. There is no need to compare it with the original embedded logo. The mere fact that the logo is visible is enough to prove the presence of watermark.

Table 1. PRGS vs. Binary Logo Watermarks

PRGS		**Binary Logo Watermarking**	
Advantages	Disadvantages	Advantages	Disadvantages
Automatic Watermark Detection	Threshold Calculation	No threshold calculation	Manual detection by visual inspection
	Use of original watermark for detection	No need of using original watermark for detection	
		Contextual relationship amongst the watermark logo	

The advantages and drawbacks of either approaches is described in Table 1. The paper is organized as follows. In Section 2, we discuss some existing watermarking schemes (based on wavelet) which embed binary watermarks. We specifically discuss some quantization based algorithms. A detailed discussion and critical analysis is provided for the existing schemes. In Section 3, we describe the proposed watermarking scheme. We first outline the procedure of watermark generation followed by watermark embedding and extraction algorithm. In Section 4, we discuss the experimental setting where we specify the attacks and its intensity which would be used to test the robustness of the proposed watermarking scheme. In Section 5, results obtained after each attack are described in detail and a conclusion is drawn as to how our algorithm resists these attacks. Section 6 concludes the paper.

2 Existing Work

In this section we discuss some wavelet based watermarking algorithms. We classify these algorithms based on their decoder requirements as blind detection or non-blind detection. Most of the watermarking schemes surveyed in this section use a binary logo as a watermark. The size of the watermark is smaller compared to the host image.

In [3], Hsu and Wu present a wavelet based watermarking scheme which embeds a binary logo as a watermark. The watermark is embedded in the mid frequency components of the wavelet sub-bands. This scheme is resistant to common image processing attacks only. Its robustness against geometric distortions is not discussed. The main drawback of this algorithm is its non-blind nature i.e. the original image is required for detecting the presence of watermark.

Lu et al. [4] present a robust watermarking scheme based on image fusion. The algorithm is a non-blind watermarking algorithm which embeds grey-scale image and binary image as watermarks. The watermark strength is modulated based on Just Noticeable Distortion (JND) threshold. All the coefficients in the LL, HL, LH, and HH subband at all the four levels are used to embed the watermark. The algorithm is shown to be robust against the following attacks: Blurring, Median Filtering, Re-scaling, JPEG compression, EZW compression, Jitter Attacks, Collusion Attacks, Rotation, Stirmark Attacks, unZign Attack, a combination of above attacks were tested. However the main issue with this algorithm is its non-blind nature which limits its application.

Raval and Rege [5] present a non-blind watermarking scheme where two binary watermarks are embedded in LL_2 and HH_2 sub-band. All the coefficients in the LL_2 and HH_2 subband are used. After performing a two level decomposition of the host image (I), the binary watermark is embedded in the LL_2 and HH_2 subband by additive embedding. It has been shown that watermarks embedded in LL_2 subbands are robust to one set of attacks (filtering, lossy compression, geometric distortions) while those embedded in HH_2 subbands are robust to another set of attacks (histogram equalization, gamma correction, contrast and brightness adjustment and cropping). However the use of uniform scaling parameter results in some visible artifacts. It should have been a good idea to consider variable scaling factors for different sub-bands.

Tao and Eskicioglu [6] conduct a comparative study to find out the effects of embedding watermarks in the first and second level decomposition. The authors suggest that embedding in the first level is advantageous because it offers more coefficients for modification and the extracted watermarks are more textured and have better subjective visual quality. The technique uses variable scaling parameters for different subbands at different decomposition levels. Their main observations are LL_1 and LL_2 bands are robust against JPEG compression, Blurring, Gaussian Noise, Scaling, Cropping, Pixilation and Sharpening. HH_1 and HH_2 bands are robust against Histogram Equalization, Intensity Adjustment, and Gamma Correction. HL_1, HL_2 and LH_1, LH_2 also show similar robustness. As with the other techniques the main issue with this algorithm is the non-blind nature, original image is required for extracting the watermarks.

Ganic and Eskicioglu [7] inspired by Raval and Rege [5] propose another watermarking scheme based on DWT and Singular Value Decomposition (SVD). They argue that the watermark embedded by using [5] scheme is visible in some parts of the image especially in the low frequency areas, which reduces the commercial value of the image. Hence they generalize their technique by using all the four sub-bands and embedding the watermark in SVD domain.

All the algorithms discussed so far require the original image for detecting the presence of watermark which is a major drawback and is not feasible in all scenarios. Hence we now discuss some blind watermarking algorithms which embed an image logo as a watermark.

In [1] Tsai et al. improve the scheme proposed in [3] by presenting a scalar quantization based blind watermarking scheme which embeds a binary logo as a watermark and the offer blind detection. They embed the watermark in the middle and low frequency components of the wavelet sub-bands i.e. all sub-bands except LL subband. All the selected coefficients are quantized by a constant factor which is a main issue with this algorithm because certain high texture rich regions within an image can tolerate large modifications (quantization step sizes) because of their inherent high texture masking capacity and hence can be strongly watermarked. At the same time smooth regions have a comparatively lower masking capacity and hence should be quantized using smaller step sizes. This algorithm shows robustness against JPEG compression only. It's robustness against geometric attacks and other image processing attacks is not discussed.

In [8] Barni et al. present wavelet based watermarking scheme which incorporates HVS to modulate the strength of the watermark according to the local characteristics. The watermark is not a binary logo but it is a binary PRGS. The watermark is embedded in HH_1, HL_1 and LH_1 subbands. This scheme is robust against JPEG compression, cropping and morphing.

In [9] Meerwald present a quantization based watermarking scheme in the JPEG2000 coding pipeline. The watermarks are embedded in all the sub-bands prior to the entropy coding stage. The scheme is only robust against a small set of attacks like JPEG, JPEG2000, Blur and Sharpening.

In [2] Chen et al. present another quantization based watermarking scheme which improves on the algorithm proposed in [1] by incorporating variable quantization based on HVS similar to [8]. They embed the watermark in the approximate subband of the fourth level wavelet decomposition i.e. the LL_4.

Based on the survey we identified the following issues with the existing watermarking schemes are:

- Do not offer subjective and objective detection simultaneously in one watermarking scheme.
- Binary logo watermarking schemes do not offer objective detection.
- Existing solutions do not provide an alternative detection mechanism in case the objective detection fails or is considered incorrect.

In order to address these issues we proposed a new watermarking scheme termed as bar-code watermarking. The basic idea behind bar-code watermarking is to represent the PRGS watermark in a binary logo and make it machine readable. The machine readability is achieved by representing the PRGS watermark as a bar-code. For example 1010101010101010 can be represented as . The proposed approach serves two main purposes firstly it could be used for objective watermark detection using correlation and secondly it could also be used for subjective watermark detection in case the objective detection fails. The extracted watermark can be visually inspected to prove the presence of the watermark.

3 Barcode Watermarking

In this paper we present a multi-purpose watermarking scheme that can offer subjective as well as objective watermark detection. The proposed scheme is termed as bar-code watermarking. The scheme is also shown to be robust against a wide range of attacks. In contrast to the schemes proposed earlier, our scheme higher detection capability because the decoder can be used for subjective and objective detection. Our watermarking scheme is divided into three steps, firstly watermark generation step followed by watermark embedding step and finally extraction step.

3.1 Bar-Code Binary Logo Watermark (BBLW) Generation

Inputs: PRGS watermark W
Output: Bar-code Binary Logo Watermark W_b

The process of watermark generation is shown in the Table 2. The PRGS watermark bits are represented in a bar-code format. Each bar (white or black) represent one bit. A black bar represents a binary bit '1' whereas a white bar represents a binary bit '0'. We generated a bar-code binary logo of the following dimensions – 64 x 64. In this logo each bar is 8 x 4 (height x width) pixels in size. Hence one row can represent 16 bits of information. After each row we leave one row blank (6 x 64 pixels). This improves the visual quality of the BBLW which might be necessary if subjective detection is desired.

Table 2. PRGS vs. Binary Logo Watermarks

PRGS watermark (W)	Bar-coded representation of PRGS watermark
10101010101010	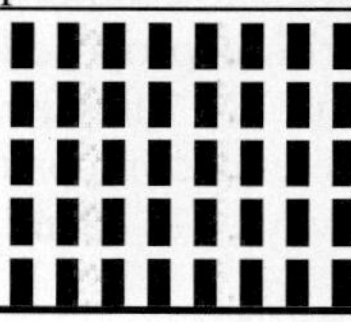
10101010101010	
10101010101010	
10101010101010	
10101010101010	

3.2 Embedding Algorithm

Inputs: Original Image (I), BBLW (W_b)*, Secret Keys (K)*
Output: Watermarked Image (I_w)

The detail approach is described as follows:

Step 1. Generate the BBLW using steps described in section 3.1.
Step 2. Permute the BBLW using the permutation function *f(.)* and permutation key *(P)* to increase the security of the watermark - W_b^P.
Step 3. The BBLW can be embedded in an image by using any binary logo embedding algorithm. In this paper we used the robust logo embedding algorithm presented by the authors in [10] to embed the binary logo *L*. The detailed algorithm is discussed in the Appendix A. The basic sub steps are:

- Decompose the original image *I* by one level wavelet transform to obtain LL_1, LH_1, HL_1 and HH_1 subbands using Haar Wavelet Filter.

- For each sub-band except the LH_1 sub-band, starting at the top left corner divide the wavelet coefficients into non-overlapping blocks of 8x8 and calculate the mean intensity values of each block.
- Construct the quantization table *T*.
- Quantifying all the blocks in LH_1, HL_1 and HH_1 using HVS threshold to represent the BBLW W_b.
- Apply inverse wavelet transform to embed the watermark logo.

Step 4. The output is the watermarked image I_w.

3.3 Extraction and Detection Algorithm

Inputs: Watermarked Image (I_w), Secret Keys (K)
Output: BBLW (W_b)

The detail approach is described as follows:

Step 1. Load the watermarked image I_w
Step 2. Using the extraction algorithm proposed in [10] extract the BBLW. The sub steps are:

- The watermarked image I_w is decomposed by one level wavelet transform to obtain LL_1, LH_1, HL_1 and HH_1.
- For each sub-band except the LL sub-band, starting at the top left corner we divide the sub-band into non-overlapping blocks of 8x8 and calculate the mean intensity values of the wavelet coefficients.
- Compare these values with the quantization table T to generate the BBLW
- Inverse permute the BBLW (W_b^P) to recover the original BBLW (W_b).

Step 3. The BBLW is now parsed to recover the PRGS . The sub steps are:

- Consider the first block of pixel (8x4) beginning from 1st row and 1st column
- Calculate the number of black pixels and white pixels with in that block
- *If* the black pixels are more than a specific threshold (T_h)
  - The block under consideration represents 1
  - Proceed to the next block
- *Else if* the white pixels are more than a specific threshold (T_h)
  - The block under consideration represents 0
  - Proceed to the next block

Step 4. Compare it with the original PRGS and calculate correlation coefficient to detect the presence of the watermark.

- *If* the correlation is weak or the watermark cannot be detected then
  - The extracted logo can be visually inspected.
  - *If* the bar-code pattern exists then
    Image is watermarked.

4 Experimental Setting

In the experiments that we conducted we used the four original images as shown in Table 3. The size of the original image is 1024x1024 pixel grey scale image whereas

Table 3. Original Images used for watermarking

Lena	Baboon	F-16	Pepper
	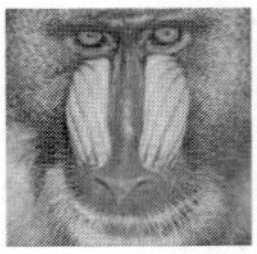		

the size of the watermark logo is 64x64 pixels. We used Haar Wavelet filter to decompose the image in the wavelet domain.

The watermark logo W_b and the permuted watermark W*b that is used in the experiments is shown in Table 4. The watermarked image is as shown in Table 5. There are no visible artifacts because the wavelet coefficients are quantized under the HVS constraints; secondly the wavelet coefficients belong to the detailed subbands (LH_1, HL_1 and HH_1) and quantizing those results in the implicit perceptual masking.

Table 4. Watermarks used in Experiments

Barcode Watermark	Permuted Watermark

The entire watermark information is hidden along the edges and corners. The proposed algorithm is shown to be robust against ten major attacks including watermark removal and synchronization removal attacks. Although distortions exist the watermark is still visually recognizable (subjective detection) and statistically detected (PSNR values).

Table 5. Watermarked Images

Lena	Baboon	F-16	Pepper
	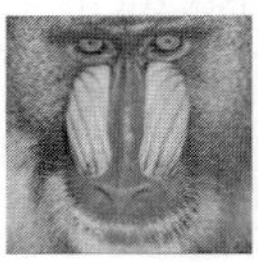		

Table 6. List of attack applied on watermarked images

Attack Name	Attack Description
Gamma Correction	Increase gamma level of image by 110, 120, 130, 140, 150%.
JPEG	Perform JPEG compression on image QF 90, 80, 70, 60, and 50.
JPEG 2000	Perform JPEG 2000 compression QF 90, 80, 70, 60, and 50.
Contrast	Increase contrast of image by 15, 32, 52, 74, 100%
Salt & Pepper	Apply a salt & pepper filter to image. Noise density 0.001, 0.002, 0.003, 0.004 and 0.005.
Row Column Blanking	Blank rows and columns in image. Blank 5, 10, 20, 30 and 40 rows and columns
Row-Column Copying	Copy rows and columns in image to the adjacent row or column. Blank 5, 10, 20, 30 and 40 rows and columns
Cropping	Crop image smaller by four block sizes, five times successively.
Rotate 90, 180	Rotate the image by 90 or 180 degrees clockwise.

We attacked the watermarked image with the following attacks; the details of the attacks are listed in Table 6.

5 Experimental Results

In this section we discuss the experimental results that we gathered by running our prototype. We used watermark shown in Table 4 to embed in four images. The extracted watermarks are shown in the following Table 7.

Table 7. Watermarked Images

Lena	Baboon	F-16	Pepper
	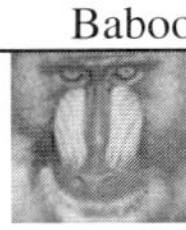	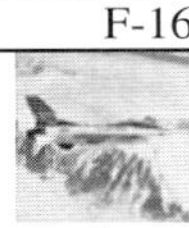	
Gamma Correction			
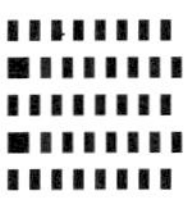		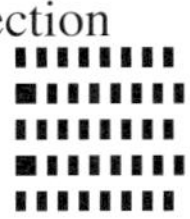	
JPEG			

Table 7. (*continued*)

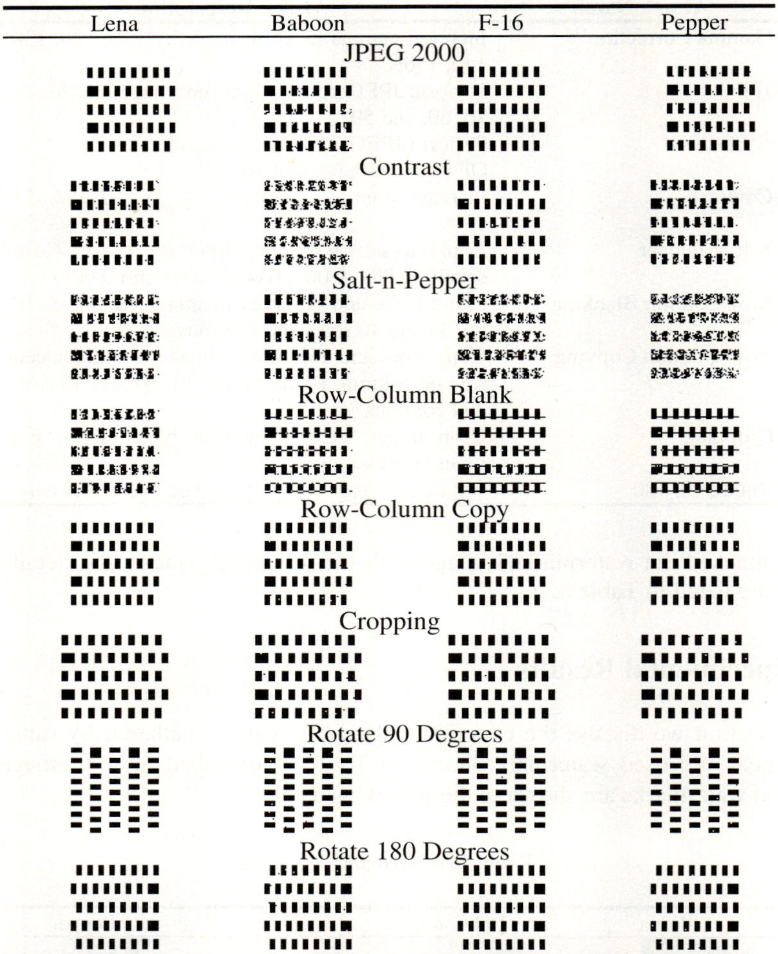

6 Conclusion

In this paper, we present a bar-code watermarking approach which can offer objective as well as subjective detection. The PRGS sequence watermark is represented as a bar-code on a binary logo. This bar-code binary logo is then embedded in the host image which is to be watermarked. The proposed approach serves two main purposes firstly it could be used for objective watermark detection using correlation and secondly it could also be used for subjective detection (visual inspection) in case the objective detection fails.

References

1. Tsai, M.J., Yu, K.Y., Chen, Y.Z.: Joint Wavelet and spatial transformation for digital watermarking. IEEE Transactions on Consumer Electronics 46, 241–245 (2000)
2. Chen, T.Z., Horng, G., Wang, S.H., Robust, A.: Wavelet Based Watermarking Scheme using Quantization and Human Visual System Model. Proceedings of the Pakistan Journal of Information and Technology 2, 212–230 (2003)
3. Hsu, C.T., Wu, J.L.: Multi-resolution Watermarking for Digital Images. IEEE Transactions on Circuits and System—II Analog and Digital Signal Processing 45, 1097–1101 (1998)
4. Lu, C.S., Huang, S.-K., Sze, C.-J., Liao, H.-Y.: A new watermarking technique for multimedia protection. Presented at Multimedia Image and Video Processing, Boca Raton, FL (2001)
5. Raval, M.S., Rege, P.P.: Discrete wavelet transform based multiple watermarking scheme. In: Proceedings of the Convergent Technologies for the Asia-Pacific Region, Bangalore, India (2003)
6. Ganic, E., Eskicioglu, A.M.: Robust digital watermarking: Robust DWT-SVD domain image watermarking: embedding data in all frequencies. In: Proceedings of the 2004 Multimedia and Security Workshop on Multimedia and Security (2004)
7. Barni, M., Bartolini, F., Piva, A.: Improved Wavelet-based Watermarking Through Pixel-Wise Masking. IEEE Transactions on Image Processing 10, 783–791 (2001)
8. Meerwald, P.: Digital Image Watermarking in the Wavelet Transform Domain, University of Salzburg (2001)
9. Lewis, A.S., Knowles, G.: Image Compression using 2-D Wavelet Transform. IEEE Transactions on Image Processing 1, 244–250 (1992)
10. Potdar, V., Han, S., Chang, E.: Self Image Logo Embedding – A Robust Image Watermarking Algorithm in Wavelet Domain, to appear in International Journal of Information Security and Privacy (2007)

Appendix A

```
IMPORT: Image of attacked barcode
EXPORT: Boolean indicating whether barcode is readable
METHOD: Boolean checkBarcode( image, reference)
Variables in terms of average white pixels in each bar of
a perfect barcode
   –  maxBlack = 0      %(will hold the highest average of
      all the bars that are supposed to be black)
   –  minWhite = 1      %(will hold the lowest average of
      all the bars that are supposed to be white)
   –  maxX = 0.5        %(will hold the highest average
      of all the bars that are supposed to be X)
   –  minX = 0.5        %(will hold the lowest average of
      all the bars that are supposed to be X)
for each row in image
for each bar in row
average = average of current bar in image
```

```
  if reference bar is:
    :black
      if average > maxBlack
      then maxBlack = average
      end if
    :white
      if average < minWhite
      then minWhite = average
      end if
    :X
      if average > maxX
      then maxX = average
      end if
      if average < minX
      then minX = average
      end if
    end if
  end for
  end for
  if maxBlack >= minX OR minWhite <= maxX
    then readable = false
    else readable = true
  return readable
%(if the barcode is readable, the appropriate threshold
values for black bars and white bars can be found in
between maxBlack and minX, and maxX and minWhite
respectively)
```

Forward Secure Threshold Signature Scheme from Bilinear Pairings

Jia Yu[1], Fanyu Kong[2], and Rong Hao[1,2]

[1] College of Information Engineering, Qingdao University, 266071 Qingdao, China
{yujia,hr}@qdu.edu.cn
[2] Institute of Network Security, Shandong University, 250100 Jinan, China
phd_kong@yahoo.com

Abstract. A forward secure threshold signature scheme from bilinear pairings is presented in this paper. Compared with previous forward secure threshold signature schemes against malicious adversary, this scheme needs very few interactions and is very efficient. A new interactive zero-knowledge proof protocol is presented and its non-interactive version can verify the validity of part signatures in this scheme. At last, we prove that the scheme is robust and forward secure in the random oracle model.

1 Introduction

Exposure of secret keys is one of the greatest threats to the security of a digital signature. Therefore, how to deal with the problem of secret key exposure in signatures is very important. Threshold signature is used to void secret key exposure. In a $(t+1, n)$ threshold signature[1, 2], a secret key is distributed into n servers, and each server has a share of the secret key. Only more than t servers can jointly generate signatures. In comparison, forward secure signature[3~5] can reduce the damage of secret key exposure. In this paradigm, the whole lifetime of signature is divided into several time periods, the secret key is updated in each period by a one-way function, at the same time, the old key is destroyed. As a result, even if the current secret key is exposed, the adversary can't forge signatures for past time periods. Forward secure threshold signature combines the merits of the both kinds of signatures, as a result, it satisfies that if an adversary breaks into no more than t servers, she can't forge any signature; even if an adversary breaks into more than t servers, she can't forge signatures pertaining to previous time periods.

Related works. Abdalla *et al.* [6] firstly present a forward secure threshold signature scheme against malicious adversary based on the scheme in [3]. However, in their scheme, the size of both the public key and the secret key is very large, what's more, the scheme needs a lot of interactions because distributed multiplication of many values protocol is used. Distributed multiplication of many values protocol is very inefficient, and it is still an open problem to improve its efficiency [6]. Following by

Y. Wang, Y. Cheung, and H. Liu (Eds.): CIS 2006, LNAI 4456, pp. 587–597, 2007.

Abdalla's work, another forward secure threshold signature with proactive property [7] is suggested, which needs shorter keys, however, has lower efficiency. Wang *et al.* [8] point out the scheme in [7] is insecure. Chu *et al.* present a forward secure threshold signature scheme with weak security as an extension of his main work [9], but it can't tolerate malicious adversary and has not any proofs of forward security.

Our contribution. Based on [5], a forward secure threshold signature scheme *FTS* from bilinear pairings is presented in this paper. We name it as scheme *FTS*.

In addition, we present a new interactive zero-knowledge proof protocol named as *Proof-VS*, and prove that it is complete, sound and zero-knowledge. Then we convert *Proof-VS* into a non-interactive version *NIProof-VS* which is used to verify the validity of part signatures in our scheme by using a collision-resistant hash function. With necessary changes, *NIProof-VS* can be used in other threshold schemes from pairings effectively, too. Note that scheme *FTS* can void using distributed multiplication of many values thanks to using bilinear pairings.

Scheme *FTS* is very efficient. There are only once interaction in update algorithm and twice interactions in signing algorithm in this scheme. The running time of both the key generation and the key update algorithm is independent of the total number of time periods T in the scheme. And the signing and verifying costs are only logarithmic in T. The new scheme is robust against malicious adversary. Finally, we prove it is forward secure in the random oracle model assuming CDH problem is hard.

Organization. In section 2, we introduce the preliminaries of our work, including communication model, definition and related mathematical background. The presented zero-knowledge proof protocol and the concrete description of the scheme are given in Section 3. We compare the efficiency of our scheme with related schemes and provide the security proof of our scheme in section 4 and 5, respectively. In section 6, further discussion is given. Finally, we conclude this paper in the last Section.

2 Preliminaries

2.1 Model and Definition

(1) Communication Model

There exists a trusted dealer during the key generation phase. We assume that the participants in our scheme include a set of n players $\{1,2,\ldots,n\}$ who are connected by a broadcast channel. Additionally, they can securely communicate over private point-to-point channels. Furthermore, the system works in a synchronous communication model; that is, all participating players have a common clock and, thus, can send their messages simultaneously in a particular round of a protocol. Finally, the whole lifetime of signature is divided into T time periods. At the end of each time period, the participants update their shares all together.

(2) Forward Secure Threshold Signature Scheme

Definition 1 (Key-evolving threshold signature scheme). A key-evolving threshold signature scheme is a quadruple of algorithms, *FTS(t,s,n)=(FTS.GEN, FTS.UPD, FTS.SIG, FTS.VER)*, where, t is the maximum number of corrupted players; s is the minimum number of honest players so that signature computation is feasible; n is the total number of players,

FTS.GEN: the key generation algorithm, inputs a security parameter $k \in N$ and the total number of time periods T, and generates a public key PK and the initial shares of secret key for all players.

FTS.UPD: the secret key update algorithm, inputs the current time period j, and generates a share $SK_{j+1}^{(i)}$ for each player i in the algorithm for the next time period.

FTS.SIG: the signing algorithm, inputs the current time period j and a message M, and the participant players jointly generate a signature <*j*, tag> of M for period j.

FTS.VER: the verification algorithm, inputs the public key PK, a message M and a signature <*j*, tag>, and returns 1 if <*j*, tag> is a valid signature of M or 0, otherwise.

$SK_j^{(i)}$ is a share player i holds in period j. Assume that $SK_j^{(i)}$ always contains the value j and the total number of time periods T. If <*j*, tag> is a valid signature generated in *FTS.SIG* algorithm, then *FTS.VER*(*M*, <*j*, tag>)=1.

The adversary model in ROM. The adversary F chooses players to corrupt at the beginning of the game. She runs in three stages: in the chosen-message attack (cma) phase, F has access to the signing oracle, and can query to obtain the signature of any message she selects under the current secret key. At the end of each time period, the adversary can choose whether to stay in the same phase or switch to the over-threshold phase. In the over-threshold phase, for a particular time period b, the adversary may corrupt a set of players of size t+1 or greater. It means F can learn the secret key. In the forgery phase, the adversary outputs her forgery, i.e. a signature message pair. We consider an adversary successful if she forges a signature of some new message for some period prior to the time period b. The adversary is allowed to query a random oracle H corresponding to a collision-resistant hash function.

Definition 2 (Forward secure threshold signature scheme). A key-evolving threshold signature scheme is a forward secure threshold signature scheme if there is no such an adversary described above that can forge a signature <*j*, tag> for some new message M *s.t.* *FTS.VER*(*M*, <*j*, tag>)=1 and $j<b$.

2.2 Cryptographic Assumptions

Let G_1 and G_2 be two groups of some prime order q, where G_1 is represented additively and G_2 is represented multiplicatively. And let $P \in G_1$ be a generator of G_1. A bilinear pairing is an efficiently computable map $e: G_1 \times G_1 \rightarrow G_2$, which satisfies:

1. Bilinear: For all $P,Q \in G_1$ and $a,b \in Z$, there is $e(aP,bQ) = e(P,Q)^{ab}$.
2. Non-degenerate: The map does not send all pairs in $G_1 \times G_1$ to the identity in G_2.
3. Computable: There is an efficient algorithm to compute $e(P,Q)$ for any $P,Q \in G_1$.

Decision Diffie-Hellman (DDH) problem: Given (P,aP,bP,cP), where $a,b,c \in Z_q$, decide whether $c = ab$ in Z_q. Computation Diffie-Hellman (CDH) problem: Given (P,aP,bP), where $a,b \in Z_q$, compute abP.

Definition 3 (GDH group). A prime order group G is a GDH group if DDH problem can be solved in polynomial time but no probabilistic algorithm solves CDH problem.

The Weil and Tate pairings are practical example of the bilinear pairing. Using the Weil or Tate pairing, certain elliptic curves can be used as GDH groups.

IG is a GDH parameter generator if only it takes security parameter k, outputs two groups G_1 and G_2 and an admissible pairing $e: G_1 \times G_1 \rightarrow G_2$.

3 The Forward Secure Threshold Signature Scheme

3.1 Building Blocks

Let G be a cyclic group of some prime order q, where G is represented additively. Let $P_i (i = 0...n)$ be the generators of G.

(1) The zero-knowledge proof protocols we present

Prover P wants to convince verifier V that she knows the values $b_i (i = 1...n)$ that satisfy $G_i = b_i P_0 (i = 1...n), H' = \sum_{i=1}^{n} b_i P_i$.

Firstly, we give an interactive protocol $Proof-VS(P_0; P_1,..., P_n; G_1,..., G_n; H')$:

①P selects $w_i \in_R Z_q (i = 1...n)$, computes $E_i = w_i P_0 (i = 1...n)$ and $F = \sum_{i=1}^{n} w_i P_i$, and sends these values to V.

②V randomly chooses $c \in_R Z_q$, and sends it to P.

③P computes $r_i = w_i - b_i c, (i = 1...n)$, and sends them to V.

④V verifies: $E_i \stackrel{?}{=} r_i P_0 + cG_i (i = 1...n)$ and $F \stackrel{?}{=} cH' + \sum_{i=1}^{n} r_i P_i$. If equations are right, V believes P; otherwise, doesn't.

Theorem 1. *Proof-VS* is complete, sound and zero-knowledge.

Proof. (Sketch)

(1)Completeness : If P and V are honest and P knows b_i, then the following both equations are right:

$$E_i = w_i P_0 = (r_i + b_i c) P_0 = r_i P_0 + cG_i, (i = 1...n),$$

$$F = \sum_{i=1}^{n} w_i P_i = \sum_{i=1}^{n} (r_i + b_i c) P_i = cH' + \sum_{i=1}^{n} r_i P_i.$$

So V believes P.

(2)Soundness: If P doesn't know some b_i, after P sends E_i and F to V, and then gets c from V, P is only able to guess r_i. The probability that P makes V believe him is $1/q$ at most. Therefore the soundness can be satisfied.

(3)Zero-knowledge: We can construct a simulator S to simulate the view of any verifier. S selects $c' \in_R Z_q$ and $r_i' \in_R Z_q (i = 1...n)$. She computes $E_i' = r_i' P_0 + c' G_i$,

$(i=1...n)$ and $F'=c'H'+\sum_{i=1}^{n} r_i' P_i$. The distributions of E_i', F', c_i' and r' are statistically indistinguishable from those of E_i, F, c, r_i in the real view.

Then, convert *Proof-VS* into a non-interactive version by a collision-resistant hash function: $H: G \to Z_q$. The protocol $NI\,Proof-VS(P_0; P_1,..., P_n; G_1,..., G_n; H')$ is described as follows:

①P selects $w_i \in_R Z_q (i=1...n)$ at random, and computes $E_i = w_i P_0 (i=1...n)$, $F=\sum_{i=1}^{n} w_i P_i$, $c = H(P_0 \| P_1 \| ... \| P_n \| G_1 \| ... \| G_n \| H' \| E_1 \| ... \| E_n \| F)$, and $r_i = w_i - b_i c, (i=1...n)$. Then sends $c, r_i (i=1...n)$ to V.

②V verifies:

$$c \stackrel{?}{=} H(P_0 \| P_1 \| ... \| P_n \| G_1 \| ... \| G_n \| H' \| r_1 P_0 + cG_1 \| ... \| r_n P_0 + cG_n \| cH' + \sum_{i=1}^{n} r_i P_i)$$

If the equation is right, V believes P; otherwise, doesn't.

(2) Distributed random secret generation (*Joint-RVSS*) protocol

All players jointly and verifiably generate a random secret ρ and each player *i* has a share ρ_i of the secret. Any *t*+1 players can reconstruct the secret ρ, however, *t* players can't get any useful message about it. The public commits include ρP_0 and $\rho_i P_0 (i=1...n)$. We use the *Joint-Exp-RSS* protocol in [10] as the *Joint-RVSS* protocol in our scheme. So we will use the security results of it to prove the security of our threshold signature scheme. As is proved in [10], the view of an adversary corrupting *t* players can be simulated when the commit ρP_0 is taken as input. Here we skip the detailed descriptions of this protocol and its security proof.

3.2 Notations

Our scheme uses a binary tree structure similar to that in [5] which is a variant of the tree structure used in the HIBS scheme in [11]. If we use a full binary tree with depth l, then the number of time periods is $T = 2^{l+1} - 1$ (labeled 0 through *T*-1). Each node of the tree is associated with one time period. Let $w^0 = \varepsilon$, where ε denotes an empty string. Let w^j denote the node associated with period *j*. Let $w^j 0$ ($w^j 1$) be the left (right) child node of w^j, $w^j |_k$ be a *k*-prefix of w^j. Associate all nodes of the tree with the time periods according to the pre-order traversal: Begin with root node w^0. If w^j is an internal node, then $w^{j+1} = w^j 0$, if w^j is a leaf node and $j < T-1$, then $w^{j+1} = w'1$, where w' is the longest string such that $w'0$ is a prefix of w^j.

The secret share $SK_j^{(i)}$ player *i* holds in period *j* is a set which is composed of the node secret share $S_{w^j}^{(i)}$ and the secret shares of the right siblings of the nodes on the path from the root to w^j. That is, whenever $w'0$ is a prefix of w^j, $SK_j^{(i)}$ contains the share $S_{w'1}^{(i)}$ of secret key of node $w'1$. The secret share $SK_j^{(i)}$ is organized as a stack $ST^{(i)}$ of the shares of node secrets when player *i* runs the key update algorithm at the end of period *j*. At that time $S_{w^j}^{(i)}$ lies in the top of $ST^{(i)}$. Firstly pop the current node secret share $S_{w^j}^{(i)}$ off the stack, then update as follows:

1. If w^j is an internal node, generate the secret shares $S_{w^j0}^{(i)}$ and $S_{w^j1}^{(i)}$ of w^j0 and w^j1, respectively. And then push $S_{w^j1}^{(i)}$ and $S_{w^j0}^{(i)}$ onto the stack orderly. The new top is $S_{w^j0}^{(i)}$ and indeed $w^{j+1} = w^j0$. Erase $S_{w^j}^{(i)}$ at last.
2. If w^j is a leaf, erase $S_{w^j}^{(i)}$. The next share on top of the stack is $S_{w^{j+1}}^{(i)}$.

3.3 Description of Our Scheme

Let IG be a GDH parameter generator for which the GDH assumption holds. Our forward security threshold signature scheme is constructed as follows:

(1) *FTS.GEN* : Input a security parameter *k*, the total number of time periods $T = 2^{l+1} - 1$ (l is the depth of the binary tree).

①Run IG (1^k) to generate groups G_1 and G_2 of some prime order q and an admissible pairing $e: G_1 \times G_1 \to G_2$.

②Select a random generator $P \in G_1$ and a random secret $\alpha \in Z_q$, and set $Q = \alpha P$. Choose $a_i \in_R Z_q (i = 1...t)$, set $f(x) = \alpha + \sum_{i=1}^{t} a_i x^i \pmod q$, and then compute $\alpha_i = f(i), (i = 1...n)$.

③Choose cryptographic hash functions $H: G_1 \to Z_q$, $H_1: \{0,1\}^* \to G_1$, $H_2: \{0,1\}^* \times \{0,1\}^* \times G_1 \to G_1$.

④The public key is $PK = (G_1, G_2, e, P, Q, l, H, H_1, H_2)$. Compute and broadcast $R_\varepsilon^{(i)} = \alpha_i P (i = 1...n)$. Send share α_i to player $i (i = 1...n)$ secretly. Each player $i (i = 1...n)$ computes $SN_\varepsilon^{(i)} = \alpha_i H_1(\varepsilon)$, and then pushes $S_\varepsilon^{(i)} = (SN_\varepsilon^{(i)})$ onto stack $ST^{(i)}$.

(2) *FTS.UPD*: Input the current time period k. Let $w = w_1 ... w_n$ denote the node corresponding to k. Firstly each player $i (i = 1...n)$ pops the node secret share $S_w^{(i)}$ off the stack $ST^{(i)} = SK_k^{(i)}$, and then does as follows:

①If w is an internal node, parses $S_w^{(i)} = (R_{w|_1}, R_{w|_2}, ..., R_{w|_{n-1}}, R_w, SN_w^{(i)})$. By executing twice $Joint-RVSS$ simultaneously, all players jointly generate two random values $\rho_{w0}, \rho_{w1} \in Z_q$. Player i gets shares $\rho_{w0}^{(i)}, \rho_{w1}^{(i)} \in Z_q$ and public commits $R_{w0} = \rho_{w0} P$, $R_{w1} = \rho_{w1} P$, $R_{w0}^{(j)} = \rho_{w0}^{(j)} P$, $R_{w1}^{(j)} = \rho_{w1}^{(j)} P$, where $j = 1,...,n$. Player i then computes $SN_{w0}^{(i)} = SN_w^{(i)} + \rho_{w0}^{(i)} H_1(w0)$, and $SN_{w1}^{(i)} = SN_w^{(i)} + \rho_{w1}^{(i)} H_1(w1)$. She erases $S_w^{(i)}$ and pushes $S_{w1}^{(i)} = (R_{w|_1}, R_{w|_2}, ..., R_{w|_{n-1}}, R_w, R_{w1}, SN_{w1}^{(i)})$ and $S_{w0}^{(i)} = (R_{w|_1}, R_{w|_2}, ..., R_{w|_{n-1}}, R_w, R_{w0}, SN_{w0}^{(i)})$ onto the stack $ST^{(i)}$ orderly at last.

②If w is a leaf, then only erases $S_w^{(i)}$.

(3) *FTS.SIG* : Input the time period k and a message M. Let $w = w_1 ... w_n$ denote the node corresponding to period k . Firstly each participant player i reads the node secret share $S_w^{(i)}$ from the top of the stack $ST^{(i)} = SK_k^{(i)}$, and then does as follows:

①Parses $S_w^{(i)} = (R_{w|_1}, R_{w|_2}, ..., R_{w|_{n-1}}, R_w, SN_w^{(i)})$. All players jointly generate a random secret $r \in Z_q$ by executing $Joint-RVSS$. Player i gets the share $r^{(i)} \in Z_q$ and the public commits $U = rP$, $U^{(j)} = r^{(j)}P$, where $j = 1,...,n$.

②Then player i computes $P_M = H_2(M, k, U)$, $FS^{(i)} = SN_w^{(i)} + r^{(i)}P_M$, and executes $NI\,Proof - VS(P; H_1(\varepsilon), H_1(w|_1),..., H_1(w|_n), P_M ; R_\varepsilon^{(i)}, R_{w|_1}^{(i)},..., R_{w|_n}^{(i)}, U^{(i)}; FS^{(i)})$ in order to prove the part signature $FS^{(i)}$ which she provides satisfies that $FS^{(i)} = \alpha_i H_1(\varepsilon) + \sum_{m=1}^{n} \rho_{w|_m}^{(i)} H_1(w|_m) + r^{(i)}P_M$, and these α_i , $\rho_{w|_m}^{(i)}, (m = 1...n)$ and $r^{(i)}$ satisfy $R_\varepsilon^{(i)} = \alpha_i P$, $R_{w|_m}^{(i)} = \rho_{w|_m}^{(i)} P, (m = 1...n)$, $U^{(i)} = r^{(i)}P$. If the verification passes, it means the participant player i provides a valid part signature.

③Any set B of t+1 players who pass the verification of *NIProof-VS*, then compute $FS = \sum_{i \in B} C_{Bi} FS^{(i)}$ and publish signature $<k, \sigma = (U, FS)>$ and $R_{w|_m} (m = 1,...,n)$.

(4) *FTS.VER* : Input a message M and a signature $<k, \sigma = (U, FS)>$ and $R_{w|_m} (m = 1,...,n)$. Let $P_M = H_2(M, k, U)$. Return 1 if

$$e(P, FS) = e(Q, H_1(\varepsilon)) \cdot \prod_{m=1}^{n} e(R_{w|_m}, H_1(w|_m)) \cdot e(U, P_M)$$

or 0, otherwise.

4 Efficiency Comparisons

The complexity analysis is considered in terms of T according to the method in [5]. Therefore, the complexity of all computations independent of T is $O(1)$. l' is a security parameter in [6, 7].

Compare the efficiency of our scheme with the schemes against malicious adversary in [6, 7] in Table 1. The running time of both key generation and key update algorithms in our scheme is independent of T, so the complexity is $O(1)$, as opposed to $O(1)T$ in [6] and $O(1)l'T$ in [7]. Signing and verifying in our scheme can all be finished in $O(1)\log T$ time. So their costs are only linear in $\log T$. The efficiency of verifying algorithm, to some extent, depends on the efficiency of pairing computation. With a good pairing computation algorithm, we can have an efficient verifying algorithm.

The total interactions in our scheme are the fewest in the three schemes, too. There is no interaction in our key generation algorithm. Key update algorithm will execute twice *Joint-RVSS* simultaneously, but only needs once interaction. In signing algorithm twice interactions are needed in total, one happens in *Joint-RVSS* and the other happens in *NIProof-VS*.

Table 1. Efficiency comparisons

	The scheme in [6]	The scheme in [7]	Our scheme
FTS.GEN time and interactions	$O(1)T$	$O(1)l'T$	$O(1)$
	0	1	0
FTS.UPD time and interactions	$O(1)T$	$O(1)l'T$	$O(1)$
	1	2	1
FTS.SIG time and interactions	$O(1)T$	$O(1)l'T$	$O(1)\log T$
	$2l'$	2	2
FTS.VER time	$O(1)T$	$O(1)l'T$	$O(1)\log T$

5 Security Analysis

Theorem 2. Let $PK=(G_1,G_2,e,P,Q,l,H,H_1,H_2)$ and $SK_0^{(i)}=S_\varepsilon^{(i)}(i=1...n)$ be the public key and the shares generated by *FTS.GEN*, respectively; Let the shares of secret key be updated by *FTS.UPD*; Let $<k,\sigma=(U,FS)>$ and $R_{w|_m}(m=1,...,n)$ be a signature generated by *FTS.SIG* on input a message M for period k. Then *FTS.VER*(*M*, <*k*,(*U*,*FS*)>=1.

Proof

$$\begin{aligned}
e(P,FS) &= e(Q,H_1(\varepsilon))\cdot\prod_{m=1}^{n} e(R_{w|_m},H_1(w|_m))\cdot e(U,P_M)\\
&= e(\alpha P,H_1(\varepsilon))\cdot\prod_{m=1}^{n} e(\rho_{w|_m}P,H_1(w|_m))\cdot e(rP,P_M)\\
&= e(P,\alpha H_1(\varepsilon))\cdot\prod_{m=1}^{n} e(P,\rho_{w|_m}H_1(w|_m))\cdot e(P,rP_M)\\
&= e(P,\alpha H_1(\varepsilon)+\sum_{m=1}^{n}\rho_{w|_m}H_1(w|_m)+rP_M)\\
&= e(P,\sum_{i\in B}(C_{Bi}\alpha_i H_1(\varepsilon)+\sum_{m=1}^{n}C_{Bi}\rho_{w|_m}^{(i)}H_1(w|_m)+C_{Bi}r^{(i)}P_M))\\
&= e(P,\sum_{i\in B}C_{Bi}FS^{(i)})\\
&= e(P,FS)
\end{aligned}$$

Theorem 3. The *FTS* scheme is a key-evolving (*t*,*s*,*n*) -threshold signature scheme against malicious adversary for $s\geq t+1$, $n\geq 2t+1$.

Proof. (Sketch) It is because *NIProof-VS* and *Joint-RVSS* protocols can detect the dishonest players in the protocol and s honest players can make *FTS.UPD* and *FTS.SIG* algorithms be executed properly for $s\geq t+1$, $n\geq 2t+1$. According to theorem 2, the scheme can tolerant a malicious adversary corrupting t players.

Theorem 4. The *FTS*(*t*,*s*,*n*) scheme is a forward secure threshold signature scheme in the random oracle model in the presence of malicious adversary for $s\geq t+1$, $n\geq 2t+1$.

Proof. (Sketch) The security of our threshold scheme is based on CDH assumption. Because *FS.PKE* [5] is forward secure, assuming that CDH problem is hard, we only need prove our scheme is forward secure as long as *FS.PKE* is forward secure.

Let *F* be an adversary working against the security of *FTS*. *F* runs in three stages: the chosen-message attack phase, cma; the over-threshold phase, overthreshold; and the forgery phase, forge. We want to construct an algorithm *I* against the security of $FS.PKE$ using *F* as a subroutine. *I* works in three stages: the chosen-message attack phase, cma; the break-in phase, breakin; and the forgery phase, forge. *I* has access to both a singing oracle SIG' and a hashing oracle H_2'.

In the cma phase, *F* is allowed to make queries to a signing oracle $FTS.SIG$ and a hash oracle H_2. Therefore, we need to simulate both of these oracles. In doing so, we have to simulate *F*'s view $VIEW_F$ of the protocol. W.l.o.g. assume that the adversary *F* corrupts players $1...t$.

The simulation of $VIEW_F$ in *FTS.GEN*: Because $f(x)$ is a random polynomial in Z_q, α_i is a random value in Z_q. That is, $SN_\varepsilon^{(i)}$ is distributed uniformly in G_1. We can pick values for $\alpha_i (i=1...t)$ at random from Z_q. And then compute $SN_\varepsilon^{(i)}$, $R_\varepsilon^{(i)}$ $(i=1...t)$. For each $R_\varepsilon^{(j)} (j=t+1...n)$, compute $R_\varepsilon^{(j)} = \alpha_j P = (\lambda_{j,0} \cdot \alpha + \sum_{i=1}^{t} \lambda_{j,i} \cdot \alpha_i)P$ $= \lambda_{j,0}Q + \sum_{i=1}^{t} \lambda_{j,i} \cdot R_\varepsilon^{(i)}$, where $\lambda_{j,i}$ is computable Lagrange interpolation coefficient.

The simulation of $VIEW_F$ in *FTS.UPD*: Because the shares of secrets ρ_{w0}, ρ_{w1} are distributed uniformly in Z_q, we can pick random values $\rho_{w0}^{(i)}, \rho_{w1}^{(i)} (i=1...t)$ in Z_q for *F*. It is easy to compute $SN_{w1}^{(i)}, SN_{w0}^{(i)}$ and provide them to *F*. According to the security proof of $Joint-RVSS$, taking as input R_{w0}, R_{w1}, we can simulate the $Joint-RVSS$ protocol to get $VIEW_F$ including $R_{w0}^{(i)}, R_{w1}^{(i)} (i=1...n)$ in this protocol.

The simulation of signing oracle *FTS.SIG*: For each query <*M*, *k*> made by *F*, query SIG' oracle and get signature <*k*, (*U*, *FS*)>. Then return <*k*, (*U*, *FS*)> to *F* as the answer to her signing query.

The simulation of H_2 hash oracle: For each query (*M*, *k*, *U*) made by *F*, query H_2' oracle, and then give the answer to *F* directly.

The simulation of $VIEW_F$ in *FTS.SIG*: For a message <*M*, *k*>, take as input *U* got from query *FTS.SIG* oracle to simulate the *Joint-RVSS* protocol, therefore, we can get $VIEW_F$ including $U^{(i)} = r^{(i)}P$ $(i=1...n)$ in the protocol. $H_2(M,k,U)$ can be got by querying H_2 hash oracle and $FS_i (i=1...t)$ can be computed according to $r_i (i=1...t)$. $SN_w^{(i)}$ and $R_w^{(i)}$ $(i=1...t)$ can be got from simulation of *FTS.UPD*. With *FS* obtained from the query of the signing oracle *FTS.SIG*, we can compute $FS_i (i=t+1...n)$ which *F* views by the same means of Lagrange interpolation in simulation of *FTS.UPD*. Simulate the *NIProof-VS* protocol at last.

In the break-in stage: When *F* has finished cma stage and decides to switch to over-threshold stage *b*, we run *I* in break-in stage. So we can get current secret key SK_b and provide it to *F*.

In forge stage: When *F* finishes her break-in stage, she can construct a forged signature $< k,(U,FS) >$ and $R_{w1_m} (m=1,...,n)$ for $< M,k >$, $(k < b)$ to *I*. Finally, *I* outputs $< k,(U,FS) >$ and $R_{w1_m} (m=1,...,n)$ as her forgery.

It means that there must be an algorithm *I* against the forward security of *FS.PKE* if there exists an adversary *F* working against the forward security of our *FTS* scheme. When CDH problem is hard, *FS.PKE* is forward secure according to the security theorem 1 in [5]. In another word, there is no PPT algorithm against the forward security of *FS.PKE*. So there is no PPT adversary against the forward security of the *FTS* scheme. According to definition 2 and theorem 3, the *FTS*(t,s,n) scheme is a forward secure threshold signature scheme in the random oracle model in the presence of malicious adversary for $s \geq t+1$, $n \geq 2t+1$.

6 Further Discussion

(1) Proactive security
We can add proactive security to this scheme. Proactive secret sharing has been presented in [12]. In the paradigm, shares are periodically renewed without change the secret key. Therefore, the shares got by the adversary in one period are useless after they are renewed. Nikov and Nikova [13] point out scheme [12] is insecure against a mobile adversary. We can apply similar method to this scheme to get proactive security against static adversary. Because of limited space, the concrete content is neglected here.

(2) Storage space
In this scheme, the secret share size and the signature size are not independent to the total time periods *T*, but have log*T* complexities. Fortunately, our scheme is based on the bilinear parings that are constructed from certain elliptic curve. Thus the scheme works on a small finite field and has smaller storage space than other schemes as long as the total number of time periods is not very large.

7 Conclusion

A forward secure threshold signature scheme from bilinear pairings is given in this paper, which is the extended version of [14]. The scheme is very efficient and needs very few interactions. As an additional result, we present an interactive zero-knowledge proof protocol and convert it into a non-interactive protocol in order to verify the validity of part signatures in the scheme. The scheme is robust and forward secure assuming CDH problem is hard.

Acknowledgement

We would like to thank anonymous referees of 2006 International Conference on Computational Intelligence and Security (CIS'06) for the suggestions to improve this paper. This work is supported by the National High-Tech R & D Program (863 Program) of China.

References

1. Desmedt, Y., Frankel, Y.: Threshold cryptosystems. In: Brassard, G. (ed.) Advances in Cryptology - CRYPTO '89. LNCS, vol. 435, pp. 307–315. Springer, Heidelberg (1990)
2. Shoup, V.: Practical threshold signature. In: Preneel, B. (ed.) Advances in Cryptology - EUROCRYPT 2000. LNCS, vol. 1807, pp. 207–220. Springer, Heidelberg (2000)
3. Bellare, M., Miner, S.: A forward-secure digital signature scheme. In: Wiener, M.J. (ed.) Advances in Cryptology - CRYPTO '99. LNCS, vol. 1666, pp. 431–448. Springer, Heidelberg (1999)
4. Itkis, G., Reyzin, L.: Forward-secure signatures with optimal signing and verifying. In: Kilian, J. (ed.) Advances in Cryptology - CRYPTO 2001. LNCS, vol. 2139, pp. 499–514. Springer, Heidelberg (2001)
5. Kang, B.G., Park, J.H., Halm, S.G.: A new forward secure signature scheme. Cryptology ePrint Archive, Report 2004/183 (2004)
6. Abdalla, M., Miner, S., Namprempre, C.: Forward-secure threshold signature schemes. In: Naccache, D. (ed.) Topics in Cryptology - CT-RSA 2001. LNCS, vol. 2020, pp. 441–456. Springer, Heidelberg (2001)
7. Tzeng, Z.J., Tzeng, W.G.: Robust forward signature schemes with proactive security. In: Kim, K.-c. (ed.) Public Key Cryptography. LNCS, vol. 1992, pp. 264–276. Springer, Heidelberg (2001)
8. Wang, H., Qiu, G., Feng, D., Xiao, G.: Cryptanalysis of Tzeng-Tzeng Forward-Secure Signature Schemes. IEICE Transactions on Fundamentals of Electronics, Communications and Computer Sciences E89-A(3), 822–825 (2006)
9. Cheng-Kang Chu, Li-Shan Liu, Wen-Guey Tzeng. A threshold GQ signature scheme. Cryptology ePrint Archive, Report 2003/016 (2002)
10. Gennaro, R., Jarecki, S., Krawczyk, H., Rabin, T.: Secure distributed key generation for discrete-log based cryptosystems, Advances in Cryptology-Eurocrypt'99. In: Stern, J. (ed.) Advances in Cryptology - EUROCRYPT '99. LNCS, vol. 1592, pp. 295–310. Springer, Heidelberg (1999)
11. Gentry, C., Silverberg, A.: Hierarchical ID-based cryptography, Advances in Cryptology-Asiacrypt 2002. In: Zheng, Y. (ed.) Advances in Cryptology - ASIACRYPT 2002. LNCS, vol. 2501, pp. 548–566. Springer, Heidelberg (2002)
12. Herzberg, A., Jarecki, S., Krawczyk, H., Yung, M.: Proactive Secret Sharing, or: how to cope with perpetual leakage, Advances in Crytptolgy-Crypto'95. In: Coppersmith, D. (ed.) Advances in Cryptology - CRYPTO '95. LNCS, vol. 963, pp. 339–352. Springer, Heidelberg (1995)
13. Nikov, V., Nikova, S.: On proactive secret sharing schemes. In: Handschuh, H., Hasan, M.A. (eds.) Selected Areas in Cryptography. LNCS, vol. 3357, pp. 314–331. Springer, Heidelberg (2004)
14. Yu, J., Kong, F., Hao, R.: A New Forward Secure Threshold Signature Scheme. In: International Conference on Computational Intelligence and Security 2006, pp. 1243–1246. IEEE Press, New York (2006)

Low-Cost Authentication Protocol of the RFID System Using Partial ID

Yong-Zhen Li[1], Yoon-Su Jeong[1], Ning Sun[1], and Sang-Ho Lee[2,*]

[1] Department of Computer Science, Chungbuk National University, Cheongju, Chungbuk, Korea
{lyz2003,jeong75,sunn}@chungbuk.ac.kr

[2] School of Electrical & Computer Engineering, Chungbuk National University, Cheongju, Chungbuk, Korea
shlee@chungbuk.ac.kr

Abstract. Previous RFID techniques cause serious privacy infringements such as excessive information exposure and user's location information tracking due to the wireless characteristics and the limitation of RFID systems. Especially the information security problem of read only tag has been solved by physical method. In this paper, we propose a low-cost mutual authentication protocol which can be adapted to read-only tag using XOR computation and Partial ID concept. The proposed protocol is secure against reply attacking, eavesdropping, spoofing attacking and location tracking, therefore it can be used to support secure and low cost RFID system.

1 Introduction

Recently, low-cost radio frequency identification (RFID) has been attracting more and more interests from both industry and academic fields. It has gained wide range adaptation for low-cost and ubiquitous computing applications, such as location tracking, access control and environmental conditions monitoring [1].

An important security concern of RFID tag is that stores inventory labeled with unprotected tags which may be monitored by unauthorized readers. Another privacy concern is that individuals may be tracked through RFID tags labeled on the carried objects. A secure RFID system has to avoid eavesdropping, traffic analysis, spoofing and denial of service, for it has large read range and no visible requirement. There have been some approaches to the RFID security and privacy issues: including killing tags at the checkout, applying a read/write able memory, physical tag memory separation, hash encryption, random access hash, and hash chains [2, 7], etc.

About these concerns the RFID technique become the setbacks to the embodiment of RFID, and the various privacy problems should be solved beforehand for the successful industrialization. Therefore, the researches regarding authentication protocol are now proceeding actively to protect the information stored

* Corresponding author.

Y. Wang, Y. Cheung, and H. Liu (Eds.): CIS 2006, LNAI 4456, pp. 598–604, 2007.

in the tag and resolve the security problems such as location tracking of the tag [3,4,5].

This paper is organized as follows. The related works of authentication protocols for RFID system are introduced in section 2. Our proposed approach is given in section 3. In section 3, we define the assumption. The basic idea and working mechanism are presented based on our assumption. In Section 4, protocol analysis of the proposed authentication protocol is given. Finally, we give a conclusion in section 5.

2 Authentication Protocols for RFID System

2.1 Hash Lock

The Hash Lock scheme [1] stores the hash of a random key K as the tag's meta-ID, i.e. meta-ID = h(K). When queried by a reader, the tag transmits its meta-ID which is forwarded to the back-end database. The database and the reader eventually respond with K. The tag hashes the key and compares it with the stored meta-ID. If the values match, it unlocks itself and offers its full functionality to the nearby readers. Although this scheme offers good reliability at low cost, an adversary can easily track the tag via its meta-ID. Furthermore, since the key K is sent in the clear way, an adversary upon capturing the key can later spoof the tag to the reader.

2.2 Randomized Hash-Lock

A similar randomized version in [2] attempts to disguise the ID so that tag output is not fixed over time. Upon query, the tag responds with the pair (r, h(ID, r)), where r is a randomly generated number. Although this scheme deters tracking, it requires brute force search for known IDs in the database until it finds one that matches the signature (r, h(ID, r)). Even though this is an issue for large databases, it is also possible to apply the following operation using very simple attack: An adversary can first query the tag to learn a valid pair (r, h(ID, r)). Then it can impersonate the tag by forwarding these values to a legitimate reader. This is a serious security flaw as the reader will identify the tag. In addition, this scheme allows the location history of the tag to be traced if the tag itself is compromised. Hence forward secrecy is not guaranteed.

2.3 Hash Chain

In [6], the authors devise a scheme that uses a low cost hash-chain mechanism to defeat the tracing problem and ensure forward security in tag transactions. The basic idea is to modify the identifier each time the tag is queried so that the tag is recognized by authorized parties only. The scheme uses two hash functions, one to refresh the secret in the tag, the other to make responses of the tag untraceable by eavesdroppers. However, the scalability of the previous scheme creates a problem since as it requires exhaustive search in the back-end database to locate the ID of the tag. Although in [5] a time-space memory tradeoff is presented that reduces the scalability problem, perhaps more important from a security point of view is that an attacker can still query the tag then replay the tags response to authenticate itself to a valid reader.

2.4 Re-encryption

Phillippe Golle et al [9]. Suggest a privacy solution called universal re-encryption mix-net (URM), which is based on mix-net a mix-net is a network based on public cryptography. Initially, more than one message (all encrypted with the network's public key) is posted to the network. The network picks up all the messages, decrypts them, and delivers them to their destination. The trick is that the messages are not delivered in the same order they are picked up. Only the network knows how the messages are mixed, so it is not possible for the receiver (or outsiders listening on the wires) to determine who send what message, and who they send it to.

2.5 XOR Based Protocol

In [10, 11], a security model is proposed that introduces a challenge-response mechanism which uses no cryptographic primitives (other than simple XORs). One of the key ideas in this work is the application of pseudonyms to help enforce privacy in RFID tags. Each time the tag is queried, it releases the next pseudonym from its list. In principle, then, only a valid verifier can tell when two different names belong to the same tag. Of course, an adversary could query a tag multiple times to harvest all names so as to defeat the scheme. So, the approach described involves some special enhancements to prevent this attack. First, tags release their names only at a certain (suitably slow) prescribed rate. Second, pseudonyms can be refreshed by authorized readers. Although this scheme does not require the tags to perform any cryptographic functions (it uses only XOR operations) the protocol involves four messages and requires updating the keys and pads with new secrets, and an operation which may be costly and difficult to realize.

3 Proposed Authentication Protocol

3.1 The Initialization Stage

In the initialization stage of our proposed protocol some computation and initialization of values in the tag should be performed, reader and database are established on the basis of the EPC standard as a preparation step to perform the proposed protocol:

1) Furnish every tag each own secret information, SID (secure ID);
2) Install the random number generator in the reader, which can generate similar random numbers;

3) Store the secret information of all the tags in the database;
4) The length of the PID used for a mutual authentication of the reader and is not less than half of the SID length.

3.2 The Detail of Proposed Protocol

The proposed protocol is composed of 11 steps as shown in the figure 1.

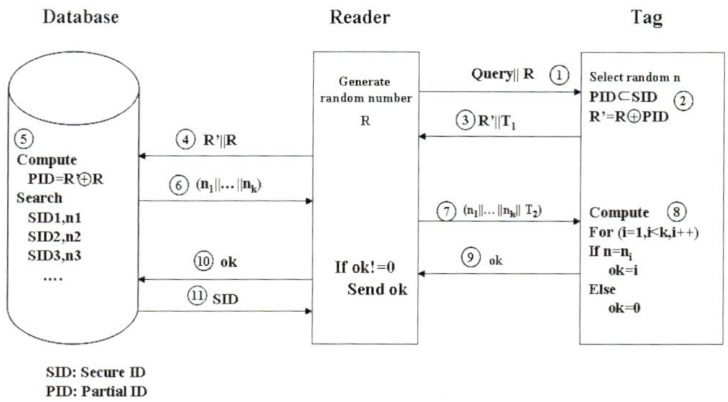

Fig. 1. The Proposed Protocol

The followings are the detail descriptions of the proposed protocol.

1) The reader generates the random numbers and sends them to the tag along with the inquiry information;
2) When the tag receives the query from the reader, the tag selects the PID which's length determined randomly and calculates R' by XORing the random number R received from the reader;
3) The tag sends the calculated R' and the time stamp T1 to the reader;
4) The reader sends R and R' to the database;
5) The database calculates the tag's PID by XORing R and R' received from the reader. Then the database searches every tag's SID which includes this PID as a partial aggregation and collects the start location information of PID in each searched SID; acknowledges the tag as a disguised one, if there is no SID including the PID as a result of search;
6) The database sends the collected start location informations to the reader;
7) The reader adds the time stamp T2 to the start location information of the PID received from the database and sends it to the tag;
8) The tag looks for the information identical to the PID start location information which received from the database; acknowledges the reader disguised if there is no information identical to the PID start location information;
9) The tag sends to the reader the PID sequence number i received above, if it finds a start location identical to the PID start location. Otherwise, it sends to the reader the no Find information;

10) The reader sends to the database the information received from the tag, if it is sequence number i. Then it terminates the protocol if it receives the no Find information; and
11) The database determines the tag's SID based on the sequence number received from the tag and provides the related information for the reader.

4 Analysis

4.1 Security Analysis

Safety Against Reply Attack. There are two kinds of attacks; resend attacks disguised as a reader and a tag. In case of disguising as a reader, the attacker eavesdrops on the message sent from the reader to the tag and resends it. In the proposed protocol, the resend attack is prevented by establishing the valid time stamps T1 and T2.

Safety Against Spoofing Attack. In most cases, the symmetry key cipher technique is used to guarantee the secrecy of sent messages. However, it costs too much to use such cipher techniques because the storing space and computation capability of RFID tag is limited. In the proposed protocol, the secrecy of the messages sent and received during the authentication step is guaranteed, by concealing and sending the sent message (PID) through the bit computation with random numbers. That is, the PID of the sent tag can be calculated, only if the random number and its own PID information are known. It is safe against the message eavesdropping attack, because it is impossible to calculate the tag's overall SID even though the PID is exposed.

Safety Against Location Tracking. The messages sent and received between the tag and the reader is transmitted as different messages each time during all the authentication steps. It is impossible to track the tag's location through the current unchanged messages, because different messages are exchanged each time due to the sending of the randomly selected PID. However, the tag's location can be estimated even though different messages are sent each time, in case the tag's SID is known. The tag tracking for a special purpose (legal investigation) becomes possible through the administrator's authorization;

Protection of User's Privacy. The user's privacy mainly means the leakage of location information or tag information of the tag's owner. As explained above, the user's privacy is guaranteed, because the exposure of tag location and the leakage of tag information can be prevented by the same reader's sending the different authentication message each time using the information concealment and the PID based on the random numbers, in spite of the authentication for the same tags.

Protocol	[1]	[2]	[6]	[9]	[10,11]	Our scheme
Spoofing	X	X	X	O	O	O
Replay	X	X	X	O	O	O
Location tracking	X	O	O	O	O	
Privacy	X	X	O	O	O	O

As a result of comparison and analysis of current authentication techniques, we know that the proposed protocol expands safety capabilities in comparison with the previous techniques. As shown in the table 1, we know that the proposed protocol is safe against various attacks.

4.2 Efficiency

In the RFID system, power consumption, processing time, memory space and number of gates work as main variables. Therefore, it is very important to decrease the above 4 elements in embodying the low-cost RFID system. According to the previous techniques, it costs much mainly in embodying the hash function and cipher symmetry key algorithm. The table 2 shows a result of comparing and analyzing the Juels[10] and Eun-young[11] techniques and proposed protocol.

	Juels[10]	*Eunyoung*[6,9]	Our Scheme
Memory	k*L	2L	1L
Computation	4k (XOR)	8(XOR)+4(+)	4(XOR)
Write Op	k*L	L	Unused

k: number of secure key(4 or 5); + : module addition;
L: Length of SID

As shown in the table 2, the proposed protocol makes the tag's computation quantity evidently down to 8 times comparison with Eun-Young technique which is the most efficient before[11]. And also it decreases memory requirement (from 2L to L) to half than of Eun-Youngs. Furthermore, in the proposed protocol, the write operation is not needed in tags during the authentication procedure. Therefore, the proposed protocol is appropriate to embody the system of distribution management, livestock management and merchandise management requiring the RFID system of low cost.

5 Conclusions

Recently, the RFID technique has been utilized for various aspects of society, because it has advantages over the current bar-code technique as faster recognition speed, bigger storage space and wireless recognition. But the current RFID system brings about new safety problems like cost, safety weakness of wireless environment and privacy infringement. Especially, the RFID system using the tag only for reading resolves the information protection problem simply in the physical manner. This paper proposes the mutual authentication protocol of low cost which is safe against various attacks and also applicable to the read-only tag, using the simple XOR computation and PID. Furthermore our proposed authentication protocol decreases memory requirement half than of the Eun-Young arithmetic, and the bit computation overhead decreases to 1/12. Furthermore, in the proposed protocol, the write operation is not needed during the authentication procedure. It is proved through the comparison and analysis of the previous techniques the proposed authentication protocol requires less resource consumption and resolves the problems such as eavesdropping, disguise and privacy infringement in comparison with the previous protocols.

References

1. Weis, S. A.: Radio-frequency identification security and privacy, Master's thesis, M.I.T (2003)
2. Weis, S.A., Sarma, S., Rivest, R., Engels, D.: Security and privacy aspects of low-cost radio frequency identification systems. In: Hutter, D., Müller, G., Stephan, W., Ullmann, M. (eds.) Security in Pervasive Computing. LNCS, vol. 2802, pp. 201–212. Springer, Heidelberg (2004)
3. Juels, A., Pappu, R.: Squealing Euros: Privacy protection in RFID-enabled banknotes. In: Wright, R.N. (ed.) Financial Cryptography. LNCS, vol. 2742, pp. 103–121. Springer, Heidelberg (2003)
4. Molnar, D., Soppera, A., Wagner, D.: A scalable, delegatable pseudonym protocol enabling ownership transfer of RFID tags. In: Preneel, B., Tavares, S. (eds.) Selected Areas in Cryptography-SAC 2005. LNCS, Springer, Heidelberg (2005)
5. Henrici, D., Muller, P.: Hash-based Enhancement of Location Privacy for Radio-Frequency Identification Devices using Varying Identifiers. In: Proceedings of the Second IEEE Annual Conference on Pervasive Computing and Communications Workshop, PERCOMW '04, pp. 149–153. IEEE, New York (2004)
6. Ohkubo, M., Suzuki, K., Kinoshita, S.: A Cryptographic Approach to 'Privacy-Friendly' tag, RFID Privacy Workshop (November 2003)
7. Yoshida, J.: RFID Backlash Prompts 'Kill' Feature, EETimes, April 28 (2003)
8. Juels, A., Rivest, R. L. Szydlo, M.: The Blocker Tag: Selective Blocking of RFID Tags for Consumer Privacy, 10th ACM Conference on Computer and Communications Security, CCS 2003, pp. 103–111 (2003)
9. Golle, P., Jakobsson, M., Juels, A., Syverson, P.: Universal re-encryption for mixnets. In: Okamoto, T. (ed.) Topics in Cryptology – CT-RSA 2004. LNCS, vol. 2964, pp. 163–178. Springer, Heidelberg (2004)
10. Juels, A.: Minimalist cryptography for low-cost RFID tags. In: Blundo, C., Cimato, S. (eds.) Security in Communication Networks. LNCS, vol. 3352, pp. 149–164. Springer, Heidelberg (2005)
11. Choi, E.Y., Lee, S.M., Lee, D.H.: Efficient RFID Authentication protocol for Ubiquitous Computing Environment. In: Enokido, T., Yan, L., Xiao, B., Kim, D., Dai, Y., Yang, L.T. (eds.) Embedded and Ubiquitous Computing – EUC 2005 Workshops. LNCS, vol. 3823, pp. 945–954. Springer, Heidelberg (2005)

A VLSI Implementation of Minutiae Extraction for Secure Fingerprint Authentication

Sung Bum Pan[1], Daesung Moon[2], Kichul Kim[3], and Yongwha Chung[4,*]

[1] Dept. of Control & Instrumentation Eng., Chosun University, Korea
sbpan@chosun.ac.kr
[2] Biometrics Technology Research Team, ETRI, Korea
daesung@etri.re.kr
[3] Dept. of Electrical & Computer Eng., University of Seoul, Korea
kkim@uos.ac.kr
[4] Dept. of Computer & Information Science, Korea University, Korea
ychungy@korea.ac.kr

Abstract. To heighten the biometrics security level, the biometrics feature extraction and verification need to be performed within smart cards, not in external card readers. However, the smart card chip has very limited processing capability, and typical fingerprint feature extraction and verification algorithms may not be executed on a state-of-the-art smart card. Therefore, this paper presents an System-on-Chip(SoC) implementation of the fingerprint feature extraction algorithm which can be integrated into smart cards. To implement the ridge-following algorithm onto resource-constrained SoCs, the algorithm has been modified to increase the efficiency of the hardware. Each functional block of the algorithm has been implemented in hardware or in software by considering its computational complexity, cost and utilization of the hardware, and efficiency of the entire system. The proposed system operated in 50MHz, and 20~50 minutiae could be extracted from typical 248×292 fingerprint images in real time with small area(97K gates). Our current implementation, developed as an IP for SoCs with ARM CPU and AMBA bus, can also be used in many other smart card configurations. Also, hardware for minutiae matching can be easily integrated into the proposed minutiae extraction hardware to execute the overall fingerprint authentication within the smart card chip, removing the possibility of leaking any biometric information.

Keywords: fingerprint authentication, minutiae extraction, VLSI, SoC.

1 Introduction

Traditionally, verified users have gained access to secure information systems, buildings, or equipment via multiple PINs, passwords, smart cards, and so on. However, these security methods have important weakness that can be lost, stolen, or forgotten. In recent years, there is an increasing trend of using **biometrics**, which

* Corresponding author.

Y. Wang, Y. Cheung, and H. Liu (Eds.): CIS 2006, LNAI 4456, pp. 605–615, 2007.

refers the personal biological or behavioral characteristics used for verification. The **fingerprint** is chosen as the biometrics for verification in this paper. Fingerprint-based identification has been known and used for a very long time. Owing to their uniqueness and immutability, fingerprints are today the most widely used biometric features[1].

A problem common to all biometric systems including fingerprint is that unauthorized use of biometric information is very easy[2]. For example, a fingerprint can be acquired from objects touched by the person. Originally, fingerprint personal authentication was put to practical use on the precondition of a close range or face-to-face interface. Therefore, protecting the privacy of fingerprint information has not been given sufficient consideration. In the near future, however, the **security** as well as the **privacy** requirements should be satisfied for large-scale user authentication services.

For example, in a typical *sensor-client-server model*[2] for remote user authentication, the sensor captures a fingerprint image, the client extracts some features from the image, and finally the server compares the extracted features with the fingerprint templates stored in a central database. In this model, many of the possible attacks in fingerprint authentication systems were identified[3]. Thus, **security issues** ensure that the opponents will neither be able to access the individual information/measurements nor be able to pose as other individuals by electronically interjecting stale and fraudulently obtained fingerprint measurements into the system. When the system and/or its communication channels are vulnerable to open physical access, cryptographic methods should be employed to protect the fingerprint information[4]. However, the fingerprint *sensor* may have a low-end processor for low-cost implementations, and it may not be possible for such low-end processors to apply the standard cryptographic techniques to the overall fingerprint images in real-time. Furthermore, compared to the server possibly protected by security experts, the *client* maintained by an individual user is more vulnerable to several attacks such as Trojan horse. Finally, with the central storage of the fingerprint templates in the *server*, there are open issues of misuse of the fingerprint templates such as the **'Big Brother' problem**. To solve these open issues, the database may need to be distributed to millions of smart cards for large-scale applications such as national ID, driver license, and border control systems[5-10].

Most of the current implementations of the solution have a common characteristic that the biometric authentication process is accomplished out of a smart card introducing the risk of leaking out biometric information. This system is called **Store-on-Card**[5], because the smart card is used only as a storage device to store the biometric pattern. For example, in a store-on-card for fingerprint verification, the fingerprint pattern stored in the smart card needs to be released to a potentially insecure external card reader to be compared with an input fingerprint pattern.

To heighten the security level, the verification operation needs to be performed within smart cards, not in external card readers. This system is called as **Match-on-Card** method, and some results based on either software or hardware design have been reported[8,9]. Note that standard PCs, on which typical biometric verification systems operate, have 2GHz CPU and 256Mbytes memory. On the contrary, a state-of-the-art smart card chip(5mm×5mm) can employ 32-bit ARM7 CPU at most. Since such a smart card chip has very limited processing capability, typical biometric verification algorithms may not be executed even on a state-of-the-art smart card successfully. To reduce the required memory space significantly, a memory-efficient fingerprint matching algorithm was developed by doing more computation with a special data structure[8].

To heighten the security level further, however, the overall authentication operations including the most time-consuming step, **feature extraction**, need to be performed within smart cards[6, 10]. Because of the resource restrictions of smart cards, it is even more challenging to execute the feature extraction on a smart card. If a fingerprint sensor is equipped on a smart card, called as **Sensor-on-Card**, and the feature extraction can be executed in the smart card, then the security and privacy problems regarding fingerprint information can be avoided.

In this paper, we present a hardware architecture for the fingerprint feature extraction which can be implemented on a smart card chip. Instead of typical fingerprint feature extraction systems employing binarization and thinning processes, we adopt an algorithm directly following ridgelines without the time-consuming processes[11]. In addition to time saving, the **ridge following** algorithm can avoid many extraction errors for low quality fingerprint images and degradation of the accuracy. However, the algorithm did not consider a smart card as its execution environment, and the computational requirement of the algorithm makes it hard to implement it on **SoC**(System-on-Chip)s by using software only. We first modify the algorithm to increase the efficiency of hardwares. Each functional block of the algorithm has been carefully implemented in hardware or in software by considering its computational complexity, cost and utilization of the hardware, and efficiency of the entire system. The fingerprint feature extraction system has been developed as an IP for SoCs, hence it can be used on many kinds of SoCs for smart cards. To the best of our knowledge, there has been no previous work reported for a hardware-based fingerprint authentication embedded into a smart card chip.

The rest of the paper is structured as follows. Section 2 explains a typical fingerprint authentication system and the feature extraction. Section 3 describes the hardware architecture of the feature extraction, and Section 4 shows experimental results. Conclusions are given in Section 5.

2 Fingerprint Authentication

A typical fingerprint authentication system has two phases: *enrollment* and *verification*. In the off-line enrollment phase, an enrolled fingerprint image is preprocessed, and the salient features derived from the fingerprint ridges, called *minutiae*, are extracted and stored. In the on-line verification phase, the similarity between the enrolled minutiae pattern and the input minutiae pattern is examined. Note that we use a typical representation of the minutiae such as x and y coordinates and angles of the ridge endings and bifurcations in the fingerprint image[1].

In general, there are three stages involved in the verification phase[1]: Image Pre-Processing, Minutiae Extraction, and Minutiae Matching. **Image Pre-Processing** refers to the refinement of the fingerprint image against the image distortion obtained from the fingerprint sensor. It consists of three processes. The *binary conversion* or *binarization process* applies a low-pass filter to smooth the high frequency regions of the image and threshold to each sub-segment of the image. The *thinning process* generates a one-pixel wide skeleton image by considering each pixel with its neighbors. In the *positioning process*, the skeleton is transformed and/or rotated so that valid minutiae information can be extracted. **Minutiae Extraction** refers to the extraction of features in the fingerprint image. After this stage, some of the minutiae are detected and stored into a pattern file, which includes the position, orientation, and type(ridge ending or bifurcation) of the minutiae. Based on the minutiae, an input fingerprint is compared with the enrolled database in **Minutiae Matching** stage.

Note that Image Pre-Processing and Minutiae Extraction stages require a lot of integer computations, and the computational workload of both steps occupies 96% of the total workload of the fingerprint authentication[7]. Thus, it is reasonable to assign the time-consuming steps to the client, rather than to the resource-constrained sensor. This kind of task assignment can be found in a combination of a smart card and a card reader[5,8]. That is, the time-consuming stages are assigned to the more powerful card reader, rather than the resource-constrained smart card. Also, many of the possible attacks in fingerprint authentication systems were identified[2,3]. And, a security protocol which is easy, fast, and inexpensive to protect all these attacks has not been reported yet. As we mentioned in Section 1, integrating all the required resources such as a fingerprint sensor into a smart card and executing all the computations within the smart card can be an ultimate solution for the security and privacy problems.

In [11], a direct gray scale minutiae detection algorithm was proposed to handle low-quality fingerprints with low computational complexity. Actually, the problem of automatic minutiae extraction has been thoroughly studied, but never completely solved. The main difficulty is that fingerprint quality is often too low; noise and contrast deficiency can produce false minutiae and hide valid minutiae. In [11], the features were extracted directly from the gray scale image without binarization and thinning for the following reasons: a lot of information may be lost during the binarization process, binarization and thinning are time-consuming, the binarization techniques proved to be unsatisfactory when applied to low-quality images.

The basic idea was to **follow the ridge lines** on the gray scale image by "sailing" according to the fingerprint directional image. A set of starting points is determined by superimposing a square-meshed grid on the gray scale image. For each starting point, the algorithm keeps following the ridge line until they terminate or intersect other ridge lines(*minutiae detection*). A labeling strategy is adopted to examine each ridge line only once and locate the intersections between ridge lines. The results achieved were compared with those obtained through some methods based on image binarization. In spite of a greater conceptual complexity, the proposed algorithm performed better both in terms of efficiency and robustness. The low computational complexity can make this method particularly suitable for applications where efficiency is a primary issue(i.e., on-line access control, low-cost biometric systems, etc.). However, the algorithm did not consider a smart card as its execution environment, and the computational requirement of the algorithm makes it hard to implement it on SoCs by using software only. In the following, we will present a hardware architecture for the fingerprint feature extraction which can be implemented on a smart card chip.

3 Hardware Implementation of Minutiae Extraction

3.1 Hardware-Software Partition

To implement the ridge following algorithm into an SoC, we need to partition each component of the algorithm into hardware and software and define the interface between them. As shown in Fig. 1(a), the given algorithm is divided into two parts: selection of a starting point and ridge following. The **selection of a starting point** is performed by 1) selection of a starting point from intersection points(*starting point*), 2) angle computation at the intersection points(*angle computation*), 3) set a section based on the computed angle and the coordinates of the intersection points(*section set*), 4) detection of a max pixel through mask operations within the section selected(*max detection*), 5) check whether the max pixel is from the preceding ridge following(*new starting point?*), 6) angle computation at the max pixel(*angle computation*), 7) repeat 1) for the coordinate followed by the preceding computation. On the contrary, the **ridge following** is performed by 1) position selection from the max pixel in the direction of φ at the distance of μ(*move*), 2) set a section based on the moving point in the direction of $\varphi + \pi/2$(*section set*), 3) detection of a max pixel through mask operations(*max detection*), 4) check whether a minutia is found(*new minutiae?*), 5) repeat 1) after the angle computation at the max pixel and the auxiliary image update if a minutia is not found, 6) selection of a new starting point if a minutia is found.

In the given algorithm, we know that the order of angle computation, section set, and max detection is the same for both parts. Also, those steps(angle computation, section set, and max detection) are the most time consuming steps in the given algorithm. Therefore, it is natural to implement those steps in hardware.

To utilize the hardware block efficiently, we modify the given algorithm. As shown in Fig. 1(b), the selection of a starting point is performed by 1) angle computation, 2) section set/max detection, 3) angle computation, 4) decision for a max pixel, and the ridge following is performed by 1) move for setting a new section, 2) section set/max detection, 3) angle computation, 4) decision for a max pixel, 5) auxiliary image update. By modifying the given algorithm in this way, the angle computation and the section set/max detection which require a lot of structured computations can be implemented in hardware. And, the transition from hardware to software during the algorithm execution is occurred at the angle computation, and this fact leads to an efficient implementation of the whole system. Note that, our modification re-orders the execution flow of the given algorithm for an efficient implementation, and it does not produce different results from the given algorithm.

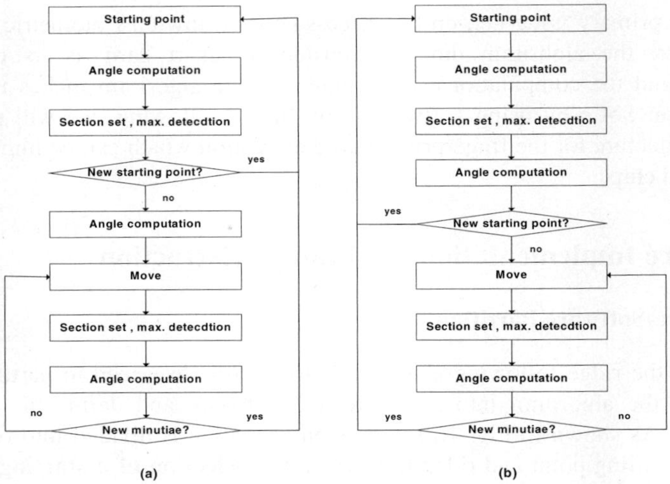

Fig. 1. (a) Flow Diagram of the Ridge Following Algorithm[11] (b) Modified Flow Diagram for Hardware Implementation

The minutiae extraction block and the auxiliary image update block are implemented in software, and the final partition between hardware and software is shown in Fig. 2.

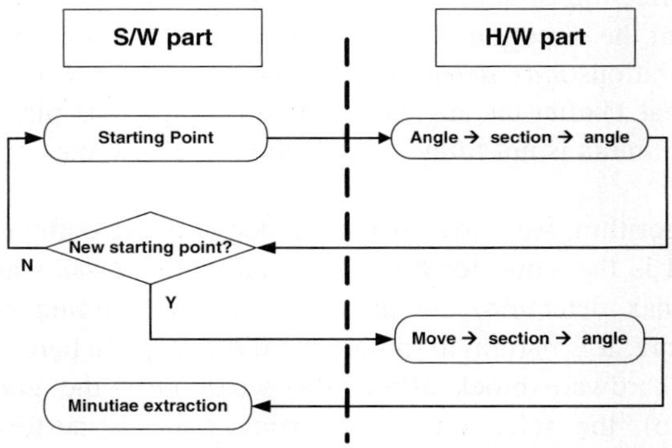

Fig. 2. Partition into Hardware and Software

In the ridge following algorithm, the computation of angles at a given point is a complicated process and needs arctangent or square root computations. Thus, in [11], the angle computation is divided into two substeps. In the pre-processing substep, the direction for each 8×8 block of a given image is pre-computed. During the ridge following substep, the Lagrangian interpolation method is employed to reduce the computation time significantly. In our implementation, the pre-processing substep and the ridge following substep are executed in software and hardware, respectively.

3.2 Hardware Architecture

The **move block** reads the coordinates and the direction of the max pixel and computes the coordinate of a μ-pixel move under the direction. It needs one multiplication and one addition to compute the coordinate of the pixel, and stores the necessary cosine and sine values in ROM. For effective hardware implementation, it stores a move location instead of cosine and sine values. Since the parameter μ is independent of input, the values of $\mu \times \cos\varphi$ and $\mu \times \sin\varphi$ can be obtained by the direction(φ). Based on the simulation results, the optimum value of μ was found to be 3 in implementing the ROM-based hardware design and the overall move path can be one of the 26 possibilities. Thus, according to the input φ, we can decide the direction as one of the 26, and this characteristic can make the hardware effective for fast computation.

After computing the starting and end points along the perpendicular direction of the ridge based on the given coordinate, **Section & Maximum Detection block** determines the coordinates of the section connecting the two points and its neighboring sections by using the Bresenham algorithm. Then, for the computed section, it performs mask operations, determines the max pixel, and checks the β condition. The block consists of following subblocks.

1) Section Subblock
Section subblock determines the coordinates of the section connecting the two points and its neighboring sections by using the Bresenham algorithm. Based on a simulation, we found σ=7 was optimum with μ=3. Because the coordinates of the section ranges from -7 to 7 based on the input coordinate, the results of the Bresenham algorithm repeat eight patterns within 45 degree. Thus, for the eight patterns within $0° < \theta < 45°$, the results of the Bresenham algorithm are pre-stored in ROM and processed by using MUX and ALU. The processed results are stored in the register file.

2) Maximum Detection Subblock
After performing the two-level mask operations, the coordinate of a max pixel and the β parameter need to be checked. The first mask operation computes an average of pixels corresponding to the section computed, and the second mask operation applies a mask of length 7. At each clock, the gray level values of the section are read from the memory and the average value is computed using an accumulator. The second mask operation is performed using the register bank. If a new max value is computed, then the new value is stored. Finally, the sectioning_register_file is read to get the coordinates of a max pixel. At this moment, the β parameter is used, and we set β to 30° through many experiments.

The **angle block** computes the direction of a pixel found in the section and max detection block. It reads the pre-computed angle for the 8×8 block from the memory, and derives the proceeding direction at the location computed by Lagrangian interpolation.

3.3 Overall Implementation

The overall hardware for minutiae extraction consists of a *master* block, a *slave* block, and a *core* block. The slave block can be written and/or read passively, whereas the master block can perform data transmissions actively. The slave block also interfaces the register file and the outside world. The software module writes some information necessary for the computation to the register file through the interface.

To start the ridge following, a pixel location which can be a starting point is given. At the initial communication between hardware and software modules, a starting address of the pre-computed angles for each 8×8 image block is also given. According to the input of the register file, the hardware module performs either the starting point decision or the ridge following. The coordinate and the angle computed are written back to the register file, and an interrupt causes the software module to execute the necessary operations. The master block inputs the necessary pixel values to the hardware module. The pre-computed angle values and the pixel values necessary for the angle computation and the sectioning are written to memory by the master block. The core block consists of 1) move block, 2) section and max detection block, 3) angle block, and there is a control block to control these three blocks. The move block is used not for the starting point decision, but for the ridge following. Fig. 3 shows a flow diagram of this hardware module.

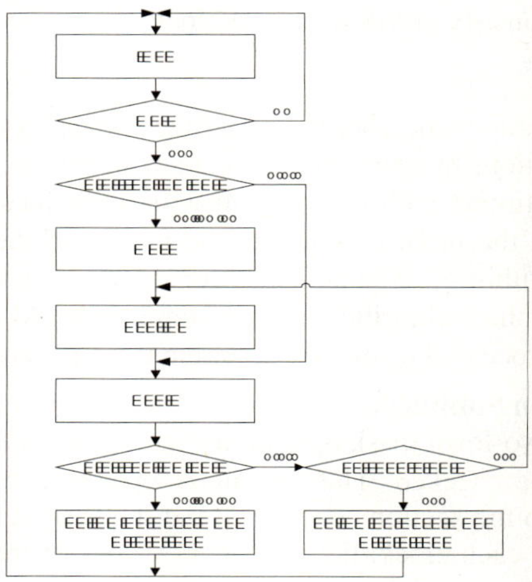

Fig. 3. Flow Diagram of the Hardware Implementation

The software module performs the angle computations of size 8×8 for Lagrangian interpolation and writes the computed values to the memory. After the hardware is initiated, the master block stores these angles to the internal memory of the hardware module. The flow diagram for starting point decision is: angle computation → section1(compute the address of the gray level) → data get → section2(decide max point) → angle computation. On the contrary, the flow diagram for ridge following is: move → section1(compute the address of the gray level) → data get → section2(decide max point) → angle computation. Once the hardware module completes one execution, the software module decides whether to select a new starting point or to execute the ridge following algorithm. A new staring point was decided by comparing an auxiliary image maintained in the software module with the result of the starting point decision obtained from the hardware module. After receiving the result of the ridge following from the hardware module, the software module decides whether to continue executing the ridge following by using the auxiliary image.

4 Experimental Results

The developed design was evaluated by using an emulator board consisting of CPU, memory, FPGA as shown in Fig. 4. The minutiae extraction system considered SoCs such as smart cards, and a low-power, general 32-bit RISC processor *ARM940T* was selected as our CPU. Also, *AMBA*(Advanced Microcontroller Bus Architecture) *AHB*(Advanced High-performance Bus)[12] was selected as our on-chip system bus because it was expected to be widely used for ARM-based smart cards. *Xilinx Virtex V2000EFG680* and *Vxworks* were selected as FPGA and OS, respectively. A host PC providing an environment for program development and simulation was connected to the developed system through Ethernet. We conducted design of hardware, debugging, and design of software simultaneously.

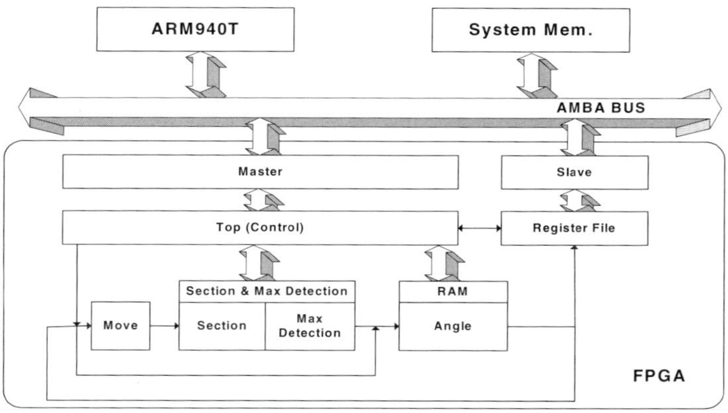

Fig. 4. An Environment for Hardware Development and Hardware Functional Blocks

The hardware blocks were design by using VHDL. The VHDL program was synthesized after functional simulation, and the synthesized results were used for validating the function blocks and evaluating the cost, complexity, and performance of the hardware. Software development was performed in *Tornado* integrated environment for Vxworks. After eliminating hardware executable portions from the software-based minutiae extraction program, we added a module for hardware integration. Once the validations of each hardware and software were completed, an integrated simulation was conducted. Finally, the quality of the minutiae extraction was evaluated and compared with that of the software-based minutiae extraction program.

Table 1. Required Resources on Xilinx Virtex V2000EFG680

Number of Slices	1,826 out of 19,200 (9%)
Number of Slice Flip Flops	1,183 out of 38,400 (3%)
Total Number 4 input LUTs	2,974 out of 38,400 (7%)
Number used as LUTs	2,846
Number used as a Route-Thru	128
Number of Block RAMs	4 out of 160 (2%)
Total Equivalent Gate Count for Design	97,054

Table 1 shows the characteristics of the hardware module. When the system operated in 50MHz, 20~50 minutiae can be extracted from typical 248×292 fingerprint images in 2~4 seconds using a small area(97K gates). Most of the execution time was for the direction computation for each 8×8 image block in Image Pre-Processing. This was because computing arctangent and square root took times without a math-coprocessor in ARM940T. In the near future, the clock rate can be improved, and then a real-time execution can be achieved.

5 Conclusions

In this paper, we have presented an SoC implementation of fingerprint minutiae extraction which can be employed in a smart card chip. To implement the ridge-following algorithm onto resource-constrained SoCs, the algorithm has been modified to increase the efficiency of hardwares. Each functional block of the algorithm has been implemented in hardware or in software by considering its computational complexity, cost and utilization of the hardware, and efficiency of the entire system.

The performance evaluation shows that our design can make the time consuming minutiae extraction executable on an area-constrained smart card. Since the fingerprint feature extraction system has been developed as an IP for SoCs with ARM CPU and AMBA bus, it can be used on many kinds of SoCs for smart cards. Also, hardware for minutiae matching[9] can be easily integrated to execute the overall fingerprint authentication within the smart card chip, removing the possibility of leaking any biometric information.

Acknowledgement

This research was supported by the MIC(Ministry of Information and Communication), Korea, under the Chung-Ang University HNRC-ITRC(Home Network Research Center) support program supervised by the IITA(Institute of Information Technology Assessment).

References

1. Maltoni, D. et al.: Handbook of Fingerprint Recognition. Springer, Heidelberg (2003)
2. Bolle, R., Connell, J., Ratha, N.: Biometric Perils and Patches. Pattern Recognition 35, 2727–2738 (2002)
3. Ratha, N., Connell, J., Bolle, R.: An Analysis of Minutiae Matching Strength. In: Proc. of AVBPA 2001, pp. 223–228 (2001)
4. X9.84: Biometrics Information Management and Security For The Financial Services Industry. ANSI (2000)
5. Moon, Y. et al.: Collaborative Fingerprint Authentication by Smart Card and a Trusted Host. Electrical and Computer Engineering 1, 108–112 (2000)
6. Hachez, G., Koeune, F., Quisquater, J.: Biometrics, Access Control, Smart Cards: A Not So Simple Combination. In: Proc. of 4th Working Conf. on Smart Card Research and Advanced Applications, pp. 273–288 (2000)
7. Moon, D., et al.: Performance Analysis of the Match-on-Card System for the Fingerprint Authentication. In: Proc. of International Workshop on Information Security Applications, pp. 449–459 (2001)
8. Pan, S. et al.: An Ultra-Low Memory Fingerprint Matching Algorithm and Its Implementation on a 32-bit Smart Card. IEEE Tr. Consumer Electronics 49(2), 453–459 (2003)
9. Kim, M., et al.: A Hardware Implementation for Fingerprint-based Match-on-Card. In: Proc. of International Workshop on Information Security Applications, pp. 743–752 (2003)
10. Rila, L., Mitchell, C.: Security Analysis of Smartcard to Card Reader Communications for Biometric Cardholder Authentication. In: Proc. of CARDIS, pp. 19–28 (2002)
11. Maio, D., Maltoni, D.: Direct Gray-Scale Minutiae Detection in Fingerprints. IEEE Trans. on Pattern Analysis Machine Intelligence 19(1), 27–40 (1997)
12. ARM limited: AMBA Specification, Rev. 2.0 (1999)

Image-Adaptive Watermarking Using the Improved Signal to Noise Ratio

Xinshan Zhu

Institute of Computer Science & Technology of Peking University,
Beijing 100871, China
zhuxinshan@icst.pku.edu.cn

Abstract. The two conflicting requirements of watermark invisibility and robustness are both required in most applications. The solution is to utilize a suitable perceptual quality metric (PQM) for watermarking correctly. This paper develops a new quality metric, the improved signal to noise ratio (iSNR). The improvement is done in the following two aspects: 1) SNR manifests much better performance in an image block of small size than in a whole image; 2) the average luminance and gradient information are added into SNR. Next, we propose a new adaptive watermarking framework based on the localized quality evaluation, which divides the cover data into nonoverlapping blocks and assigns an independent distortion constraint to each block to control the quality of it. In comparison with ones based on the global quality evaluation, the new one exploits the localized signal characteristics sufficiently while guaranteeing the localized watermark invisibility. Then, a specific implementation of the above framework is developed for image applying iSNR as the quality metric in the sense of maximizing the detection value. Experimental results demonstrate that the proposed watermarking performs very well both in robustness and invisibility.

1 Introduction

Image watermarking [1] has been shown as a valid solution to the problem of image copyright protection. To this aim, the most important features a watermarking technique should exhibit are unobtrusiveness and robustness. However, the two basic requirements conflict with each other. To deal with the problem, many perceptual quality metrics are introduced into watermarking in previous works.

Peak signal to noise ratio (PSNR) and SNR are used widely to measure the difference distortion between two signals. However, they are not suitable for estimating image quality [2], although they are still in many existing watermarking.In [3], Voloshynovskiy et al. proposed the weighted PSNR, which exploits the local image variance. They announced that the improvement of wPSNR is prominent. Presently more attention is paid to human visual model (HVM) [1]. Usually, the just noticeable difference (JND) is defined in HVM, which is used to estimate the smallest discernible amount of change at each pixel or coefficient in transform domain [4,5].

Y. Wang, Y. Cheung, and H. Liu (Eds.): CIS 2006, LNAI 4456, pp. 616–625, 2007.

In applying distortion measures, Perceptually shaped watermarking (PSW) is a typical scheme [6]. A watermark signal is shaped through weighting its each component with JND. A global gain factor is used to adjust adaptively the watermark strength under the given global distortion constraint. Many other algorithms follow the scheme [7,8]. In [9], the optimal use of perceptual models was presented. Two alternative optimal behaviors for the embedder are specified as follows: 1) maximizing the robustness of an embedded mark, while maintaining a constant perceptual distance. 2) minimizing perceptual distance while maintaining a constant robustness. Zhu et al. [10] utilized the linear prediction synthesis filter to shape the watermark signal, whose parameters are derived from a set of JND's. These algorithms are all designed under a global constraint specified by some distortion measure, while the localized image quality is disregarded.

The goal of this paper is to improve SNR and develop a new adaptive watermarking framework to achieve a better tradeoff between the requirements of invisibility and robustness. The remainder of this paper is structured as follows: Section 2 presents the improved SNR. In Section 3, we describe a new adaptive watermarking framework based on localized quality evaluation. A specific implementation of it is developed for image utilizing iSNR in Section 4. A serial of tests are done to evaluate our algorithm in Section 5. Finally, Section 6 concludes.

2 The Improved Signal to Noise Ratio

As a signal distortion measure, SNR is widely used in the fields of signal processing, image processing and information theory, etc.. For a two-dimensional image, SNR is defined as

$$SNR = \frac{\sum\limits_{i,j} x(i,j)^2}{\sum\limits_{i,j} (x(i,j) - x'(i,j))^2} \tag{1}$$

where $x(i,j)$ represents a pixel, whose coordinates are (i,j), in the original, undistorted image, and $x'(i,j)$ represents a pixel, whose coordinates (i,j), in the distorted (watermarked) image [2]. And it is also usually expressed in decibels (dB), i.e., $SNR(dB) = 10\log_{10}(SNR)$.

However, it is well known that SNR performs badly in estimating the perceptual quality of image. From Equation (1), SNR penalizes the visibility of noise of each pixel equally, which is not consistent with human vision [3]. Using it to quantify the distortion caused by watermark embedding might therefore result in misleading the design of watermarking [2]. Presently, many existing human visual models (HVM) are applying successfully in such respect. But to improve SNR is still very significant and possible. The quadric form of SNR has some exclusive advantages for signal processing.

In [3], Voloshynovskiy proposed the weighted PSNR (wPSNR), which made use of different weight for the noise of different pixel by consideration of the

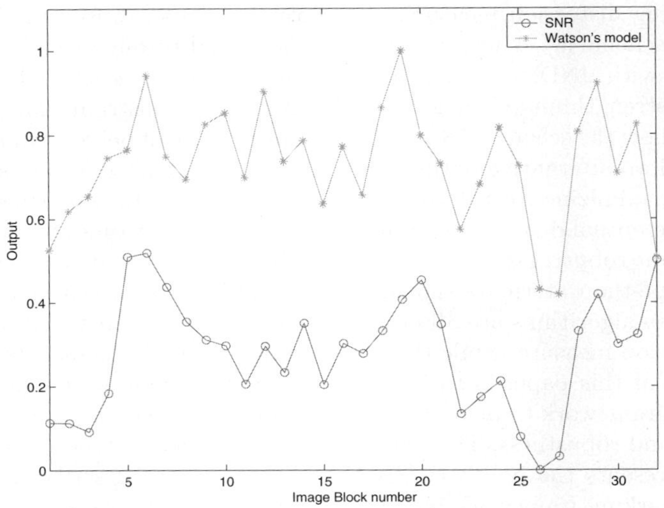

Fig. 1. Comparing SNR with Watson's model on local image quality estimation. This figure shows the scaled reciprocal values of SNR and PD values of the 32 blocks of the 1st row of 'Lena'.

local image variance. Unlike the idea of wPSNR, first we notice SNR does well on estimation of perceptual quality of an image block of small size. Intuitively, this is because the visibility of each pixel in one small region is approximately equal. Such a viewpoint is also proved right by experiments. Between the original 'Lena' image and its noised version, the perceptual quality of each image block of size 8×8 is estimated by SNR and perceptual distance (PD) of Watson's model [4] respectively. For convenience of comparison, the reciprocal values of SNR are scaled into the range from 0 to 1 and then are displayed in Fig. 1 together with PD values. Fig. 1 obviously illustrates that SNR almost does as well as the HVM on perceptual quality estimation of small region.

In what follows, attention is paid to modify the definition of SNR. First, let us analyze its original definition. Suppose $\bar{x} = \frac{1}{MN}\sum_{i,j} x(i,j)$ and $S^2 = \frac{1}{MN}\sum_{i,j}(x(i,j) - \bar{x})^2$, where M and N denote the number of row and column of an image respectively. Then Equation (1) is transformed into Equation (2).

$$SNR = \frac{MN(S^2 + \bar{x}^2)}{\sum_{i,j}(x(i,j) - x'(i,j))^2} \tag{2}$$

In Equation (2), S^2 describes gradient information of image, i.e., image texture, which can be seen clearly from the following analysis. Suppose $\nabla^2 = \frac{1}{6MN}\sum_{i,j}\sum_{m=0}^{1}\sum_{n=0}^{1}(x(i,j) - x(i+m, j+n))^2$, where $x(i+m, j+n)$ is replaced by $x(i+m, j+n-N)$ when its horizontal coordinate exceeds image size and so does it for vertical coordinate. Therefore, we have

$$S^2 = \nabla^2 + \frac{1}{3MN}[\sum_{i,j} x(i,j)(x(i+1,j) + x(i,j+1) + x(i+1,j+1)) - \bar{x}^2] \quad (3)$$

If the pixels are mutually independent, the difference between the last two terms in Equation (3) is zero in statistical sense. In other words, S^2 approximately expresses the average gradient energy of image. Actually, S^2 represents the average gradient energy between pixels and their mean value (see its definition). Hence, by consideration of the masking effect of image gradient, it is reasonable to substitute S^2 in Equation (2) with ∇^2. Additionally, $\bar{x}$ expresses the average luminance of image. Based on the consideration that the eye is less sensitive to noise in those areas with high or low brightness [5,8], the factor $\bar{x}^2$ in Equation (2) should be modified as $(\bar{x} - 128)^2$ (the mean pixel brightness is 128). Finally, the improved SNR is represented by

$$iSNR = \frac{MN[\nabla^2 + (\bar{x} - 128)^2]}{\sum_{i,j} (x(i,j) - x'(i,j))^2} \quad (4)$$

The iSNR will be used to measure the perceptual quality of an image block, but not the whole image. We suggest that the appreciate block size is 3×3 or 5×5, which is usually used as the size of spatial filtering mask. The left problem is how to evaluate the perceptual quality of the whole image. The optional strategy is to compute some statistical variable of all local iSNR values, e.g., the mean value, or even to see their distribution directly. We believe that is flexible for a specific application.

3 Adaptive Watermarking Based on Localized Quality Evaluation

In previous works, the distortion resulted from watermarking was usually measured globally. However, some experimental results [3] showed that even if the global distortion condition is satisfied, it is possible that watermark is visible at some local positions. To deal with the problem, we propose a new adaptive watermarking framework based on localized quality evaluation with PQM here.

The general embedding procedure is described detailedly as follows and shown in Fig. 2.

1) Generate a watermark signal W for the embedded message M.
   The host signal X_o is sometimes required or not in the process. And for the sake of security, the generation of W usually depends on the cryptographic key K.
2) Partition X_o into p nonoverlapping small blocks, $X_o = X_1 \| X_2 \| \cdots \| X_p$. The same operation is also carried out on W, $W = W_1 \| W_2 \| \cdots \| W_p$.

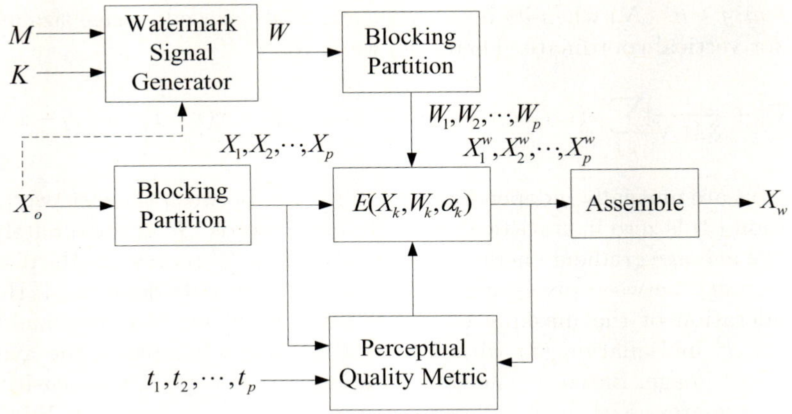

Fig. 2. The general embedding procedure of an adaptive watermarking based on localized quality evaluation

3) Choose a suitable PQM and set an acceptable distortion constraint for each block.
4) Embed each watermark signal block into the corresponding host signal block.
   For block X_k, an optimal embedding function $E(\cdot)$ is obtained through maximizing the robustness while maintaining a constant distortion. An additional gain factor α_k is applied to adjust localized watermark strength to meet the given distortion constraint. Thus, the watermarked signal block X_k^w is generally expressed as $X_k^w = E(X_k, W_k, \alpha_k)$.
5) Assemble all the watermarked blocks to form the watermarked signal, i.e., $X_w = X_1^w \| X_2^w \| \cdots \| X_p^w$.
   According to the embedding strategy, the perceptual quality of each watermarked signal block is controlled by the corresponding localized distortion condition. As a result, the localized watermark invisibility is obtained if each localized distortion condition is set reasonably, so the drawback of the existing adaptive watermarking is overcome. Additionally, each block has its own gain factor, which allows us to adjust the localized signal quality independently. It is believed that the strategy can achieve an optimal tradeoff between watermark invisibility and robustness.

4 A Specific Implementation: iSNR-Based Image Adaptive Watermarking

The proposed locally adaptive watermarking framework is easily combined with the existing watermarking. In this section, we will present a specific implementation for image with the proposed iSNR as the distortion measure. The watermark embedding is directly operated in the spatial domain.

Let X_o denote the original gray-scale image of size $M \times N$. The watermark signal, W is generated by a random number generator, which is initialized with a seed that depends on the cryptographic key K. Without loss of generality, we assume that watermark signal has the same size as the host image.

The original image is divided into nonoverlapping blocks of size $L \times L$, $X_o = X_1 \| X_2 \| \ldots \| X_p$, where $X_k, 0 \leq k \leq p$, is a macroblock of $L \times L$ pixels. If p is not a whole number, extra pixels are truncated, i.e., $\lfloor M/L \rfloor \times \lfloor N/L \rfloor$. The same operation is also performed on the watermark signal.

On the image block X_k, we compute the statistic variable ∇_k^2 and $\bar{x}_k^2$ according to their definitions in Section II respectively. Under the distortion constraint $iSNR = t_k$, we obtain

$$\frac{L^2(\nabla_k^2 + (\bar{x}_k - 128)^2)}{\sum\limits_{(i,j)\in X_k} (x'(i,j) - x(i,j))^2} = t_k \tag{5}$$

where $x'(i,j)$ is the pixel value of the watermarked image X_w corresponding to $x(i,j)$. In this work, we consider the case of maximizing the linear correlation ρ_k between X_k^w and W_k, i.e.,

$$\rho_k = \frac{1}{L^2} \sum_{(i,j)\in X_k} x'(i,j) w(i,j) \tag{6}$$

where $w(i,j)$ denotes the component at coordinate (i,j) in the kth block, W_k.

Obviously, this is a constrained optimization problem. Combining Equation (5) and (6), a Lagrange equation can be constructed and solved to yield

$$x'(i,j) = x(i,j) + \alpha_k w(i,j) \quad (i,j) \in X_k \tag{7}$$

where

$$\alpha_k = \sqrt{\frac{L^2(\nabla_k^2 + (\bar{x}_k - 128)^2)}{t_k \sum\limits_{(i,j)\in X_k} w(i,j)^2}} \tag{8}$$

Finally, the global embedding function is represented by

$$x'(i,j) = x(i,j) + \sum_{k=1}^{p} I_{X_k}(i,j) \alpha_k w(i,j) \tag{9}$$

where $I_{X_k}(i,j)$ represents indicator function, that is

$$I_{X_k}(i,j) = \begin{cases} 1, & (i,j) \in X_k \\ 0, & \text{else} \end{cases}$$

Equation (9) is obtained in case that the acceptable distortion in each block is specified by iSNR, which differs from many existing watermarking under only one global distortion constraint. We call such a scheme as iSNR-based spread spectrum (iSNR-SS). It allows us to exploit local image characteristics sufficiently for watermark embedding, because each localized gain factor α_k is determined by the localized image information (see Equation (8)). So it is possible to guarantee localized watermark invisibility while enhancing detection value.

5 Experimental Results

The presented watermarking has been extensively tested on various standard images and attempting different kinds of attacks: in this section some of the most significant results will be shown. For the experiments presented in the following, the size of image block is set to 5×5.

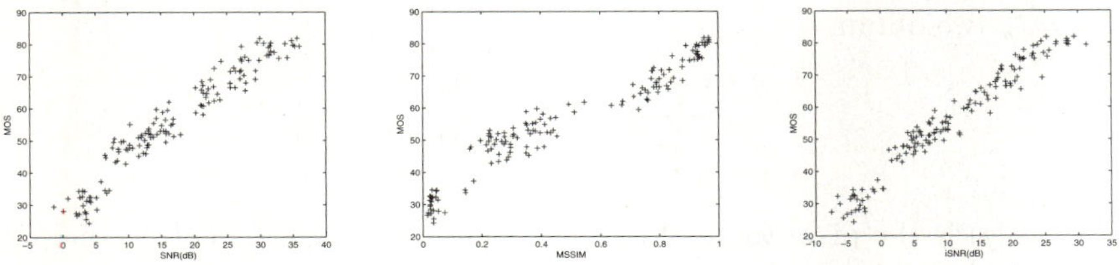

(a) (b) (c)

Fig. 3. Scatter plots of subjective mean opinion score (MOS) versus model prediction. (a) SNR; (b) MSSIM (using the same parameters as [11]); (c) iSNR.

In order to manifest the performance of iSNR, we tested it on the image database composed of White Gaussian noised images [12]. The database is adopted, because the distortion resulted from watermarking is usually modeled as white noise. For each image, we compute a mean iSNR index of all localized ones to evaluate the overall image quality. Other quality assessment models used for comparison include SNR and mean structural similarity (MSSIM) [11]. The scatter plot of Mean opinion score (MOS) versus model prediction for each model is shown in Fig. 3. Fig. 3 illustrates that the iSNR supplies remarkably better prediction of the subjective scores than SNR and MSSIM.

Watermark invisibility is evaluated on images of Airport, Baboon and Peppers. The localized iSNR for these three watermarked images are 40 dB, 35 dB, and 30 dB, respectively. In Fig. 4 (a), the original images are presented, while in Fig. 4 (b), the watermarked copies are shown: the images are evidently undistinguishable, in particular, while the iSNR is lower than 35 dB, which is the empirical value for the image without any perceivable degradation. It is because the localized image quality is also controlled by iSNR in iSNR-SS watermarking and the iSNR can mask watermark signal better with consideration of the average luminance and gradient information. The masking effectiveness of iSNR can be appreciated from Fig. 4 (c), where the absolute difference between the original image and the watermarked one, magnified by a factor 10, is shown: it is evident that the watermark is reshaped into high activity regions and around edges.

Simulation results of iSNR-SS for some attacks, including JPEG compression, additive noise, low-pass filtering, and cropping, are shown in Table 1 together with ones of PSW [6]. For fair comparison, the iSNR for all the watermarked images is set to 30 dB. The threshold used for detection is 0.83 calculated with

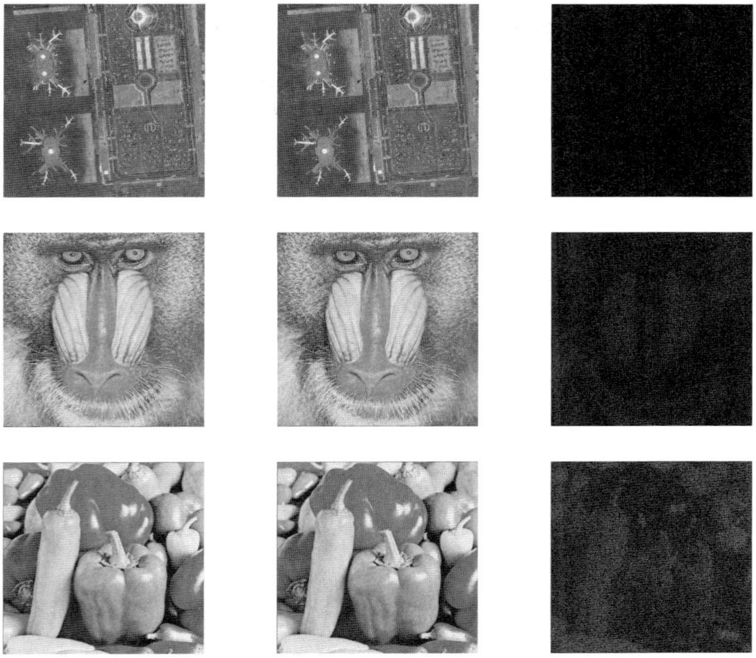

(a) (b) (c)

Fig. 4. (a) The Original images, 'Airport' (the 1th row), 'Baboon' (the 2th row) and 'Peppers' (the 3th row); (b) The watermarked copies; (c) the corresponding watermarks, magnified by a factor 10

Table 1. Simulation results under different attacks. The parameters in the second row mean quality factor, noise variance, and filter width, and the size of cropped corresponding to attacks. The outputs are detection values, i.e., linear correlation.

Image	Scheme	compression			Gaussian noise			filtering			cropping		
		80	50	20	13	32	45	0.4	0.6	0.8	128*128	96*96	64*64
Airport	iSNR-SS	2.24	1.38	0.82	1.93	1.79	1.52	2.50	1.38	0.89	3.44	2.94	3.04
	PSW	2.10	1.30	0.75	3.23	3.10	2.44	2.38	1.52	1.23	3.95	3.35	2.99
Baboon	iSNR-SS	2.89	1.77	1.09	2.35	1.97	2.02	3.04	1.63	1.01	3.10	3.24	3.66
	PSW	2.5	1.68	1.29	3.56	3.16	3.03	4.72	2.44	1.51	3.68	3.63	3.52
Peppers	iSNR-SS	1.65	0.83	0.27	2.53	1.97	1.67	2.87	1.45	0.83	3.12	3.06	2.73
	PSW	1.93	0.83	0.52	2.00	1.53	1.63	2.41	1.65	1.34	3.20	3.39	3.43

the given false positive possibility $P_{fp} = 10^{-8}$ [10]. These results allow us to test the resilience of the watermark against the loss of information. It can be clearly observed that the robustness of iSNR-SS is almost as good as PSW under all four attacks, in particular, JPEG compression and filtering (many spatial domain methods are defeated by them). However, the computation cost of iSNR-SS is much lower than PSW. Moreover, the localized perceptual quality of the watermarked images by iSNR-SS is better than PSW even under the same distortion measure. The results also reflect the fact that the iSNR is a valid spatial masking model.

6 Conclusion

This paper presented the iSNR, which sufficiently took the image characteristics into account including the average luminance and gradient information. Both theoretical analysis and simulation results show the iSNR performs very well. Then we developed a new adaptive watermarking framework based on local quality evaluation. Better local watermark invisibility is achieved through setting an acceptable local distortion bound with one PQM. At the same time, the framework allows us to adjust local embedding strength independently, so local signal characteristics are exploited sufficiently to enhance the robustness. Thereafter, a specific implementation using the iSNR, iSNR-SS is proposed for image. Experimental results illustrated that iSNR-SS attains an optimal trade-off between fidelity and robustness.

Acknowledgments. This work was supported by China Postdoctoral Science Foundation under Grant No. 20060390009.

References

1. Cox, I., Miller, M.L.: A review of watermarking and the importance of perceptual modeling. In: Proc. Electronic Imaging (1997)
2. Kutter, M., Petitcolas, F.A.P.: A fair benchmark for image watermarking systems. In: de Boer, F.S., Bonsangue, M.M., Graf, S., de Roever, W.-P. (eds.) Formal Methods for Components and Objects. LNCS, vol. 3657, Springer, Heidelberg (2005)
3. Voloshynovskiy, S., Pereira, S., Iquise, V., Pun, T.: Attack modelling: Towards a second generation watermarking benchmark. Signal Processing, Special Issue 81, 1177–1214 (2001)
4. Watson, A.B.: Dct quantization matrices optimized for individual images. Human Vision, Visual Processing, and Digital Display IV SPIE-1913, 202–216 (1993)
5. Lewis, A.S., Knowles, G.: Image compression using the 2-d wavelet transform. IEEE Trans. Image Processing 1, 244–250 (1992)
6. Podilchuk, C., Zeng, W.: Image-adaptive watermarking using visual models. IEEE J. Selected Areas Comm. 16, 525–539 (1998)
7. Kirovski, D., Malvar, H.S.: Spread-spectrum watermarking of audio signals. IEEE Transactions on Signal Processing 51, 1020–1033 (2003)
8. Barni, M., Bartolini, A.P.F.: Improved wavelet-based watermarking through pixel-wise masking. IEEE Transactions on Image Processing 10, 783–791 (2001)
9. Cox, I.J., Miller, M.L., Bloom, J.A. (eds.): Digital Watermarking. Academic Press, San Francisco (2002)
10. Zhu, X.S., Wang, Y.S.: Better use of human visual model in watermarking based on linear prediction synthesis filter. In: Cox, I., Kalker, T., Lee, H.-K. (eds.) Digital Watermarking. LNCS, vol. 3304, pp. 66–76. Springer, Heidelberg (2005)

11. Wang, Z., Bovik, A.C., Sheikh, H.R., Simoncelli, E.P.: Image quality assessment: from error visibility to structural similarity. IEEE Transactions on Image Processing 13, 600–612 (2004)
12. Sheikh, H.R., Wang, Z., Bovik, A.C., Cormack, L.K.: Image and video quality assessment research at live. [Online] Available: http://live.ece.utexas.edu/research/quality/

New Malicious Code Detection Based on N-Gram Analysis and Rough Set Theory

Boyun Zhang[1,2], Jianping Yin[1], Jingbo Hao[1], Shulin Wang[1], and Dingxing Zhang[1]

[1] School of Computer Science, National University of Defense Technolgy, Changsha 410073, China
{hnjxzby,dingxingzhang}@yahoo.com.cn, {jpyin,hjb}@nudt.edu.cn, jt_slwang@hnu.cn

[2] Department of Computer Science, Hunan Public Security College, Changsha 410138, China

Abstract. Motivated by the standard signature-based technique for detecting viruses, we explore the idea of automatically detecting malicious code using the N-gram analysis. The method is based on statistical learning and not strictly dependent on certain viruses. We propose the use of rough set theory to reduce the feature dimension. An efficient implementation to calculate relative core, based on positive region definition is presented also. The k nearest neighbor and support vector machine classifiers are used to categorize a program as either normal or abnormal. The experimental results are promising and show that the proposed scheme results in low rate of false positive.

1 Introduction

Since the appearance of the first computer virus in 1986, a significant number of new viruses have appeared every year. This number is growing and it threatens to outpace the manual effort by anti-virus experts in designing solutions for detecting them and removing them from the system [1]. Excellent technology exists for detecting known viruses. Programs such as Norton Anti-Virus are ubiquitous. These programs search executable code for known patterns. One shortcoming of this method is that we must obtain a copy of a malicious program before extracting the pattern necessary for its detection.

And then there have been few attempts to use machine learning and data mining for the purpose of identifying new or unknown malicious code [2-4]. In addition there are other methods of guarding against malicious code, such as object reconciliation, which involves comparing current files and directories to past copies. One can also compare cryptographic hashes. These approaches are not based on data mining.

In this paper, we explore solutions based on machine learning and not strictly dependent on certain viruses. It would not be feasible to design a general anti-virus tool that could replace a human expert or be as reliable as the exact solutions for known viruses, but such a solution would be of a great benefit in warning against new viruses, in aiding experts in finding a good signature for a new virus, and in adaptable solutions for different users.

Y. Wang, Y. Cheung, and H. Liu (Eds.): CIS 2006, LNAI 4456, pp. 626–633, 2007.

In the following sections, we first detail the feature selection based on N-gram and Information Gain, and then a new feature reduction method by using rough set theory is proposed. Section 3 shows the experiment results. We state our plans for future work in Section 4.

2 Detection Engine

2.1 Feature Extraction

The idea of using n-grams for malicious code analysis is not new [1, 5], but we did not find many reported results. Before extracting features of each file, we first introduce n-gram analysis. An n-gram [6] is a subsequence of *N* consecutive tokens in a stream of tokens. N-gram analysis has been applied in many tasks, and is well understood and efficient to implement. By converting a string of data to n-grams, it can be embedded in a vector space to efficiently compare two or more streams of data. Alternatively, we may compare the distributions of n-grams contained in a set of data to determine how consistent some new data may be with the set of data in question. An n-gram distribution is computed by sliding a fixed size window through the set of data and counting the number of occurrences of each "gram".

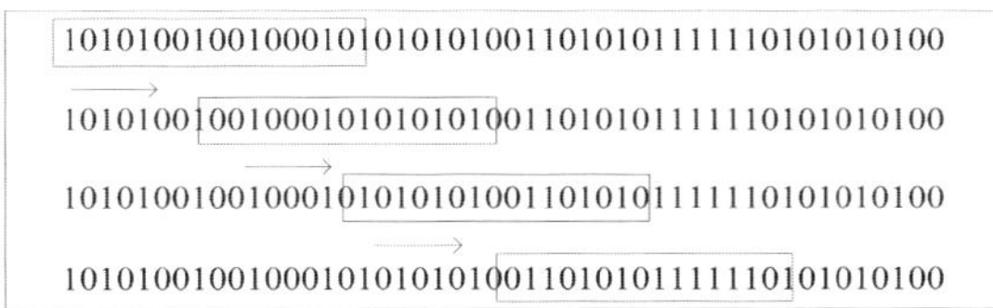

Fig. 1. Sliding window (window size=2 Byte)

Table 1. Feature Frequency Matrix. (*n*=2)

Samples	Features					
	0080	61C3	638D	9090	E020	…
Win32.Alcaul.a	2	4	21	8	79	
Win32.Alcaul.b	45	6	40	7	20	
Win32.Alcaul.c	11	11	18	8	14	
Win32.Alcaul.e	7	0	12	6	25	
Win32.Alcaul.f	9	20	15	5	27	…
Win32.Alcaul.g	11	0	17	3	20	
Win32.Alcaul.h	19	17	48	4	29	
…	…	…	…	…	…	

Figure 1 displays an example of a 2-byte window sliding right one byte at a time to generate each 2-gram. Each 2-gram is displayed in the highlighted "window". The choice of the window size depends on the application. First, the computational complexity increases exponentially as the window size increases. Data is considered a stream of tokens drawn from some alphabet. If the number of distinct tokens (or the size of the alphabet) is *X*, then the space of grams grows as X^N. In this work, we focus initially on 2-gram analysis of binary values of PE format file. After the preliminary processing, the frequency matrix of data set is obtained. An example of frequency matrix is shown in table1 of our experiment.

2.2 Feature Selection Based on IG

For feature selection in our approach we adopt correlation measures based on the information theoretical concept of entropy, a measure of the uncertainty of a random variable. The distinguishing power of each feature is derived by computing its information gain (IG) based on its frequencies of appearances in the malicious class and benign class. Features with negligible information gains can then be removed to reduce the number of features and speed the classification process.

The entropy of a variable X is defined as:

$$H(X) = -\sum_i P(x_i)\log_2(P(x_i)), \tag{1}$$

And the entropy of X after observing values of another variable Y is defined as:

$$H(X \mid Y) = -\sum_j P(y_j)\sum_i P(x_i \mid y_j)\log_2(P(x_i \mid y_j)), \tag{2}$$

where $P(x_i)$ are the prior probabilities for all values of X, and $P(x_i \mid y_j)$ is the posterior probabilities of x_i given the values of y_j. The amount by which the entropy of X decreases reflects additional information about X provided by Y is called information gain, given by

$$IG(X \mid Y) = H(X) - H(X \mid Y). \tag{3}$$

Information gain tends to favor variables with more values and can be normalized by their corresponding entropy.

For our problem, the expected entropy calculated as:

$$\begin{aligned} H(X) = -[&P(x\ is\ normal)\cdot\log_2 P(x\ is\ normal) \\ &+ P(x\ is\ abnormal)\cdot\log_2 P(x\ is\ abnormal)]. \end{aligned} \tag{4}$$

If the data set is further partitioned by feature y_i, the conditional entropy $H(X \mid y_i)$ is calculated as:

$$\begin{aligned} H(X \mid y_i) = &-P(y_i = 0)\cdot[P(x\ is\ normal \mid y_i = 0)\cdot\log_2 P(x\ is\ normal \mid y_i = 0) \\ &+ P(x\ is\ abnormal \mid y_i = 0)\cdot\log_2 P(x\ is\ abnormal \mid y_i = 0)\ ] \\ &- P(y_i = 1)\cdot[\ P(x\ is\ normal \mid y_i = 1)\cdot\log_2 P(x\ is\ normal \mid y_i = 1) \\ &+ P(x\ is\ abnormal \mid y_i = 1)\cdot\log_2 P(x\ is\ abnormal \mid y_i = 1)\ ]. \end{aligned} \tag{5}$$

where $y_i = 0$ denotes that the feature y_i do not appear in the samples, $y_i = 1$ denotes that the feature y_i appears in the samples.

The information gains for each feature are detailed in table 2.

Table 2. The Information Gain of Features. (n=2)

Features	Benign Sample Set		Malicious Sample Set		Information Gain
	y_i=1	y_i=0	y_i=1	y_i=0	
FF84	98	11	92	0	0.000954615
4508	106	3	85	7	0.000387123
FDFF	109	0	89	3	0.001103624
F33C	101	8	76	16	0.002371356
BF28	94	15	91	1	0.000767842
...	...	...	...	...	...

2.3 Using Rough Set Theory to Reduce Feature

Because the n-grams obtained from the method above is redundant, we should firstly reduce the feature dimension of our detection model as a preprocessing step. Here we use RST to reduce the feature dimension.

As we know that Rough Set Theory (RST) offers two fundamental concepts to deal with this particular problem: reduct and core. These concepts are generalized to families of equivalence relations. Some algorithms have been proposed to calculate reducts and core. Based on discernibility matrix and functions an algorithm to obtain core and reducts is defined [7]. However these routines are space and time consuming in practice for real world databases, thus, the need for an alternative implementation to improve and make more efficient large database processing. In this paper an efficient implementation to calculate relative core, based on positive region definition is presented. Our method of implementation takes into account the following considerations:

When checking if an equivalence relation $R \in P$ is Q-indispensable, where P and Q are families of equivalence relations $POS_{IND(P)}(IND(Q))$ is considered as a set of equivalence classes. In this case, indispensability is verified based on comparisons within the respective equivalence classes.

Verification is done in an incremental way, thus reducing calculation time when the equivalence relation is Q-indispensable. Comparisons between sets are time-consuming if we do it in a naive form -that is, each element at a time. When the positive region is considered as a set of equivalence classes, some properties are satisfied so that comparison within sets, then the calculation could be simplified based on its cardinalities. In our experiments an algorithm to calculate reducts based on the improved method is detailed in alg1.

2.4 Classification Method

Malicious code detection can be look as a binary classification problem. We use K Nearest Neighbor (KNN) and Support Vector Machine (SVM) classifiers to conduct the detection. The proposed detection procedure details as follow steps: 1) Dumping Hex-decimal byte sequence from malicious and benign PE format files. 2) Slicing each Hex sequence into gram by n –the size of sliding window. 3) Selecting feature based on the Information Gain of each feature. 4) Reducing the feature dimension by using Rough Set Theory. 5) Training and checking the classifiers. And the detailed step is shown in figure 2.

```
Reducts( P,Q )
Input:  P, Q families of equivalence relations.
Output: R, R is a Q-reduct of P

 Call  Core(P,Q)
R ← {R ∈ P | R is not marked}
 if R = ∅ then
        return {P}
 else
        return ∪_{R∈P} {Reducts(P − {R}), Q)}
 end

Procedure Core( P,Q )
input:  P, Q families of equivalence relations
Output: R ∈ P , Q-indispensable are marked
  indP ← U/IND(P)
  indQ ← U/IND(Q)
  for ∀W ∈ IND(Q) do
       m ← LowerCard(U / IND(P), W)
       for  ∀R ∈ P , not marked  do
            n ← LowerCard(U / IND(P − {R}), W)
            if m ≠ n then
               mark R
            end
       end
  end

Procedure LowerCard( P,W )
Input: P partition , W ⊆ U .
Output: |IND(P)W|
  cardinality ← 0
  for ∀S ∈ P do
       if S ⊆ W then
            cardinality ← cardinality +|S|
       end
  end
  return cardinality
```

Alg 1. Feature reduction Algorithm

In reality, it is likely to be impossible to collect all normal variations in behavior, so we must face the possibility that our normal database will provide incomplete coverage of normal behavior. If the normal were incomplete, false positives could be the result. Moreover, the inaccuracy of each classifier itself also needs to set some judge rules to improve the performance of the detecting systems. So our method is preliminary.

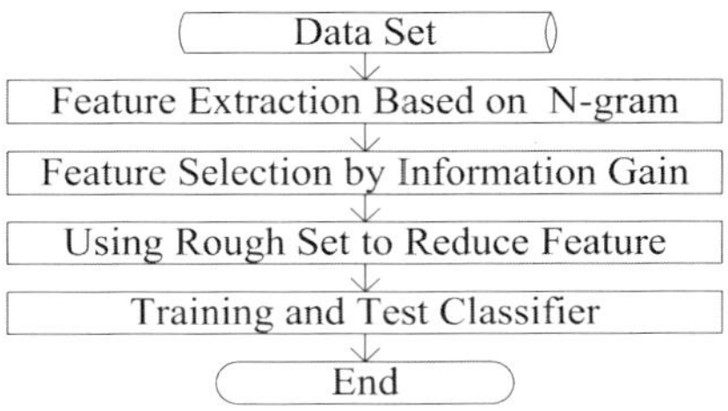

Fig. 2. Detection Procedure

3 Experiments

We collected 201 distinct Windows executable files (92 malicious code, and 109 benign codes) and labeled by a commercial virus scanner with the correct class label (malicious or benign) for our method. The total malicious code size is 3,614,242 byte, and benign code 5,765,650 bytes.

During the experiment, we use the software- Ngrams[8], LIBSVM[9] and RSES[10]. Ngrams tool is used in building byte n-gram profiles with parameters $8bit \le n \le 16bit$, and $20 \le L \le 4000$, where L is the number of features. RSES and LIBSVM tools are used to reduce feature and conduct classification. To evaluate our system we were interested in several quantities: False Negative (FN), the number of malicious executable examples classified as benign; False Positives (FP), the number of benign programs classified as malicious executables.

The experiment result shows in table 3. The results are very encouraging- for SVM classifier, it achieving accuracy of about 96% for several parameter configurations. The result shows a fact that the dataset can be represented as two 2-gram profiles, and be successfully used in the classification.

In another experiment [11], we had used a method based on Fuzzy Pattern Recognition algorithm (FPR) to classify virus. That algorithm had the lowest false positive

Table 3. Experiment Results

Number of features		KNN(%)		SVM(%)	
Before Reduction	After Reduction	FN rate	FP rate	FN rate	FP rate
20	17	18.48	13.04	13.76	10.87
50	39	19.57	15.22	13.76	11.96
100	76	11.96	10.87	7.34	7.61
200	153	9.78	9.78	5.50	6.52
500	385	8.70	7.61	*4.59*	*3.26*
1000	769	9.78	8.70	4.59	5.43
1500	1071	8.70	8.70	5.50	4.35
2000	1428	10.87	7.61	5.50	5.43
3000	2140	9.87	9.78	6.42	6.52
4000	2669	9.87	8.70	5.50	5.43

rate, 4.45%. The present method has the lowest false positive rate, 3.26%, which has better detection rates than the algorithm based on FPR. Notice that the detection rates of these two methods are nearly equal, but the FPR algorithm uses more training samples than the present method. This shows that our method is fit to detect malicious code when the gather of samples is difficult.

4 Conclusion

The present paper proposes the use of n-gram analysis in the area of anti-virus to make it more suitable as on-line detection system. In order to have a faster response from scanner, number of features should be minimized without affecting the classification power of the system. In the experiment we use rough set theory to reduce features that discard redundant attribute values. Experiment result shows that the present method could effectively use to discriminate benign and malicious PE format programs. The method achieves high rate of accuracy. Future work include testing this method over a larger set of malicious and benign executables for a fully evaluation of it. In addition with a larger data set, we plan to evaluate this method on different types of malicious codes such as Macros and Visual Basic scripts.

Acknowledgment

This work was supported in part by the National Natural Science Foundation of China under Grant No.60373023 and the Scientific Research Fund of Hunan Provincial Education Department of China under Grant No.05B072.

References

1. Kephart, J., Arnold, W.: Automatic Extraction of Computer Virus Signatures. In: Proceedings.of the 4th Virus Bulletin International Conference, Abingdon, pp. 178–184 (1994)
2. Lo, R., Levitt, K., Olsson, R.: MCF: A Malicious Code Filter. Computers and Security 14, 541–566 (1995)
3. Tesauro, G., Kephart, J., Sorkin, G.: Neural networks for computer virus recognition. IEEE Expert. 8, 5–6 (1996)
4. Schultz, M., Eskin, E., Zadok, E., Stolfo, S.: Data mining methods for detection of new malicious executables. In: Proceedings of the, IEEE Symposium on Security and Privacy, Los Alamitos, pp. 38–49 (2001)
5. Kephart, J.: A Biologically Inspired Immune System for Computers, In: Proceedings of the Fourth International Workshop on Synthesis and Simulation of Living Systems, Massachusetts, pp. 130–139 (1994)
6. Damashek, M.: Gauging similarity with n-grams: language independent categorization of text. Science. 267, 843–848 (1995)
7. Skowron, A., Rauszer, C. (eds.): Intelligent decision support: Handbook of applications and advances of the Rough Set Theory. Kluwer Academic Publishers, Boston (1992)
8. Perl package Text::Ngrams: http://search. cpan. org /author /vlado /Text-Ngrams-0.03 N grams.pm

9. LIBSVM Tools Home Page: http://www.csie.ntu.edu.tw/ cjlin/
10. RSES Tools Home Page: http://logic.mimuw.edu.pl/ rses
11. Zhang, BY., Yin, JP., Hao, JB.: Using Fuzzy Pattern Recognition to Detect Unknown Malicious Executables Code. In: Wang, L., Jin, Y. (eds.) Fuzzy Systems and Knowledge Discovery. LNCS (LNAI), vol. 3613, pp. 629–634. Springer, Heidelberg (2005)

An Efficient Watermarking Technique Using ADEW and CBWT for Copyright Protection

Goo-Rak Kwon, Seung-Won Jung, and Sung-Jea Ko

Department of Electronics Engineering, Korea University
5-1 Anam-Dong, Sungbuk-ku, Seoul 136-701, Korea
Tel. +82-2-3290-3228
{grkwon,swjung,sjko}@dali.korea.ac.kr

Abstract. In this paper, we propose an efficient watermarking technique using adaptive differential energy watermarking (ADEW) and cross binding wavelet tree (CBWT) for copyright protection. The ADEW embeds a secret bit string using the reference threshold with experimental statistics. The proposed method not only takes advantage of the ADEW's error resilience but corrects a secret bit string by using ECC after error occurrence. Experimental results indicated that the proposed method provides better robustness against attacks than the conventional DEW approaches.

1 Introduction

Digital watermarking is increasingly demanded for protecting or verifying the original image ownership. Over the last decade, watermarking has been developed to a large extent for copyright protection of digital contents [1,2,3,4]. Since Cox et al. [5] proposed a novel watermarking strategy using spread-spectrum technique, there have been many researches inspired by methods of image coding and compression. These works are robust to image noise and spatial filtering, but show severe problems to geometric distortions. To solve these problems, Langelaar et al. [6] introduced a blind method called differential energy watermarking (DEW). A macroblock (MB) with 16×16 size which consists of discrete cosine transform (DCT) blocks with 8×8 size is divided into two parts to embed a watermark bit. High frequency DCT coefficients are selectively discarded to produce an energy difference in the two parts of the same MB. In the same method, Wang [7] proposed a watermarking scheme that embeds a watermark into a pair of trees [8,9] using wavelet transform (WT). The total energy of a tree is selectively reduced according to the watermark bit until the remained energy is below the other's. However, this scheme has a serious problem. When the energy difference between two trees is large, the degradation of the image quality cannot be avoided. In fact, most transformed image has the pairs of trees with a high energy difference.

In this paper, we propose an adaptive wavelet tree based blind watermarking scheme. The wavelet coefficients of the image are grouped into two pairs of wavelet trees which are bound crosswise. Each watermark bit which is encoded

Y. Wang, Y. Cheung, and H. Liu (Eds.): CIS 2006, LNAI 4456, pp. 634–641, 2007.

by ECC [4] is embedded into two pairs of wavelet trees. To embed a watermark bit into the two pairs which are composed in CBWT, the energy of each tree is selectively discarded by ADEW.

The rest of this paper is organized as follows. In Sect. 2, the proposed watermarking algorithm is explained in detail. In Sect. 3. the experimental results are shown. Finally we present the conclusion of our experiments in Sect. 4.

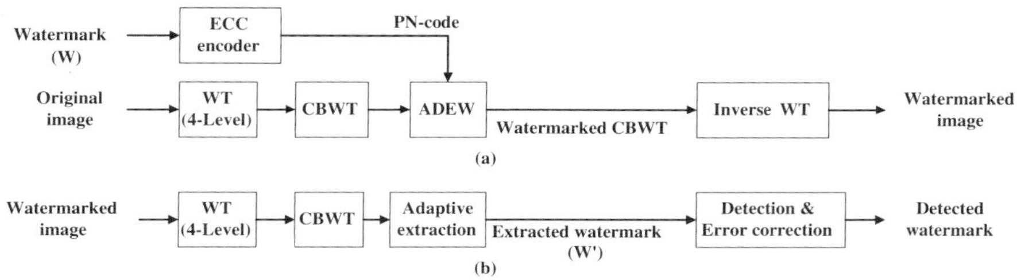

Fig. 1. Block diagram of proposed watermarking system: (a) Watermark encoder. (b) Watermark decoder.

2 Proposed Watermarking Scheme

Figure 1 illustrates the overall block diagram of the proposed watermarking system. Figure 2(a) shows the proposed watermark encoder. The watermark is changed to a PN-Code which is a watermark bit of ± 1. The original image is transformed into wavelet coefficients using WT. CBWT groups the wavelet coefficients into two pairs of trees shown in Sect. 2.1. The PN-code is embedded into the two pairs by using ADEW. The proposed CBWT and ADEW are later described in Sects. 2.1 and 2.2, respectively. Figure 2(b) represents the extraction procedure in the watermark decoder.

2.1 Proposed CBWT

Before explaining CBWT in detail, we introduce the energy difference, D, for both the conventional method and the proposed method. $D = |E_A - E_C|$ is used for the Wang's method and $D = |(E_A + E_B) - (E_C + E_D)|$ for the proposed method, as shown in Fig 3. The energy rate, R_E, between the Wang's method and the proposed CBWT is shown in Fig. 2. In the Wang's method, R_E is given by

$$R_E = \begin{cases} \frac{E_A}{E_C}, & if\ E_A \geq E_C \\ \frac{E_C}{E_A}, & otherwise. \end{cases} \quad (1)$$

In the proposed method, R_E is given by

$$R_E = \begin{cases} \frac{E_A+E_B}{E_C+E_D}, if (E_A + E_B) \geq (E_C + E_D) \\ \frac{E_C+E_D}{E_A+E_B}, otherwise. \end{cases} \quad (2)$$

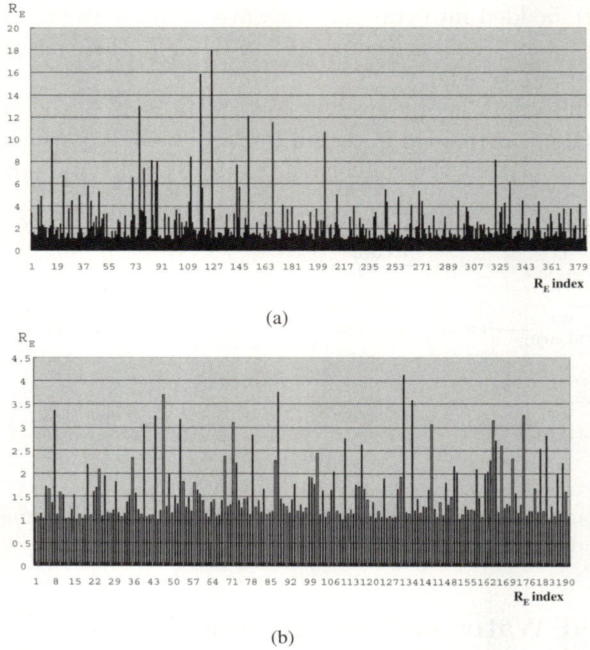

Fig. 2. The energy rate: (a) Wang's method. (b) Proposed method. (Test image is "LENNA" with size of 256×256).

Note that the highest R_E is about 18 in the Wang's method (see Fig. 2(a)). Figure 2(b) shows that the proposed method has the peak value that is close to 4. Here, R_E, which is related to D, is an important factor in determining the

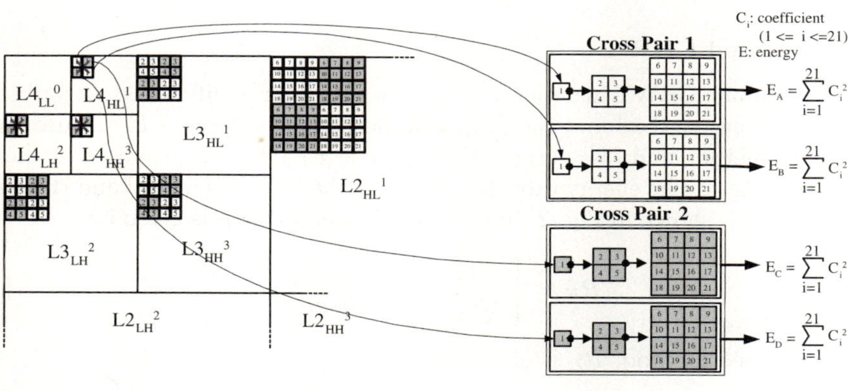

Fig. 3. An example of the proposed CBWT and the calculation of the energy by using wavelet coefficients

number of coefficients that should be eliminated in DEW. If the energy difference of wavelet trees is high, a lot of wavelet coefficients should be removed, which results in the degradation of the original image. On the other hand, if the energy difference of wavelet trees is low, a lot of wavelet coefficients which should be removed can be minimized. Thus, the original image is slightly damaged.

Figure 3 shows an example of the proposed CBWT. In this case, we use 4-level WT with 13 subbands. We use the coefficients in subbands $L4^1_{HL}$, $L4^2_{LH}$, and $L4^3_{HH}$ as roots to form wavelet trees [9]. CBWT binds the four trees crosswise which are located adjacent to two pairs. By binding the four trees crosswise into two pairs, the energy difference of two pairs can be reduced.

2.2 Proposed ADEW and Adaptive Extraction

To embed a watermark bit into the two pairs which are composed in CBWT, the energy of each tree is selectively discarded by DEW. However, if DEW is applied on the two pairs which have the high energy difference, the image should be damaged. Therefore, to preserve the image, we propose the ADEW in Fig. 4(a). The procedure of ADEW is as follows:

1. Calculate each energy of wavelet trees.
2. Obtain D between CBWT and compare D with threshold T.
3. If $D > T$, skip to embed W in CBWT.
4. Otherwise, embed W in CBWT.

Figure 4(b) shows the adaptive extraction as follows:

1. Calculate each energy of wavelet trees.
2. Obtain D between CBWT and compare D with threshold T.
3. If $D > T$, skip to extract W from CBWT.
4. Otherwise, extract W from CBWT.

In the embedding watermark process, the total energy of discarding trees is reduced until the remained energy is below the other's to use the reference

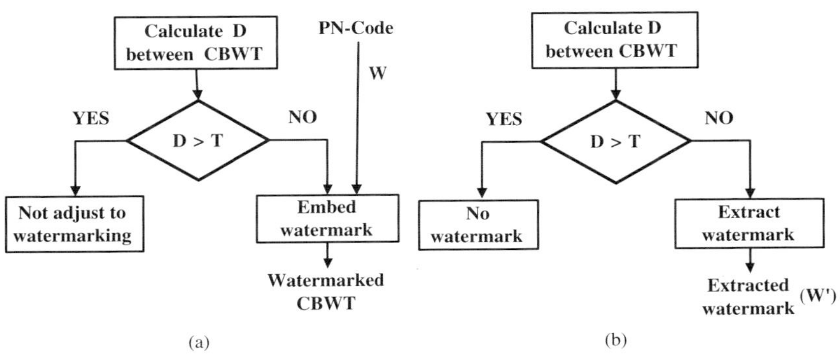

Fig. 4. The proposed ADEW: (a) ADEW. (b) Adaptive extraction.

threshold, T_r, with experimental statistics. In this letter, the reference threshold corresponding to PSNR = 35dB and PSNR = 40dB are, respectively, $T_r = 9$ and $T_r = 14$. In the same way, the adaptive extraction is applied when the energy difference of them is smaller than the threshold. Here, T_r provides a tradeoff between robust watermarking and quality of the watermarked image.

2.3 Proposed Detection Process

In Fig. 1(b), W is the number of inserting watermark bits and W' is the number of extracted watermark bits. After the adaptive extraction extracts W', the detection process compares W' with the original W. The normalized correlation between W and W' is computed. The normalized correlation coefficient, ρ_1, should be increased or decreased according to the number of bits in W and the degree of the attack. In the conventional method, ρ_1 is defined as,

$$\rho_1 = \frac{W \cdot W'}{\sqrt{W' \cdot W'}}. \tag{3}$$

However, the value calculated by (5) may change depending on the length of the vector. In order to solve this problem, we define the percentage of the remained watermark against the attack as a measure of correlation between W and W' as follows:

$$\rho_2 = \frac{W \cdot W'}{\sqrt{W' \cdot W'}} / \frac{W \cdot W}{\sqrt{W \cdot W}}, \tag{4}$$

where $\frac{W \cdot W}{\sqrt{W \cdot W}}$ means the self-similarity. If the similarity value is greater than a threshold value in [7], we detect the existence of the watermark. The choice of the normalized correlation coefficient (ρ_2=0.23) depends on the desired false positive probability. The watermark from CBWT is extracted by adaptive extraction. W' is detected and corrected by error correction [11].

The proposed detection process distinguishes the watermark in watermarked image by using the similarity between the original watermark and the extracted watermark.

3 Experimental Results

In order to evaluate the performance of the proposed method in terms of watermark capacity, robustness, and visual quality impact, we tested the extracted watermark using CBWT and adaptive DEW.

For experiments, the proposed method was compared with the Wang's method using 100 randomly collected images. The spatial resolution of collected images is 256×256.

Figures 5(b) and (c) show that the watermark is embedded into "LENNA" test image by Wang's and proposed methods. The proposed method outperforms the Wang's method in image quality while preserving the same watermark payload.In tables 1 and 2, we compared the proposed method with that in [7] using the

Fig. 5. Test image: (a) Original LENNA. (b) Watermarked LENNA with PSNR = 30.05dB. (Wang's method [7]) (c) Watermarked LENNA with PSNR = 40.08dB. (Proposed method).

100 randomly collected images. Here, #Img. represents the number of images where the watermark was correctly detected and Corr. indicates the degree of the correlation between the original watermark and the extracted watermark in (5). The normalized correlation coefficient, ρ_1, should be increased or decreased according to the number of bits in W and the degree of the attack. In the conventional method, ρ_1 is defined as,

$$\rho_1 = \frac{W \cdot W'}{\sqrt{W' \cdot W'}}. \tag{5}$$

The choice of the normalized correlation coefficient (ρ_1=0.22) depends on the desired false positive probability. In our experiment, to protect the copyright, the excessive skip process in ADEW should be avoided. Therefore, we use 184bits for watermark in payload. The details of the attacks used and the corresponding results are as follows:

- Median and Gaussian filter: After these attacks, the collected images are blurred or unsharpened on the edges.
- Noise addition: The attacker may apply one or more watermark using the same wavelet tree technique.
- SPIHT [8]: The performance of the proposed method is better than that of Wang's method in terms of PNSR and correlation.
- JPEG [10]: Wang's method can not detect the W in watermarked image.
- Removal of bitplane: This attack is done by removing LSBs of wavelet trees.
- Rotation and Scaling: In Table 2, these have less effect on the W extraction on the test images.
- Pixel shift: This affects most watermark extraction in most collected images.

Through simulations, we can find that the proposed method is more robust against signal processing and geometric attacks.

Table 1. Performance under signal processing attacks

	Ref. [7]		Proposed method	
	#Img.	Corr.	#Img.	Corr.
No attack	100	1.00	100	1.00
Median 2×2	93	0.35	97	0.67
Median 3×3	90	0.31	97	0.66
Median 3×3	83	0.26	97	0.66
Gaussian filter	96	0.64	98	0.70
Noise addition	96	0.64	98	0.88
SPIHT				
- Bitrate = 0.3	21	0.13	59	0.71
- Bitrate = 0.5	76	0.27	87	0.72
- Bitrate = 0.7	85	0.27	94	0.80
JPEG (QF = 30)	37	0.15	98	0.71
JPEG (QF = 40)	75	0.23	97	0.73
JPEG (QF = 50)	83	0.26	98	0.82
JPEG (QF = 70)	93	0.57	98	0.86
JPEG (QF = 90)	100	1.00	100	0.93

Table 2. Performance under geometric distortion attacks

	Ref. [7]		Proposed method	
	#Img.	Corr.	#Img.	Corr.
Removal of bitplane 1	100	1.00	100	1.00
Removal of bitplane 2	100	1.00	100	0.98
Removal of bitplane 3	100	0.99	100	0.92
Removal of bitplane 4	92	0.52	98	0.92
Removal of bitplane 5	30	0.11	97	0.71
Pixel shift 2	84	0.28	95	0.67
Pixel shift 3	92	0.34	96	0.64
Pixel shift 4	89	0.29	96	0.72
Pixel shift 5	83	0.28	95	0.62
Rotation 0.25°	90	0.37	91	0.59
Rotation 0.5°	89	0.29	91	0.60
Rotation 0.75°	83	0.26	91	0.56
Rotation 1°	82	0.24	91	0.56
Rotation -0.25°	91	0.32	92	0.60
Rotation -0.5°	83	0.23	92	0.61
Rotation -0.75°	82	0.24	92	0.59
Rotation -1°	32	0.16	92	0.59
Scaling 0.5×	91	0.48	93	0.66
Scaling 0.8×	90	0.41	93	0.64

4 Conclusions

This paper has proposed an efficient watermarking technique using ADEW and CBWT for copyright protection. The watermark strength and spread of the watermark into CBWT are controlled by wavelet tree energy. The proposed method is highly robust to most popular intentional attacks. Simulation results show that the proposed method not only has the transparency and the robustness for copyright protection from illegal duplication and mass distribution but also preserves the image quality which is very important in some security applications.

Acknowledgments

This research was supported by Seoul Future Contents Convergence (SFCC) Cluster established by Seoul Industry-Academy-Research Cooperation Project.

References

1. Langelaar, G. C., Setyanwn, I., and Lagendijk, R. L.:Watermarking digital image and video data, a state-of-the-art overview. IEEE Signal Processing Mag, pp. 20–46 (2000)
2. Special Issue on Digital Watermarking. IEEE Signal Process. Mag. 17 (2000)
3. Kaewkamnerd, N., Rao, K.R.: Wavelet based image adaptive watermarking scheme. Electron. Lett. 36, 312–313 (2000)
4. Zeng, W., Liu, B.: A statistical watermark detection technique without using original images for resolving rightful ownerships of digital images. IEEE Trans. Image Processing 8, 1534–1548 (1999)
5. Cox, I.J., Kilian, J., Leighton, F.T., Shamoon, T.: Secure spread spectrum watermarking for multimedia. IEEE Trans. Image Processing 6, 1673–1687 (1997)
6. langelaar, G.C., Langendijk, R.L.: Optimal differential energy watermarking of DCT encoded images and video. IEEE Journal on Selected Areas in Comm. 12, 525–539 (1998)
7. Wang, S.-H., Lin, Y.-P.: Wavelet tree quantization for copyright protection watermarking. IEEE Trans. Image Processing 13, 154–165 (2004)
8. Said, A., Pearlman, W.A.: A new, fast, and efficient image codec based on set partitioning in hierarchical trees. IEEE Trans. Circuits Syst. Video Technol. 6, 243–250 (1996)
9. Shapiro, J.M.: Embedded image coding using zerotrees of wavelet coefficients. IEEE Trans. Signal Processing 41, 3445–3462 (1993)
10. Wallace, G. K.:The JPEG still picture compression standard. Commun. ACM (1991)
11. Hamming, R.W.: Error detecting and error correcting codes. The Bell System Technical Journal 29, 147–160 (1950)

An Image Protection Scheme Using the Wavelet Coefficients Based on Fingerprinting Technique

Jin-Wook Shin[1], Ju Cheng Yang[2], Sook Yoon[3], and Dong-Sun Park[2]

[1] Advanced Graduate Education Center of Jeonbuk for Electronics and Information Technology-BK21
jwshin@chonbuk.ac.kr
[2] Dept. of Infor. & Comm. Eng., Chonbuk Nat'l University, Jeonju, Jeonbuk, 561-756, Korea
yangjucheng@hotmail.com, dspark@chonbuk.ac.kr
http://multilab.chonbuk.ac.kr
[3] Major in Multimedia Eng., Division of Inform. Eng., Mokpo National University Jeonnam, 534-729, Korea
syoon@mokpo.ac.kr

Abstract. Various technologies have been used to protect the copyrights of digital contents from illegal or unintentional attacks. Watermarking methods protect digital contents by embedding a watermark message into them. However, since conventional watermarking algorithms change original digital contents to embed digital watermarks using various embedding methods, they result in the degradation of digital contents and decrease the fidelity of digital contents. A fingerprinting technique can be also used for protecting digital contents. However this method may have high computational complexity to generate unique features for digital contents. In order to provide the excellent fidelity, the proposed technique distributes original digital contents without any change like fingerprinting technique and just generates the content-associated information, which is combined wavelet coefficients with copyright message and used to extract copyright message afterward. Experimental results show that the proposed method outperforms an existing method for various signal processing attacks.

1 Introduction

Recently, the production and spread of digital multimedia contents such as text, picture, MP3, and video have been rapidly progressed owing to the popularity of Internet and development of digital technology. In addition, digital contents can be easily pirated through their illegal copies, modifications, and distributions. Therefore, digital contents providers and makers have tried to find optimal solutions to protect their products. As solutions, cryptography, watermarking and fingerprinting techniques have been applied to protect intellectual property rights.

Watermarking technologies[1,2] protect intellectual property rights of digital contents by hiding watermark messages such as user's information or various information about contents into the original contents. The watermarking techniques

Y. Wang, Y. Cheung, and H. Liu (Eds.): CIS 2006, LNAI 4456, pp. 642–651, 2007.

can be divided into spatial domain-based watermarking and frequency domain-based watermarking. A typical method among spatial domain-based watermarking techniques is to change the least significant bits of original contents[3]. In order to insert a watermark message in frequency domain, an original content is transformed to the frequency domain through DFT[4], DCT[5], Wavelet[6,7] et al, and then a watermark message is embedded into the space of coefficients of its transform. These methods are so robust that a watermark message is not corrupted by simple attacks. However, these algorithms are more complex and require much more processing time than spatial domain-based algorithms.

A fingerprinting technique[8], included in MPEG-21 part11, extracts unique features from digital contents using computer vision techniques, saves them in a database, and uses them when there is a need to prove the identification of the digital contents. Since this method distributes the original contents without modifying any values, it may endure more changes during distribution. However, this technique is usually time-consuming due to the high computational complexity implementing computer vision techniques.

In this paper, we introduce about a new type of information, called content-associated information, and propose the technique for its generation using wavelet transform and extraction of a copyright message. In addition, in the proposed scheme we distribute an original content without any reformation such as fingerprinting technique.

This paper is organized as follows. In Section 2, a general watermarking and a fingerprinting model is presented. The proposed algorithm for generation of content-associated information and extraction of copyright message using wavelet transform is described in Section 3. Finally, experimental results and conclusion are reported in Section 4 and 5, respectively.

2 Related Works

2.1 Watermarking

In typical watermarking systems, a watermark message that contains information on manufacturers or authorized users is embedded in the digital contents and then distributed to the outside world. The embedded watermark message should not be perceivable not to degrade the quality of the digital contents. The embedded watermark message can be extracted to resolve legal disputes on the digital contents such as illegal copy, modification and distribution.

A typical watermarking system consists of an embedder and a detector. The embedder embeds a watermark message to an original content and the watermarked content is distributed. The watermarked content can be modified by various signal processing operations or malicious attacks. The watermark detector extracts a watermark message from the corrupted version of the watermarked contents. Various techniques have been developed for the better performance depending on the specific applications[9].

The properties required for a watermarking system can be varied according to the applications. Some properties including fidelity, robustness, computational complexity, and informed/blind detection can be found in Cox[1].

2.2 Fingerprinting

Like watermarking system, a fingerprinting technique[8] can be also used to protect digital contents from illegal uses. The main difference between two methods is in that a fingerprinting system extracts features from digital contents and uses the features for identifying the digital contents while a watermarking system embeds an external watermark message in the digital contents and uses the embedded watermark for identifying the digital contents.

The conceptual block diagram of a fingerprinting system is shown in Fig. 1. It consists of two fingerprint generators and a comparison part. The technique usually employs computer vision techniques to generate invariant fingerprints from the digital contents.

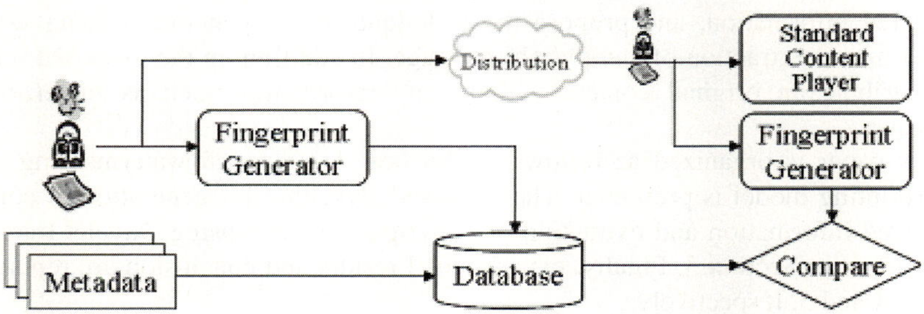

Fig. 1. Fingerprinting model

The generated features are stored in a database and then can be used for comparison whenever a legal dispute happens. As shown in the Fig. 1, the fingerprinting technique does not embed any information in the digital contents. The digital contents are not modified and distributed to outside with no degradation of quality. However, since this technique usually uses time-consuming technique to find unique fingerprint, it is very hard to apply them to real time applications.

3 The Combination of Wavelet Coefficients and Copyright Message

A general watermarking scheme usually uses spatial domain or frequency domain to embed watermark message. Since the conventional watermark methods change their contents to hide a copyright message, the quality degradation of the contents is occurred.

A fingerprinting technique works by extracting its characteristics to protect contents. Since this method distributes the original contents without modifying any values, it may endure more changes during distribution. However, this technique is usually time-consuming to extract unique features using computer vision techniques.

In this paper, we propose a novel copyright protection technique for digital images using positive features of both watermarking and fingerprinting techniques. The proposed method uses content-associated information that combines wavelet coefficients of original image with copyright message as shown in Fig. 2. And then, the original image is distributed without any modification like fingerprinting technique. Therefore, there is no degradation of contents quality in the proposed method. Fig. 2 shows the proposed model which consists of wavelet transform block, content-associated information generator/extractor and pseudo random number generator(PRNG).

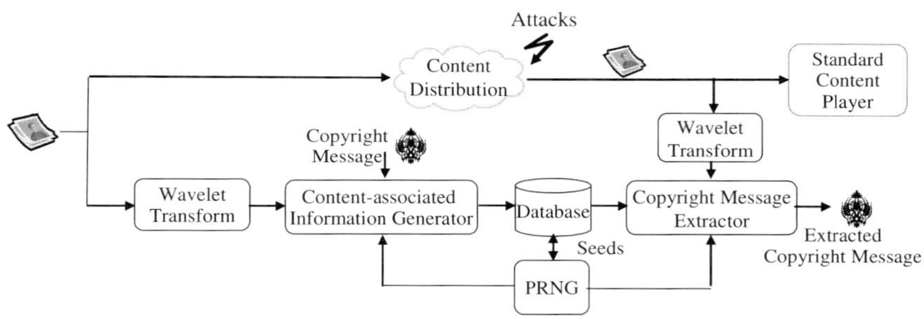

Fig. 2. Proposed model

The proposed scheme is different from conventional watermark algorithms in that a copyright message is not directly embedded into content. Besides, the proposed mechanism using content-associated information to extract a copyright message is distinguished from fingerprinting technique[8] that only uses extracted features from contents. The generated content-associated information is stored in a certified DB and used to identify content later.

3.1 Selection of Wavelet Coefficients

Wavelet techniques[10] have been studied on image retrievals, image compressions, and digital watermarking, since the wavelet transform has low computational complexity, fast processing time, and no blocking effect. Watermarking techniques using the wavelet transform have robustness to signal processing attacks[6, 7].

In this paper, wavelet coefficients are used to make the content-associated information. Fig. 3 shows multi-resolution wavelet transform and their group coefficients.

A pseudo random number generator is used to select layer and position of wavelet coefficients. We actually use only sign information to generate content-associated information. In Fig. 3, a coefficient in the lower layer represents four coefficients of its upper layer. In the proposed scheme, the relationship of the lower layer and its upper layer is not considered in order to reduce the time needed to select coefficients.

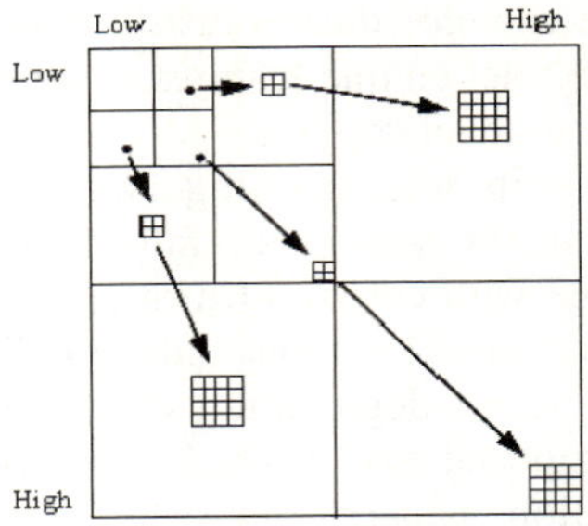

Fig. 3. Wavelet decomposition and its grouping coefficients

3.2 Generation of Content-Associated Information Using Wavelet Coefficient

In the proposed algorithm, the content-associated information is generated by combining a copyright message with wavelet coefficients of an original content. The created content-associated information is stored in a database and used to extract a copyright message in the future. Finally, the original content is distributed without any modification.

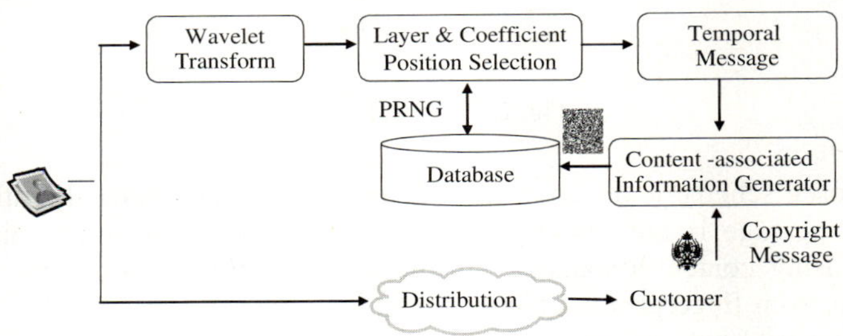

Fig. 4. Generation of content-associated information

In this system, let us define that an original content is X, pseudo random number K, and a copyright message is W. Fig. 4 shows the generation of the content-associated information. It consists of a wavelet transform, a position selection part to select position of layer and coefficient using three random sequences that generated from the random number generator, temporal message is made from the sign information of coefficients and Content-associated information generator

The original content, X, is a gray-level image with 8 bits per pixel and contains $X_H \times X_W$ pixels and the copyright message, $W(W_H , W_W)$, is assumed to be a binary image with one bit per pixel. The generation steps are follows:

Step 1 : Select a layer and its coefficient positions in the selected layer.
In first step, to obtain the above information, three random sequences are needed; namely, a sequence to select a layer and two sequences to choice one coordinate (x, y) on that layer.

Step 2 : Make a temporal message(a binary image).
In step 2, a temporary message T is obtained from the sign of coefficients, as described in Eq. (1).

$$T=\left\{t_k = \begin{cases} 1 & if\ C_l(x_k, y_k) \geq 0 \\ 0 & if\ C_l(x_k, y_k) < 0 \end{cases} \middle| \ k = 0,1,\ldots,n-1 \right\} \tag{1}$$

Where n is $(W_H \times W_W) - 1$, C_l coefficient value at level l.

Step 3 : Operate Exclusive-*OR* with the temporary message and copyright message.
Finally, the content-associated information is generated by Exclusive-*OR* operation of the temporary image, T, obtained from Eq. (1) and copyright message, W, as shown in Eq.(2).

$$\text{Contents Associated Information}(x,y) = W(x,y) \oplus T(x,y) \tag{2}$$

The finally generated content-associated information, *CAI*, and seeds for random number generator are saved in a database and used to restore a copyright message later.

3.3 Extraction of Copyright Message

The digital contents received from Internet or other several media can be damaged by noise or malicious attacks. Due to the degradation of digital contents, a copyright message can also be affected. The extraction process of a copyright message from the received content is similar to the method that generates content-associated information.

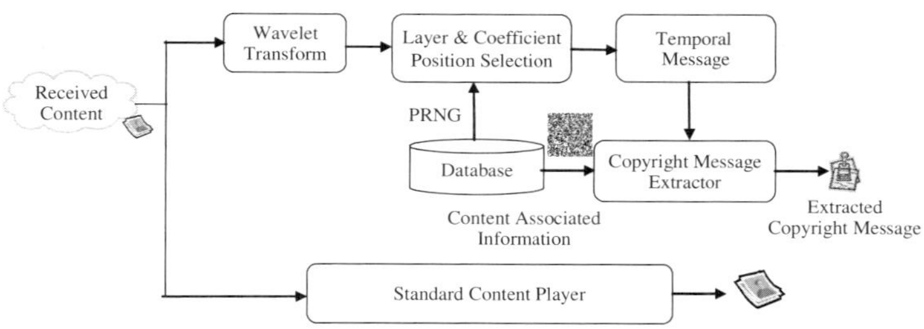

Fig. 5. Extraction of copyright message

Fig. 5 shows that a copyright message is extracted from a combination of a temporary message, using sign of coefficients generated from the wavelet transform, and content-associated information in the database.

When the received image is X' and temporary message, T'(binary image), the extracted copyright message, $W'$is described as shown in Eq.(3).

$$W' = CAI(x,y) \oplus T'(x,y) \tag{3}$$

If there is no degradation during the distribution, an original copyright message is equal to extracted one.

4 Experimental Results

Various performance measures in watermarking or fingerprinting systems can be used dependently on the types of applications. To evaluate the performance of the proposed method, we used a popular benchmark test called Stirmark[11]. Bit Correct Ratio (*BCR*) defined in Eq. 4[9] is mostly used to show the correctness of the extracted copyright message.

$$BCR = \left(1 - \frac{\sum_{i=0}^{W_H} \sum_{j=0}^{W_W} \overline{w_{i,j} \oplus w'_{i,j}}}{\mathrm{W_H} \times \mathrm{W_W}} \right) \times 100\ \% \tag{4}$$

In this equation, a copyright message has $W_H \times W_W$ elements.

(a) Lena (b) Baboon

(c) Copyright image (d) Content-associated image of *(a)*

Fig. 6. Original images and its content-associated image

In this experiment, we used the *Lena* and *Baboon* images with 8 bits per pixel and 512 × 512 elements for the original content and 64 × 64 binary image for the copyright message. Fig. 6 shows the original *Lena* and *Baboon*, a binary copyright image and its generated content-associated image of Fig.6 (a), respectively.

Many useful random number generators have been proposed [12, 13, 14]. However, we used the random number generator of *Visual C* program to select layer and wavelet coefficients. We made an experiment with the attacked images using Stirmark and histogram equalization images.

Firstly, histogram equalization process was used to alter the original image *Lena* and *Baboon*. The extracted copyright messages and theirs BCRs are shown in Fig. 7, respectively.

(a) Histogram equalization

(b) BCR : 97.3%

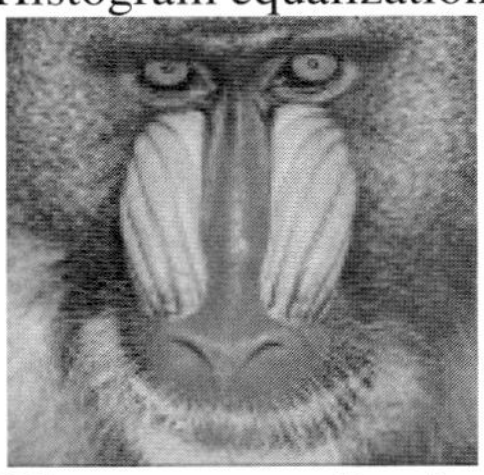

(c) Histogram equalization

(d) BCR : 98.1%

Fig. 7. Histogram equalization and its extracted copyright message

Fig. 8 shows the copyright messages and theirs BCRs extracted under the attack using median filter which its window size is 9×9.

(a) Lena BCR : 95.74%

(b) Baboon BCR : 90.96%

Fig. 8. Copyright messages extracted under median filtering attack

The extracted copyright message and its BCR of scaling process that resized image from the shrunken image(75% of original size) are showed in Fig. 9, respectively.

(a) Lena BCR : 97.2%

(b) Baboon BCR : 97.1%

Fig. 9. Copyright messages extracted under scaling attacks

We also made an experiment on rotation with 5°-rotated image in Fig. 10. According to the rotation results, the proposed method using wavelet algorithm has poor BCRs.

(a) Lena BCR : 57.2% (b) Baboon BCR : 57.6%

Fig. 10. Extracted copyright message from rotation

We analyzed the results of the proposed algorithm the following aspects.

A. Fidelity
A general watermark system requires the modification of pixel values to embed a watermark message in the spatial domain or frequency components in the frequency domain. This degrades the fidelity of the digital contents. However, the proposed method does not change the original contents as in the fingerprinting technique, therefore it keeps the fidelity to 100%.

B. Complexity
Except processing time for wavelet transform to get wavelet coefficients, the proposed method is very faster than fingerprinting technique because it uses Exclusive-*OR* operations. Therefore, it can be used in real-time applications such as Internet broadcast monitoring.

C. Robustness
The algorithm showed good results average 97.3 %, 96.6% and 96.6% in histogram equalization, smoothing and compression, respectively. The main reason is no change of original image. However, it had low *BCR* under the rotational attack since the horizontal, vertical and diagonal coefficients are deformed according to rotation ratio due to properties of wavelet operation.

5 Conclusion

In this paper, we suggested a method that creates content-associated information using wavelet coefficients. The content-associated information obtained from the combination of an original image and a copyright message is stored into a database and can be used to extract a copyright message in any dispute or monitoring. Since, in the proposed system, an original content is distributed without changing any of its content, no degradation is occurred.

We evaluated the proposed scheme using various attacked images. The proposed scheme has satisfactory BCR, more than average 96.4% in signal processing attacks such as histogram equalization, compression, and median filtering. In addition, the computational time of the proposed method is very faster than that of fingerprinting technique. However, the proposed algorithm had not good results in geometric attacks such as rotation.

We will further study about the algorithms which can search content-associated information effectively and the robust algorithms against geometric attacks

Acknowledgment. This work was supported by the second stage of Brain Korea 21 Project.

Reference

1. Cox, Ingemar, J.: Digital Watermarking(Multimedia Information and System). Morgan-Kaufmann, San Francisco (2002)
2. Huang, H., Hang, H., Pan, J.: An Introduction to Watermarking Techniques, Series on Innovative Intelligence, vol. 7, pp. 3–39. World Scientific Publishing Co. Pte. Ltd, Singapore (2004)
3. Schydel, R.G.V., Tirkel, A.Z., Osborne, C.F.: A Digital Watermark. In: Proceeding of the International Conf. on Image Processing, Austin, pp. 86–90. IEEE Press, New York (1994)
4. Huang, H., Pan, J., Hang, H.: Watermarking Based on Transform Domain, Series on Innovative Intelligence, vol. 7, pp. 147–163. World Scientific Publishing Co. Pte. Ltd, Singapore (2004)
5. Deng, F., Wang, B.: A Novel Technique for Robust Image Watermarking in the DCT Domain, IEEE Int. Conf. Neural Networks and Signal Processing (2003)
6. Chang, C., Lin, I.: Robust Image Watermarking Systems Using Neural Networks, Series on Innovative Intelligence, vol. 7, pp. 395–427. World Scientific Publishing Co. Pte. Ltd, Singapore (2004)
7. Zhang, X., Lo, K., Freng, J., Wang, D.: A Robust Image Watermarking Using Spatial-Frequency Feature of Wavelet Transform. In: Proceeding of ICSP 2000(2000)
8. ISO/IEC 21000-11. Information technology-Multimedia framework(MPEG-21)-Part11:Evaluation Tools for Persistent Association Technologies
9. Nikolaidis, N., Pitas, I.: Benchmarking of Watermarking Algorithms, Series on Innovative Intelligence, vol. 7. World Scientific Publishing Co. Pte. Ltd, Singapore (2004)
10. Lee, S.-h., Yoon, D.-h.: Introduction to the Wavelet Transform, JinHan Press(2003)
11. http://www.petitcolas.net/fabien/watermarking/stirmark/
12. Heidari-Bateni, G., McGillem, C.D.: A Chaotic Direct-Sequence Spread-Spectrum Communication System. IEEE Trans. on Comm. 42(2/3/4), 1524–1527 (1994)
13. Bernstein, G.M., Lieberman, M.A.: Secure random number generation using chaotic circuits. IEEE Trans. Circuits Syst. 37, 1157–1164 (1990)
14. Blum, L., Blum, M., Shub, M.: A simple unpredictable pseudo-random number generator. SIAM Journal on Computing 15, 364–383 (1986)

iOBS3: An iSCSI-Based Object Storage Security System

Huang Jianzhong, Xie Changsheng, and Li Xu

Wuhan National Laboratory for Optoelectronics,
Huazhong University of Science and Technology, Wuhan, Hubei, P.R. China 430074
husthjz@126.com, csxie@263.net, lixu_cn@163.com

Abstract. With the growing importance of data, networked storage of high performance and strong security has become a hotspot of research. Aiming at the goals, an iSCSI-based object storage security system (iOBS3) adopting OSD command sets has been proposed in this paper. Firstly, incurring to the block I/O channel of iSCSI and the security method within OSD, iOBS3 can achieve high-speed bandwidth of block I/O and access control capability of object I/O; secondly, iOBS3 enhances its transfer security by employing IPSec at IP layer or SSL above TCP layer; thirdly, iOBS3 greatly improves the I/O speed using zero-copy TCP at initiator-side. The experimental results indicate iOBS3 can achieve high throughput, in the meantime guaranteeing both the transmission and storage security.

1 Introduction

With the development of networking technology and exponential expansion of digital information, networked storage becomes more and more important, and many related technologies appear, e.g. FC-SAN, NAS.

FC-SAN has some security vulnerabilities such as unauthenticated access, idle host scanning, data sniffer, and so on. FC-SAN hasn't been broadly accepted because of its high cost and poor interoperability. On the contrary, IP storage (e.g. iSCSI, IP-SAN, NAS) is regarded as the substitute of FC infrastructure due to its low TCO and mature interconnecting, but IP storage also encounters many security threats, such as information disclosure, denial of services, etc.

Object-based storage has the performance scalability of SAN and the cross-platform interoperability of NAS. Herein, we designed and implemented an iSCSI-based Object Storage Security System (iOBS3) based on the command sets of Object-based Storage Device (OSD) and zero-copy optimization. Relative to iSCSI, iOBS3 exhibits certain security advantages as follows: firstly, Enhancing the security, its essential idea is to transfer OSD commands using iSCSI protocol, so to separate the transfer security from access control; secondly, Adopting the IPSec or SSL protocol and boosting the security, it is a beneficial supplement to the common CHAP security measure; thirdly, Implementing the zero-copy TCP via page remapping between kernel buffer and user process virtual memory at the socket layer, thus reducing the number of data copy and saving extra overhead.

The remainder of the paper is organized as follows. Section 2 describes the related technologies. Section 3 details the design of iOBS3. Section 4 presents the

Y. Wang, Y. Cheung, and H. Liu (Eds.): CIS 2006, LNAI 4456, pp. 652–660, 2007.

experimental results and the quantitative analysis. Finally section 5 gives the summary of the paper.

2 Related Technologies

2.1 OSD

The research of object-based storage can track back to the NASD project [1]. The interface of NASD is based on the file I/O access, but NASD introduces the concept of object. Currently SNIA has founded a task workgroup named OSD-TWG and submitted the OSD commands to T10 committee as a working draft [2].

Table 1. CAPKEY security methods and threats thwarted

Threats	CAPKEY (over secure channel) No	Yes
Forgery or alteration of credential	Yes	Yes
Unauthorized use of credential	Yes	Yes
Replay of command or status	No	Yes
Alteration of command or status	No	Yes
Replay or alteration of data	No	Yes
Inspection of command, status or data	No	Yes

The OSD draft defines four security methods: NOSEC, CAPKEY, CMDRSP, and ALLDATA. Here the CAPKEY security method can be used in secure channel or non-secure channel. Each OSD security method can address one or more specific security threats. Table 1 lists some security threats, which can be thwarted by CAPKEY security method.

2.2 iSCSI and Its Implement

iSCSI is a SCSI transport protocol that maps the SCSI family of protocols onto TCP/IP. Namely, iSCSI protocol encapsulates the SCSI block commands into IP

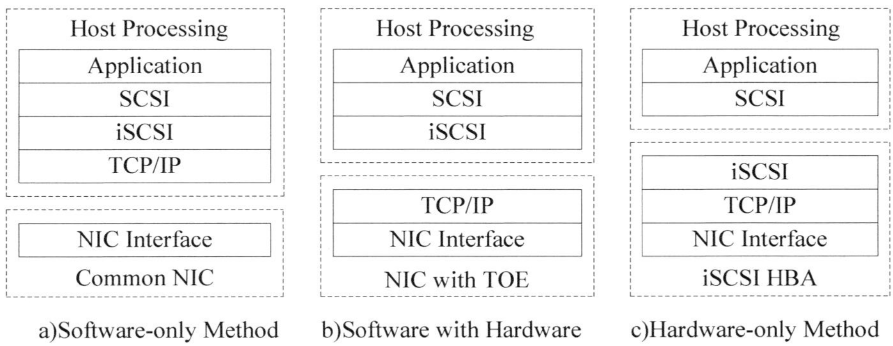

Fig. 1. iSCSI end-point methods comparison

packets for transmission over IP network, and decapsulates SCSI commands from iSCSI commands at the receiver side. In iSCSI, SCSI commands can be transparently transferred over IP, and remote device can be accessed as if it is a local SCSI disk [3].

iSCSI end-point (i.e. iSCSI initiator or target) can be implemented via one of the following solutions: software-only, software with hardware assistance, or hardware-only solution, as shown in Fig. 1. Generally, hardware-only solution costs highly but it may exhibit the highest performance among them.

iOBS3 encapsulates, transfers and interprets the OSD command sets using software-only solution due to its low-cost and flexibility.

2.3 IPSec and SSL

IPSec usually sets up a secure channel between the communicating entities to obtain transfer security using the Authentication Header (AH) or the Encapsulating Security Payload (ESP), and provides protection for IP and/or upper layer. Both AH and ESP are algorithm-independent, so iOBS3 adopts keyed MD5 in AH [4].

Both AH and ESP support two modes: transport mode and tunnel mode. In transport mode, AH and ESP primarily provide protection for upper layer protocols. In tunnel mode, AH and ESP are applied to tunneled IP packets.

Secure Socket Layer (SSL) protocol is widely deployed to keep communication between clients and servers secure, ensuring Internet security [5][6].

The SSL protocol includes two sub-protocols: the SSL record protocol and the SSL handshake protocol. SSL lies between the reliable connection-oriented network layer (e.g. TCP) and the application layer (e.g. HTTP), and offers secure communication using mutual authentication, digital signatures, and encryption.

2.4 Zero-Copy Optimization

There are three zero-copy methods: Page Flipping, Scatter/Gather API, and Direct Data Placement (DDP). In page flipping, NIC can not only split headers and coalesce payloads to fill aligned buffer pages, but also recognize upper-level protocol (ULP) headers. In scatter/gather API mode, NIC can demultiplex packets and place data anywhere in buffer pool for recipient. In DDP, NIC steers payload directly to the application buffers according to the ULP headers. An example of DDP is RDMA[7].

From the viewpoint of price, the DDP method costs the highest though its function is the strongest. The operation of data copying between different buffers in TCP/IP communications may introduce additional overhead, thus iOBS3 implements the zero-copy TCP using page flipping mode.

3 Design and Implement of iOBS3

iOBS3 consists of two components: iOBS3 initiator and iOBS3 target. The iOBS3 initiator is a data consumer, which intercepts I/O requests from high-level file system and encapsulates them into iSCSI Protocol Data Units (PDUs), then sends the iSCSI PDUs out from NIC. The target acts as a data provider, which constructs SCSI commands from iSCSI PDUs and delivers them to SCSI device.

We recompose the iSCSI protocol to make it suitable for OSD command sets, and add OSD interpreting program to iSCSI target thus acting as the iOBS3 target, then adopt the IPSec and SSL protocol respectively to improve the transfer security, lastly implement the zero-copy TCP at iOBS3 initiator-side to optimize the data copying between kernel buffers and user process virtual memory.

3.1 Delivering OSD Commands Using iSCSI

OSD is used to provide efficient operation of I/O logical units that manage the allocation, placement, and accessing of objects which are variable-size data-storage containers. All OSD commands require direct-data access and use both the Data-In Buffer and Data-Out Buffer, that is, the transfer protocol must allow bidirectional data transfer. Therefore iOBS3 adopts iSCSI protocol to deliver OSD command sets.

iOBS3 behaves differently from iSCSI: it modifies the SCSI driver and provides OSD SCSI command sets with extended command descriptor blocks (CDBs), and the modified SCSI driver acts as an OSD driver at SCSI upper layer; in addition, it adds OSD command sets interpreter into remote iSCSI target, acting as an iOBS3 target.

The iOBS3 target includes OSD command processing layer, target file-system layer and block encapsulation layer, and supports the CAPKEY security method, which guarantees the integrity of the credential (see Table 1).

3.2 iOBS3 Using IPSec or SSL

iOBS3 regards the OSD commands as the extension of SCSI commands, theoretically separating transmission security from access control mechanism. There are two ways to enhance the transfer security: reducing the unauthorized access and minimizing the probability of being tampered. The former usually employs LUN masking and CHAP, and the latter usually adopts encryption or authentication method (e.g. IPSec or SSL) to keep data packet secure.

MD5 is a one-way hash function that can generate 128 bits of the message digest, which is enough for the IPSec. Here iOBS3 uses keyed MD5 to authenticate in AH protocol. The protocol model of iOBS3 using IPSec is shown at Fig. 2(a).

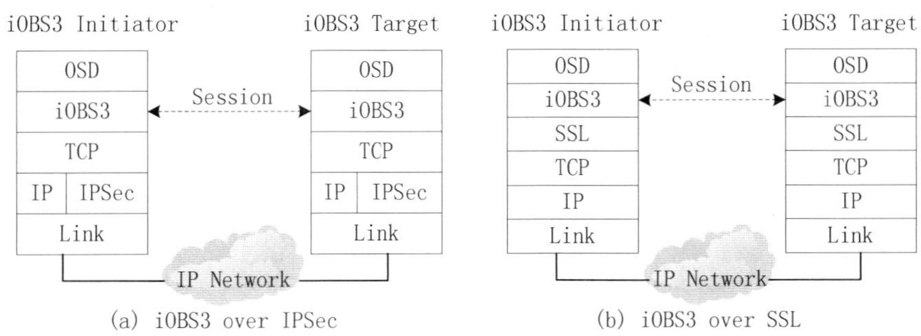

Fig. 2. Protocol stack of iOBS3 over IPSec or over SSL

Since iOBS3 end-point (i.e. initiator or target) is a 5-Layer entity, SSL can be placed between the iOBS3 layer and the TCP/IP layer. SSL involves such functions as authentication, integrity, confidentiality and replay-protection. Relative to IPSec, SSL can provide finer security to end users owing to its end-to-end security. The protocol stack of iOBS3 over SSL is given in Fig. 2(b).

3.3 Zero-Copy TCP

As mentioned above, conventional TCP/IP communication needs data copying between kernel buffers and user process virtual memory at the socket layer, resulting in a high overhead. Page remapping is a method, which can reduce or eliminate the extra operation of copying. Additionally, the page-remapping scheme should preserve the copy semantics of the existing socket interface.

During the implement of zero-copy TCP (i.e. zcTCP), we adopt some delicate skills: we first assume each packet payload is the integral multiple of the page size of operating system, keeping the store buffer naturally aligned on page boundaries; then the NIC of the receiver divides the TCP headers and payload into buffers, leaving the payload page-aligned. The sending host explicitly separates header from the payload of packet and constructs receiving 'mbuf' chains.

The packet assembly/disassembly is an intensive operation, and the transmission overhead associated with the Ethernet packet is a smaller proportion comparing to a common frame. In order to increase the I/O bandwidth of iOBS3, we apply the mode of Jumbo Frame to the zcTCP.

4 Experimental Tests

4.1 Test Environment

Fig. 3 illustrates the test environment, and Table 2 lists the hardware detail of test machines. The test tool is IOMeter.

The machines of initiator, target and IOMeter console are connected to a 100Mbps Ethernet switch. The initiator and IOMeter console need running the 'Dynamo' program to generate workload. The shell script in the initiator is 'dynamo -i 192.168.83.127 -m 192.168.83.126'.

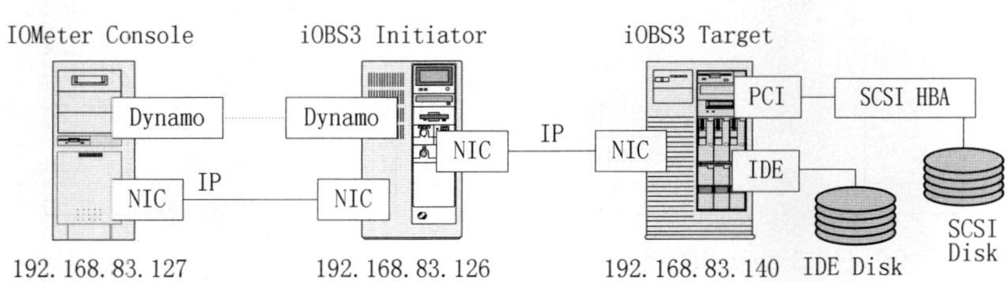

Fig. 3. Test environment of iOBS3

Table 2. Hardware environment of testbed

	CPU(GHz)	IDE Disk	SCSI Disk	NIC
Console	P4 2.0	ST380011A	N/A	Realtek RTL8139
Target	P4 3.06	ST340016A	DPSS318350	Dlink DGE550 sx
Initiator	C4 2.4	MX6Y080L0	N/A	Realtek RTL8139

To focus on performance testing, we used the long-term key in CAPKEY method, and adopted keyed MD5 as the packet authentication algorithm in IPSec AH tunnel mode. We adopted Linux of kernel 2.4.20-8 as test-bed, Freeswan 2.06 [8] to enable IPSec and OpenSSL 0.9.8 [9] to support SSL.

4.2 Test Method

To study the performance of each security measure, we have conducted such contrastive tests: ①iSCSI R/W; ②iOBS3 R/W without packet level security; ③iOBS3 R/W over IPSec AH or SSL; ④iOBS3 R/W over IPSec AH or SSL using zcTCP. We can obtain the performance effect of zcTCP by comparing ③ with ④.

Here we pay attention to the following three metrics: the transfer rate of iOBS3, the mean response latency of iOBS3, and the CPU overhead. The experimental results are illustrated in Fig. 4, 5, and 6.

4.3 Results and Analysis

1) Test of Block I/O Operation

We compare the experimental result of iOBS3 with that of iSCSI and know that iOBS3 degrades from 21% to 33% relative to iSCSI (shown in Fig. 4). In addition, the throughput of iOBS3 drops from 5% to 12% using IPSec, which means that IPSec slightly degrades the performance of system and MD5 is high-throughput.

After adopting zcTCP scheme, the throughput of iOBS3 has increased. The performance of iOBS3 adopting IPSec and zcTCP is comparable with that of iSCSI. It is obvious that the improvement grows remarkably when the block size is 4KB or 8KB, corresponding to the fact that the page size of iOBS3 is 4KB. For the small block request, the performance improves faster as block size increases.

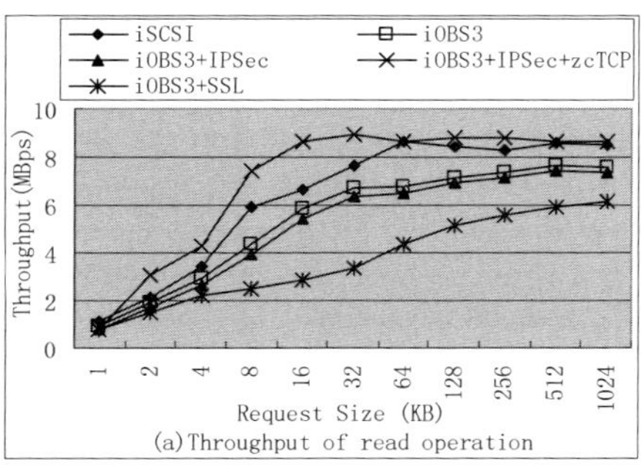

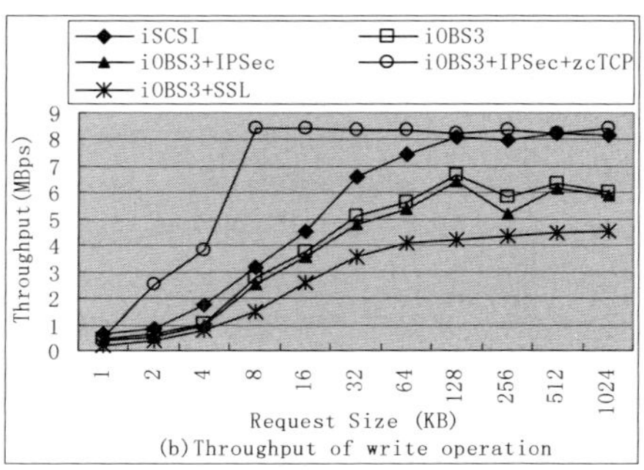

Fig. 4. Performance view of block read and block write

2) Mean Response Latency

Fig. 5 shows the mean response latency of write operation in iSCSI and iOBS3 respectively. The data indicates the mean response latency of iOBS3 is more than that of iSCSI, which indirectly reflects the assertion that the deployment of security measure usually leads the degradation of performance [10].

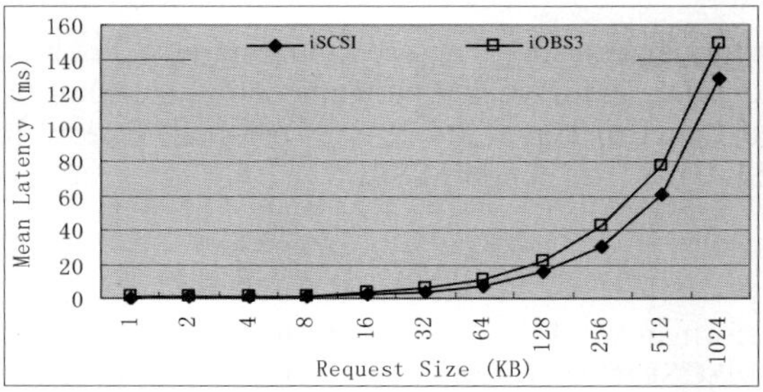

Fig. 5. Mean response latency of block I/O write

3) CPU Overhead of Different Schemes

Fig. 6 illustrates the CPU overhead of iOBS3 in four cases: 1) without security scheme; 2) using IPSec; 3) using SSL; 4) using IPSec and zcTCP concurrently. From the figure, it shows that the extra CPU overhead caused by IPSec is from 11% to 34% in reading, and from 15% to 21% in writing. As to SSL, it is from 19% to 57% in reading, and from 20% to 70% in writing.

After quantitative analysis, it indicates that zcTCP can reduce CPU overhead from 10% to 40%. Meanwhile, zcTCP causes extra CPU overhead when requesting small block, because it can't keep the page boundary aligned.

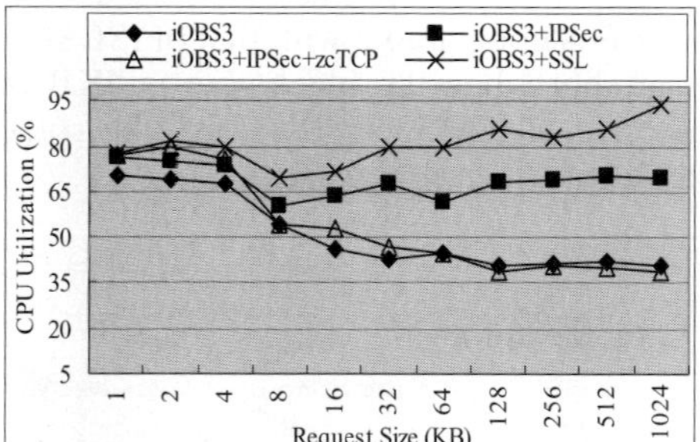

(a) CPU utilization of read operation

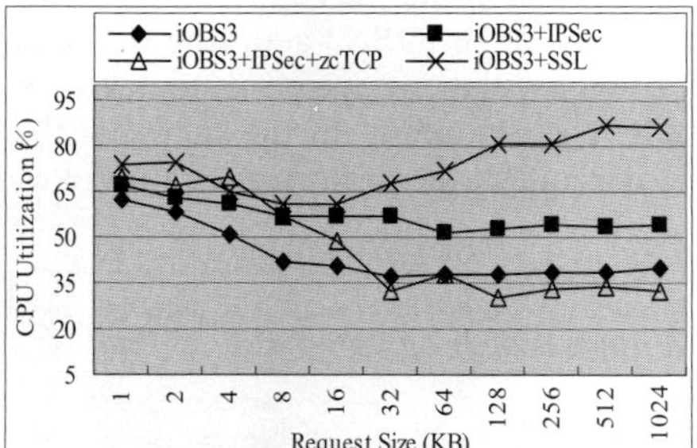

(b) CPU utilization of write operation

Fig. 6. CPU utilization in block read and block write

4) Qualitative Analysis

It is reasonable to believe that iOBS3 combining CAPKEY method and IPSec/SSL can defend all kinds of threats listed in Table 1. We implement iOBS3 and zcTCP using software-only method because its cost is the least.

The performance of iOBS3 degrades relative to iSCSI because of extra security processing overhead. For example, the OSD commands must be decapsulated into the SCSI commands by the OSD interpreter, and must be executed by SCSI device, which needs extra steps.

The zcTCP makes use of the page remapping, which reduces the amount of switches between the kernel buffer and user memory, avoiding or eliminating the CPU scheduling overhead of data copying.

5 Summary

Herein, we designed and implemented an object-based storage security system, which delivers OSD command sets using iSCSI protocol. This approach separates transmission security from access control in principle, which allows to improve the storage security via storage and to boost the transfer security via network security protocol (e.g. IPSec or SSL). The experimental results demonstrate that the performance of iOBS3 adopting IPSec and zcTCP is comparable with that of iSCSI, but iOBS3 is an object-based solution and guarantees stronger security.

Though improving the I/O bandwidth, zcTCP itself consumes some CPU resource. Employing dedicated RDMA network interface controllers (RNICs) can offload CPU processing. In the future, we hope to apply RNICs to iOBS3, and pay attention to the security of RDMA, because the IP-based RDMA applications generally expose the storage system to the IP networks, which is a new security issue.

Acknowledgments

This work is supported by both National Project on Key Basic Research Project of P. R. China (973 Program) under the grant No. 2004CB318203 and Natural Science Foundation of P. R. China under the Grant No. 60603074.

References

1. Gibson, G.A., Nagle, D., Amiri, K., Chang, F.W., Feiberg, E.M.: File Server Scaling with Network Attached Secure Disks. In: Proc. of the ACM ICMMCS, pp. 272–284 (1997)
2. Weber, R.O.: SCSI Object-Based Storage Device Commands-2 (OSD-2). Document Number: ANSI/INCITS 400-2004, (2004), http://www.t10.org/drafts.htm
3. Xie, C.S., Fu, X.L., Han, D.Z.: The Study and Implementation of an iSCSI-based SAN. Journal of Computer Research and Development (in Chinese) 40, 246–251 (2003)
4. Deering, S., Hinden, R.: Internet Protocol, Version 6 (IPv6) – Specification, ISI, RFC 2460, (1998), http:// www.arin.net/reference/rfc/rfc2460.txt
5. Tang, S.Y., Lu, Y.P., Du, H.C.: Performance Study of Software-based iSCSI Security. In: Proc. of the first International IEEE Security in Storage Workshop (2002)
6. Mraz, R.: Secure Blue: An Architecture for a Scalable, Reliable High Volume SSL Internet Server. In: Proc. of 17th Annual Conference on Computer Security Applications, pp. 391–398 (2001)

7. Culley, P., Garcia, D., Hilland, J.: A RDMA Protocol Specification, IETF Internet Draft, draft-hilland-iwarp-00 (2003)
8. FreeSWAN documentation, IPSec Protocol, http://www.freeswan.org/
9. Engelschall, R.S.: OpenSSL Project, http://www.openssl.org/
10. Singh, A., Voruganti, K., Gopisetty, S., Pease, D., Duyanovich, L., Liu, L.: Security vs Performance: Tradeoffs using a Trust Framework. In: Proc. of 13th NASA Goddard/22nd IEEE Conference on Mass Storage and Technologies (2005)

An Efficient Algorithm for Clustering Search Engine Results

Hui Zhang, Bin Pang, Ke Xie, and Hui Wu

National Laboratory of Software Development Environment
Beihang University
Beijing 100083, China
{hzhang,pangbin,xieke,wuhui}@nlsde.buaa.edu.cn

Abstract. With the increasing number of Web documents in the Internet, the most popular keyword-matching-based search engines, such as Google, often return a long list of search results ranked based on their relevancy and importance to the query. To cluster the search engine results can help users find the results in several clustered collections, so it is easy to locate the valuable search results that the users really needed. In this paper, we propose a new Key-Feature Clustering (KFC) algorithm which firstly extracts the significant keywords from the results as key features and cluster them, then clusters the documents based on these clustered key features. At last, the paper presents and analyzes the results from experiments we conducted to test and validate the algorithm.

1 Introduction

With the rapid growth of information in the Internet, people usually use the search engine, such as Google, to retrieve the information they are interested in. Most users usually input one or two simple keywords into the search engine that always make the search engine return too many results. Google returns the results in a page-ranked order and people usually browse the first few pages, thus, some valuable results might be ignored for the reason that they are not in the first few pages. The search engine also neglects the context and the semantic of the keywords.

It is a good idea to cluster the results automatically, so people can easily select the search results they really need from the clusters. Search results in the same cluster have high similarity while large difference exists among different clusters. In recent years, several achievements have been made in clustering the search engine results, mainly in three approaches. The first approach is to take the advantage of the Hits and PageRank algorithms [1], which analyzes the hyperlinks among the web pages and then clusters the pages with similar features into the same bunch. The second approach, proposed by Huajun Zeng et al [2], applies Text Clustering [3] into clustering search engine results. This approach encodes each result into a vector set, then uses text-clustering algorithm to cluster the results. In addition, Po-Hsiang Wang [4] proposed an algorithm that takes advantage of users' response to optimize the order of clustering results: the larger number of users interested in the specific results,

Y. Wang, Y. Cheung, and H. Liu (Eds.): CIS 2006, LNAI 4456, pp. 661–671, 2007.

the topper order the results will be placed in. By applying some ideas from Text Clustering [3], this paper proposes a novel topic-oriented algorithm to cluster the results, so user can choose the results from the clustered results and make the results more accurate to the user.

2 Design of Clustering Algorithm

At present, most clustering algorithms are based on the document Vector Space Model [5] (VSM). These algorithms are easy to implement, however the meaning of each cluster is not clear to users. They merely vectorize the search results, and cluster the search results to the same bunch if the similarity of them is larger than a certain threshold. Consequently, the clustering results are inaccurate and the algorithm is inefficient, so they are seldom applied in the commercial search engines.

The approach we proposed ensures the efficiency of clustering with lower algorithm complexity. The topic of a document mainly depends on the high frequency-terms (stop-words not included) in the document. So based on these high-frequency terms, the documents can be clustered into different groups based on different topics. According to the appearances of the terms in the documents, the similarities among different documents are computed and documents are clustered using heuristic rules. The flowchart of the algorithm is shown in Fig. 1.

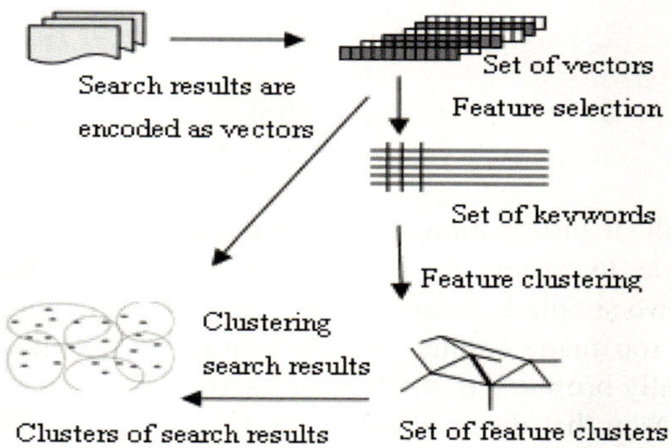

Fig. 1. Flowchart of algorithm

We assume that each search result returned by the search engine for a certain query is an independent cluster unit, and the more frequently one word occurs in a search result, the higher importance it gains. So we can regard these high-frequency words as the key features of a document and use them to feature the documents. There are some characteristics of a single feature, such as the keyword's frequency inside a search result, and the frequency of the search result that the keyword occurs in the search result collection. There are some relationships between two different features, such as the number of search results in the search result collection and respective frequency in the search results in which both features appear. After the selected search results have been encoded as vectors, feature selection, feature clustering, weight computation and search result clustering will be applied according to the clustering algorithm.

3 Feature Selection

A search result is represented as a N-dimension vector shown in Fig. 2. The vector records the frequencies that different keywords appear in the corresponding search result.

Keyword_1	Keyword_2	. . .	Keyword_N
frequency_1	frequency_2	. . .	frequency_N

Fig. 2. The keyword vector of the corresponding search result

In Fig.2, Keyword_i ($1 \leq i \leq N$) represents a certain word; N is the total number of indexed terms in the system; frequency_i (frequency_i > 0) is the frequency that Keyword_i appears in the corresponding search result.

Many keyword vectors corresponding to search results can generate a vector set. After calculating the frequency of each word, we choose the first P percent high-frequency words as key features of a search result.

To get the proper value of P, we conducted 1003 query-request in the experiment. The statistical analysis of frequencies was applied on the simulation results. All keywords were ranked by the frequency. X represents the ratio of first high-ranked keywords (the number of high-ranked keywords / the total number of keywords), Y

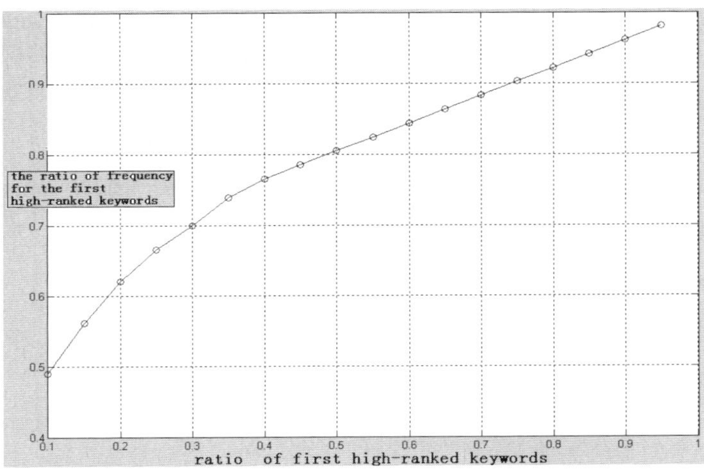

Fig. 3. The relationship between the ratio of first high-ranked keywords and the ratio of frequency for the first high-ranked keywords

represents the ratio of frequency for the first high-ranked keywords (the sum frequency of high-ranked keywords /total frequency), the relationship between X and Y is shown as Fig. 3.

As seen from Fig.3, we find that 25% high-frequency keywords occupy 67% of total frequencies, which are of great significance to the topic extraction, so proper value of P here is 25.

4 Automatic Clustering

4.1 Feature-Feature Weight Computation

We use the idea of Term Frequency * Inverted Document Frequency (TF*IDF) [5] to calculate the weight of features. The assumption we make can be summarized as follows.

$SearchR$ represents the set of search result vectors. $SearchR=\{SR_1.SR_2,...,SR_{total}\}$ (*total* is the number of search results which will be clustered), and SR_i ($1 \le i \le total$) represents a search result vector. $SR_i =$ {(Keyword_1, Frequency_ 1) ,(Keyword_2, Frequency_2), ..., (Keyword_n, Frequency_n)} $(n \in N)$, $\text{Frequency}_j (1 \le j \le n)$ represents the frequency that keyword Keyword__j appears in the search result SR_i.

$CharacterCluster$ is the feature set selected from the first P percent high-frequency words mentioned in the section 3.

k_i 、 $k_j \in CharacterCluster$ （ $k_i \neq k_j$ ） . Ti 、 T_j represent the total frequency of k_i、 k_j that appears in the $SearchR$ respectively.

TR_i 、 TR_j represent the numbers of vectors in $SearchR$ that contains k_i、 k_j respectively. TRS_{ij} represents the numbers of vectors in $SearchR$ that k_i and k_j appear simultaneously.

ST_i 、 ST_j represent respectively the frequency that k_i and k_j appears in the vectors that k_i and k_j appear simultaneously

The weight between k_i and k_j is defined as follows:

$$Weight_{ij} = (f_{k_i}(k_j) + f_{k_j}(k_i)) / 2 \quad (1)$$

$f_{k_i}(k_j)$ and $f_{k_j}(k_i)$ are computed as follows:

$$f_{k_i}(k_j) = \alpha \times (ST_i / T_i) + \beta \times (TRS_{ij} / TR_i) \quad (2)$$

$$f_{k_j}(k_i) = \alpha \times (ST_j / T_j) + \beta \times (TRS_{ij} / TR_j) \quad (3)$$

Here, $\alpha + \beta = 1$, and we assign $\alpha=0.3$ and $\beta=0.7$.

4.2 Feature Clustering

4.2.1 Algorithm

According to Eq.1, the feature-feature weights are calculated to quantify the correlation between every two features, as shown in Fig. 3. Weight_ij ($1 \le i, j \le N$) describes the correlation between K_i and K_j.

	K_1	K_2	K_3	...	K_N
K_1		Weight_12	Weight_13	...	Weight_1N
K_2			Weight_23	...	Weight_2N
...					...
K_N					

Fig. 4. Feature-feature weight matrix

The goal of the feature clustering is to ensure that features in the same cluster are more relevant while features in different clusters are irrelevant. The relationship between two features is proportional to the value of the feature-feature weight. The similarity of features in a cluster can be measured by the standard deviation of feature-feature weights. In this paper, Key-Feature Clustering (KFC) algorithm is proposed, which combines the feature-feature weights and the standard deviation of feature-feature weights in one cluster. The KFC maximizes the feature-feature weights and minimizes their standard deviation in one cluster. The assumption we make to describe the algorithm can be summarized as follows:

$S=\sqrt{\sum_{j=i+1}^{n}\sum_{i=1}^{n-1}\frac{(Value_{ij}-\overline{Value})^2}{\frac{n(n-1)}{2}-1}}$ is the standard deviation of feature-feature weights in a cluster. $\{sk_1, sk_2, ..., sk_n\}$ is the feature set of a cluster. $Value_{ij}$ is the feature-feature weight between feature sk_i and sk_j.

$$\overline{Value}=\frac{2}{n(n-1)}\sum_{j=i+1}^{n}\sum_{i=1}^{n-1} Value_{ij}$$

f_{con} is a threshold of feature-feature weight when merging a new feature to one cluster.

$Sort = \{Sort_1, Sort_2, ..., Sort_l\}$ is the set of clusters. S_{hi} $(1 \le i \le n)$ is a feature of cluster $Sort_h$. $Sort_h = \{S_{h1}, S_{h2}, ..., S_{hn}\}$ $(1 \le h \le l)$.

$sortTemp$ represents a cluster, $tempSD$ represents a standard deviation of feature-feature weights in a cluster.

Our algorithm is composed of 4 steps:

a. Initialize $Sort$ as empty value;

b. Initialize a cluster: Select two features whose feature-feature weight is the greatest in the matrix shown in Figure.4. Calculate f_{con} of these two features, and then remove these two features from the unselected feature set. Select a new feature which meets two conditions: (1) The feature-feature weight between the new feature and each initial feature is greater than f_{con} ; (2) The feature-feature weights standard deviation of three features is the smallest. These three features form the initial cluster $sortTemp$. Remove this new selected feature from the unselected feature set and recompute the f_{con} and feature-feature weights standard deviation S of $sortTemp$.

c. Select a new feature: for any feature X that has not been selected, if the feature-feature weight between any feature in $sortTemp$ and X is greater than f_{con}, the standard deviation of $sortTemp \cup \{ X \}$ is calculated, which is marked as $tempSD$. If $tempSD < S$, feature X is merged to the cluster $sortTemp$, then S and f_{con} are updated. Remove feature X from the unselected feature set, and skip to step c. Else skip to step d.

d. Add cluster $sortTemp$ to the cluster set $Sort$. If all features have been merged to the relevant clusters, algorithm terminates. Else skip to step b.

4.2.2 Analysis and Adjustment of Parameters

The threshold f_{con} is a key factor that impacts the accuracy of the clustering. Experience has shown that the more keywords the user inputs for querying, the more clearly the topic is. So the number of keywords inputted is important, and take the information of specific cluster into account, f_{con} is computed as Eq.4.

$$f_{con} = g(KeyWords\_Number) * \overline{Value} \tag{4}$$

$\overline{Value}$ is the mean value of feature-feature weights of features already in this cluster. $KeyWords\_Number$ is the number of the inputted keywords. We consider $KeyWords\_Number$ as three conditions: $KeyWords\_Number \leq 2$, $KeyWords\_Number = 3$ and $KeyWords\_Number \geq 4$. For each condition, we conducted experiments when the value of $g(KeyWords\_Number)$ was set to 0.50, 0.55, 0.60, 0.65, 0.70, 0.75, 0.80, 0.85, 0.90 and 0.95. By analyzing the results of these experiments, we have the following equation:

$$g(KeyWords\_Number) = \begin{cases} 0.60, KeyWords\_Number \leq 2 \\ 0.65, KeyWords\_Number = 3 \\ 0.70, KeyWords\_Number \geq 4 \end{cases} \tag{5}$$

5 Weight Computation Between Clustered Features and Search Results

In section 4.2, we cluster the features to form a cluster set, and each cluster is a set of keywords. Each search result is represented as an N-dimensional vector of keywords. In this section, we improve Term Frequency * Inverted Document Frequency (TF * IDF) [4] to calculate the weight between each feature cluster and search result. Such weight is the primary parameter to cluster search results.

The assumptions we made can be summarized as follows.

$VR_i = V(I_{k_i}, I_{k_2}, ..., I_{k_n})$ represents the vector of weights between search result SR_i and features. I_{ji} is the weight between search result SR_i and feature K_j;

TRI_{ji} represents the frequency that feature K_j appears in search result SR_i;

SRI_i represents the total frequency that all features appear in SR_i;

TR_i represents the number of search results in which feature k_i appears;

$Total$ represents the sum of all search results;

Other assumptions are the same as we made previously.

The equation used to calculate the weight is shown as follows:

$$I_{ji} = \log(1 + TRI_{ji} / SRI_i) \times \log(Total / TR_i) \quad (6)$$

6 Search Results Clustering

The weight between one search result and each feature calculated in the 5th Section reflects the relevancy between this feature and the search result. The higher the weight is, the more important the feature is to the corresponding search result. Otherwise, the feature is less important. In this section, we apply the K-Nearest Neighbors (KNN) algorithm [6] and introduce the voting-method into the clustering algorithm. The assumption we make in the algorithm can be summarized as follows:

$VSRI_{h,i}(I_{e_{hj}}) \in \{0,1\}$ represents the weight between the search result SR_i and the feature $I_{e_{hj}}$ in the cluster $Sort_h$;

$VSR_i(VSRI_{h,i}(I_{e_{h1}}), VSRI_{h,i}(I_{e_{h2}}), ..., VSRI_{h,i}(I_{e_{hn}}))$ represents the weight sequence between the search result SR_i and each feature in cluster $Sort_h$;

$VBSR_{h,i} = V(Sort_h, SR_i) \in \{0,1\}$ represents the belonging-relationship between search result SR_i and the cluster $Sort_h$; Value 0 represents that SR_i does not belong to $Sort_h$, while value 1 represents that SR_i belongs to $Sort_h$;

$WSR_i = \{VBSR_{1,i}, VBSR_{2,i}, ..., VBSR_{h,i}\}$ represents the weight sequence between search result SR_i and each cluster in the cluster set;

According to the assumptions we made, the algorithm is shown as follow:

$$VSRI_{h,i}(I_{e_{hj}}) = \begin{cases} 1, \text{in } VR_i, & I_{e_{hj}} \neq 0 \\ 0, \text{in } VR_i, & I_{e_{hj}} = 0 \end{cases} \tag{7}$$

Note: $VSRI_{h,i}(I_{e_{hj}}) = 0$ means that the frequency that keyword K_j appears in the search result SR_i is 0 or keyword K_j appears in all search results.

$$VBSR_{h,j} = \begin{cases} 1, \sum_{j=1}^{n} VSRI_{h,i}(I_{e_{hj}}) \big/ n \geq 0.6 \\ 0, \sum_{j=1}^{n} VSRI_{h,i}(I_{e_{hj}}) \big/ n < 0.6 \end{cases} \tag{8}$$

Note: The Equation (8) means that, if the mean $VSRI_{h,i}(I_{e_{hj}})$ value is higher than a threshold, the features of search result SR_i are most similar to cluster $Sort_h$. In this section, the threshold is 0.6.

7 Analysis of Algorithm

We analyze the algorithm in complexity and accuracy by using the same test data as in the Section 5, i.e. 1003 inquiry requests. The statistics is shown in Fig. 4.

The statistical item	Value
number of keywords in each search result	27
frequency of keywords in each search result	35
mean number of keywords in all results of each search	978
mean number of cluster features in each search result	17

Fig. 5. The statistical data

In traditional method, each sample is represented as a M-dimensional vector (M is the total number of index terms in the system) which includes massive features. For example, in experiments we conducted, the average number of keywords in a text document is 978 as shown in Fig.5. In order to improve efficiency of the algorithm, optimization is made both in time and space complexity. In the algorithm, we only select the 25% high-frequency keywords as features of a search result.

Another analysis we made is the accuracy of clustering. More than 100 search results were used to analyze the number of clusters that generated by the algorithm, as shown in Fig. 6.

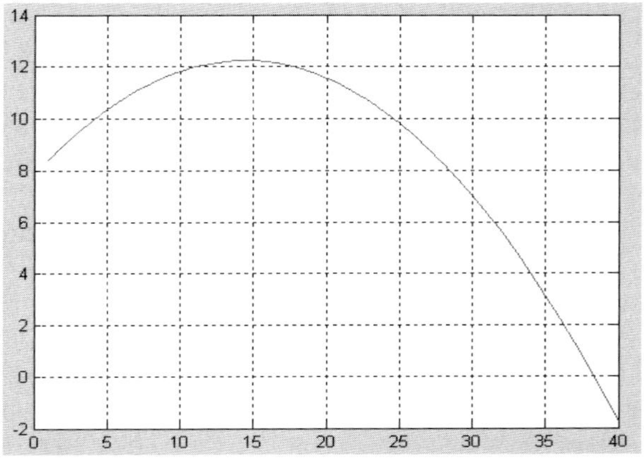

Fig. 6. The cluster statistics of selection more than 100 search results (The X-axis of these charts is the number of clusters, while the Y-axis is the times of query. The expected number of clusters is between 10 and 20).

It can be seen from Fig. 6 that when X- axis distributes between [10, 20], the Y-axis has the largest values. It means that in most searches, the number of clusters is between 10 and 20 which we expected. Compared to the traditional KNN [6] clustering algorithm, this algorithm does not require the initial clustering number, and can automatically control the threshold when a new feature is added.

The main goal of this algorithm is to discover the topics of the result collection, which helps users to obtain much more precise results. In many practical cases, one search result often contains more than one topic, thus one search result should appear in many different topic-based clusters. The algorithm we proposed has this important effectiveness while many traditional clustering algorithms haven't.

We also compared KFC Algorithm with the traditional CURE Algorithm [11] by mean similarity within a cluster (mean similarity between cluster centroid and search results within a cluster) and mean similarity between clusters(mean similarity between cluster centroid), as shown in Fig. 7 and Fig. 8.

The experiments show that the curves of CURE Algorithm and KFC algorithm have similar trend, but CURE Algorithm performs better than KFC Algorithm with greater mean similarity within a cluster as shown in Fig.7, while KFC Algorithm performs better than CURE Algorithm with greater mean similarity between clusters as shown in Fig.8. So KFC Algorithm can be used in the applications with lower time and space complexity when processing large amount of data.

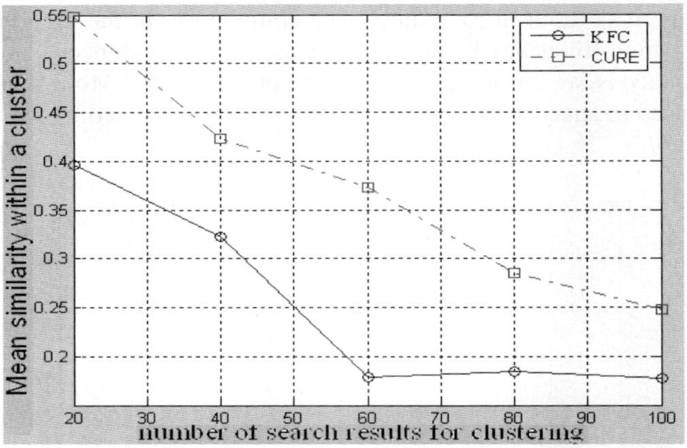

Fig. 7. Mean similarity within a cluster

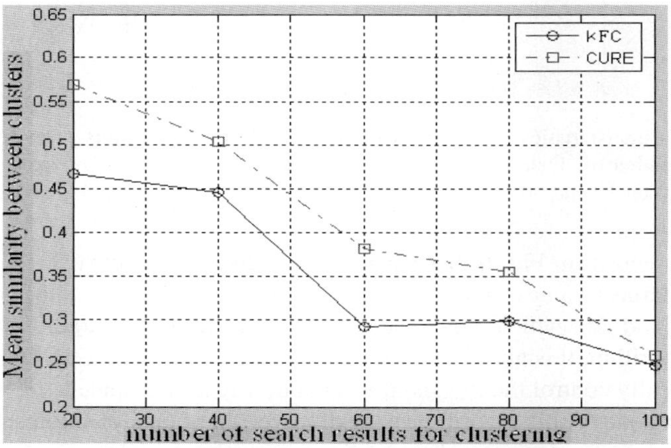

Fig. 8. Mean similarity between clusters

8 Conclusion and Future Works

In this paper, we introduce the novel KFC algorithm which firstly extracts the significant keywords from search results as key features and cluster them, then clusters the documents based on these clustered key features. We conduct several experiments to determine the proper value of the parameters in the algorithm.

In comparing with the traditional clustering algorithm, the KFC algorithm is more efficient when clustering the large amount of search engine results. How to make the clustering results independent to the test data is still worthy of further research. In the future research, we will apply the semantics into our algorithm and use priori-knowledge for more accurate and reasonable results clustering.

References

1. Wang, Y., Kitsuregawa, M.: Use Link-based Clustering to Improve Web Search Results. IEEE, New York (2002)
2. Zeng, H.-J., He, Q.-C.,Chen, Z., Ma, W.-Y., Ma, J.: Learning to Cluster Web Search Results
3. Hotho, A., Maedche, A., Staab, S.: Ontology-based Text Document Clustering
4. Wang, P.-H., Wang, J.-Y., Lee, H.-M.: Query Find: Search Ranking Based on Users' Feedback and Expert's Agreement. IEEE, New York (2004)
5. Yuliang, G., Jiaqi, C., Yongmei, W.: Improvement of clustering algorithm in chinese web retrieva [J]. Computer engineering and design,2005.10
6. Lixiu, Y., Jie, Y., Chenzhou, Y., Nianyi, C.: K Nearest Neighbor(KNN) Method Used in Feature Selection [J]. Computer and applied chemistry,2001.3
7. Xiaoying, D., Zhanghua, M., et al.: The retrieval use and service of internet information resource[J]. Beijing University Press, 2003.7
8. Xiaohui, Z. et al.: INFORMATION DISCOVERY AND SEARCH ENGINE FOR THE WORLD-WIDE WEB. MINI-MICRO SYSTEMS 6, 66–71 (1998)
9. Jianpei, Z., Yang, L., Jing, Y., Kun, D.: Research on Clustering Algorithms for Search Engine Results[J].Computer Project,2004.3
10. Sai, W., Dongqing, Y., Jinqiang, H.,ming, Z., Wenqing, W., Ying, F.: WRM: A Novel Document Clustering Method Based on Word Relation[J]
11. Guha, S., Rastogi, R., Shim, K.: CURE: An Efficient Clustering Algorithm for Large Databases. In: Proceedings of the, ACM SIGMOD international conference on Management of data, pp. 73–84, Washington, USA, 1998 (1998)

Network Anomalous Attack Detection Based on Clustering and Classifier

Hongyu Yang[1,2], Feng Xie[3], and Yi Lu[4]

[1] Information Technology Research Base, Civil Aviation University of China
Tianjin 300300, China
[2] Tianjin Key Lab for Advanced Signal Processing, Civil Aviation University of China
Tianjin 300300, China
yhyxlx@hotmail.com
[3] Software Division, Inst. of Computing Tech., Chinese Academy of Science
Beijing 100080, China
xiefeng@software.ict.ac.cn
[4] Security and Cryptography Laboratory, Swiss Federal Institute of Technology
(EPFL), CH-1015 Lausanne, Switzerland
yi.lu@epfl.ch

Abstract. A new approach to detect anomalous behaviors in network traffic is presented. The network connection records were mapped into different feature spaces according to their protocols and services. Then performed clustering to group training data points into clusters, from which some clusters were selected as normal and known-attack profile. For those training data excluded from the profile, we used them to build a specific classifier. The classifier has two distinct characteristics: one is that it regards each data point in the feature space with the limited influence scope, which is served as the decisive bounds of the classifier, and the other is that it has the "default" label to recognize those novel attacks. The new method was tested on the KDD Cup 1999 data. Experimental results show that it is superior to other data mining based approaches in detection performance, especially in detection of PROBE and U2R attacks.

1 Introduction

The goal of intrusion detection is to detect security violations in information systems. It is a passive approach to security as it monitors information systems and raises alarms when security violations are detected. There are generally two types of approaches taken toward network intrusion detection: *misuse detection* and *anomaly detection.*

In supervised anomaly detection, given a set of normal data to train from, the goal is to determine whether the test data belongs to normal or to an anomalous behavior. Recently, there have been several efforts in designing supervised network-based anomaly detection algorithms, such as ADAM [1]. Unlike supervised anomaly detection where the models are built only according to the normal behavior on the network, unsupervised anomaly detection attempts to

Y. Wang, Y. Cheung, and H. Liu (Eds.): CIS 2006, LNAI 4456, pp. 672–682, 2007.

detect anomalous behavior without using any knowledge about the training data. Unsupervised anomaly detection approaches are usually based on statistical approaches [2], clustering [3,4,5,6], outlier detection schemes [7,8], etc.

In this paper, we introduce a novel data mining based framework for anomaly detection, which uses clustering and classification algorithms to automatically detect the known and new attacks against computer networks and systems. We evaluated our system over KDD Cup 1999 data [9], which is a very popular and widely used intrusion attack data set. Experimental results show that our approach is really very competitive with respect to other approaches

2 System Design

Our aim is to justify the network connections normal or intrusive, which means we would reconstruct the network packets and extract features that describe the higher-level interactions between end hosts. Our scheme is divided into two phases. In training phase, we construct the normal profile and known-attack profile from the labeled training data, respectively. When detecting, our system classify the incoming connection as normal, known-attack or anomaly.

2.1 Framework

We use a combination of clustering and classification to discover attacks in a tcpdump audit trail. In our framework, the training set needs to be labeled or attack-free. If the data set includes the labeled attacks, we could get the known-attack profile. Otherwise, we only have the normal profile. When training is finished and detection model is built, we can use it to discriminate the new incoming connection on line. The purpose of clustering is to model the normal and known-attack network behaviors. We think the connections of the same type are more resemble statistically, which means these data are more easily clustered together. Therefore, we can use the centroid of a cluster to represent all members within that cluster, which will reduce the mass of raw data markedly.

For those ambiguous data in sparse space, we need a classifier to deal with them. Other than traditional classifiers, our classifier has the ability to classify a connection record as "anomaly". It is important to note that there is no "anomaly" class in training set, in which all examples belong to either "normal" class or "known-attack" class. Generally speaking, the traditional classifier only labels the data as known categories that are presented in the training set. However, we let the classifier include a "default" label by which the classifier expresses its inability to recognize the class of the connection as one of the known classes. Of course, the "default" label is "anomaly" in our algorithm. Our later experimental results will show that this is a very efficient way to detect the novel attacks that keep unseen before.

Thus, the system is ready to detect intrusions. First, the raw network packets are reconstructed to a connection and correspondingly preprocessed according to its protocol and service. Then it is compared with the profile modeled in the training phase. If it exists in the profile, we will label it as the matched type. Otherwise, it will be fed to the classifier, which will label it as normal, known attack, or anomaly. Finally, when the number of data labeled as known-attack or anomaly surpasses a threshold, an analysis module using the association algorithms will deal with the vast data in order to extract the frequent episodes and rules.

2.2 Feature Space and Attributes Deals

Feature Spaces

We map the connection records from the audit stream to a feature space. The feature space is a vector space of high dimension. Thus, a connection is transformed into a feature vector. We adopt 8 feature spaces according to the protocol and service of the connection. That is, we choose the different attributes for the connections with different services. An important reason is that different services usually have the specific security-related features. For example, the attributes of an HTTP connection are different from those of an FTP connection. The eight services include HTTP, FTP, SMTP, TELNET, FINGER, UDP, ICMP and OTHER, in which OTHER service is default. So, even if a new service occurs in the data stream for the first time, it can be simply regarded as OTHER service without reconfiguring the system.

Distance Function

In order to describe the similarity of two feature vectors, we use the Euclidean distance as our measure function:

$$d(v_i, v_j) = \sqrt{\sum_{k=1}^{\|v_i\|} (v_i^{(k)} - v_j^{(k)})^2} \tag{1}$$

where both v_i and v_j are feature vectors in the vector space $\Re^n$ of the same dimensions. $v_i^{(k)}$ represents the kth component of vector v_i, and $\|v_i\|$ means the dimensions of v_i, i.e. n.

Apparently, the distance between the two vectors is in reverse proportion to the similarity between them. For simplicity, we suppose each component of a vector is the same weight.

Discrete and Continuous Attributes

There are two attribute types in our connection records. One is discrete, i.e. nominal, and the other is continuous. Since the number of normal instances usually vastly outnumbers the number of anomalies in training data set and in anomaly detection values that are observed more frequently are less likely to be anomalous, we represent a discrete value by its frequency. As a result, discrete attributes are transformed to continuous ones. For a continuous attribute, we adopt the "cosine" normalization to quantize the values. Furthermore, the values of each attribute are normalized to the range [0,1] to avoid potential scale problem. The whole normalization processes include two steps: the first step is normalization of each continuous attribute,

$$v_i^{(k)'} = \frac{v_i^{(k)}}{\sqrt{\sum_{j=1}^{\|D\|} (v_j^{2(k)})}} \tag{2}$$

where $\|D\|$ represents the total number of vectors in the training set D. And the second step is the normalization of the feature vector. Note that we don't regard those transformed from discrete attributes in this step.

$$v_i^{(k)'} = \frac{v_i^{(k)}}{\sqrt{\sum_{k=1}^{\|v_i\|} (v_i^{2(k)})}} \tag{3}$$

2.3 Clustering and Profile Selection

At present, we use standard k-means algorithm [10] as our clustering approach. K-means is a centroid-based clustering with low time complexity and fast convergence, which is very important in intrusion detection due to the large size of the network traffic audit dataset.

Each cluster in profile can be simply expressed as a centroid and an effect influence radius. So a profile record can be represented as the following format:

$$\langle\ \textit{\textbf{centroid}},\ \textit{\textbf{radius}},\ \textit{\textbf{type}}\ \rangle$$

Centroid is a centric vector of the cluster, *radius* refers to influence range of a data point (represented as the Euclidean distance from the centroid), and *type* refers to the cluster's category, e.g. normal or attack. We can determine whether a vector is in the cluster or not only by computing the distance between the vector and the centroid and comparing the distance with the radius. If the distance is less than radius, we consider that the vector belongs to the cluster. And then we can label the vector as the cluster's type. Therefore, the whole search in the profile only includes several simple distance calculations, which means we can deal with the data rapidly.

Of course, not all clusters can serve as the profile. Some maybe include both normal and attack examples and not fit for the profile apparently. It is necessary to select some clusters according to a strategy. At present, we use the following conditions as our selection criterion.

Condition 1: *The number of examples in the cluster as the profile must surpasses a threshold.*

Condition 2: *The purity of the cluster as the profile must surpasses a threshold.*

Condition 3: *The density of the cluster as the profile must surpasses a threshold.*

Cond.1 emphasizes the confidence of the cluster as the profile. We think one cluster with more examples often means more stable and more representative. On the contrary, a little cluster, e.g. there are only 5 examples in it, is distinctly not fit for a profile.

In ***cond.2***, the purity of a cluster refers to percentage of majority examples in the cluster. Formally, it can be represented as follows:

$$Purity(X) = \frac{Number\ of\ Majority\ Examples}{Total\ Number\ of\ Examples\ in\ Cluster\ X}$$

A majority example is an example that belongs to the most frequent class in the cluster. The higher the purity is, the better the cluster is served as a profile. A cluster with small purity means that there are many attacks with different types in the cluster, so we don't select such cluster as our profile. Instead, we use them as the training set for classifier.

Cond.3 is less important than the first two conditions. Usually, most clusters meet this condition by nature. Here, we just use it to prevent those sparse clusters. For a cluster with low density, it is possible that some novel attacks will lie in it. So we think the sparse cluster is not fit for the profile.

After the clusters are selected for the profile, we put them into the profile repository. The basic contents include *centroid*, *radius* and *type*. Here, we use the type of majority examples in one cluster as the whole cluster's type regardless of the minority examples.

Parameters Determination

There are 4 parameters determining the profile selection: the number of clusters K, the *size*, *purity* and *density* of cluster. It is rather difficult to decide how to set these values to let the system be the best. But according to the experimental results, we found even if these parameters are set simply, the system can achieve a good performance. Intuitively, we hope the *size* is equal to the average size of cluster, i.e. the parameter *size* = the total number of samples in training set/the parameter K. In contrast to K, the parameter *size* is meaningful and set more easily. The larger size means the cluster is more stable and, unfortunately, the number of cluster satisfying the condition is less. Therefore, the value is set to 200 in our experiment. Accordingly, the parameter K is also determined. The parameter *purity* is very easy to set. This value decides the quality of cluster directly. If it is too little, many mixed clusters will be served as profile which will reduce the final detection. In the following experiment, we fixed it as 0.98. Finally, for simplicity, the parameter *density* is defined as the scale of the number of samples in the cluster to the radius of such cluster.

2.4 Influence-Based Classifier

There are many classification algorithms, such as Naive Bayes and decision tree, but they all don't support the "default" label in itself. Therefore, we present a new algorithm to address this problem, which is called influence-based classification algorithm in which we introduce the concept of data field and influence. We view the whole feature space as a large data field, in which every object interacts with each other. We use a function to quantify the influence of an object, which is called influence function. We adopt the Gaussian function to measure it. Denote the N-dimension feature space by $\Re^n$. So, the influence function can be represented as follows:

$$f_y(x) = \phi(x, y) = e^{-\frac{d^2(x,y)}{2\sigma^2}} \tag{4}$$

where $x, y \in \Re^n$, $f_y(x)$ means the influence function of a data object y. $d^2(x, y)$ is the square of the distance between x and y, while σ is called influence factor determining the influence scope of y.

The influence function of a dataset $D \subset \Re^n$ is defined as the sum of the influence functions of all data objects in D.

$$f_D(x) = \sum_{y \in D} f_y(x) = \sum_{y \in D} e^{-\frac{d^2(x,y)}{2\sigma^2}} \tag{5}$$

As we know, for a Gaussian distribution, rough 99.7% of the values fall within 3σ margin, which is the famous "3σ criterion". That is, the influence scope of a data object is rough equal to 3σ. So, in our algorithm, we only focus on those objects inside this range and ignore others. The whole algorithm is illustrated in Fig. 1.

Input: a sample P to be labeled, the influence factor σ, and the training set D
Output: Label P as normal, known-attack or anomaly
Begin
1. normalize P;
2. $f_+ \leftarrow 0$, $f_- \leftarrow 0$;
3. **for each** sample Q in D
4.   **if** $d(P, Q) > 3\sigma$ **continue**;
5.   compute the influence at P generated by Q and add it to f_+ **if** Q is normal, otherwise add it to f_-;
    endfor
6. **if** $f_+/(f_- + f_+) > T_N$ label P as normal;
7. **else if** $f_-/(f_- + f_+) > T_A$ label P as known-attack;
8. **else** label P as anomaly.
End.

Fig. 1. Influence-based Classification Algorithm

3 Experiment and Result

In the experimentg, we handled 10% of the whole KDD'99 dataset [9] corresponding to 494019 training connections and 311029 testing connections. Fig. 2 shows the results of our experiments, in which there are 5 ROC curves, 4 curves corresponding to 4 categories of attacks respectively, i.e. PROBE, DOS, U2R and R2L, and the left one corresponding to the overall attacks. "PROBE (4166)" denotes there are 4166 probing examples in the test set. Also, "OVERALL (250436/60593)" means there are total 250436 attacks and 60593 normal examples in the test set, and the corresponding curve describes the overall detection performance of our system. Furthermore, we list the more detailed results including each attack name, category, total number in the testing set and corresponding detection rate at the false alarm rate of 0.7% (stated in Table 1).

Table 1. The detection performance of all attacks in the test set. "*" means the attack type is novel, i.e. it doesn't occur in the training set. Note that the false alarm rate is 0.7%, TOTAL means the total number of attacks with the same category in the test set and TDR denotes true detection rate.

ATTACK NAME	TOTAL (TDR)	ATTACK NAME	TOTAL (TDR)	ATTACK NAME	TOTAL (TDR)	ATTACK NAME	TOTAL (TDR)
portsweep (PROBE)	*354 (99.72%)*	smurf (DOS)	*164091 (100%)*	udpstorm* (DOS)	*2 (100%)*	processtable* (DOS)	*759 (94.20%)*
satan (PROBE)	*1633 (99.88%)*	pod (DOS)	*87 (98.85%)*	xterm* (U2R)	*13 (84.62%)*	snmpgetattack* (R2L)	*7741 (0%)*
nmap (PROBE)	*84 (100%)*	neptune (DOS)	*58001 (99.97%)*	apache2* (DOS)	*794 (58.94%)*	snmpguess* (R2L)	*2406 (0.04%)*
ipsweep (PROBE)	*306 (99.02%)*	land (DOS)	*9 (100%)*	mailbomb* (DOS)	*5000 (12.20%)*	guess_passwd (R2L)	*4367 (14.88%)*
saint* (PROBE)	*736 (99.05%)*	teardrop (DOS)	*12 (83.33%)*	Perl (U2R)	*2 (100%)*	buffer_overflow (U2R)	*22 (95.45%)*
mscan* (PROBE)	*1053 (99.24%)*	back (DOS)	*1098 (99.36%)*	phf (R2L)	*2 (50%)*	loadmodule (U2R)	*2 (100%)*
rootkit (U2R)	*13 (23.08%)*	ps* (U2R)	*16 (68.75%)*	xlock* (R2L)	*9 (44.44%)*	warezmaster (R2L)	*1602 (63.05%)*
sendmail* (R2L)	*17 (17.65%)*	ftp_write (R2L)	*3 (66.67%)*	multihop (R2L)	*18 (61.11%)*	httptunnel* (U2R)	*158 (84.18%)*
xsnoop* (R2L)	*4 (50%)*	named* (R2L)	*17 (35.29%)*	worm* (R2L)	*2 (0%)*	sqlattack* (U2R)	*2 (100%)*
imap (R2L)	*1 (100%)*	-	-	-	-	-	-

It is shown that the performance of detection of PROBE and DOS attacks of the system is superior to that of other attacks, especially detection of R2L attacks. We analyzed the results in detail and found the reason for the low detection rate for R2L attacks. Both PROBE and DOS attacks often have the distinct traffic characteristic while U2R and R2L are more similar to normal examples. Especially, two R2L attack types (*snmpgetattack* and *snmpguess*) are hardly detected, which account up rough 63% of all R2L attacks. In fact, they are almost identical with normal examples and hardly detected only by the connection information. This means the detection rate for R2L attacks would reach 37% at most no matter what the false alarm rate is. Therefore, in Fig. 2, the detection rate for R2L attacks keeps stable (about 36.6%) when false positive rate surpasses 2.8%. Excluding these two types, our system can detect other attacks with the interesting detection and false alarm rates.

Fig. 3 shows the discrimination of the test data graphically, in which X axis denotes the number of testing samples with different categories, while Y axis denotes the ratio of the influence at a testing point produced by the normal samples to those produced by all samples, i.e. $f_+/(f_+ + f_-)$. For simplicity, we call the ratio value as the positive influence ratio. If the influence at a point in the data field is zero, we let the value be 0.5. Considering the mass of DOS attacks, we only use a little part of them, but keep all other attacks. Note that the value *cutoff 1* and *cutoff 2* are all thresholds, respectively corresponding to $(1-T_A)$ and T_N in Fig. 1. In the experiment, we found that they were insensitive, which means they are easy to set and don't affect the final results too much. Meanwhile, we found the obtained values mostly focused on 0, 1 and 0.5. That is, these samples could be discriminated easily. For example, there are rough 99.2% of total 60593 normal samples, of which the positive influence ratio are equal to 1. We, however, also can see that a few attacks are mislabeled, in which most are *snmpgetattack* and *snmpguess* (they are labeled in the figure too).

Fig. 4 shows the average positive influence ratio of all samples in this test set. Clearly, the average ratio of normal samples is distinct from that of intrusions excluding *snmp* attacks. Note that the values of novel attacks are mostly approximate to 0.5 according to our algorithm.

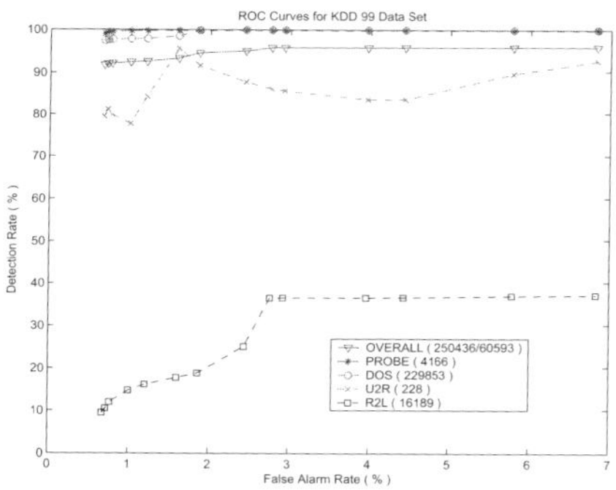

Fig. 2. The performance of proposed system. The curves are obtained by varying the influence factor σ.

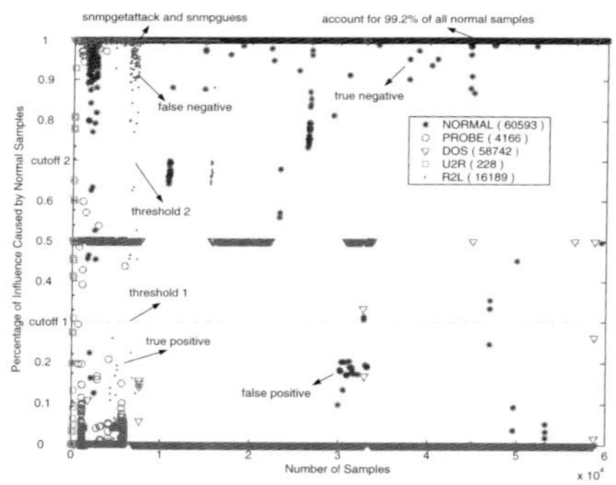

Fig. 3. The distribution of positive influence ratio of all samples in testing set. We omit a lot of DOS attacks. cutoff 1 and cutoff 2 are thresholds deciding the class of data.

Furthermore, we have compared our approach with other proposed methods, of which some participated in the task of KDD Cup. Since KDD Cup is concerned with multi-class classification but we are only interested in knowing whether the record is normal or anomalous, we have converted the results of those methods into our format. Specifically, the detection rate measures the percentage of intrusive connections in the test set that are labeled as known-attack or anomaly,

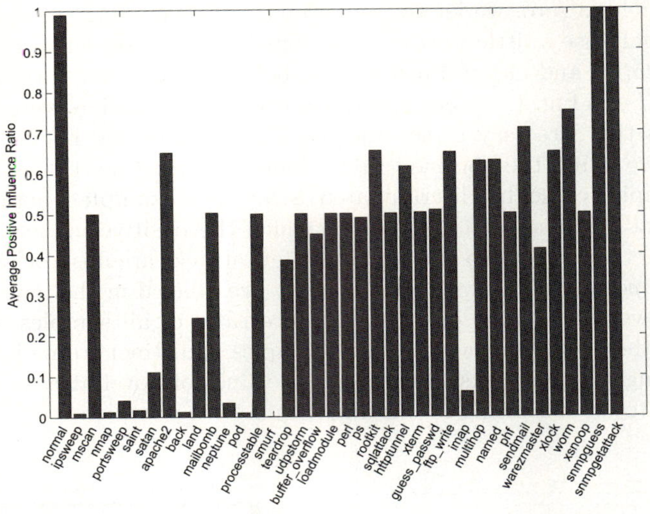

Fig. 4. The average positive influence ratio of all samples in test set in KDD Cup data

Table 2. Comparison of our system with other approaches

METHOD	FAR	PROBE	DOS	U2R	R2L
Our approach	0.7%	**99.5%**	**97.92%**	**81.14%**	10.44%
C5 Bagged Boosting	0.55%	87.73%	97.7%	26.32%	10.27%
Kernel Miner	0.55%	89%	97.57%	22.37%	7.38%
NN	**0.45%**	83.3%	97.3%	8.33%	2.5%
Decision Tree	0.5%	77.92%	97.24%	13.6%	0.52%
Naive Bayes	2.32%	88.33%	96.65%	11.84%	8.66%
PNrule	0.5%	78.67%	97%	14.47%	**10.8%**

without considering whether they are classified into the correct intrusion categories. The results are shown in Table 2, in which FAR means false alarm rate. The best results are highlighted by bold face. It can be seen that our system outperforms others significantly, especially in detection of PROBE and U2R attacks, while false alarm rate is comparable to the other approaches.

Table 3. The example distribution of 3 subsets in 3-fold cross validation experiments

Subsets	NORMAL	PROBE	DOS	U2R	R2L
A	52602	2940	204790	16	4755
B	52599	2987	207168	146	5213
C	52670	2346	209344	118	7347

Table 4. The grouping in 3-fold cross validation experiment

-	Training Set	Test Set
Group 1	A + B	C
Group 2	A + C	B
Group 3	B + C	A

Table 5. Results of 3-fold cross validation. We lists the detection performance at 5 different levels of false alarm rate, and P, D, U and R refers to detection rate of PROBE, DOS, U2R and R2L, respectively.

FAR	0.005				0.007				0.01				0.015				0.025			
TDR	P	D	U	R	P	D	U	R	P	D	U	R	P	D	U	R	P	D	U	R
Group 1	*.81*	*.99*	*.57*	*.51*	*.87*	*.99*	*.75*	*.52*	*.88*	*.99*	*.83*	*.53*	*.89*	*.99*	*.96*	*.53*	*.89*	*.99*	*.96*	*.53*
Group 2	*.84*	*.97*	*.72*	*.41*	*.89*	*.99*	*.77*	*.50*	*.95*	*.99*	*.90*	*.52*	*.97*	*.99*	*.98*	*.54*	*.97*	*.99*	*.98*	*.54*
Group 3	*.93*	*.99*	*.82*	*.45*	*.97*	*.99*	*1.0*	*.54*	*.98*	*.99*	*1.0*	*.55*	*.98*	*.99*	*1.0*	*.55*	*.98*	*.99*	*1.0*	*.55*

In addition to regular evaluations above, we have performed the 3-fold cross validation, i.e. we incorporated the original training and testing sets into one set, and randomly split it into 3 subsets of approximately equal size. Afterwards, we trained the model 3 times, each time leaving out one of the subsets from training, but using only the omitted subset to compute detection rate and false alarm rate. In these subsets, we let some attacks only occur in one subset intentionally in order that these attacks could be regarded as novel attacks when the subset was used as test set. The sample distribution of 3 subsets and experiment grouping are shown in Table 3 and Table 4, respectively. and the experimental results are shown in Table 5.

4 Conclusion

Indeed, the proposed framework is a supervised system including the benefit of clustering and classification. Compared with another famous supervised system ADAM which use frequent episodes to build the normal profile, we adopt clusters as system profile. We deem that this method characterizes the network behaviors better and more precise. In addition, we can get not only normal profile but also known-attack profile if the training data set includes the attack samples. As far as detection performance is concerned, our system can find many categories attacks while ADAM is devised to detect only PROBE and DOS attacks.

We adopt a influence-based classification algorithm to perform the final detection. Specifically, we view the whole feature space as data field, in which each point has a limited influence on others. So, we use the influence to discriminate the data. The experimental results show the approach is effective.

Acknowledgement

This work was supported in part by grants from the Major Project of High-Tech Research and Development Program of China (20060112A1037), Natural Science Foundation of Tianjin (06YFJMJ00700), the Research Foundation of CAUC (05YK12M) and the Open Foundation of Tianjin Key Lab for Advanced Signal Processing. We would like to thank those organizations and people for their supports.

References

1. Barbara, D., Couto, J., Jajodia, S., Wu, N.: ADAM: A Testbed for Exploring the Use of Data Mining in Intrusion Detection. SIGMOD Record (2001)
2. Ye, N., Chen, Q.: An Anomaly Detection Technique Based on a Chi-Square Statistic for Detecting Intrusions into Information Systems. Quality and Reliability Engineering International 17(2), 105–112 (2001)
3. Eskin, E., Arnold, A., Prerau, M., Portnoy, L., Stolfo, S.J.: A Geometric Framework for Unsupervised Anomaly Detection: Detecting Intrusions in Unlabeled Data. In: Proc. Of Application of Data Mining in Computer Security, Kluwer, Dordrecht (2002)
4. Leung, K., Leckie, C.: Unsupervised Anomaly Detection in Network Intrusion Detection Using Clusters. In: Proc. of 28th Australasian Computer Science Conference (ACSC), Newcastle, Australia, pp. 333–342 (2005)
5. Oldmeandow, J., Ravinutala, S., Leckie, C.: Adaptive Clustering for Network Intrusion Detection. In: Proc. of the 3th International Pacific-Asia Conference on Knowledge Discovery and Data Mining (PAKDD) (2004)
6. Portnoy, L., Eskin, E., Stolfo, S.: Intrusion Detection with Unlabeled Data Using Clustering. In: Proc. of ACM CSS Workshop on Data Mining Applied to Security (2001)
7. Ertoz, L., Eilertson, E., Lazarevic, A.: The MINDS - Minnesota Intrusion Detection System. In: Proc. Of Workshop on Next Generation Data Mining (2004)
8. Ramaswamy, S., Rastogi, R., Shim, K.: Efficient Algorithms for Mining Outliers from Large Data Sets. In: Proc. Of the ACM SIGMOD Conference (2000)
9. KDD Cup 1999 Data (2006), http://kdd.ics.uci.edu/databases/kddcup99/kddcup99.html
10. MacQueen: Some Methods for Classification and Analysis of Multivariate Observations. In: Proc. 5th Berkeley Symposium on Mathematical Statistics and Probability, pp. 281–297 (2001)

Fair Reputation Evaluating Protocol for Mobile Ad Hoc Network*

Zhu Lei[1], DaeHun Nyang[1], KyungHee Lee[2], and Hyotaek Lim[3]

[1] Information Security Research Laboratory, INHA University
[2] Department of Electrical Engineering, The University of Suwon
[3] Division of Computer Information Engineering, Dongseo University
koudai@seclab.inha.ac.kr, nyang@inha.ac.kr, khlee@suwon.ac.kr, htlim@dongseo.ac.kr

Abstract. Ad hoc network is a society of nodes who work in cooperative manner in accordance with self regulatory protocol. So reputation and trust should be built up and selfishness be dealt with a proper regulatory protocol. Selfish nodes are those which do not behave as the protocol specifies, with a wish to conserve power. This paper proposes an environmental compensation algorithm to the General Reputation Model. The algorithm provides a scheme as a mean to mitigate the detrimental effect of selfish nodes. And it deals for the first time with the security -the environment's influence on nodes' behavior. It also shows how to establish trusts in different areas with different environmental characteristics.

Keywords: Security, Ad Hoc, Environment, Trust.

1 Introduction

Reputation systems have been proposed for a variety of applications. Selection of good partners in a peer-to-peer communications and choice of faithful trade partners in online auctioning are among those. Under the mobile ad hoc networking architecture, the detection of misbehaving nodes provides the basis of reputation system.

There is a trade off between efficiency in using the available information and robustness against false ratings. If the ratings are made by others, the reputation system can be vulnerable to false accusations or praise. If it is established on the basis of one's own experience only, it does not provide a comprehensive rating neglecting other's experiences.

The goal of our model is to make neighborhood survailence systems both robust against selfishness and efficiency in detecting misbehavior. Our proposal is making use of all the available information, i.e. both positive or negative, and one's own or other's. And to guarantee the robustness of the reputation system, we show a way to deal with false ratings.

* This research was supported by the MIC(Ministry of Information and Communication), Korea, under the ITRC(Information Technology Research Center) support program supervised by the IITA(Institute of Information Technology Advancement)(IITA-2006-C1090-0603-0028).

Y. Wang, Y. Cheung, and H. Liu (Eds.): CIS 2006, LNAI 4456, pp. 683–693, 2007.

2 The Reputation Methods in Mobile Ad Hoc Networks

The use of reputation systems in many different areas is increasing, not least because of their widely publicised use in online auctions and product reviews, see, for example eBay and Amazon [14]. Mui et al. [13] gave many examples of how reputation systems are used.

Reputation systems are used to decide whom to trust, and whom to encourage trustworthy behaviour. Resnick and Zeckhauser [12] identified three goals for reputation systems:

1. To provide information to distinguish between a trustworthy principal and an untrustworthy principal,
2. To encourage principals to act in a trustworthy manner, and
3. To discourage untrustworthy principals from participating in the service the reputation mechanism is present to protect.

Two reputation mechanisms that have been proposed to help protect ad hoc routing are the Cooperation of Nodes: Fairness in Dynamic Ad-Hoc NeTworks (CONFIDANT) protocol [1], and the Collaborative Reputation Mechanism(CORE) protocol [2], which work in a similar way.

But both of them have some problems. For example, by placing more weight on past behaviour, CORE scheme is vulnerable to an attack where a node can build up a good reputation before behaving maliciously for a period. Attacks involving 'building up credit' before behaving selfishly have less effect in CONFIDANT, as good behaviour is not rewarded, so all nodes are always under suspicion of bad behaviour. However, this makes CONFIDANT less tolerant of failed nodes, which may be exhibiting failed behaviour due, for example, to loss of power.

3 The General Reputation Method

3.1 Assumptions

We assume certain things:

- Each node has a unique id.
- Links are bidirectional.
- Nodes do not have a prior "trust" relationships.
- All nodes give correct reputation to others.
- Misbehaving nodes do not forward data packets, but act correctly for everything else(which is selfishness).
- There are no malicious nodes (who want to destroy the network).

3.2 Direct Trust (DT)

When we want to know if we can trust some node B, we can route some packets via B and see (by sniffing in promiscuous mode) if B forwards them correctly.

The fraction of correctly forwarded packets in relation to the total amount of packets then gives us some idea on how trustworthy B is.

$$DT(A, B) = \frac{\sharp forwarded}{\sharp sent} \qquad (1)$$

$\sharp$ forwarded = number of packets (coming from A) correctly forwarded by B.
$\sharp$ sent = number of packets sent to B (by A).

3.3 Indirect Trust (IDT)

What happens if a new node comes? If A now wants to get references for B, he creates a reputation request, sets himself as source, sets B as target and broadcasts it to his neighbors (ttl = 1). Every node N receiving this request then looks if he has a direct trust value for B and if yes creates a reputation reply (from him to A) which is carrying this value. After some time A can then combine the received values to a reputation value for B:

$$IDT(A, B) = \frac{\sum_{i=1}^{n} DT(A, N_i) \times DT(N_i, B)}{n} \qquad (2)$$

N_i : node A's i-th neighbor node

This indirect trust value depends on when it is calculated and how many answers (route replies) have been received (and from whom). The question is how we combine all the *direct trust values* from the reputation replies together to one *indirect trust value*. One possibility is to weight them with the *direct trust values* we have (as in equation(2)). Another possibility is to look at the answers and compare them.

3.4 Reputation

Now we have some direct trust values and some indirect trust values. They can be combined in the following way:

$$REP(A, B) = \omega \times DT(A, B) + (1 - \omega) \times IDT(A, B) \quad (0 < \omega < 1) \qquad (3)$$

ω : the weight we put on DT(A,B).

4 Reputation Compensation Protocol

There are a lot of reputation methods for mobile ad hoc networks. But none of them had concerned about environment's influence on the behavior of nodes yet. For example, consider that the network is formed by several parts. Each part has different environment (it's easy for nodes to communicate with each other when they are in flat areas compare to hilly fields). If we use the same rule to all nodes, obviously it's unfair. Some nodes may be punished not because they misbehaved, but for the environmental reason that forces they have low trust value.

We propose a new method in order to compensate those nodes who are in the bad areas. This method can be applied to other protocols such as CONFIDANT[1] or CORE[2]. We take the general reputation protocol as an example to show how the environment can affect the nodes' behavior.

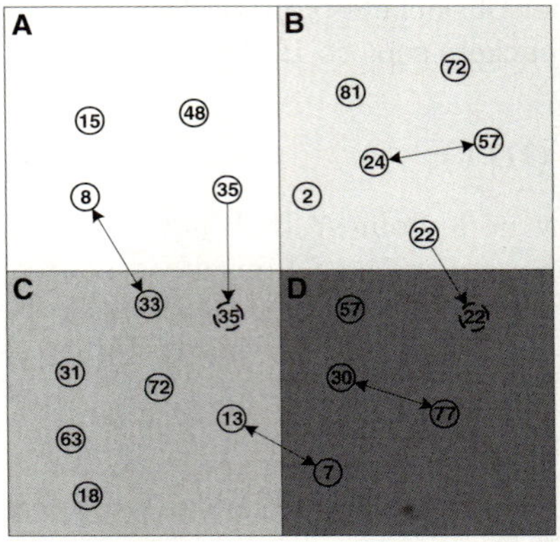

Fig. 1. The Network Model

In our scheme, the whole network would be divided into several parts depending on their environment. See Figure 1 as an example. The whole network is divided into four parts: A, B ,C and D. Within each part, environment is all the same(nodes have the same radio coverage or other parameters. The environment has the same influence on each node). Suppose the part A is the best environment for nodes to communicate with each other, the part B is the second, then the part C, the area of the part D is the worst amongst these four parts. So nodes in this part are hardest to communicate with each other. Take node No.8 and node No.33 for example, and assume that node No.33 is in the worse part. Then it may have a higher packet drop rate because of the environment's influence not because of its own wish. Then if node No.8 calculate node No.33's *direct trust* value, it may have a low *direct trust* value. Node No.33's *reputation* value may below the threshold and be considered as a misbehaving node(So as node No.13 etc.). So we must have a method to compensate the nodes that are in the "bad" part of the network.

4.1 Compensated Direct Trust(CDT)

The compensated direct value would be like this:

$$CDT(A, B) = \alpha_{A,B} \times \frac{\sharp forwarded}{\sharp sent} \tag{4}$$

α : the compensating factor to direct trust value

Situation 1. **Nodes in the same part**

Because node No.24 and No.57 are in the same part, they share the same environment. Then it's no need to compensate them. Thus, for them, the α value would be 1(The same for node No.30 and No.77).

Situation 2. **Nodes in the different parts**

Now, concern about node No.8 and No.33. They are in the different parts. Obviously 33 has a worse environment. Then we have to compensate it(The same for node No.13 and No.7). Also, when node No.35 and No.22 move to other part, their α value should be changed.

The α value would be like this:

$$\alpha_{A,B} = \frac{avg\ A}{avg\ B} \tag{5}$$

$avg\ A$: average reputation values of the nodes belonging to the part of A
$avg\ B$: average reputation values of the nodes belonging to the part of B

4.2 CIDT and CREP

Since the α value has already been added in the $DT(A, N_i)$ and $DT(N_i, B)$, it's no need to compensate the *indirect trust value* and the *reputation value* with α.

Then compensated CIDT and CREP are following:

$$CIDT(A, B) = \frac{\sum_{i=1}^{n} CDT(A, N_i) \times CDT(N_i, B)}{n} \tag{6}$$

and

$$CREP(A, B) = \omega \times CDT(A, B) + (1 - \omega) \times CIDT(A, B) \quad (0 < \omega < 1) \tag{7}$$

ω : the weight we put on CDT(A,B).

5 The Whole Scenario

The whole network is divided into several parts according to the environment. A node maintains a direct trust table which consists of entries for every neighbor and their direct trust value for performing a certain function. Nodes temporarily send *DT_update* message, which contains the source node 's direct trust value of other nodes and its own α value. On receiving this message, other nodes check sender's id and see if it is misbehaving or not. If the sender is dependable, nodes will accept the message and then update other nodes' indirect trust value (the most voted) and calculate other nodes' reputation value. The reputation value *rep*, is initially set to the variable *startdtv* (start direct trust value)

When a node requests a service from a neighbor, it gives the neighbor x opportunities to respond, where initially x is equal to *startdtv*. If the response is positive, x is increased by *cv* (change value). While x is positive, the value of x should be returned to the initial starting value after a timeout period, and thus, the value has to be earned again. After a certain number of consecutive timeout periods where no negative behavior has occurred, the *rep* value should be increased by *cv*.

Where there is no response or the response is negative, x is decreased by $2cv$. The node should keep trying until x reaches zero, then the corresponding *direct trust value* is decreased by $2cv$. In this event, the node should look to request the service from a different node. If later on, the node wishes to try and request the service from the same neighbor again, it performs the same algorithm, where the *rep* value is less and thus the number x of opportunities is now less, i.e. the neighbor is given less chances. The node should perform exponential back off to allow the neighbor to recover from any temporary problems(i.e. suddenly lose power). Neighbor nodes should be given some chance of recovery. Thus, if a node has no other option but to try a selfish node, the node can just request the service with an initial x value of 1. This, along with a decreasing *direct trust value*, results in less resources being wasted on a neighbor who is selfish or failed. Also, to discourage unwanted behavior, service requests from nodes with reputation values below a threshold should be ignored.

5.1 Which Nodes Are Misbehaving?

First, we need to observe that it is not possible for us to differentiate the different types of misbehavior. We cannot say if a node is misbehaving because he is malicious, just selfish, has no battery left and so on. We - in the following - just try to somehow determine which nodes are misbehaving without too many false positives.

In 4.2, we calculated trust values. But how to use them? When do we trust a node for routing packets?

The idea is to exclude misbehaving nodes from the network. Nobody wants to send his packets via a misbehaving node where one can not be sure if it reaches its destination (unchanged), but when nobody sends packets via misbehaving nodes they are relieved from the burden of forwarding packets, and therefore rewarded for their misbehavior. Many proposed protocols work like this, but we do not want to encourage misbehavior. We want to enforce cooperation. This can be achieved by dropping packets of misbehaving nodes by the other nodes (instead of forwarded). In this way, misbehaving nodes are completely excluded from the network. Because we want to give misbehaving nodes a chance of changing their behavior, we will route some of our packets through them (so that we can monitor their behavior), but we will not forward packets for them.

How do we determine if a node is misbehaving? A trust value can be small if a node dropped packets, but also if they never reached him or if we have not seen the correct forwarding. For the forwarding of packets it does not matter why a node has a small trust value. We, therefore, choose nodes with high trust values to maximize the probability of reaching the destination. In the other case we want to drop packets of misbehaving nodes only.

All this can not be achieved at 100%, but the errors should be minimized. So we need some thresholds. However, we use α value to compensate nodes in bad environment, so the whole network can use the same threshold. Where all nodes with $CREP < \tau$ will be treated as misbehaving.

5.2 The Bottleneck Problem

We use reputation system in order to find a relatively stable route to the destination. However, if a node has a high reputation and all the nodes want to send their packets through it, the congestion would happen, and it would be the bottleneck of the network. The route is "safe" but may not be efficient at all.

We use the following rule to select node:

- PDR_x : node x's packet drop rate
- $avg(PDR_x)$: average packet drop rate of the part the node x belongs to
- REP_x : node x's reputation value
- $avg(REP_x)$: average reputation value of the part the node x belongs to

If $\frac{PDR_x}{avg(PDR_x)} > \frac{REP_x}{avg(REP_x)}$, we shouldn't give too much bandwidth to this node. Else $\frac{PDR_x}{avg(PDR_x)} \leq \frac{REP_x}{avg(REP_x)}$, we can give more bandwidth to this node

6 Performance Analysis

To evaluate our protocol, we run NS-2 simulations with our implementation[10].

6.1 Definitions

- Original DSR : The original DSR protocol without reputation systems
- General : The DSR protocol with the general reputation scheme
- Compensated : The DSR protocol with the reputation compensation protocol
- Goodput : The ratio of received to sent packets
- Overhead : The ratio of number of reputation messages to routing messages

We simulated our protocol with the following parameters: Area 1000m $\times$ 1000m,Placement is uniform, Application is CBR, The number of nodes is 100, Maximal speed is 50 m/s, Packet size is 128 B, Pause time is 0,Percentage of Selfish nodes is 20%, Weight $\omega = 0.5$, and finally, Threshold τ is 0.4.

6.2 Simulation Results

Figure 2 shows the number of nodes are convinced to be misbehaving node varying the simulation time. We set 20 selfish node in Figure 2(a) and 40 in Figure 2(b). It's obvious the reputation compensation scheme is better than the general scheme. The reputation compensation scheme can catch out every selfish node without treating other good node unjustly. However, the general scheme consider almost 80% of nodes are selfish node because it has no compensation

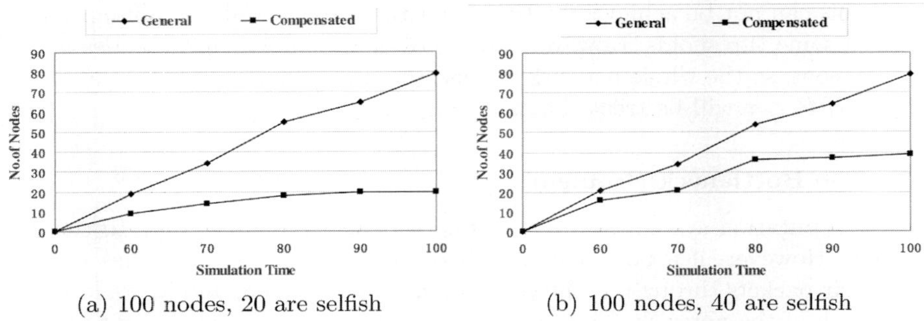

Fig. 2. No.of nodes are convinced to be selfish versus time

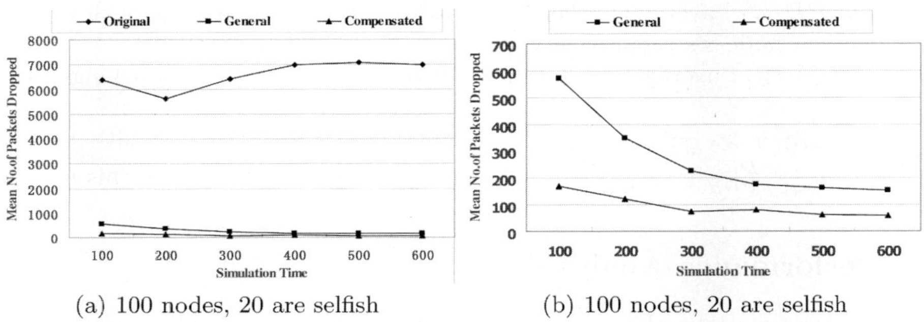

Fig. 3. Mean No.of packets dropped versus time

to nodes in the bad parts. So when they communication with other nodes and would be convinced to be bad.

Figure 3 shows mean number of packets dropped varying the simulation time. In the original DSR protocol, there are about 7000 packets dropped due to the selfish node. And both of the general and the reputation compensation scheme have a far better result than the original scheme. They just dropped a few packets because they can detect selfish nodes effectively. Then we take the general and the reputation compensation part out of the Figure 3(a). As showing in Figure 3(b), the reputation compensation scheme has a better performance than the general scheme because fewer nodes are convinced to be selfish.

Figure 4 shows mean number of packets dropped versus the percentage of selfish nodes. We can see that in the original DSR, even a small percentage of selfish nodes can work havoc. There is not much difference in the number of intentionally dropped packets as the percentage of selfish nodes increases. This can be explained by the fact that it does not matter where on the path a packet is lost. Our scheme still keeps the number of deliberately dropped packets low even in a very hostile environment as given by more than half the population acting selfishly - given that there are enough nodes to provide harmless alternate partial paths around selfish nodes.

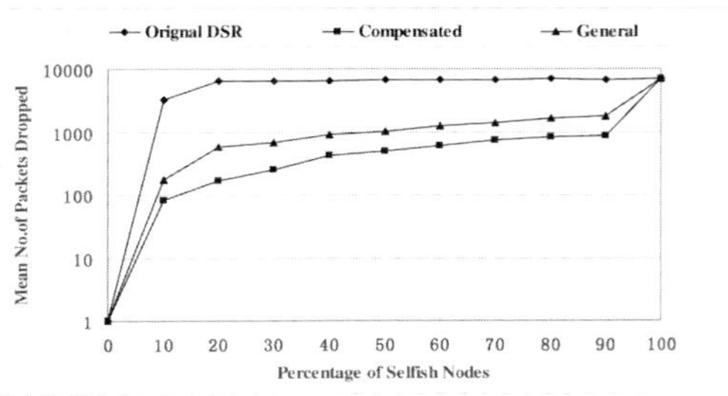

Fig. 4. Mean No.of packets dropped versus percentage of selfish nodes, 100 nodes, 20 are selfish

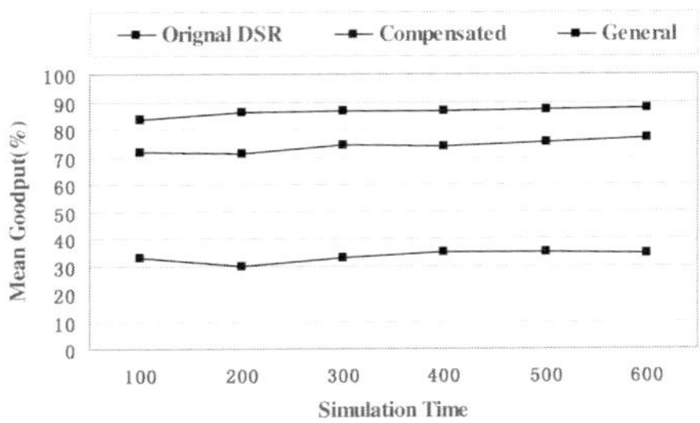

(a) 100 nodes, 20 are selfish

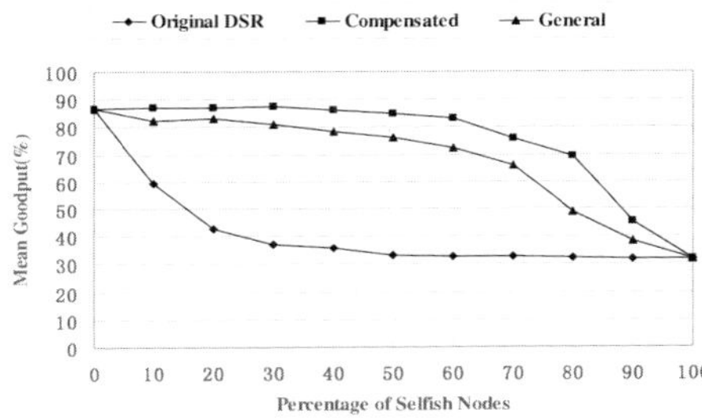

(b) 100 nodes

Fig. 5. Mean Goodput versus time and percentage of selfish nodes

Figure 5(a) shows mean goodput varying the simulation time. The original DSR has a very bad performance, and the mean goodput is between 30% to 40%. The general protocol has a better performance, and the mean goodput is between 70% to 80%. Then the reputation compensation protocol has the best performance at the end of the simulation, and it almost reaches 90%.

Figure 5(b) shows mean goodput versus the percentage of selfish nodes. Obviously, our scheme has a better performance. The goodput of the original DSR

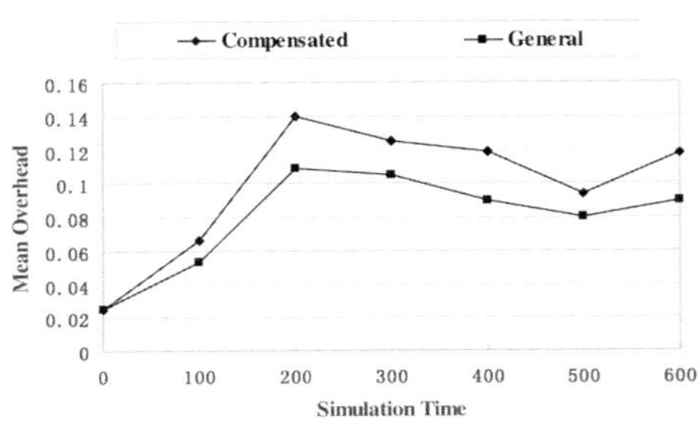

Fig. 6. Mean Overhead, 100 nodes, 20 are selfish

decreases sharply from the beginning and then decreases steadily. But our scheme keeps steadily at the beginning even half of nodes are selfish.

Figure 6 shows mean overhead varying the simulation time. Always when adding a new protocol, the overhead caused should not be too large. Our protocol adds less than 15% overhead but gain more than 50% in mean goodput, so that our protocol is worth to be added.

7 Conclusion

This paper tried to show how to incorporate reputation, trust and selfishness into the cooperative protocol of ad hoc networking. Its significance also lies in not only suggesting the reputation model, but also showing that its performance is promising.

The paper also proposed the General Reputation Model for mitigating detrimental effect of selfish nodes. To the model, we added the environmental influence attribute on nodes behavior and showed how it worked. The simulation by DSR proved our reputation- based trust management significantly improved the performance with a small amount of overhead increment. Goodput in a setup with 20% selfish nodes can be improved more than 50%, causing less than 15% overhead.

References

1. Buchegger, S., Le Boudec, J.-Y.: Performance Analysis of the CONFIDANT Protocol (Cooperation Of Nodes: Fairnes. In Dynamic Ad-hoc NeTworks). In: Proceedings of IEEE/ACM Symposium on Mobile Ad Hoc Networking and Computing (MobiHOC), Lausanne, CH (June 2002)
2. Michiardi, P., Molva, R.: Core: A Collaborative Reputation mechanism to enforce node cooperation in Mobile Ad Hoc Networks. In: Proceedings of the IFIP TC6/TC11 Sixth Joint Working Conference on Communications and Multimedia Security: Advanced Communications and Multimedia Security, pp. 107–121 (September 26-27, 2002)
3. Buchegger, S., Boudec, J.-Y.L.: Nodes bearing grudges: Towards routing security, fairness, and robustness in mobile ad hoc networks. In: Proceedings of the Tenth Euromicro Workshop on Parallel, Distributed and Network-based Processing, Canary Islands, pp. 403–410. IEEE Computer Society, Los Alamitos (2002)
4. Pirzada, A. A., McDonald, C.: Establishing trust in pure ad-hoc networks. ACM International Conference Proceeding Series; Vol. 56. In: Proceedings of the 27th conference on Australasian computer science - Volume 26
5. Dewan, P., Dasgupta, P., Bhattacharya, A.: On Using Reputations in Ad hoc Networks to Counter Malicious Nodes. QoS and Dynamic Systems in conjunction with IEEE ICPADS Newport Beach, USA (2004)
6. Marti, S., Giuli, T.J., Lai, K., Baker, M.: Mitigating Routing Misbehaviour in Mobile Ad Hoc Networks. In: Proceedings of the Sixth Annual International Conference on Mobile Computing and Networking MobiCom (2000)
7. IETF MANET Working Group Internet Drafts. `http://www.ietf.org/ids.by.wg/manet.html`

8. Broch, J., Johnson, D.B., Maltz, D.A.: The dynamic source routing protocol for mobile ad hoc networks. Internet-Draft Version 03, IETF (October 1999)
9. Zhou, L., Haas, Z.J.: Securing ad hoc networks. IEEE Network Magazine, vol. 13(6)(November/ December 1999)
10. The Network Simulator - ns-2 (2002), http://www.isi.edu/nsnam/ns/
11. The CMU Monarch Project. The CMU Monarch Projects Wireless and Mobility Extensions. (October 12, 1999) http://www.monarch.cs.rice.edu/cmu-ns.html
12. Resnick, P., Zeckhauser, R.: Trust among strangers in internet transactions: Empirical analysis of ebays reputation system. In: Baye, M. (ed.) Advances in Applied Microeconomics: The Economics of the Internet and E-Commerce, vol. 11, pp. 127–C157. Elsevier Science Ltd, Amsterdam (November 2002)
13. Mui, L., Mohtashemi, M., Halberstadt, A.: Notions of reputation in multi-agents systems: a review. In: Gini, M., Ishida, T., Castelfranchi, C., Johnson, W. (eds.) Proceedings of the first international joint conference on Autonomous agents and multiagent systems, Bologna, Italy, July 15-C19, 2002, ACM Press, New York (2002)
14. Resnick, P., Zeckhauser, R., Friedman, E., Kuwabara, K.: Reputation systems. Communications of the ACM, 43(12), 45–C48 (2000)

Multisensor Real-Time Risk Assessment Using Continuous-Time Hidden Markov Models

Kjetil Haslum and Andr Årnes*

Center for Quantifiable Quality of Service in Communication Systems**
Norwegian University of Science and Technology
O.S. Bragstads plass 2E, N-7491 Trondheim, Norway
{haslum,andrearn}@q2s.ntnu.no

Abstract. The use of tools for monitoring the security state of assets in a network is an essential part of network management. Traditional risk assessment methodologies provide a framework for manually determining the risks of assets, and intrusion detection systems can provide alerts regarding security incidents, but these approaches do not provide a real-time high level overview of the risk level of assets. In this paper we further extend a previously proposed real-time risk assessment method to facilitate more flexible modeling with support for a wide range of sensors. Specifically, the paper develops a method for handling continuous-time sensor data and for determining a weighted aggregate of multisensor input.

1 Introduction

With the complexity of technologies in todays society, we are exposed to an increasing amount of unknown vulnerabilities and threats. For a system or network administrator, it is vital to have access to automated systems for identifying risks and threats and for prioritizing security incidents. In this paper we study and extend a previously proposed system for real-time risk assessment. The proposed system computes a quantitative risk measure for all assets based on input from sensors such as network-based intrusion detection systems (IDS). The approach was first proposed in [1], and it has been validated using simulations in [2] and real-life data in [3]. During this work, several open research issues have been identified. There is a need for more flexible security state modeling, and the wide range of potential sensor types require different modeling schemes. In particular, a typical signature-based IDS can be much better modeled using a continuous-time hidden Markov model (HMM) than the discrete-time HMM in [1].

* AndrÅrnes is currently with the High-tech Crime Division of the Norwegian Criminal Investigation Service, Postboks 8163 Dep, N-0034 Oslo, Norway.

** The Centre for Quantifiable Quality of Service in Communication Systems, Centre of Excellence, is appointed by the Research Council of Norway, and funded by the Research Council, NTNU, UNINETT, and Telenor.

Y. Wang, Y. Cheung, and H. Liu (Eds.): CIS 2006, LNAI 4456, pp. 694–703, 2007.

The contributions of this paper consist of a method for continuous-time estimation using transition rates rather than transition probabilities, as well as a method for computing risk as a weighted sum of sensor input, taking into consideration the fact that some sensors are statistically more reliable and significant than others.

In Section 2 we revisit the proposed risk assessment approach and provide explanations of the necessary terminology. In Section 3 and 4 we present various ways of HMM modeling for a flexible real-time risk assessment system, with particular focus on continuous-time HMMs and the aggregation of input from multiple sensors. In Section 5 we discuss the results and provide directions for further work.

2 Real-Time Risk Assessment

Risk assessment is typically a manual analysis process based on standardized frameworks, such as those recommended by NIST [4] and AS/NZS [5]. Such methodologies are suitable for evaluating threats and vulnerabilities, but they are not designed to support operational network management. A notable exception is the real-time risk assessment system presented in [6], which introduces a formal model for real-time characterization of the risk faced by a host. In [1], we presented another real-rime risk assessment system employing HMMs. An HMM enables the estimation of a *hidden* state based on *observations* that are not necessarily accurate. An important feature of this approach is that it is able to model the probability of false positives and false negatives associated with the observations. The method is based on Rabiner's work on HMMs [7]. This section reviews the model presented in [1]. Some adaptations have been introduced for the purpose of this paper.

The target of the risk assessment is a generic computer network, consisting of *assets*. Unknown factors in such a network may represent *vulnerabilities* that in turn can be *exploited* by a malicious attacker or computer program, causing *unwanted incidents*. The potential exploitation of a vulnerability can be described as *threats* to the assets. The *risk* of the network is evaluated as the probability and consequence of unwanted incidents. The consequences of an unwanted incident is referred to as the *cost* of the incident. As in [1], we assume a multiagent system architecture consisting of *agents* and *sensors*. A *sensor* typically refers to an IDS, but it could be any information-gathering program or device capable of collecting security relevant data, such as logging systems, virus detectors, honeypots, and network sniffers using sampling or filtering. The main task of a sensor is to gather information about the security state of assets and to send standardized observation messages to the agents. An *agent* is responsible for performing real-time risk assessment based on data collected from a number of sensors. The multiagent architecture has been chosen for its flexibility and scalability, in order to support future applications, such as distributed automated response.

Assume that the security of an asset can be modeled by N states, denoted $S = \{s_1, \ldots, s_N\}$. Due to security incidents such as attack attempts and compromises,

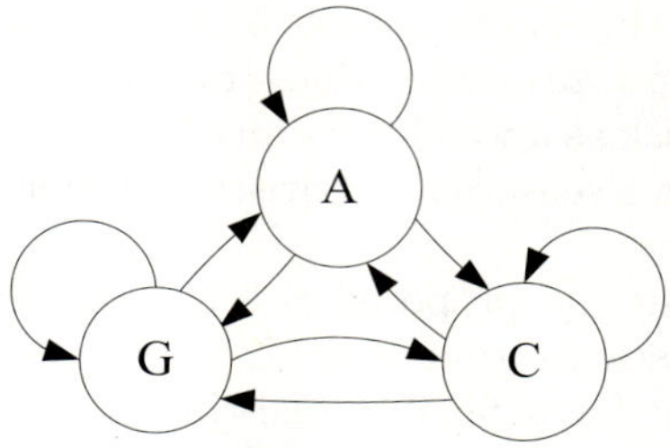

Fig. 1. Fully connected Markov model

the security state of an asset will change over time. The sequence of states visited is denoted $X = x_1, \ldots, x_T$, where $x_t \in S$ is the state visited at time t. As in [1], we assume that the state space can be represented by a fully connected Markov model with the states G (good), A (under attack), and C (compromised), i.e., $S = \{G, A, C\}$, as shown in Fig. 1. State G means that the asset is up and running securely and that it is not subject to any kind of attack activity. As an attack against an asset is initiated, it will move to security state A. An asset in state A is subject to an ongoing attack, possibly affecting its behavior with regard to security. Finally, an asset enters state C if it has been successfully compromised by an attacker. It is then assumed to be completely at the mercy of an attacker and subject to any kind of confidentiality, integrity, and/or availability breaches. The risk-assessment method is general and independent of the specific states used. Two alternative ways of modeling the security states of assets are presented in Fig. 2(a) and 2(b). In Fig. 2(a) we show how an asset can be represented by three separate Markov models indicating the security state with respect to *confidentiality*, *integrity*, and *availability*. In Fig. 2(b) we show a left-right model, where the asset can only transfer to a more serious state, with C as an absorbing state.

The risk *observation messages* are provided by the K sensors monitoring an asset, indexed by $k \in \{1, \ldots, K\}$. An observation message from sensor k can consist of any of the symbols in the observation symbol set $V^k = \{v_1^k, \ldots, v_M^k\}$. Different sensor types may produce observation messages from different observation symbol sets. We assume that the observation messages are independent, i.e., an observation message will depend on the asset's current state only and not on any previous observation messages. The *sequence* of messages received from sensor k is denoted $Y_t^k = y_1^k, \ldots, y_t^k$, where $y_t^k \in V^k$ is the observation message received from sensor k at time t. For the purpose of this paper, we assume an observation symbol set $V^k = \{g^k, a^k, c^k\}, \forall k$, corresponding to the states in $S = \{G, A, C\}$. Based on the observation messages, an agent performs real-time risk assessment. As one cannot assume that it is possible to resolve the correct state of the monitored assets at all times, the observation symbols are probabilistic functions of the asset's security state. The asset's true state is *hidden*, consistent with the basic idea of HMM [7].

For each sensor k monitoring an asset, there is an HMM described by the parameter vector $\lambda^k = (\mathbf{P}, \mathbf{Q}^k, \pi)$. $\mathbf{P} = \{p_{ij}\}$ is the state transition probability

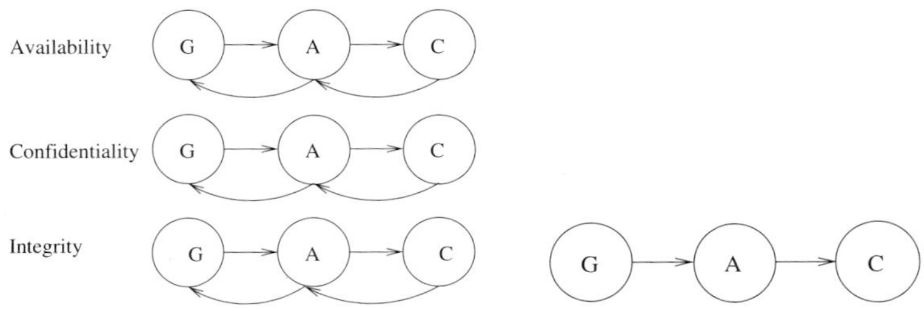

(a) A risk model consisting of tree submodels

(b) A pure birth process

Fig. 2. Alternative security state models

distribution matrix for an asset, where $p_{ij} = P(x_{t+1} = s_j | x_t = s_i), 1 \leq i, j \leq N$. Hence, p_{ij} represents the probability that the asset will transfer into state s_j next, given that its current state is s_i. $\pi = \{\pi_i\}_{i \in S}$ is the initial state distribution for the asset. Hence, $\pi_i = P(x_1 = s_i)$ is the probability that s_i was the initial state of an asset.

For each asset, there are K observation symbol probability distribution matrices, one for each sensor. Each row i in the observation symbol probability distribution matrix $\mathbf{Q}^k = \{q_i^k(m)\}$ is a probability distribution for an asset in state s_i over the observation symbols from sensor k, whose elements are $q_i^k(m) = P(y_t^k = v_m^k | x_t = s_i), 1 \leq i \leq N, 1 \leq k \leq K, 1 \leq m \leq M$. The element $q_i^k(m)$ in $\mathbf{Q}^k$ represents the probability that sensor k will send the observation symbol v_m^k at time t, given that the asset is in state s_i at time t. $\mathbf{Q}^k$ therefore indicates sensor k's false-positive and false-negative effects on the agents risk assessments.

The π vector and the $\mathbf{P}$ matrix describe the initial state and the security behavior of an asset, and they must be the same for all sensors monitoring the same asset. Since each sensor may produce a unique set of observation symbols, the $\mathbf{Q}^k$ matrix depends on the sensor k. For each sensor the agent updates the probability distribution $\gamma_t^k = \{\gamma_t^k(i)\}$, where $\gamma_t^k(i) = P(x_t = s_i | Y_t^k)$, by using the method presented in [1]. In [1], the risk of an asset was then evaluated as $\mathcal{R}_t^k = \sum_{i=1}^{N} \gamma_t^k(i) \mathcal{C}(s_i)$, where t is the time of the evaluation, k is the sensor used, and $\mathcal{C}(s_i)$ describing the cost due to loss of confidentiality, integrity, and availability for each state of an asset. In Section 4 we present a new method for multisensor assessment using a weighted sum of the results from multiple sensors.

3 Continuous-Time Markov Chains

There is a multitude of sensors that can provide security relevant information, such as IDS, network logs, network traffic measurements, virus detectors, etc. In our previous work, we have only considered the use of discrete-time HMMs, but we have seen the need for continuous-time HMMs allowing for transition rates rather than probabilities. The two HMM types complement each other, and they are suitable for different types of sensors. Let us consider some example sensor types. A signature based IDS matches network traffic (network IDS) or host activity (host IDS) with signatures of known attacks and generates alerts. Virus detection systems use a similar technique. The alert stream of a signature based IDS is typically highly varying, and a continuous time HMM approach is preferable. An active measurement systems can be used to perform periodical measurements of the availability of hosts and services, for example based on delay measurements. Such a measurement system is an example of an active sensor suitable for a discrete-time HMM that is updated periodically. An anomaly based IDS uses statistical analysis to identify deviation from a behavior that is presumed to be normal. Such a sensor could be used with either a continuous- or a discrete- time model. If the sensor is used to produce alerts in case of detected anomalies, it can be used in a fashion similar to the signature based sensors. If the sensor is used to compute a measure of the normality of a network or system, it can be used as a basis for periodic computations using a discrete time model.

We assume that a continuous-time Markov chain $(x(t), t \geq 0)$ can be used to model the security of an asset. The model consists of the set of states $S = \{s_1, \ldots, s_N\}$, the initial state distribution π, and a transition rate matrix $\mathbf{\Lambda} = \{\lambda_{ij}\}$, $1 \leq i, j \leq N$. When the system is in state s_i, it will make λ_{ij} transitions to state s_j per time unit. The time spent in state s_i is exponentially distributed with mean u_i^{-1} (sojourn time), where $u_i = \sum_{j \neq i} \lambda_{ij}$ is the total rate out of state s_i. The rate in and out of a state must be equal and therefore $\sum_j \lambda_{ij} = 0$, where $\lambda_{ii} = -u_i$ represent the rate of transitions into state s_i. The new HMM for sensor k, based on the transition rates, is then $\lambda^k = (\mathbf{\Lambda}, \mathbf{Q}^k, \pi)$.

The time between observations is not constant, so for each new observation, a transition probability matrix $\mathbf{P}(\Delta_t) = \{p_{ij}(\Delta_t)\}$ have to be calculated, where Δ_t is the time since last observation was received. Suppose that the process $x(t)$ is in state s_i at time t, then the probability that the process is in state s_j at time $t + \Delta_t$ is given by $p_{ij}(\Delta_t) = P(x(t + \Delta_t) = s_j | x(t) = s_i)$. If the transition probability from state s_i to s_j is independent of t, the process is said to be a homogeneous Markov process. The transitions probability matrix $\mathbf{P}(\Delta_t)$ can be calculated by

$$\mathbf{P}(\Delta_t) = e^{\mathbf{\Lambda} \Delta_t},$$

and approximated by

$$\mathbf{P}(\Delta_t) \approx \lim_{n \to \infty} \left(\mathbf{I} + \mathbf{\Lambda} \frac{t}{n} \right)^n . \tag{1}$$

More details on computing the transition probability matrix can be found in [8], pages 388 – 389.

Example 1. Consider a network with continuous-time sensors monitoring a central server. Through a manual risk assessment process, the administrators have estimated the initial state distribution and the transition rates for the system per day. Given a set of states $S = \{G, A, C\}$, the transition rate matrix is set to

$$\mathbf{\Lambda} = \begin{pmatrix} \lambda_{GG} & \lambda_{GA} & \lambda_{GC} \\ \lambda_{AG} & \lambda_{AA} & \lambda_{AC} \\ \lambda_{CG} & \lambda_{CA} & \lambda_{CC} \end{pmatrix} = \begin{pmatrix} -1.1 & 1.0 & 0.1 \\ 4 & -5 & 1 \\ 3 & 1 & -4 \end{pmatrix}.$$

As noted above, the values indicate the transition rate per day. However, the numbers in the diagonal of the matrix is the rate into the state, which is equal to the sum of the rates out of the state. The first row represents the rates in and out of state G, indicating that the rate of transitions to state A (1 transition per day) is greater than the rate of transitions to state C (0.1 transitions per day). The bottom row of the matrix represents state C, and it indicates that the most probable development is a return to state G due to a successful repair.

First, we calculate the rate at which the system leaves each state

$$\begin{aligned} u_G &= \lambda_{GA} + \lambda_{GC} = 1 + 0.1 = 1.1 = -\lambda_{GG}, \\ u_A &= \lambda_{AG} + \lambda_{AC} = 4 + 1 = 5 = -\lambda_{AA}, \\ u_C &= \lambda_{CG} + \lambda_{CA} = 3 + 1 = 4 = -\lambda_{CC}. \end{aligned}$$

From this we can calculate the sojourn time for each state

$$u_G^{-1} = \frac{10}{11},\ u_A^{-1} = \frac{1}{5},\ u_C^{-1} = \frac{1}{4}.$$

If observations are received at $t_0, t_1, t_2, t_3 = 0, 0.01, 0.11, 0.13$, we have to calculate the time between successive observations $\varDelta_l = t_l - t_{l-1}$. This gives

$$\varDelta_1, \varDelta_2, \varDelta_3 = 0.01, 0.1, 0.02.$$

If we apply Equation 1 for computing the transition probabilities, using $n = 2^{10} = 1024$ in the approximation, we get the following transition matrix

$$\mathbf{P}(\varDelta_1) = \mathbf{P}(0.01) = \begin{pmatrix} 0.9893 & 0.0097 & 0.0010 \\ 0.0390 & 0.9515 & 0.0096 \\ 0.0294 & 0.0097 & 0.9609 \end{pmatrix},$$

$$\mathbf{P}(\varDelta_2) = \mathbf{P}(0.1) = \begin{pmatrix} 0.9133 & 0.0752 & 0.0114 \\ 0.3102 & 0.6239 & 0.0659 \\ 0.2497 & 0.0752 & 0.6750 \end{pmatrix},$$

$$\mathbf{P}(\varDelta_3) = \mathbf{P}(0.02) = \begin{pmatrix} 0.9791 & 0.0188 & 0.0021 \\ 0.0759 & 0.9058 & 0.0184 \\ 0.0578 & 0.0188 & 0.9234 \end{pmatrix}.$$

We see from the matrices above that the probability of transferring to another state increases as the period between observations $\varDelta$ increases. For the special case $\varDelta = 0$, the probability of staying in the same state would be 1. Furthermore, we can see from the matrices that the rows sums to 1, as expected for a probability distribution. The computations were performed in Matlab. Only 10 matrix multiplications were necessary in order to compute a matrix to the power of 1024.

4 Multisensor Quantitative Risk Assessment

Following the terminology in [5], risk can be measured in terms of *consequences* and *likelihoods*. A consequence is the qualitative or quantitative outcome of an event, and the likelihood is the probability of the event. To perform risk assessment, we need a mapping: $\mathcal{C} : S \to \mathbb{R}$, describing the cost due to loss of confidentiality, integrity, and availability for each state of an asset.

The risk $\mathcal{R}_t = E[\mathcal{C}(x_t)]$ is the expected cost at time t, and it is a function of the hidden state x_t of an asset. The only information available about x_t is the distribution γ_t estimated by the HMM. The risk $\mathcal{R}_t^k$ estimated by sensor k is based on the observations Y_t^k from sensor k

$$\mathcal{R}_t^k = E[\mathcal{C}(x_t)|Y_t^k] = \sum_{i=1}^{N} \gamma_t^k(i)\mathcal{C}(s_i),$$

and the estimated variance $\sigma_t^2(k)$ of $\mathcal{R}_t^k$ is

$$\sigma_t^2(k) = Var[\mathcal{R}_t^k] = \sum_{i=1}^{N} \gamma_t^k(i)(\mathcal{C}(s_i) - \mathcal{R}_t^k)^2.$$

A new estimate of the risk $\mathcal{R}_t^0$ based on observations from all the K sensors, is formed by taking a weighted sum of the estimated risk from each sensor. Assuming the estimated risk from each sensor to be unbiased and independent random variables, we can then use the inverse of the variance as weights to get an unbiased minimum variance estimator of the risk. This can be shown by applying the Lagrange multiplier method, see Appendix A.

$$\begin{aligned} \mathcal{R}_t^0 &= E[\mathcal{C}(x_t)|Y_t^1, Y_t^2, \dots, Y_t^K] \\ &= \frac{\sum_{k=1}^{K} (\sigma_t^2(k))^{-1} \mathcal{R}_t^k}{\sum_{k=1}^{K} (\sigma_t^2(k))^{-1}}, \end{aligned} \tag{2}$$

and the variance $\sigma_t^2(0)$ of $\mathcal{R}_t^0$ can be estimated as follows

$$\sigma_t^2(0) = Var[\mathcal{R}_t^0] = \frac{1}{\sum_{k=1}^{K} \frac{1}{\sigma_t^2(k)}}. \tag{3}$$

A derivation of equation 3 is shown in Appendix A.

Example 2. Consider the same network as in Example 1. Assume that the server is monitored by two different sensors with the following states and cost values

$$\begin{aligned} S &= \{G, A, C\}, \\ \mathcal{C} &= (\mathcal{C}(G), \mathcal{C}(A), \mathcal{C}(C)) = (0, 5, 20). \end{aligned}$$

At time t, assume that the two HMMs of the two sensors have the following estimated state distributions

$$\gamma_t^1 = (0.90, 0.09, 0.01),$$
$$\gamma_t^2 = (0.70, 0.20, 0.10).$$

We are interested in finding an estimator for the risk of the monitored asset based on the input from the two sensors. As this estimator should have as little variance as possible, we wish to give more weight to the sensor with the best estimate, i.e., the sensor with the least variance. The weight is computed as the inverse of the variance from the two sensors. We compute the mean and variance of the risk from each sensor

$$\begin{aligned}
\mathcal{R}_t^1 &= 0.9 \times 0 + 0.09 \times 5 + 0.01 \times 20 = 0.650, \\
\mathcal{R}_t^2 &= 0.7 \times 0 + 0.2 \times 5 + 0.1 \times 20 = 3.000, \\
\sigma_t^2(1) &= 0.9(0 - 0.65)^2 + 0.09(5 - 0.65)^2 \\
&\quad + 0.01(20 - 0.65)^2 = 5.826, \\
\sigma_t^2(2) &= 0.7(0 - 3)^2 + 0.2(5 - 3)^2 + 0.1(20 - 3)^2 \\
&= 36.00.
\end{aligned}$$

We now combine the risk from each sensor to get a minimum variance estimate of the risk

$$\begin{aligned}
\mathcal{R}^0 &= \frac{\frac{1}{5.8275}0.65 + \frac{1}{36}3}{\frac{1}{5.8275} + \frac{1}{36}} &= 0.977, \\
\sigma_t^2(0) &= \frac{1}{\frac{1}{5.8275} + \frac{1}{36}} &= 5.016.
\end{aligned}$$

We see that the mean for the weighted risk is close to the mean for sensor 1. This is intuitive, as sensor 1 has the least variance. We can also see that the variance of the weighted risk is smaller than that of the individual sensors.

5 Conclusions and Further Work

We have addressed several issues to improve the proposed method for real-time risk assessment. The rate-based assessment is proposed as an alternative for some common sensors, and the weighted multisensor risk assessment method provides a mechanism for integrating sensors with varying accuracy and reliability into the system. The mechanisms proposed in this paper should be implemented and tested using real-life data and simulations, as previously done in [3]. Another issue that still remains is the problem of parameter estimation and learning. It is possible to set the model parameters using expert knowledge, but this is a cumbersome process, and it would be preferable to automate the process of estimating and learning the parameters.

References

1. Årnes, A., Sallhammar, K., Haslum, K., Brekne, T., Moe, M.E.G., Knapskog, S.J.: Real-time risk assessment with network sensors and intrusion detection systems. In: International Conference on Computational Intelligence and Security (CIS) (2005)
2. Årnes, A., Sallhammar, K., Haslum, K., Knapskog, S.J.: Real-time risk assessment with network sensors and hidden markov model. In: Proceedings of the 11th Nordic Workshop on Secure IT-systems (NORDSEC 2006) (2006)
3. Årnes, A., Valeur, F., Vigna, G., Kemmerer, R.A.: Using hidden markov models to evaluate the risk of intrusions. In: Proceedings of the 9th International Symposium on Recent Advances in Intrusion Detection, RAID 2006, Hamburg, Germany, pp. 20–22, (September 2006)
4. Stonebumer, G., Goguen, A., Feringa, A.: Risk management guide for information technology systems, National Institute of Standards and Technology, special publication pp. 800–830 (2002)
5. Standards Australia and Standards New Zealand: AS/NZS 4360: 2004 risk management (2004)
6. Gehani, A., Kedem, G.: Rheostat: Real-time risk management. In: Proceedings of the 7th International Symposium on Recent Advances in Intrusion Detection, RAID, Sophia Antipolis, France, September 15 – 17, 2004., Springer pp. 296–314 (2004)
7. Rabiner, L.R.: A tutorial on hidden markov models and selected applications in speech recognition. Readings in speech recognition, pp. 267–296 (1990)
8. Ross, S.M.: Introduction to Probability Models, 8th edn. Academic Press, New York (2003)

A Minimum Variance Estimator

Assume that we have K independent random variables $(x_k,\ k = 1, \ldots, K)$ with the same mean μ, and variance $Var[x_k] = \sigma_k^2$. A new random variable $x = \sum_{k=1}^{K} a_k x_k$ is constructed from $(x_k\ k = 1, \ldots, K)$, this new random variable should be unbiased $E[x] = \mu$ and have minimum variance

$$Var[x] = Var[\sum_{k=1}^{K} a_k x_k] = \sum_{k=1}^{K} a_k^2 Var[x_k] = \sum_{k=1}^{K} a_k^2 \sigma_k^2,$$

$$E[x] = E[\sum_{k=1}^{K} a_k x_k] = \sum_{k=1}^{K} a_k \mu = \mu \Rightarrow \sum_{k=1}^{K} a_k = 1$$

To find the optimal weights $(\bar{a}_k,\ k = 1, \ldots, K)$ we apply the Lagrange multiplier method to to minimise the performance index $f(a_1, a_2, \ldots, a_K) = \sum_{k=1}^{K} a_k^2 \sigma_k^2$, under the restriction $g(a_1, a_2, \ldots, a_K) = \sum_{k=1}^{K} a_k - 1 = 0$. This is done by solving the equation $\nabla f = \lambda \nabla g$, where ∇f denotes the gradient of f. This is equivalent to the following sets of partial differential equations

$$\frac{\partial}{\partial_{a_k}} \left[f + \lambda g \right]_{a_k = \bar{a}_k} = 0,\ (k = 1, \ldots, K),$$

$$\frac{\partial}{\partial_{a_k}} \left[\sum_{l=1}^{K} a_l^2 \sigma_l^2 + \lambda (\sum_{l=1}^{K} a_l - 1) \right]_{a_k = \bar{a}_k} = 0,\ (k = 1, \ldots, K). \tag{4}$$

When we take the derivatives we end up with the following set of lineare equations $2\bar{a}_k\sigma_k^2 + \lambda = 0$, with the solution $\bar{a}_k = -\frac{\lambda}{2\sigma_k^2}$, and $\lambda = \frac{-2}{\sum_{k=1}^{K}\frac{1}{\sigma_k^2}}$. This gives us the optimal weights

$$\bar{a}_k = \frac{\frac{1}{\sigma_k^2}}{\sum_{k=1}^{K}\frac{1}{\sigma_k^2}},$$

and the variance

$$Var[x] = \sum_{k=1}^{K}\left(\frac{\frac{1}{\sigma_k^2}}{\sum_{k=1}^{K}\frac{1}{\sigma_k^2}}\right)^2 \sigma_k^2 = \frac{1}{\sum_{k=1}^{K}\frac{1}{\sigma_k^2}}.$$

A Load Scattering Algorithm for Dynamic Routing of Automated Material Handling Systems

Alex K.S. Ng, Janet Efstathiou, and Henry Y.K. Lau

University of Oxford, the University of Hong Kong
{alex.ng, janet.efstathiou}@eng.ox.ac.uk, hyklau@hku.hk

Abstract. An agent-based dynamic routing strategy for a generic automated material handling systems (AMHS) is developed. The strategy employs an agent-based paradigm in which the control points of a network of AMHS components are modelled as cooperating node agents. With the inherent features of route discovery a set of shortest and near-shortest path, an average-flow route selection algorithm is developed to scatter the load of an AMHS. Their performance is investigated through a detailed simulation study. The performance of the proposed dynamic routing strategy is benchmarked with the shortest path algorithm. The results of the simulation experiments are presented and their performance compared under a number of performance indices including the hop count, flow and ability to balance network loading.

1 Introduction

The performance of an automated material handling system (AMHS) can often be measured by its ability to undertake efficient material flow. AMHS are commonly found in distribution centres, cargo terminals and logistics infrastructures where movement of cargo and goods under particular routing strategy is a major factor that determines their performance. Such routing strategy determines the movement of a shipment from a source location to a destination location.

Existing routing strategies that aim at minimizing the transit time and scalability often use static routing information based on heuristics such as shortest-distance for assigning routes for shipments. Static routing information that is stored in routing tables is computed every time when the system layout is modified or its operation changed. These strategies generate routing solutions that may not reflect the current status of the system and fails to consider changes such as arrival pattern and congestion in the operating environment.

As a result, these strategies often produce sub-optimal solutions by moving shipment to a destination through highly congested paths while other less congested paths are available. As a consequence, shipment may spend more time than actually needed that lowering the efficiency of the whole system. From a system prospective, this unbalanced utilization of system resources often leads to bottlenecks. To enable efficient and robust material flow, and scalable system configuration, a dynamic routing approach is essential.

In this paper, a routing algorithm for determining the best route for scattering material flow under a dynamic operating environment is introduced. The algorithm

Y. Wang, Y. Cheung, and H. Liu (Eds.): CIS 2006, LNAI 4456, pp. 704–713, 2007.

making used of an agent-based control architecture that an AMHS is modelled as a set of generic automated equipment/units in the structure of network connecting by unidirectional links. In other words, individual node represents system control points where shipment flows are controlled and the unidirectional links represent the physical path between system control points.

Under the proposed strategy, a generic AMHS network is modelled as a network of material handling sub-systems that is modelled by a graph $G(N, L)$ where N is the set of autonomous node agents representing the decision or control points of the AMHS while L is the set of unidirectional links of shipment flow paths that connects different control points such that $n_1, n_2, \ldots, n_{m-1}, n_m$ are the set of node agents and $l_1, l_2, \ldots, l_{k-1}, l_k$ are the set of multi-dimensional link vectors. Figure 1 shows a generic AMHS network. The nodes represent individual system control points and the links represents the physical path between control points. Each node can only obtain information from the neighbouring nodes so it forms the transmission range of each node.

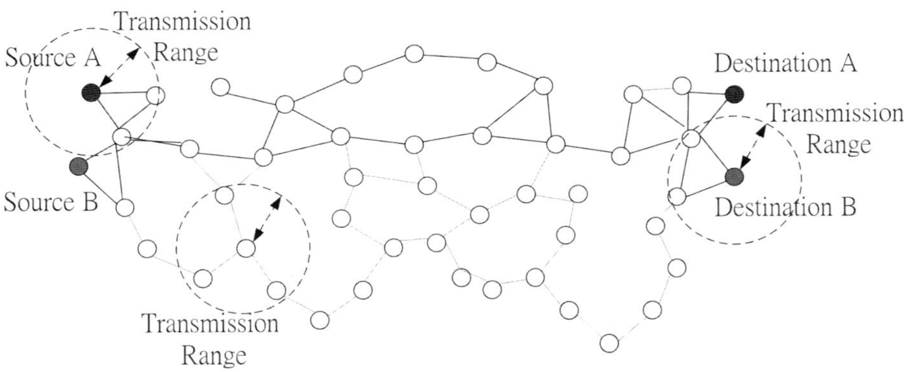

Fig. 1. A generic AMHS network

Under this abstraction, the AMHS routing problem can be mapped to a network routing problem where shipment is moved from origin nodes to destination nodes via a network of intermediate automated equipment of which the objective is to determine the best route under a set of dynamically changing constraints. In this paper, we quantify the best route by the hop count of the material flow and the balance of equipment utilization.

Following the introduction, Section 2 reviews the existing dynamic routing algorithms. Section 3 presents our proposed average-flow routing algorithm. Section 4 presents the simulation results. Section 5 concludes the contribution of this paper.

2 AMHS Dynamic Routing Architecture

In an automated material handling system, the control of material flow is often determined by its routing strategies. These strategies can be classified broadly into static and dynamic routing strategies.

Static routing strategies employ conventional static routing tables that contain pre-computed routes for each origin-destinations pair that are generated by heuristics such as shortest distance heuristics or minimum utilization of resources. One limitation of the static routing strategies is that they failed to consider the current status of the routing network and hence results in ineffective routing decisions and poor resources utilization [1]. In order to overcome the inflexibility of static routing, dynamic routing approaches are developed with a view to improve equipment utilization and reduction in running costs.

Dynamic routing can be achieved by exchanging real-time network information to determine an optimal route from a large number of possible choices. Distributed state-dependent real-time dynamic routing approach can further be divided into proactive routing scheme and reactive routing scheme.

Proactive routing scheme such as Optimized Link State Routing (OLSR) [2] and Global State Routing (GSR) [3] computes routes to all destinations at start-up and maintains these routes using a periodic route update process. These scheme aims to maintain a global view of the network topology. Reactive routing scheme such as Adaptive Distance Vector routing (ADV) [4] and Dynamic Source Routing (DSR) [5] computes routes as required by a source location through a discovery process. The

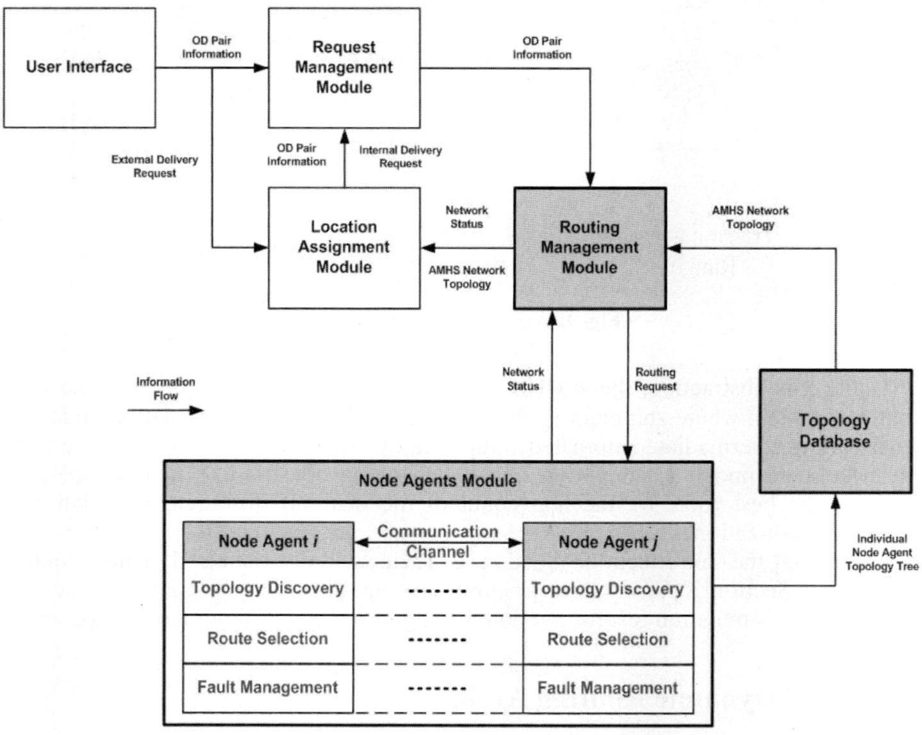

Fig. 2. The Conceptual framework of the proposed dynamic routing strategy

scheme aims to reduce the control overhead due to periodic network update by maintaining the current network state only in route discovery. When an optimal route is produced for an OD pair, the route is used repeatedly until it is not viable. The scheme is more efficient than proactive schemes in a highly dynamic operating environment. As the quality of a particular route may fluctuate over time, the optimality of the routing may not be maintained, resulting in limited efficiency and scalability for large-scale networks.

The proposed framework (Figure 2) consists of 6 modules including User Interface, Request Management Module, Location Assignment Module, Routing Management Module, Topology Database, and Node Agents Module.

The Node Agent Module is the key to the routing framework consisting of a set of distributed homogeneous node agents. These node agents are responsible for the selection of routes given the origin-destination (OD) requests that are generated by the Routing Management Module, and for updating the network status. Node agents are autonomous in nature and can be geographically distributed in an AMHS network in which routing decisions are made through their cooperation. By sharing of network information, node agents acquire resources and generate feasible routing solutions in a dynamic operating environment. With these node agents, the framework exhibits three key features, namely, (a) route discovery, (b) route selection, and (c) fault detection and restoration. In this paper, we focus on route discovery and route selection.

The Request Management Module receives external and internal delivery requests and process the OD information for the Routing Management Module for route assignment. The Routing Management Module is responsible for coordinating the movement of the shipment. OD information is validated by consulting the latest AMHS network topology obtained from the Topology Database. Validated OD requests are sent to the Node Agent Module. Changes in the Topology Database will result in the update of the Location Assignment Module by the Routing Management Module. The Topology Database stores configuration information of an AMHS network for the Routing Management Module and the Location Assignment Module. The Location Assignment Module computes the destination location for a delivery request. Decisions are made on the basis of the current network status obtained from the Routing Management Module. The User Interface provides channels for information exchange.

Considering these dynamic routing schemes, the reactive approach is most computational efficient for dynamic routing in an integrated AMHS. In particular, the routing between OD pairs is on-demand and is determined by the current system status that the most efficient solution can be computed. With the availability of transmitting flow status of each node, an on-demand routing algorithm for AMHS can be achieved (Figure 3).

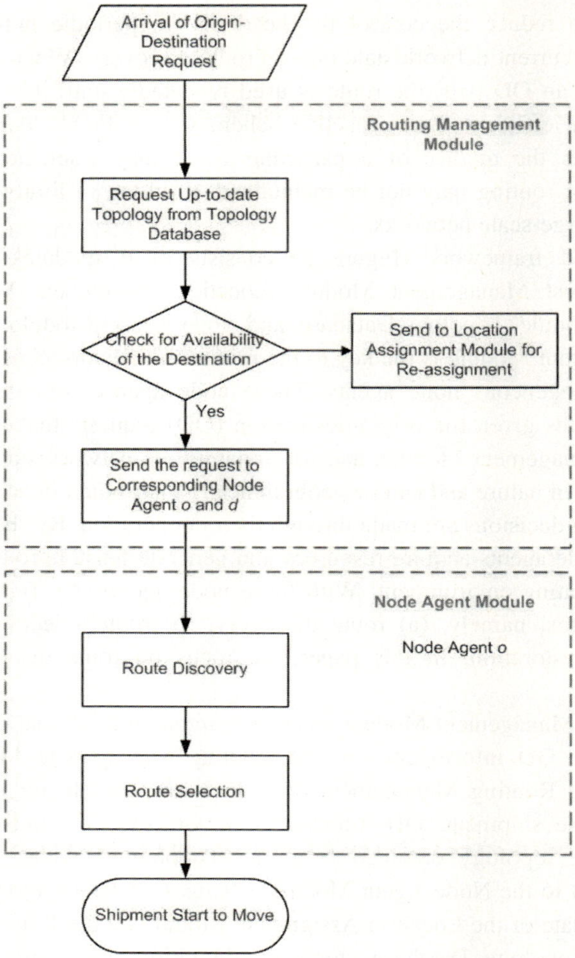

Fig. 3. High level decision logic of the routing framework

3 Route Selection

In dynamic routing, route selection is an important issue for integrated AMHS. The main objective of route selection is to select a feasible route that achieves the most efficient resource utilization with minimum travelling distance and costs [6]. Existing routing algorithms use the shortest distance heuristic as the criteria for route selection, for example for routing of vehicles [7], and routing of communication networks [8] by using different shortest path algorithms such as Dijkstra's algorithm and Belhnan-Ford [9]. However, these algorithms require a centralized control scheme.

In our control architecture, the agent needs to gather network information from others control points to work out the best route. Two major strategies, namely, the utilization-based and distance-based strategies are commonly adopted. Utilization-based route selection strategies aim to select the best route such that the utilization of the network is balanced (e.g. [10]-[12]). Distance-based route selection strategies select routes with the shortest distance for a delivery request [11]. By nature of the algorithm, neither distanced-based nor utilization-based route selection strategies can best balance of the network utilization and minimize the distance-related network costs. Hence, different hybrid strategies are developed including Widest-Shortest Path (WSP) [13] that selects a path with the minimum distance in terms of hop count among all possible routes and Shortest Widest Path strategies (SWP) [14] that finds a path with the lowest utilization.

However, these strategies cannot sufficiently fulfil the requirements of route selection of an AMHS network, where congestion and cycle time are the prime concerns. SWP sometimes select a route which distance is too long, while WSP may select a route via congested node(s) [6]. In order to minimize the cycle time and balance the equipment utilization, strategies that combine these two objectives with novel routing selection algorithm should be used.

Node agents use a two-stage route selection algorithm for selecting the best route. Our approach incorporates the use of shortest path and least flow. Our algorithm is divided into two stages, possible shortest path discovery and least flow selection. In the stage of possible shortest path discovery, the origin node broadcast the request of route to its neighbouring nodes with the information of destination nodes in the message header. The neighbouring nodes will evaluate the destination nodes of the request message. If they are not the destination nodes, they will pass the messages to their neighbours. This process will continue until that the request message have reached the destination nodes.

When the destination node receives the request message, it will reply the source nodes via the intermediates recorded in the request messages. In the reply message, the intermediate nodes include their updated flow status. In this route recovery process, a number of request messages arrive in the destination node via different intermediate nodes. The destination node reply to these messages up to an pre-defined upper bound, for example six request messages and the origin nodes wait for the return of reply message up to an pre-defined upper bound, for example reply messages with 2 extra hop counts than the first coming message or 180 seconds. Any reply message beyond the first six messages will be rejected and any messages exceeding the time limit will be died. This upper bound limit is designed to limit the possible route candidates and reduced the pending due to the route discovery process. Once the origin node receives all the potential route candidates, these candidates are evaluated by the average-flow algorithm. In this paper, a novel evaluation criterion to scatter the flow of routes, namely average operational flow, in the network is presented. Average operational flow is the sum of individual load along the route divided by the hop count. Equation 1 shows the definition of average operational flow, $B(N,r)$.

$$B(N,r) = \frac{\sum_{k \neq i, k \neq j} L_k^{i \to j}}{H} \tag{1}$$

where i is the origin node, j is the destination node, k is the intermediate node, $L_k^{i \to j}$ is the flow of intermediate links from origin node i to destination node j via node k and H is the hop count that is the number of links from origin node i to destination node j. Average operational flow describes the load of links in the routes. When route passes through heavily loaded links in the network, the average operational flow of the route increase and make the route less desirable due to the possible congestion on heavily loaded nodes. In this paper, average operational flow of each potential route candidate is compared and the route with the smallest average operational flow is selected.

Intuitively, the stage of possible shortest route discovery produces a set of possible candidates with shortest and near-shortest paths. By the mechanism of broadcasting the request message to the neighbouring nodes, the first arrival message to the destination node is the message via the shortest path. With the consideration of a set of routes longer the shortest path, this algorithm include a set of routes with reasonable distance, which is the optimal set against the travelled distance. If the shortest path is selected, the route of two OD pairs may overlap completely which produces congestion (Figure 4). In this algorithm, the shortest path may not be selected due to the heavy flows.

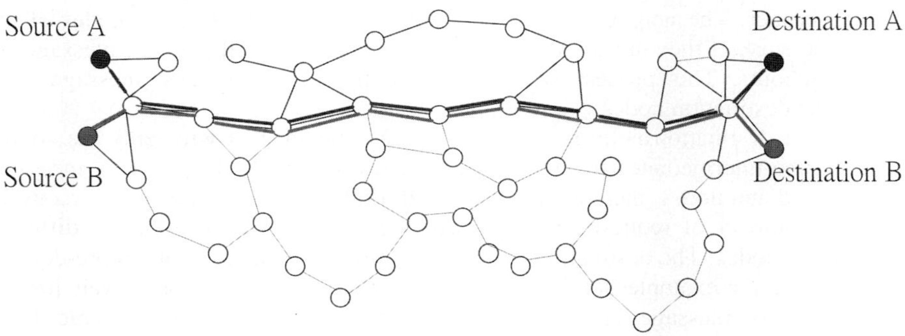

Fig. 4. Routing algorithm with shortest path

In the second stage of the algorithm, the optimal set of routes is evaluated by the average operational flow. With the consideration of novel flow parameter along the route, the heavily congested route will be ruled out and the least congested route in the optimal set is selected. If the least flow route is selected from all possible routes, the selected route may take a longer path to reach the destination and cause a longer travelling time (Route B2 in Figure 5). This selection is not optimal against both parameters of shortest path and least flow. With the proposed algorithm, this problem is modelled into a multi-criterion optimisation problem that the optimal route is selected against both parameters of path distance and least flow (Route B1 in Figure 5).

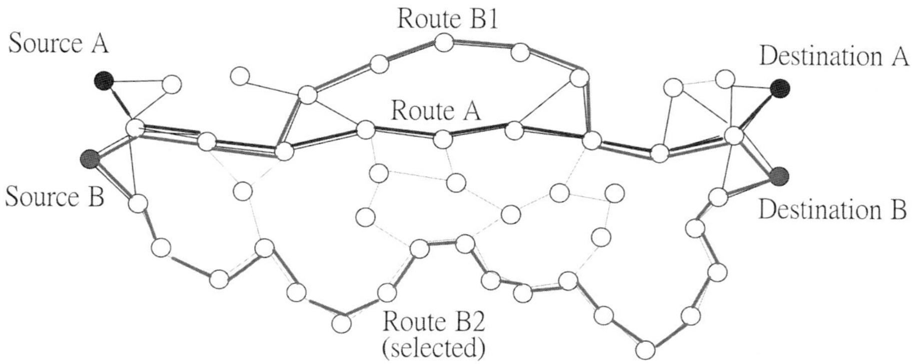

Fig. 5. Routing algorithm with least flow

4 Simulation Results

In this paper, a MATLAB simulator is developed to realize the proposed average flow route selection algorithm. Figure 6 shows a schematic diagram of MATLAB AMHS simulator.

In this simulator, an AMHS system is modelled as a network that the adjacency matrix is defined in the Topology module. The flow of the system is inputted by the Flow module. The Routing module specified the routing selection algorithm of the system. The Performance Indicator module produces the plots of the simulated systems. In this paper, a simple network of 20 nodes is simulated against two algorithm, namely shortest path algorithm and average flow routing algorithm with three different values of possible shortest route discovery parameter which are either shortest path plus one, two or three. In these simulations, the possible set of route candidates are selected either from the shortest path, an extra hop longer, two hops longer or three hops longer. The simulated network requires transporting 50 overall shipments per unit time with individual resource rated at 20 shipments per unit time.

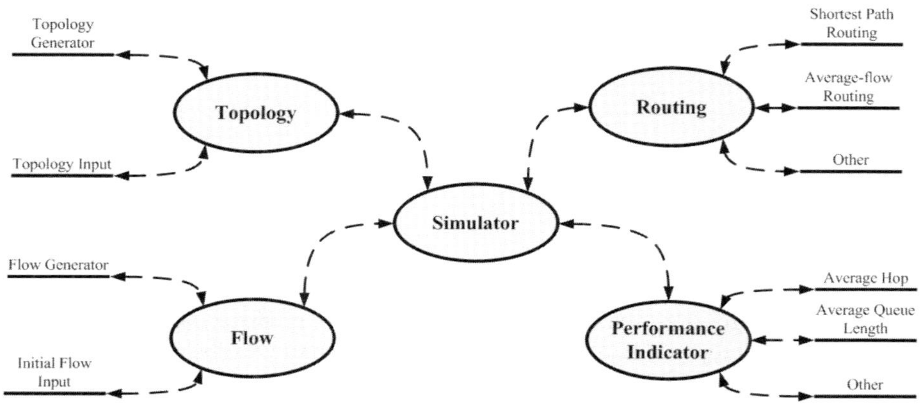

Fig. 6. Schematic diagram of MATLAB AMHS network simulator

In the simulation results, Figures 5a, 6a and 7a show the difference in hop count between average-flow routing algorithm and shortest path routing algorithm. The difference in hop count is calculated by the Equation 2.

$$\textit{Difference in hop count} = H_{af} - H_{sp} \tag{2}$$

where H_{af} is the hop count of routes using average-flow algorithm and H_{sp} is the hop count of routes using shortest path algorithm. The difference in hop count is always positive as the shortest path route is the lower bound of the hop count. If the difference is smaller, the shorter is the travelled distance via routes.

$$\textit{Difference in hop count} = \frac{Q_{sp} - Q_{af}}{Q_{sp}} \tag{3}$$

where Q_{af} is the queue length of routes using average-flow algorithm and Q_{sp} is the queue length of routes using shortest path algorithm. The difference in queue is always positive showing that there are improvements of reducing the queue by the average-flow algorithm. If the difference is greater, the smaller is the queue length of each node.

Table 1 shows the comparison between average-flow algorithm and the shortest path algorithm. By comparing the maximum queue length between two algorithms, the average-flow algorithm reduced the maximum queue by 18-, 11- and 34-fold respectivly. By comparing the sum of queue length between two algorithms, the average-flow algorithm reduced the sum of queue length by 12-, 19- and 27-fold respectively.

Table 1. Comparison between average-flow algorithm with shortest path algorithm

	Queue Length				Difference in Hop Count	Difference in Queue Length
	Shortest path algorithm		Average-flow algorithm			
	Maximum	sum	maximum	Sum	Sum	Sum
Shortest path + 1	76	3109	4	236	34	2873
Shortest path + 2	107	8256	9	403	101	7853
Shortest path + 3	210	15328	6	549	448	14779

5 Conclusion

In this paper, an AMHS system is modelled as a network of sub-systems that the shipments of cargos are achieved by the routing of self-organized control agents. The novel routing is proposed that the algorithm is divided into two stages: possible route discovery and route selection. In this algorithm, the shortest and near-shortest paths are selected as the candidates of potential routes which are evaluated by their current flow. The route with the least flow is selected to transport the shipment from the origin node to destination node. A MATLAB AMHS simulator is developed to investigate the proposed algorithm. The simulation results show that the average queue of the system is improved by 9.85% with the increment of hop count of 2.24%. The maximum and average queue length of nodes can be reduced by 34- and 27-fold respectively. These reductions of queue length can reduced the queue of nodes and prevent the queue cascading to other nodes. Further simulations will be conducted to investigate the average-flow algorithm with a large scale AMHS and queue cascading effect.

References

1. Ash, G.R.: Dynamic Routing in Telecommunication Networks. McGraw-Hill, New York (1998)
2. Jacquet, P., Muhlethaler, P., Clausen, T., Laouiti, A., Qayyum, A., Viennot, L.: Optimized link state routing protocol for ad hoc networks. Proceedings of IEEE Multi Topic Conference: Technology for the 21st Century, pp. 62 – 68 (2001)
3. Chen, T., Gerla, M.: Global State Routing: A new routing scheme for ad hoc wireless networks. In: Proceedings of IEEE International conference of communication (1998)
4. Boppana, R. V., Konduru, S. P.: An adaptive distance vector routing algorithm for mobile, ad hoc networks. In: Proceedings of 20th Annual Joint Conference of the IEEE Computer and Communications Societies, vol. 3, pp. 1753–1762 (2001)
5. Wang, L., Zhang, L. F., Shu, Y. T., Dong, M.: Multi-path source routing in wireless ad hoc networks. Proceedings of Canadian Conference on Electrical and Computer Engineering, vol. 1, pp. 479–483 (2000)
6. Marzo, J. L., Calle, E., Scoglio, C., Anjali, T.: QoS online routing and MPLS multi-level protection: A survey. IEEE Communications Magazine, pp. 126–132 (2003)
7. Wang, F.K., Lin, J.T.: Performance evaluation of an automated material handling system for a wafer fab. Robotics and Computer Integrated Manufacturing 20, 91–100 (2004)
8. Griss, M.L., Pour, G.: Accelerating development with agent components. IEEE Computation Magazine 35(5), 37–41 (2002)
9. Evans, J. R., Minieka, E.: Optimization Algorithms for Networks and Graphs. M. Dekker, New York, 2nd edition (1992)
10. Chen, Z., Berger, T.: Performace Analysis of Random Routing algorithm for n-D connected networks. In: Proceedings of the IEEE Region 10 Annual International Conference '93, pp. 233–236 (1993)
11. Qi, W. D., Dong, M., Shen, Q. G., Chen, H.: How smooth is Smoothed Round Robin. In: Proceedings of International Conference on Communication Technology 2003, pp. 421–428 (2003)
12. Gokhale, S. S., Tripathi, S. K.: Routing metrics for best-effort traffic. In: Proceedings of Eleventh International Conference on Computer Communications and Networks, pp. 595–598 (2002)
13. Elsayed, K.M.F.: A framework for end-to-end deterministic-delay service provisioning in multiservice packet networks. IEEE Transactions on Multimedia 7(3), 563–571 (2003)
14. Sobrinho, J.L.: Algebra and algorithms for QoS path computation and hop-by-hop routing in the Internet. IEEE/ACM Transactions on Networking 10(4), 541–550 (2002)

Software Agents Action Securities

Vojislav Stojkovic[1] and Hongwei Huo[2]

[1] Morgan State University, Computer Science Department, CA205
1700 East Cold Spring Lane, Baltimore, MD 21251, USA
stojkovi@jewel.morgan.edu

[2] Xidian University, School of Computer Science and Technology
Xi'an 710071, China
hwhuo@mail.xidian.edu.cn

Abstract. Software agents may interact with other agents (including software agents, machines, and human beings), ask for services from other agents, and/or give services to other agents. Software agent security ensures that a software agent can protect its information and services. This paper presents some aspects of software agents securities and focuses on software agents action securities.

1 Introduction

Many years long trend in the software leads to design small, modular pieces of code, where each module performs a well-defined, focused task. Software agents are the latest product of that trend. Software agents are programmed to interact with other agents (including software agents, machines, and human beings), ask for services from other agents, and/or give services to other agents. Software agents act autonomously with prescribed backgrounds, beliefs, and operations. For more on software agents see [2, 3, 4].

A multiagent system, as defined by Weiss in [7], is a system of agents. It can access and manipulate diverse data such as data on the Internet.

An infrastructure to support multiagent system must provide two types of security:

- the infrastructural security and
- the agent security.

The infrastructural security ensures that an agent cannot cover-up as another agent. The agent security ensures that an agent can protect its information and services.

In the last few years agent security is one of the most important and active field of Agents.

The agent security can be split into two components:

- agent data security and
- agent action security.

For more on computer security see [1] and software security see [6].

Y. Wang, Y. Cheung, and H. Liu (Eds.): CIS 2006, LNAI 4456, pp. 714–724, 2007.

IMPACT (Interactive Maryland Platform for Agents Collaborating Together), an experimental agent infrastructure that translates formal theories of agents into a functional multiagent system that can extend legacy software code and application specific or legacy data structures has great influence on our work. We have tried to elevate Subrahmanian's [5] work on software agents action security making it more formal for scientific, more understandable for education purposes, and all together more applicable.

Agent data security is based on the following data security principle: there may be restrictions on how one agent may read, write, or manipulate data of another agent.

Agent action security is based on the following action security principle: there may be restrictions on how one agent may use actions of another agent.

The ability to build agents on the top of arbitrary pieces of code – the disparate diverse data sources and software packages is critical to agents enterprise.

2 Agents

An agent is a persistent goal-oriented entity that may move between hosts (environments - worlds) in response to changes in requirements such as security, efficiency, and cost.

Hosts, by the rule, are limited in the computational resources such as processor time, memory, network bandwidth, and etc.

An agent, as defined by Russel and Norvig in [3], must be capable of autonomous actions at host (in environment) in order to satisfy its design objectives.

An intelligent agent is a complex computer system that is capable of flexible autonomous actions in an environment in order to satisfy its objectives and has the properties conceptualized and/or implemented using concepts such as knowledge, belief, choice, decision, capability, intention, obligation, commitment, etc.

An agent model is characterized by the fact that it is possible to develop (write, construct, make, build, etc.) independent agents (units, routines, functions, modules, pieces of code, systems, machines, etc.) to do something with some purposes. This approach asserts that agents are self-contained, though they may contain references to other agents.

An agent can be implemented as:

- an agent architecture or
- an agent function.

An agent architecture is a classical approach to building agents viewing them as a type of knowledge based system. Typically it includes data structures and operations on data structures.

A function/action rule R is a clause of the form

$$\text{R: A} \leftarrow L_1, L_2, ..., L_m$$

where:
- A is an action status atom;
- L_i, $1 \leq i \leq m$, is either an action status atom or a code call atom, each of which may be preceded by a negation operator $\neg$.

An agent function/action rule maps atoms/percept from an environment to an action. It uses some internal data structures updated as a new percept arrives. These data structures are operated on by the agent's decision-making procedures to generate an action choice, which is then passed to the architecture to be executed.

An agent program is a finite collection of agent functions/action rules. An agent program runs on a computing device, called architecture.

The architecture might be:
- a computer
- a special-purpose hardware for certain tasks
- a software that provides a degree of insulation between the computer and the agent program.

The architecture:
- makes the percepts from the sensors available to the agent program
- runs the agent program
- feeds the agent program's action choices to the effectors as they are generated.

The relationship among agent, architecture, and agent program can be expressed as:

$$\text{agent} = \text{architecture} + \text{agent program}$$

3 Agents Action Securities

An agent must have an action policy or an action strategy.

An agent may be:
- obliged to take certain actions
- permitted to take some actions
- forbidden to take another actions.

Agent action security specifies:
- what an agent obliged to do
- what an agent permitted to do
- what an agent forbidden to do
- how an agent selects a sequence of actions to achieve, obligations, permissions, and restrictions.

Agent action security has the set of operators

$$\text{O, P, F, W, Do, ...}$$

where:
- O means Oblige
- P means Permit
- F means Forbidden
- W means Waived-Obligation
- Do means Do/take action.

The sequence ActionSecurity(agentA, agentB) is the sequence of action securities of the agent A for the agent B.
⟨ action security sequence ⟩ ::= ⟨ action security ⟩; ⟨ action security⟩;
⟨ action security ⟩ ::= ⟨ action security statement ⟩

An action security statement has two syntax forms:
⟨action security statement⟩ ::=
⟨forbidden action sequence⟩
[
⟨repair action sequence⟩
where ⟨code call condition⟩
]
|
⟨forbidden action sequence⟩
when ⟨code call condition⟩
[
⟨repair action sequence⟩
where ⟨code call condition⟩
]

The repair part of the action security statement is the optional.
⟨repair action sequence⟩
where ⟨code call condition⟩

A forbidden action sequence is a sequence of f-actions that leaves the agent in the state that makes code call condition true.
⟨forbidden action sequence⟩ ::= **forbid** ⟨f-action sequence⟩
⟨f-action sequence⟩ ::= ⟨action sequence⟩

An action sequence is a regular expression consists of actions composed with the operators:
- ";" - binary infix sequence operator
- "|" - binary infix alternative operator and
- "*" - unary postfix closure operator.

An action sequence can be nested arbitrarily.

⟨action sequence⟩ ::= ⟨action⟩ { ⟨sequence operator⟩ ⟨action⟩ }
⟨action⟩ ::= ⟨term⟩ { ⟨alternative operator⟩ ⟨term⟩ }
⟨term⟩ ::= ⟨term⟩ ⟨closure operator⟩ { ⟨closure operator⟩ }
⟨term⟩ ::= "(" ⟨action⟩ ")"
⟨sequence operator⟩ ::= ";"
⟨alternative operator⟩ ::= "|"
⟨closure operator⟩ ::= "*"

An action is defined by action name and action arguments.
⟨action⟩ ::= ⟨action name⟩ "(" ⟨action arguments⟩ ")"
⟨action name⟩ ::= ⟨name⟩

⟨action arguments⟩ ::= ⟨action argument⟩ {”,” ⟨action argument⟩ }
⟨action argument⟩ ::= ⟨argument⟩

Names and arguments are further defined by the syntax of the appropriate programming language or operating system language.

An action argument may be unspecified. An underscore symbol ”_” on the place of an action argument means that the action argument is unspecified.

Example of an action sequence

The action sequence
open(_ , rw); read(_)*; write(_)
means:
- open a file in rw(read/write) mode
- perform zero or more read operations
- perform a write operation.

Example of a forbidden action sequence

forbid open(_ , rw); read(_)*; write(_)

means that the following action sequences are forbidden.
open(_ , rw); read(_)*; write(_)
⟨repair action sequence⟩ ::= **repair** ⟨r-action sequence⟩
⟨r-action action sequence⟩ ::= ⟨action sequence⟩

A code call condition is a conjunction of code call atoms.
⟨code call condition⟩ ::= ⟨code call atom⟩ { & ⟨code call atom⟩}

A code call condition is a logical expression that access the data of heterogeneous software sources using the pre-existing external application program interface (API) function calls provided by the appropriate software package.

A code call condition is a generic query language that can span multiple abstractions of software code.
⟨code code atom⟩ ::= in(X, ⟨ code call ⟩) | not_in(X, ⟨ code call ⟩)
X ::= ⟨variable symbol⟩ | ⟨object⟩

A code call atom has a Boolean value. A code call atom may be thought of as a special type of a logical atom.

in(X, ⟨code call⟩ has the value true, if X can be set to a pointer to one of the objects in the set of objects returned by executing the code call.

not_in(X, ⟨code call⟩) has the value true, if X is not in the set returned by code call or if X cannot be set to a pointer to one of the objects in the set of objects returned by executing the code call.
⟨repair action sequence⟩
where ⟨code call condition⟩
only exists as the part of the action security statement.

The repair action sequence may provide:
- an alternative services or
- a repair service.

The action security statements

forbid α_1; α_2; ...; α_m
repair β_1; β_2; ...;β_n **where** χ_1 & χ_2 & ...& χ_v

or

forbid α_1; α_2; ...; α_m **when** χ'_1 & χ'_2 & ...& χ'_u
repair β_1; β_2; ...;β_n **where** χ_1 & χ_2 & ...& χ_v

replace the last element α_m of the f-action sequence α_1; α_2; ...; α_m by the r-action sequence β_1; β_2; ...;β_n. $\alpha_m \leftarrow \beta_1$; β_2; ...;β_n.

Example of an alternative service

A forbidden action - unix command ls, that would let to the agent B to see the whole content of the current directory, may be replaced by a restricted action - unix command ls filename1 filename2, that would let to the agent B to see the only allowed files filename1and filename2.

This scenario may be achieved with the following action security statement.

forbid ls **repair** ls filename1 filename2 **where** χ.

Example of a repair service

The agent A is willing to manipulate files upon requests from the agent B, with the limitation that one file may be simultaneously open. In case of violations, the agent A may be cooperative and close the first file before opening the second file.

This scenario may be achieved with the following action security statement

forbid
open(_ , _);
(read(_ , _) | write(_ , _))*;
open(_ , _)
repair close(OldFile); open(NewFile, Mode)
where
in(oldFile, A: OpenFileTable(b)) &
O open(NewFile, Mode)

The logical expression

in(oldFile, A: OpenFileTable(b)) & O open(NewFile, Mode)
is the code call condition.

in(oldFile, A: OpenFileTable(b)) is the code call atom.

oldFile is the object of the output type of the code call.

A: OpenFileTable(b) is the code call. The code call atom in(oldFile, A: OpenFileTable(b)) succeeds because oldFile can be set to a pointer to one of the objects of the set of objects returned by executing the code call A: OpenFileTable(b).

O open(NewFile, Mode) is an action status atom and means that the agent is obliged to take action open(NewFile, Mode).

O is the oblige operator. The value of a code call atom is a Boolean values.

Example of the action security statement alternative syntax form

The agent AutomaticTellerMachine should obey a request from the agent Customer to withdraw money from the agent AutomaticTellerMachine only if the request to withdraw money does not put the CustomerBalance to be smaller than the minimum Balance.

Suppose that the minimum Balance is minBalance. If the CurrentBalance is already at the minBalance, a request to move the CurrentBalance to a lower balance must be ignored-rejected.

The sequence of action securities of the agent AutomaticTellerMachine for the agent Customer, ActionSecurity(AutomaticTellerMachine, Customer), must has an action security defined by an action security statement such as

forbid setBalance(CurrentBalance)
  when
    in
    (Withdraw, AutomaticTellerMachine: getWithdraw())
     &
    CurrentBalance-Withdraw < minBalance

No repair action is specified. The forbidden action setBalance(CurrentBalance) is ignored.

4 Agent Security Package

An Agent security package consists of the following and many other functions:
- CompileActionSecurityStatement
- Forbidden
- Done.

4.1 CompileActionSecurityStatement Function

An action security statement S_i,

forbid α_1^i; α_2^i; ... ; α_m^i
  repair β_1^i; β_2^i; ... ; β_n^i **where** χ_1^i& χ_2^i& ... & χ_v^i
or

forbidα^i_1; α^i_2; ... ; α^i_m **when**χ'^i_1& χ'^i_2& ... & χ'^i_u
repair β^i_1; β^i_2; ... ; β^i_n **where**χ^i_1&χ^i_2& ... & χ^i_v

can be compiled into the pair
(finite automaton, sequence of action rules) = $(FA, R_1, R_2, ..., R_w)$,
where i = 1, 2, ...

Sequence of action rules $R_1; R_2; ...; R_w$ replaces the last action of the i-th f-action sequence , α^i_m, with the i-th r-action sequence β^i_1; β^i_2; ... ; β^i_n

$\alpha^i_m \leftarrow \beta^i_1$; β^i_2; ... ; β^i_n

The input of the finite automaton FA is the sequence of action security statement

$S_1; S_2; ...; S_i; ...; S_j;$

The output of the finite automaton FA is the index i of the security statement S_i, if the security statement S_i includes the recognized the f-action sequence

α^i_1; α^i_2; ... ; α^i_m. $\delta(S_1; S_2; ...; S_i; ...; S_j; ...) = i$

δ function is the transition function of the finite automaton FA.

δ function is defined by δ' function which is the transition function of the finite automaton FA'.

The input of the finite automaton FA' is an action security statement S.

The output of the finite automaton FA' is true - accepted, if the security statement S includes the recognized the f-action sequence.

The output of the finite automaton FA' is false - rejected, if the security statement S includes the recognized the f-action sequence.

δ'(S) = boolean constant

δ' function has to "cover" all f-action sequences and it is a complex function.

The CompileActionSecurityStatement function constructs the finite automata FA.

The CompileActionSecurityStatement function produces for the action security statement S_i

forbid α^i_1; α^i_2; ... ; α^i_m
repair β^i_1; β^i_2; ... ; β^i_n **where** χ^i_1&χ^i_2&...&χ^i_v

the following rules

WX $\leftarrow$
O X &
in(i, SecurityPackage(a): Forbidden(X))

O α_j $\leftarrow$
O X &
in(i, SecurityPackage(a): Forbidden(X)) & χ^i_1&χ^i_2&...&χ^i_v

where $i, j = 1, ..., n$.

The first rule blocks the last action X of the forbidden sequence.

The other rules trigger the repair actions α_j, whose parameters may have been instantiated by evaluating $\chi_1^i \& \chi_2^i \& \ ... \ \& \ \chi_v^i$.

Two rules are triggered only when action X completes an instance of α_1^i; α_2^i; ... ; α_m^i, as checked by in(i, SecurityPackage(a): Forbidden(X)).

This check is performed only on the action X that are obligatory because OX holds and hence about to be executed.

The CompileActionSecurityStatement function produces for the action security statement S_i

forbid α_1^i; α_2^i; ... ; α_m^i **when**$\chi'^i_1 \& \ \chi'^i_2 \& \ ... \ \& \ \chi'^i_u$
  repair β_1^i; β_2^i; ... ; β_n^i **where**$\chi_1^i \& \chi_2^i \& \ ... \ \& \ \chi_v^i$

the following rules

WX ←
  O X &
  in(i, SecurityPackage(a): Forbidden(X)) & $\chi'^i_1 \& \ \chi'^i_2 \& \ ... \ \& \ \chi'^i_u$

O α_j ←
  O X &
  in(i, SecurityPackage(a): Forbidden(X)) & $\chi_1^i \& \chi_2^i \& ... \& \chi_v^i$ &
    $\chi'^i_1 \& \ \chi'^i_2 \& \ ... \ \& \ \chi'^i_u$

where $i, j = 1, ..., n$.

4.2 Forbidden Function

The output of the finite automaton FA, the index i, can be read with the function Forbidden.

The Forbidden(Action) function provides the action Action to the input of the finite automaton.

If the last executed action is followed by Action and constitutes an instance of the regular expression specified in the i-th statement, then the index i is returned.

If the sequence matches two or more statements, then the least index i is returned.

If no statement is matched, then the OK value is returned. The finite automaton's state is then restored to the previous value (i.e., the effects of Action are undone). and one after.

4.3 Done Function

The Done(Action) function tells to the finite automaton that the Action action has been executed.

5 Implementation

The Agent Security Package is implemented in the C programming language. The most important parts of the Agent Security Package - finite automata may be implemented:
- from the scratches using the C programming language
- from the specifications using the well-known lexical analyzer generators such as lex or flex.

The main concern is on the uncertain nature of Forbidden: it must be possible to try Action and then to go back to the previous state of the finite automaton, in order to verify other possible actions Action. For that purpose, it will be enough to store the index of the previous state and provide a statement that replaces the current state index with the previous one.

6 Conclusion

Integrating security throughout the whole software is one of today's challenges in software engineering research and practice. A challenge so far has proved difficult to meet. The major difficulty is that providing security does not only require to solve software problems but also hardware, infrastructure, and organization problems.

This makes the usage of traditional software engineering methodologies difficult or unsatisfactory.

This paper presents some aspects of software agents security and focuses on software agents action security.

7 Future Work

Our future short-term research will be focused on:

(1) Formal definition/specification/characterization of software agents.

Parameters that typically have been used to characterize a software agent are: ongoing execution, autonomy, adaptiveness, intelligence, awarenenes, mobility, anthromorphism, reactivity, course of action evaluation, communication ability, planning, and negotiation.

It is a challenge to connect characterizations and security of software agents.

(2) Deontic logic.

The operators: Permit, Forbidden, Oblige, Waived- Obligation, and Do/take action are elements of deontic logic.

(3) Logic and nonmonotonic logic programming.

Semantics of agent programs are closed tied to semantics of logic and non-monotonic logic programs.

The expecting results may be very useful for theory and practice of software agents security.

Our future long-term research will be focused on design/implementation of a framework for modeling, simulation, visualization, and analyzing software agent security and in general software security.

We are sure that results will have a big influence on the theory and practice of algorithms, data structures, programming languages, programming languages processor design, operating system design, and etc.

Our education task is to enter into Information Assurance & Computer Security undergraduate and graduate Curriculum the following (at least as elective) courses:
- Agent Theory
- Agent-oriented Programming
- Agent Security
- (Deontic, Nonmonotonic, Temporal, and etc.)Logic
- Logic and Nonmonotonic Logic Programming
- Modeling and Simulation
- Visualization.

Acknowledgement. This research was supported by MSU, SCMNS, Computer Science Department's "Information Assurance and Computer Security" Project Grant.

References

1. Bishop, M.: Computer Security - Art and Science. Addison-Wesley, Boston,Massachusetts (2003)
2. Huhns, M.N., P., M.: Readings in Agents. Morgan Kaufmann Publishers Inc, San Francisco, California (1997)
3. Russell, S., Norvig, P.: Artificial Intelligence: A Modern Approach. Prentice Hall, Englewood Cliffs, New Jersey (1995)
4. Stojkovic, V., Lupton, W.: Software Agents - A Contribution to Agents Specification. ISECON 2000, Information System Education; Philadelphia, Pennsylvania (2000)
5. Subrahmanian, V.S., Bonatti, P., Dix, J., Eiter, T., Kraus, S., Ozcan, F., Ross, R.: Heterogeneous Agent Systems. MIT Press, Cambridge, Massachusetts (2000)
6. Viega, J., McGraw, G.: Building Secure Software - How to Avoid Security Problems the Right Way. Addison-Wesley, Boston, Massachusetts (2002)
7. Weiss, G.: Multiagent Systems: A Modern Approach to Distributed Artificial Intelligence. The MIT Press, Cambridge, Massachusetts (1999)

A Key Distribution Scheme Based on Public Key Cryptography for Sensor Networks

Xiaolong Li[2], Yaping Lin[3], Siqing Yang[1], Yeqing Yi[2], Jianping Yu[2], and Xinguo Lu[2]

[1] Department of Computer, Hunan Institute of Humanities, Science and Technology, Loudi, 417000, China
siqingy@163.com
[2] School of Computer and Communication, Hunan University, Changsha, 410082,China
xiaolong-lee@163.com
[3] School of Software, Hunan University, Changsha, 410082, China
yplin@hnu.cn

Abstract. This paper takes advantages of symmetrical key and asymmetrical key technologies, and proposes a key distribution scheme based on public key cryptography. This scheme does not need to pre-distribute pair-wise keys. Pair-wise key is established between two nodes after deployment according to a specific route algorithm. The scheme can guarantee there is a direct pair-wise key between two nodes that need communication frequently. As a result, it will decrease communication overhead. Both analytical results and simulation results demonstrate that the scheme can save memory usage, and in the scenario of large and dense deployment, the scheme achieves a higher level of connectivity and robustness.

1 Introduction

Sensor network is one kind of wireless ad-hoc networks with small memory storage, limited computation ability and energy power [1]; therefore, in the most research on sensor security, symmetrical key technology is applied data set [2,3,4], which has the characteristic of simple computation and small communication overhead. However, according to symmetrical key cryptography scheme, there are pair-wise keys between any two directly communicating nodes, because of limitation on the memory, which results in the case that any node can directly communicate with a few nodes among neighbors. These techniques are not able to achieve a perfect connectivity. The use of public key cryptography can solve the above problem. Although several papers data set [5,6] prove that public key infrastructure is viable on MICA2 [7], it will bring the higher computational complexity and communication overhead.

Motivated by these reasons, this paper takes advantages of symmetrical key and asymmetrical key technologies, and proposes a key distribution scheme based on public key cryptography. Keys are established between communicating nodes

Y. Wang, Y. Cheung, and H. Liu (Eds.): CIS 2006, LNAI 4456, pp. 725–732, 2007.

according to routing information, so the scheme has better level of connectivity and robustness. Both analytical results and simulation results demonstrate that this scheme is proper to large-scale, dense sensor networks, in which environment the scheme achieves a higher level of connectivity and robustness.

The remainder of this paper is organized as follows. In section II, we simply describe the techniques of this model and in section III, we give details of the key distribution scheme based on public key cryptography. Experimental simulations are presented in section IV and we conclude this paper in section V.

2 The Techniques of This Scheme

We simply describe the techniques adopted in this scheme: Two-Party Key Exchange algorithm (TPKE) and Hash function.

TPKE algorithm needs the exchange of two sensor nodes' public keys. One node's own private key and the other node's public key can produce a shared key that is the pair-wise key of both nodes (depicted in figure 1). If we adopt $Diffee-Hellman$ key exchange algorithm, shared key equals $k_{B1}^{k_{A2}} \bmod q$ and $k_{A1}^{k_{B2}} \bmod q$ (q is a large prime number).

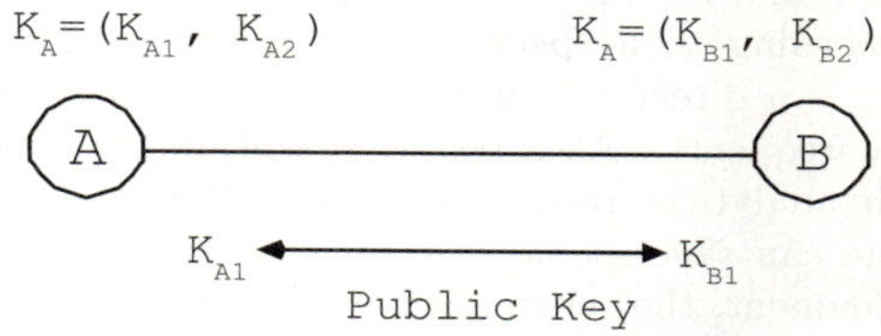

Fig. 1. Two-party public key exchange

At present one-way Hash function includes MD5, SHA_1, etc. For arbitrary size pair-wise key x, Hash function can process a variable length message into a fixed-length output(the output of MD5 is 128 bits meanwhile the output of SHA_1 is 160 bits). The implementation of WH-16 in [8] only consumes 2.95μW at 500 kHz. It can therefore be integrated into a self-powered device and achieve perfect serialization in the hardware implementation.

3 The Key Distribution Scheme

Before presenting the key distribution scheme, let us introduce the following definitions:

Definition 1: neighboring nodes based on routing algorithm. Adopting a specific routing algorithm, any node A is impossible to send data to some of neighboring nodes. We define the rest of neighboring nodes as A's neighboring nodes based on the routing algorithm. Depicted by figure 2: adopting on Angle-based Dynamic

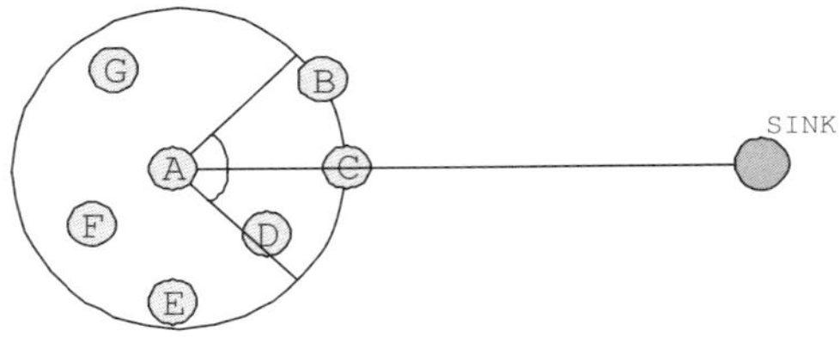

Fig. 2. A's neighboring nodes based on *ADPC* when route angle= θ

Path Construction algorithm [9], when the route angle=θ, nodes B, C, emphD are A's neighboring nodes based on ADPC.

Definition 2: the serial number of neighboring nodes based on routing algorithm. Given any node A, through a specific routing algorithm, A calculates which of all the neighboring nodes based on the routing algorithm is the next hop node, and we define the node as A's 1st neighboring node based on the routing algorithm, whose serial number is 1. Then except for the node, A calculates which is the next hop node, and we define the node as A's 2nd neighboring node based on the routing algorithm, whose serial number is 2. We induce the serial number of neighboring nodes else from the above principle. Depicted by figure 2: node C is A's 1st neighboring nodes based on ADPC.

In this scheme we make the following assumptions:

1)Thousands of nodes are deployed in a large-scale region of interest. The sensor nodes are *not* grouped into clusters, in other words, the sensor network is flat.

2)All nodes are *stationary* after deployment.

3)A specific routing algorithm is established prior to deployment.

Before deploying all nodes, we pre-distribute among the nodes same data, including a large prime number q and a key generator. We also integrate the same Hash function into any node, or strap on sensor node some same kind of hardware to achieve Hash function. For any shared key between two nodes generated by TPKE, both of the two nodes calculate h(shared key) and store it as the pair-wise key between the two nodes.

Sensor nodes will send packets along certain route path to Sink node. If different routing algorithms are adopted, corresponding route paths from any node A to Sink node may not be same. In other words, corresponding times that node A sends data to its each neighboring nodes might not be same based on different routing algorithm. The scheme is as follows:

Step 1: Given any node A, node A broadcasts inquiry packets and checks which are its neighboring nodes. After its neighboring nodes receive the inquiry packets, they will send their node IDs to node A.

Step 2: Initialize i=1. A calculate the serial number of Neighboring Nodes based on the User-specified Routing algorithm (NNUR).

Step 3: A selects A's ith neighboring node based on the routing algorithm. If the node satisfies conditions: the node has less than m pair-wise keys and has not established the pair-wise key with A, then go to step 4, otherwise jump to step 5.

Step 4: A pair-wise key is established between the node and node A by TPKE. Both the node and node A store the pair-wise key. Take figure 2 for example. when i=1, and if node C satisfies conditions, A will establish a pair-wise key with C.

Step 5:i++. Repeat step 3 till A store m (m is a system parameter) pair-wise keys or all NNURs store m pair-wise keys, then stop.

Before executing experimental simulations of the key distribution scheme, we estimate the times of operating TPKE of whole sensor networks.

Theorem 1: N sensor nodes are randomly deployed in the L^*L fields, and the communication range of each node is r. Assume M is a fixed value, and any node $($A)'s neighboring node is its NNUR with a probability $\frac{1}{K}$, the total times of operating TPKE algorithm after deployment will be less than:

$$1N * C_{N-1}^{1} p^1 q^{N-2} + \cdots + MN * C_{N-1}^{M} p^M q^{N-1-M} + \cdots + MN * C_{N-1}^{N-1} p^{N-1} q^0 \tag{1}$$

$$p = \frac{1}{K}\frac{\pi r^2}{L^2}, q = 1 - \frac{1}{K}\frac{\pi r^2}{L^2} \tag{2}$$

Proof: Consider any node A. A randomly deployed node is in the radio transmission range of A with the probability of $\frac{\pi r^2}{L^2}$. Hence, the node is A's NNUR with $\frac{1}{K}\frac{\pi r^2}{L^2}$. Among N-1 nodes there are i nodes in A's communication range with the probability of $C_{N-1}^{i} p^i q^{N-1-i}$.$\Rightarrow$ The number of nodes that have one NNUR is $< N * C_{N-1}^{1} p^1 q^{N-2}$.$\cdots$. Similarity, the number of nodes that have M NNURs is $< N * C_{N-1}^{M} p^M q^{N-1-M}$.$\cdots$. $\Rightarrow$ The total times of the nodes that have one NNUR operating TPKE algorithm after deployment are $< N * C_{N-1}^{1} p^1 q^{N-2}$.$\cdots$. Similarity, the total times of nodes that have M NNURs operating TPKE are $< M*N*C_{N-1}^{M} p^M q^{N-1-M}$.$\cdots$. Because of memory limitation, the total times of the nodes that have $M+1$ NNURs operating TPKE algorithm are $< M * N * C_{N-1}^{M+1} p^{M+1} q^{N-2-M}$.$\cdots$. We add all times of all nodes in the networks, and prove theorem 1 is correct.

4 Experimental Simulations

In this section, we give simulations to study the characteristics of the key distribution scheme. Experiment 1 illustrates the relationship between m and isolated nodes. Through experiment 2, we investigate the impact of m on among all nodes the percentage of nodes, which have established pair-wise keys with their ith neighboring nodes. In the simulations, 5000 sensor nodes are randomly

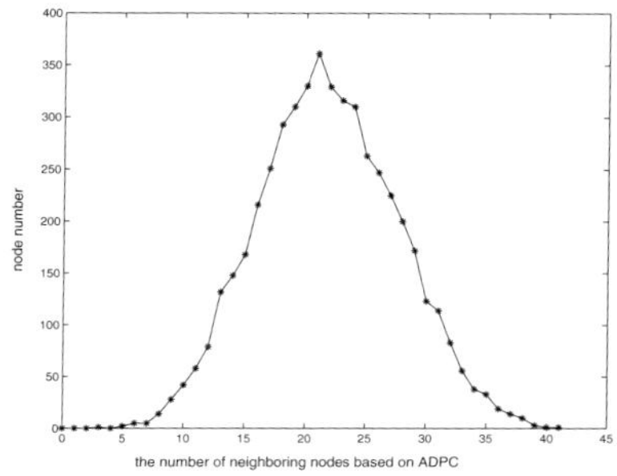

(a) in 500m*500m field

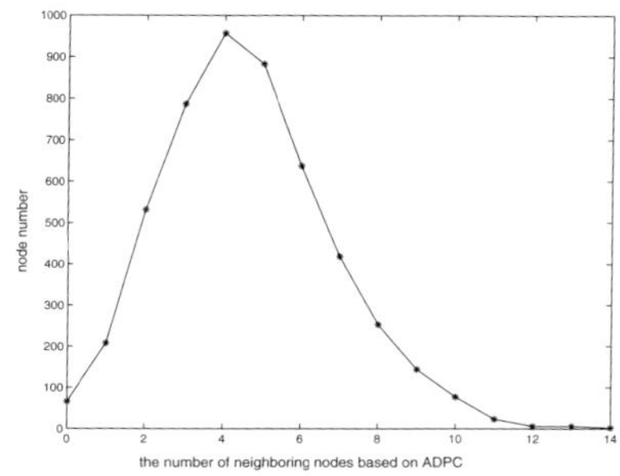

(b) In 1000m*1000m field

Fig. 3. In 500m*500m and 1000m*1000m-two field above, the node number vs. the number of neighboring nodes based on ADPC

deployed to 500m*500m and 1000m*1000m fields, and the communicating range of each node is 40m. The route angle is 90 degree under the distributed ADPC routing algorithm. All the sensor nodes establish pair-wise keys under the ADPC routing algorithm. By figure3, we present the relationship between the number of neighboring nodes based on ADPC and the corresponding node number when the Sink is at (0, 0).

4.1 Experiment 1

From figure3 we notice that the curve is almost a exponential distribution, and the parameter λ is equal to $\frac{1}{K}$ of neighboring nodes when the nodes are evenly distributed. When all nodes are deployed as in figure 3.a, we can find the relationship between m and k in table I: k is the number of isolated nodes. When m goes up from 1 to 2 and 3, the number of isolated nodes decreases greatly, and the isolated nodes disappear when $m \geq 4$. When all nodes are deployed as in figure 3.b, the relationship between m and k is as shown in table II. When m goes up from 1 to 2, 3 and 4, the number of isolated nodes decreases greatly. Increasing m when $m \geq 4$, the number of isolated nodes has not changed obviously. Through figure 3, while the sensor networks is dense, even m is small, the isolated number is approximately to 0; while the sensor networks is sparse, it has no effect to decrease the isolated nodes through increasing m while m is more than a certain number. Compared to table I and II, when m is a fixed value, the connectivity in dense sensor networks is better than in sparse sensor networks.

Table 1. In 500m*500m field, m vs. the number of isolated nodes

m	1	2	3	4	5	6	7	8	9	10
k	126	6	1	0	0	0	0	0	0	0

Table 2. In 1000m*1000m field, m vs. the number of isolated nodes

m	1	2	3	4	5	6	7	8	9	10
k	678	192	92	56	53	52	51	50	50	49

4.2 Experiment 2

If any node A gets measurement data, the node will sends the data to its 1st NNUR as long as the node is live. If A and A's 1st NNUR have established a pair-wise key, they will not seek a key-path. If A's 1st NNUR has failed, A has to send data to A's 2nd NNUR. When A's 1st and 2nd NNUR have failed, A will send data to its 3rd neighboring node. Similarly A will send data to another NNUR else. So an node setting up the pair-wise keys with its ith NNUR shows the robustness of the node, accordingly, and all nodes setting up the pair-wise keys with their ith NNUR shows a level of robustness of the sensor network .

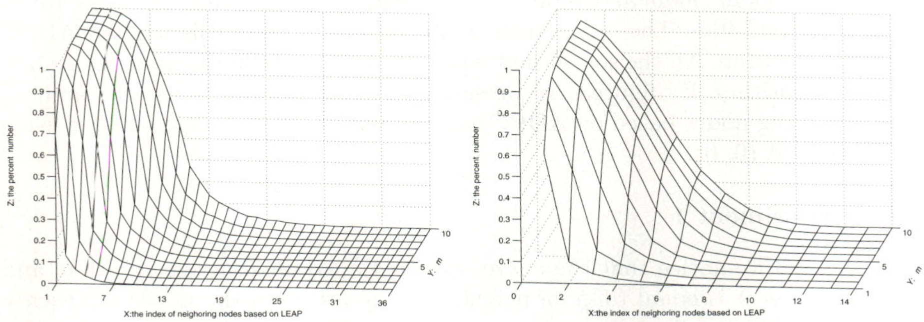

(a) in 500m*500m field (b) in 1000m*1000m field

Fig. 4. In 500m*500m and 1000m*1000m-two field above, the relation between m and the percents of nodes which has established pair-wise keys with its ith neighboring nodes based the routing algorithm

Figure 4.a presents the relation between m and the percentage of nodes which have established pair-wise keys with their ith neighboring nodes based ADPC in the 500m*500m field. From figure 4.a, when m=1, the percentage of nodes which have established pair-wise keys with their 1st neighboring nodes based on ADPC is 70%; m=3, the percentage is 95%. When m=5, the percentage of nodes which have established pair-wise keys with their 2nd neighboring nodes based on ADPC is more than 95%. When m=10, the percentage of nodes which have established pair-wise keys with their 5th neighboring nodes based on the routing algorithm is more than 95%.

Figure 4.b presents the relation between m and the percentage of nodes which have established pair-wise keys with their ith neighboring nodes based on ADPC in the 1000m*1000m field. When m=1, the percentage of nodes which have established pair-wise keys with their 1st neighboring nodes based on ADPC is

61%; m=3, the percentage is 90%. When $m \geq 8$, the percentage hardly changes if increasing m, which is about 95%, and the percentages of nodes which have established pair-wise keys with their ith neighboring nodes based on ADPC elsewhere change so little. Compared to figure 4.a and figure 4.b, when m is a fixed value, the robustness in dense sensor networks is better than in sparse sensor networks.

5 Conclusion

Because of taking advantages of symmetrical key and asymmetrical key technologies, the key distribution scheme based on public key cryptography don't need to pre-distribute pair-wise keys, and pair-wise key is established between two nodes after deployment according to a specific routing algorithm. As a result, the scheme is able to guarantee that there is a pair-wise key between two nodes needing to frequently directly communicate, which will decrease communication overhead. And no pair-wise key among two nodes without direct communication will save memory usage. Experimental simulations demonstrate that this scheme can save memory usage, and in the scenario of large and dense deployment, this scheme achieves a higher level of connectivity and robustness. Even if m is smaller, the connectivity is satisfying. For a large-scale, sparse sensor network, if they need it to provide high connectivity, m must be relatively bigger. The level of its robustness hardly increase if continuing to increase the value of m.

For large-scale, dense sensor networks, although increasing the value of m will correspondingly improve the connectivity and robustness, the bigger the m, the complex the computation is and the communication overhead increase as well. We are currently investigating for proper m in the demanding of a certain level of connectivity and robustness for different distributed sensor networks.

References

1. Pottie, G., Kaiser, W.: Wireless Sensor Networks. Communications of the ACM 43, 51–58 (2000)
2. Eschenauer, L., Gligor, V.: A key-management scheme for distributed sensor networks. In: Proc. of the 9th ACM Conference on Computer and Communication Security, pp. 41–47 (2002)
3. Chan, H., Perrig, A., Song, D.: Random key pre-distribution schemes for sensor networks. In: IEEE Symposium on Security and Privacy, pp. 197–213 (2003)
4. Liu, D., Ning, P., Li, R.: Establishing Pairwise Keys in Distributed Sensor Networks. In: IEEE Symposium on Security and Privacy, pp. 1–35 (2004)
5. Malan, D.J., Welsh, M., Smith, M.D.: A public-key infrastructure for key distribution in TinyOS based on elliptic curve cryptography. In: Proc. of 1st IEEE Communications Society Conference on Sensor and Ad Hoc Communications and Networks (Secon2004) (2004)
6. Gaubatz, G., Kaps, J.P., Sunar, B.: Public Key Cryptography in Sensor Network-Revisited. In: the Proc. of the 1st European Workshop on Security in Ad-Hoc and Sensor Networks(ESAS) (2004)

7. Crossbow Technology Inc. Wireless sensor networks (2005), `http://www.xbow.com/`
8. Kaps, J.P., Yuksel, K., Sunar, B.: Energy Scalable Universal Hashing. IEEE Transactions on Computers 54, 1484–1495 (2005)
9. Choi, W., Das, S.K., Basu, K.: Angle-based Dynamic Path Construction for Route Load Balancing in Wireless Sensor Networks. In: the Proc. of IEEE Wireless Communications and Networking Conference(WCNC) (2004)

Collision-Resilient Multi-state Query Tree Protocol for Fast RFID Tag Identification

Jae-Min Seol and Seong-Whan Kim

Department of Computer Science, University of Seoul, Jeon-Nong-Dong, Seoul, Korea
Tel.: +82-2-2210-5316; Fax: +82-2-2210-5275
seoleda@hotmail.com, swkim7@uos.ac.kr

Abstract. RFID (radio frequency identification) is a RF based identification system, where RF reader reads (and writes) data from each entity (RF tag). Upon request from reader, tags in reader's accessible RF range will respond, and if the number of tags is larger than 2, the reader cannot identify tags (collision). To avoid the collision, there are two previous approaches: ALOHA based and binary tree algorithm. However, they are essentially collision avoidance algorithms, and require much overhead in retransmission time. In this paper, we present collision recovery scheme for RFID system. It uses 20 symbols, and each symbol is 16-bit vectors derived from (16, 4, 1)-BIBD (balanced Incomplete Block design) which is resilient to collision. Although our scheme can decrease the total number of support users, it shows good performance even with low SNR region.

1 Introduction

RFID (radio frequency identification) is a RF based identification system. RFID system is easier to use than magnetic card and bar code. The RFID has high potential such as supply chain management, access control with identification card, and asset tracking system. As shown in Figure 1, RFID system is composed of a reader (transceiver) and tags (transponder), where RF reader reads and writes data from each entity (RF tag).RFID Reader (transceiver): supplies energy for a tag using RF (radio frequency), requests information about tag and interpret received signal. RFID Tag (transponder) responds to reader and it has unique identification information. As shown in Figure 1, all tags in reader's radio range, will respond to request of readers simultaneously. Without collision resolution, the reader can not identify tag, when 2 or more tags are in its radio range.

To prevent collision in RFID system, there are two previous researches: (1) multiple access protocol which is known to ALOHA from networking, and (2) binary tree algorithm, which is relatively simple mechanism [1]. The ALOHA is a probabilistic algorithm, which shows low throughput and low channel utilization. To increase the performance, slotted ALOHA (time slotted, frame slotted, or dynamic frame slotted) protocol is suggested. Binary tree algorithm is a deterministic algorithm, which detects the location of bit conflict among tags, and partitions tags into two groups recursively until there are no collision. It requires as many as the length of ID to identify one tag in worst case.

Y. Wang, Y. Cheung, and H. Liu (Eds.): CIS 2006, LNAI 4456, pp. 733–742, 2007.

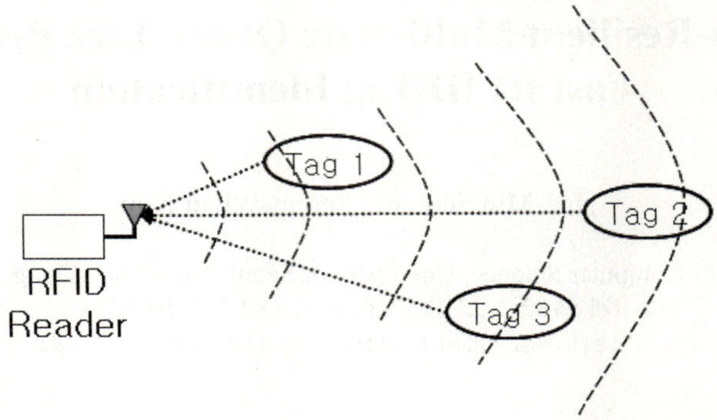

Fig. 1. Multiple tag identification in RFID system

Request signal also supplies energy for passive tags to make them respond to reader, and the strength of response signal sent by the tag is much smaller than the power of reader's request signal. To improve the signal to noise ratio of received signal from tags, we can use a direct sequence spreading, which spreads or repeats small energy, and increases the total received energy from tag to reader. Whereas typical direct sequence spreading technique assigns unique chipping sequence to users or devices and modulate its own sequence, we assign a chipping sequence to each unique symbol which can be differentiated for each others. In this paper, we propose a direct sequence spreading scheme based on collision resilient code symbols In this paper, we propose a variation of query tree algorithm, but has collision free factor. When there are less than k responding tags in reader's radio range, our protocol can identify the tags without any re-transmission. In section 2, we review previous approaches for tag collision, and propose our scheme with simulation results in section 3 and section 4. We conclude in section 5.

2 Related Works

To avoid collusion and share limited channel in communication system, there are many multiple access techniques - space division multiple access (SDMA), Frequency domain multiple access (FDMA), time domain multiple access (TDMA), code division multiple access (CDMA). But, these techniques assume that each user can use channel continuously, and are not suitable for RFID system. In RFID system, there two type of collision resolution scheme: (1) Probabilistic algorithm, which is based on ALOHA. (2) Deterministic algorithm which detects collided bits and splits disjoint subsets of tags. There are two open standards from ISO and EPC organizations. ISO 18000-6 family standard uses probabilistic algorithm which is based on ALOHA procedure, and EPC family standard uses deterministic algorithm.

2.1 Probabilistic Algorithm

The ALOHA is very simple procedure, a reader requests ID, tags will randomly send their data. When collision occurs, they wait random time and retransmit. To enhance performance, they will uses switch off, slow down and carrier sense [2]. In slotted

ALOHA, time is divided in discrete time slot, and a tag can send its data at the beginning of its pre-specified slot. Although the slotted ALOHA can enhance the channel utilization and throughput, it cannot guarantee the response time when there are many tags near reader. To guarantee the response time, frame slotted ALOHA is proposed. In this scheme, all the tags response within frame size slots. As the frame size is bigger, the probability of collision gets lower, but the response time gets longer. Figure 2 shows frame slotted ALOHA procedure. 5 tags will randomly select one slot from 3 (frame size). In this case, tag 1 and tag4 and tag 2 and tag 5 will collide by pigeonhole principle. When frame size equals to the number of tags, this scheme shows best high throughput [3].

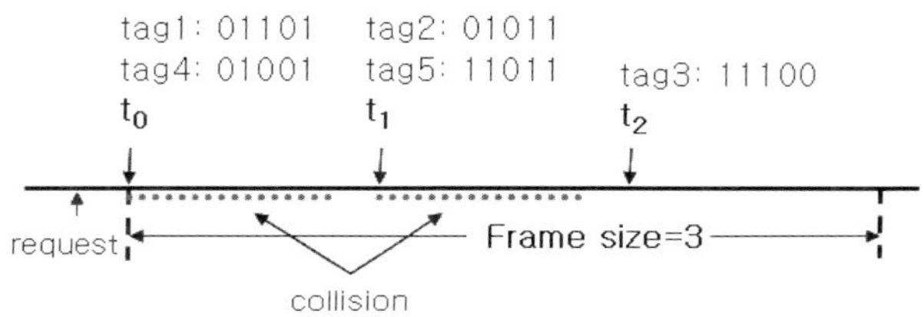

Fig. 2. The example of frame slotted ALOHA procedure

In [3, 4], they suggest dynamic frame slotted ALOHA algorithm, which estimate the size of tags and dynamically change frame size. ALOHA based protocol, however, cannot perfectly prevent collisions. In addition, they have the tag starvation problem, where a tag may not be identified for a long time [6].

2.2 Deterministic Algorithm [5, 6, 7]

Deterministic algorithm, which has no starvation problem, is most suitable for passive tag applications. It is categorized into binary tree protocol and query tree protocol. Both of these protocols require all tags response at the same time and the reader identify corrupted bits [6]. In binary tree protocol, the tag has a register to save previous inquiring result. It has disadvantage of complicated tag implementation, and the tag in overlapped range of two readers will show incorrect operation. Query tree protocol does not require tag's own counter. Instead of using counter, the reader transmit prefix and tags are response their rest bits. The query tree protocol is memory-less protocol and tags has low functionality. However, it is slower than binary tree protocol for tag identification.

Figure 3 shows the difference between binary tree algorithm and query tree algorithm. In binary protocol [5], a reader broadcast 0 at t_0, two tags whose IDs 0001 and 0011 will transmit next bit whose data are all 0 and increase their counters. Next time t_1, the reader broadcast 0 (second bit data), and the two tags 0001 and 0011 also responds next bit and increase their counter. But, at this time, the reader detects collision. At t_2, the reader broadcast 0 (third bit data) only 0001 transmits its data, in this step, 0011 reset it counter.

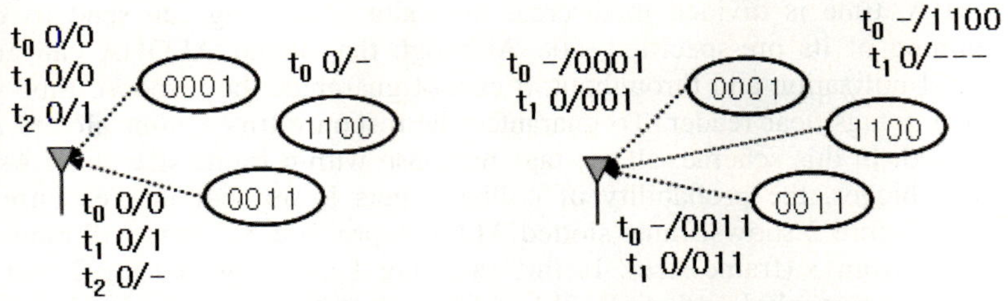

(a) The tags store previously request, matched tag will next one bit (b) When the reader send prefix, matched tags response rest ID.

Fig. 3. The difference between binary tree algorithm (a) and query tree algorithm (b)

In query tree protocol [6] as shown in Table 1, the reader requests their ID with no prefix, and all tags transmit their IDs. As a result, received four bits are totally corrupted. Next, the reader requests it with prefix 0, 0001 and 0011 transmit their bits [0X1]. The reader can know third bit is in collision, it request ID with prefix 000 and only one tag whose ID is 0001 transmit fourth bit as one.

Table 1. Detailed Procedure of query tree protocol

Time	**Reader request**	**Tag response**	**Note**
t_0	null	Tag_1: 0001	All tags reply with their IDs, as a result, the reader knows that all bits are collusion.
		Tag_2: 0011	
		Tag_3: 1100	
t_1	0	Tag_1: 001	Tag 1 and tag 2 who match prefix 0 replies with their remaining IDs. - : means not response
		Tag_2: 011	
		Tag_3: -	
t_2	000	Tag_1: 1	Tag 1 who matches prefix 000 reply with its last bit. Tag 1 identified.
		Tag_2: -	
		Tag_3: -	

3 Collision Resilient Multi-state Query Tree Scheme

In this paper, we propose multiples query tree algorithm. Even there are two or more tags in radio range we represent multiple tag identification scheme no more than two transmission using the balanced incomplete block design (BIBD).

Figure 4 shows the idea of collision recovery scheme. In the error correction code scheme, the distance of any symbols should be at least D. and if the received signal is closer to one symbol than D/2, it will be corrected. However, the received symbol is far from any symbol, it will be error. In error correction code, there are no reasons to be equal distances for all pair of symbols. The important thing is that minimum distance. But, if the distance of every pair of symbols equals, some regions can be defined as collision recovery region. The collision resilient symbol means that the

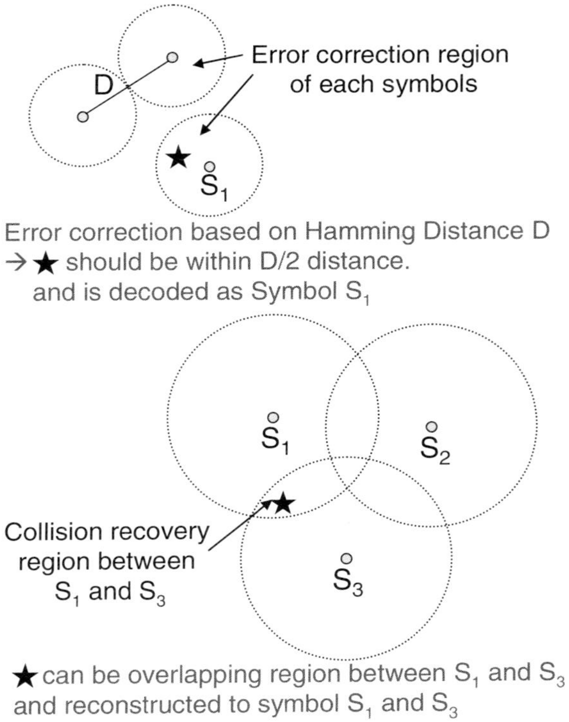

Fig. 4. Collision recovery vs. error correction code for collision resilience

distance of arbitrary two symbols is same. Therefore, if the received symbol is same distant with any original symbols, we can reconstruct originally sent signals.

In Figure 4, when symbol S_1 and S_3 are under collision, the signal may have same distance with them. Therefore, we can reconstruct originally sent signal. In this sense, if the received symbol is same distance of any original symbols, we can reconstruct originally sent signals. And under noisy environment, it is hard that the star mark gets closer to S2 then other symbols. To make a resilient symbol, we suggest collusion resilient symbol using balanced incomplete block design,

3.1 Collision Resilient Symbol Design

The definition of (v, k, λ)-BIBD code is set of k-element subsets (blocks) of v-element set χ, such that each pair of elements of χ occurs together in exactly λ blocks. The (v, k, λ)-BIBD has total of $n= \lambda (v^2-v)/(k^2-k)$ blocks, and we can represent (v, k, λ)-BIBD code an v*n incident matrix, where C(i,j) is set to 1 when the i-th element belongs to the j-th block and set to 0 otherwise [8].

Figure 5 shows the example of (7, 3, 1)-BIBD which can identify up to 3 symbols at one transmission. For example, when the 1st, 2nd and 3th symbols (column) collide, the first bit remains one. On the contrary, if one bit is set to one and the others are

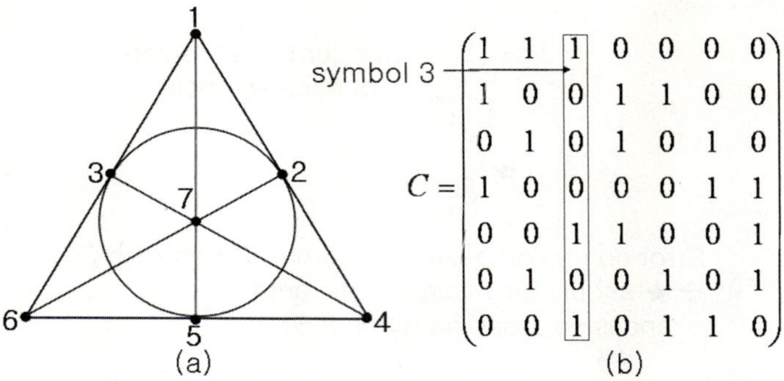

Fig. 5. Geometric (a) and incident matrix (b) representation of (7, 3, 1)-BIBD

collapsed, the reader knows that what three symbols really sent. If one or more bits are not corrupted, we can make partition into two disjoint subsets and the one has less than 3 tags and it has unique elements. e.g) when third bit is 1, the subset has first, sixth and seventh symbols. In Figure 5, (7, 3, 1)-code can represent only 7 symbols and identify up to 3 symbols within one transmission, we can redesign the parameter (v, k). (16, 4, 1)-BIBD can support n = (16*15)/4*3=20 symbols.

Although it lacks supported tags, it has strong advantage in identification speed, low power consumptions and robustness under low SNR region. To solve the small number of tags and compatibility with the electronic product code, we can compose of multiple BIBD codes. For instance, 32bits are divide into two 16 bits, and two 16 bits are (16, 4, 1)-BIBD codes, to support 20*20 users, or adopt hybrid scheme where small part uses BIBD scheme for compatible EPC Global Code.

3.2 Multi-state Query Tree Protocol

To identify tags, we suggest multiple state query tree protocol, which is variation of query tree protocol. The query tree algorithm consists of rounds of queries and response. In each round the reader asks the tags whether and of their IDs contains a certain prefix. If more than one tag answer, then the reader knows that there are at least two tags having that prefix. The reader then appends symbol 1, 2, ··· or 20 to the prefix, and continue to query for longer prefix. When a prefix matches a tag uniquely, that tag can be identified. Therefore, by extending the prefixes until only one tag's ID matches, the algorithm can discover all the tags.

In the query tree protocol, a reader detects collision bit by bit. But in our scheme can detect collision with 16 bit vector symbols which have twenty symbols. And all tags which are matched the prefix, transmit their remained bits in query tree protocol, but in multiple states query tree protocol, they transmit their next one symbol which is 16 bits. The following describes the protocol:

```
Set the prefix empty
Begin until
    rx-signal = request (with the prefix)
    If (rx-signal is no response ) then
          If (the prefix is not empty) then
                delete last symbol in the prefix
          Else
                no response with empty prefix
          Endif
    Else
          Symbol = decode (the rx-signal)
          add symbol in to end of the prefix
    Endif
    If (size of prefix == size of tags symbol) then
          ensure that existence of the tag and
          make it not response
          delete last symbol in the prefix
    Endif
Until (there are no response with empty prefix)
```

Suppose that the RFID system use 48 bits for IDs, which consist of three symbols and supports 8000 tags. Each tag has unique path in the query tree and its depth is 3. Therefore we can identify one tag at most 3 times transmission. When a reader request next symbol with prefix, the tags transmit their next 16-bit symbols and the prefix matches with one tag's all symbol, the tag must send conform message. For example, there 4 tags whose ID are [4 18 5], [4, 18, 7], [8, 9, 2], [6 8 3] in the reader, the readers requests command bellows:

	Reader request	Tags response		Reader request	Tags response
1	null	[4]	2	[4]	[18]
3	[4 18]	[5]	-	[4, 18, 5]	Identified
4	[4 18]	[7]	-	[4, 18, 7]	Identified
5	[4 18]	null	6	[4]	Null
7	null	[8]	8	[8]	[9]
9	[8 9]	[2]	-	[8 9 2]	Identified
10	null	[6]	11	[6]	[8]
12	[6 8]	[3]	-	[6 8 3]	Identified
13	[6 8]	Null	14	[6]	Null
15	null	Null			

To support 8000 tags, the other protocol needs 13 bits (8192 tags) and 13 iterations to identify one tag in worst case but our scheme needs only 3 iterations in worst case.

4 Experimental Results

In our experimentation, we assume AWGN (additive white Gaussian noise) model without fading for radio channel, and used (16, 4, 1) BIBD code to identify maximum 20 symbols (i.e. 20 = 16*(16-1)/(4*(4-1))) for collision case. We repeat 10,000 times randomly select symbols and collides. We assume that when reader transmits RF with power 1, tags will share fairly 1/k. Figure 6 shows the symbol error rate over various RF channel environments (signal to noise ratio between tags and reader). Our scheme shows better ID identification over increased SNR, and it gets worse as the number of symbols in a RF reader zone and SNR decreases. Simulation results show that we can achieve successful identification for maximum 4 symbols using (16, 4, 1) BIBD code. Mathematically, (16, 4, 1)-BIBD can 4 symbols at once, interference and fading degrade performance when 4 symbols. Depending on the RF environments, we can choose the parameter (v, k, λ) for better coverage and symbol identification performance.

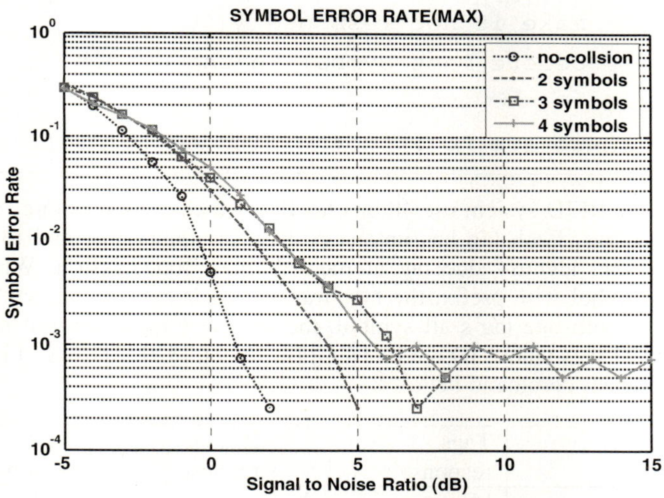

Fig. 6. Symbol Error Rate, using (16, 4, 1)-balanced incomplete block design

Figure 7 shows that our scheme has no degradation of performance when the power of signal is bigger then noise and operates well even extremely low signal to noise ratio (SNR). It support 6.4*10^7 tags. When 100 tags are one reader range under low SNR (-5dB), our scheme needs 6*10^4 bits between reader and tags to identify all tags. According to protocol for 900Mhz class 0 RFID [5], the transmission

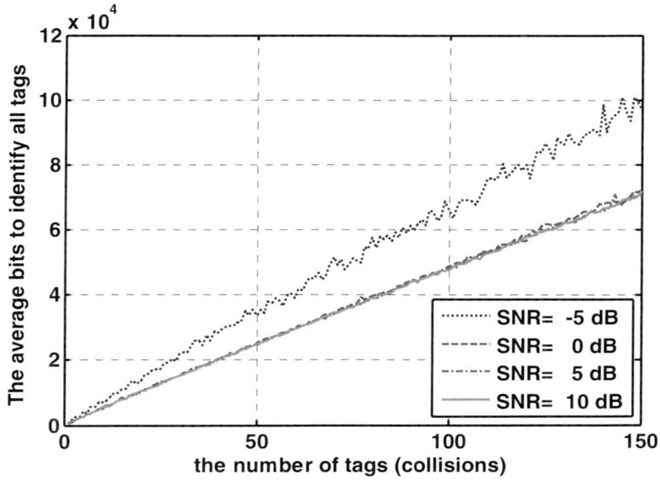

Fig. 7. The tag identification performance using 6 symbols (16*6=96 bits) for one tag

time between reader and tag is 12.5 microsecond, Our scheme can identify 100 tags within 0.75 (6*10^4*12.5*10^-6) second. Although it wastes bits, the identification speed is very fast. It can be adopted small/medium domain real time tracking system.

5 Conclusions

RFID requires efficient collision recovery scheme. Traditional query tree protocol is bit based and requires slower singularization for big tag population. In this paper, we proposed a collision detection and recovery algorithm for RFID tag collision cases. We designed the basic code using (v, k, λ) BIBD (balanced incomplete block design) code, and it can identify symbols when up to k symbols are collapsed. Our scheme does not require re-transmission, which costs power consumption. We simulated our scheme over various radio environments using AWGN channel model. Our scheme shows good collision detection and ID recovery (average k symbols for bad radio environments).

Reference

1. Finkenzeller, K.: RFID Handbook, Fundamentals and Application in Contact-less Smart Card and Identification, 2nd edn. John Wiley & Sons Ltd, New York (2003)
2. Parameters for Air Interface Communications at 13.56MHz, RFID Air Interface Standards. ISO/IEC 18000 Part 3 (2005)
3. Cha, J., Kim, J.: Novel Anti-collision Algorithm for Fast Object Identification in RFID System. IEEE Conf. on Parallel and Distributed System 2, 63–67 (2005)
4. Vogt, H.: Multiple object identification with passive RFID tags. IEEE Conf. on System, Man and Cybernetics 3, 6–9 (2002)

5. Draft protocol specification for a 900MHz Class 0 Radio Frequency Identification Tag. MIT Auto-ID Center (2003)
6. Myung J., Lee W.: An Adaptive Memoryless Tag Anti-Collision Protocol for RFID Networks. IEEE Conf. on computer communication, Poster Session, Miami, Florida (2005)
7. Zhou F., Chen C., Jin D., Huang C., Min H.: Evaluation and Optimizing Power Consumption of Anti-Collision Protocols for Applications in RFID System. In: Proc. Of Int'l Symposium on Low Pwer electronics and Design, pp. 357–362 (2004)
8. Colbourn, C., Dinitz, J.: The CRC Handbook of Combinatorial Design. CRC Press Inc, Boca Raton (1996)
9. Staddon, J., Stinson, D., Wei, R.: Combinatorial properties of frameproof and traceability codes. IEEE Trans. on Information theory 47, 1042–1049 (2001)

Toward Modeling Sensor Node Security Using Task-Role Based Access Control with TinySec

Misun Moon, Dong Seong Kim, and Jong Sou Park

Network Security and System Design Lab., Hankuk Aviation University, Seoul, Korea
{ulitawa, dskim, jspark}@hau.ac.kr

Abstract. There is a TinySec in TinyOS to provide integrity and confidentiality of message for Wireless Sensor Network (WSN). However, TinySec employs a simple group key management, so if a sensor node is compromised by an adversary, overall sensor nodes in the network are likely to be compromised. Therefore, we propose a new access control methodology for WSN, based on Task-Role Based Access Control (T-RBAC). T-RBAC has been successfully applied to many different kinds of security applications. T-RBAC has also capability to provide flexible authentication and authorization to the system. We present the design and implementation results on our approach, and we show security analysis and comparison results show the feasibility of our approach.

1 Introduction

Wireless Sensor and Actor Networks (WSANs) [1] can be an integral part of systems such as battlefield surveillance and micro climate control in buildings, nuclear, biological and chemical attack detection, home automation and environmental monitoring. WSANs is also a sensor network based on ad-hoc network. There is a TinySec in TinyOS to provide integrity and confidentiality of message for Wireless Sensor Network (WSN). However, TinySec employs a simple group key management, so if a sensor node is compromised by an adversary, overall sensor nodes in the network are likely to be compromised. So, we need to consider the security problem after a sensor node is compromised. Of course, other key management protocols, including key pre-distribution, can minimize the key compromization problem. This is not enough solution in terms of access control of resource in sensor nodes in the network.

Accordingly, we focus on access control for sensor nodes in sensor networks. We adopt a Task-Role Based Access Control (T-RBAC) [5] for access control. We assume that operating system of most sensor nodes is based on components, which executing a task. T-RBAC is proper for sensor node access control because task is factor of T-RBAC. Also, T-RBAC is more dynamic than Role Based Access Control (RBAC) [4]. Hence, T-RBAC is appropriate on our approach. The next section presents our proposed architecture.

Y. Wang, Y. Cheung, and H. Liu (Eds.): CIS 2006, LNAI 4456, pp. 743–749, 2007.

2 Proposed Architecture

2.1 Overall Structure

Our proposed architecture is built on Wireless Sensor and Actor Networks (WSANs). In WSANs, the phenomena of sensing and acting are performed by sensor and actor nodes. Sensor nodes are low-cost, low power devices with limited sensing, computation, and wireless communication capabilities. Actor nodes are resource rich node equipped with better processing capabilities, higher transmission powers and longer battery life. In other words, actor nodes have higher capabilities and can act on large areas. WSANs have the following unique characteristics. One is 'Real-time requirement ', the other is 'Coordination'. Coordination provides the transmission of event features from sensors to actors. After receiving event information, actors need to coordinate with each other in order to make decisions on the most appropriate way to perform the action. Sensor nodes transmit their readings to the actor nodes, and route data back to the sink. Sink monitors the overall network and communicates with the task manager node and sensor/actor nodes. But traditional Wireless Sensor Network (WSN) has sink as central controller of all sensor nodes. Our proposed architecture has 3 phases.

1) Neighbor nodes discovery and network formation
2) Authentication with membership lists
3) Access Control and Authorization based on Task-Role Based Access Control (T-RBAC)

Neighbor nodes discovery and network formation. Sensor nodes and actor nodes are deployed in monitoring fields. We assume that all actor nodes are secure against any kinds of attacks and adversary cannot insert any malicious actor nodes in networks. If malicious or compromised actor nodes on purpose are inserted by attacker, all WSANs may be compromised. The problem is out of scope of this paper. Actor nodes send its information to both other actor nodes and sensor nodes within its transmission range. Sensor nodes select nearest actor node and send its information (e.g. sensor node ID) to the actor node. Actor nodes collect sensor node's information and then make membership lists. The WSANs are formatted like this way.

Authentication with membership lists. After network formation, actor nodes send group key and membership list to sensor nodes within its transmission range using SPINs proposed by A. Perrig *et al.* [6] in secure way. The membership lists include sensor node's ID and role information. The sensor nodes belong to same actor nodes share common membership list.

Access Control and Authorization based on Task-Role Based Access Control (T-RBAC). Sensor nodes which want to run task or to get service send message to other nodes. The message includes sender's ID, task information to run and authority value. To authorize sender, receiver finds Role ID with sender's ID in list. And if sender's ID has Role ID, it goes to next step. A receiver checks whether task information and authority value in message is available. We use T-RBAC for this access control. In section 2.3, we will explain T-RBAC.

2.2 Authentication on Network

We propose an algorithm which adopts SPINs [6] for RBAC on MANET [3] due to authentication of node on network. Actor node manages sensor nodes for membership list. RBAC on MANET uses certification to manage membership of its network or group. But sensor node has small energy, storage, computation and community capacity. But the certification needs large resources, so we use group key of network based on SPINs because group key is very simple and if it is exposed it can affect whole network. SPINs provides secure transmission information such as group key that shared to maintain membership.

But though each node joins to network and has membership list, node can be compromised and can attempt illegal access to other nodes. Therefore, it is necessary to consider sensor nodes security.

Actor nodes play role of group leader to maintain membership and to announce changed information of network.

2.3 T-RBAC Based Access Control in WSAN

This architecture uses T-RBAC [5] model for access control. Figure 1 shows T-RBAC model of this architecture.

T-RBAC module is located on each sensor nodes and T-RBAC module has URA (User Role Assignment) policy that shares with authentication module of membership management module on network. Nodes have role information of other nodes that had same membership [3].

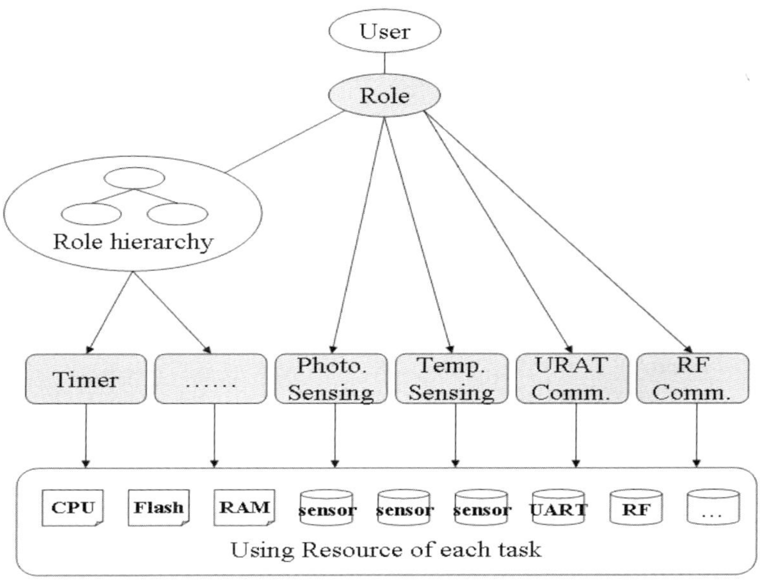

Fig. 1. T-RBAC Model for Proposed Approach

'User' means each sensor node and 'Role' means assigned role of each sensor node. T-RBAC model assigns 'Task' to 'Role'. Gray rectangles are 'Task' of sensor nodes and each 'Task' uses one or more resources of sensor nodes [5].

Each sensor node runs programs and task, which uses resource of sensor nodes. There are some kinds of sensors, communication modules and so on. Each resource can be drove by tasks or sensor node operating systems.

3 Design and Implementation

We design proposed approach on TinyOS. TinyOS is designed only for sensor nodes with resource constraints such as low power consumption, low power communication, efficient memory and process management. TinyOS has TinySec -secure link layer module- to provide access control, integrity, and confidentiality.

If TinySec [2] is compromised, sensor node cannot countermeasure against attacks and cannot guarantee confidentiality, integrity of data collected in sensor nodes. But, access control in TinySec is just sharing the group key to distinguish nodes in same area, not security as protection from attack. If key is exposed by adversary's eavesdropping attack, WSANs is not secure and compromised sensor node is not available. Therefore more fine grained access control approach is necessary to guarantee availability of sensor node [2].

```
Msg_recv_process(struct recv_msg)
{
  u08 rid;
  u04 tid, aid;

  if(recv_msg.gid is not same with my gid)
    call rejection routine;

  rid = search role(recv_msg.nid in role table);
  if(!rid)
    call rejection routine;
  else{
    aid = search authority(rid, recv_msg.tid);
    if(!aid or aid is not same with recv_msg.aid)
      call rejection routine;
    else
      provide service;
  }
}
```

```
gid : network ID
rid : role ID
nid : node ID
tid : task ID
aid : authority ID
```

Fig. 2. Pseudo Code of Proposed Approach

Figure 2 shows proposed architecture's algorithm of this paper. When a sensor node gets the message, in order to check packet that is normal and secure, the message is passed to authentication process based on SPINs [6]. After authentication module of sensor node checks whether packet is secure or not, access control module extracts information from packet for access control that requesting user can access to task or resource.

3.1 Network Environment

We use WSAN [1] architecture for network environment. There are a number of sensor nodes and some actor nodes. Each actor node has information of sensor nodes that transmit their sensing value to actor node to send their reading to sink node.

We assume all sensor nodes have own ID which is unique in network. ID means identifier and system use ID as information for access control. And we also assume sensor nodes are fixed at deploying time. Sensor nodes are able to move because human or animals can move. But then we assume that nodes collect data in fixed location. Each sensor nodes have role-table, task-authority-table for T-RBAC module that access control by role, task and authority of that.

3.2 Message Format

TinyOS uses packet structure which size is 36 bytes. The message format of TinyOS is {Dest(2b), L(1b), M(1b), G(1b), Data(0-29b), CRC(2b)}. Dest means destination address field, L is message length field, M is AM (Active Message) type field, G is group field, Data is data field and CRC is CRC field. 'G' value is base to adjudicate whether receiver gets broadcasting message [7].

We define message format for applying our access control model to TinySec. TinySec has two modes and respective modes have own message format. One is authentication mode {Dest(2b), L(1b), M(1b), Src(2b), Ctr(2b), Data(0-29b), MAC(4b)} and other one is authentication/encryption mode {Dest(2b), L(1b), M(1b), Data(0-29b), MAC(4b)}. And two mode are also different each other [7].

We defined new message format by combining and modifying TinySec message format. Our message format is {Dest(2b), L(1b), M(1b), Src(2b), Ctr(2b), N(1b), T(1b), Data(0-29b), MAC(4b)}. There are two new field and other fields are same with original TinySec message. 'N' value is used in first search process, and it is value shared between nodes of network. This process examines whether node exist, and if not, refuse request. Though 'T' field is divided again, these are information for task in high position 4 bit, authority requested to access in low position 4 bit. Also, draw information for node that do task public ownership request using 'Src' field cost including address of sauce node that is defined originally in message rescue and examine role accordingly and foretell request acceptance and rejection.

3.3 Role and Task-Authority

Role consists of 4 levels (0x00, 0x01, 0x02, 0x03) in this system. One actor node makes or has membership list. Each sensor node has 16 bit unique ID and one role. And each sensor node receives this data from actor node with group key ('gid') and membership list (pair of 'rid' and 'nid') periodically.

Also, sensor node has task ID information. Each task on a sensor node such as Timer, Sensing and Communication is assigned 'tid'. And there is 'aid' which is similar to Linux system. These 'tid', 'aid' make small size of information covering many cases.

For example, if 'nid' 0x0001 requests executing ('aid'=1) photo sensor ('tid'=4), 0x0001 will send message <0x0001, 0x41>. Then the node that receives message compare to information it has. If request is appropriate, it will be accepted.

4 Security Analysis and Discussion

4.1 Security Analysis

We make example for explanation how our approach can countermeasure several attacks.

Eavesdropping – Exposure Group Key. Malicious node can acquire 'gid' through eavesdropping. In this case, when malicious node requests some access T-RBAC module checks whether node id of malicious node is in membership list or not. If it is not in list, request is rejected. And though malicious node can get access authority, it is impossible that malicious node requests correct authority of executing task.

DoS Attack – Misdirection. This attack prevents transmitting data by forwarding to wrong routing route. This attack can make data outflow by sending to other adversary or make paralysis communication by sending whole traffic to specific node. In this case, actor node sends adversary node id to sensor nodes. Then each sensor node doesn't receive message from adversary, and when network make re-configuration routing except adversary node.

DoS Attack – Flooding. This attack is occurred on connect-oriented communication. Adversary sends 'SYN packet' to one node continuously, it can make paralysis of communication because almost nodes of sensor network participate in routing. If network detects attack, actor node broadcasts attack and adversary ID to sensor nodes. Then sensor nodes controlled under that actor node can be protected as they don't receive message from adversary and don't respond.

4.2 Comparison

TinySec provides access control by group key fixed on deploying time, confidentiality and integrity by IV (Initial Vector) and counter. But if adversary catches group key through eavesdropping and interrupt communication between each node (i.e. intercept message, efficient routing, incorrect message transmission, and DoS attack), network cannot ensure network availability.

Our approach can maintain these vulnerabilities by using T-RBAC. After actor node including detection module finds which node causes problem, it broadcasts information of that node to other member nodes. Then, each member node is aware of attack on this network, and they control access of attacker. This way reduces violation propagation, and then it improves availability of each sensor node and network.

Table 1. The comparisons of TinySec and proposed approach

	TinySec	Proposed Approach
Method	Encryption, Authentication, Access Control by group key	Encryption, Authentication, **Access Control by T-RBAC**
Flexibility	-	Modify role information or authority for access resource
Extensibility	Key-redistribution	**Add 1 entry to membership list**
Defense against attack	Not available	Defense against key exposure and DoS attack

5 Conclusion and Future Works

Existing sensor node security methods mostly focus on ensuring confidentiality and integrity, and authentication way through group key or key pre-distribution. But, by sensor network's feature, if one node is compromised, it can be expanded by broadcast. To secure network from this violation, we need sensor node security methods. In this thesis, we proposed sensor node security approach using T-RBAC. This approach reduces violation propagation through node security, even if network or node is attacked by adversary, it can increase whole network availability as it increases a number of available node.

Acknowledgement

This research was supported by the MIC(Ministry of Information and Communication), Korea, under the ITRC(Information Technology Research Center) support program supervised by the IITA(Institute of Information Technology Assessment) (IITA-2006-C1090-0603-0027).

References

1. Akyildiz, I.F., Kasimoglu, I.H.: Wireless Sensor and Actor Networks: Research Challenges. Ad Hoc Networks 2(4), 351–367 (2004)
2. Karlof, C., Sastry, N., Wagner, D.: TinySec: User Manual, http://www.tinyos.net
3. Keoh, S. and Lupu, E.: An Efficient Access Control Model for Mobile Ad-Hoc Communities, 2nd Int. Conf. on Security in Pervasive Computing, pp. 210–224 (2005)
4. Lee, H.H.: A Frmework for Application Design and Execution in Dynamic Role-Based Access Control Model, Chonnam Univ. Department of Computer Science and Statistics Ph. D dissertation (2000)
5. Oh, S., Park, S.: Task-role-based access control model, Information Systems, 28(6), 533–562 (2003)
6. Perrig, A., Szewczyk, R., Wen, V., Culler, D., Tygar, J. D.: SPINS: Security Protocols for Sensor Networks. In: Proc. of 7th Annual Int. Conf. on Mobile Computing and Networks (2001)

An Intelligent Digital Content Protection Framework Between Home Network Receiver Devices

Qingqi Pei[1], Kefeng Fan[1,2], Jinxiu Dai[1], and Jianfeng Ma[1]

[1] Key Laboratory of Computer Networks and Information Security(Ministry of Education), Xidian University, Xi'an 710071, China
{qqpei,jxdai}@xidian.edu.cn, ejfma@hotmail.com.cn
[2] Advanced DTV Testing Center of MII, China Electronics Standardization Institute, Beijing 100007, China
fankf@cesi.ac.cn

Abstract. This paper presents an intelligent digital content protection framework for various digital interfaces in consumer electronics device, named universal content protection system (UCPS).The UCPS system aims at achieving three aspects. First, it is to achieve secret transmission of audiovisual content between the interfaces in valid devices. Second, it is to achieve the integrality between the related control information in the valid devices. Third, it is to maintain the integrality of the system. The proposed framework can be have been implemented as a security core which can be transplanted to the digital interfaces including the POD-Host, HDMI, DVI, USB, IEEE 1394 used in the home network receiver devices.

1 Introduction

The worldwide digital consumer media content protection market is poised to generate tremendous profits. This growth was driven largely by the more mature digital pipelines: digital pay TV and DVD. New digital pipelines, like mobile networks and internet media services, as well as more sophisticated digital content protection for existing pipelines are to offer significant growth prospects throughout the forecast period. Services like HDTV, video-on-demand, and secure media download have begun to find commercial success and are creating new opportunities across the value chain. Additionally, newly implemented standards for secure digital broadcast and recording, like the broadcast flag, DTCP[1] and HDCP[2], are clearing the way for a wave of growth in digital terrestrial broadcast and digital recording devices.

In the entertainment world, original multimedia content (e.g., text, audio, video and still images) is made available for consumers through a variety of channels. Modern distribution systems allow the delivery of content to millions of households every day. Although legal institutions exist for protecting intellectual property (trademarks and patents) owned by content creators, complimentary technical measures are needed to sustain financial returns. Protection of digital multimedia content therefore appears to be a new and crucial problem for which immediate solutions are needed. Three

Y. Wang, Y. Cheung, and H. Liu (Eds.): CIS 2006, LNAI 4456, pp. 750–757, 2007.

major industries have a great interest in this problem, which include motion picture industry, consumer electronics (CE) industry, and information technology (IT) industry. The content owners are the motion picture studios. Their content (movies) is displayed or recorded on devices manufactured by CE companies. The IT industry manufactures computing devices, such as personal computers, which can also be used to display and store content.

In this paper, we propose a new concept, home network receiver device (HNCD), which is defined as the receivers, such as digital TV, Set-top Box (STB), DVD players that can be constructed a home network. In order to protect the copyrights of contents in various digital interfaces of CE devices, an intelligent content protection system, named Universal Content Protection System (UCPS), is introduced, The system design is based on cryptography algorithm, which mainly includes stream cipher, ECC, authentication protocol, grouping cipher, RNG, and Hash (SHA-256). UCPS is secure, reliable, and efficient:

1. UCPS can be integrated into the traditional conditional access system to achieve the complete protection.
2. The possible devices for UCPS can be various CE devices such as PCs, STB, and so on.
3. Content provider can restrict the reuse of the protected content by binding a usage with the entitlement.

2 Background

Table 1 shows the current digital content protection technology specifications for CE devices[3],[4], in which 4C means four companies. The inclusion of digital interfaces in receiver leads to the establishment of home networks. Up till now content protection in home networks, e.g., the 5C scheme[5], has mainly focused on physical link and storage protection. However, there is a growing awareness that content protection and especially DRM should be addressed at the middleware of at the application layer.

First, a copy protection system architecture (CPSA) that combines 4C media protection with 5C link protection technologies to provide a protected home network[4]. Second, rather than exploiting media and link protection, SmartRight[6] builds upon the conditional access approach. Each device in the home network is equipped with a smart card that contains the key to decrypt the encrypted content stream. Upon entrance in the home the STB replaces the ECM of the CA stream with a local ECM (LECM). This LECM is unique to the home network and in such a way the content is "bound" to this specific home network. Third, the Philips Researchers explore various solutions for an AD implementation. One of these is the device-based AD, which defines an AD as a collection of devices belonging to a specific household [7]. The system is neither targeted to a specific content delivery channel nor to a specific content type. In this way only the device can access the content by using its private key. By using a key hierarchy, laborious reencryption of the content itself can be avoided. Finally, the IBM home network protection scheme xCP based on broadcast encryption [8] as another alternative home network protection scheme [9].

3 Proposed Content Protection Framework

The UCPS system comprises two parts: the descriptor embedded in the head end named by UCPS-Flag and the content protection part named by UCPS-CP which is our focus.

Table 1. Existing main digital content protection technology specifications

	Security System	Licensers	Application
1	DTCP	DTLA, LLC	Output
2	HDCP	DCP, LLC	Output
3	D-VHS	JVC	Recording
4	MagicGate	Sony	Recording
5	CPRM	4C Entity, LLC	Recording
6	TiVoGuard	TiVo	Recording
7	Vidi	Philips and HP	Recording for+ R/RW
8	WM-DRM	Microsoft	Digital rights management
9	Helix-DRM	RealNetworks	Digital rights management
10	SmartRight	Thomson	Digital rights management

Therefore, we use UCPS to replace the UCPS-CP. The protection for the digital interfaces in the home network receivers may need three procedures including authentication, encryption and system renewing/revocation. In addition, three kinds of modules need to be designed as shown in Fig. 1, with respective picture patterns.

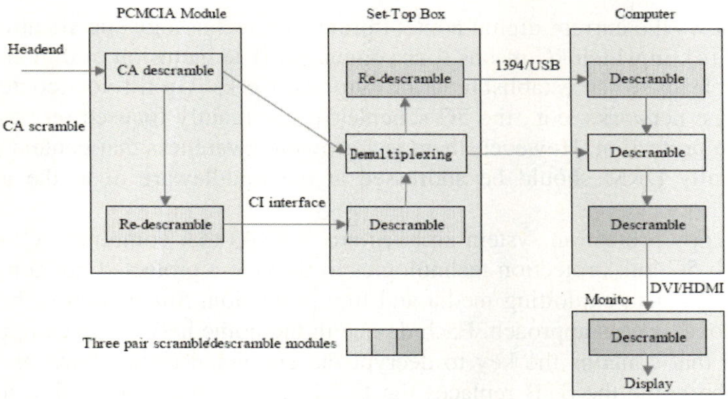

Fig. 1. The implementation of the unified content protection framework

UCPS framework consists of three parts: data, algorithm, and protocol. Data contains all the cipher keys needed to be protected by the hardware, the public data that can not be tampered, and the state information. The algorithm includes the basic algorithms such as the signature, verification, encryption, and decryption, etc. These algorithms need physical security to prevent being tampered. The protocol is the function module implemented in the application layer. The protocol stack structure of UCPS is described as Table 2.

Table 2. Hierarchical structure of protocol stack in UCPS devices

Application Layer	Protocol
Transaction Layer, Session Layer	Interface
Link Layer	
Physical Layer	Data, Algorithm

3.1 Authentication and Key Setup

Authentication consists of four kinds: full mutual authentication, full one-way authentication, mutual re-authentication, one-way re-authentication. Two or all of the protocols can be chosen to be implemented in different interfaces. Secret key establishment and confirmation are accomplished in the authentication process. Secret key confirmation is divided into two parts: mutual confirmation and one-way confirmation. The established key after authentication is named by the main secret key, which can be generated into encrypted key and integrality checkout key.

Authentication and secret key setup rely on a relatively close PKI. Any two of the UCPS modules can establish trust relations through verifying the certificate chain. Fig.2 shows the PKI trust model of two levels CA(certificate authority).The authentication protocol can assure the trust relation being right established. Meanwhile, it finishes the setup and confirmation of the shared key to prevent the attack of hackers. The generation of the certificate requires to be formatted according to format of the certificate. And then, the formatted message is signed by the ECC signature algorithm.

The core technologies of authentication and the key exchange protocol are to

1. establish the trust relations using public certificate
2. guarantee the verdure achieve the mutual and one-way authentication using inquiry- response for the protocol.
3. set up the shared key using Diffie-Hellman secret key exchange method[10].

Each UCPS module must store a certificate list. The root certificate stored in UCPS module by itself is used to verify the validity of the received certificate list. Hence, the credibility of the certificate is confirmed. Furthermore, the public key of the device certificate is used to verify the real-time signed message. Correspondingly, the entity authentication is achieved. The protocol runs on the application layer, which crosses the main program of the application layer and can be invoked to finish the authentication, information collection, system integrity renewing, data transmission, and secret data transmission.

The authentication protocol finishes authentication, shared key setup, and shared key confirmation. That contains four kinds, each of which includes 2-3 rounds message transmission. Each round message of each kind of authentication protocol has specific flag information, which includes

$$\text{Protocol type} \parallel \text{protocol sub type} \parallel \text{protocol round}$$

Where protocol type indicates the protocol is AKE(authentication key exchange) protocol, the sub type indicates the type of the four kinds, the protocol round indicates the round of additional message in this type protocol.

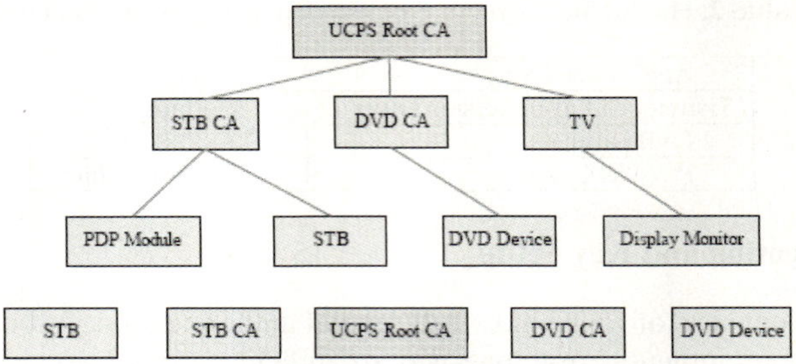

Fig. 2. PKI trust model of two levels CA

3.2 Secure Transmission

The encrypted key and integrality key are used and updated in the transportation process to achieve the secret transmitting of audio, video content, and control information related to the content. Integrality transportation of control information mainly involves control information transportation protocol, which is used in the single data packet comprised much control information. After the authentication and secret key exchange, the communicating entities both have 256 bits share main key.

The invalid device is revoked to maintain the integrity of the system, which can be achieved by the query of CRL (certification revocation list). There are three kinds of CRL queries. First, the temporal ID of the link device is reported to the front network, by which CRL query is achieved and return to the query result by the down channel. Second, the local storage CRL is queried to get the query result. Third, the validity record list of the ID in local device is queried, whose query result is as the CRL query result. In the proposed module, for the sake of many kinds of interfaces and the big difference in the application environment, it is therefore that the integrity of the system is ensured by the different techniques.

4 UCPS-Based DRM Between Home Networks Receiver Devices

Based on the proposed UCPS security core concept, we have developed a digital rights management system for the home network. Fig.3 depicts an illustrative example of such a chain, where for the sake of clarity analog connections are not shown. The strength and completeness of the chain depends on more than just the individually developed links. By promoting the development of a comprehensive, compatible content protection system, this architecture stands to benefit content owners, content providers, device manufacturers, and above all consumers. The UCPS can provide the encryption mechanism to the different receivers in a home network. In the receiver and the recordable devices terminal, the UCPS also can provide the authorized decryption methods to achieve playing and recording the encrypted data stream. The receiver devices receive content from a variety of sources, including cable operators, satellite or terrestrial broadcasters, and telephony centers. Pre-recorded media is also considered to be a content source.

A commonality of all these sources is that they protect the content in some private way before delivery. Examples are the protection provided by the DirecTV Digital Satellite System (DSS) system and the Content Scramble System (CSS) for DVDs. When the scrambled content reaches the boundaries of the network, an authorized access device (a DSS set-top box) descrambles the stream, and makes it available for display or storage. The content then has to be sent to a display or storage device. A global copy protection framework needs to address two problems: protection of content in transmission and protection of content in storage. Copy protection technologies and tools are used to prevent unauthorized access. The proposed approaches can offer an intelligent solution that handles both of the transmission and storage.

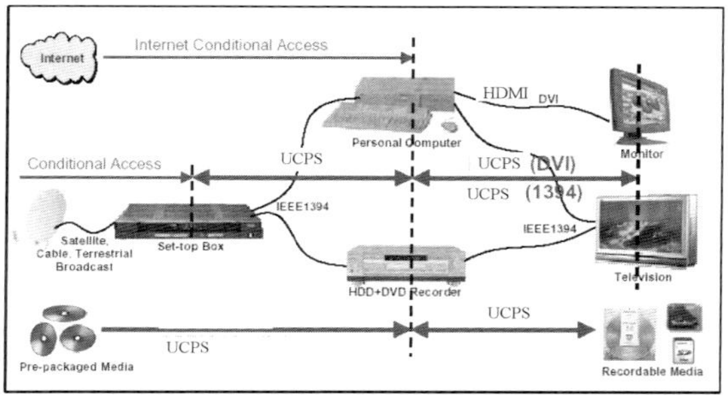

Fig. 3. An illustrative example of UCPS used in the home network

5 System Analysis

As above described, the purpose of the proposed framework is as follows. First, the audiovisual content in the valid devices can be secretly transmitted. Second, the control information of the content can be transported with intactness.

The validity of the devices is embodied by the authentication protocol, which ensures the validated devices have the certificate signed by the CA in UCPS system and the corresponding secret key in the device. The validity of the certificate is guaranteed by the validity of the certificate subscribe link. The enforceability is guaranteed by the ECC signing algorithm in certificate, whose validity is ensured by detecting the system integrity information. The secret key is obtained in terms of authorized terms. The manufacturers obtained the secret key can produce the valid devices.

Secure transmission is characterized by the secure transportation. The final security depends on encryption algorithm. The length of the ciphertext counter is 32bits. Therefore, encryption key and integrity key can be changed once after encrypted 4G bit plaintext data each time. The length of encryption key is 128bits, which can ensure the secure transportation of 4G data. When the transfer rate is 5Gbps, 4G data needs 0.8 second to be transferred. Considering that the random number is 128 bits, the time for each cycle is about $0.8 \times 2^{18} = 8.6 \times 10^{30}$ years. Therefore, the cycle event can not happen in the lifetime and can provide the enough secret key for the secret transmission.

The integrated transmission is achieved by the secure transmission. The difference lies in the integrality key. The security depends on the security of Hash (SHA-256)

and the security strength of the encryption algorithm. The key thing of the system integrity is the acquisition of CRL, whose security depends on update frequency and the security of the CRL. The security of signature depends on the signature algorithm, in which we use ECC in GF(P) with a length of 192 bits. That is absolute safe. The security of our proposed system is based on the secret of the key, which is irrelevant to the algorithm itself.

6 Discussions and Conclusions

While home network content sharing has brought an innovative digital experience to the users, it is still crucial to protect the rights of copyright holders of the shared contents on the home network. Since it is quite easy for people to send digital contents to the public through the internet, it is important to adopt strong DRM (digital rights management) system. Before we started developing the UCPS for the home network receivers, we decided two major items of DRM policy as follows.

1) Authorized domain

The content may be constrained within an AD. Meanwhile, the authorized usage meta-data named Usage State Information (USI) is tightly bound to the content.

2) Copy control information

CCI is embedded in the content stream and transmitted with the content. If the completeness of the content is ensured by the encryption algorithm, the completeness of CCI is ensured. All the CCI of this frame must be offered by the source device to construct the CCI record. Hence, the verification protocol of CCI is executed.

We developed the digital content protection system by the proposed framework for the home network receivers, which can prevent being replicating and distributed. The proposed technology can provide the encryption mechanism to the existing digital interfaces of the home network receivers, which can encrypt the transparent content stream. The receiver and recordable device terminals can provide the authorized decryption method to play and record the encrypted data stream. The requirements for UCPS are follows: 1) Consensus is needed. 2) To reach a common set of goals, the participating industries need to agree on certain legal and technical issues.3) be licensed to the hardware manufacturers. 4) Includes an effective technological measure. 5) The measure must permit legal enforcement against circumvention. 6) Provides transmission and storage protection. 7) Is renewable. 8) Low complexity and low cost.

The system has low complexity in implementation, operation, maintenance and administration. Our next step may include establish the UCPS certificate management system and the corresponding compliance testing system to ensure the interoperability among the different receiver devices, enhance the storage and link protection to support digital rights management, and develop a solution to close the analog whole.

Acknowledgment

The authors wish to thank Prof. Jianhua Ge and Prof. Yumin Wang from Xidian University, Xi'an, China, for their useful technological support. This work has been Supported by the National Natural Science Foundation of China Under Grant No. 60672112, the Graduate Innovation Fund, Xidian University under Grant No. 05001, and the National Natural Science Foundation of China Under Grant No. 60633020.

References

1. Digital Transmission Content Protection Specification Revision 1.3, January 7, (2004) Available at http://www.dtcp.com
2. High-bandwidth Digital Content Protection System?Revision 1.1, (June 9, 2003) Available at http:// www.digital-cp.com
3. Lin, E.I., Eskicioglu, A.M., Lagendijk, R.L., Delp, E.J.: Advances in digital video content protection. Proceedings of the IEEE 93, 171–183 (2005)
4. Jonker, W., Linnartz, J.-P.: Digital rights management in consumer electronics products. Signal Processing Magazine, IEEE 21(2), 82–91 (2004)
5. 5C digital transmission content protection white paper. [Online].Available: http://www.dtcp.com
6. [Online]. Available: http://www.smartright.org
7. van den Heuvel, S.A.F.A., Jonker, W., Kamperman, F.L.A.J., P.J. 11. Lenoir: Secure Content Management in Authorised Domains. Int. Broadcasting Conv (IBC, Amsterdam, The Netherlands, pp. 467–474 (2002)
8. Lotspiech, J., Pestoni, F., Nusser, S.: Broadcast encryption's bright future. IEEE Computer 35(8), 57–63 (2002)
9. IBM response to DVB-CPT cfp for content protection and copy management: xCP cluster Protocol, DVB-CPT-716, (October 2001)
10. Diffie, W., Hellman, M.E.: New directions in cryptography. IEEE Trans. Inf. Theory IT-22(6), 644–654 (1976)

An Efficient Anonymous Registration Scheme for Mobile IPv4

Xuefei Cao[1], Weidong Kou[1], Huaping Li[1], and Jie Xu[2]

[1] Chinese National Key Lab of Integrated Service Networks, Xidian University, Xi'an, Shannxi 710071, China
{xfcao, wdkou, hpli}@mail.xidian.edu.cn
[2] Information and Control Engineering School, Xi'an University of Architecture & Technology, Xi'an Shannxi 710055, China
xdxj123@sohu.com

Abstract. With the develop of wireless networks, user anonymity are of growing concern. A key problem in the anonymous Mobile IP registration is how to minimize the registration delay while improve the security. This paper solves this problem by the non-interactive authentication from pairings in the identity-based cryptography. The main idea behind our scheme is to minimize both the on-line pairing operation time and the inter-domain communication round trip time based on the dynamic one-way authentication key. Analysis shows that the registration delay is reduced to 39.2001mswhile the improved security attributes including mutual tri-partite authentication, local key generation, stolen-verifier attacker and user privacy are provided in our scheme.

1 Introduction

Mobile IPv4 is used as third layer protocol in the Beyond Third Generation(B3G) wireless networks to provide seamless data transmission for mobile nodes when they leave their home network and roam in foreign networks [1]. In Mobile IPv4, a *mobile node*(MN) is provided with a *home agent* (HA) and a *home address* in his/her home network. When the MN roams to a visiting network, he/she obtains a new address, i.e. *Care-of-Address* (COA) and registers the COA during Mobile IP registration at his/her HA. Then the HA will redirect the data packet destined to the MN's *home address* to MN's *foreign agent* (FA) at the visiting network and finally to the mobile node's COA.

Anonymity are of growing concern to end users [3]. It is wanted that Mobile IP registration can satisfy user anonymity so that for one thing, MN can enjoy seamless data transfer wherever he/she is; for the other thing, an untrusted party can not track MN's location, or identify calls made to or from MN by eavesdropping on the radio path. Further, considering the risks existing in open wirelss networks, Mobile IP registration should also satisfies the following requests [2]:

R1. Mutual authentication between MN, HA and FA.
R2. Local Key generation, i.e. MN, FA and HA can generate session keys locally so that they can be sure of the security of the session keys.

Y. Wang, Y. Cheung, and H. Liu (Eds.): CIS 2006, LNAI 4456, pp. 758–766, 2007.

R3. Resistant to Verifier-Stolen attack, i.e. there is no need for HA to maintain MN's verifier or password or pseudonym, otherwise HA will become the bottleneck of system security.
R4. Non-repudiation of accountting information.

What's more, Mobile IP registration scheme should be effective because that MN is always power-limited and that the wireless communication channel is bandwidth-limited.

Many Mobile IP registration schemes [4,5,6,7,9,10] were proposed based on traditional Certificate-based Public Key Cryptology (CA-PKC). However, those schemes is not efficient in terms of bandwidth because the transfer of public key certificate consumes extra bandwidth. Recent Mobile IP registration schemes[8,11] replaced CA-PKC with Identity-Based Public Key Cryptosystem (ID-PKC) to reduce the security cost and throughput. However, those schemes are not efficient because they require intensive bilinear paring operation which is the most costly operation among all the available cryptographic applications [12]. What's more, except for [8], none of the previous schemes realizes both anonymity and the security requirement listed above. In this paper, we propose an anonymous Mobile IP registration which is both efficient and secure.

In our scheme, non-interactive authentication from pairings in ID-PKC [13] is employed in our scheme to reduce both inter-domain round trip time (RTT) and on-line pairing operation time. Authentication between MN and HA is Password-based which helps to minimize the computation overhead of MN. In contrast to the *Verifying the Pre-shared Secret* method in [6,11], our method is resistant to Verifier-stolen attack because HA can compute MN's verifier by itself. The main features of our scheme include user anonymity, improved security and efficiency.

The remainder of the paper is as follows: Section 2 introduces the preliminaries; Section 3 describes our proposed scheme, followed by the performance and security analyses in Section 4; Section 5 concludes the paper.

2 Preliminaries

We will introduce in this section the preliminaries on which to base our scheme.

2.1 Trust Model

The current RFC 2002 [1] proposed the trust model of Mobile IP registration. RFC 2002 supports HA and the FA in providing Mobile IP services to MN. HA is the trusted server of MN, a long-term Security Association(SA) is established between MN and HA. When MN roams to a visiting network, which has had business agreement with MN's home network, a certain FA should provide network services to MN. MN has to register his/her COA at HA in order to maintain continuity of communication while he/she is away form his/her home network.

2.2 Bilinear Pairngs

Let $\mathbb{G}_1$and $\mathbb{G}_2$ be additive and multiplicative cyclic groups of prime order q, respectively, and let P be an arbitrary generator of $\mathbb{G}_1$. Bilinear paring e : $\mathbb{G}_1 \times \mathbb{G}_1 \rightarrow \mathbb{G}_2$ is a map with following properties:

1. Bilinear: For $R, S \in \mathbb{G}_1$, $a, b \in \mathbb{Z}_q^*$, $e(aR, bS) = e(bR, aS) = e(R, S)^{ab}$.
2. Non-degenerate: $e(P, P) \neq 1_{\mathbb{G}_2}$.
3. Computable: There exists an efficient algorithm to compute $e(R, S)$ for all $R, S \in \mathbb{G}_1$.

The following problem is assumed intractable on $\mathbb{G}_1$.

Computational Diffie-Hellman Problem: For $a, b \in \mathbb{Z}_q^*$, given an instance $\{P, aP, bP\}$, compute abP.

2.3 Non-interactive Authenticated Key Agreement in ID-Based Cryptosystem

Identity-based Cryptology (ID-PKC) [14] is a form of public key cryptography in which the identity information of a user functions as his/her public key. A Trusted Authority (TA) which is trusted by all the users is responsible for generating the users' private keys. In ID-PKC, the user's public key can be obtained and used without a CA-based certificate; this simplifies the certificate management. Another inherent advantage of ID-PKC is that two users can share an authentication key non-interactively[13]. To consummate the advantage in our proposed scheme, ID-PKC should consist of two basic operation `Setup` and `Private-key-extraction` such that:

`Setup`. A Trusted Authority (TA) takes security parameter k as input and returns the system parameters params and master-key such that:

1. Specifies $\mathbb{G}_1, \mathbb{G}_2, q, e, P$ as described in Section 2.2.
2. Selects a master-key s uniformly at random from $\mathbb{Z}_q^*$ and sets the system pubic key $P_0 = sP$.
3. Chooses two hash functions $H_1 : \{0,1\}^* \rightarrow \mathbb{G}_1$ and $H : \{0,1\}^* \rightarrow \mathbb{Z}_q^*$.

TA then publishes the system parameters $\langle \mathbb{G}_1, \mathbb{G}_2, q, e, P, P_0, H_1, H \rangle$.

`Private-Key-Extract`. TA calculates $Q_{ID_A} = H_1(ID_A)$, where ID_A is an identifier associated uniquely with user A. The TA then sends the private key $S_A = sQ_A$ to A via a secure channel.

In such a system, two users A and B can authenticate each other by non-interactive key k_{AB} between them.

$$k_{AB} = e(S_A, Q_B)e(Q_A, S_B)$$

3 Proposed Scheme

3.1 System Initialization

Before we introduce the system initialization, we first introduce the notations in use: N and T are 128bits nonce and timestamp, respectively; ID_A and IP_A are user A's unique identifier and IP address, respectively; k_{A-B} is secret key between user A and user B; $H(k,m)$ is a hash function of message m with a secret key k as parts of its input; $Enc(k,m)$ is encryption of message m under secret key k using a secure symmetric encryption algorithm such as AES, $Sig(S,m)$ is signature of message m under private key S.

System initialization establishes the security association (SA) between HA and FA, and SA between HA and MN.

The SA between HA and FA is established by a globally Trusted Authority (TA) who sets up system as described in Section 2.3. Being clients of TA, HA and FA are provided by TA with secret keys S_{HA} and S_{FA} respectively. HA and FA are also provided with system parameters$\langle \mathbb{G}_1, \mathbb{G}_2, q, e, P, P_0, H_1, H \rangle$.

To setup SA for its clients, HA firstly chooses a secret number $r \in \mathbb{Z}_q^*$ at random and computes his public key $k_{pub} = rP$. HA then publicizes $\langle k_{pub}, P, ID_{HA}, IP_{HA}, H, q$ as system parameters. For a qualified MN with identifier ID_{MN}, the SA between HA and MN is established as follows:

1. MN sends ID_{MN},IP_{MN} to HA.
2. HA computes $k_{MN-HA} = H(r, ID_{MN})$ and sends k_{MN-HA} to MN via a secure channel.
3. HA accepts MN with identifier ID_{MN} and home address IP_{MN} as an authorized client.

3.2 Mobile IP Registration

As shown in Fig.1, our Mobile IP registration is described in detail as follows:

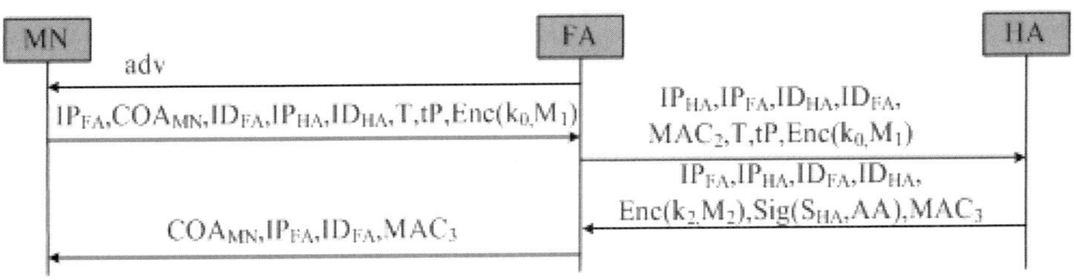

Fig. 1. Efficient Anonymous Mobile IP Registration Scheme

1. FA broadcasts periodically the routing advertisement adv which includes ID_{FA},IP_{FA}.
2. On receiving adv, MN do the following:

(a) choose at random $t \in \mathbb{Z}_q^*$, computes tP and the temporal session key $k_0 = tk_{pub} = trP$.
(b) obtain current timestamp T, computes and stores authentication key $k_1 = H(k_{MN-HA}, T)$
(c) computes message authentication code $MAC_1 = H(k_1, ID_{MN} \| IP_{MN} \| COA_{MN})$
(d) encrypts $M_1 = ID_{MN} \| IP_{MN} \| COA_{MN} \| MAC_1$ with k_0.

3. MN→FA: COA_{MN}, IP_{FA}, ID_{FA}, IP_{HA}, ID_{HA},T, tP, $Enc(k_0, M_1)$.
4. On receiving message from MN, FA do the following:
   (a) computes authentication key between HA and FA $k_2 = H_2(T, e(S_{FA}, H1(ID_{HA})))$
   (b) computes $MAC_2 = H(k_2, ID_{FA} \| ID_{HA} \| COA_{MN})$.
5. FA→HA: IP_{HA}, IP_{FA}, ID_{HA}, ID_{FA}, MAC_2,T,tP, $Enc(k_0, M_1)$.
6. On receiving message from FA, HA do the following:
   (a) computes $k_0 = rtP$ with its secret key r.
   (b) Decrypts $Enc(k_0, M_1)$ for ID_{MN}, IP_{MN},COA_{MN} and MAC_1 with k_0.
   (c) computes k_{MN-HA} with ID_{MN} and r.
   (d) computes k_0 with k_{MN-HA} and T.
   (e) checks the integrity of MAC_1 by reconstructing MAC_1 with k_1.
   (f) computes $k_2 = H(T, e(H_1(ID_{FA}, S_{HA})))$ with S_{HA}.
   (g) checks the integrity of MAC_2 by reconstructing MAC_2 with k_2.
   (h) if both the check on MAC_1 and MAC_2 pass, authorizes MN and FA respectively, updates the care-of-address binding of MN. Generates accounting acknowledgement AA of MN for FA with its private key S_{HA}.
   (i) encrypts $M_2 = COA_{MN} \| ID_{HA} \| k_1$ with k_2.
   (j) computes $MAC_3 = H(k_0, ID_{MN} \| ID_{FA} \| IP_{FA})$.
7. HA→FA: IP_{FA},IP_{HA},ID_{FA},ID_{HA},$Enc(k_2, M_2)$, $Sig(S_{HA}, AA)$, MAC_3.
8. On receiving message from HA, FA decrypts $Enc(k_2, M_2)$ with k_2, checks the integrity of COA_{MN} and ID_{HA} included in M_2. If the check passes, FA authorizes HA and MN, then FA stores k_1 for future communication with MN and k_2 for future communication with HA.
9. FA→MN: COA_{MN}, IP_{FA}, MAC_3.
10. On receiving message from HA, MN checks the integrity of MAC_3, if the check passes, MN authenticates FA and HA. k_0 is used for MN's future communication with HA and k_1 for MN's future communication with FA.

4 Evaluation

4.1 Security Features

Our scheme satisfies the following security requirements:

R1. Mutual authentication between MN, HA and FA: The mutual authentication between HA and FA is based on dynamic authentication key k_2. By the bilinearity of pairing, $e(S_{FA}, H_1(ID_{HA})) = e(H_1 ID_{FA}, S_{SA}) = K$, no one except HA,FA and TA is able to generate K. TA is trusted not to abuse its knowledge of master key s. The generation of k_2 requires both K and timestamp T, which helps to deter against reply attack.Therefore, HA and FA can use k_2 to authenticate each other.

The mutual authentication between HA and MN is based on dynamic authentication key k_0 and k_1. $k_{MN-HA} = H(r, ID_{MN})$ is known only to HA and MN, k_1 is generated based on k_{MN-HA} and timestamp T, therefore, MN can authenticate itself to HA based on k_1. $k_0 = tk_{pub} = rtP$ is generated based on HA's public key k_{pub}, only HA can compute k_0 given tP, therefore, MN authenticates HA based on k_0.

The mutual authentication between MN and FA is realized based on MN's and FA's trust towards HA. HA is believed to be an honest agent, which is similar to the case in commercial applications. HA will not send $Enc(k_2, M_2)$ to FA if HA can not authenticate MN, therefore FA authenticate MN via HA. The same is with MN's authentication to FA. HA will not send MAC_3 to MN if HA can not authenticate FA, thus MN authenticates FA via HA.

R2. Session keys can be generated locally. In the available Mobile IP registration schemes [4,5,6,9] session keys $k_0(k_{MN-HA})$, $k_1(k_{MN-FA})$, and $k_2(k_{MN-FA})$ are distributed by HA. However, in our protocol, the session keys k_0, k_1, k_2 can be generated locally, thus improves the security of the session keys.

R3. In our scheme, there is no need for HA to maintain MN's verifier k_{MN-HA} because HA can compute k_{MN-HA} from its secret key r. HA only need to keep its secret r which reduce the HA's maintaining overhead.

R4. Non-repudiation: HA's signature of the account acknowledgement is included to provide the non-repudiation.

R5. Anonymity and location privacy of MN: MN's identifier is not transmitted in plaintext, only HA can extract MN's true identity.

The security comparison of different schemes are given in Table 1. In the table, $\surd$ means "satisfied" while \ means "not satisfied". From Table 1, we can see that only our scheme and scheme in [8] satisfies all the security requirements **R1 R5** listed above.

Table 1. Security comparison of different Mobile IP registration sechemes

	R1	**R2**	**R3**	**R4**	**R5**
Scheme in [4]	√	\	√	√	\
Scheme in [5]	√	\	\	√	\
Scheme in [6]	√	\	\	√	\
Scheme in [7]	√	√	\	√	\
Scheme in [8]	√	√	√	√	√
Our scheme	√	√	√	√	√

4.2 Performance

In this part, we evaluate the performance of different Mobile IP registration schemes according to the experimental data directly from the previous works [15,16]. The hardware platform for home or foreign agent servers is an AMD Opteron 1.6 GHz processor under Linux 2.4.21; the one for MN is a 206MHz StrongARM processor under Windows CE pocket PC 2002. 1024bits RSA, 128bits DES, 160bits SHA-1, the ID-based algorithms of [7] and the Tate pairing are employed. The IP address, identifier, nonce and timestamp in our scheme is 128bits in length recpectively; Point in group $\mathbb{G}_1$ is 160bits in length; Public key certificate is 256bytes in length. The data rate of wireless link is 2Mbps, the propagation time is 0.5ms. The cryptography operation time of the agent server is obtained from [17,18]; the time for MN is obtained from [19,20]; Table 2 lists the running time of cryptology operations of server and MN respectively.

Table 2. Running time of different cryptology operations

	RSA sign/ decrypt	RSA verify/ encrypt	ID sign/ decrypt	ID verify/ encrypt	DES	SHA	Tate pairing	Scalar multi-plication
MN	78.3	5.01	376.24	355	0.0367	0.19	355	10.62
Server	2.07	0.07	4.74	3.16	6e-4	2e-4	3.16	0.79

We adopt the method in [11] to compute the registration delay of our scheme:

$$\begin{aligned} delay = {} & [k_0]_{MN} + [tP]_{MN} + 2[SHA]_{MN} + [DES]_{MN} + [Message]_{MN-FA} + \\ & [Paring]_{FA} + 2[SHA]_{FA} + [Message]_{FA-HA} + \\ & [k_0]_{HA} + 2[DES]_{HA} + 6[SHA]_{HA} + [Pairing]_{HA} + [Message]_{HA-FA} + \\ & [DES]_{FA} + [Message]_{FA-MN} + [SHA]_{MN} = 39.2001ms \end{aligned}$$

Similarly, the registration delay of the other Mobile IP registration schemes can be computed: 117.114ms for scheme in [4]; 103.9831ms for scheme in [5]; 24.5399ms for scheme in [6]; 20.4039ms for scheme in [7] and 762.0208ms for scheme in [8]. The comparison result is shown in Fig.2. Due to the space limit, the registration delay of scheme [8] is not illustrated accurately in Fig. 2. From the comparison in running time, it can be seen that our scheme is efficient. Although the registration delay of our scheme is a little longer than that of scheme in [6] and [7], our scheme is provides better security attributes and the extra efficiency cost of our scheme is trivial compared with the security features improved.

The registration delay of our scheme is drastically reduced for two reasons: First, the employment of non-interactive key agreement from pairings minimize both the inter-domain round trip time and on-line paring operation time; second, hash functions and symmetric encryption are used instead of asymmetric cryptology operation.

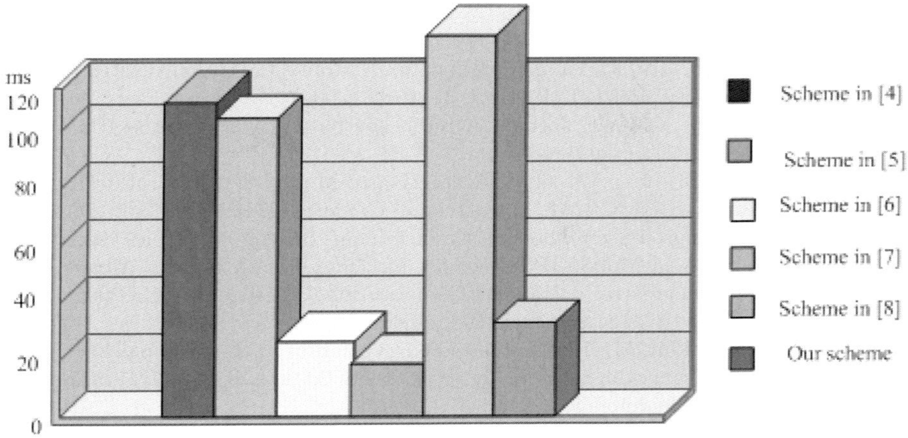

Fig. 2. Comparison result of the registration delay of different schemes

5 Conclusion

In this article, we have proposed an efficient anonymous Mobile IP registration scheme from pairings. In our scheme, anonymity and location privacy of end user is provided with other improved security features including (1) mutual tri-party authentication between MN,FA and HA (2) local key generation and (3) resistant to verifier-stolen attack. Further, our scheme is effective with an registration delay of 39.2001ms because non-interactive authentication based on pairings is employed. Therefore, our scheme is a suitable candidate for the future real-time mobile communication where high grade of security is required and the terminal is power-limited. Our future work is the research on the optimized session set-up between MN and its correspondent node.

References

1. RFC,: IP Mobility Support (IPv4) (2002), `http://www.ietf.org/rfc/rfc2002.txt`
2. Wang, H., Zheng, S.: The security issues and countermeasures in Mobile IP. In: Proceedings of, International Conferences on Info-tech and Info-net(ICII 2001). IEEE, New York, pp. 122–127 (2001)
3. Ateniese, G., Herzberg, A., Krawczyk, H., Tsudik, G.: Untraceable Mobility or How to Travel Incognito. Comput. Netw 8, 871–884 (1999)
4. Jacobs, S.: Mobile IP Public Key Based Authentication, Internet Draft, draft-jacobs-mobileip-pki-auth-00.txt, Work in progress (1998)
5. Chung, S., Chae, K.: An Efficient Public Key-based Authenticaiton with Mobile IP in E-Commerce. In: Proceedings of the International Conference on Parallel and Distributed Systems, IEEE Press, New York (2000)
6. Lam, S.: Mobile-IP Registration Protocol: A Security Attack and New Secure Minimal Pubic-key Based Authentication. In: Proceedings of the 1999 International Symposium on Parallel Architectures, IEEE, New York (1999)

7. Wang, L., Yang, B.: A Timestamp Based Registration Protocol in Mobile Ip. Journal of Xidian Universiy 5, 777–780 (2004)
8. Zhang, S., Xu, G., Hu, Z., Yang, Y., Zhou, X.: A Mobile IP Authenticaiton Protocol Based on Identitty. Journal of BUPT 3, 86–88 (2005)
9. Zao, J., Kent, S., Gahm1, Joshua: A publickey based secure Mobile IP. Wireless Networks 5, 373–390 (1999)
10. Chou,CY. Min,SH. Jian,WL.et al: A Solution to Mobile IP Registration for AAA. In: Proceedings of 7th CDMA International Conference, IEEE, Seoul (2002)
11. Kwang, C.: ID-Based Secure Session Key Exchange Scheme to Reduce Registration Delay with AAA in Mobile IP Networks. In: Sunderam, V.S., van Albada, G.D., Sloot, P.M.A., Dongarra, J.J. (eds.) Computational Science – ICCS 2005. LNCS, vol. 3515, pp. 510–C518. Springer, Heidelberg (2005)
12. Boneh, D., Franklin, M.: Identity-based encryption from the Weil pairing. In: Kilian, J. (ed.) Advances in Cryptology - CRYPTO 2001. LNCS, vol. 2139, pp. 213–C229. Springer, Heidelberg (2001)
13. Sakai, R., Ohgishi, K. and Kasahara, M.: Cryptosystems based on pairing. In: The 2000 Sympoium on Cryptography and Information Security (2000)
14. Shamir, A.: Identity-base cryptosystems and signature schemes. In: Proc. of Crypto '84, Springer, Heidelberg (1985)
15. Hess, A., Shafer, G.: Performance Evaluation of AAA/Mobile IP Authentication. In: Proceedings of 2nd Polish-German Teletraffic Symposium, Gdansk, Springer, Heidelberg (2002)
16. McNair, J., Akyldiz, I.F., Bender, M.D.: An inter-system handoff technique for the IMT-2000 system. In: INFOCOM 2000, IEEE, New York (2000)
17. Paulo, S. L. M., Barreto.: Efficient Pairing Computation on Supersingular Abelian Varieties. In: Cryptography ePrint Archive, Report (2004), `http://eprint.iacr.org/2004/375.pdf`
18. Wei, D.: `http://www.eskimo.com/~weidai/benchmarks.html`
19. Bertoni, G.M., Chen, L. Harrison, K.A. Pelosi, G.: Computing Tate pairing on smart cards. `http://www.st.com/stonline/products/families/smartcard/ches2005v4`
20. Patroklos, G.: Performance Analysis of Cryptographic Protocols on Handheld Devices. In: TCD-CS-2003-46.pdf (2003), `https://www.cs.tcd.ie/publications/techreports/reports.03/`

An Elliptic Curve Based Authenticated Key Agreement Protocol for Wireless Security

SeongHan Shin, Kazukuni Kobara, and Hideki Imai

Research Center for Information Security (RCIS)
National Institute of Advanced Industrial Science and Technology (AIST)
1-18-13 Sotokanda, Chiyoda-ku, Tokyo 101-0021 Japan
{seonghan.shin,kobara_conf,h-imai}@aist.go.jp
http://www.rcis.aist.go.jp/

Abstract. When we consider wireless security, it is strongly preferable to use password-based authentication and the elliptic curve based Diffie-Hellman protocol since the former provides a user-friendly authentication method and the latter is an efficient key agreement protocol. However, this combination does not necessarily guarantee security against off-line dictionary attacks (especially, "partition attacks"). In this paper, we propose an elliptic curve based authenticated key agreement (called EC-AKA) protocol that is secure against partition attacks as well as suitable for the following situation: (1) a client, who communicates with many different servers, remembers only one password and has insecure devices; (2) the counterpart servers are not perfectly secure against several attacks; (3) neither PKI (Public Key Infrastructures) nor TRM (Tamper-Resistance Modules) is available. The EC-AKA protocol is secure under the elliptic curve Diffie-Hellman problem in the random oracle model. We also show that the EC-AKA protocol achieves more strengthened security properties and efficiency compared with the existing protocols (employed in the IEEE 802.1x).

1 Introduction

The rapid advance of wireless technology has brought much attention from many researchers who, at the same time, have expressed concerns about security. As we know, the most fundamental security goals are authentication that is a means to verify who is communicating with whom or whether a party is a legitimate one, and confidentiality that is a means to protect messages exchanged over open networks (i.e., the Internet). One of the ways to achieve such security goals is to use an authenticated key agreement (AKA) protocol by which the involving parties authenticate each other and then share a common session key to be used for their subsequent secure channels. Up to now, many AKA protocols have been proposed where some take advantage of PKI (Public Key Infrastructure) and others are based on a secret shared between the parties (e.g., human-memorable password).

Compared to the wired networks, wireless ones typically place severe restrictions on designing such cryptographic protocols. Main obstacles include: client's

Y. Wang, Y. Cheung, and H. Liu (Eds.): CIS 2006, LNAI 4456, pp. 767–777, 2007.

mobile devices have constraints on available power consumption, followed by restriction of computing power; mobile devices are easy to be lost or stolen due to a holder's carelessness; wireless communications are more prone to interception than wired ones; communication bandwidth is already limited; and it is difficult to keep some information secure on mobile devices, and so on.

For efficiency, one can use elliptic curve groups whose use in public key cryptography was first proposed by Koblitz [1] and Miller [2] [1]. This is because public key schemes based on elliptic curve groups typically have lower processing requirements, and can achieve the same level of security with considerably shorter key sizes than counterparts based on the more traditional RSA and standard discrete logarithm settings. Such elliptic curve cryptographic systems and protocols are ideal for wireless environments where processing power, time and/or communication bandwidth are at a premium.

Therefore, when we consider wireless security it is strongly preferable to use password-based authentication and the elliptic curve based Diffie-Hellman protocol since the former provides a user-friendly authentication method and the latter is an efficient key agreement protocol. However, this combination sometimes results in insecurity against a special kind of off-line dictionary attacks known as "partition attacks". That is, the direct elliptic curve analogs of password-based AKA protocols are insecure against partition attacks (see [3]). Here is a simple example: given an affine point $(\mathcal{X}, \mathcal{Y})$ on an elliptic curve E, the $\mathcal{Y}$-coordinate may be used for an attacker to exclude invalid password candidates by executing a password-based AKA protocol once so that the attacker can sieve out the correct password at a logarithm rate.

1.1 Our Contributions

The first motivation of this work is to thwart partition attacks in an elliptic curve based AKA protocol. And the second motivation comes from the fact that the leakage of stored secrets is a more practical risk rather than breaking a well-studied cryptographic hard problem (e.g., the discrete logarithm problem). In order to deal with this problem, we consider the following situation: (1) a client, who communicates with a variety of servers, remembers only one password and has *insecure* devices (e.g., mobile phones or PDAs) with built-in memory capacity; (2) the counterpart servers are not perfectly secure against several attacks (e.g., virus or hacker); (3) neither PKI nor TRM is available.

In this paper, we propose an AKA (called EC-AKA) protocol based on the elliptic curve Diffie-Hellman protocol that is an analog of the original Diffie-Hellman protocol [4]. The EC-AKA protocol is suitable for the above situation in that it is secure against leakage of stored secrets from a client and servers, respectively, as well as secure against partition attacks. We prove that the EC-AKA protocol is provably secure in the random oracle model with the reduction to the elliptic curve Diffie-Hellman problem. Moreover, we show that the EC-AKA

[1] They observed that the discrete logarithm on elliptic curves over finite fields appeared to be intractable and hence ElGamal encryption and signature schemes have natural counterparts on these curves.

protocol achieves more strengthened security properties and efficiency compared with the existing password-based AKA protocols (e.g., [3,5]). Note that the authenticity of the EC-AKA protocol is based on password and an additional stored secret which might seem to be similar to that of EAP-FAST. However, the obvious distinction between the two protocols is that the EC-AKA protocol remains secure even if the stored secret on client's side is leaked out to an attacker while EAP-FAST does not.

2 An Elliptic Curve Based Authenticated Key Agreement (EC-AKA) Protocol

2.1 Preliminary

Here we consider an elliptic curve E defined over the field $GF(p^m)$, with either $p \geq 2^{160}$ and $m = 1$ or $p = 2$ and $m \geq 160$, where $q = p^m$ and p is a prime. For example, the curve in short Weierstrass form is

$$E : \mathcal{Y}^2 = \mathcal{X}^3 + a\mathcal{X} + b. \tag{1}$$

As shown in the literature [7], we can define an additive (abelian) group in the set of points on this curve (taken together with the point at infinity O). Let G_1 and G_2 be two generators of order q (i.e., $qG_1 \equiv qG_2 \equiv O \bmod p^m$) chosen from the points on E. This is the group where the elliptic curve discrete logarithm problem (EC-DLP) is defined: given two points G_1 and H on E it is hard to find an integer e such that $H \equiv e \cdot G_1$. On the other hand, the e multiple of G can be readily computed by using a method similar to the "square-and-multiply" for exponentiation in $GF(p)$.

Let k denote the security parameter for hash functions (say, 160 bits). Let N be a dictionary size of passwords (say, 36 bits for alphanumerical passwords with 6 characters). Let $\{0,1\}^\star$ denote the set of finite binary strings and $\{0,1\}^k$ the set of binary strings of length k. Let "$||$" denote the concatenation of bit strings in $\{0,1\}^\star$. Let us define secure one-way hash functions. While $\mathcal{H} : \{0,1\}^\star \rightarrow \mathbb{Z}_q^\star \backslash \{1\}$ denotes a full-domain hash (FDH) function, the other hash functions are denoted $\mathcal{H}_j : \{0,1\}^\star \rightarrow \{0,1\}^k$ for $j = 1, 2, 3$ and 4. Here $\mathcal{H}$ and $\mathcal{H}_j$ are distinct random functions one another. Let $\mathcal{C}$ and $\mathcal{S}$ be the identities of client and server, respectively, with representing each ID $\in \{0,1\}^\star$ as well.

2.2 The Protocol

In this subsection, we propose the EC-AKA protocol in detail (see Fig. 1 and 2).

During the initialization phase, server $\mathcal{S}$ sends its elliptic curve parameter param, which is generated in a form (E, q, G_1, G_2), to the client. The latter picks a secret value s_1 randomly chosen from $\mathbb{Z}_q^\star$ and registers securely a verification data v_1 to server $\mathcal{S}$ where pw is the client's password. Then client $\mathcal{C}$ remembers his password pw *and* additionally stores the secret value s_1 as well as the parameter param on insecure devices that may happen to leak s_1 and param in the end.

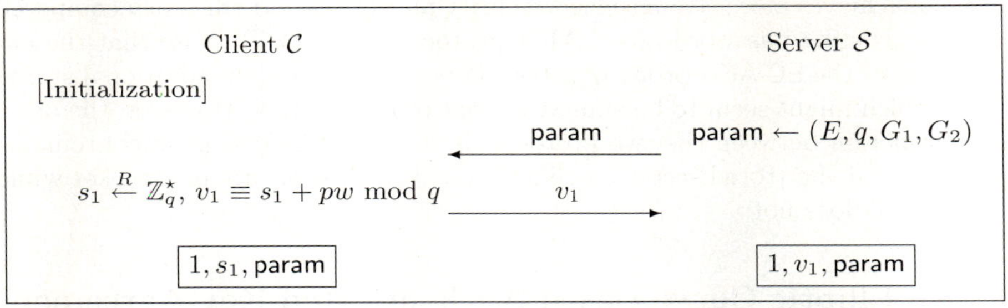

Fig. 1. The initialization of EC-AKA protocol where the enclosed values in rectangle represent stored secrets of client and server, respectively

The server $\mathcal{S}$ also stores the verification data v_1 and its parameter param on its databases both of which may be leaked out. Finally, they set a counter j as 1.

In the j-th ($j \geq 1$) execution of the EC-AKA protocol, client $\mathcal{C}$ should recover the verification data v_j by adding the secret value s_j with the password pw. With a randomly chosen value x from $\mathbb{Z}_q^\star$, the client computes the Diffie-Hellman public value X and calculates Z using a mask generation function as the addition of X with $W \cdot G_2$ where W is a full-domain hash of (j, v_j). Then client $\mathcal{C}$ sends $(\mathcal{C}, j, Z)$ to server $\mathcal{S}$. If the received counter j is incorrect, the server terminates the protocol. Otherwise, server $\mathcal{S}$ extracts X' from this masked Diffie-Hellman public value Z with $W \cdot G_2$. If the resultant value is a quadratic non-residue, the server terminates the protocol. The latter computes not only the Diffie-Hellman public vale $Y \equiv y \cdot G$ with a randomly chosen value y from $\mathbb{Z}_q^\star$ but also the keying material $K_{\mathcal{S}} \equiv y \cdot X'$ that is used to compute its authenticator $V_{\mathcal{S}}$ and a session key SK_j. Upon receiving $(\mathcal{S}, Y, V_{\mathcal{S}})$ from the server, client $\mathcal{C}$ computes the keying material $K_{\mathcal{C}}$ from Y and then generates his authenticator $V_{\mathcal{C}}$ and a session key SK_j, as long as the authenticator $V_{\mathcal{S}}$ is valid, before sending $V_{\mathcal{C}}$ to server $\mathcal{S}$. If the authenticator $V_{\mathcal{C}}$ is valid, server $\mathcal{S}$ actually computes a session key SK_j. At the end of the j-th protocol execution, client $\mathcal{C}$ (resp., server $\mathcal{S}$) refreshes s_j (resp., v_j) to a new one $s_{(j+1)}$ (resp., $v_{(j+1)}$) for the next session.

Remark 1. In order to prevent the invalid-curve attacks [6], both of client and server should check that a received point does indeed lie on the elliptic curve (e.g., by using formulas for the addition law that use both coefficients a and b of the equation of the elliptic curve).

3 Security

First, we give a clue about why the proposed EC-AKA protocol is secure against partition attacks.

Before the EC-AKA protocol execution, the client and the server can agree on the $\mathcal{Y}$-coordinate on curve E with a single bit $(+, -)$. Here we assume that the sign is $+$. Let us think of Z in the first flow of Fig. 2: $Z \equiv X + W$. In this

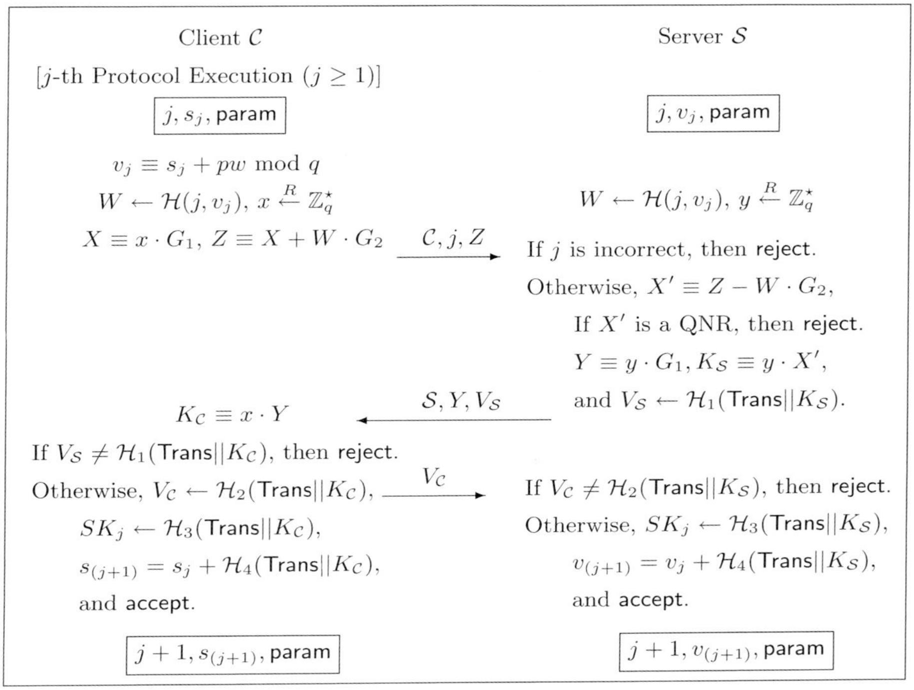

Fig. 2. The j-th execution of EC-AKA protocol where the enclosed values in rectangle represent stored secrets of client and server, respectively, and $\mathsf{Trans} = \mathcal{C}||\mathcal{S}||j||Z||Y$

case, an attacker can try the possible password candidates in order to get the de-masked value X'. If X' is a quadratic non-residue, the attacker can exclude the password candidates used. From Hasse's theorem [7], the number of such values X' is in the range $[(q+1)/2 - \sqrt{q}, (q+1)/2 + \sqrt{q}]$. Hence the attacker can reduce the dictionary size by roughly half with such partition attack. That means the password can be sieved out to be correct one, given a number of protocol runs, at a logarithmic rate to the dictionary size.

However, the client in the EC-AKA protocol sends Z computed with an additional mask $W \cdot G_2$. Suppose an attacker who tries a guessed password on Z. The attacker cannot determine whether the guessed password is correct or not since all of the Legendre symbols $\left(\frac{X'}{q}\right)$ are quadratic residues. Thus the EC-AKA protocol is secure against partition attacks. This technique used in the EC-AKA protocol is quite different from [3] in that the latter ensures that any candidate $\mathcal{X}$-coordinate observed by an attacker is valid by utilizing an elliptic curve and its twisted one in order to obviate partition attacks.

3.1 Model and Security Notion

Here we introduce the model based on [8] and security notion.

The Model. We denote by $\mathcal{C}$ and $\mathcal{S}$ two parties that participate in the key exchange protocol P. Each of them may have several instances called oracles involved in distinct, possibly concurrent, executions of P where we denote $\mathcal{C}$ (resp., $\mathcal{S}$) instances by $\mathcal{C}^i$ (resp., $\mathcal{S}^j$), or by $\mathcal{U}$ in case of any instance. During the execution of P, an adversary has the entire control of the network and additionally has access to the parties' stored secrets where the latter simulates *insecure* devices and databases. Let us show the capability of adversary $\mathcal{A}$ each query captures:

- $\mathsf{Execute}(\mathcal{C}^i, \mathcal{S}^j)$: This query models passive attacks, where the adversary gets access to honest executions of P between $\mathcal{C}^i$ and $\mathcal{S}^j$ by eavesdropping.
- $\mathsf{Send}(\mathcal{U}, m)$: This query models active attacks by having $\mathcal{A}$ send a message to instance $\mathcal{U}$. The adversary $\mathcal{A}$ gets back the response $\mathcal{U}$ generates in processing the message m according to the protocol P. A query $\mathsf{Send}(\mathcal{C}^i, \mathtt{Start})$ initializes the key exchange protocol.
- $\mathsf{Reveal}(\mathcal{U})$: This query handles the misuse of the session key by any instance $\mathcal{U}$. The query is only available to $\mathcal{A}$ if the instance actually holds a session key and the latter is released to $\mathcal{A}$.
- $\mathsf{Leak}(\mathcal{U})$: This query handles the leakage of the "stored" secrets by any instance $\mathcal{U}$. The adversary $\mathcal{A}$ gets back (s_j, param) and (v_j, param) where the former (resp., the latter) is released if the instance corresponds to $\mathcal{C}^i$ (resp., $\mathcal{S}^j$).
- $\mathsf{Test}(\mathcal{U})$: The Test-query can be asked at most once by the adversary $\mathcal{A}$ and is only available to $\mathcal{A}$ if the instance $\mathcal{U}$ is "fresh" in that the session key is not obviously known to the adversary. This query is answered as follows: one flips a (private) coin $b \in \{0, 1\}$ and forwards the corresponding session key SK ($\mathsf{Reveal}(\mathcal{U})$ would output) if $b = 1$, or a random value except the session key if $b = 0$.

Security Notion. The adversary $\mathcal{A}$ is provided with random coin tosses, some oracles and then is allowed to invoke any number of queries as described above, in any order. The aim of the adversary is to break the privacy of the session key in the context of executing P. The AKE security is defined by the game $\mathbf{Game}^{\mathsf{ake}}(\mathcal{A}, P)$, in which the ultimate goal of the adversary is to guess the bit b involved in the Test-query by outputting this guess b'. We denote the AKE advantage, by $\mathsf{Adv}_P^{\mathsf{ake}}(\mathcal{A}) = 2\Pr[b = b'] - 1$, as the probability that $\mathcal{A}$ can correctly guess the value of b. The protocol P is said to be (t, ε)-AKE-secure if $\mathcal{A}$'s advantage is smaller than ε for any adversary $\mathcal{A}$ running time t.

3.2 Elliptic Curve Diffie-Hellman Assumption

A (t, ε)-$\mathsf{ECDH}_{G,\mathbb{G}}$ attacker, in a finite cyclic group $\mathbb{G}$ of prime order q with G as a generator, is a probabilistic machine $\mathcal{B}$ running in time t such that its success probability $\mathsf{Succ}_{G,\mathbb{G}}^{\mathsf{ecdh}}(\mathcal{B})$, given random elements aG and bG to output abG, is greater than ε. We denote by $\mathsf{Succ}_{G,\mathbb{G}}^{\mathsf{ecdh}}(t)$ the maximal success probability over every adversaries running within time t. The ECDH-Assumption states that $\mathsf{Succ}_{G,\mathbb{G}}^{\mathsf{ecdh}}(t) \leq \varepsilon$ for any t/ε not too large.

3.3 Security Proofs

Suppose an active attacker $\mathcal{A}$, who gets the client's stored secret, is willing to break the semantic security of the EC-AKA protocol. The protocol is said to be secure if, when passwords are chosen from a dictionary of size N, $\mathsf{Adv}_P^{\mathsf{ake}}(\mathcal{A}) \leq O(q_s/N) + \varepsilon(\cdot)$ for some negligible function $\varepsilon(\cdot)$ in the security parameter. The first term represents the fact that the attacker can do no better than guess a password during each interaction to the parties where q_s is the number of queries to the Send-oracle.

Theorem 1. *The* EC-AKA *protocol is* provably secure *against an attacker, who asks the* $\mathsf{Leak}(\mathcal{C}^i)$*-query, in the random oracle model [9] if the elliptic curve Diffie-Hellman (*ECDH*) problem is hard.*

Proof. We prove this theorem by contradiction. Here we assume that the EC-AKA protocol is insecure in the sense that the attacker $\mathcal{A}$ can distinguish the key given by the Test-oracle. With the elliptic curve Diffie-Hellman instance as input, we show that an algorithm $\mathcal{B}$ can compute the Diffie-Hellman key by using the attacker $\mathcal{A}$ as a subroutine.

The algorithm $\mathcal{B}$ is given the ECDH instance $(G, P = aG, Q = bG)$ and should simulate all of the queries from attacker $\mathcal{A}$. When $\mathcal{A}$ asks a hash-query $\mathcal{H}_j(q)$, such that a record (j, q, r) appeared in the $\mathcal{H}_j$-oracle, the answer is r. Otherwise, answer r is chosen randomly from $\{0, 1\}^k$ and the record (j, q, r) is added to the $\mathcal{H}_j$. Now, algorithm $\mathcal{B}$ sets $(G_1 = G, G_2 = Q)$, feeds it to attacker $\mathcal{A}$, and then simulates the protocol as usual. When $\mathcal{A}$ asks a $\mathsf{Send}(\mathcal{S}^j, *)$-query, $\mathcal{B}$ computes Y as follows: $Y \equiv yP$. We can easily see that the simulation is perfectly indistinguishable in the view of $\mathcal{A}$ since there exists a unique discrete logarithm for Y. After seeing a hash-query $\mathcal{H}_j(q)$ asked by $\mathcal{A}$, $\mathcal{B}$ can solve the ECDH problem with non-negligible probability. Let $W_i = \mathcal{H}(q_i)$ and $K_i = \mathsf{ECDH}_{G,\mathbb{G}}((Z - W_iG_2), Y) = \mathsf{ECDH}_{G,\mathbb{G}}(Z, Y) + \mathsf{ECDH}_{G,\mathbb{G}}(-W_iG_2, Y)$ such that the tuple (Z, Y, K_i) is in $\mathcal{H}_j$. With probability $1/q_h^2$, $\mathcal{B}$ can compute the Diffie-Hellman key $\mathsf{ECDH}_{G,\mathbb{G}}((W_0 - W_1)Q, yP) = K_1 - K_0$ since B already knows y, W_0 and W_1. The running time of $\mathcal{B}$ is the running time of $\mathcal{A}$ plus some constant time for modular multiplication. This concludes the proof.

Of course, the attacker can do on-line dictionary attacks with the success probability $O(q_s/N)$. But, notice that the EC-AKA protocol doesn't allow even on-line attacks without any leakage of stored secrets since the authentication depends on the strong secret v_j like [10,11].

Suppose an active attacker, who gets the server's stored secret, is willing to break security of the EC-AKA protocol by impersonating the compromised server. In that case, we cannot avoid this impersonation attack as all of the authentication protocols cannot. However, we can say the following theorem.

Theorem 2. *The* EC-AKA *protocol is* secure *against an attacker, who asks the* $\mathsf{Leak}(S^j)$*-query, unless the attacker do the server impersonation attack within a limited time period.*

Table 1. Classification and comparison of AKA protocols

Protocols	Client's possessions			Extension*1
	Password	Stored Secret	Public Info.	
EAP-MD5, LEAP	√			impossible
PAKE [3,5]	√			impossible
MA-DHKE*2 [13]	√		√	impossible
EAP-SIM [14]		√		possible*3
EAP-FAST	√	√		impossible
EC-AKA	√	√		possible*3
EAP-TLS		√	√	possible
EAP-TTLS, PEAP	√	(√)*4	√	impossible

*1: Whether or not each protocol can be extended to the multiple server scenario (with only one password).

*2: Mutual Authentication and Diffie-Hellman Key Exchange of Section 3.4.

*3: The number of stored secrets grows linearly to the number of servers.

*4: Optional.

We assume that the EC-AKA protocol runs at a fixed time period (e.g., a day) and an attacker obtains the secret (i.e., v_j) at that time. In this case, if the update of v_j between the client and the server is completed before the attacker does, the latter cannot do the impersonation attack any more because v_j is no longer valid.

4 Comparison

In this section, we compare the EC-AKA protocol with the existing AKA protocols (including EAP methods [12]). In Table 1, we classify each protocol in the viewpoint of which kind of information is needed for client authentication. Table 2 shows the comparative result of security properties when the leakage of stored secrets happen in each protocol. Though both the EAP-FAST and EC-AKA protocols are based on the password and additional secret stored on client's devices, the former is not adequate for multiple sever scenario and insecure against the leakage of stored secrets.

Efficiency, as well, is very important when considering practical applications for mobile devices with restricted computing power and wireless networks having limited bandwidth. As for communication overhead, we represent the points on the elliptic curve in a compressed form: given an affine point $(\mathcal{X}, \mathcal{Y})$ the $\mathcal{X}$-coordinate requires n bits where n is the bit length of the underlying field and the $\mathcal{Y}$-coordinate is represented by one bit in order to distinguish two solutions of a quadratic equation. In addition, the length of identities and counter is excluded. Table 3 indicates that the EC-AKA protocol is more efficient mainly in terms of computation costs of client and communication overheads compared to [3,5].

Table 2. Comparison of AKA protocols in a situation where no perfect TRM is available

Protocols	Security*1 (of password)		
	on communications	against the leakage of stored secrets	
		from client $\mathcal{C}$	from server $\mathcal{S}$
EAP-MD5, LEAP	△*2	○	X (△*2)
PAKE [3,5]	○	○	X (△*2)
MA-DHKE [13]	○	○	△*2
EAP-SIM [14]	○	X	X
EAP-FAST	○	X	X
EC-AKA	○	○*3	○*3
EAP-TLS	○	X	X
EAP-TTLS, PEAP	○	○	X (△*2)

*1: ○ guarantees the security of password against both on-line and off-line dictionary attacks. △ guarantees the security of password against on-line, but not off-line attacks. X guarantees the security of password against neither on-line nor off-line attacks.
*2: A client registers password verification data computed with a particular one-way function of the password, $f(pw)$, at the server instead of pw.
*3: Information-theoretically secure.

Table 3. Comparison of elliptic curve based AKA protocols, which do not rely on PKI, in terms of efficiency

Protocols	Computation costs of client*1	Communication overhead*2	The number of flows
EC-EKE [3]	$4Mul$, $[3Mul]$ *3	100 Bytes	3
PAKE-EC [5]	$5Mul$, $[3Mul]$ *3	160 Bytes	4
EC-AKA	$4Mul$, $[3Mul]$	60 Bytes	3

*1: Mul denotes the number of modular multiplications and the figures in the brackets are the remaining costs after pre-computation.
*2: For the minimum security parameters recommended for use in current practice: $|q| = |\mathcal{H}| = 160$ (for the elliptic curve Diffie-Hellman protocol and hash functions).
*3: $2Mul$ are needed for checking the group order.

5 Conclusions

When we consider wireless security, a combination of password-based authentication and the elliptic curve Diffie-Hellman protocol is strongly preferable mainly because it not only does not require any security infrastructure, but also provide computation and communication efficiency. However, such combination does not necessarily guarantee security against a special kind of off-line dictionary attacks, known as "partition attacks".

As one of the solutions for wireless security, we have proposed an elliptic curve based AKA (EC-AKA) protocol secure against partition attacks as well as suitable for the following situation: (1) a client, who communicates with many different servers, remembers only one password and has insecure devices (e.g., mobile phones or PDAs); (2) the counterpart servers are not perfectly secure against several attacks (e.g., virus or hacker); (3) neither PKI nor TRM is available. The authenticity of the EC-AKA protocol is based on the client's relatively short password and an additional secret stored on insecure devices. We proved that the EC-AKA protocol is provably secure in the random oracle model with the reduction to the elliptic curve Diffie-Hellman problem. In addition, we analyzed its several security properties and efficiency while comparing with the existing AKA protocols (employed in the IEEE 802.1x [15]).

Acknowledgments. The authors appreciate anonymous reviewers for their helpful comments.

References

1. Koblitz, N.: Elliptic Curve Cryptosystems. Mathematics of Computation 48, 203–209 (1987)
2. Miller, V.: Use of Elliptic Curves in Cryptography. In: Williams, H.C. (ed.) Advances in Cryptology. LNCS, vol. 218, pp. 417–426. Springer, Heidelberg (1986)
3. Boyd, C., Montague, P., Nguyen, K.: Elliptic Curve based Password Authenticated Key Exchange Protocols. In: Varadharajan, V., Mu, Y. (eds.) Information Security and Privacy. LNCS, vol. 2119, pp. 487–501. Springer, Heidelberg (2001)
4. Diffie, W., Hellman, M.: New Directions in Cryptography. IEEE Transactions on Information Theory IT-22(6), 644–654 (1976)
5. Wong, D.S., Chan, A.H., Zhu, F.: Password Authenticated Key Exchange for Resource-Contrained Wireless Communications. In: Lorenz, P., Dini, P. (eds.) Networking - ICN 2005. LNCS, vol. 3421, pp. 827–834. Springer, Heidelberg (2005)
6. Antipa, A., Brown, D., Menezes, A., Struik, R., Vanstone, S.: Validation of Elliptic Curve Public Keys. PKC 2003. In: Desmedt, Y.G. (ed.) Public Key Cryptography - PKC 2003. LNCS, vol. 2567, pp. 211–223. Springer, Heidelberg (2002)
7. Blake, I.F., Seroussi, G., Smart, N.P.: Elliptic Curves in Cryptography. In: Jantke, K.P. (ed.) Analogical and Inductive Inference. LNCS, vol. 265, Springer, Heidelberg (1987)
8. Bellare, M., Pointcheval, D., Rogaway, P.: Authenticated Key Exchange Secure against Dictionary Attacks. In: Preneel, B. (ed.) Advances in Cryptology - EUROCRYPT 2000. LNCS, vol. 1807, pp. 139–155. Springer, Heidelberg (2000)
9. Bellare, M., Rogaway, P.: Random Oracles are Practical: A Paradigm for Designing Efficient Protocols. In: ACM CCS'93, pp. 62–73. ACM Press, New York (1993)
10. Bellare, M., Rogaway, P.: Entity Authentication and Key Distribution. In: Stinson, D.R. (ed.) Advances in Cryptology - CRYPTO '93. LNCS, vol. 773, pp. 232–249. Springer, Heidelberg (1994)
11. Shoup, V.: On Formal Models for Secure Key Exchange. IBM Research Report RZ 3121 (1999), `http://eprint.iacr.org/1999/012`
12. IETF (Internet Engineering Task Force).: PPP Extensible Authentication Protocol (EAP). RFC 2284 (1998)

13. Halevi, S., Krawczyk, H.: Public-Key Cryptography and Password Protocols. In: ACM Transactions on Information and System Security, vol. 2(3), pp. 230–268. ACM Press, New York (1999)
14. Haverinen, H., Salowey, J.: Extensible Authentication Protocol Method for GSM Subscriber Identity Modules (EAP-SIM) (2004) `draft-haverinen-pppext-eap-sim-16.txt`
15. IEEE 802.1x.: Port Based Network Access Control. IEEE, `http://www.ieee802/org/1/pages/802.1x.html`

An Efficient and Secure RFID Security Method with Ownership Transfer

Kyosuke Osaka[1], Tsuyoshi Takagi[1], Kenichi Yamazaki[2], and Osamu Takahashi[1]

[1] Future University-Hakodate 116-2, Kamedanakano, Hakodate, 041-8655, Japan
[2] NTT DoCoMo, Inc. 3-5, Hikarinooka, Yokosuka, 239-8536, Japan

Abstract. Radio Frequency Identification (RFID) has come under the spotlight as technology supporting ubiquitous society. But now, we face several security problems and challenges in RFID systems. Recent papers have reported that RFID systems have to achieve the following requirements: (1) Indistinguishability, (2) Forward Security, (3) Replay Attack resistance, (4) Tag Killing resistance, and (5) Ownership Transferability. We have to design RFID system that achieves the above-mentioned requirements. The previous security methods achieve only some of them individually, and no RFID system has been constructed that achieves all requirements. In this paper, we propose an RFID security method that achieves all requirements based on a hash function and a symmetric key cryptosystem. In addition, our proposed method provides not only high-security but also high-efficiency.

1 Introduction

RFID has been used by manufacturing management, custody control, management of humans and farm animals, arrangement of books at some libraries, etc. From now, intended purpose of RFID will be diversified, and will be used in every nook and cranny. But now, we face several security problems and challenges in RFID systems.

We consider that the RFID system is constructed as Tag, Reader, and Database. The security problems in RFID system arise from the following: data transmission between Tag and Reader is unencrypted, Tags provide no tamper resistant because Tags are inexpensive micromini devices. Hence Tag and Reader communicate with each other in insecure channel. Therefore, we face new threats in the RFID systems. Recent papers have reported that RFID systems have to achieve the following requirements: (1) the security that the adversary cannot distinguish output of Tag (Indistinguishability [4]), (2) the security that past data are secure even if present data on Tag leaked out to the adversary (Forward Security [4]), (3) the security against the attack that the adversary spoofs as legitimate Tag (Replay Attack resistance [5]), (4) the security against the attack that broadcasts large amount of Query to Tag, then stops its services (Tag Killing resistance [2]), (5) ownership is transferable without invasion of owner's privacy (Ownership Transferability [6]). The previous security methods have

Y. Wang, Y. Cheung, and H. Liu (Eds.): CIS 2006, LNAI 4456, pp. 778–787, 2007.

been proposed to achieve only some of the above-mentioned requirements individually [1,3,4,5,6,7,8,9,10]. No RFID system has been constructed that achieves all requirements.

In this paper, we propose an RFID security method, that achieves all requirements, based on a hash function and a symmetric key cryptosystem. Proposed method provides not only high-security but also high-efficiency.

This paper is constructed as follows: Section 2 describes the RFID security systems and security requirements. It also reviews the previous security methods. Section 3 describes protocol and security of the proposed method. It also compares the security and efficiency of the proposed method with those of the previous security methods. Section 4 describes conclusion.

2 RFID Security Systems

RFID security system consists of the three components (Tag, Reader, and Database). We describe the protocol of the RFID security system treated in this paper.

Database holds the unique IDs of each Tag, and administrates the information related to the ID (e.g. time and location, manufacturer name, ownership, etc.). We call it $Info(ID)$. During the protocol, the IDs are secretly held by only Database all of the time, and the IDs are cryptographically converted and distributed outside Database. We call the converted IDs $OutConv.ID^{(j)}$ corresponding to the IDs, where j is the number of communication starting with $j = 1$. In summary $OutConv.ID^{(j)}$ is the j-th converted ID distributed outside Tag. Database is securely connected only to Reader, and tries to find the ID based on $OutConv.ID^{(j)}$. And then, Database gives $Info(ID)$ to Reader.

Reader is able to read/write the data on Tag via insecure radio-frequency transmission channel. Reader broadcasts $Query$ and if necessary, also some data (e.g. random number) to Tag. Reader also requests $Info(ID)$ to Database.

Tag holds cryptographically converted ID. We call it $InConv.ID^{(i)}$, where i is the number of update starting with $i = 1$. In summary $InConv.ID^{(i)}$ is the i-th updated ID. In some RFID security methods, Tag also recomputes and updates the $InConv.ID^{(i)}$. Tag computes and transmits to Reader $OutConv.ID^{(j)}$ based on the $InConv.ID^{(i)}$ and some data (e.g. random number, count number). Generally i is not equal to j, but some security methods satisfy $i = j$ [1,4].

Recall that Tags are memory-constraint and low-energy devices, so that data transmission between Tag and Reader is unencrypted, and Tags provide no tamper resistant. Hence we have to deal with new security problems and challenges in RFID system that have not been considered in the conventional security systems.

2.1 Security Requirements

Here, we prepare some notations. $A \xrightarrow{x} B$ is a transmitting map of data x from entity A to B. $x * y \mapsto z$ is a converting map from data x and y to z by operation "$*$". $C(x) \mapsto y$ is a converting map from data x to y by function C.

Entity A, B are either Tag, Reader, or Database. Data x, y, z are either $Query$, random number r, ID, $InConv.ID^{(i)}$, $OutConv.ID^{(j)}$, or $Info(ID)$.

In this paper, we address the following five security requirements as the security of RFID systems:

Indistinguishability (IND) [4]**:** Indistinguishability is the security that the adversary cannot distinguish output of Tag. To this end, indistinguishability satisfies the following conditions:

1. Even if the adversary obtains several $OutConv.ID^{(j)}$ (and other data) from different Tags, the adversary cannot distinguish which Tag output them,

   $OutConv.ID^{(j)} \neq OutConv.ID'^{(j)}$ for $ID \neq ID'$.

2. Even if the adversary obtains several $OutConv.ID^{(j)}$ (and other data) from same Tag, the adversary cannot distinguish the same Tag output them,

   $OutConv.ID^{(j)} \neq OutConv.ID^{(j')}$ for $j \neq j'$.

Forward Security (FS) [4]**:** Forward security tries to achieve the following condition: even if present data $InConv.ID^{(i)}$ on Tag leaked out to the adversary, past data $InConv.ID^{(j)}$ with $j < i$ are still secure (In some security methods, Tag also holds some data, e.g. secret key, random number, count number, etc.). In the other words, forward security must satisfy that there exist no adversary A such that,

$A(InConv.ID^{(i)}) \not\rightarrow InConv.ID^{(j)}$ for $j < i$.

Note that Tags are memory-constraint and low-energy devices, so that Tags provide no tamper resistant. Hence the adversary could obtain the $InConv.ID^{(i)}$ from Tag.

Replay Attack resistance (RA) [5]**:** Replay attack is the attack that the adversary spoofs as legitimate Tag. The adversary first eavesdrops and obtains the $OutConv.ID^{(j)}$ between Reader and Tag. The adversary then tries to spoof as the legitimate Tag, by transmitting the obtained $OutConv.ID^{(j)}$ to Reader,

Adversary's Tag $\xrightarrow{OutConv.ID^{(j)}}$ Reader.

Replay Attack resistance is a requirement that have resistance to this attack.

Tag Killing resistance (TK) [2]**:** Tag killing is the attack that broadcasts large amount of $Query$ to targeted Tag, then stops its services. For instance, if Tag need to store random number per each authentication, Tag's memory will be exhausted and will stop its services by Tag Killing,

Adversary's Reader $\xrightarrow{\text{large amount of } Query}$ Tag.

Tag Killing resistance is a requirement that have resistance to this attack.

Ownership Transferability (OT) [6]**:** In this paper, we denote persons possessing Tag by *owner*, and denote the Tag's ownership by *ownership*. When *ownership* is transferred, present *owner* A might have to transmit the necessary data (e.g. ID, $Info(ID)$, etc.) to new *owner* B (e.g. A : manufacturer, B : wholesaler). Ownership Transferability is a requirement that violations of present and new *owner*'s privacy do not arise even if the present *owner* gives necessary data to new *owner*.

2.2 Previous Security Methods

In this section, we review some previous security methods, their security flaws, and their improved variations. In what follows, let N be the number of Tag, let M be the hash chain size which is a computable upper limit of hash operation on Tag provided in [1,4].

Ohkubo Scheme [4]**:** Ohkubo et al. proposed a scheme that computes the hash value of the $InConv.ID^{(i)}$ per each $Query$ using two hash functions H and G,

$$H(InConv.ID^{(i)}) \mapsto InConv.ID^{(i+1)},$$
$$G(InConv.ID^{(i)}) \mapsto OutConv.ID^{(i+1)}.$$

This scheme achieves indistinguishability and forward security due to the collision resistant property and one-wayness of hash functions, respectively. Database requires NM computations of hash function for the searching cost of ID.

Efficient Ohkubo Scheme [4]**:** Ohkubo et al. also proposed a scheme that the searching cost of ID in Database is more efficient than Ohkubo scheme. Tag transmits communication number j in addition to the $OutConv.ID^{(j)}$ to Reader,

$$\text{Tag} \xrightarrow{OutConv.ID^{(j)},\ j} \text{Reader}.$$

Then the computations of hash function in Database reduce to N from NM due to the transmitted j. Moreover, this scheme is secure against the replay attack by the communication number j. This scheme however achieves no indistinguishability, because the adversary might be able to distinguish output of Tag due to the regularly changed j.

Modified Ohkubo Scheme [1]**:** Avoine et al. proposed a more secure scheme than Ohkubo scheme. Reader broadcasts random number r with $Query$ to Tag. Then Tag computes the $OutConv.ID^{(i+1)}$ from the $InConv.ID^{(i)}$ and the r,

$$\text{Reader} \xrightarrow{Query,r} \text{Tag},$$
$$H(InConv.ID^{(i)}) \mapsto InConv.ID^{(i+1)},$$
$$G(InConv.ID^{(i)} \oplus r) \mapsto OutConv.ID^{(i+1)}.$$

$\oplus$ is a XOR operation. This scheme achieves indistinguishability and forward security due to the collision resistant property and one-wayness of hash functions, respectively. Moreover, this scheme is secure against the replay attack due to the XOR operation between the $InConv.ID^{(i)}$ and the r which are changed per each *Query*. Database requires NM computations of hash functions for the searching cost of ID.

Unidentifiable Anonymous ID Scheme [3]**:** Kinoshita et al. proposed a scheme that the $InConv.ID^{(i)}$ is converted by a symmetric key cryptosystem. In this scheme, the $InConv.ID^{(i)}$ is also distributed outside Tag,

$$\text{Tag} \xrightarrow{InConv.ID^{(i)}} \text{Reader}.$$

In additional phase, Reader writes the $InConv.ID^{(i+1)}$ by new symmetric key into Tag to improve security,

$$\text{Reader} \xrightarrow{InConv.ID^{(i+1)}} \text{Tag}.$$

Even if the $InConv.ID^{(i)}$ leaked out, neither ID nor $InConv.ID^{(j)}$ $(j < i)$ leaks out to the adversary who have no past symmetric keys. Therefore, this scheme achieves forward security. Moreover, this scheme is secure against the tag killing due to the following two reasons: Tag has no computable upper limit such as hash chain size [1,4]. Tag requires no new memory per each *Query* for random number such as Challenge-Response scheme [5,7,8,9,10]. Database requires only 1 computation for the decryption of ID.

Ownership Transfer Scheme [6]**:** Saito et al. proposed a scheme that ownership is transferable. Tag holds no $InConv.ID^{(i)}$ but holds ID, a symmetric key, and count number C incremented per each *Query*. Tag computes the $OutConv.ID^{(j)}$ from the ID, the symmetric key, and the count number C,

$$E_k(\text{ID}\|C) \mapsto OutConv.ID^{(j)}.$$

E_k is a encryption function by a symmetric key k, and operation "$\|$" is a concatenation operation. This scheme is able to transfer ownership by changing the symmetric key k. Moreover, this scheme achieves indistinguishability due to the concatenation operation between the ID and the C incremented per each *Query*. In addition, this scheme is secure against the tag killing due to the same reason as unidentifiable anonymous ID scheme. This scheme however achieves no forward security because Tag always holds the ID. Recall that Tags provide no tamper resistant, the adversary therefore could obtain the ID by tampering. Saito et al. considered that this scheme is constructed by Tag, Reader, and trusted third party. Therefore, there is no description about Database.

3 Proposed Method

In this section, we propose an RFID security method, achieves all requirements, based on a hash function and a symmetric key cryptosystem.

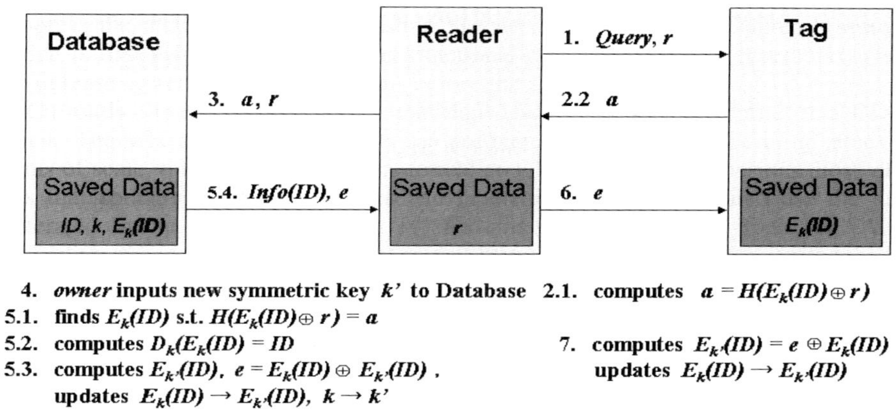

Fig. 1. Authentication Process

3.1 Protocol of the Proposed Method

Our protocol consists of three processes, namely writing process, authentication process, and ownership transfer process.

Writing process is a process to write the $InConv.ID^{(i)}$ into Tag. In this process, manufacturer generates a symmetric key k, and writes $E_k(ID)$, which is converted ID by the symmetric key k, into Tag. In proposed method, the $E_k(ID)$ is corresponding to the $InConv.ID^{(i)}$.

Authentication process is a process to authenticate transmitted data from Reader, and gives $Info(ID)$ to Reader. In proposed method, hash value a of hash function H is corresponding to the $OutConv.ID^{(j)}$.

Ownership transfer process is a process to transfer ownership without invasion of present and new owner's privacy by changing the symmetric key. In ownership transfer process, necessary data (e.g. symmetric key, ID, $Info(ID)$, etc.) to transfer ownership are transmitted.

In the following, we present the three processes of the proposed method:

Writing Process

Manufacturer generates a symmetric key k and writes $E_k(ID)$, which is converted ID by the symmetric key k, into Tag,

Manufacturer's Reader $\xrightarrow{E_k(ID)}$ Tag.

Authentication Process

This process is shown as Fig.1.

1. Reader broadcasts $Query$ and a random number r to Tag,

   1. Reader $\xrightarrow{Query,r}$ Tag. [-2pt]

2. Tag computes and transmits to Reader hash value a of hash function H,

   2.1. $H(E_k(ID) \oplus r) \mapsto a$,
   2.2. Tag $\xrightarrow{a}$ Reader.

3. Reader transmits the hash value a and the r to Database,

   3. Reader $\xrightarrow{a,r}$ Database.

(I) Phase without changing a symmetric key

4. Firstly, Database tries to find $E_k(ID)$ which satisfies $H(E_k(ID) \oplus r) = a$ for both a and r received from Reader. Secondly, Database obtains ID by doing decryption of $E_k(ID)$ by decryption function D_k. Finally, Database finds and transmits to Reader $Info(ID)$,

   4.1. find $E_k(ID)$ s.t. $H(E_k(ID) \oplus r) = a$,
   4.2. $D_k(E_k(ID)) \mapsto ID$,
   4.3. Database $\xrightarrow{Info(ID)}$ Reader.

(II) Phase with changing a symmetric key

4. *Owner* inputs new symmetric key k' to Database in secure channel.
5. Firstly, Database tries to find $E_k(ID)$ which satisfies $H(E_k(ID) \oplus r) = a$ for both a and r received from Reader. Secondly, Database obtains ID by doing decryption of $E_k(ID)$, then Database finds $Info(ID)$. Then Database encrypts ID by new symmetric key k'. Thirdly, Database computes $e = E_k(ID) \oplus E_{k'}(ID)$. Then Database updates both saved data from k to k' and from $E_k(ID)$ to $E_{k'}(ID)$. Finally, Database transmits $Info(ID)$ and the e to Reader,

   5.1. find $E_k(ID)$ s.t. $H(E_k(ID) \oplus r) = a$,
   5.2. $D_k(E_k(ID)) \mapsto ID$,
   5.3. $E_k(ID) \oplus E_{k'}(ID) \mapsto e$,
   5.4. Database $\xrightarrow{Info(ID),e}$ Reader.

6. Reader transmits the e to Tag,

   6. Reader $\xrightarrow{e}$ Tag.

7. Tag computes $E_{k'}(ID)$ from e and $E_k(ID)$, and updates the saved data from $E_k(ID)$ to $E_{k'}(ID)$,

   7. $e \oplus E_k(ID) \mapsto E_{k'}(ID)$.

Ownership Transfer Process

1. Present *owner* changes a symmetric key k to new symmetric key k' in order to prevent invasion of own privacy. Then present *owner* gives necessary data (e.g. k', ID, $Info(ID)$, etc.) to new *owner* in secure channel.

2. New *owner* changes the received symmetric key k' to new symmetric key k'' in order to prevent invasion of own privacy. And then new *owner* will use k'' as own symmetric key.

3.2 Security of the Proposed Method

In this section, we analyze the security of the proposed method.

Indistinguishability(IND): The hash value a, which is output from Tag per each *Query*, is indistinguishable due to the hash operation between the random number r and the $E_k(ID)$. Proposed method therefore satisfies as follows,

1. $H(E_k(ID) \oplus r) \neq H(E_k(ID') \oplus r)$ for $ID \neq ID'$.
2. $H(E_k(ID) \oplus r) \neq H(E_k(ID) \oplus r')$ for $r \neq r'$.

The $e = E_k(ID) \oplus E_{k'}(ID)$, which is transmitted to Tag, is also indistinguishable from next interaction $e' = E_{k'}(ID) \oplus E_{k''}(ID)$ due to the XOR operation,

$(E_k(ID) \oplus E_{k'}(ID)) \neq (E_{k'}(ID) \oplus E_{k''}(ID))$
for k, k', and k'' are pairwisely different.

Therefore, proposed method achieves the indistinguishability.

Forward Security (FS): Even if the $E_{k'}(ID)$ leaked out, neither ID nor $E_k(ID)$ leaks out to the adversary who have no past symmetric keys,

$A(E_{k'}(ID)) \not\mapsto E_k(ID)$ for k' is a preset key, k is a past key.

Therefore, proposed method achieves the forward security.

Repay Attack resistance (RA): The r' broadcasted by legitimate Reader and the eavesdropped r are different. Hence $H(E_k(ID) \oplus r)$ and $H(E_k(ID) \oplus r')$ are also different due to the collision resistant property of hash functions. The adversary therefore cannot spoof as legitimate Tag,

$H(E_k(ID) \oplus r) \neq H(E_k(ID) \oplus r')$ for $r \neq r'$.

Therefore, proposed method is secure against the replay attack.

Tag Killing resistance (TK): Tag has no computable upper limit such as hash chain size [1,4], Tag requires no new memory per each *Query* for random number such as Challenge-Response scheme [5,7,8,9,10]. Therefore, proposed method is secure against the tag killing.

Ownership Transferability (OT): Proposed method is able to transfer the *ownership* without invasion of present and new *owner*'s privacy by changing a symmetric key which encrypts ID. Therefore, proposed method achieves the ownership transferability.

Remark 1. We considered another way based on the efficient Ohkubo scheme to achieve all security requirements. Previous hash chain methods [1,4] have

Table 1. Security Comparison (○: achievable, ×: non-achievable)

Security Methods	IND	FS	RA	TK	OT
Ohkubo Scheme [4]	○	○	×	×	×
Efficient Ohkubo Scheme [4]	×	○	○	×	×
Modified Ohkubo Scheme [1]	○	○	○	×	×
Unidentifiable Anonymous ID Scheme [3]	×	○	×	○	×
Ownership Transfer Scheme [6]	○	×	×	○	○
Proposed Method	○	○	○	○	○

Table 2. Efficiency Comparison

	Computation Time		
Security Methods	Tag	Reader	Database
Ohkubo Scheme [4]	2 T_H	No Time	NM T_H
Efficient Ohkubo Scheme [4]	2 T_H	No Time	N T_H
Modified Ohkubo Scheme [1]	2 T_H + 1 T_{XOR}	1 T_{RNG}	NM T_H
Unidentifiable Anonymous ID Scheme [3]	No Time	No Time	1 T_{SKC}
Ownership Transfer Scheme [6]	1 T_{CUM} + 1 T_{SCK}	No Time	No Data
Proposed Method	1 T_H + 1 T_{XOR}	1 T_{RNG}	N T_H + 1 T_{SKC}

following two demerits: Tag only can update $InConv.ID^{(i)}$ until hash chain size M (i.e. $i \leq M$). They cannot make M larger because the searching cost of ID in Database depends on M. Previous hash chain methods are therefore vulnerable against the tag killing. However in this method, the searching cost of ID in Database does not depend on M by encrypting j used in efficient Ohkubo scheme. Therefore, we can make M larger because the searching cost of ID in Database does not depend on M. This method is therefore secure against the tag killing. Moreover, this method is able to transfer *ownership* by changing a symmetric key which encrypts j.

3.3 Comparison with Previous Methods

In this section, we compare the security and efficiency of the proposed method with those of the previous security methods appeared in Section 2.2.

Table 1. shows the comparison in the sense of security described in Section 2.1. None of the previous security methods achieve all requirements, but the proposed method achieves all requirements.

Table 2. discusses the efficiency using the speed of the hash function T_H, the XOR operation T_{XOR}, the random number generation operation T_{RNG}, concatenation operation T_{CUM}, and the encryption/decryption by a symmetric key cryptosystem T_{SKC}. Those parameters for estimating the computation time have been used in the previous papers. Let N be the number of Tag, and let M be the hash chain size.

The speed of the proposed method is faster than previous security methods except unidentifiable anonymous ID scheme. In this paper, we consider that memory is not a big deal because the required memory of the proposed method is comparable with previous security methods.

4 Conclusion

In this paper, we proposed an RFID security system that achieves several security requirements: the indistinguishability, the forward security, the replay attack resistance, and the tag killing resistance. Further, the proposed method allows the ownership transferability. None of the previous security methods has achieved all the above-mentioned requirements. Finally the proposed method is reasonably efficient comparing with the previous security methods, e.g. the searching cost of ID in Database is the order of the number of Tag.

References

1. Avoine, G., Dysli, E., Oechslin, P.: Reducing Time Complexity in RFID Systems. In: Preneel, B., Tavares, S. (eds.) Selected Areas in Cryptography. LNCS, vol. 3897, pp. 291–306. Springer, Heidelberg (2006)
2. Han, D.G., Takagi, T., Kim, H.W., Chung, K.I.: New Security Problem in RFID Systems Tag Killing. In: Gavrilova, M., Gervasi, O., Kumar, V., Tan, C.J.K., Taniar, D., Laganà, A., Mun, Y., Choo, H. (eds.) Computational Science and Its Applications - ICCSA 2006. LNCS, vol. 3982, pp. 375–384. Springer, Heidelberg (2006)
3. Kinoshita, S., Hoshino, F., Komuro, T., Fujimura, A., Ohkubo, M.: Low-cost RFID Privacy Protection Scheme. IPSJ Journal 45(8), 2007–2021 (2004) (In Japanese)
4. Ohkubo, M., Suzuki, K., Kinoshita, S.: Cryptographic Approach to Privacy Friendly Tags. In: RFID Privacy Workshop, MIT, Cambridge, MA (2003)
5. Rhee, K., Kwak, J., Kim, S., Won, D.: Challenge-Response based RFID Authentication Protocol for Distributed Database Environment. In: Hutter, D., Ullmann, M. (eds.) Security in Pervasive Computing. LNCS, vol. 3450, pp. 70–84. Springer, Heidelberg (2005)
6. Saito, J., Imamoto, K., Sakurai, K.: Reassignment Scheme of an RFID Tag's Key for Owner Transfer. In: Enokido, T., Yan, L., Xiao, B., Kim, D., Dai, Y., Yang, L.T. (eds.) Embedded and Ubiquitous Computing – EUC 2005 Workshops. LNCS, vol. 3823, pp. 1303–1312. Springer, Heidelberg (2005)
7. Weis, S.A., Sarma, S.E., Rivest, R.L., Engels, D.W.: Security and Privacy Aspects of Low-Cost Radio Frequency Identification Systems. In: Hutter, D., Müller, G., Stephan, W., Ullmann, M. (eds.) Security in Pervasive Computing. LNCS, vol. 2802, pp. 201–212. Springer, Heidelberg (2004)
8. Kang, J., Nyang, D.: RFID: Authentication Protocol with Strong Resistance against Traceability and Denial of Service Attacks. In: Molva, R., Tsudik, G., Westhoff, D. (eds.) Security and Privacy in Ad-hoc and Sensor Networks. LNCS, vol. 3813, pp. 164–175. Springer, Heidelberg (2005)
9. Molnar, D., Wagner, D.: Privacy and Security in Library RFID: Issues, Practices, and Architectures. In: ACM CCS, pp. 210–219. ACM Press, New York (2004)
10. Henrici, D., Müller, P.: Hash-based Enhancement of Location Privacy for Radio-Frequency Identification Devices using Varying Identifiers. In: Henrici, D., Müller, P. (eds.) PerSec 2004, pp. 149–153. IEEE Computer Society, New York (2004)

Security and Privacy on Authentication Protocol for Low-Cost RFID

Yong-Zhen Li[1], Young-Bok Cho[1], Nam-Kyoung Um[1], and Sang-Ho Lee[2,⋆]

[1] Department of Computer Science, Chungbuk National University, Cheongju, Chungbuk, Korea
{lyz2003,bogi0118,family}@chungbuk.ac.kr
[2] School of Electrical & Computer Engineering, Chungbuk National University, Cheongju, Chungbuk, Korea
shlee@chungbuk.ac.kr

Abstract. The Radio Frequency Identification (RFID) is an automatic identification system, relying on storing and remotely retrieving data about objects we want to manage using devices called RFID tag. Even though RFID system is widely used for industrial and individual applications, RFID tag has a serious privacy problem, i.e., traceability. To protect the users from tracing and also to support Low-cost RFID, we propose an authentication protocol which can be adopted for read-only RFID tag using XOR computation and Partial ID concept. The proposed protocol is secure against reply attacking, eavesdropping, and spoofing attacking so that avoiding the location privacy exposure.

1 Introduction

The Radio Frequency Identification (RFID) is an automatic identification system, relying on storing and remotely retrieving data about objects we want to manage using devices called RFID tag. A secure RFID system has to avoid eavesdropping, traffic analysis, spoofing and denial of service, as it has large read range and no line of sight requirement. There have been some approaches to the RFID security and privacy issues, including killing tags at the checkout, applying a read/write able memory, physical tag memory separation, hash encryption, random access hash, and hash chains [1].

The RFID technique, however, causes the serious privacy infringement, such as excessive information exposure and user's location information tracking, due to the wireless characteristics because it is easy to be recognizable without the physical contact between the reader and the tag while the tag information is sent[3,4]. These concerns become the setbacks to the embodiment of RFID, and the various privacy problems should be solved beforehand for the successful industrialization. Therefore, the research regarding the authentication protocol are now proceeding actively to protect the information stored in the tag and resolve the safety problems such as the location tracking of the tag [4].

⋆ Corresponding author.

Y. Wang, Y. Cheung, and H. Liu (Eds.): CIS 2006, LNAI 4456, pp. 788–794, 2007.

This paper is organized as follows. We describe RFID security and privacy problems in section 2. Then our approach is proposed in section 3. In this section, the assumption is stated. Under this assumption, the basic idea is presented and the working mechanism is detailed. We compare our scheme with other schemes about security and efficiency in Section 4. In the final section, we provide a summary of our work.

2 RFID Security and Privacy

2.1 Privacy

Privacy and cloning of tag must be solved for proliferation of RFID technology. Because everyone can query to a low-cost tag (which doesn't have an access control function, e.g., Class I tag) without recognition of the tag holder, privacy must be considered [1,5].

One of privacy problems is the information leakage on user's belongings. People don't want that their personal things are known to others. For example, exposure of expensive products can make a tag holder be a victim of a robber. A personal medicine known to another throws the user into confusion. Even though the information leakage problem is significant, it's easy to solve. It can be solved just by using the anonymous ID's that DB only can match with the real product codes [1,4].

Another problem about the user privacy is a user tracing problem. By tracing tag, adversary can chase and identify the user. If adversary installs a vast amount of R's at a wide area, each individual person's location privacy is violated by adversary. The user tracing problem is hard to solve, because we must update every response of tag in order to evade a pursuer while a legitimate user can identify tag without any inconvenience. Moreover, this job must be performed by tag with small computational power [5,12].

2.2 Authentication

For the security and privacy problems in RFID, we usually solve the mutual authentication between tag and reader by the approaches of random ID, hash or cryptography. In the following we will introduce several general RFID authentication protocols.

Hash Lock. The scheme [1] stores the hash of a random key K as the tag's meta-ID, i.e. meta-ID = h(K). When queried by a reader, the tag transmits its meta-ID. The database and the reader respond with K. The tag hashes the key and compares it to the stored meta-ID. Although this scheme offers good reliability at low cost, an adversary can easily track the tag via its meta-ID for its a certain value. Furthermore, since the key K is sent in the clear way, an adversary capturing the key can later spoof the tag to the reader.

Randomized Hash Lock. The scheme [1] is that each tag has its own ID and a random number generator to make its constant variable randomized. The tag picks pseudo random number r uniformly and calculates c = hash(ID —— r) as the tag's unique identification for every session. The tag transmits its c and r to a back-end server by way of the reader. By the way of comparing c with the construction of r and all IDs that are stored in database of the server, the server authenticates itself by sending the unique identifier ID back to the tag.

Hash Chain. In [6], Okubo et al. proposed hash-chain based authentication protocol which protects users' location privacy and anonymity. They claim that their scheme provides strong forward security. However, hash-chain calculation must be burden on low-cost RFID tags and gives back-end servers heavy calculation loads.

Re-encryption. The method uses public key cryptosystem[9]. Tag data is re-encrypted when a user requires using the data transferred from an external unit. As public key encryption needs high computation cost, a tag cannot process for itself. Thus, this job is generally processed by a reader. Each tag data is randomly shown until next session, the attacker eaves dropping the tag data cannot trace the tag for long-term period. However, this method has difficulty to frequently refresh each tag's data since the encrypted ID stored on tag is constant so that user location privacy is compromised. This job is processed by users (or tag bearers) and is considered impractical.

Low-Cost Authentication. In [10, 11], a security model is proposed that introduces a challenge-response mechanism which uses no cryptographic primitives (other than simple XORs). One of the key ideas in this work is the application of pseudonyms to help enforce privacy in RFID tags. Each time the tag is queried, it releases the next pseudonym from its list. In principle, then, only a valid verifier can tell when two different names belong to the same tag. Of course, an adversary could query a tag multiple times to harvest all names so as to defeat the scheme. So, the approach described involves some special enhancements to help prevent this attack. First, tags release their names only at a certain prescribed rate. Second, pseudonyms can be refreshed by authorized readers. Although this scheme does not require the tags to perform any cryptographic functions (it uses only XOR operations), the protocol involves four messages and requires updating the keys and pads with new secrets.

3 Proposed Authentication Protocol

3.1 The Initialization Stage

At first, make every tag each own secret information, SID (secure ID), and store the corresponding information to the database; Secondly, install in the reader the random number generator which can generate pseudo random numbers; Finally, establish the random length of the PID used for a mutual authentication of the next reader and tag; We find that the length of n1 and n2 has the $2L \geq n1 + n2 \geq L/2$property.

3.2 The Detail of Proposed Protocol

The proposed protocol comprises of 4 steps as shown in the figure 1.

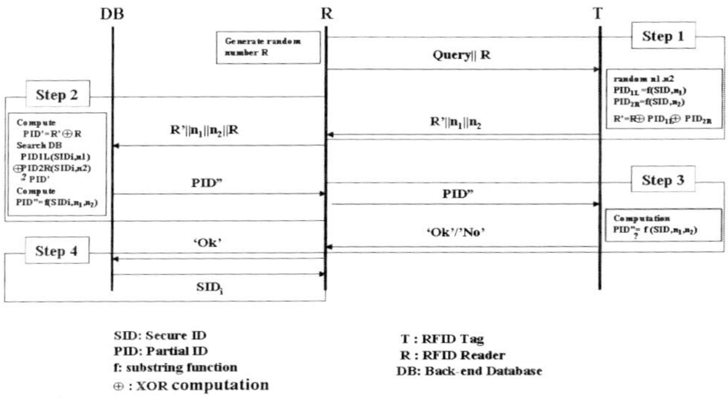

Fig. 1. Proposed protocol

Step 1 : Generating PID

- The readers generate the random number and send them to the tag along with the inquiry information.
- In its own SID, the tag selects 2 PIDs, and each length of PIDs is determined randomly. PID_{1L} is selected from the start location of SID, and PID_{2R} is from the end. Then calculate R by XORing PID_{1L}, PID_{2R} and R received from the reader.
- The tag sends to the reader the calculated R and two parameters n_1,n_2, which respectively mark the length of PID_{1L}, and PID_{2R}.

Step 2 : Searching SID and Tag Authentication

- The reader sends to the database the random number R generated above and R received from the tag and n1, n2.
- The database calculates the tags PID, by XORing R and R received from the reader; And by using the calculated PID, the database searches for the every tags SID making this PID exactly equal to the value XORing PID_{1L} (selecting the part from the start location of SIDi to the location of n1) and PID_{2R}(selecting the part from the location of n2 to the end location of SIDi) and collects the value of PID, which is selected from the location of n1 to the location of n2 in the searched SIDs; acknowledges the tag as a disguised one, if there is no SID filling the requirements of the PID as a result of search.
- Sends to the reader the collected PID values;

Step 3 : Reader Authentication

- The reader sends the collected PID values to the tag;
- The tag judges if the value of selected in SID from the location of n_1 to the location of n_2 is identical to the PID values received from the database; acknowledges the reader disguised if they are not identical;

- The tag sends to the reader the PID Ok, if it finds PID identical to the value of selected in SID from the location of n_1 to the location of n_2. Otherwise, it sends to the reader the no find information;

Step 4 : Return Result

- The reader sends to the database the information received from the tag, if it is Ok. And it terminates the protocol if it received the No find information;
- The database provides the collected SID information for the reader.

4 Analysis

4.1 Security Analysis

Safety Against Location Privacy. The user's privacy mainly means the leakage of location information or tag information of the tag's owner. The messages sent and received between the tag and the reader is transmitted as different messages each time during all the authentication procedures. It is impossible to track the tag's location through the previous unchanged messages, because different messages are exchanged each time due to the sending of the randomly selected PID. However, the tag's location can be estimated even though different messages are sent each time, in case the tag's SID is known. The tag tracking for a special purpose (legal investigation) becomes possible through the administrator's authorization;

Safety Against Spoofing Attack. In most cases, the symmetry key cipher technique is used to guarantee the secrecy of sent messages. However, is costs too much to use such cipher techniques because the storing space and computation capability of RFID tag is limited. In the proposed protocol, the secrecy of the messages sent and received during the authentication procedure is guaranteed, by concealing and sending the sent message (PID) through the bit computation with random numbers. That is, the PID of the sent tag can be calculated, only if the random number and its own PID information is known. It is safe against the message eavesdropping attack, because it is impossible to calculate the tag's overall SID even though the PID is exposed.

Safety Against Reply Attack. There are two kinds of attack; resend attacks disguised as a reader and as a tag. In case of disguising as a reader, the attacker eavesdrops on the message sent from the reader to the tag and resends it. In the proposed protocol, the resend attack is prevented by establishing the pseudo random number R, n1 and n2.

Through the above security analysis, we can know that the authentication protocol proposed in this paper solve the secure problems of spoofing attack, reply attack and user location tracking.

4.2 Efficiency

In the RFID system, power consumption, processing time, memory space and gate number work as main variables. Therefore, it is very important to decrease the above 4 elements in embodying the RFID system of low cost. Comparing the hash and cryptography approaches, which both cost 20,000 30,000 gate numbers, the Juels and Eunyoung approaches only cost 500 5000 gate numbers. So we need only compare our scheme with the more efficient methods. The table 1 shows a result of comparing and analyzing the Juels[10] and Eun-young[11] techniques and proposed protocol.

	Juels[10]	*Eunyoung*[6,9]	Our Scheme
Memory	k*L	2L	1L
Computation	4k (XOR)	8(XOR)+4(+)	4(XOR)
Write Op	k*L	L	Unused

k: number of secure key(4 or 5); + : module addition;
L: Length of SID

As shown in the table 1, the proposed protocol makes the tag's computation quantity evidently decrease in comparison with the Juels and Eun-Young techniques [10,11]. Also our protocol decreases memory requirement to half (from 2L to L) of the Eun-Young arithmetic, and the chief bit computation decreases to 1/3 (8(XOR)+4(+)4(XOR)). Furthermore, the write operation is not needed in tags during the authentication procedure. Besides, in the RFID system, it is not realistic to reserve the additional space for writing computation and storage. And while the information protection of RFID system using the tag only for reading is previous possible through the physical approach, it is so through the software method in the proposed protocol, which is an evidence of superiority over the previous techniques.

5 Conclusions

Previous RFID techniques cause serious privacy infringements such as excessive information exposure and user's location information tracking due to the wireless characteristics and the limitation of RFID systems. Especially the information security problem of read-only tag has been solved by physical method. This paper proposes the mutual authentication protocol of low cost using the simple XOR computation and PID concept, which is applicable to the fields of logistics activity, medicine transfer management with the read-only tag. Furthermore proposed authentication protocol decreases memory requirement to half of the Eun-Young arithmetic, and the chief bit computation is decreased to 1/3. Furthermore, the write operation is not needed in tags during the authentication procedure. Therefore the proposed protocol supports major desirable security features of RFID systems such as implicit mutual authentication, traffic encryption and privacy protection.

References

1. Weis, S.A., Sarma, S., Rivest, R., Engels, D.: Security and privacy aspects of low-cost radio frequency identification systems. In: Hutter, D., Müller, G., Stephan, W., Ullmann, M. (eds.) Security in Pervasive Computing. LNCS, vol. 2802, pp. 201–212. Springer, Heidelberg (2004)
2. Juels, A., Pappu, R.: Squealing Euros: Privacy protection in RFID-enabled banknotes. In: Wright, R.N. (ed.) FC 2003. LNCS, vol. 2742, pp. 103–121. Springer, Heidelberg (2003)
3. Molnar, D., Soppera, A., Wagner, D.: A scalable delegatable pseudonym protocol enabling ownership transfer of RFID tags. In: Preneel, B., Tavares, S. (eds.) Selected Areas in Cryptography-SAC 2005. LNCS, Springer, Heidelberg (2005)
4. Henrici, D., Muller, P.: Hash-based Enhancement of Location Privacy for Radio-Frequency Identification Devices using Varying Identifiers. In: Proceedings of the Second IEEE Annual Conference on Pervasive Computing and Communications Workshop, PERCOMW '04, pp. 149–153. IEEE Computer Society Press, Los Alamitos (2004)
5. UHF wireless tag, Auto-ID Center, http://www.autoidcenter.org/research/mit-autoid-tr007.pdf
6. Ohkubo, M., Suzuki, K., Kinoshita, S.: A Cryptographic Approach to 'Privacy-Friendly' tag, RFID Privacy Workshop (November 2003)
7. Yoshida, J.: RFID Backlash Prompts 'Kill' Feature, EETimes, (April 28 2003)
8. Juels, A., Rivest, R.L., Szydlo, M.: The Blocker Tag: Selective Blocking of RFID Tags for Consumer Privacy. In: 10th ACM Conference on Computer and Communications Security, CCS 2003, pp. 103–111 (2003)
9. Golle, P., Jakobsson, M., Juels, A., Syverson, P.: Universal re-encryption for mixnets. In: Okamoto, T. (ed.) CT-RSA 2004. LNCS, vol. 2964, pp. 163–178. Springer, Heidelberg (2004)
10. Juels, A.: Minimalist cryptography for low-cost RFID tags. In: Blundo, C., Cimato, S. (eds.) SCN 2004. LNCS, vol. 3352, pp. 149–164. Springer, Heidelberg (2005)
11. Choi, E.Y., Lee, S.M., Lee, D.H.: Efficient RFID Authentication protocol for Ubiquitous Computing Environment. In: Enokido, T., Yan, L., Xiao, B., Kim, D., Dai, Y., Yang, L.T. (eds.) International Workshop on Security in Ubiquitous Computing Systems - secubiq 2005. LNCS, vol. 3823, pp. 945–954. Springer, Heidelberg (2005)
12. Avoine, G.: Radio frequency identification: adversary model and attacks on existing protocols, Technical Report LASEC-REPORT-2005-001, EPFL, Lausanne, Switzerland (September 2005)

Securing Overlay Activities of Peers in Unstructured P2P Networks*

Jun-Cheol Park[1] and Geonu Yu[2]

[1] Department of Computer Engineering
Hongik University, Seoul 121-791, Korea
jcpark@cs.hongik.ac.kr
[2] MD Development Group, LG Electronics
Pyungtaik, Kyunggi-Do 451-713, Korea
geonu@lge.com

Abstract. This paper discusses how to secure overlay activities of peers on overlay level messages exchanged in unstructured P2P networks. We identify some attacks that can be effectively handled by appropriate cryptographic means. We then give a detection method against those attacks including message modification, replay attack, and message generation with wrong information. The method presumes the existence of a set of CAs, which are consulted when peers are newly joining the network and otherwise uninvolved in the peer activities. We also address the attack of a peer's illegal dropping of relaying messages, which is hard to be traced to its doer even with the assist of cryptographic means. We propose an audit and topology adaptation technique to confine and weaken the ill effect of such an attack on other peers in the network. We demonstrate the effectiveness of the technique using a modified GnutellaSim [14] simulator with respect to various metrics. Being based upon a generic overlay model, the proposed techniques can be applied to any unstructured P2P network either separately or all together.

1 Introduction

P2P networks[1,7,6,9] exhibit a weakness in identifying accountability of selfish or malicious acts because of the open, flat, and autonomous nature of such networks. The network peers must be considered untrusted participants and nothing can stop a peer from executing its own code rather than the common program given to all peers. A P2P network must be robust against active attacks(for example, message corruption/replay, impersonation, ID spoofing, uploading a virus file with a disguised name, etc) by a single peer or a group of colluding peers. This paper focuses on active attacks on peers' overlay activities regarding message exchanges in unstructured P2P networks.

We first identify some attacks on peers that can be effectively detected by appropriate cryptographic means. To the attacks, we present a cryptographic method for detecting such attacks. It presumes the existence and help of a set

* This work was supported by the 2006 Hongik University Research Fund.

Y. Wang, Y. Cheung, and H. Liu (Eds.): CIS 2006, LNAI 4456, pp. 795–805, 2007.

of trusted entities, called CAs. A CA is consulted when a peer newly joins the network. In the process, we assume that the peer, if approved, securely obtains an ID, a public/private key pair, and a certificate signed by the CA. It should be noted that the CAs are uninvolved in the usual activities of the peers. The method detects and deters message modification, replay attack, and message generation with wrong information. The paper also addresses the problem of a peer's illegal dropping of relaying messages. We present a technique that allows a peer to determine at which *direction* selfish or malicious peers, if any, reside and then to adapt its overlay connections to keep the peer away from the directed area. Any peer can execute this *audit* process by issuing a query(request), which is a normal action of the peer causing no extra overhead. The proposed techniques in this paper are for somewhat orthogonal problems and thus can be used either separately or together. They detect and deter various attacks on overlay activities of peers dealing with messages.

This paper is organized as follows. In the next section, we give a P2P overlay model on which the proposed techniques are based. In section 3, we present how to secure some overlay peer activities via cryptographic means using a message format suggested for this sake. In section 4, we give an active audit and topology adaptation technique for defending message dropping by relaying peers. Some simulation results follow for demonstrating the practicality of the approach. We give related work in section 5 and conclude the paper in section 6.

2 P2P Overlay Model

For the presentation of the techniques, we give an overlay model that specifies generic overlay activities of peers and topology adaptation.

2.1 Peer Overlay Activities

We stipulate the existence of a set of CAs as in public key based infrastructure. When a peer wants to join the network, it first needs to contact a CA that provides the peer, if approved, with an ID, a public/private key pair, and a certificate issued by the CA. Once owning an ID and related things, a peer needs to contact no CAs, which are, as a result, uninvolved in usual overlay activities of peers.

When a peer leaves the network, it may cause some existing peers to be poorly connected or disconnected from the remaining network. These peers may want to be connected with a few more peers. Each P2P overlay network has its own protocol to adapt its topology on the fly, and our overlay model does not assume any particular procedure for this.

While in online, each peer sends and receives messages as specified in the application protocol. The model specifies two message types: request and response. In file searching, for example, each peer can issue a query (request) and wait for the queryhits (responses) from other peers that have the required file. The model assumes that these messages should travel the overlay through the peers on the network. The overlay activities of peers include the generation, relaying, responding, and discarding of peer messages.

2.2 Topology Adaptation

The P2P overlay topology is formed in either an *unstructured* way or a *structured* way. Recently many research focused on the DHT(Dynamic Hash Table)-based structured P2P networks [10,11,12]. In these networks, queries can be efficiently routed to the node that has the desired file because of the tight mapping between a file and its location. But, they are yet to be shown to scalably implement techniques for keyword searching, which are common on current file sharing systems. Also, compared to unstructured networks, these networks are less resilient when nodes are joining and leaving at a high rate. In unstructured networks, the overlay topology is made in an ad-hoc way and the storage of data is completely unrelated to the overlay topology. Unstructured networks can easily accommodate a highly transient node population due to frequent joins and leaves of nodes. However, it is hard to efficiently find the desired files without distributing queries widely(e.g. flooding). The current most popular P2P applications still operate on unstructured overlay networks.

An unstructured overlay topology can be adjusted on the fly to improve efficiency and thus the scalability of the network. Besides efficiency, search(the most important service in resource(e.g. file) sharing) quality for peers becomes yet another reason for topology adaption in unstructured P2P networks.

3 Cryptographic Means for Securing Some Peer Overlay Activities

A peer in an overlay network is supposed to participate in the online activities among the peers in the network. Among others, we focus on those activities dealing with messages exchanged including message generation, relaying, and responding. These are the most basic activities of peers for fulfilling the purpose of any P2P application in use.

Before presenting attacks and defenses in detail, we devise a message format that is essential in detecting illegal modification on the message content. Figure 1 shows the message format that contains the data and the additional information to be sent together.

The *message ID* is a unique ID assigned to the message by the source(with *peer ID*). Each message is identified with its *message ID* and *peer ID*. Thus it would be fine for two messages with different sources to have the same *message ID*. The *deadline* specifies the lifetime of the message. After the *deadline*, no peer is allowed to forward the message. The *type* field says whether the message is a request(e.g. query) or a response(e.g. queryhit). According to the value of *type* field, the *in response to* field becomes a null value(if the message is a request) or the hash of the request that invoked this response(if the message is a response). The *payload* is self-explanatory. Taken together, those are the data the source

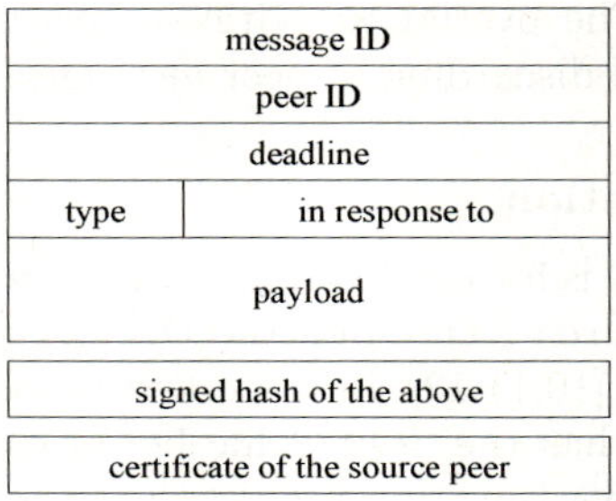

Fig. 1. Message Format

peer wants to transmit. In addition, the signature on the hash of the whole data is computed and attached, where the signing is performed by the private key of the source peer. Finally, the certificate of the source peer issued by a CA is also attached.

When a peer receives a message from one of its neighbor peers, it verifies the message as follows. It first checks the validity of the certificate, which is easy provided it knows the public key of the CA. No one is able to fabricate a certificate that will pass this test unless the private key of the CA is stolen. Then the peer checks the integrity of the signed hash part using the public key enclosed in the certificate. It verifies the signature and tests if the decrypted hash matches to the hash value computed over the data part of the message received. The peer stops if and when any test step fails and discards the message. Even though a message has passed all the tests, it would not be forwarded further by the peer if the message's deadline has reached.

Below are some active attacks on peers' overlay activities and defenses.

- *Tampering with Relaying Messages*: Suppose a message is tampered with by a peer. For the modification of either the payload or any of the fields(*message ID*, *peer ID*, *deadline*, *type*, and *in response to*), the signed hash of the data part will not match to the modified data unless the altered part happens to generate the exact same hash. However, the feasibility of obtaining a text that produces a given hash value is negligible since the hash function is one-way. Similarly, the modification of the signed hash of the message is detectable. In case the data part and the signed hash are modified together, the signature won't be verified by the public key in the certificate. The certificate is also subject to change, but the change will be detected since the testing peer is assumed to know the public key of the CA, who issued the certificate. The point is that the certificate, not just the public key that can be easily replaced without being noticed, of the source peer is to be attached to every message the peer generates.
- *Providing False/Wrong Information Purposely*: Suppose a peer issues a query message including a question that the peer already knows the answer(e.g., a reputation value of a target peer that the source peer knows well and trust).

When a "wrong"(believed to be wrong by most peers in the network) answer arrives to the source peer, it can report a complaint with the answer as an evidence. Thanks to the signature on the message content and the source's certificate, no peer can fabricate a bogus message that looks as if some other peer has generated it. So the evidence must be very strong and would discourage any peer from telling a lie.

– *Replay Attack*: Replay attack is a kind of illegal usage of a message for such an instance that the message's distribution is not expected by the network and thus prohibited. One plausible motivation for the attack is to disgrace the source peer's reputation for flooding the stored message into the network and abusing the network resources. Our prevention against this attack is the use of absolute time as the deadline, which is covered by the source's signature. Unlike the TTL or hop limit as in IPv4 or IPv6, the deadline set by the source does not have to be updated at each peer, and thus can be protected by the source peer's encryption. Because of clock drifts among the peers, however, it is essential to give some margin to the deadline value when setting it.

4 Active Topology Adaptation for Defending Message Dropping

In this section, we propose an audit and topology adaptation technique to confine and weaken the effect of illegal message dropping on honest peers.

4.1 Request(Query) Table Format

Before we go into detail, we need to identify a list of message types - borrowed from the Gnutella [13] protocol - used in the presentation of the technique. Note that the list contains only the most basic and essential types that must be present in almost every unstructured P2P network.

– *Query*: used to search for a certain resource(e.g., file)
– *QueryHit*: used to carry a positive response to a *Query*
– *Bye*: used to gracefully close a connection to a neighbor

A peer can transmit a *Query* to its neighbors in order to observe how many *QueryHits* to the query are returned. The content of *Query* can be chosen such that the average number of responses(hits) to the query is stabilized in the target network. *QueryHit* messages would be returned along the same path in reverse order that carried the *Query* message. This ensures that only those peers that forwarded the *Query* message will see the matching *QueryHit* message. Each peer of a P2P network has a separate query table for maintaining its *injected* queries. In addition to the query table, each peer needs to store and maintain the live P2P overlay connections from it.

Format. An injected *Query* message is represented by an entry *(nbr, msgid, hits, threshold, deadline)*. *nbr* represents the neighbor of the source to which to forward the message. *msgid*, *hits*, *threshold*, and *deadline* are the message id, the number of *QueryHits* received, the expected number of hits to arrive, and the deadline for accepting the hits, respectively.

4.2 Audit and Topology Adaptation

The intuition behind the *audit* is that the number of responses(hits) returned to a query can serve as an indicator to the reliability of the relaying paths in the overlay. Consider a query whose average number of hits is known per neighbor link within a certain radius(TTL) in an overlay network. If the number of hits received through a particular neighbor is far less than the expected threshold value, it is very much likely that a peer or a group of peers are responsible for not forwarding the query and/or its response(s). The offender in this case is not necessarily the neighbor of the query's source, because it is also possible for a peer or a group of peers residing far from, but still within the query's TTL range, of the source to act selfishly or maliciously.

Assume that a peer x selects a P2P connection (x, y) and a query content for auditing the reliability of the forwarding paths via the neighbor y.

Insert. An injection of the *Query* to the direction of the peer y produces a new entry in the query table of the peer x. The new entry is a tuple *(y, id, 0, k, d)*, where k and d are such that k hits are expected to arrive by the time d.

Update. Each arrival of a matching *QueryHit* to x increments the value on the appropriate *hits* field by one.

Each peer looks into its query table periodically. For each entry e = *(dst, id, hits, threshold, deadline)* in a query table, the peer does the following. If e is unresolved, i.e., *hits* < *threshold* holds at the *deadline*, the peer essentially closes the link toward the *dst* by transmitting a *Bye* message to the *dst*. Then the peer tries to connect to a randomly selected peer as a new neighbor of it.

4.3 Experiments

We take the GnutellaSim [14] simulator for Gnutella - one of the most popular P2P networks - system and make some modification to incorporate the procedure. Using various performance metrics, we show that the proposed technique effectively isolates malicious peers from others without much impact on the service quality of normal peers.

Simulation Set. We use a modified GnutellaSim(version 2.26) that implements the Gnutella protocol version 0.4 describing a flooding-based search on a pure unstructured overlay.

The network topology generated in each simulation is a random graph with node degrees ranging from 1 upto 4. The size of the network is 1200. A simulation run ends at 1000 seconds starting from 0. When a new peer joins the network somewhere between 0 and 100 seconds, it first contacts a central server to get a list of online peers and tries to connect to some peers in the list. The server is responsible for maintaining the identities of the online peers. A peer starts from the "online" state and switches between the "online" state and the "offline" state during the simulation(the average time between the switches is set to 1000 seconds). While online, it switches between "active" state and "idle" state. It sends a query in the "active" state, and only serves as a forwarder in the "idle" state. Each peer in the "active" state sends a query in the rate of every 100 seconds. After receiving responses to its query(TTL set to 4), a peer goes to either the "offline"(with probability 0.1) state or the "idle"(with probability 0.9) state. A peer can be either a *normal* peer or a *malicious* peer, but not both. A malicious peer always drops a relaying message and returns a "fake" query hit to a query. The portions of malicious peers used in the simulated network are 0%, 5%, 10%, and 15%, respectively. When a peer, either malicious or not, loses a connection, it actively tries to reconnect to a new peer picked randomly from the central server's list.

Simulation Results. To estimate the degree of separation of malicious peers, we use the number of fake query hits received as a major metric. We consider the number of query hits received as well, because it needs to ensure a peer to get a reasonable number of query hits even when the procedure is in effect.

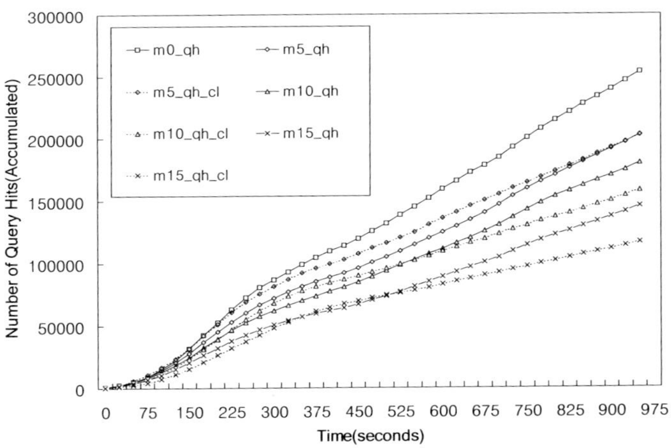

Fig. 2. The Number of Query Hits(Accumulated)

Figure 2 shows the number of accumulated query hits received during a simulation run. The scripts in the figure read as follows: in mX_[f]qh[_cl], "X" is a number 0, 5, 10, or 15 representing the portion of malicious peers in the network, "f" stands for fake, "qh" means queryhit, and "cl" stands for closing(blocking) connection, i.e., the procedure applied. We see that the technique reduces the number of query hits. It is because the closing of connections makes even the normal query hits unreachable to their destinations. Note that as the portion of malicious peers is getting larger, the reduction is more noticeable.

Figure 3 shows the number of accumulated fake query hits received during a simulation run. The fake query hits are reduced in all three runs(X= 5, 10, 15), compared to the bare runs, as time evolves. The reduction is more evident as the portion of malicious peers is getting smaller.

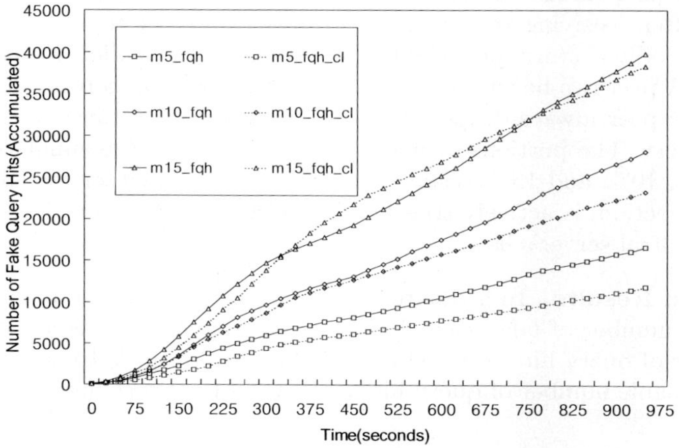

Fig. 3. The Number of Fake Query Hits(Accumulated)

In Figure 4, we show the number of degree changes for normal peers("n" in the scripts) and malicious peers("m" in the scripts), respectively. As expected, the degree change(i.e. close or reconnection) happens more frequently at malicious peers, which indicates the instability of those peers in terms of their peer connections. Figure 5 shows the number of link closings occurred over time. After the peaks at about time 200, which corresponds to sometime after the bootstrapping phase(0 to 100), each case(X= 5, 10, 15) goes to a steady state where the number of link closings varies not much. This indicates that the malicious peers remain to be poorly connected to normal peers provided the number of peers in the network is stabilized.

Discussion. Among others, we observe that (1) the reduction ratio of the number of fake query hits is larger than that of the number of query hits, (2) the connection state of a malicious peer is unstable compared to that of a normal peer, that is, the average number of degree changes of a malicious peer is always larger than that of a normal peer, and (3) the number of link closings, which is proportional to the connectivity of malicious peers with normal peers, is rapidly reduced and does not change much thereafter. If a peer is located close to a malicious peer, it is likely that the former would close its link toward the latter before other peers do so. Accordingly, when applying the proposed technique, it

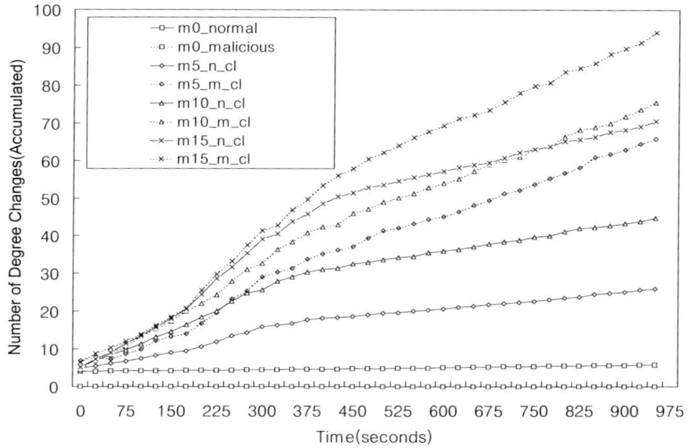

Fig. 4. The Number of Degree Changes(Accumulated)

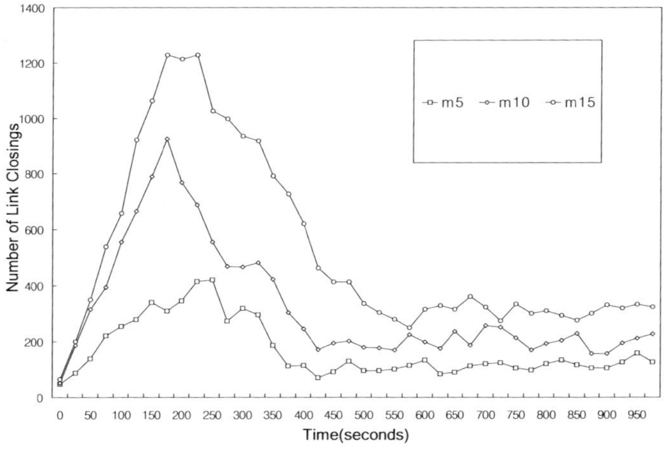

Fig. 5. The Number of Link Closings

would be more effective for each peer to repeat the audit process by issuing a series of queries with an incremented TTL value each time, if possible.

5 Related Work

Various cryptographic algorithms and protocols are employed to provide security in the context of P2P networks. Self-certifying data [8] is data whose integrity can be verified by the peer retrieving it. Information dispersal algorithm [15] encodes a file into m blocks, of which any n of them are sufficient to reassemble the original file. Similarly, the secret sharing scheme [16] can specify the minimum number of parts, from which the original key before splitting is obtainable. Unlike these works, the cryptographic work in this paper has different problem domain of securing routing and forwarding of overlay messages.

Many research has been published on the formation of P2P overlays for *efficiency*[3,4]. To increase the search efficiency in unstructured P2P networks, [3] proposed a topology adaptation and flow control algorithm. The algorithm assists that queries flow towards the node with sufficient capacity to handle them. Another topology adaptation technique [4] is proposed for the Gnutella network. It ensures that most nodes will be at a short distance from high capacity nodes. The adaptation technique, when used together with other techniques, results in a significant performance improvement over the original Gnutella protocol. The audit and adaptation technique in this paper has a different design goal of isolating malicious peers from others in the network. The work in [2] dealt with the *non-cooperation* problem, where peers do not forward queries to neighbors if they are potential competitors. It uses an economic protocol for buying and selling of the right-to-respond to each query. So peers cooperate in the operation of P2P networks to increase their economic gains. The approach in this paper is to isolate and punish, rather than give direct incentives[5] to cooperate, the non-cooperating peers in a P2P network.

6 Conclusion

For some attacks feasible while the peers are communicating over the overlay, we proposed a novel message structure and a preventive technique for effectively deterring message modification, replay attack, and message generation with wrong information. The trusted CAs assumed in the technique are not involved in the usual overlay activities of peers. Another attack considered in this paper is for a peer to drop relaying messages illegally for its own benefit (e.g. refuse to forward a bid request to possible competitors in an online P2P auction), which is hard to be traced to its responsible peer. We presented a technique that allows each peer to determine at which direction selfish or malicious peers, if any, reside and to adjust its overlay connections on the fly to avoid the direction. It would urge the peers to abstain from cheating in terms of message relaying. We implemented the technique on the GnutellaSim [14] simulator and demonstrated its practicality using various metrics.

The proposed techniques, used either separately or together, would serve a strong deterrent to various active attacks on overlay activities of peers dealing with messages.

We plan to evaluate the performance overhead of the proposed cryptographic technique. It would be also interesting to investigate an extension of the adaptation technique for allowing search schemes other than the unbiased flooding and more diverse peer activity models.

References

1. Androutsellis-Theotokis, S., Spinellis, D.: A Survey of Peer-to-Peer Content Distribution Technologies. ACM Computing Surveys, 36(4) (2004)
2. Yang, B., Kamvar, S.D., Garcia-Molina, H.: Addressing the Non-Cooperation Problem in Competitive P2P Systems. In: Proc. Workshop on Economics of Peer-to-Peer Systems (2003)
3. Lv, Q., Ratnasamy, S., Shenker, S.: Can Heterogeneity Make Gnutella Scalable? In: Proc. Int'l Workshop on Peer-to-Peer Systems (2002)
4. Chawathe, Y., Ratnasamy, S., Breslau, L., Lanham, N., Shenker, S.: Making Gnutella-like P2P Systems Scalable. In: Proc. ACM SIGCOMM'03, August (2003)
5. Zhao, J., Lu, J.: Pyramid: Building Incentive Architecture for Unstructured Peer-to-Peer Network. In: Proc. Advanced Int'l Conf. on Telecommunications and Int'l Conf. on Internet and Web Applications and Services(AICT/ICIW'06) (2006)
6. Marti, S., Garcia-Molina, H.: Taxonomy of Trust: Categorizing P2P Reputation Systems. COMNET Special Issue on Trust and Reputation in Peer-to-Peer Systems (2005)
7. Risson, J., Moors, T.: Survey of Research Towards Robust Peer-to-Peer Networks: Search Methods. In: TR UNSW-EE-P2P-1-1, Univ. of New South Wales, Australia (2004)
8. Castro, M., Druschel, P., Ganesh, A., Rowstron, A., Wallach, D.: Secure Routing for Structured Peer-to-Peer Overlay Networks. In: Proc. Usenix Symp. on Operating Systems (2002)
9. Dewan, P., Dasgupta, P.: Securing P2P Networks Using Peer Reputations: Is there a silver bullet? In: Proc. IEEE Consumer Communications and Networking Conf. (CCNC2005), USA (2005)
10. Stoica, I., Morris, R., Liben-Nowell, D., Karger, D., Kaashoek, M.F., Dabek, F., Balakrishnan, H.: Chord: A Scalable Peer-to-Peer Lookup Protocol for Internet Applications. IEEE/ACM Tr. on Networking 11(1) (2003)
11. Ratnasamy, S., Francis, P., Handley, M., Karp, R., Shenker, S.: A Scalable Content-Addressable Network. In: Proc. ACM SIGCOMM'01 (2001)
12. Rowstron, A., Druschel, P.: Pastry: Scalable, Distributed Object Location and Routing for Large-scale Peer-to-Peer Systems. In: Proc. IFIP/ACM Int'l Conf. Distributed Systems Platforms(Middleware 2001) (2001)
13. Gnutella Website, `http://www.gnutella.com`
14. He, Q., Ammar, M., Riley, G., Raj, H., Fujimoto, R.: Mapping Peer Behavior to Packet-level Details: A Framework for Packet-level Simulation of Peer-to-Peer Systems. In: Proc. ACM/IEEE Int'l Symp. on Modeling, Analysis and Simulation of Computer and Telecommunication Systems (2003)
15. Rabin, M.: Efficient Dispersal of Information for Security, Load Balancing and Fault Tolerance. Journal of the ACM 36(2) (1989)
16. Shamir, A.: How to Share a Secret. Communications of the ACM 22 (1979)

Security Contexts in Autonomic Systems

Kaiyu Wan and Vasu Alagar

Department of Computer Science and Software Engineering
Concordia University
Montreal, Canada
{ky_wan,alagar}@cse.concordia.ca

Abstract. Autonomic Computing Systems (ACS) are expected to achieve the same level of self-regulation and pervasiveness as human autonomic systems. Because of the features of ACS, the traditional security model can not be applied to ACS any more. The goal of our research is to develop a context-based security model and architecture for ACS. Our focus is on self-protection feature of ACS. The self-protection feature is enforced through *security contexts* that we define. By taking security contexts into account, security policies can dynamic change in order to cope with new environment.

1 Introduction

As the costs of system hardware and software have decreased, the costs of the human resources devoted to system administration have continued to grow, and therefore constitute a steadily larger fraction of information technology costs. The autonomic computing initiative is aimed at addressing these increasing costs by producing computing systems that require less human effort to administer. The concept of *Autonomic Computing*(AC) was first expressed by Paul Horn [8] as "an approach to self-managed computing systems with a minimum of human interference". Consequently, Autonomic Computing Systems (ACS) are expected to achieve the same level of self-regulation and pervasiveness as human autonomic systems. ACS have the ability to manage themselves, monitor themselves, recover from failures and repair themselves, and adapt to changes in its environment in accordance with the policies governing the system. Examples of such systems include IBM Trivoli Management Suite [13], SUN Microsystems - N1 [16,17], Hewlett-Packard's Adaptive Enterprise [9], and Microsoft's Dynamic Systems Initiative [12].

The most important characteristics of ACS, as defined by Paul Horn [2] are as follows:

- *Self-configuring:* ACS must adapt automatically to the dynamically changing environments.
- *Self-healing:* ACS must detect, diagnose, and recover from any damage that occurs.
- *Self-optimizing:* ACS must monitor and tune resources automatically.
- *Self-protection:* ACS must detect and guard itself against damage from accidents, equipment failure, or outside attacks by hackers and viruses.

Y. Wang, Y. Cheung, and H. Liu (Eds.): CIS 2006, LNAI 4456, pp. 806–816, 2007.

As Chess remarked in [4], like any other significant computing system, ACS need to be secure. All the traditional issues familiar to computer security researchers will arise in ACS, for example, the improvement of cryptographic algorithms in order to make them more resistent to hackers, implementation of new authentication methods and designing access control mechanisms, etc. In traditional security systems, the security policy is pre-configured to a static behavior and can not be seamlessly adapted dynamically to new constraints. However, because of the features of ACS, the static security policy can not be applied to ACS. For instance, many ACS will use new techniques and new architectures whose security implications are not yet well understood. Autonomic systems should not rely on anomalous behavior caused by static security compromises being noticed by humans, if they are to benefit from reduced human administration costs. Moreover many autonomic systems are expected to deal with a constantly changing set of other systems as suppliers, customers, and partners, they need flexible new methods for detecting attacks and recovering from security incidents automatically. Apparantly, the traditional security model can not be applied to ACS any more.

The goal of our research is to develop a context-based security model and architecture for ACS. Our focus is on self-protection feature of ACS. The self-protection feature is enforced through *security contexts* that we define. By taking security contexts into account, security policies can dynamic change in order to cope with new environment.

Self-protection in ACS requires self-awareness (internal monitoring) and context-awareness (external monitoring). By being aware of its internal state and its external situation which includes service requirements and potential threats, the system adapts itself according to system policies in a timely fashion. That is, it provides the right services at the right time to the right clients, detects hostile intrusive behavior of external agents and takes actions to safeguard the system status and integrity, and correctly fulfills the system obligations in order to assure privacy aspects of clients. These three aspects involved in self-protections are formalized using security contexts in the proposed architecture. As a preliminary to such an investigation we review in Section 2 basic concepts on context, context-awareness, self-awareness as applicable to security, and privacy issues. The rest of the paper is organized as follows: Security contexts are introduced in Section 3. The architecture for ACS is discussed in Section 4. The paper is concluded in Section 5 where implementation issues and future works are given.

2 Self-awareness and Context-Awareness

Awareness induces the system elements to take an active role and becoming proactive. As an example, a cell phone that is aware of its surroundings may not beep and automatically send a reply to the caller to call at a later time. Typically, a system that is aware of it's internal states (self-awareness) and its environment (context-awareness) will automatically provide access to any and all information that may be relevant to a service request, and facilitate communication among the groups of users involved in the fulfillment of the task. In this section we restrict our discussion to awareness that is relevant for self-protection.

2.1 Self-awareness

ACS must be aware of its internal state, in particular the critical states that must be protected. At any instance the state of the system is defined by the following information:

1. *Users* are the subjects (users, and other clients such as program calls) who are active in the system. Each subject must belong to a category, based on the roles of subjects. The system maintains a database of user categories and identification of users in each category. By constantly updating the database the system is aware of the subjects active at any instance.
2. *Data* are the objects (files, email documents, policy documents, customer records, facsimile documents) that are under use, and whose access is controlled by business policy (security and privacy policy). Each data item that needs to be protected is assigned to one or more categories. With each category a label indicating the level of security is attached.
3. *Permission* For each object in the system and for each user an access list exists that specifies explicitly the actions that the user can perform on the object.
4. *Obligation* are the set of mandatory rules specifying the system action (response) after fulfilling the user request consistent with the permission.

The system changes its state in the following manner:

- A user accesses the system to perform one or more actions. The user must indicate the *purpose* behind each activity. For instance, the user requesting to view an email document in the system may indicate the purpose as "legal". Depending upon the category to which user belongs and the security label of the item to be viewed, the activity may be allowed or denied. If the request to view the email document is granted, and it's presence in the system violates the business policy the obligatory rule will be applied.
- User categories change, users are added/deleted from the system.
- Data categories change, data are added/deleted from the system.
- Permission list and Obligations are modified.

The system is initialized with initial state information. Subsequently, it automatically follows through its state changes and keeps a record of the history of state changes. Thus the system knows its past as well as its present.

2.2 Context-Awareness

Context is a rich concept often used by linguists and philosophers to refer to different worlds of discourse of interest. It's usage in computing was first in Artificial Intelligence (AI) studies [14,7]. Their goal was to use context in natural language processing, hence the meaning of context was tacitly understood but not defined. Although rich concepts defy precise definition, a formal definition of it, albeit only approximate, is required for a rigorous development of context-aware systems. Several formal approaches based on logic to reason about contextual knowledge is discussed in [1]. Dey [6] discussed context representation informally while discussing its role in ubiquitous computing.

Recently, a formal definition of context, and a context calculus for context-aware applications have been introduced in [18]. Wan [19] has introduced context as a first class object in Intensional Programming and has shown the expressive power of that language for programming different applications. We review this formalization in Section 3 and introduce security contexts.

The distinguishing features of a context-awareness are *perception* and *adaptation*. In order to be context-aware, the system maintains an internal model of user's needs, preferences, and privacy requirements. The perception feature makes the system aware of the entities in the region of its governance, and triggers context-driven interaction among the entities. The nature of interaction is in general heterogeneous, with varying levels of synchrony, concurrency, and delay. However, the system is to be fully controlled and guided by the time-varying contextual conditions and system's progress should remain both predictable and deterministic. In order to achieve determinism and predictability, the system adapts to the stimuli from its environment by learning the changing relationship among the entities and acting to fulfill the intentions expressed by the entities. That is, based upon its internal representation and changes perceived in its environment the system must reason about the appropriate action to be taken and takes it in a timely manner. For example, if a user logs in to transact on-line banking from a location which is different from the location indicated in the profile of the user maintained by the system, the system could interrogate the user with questions in the user profile. When the user's answers to the questions match the answers in the user profile the user is authenticated, otherwise the user's identity is unknown to the system. If the user is successfully authenticated, the obligation rule, if it exists, will be applied to update the current context (location) of the user. In general, the system reconstructs contexts based on the information it gathers from the possible worlds defined by five distinguished *dimensions*, which we call W5:

- [*perception*]- *who* provides the service and who requires the service?
- [*interaction*]- *what* service is required?
- [*locality*]- *where* to provide the service?
- [*timeliness*]- *when* to provide the service?
- [*reasoning*]- *why* an action is required?

Typically, the system will obtain context information from sensors, or infer from user input, or use external Personal Information Management Systems. From the collected data, the system must accurately determine the environmental context as well as the intentions of the user in that context. Hence, context-awareness require *inferencing* and *learning*. These two features are naturally inherent in agents. That is another major reason that we are proposing an agent-based architecture for ACS.

3 Security Contexts

We propose three primitive security categories: *Internal Security Category* (ISC), *Boundary Security Category* (BSC), and *External Security Category* (ESC). All contexts in a primitive security category have the same structure. Context operators when applied to security contexts in one primitive category produce a security context in the same primitive category. Context operators when applied to security contexts from different primitive categories will generate a context in one of the non-primitive (mixed) security categories IBSC, IESC, BESC, IBESC. The category IBSC contains security contexts obtained by combining one or more security contexts from ISC and BSC. Similar interpretation is given to the other mixed security categories.

3.1 Context Definition

Context is a reference to some world phenomena. Hence, the context information is in general *multidimensional*, where in each dimension there exists several choices to be considered. In each dimension, there are several possible ways to represent information. We say information in each dimension is *tagged*. The tags may sometimes be the actual information itself.

Let $DIM = \{d_1, d_2, \ldots, d_n\}$, denote a finite set of dimensions, and $TAG = \{X_1, \ldots, X_r\}$ denote the set of tag sets. The function $f_{dimtotag} : DIM \rightarrow TAG$ associates with every $d_i \in DIM$ exactly one tag X_j in TAG. Consider the relations

$$P_i = \{d_i\} \times f_{dimtotag}(d_i) \quad 1 \leq i \leq n$$

A context c, given $(DIM, f_{dimtotag})$, is a finite subset of $\bigcup_{i=1}^{n} P_i$. The *degree* of the context c is $\mid \Delta \mid$, where $\Delta \subset DIM$ includes the dimensions that appear in c. The concrete syntax for a context is $[d_1 : x_1, \ldots, d_n : x_n]$, where $d_1, \ldots, d_n$ are dimensions, and $x_i \in f_{dimtotag}(d_i)$. As an example, a location context can have four dimensions $GPS, TIME, NS, EW$. Let the tag set for GPS be identical to the value determined automatically by the geographical positioning system and the tag set for $TIME$, NS, and EW be positive integers. Thus, the context $c = [GPS : NYC, TIME : 10, NS : 12, EW : 3]$ gives the space time coordinates in New York city at time 10 of the location which is the intersection of 12th north-south street and 3rd east-west avenue. The context c may refer to a building in that location or to an event that happens at that corner or to a set of vehicles at that intersection. In the following discussion/examples we may skip stating the type of tag sets.

3.2 Structure of Security Categories

The dimensions for contexts in a security category are determined by system designers. For the purpose of illustration we suggest below what we regard as the important dimensions in which information must be represented.

A context in ISC should provide information to protect the internal state of the system. Assume that $UC = \{UC_1, \ldots, UC_m\}$ is the set of user categories as determined by user roles. Let $DC = \{DC_1, \ldots, DC_k\}$ be the set of data categories which are to be protected. We regard UC_i's and DC_js as dimensions. Let PC denote the purpose dimension. Assume that the tag set along each UC_i is the set of user names, the tag set along each DC_i can be the set of integers (pointers to files), and the tag set for PC is {Legal, Administrative, Marketing}. An example of ISC context is $[UC_1 : u, DC_1 : j, PC :$ Legal$]$, meaning that user u is allowed to access the data referenced by j in category DC_1 for legal purposes.

A context in ESC should provide information on the environment in which the system functions. The relevant dimensions can be considered are LOC, $TIME$, WHO, $WHAT$, $WHERE$, $WHEN$, WHY which correspond respectively to the location from where service is requested, the date/time at which the service request is made, the user requesting the service, the nature of service, the location where the service should be provided, the date/time by which the service should be given, and the reason for requesting the service. An example of ESC context is $[LOC$: Beijing, $TIME$: $d_1, WHO : Alice, WHAT$: file transfer, $WHERE : Shanghai, WHEN : d_2$, WHY : Auditing].

A context in BSC category exists on system boundary, the firewall that separates the inside of the system from its users. Following the standards used in [5], we define a boundary security context having the dimensions $NAME$, SP,(security policy) IF(interface), $CLASS$ (context membership class), and $CURL$(configuration file URL). The tag set for $NAME$ consists of names of users, including the administrator as the distinguished user in the system. The tag set for SP consists of pointers (integers) to the policy base. The tag set for IF consists of VLAN numbers (can be a range of integers). The tag set for $CURL$ consists of the URLs (such as disk://C/bsc/filename) from which the firewall loads the context configuration. The tag set for $CLASS$ is $\{default, bronze, silver, gold\}$. Each class is assigned a set of resources and has a resource limit as set by the system administrator. Contexts in different classes may share a resource, but to different degree of utilization. For example, contexts in "gold" and "default" classes have unrestricted access to system resources. An example of BSC context is $[NAME : Admin, SP : NULL, IF : vlan100, IF : vlan120, CLASS : gold, CURL : root]$. Any user who gets access to the above context gets the privileges of the system administrator. The BSC contexts are usually configured by the system administrator to optimize resource utilization and system protection. The configuration may be changed periodically by the system administrator. This task may be done by an agent in the autonomic system. The context configuration must itself be protected, lest it may be compromised by an intruder.

3.3 Security Context Sets

A security context in which a dimension name is repeated, as in $[NAME : Admin, SP : NULL, IF : vlan100, IF : vlan120, CLASS : gold, CURL : root]$, is equivalent to the set of contexts $\{[NAME : Admin, SP : NULL, IF : vlan100, CLASS : gold, CURL : root], [NAME : Admin, SP : NULL, IF : vlan100, IF : vlan120, CLASS : gold, CURL : root]\}$. The Box notation introduced by Wan [19] can be used to represent a set of contexts that satisfy a specific property. For example, if two users $Alice$ and Bob are in the same user categories who share the same set of security policies and the interface in BSC uses the VLANs in the range $100, \ldots, 200$ the BSC contexts are represented as $Box[\Delta_e \mid p] = \{s \mid s = [NAME : u, SP : j, IF : v, CLASS : silver, CURL : path] \wedge (u = \text{Alice} \vee u = \text{Bob}) \wedge v \geq 100 \wedge v \leq 200\}$, where Δ_e is the set of dimensions associated with BSC contexts. Notice that the predicate part determines the tag values for $NAME$ and IF.

3.4 Applying Security Contexts

All incoming (service request) and outgoing (service providing) traffic are classified and automatically routed through the appropriate BSC context. The sequence of security checks on a service request is :

classify at the fire-wall $\Rightarrow$ route through BSC $\Rightarrow$ apply ISC to request.

The sequence of security checks on an outgoing traffic is :

apply ESC to system response $\Rightarrow$ classify at the fire-wall $\Rightarrow$ route through BSC.

A service request (provision) is fulfilled by executing a sequence of atomic actions. Each atomic action, considered as a pair $\langle operation, data \rangle$, is evaluated at security contexts as follows:

1. *Service Request*
   - (Fire-wall) Based upon the user who requests the service and the action specification in the request, the fire-wall chooses the appropriate BSC context (using $NAME$) and loads it from $CURL$.
   - (BSC) One of the servers in the interface IF of the context should authenticate the user. If the authentication fails service is denied. If the authentication succeeds the security policy SP of the context is applied. For example, a policy may be "user must be at least 18 years of age to receive the service requested". The result of this application is either "Allow" or "Deny". If the permission is granted, the request is taken up for internal processing.
   - (ISC) From the request the system extracts the ESC context. As an example, if the ESC context is $[LOC$: Beijing, $TIME : d_1, WHO : Alice, WHAT$: file transfer, $WHERE : Shanghai, WHEN : d_2, WHY$: Auditing$]$, the system constructs the context $[WHO : Alice, WHAT$: file transfer, WHY : Auditing$]$ (see below). The constructed context is compared with the ISC contexts. If there is a match, then the action requested by $Alice$ is authorized, otherwise denied.
2. *Service Provision* We discuss only the obligation issue here, namely the action that the system should mandatorily perform after applying certain rules associated with service request.
   - (Notify the user) Notification is a privacy-policy related obligation. For example, whenever the credit information changes the system may be required to inform the client. Notification involves the sequence :
     apply ESC to system response $\Rightarrow$ classify at the fire-wall
     $\Rightarrow$ route through BSC,
     of security checks. The security actions at the fire-wall and at BSC contexts are quite similar to what is described for service request. Applying ESC to system response has the following steps: (1) From ESC context, the system determines where and when to provide the service/response. (2) From user preferences the system determines how much and/or in what form the information should be provided.
   - (State Change) After servicing a request some data items may have to be deleted, or modified, or archived. For instance, if the service request is "move the personal file of Alice from Engineering to Medical School", the personal file at the Engineering school must be deleted after fulfilling the request.

3.5 Context Modification

Contexts can change dynamically in the system. This is instrumented through the context toolkit discussed in [19]. The toolkit includes standard binary operators that take contexts as operands and returns a context, and a few others as explained in Table 1. It also provides precedence rules for evaluating context expressions, and operators for sets of contexts. For example, the extraction of context in step 2 under *service request* discussed above is carried out using the projection (↓) operator: $[LOC : \text{Beijing}, TIME : d_1, WHO : Alice, WHAT : \text{file transfer}, WHERE : Shanghai, WHEN : d_2, WHY : \text{Auditing}] \downarrow \{WHO, WHAT, WHY\}$.

Table 1. Context Operators

operator name	symbol	meaning
Union	$\sqcup$	Set Union
Intersection	$\sqcap$	Set Intersection
Difference	$\ominus$	Set Difference
Subcontext	$\subseteq$	Subset
Supcontext	$\supseteq$	Superset
Override	$\oplus$	Function overwrite
Projection	$\downarrow$	Domain Restriction
Hiding	$\uparrow$	Range Restriction
Undirected Range	$\rightleftharpoons$	Range of simple contexts with same domain
Directed Range	$\rightharpoonup$	Range of simple contexts with same domain

4 Architecture for Autonomic Computing Systems

A generic architecture for context-based security in ACS is shown in Figure 1. Only the minimal software architecture is provided so that it can be easily extended to build more specific applications. In addition, context toolkit and protected resources are loosely coupled so that adding or removing of new resources and modifying their respective

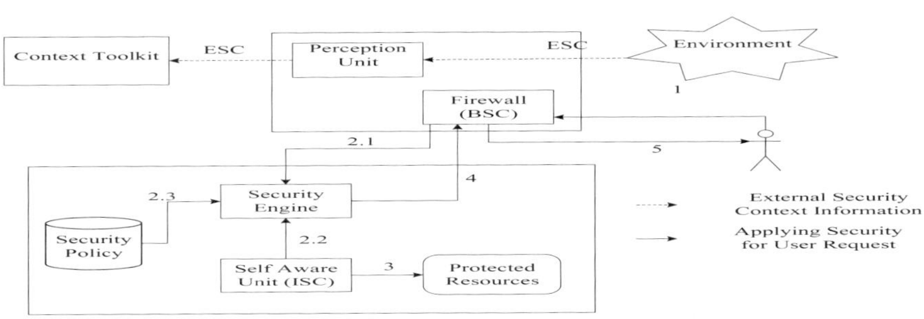

Fig. 1. Generic Architecture for Context-Based Security in ACS

access policies can be achieved in a transparent manner. The security policy base is pre-defined by system administrators at the first place. In order to change these security policies at run-time, additional reasoning or learning components are needed, which is another interesting research topic to be investigated. The procedure of applying security policy is described as follows:

1. User request;
2. The following steps may be done concurrently;
   2.1. Firewall forwards user request after applying BSC;
   2.2. Security engine collects ISC from internal system state;
   2.3. Security engine refers to security policy base;
3. Security engine applies security policy relevant to security contexts to protected resources;
4. Security engine sends the result to the user through firewall;
5. Firewall applies BSC and forwards the result to the user.

Currently, there are two major approaches for providing an architecture for ACS, i.e. *Adaptive Multi-Agent Systems* and *Architecture Design-Based Autonomic Systems.* In the former approach, agents within an autonomic system are proactive and possess social abilities. There exist agents in the system that implement self-management [15]. Since there is no centralized monitoring mechanism, agents must monitor themselves and each agent is autonomic. In the latter approach, individual component is not autonomic. Instead, the infrastructure which handles the autonomic behavior within the system uses the architectural description model to monitor, reason about the running system, and determine appropriate adaptive actions [11]. Compared to the architecture design-based approach, adaptive multi-agent systems have several advantages, the most important being the distributed nature of the system that can scale-up to handle large practical application systems. Consequently we have decided to use multi-agent systems for providing ACS architecture. In our approach, a multi-agent sytem has three vertical layers shown in Figure 2. Informally, these layers correspond to *Human Interface Layer* (HIL), *Middle Agent Layer* (MAL), and *Task Agent Layer*(TAL). The functionality of the agents on each layer is as follows:

- On the HIL layer, Human Interface Agents(IA) provides user interface and helps user to represent their requirements to the systems.
- On the MAL layer, the MA analyzes requirements and decides the configurations consisting of the Task Agents (TA) chosen from the third layer and distributes the sub-tasks to the TAs. Firewall unit and context perception unit are considered to be MAs.
- On the TAL layer, the TAs fulfill the given subtasks and inform the results to the MA. Since there are four important features of ACSs, four different TAs are designed to fulfil these features separately. Meanwhile, there is a context toolkit agent to construct and deconstruct contexts and a security agent to deal with security requirements.
- The MA incorporates the results from the TAs and gives the feedback to the IA.

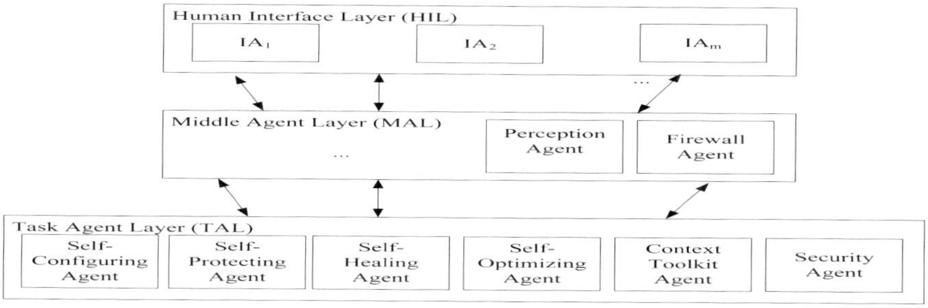

Fig. 2. Vertical Layering of Multi-agent System

5 Conclusion

In this paper, we investigate the security issues in ACSs. The security of ACS is enforced through *security contexts* that we define and the security model we provide. By taking security contexts into account, security policies can dynamic change in order to cope with new environment. We also investigate the implementation of secure ACSs based on the adaptive multi-agent systems.

As Chess concluded in his paper [4], there are several opening challenges to be investigated for security in ACSs. In particular, we would like to further our research on investigating the possibility of dynamic security policies to deal with fraud and persuasion. Investigating languages for communicating and negotiating about the security and privacy states and policies is among our research interests too.

References

1. Akman, V., Surav, M.: Steps toward formalizing context. AI Magazine 17(3), 55–72 (1996)
2. IBM White Paper.: Autonomic Computing Concepts. Available at: `http://www-03.ibm.com/autonomic/pdfs/AC_Concepts.pdf`
3. Bantz, D.F. et al.: Autonomic personal computing. IBM Systems Journal 42(1), 165–176 (2003)
4. Chess, D.M., Palmer, C.C., White, S.R.: Security in an autonomic computing enrironment. IBM SYSTEM JOURNAL 42(1) (2003)
5. CISCO White Paper.: Managing Security Contexts. Available at: `http://www.cisco.com/univercd/cc/td/doc/product/lan/cat6000/mod_icn/fwsm/fwsm_2_2/fwsm_cfg/context.htm`
6. Dey, A.K.: Understanding and Using Context. Personal and Ubiquitous Computing Journal 5(1), 4–7 (2001)
7. Guha, R.V.: Contexts: A Formalization and Some Applications. Ph.d thesis, Stanford University (1995)
8. Horn, P.: Automatic Computing: IBM's Perspective on the State if Information technology. IBM Corporation (October 15, 2001)
9. Packard, H.: HP's Darwin Reference Architecture Helps Create tighter Linkage Between Business and IT. Available at: `http://www.hp.com/hpinfo/newsroom/press/2003/030506b.html`

10. Lin, P., MacArthur, A., Leaney, J.: Defining Autonomic Computing: A Software Engineering Perspective. In: Proceedings of the 2005 Australian Software Engineering Conference (ASWEC'05), IEEE, New York (2005)
11. McCann, J.A., Huebscher, M.C.: Evaluation issues in autonomic computing. In: Proceedings of the Grid and Cooperative Computing Workshops (GCC), pp. 597-608 (2004)
12. Microsoft White Paper.: Microsoft Dynamic Systems Initiative. Available at: `http://download.microsoft.com/download`
13. Murch, R.: Autonomic Computing. In: Prentice Hall Professional Technical Reference, IBM Press, pp. 235–245 (2004)
14. McCarthy, J., Buva, S.: Formalizing Context(expanded notes). In: Technical Note STAN-CS-TN-94-13, Computer Science Department, Stanford University, Stanford, CA (1994)
15. Sterritt, R., Bustard, D.W.: Towards an Autonomic Computing Environment. In: Proceedings of DEXA Workshops, pp. 699–703 (2003)
16. Sun Microsystems White Paper.: Sun Cluster Grid Architecture (2002), Available at `http://whitepapers.silicon.com`
17. Sun Microsystems White Paper.: ARCO, N1 Grid Engine 6 Accounting and Reporting Console (2005) Available at: `http://www.sun.com/software/gridware/ARCO_whitepaper.pdf`
18. Wan, K., Alagar, V.S., Paquet, J.: An Architecture for Developing Context-aware Systems. LNCS, pp. 48–61. Springer, Heidelberg (2005)
19. Wan, K.: Lucid Enriched with Context. Ph.D Thesis, Concordia University (May 2006)

Knowledge Structure on Virus for User Education

Madihah Saudi[1] and Nazean Jomhari[2]

[1] Faculty Science and Technology,
Islamic Science University of Malaysia(USIM),
Bandar Baru Nilai, 71800 Nilai, Negeri Sembilan, Malaysia
madihah@admin.kuim.edu.my
[2] Faculty of Computer Science & IT
University of Malaya
50603 Kuala Lumpur, Malaysia
nazean@um.edu.my

Abstract. There are many factors contribute to the virus spread and infection. One of the big challenges in confronting computer viruses is to educate user. It needs a lot of effort to educate user about computer virus. The researchers have produced ECOVP which is to help user handle virus problem and the targets users including home user, non-IT literature background and IT personnel needs in handling virus incident. Researchers had studied what are the information needs to be process, so we could use them to generate the knowledge on how to handle the virus problem. We had identified seven important criteria for user need to understand in capable for them facing the computer virus. However, this paper is focusing on virus attack on Windows platform only.

Keywords: virus, user education, symptom, propagation, mechanism trigger, payload, severity, operating algorithm, virus type.

1 Introduction

From Symantec website, worm is defines as program that replicate itself from system to system without the use of a host file. As for Trojan Horse it is refers as an impostors, files that claim to be something desirable but, in fact, are malicious[1]. Viruses are in contrast to worms, which require the spreading of an infected host file. A very important distinction between Trojan horse programs and viruses is that they do not replicate themselves. Trojan Horse contains malicious code that when triggered could caused loss, or even theft, of data. In order for a Trojan horse to spread, it is must for the Trojan horse program to be executed in the victim's host.

From the reference to [1], [2], [3], [4] and research made by the researchers, the differences between virus, worm and Trojan horse is summarized in the Table 1. As conclusion worm and virus are very similar to one another but are technically different in the way that they replicate and spread through a system. As for Trojan Horse its capability to control PC remotely makes it different from worm and the virus.

Y. Wang, Y. Cheung, and H. Liu (Eds.): CIS 2006, LNAI 4456, pp. 817–823, 2007.

Table 1. The Differences between Virus, Worm and Trojan Horse

Virus	Worm	Trojan Horse
Non self replicate	Self replicate	Non self replicate
Produce copies of themselves using host file as carriers	Do not produce copies of themselves using host file as carriers (independent program)	Do not produce copies of themselves using host file as carriers (independent program)
Cannot control PC remotely	Cannot control PC remotely	Can control PC remotely
Can be detected and deleted using antivirus	Can be detected and deleted using antivirus	Sometimes cannot be detected and deleted using antivirus

2 The Needs of User Education on Handling Computer Virus

User education is as important as anti-virus software. Training users in safe computing practices, such as not downloading and executing unknown programs from the Internet, would slow the spread of viruses [5].

Quoted from Symantec press release on September 27th 2004 at Cupertino, California[6], it stated that many employees in today's workforce are not aware that they play an important role in their organization's security. In other word, it is the lack of user awareness among the employees. According to META Group research, 75 percent of organizations identify a lack of user awareness as moderately or severely reducing the effectiveness of their current program. Additionally, 66 percent cite executive awareness as a concern.

Another survey conducted by the Chinese Ministry of Public Security shows that approximately 85 percent of computers in the country were infected with a virus on 2003. As one of initiatives, to help China to countermeasure this problem, Sophos the anti virus company is doing its part by sharing information about safe computing and how businesses can best protect themselves from virus attack[7]. Sophos is doing its part to increase user education about security threats in China.

Until today there are still many people click on email attachment from untrusted source. Who should be blamed? So, user needs guidance to avoid from being infected by the virus, worm, Trojan Horse or spyware.

3 Structuring Knowledge on Computer Virus

The domain knowledge of this project is the computer viruses on Windows platform. It is part of the malicious code. This domain knowledge consists of two main parts. So how can we classify the virus information? In order to retrieve important information related with the computer viruses for the usage of the ECOVP system, the structure of the computer viruses classification that was proposed by the researchers was used for the system.

There are thousands of variations of viruses, the classification of computer viruses[8] can be done via several ways which are based on the type of host victim, the type of infection technique and the special virus features. A common tripartite model of a computer virus structure consists of three parts [8]; Infection mechanism, Trigger and Payload. For this project, based on researcher observation and research, to ensure the system for this project is structured and easy to be implemented, using the Marko Helenius's as the basis concept in computer virus classification, the computer virus classification in this project is classified based on:

- The *Infection mechanisms.*
- The *Operating algorithm.*
- The *Payload*

Figure 1 is the computer viruses classification for this project. From this virus classification, later seven main features are extracted and the seven main features are verified and identified to be included as the problem descriptor for the proposed system.

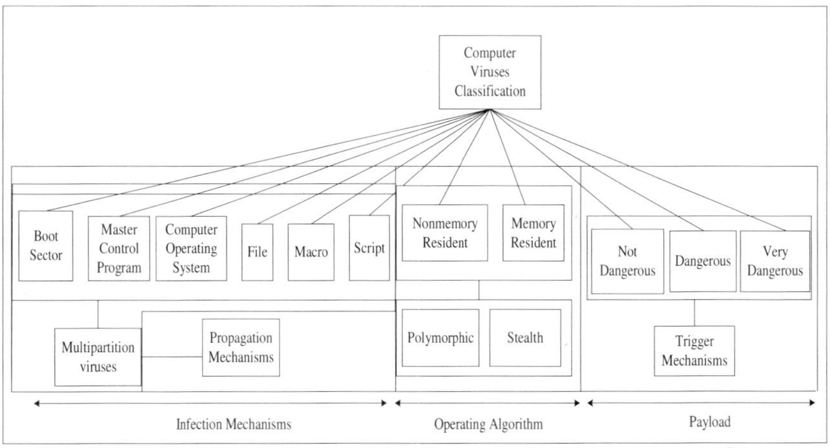

Fig. 1. Virus Classification for ECOVP System

Another form of classification of computer viruses [9] is based on the three ways a virus may add itself to host code as a shell, as an add-on and as an intrusive code. As for Marko Helenius[10], he classified computer viruses into four basic classes by infected objects. The computer viruses are classified into boot sector viruses, file viruses, macro viruses, script viruses and multipartition viruses.

This information was used by the researcher to ensure the system is capable to produce the required solution. The infection mechanisms, operating algorithm and payload can be divided into more specific parts in order to fulfill user needs.

The whole virus classification diagram for ECOVP system was illustrated in Figure 1 while the input and output process illustrated in Figure 2. The information virus classification is sub categorize into seven main features which are used as the input or also known as the problem from the user. The seven features are symptom, propagation, trigger mechanism, payload, severity, operating algorithm and virus type. How do we derived these seven important criteria in ECOVP was explained in Figure 3.

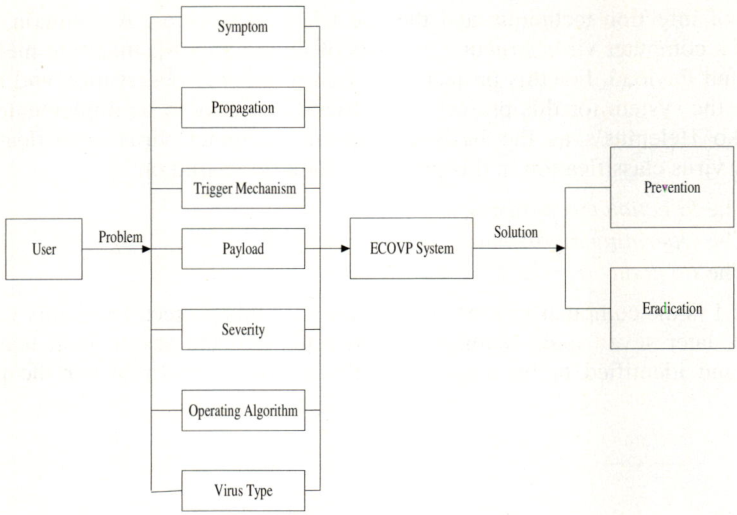

Fig. 2. Input problem and output solution

The problem which is the input from user, contributes to variety of solution where the solution consists of the prevention and eradication procedure. The input from a user which is also known as the problem consists of symptom, propagation, mechanism trigger, payload, severity, operating algorithm and virus type.

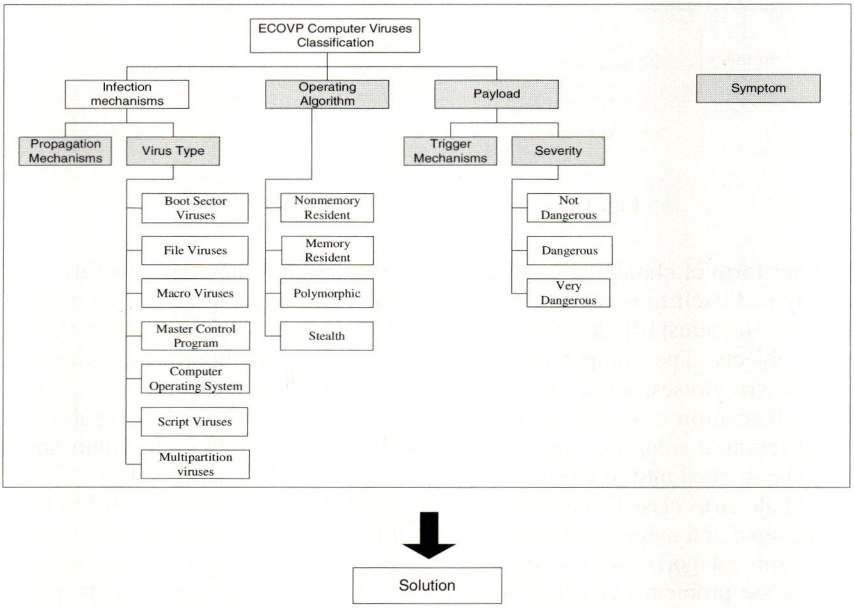

Fig. 3. Problem derivation features

The problem features stated above are derived from the virus classification. For each of the main features it consists of the infection mechanisms, operating algorithm and payload can be divided into more specific parts as illustrated in Figure 3. The highlighted was the main features that user have to key in the data into the system to get the eradication and prevention solution.

Referring to Figure 3, below is the details explanation of the figure:

- The top box which consists of the ECOVP computer viruses classification is the computer virus classification made by the researchers which was extracted from Figure 1, while Figure 2 summarized the computer viruses classification for ECOVP system. From the ECOVP computer viruses classification, six main features that are used for the ECOVP system are extracted.
- The ECOVP Computer Viruses Classification is categorized based on three main categories which are the infection mechanisms, operating algorithm and payload. Each of these main categories has its own feature. Then these three main categories are extracted and are put in the middle box.
- In the middle box, from these three main categories, for infection mechanisms, it is subcategorized into two categories which are the virus type and propagation mechanisms. These two categories contribute as the main features in the ECOVP system. The virus type consists of boot sector viruses, file viruses, macro viruses, master control program, computer operating system and multipartition viruses features.
- The operating algorithm is extracted as one of the main feature for ECOVP system. The operating algorithm consists of nonmemory resident, memory resident, polymorphic and stealth.
- As for the payload, it is subcategorized into severity and trigger mechanisms which contribute as the main features for ECOVP system. The severity consists of non dangerous, dangerous and very dangerous features. Even though the payload has been subcategorized, still the payload is chosen as one of the main feature in the ECOVP system due of its importance roles in identifying the solution.
- Another feature that is included as the problem descriptor is the symptom of the viruses. The symptom is not derived from the ECOVP computer viruses classification. It is chosen as one of the main features because it is one of the main important features needs to be identified by the user as the problem descriptor of the system.
- From these seven main features the solution which consists of the prevention and eradication is derived. These seven main features play important role to determine the solution that will be displayed to user.

4 Solution

A solution consists of the prevention procedure and eradication procedure. As illustrated in Figure 5, the solution is consists of the prevention and eradication procedure. The solution is also part of the domain knowledge. Based on the questionnaire conducted, most of the user interested to know the prevention and the eradication procedure when confronting the virus incident. The prevention and eradication for this system is defines as:

a. Prevention: This procedure is to avoid and prevent the virus from the entire system completely.
b. Eradication: This procedure is to remove the virus from the entire system completely.

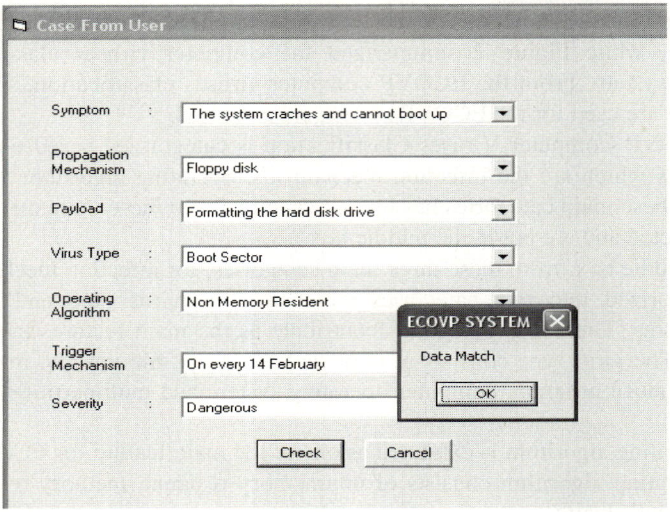

Fig. 4. Match Search

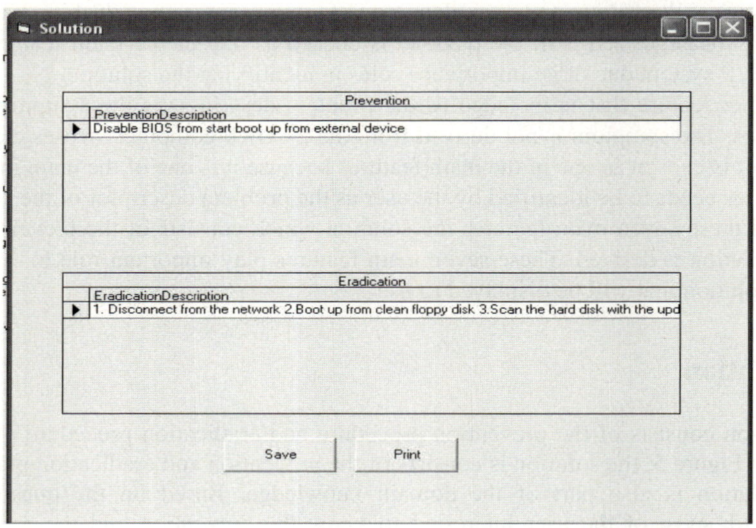

Fig. 5. Match Solution

The solution given in this system is based on the solution provided in anti virus advisories, computer viruses book and MyCERT advisories. The anti virus advisories are from the Symantec anti virus, Trend Micro antivirus and F-Secure anti virus.

5 Conclusion

The derivation of the seven important elements was based on Marko Helenius who is the experts on virus. The seven features are symptom, propagation, mechanism trigger, payload, severity, operating algorithm and virus type. This information is very important in identifying the eradication and prevention solution in handling virus. If user could not understand the term, this system is capable to offer support if user wants to know more detailed on contextual information on each term by moving the mouse to the label of the problem descriptor and the explanation of each label is displayed. Hope this system would help computer user in handling virus especially on Windows platform.

References

1. Symantec.: What is the difference between viruses, worms, and Trojans? (1999) [Online]. Available: http://service1.symantec.com/SUPPORT/nav.nsf/docid/1999041209131106
2. Saudi, M.: Combating Worms Outbreaks: Malaysia Experience (Common Ground). International Journal of Learning (Common Ground) 12(2), 295–304 (2006)
3. Resnet.: The Difference Between a Trojan Horse, Virus and a Worm. (2004). [Online]. Available: http://www.lasalle.edu/admin/it/portal/virus_updates/trojan_horse_virus_worm.htm
4. Microsoft: What is a virus, worm, or Trojan Horse? (May 23, 2005) [Online]. Available: http://www.microsoft.com/athome/security/viruses/intro_viruses_what.mspx
5. Antivirus.world.com.: How Does Anti-Virus Software Work? (August 23, 2005) [Online]. Available: http://www.antivirusworld.com/articles/antivirus.php
6. Symantec: Symantec Education Services Program Emphasizes Employee Training for Improved Security Posture (September 27, 2004) [Online]. Available: http://www.symantec.com/press/2004/n040927.html
7. Sophos.: China Crisis: Computer Viruses Rampant Says Survey. (October 21, 2003) [Online]. Available: http://www.sophos.com/virusinfo/articles/chinavirus.html
8. Martin, R.: FAQ der VIRUS.GER: Version 2.3. (1997) [Online]. Available: http://www.virushelpmunich.de/faq/faq
9. Spafford, E.H.: Computer Viruses as Artificial Life. Artificial Life 1(3), 249–265 (1994)
10. Helenius, M.: A System to Support the Analysis of Antivirus Products' Virus Detection Capabilities. PhD Dissertation, Department of Computer and Information Sciences, University of Tampere (2002)

An Efficient Anonymous Fingerprinting Protocol*

Yang Bo[1], Lin Piyuan[1], and Zhang Wenzheng[2]

[1] College of Information, South China Agricultural University,
Guangzhou, 510642, China
byang@scau.edu.cn
[2] National Laboratory for Modern Communications,
Chengdu, 610041, China

Abstract. Fingerprinting schemes are technical means to discourage people from illegally redistributing the digital data they have legally purchased. These schemes enable the original merchant to identify the original users of the digital data. Anonymous fingerprinting schemes allow a seller to fingerprint information sold to a user without knowing the identity of the user and without the seller seeing the fingerprinted copy. Finding a (redistributed) fingerprinted copy enables the seller to find out and prove to third party whose copy it was. In this paper, we propose a new scheme of anonymous fingerprinting by using electronic wallet, in which, the user doesn't need making a computationally expensive zero-knowledge proof, on finding a fingerprinted copy, the seller can directly determine the redistributor by a simple computation without the help of a registration authority and without making a search for the redistributor's public key in purchase record. In addition, our scheme can prevent the collusion of merchant and registration center to make false-accusation to honest users. By using electronic wallet, our scheme can be integrated with electronic payment system.

1 Introduction

Fingerprinting schemes are cryptographic techniques to support the copyright protection of digital data. It is assumed that users obtain data in digital form and can copy them. Users who redistribute copies disregarding the copyright conditions are called traitors. Fingerprinting schemes discourage traitors by enabling the original merchant to identify a traitor who originally purchased the data item.

Classical fingerprinting schemes [1, 2] are symmetrical in the sense that both the seller and the user know the fingerprinted copy. Even if the seller succeeds in identifying a dishonest user, the seller's previous knowledge of the fingerprinted copies means that they cannot be used as proof of redistribution in front of third

* This work is supported by the National Natural Science Foundation of China under Grants 60372046, 60573043 and the Foundation of National Laboratory for Modern Communications under Grant 9140c1108010606.

Y. Wang, Y. Cheung, and H. Liu (Eds.): CIS 2006, LNAI 4456, pp. 824–832, 2007.

parties. In [3], an asymmetric fingerprinting scheme was proposed, in which only the user knows the fingerprinted copy. The drawback of this solution is that the seller knows the user's identity even if the user is honest; such buyer-profiles are very appealing to commercial misuse. Thus it is desirable for buyers to be capable of purchasing fingerprinted digital items anonymously and remain anonymous as long as they do not distribute the digital contents illegally. In [4], the concept of anonymous fingerprinting was introduced; the principle is that the seller does not know the fingerprinted copy or the user's identity. On finding a fingerprinted copy, the merchant needs the help of a registration authority to identify the redistributor.

The proposed scheme by Josep Domingo-Ferrer in [5] is the first concrete anonymous fingerprinting scheme, in which a seller needs no help to identify the dishonest user. But the seller does much computation in the identification process, if the purchase record of users is $O(N)$ in size, it needs averagely $O(N/2)$ exponential computations for the seller. Since then, various anonymous fingerprinting schemes have been proposed in [6-9]. Domingo's scheme was improved by Chanjoo Chung etc. in [6], with efficient identification of redistributor. In [7], group signature was used to construct an anonymous fingerprinting scheme that could offer the user's anonymity and unlinkability. In [8], an anonymous fingerprinting scheme was presented by using the blind version of a modification of DSA signature scheme together with cut-and-choose technique. A scheme based on bilinear Diffie-Hellman was proposed in [9], the added cost of the scheme is the need for paring operations, which is computationally expensive, because paring is known to be a costly operation.

Against the collusion attack, c-secure code was studied in many papers [1, 10-12]. In [10], based on the Chinese Remainder Theorem, a new c-secure code for larger c and n(the length of the code) was constructed. In [11], the problem of collusion-secure fingerprinting, when marks were binary and coalition is of size 2, was researched. In [12], the authors proposed binary fingerprinting codes secure against size-t coalitions which enable the seller to recover at least one of the users from coalition with probability of error $\exp(-\Omega(n))$ for $M = \exp(\Omega(n))$ (M denotes the total number of users).

In this paper, we propose a scheme for anonymous fingerprinting by using electronic wallet. Its advantages are as follows. Firstly, the user doesn't need making a computationally expensive zero-knowledge proof like the schemes in [6-9]. Secondly, on finding a fingerprinted copy, the seller can directly determine the redistributor by a simple computation without the help of a registration authority and without the search to the purchase record to be done. Thirdly, our scheme can prevent the collusion of merchant and registration center to make false-accusation to honest users because the link of user's real identity with anonymous identity is made by user's smart card instead of by a registration center as in [5,9]. In addition, by using electronic wallet, our scheme can be integrated with electronic payment system[14].

An electronic wallet is made of two parts:

- A small hand-held computer or the user's PC, indicated by C.
- A tamper-resistant card (such as a smart card) issued by the bank, indicated by S.

The electronic wallet works in such a way that S and C condition each other. S will not work if the user deviates from prescribed protocols or change any information in its database. And S cannot communicate directly with outside world, all information which enters or leaves S must pass through C to prevent S from leaking user's private information during a transaction (e.g. the identity of the user).

2 The Construction of Fingerprinting Protocol

The scheme consists of four subprotocols described below, in which there are five parties (a user U, a merchant M, a bank B, a registration center RC and an arbiter A.) The bank is responsible for managing and issuing smart cards to users. The users must apply for the smart cards with their real identifications. In registration protocol, the user sends his registration request, and his anonymous identity is generated by his smart card S. In fingerprinting protocol, the user purchases data item with his anonymous identity, in which the user and merchant perform a secure two-party computation. The user obtains the fingerprinted data information only when user-related information passes verification. On finding a fingerprinted copy, the seller can directly determine the redistributors in the identification protocol.

In our scheme, we let p, q be two large primes, satisfying $q|\,(p-1)$, $g,\ g_1,\ g_2 \in Z_p^*$ of multiplication order q, the computation of the discrete logarithm modulo p to the base $g,\ g_1,\ g_2$, respectively, is assumed to be intractable.

2.1 Opening an Account

Let $x_B \in_R Z_q,\ h_B = g^{x_B} \pmod p$ be respectively secret key and public key of bank, and the computation of the discrete logarithm modulo p to the base h_B is assumed to be intractable. To open an account with B and apply for a smart card from B, U first identifies himself to B, B then issues to U a tamper-resistant smart card, S, which has stored the descriptions of Z_q and Z_p , B's secret key x_B and a signature generation function $Sig_{x_B}(\cdot)$. The public verification function $Ver_{h_B}(\cdot,\cdot)$ of the signature generation function $Sig_{x_B}(\cdot)$ satisfies:

$$\forall m, s: \quad Ver_{h_B}(m, s) = 1 \Leftrightarrow s = Sig_{x_B}(m)$$

In this paper, all signature algorithms are supposed to be secure. The protocol is given in Fig. 1.

2.2 Registration

Let $x \in_R Z_q,\ h = g^x \pmod p$ be respectively secret key and public key of RC, also the computation of the discrete logarithm modulo p to the base h is assumed

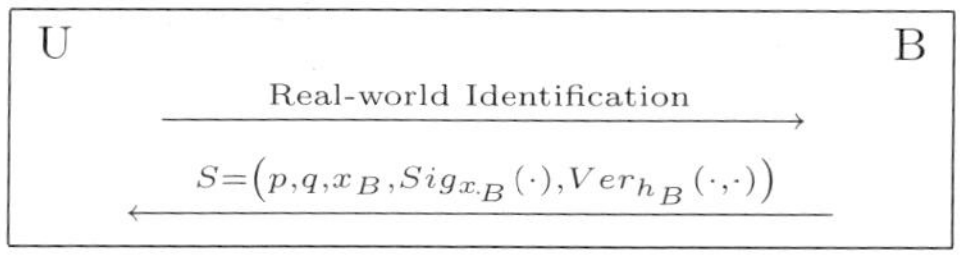

Fig. 1. Opening an account

to be intractable. And let $Sig_x(\cdot)$ and $Ver_h(\cdot,\cdot)$ be respectively secret signature generation function and the public verification function. The verification function is 1 if and only if the signature passes the verification.

The registration protocol is given in Fig. 2, where S indicates U's smart card. U, under his real identity, first sends his registration request to RC. RC generates x_p, y_p and the signature S_p on y_p, in which y_p will be used as U's public identity. After verifying RC's signature on y_p, U inputs x_p and S_p into his smart card S. S generates x_A, $d = h^{x_A} \pmod p$ and signature S_d on d . After receiving x_A, d and S_d , U generates his anonymous identity that is unlinkable with U's real identity.

In our scheme, the value x_A , which is used as the link of user's public identity with his anonymous identity, is generated and signed by user's smart card instead of by user own as in [5,9]. If the user generates his anonymous identity y_A by forged x_A , it will not pass the checks in fingerprinting protocol, see 3.1 security

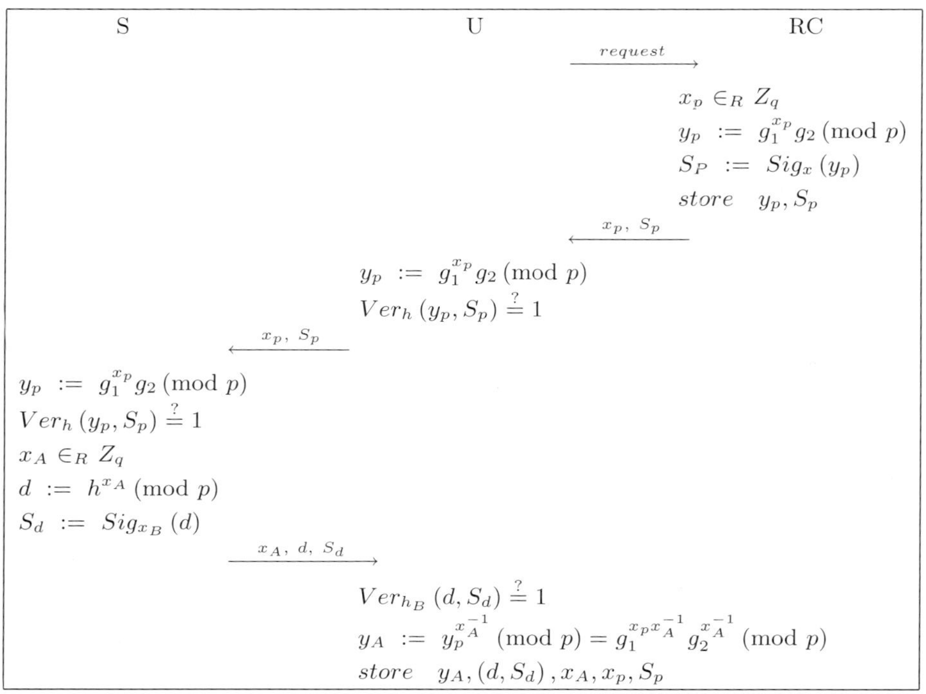

Fig. 2. User's registration with registration center

for the merchant. So it is not necessary for user convinces RC in zero-knowledge of possession of x_A.

2.3 Fingerprinting

Let *item* be the original information to be fingerprinted,*text* be a string describing the purchase item and licensing conditions,(sk_{text}, pk_{text}) be user's key pair to be used for signing *text* from an arbitrary signature scheme.

Fingerprinting protocol is given in Fig. 3.

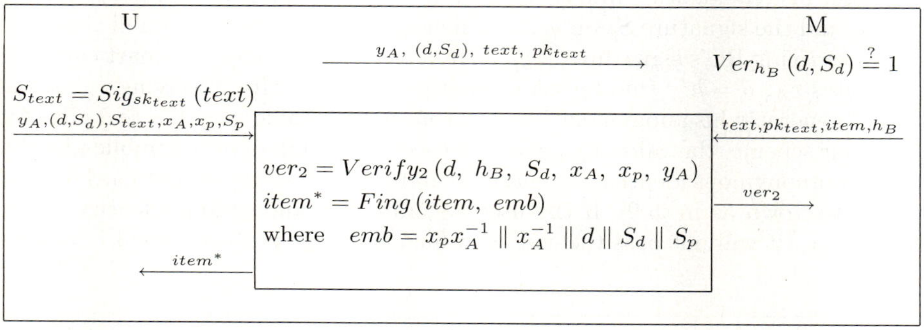

Fig. 3. Opening an account

In this protocol, U first gives $y_A, (d, S_d), text, pk_{text}$ to M, in which y_A and S_d are U's anonymous identity and S's signature on d respectively. Then U computes the signature S_{text} on $text$ with the secret key sk_{text}, S_{text} is not sent to M. After verifying the signature S_d, M and U enter a secure two-party computation[13] that is shown by an internal square in Fig. 3. U's inputs are $y_A, (d, S_d), S_{text}, x_A, x_p$ and S_p. M's inputs are $text, pk_{text}, item$ and h_B. $Ver_{pk_{text}}$is the verification function of signature S_{text} on $text$ using the public key pk_{text}, its output ver_1 is only seen by M which is 1 if and only if the signature verification succeeds. The output ver_2 of $Verify_2$ is also only seen by M, which is 1 if and only if the four checks listed below succeed:

(1) $d = h^{x_A} \pmod p$,
(2) $Ver_{h_B}(d, S_d) = 1$,
(3) $y_A^{x_A} = g_1^{x_p} g_2 \pmod p$,
(4) $y_p := g_1^{x_p} g_2 \pmod p, Ver_h(y_p, S_p) = 1$

If and only if both ver_1 and ver_2 are 1, U obtains the fingerprinted information $item^*$ that is only seen by U, where $Fing$ is a classical fingerprinting algorithm used to embed emb into the original information $item$, $emb = x_p x_A^{-1} \parallel x_A^{-1} \parallel d \parallel S_d \parallel S_p$.

2.4 The Identification Protocol

On finding a redistribution copy, M extracts emb and obtains x_A^{-1}, further x_A and $x_p = x_p x_A^{-1}/x_A^{-1}$. So M can obtain $y_p = g_1^{x_p} g_2 \pmod p$. M constructs a redistribution proof (y_p, x_A, d, S_d, S_p) and sends the proof to the arbiter A. A verifies $Ver_{h_B}(d, S_d) \stackrel{?}{=} 1$, $Ver_h(y_p, S_p) \stackrel{?}{=} 1$ and $d \stackrel{?}{=} h^{x_A} \pmod p$. If the verifications are passed, A finds U guilty of redistribution.

3 Security and Efficiency

3.1 Security for the Merchant

The merchant's security requirement is that the user can not obtain the fingerprinted information by forged anonymous identity, otherwise the merchant can not identify a traitor. This requirement can be satisfied in our protocol. In the fingerprinting protocol, user's inputs to a secure two-party computation are $y_A, (d, S_d), S_{text}, x_A, x_p$ and S_p, in which y_A is user's anonymous identity. Because of $y_A = g_1^{x_p x_A^{-1}} g_2^{x_A^{-1}} \pmod p$, the user can forge y_A by one of three ways: (1) forging x_A, (2) forging x_p, and (3) finding $x_1, x_2 \in Z_q$ with $x_1 \neq x_p x_A^{-1}$ and $x_2 \neq x_A^{-1}$ such that $y_A = g_1^{x_1} g_2^{x_2} \pmod p$. The user can not forge x_A, this is because forged x_A and $d = h^{x_A}$ (mode p) will not pass the verification$Ver_{h_B}(d, S_d)$ unless the user can break the signature algorithm $Sig_{x_B}(\cdot)$. Because x_p satisfies $y_A^{x_A} = g_1^{x_p} g_2 \pmod p$, the user cannot forge x_p unless he can solve the discrete logarithm problem. The third way to forge y_A is to solve a representation problem, which is equivalent to the existence of an algorithm solving the discrete logarithm problem [15]. Therefore, all the three ways to forge y_A are infeasible.

So, in the identification protocol, the merchant can identify the redistributors if both ver_1 and ver_2 are 1.

Representation-problem: Let $h_0, h_1, \ldots, h_v$ be elements of Z_p^* so that $h_j = g^{r_j}$ for $j = 0, \ldots, v$ with $r_0, r_1, \ldots, r_v \in Z_q$. For a certain element $y = g^b$ of Z_p^* a representation of y with respect to the base $h_0, h_1, \ldots, h_v$ is a $(v+1)-$vector $\overline{\delta} = \langle \delta_0, \ldots, \delta_v \rangle$ such that $y = h_0^{\delta_0} \ldots h_v^{\delta_v}$. It is well known (see [15]) that obtaining representation of a given y with respect to some base $h_0, h_1 \ldots, h_v$ is as hard as the discrete logarithm problem over Z_p^*.

3.2 Anonymity for the User

In fingerprinting protocol, the merchant M obtains $y_A, (d, S_d), text, pk_{text}$, in which $text, pk_{text}$ are irrelevant to user's identity information, the way for the merchant to obtain user's real identity is computing $y_p = y_A^{x_A} \pmod p$ or $y_p = g_1^{x_p} g_2 \pmod p$, this requires to know x_A or x_p. If secure two-party computation is feasible, M cannot obtain x_A and x_p from two-party computation. The only way for M is computing x_A from $d = h^{x_A} \pmod p$. Because of the difficulty of computing discrete logarithm, it is infeasible to compute x_A from d.Therefore it is infeasible for the merchant to compute user's real identity.

3.3 Security of the User

The user's security requirement can be formulated as follows: Consider a user U who correctly follows the protocols and keeps the obtained results secret, in particular the data item bought. No matter what the other parties do, the honest user cannot be found guilty of illegal redistribution.

Case 1: the merchant cannot make a false-accusation to the honest user.

In fingerprinting protocol, M can only obtain U's $y_A, (d, S_d), text, pk_{text}$, if he wants to make a false-accusation to this user, he must construct a redistribution proof (y_p, x_A, d, S_d, S_p). The only way is to forge x_A satisfying $d = h^{x_A} \pmod p$ and $Ver_{h_B}(d, S_d) = 1$, then to forge x_p satisfying $y_A^{x_A} = g_1^{x_p} g_2 \pmod p$ and $Ver_h(y_p, S_p) = 1$ in which $y_p = g_1^{x_p} g_2 \pmod p$. It needs computing discrete logarithm, which is intractable.

Case 2: RC cannot make a false-accusation to the honest user.

In registration protocol, RC generates x_p, y_p and S_p for U. If U is a redistributor, RC can obtain x_A^{-1}, d and S_d from *emb*, therefore RC can also construct a redistribution proof (y_p, x_A, d, S_d, S_p). Otherwise, RC can only obtain x_A and d by forgeing, but RC cannot forge S_d satisfying $Ver_{h_B}(d, S_d) = 1$ unless he can break the signature algorithm $Sig_{x_B}(\cdot)$.

Because q is a large prime, x_A is randomly selected in Z_q, the probability of the event that x_A forged by RC is same as x_A selected by U, that is RC can make a false-accusation to U, is negligibly small.

Case 3: RC cannot collude with M to make a false-accusation to the honest user.

RC knows the user's x_p, y_p and S_p, M knows the user's $y_A, (d, S_d)$, but they cannot construct a redistribution proof (y_p, x_A, d, S_d, S_p) to the honest user, even they collude, unless they can know x_A satisfying $d = h^{x_A} \pmod p, Ver_{h_B}(d, S_d) = 1$ and $y_A^{x_A} = g_1^{x_p} g_2 \pmod p$, which needs computing discrete logarithms.

Case 4: RC cannot collude with a malicious user to make a false-accusation to the honest user.

A malicious user cannot know the correspondence between the honest user's public identity with anonymous identity, even if the malicious user collude with RC. So it is similar to case 3.

3.4 Efficiency

Our scheme is more efficient than other available schemes in terms of computation complexity and communication complexity. Table 1 and table 2 show the comparisons. Similarly to [9], we use E to denote the cost of modular exponentiation, M the cost of modular multiplication, S the cost of the point multiplication on an elliptic curve, P the cost of the paring on an elliptic curve, A the cost of point addition on an elliptic curve, R the number of rounds in given protocol, and N the number of public key in directory.

Table 1. The comparison of computation complexity in three previous schemes with ours

Protocol	SCHEME [5]	SCHEME [6]	SCHEME [9]	Our scheme
Zero-knowledge proof	yes	yes	yes	no
Registration	6E+1M	7E+2M	4S+4P+1A	5E+2M
Fingerprinting	5E+1M	4E+2M	2S+1P	3E+2M
Identification	3E+N/2+2M	(3+1)E+2M	1S+2P	1E+1M

Table 2. The comparison of computation complexity in three previous schemes with ours

Protocol	SCHEME [5]	SCHEME [6]	SCHEME [9]	Our scheme
Registration	4R	2R	3R	3R
Fingerprinting	6R	6R	6R	6R
Identification	$\frac{N}{2}$R	$\frac{N}{2}$R	$\frac{N}{2}$R	1R

4 Conclusion

We have described a scheme for anonymous fingerprinting and analysized its security, it is shown the scheme is efficient and secure.

References

1. Boneh, D., Shaw, J.: Collusion-secure Fingerprinting for Digital Data. In: Coppersmith, D. (ed.) Advances in Cryptology - CRYPTO '95. LNCS, vol. 963, pp. 452–465. Springer, Heidelberg (1995)
2. Blakley, G.R., Blakley, G.R., Meadows, C., Purdy, G.B.: Fingerprinting Long Forgiving Message. In: Williams, H.C. (ed.) Advances in Cryptology. LNCS, vol. 218, pp. 180–189. Springer, Heidelberg (1986)
3. Pfitzmann, B., Schunter, M.: Asymmetric Fingerprinting. In: Nagl, M. (ed.) Graph-Theoretic Concepts in Computer Science. LNCS, vol. 1017, pp. 84–95. Springer, Heidelberg (1995)
4. Pfitzmann, B., Waidner, M.: Anonymous Fingerprinting. In: Fumy, W. (ed.) Advances in Cryptology - EUROCRYPT '97. LNCS, vol. 1233, pp. 88–102. Springer, Heidelberg (1997)
5. Domingo-Ferrer, J.: Anonymous Fingerprinting of Electronic Information with Automatic Identification of Redistributor. IEE Electronics Letters 13, 1303–1304 (1998)
6. Chung, C., Choi, S., Choi, Y., Won, D.: Efficient Anonymous Fingerprinting of Electronic Information with Improved Automatic Identification of Redistributor. In: Won, D. (ed.) Information Security and Cryptology - ICISC 2000. LNCS, vol. 2015, pp. 221–234. Springer, Heidelberg (2001)
7. Camenish, J.: Efficient Anonymous Fingerpriting with Group Signature. In: Okamoto, T. (ed.) Advances in Cryptology - ASIACRYPT 2000. LNCS, vol. 1976, pp. 415–428. Springer, Heidelberg (2000)

8. Wang, Y., Lu, S., Liu, Z.: A Simple Anonymous Fingerprinting Scheme based on Blind Signature. In: Qing, S., Gollmann, D., Zhou, J. (eds.) Information and Communications Security. LNCS, vol. 2836, pp. 260–268. Springer, Heidelberg (2003)
9. Kim, M., Kim, J., Kim, K.: Anonymous Fingerprinting as Secure as the Bilinear Diffie-Hellman Assumption. In: Deng, R.H., Qing, S., Bao, F., Zhou, J. (eds.) Information and Communications Security ICICS 2002. LNCS, vol. 2513, Springer, Heidelberg (2002)
10. Hirofumi Muratani, A., Muratani, H.: A Collusion-Secure Fingerprinting Code Reduced by Chinese Remaindering and Its Random-Error Resilience. In: Moskowitz, I.S. (ed.) Information Hiding - IH 2001. LNCS, vol. 2137, pp. 301–305. Springer, Heidelberg (2001)
11. Cohen, G., Litsyn, S., Zemor, G.: Binary Codes for Collusion-Secure Fingerprinting. In: Kim, K.-c. (ed.) Information Security and Cryptology - ICISC 2001. LNCS, vol. 2288, pp. 178–185. Springer, Heidelberg (2002)
12. Barg, A., Blakley, G.R., Kabatiansky, G.A.: Digital Fingerprinting Codes: Problem Statements, Construction. Identification of Traiors. IEEE Transaction on Information Theory 49(4), 852–865 (2003)
13. Chaum, D., Damgaard, I.B., van de Graaf, J.: Multiparty computations ensuring privacy of each party's input and correctness of the result. In: Pomerance, C. (ed.) Advances in Cryptology - CRYPTO '87. LNCS, vol. 293, pp. 87–119. Springer, Heidelberg (1988)
14. Bo, Y., Dongsu, L., Yumin, W.: An Anonymity- Revoking e-Payment System with Smart Card. International Journal on Digital Libraries 3(4), 291–296 (2002)
15. Brands, S.: Off-Line Cash Transfer by Smart Cards. Technical Report CS-R9455,CWI(Centre for Mathematics and Computer Science), Amsterdam (1994) Available at http://www.cwi.nl/static/publications/reports/CS-R9455

Senior Executives Commitment to Information Security – from Motivation to Responsibility

Jorma Kajava[1], Juhani Anttila[2], Rauno Varonen[3], Reijo Savola[4], and Juha Röning[5]

[1] University of Lapland, P.O. Box 122, FIN-96101 Rovaniemi
[2] Quality Integration, Rypsikuja 4, FIN-00660 Helsinki
[3] University of Oulu, P.O. Box 7200, FIN-90014University of Oulu
[4] VTT Technical Research Centre of Finland, P.O. Box 1100, FIN-90571 Oulu
[5] University of Oulu, P.O. Box 4500, FIN-90014 University of Oulu, Finland
Jorma.Kajava@ulapland.fi, Juhani.Anttila@telecon.fi,
Rauno.Varonen@oulu.fi, Reijo.Savola@vtt.fi, Juha.Roning@oulu.fi

Abstract. For senior executives, information security is a basic requirement for business success. Yet, despite being well-motivated, top managers often have only a superficial understanding of information security, which may lead them to make decisions that are not conducive to raising the organization's security level. Enhancing information security awareness among all employees has been found necessary, but the key to success is raising the awareness level of senior management. Playing a decisive role, they must assume overall responsibility for information security. The question is how to achieve this in an efficient and natural way.

1 Introduction

Attitudes toward information security vary. Everyone knows the fundamentals, but few have a deeper understanding of it. Some time ago, an extensive survey, conducted in a Finnish company, indicated that although all employees were well-motivated, senior management lacked the necessary information security management skills. This was evidenced by the fact that an external consultant managed to convince the top management to agree to a work safety study without asking experts on the company payroll, who anticipated a better information security solution. Examples such as this one can be found also in governmental offices and at univiersities.

Our work aims at elucidating the significance of senior management in the promotion of organizational information security. A great number of organizations boast extensive security awareness programmes, but the top management often shies away from them. Damage caused by an individual employee may have far-reaching consequences for a company, but when damage is inflicted by senior management, the effects may be devastating. Thus, it is important to get top managers to endorse the adopted information security solutions whole-heartedly, which involves not only being motivated to follow security principles, but also accepting the responsibilities that go with the highest positions.

As its starting-off point, this paper takes the new international standard ISO 17799 [1] However, as we are dealing with a serious issue, standards are not sufficient, we must advance from a discussion on standards to a change in culture [6].

Y. Wang, Y. Cheung, and H. Liu (Eds.): CIS 2006, LNAI 4456, pp. 833–838, 2007.

2 Day to Day Business

Business life tends to value ease-of-use more than security. A change of values occurs often only after a serious mishap, although only part of the damage may be expressed directly in terms of money.

The prevailing view seems to be that information security produces costs, not profit. Unless we change our way of thinking, we will soon find that the cost of doing nothing is even higher. As indicated by our survey, there are great deficiences in the management of information security, particularly as regards the commitment of senior managers. To remedy this situation, we must find the means of gaining this commitment, before some hostile party forces the change.

As a rule, information security management is seen from the viewpoint of large corporations. In today's world, however, we must become cognizant of the fact that business is based on networking. Even giant corporations are not islands, they are connected with other, smaller companies through subcontracting and outsourcing, for instance. As a result, negligence in the management of information security, even when it occurs several nodes down from some large corporation, may nevertheless affect it through the network. Commitment to information security is therefore of utmost importance for the entire network. By their commitment, corporate managers help pave the way towards the information society.

3 Commitment of Senior Executives

Ultimate responsibility for managing information security is borne by corporate management, which provides the resources and sets the requirements on the basis of which the IT security manager promotes and coordinates security activities. A lively discussion has been going on for some time now on the commitment of senior management to information security.

The objects and activities of information security must be in line with the organization's business objectives and the requirements imposed by them. Senior management must take charge of this and provide visible support and show real commitment. To do this, they have to understand the seriousness of the threat that information risks pose to corporate assets. Further, they need to ensure that middle management and other staff fully grasp the importance of the issue. The organization's information security policy and objectives must be known by corporate employees as well as by external partners.

Information security policy represents the position of senior management toward information security, and sets the tone for the entire organization. It is recommended that coordinating the organization's information security policy should be the responsibility of some member of top management.

Encouragement should be given to the extensive application of information security within the organization and among its stakeholder groups to make certain that problems are dealt with in an efficient and regular manner. When necessary, external professional assistance should be sought to keep abreast of advances, standards and values in the field. At the same time, this enables establishing forms of collaboration for potential security breaches.

The key component of information security work is the visible support and engagement of senior management. In practical terms, this commitment involves allocating necessary funding to information security work and responding without delay to new situations. Nevertheless, swelling the size of the information security organization is unwise, for a small organization is often more flexible and faster on the draw. A better alternative to enlarging security staff is to enhance information security skills and knowledge at all levels of the organization, because that is where the actual work processes are. Yet another way of showing management commitment is participation in a range of information security-related events, which serves to underline the importance attached to the topic.

4 Evidence Supplied by Surveys

We became aware of the sensitive nature of the topic in 2002, when several reports were published highlighting the commitment of senior management to corporate information security solutions. Of particular interest was the report stating that the commitment level among Finnish managers was slightly above 20 percent [5]. This finding provided a good starting point for a national discussion. When the result was explained to a groups of Austrian researchers, they congratulated us on the high percentage rate. This was a little confusing, as the title of the original paper declared that information security does not interest corporate management. Moreover, the paper went on to point out that only two managers out of ten have realized that information security is of strategic value to their company. And yet this survey involved 50 companies among the top 500 businesses in Finland listed by business magazines. The crucial question was: how is this result to be understood and evaluated objectively.

One central issue identified by the survey was that merely 11 of the 50 largest companies had an information systems manager or a corresponding person in the management team. This is a far cry from showing commitment, and is undoubtedly reflected in corporate attitudes and practices. Thus, the sentiments implied in the title of the paper, information security does not interest corporate management, describe the situation spot on, because smaller companies display even less commitment.

At around the same time, we conducted a survey in a Northern Finnish company with 500 employees. It turned out that all members of the fairly large management team as well as key personnel were well-versed in information security and its attendant risks. Yet, although they were motivated to deepen their knowledge and hone their skills, we were left wondering, whether they had internalized their own roles in the management of information security [6].

What does commitment to security work entail? A key factor is enthusiasm, "getting personally involved", believing in what you are doing. Another important factor is providing resources for the work. Everyone must also know who is responsible for taking decisions and directing activities. On this road, the first step involves motivation and gaining an understanding of information security. Obtaining funding serves to anticipate future needs and has far-reaching consequences, but training staff and winning their support are equally important.

At the management team level, the delicate issue of authority and responsibility often leads to conflict. Authority should be exercised in a manner that promotes performance even under difficult circumstances. Responsibilities stand in relief when things go wrong and a mishap occurs. Authority and responsibilities are also necessary during the following recovery period, and should be considered in advance.

Most information security breaches and violations take place within the organization, by its own staff, who are involved either wittingly or unwittingly. Incidents of this type show how important it is that the person charged with coordinating information security really has the support of the senior management and act with their authorization. Although it may be disconcerting, action must be taken to prevent insider abuse before anything serious happens.

5 Information Security Awareness Programmes

Success in information security management, as stated in the ISO/IEC 17799 standard (2005) [1], demands two things: commitment of senior management and provision of information security awareness programmes to all staff. The contents of such a programme were outlined already in earlier documents of the ISO/IEC JTC 1/SC 27/WG 1. In 2002 - 2004, we have applied this information to create an intranet-based learning environment for information security [3].

An information security awareness programme may incorporate at least the following topics:

- factors that influence organizational information security policy together with such extensions to the policy, guidelines, directives and risk management strategy that enable a deeper understanding of risks and security measures,
- implementing the information security programme/plan and verifying the effects of security measures,
- basic data protection requirements,
- a classification scheme for protection of information,
- a reporting procedures for information security breaches, attempts thereof and investigation of such breaches,
- the significance of security extensions to end users and the entire organization,
- work procedures, responsibilities and job descriptions,
- security audits and checks,
- managing activities and organizational structures,
- explaining effects of unauthorized activities.

There are several avenues of obtaining guidelines on information security training. It may be confusing for some employees that they receive security-related information from several sources or through many different channels. In larger organizations, the implementation of information security programmes is coordinated by IT security managers. Nevertheless, these awareness programmes are invariably the responsibility of senior management in order to integrate the approach with the genuine business needs.

6 Promoting a Culture of Security

An approach that considers the best interests of all participants and the characteristics of information systems, networks and associated services can be both efficient and secure [7].

The OECD approach comprises nine principles that deal with awareness, responsibility, response, ethics, democracy, risk assessment, security design and implementation, security management and reassesment: "*Security management should be based on risk assessment and should be dynamic, encompassing all levels of participants' activities and all aspects of their operations. It should include forward-looking responses to emerging threats and address prevention, detection and response to incidents, systems recovery, ongoing maintenance, review and audit. Information system and network security policies, practices, measures and procedures should be coordinated and integrated to create a coherent system of security. The requirements of security management depend upon the level of involvement, the role of the participant, the risk involved and system requirements.*" [7].

In addition, the OECD guidelines state that fostering a culture of security requires both leadership and extensive participation. Security design and management should be an important element in corporate management, and all participants must appreciate the value of security. The principles set up by the OECD form a foundation for promoting a culture of security across the society. All participants must assimilate and promote this culture as a way of thinking about, assessing and implementing information systems and networks.

Organizations are exhorted to adopt a proactive approach to information security. Business is likely to suffer if senior management has insufficient knowledge of security. This state of affairs poses a severe threat not only to the organization's reputation, but to its entire business and existence.

This paper seeks to emphasize the role of senior management in the creation of organizational culture of security. A solution that is custom-tailored to a particular organization is only applicable to that organization. This raises the issue of how general principles and standards could be utilized to create an approach to information security and security management that is adaptable to different organizations with certain adjustments. This leads us to propose that the starting point for an information security awareness model designed for senior management should incorporate the following aspects: senior management

- must understand their own roles as business leaders. A better grasp of information security in fact facilitates their work, as it enables them to set policy objectives and take a leading role also in security;
- should define what the critical assets are that must be protected. For that, they need to have a basic understanding of information classification; and
- must pledge a holistic commitment to information security, manifested, for example, by active participation in business continuity planning.

7 Conclusions

We have discussed one of the most remarkable practical-level problems of information security management in organizations: the lack of senior management commitment to information security.

This problem is difficult to solve because many professionals think that it is not a good idea to "teach" their managers, or "preach" to them. However, if the information security awareness of senior management of a company is at too low level, the consequences might be very dramatic to the business of the company. Products – goods and services – with poor information security solutions can be very easily voted out of the market by consumers. In addition, co-operation partners can vanish after they realize that a company is not paying enough attention to its information security management and the key persons – the senior management is not committed.

References

1. ISO/IEC 17799:2005: Information Technology – Security Techniques – Code of Practice for Information Security Management, ISO, Geneve (2005)
2. ISO/IEC 27001:2005: Information Technology – Security Techniques – Information Security Management Systems – Requirements, ISO, Geneve (2005)
3. Heikkinen, I., Ramet, T. (eds.): E-Learning as a Part of Information Security Education Development from Organisational Point of View. Oulu University, Oulu, Finland (2004) (In Finnish)
4. Kajava, J.: Critical Success Factors in Information Security Management in Organizations: The Commitment of Senior Management and the Information Security Awareness Programme. Hallinnon tutkimus – Administrative Studies, vol. 22(1) Tampere (2003)
5. Kajava, J., Varonen, R., Tuormaa, E., Nykänen, M.: Information Security Training through eLearning - Small Scale Perspective. In: VIEWDET 2003, pp. 26–28. Vienna, Austria (2003)
6. Lempinen, H.: Security Model as a Part of the Strategy of a Private Hospital. University of Oulu, Finland (2002) (In Finnish)
7. OECD, OECD Guidelines for the Security of Information Systems and Networks – Towards a Culture of Security, OECD Publications, Paris, France, p. 29 (2002)

A Hierarchical Key Distribution Scheme for Conditional Access System in DTV Broadcasting

Mengyao Zhu, Ming Zhang, Xiaoling Chen, Ding Zhang, and Zhijie Huang

Department of Information Science & Electronic Engineering, Yuquan Campus, Zhejiang University, Hangzhou 310027, China
zmengy@zju.edu.cn

Abstract. A variety of subscriptions in Conditional Access System (CAS) of DTV broadcasting network bring complexity to the key distribution scheme. In this paper, an innovation of hierarchical key distribution scheme for CAS in DTV broadcasting is proposed to reduce the computation of encryption and the number of messages for key refreshment. Compared with the conventional key distribution schemes, no encrypted message is distributed for key refreshment when a subscriber leaves. Further more, our hierarchical tree of key can provide a lot more dynamic management, from which broadcasters can improve efficiency in managing program channels.

1 Introduction

With the development of modern technologies in Digital Television (DTV) broadcasting, the broadcaster provides enormous programs to satisfy the increasing and varied demands of the viewers. Conditional access system (CAS) is a pivotal technique in DTV broadcasting network, which provides different programs according to the variety of viewer's demand and brings financial revenue to the operators.

The existing CAS modes can be classified into two groups: Pay-Per-Channel (PPC), which means that subscribers pay for a package of program channel for a period of time, and Pay-Per-View (PPV), which means that subscribers pay for each single program (for example, movies).

The broadcaster introduces CAS to ensure the access rights of the authorized users and forestall unauthorized access. The transmitted programs are scrambled to make the programs unintelligible with a pseudo-random sequence (PRSG), which is initialized by Control Word (CW). The authorized users can descramble the scrambled program if they are holding the CW. Because of real-time requirement in DTV broadcasting, CAS employs symmetric key cryptography for high speed scramble and descramble. The security of scramble cryptography is improved by means of changing CW periodically. Distribution of CW in the DTV broadcasting network risks the illegal attacks, therefore, the key distribution scheme is proposed for distribution of encrypted CW which can only be decrypted by the authorized users.

We presume that the scramble cryptography is secure enough if CW is renewed once per 5 ~ 20 seconds. So the security of CAS merely depends on key distribution scheme. One problem of key distribution scheme is that updating keys causes heavy

Y. Wang, Y. Cheung, and H. Liu (Eds.): CIS 2006, LNAI 4456, pp. 839–846, 2007.

load on DTV broadcasting network. Several key distribution schemes proposed recently can partially reduce the traffic load of the broadcasting network, but far from settling the problem.

In this paper, we propose a novel non-updating hierarchical key distribution scheme for CAS. The contents are organized as below. Section 2 discusses the conventional key distribution schemes. Section 3 proposes our key distribution scheme in detail. Section 4 analyzes performance and security issues. Finally, conclusions are given in section 5.

2 Related Works

In 1992, a three-level key distribution scheme, shown in Fig.1, was proposed in ITU Recommendation 810 [1], in which the three-level key scheme is defined as Control Word (CW), Authorization Key (AK), and Distribution Key (DK).

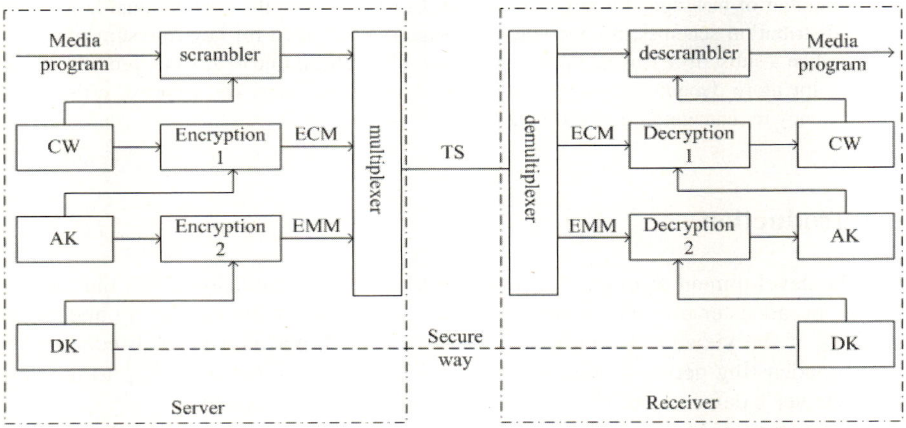

Fig. 1. Three-level key distribution scheme

At the server end, firstly, CW is used to initialize the pseudo-random sequence generator (PRSG) for scrambling the media programs, and then unintelligible media programs form the transport package. After that, AK is used to encrypt the CW, and the cipher text of CW is packed in Entitlement Control message (ECM). Finally, AK is encrypted by DK, and the cipher text of AK is packed in Entitlement Management message (EMM). DK should be transmitted in a secure way, such as a smart card or telecommunication. The scrambled media program transport package, ECM and EMM are multiplexed in Transport Stream (TS).

In the receiver's Set-Top Box (STB), authorized subscriber uses his/her DK to decrypt EMM to recover AK, and AK can be used to decrypt ECM to recover CW, then CW initializes the PRSG to obtain the descrambled programs.

For a three-level key scheme, to make sure the subscriber can not descramble the unintelligible programs by using his/her overdue AK, AK must be renewed after the subscriber leaves. Refreshment of AK requires distributing AK with DK to each subscriber separately. The refreshment of AK is time-consuming and shall cause heavy traffic load on the broadcasting network. Another drawback is that, the scheme can not be managed dynamically i.e. adding or deleting channels without system reconstruction. Therefore it is not suitable for PPV channel.

As an improvement, a key distribution scheme with one more level than three-level key distribution was proposed by J. W. Lee [2], in 1996. A Group Key (GK) is added to the key distribution scheme in which partial subscribers sharing the same GK intend to reduce load when AK is renewed. However if a large number of subscriber groups exist, there is still heavy load on broadcasting network. Tu, Laih and Tung [3], in 1999, proposed a modified scheme to reduce the refreshment of AK which is also based on four-level key distribution scheme. What's more, they put forward a dynamic management for PPV channel. Recently, several papers work on further reducing key refreshment and improving program channel management dynamically [4], [5], [6].

3 Hierarchical Key Distribution Scheme for CAS

In the proposed key distribution scheme, we adopt a four-level hierarchical key scheme, which includes CW, AK, GK, and DK. CW is used to initialize PRSG. AK encrypts different CW for each channel. GK is used to deduce AK which belongs to the group of GK. DK is generally stored in user's smart-card, and used to encrypt GK or AK.

3.1 Hierarchical Tree of Group Key

A top-down structure for the hierarchical key generation was proposed by Akl and Taylor [7], in 1982. A modified scheme using the one-way hash functions was proposed by Yang and Li [8], in 2004. Based on the two papers above, our top-down structure for the hierarchical key generation using one-way hash functions is adopted in this paper.

We divide the program channels into groups, and form higher level groups by lower level groups. An actual example is given below.

There are many program channels available in Hangzhou DTV broadcaster, and these channels are usually divided into several groups, such as sports group G1, news group G2, and movie group Gi. Furthermore, news group G2 can be divided into several sub-groups (e.g., international news sub-group G21, domestic news sub-group G22, and local news sub-group G23), movie group Gi can also be divided into several sub-groups (e.g., Hong Kong movie sub-group Gi1, Hollywood movie sub-group Gix etc.). The further subdivision can be done if necessary. Subscribers can subscribe either some groups or some channels individually. Fig. 2 below shows the hierarchical tree of groups.

At the Server end, the GK of the hierarchy is generated as below.

a) Two large primes p and q are chosen, make $n = pq$;
b) A set of relative primes is $\{m_1, m_2, \ldots, m_u\}$, where u is the maximum number of direct child groups (e.g. G_{21} is direct child group of G_2 in Fig. 2) in the hierarchy. These primes are publicly known.
c) GK_0 of group G_0 is assigned an arbitrary key.

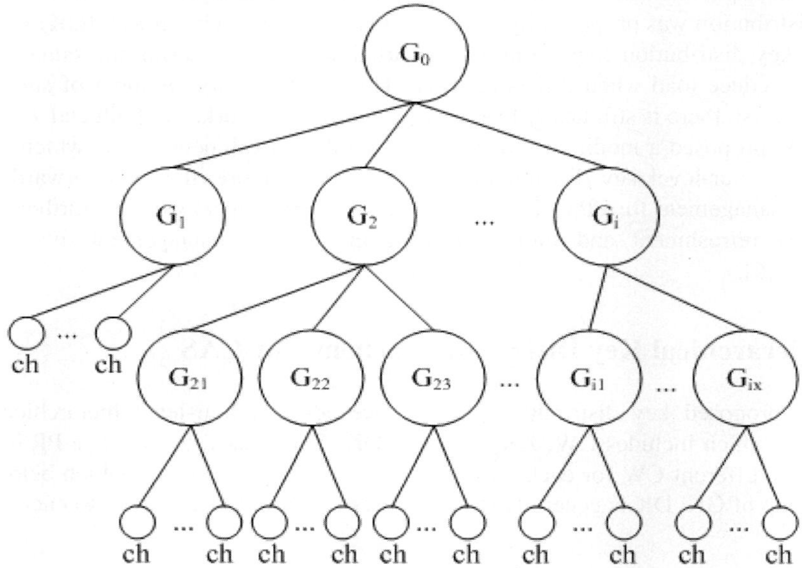

Fig. 2. The hierarchical tree of groups and channels

The child group key GK_j has one direct parent group whose key is GK_k; and if GK_j is the i-th (from left to right) direct child group of GK_k, e.g. G_{23} is the 3rd direct child group of G_2 in Fig. 2. Then

$$GK_j = GK_k^{m_i} \bmod(n) \tag{1}$$

The lowest groups in the hierarchical tree can also contain several program channels, which means AK_{ch} can be derived from lowest group GK_l, e.g. G_1, G_{23} and G_{i1} etc. in Fig.2 are lowest group, assuming AK_{ch} is the i-th channel (from left to right) of GK_l,

$$AK_{ch} = GK_l^{m_i} \bmod(n) \tag{2}$$

Because of the complexity of factoring large prime numbers, one owning child group key GK_j can not deduce its parent group key or brother group key, because $\{m_1, m_2, \ldots, m_u\}$ is a set of relative primes.

3.2 Key Distribution Method

There is one problem with distributing GK to different subscribers. We propose a key distribution method based on the paper of MA Hua [9].

At the server end, the key distribution is in this method,

1. Generate two large primes p and q;
2. Let n = pq, and let m = (p-1)(q-1);
3. Choose a number e, coprime to m, <e, n> is a public key;
4. Find d, such that de % m = 1, <d, n> is a private key;

We employ a symmetric encryption algorithm in which E_{sk} stand for an encryption and D_{sk} stand for a decryption. sk is a common secret key:

A. Server chooses a set of different primes $x_1, x_2, \ldots, x_m$, x_i is privately known by subscriber i, and $X = x_1 x_2 \ldots x_m \bmod (n)$;

B. $k = X^d \bmod (n)$, and is publicly known;

C. p_0 is an arbitrary value, and

$$sk = p_0^{X} \bmod(n) \tag{3}$$

D. Cryptograph is $M = E_{sk}$ (GK);

At the user end, $\langle x_i, d, n \rangle$ is a private key stored in user's smart-card, GK is recovered by the following method:

1) sk is recovered by

$$sk = p_0^{x_i (k / x_i^{d})^{e} \bmod(n)} \bmod(n) \tag{4}$$

2) M is decrypted by sk, $GK = D_{sk}$ (M);

We proof that the sk recovered is exactly the same to the one generated at the server end:

$$\begin{aligned} \text{Eq.}(4) &= p_0^{x_i (k / x_i^{d})^{e} \bmod(n)} \bmod(n) \\ &= p_0^{x_i (X^d / x_i^{d})^{e} \bmod(n)} \bmod(n) \\ &= p_0^{x_i (X^{de} / x_i^{de}) \bmod(n)} \bmod(n) \\ &= p_0^{X} \bmod(n) \\ &= \text{Eq.}(3) \end{aligned} \tag{5}$$

AK_{ch} is deduced from GK, together with sk, $\langle AK_{ch}, sk \rangle$ is the AK which is used to decrypt CW. When a subscriber j is leaving, server computes X without x_j. The k is regenerated because of the change of X, and sk recomputed by the rest of subscribers, but AK_{ch} does not need to be changed. When a subscriber joins, AK_{ch} needs to be distributed to the subscriber.

Because k is broadcasted in public, subscribers sharing a common GK need a corresponding k. Server can rapidly respond to Subscriber's leaving and joining by periodic (usually in 10 ~ 20 seconds) computing and transmitting of k. Generally, n is

1024 ~ 2048 bit, and so is k. We assume that k is regenerated in 10 seconds, so the overhead of bandwidth is 0.1 ~ 0.2 kbps.

AK combines asymmetric and symmetric encryption. To ensure the safety, the key of symmetric encryption is renewed in 10 ~ 20 seconds, so the security of our scheme is equivalent to RSA [10] cryptography.

The frequent computation of k is suitable for PPV channel, because the privilege is revoked when the subscription of a single program is over.

3.3 Dynamic Management

Dynamic management here means adding, deleting and changing groups or channels, which is a useful method for server to manage the program channels or groups, especially for PPV channels.

Deleting a group or channel D from parent group P takes the following steps: service provider changes the D's key value to an arbitrary value, so D is no longer available, because no one knows D's key. Then we can call D an empty group. The brother groups or channels, which have the same parent group with D, need not to regenerate their keys.

Adding a group or channel R to parent group P is in this way: if there is an empty group or the number of child groups/channels of P is less than u, then R's key value can be derived from P's, else find m_{u+1}, which is a relative prime to $\{m_1, m_2, \ldots, m_u\}$, make it publicly known. Then we can derive R's key from P's. The key of brother groups or channels of R need not to be regenerated.

Changing a group or a channel can be divided into adding and deleting operation.

4 Analysis and Comparison

In the three-level key distribution scheme [1], each refreshment of AK needs to distribute AK encrypted by DK to each subscriber directly, so there are S*C (refer to Table 1) messages to be encrypted and broadcasted. In the Tu's scheme [3], subscribers are grouped together according to their subscribed channels. The subscribers in the same group share the same DK. For AK and GK refreshment, the number of encrypted and broadcasted messages equals to M*G (refer to Table 1).

In our scheme, AK is deduced from the hierarchical tree of GK. Therefore, GK is encrypted and broadcasted to subscribers instead of AK. The users who subscribe those channels can decrypt the GK and recover the AK. Compared with the schemes above, only G (refer to Table 1) messages are encrypted and broadcasted.

What's more, our scheme provides a flexible control of subscriptions. As row 4 in Table 1 shows, when a subscriber leaves, K*T (refer to Table 1) messages are encrypted and broadcasted in the ITU's three-level key distribution scheme, and in the Tu's scheme [3], K (refer to Table 1) messages are encrypted and broadcasted. No message broadcasting is required in our scheme, and server responds to the subscription in time (generally in 10 ~ 20 seconds), because subscriber's decrypted key is derived from a public message.

Table 1. Comparison of message transmitted

Opetions/Scheme	**ITU's Scheme**	**Tu's Scheme**	**Ours' scheme**
AK and GK refreshment	*S*C*	*M*G*	*G*
subscriber's Joining	*1*	*1*	*1*
subscriber's Leaving	*K*T*	*K*	*0*

S: number of subscribers
M: number of subscriber groups
C: number of channels
G: number of channel groups
K: number of subscribers in a subscriber group
T: number of channels in a subscriber group

On the other hand, our scheme employs a hierarchical tree of GK for dynamic managing channels and groups, adding or deleting channels/groups will not cause regeneration of GK or AK. In the T. Jiang's scheme [4], regeneration of GK and AK is ineluctable for all the ancestor groups.

5 Conclusions

In this paper, we proposed a hierarchical key distribution scheme for CAS in the DTV broadcasting. Our schemes can greatly reduce the computation complexity of encryption and the number of messages for key refreshment, with high efficiency and security. Further more, there are notable advantages of an improved dynamic management in program channels and subscribers.

Compared with related schemes above, our scheme is efficient and flexible in either PPC or PPV channel. In conclusion, it is a feasible scheme in the DTV broadcasting.

References

1. ITU-R Rec. 810: Conditional-Access Broadcasting Systems, (1992)
2. Lee, J.W.: Key Distribution and Management for Conditional Access System on DBS. In: Proc. Int. Conf. Cryptology and Information Security, pp. 82–86 (1996)
3. Tu, F., Laih, C., Tung, H.: On Key Distribution Management for Conditional Access System on Pay-TV System. IEEE Transactions on Consumer Electronics 45(1), 151–158 (1999)
4. Jiang, T., Zheng, S., Liu, B.: Key Distribution Based on Hierarchical Access Control for Conditional Access System in DTV Broadcast. IEEE Transactions on Consumer Electronics 50(1), 225–230 (2004)

5. Huang, Y., Shieh, S., Ho, F., Wang, J.: Efficient Key Distribution Schemes for Secure Media Delivery in Pay-TV Systems. IEEE Transactions On Multimedia 6(5), 760–769 (2004)
6. Liu, B., Zhang, W., Jiang, T.: A Scalable Key Distribution Scheme for Conditional Access System in Digital Pay-TV System. IEEE Transactions on Consumer Electronics 50(2), 632–637 (2004)
7. Akl, S.G., Taylor, P.D.: Cryptographic Solution to A Multilevel Security Problem. In: Proc. Crypto-82, 249th edn. Santa Barbara, CA, August 23-25, pp. 23–25 (1982)
8. Yang, C., Li, C.: Access Control in A Hierarchy Using One-Way Hash Functions. In: Computers & Security, pp. 659–664 (2004)
9. Hua, M., Zheng-wen, C.: A Traitor Tracing Scheme Based on RSA. Journal of Xidian University 31(4), 611–613 (2004)
10. Rivest, R.L., Shamir, A., Adleman, L.: A Method for Obtaining Digital Signatures and Public-Key Cryptosystems. Communication of the ACM 21(2) (1978)

Combining User Authentication with Role-Based Authorazition Based on Identity-Based Signature

Jin Wang[1], Jia Yu[1,2], Daxing Li[1], Xi Bai, and Zhongtian Jia[1,3]

[1] Institute of Network and Information Security, Shandong University, Jinan 250100, China
[2] College of Information Engineering, Qingdao University, Qingdao 266071, China
[3] School of Information Science and Engineering, Jinan University, Jinan 250022, China
{wangjin06,jiayu}@mail.sdu.edu.cn, xibai@email.jlu.edu.cn

Abstract. Authentication and authorization are crucial for ensuring the security of information systems. Role-based access control (RBAC) can act as an efficient method of managing authorization of system resources. In this paper, we apply identity-based signature (IBS) technique to cryptographically provide user authentication and role-based authorization. To achieve this, we first extend the RBAC model to incorporate identity-based cryptography. Our access control architecture is derived from an identity-based signature scheme on bilinear pairings and eliminates the use of digital certificates. In our suggestion, the manager checks the validity of a user's identity and user's activated roles simultaneously by verifying a corresponding signature, thus the user authentication and role-based authorization procedures can be combined into one operation. We also prove the security of the proposed scheme in the random oracle model.

1 Introduction

1.1 Background and Related Work

In proportion to the spread of computation and communication technologies, how to provide security services, especially authentication and authorization , is becoming even more crucial than ever.

Role-Based Access Control. Role-based access control [1,2] is an effective access control method for protecting information and resources in large-scale and enterprise-wide systems. In RBAC, access rights (*permissions*) are associated with *roles*, and *users* are assigned appropriate roles thereby acquiring the corresponding permissions. Moreover, RBAC allows for roles and permissions to be activated within a user's *session*, thus access privileges can be given only when required. RBAC provides administrators with a means of managing authorization of system resources. In the implementation phase, access control should

Y. Wang, Y. Cheung, and H. Liu (Eds.): CIS 2006, LNAI 4456, pp. 847–857, 2007.

be strong and efficient based on user authentication information, so the RBAC mechanism often requires user authentication as a prerequisite.

Identity-based Cryptography. Certificate-based PKI (Public Key Infrastructure)[11] is widely applied to provide user authentication, but there exists grievous management cost expanding problems for public key certificates. Identity-based cryptography (IBC) can eliminate the need for certificates and overcome those hurdles of PKI by allowing a user's public key to be derived from its identity, such as an email address. The idea of identity-based cryptography was first introduced by Shamir [3], and the first practical identity-based encryption scheme was proposed by Boneh and Franklin [4] based on bilinear pairings. Identity-based cryptosystem fits very well to cryptographically support RBAC. Firstly, it is possible to use arbitrary string values, including a user's identity, a role's identity as a public key. And secondly, a user can just get the corresponding private key from the PKG (Private Key Generator) if the user is currently playing the requested role. There is no need to share or store any certificates of the user.

Related Work. There have been several approaches about cryptographic support of access control involving identity-based cryptography. Smart presents a simple mechanism [5] to drive access control to broadcast encrypted data using a variant of identity-based encryption scheme. Nali et al. [6] extend a mediated identity-based encryption scheme to support RBAC. But due to the encryption-based access control method, previous approaches cannot support flexible access rights, and are not suitable for widely application environment.

1.2 Our Contribution

In this paper, we propose a scheme that cryptographically provides user authentication and role-based access control for large organizations based on identity-based signature (IBS) technique. To achieve this, we extend the elements *user* and *role* in RBAC model [1,2] to cooperate with identity-based cryptography. Our suggestion is that each role is associated with a pair of public/private keys. Each user uses his/her identity as a public key, and has a set of private keys (called *assigned key*) corresponding to the roles assigned to him/her. A role's private key is used to generate a user's assigned key while the administrator assigns this role to the user. Our access control architecture is based on a pairing-based identity-based signature scheme [7]. In our proposed scheme, the manager can check the validity of a user's identity and activated roles by verifying the user's signature, so there is no need to authenticate users in an independent procedure.

The rest of this paper is organized as follows. Section 2 introduces some related preliminary information; Section 3 presents our RBAC scheme based on identity-based signature; in Section 4 we analyze the security of the proposed scheme; we conclude in Section 5.

2 Preliminaries

In this section, we briefly review some of the properties of bilinear pairings, and recall an identity-based signature scheme proposed by Cha and Cheon[7], which is the basis of our proposed scheme.

2.1 Bilinear Pairings and Gap Diffie-Hellman Groups

Bilinear Pairing. Let G_1 be an additive group of prime order q and G_2 be a multiplicative group of the same order q. A bilinear pairing is a map $\hat{e}$: $G_1 \times G_1 \rightarrow G_2$, with the following properties.

1 *Bilniearity:* $\hat{e}(aP, bQ) = \hat{e}(P, Q)^{ab}$, for all $P, Q \in G_1$, $a, b \in Z_q^*$;
2 *Non-degeneracy:* There exist $P, Q \in G_1$, such that $\hat{e}(P, Q) \neq 1$;
3 *Computability:* There is an efficient algorithms to compute $\hat{e}(P, Q)$ for all $P, Q \in G_1$.

At the same time, we are interested in the following mathematical problems. Let P, Q be elements of G_1 and a, b, c be elements of Z_q^*.

Discrete Logarithm Problem (DLP). Given P, Q, find an integer n such that $P = nQ$, where such n exists.

Computational Diffie-Hellman Problem (CDHP). Given (P, aP, bP), compute abP.

Decisional Diffie-Hellman Problem (DDHP). Given (P, aP, bP, cP), decide whether $c = ab$ in Z_q^*.

We call G a GDH group if DDHP can be solved in polynomial time but no probabilistic algorithm can solve CDHP with non-negligible advantage within polynomial time. Such group can be found on super singular or hyper elliptic curves over finite field. The Weil pairing and the Tate pairing [13] are admissible applications satisfying the properties mentioned above.

2.2 Identity-Based Signature

An Identity-based signature scheme consists of four phases namely *Setup*, *Extract*, *Sign*, and *Verify*. The PKG initializes the system in the Setup phase by generating the system public parameters. The PKG also chooses a master key and keeps it secret. The master key is used in the Extract phase to calculate private keys for the participating users in the system. A signer signs a message in the Sign phase using a private key given by PKG corresponding to his/her identity. To verify a signature of a user with identity ID, a verifier just uses ID in the Verify phase. An identity-based signature scheme proposed by Cha and Cheon[7] is introduced as follows.

Setup: The PKG specifies two groups G_1 and G_2 of prime order q, a generator P of G_1, a bilinear map $\hat{e}$: $G_1 \times G_1 \rightarrow G_2$, and two hash functions $H_1 : \{0, 1\}^* \rightarrow G_1$

and $H_2 : \{0,1\}^* \times G_1 \rightarrow Z_q^*$. It also chooses $s \in Z_q^*$ randomly as its master secret key and computes the global public key P_{pub} as sP.
System params:$\langle G_1, G_2, \hat{e}, P, P_{pub}, H_1, H_2 \rangle$. Master-key: $\langle s \rangle$.

Extract: The PKG verifies the given identity ID, and computes the secret key for the identity as $S_{ID} = sH_1(ID)$. The component $Q_{ID} = H_1(ID)$ plays the role of the corresponding public key.

Sign: To sign a message $m \in \{0,1\}^*$ using the private key S_{ID}, the signer chooses $r \in Z_q^*$ randomly and calculates:

1 $U = rQ_{ID}$
2 $h = H_2(m, U)$;
3 $V = (r + h)S_{ID}$.

Signature: $\sigma = \langle U, V \rangle \in G_1 \times G_1$.

Verify: To verify a signature $\sigma = \langle U, V \rangle$ for an identity ID on a message m, a verifier checks whether $(P, P_{pub}, U + hQ_{ID}, V)$ is a valid Diffie-Hellman tuple. This can be accomplished by the equation below: $\hat{e}(P, V) = \hat{e}(P_{pub}, U + hQ_{ID})$. Notice that this check can be performed because of the assumption that the group G_1 is a GDH group.

3 Our RBAC Scheme Based on IBS

In this section we present a scheme that cryptographically enforces user authentication and role-based access control based on the extension of above Cha-Cheon's scheme. Hereafter we refer our proposed scheme as IRBAC (Identity& Role Based Access Control) scheme.

3.1 Notations

We extend the elements *user* and *role* in RBAC model [1,2] to cooperate with identity-based cryptography.

- **User:** In our suggestion, each user can be represented as $u = \langle ID, USKS \rangle$. ID is an identity information of the user and is used as a public key. $USKS = \{S_{IDr_1}, ..., S_{IDr_n}\}$ represents a set of *assigned keys* corresponding to the roles assigned to the user.
- **Role:** A role is described as a set of permissions to access system resources, each role can be represented as $r = \langle rpk, rsk \rangle$. rpk and rsk are defined as a pair of public/private keys belonging to the role, where rsk is randomly chosen from Z_q^* and $rpk = rsk \cdot P$. Here our system parameters are identical to Cha-Cheon's scheme, where P is a generator of G_1. Each role can be considered as be associated with a PKG, which generates user's assigned key as a function of its rsk and a user's identity while assigning the role to the user.

3.2 System Architecture

The entities participating in the scheme and their responsibilities are described as follows.

- **System Manager (SM):** The SM is responsible for generating system parameters and defining roles. When a new role is added in the system, the SM generates a public/private key pair for the role, and keeps the private role key secret.
- **Role Manager (RM):** The RM is responsible for assigning roles to users. As mentioned above, each role is corresponding to a PKG as in the IBS scheme, but it is unpractical to build as many PKGs as roles. In our scheme, the RM receives all of the role's private keys securely from the SM and uses them to issue assigned keys while assigning corresponding roles to users.
- **Access control Enforcement Facility (AEF)** and **Access control Decision Facility (ADF):** The AEF and the ADF are responsible for managing the system's resources. The AEF mediates access request, and passes the user's notation to the ADF. The ADF makes the access control decisions based on the system security policies. The AEF enforces access decisions made by the ADF.

3.3 Framework

Definition 1. *Our scheme is specified by five algorithms (Gen_{Sys}, Add_{Role}, $Asgn_{User}$, Gen_{Sig} and $Auth_{User}$) such that:*

- Gen_{Sys}: *It takes as input the security parameter k, and returns system parameters.*
- Add_{Role}: *It takes as input a new role's identity. It generates a pair of public/private keys for the role.*
- $Asgn_{User}$: *It takes as input a user $\mathcal{A}$'s identity and a role r_i's private key. It assigns r_i to $\mathcal{A}$, that is, it generates an assigned key for $\mathcal{A}$ corresponding to r_i.*
- Gen_{Sig}: *It takes as input $\mathcal{A}$'s identity, a set of assigned keys of $\mathcal{A}$ and an access request message Q. It generates a signature on Q for $\mathcal{A}$.*
- $Auth_{User}$: *It takes as input $\mathcal{A}$'s identity, a set of roles' public keys, an access request message Q and a signature for $\mathcal{A}$. It decides to allow $\mathcal{A}$'s access request or not.*

3.4 IRBAC Scheme

Our proposed scheme is driven from Cha-Cheon's identity-based signature scheme [7], we describe each algorithms of our scheme. We assume that all the users agree on a set of public parameters. The RM generates system parameters as follows.

Gen$_{Sys}$: the SM
Chooses a generator P of G_1, two hash functions $H_1 : \{0,1\}^* \rightarrow G_1$ and H_2 :

$\{0,1\}^* \times G_1 \rightarrow Z_q^*$. The SM also picks its master key $s \in Z_q^*$ at random and computes the system public key $P_{pub} = sP$.
The system public parameters are $params = \langle P, P_{pub}, H_1, H_2 \rangle$.

When a role r_i is added to the system, The SM carries out Add$_{Role}$ as follows.

Add$_{Role}$: The SM
1. Picks a random $s_i \in Z_q^*$ as r_i's private key, and sets $P_i = s_i P$ as r_i's public key. If s_i is equal to other existing role's private key, the RM randomly picks another value from Z_q^* as r_i's private key.
2. Assigns specified permissions to r_i.The SM maintains a permission-assignment list (PAL) to record the assignment relationships between roles and permissions.
3. Sends (s_i, P_i) to the RM via secure channel.

In order to authorize users to access system resources, the RM must issue assigned keys stating the roles being granted. If a user A with identity ID_A wants to be a member of role r_i, he submits the request message to the RM. To assign r_i to A, the RM carries out Asgn$_{User}$ as follows:

Asgn$_{User}$: The RM
1. Checks validity of A's identity.
2. Computes $Q_{ID_A} = H_1(ID_A)$.
3. Generates A's assigned key corresponding to $r_i : S_{ID_A r_i} = s_i Q_{ID_A}$, where s_i is r_i's private key.
4. Sends $S_{ID_A r_i}$ to A via secure channel.

We suppose that A wants to access system resources, he initiates a session by interacting with the AEF. Then A performs Gen$_{Sig}$ as follows.

Gen$_{Sig}$: A
1. Selects a role or role set to activate in the current session, assume the activated role set is $AR = \{r_1, ..., r_k\}$.
2. Generates the query message Q and the signature $SigQ$ on Q using assigned keys corresponding to AR. Let $Q = ID_A|AR|p$, where ID_A is A's identity, p is the permission that A wants to enforce. To generate the signature on Q, A chooses a random number $r \in Z_q^*$ and computes:

a) $U = rQ_{ID_A}$.
b) $h = H_2(Q, U)$.
c) $S_{ID_A AR} = \sum_{i=1}^{k} S_{ID_A r_i}$, where $S_{ID_A r_i}$ is an assigned key of A corresponding to the role r_i.
d) $V = (r + h) S_{ID_A AR}$.

Signature: $SigQ = \langle U, V \rangle$.
3. Submits Q and $SigQ$ to the AEF.

After receiving Q and $SigQ$, the AEF and the ADF carries out Auth_{User} as follows.

Auth$_{User}$: The AEF

1. Checks the validity of $SigQ$ using ID_A and the public keys of $r_1, ..., r_k$. This can be accomplished by the equation below:

$\hat{e}(P, V) = \hat{e}(P_{AR}, U + hQ_{ID_A})$, where $h = H_2(Q, U)$, $P_{AR} = \sum_{i=1}^{k} P_i$, P_i is the public key of the role r_i.

2. The ADF maintains a permission-assignment list (PAL) to record the assignment relationships between roles and permissions. If $SigQ$ is valid, the ADF retrieves permissions assigned to the roles of AR, and makes the decision whether Alice's request should be allowed or denied according to the assigned permissions and system security policies. The ADF returns the decision to the AEF, and then the AEF enforces the ADF's decision.

For any valid signature produced by a user, we obtain

$$\begin{aligned}
&\hat{e}(P_{AR}, U + hQ_{ID}) \\
&= \hat{e}(\sum_{i=1}^{k} P_i, rQ_{ID} + hQ_{ID}) \\
&= \hat{e}(\sum_{i=1}^{k} sP, (r + h)Q_{ID}) \\
&= \hat{e}(P, (r + h)\sum_{i=1}^{k} s_i Q_{ID}) \\
&= \hat{e}(P, (r + h)S_{IDAR}) \\
&= \hat{e}(P, V)
\end{aligned}$$

So the correctness of our scheme can be easily verified.

Of course, we can choose other identity-based signature schemes as the basic signature scheme, such as [8,9,10].

3.5 Discussion

Our scheme has several advantages over the previous approaches [5,6]. Firstly, our scheme prevents a service from having to provide system resources to any users in an encrypted form, which can be an expensive task. Secondly, since the encryption-based access control method is avoided, our scheme fulfills the requirement of supporting multiple types of operations and objects in RBAC model. And thirdly, in our scheme, both aspects of the user authentication and checking the activated role's validity can be combined into one operation of verifying a signature of the user, so there is no need to check the user's identity in an independent procedure.

4 Security Analysis

4.1 Authenticity

Since an assigned key is generated as a function of a role's private key and a user's identity, it is uniquely corresponding to the user and the assigned role. The signature $SigQ$ is generated using the sum of assigned keys corresponding to the roles activated by the user, so the validity of $SigQ$ can prove the user's possession of the activated roles and authenticate the user's identity. There is no need to check the user's ID in an independent procedure.

4.2 Unforgeability

Our IRBAC scheme can be regarded as an identity-based signature scheme with multiple PKGs, each PKG is associated with a role. In order to activate role set $AR = \{r_1, ..., r_k\}$, a user has to generate a valid signature using the sum of assigned keys corresponding to all the roles of AR on the user's ID. We use similar technique in [7] to prove the unforgeability of our scheme. Suppose the hash functions H_1 and H_2 are random oracles. The following attack model appropriate to IRBAC scheme may be considered.

Definition 2. *We say that our IRBAC scheme is secure against existential forgery under adaptively chosen message and ID attack if no polynomial time adversary $\mathcal{A}$ has a non-negligible advantage against challenger $\mathcal{C}$ in the following game:*

1. Assume that performing specified permissions need to activate roles set $AR = \{r_1, ..., r_k\}$. Adversary $\mathcal{A}$ first chooses $k-1$ roles of AR which it wants to corrupt. Without loss of generality, let $SR = \{r_2, ..., r_k\}$ be the roles chosen by $\mathcal{A}$. $\mathcal{C}$ runs the System Setup algorithm and the resulting system parameters are given to $\mathcal{A}$.
2. $\mathcal{A}$ issues a number of the following queries as it wants, every request may depend on the answers to the previous ones:
*- **Hash Function Query:** $\mathcal{C}$ computes the value of the hash function for the requested input and sends the value to $\mathcal{A}$.*
*- **Extract Query:** $\mathcal{A}$ can issue two type of extract queries:*

a) $\mathcal{A}$ selects an identity ID and a role $r_i \in AR$, $\mathcal{C}$ returns the corresponding assigned key S_{IDr_i} which is obtained by running $Asgn_{User}$ algorithm.

b) $\mathcal{A}$ selects an identity ID, $\mathcal{C}$ returns the sum of all of assigned keys $\sum_{i=1}^{k} S_{IDr_i}$ (with $r_i \in AR$).

*- **Activate Query:** Given an identity ID and a message m, $\mathcal{C}$ returns a signature which is obtained by activating all the roles of AR, namely the signature is generated using the sum of all of assigned keys $\sum_{i=1}^{k} S_{IDr_i}$ (with $r_i \in AR$).*

3. $\mathcal{A}$ submits a target identity ID, such that ID is not equal to any input of Role Extract queries, and receives from $\mathcal{C}$ $k-1$ assigned keys S_{IDr_i} (with $r_i \in AR$) corresponding to the target ID.
4. Finally, $\mathcal{A}$ outputs (ID, m, σ), where ID is target identity chosen in phase 3, m is a message and σ is a signature such that (ID, m) is not equal to any input of Activate queries. $\mathcal{A}$ wins the game if σ is a valid signature of m using the sum of all assigned keys $\sum_{i=1}^{k} S_{IDr_i}$ (with $r_i \in AR$).

Our IRBAC scheme is based on Cha-Cheon's identity-based signature scheme, and Cha-Cheon's scheme is completely secure against existential forgery under adaptively chosen message and ID attack [7] in the random oracle model assuming the hardness of CDHP. The security proof of Cha-Cheon's scheme is given in [7].

Theorem 1. *Suppose that there exists a polynomial-time adversary $\mathcal{A}$ that can attack our scheme in the game described in Definition 2 with a non negligible advantage $Adv^{IRBAC}(\mathcal{A})$. Then we have an adversary $\mathcal{B}$ that is able to gain advantage $Adv^{CCIBS}(\mathcal{B}) = Adv^{IRBAC}(\mathcal{A})$ against Cha-Cheon's scheme under the adaptively chosen message and ID attack model.*

Proof. We use $\mathcal{A}$ to build algorithm $\mathcal{B}$ that can attack Cha-Cheon's scheme under the adaptively chosen message and ID attack model.

1. At first, $\mathcal{B}$ receives a random system parameter $K_{pub} = \langle G_1, G_2, \hat{e}, P, P_{pub}, H_1, H_2\rangle$, which is generated by its challenger of Cha-Cheon's scheme. The system private key s is kept unknown to $\mathcal{B}$. $\mathcal{B}$ works by simulate $\mathcal{A}$'s environment as follows. $\mathcal{B}$ chooses $a \in Z_q^*$ randomly, and supplies $\mathcal{A}$ with the IRBAC system parameters $\langle G_1, G_2, \hat{e}, P, aP, H_1, H_2\rangle$, where $G_1, G_2, \hat{e}, P, H_1, H_2$ are taken from K_{pub}. $\mathcal{B}$ informs $\mathcal{A}$ the role set $AR = \{r_1, ..., r_k\}$ to be activated. $\mathcal{A}$ chooses $k-1$ roles in AR it wants to corrupt, let $SR = \{r_2, ..., r_k\}$ be the roles chosen by $\mathcal{A}$. Then $\mathcal{B}$ randomly selects $s_i \in Z_q^* (i = 2, ..., k)$ as r_i's private key$(i = 2, ..., k)$, the corresponding role public key is $P_i = s_iP (i = 2, ..., k)$. Let r_1's private key $s_1 = s - \sum_{i=2}^{k} s_i$, public key $P_1 = P_{pub} - \sum_{i=2}^{k} P_i$. s_1 is kept unknown to $\mathcal{B}$. $\mathcal{B}$ sends $P_i (i = 1, ..., k)$ to $\mathcal{A}$.
2. $\mathcal{A}$ has access to the random H_1, H_2, Extract and Activate oracles. H_1 and H_2 are taken from Cha-Cheon's scheme, for every query made by $\mathcal{A}$ to random oracles H_1 and H_2, $\mathcal{B}$ forwards it to its challenger and sends the answer back to $\mathcal{A}$. $\mathcal{B}$ simulates the Extract oracle and Activate oracle as follows.

Extract-queries

a) $\mathcal{A}$ chooses a new ID_j, a role $r_i \in AR$, and issues an assigned key extract query. If $r_i \neq r_1$, $\mathcal{B}$ reply to $\mathcal{A}$ with $S_{ID_jr_i} = s_iH_1(ID_j)$. Otherwise, $r_i = r_1$, $\mathcal{B}$ forwards ID_j as its extract query to its challenger and gets the reply $S_{ID_j} = sH_1(ID_j)$. $\mathcal{B}$ computes $S_{ID_jr_1} = (s - \sum_{i=2}^{k} s_i)H_1(ID_j) = S_{ID_j} - \sum_{i=2}^{k} s_iH_1(ID_j)$, and returns $S_{ID_jr_1}$ to $\mathcal{A}$.

b) When $\mathcal{A}$ chooses a new ID_j , and query the sum of assigned keys corresponding to AR, $\mathcal{B}$ first forwards it to its Extract oracle and gets the reply $S_{ID_j} = sH_1(ID_j)$. $\mathcal{B}$ computes the sum of assigned keys $S_{ID_j}r_i$(with $r_i \in AR$) as: $S_{ID_jAR} = \sum_{i=1}^{k} S_{ID_jr_i} = \sum_{i=1}^{k} s_iH_1(ID_j) = sH_1(ID_j) = S_{ID_j}$, so $\mathcal{B}$ returns S_{ID_j} to $\mathcal{A}$.

Activate-queries
When $\mathcal{A}$ chooses (ID_j, m), and makes a query to the Activate oracle, since the signing structure of IRBAC is identical to Cha-Cheon's scheme and $S_{ID_jAR} = S_{ID_j}$, $\mathcal{B}$ forwards (ID_j, m) as its sign query to its challenger of Cha-Cheon's scheme, and returns the reply to $\mathcal{A}$.
3. At some point, $\mathcal{A}$ submits a target identity ID*. $\mathcal{B}$ generates $k-1$ assigned keys for ID* corresponding to SR as $S_{ID^*r_i} = s_iH_1(ID^*)(i = 2, ..., k)$, then sends $S_{ID^*r_i}(i = 2, ..., k)$ to $\mathcal{A}$. $\mathcal{B}$ also regards ID* as its own target identity.
4. Finally, $\mathcal{A}$ outputs (ID^*, m^*, σ^*). $\mathcal{B}$ also takes (ID^*, m^*, σ^*) as its output because $S_{ID^*AR} = sH_1(ID^*) = S_{ID^*}$ and IRBAC uses an identical signing structure to Cha-Cheon's scheme. From $\mathcal{A}$'s viewpoint, the above simulation is indistinguishable from the real protocol, and $\mathcal{B}$ is successful only if $\mathcal{A}$ is successful. Thus $Adv^{CCIBS}(\mathcal{B}) = Adv^{IRBAC}(\mathcal{A})$.

5 Conclusion

In this paper, we apply identity-based signature technique to address user authentication problem in the role based access control systems. To achieve this, we extend the elements *user* and *role* in RBAC model to cooperate with identity-based cryptography. In our scheme, the manager can check the validity of a user's identity and activated roles simultaneously by verifying the user's signature, so the independent authentication procedure is eliminated. As we know our scheme is the first scheme that realizes user authentication and role-based access control in one operation using identity-based signature technique.

References

1. Sandhu, R., Coyne, E.J., Feinstein, H.L., Youman, C.E.: Role-Based Access Control Models. IEEE computer 29(2), 38–47 (1996)
2. Ferraiolo, D.F., Sandhu, F., Gavrila, S., Kuhn, D.R., Chandramouli, R.: Proposed NIST Standard for Role-Based Access Control. In: ACM Trans. Information and System Security, vol. 4(3), pp. 224–274. ACM Press, New York (2001)
3. Shamir, A.: Identity-based cryptosystems and signature schemes. In: Blakely, G.R., Chaum, D. (eds.) Advances in Cryptology. LNCS, vol. 196, pp. 47–53. Springer, Berlin Heidelberg New York (1984)
4. Boneh, D., Franklin, M.: Identity-based encryption from the Weil pairing. In: Kilian, J. (ed.) Advances in Cryptology - CRYPTO 2001. LNCS, vol. 2139, pp. 213–229. Springer, Heidelberg (2001)

5. Smart, N.P.: Access control using pairing based cryptography. In: Joye, M. (ed.) Topics in Cryptology - CT-RSA 2003. LNCS, vol. 2612, pp. 111–121. Springer, Heidelberg (2003)
6. Nali, D., Adams, C., Miri, A.: Using mediated identity-based cryptography to support role- based access control. In: Zhang, K., Zheng, Y. (eds.) Information Security. LNCS, vol. 3225, pp. 245–256. Springer, Heidelberg (2004)
7. Cha, J., Cheon, J.H.: An Identity-Based Signature from Gap Diffie-Hellman Groups. In: Desmedt, Y.G. (ed.) Public Key Cryptography - PKC 2003. LNCS, vol. 2567, pp. 18–30. Springer, Heidelberg (2002)
8. Hess, F.: Efficient identity based signature schemes based on pairings. In: Nyberg, K., Heys, H.M. (eds.) Selected Areas in Cryptography. LNCS, vol. 2595, pp. 310–324. Springer, Heidelberg (2003)
9. Paterson, K.G.: ID-based signatures from pairings on elliptic curves. Cryptology ePrint Archive, Report 2002/004, (2002) `http://eprint.iacr.org/2002/004`
10. Sakai, R., Ohgishi, K., Kasahara, M.: Cryptosystems based on pairing. In: Symposium on Cryptography and Information Security-SCIS'00 (2000)
11. Public-Key Infrastructure(X.509), `http://www.ietf.org/html.charters/pkixcharter.html`
12. Boneh, D., Lynn, B., Shacham, H.: Short signatures from the Weil pairing. In: Boyd, C. (ed.) Advances in Cryptology - ASIACRYPT 2001. LNCS, vol. 2248, pp. 514–532. Springer, Heidelberg (2001)

Modeling and Simulation for Security Risk Propagation in Critical Information Systems*

Young-Gab Kim[1], Dongwon Jeong[2], Soo-Hyun Park[3], Jongin Lim[1], and Doo-Kwon Baik[4]

[1] Graduate School of Information Management and Security, Center for Information Security Technologies (CIST), Korea University, 1, 5-ga, Anam-dong, SungBuk-gu, 136-701, Seoul, Korea
{always,jilim}@korea.ac.kr

[2] Dept.of Informatics & Statistics, Kunsan National University San68, Miryong-dong, Gunsan, Jeolabuk-do, 573-701, Korea
djeong@kusan.ac.kr

[3] School of Business IT, Kookmin University, 861-1, Chongnung-dong. SungBuk-gu, Seoul, Postfach 136-702, Korea
shpark21@kookmin.ac.kr

[4] Department of Computer Science & Engineering, Korea University 1, 5-ga, Anam-dong, SungBuk-gu, 136-701, Seoul, Korea
baikdk@korea.ac.kr

Abstract. Existing risk propagation models are limited and inadequate for the analysis of cyber attacks caused by various threats to information systems, because of their limited focus only on one specific threat, such as a single virus or worm. Therefore, we herein propose a risk propagation model based on the Markov process, which can be applied to diverse threats to information systems. Furthermore, simulations including in case a threat occurs related with other threats are performed using five scenarios to verify the proposed model.

1 Introduction

Security risk analysis (it is also called risk assessment) is a process of evaluating the systems assets, their vulnerability to various threats, and the cost or impact of potential losses. Precise security risk analysis provides two key advantages: supporting practical security policies for organizations by monitoring and effectively protecting the critical assets of the organization, and providing valuable analysis data for future estimation through the development of secure information management [1]. Despite the considerable research relating to risk analysis, little attention has focused on evaluating the security risk propagation [1, 2, 3]. Furthermore, the existing security

* "This research was supported by the MIC (Ministry of Information and Communication), Korea, under the ITRC (Information Technology Research Center) support program supervised by the IITA (Institute of Information Technology Advancement)" (IITA-2006-(C1090-0603-0025)).

Y. Wang, Y. Cheung, and H. Liu (Eds.): CIS 2006, LNAI 4456, pp. 858–868, 2007.

risk propagation models are inadequate to apply this to the analysis of attacks caused by diverse threats because they can only be applied to specific threats such as a virus or worm. Furthermore, it is difficult to globally analyze the scope of risk propagation caused by such threats, using their interrelationships. Therefore, a previous work [4] proposed a probabilistic model for damage propagation based on the Markov process [6, 7] and on historical data collected over several years. Using the proposed model, the occurrence probability and frequency for each threat to information systems can be predicted globally, and applied to establish effective countermeasures. However, the previous work [4] only analyzed the approach method with a case study. Furthermore, simulations performed in the previous paper [5] only simulated security risk propagation for case of an independent threat. Therefore, this paper presents a modeling and simulation for security risk analysis. In addition, five scenario simulations are performed in this paper to verify the proposed model.

The sebsequent sections of this paper are organized as follows: In Section 2, the security risk propagation model that has been proposed in previous work [4] is explained. Section 3 shows the simulations for security risk propagation, including in case a threat occurs related with other threats. Section 4 shows the related work, including the worm and virus propagation model. Section 5 concludes this paper.

2 Modeling of Security Risk Propagation

In this section, the risk (or damage) propagation model based on the Markov process proposed in the previous work [4] is explained briefly. The model proposed in the previous work [4] is composed of 4 steps: Threat-State Definition, Threat-State Transition Matrix, Initial Vector, and Risk Propagation Evaluation. A more detailed description will be presented in the following subsections.

2.1 Definition of a Set of Threat-States (Step 1)

In Step 1, three tasks are performed to define the threat-states: the gathering of occurrence data of threats, threat analysis, and definition of a set of threat-states. That is, in this step, all kinds of threats are examined, the threat-occurrence data are collected and analyzed in information systems, and finally the possible threat-states can be defined. If S is a set of threat-states, S can be defined as formula (1).

$$\begin{aligned} &T = \text{a set of thresholds, } \{T_1, T_2, \ldots, T_n\} \\ &T_i = \text{a specific threat such as hacking, worm or virus} \\ &S = \text{a set of threat-states, } \{S_1, S_2, \ldots, S_i, \ldots, S_n\} \\ &S_i = \text{a pair of thresholds, } (T_\alpha, T_\beta, \ldots, T_\gamma), \\ &\qquad \text{where } \alpha, \beta, \text{ and } \gamma \text{ are each a different threat.} \end{aligned} \tag{1}$$

It is particularly important to collect reliable and numerous historical data related with the threats because such historical data is more important than other elements in the probability model based on the Markov process. Therefore, in the simulation results presented in Section 3 of this paper, statistics on hacking and virus propagation published by the Korea Information Security Agency (KISA) were used for 54 months, from January 2001 to June 2005, to ensure the reliability of the past data [8].

The definition of a threat-state task decides the threat-states by analyzing the threat-occurrence, and establishing a threshold indicating the frequency range of the threat-occurrences. Two methods are available to define the set of threat-states, according to the dependency among threats. That is, when a threat occurs independently of other threats, the set of threat-states is composed of a number of several thresholds. Conversely, when a threat occurs that is related with other threats, the set of threat-states is created with the combination of thresholds of each threat. Therefore, in the latter case, the number of threat-states and the complexity of transition matrix, which describes the probabilities of moving from one state to another, will increase in proportion with the number of threat-states.

2.2 Transition Matrix of Threat-State (Step 2)

In Step 2, the threat-state transition matrix is calculated, which is a square matrix describing the probabilities of moving from one threat-state to another. In order to obtain the transition matrix, three tasks are performed. First, threat-states are listed by mapping the threat-occurrence data of each threat into the threat-state defined in the previous step. Second, the number from one threat-state to another is counted. Finally, the matrix is constructed. The function mapping each state S to a set of thresholds is as follows:

$$\text{Threat-states: } S \rightarrow 2^{T}, \text{ a function mapping each state } S \text{ to a set of thresholds } T \qquad (2)$$

As in Step 1, the creation of a transition matrix is divided into two methods, according to the dependency among threats. When a threat occurs independently, the transition matrix can be created simply with the two tasks mentioned previously. However, when a threat occurs that is related to others, the size and complexity of the threat-transition matrix are increased, depending on the number of related threats and the threat-state defined in Step 1. Therefore, in order to reduce the complexity and size of the transition matrix, it is very important to decide the proper number of threat-states in Step 1.

If P is the transition probability matrix created in this step, it is compactly specified as the form of matrix (3). Furthermore, the entries of the matrix P satisfy the property (4).

$$P = \begin{bmatrix} P_{11} & P_{12} & \cdots & P_{1n} \\ P_{21} & P_{22} & \cdots & P_{2n} \\ \cdots & \cdots & P_{ij} & \cdots \\ P_{n1} & P_{n2} & \cdots & P_{nn} \end{bmatrix} \qquad (3)$$

$$\text{where } \sum_{j=1}^{n} P_{1j} = 1, \sum_{j=1}^{n} P_{2j} = 1, \ldots, \sum_{j=1}^{n} P_{nj} = 1 \text{ . That is, } \sum_{j=1}^{n} P_{ij} = 1, i = 1,2,\ldots,n \qquad (4)$$

Each row shows the probabilities of moving from the state represented by that row, to the other states. The rows of the Markov transition matrix therefore each add up to one.

2.3 Initial Probability (π Vector) (Step 3)

Step 3 is a process to obtain the initial probability vector, which represents the occurrence possibility of each threat-state in the initial state. In order to obtain the initial probability, the most recent threat-occurrence data are used, which can be divided by the time period such as three, six, and nine months and one year. By analyzing the most recent data, the initial probability vector is calculated using formula (5) satisfied by condition (6).

$$P(S_1 \quad S_2 \quad \dots \quad S_k \quad \dots \quad S_n) = P(\frac{\alpha}{F} \quad \frac{\beta}{F} \quad \dots \quad \frac{\gamma}{F} \quad \dots \quad \frac{\delta}{F}) \tag{5}$$

$$F = \sum_{i=1}^{n} f_i = \alpha + \beta + \dots + \gamma + \dots + \delta \tag{6}$$

where α, β, γ and δ represent the number of threat-occurrences for each state, S_1, S_2, S_k and S_n, respectively. Furthermore, the initial probability $P(S_i)$ of each state S_i satisfies the formula (7) because the sum of the initial probabilities must add up to one.

$$\sum_{i=1}^{n} P(S_i) = 1 \tag{7}$$

2.4 Prediction of Threats (Step 4)

In Step 4, the probability and frequency of the threat-occurrence that will occur in the future are estimated, using the transition matrix created in Step 2 and the initial probability vector created in Step 3. Formula (8) depicts the computation of the probability of threat-occurrence.

$$P(S_1 \quad S_2 \quad \dots \quad S_k \quad \dots \quad S_n) \begin{bmatrix} P_{11} & P_{12} & \dots & P_{1n} \\ P_{21} & P_{22} & \dots & P_{2n} \\ \dots & \dots & P_{ij} & \dots \\ P_{n1} & P_{n2} & \dots & P_{nn} \end{bmatrix} = P'(S_1 \quad S_2 \quad \dots \quad S_k \quad \dots \quad S_n) \tag{8}$$

where n is the number of threat-states, $P(S_i)$ the initial probability of each threat-state, and $P'(S_i)$ the next probability of threat-occurrence.

Finally, the Expected Frequency (*EF*) of threat-occurrence is estimated using the probability of threat-occurrence and the median for each threat-state, as formula (9).

$$EF = \sum_{i=1}^{n} P(S_i) M(S_i) \tag{9}$$

where n is the number of threat-states, $P(S_i)$ the probability of threat-occurrence for each threat-state, and $M(S_i)$ the median of each threat-state.

Further details on the creation of the Markov process-based risk propagation model are available in [4].

3 Simulation for Security Risk Propagation

As described in section 2.1 above, simulation studies require the use of an organization's historical data for some period of time. First, threat-occurrence data is gathered and analyzed, and priority is given to threats. Second, the monthly frequency and statistics of threats are obtained, as presented in Tables 1 and 2.

Table 1. Frequency and statistics of threat T_1 for each month

	Jan	Feb	Mar	Apr	May	Jun	Jul	Aug	Sep	Oct	Nov	Dec	Total
2001	85	125	70	89	85	64	65	495	268	77	51	97	1571
2002	401	119	82	59	286	417	313	298	210	465	472	990	4112
2003	1148	557	1132	934	306	450	185	544	119	137	129	96	5837
2004	154	148	118	1066	493	181	72	22	16	24	125	90	2509
2005	29	20	15	3	15	36	-	-	-	-	-	-	118

T_1 is an 'illegal intrusion using malicious applications such as Netbus and Subseven' as one of the hacking threats to an information system. This threat leaks information and interrupts the normal process in information systems.

Table 2. Frequency and statistics of threat T_2 for each month

	Jan	Feb	Mar	Apr	May	Jun	Jul	Aug	Sep	Oct	Nov	Dec	Total
2001	1	1529	2429	625	684	520	6106	5965	10772	4795	4068	3024	40518
2002	2005	1384	1306	3165	2760	1774	1706	1458	1610	3566	3028	1684	25446
2003	1361	1320	2537	2350	3704	1854	1185	9748	19682	3999	11658	8949	68347
2004	4824	5750	9820	4233	19728	22767	15228	8132	3153	2658	2319	2117	100727
2005	1832	1205	1049	648	1302	1040	-	-	-	-	-	-	

T_2 is an 'Internet Worm' as an example of a virus threat. The Internet worm is a self-replicating computer program or executable program with rapid self-propagation. The incidence of this threat has recently increased greatly, and considerable research relating to the propagation of Internet worms is processing.

The proposed model is simulated using a statistical method for comparing real-world observations and simulation output data as in the inspection approach [9], which computes one or more statistics from the real-world observations and corresponding statistics from the model output data. The two sets of statistics are then compared without the use of a formal statistical procedure. An inspection approach may provide valuable insight into the adequacy of a simulation model for certain simulations. In this Section, 5 scenarios are investigated to verify the proposed, Markov process-based, risk propagation model.

First of all, in order to verify the proposed model, the elements of the risk propagation model (that is, threat-states, initial vector, and threat transition matrix) are defined using the statistics on hacking and virus attack reported by KISA for 42 months, from January 2001 to June 2004. Next, using this model, the frequency of threat-occurrence for 1 year, from July 2004 to June 2005, is calculated. Finally, the one-year *EF* calculated from the proposed model is compared with the real frequency as presented by KISA.

Scenario 1. In *Scenario 1*, three different ranges are used to calculate the median: 1 month, an average of 2 months, and an average of 6 months. The simulation condition is as follows:

- ***Median:*** the ranges to calculate the median are divided into 3 cases: 1 month, an average of 2 months and an average of 6 months
- Initial vector: the most recent 6-month frequency data are used to calculate the initial vector. Furthermore, the initial vector is changed every month
- Threat-states transition matrix: the transition matrix is changed every 6 months

The simulation result of *Scenario 1* is presented in Fig. 1.

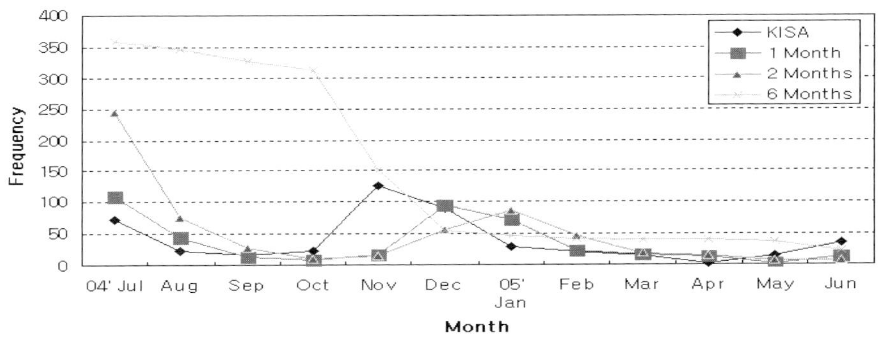

Fig. 1. Simulation result of Scenario 1

In the simulation result with 1 month set as the median range, the frequency of threat-occurrence is closer to the real frequency reported by KISA than using 2- and 6-month medians, i.e., a more precise result is obtained with a shorter range.

Scenario 2. In *Scenario 2*, three different ranges are used to calculate the initial probability vector: 3 months, 6 months, and 1 year. The simulation condition is as follows:

- Median: the most recent frequency data from the previous month are used to calculate the median. Furthermore, the median is changed every month
- ***Initial vector:*** the ranges to calculate the initial vector are divided into 3 cases: 3 months, 6 months and 1 year
- Threat-states transition matrix: the transition matrix is changed every 6 months

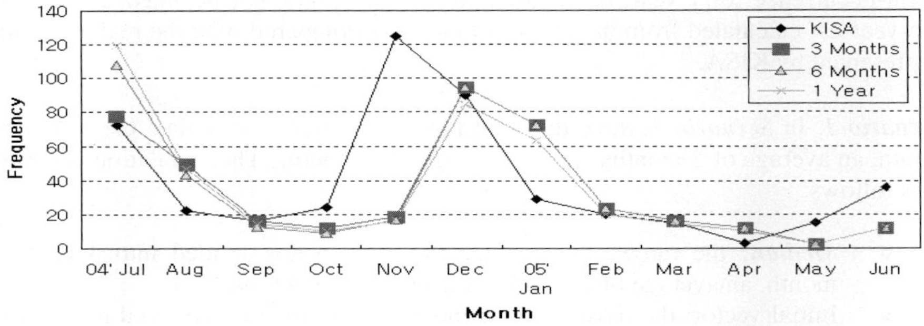

Fig. 2. Simulation result of Scenario 2

The simulation result of *Scenario 2* is presented in Fig. 2. As in *Scenario 1*, when the most recent frequency data is used as the range, the frequency of threat-occurrence is closer to the real frequency reported by KISA, i.e., a more precise result is obtained with a range of 3 months to calculate the initial vector.

Scenario 3. In this scenario, the period of changing the transition matrix is divided into 3 cases: 3 months, 6 months and 1 year. The simulation condition is as follows:

- Median: the most recent one-month frequency data are used to calculate the median. Furthermore, the median is changed every month
- Initial vector: the most recent 6-month frequency data are used to calculate the initial vector. Furthermore, the initial vector is changed every month
- ***Threat-states transition matrix:*** In order to construct the transition matrix, the periods of changing the matrix are divided into 3 cases: 3 months, 6 months and 1 year

The simulation result of *Scenario 3* is presented in Fig. 3.

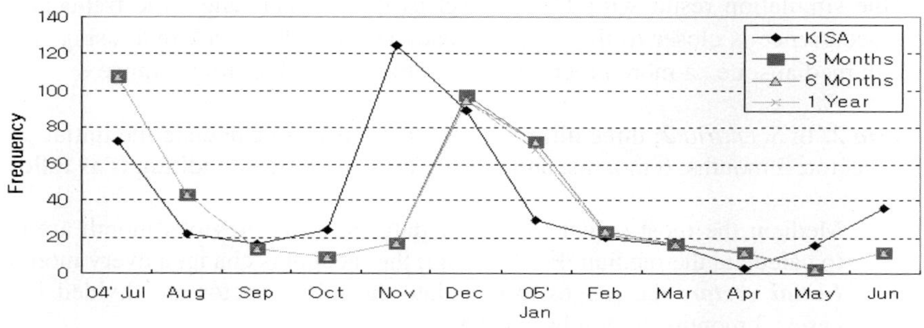

Fig. 3. Simulation result of Scenario 3

As shown in Fig. 3, the simulation results of the 3 cases are almost unaffected by the different period of changing the matrix. The period of changing the matrix hardly affects the frequency of threat-occurrence because the changes of the transition matrix are too small to create a new transition matrix, which is greatly different from the existing one.

Scenario 4. Six thresholds are applied in *Scenario 4*, unlike the previous three scenarios. The threat-states are divided into 2 cases: four threat-states and six threat-states. The simulation condition is as follows:

- Four threat-states : = S_1: 0~300, S_2: 301~600, S_3: 601~900, S_4: 901~1200
- Six threat-states := S_1: 0~200, S_2: 201~400, S_3: 401~600, S_4: 601~800, S_5: 801~1000, S_6: 1001~1200
- Median: the most recent one-month frequency data are used to calculate the median. Furthermore, the median is changed every month
- Initial vector: the most recent three-month frequency data are used to calculate the initial vector. Furthermore, the initial vector is changed every month
- Threat-states transition matrix: the transition matrix is changed every 6 months

The simulation result of *Scenario 4* is presented in Fig. 4.

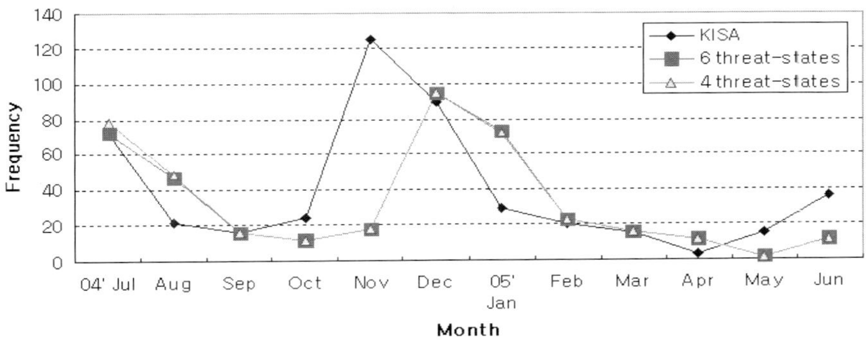

Fig. 4. Simulation result of Scenario 4

The simulation results of *Scenario 4* show a slight difference between the two cases. However, the amount of frequency data, which is applied to create the model proposed in this paper, was considered to be too small. As a result, a more precise result was obtained with a larger number of thresholds.

Scenario 5. In *Scenario 5*, the frequency of threat-occurrence is analyzed for cases of interrelated threats. The simulation condition is as follows:

- Thresholds of T_1 := H_1: 0~400, H_2: 401~800, H_3: 801~1200
- Thresholds of T_2 := W_1: 0~4000, W_2: 4001~8000, W_3: Over 8001

- Median: the most recent one-month frequency data are used to calculate the median. Furthermore, the median is changed every month
- Initial vector: the most recent 6-month frequency data are used to calculate the initial vector. Furthermore, the initial vector is changed every month
- Threat-states transition matrix: the transition matrix is changed every 6 months

The simulation result of *Scenario 5* is presented in Figs. 5 and Fig. 6.

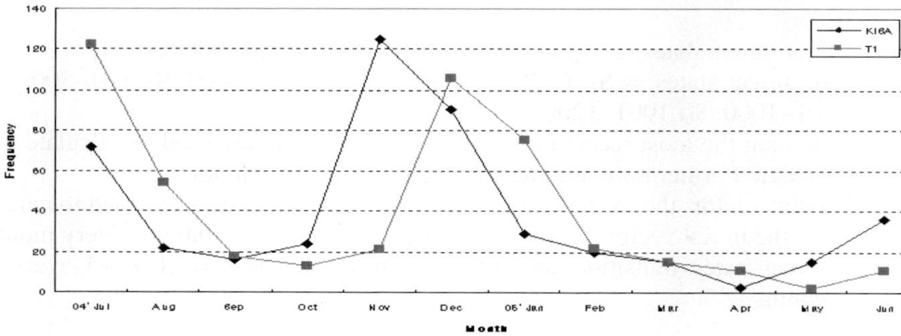

Fig. 5. Simulation result of Scenario 5 (T_1)

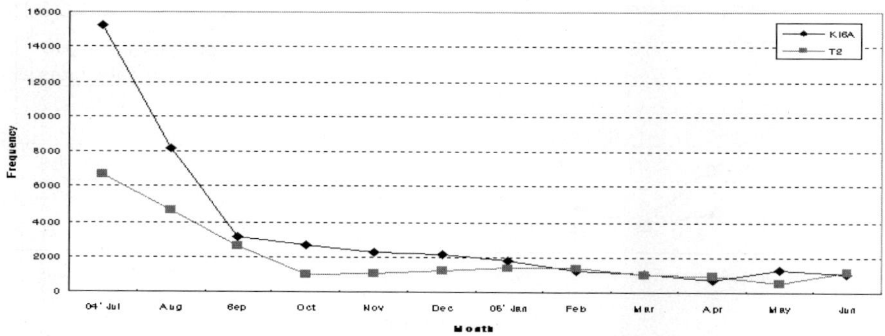

Fig. 6. Simulation result of Scenario 5 (T_2)

The number of thresholds is 4 for the independent threats of Scenarios 1 to 4, but is 3 in *Scenario 5*. That is, the simulation result of the *EF* for T_1 is different between *Scenario 5* and the previous 4 scenarios due to the different number of thresholds. From the simulation result of *Scenario 5* for T_2, the *EF* estimated by the proposed model is close to the real frequency presented by KISA.

Through the simulation result of the 5 scenarios, the *EF* estimated by the Markov process-based risk propagation model is generally close to the real frequency, except for specific months such as Nov. 2004 for T_1, due to the new emergence of malicious applications such as Netbus and Subsevens, and Jul. 2004 for T_2, due to the new emergence of an Internet worm. Further requirements are necessary to obtain a more precise estimation in the proposed model [4]. First, the estimation, which is close to the real occurrence of a threat, is decided by subdivision of the threshold, i.e., more precise data can be obtained with a larger the number of thresholds. Second, the scope of the most recent data to define the Initial Probability should be considered. Third, statistically analysis is required. In this paper, although the past data of each month is used, a more precise result can be obtained than if past data is used relative to the date or week.

4 Related Work

Several research efforts have been made to model risk propagation, especially for viruses and worms. Two classical epidemic models are initially introduced. A simple epidemic model is a simple model of an epidemic of an infectious disease in a population [10, 11,12]. It is assumed that the population consists of two types of individuals, whose numbers are denoted by the letters S and I, which are susceptible individuals, who do not presently have the disease but are susceptible, and infective individuals, who have the disease and can infect others, respectively. That is, this model assumes that each host stays in only one of two states: susceptible or infective. These are, of course, functions of time. The second epidemic model is the Kermack-Mckendrick (KM) epidemic model [9, 11, 13], which adds a third state, R (removed), into the simple epidemic model. R is the number of removed individuals, who cannot be infected by the disease or infect others with the disease. This is called an SIR model due to the S→I→R possible state transition. Various propagation models extend from these two epidemic models. Although the KM model improves the simple epidemic model by considering the possibility for some infectious hosts to either recover or die after some time, this model is not suitable for modeling worm propagation because it does not consider human countermeasures. The two-factor worm model considers the effect of human countermeasures and the congestions caused by worm scan traffic [13, 14]. In the Internet, countermeasures such as cleaning, patching, and filtering against worms will remove both susceptible and infectious hosts from circulation in the KM model. Zou et al. and Moore et al. study the effect of quarantine on the Internet level to constrain worm propagation [14, 15]. They show that an infectious host has a number of paths to a target due to the high connectivity of the Internet. Therefore, they can prevent the wide spread of a worm on the Internet level by analyzing the effect of quarantine on the Internet. Chen et al. and Vogt present a discrete-time worm model that considers the patching and cleaning during worm propagation [16, 17]. As shown previously, most risk propagation models focus on viruses and worms and therefore cannot be applied to the diverse threats faced by modern information systems.

5 Conclusion

This paper has briefly presented a probabilistic model of security risk propagation based on the Markov process, which can estimate the spread of risk when attacks occur from diverse threats as well as viruses and worms. Furthermore, the proposed model was verified by running five scenario-based simulations. The simulation results confirmed the close agreement of the *EF* estimated by the Markov process-based, risk propagation model over a one-year period with the real frequency as presented by KISA, except for two specific months: Nov. 2004 for T_1, due to the new emergence of malicious applications such as Netbus and Subsevens, and Jul. 2004 for T_2, due to the new emergence of an Internet worm. Future research will therefore need to focus on a suitable and effective method to deal with the regular appearance of a diverse range of threats to information systems.

References

1. In, H.P., Kim, Y.-G., Lee, T., Moon, C.-J., Jung, Y.-J., Kim, I., Baik, D.-K.: A Security Analysis Model for Information Systems. In: Baik, D.-K. (ed.) Systems Modeling and Simulation: Theory and Applications. LNCS (LNAI), vol. 3398, pp. 505–513. Springer, Heidelberg (2005)
2. Stoneburner, G., Goguen, A., Feringa, A.: Risk Management Guide for Information Technology Systems, NIST Special Publication 800-30, NIST (2002)
3. GAO: Information Security Risk Assetment-Practices of Leading Organizations. GAO/AIMD-00-33 (1999)
4. Kim, Y.-G, Lee, T., In, H.P., Jung, Y.-J., Kim, I., Baik, D.-K.: A Probabilistic Approach to Estimate the Damage Propagation of Cyber Attacks. In: Won, D.H., Kim, S. (eds.) Information Security and Cryptology - ICISC 2005. LNCS, vol. 3935, pp. 175–185. Springer, Heidelberg (2006)
5. Kim, Y.-G., Jeong, D., Park, S.-H., Baik, D.-K.: Simulation of Risk Propagation Model in Information Systems. In: Proc. of the 2006 International Conference on Computational Intelligence and Security (CIS 2006), pp. 1555–1558. IEEE Computer Society Press, Los Alamitos (2006)
6. Trivedi, K.S.: Probability and Statistics with Reliability, Queuing and Computer Science Applications. In: Probability and Statistics with Reliability, Queuing and Computer Science Applications, 2nd edn. WILEY Interscience, New York (2002)
7. Yates, R.D., Goodman, D.J.: Probability and Stochastic Process. 2nd edn. WILEY International, New York (2003)
8. KISA: Statistics and Analysis on Hacking and Virus, http://www.krcert.or.kr
9. Law, A., Kelton, W.: Simulation Modeling and Analysis, 3rd edn. McGraw-Hill Higher Education, New York (2000)
10. Frauenthal, J.C.: Mathematical Modeling in Epidemiology. Springer, New York (1980)
11. Deley, D.J., Gani, J.: Epidemic Modeling: An Introduction. Cambridge University Press, Cambridge (1999)
12. Staniford, S., Paxson, V., Weaver, N.: How to Own the Internet in Your Spare Time. In: Proc. of the 11th USENIX Security Symposium (Security02) (2002)
13. Zou, C.C., Gong, W., Towsley, D.: Worm Propagation Modeling and Analysis under Dynamic Quarantine Defense. In: Proc. of the ACM CCS Workshop on Rapid Malcode (WORM'03), ACM Press, New York (2003)
14. Zou, C.C., Gong, W., Towsley, D.: Code Red Worm Propagation Modeling and Analysis. In: Proc. of the proceedings of the 9th ACM Conference on Computer and Communications Security, pp. 138–147. ACM Press, New York (2002)
15. Moore, D., Shannon, C., Voelker, G.M., Savage, S.: Internet Quarantine: Requirements for Containing Self-Propagating Code. In: In: Proc. of the proceedings of IEEE INFOCOM, IEEE Computer Society Press, Los Alamitos (2003)
16. Chen, Z., Gao, L., Kwiat, K.: Modeling the Spread of Active Worms. In: Proc. of the proceedings of IEEE INFOCOM2003, IEEE Computer Society Press, Los Alamitos (2003)
17. Vogt, T.: Simulating and Optimising Worm Propagation Algorithms (2003), http://web.lemuria.org/security/WormPropagation.pdf

Information Assurance Evaluation for Network Information Systems

Xin Lü[1] and Zhi Ma[2]

[1] State Information Center, No. 58 Sanlihe Road, Beijing, 100045, China
lux@cei.gov.cn
[2] Department of Information Research, PLA Information Engineering University, Zhengzhou, 450002, China
muzinihao@hotmail.com

Abstract. In both the public and private sectors, organizations have become significantly depend over on the proper functioning of information systems. As security spending continues to rise, organizations contend that metrics initiatives will become critical to managing and understanding the impact of information security programs. This paper reviews information assurance (IA) conceptions from viewpoint of system science and analyses the construction of IA systems. An IA evaluation model is addressed in this paper, which is depicted by IA capability index, IA countermeasure index and IA cost index. This evaluation model can be used for organizations to assess their IA strategies and analyzes their security state.

1 Introduction

Rapidly advancing information-based technologies and increasingly competitive global environment have drive information into the center stage in society, government now. Information becomes the important national and organizational resource, which has natural and social properties independent of matter and energy. The most popular definition of information is a message or communication. However, a message is not information because the same message can contain information for one person and no information for another person. In 1928, Hartley defined information as the eliminated uncertainty [1]. Information can also be defined as the eliminated uncertainty or reflected variety [2]. These definitions are based on Shannon's information theory, which represents a statistical approach to information. Warren Weaver gave the three levels of problems in communication, which can be described as the technical problem, the semantic problem and the effectiveness problem. The technical problem cares about the accuracy that the symbols of communication be transmitted. The semantic problem cares about the precise that the transmitted symbols convey the desired meaning. The effectiveness concerns the pragmatics and the use or function of language. The broad research object of information science is the information acquisition, information transformation, information processing, information decision and information effectiveness.

Y. Wang, Y. Cheung, and H. Liu (Eds.): CIS 2006, LNAI 4456, pp. 869–877, 2007.

Information security is one of the cornerstones of the Information Society. Confidentiality within a virtual enterprise, integrity of financial transactions, authenticity for electronic signatures, privacy of personal information, reliability of critical infrastructure, all depend on the availability of trustworthy security mechanisms. In a popular view, information security has experienced communication security phase (COMSEC), information security phase (INFOSEC) and information Assurance phase (IA) [3,6,7,8,9]. Information assurance is about protecting information assets from destruction, degradation, manipulation and exploitation by an opponent. DOD perspective, JP 3-13 provides a widely accepted definition of IA. IA protects and defends information and information systems by ensuring their availability, integrity, identification and authentication, confidentiality, and non-repudiation [10,11]. This includes providing for the restoration of information systems by incorporating protection, detection, and reaction capabilities. IA employs technologies and processes such as multilevel security, access controls, secure network servers, and intrusion detection software. IA's Goals and Objectives are to minimize the probability of information assurance vulnerability, to minimize the damage if vulnerability is exploited and to provide methods to recover efficiently and effectively from the damage.

More important, security evaluation provide a mechanism for information systems security management and feed a process toward continuous security improvement. In section 2, we define IA model based on system science methodologies and describe the key security services, IA risks and IA countermeasures. Section 3 propose an IA evaluation model and metrics indices. Conclusions are made in section 4.

2 IA Model and IA Systems

2.1 IA Model

Information security theoretical models have been intensively studied in the last thirty years. The Bell-LaPadula Model (BLM), also called the multi-level model, was addressed by Bell and LaPadula, is one of the fundamental models of computer security, which was designed for enforcing access control in government and

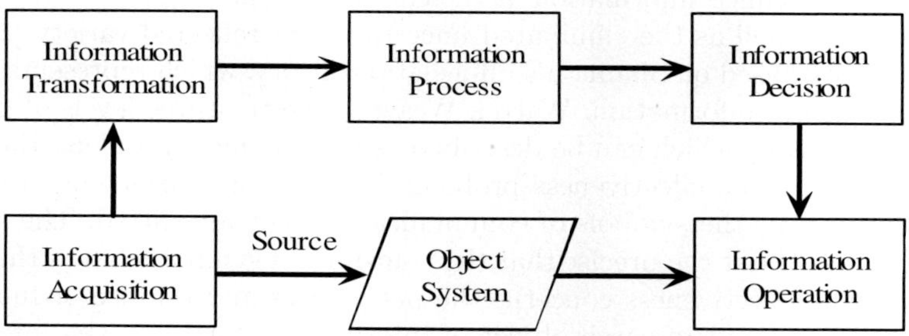

Fig. 1. Information flow in an information system

military applications [4]. In this model, subjects and objects are often partitioned into different security levels. A subject can only access objects at certain levels determined by his security level. David *et al.* proposed a very interesting and intriguing commercial security model, the Chinese Wall model [5], and showed that it couldn't be correctly represented by a Bell-LaPadula model. McCumber presented an INFOSEC model, also known as McCumber Cube model, which is always used as a structured methodology to assessing and managing security risk in IT systems [6,7]. However, McCumber Cube model is not enough to be used as an IA model because it concerns only about the states and security characters of "information". In IA model, both information and information system are the protected objects.

The word "system" is used to describe any "experience-cluster" that we can map as a set of interacting elements over time. Information system includes the entire infrastructure, personnel, organization, and components that collect, store, transmit, disseminate, and act on information. Typically a system is mapped by identifying the pathways of information flow, as well as possibly the flow of energy, matter and other variables. The information flow of an information system can be depicted as Fig.1.

In this paper, an IA system is defined as a system to provide security technology, security management and personnel to protect information and information system from destruction by all kinds of threat, such as natural threat, intentional threat and unintentional threat (see Fig.2.).

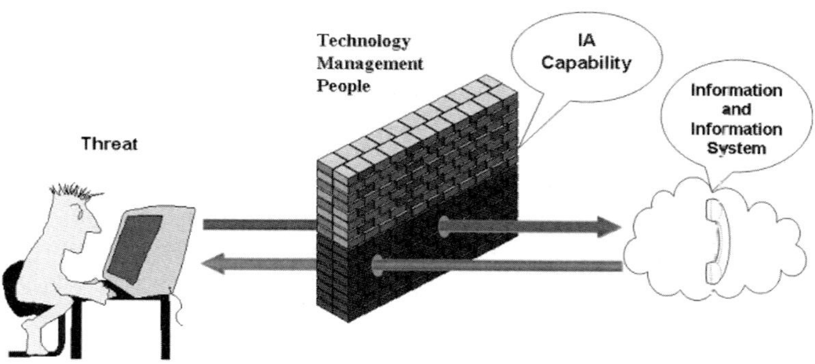

Fig. 2. IA systems

2.2 The Security Services for Information and Information System

The main object of an IA system is to provide five security services for information and information system: confidentiality, integrity, availability, authenticity and non-repudiation.

Confidentiality ensures that information is not available or disclosed to unauthorized individuals, entities, or processes.

Integrity means that data has not been altered or destroyed in an unauthorized manner.

Availability means that the information and information systems can always be timely and reliable accessible by authorized entities. Availability is regarded as a function, which is not entirely security.

Confidentiality, integrity, availability are the basic security service for an information system, which are also know as CIA model.

Authenticity indicates the corroboration that the source of data received is as claimed.

Non-repudiation requires the recipient of data to provide proof of the origin of data.

2.3 IA Risk

As is well known, information security risk of computer systems is tied to two factors: internal vulnerabilities and external threats. The internal vulnerabilities are flaws or weakness that expose the system to harm. The external threat is a intentional or unintentional event, which could destroy the system by employ one or more vulnerabilities.

2.3.1 Vulnerabilities

Vulnerability is defined as the degree to which a software system or component is open to unauthorized access, change, or disclosure of information and is susceptible to interference or disruption of system services. Fig.3 illustrates the increasing trend in Vulnerability reported by the Computer Emergency Response Team Coordination Center (CERT/CC).

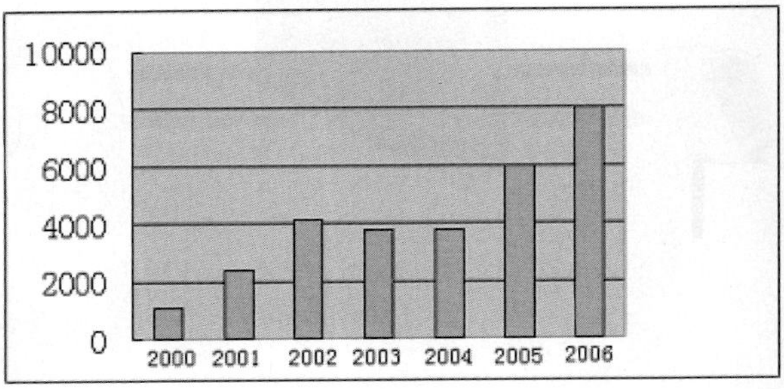

Fig. 3. Vulnerabilities reported from 2000 to 2006 by CERT/CC

2.3.2 Threat

In the context of information assurance, a threat to a system can be defined as: "a circumstance or event that has the potential to cause harm by violating security of an information system". There are several types of threat in the information world includes: the insider, the hacker, the criminal, industrial or economic espionage and the terrorists.

Recently, botnet, social engineering, phishing and Zero-day are new rising type of attacks which challenge the network protection policies and the traditional information security products.

Botnet attacks take advantage of programs that secretly install themselves on thousands of personal computers and use them to commit Internet crimes.

For a social engineering attack, an attacker uses human interaction to obtain or compromise information about organizations or their computer systems. The attackers may claim to be a new employee, repair person, or researcher and even offering credentials to support that identity.

Phishing is a form of social engineering, which is a technique used to gain personal information for purposes of identity theft and seeking financial benefits. Symantec detected 157,477 unique phishing messages in the first half of 2006, up 81 from the last six months of 2005. Home PCs were targets of 86 of security threats in the first six months of 2006, according to the Symantec report.

Zero-day attack can be defined as a virus or other exploit that takes advantage of a newly discovered hole in certain program or operating system before the software developer has made a fix available, or before they are even aware the hole exists.

2.4 IA Countermeasures

(1) Technique
Technology, in a security context now includes access control, identification and authentication,crypto systems, , system and communication protection audit and accountability, physical and environment protection, security protocols etc.

(2) Management
IA management is the process of achieving objectives using a given set of security resources. IA management includes risk assessment, planning, system and services acquisition, certification, accreditation, maintenance, policy, standards, law, procedures and so on.

(3) People
People are the most critical link in the information assurance program. This aspect of IA includes security personnel and the security of personnel. People require security awareness, education and training when designing, using, managing the information systems. IA awareness is very important in the IA process due to that most of attacks and incidents, according to FBI, are form the internal of the organizations. IA training and education is also the fundamental to development IA technology in companies and construct complete IA management systems.

3 Evaluation of IA Systems

3.1 IA Evaluation Indicator Systems

The proposed IA evaluation model includes IA capability index, IA countermeasure index and IA cost index , which is described in Fig.4.

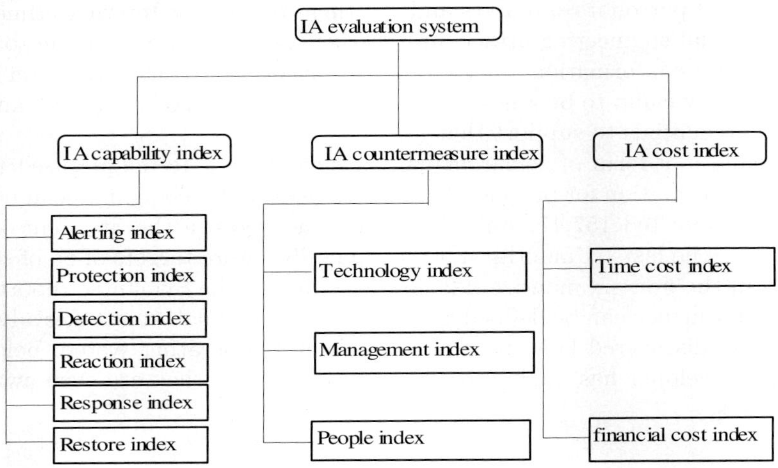

Fig. 4. IA evaluation indicator systems

3.1.1 IA Capabilities Index

In many professionals' views, information assurance can be regarded as one complete system or a process. The Alerting-Protection-Detection-Response-Restore-Counterattack (APDRRC) capability model is a true system, which is a holistic approach to deal with IA problems.

(1) Alerting, noted as *al*, means that preventing an accident or eradicating an attack before they comes. Security warning procedure and alerting organization, such as US-CERT and CN-CERT, should be established. These organizations alert users to potential threats to the security of their systems and provide timely messages about how to avoid, minimize, or recover from the damage.
(2) Protection, noted as *pr*, deals with the issues of ensuring the confidentiality, integrity, availability, authenticity and non-repudiation of information and the survivability, reliability of information systems from destruction and intrusion.
(3) Detection. Timely and exactly detection of the existence of attacker and incidents is the key to initiating restoration and attacker response. Regardless of the type of attack, the earlier an intrusion is detected, the quicker a appropriate response can be initiated. Detection can be noted as *de*.

(4) Reaction. The first task of organization, when attack is detected, is to stop the attack and to mitigate the risk to a low and accepted level. The second task is to collect evidence to facilitate legal action. The third task is to set up formal reporting procedure. Security incidents should be reported through appropriate channel as quickly as possible.Reaction can be noted as rea.

(5) Restoration. The objective of an effective reaction is to restore the availability, confidentiality, and integrity etc. of information and information systems to their original or accepted state. It requires backup strategy based on its ability to meet the organization's needs in terms of time required to restore the data and return the information system to an operational state. Restoration can be noted as res.

(6) Counterattack, by attacking the peacebreaker's system or take the legal steps to hold the peacebreaker accountable, is part of IA in some cases. Counterattack can be noted as ct.

3.1.2 IA Countermeasure Index

The IA countermeasure can be obtained from IA technology index, IA management index and IA people index.

3.1.3 IA Cost Index

In the process to build IA system, cost must be taken into account because almost all the organizations aim at obtaining the greatest return on investment. In this research, IA costs can be classified into three categories: time cost, personal cost and financial cost.

3.2 IA Evaluation Model

Following the general system theory used in Bell-La-Padula security model [12], we regard IA capability as IA, IA cost as CST, IA countermeasures as C and note time as T. Thus the state of an information system's IA state can be written as

$$y = (IA, CST, C, T) \in Y \tag{1}$$

where, $IA \in (al, pr, de, rea, res, ct)$ represents IA capabilities for certain information system, al, pr, de, rea, res, ct denote the capability of alerting, protect, detection, response, restore and counterattack respectively. $CST \in (tc, wc, fc)$ represents IA cost, which includes time cost, personal workforce and financial cost for IA system. $C \in (t, m, p)$ represents IA countermeasures, t, m, p denote technology countermeasures, management countermeasures and people countermeasures respectively.

A system's IA baseline describes the basic requirements for IA capabilities, IA cost and IA countermeasures (see Fig.5), and the baseline equation can be written as

$$f_B = F(IA_B, CST_B, C_B) \tag{2}$$

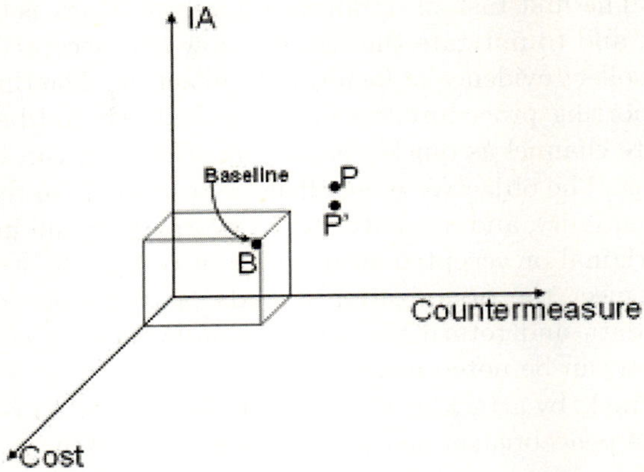

Fig. 5. IA evaluation indicator systems

When a system's IA state is P, which satisfies $f_P \geq f_B$, we say that the system satisfies the baseline requirements. Otherwise, the system does not meet the basic security requirements. For IA strategies P and P' within the same information system, if $IA_P = IA_{P'}$, $C_P = C_{P'}$ and $CST_P < CST_{P'}$, then we say that the IA strategies of P is better than the IA strategies of P'.

4 Conclusions

Along with the rapid breakthrough of information applications and the increase of information sharing, the problem of information security has become a main issue of the whole society. Theoretical model for information assurance is studied in this paper, which can be used in information security policy design for organizations. This paper proposed an IA evaluation model which is described by IA capability index, IA countermeasure index and IA cost index. This evaluation model can be used for an organization to devise IA plan and assessment the IA strategies of its information systems.

Acknowledgments. This work was supported by the Postdoctoral Science Foundation of China under Grant No.20060400048 and the Natural Science Foundation of China under Grant No.60403004.

References

1. Hartley R.V.L.: Transmission of Information. In: Bell System Techn. vol. 1928(3) 535–563
2. Shannon, C.E.: Mathematical Theory of CommunicationBSTJ1948
3. British Standards Institute, Code of practice for information security management, BS 7799, London (1999)

4. Bell, D., Padula, L.: Security Computing Systems: Mathematical Foundation and Model. MITRE Report, Bedbord, MA (1975)
5. David, F.C.B., Michael, N.: The Chinese Wall Security Policy. In: IEEE Symposium on Research in Security and Privacy, pp. 206–214 (1989)
6. McCumber, J.: Information Systems Security: A Comprehensive Model. In: Proceedings 14th National Computer Security Conference. National Institute of Standards and Technology. Baltimore, MD (October 1991)
7. Maconachy, W.V., Schou, C.D., Ragsdale, D., Welch, D.: A Model for Information Assurance: An Integrated Approach. In: Proceedings of the, IEEE Workshop on Information Assurance and Security United States Military Academy, 2001, pp. 306–310 (2001)
8. ITU X.800. Security Architecture for Open Systems Interconnection for CCITT Applications (1991)
9. National Security Agency. National Information Systems Security Glossary. NSTISSI 4009 Fort Meade, MD (Septemper 2000)
10. Information Assurance Technical Framework, National Security Agency Information Assurance Solutions Technical Directors (September 2002)
11. Zhao, Z.S.: Lectures on Information Assurance. State Key Lab of Information Security, Chinese Academy of Sciences (In Chinese) (2005)
12. Chen, X., Zheng, Q., Guan, X. et al.: Multiple behavior information fusion based quantitative threat evaluation. Computers and Security 24, 218–231 (2005)

Simulation and Analysis of DDoS in Active Defense Environment*

Zhongwen Li[1], Yang Xiang[2], and Dongsheng He[3]

[1] Information Science and Technology College,
Xiamen University
Xiamen 361005, China
lizw@xmu.edu.cn

[2] School of Management and Information Systems
Faculty of Business and Informatics Central
Queensland University
Rockhampton, Queensland 4702, Australia
y.xiang@cqu.edu.au

[3] School of Architecture Engineering,
Southwest Petroleum University
Xindu 610500, China
dongsheng_he@sina.com

Abstract. Currently there is very few data that can describe the whole profile of a DDoS attack. In this paper, the active DDoS defense system deploys a number of sub-systems, such as Flexible Deterministic Packet Marking (FDPM) and Mark-Aided Distributed Filtering (MADF). In addition, two DDoS tools, TFN2K and Trinoo, are adopted and integrated into SSFNet to create virtual DDoS networks to simulate the attacks. Then, simulation experiments are used to evaluate the performance of the active DDoS defense system. At last, we set up a model to describe the interactions between DDoS attack and defense party, which allows us to have a deep insight of the interactions between the attack and defense parties. Experiment results shows that the model can precisely estimate the defense effectiveness of the system when it encounters attacks.

1 Introduction

Nowadays there have been many DDoS defense techniques proposed such as anomaly detection, congestion control, filtering, traceback and replication. Many were proven (under some preset conditions and assumptions) to be effective, at some level, to mitigate the sufferings of victim host or network that are caused by the DDoS flood. There are also some DDoS defense systems in the literature, such as D-WARD [1] and SOS [2]. Most of the current defense systems are passive, which means the defense actions are taken only after the DDoS attacks are launched. In order to

---

* This work is supported partly by national natural science grant (50674077), Fujian natural science grant (A0410004), Guangdong natural science grant (06029667), NCETXMU 2004 program (0000-X07116), and Xiamen University research foundation (0630-E23011).

Y. Wang, Y. Cheung, and H. Liu (Eds.): CIS 2006, LNAI 4456, pp. 878–886, 2007.

suppress the attack as early as possible, we need an active DDoS defense system, which is first proposed in [3]. In the functional range of active defense approaches, the defense system can protect victims before the attacks start.

Currently there is very few data that can describe the whole profile of a DDoS attack. The MIT and UCLA data sets can not picture the whole profile of an attack in terms of scale, time, and resemblance to real attacks. In this paper, besides those data sets that contain clean training data and labeled attack data, we also use the data generated by an SSFNet simulator [4] and the embedded DDoS tools [5]. After evaluating the performance of our active DDoS defense system, we propose an analytical model based on the experiments on DDoS defense for the interactions between DDoS attack party and defense party.

The rest of the paper is organized as follows. Section 2 introduces our experiments on active DDoS defense. Section 3 provides the basic analytical model for DDoS attack and defense. Section 4 gives inconstant strengths of both parties. Section 5 draws the conclusions.

2 Experiments on Active DDoS Defense

2.1 Simulation and Metrics

The reasons of choosing a simulator to generate data are first, to obtain hardware resources such as hosts and networks could be very expensive; second, although to launch DDoS attacks in a laboratory or in a real world network and collect data could be direct, it might not be legal and practical; third, it is not easy to change real network topology to create different scenarios; and finally, it is difficult to control the attack process in a real environment because there are too many factors that can affect the result.

The distributed active DDoS defense system deploys a number of sub-systems (such as Mark-Aided Distributed Filtering (MADF) [6]). MADF gathers the intelligence by the marks in the previous scheme, by using neural networks to detect anomalies. Simulation experiments are conducted by using SSFNet simulator to evaluate the performance of the distributed active DDoS defense system. TFN2K and Trinoo [7] are integrated into SSFNet to create virtual DDoS networks to simulate the attacks . In order to simulate the DDoS attack as real as possible, we also use the real Internet topology from Cooperative Association for Internet Data Analysis (CAIDA)'s Skitter project [8]. The data set used is generated from server aroot ipv4.20040120 on 09/Jan/2004. To simplify the problem, we connect all routers by 100M network interfaces. We randomly choose the 1000 attack hosts and let the rest be legitimate clients, and let the Skitter server be the victim. Constant rate attack of 300KBps is applied to all attack hosts. According to the hop distribution (number of routers between the victim and its clients), most of the clients locate in the distance between 10 hops and 25 hops. Therefore, we deploy the FDPM [9] (Flexible Deterministic Packet Marking) encoding module at routers 10 hops from the victim, and the MADF at routers from 1 to 9 hops from the victim.

To measure the performance of the defense system we use average value of legitimate traffic passed rate (LTPR) and attack traffic passed rate (ATPR) of distributed filtering systems. Let

$$LTPR = \frac{Number\_of\_legitimate\_packets\_passed}{Number\_of\_total\_legitimate\_packets}. \quad (1)$$

$$ATPR = \frac{Number\_of\_attack\_packets\_passed}{Number\_of\_total\_attack\_packets}. \quad (2)$$

Another criterion to measure the performance is the LTPR/ATPR ratio LAR , as it is shown in formula (3).

$$LAR = \frac{LTPR}{ATPR}. \quad (3)$$

A perfect DDoS defense system can achieve this value of $+\infty$ because the denominator ATPR will reach 0. On the other hand, a worst case of defense system has this value of 0 because the numerator LTPR will reach 0. Therefore, a high LAR indicates a strong defense system. Besides the above criteria, we also introduce a network flooding ratio NFR as in formula (4) because the above criteria can only denote how good the filtering function is, but can not denote the overall defense result of a distributed defense. As we discussed before, like other distributed defense systems, MADF can be deployed at any point between the source end (one hop behind FDPM encoding module) and the victim end. A criterion is needed to measure the effectiveness of a defense system in preventing the overall network flooding caused by DDoS attacks. Unfortunately, most research that has been done so far did not pay much attention to this important criterion. Obviously, a low NFR represents a strong distributed defense to protect the whole network. Let

$$NFR = \frac{\sum_{i=1}^{n} Num\_of\_attack\_packets\_passed\_in\_router(i)}{\sum_{i=1}^{n} Num\_of\_total\_packets\_passed\_in\_router(i)} \quad (4)$$

Where n is the total number of routers in the whole network.

2.2 Evaluation

We deploy MADF at different distances from the victim and conduct experiments based on both TFN2K and Trinoo DDoS simulator tools. Random algorithms in SSFNet are used to generate legitimate traffic. After the neural network is trained, the DDoS tools are initiated to start the attack with different attack rates. Then the traffic on the deployment points is monitored. Figure 1 show the average values of LTPR and ATPR at routers located at different hops from the victim. From the figures we can see our scheme can filter out most of the attack traffic and let most of the legitimate traffic pass through. These two figures also show that both LTPR and ATPR decrease gradually as the defense systems are deployed closer to the attack source end. This proofs MADF can be deployed at any place in the protect network without sacrificing much performance because at the source end it only loses a little LTPR but decreases ATPR as well, which is one of our goals (a low ATPR).

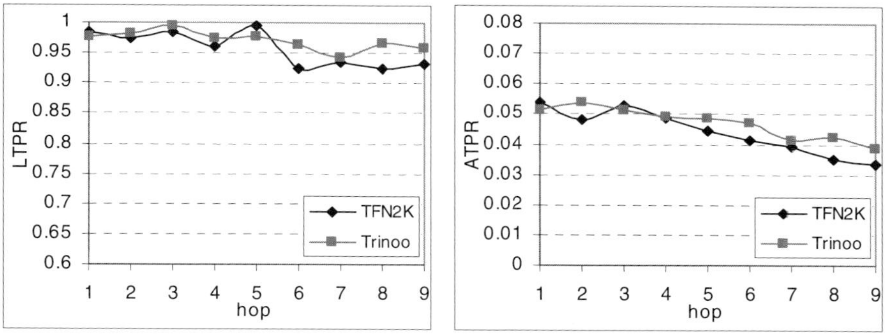

Fig. 1. Average LTPR and ATPR at different distances

Figure 2(a) shows the LTPR/ATPR ratio LAR at different routers from the victim. The value is from 18.32 to 27.71, which means a strong and precise filtering. Our system is better than many other current defense systems in terms of LAR. For example, the best LAR of Pi [10] is about 7 and the intelligent packet filtering [11] is about 18, which both are lower than MADF. Moreover, from this figure we can see the LAR becomes higher when the system is deployed closer to the attack sources (LARhop9>LARhop1). This gives the justification to support the argument of the mixture of both source end and victim end deployment instead of the traditional victim end deployment. Figure 2(b) shows the relationship between the LAR and the LTPR. The LAR increases according to the raise of the LTPR. This also proves that the system can let more legitimate traffic pass through while let less attack traffic pass through. Additionally, these 3 curves show the system can obtain higher LAR for stronger DDoS attacks (LAR300KBps> LAR100KBps).

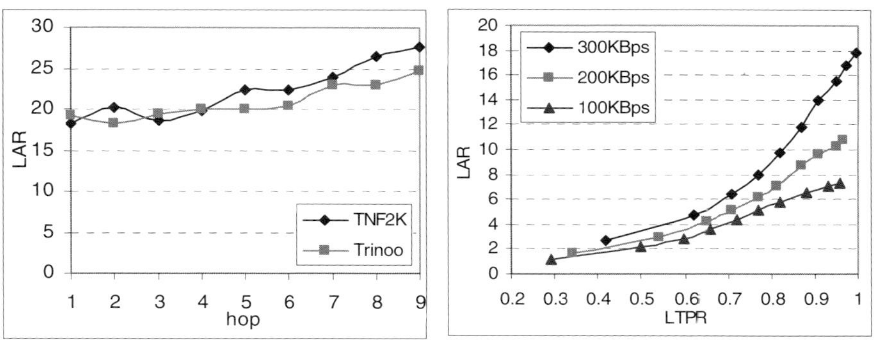

(a) (b)

Fig. 2. Analysis of LAR

By using the definition in formula (4) we obtain the network flooding ratio NFR curves of both TNF2K and Trinoo attacks at 300KBps attack rate in figure 3 When the defense system is deployed close to the victim end, most of the network is still saturated by the attack packets (0.2741 for TFN2K and 0.2845 for Trinoo at hop 1). However, when it is deployed close to the source end, this value gradually decreases to a very low level (0.0154 for TFN2K and 0.0162 for Trinoo at hop 9). Therefore, this figure shows the NFR decreases when the system is deployed closer to the attack sources. This is another justification to support argument of the mixture of both source end and victim end deployment instead of the traditional victim end deployment. Moreover, it proves if MADF is properly deployed it can not only protect the single victim but also prevent overall network congestion.

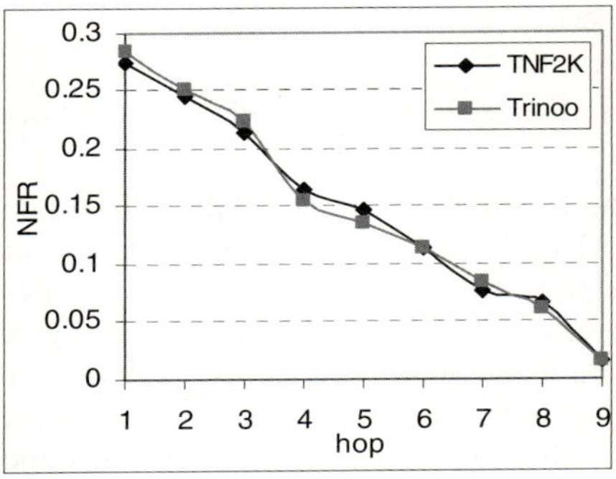

Fig. 3. NFR in the network

3 DDoS Modeling

3.1 Definitions and Assumptions

Definition 1 – strength functions. In a DDoS attack and defense scenario, there are two parties. One is the attack party X and the other is the defense party Y. Let x(t) and y(t) respectively denote the strength functions of the DDoS attack party X and defense party Y at time t. The strength function here means the function of the factors that can cause the part to win or lose. In order to simplify the problem, here we do not indicate what the factors are for each party, but just use the concept of strength function to establish the basic model. In section 3.2 we will instantiate the strength of defense as LTPR/ATPR ratio LAR.

Definition 2 – termination of the combat. The termination of the combat is defined as a stable condition after a period of time of interaction, either the attack traffic tends to a successful flood (attacker wins) or the defense system filters out most of the attack traffic (defender wins).

Assumption 1 – both x(t) and y(t) are continuous differentiable functions of time and are nonnegative. This idealization allows us to model the strength functions by differential equations. The minimum value of x(t) and y(t) is zero because any negative value has no physical meaning in practice.

Assumption 2 – the casualty rate for the attack party X is proportional to the strength of the defense party Y, and vice versa. This assumption is reasonable because in the actual cases if there are more powerful defense systems deployed then it would be less possibility for the attack party to win. On the contrary, if the attack part puts more resources such as attacking hosts then the defense party will more likely to lose. We model this assumption as these following two equations.

$$\frac{dx}{dt} = -ay, a > 0. \tag{5}$$

$$\frac{dy}{dt} = -bx, b > 0. \tag{6}$$

Where a is the rate that a defense party can mitigate the attack strength and b is the rate an attack party can deteriorate the defense strength. These two parameters are defined as attrition rates.

Assumption 3 – in this basic model the rate a and b are constant over time t and also independent on strength x and y. At the initial status t=0, we have

$$x(0) = x_0, y(0) = y_0, t = 0. \tag{7}$$

Solve the differential equation system in equation (5) and (6) by initial condition in equation (7) we have equation (8) and (9). Equation (8) can also be written as (10):

$$y(t) = y_0 \cos(\sqrt{ab}t) - x_0\sqrt{\frac{a}{b}}\sin(\sqrt{ab}t). \tag{8}$$

$$x(t) = x_0 \cos(\sqrt{ab}t) - y_0\sqrt{\frac{a}{b}}\sin(\sqrt{ab}t). \tag{9}$$

$$\frac{y(t)}{y_0} = \cos(\sqrt{ab}t) - \left(\frac{x_0}{y_0}\right)\sqrt{\frac{a}{b}}\sin(\sqrt{ab}t). \tag{10}$$

Where $y(t)/y_0$ means the normalized defense strength level, which depends on two parameters, $\sqrt{a/b}$ and $\sqrt{abt}$. The parameter $\sqrt{a/b}$ shows the relative effectiveness of the attack and defense parties. The parameter $\sqrt{ab}$ represents the intensity of the DDoS attack and defense scenario, which determines how quickly the scenario ends (defense party successes or attack party successes).

3.2 Validity of the Model

In this section we show the validity of the model by comparing the numerical performance with the experimental one. As we introduced in the previous section, the parameters a and b are obtained by the experiments then used to estimate the numerical performance.

In the model we instantiate the parameter a in equation (5) as the marking rate and solve the parameter b in equation (6) according to the experimental data. Because the above performance is the metric when the defense system approaches a stable status, the time factor in the model become not correlative with our results, and the actual correlation can be adjusted by the parameter a and b. The model is fitted with the experimental data of the attack rate 100KBps and the b can be evaluated as 8.780430744. We solve the model with parameter a and b and let the attack rate as 200KBps and 300KBps. Then the fitted LAR curves by numerical method of our model are obtained as figure 4.

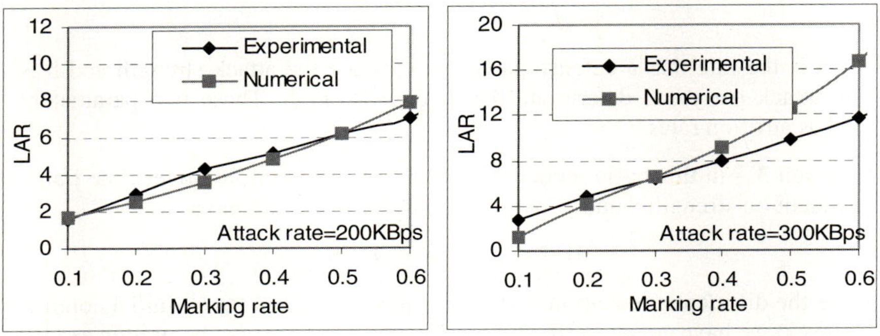

Fig. 4. Experimental and numerical curves of LAR

From figure 4 we can see when the attack rate is 200KBps the numerical curve from the model can fit very well will the experimental curve. This proves our analytical model can precisely estimate the effectiveness of the DDoS defense system under different scenarios. It is beneficial to know in advance the effectiveness of a defense system without experiencing many different real attacks. Moreover, this estimation can give a guide that how secure is the system and how much reinforcement is needed. From figure 4 when the attack rate is 300KBps the numerical curve can also fit well with the experimental curve, although more errors occur in this situation than the one of 200KBps attack rate. Actually we can expand this model with the non-constant parameters a and b to have a more flexible model (the expanded model results in better fit). However, to setup these sub-models is beyond the scope of this paper.

4 Strengths of Both Parties

Assumption 3 assumes the constant rates a and b for the basic model. However, in many real cases these rates are changing over time. Then we have $a=a(t)$ and $b=b(t)$, in which these rates become time dependent functions. In some cases the rates become not only dependent on time but also dependent on the strengths of the two parties. Then we have

$$a = a(t, x, y) \tag{11}$$

$$b = b(t, x, y) \tag{12}$$

In some cases the functions in equation (11) and (12) are dependent on the strength of opposite parties. We start the analysis with the simple assumptions as follows.

Assumption 4 – The attrition rates in both parties are dependent on the number of attack/defense points. Here the attack points can be the zombie hosts that a DDoS attacker recruit. The defense points can be the filtering sub-systems that are deployed in different places. In the real cases, it is reasonable if more points for each party result in better performance for their tasks.

Assumption 5 – Both attack and defense parties have enough resources to perform their tasks. We will not consider the factors of economics when we analyze this model.

Assumption 6 – Both attack and defense parties will not retreat and reinforce their attack/defense points. Moreover, there is no operation loss for both parties.

Then the basic model in equation (5) and (6) become

$$\frac{dx}{dt} = -gxy, g > 0 \tag{13}$$

$$\frac{dy}{dt} = -hyx, h > 0 \tag{14}$$

Integrate the above equations by the initial conditions when t=0, x=x_0 and y=y_0 we have

$$g(y - y_0) = h(x - x_0) \tag{15}$$

Let

$$K = gy_0 - hx_0 \tag{16}$$

We have

$$gy - hx = K \tag{17}$$

For the condition of K>0, the defense party wins, otherwise the attack party wins. The condition can also be written as

$$\frac{y_0}{x_0} > \frac{h}{g} \tag{18}$$

We give the solution of the strength of defense party in system of equation (13) and (14) as

$$y(t)=\frac{e^{(t(-x_0h+y_0g))}e^{\ln\left(\frac{y_0}{x_0h}\right)}(-x_0h+y_0g)}{-1+e^{(t(-x_0h+y_0g))}e^{\ln\left(\frac{y_0}{x_0h}\right)}g} \tag{19}$$

5 Conclusion

In this paper, simulation experiments are conducted by using SSFNet simulator to evaluate the performance of the distributed active DDoS defense system, which deploys a number of sub-systems, such as Flexible Deterministic Packet Marking (FDPM) and Mark-Aided Distributed Filtering (MADF). Then we propose an analytical model that can describe the interactions between the DDoS attack party and the defense party according to experiments.

References

1. Mirkovic, J., Reiher, P.: A Source-End Defense against Flooding Denial-of-Service Attacks. IEEE Transactions on Dependable and Secure Computing 2(3), 216–232 (2005)
2. Keromytis, A.D., Misra, V., Rubenstein, D.: SOS: An Architecture for Mitigating DDoS Attacks. IEEE Journal on Selected Areas in Communications 22(1), 176–188 (2004)
3. Xiang, Y., Zhou, W., Chowdhury, M.: A Survey of Active and Passive Defence Mechanisms against DDoS Attacks, Technical Report, TR C04/02, School of Information Technology, Deakin University, Australia (2004)
4. SSFNet, Scalable Simulation Framework (2005), http://www.ssfnet.org
5. Chen, R.C., Shi, W., Zhou, W.: Simulation of Distributed Denial of ServiceAttacks (Technical Report). In: TR C04/09, School of Information Technology, Deakin University, Australia (2004)
6. Xiang, Y., Zhou, W.: Mark-Aided Distributed Filtering by Using Neural Network for DDoS Defense. In: IEEE Global Telecommunications Conference 2005 (IEEE GLOBECOM 2005), IEEE Computer Society Press, Los Alamitos (2005)
7. Dittrich, D.: Distributed Denial of Service (DDoS) Attacks/tools (2005), http://staff.washington.edu/dittrich/misc/ddos/
8. Skitter project, Cooperative Association for Internet Data Analysis (CAIDA), http://www.caida.org/tools/measurement/skitter/
9. Xiang, Y., Zhou, W., Rough, J.: Trace IP Packets by Flexible Deterministic Packet Marking (FDPM) In: Proceedings of IEEE International Workshop on IP Operations & Management IPOM, pp. 246–252 (2004)
10. Yaar, A., Perrig, A., Song, D.: Pi: A Path Identification Mechanism to Defend against DDoS Attacks. In: 2003 IEEE Symposium on Security and Privacy, pp. 93–107 (2003)
11. Sung, M., Xu, J.: IP Traceback-based Intelligent Packet Filtering: A Novel Technique for Defending Against Internet DDoS Attacks. IEEE Transactions on Parallel and Distributed Systems 14(9), 861–872 (2003)

Access Control and Authorization for Security of RFID Multi-domain Using SAML and XACML

Dong Seong Kim[1], Taek-Hyun Shin[1], Byunggil Lee[2], and Jong Sou Park[1]

[1] Network Security and System Design Lab., Hankuk Aviation University, Korea
{dskim, eureka57, jspark}@hau.ac.kr
[2] ETRI (Electronics and Telecommunications Research Institute)
bglee@etri.re.kr

Abstract. The necessity of collaboration between different RFID applications domains is becoming significant. The previous works on security and privacy in RFID system, it's commonly assumed that all RFID tags belong to a single RFID system. In this paper, we propose an access control and authorization for security of RFID multi-domain. We employ Security Assertion Markup Language (SAML) and eXtensible Access Control Markup Language (XACML). SAML and XACML are well defined and applied to web security and grid security. We show the possibility of our approach through a case study.

1 Introduction

The RFID technology is one of the core technologies in ubiquitous computing era. One of main obstacles to prevent RFID technology from its proliferation is security and privacy problems. Juels [7] surveyed and summarized the previous security and privacy issues for RFID system. The security and privacy for RFID system have been studied in viewpoint of communication between RFID tags and reader. As the RFID technology is adopted in my applications such as supply chain management, enterprise resource planning, the cooperation and collaboration between different RFID domains (i.e. cross RFID domain) is becoming more important. We define that RFID multi domain is the domains that share information and cooperate each other. When two different domains need to share information, they have to authenticate a user and grant proper privilege(s) to the user. The problem can be considered as authentication and authorization in two different RFID domains. The previous approaches on security and privacy in RFID system have not considered the authentication and authorization in RFID system. Our idea is similar to multi-domain security, and single sign on (SSO). However, it is unable to apply them to our problem. In this paper, we propose an access control and authorization methodology for security of RFID multi-domain. We design an authentication and authorization on basis of on industrial standard referred as *EPCglobal network*, using Security Assertion Markup Language (SAML) and eXtensible Access Control Markup Language (XACML).

The reminder of this paper is as follows: Section 2 presents background and related work. Section 3 presents our proposed approach. Section 4 presents a case study and discussion, and Section 5 concludes this work.

The next sections introduce our approach in more detail.

Y. Wang, Y. Cheung, and H. Liu (Eds.): CIS 2006, LNAI 4456, pp. 887–893, 2007.

2 Background and Related Work

In this section, we present several related work to our approach. First, we introduce EPCglobal Network, which is most representative example of RFID networks, and it is considered as industrial standard (see figure 1). The EPC stands for 'Electronic Product Code'. The EPC Network Architecture is depicted in Figure 1 [2].

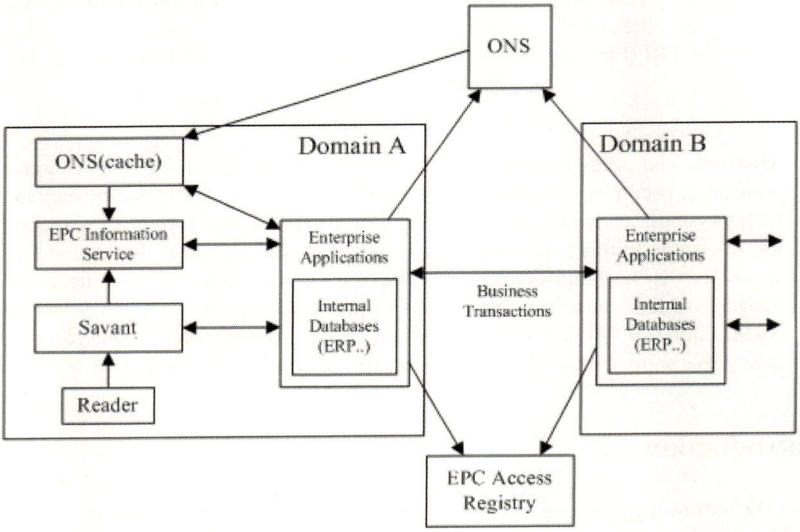

Fig. 1. EPCglobal network architecture: across Enterprises

EPCglobal Network has to provide an opportunity for trading partners to share information and massively increase the visibility of product flows within supply chains, for example, Domain A and Domain B in figure 1. It is essential that they should be done in a secure way; companies can be assured that they retain control of who has access to which subsets of their data. In vision of EPCglobal Network, they want to use common security authentication and authorization mechanisms. There are various aspects of security that need to be considered. Authentication is necessary to check who is making the request and/or who is providing the data in response. Access control is necessary to ensure whether the requestor has the correct role-based access privileges to entitle them to read (or even update) that specific information. We also surveyed some related work to authentication, access control and authorization across different domains. Microsoft's .NET passport [9] has initially started their service but it's exclusive and not popularized. The Liberty Alliance Project [8] has been trying to build open standard-based specification for federated identify and identity based web services. Additionally, grid security and web security are also related to our approach. Grid security researcher community organized the Globus Alliance [11], which is a community of organizations and individuals developing fundamental technologies behind the "Grid" which lets people share computing power, databases, instruments, and other on-line tools securely across corporate, institutional, and geographic bound-aries without sacrificing local autonomy. The web security have been developed for long time and there is a big e-business standard, OASIS [10, 12]. OASIS develops security standards needed in e-business and web services applications. There are several OASIS standards. This paper proposes an approach based on two main standards, Security Assertion Markup Language (SAML) and eXtensible Access Control Mark-up Language (XACML), focusing on general flow of authentication, access control and authorization in RFID multi-domain environments. There are a lot of researches to provide interoperability between different applications domains, based on SAML and XACML.

However, as far as we know, there are no studies for design of access control and authorization in RFID multi-domain environments. We propose access control and authorization methodology in this paper for the first time. Next section present how to apply existing SAML and XACML to RFID multi domain environment, including RFID tag, reader, and discovery service according to user's role.

3 Proposed Approach

This section presents authentication, access control and authorization methodology in RFID multi-domain. According to location of users' service request, the authentication and authorization procedures are mainly divided into two cases, single RFID domain and cross RFID domain. We omit them of single RFID domain in this paper. The flow of an authentication and authorization framework in cross RFID domain is depicted in figure 2. We assume that domain A and domain B have the trusted security association beforehand.

Let assume that a user and her name is Alice. Alice is registered, authenticated, and authorized in domain B. In this case, Alice belongs to domain B, she sends a service request with her authentication information to domain A. Alice first sends request for her authentication to domain A, not domain B. This means that authentication and authorization are delegated to domain A from domain B. This mechanism is one of the important parts in authentication and authorization framework. In this paper, we assume that Alice is able to authenticate her identification using simple authentication protocol, for example, id/password. After Alice sends service request to domain A, domain A send it to domain B. The backend system in domain B responds to domain A, with requested information, including identification and attributes of requested user (Alice). The backend system in domain A determines whether it accepts or denies the requested user. If request user is authenticated and authorized, the user is able to use services with respect to user's authorization. User may use reader or tag in domain A.

The detailed flow of authentication and authorization for the cross RFID domain is depicted in figure 3. In figure 3, there are two RFID domains. The security assertion and delegation is carried out between two domains. Each domain is consisted of AA (Attribute Authority), context handler, PAP (Policy Administration Point), PDP (Policy Decision Point), PEP (Policy Enforcement Point), PIP (Policy Information Point),

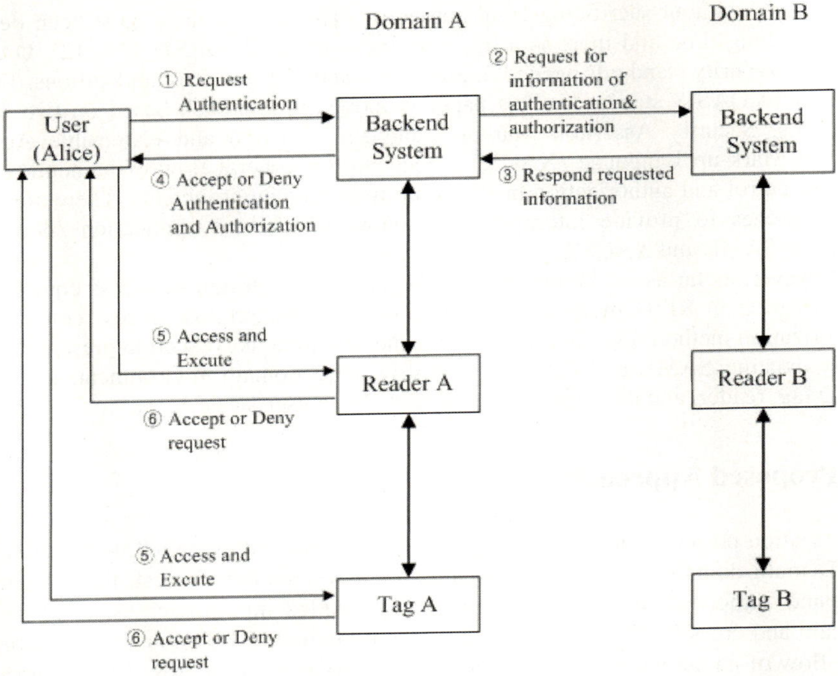

Fig. 2. Authentication, access control and authorization in cross RFID domain

and RIP (Resource Information Point).[5] AA manages user's attributes. Context handler converts decision requests in the native request format to the XACML canonical form and converts authorization decisions in the XACML canonical form to the native response format. PAP creates a policy or policy set. PDP evaluates applicable policy and renders an authorization decision. PEP performs access control, by making decision requests and enforcing authorization decisions. PIP acts as a source of attribute values. RIP provides resource context. The detail phase is described below [5]:

1. PAPs write policies and policy sets and make them available to the PDP. These policies or policy sets represent the complete policy for a specified target.
2. User (domain B) sends a request for access to the PEP(in domain A).
3. The PEP(domain A) requests SAMLAttribute-Statement to the PEP (domain B).
4. The PEP(domain B) requests SAMLAttribute-Statement to the AA(domain B).
5. The AA (domain B) response SAMLAttribute-Statement to the PEP (domain B).
6. The PEP (domain B) response SAMLAttribute-Statement to the PEP (domain A).
7. The PEP sends the request for access to the cont-ext handler in its native request format, optionally including attributes of the subjects, resource, action and environment.
8. The context handler requests the attributes from a PIP.
9. The PIP obtains the requested attributes.

10. The PIP returns the requested attributes to the con-text handler.
11. Optionally, the context handler includes the resource in the context.
12. The context handler sends the requested attributes and (optionally) the resource to the PDP. The PDP evaluates the policy.
13. The PDP returns the response context (including the authorization decision) to the context handler.
14. The context handler translates the response cont-ext to the native response format of the PEP. The cont-ext handler returns the response to the PEP.
15. If access is permitted, then the PEP permits access to the service; otherwise, it denies access.

The next section illustrates a case study and we also present some discussions.

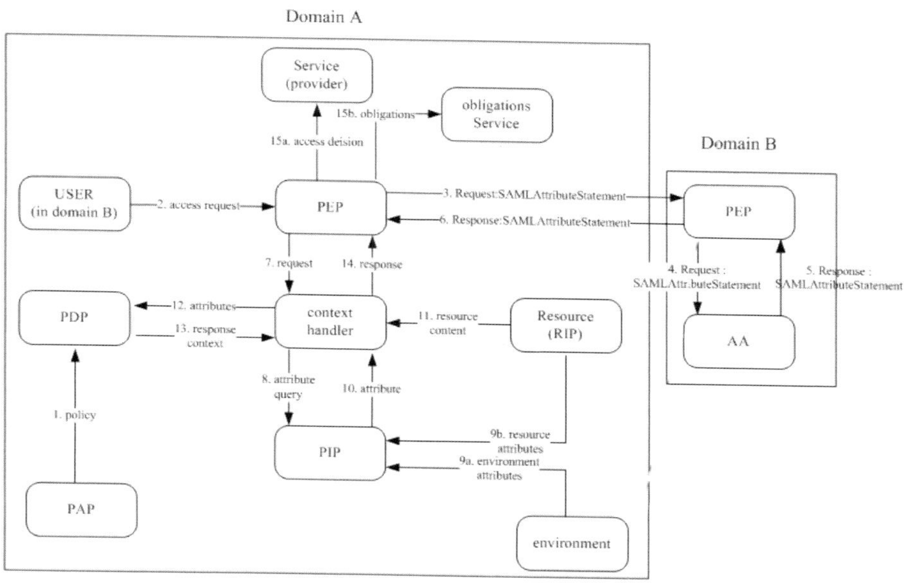

Fig. 3. A detailed flow of an authentication and authorization in RFID multi-domain

4 A Case Study and Discussion

Bob belongs to domain B. Bob want to use a service provided by domain A. Domain A requests Bob's information to domain B, then Domain A allocates a service to Bob according to its security policy. Then, Bob is able to use the service allocated by Domain A.

We have mentioned the necessity of authentication and authorization, and our approach also needs role and authorization information. The role and related authorization make it possible to provide fine-grained access control according to user's role. The table 1 shows examples of user role, authorization information in term of services in domain A. The role specification was build according to the specification of states information of EPC Class 1 Gen-2 Tags [4]. In case of a user with Role 0, Bob cannot use any type of services for RFID applications in Domain A. In case of a user with role 6, Bob can use tag, reader, and discovery services. The detailed information of tag, reader, and discovery services are summarized in table 2, 3. For example, a user with role 6 can use commands in Tag such as request random number, read, write, and etc. as well as commands in Reader such as reading tags, writing tags, and so on.

Bob belongs to domain B. Bob want to use a service provided by domain A. Domain A requests Bob's information to domain B, then Domain A allocates a service to Bob according to its security policy. Then, Bob is able to use the service allocated by Domain A.

Table 1. Examples of user role and authorization (services)

User Role/ Authorized Service	User Authorization		
	Tag	Reader	Discovery Services
Role0	N/A	N/A	N/A
Role 1/Service 1	T1-2	R1	N/A
Role 2/Service 2	T1-3	R1-2	N/A
Role 3/Service 3	T1-5	R1-2	N/A
Role 4/Service 4	T1-6	R1-3	D1
Role 5/Service 5	T1-6	R1-6	D1-2
Role 6/Service 6	T1-6	R1-6	D1-3

Table 2. Classification of RFID tags and readers services

Tags		Readers	
Services	Commands	Services	Commands
T1	Req_RN	R1	Reading Tags
T2	Read	R2	WritinTags
T3	Write	R3	Killing Tags
T4	Access	R4	Identity functions
T5	Lock	R5	Discovery functions
T6	Kill	R6	Provisioning functions

Table 3. Classification of discovery services

Services	Commands
D 1	Location EPCIS services
D 2	Caching selected EPCIS data
D 3	Enforce Authorization Policies

5 Conclusion

This paper has presented an access control and authorization to guarantee security of RFID multi-domain system. Our approach employed a combination of SAML and XACML, which are widely used in web service security technology. We have showed the detailed flow of an authentication, access control and authorization. In future works, more detail security, design and implementation issue will be presented.

Acknowledgement

This research was supported by the MIC(Ministry of Information and Communication), Korea, under the ITRC(Information Technology Research Center) support program supervised by the IITA(Institute of Information Technology Assessment) (IITA-2006-C1090-0603-0027).

References

1. About the EPCglobal Network, http://www.epcglobalinc.org/about/about_epc_network.html
2. Auto-ID Object Name Service (ONS) 1.04 Auto-ID Cent-er Working Draft 12 (August 2003), http://www.autoid labs. org
3. Barthel, H.: RFID and beyond Standards for Collabo-rative Commerce, EPCglobal, http://www.epcglobalinc.org
4. EPC Radio-Frequency Identity Protocols Class-1 Gener-ation-2 UHF RFID Conformance Requirements Specification v.1.0.2, EPCglobal Inc. (February 2005)
5. eXtensible Access Control Markup Language (XACML) Version 2.0 OASIS Standard, (February 1. 2005), http://www.oasis-open.org/
6. Fabian, B., Günther, O., Spiekermann, S.: Security Analysis of the Object Name Service for RFID. In: Security, Privacy and Trust in Pervasive and Ubiquitous Computing (July 2005)
7. Juels, A.: RFID Security and Privacy: A Research Sur-vey, Condensed version to appear in IEEE J-SAC in (2006)
8. Liberty Alliance Project, http://www.projectliberty.org/
9. Microsoft. NET passport, http://www.microsoft.com/net
10. OASIS eXtensible Access Control Markup Language (XACML) TC, http://www.oasis-open.org/
11. Overview of the Grid Security Infrastructure, http://www.globus.org/security/overview.htm
12. Technical Overview of the OASIS Security Assertion Markup Language (SAML) V1.1, OASIS Open, (May 4 , 2004) http://www.oasis-open.org
13. The EPCglobal Network Overview of Design, Benefits, and Security, EPCglobal Inc. (September 24, 2004)
14. Traub, K., et al.: EPCglobal Architecture Framework Version 1.0, (July 2005)

Generalization of the Selective-ID Security Model for HIBS Protocols

Jin Li[1], Xiaofeng Chen[2], Fangguo Zhang[3], and Yanming Wang[1,4]

[1] School of Mathematics and Computational Science
Sun Yat-Sen University
Guangzhou, 510275, China
sysjinli@hotmail.com

[2] Department of computer Science
Sun Yat-Sen University
Guangzhou, 510275, China
isschxf@mail.sysu.edu.cn

[3] Department of Electronics and Communication
Engineering, Guangzhou, 510275, China
isszhfg@mail.sysu.edu.cn

[4] Lingnan College, Sun Yat-Sen University
Guangzhou, 510275,China
stswym@mail.sysu.edu.cn

Abstract. At PKC 2006, Chatterjee and Sarkar gave a generalization of the selective-ID security model for hierarchical identity-based encryption (HIBE). Corresponding to HIBE, in this paper, a generalization of the selective-ID security model for hierarchical identity-based signature (HIBS) is first proposed. They yield a complete generalization of the selective-ID security model for hierarchical identity-based cryptosystem. We introduce two security models which allow the adversary to commit to a set of identities and in the forgery phase choose any of the previously committed identities. Two constructions of HIBS are presented which can be proved to be secure in the two models. Furthermore, one of the HIBS schemes supports an unbounded number of levels.

1 Introduction

Certificate-based public key cryptosystems use a random string to be the public key of a user. When another user wants to send a message to him, she must obtain an authorized certificate that contains his public key. This creates the certificate management problem. Identity-based cryptosystem [13], introduced by Shamir, is a public key cryptosystem where the public key can be an arbitrary string such as an email address. A private key generator (PKG) uses a master secret key to issue private keys to identities. Many identity-based signature (IBS) have been proposed such as [1,8] since shamir proposed the ID-based notion. Until 2001, Boneh and Franklin [5] proposed the first practical identity-based encryption scheme, which is provably secure in the random oracle model. However, using a single PKG is not efficient in large scale, so another research direction

Y. Wang, Y. Cheung, and H. Liu (Eds.): CIS 2006, LNAI 4456, pp. 894–902, 2007.

is hierarchical ID-based cryptosystem [11,12]. In the hierarchical version, PKGs are arranged in a tree structure, the identities of users (and PKGs) can be represented as vectors. An identity can issue private keys to its descendant identities. All the PKGs in the leaves are responsible for generating private keys for users in the corresponding domain. Canetti et al. [7] recently proposed a slightly weaker security model, called selective identity (selective-ID) IBE. In this model the adversary must commit ahead of time (non-adaptively) to the identity it intends to attack. The adversary can still issue adaptive chosen ciphertext and adaptive chosen identity queries. Later, Boneh and Boyen proposed two HIBE [2,3] without random oracles, which can only be proved to be secure in the selective-ID model as opposed to the full model considered in [10]. Corresponding to HIBE [2], the first HIBS was proposed by Chow et al. in [10], which is provably secure against existential forgery for only selective-ID, adaptive chosen message and identity attacks.

Very recently, Chatterjee and Sarkar [9] gave a generalization of the selective-ID security model for hierarchical identity-based encryption (HIBE) at PKC 2006. They presented a new security model, which allows the adversary to commit to a set of identities, not only one identity, and in the challenge phase choose any one of the previously committed identities. Two constructions of HIBE were also constructed which are secure in the two models. Furthermore, from the description of the generalization of the selective-ID security model, it will help in obtaining a unified view of the selective-ID, full and the new security models they defined.

Contributions. First, we generalize the selective-ID model and introduce two new models of security for HIBS protocols, which allow the adversary to commit to a set of identities before setup. There are two ways to view this generalization leading to the two different security models denoted by $\mathbf{M}_1$ and $\mathbf{M}_2$, respectively. In $\mathbf{M}_1$, the adversary commits to a set I^*. It can then ask for private key of any identity $ID = (I_1, \cdots, I_k)$, as long as all the I_i are not in I^*. Furthermore, in the forgery phase, it has to output a forged signature on an identity all of whose components are in I^*. The second model $\mathbf{M}_2$ is an obvious generalization of the selective-ID model for HIBS. In this case, the adversary specifies k sets $I_1^*, \cdots, I_k^*$. Then it can ask for private key of any identity ID as long as there is an i such that the ith component of ID is not in I_i^*. In the forgery phase, the adversary has to submit an identity such that for all i, the ith component of the identity is in I_i^*. Additionally, two constructions are presented which can be proved to be secure in the new security models. In fact, the new HIBS schemes are more efficient than Chow et al.'s [10] in their selective-ID security model.

Organization. The next section presents the generalization of the selective-ID HIBS security models and, briefly explains the bilinear pairing and some problems related to pairings. Section 3 gives the construction of HIBS scheme and their security analysis in security model $\mathbf{M}_1$. section 4 is the HIBS construction and its analysis in model $\mathbf{M}_2$. The paper ends with some concluding remarks.

2 Preliminaries

2.1 Security Model

Definition 1. (HIBS) *An HIBS scheme consists of four algorithms: (Setup, Der, Sign, Verify). The algorithms are specified as follows:*

- Setup. *On input a security parameter 1^k, the PKG generates $msk, param$ where msk is the randomly generated master secret key, and $param$ is the corresponding public parameter.*
- Der. *On input an identity vector $ID = (I_1, \ldots, I_k)$, where all $I_k \in \{0,1\}^*$ and the private key $d_{ID|_{k-1}}$ for its parent identity $ID|_{k-1} = (I_1, \ldots, I_{k-1})$, it returns the corresponding private key d_{ID}.*
- Sign. *On input the private key of the signer ID, d_{ID} and a message M, it outputs a signature σ corresponding to $param$.*
- Verify. *On input the signer identity vector ID, a message M and signature σ, it outputs 1 if σ is a valid signature of M corresponding to ID. Otherwise, it outputs 0.*

2.2 Security Model

We define the following oracles:

- Extraction Oracle: The Key Extraction Oracle with input ID will output the corresponding secret key d_{ID}.
- Signing Oracle: The Signing Oracle with input signer ID and message M will output a signature σ such that $\mathsf{Verify}(ID, M, \sigma) = 1$.

Chow et al. [10] defined the security notion for HIBS as existential forgery for selective-ID, adaptive chosen message-and-identity attack (EF-sID-CMIA). The adversary $\mathcal{A}$ has to commit to an identity ID^*, which will be used to challenge.

We will be interested in defining two new security models. We first present the description of the interactive game in a manner which will help in obtaining a unified view of the selective-ID, full and the new security models that we define in the following.

- *Init*: In this stage, the adversary commits to two sets S_1 and S_2 of identities. The commitment has the following restrictions.
  1. The adversary is not allowed to query extraction oracle on any identity in S_1.
  2. In the forgery stage, the adversary has to choose one of the identities from the set S_2.
- *Setup*: The simulator sets up the HIBS protocol and provides the public parameters to the adversary and keeps the master key to itself.
- *Extract*: $\mathcal{A}$ chooses an identity ID. $\mathcal{C}$ computes $\mathrm{Extract(ID)} = d_{ID}$ and sends the result to $\mathcal{A}$. The only restriction is that ID cannot be an element of S_1.
- *Sign*: $\mathcal{A}$ chooses an identity ID, and a plaintext m. $\mathcal{C}$ signs m by computing $\sigma = Sign(m, d_{ID})$ and sends σ to $\mathcal{A}$.

The adversary $\mathcal{A}$ outputs (σ^*, m^*, ID^*) where ID* and any prefix of ID*, (m^*, ID*) does not appear in any Extract query, sign query respectively. Meanwhile, ID* is an element of the set S_2. We say that $\mathcal{A}$ wins the game if the response of the Verify on (σ^*, m^*, ID*) is equal to 1. The advantage of $\mathcal{A}$ is defined as the probability that it wins.

2.3 Full Model

Suppose $S_1 = \phi$ and S_2 is the set of all identities. The adversary is not allowed to query extraction oracle on any identity in S_1. Since S_1 is empty, this means that the adversary is actually allowed to query extraction oracle on any identity, which is actually the definition of full model and is currently believed to be the most general notion of security for HIBS.

2.4 Selective-ID Model

Let $S_1 = S_2$ be a singleton set. This means that the adversary commits to one particular identity; never asks for its private key; and in the forgery phase is given the signature under this particular identity. This model is significantly weaker than the full model and is called the selective-ID model.

2.5 New Security Models

We introduce two new security models by suitably defining the sets S_1 and S_2. In our new models, (as well as the sID model), we have $S_1 = S_2$. If the HIBS is secure in the following two security models, they are defined as secure against existential forgery for general selective-ID, adaptive chosen message-and-identity attack (EF-gsID-CMIA).

Model $\mathbf{M}_1$: Let I^* be a set. We define $S_1 = S_2$ to be the set of all tuples $(I_1, \cdots, I_k)$, such that each $I_j \in I^*$.

Model $\mathbf{M}_2$: Let $I_1^*, \cdots, I_k^*$ be sets and $|I_j^*| = n_j$ for $1 \leq j \leq k$. We set $S_1 = S_2 = I_1^* = \cdots = I_k^*$. This model is a strict generalization of the sID model for HIBS. This can be seen by setting $n_1 = \cdots = n_k = 1$, i.e., $I_1^*, \cdots, I_t^*$ to be singleton sets.

The difference between models $\mathbf{M}_1$ and $\mathbf{M}_2$ is that, in $\mathbf{M}_2$, for each level of the HIBS, the adversary is allowed to independently choose the set of possible values which the corresponding component of the target identity may take. In $\mathbf{M}_1$, the set of possible values for all components are the same.

2.6 Pairings

Let G, G_T be cyclic groups of prime order p, writing the group action multiplicatively. Let g be a generator of G.

Definition 2. *A map $e : G \times G \to G_T$ is called a bilinear pairing if, for all $x, y \in G$ and $a, b \in Z_p$, we have $e(x^a, y^b) = e(x, y)^{ab}$, and $e(g, g) \neq 1$.*

Definition 3. *(CDH problem) The Computational Diffie-Hellman (CDH) problem is that, given* g,g^x,$g^y \in G$*, for unknown* $x, y \in Z_p^*$*, to compute* g^{xy}*.*

We say that the (t, ϵ)-CDH assumption holds in G if no t-time algorithm has advantage at least ϵ in solving the CDH problem in G.

3 Concrete HIBS Construction S_1

We present the HIBS scheme S_1. It can be proved to be secure in security model M_1. And it supports unbounded number hierarchical levels.

Let G be a bilinear group of prime order p. Given a pairing: $e : G \times G \rightarrow G_T$.

Setup. To generate system parameters, the algorithm selects random generators g, g_2, g_3, h_1, $\ldots$, $h_n, h \in G$, picks a random $\alpha \in Z_p$, and sets $g_1 = g^\alpha$. Define a hash function $H : \{0,1\}^* \rightarrow G$. The system parameters are $param = (g, g_1, g_2, g_3, h_1, \ldots, h_n, h, H)$ and the master key is g_2^α.

Der. To generate a private key for $ID = (I_1, \ldots, I_k) \in (Z_p)^k$, the algorithm computes as follows:

a. For any $x \in Z_p$, define $v(x) = h_1^x h_2^{x^2} \cdots h_n^{x^n}$.
b. For $1 \leq i \leq k$, compute $v(I_i) = h_1^{I_i} h_2^{I_i^2} \cdots h_n^{I_i^n}$ and $v_i = g_3 \cdot v(I_i)$.
c. Pick random $r_1, r_2, \cdots, r_k \in Z_p$ and compute $a_1 = g^{r_1}, \cdots, a_k = g^{r_k}$. Finally, output the private key as $d_{ID} = (a_0, a_1, \cdots, a_k)$, where $a_0 = g_2^x \cdot v_1^{r_1} \cdots v_k^{r_k}$.

In fact, the private key for ID can also be generated as $d_{ID} = (a_0'(v_k)^{r_k}, a_1', \ldots, a_{k-1}', g^{r_k})$ by its parent $ID_{|k-1} = (I_1, \ldots, I_{k-1})$ with secret key $d_{ID_{|k-1}}=(a_0', a_1', \ldots, a_{k-1}')$.

Sign. For a user with identity ID and private key $d_{ID} = (a_0, a_1, \ldots, a_k)$, it signs a message m as follows: Pick a random $r \in Z_p$, compute $T = g^r$ and $A = a_0 \cdot [g_3 \cdot h^{H(m)}]^r$. Finally, output the signature as $\sigma = (A, a_1, \ldots, a_k, T)$.

Verify. After received a signature $\sigma = (A, a_1, \ldots, a_k, T)$ on message m for ID$=(I_1, \cdots, I_k)$, the verifier computes $v_i = g_3 \cdot v(I_i)$ for $i = 1, \cdots, k$, and checks if the following equation holds: $e(g, A) \stackrel{?}{=} e(g_1, g_2)e(v_1, a_1) \cdots e(v_k, a_k)e(g_3 \cdot h^{H(m)}, T))$. Output 1 if it is true. Otherwise, output 0.

The correctness of the scheme is obvious. Meanwhile, it is also very efficient. Signature generation requires only two exponentiation operations in G, regardless the hierarchy depth. However, the HIBS [10], which also shares the same parameters with us, requires $(l+2)$ exponentiation operations for an l-level user. So, the new HIBS is more efficient than [10] even in the only selective-ID security model.

3.1 Security Analysis

We show that our HIBS scheme is secure against EF-gsID-CMIA.

Theorem 1. *Assuming the (t, ϵ)-CDH assumption holds in G, then our HIBS scheme is $(t', q_S, q_H, q_E, \epsilon')$-secure against EF-gsID-CMIA in security model M_1, where $t' \leq t - \Theta((q_H + q_E + q_S)t_{exp})$, $\epsilon \geq \frac{1}{q_H} \cdot (1 - \frac{q_S}{q_H}) \cdot (\epsilon' - \frac{1}{p})$, and t_{exp} is the maximum time for an exponentiation in G.*

Proof. If there exists an adversary $\mathcal{A}$ breaks the scheme in the random oracle, then we show there exists an algorithm $\mathcal{C}$ that, by interacting with $\mathcal{A}$, solves the CDH problem. Our algorithm $\mathcal{C}$ described below solves CDH problem for a randomly given instance $\{g, X = g^x, Y = g^y\}$ and asked to compute g^{xy}. The details are as follows.

Init: $\mathcal{A}$ first commits to a target identity set $I^* = (I_1^*, \cdots, I_n^*) \in Z_p^n$.

Setup: Define a polynomial in $Z_p[x]$ by $F(x) = (x - I_1^*) \cdots (x - I_n^*) = x^n + a_{n-1}x^{n-1} + \cdots + a_1 x + a_0$. These coefficients depend on the adversary's input and cannot assume any distribution on these values. For notational convenience, we define $a_n = 1$. It is obvious $F(x) \neq 0$ for any $x \notin I^*$. Meanwhile, randomly choose $b_0, b_1, \cdots, b_n$ from Z_p and define another polynomial $J(x) = b_n x^n + b_{n-1}x^{n-1} + \cdots + b_1 x + b_0$. Then we define $g_1 = X, g_2 = Y$, $g_3 = g_2^{a_0} g^{b_0}$ and $h_i = g_2^{a_i} g^{b_i}$ for $1 \leq i \leq n$. So, for any $I_i \in Z_p$, we have $v_i = g_3 \cdot h_1^{I_i} h_2^{I_i^2} \cdots h_n^{I_i{}^n} = g_2^{F(I_i)} g^{J(I_i)}$. Furthermore, $\mathcal{C}$ chooses $c, c' \in Z_p$ and defines $h = g_2^{-\frac{a_0}{c}} g^{c'}$. A hash function $H : \{0,1\}^* \rightarrow Z_p$ is also defined, which acts as random oracle in the proof. Algorithm $\mathcal{C}$ gives the public system parameters $(g, g_1, g_2, g_3, h_1, \cdots, h_n, h, H)$ to the adversary $\mathcal{A}$. The corresponding master key, which is unknown to $\mathcal{C}$, is g_2^x.

Extraction Queries: Let ID=$(I_1, \cdots, I_k)$ be the identity for private key query. Because all I_i does not belong to the set I^*, assume index t is the minimum value such that $I_t \notin I^*$. Then, $\mathcal{C}$ chooses k random values $r_1, \cdots, r_{t-1}, r'_t, r_{t+1}, \cdots, r_k \in Z_p^*$. Let $r_t = r'_t - \frac{x}{F(I_t)}$ (which is not known to $\mathcal{C}$) and output the simulated private key as $d_{ID} = (g_2^{F(I_t)} g^{J(I_t)})^{r'_t} g_1^{\frac{-J(I_t)}{F(I_t)}} \prod_{i=1, i \neq t}^{k} v_i^{r_i}, g^{r_1}, \cdots, g^{r_{t-1}}, g^{r'_t} g_1^{-\frac{1}{F(I_t)}}, g^{r_{t+1}}, \cdots, g^{r_k})$. It can be easily verified the private key computed as above is valid from the viewpoint of $\mathcal{A}$.

Hash Function Queries: $\mathcal{C}$ maintains a list $\mathcal{L}$ to store the answers of the hash oracle. Meanwhile, $\mathcal{C}$ picks a random value $s \in [1, q_H]$. If m_i is sent for H query, $\mathcal{C}$ checks the list $\mathcal{L}$. If an entry for the query is found, the same answer will be returned to $\mathcal{A}$. Otherwise, $\mathcal{C}$ will randomly choose $c_i \in Z_p$ and answer $H(m_i) = c_i$, if $i \neq s$, and stores (m_i, c_i) in $\mathcal{L}$ too. If $i = s$, $\mathcal{C}$ answers $H(m_s) = c$.

Signature Queries: After received $(m$, ID=$(I_1, \cdots, I_j))$ for signature query, if all I_i does not belong to the set I^*, the simulator just extracts the private key for ID as above and give the signature for m by using algorithm Sign. If all I_i of ID belongs to the set I^*, then $F(I_i) = 0$ for $1 \leq i \leq j$. Assume the hash function value on m always has been queried before signature query. If $H(m) = c$, $\mathcal{C}$ will abort. Otherwise, let $H(m) = c_i$ for some c_i, we have $g_3 \cdot h^{H(m)} = g_2^{(1-\frac{c_i}{c})a_0} g^{c'c_i + b_0}$. Then, $\mathcal{C}$ chooses $r_1, \cdots, r_j, r' \in Z_p^*$. Let

$r = r' + x\frac{c}{(c_i - c)a_0}$ and output the simulated signature on message m as $\sigma = ((g_3 h^{c_i})^{r'} g_1^{\frac{c(c_i c + b_0)}{a_0(c_i - c)}} g^{\sum_{i=1}^{j} J(I_i) r_i}, g^{r_1}, \cdots, g^{r_j}, g^{r'} g_1^{\frac{c}{a_0(c_i - c)}})$. It can be easily verified the signature computed as above is a valid signature from the viewpoint of $\mathcal{A}$ for $g_2^x (g_3 h^{H(m)})^r = (g_3 h^{c_i})^{r'} g_1^{\frac{c(c_i c + b_0)}{a_0(c_i - c)}}$ and $g^r = g^{r'} g_1^{\frac{c}{a_0(c_i - c)}}$, which is similar to the simulation technique of extraction query. So, $\sigma = ((g_3 h^{c_i})^{r'} g_1^{\frac{c(c_i c + b_0)}{a_0(c_i - c)}} g^{\sum_{i=1}^{j} J(I_i) r_i}$, $g^{r_1}, \cdots, g^{r_j}, g^{r'} g_1^{\frac{c}{a_0(c_i - c)}}) = (g_2^x \cdot v_1^{r_1} \cdots v_j^{r_j} [g_3 \cdot h^{H(m)}]^r, g^{r_1}, \cdots, g^{r_j}, g^r)$ is a valid simulated signature.

After the simulation, the adversary outputs a forged signature $(A^*, a_1^*, \cdots, a_l^*, T^*)$, on message m^* associated with identity $ID^* = (I_1^*, \cdots, I_l^*)$ such that each $I_i^* \in I^*$ and $m^* = m_s$. Then $F(I_i^*) = 0$ and $H(m^*) = c$. If it is a valid signature, it must satisfy $a_1^* = g^{r_1^*}, \cdots, a_l^* = g^{r_l^*}$, $T^* = g^{r^*}$, $A^* = g_2^x \cdot \prod_{i=1}^{l} v_i^{r_i^*} (g_3 h^{H(m^*)})^{r^*} = g^{xy} \cdot T^{*cc' + b_0} \prod_{i=1}^{l} a_i^{*J(I_i^*)}$, for some unknown $r_1^*, \cdots, r_l^*, r^*$. So, we can extract $g^{xy} = A^* / (T^{*(b_0 + cc')} \prod_{i=1}^{l} a_i^{*J(I_i^*)})$ and solves the CDH problem. Since H is a random oracle, the probability that the output m^* of $\mathcal{A}$ is valid without any query of $H(m^*)$ is at most $\frac{1}{p}$. Meanwhile, $\mathcal{C}$ does not abort in signature query with probability not less than $(1 - \frac{1}{q_H})^{q_S}$, and $(1 - \frac{1}{q_H})^{q_S} \geq 1 - \frac{q_S}{q_H}$. So, we have $\epsilon \geq \frac{1}{q_H} \cdot (1 - \frac{q_S}{q_H}) \cdot (\epsilon' - \frac{1}{p})$.

4 Concrete HIBS Construction S_2

In this section, an HIBS scheme that can be proved to be secure in model S_2 is constructed. The description of HIBS S_2 is similar to that of S_1. We describe it as follows:

Setup. Let G be a bilinear group of prime order p. Given a pairing: $e : G \times G \to G_T$. Define the maximum depth of the HIBS to be l. Additionally, a tuple $(n_1, \cdots, n_l)$ of positive integers is required. To generate system parameters, the algorithm selects random generators g, g_2, g_3', h, $(g_{3,1}, \cdots, g_{3,l})$, $h_{i,j} \in G$, where $1 \leq i \leq l$ and $1 \leq j \leq n_i$, picks a random $\alpha \in Z_p$, and sets $g_1 = g^\alpha$. Define a hash function $H : \{0,1\}^* \to G$. The system parameters are $param = (g, g_1, g_2, g_3', h, (g_{3,1}, \cdots, g_{3,l}), h_{i,j}$, where $1 \leq i \leq l$ and $1 \leq j \leq n_i$, $H)$ and the master key is g_2^α.

Der. To generate a private key for $ID = (I_1, \ldots, I_k) \in (Z_p)^k$, the algorithm computes as follows:

a. For any $x \in Z_p$, define $v(i, x) = h_{i,1}^x \cdots h_{i,n_i}^{x^{n_i}}$. Given an identity ID$=(I_1, \cdots, I_k)$, define $v_i = g_{3,i} \cdot v(i, I_i)$.
b. For $1 \leq i \leq k$, compute $v(i, I_i) = h_{i,1}^{I_i} h_{i,2}^{I_i^2} \cdots h_{i,n_i}^{I_i^n}$ and $v_i = g_{3,i} \cdot v(i, I_i)$.
c. Pick random $r_1, r_2, \cdots, r_k \in Z_p$ and compute $a_1 = g^{r_1}, \cdots, a_k = g^{r_k}$. Finally, output the private key as $d_{ID} = (a_0, a_1, \cdots, a_k)$, where $a_0 = g_2^x \cdot v_1^{r_1} \cdots v_k^{r_k}$.

In fact, the private key for ID can also be generated as $d_{ID} = (a_0'(v_k)^{r_k}, a_1', \ldots, a_{k-1}', g^{r_k})$ by its parent $ID_{|k-1} = (I_1, \ldots, I_{k-1})$ with secret key $d_{ID_{|k-1}} = (a_0', a_1', \ldots, a_{k-1}')$.

Sign. For a user with identity ID and private key $d_{ID} = (a_0, a_1, \ldots, a_k)$, it signs a message m as follows: Pick a random $r \in Z_p$, compute $T = g^r$ and $A = a_0 \cdot [g_3' \cdot h^{H(m)}]^r$. Finally, output the signature as $\sigma = (A, a_1, \ldots, a_k, T)$.

Verify. After received a signature $\sigma = (A, a_1, \ldots, a_k, T)$ on message m for ID=$(I_1, \cdots, I_k)$, the verifier computes $v_i = g_{3,i} \cdot v(i, I_i)$ for $i = 1, \cdots, k$, and checks if the following equation holds: $e(g, A) \stackrel{?}{=} e(g_1, g_2)e(v_1, a_1) \cdots e(v_k, a_k)$ $e(g_3' \cdot h^{H(m)}, T)$. Output 1 if it is true. Otherwise, output 0.

Theorem 2. *The HIBS scheme is $(t', q_S, q_H, q_E, \epsilon')$-secure against EF-gsID-CMIA in security model M_2, if the (t, ϵ)-CDH assumption holds in G, where $t' \leq t - \Theta((q_H + q_E + q_S)t_{exp})$, $\epsilon \geq \frac{1}{q_H} \cdot (1 - \frac{q_S}{q_H}) \cdot (\epsilon' - \frac{1}{p})$, and t_{exp} is the maximum time for an exponentiation in G.*

Proof. The security reduction for S_2 in model $\mathbf{M}_2$ is similar to that of S_1 in model M_1, which is omitted here.

5 Conclusion

A generalization of the selective-ID security model for hierarchical identity-based signature (HIBS) is proposed in this paper. Combined with generalization of the selective-ID security model for HIBE protocols [9] proposed at PKC 2006, they yield a complete generalization of the selective-ID security model for hierarchical identity-based cryptosystem. We introduce two security models which allow the adversary to commit to a set of identities and in the forgery phase choose any of the previously committed identities. Additionally, two constructions of HIBS are presented which can be proved to be secure in the two models.

Acknowledgments

This work is supported by the National Natural Science Foundation of China (No. 60503006 and No. 10571181). The first author is also supported by KaiSi Grant.

References

1. Bellare, M., Namprempre, C., Neven, G.: Security Proofs for Identity-based Identification and Signature Schemes. In: Cachin, C., Camenisch, J.L. (eds.) Advances in Cryptology - EUROCRYPT 2004. LNCS, vol. 3027, pp. 268–286. Springer, Heidelberg (2004)
2. Boneh, D., Boyen, X.: Efficient Selective-ID Secure Identity-Based Encryption Without Random Oracles. In: Cachin, C., Camenisch, J.L. (eds.) Advances in Cryptology - EUROCRYPT 2004. LNCS, vol. 3027, pp. 223–238. Springer, Heidelberg (2004)
3. Boneh, D., Boyen, X.: Secure Identity Based Encryption Without Random Oracles. In: Franklin, M. (ed.) Advances in Cryptology – CRYPTO 2004. LNCS, vol. 3152, pp. 443–459. Springer, Heidelberg (2004)

4. Boneh, D., Boyen, X., Goh, E.-J.: Hierarchical Identity Based Encryption with Constant Size Ciphertext. In: Cramer, R.J.F. (ed.) Advances in Cryptology – EUROCRYPT 2005. LNCS, vol. 3494, pp. 440–456. Springer, Heidelberg (2005)
5. Boneh, D., Franklin, M.: Identity-Based Encryption from the Weil Pairing. In: Kilian, J. (ed.) Advances in Cryptology - CRYPTO 2001. LNCS, vol. 2139, pp. 213–229. Springer, Heidelberg (2001)
6. Boneh, D., Katz, J.: Improved Efficiency for CCA-Secure Cryptosystems Built Using Identity-Based Encryption. In: Menezes, A.J. (ed.) Topics in Cryptology – CT-RSA 2005. LNCS, vol. 3376, pp. 87–103. Springer, Heidelberg (2005)
7. Canetti, S.H., Katz, J.: Chosen-ciphertext security from identity-based encryption. In: Cachin, C., Camenisch, J.L. (eds.) Advances in Cryptology - EUROCRYPT 2004. LNCS, vol. 3027, pp. 207–222. Springer, Heidelberg (2004)
8. Cha, J.C., Cheon, J.H.: An identity-based signature from gap Diffie-Hellman groups. In: Desmedt, Y.G. (ed.) Public Key Cryptography - PKC 2003. LNCS, vol. 2567, pp. 18–30. Springer, Heidelberg (2002)
9. Chatterjee, S., Sarkar, P.: Generalization of the Selective-ID Security Model for HIBE Protocols. In: Yung, M., Dodis, Y., Kiayias, A., Malkin, T.G. (eds.) Public Key Cryptography - PKC 2006. LNCS, vol. 3958, pp. 241–256. Springer, Heidelberg (2006)
10. Sherman, S.M., Chow, L.C.K., Hui, S.M.: Yiu, and K. In: Lopez, J., Qing, S., Okamoto, E. (eds.) Information and Communications Security. LNCS, vol. 3269, pp. 480–494. Springer, Heidelberg (2004)
11. Gentry, C., Silverberg, A.: Hierarchical ID-Based Cryptography. In: Zheng, Y. (ed.) Advances in Cryptology - ASIACRYPT 2002. LNCS, vol. 2501, pp. 548–566. Springer, Heidelberg (2002)
12. Horwitz, J., Lynn, B.: Toward Hierarchical Identity-Based Encryption. In: Knudsen, L.R. (ed.) Advances in Cryptology - EUROCRYPT 2002. LNCS, vol. 2332, pp. 466–481. Springer, Heidelberg (2002)
13. Shamir, A.: Identity-based cryptosystems and signature schemes. In: Blakely, G.R., Chaum, D. (eds.) Advances in Cryptology. LNCS, vol. 196, pp. 47–53. Springer, Heidelberg (1985)

Discriminatively Learning Selective Averaged One-Dependence Estimators Based on Cross-Entropy Method

Qing Wang[1], Chuan-hua Zhou[1,2], and Bao-hua Zhao[2]

[1] School of Management Science and Engineering, Anhui University of Technology, Ma'anshan 243002, China
{wangq, chzhou}@ahut.edu.cn

[2] Department of Computer Science and Engineering, University of Science and Technology of China, He'fei 230026, China
bhzhao@ustc.edu.cn

Abstract. Averaged One-Dependence Estimators [1], simply AODE, is a recently proposed algorithm which weakens the attribute independence assumption of naïve Bayes by averaging all the probability estimates of a collection of one-dependence estimators and demonstrates significantly high classification accuracy. In this paper, we study the selective AODE problem and proposed a Cross-Entropy based method to search the optimal subset over the whole one-dependence estimators. We experimentally test our algorithm in term of classification accuracy, using the 36 UCI data sets recommended by Weka, and compare it to C4.5[5], naïve Bayes, CL-TAN[6], HNB[7], AODE and LAODE[3]. The experiment results show that our method significantly outperforms all the other algorithms used to compare, and remarkably reduces the number of one-dependence estimators used compared to AODE.

1 Introduction

A Bayesian network classifier is a probability classification model which consists of a structural model and a set of conditional probabilities and uses the maximum posterior probability (MAP) to predict the class label. Learning a Bayesian network classifier is a process of constructing a special classifier from a given set of training examples with class label. Assuming that $<A_1,A_2,\dots,A_n>$ are n attributes, and a training instance is represented by a vector $<a_1,a_2,\dots,a_n>$, where a_i is the value of the i-th attribute A_i. These attributes will be used collectively to predict the class value c of the class variable C using MAP. Thus, the Bayesian network classifier can be defined as:

$$\arg\max_{c\in C} P(c)P(a_1,a_2,\dots,a_n \mid c) \tag{1}$$

Assuming that all the attributes are independent from each other given the class, we got Eq.(2), which is called naïve Bayesian classifier, or naïve Bayes.

$$\arg\max_{c\in C} P(c)\prod_{i=1}^{n} P(a_i \mid c) \tag{2}$$

Y. Wang, Y. Cheung, and H. Liu (Eds.): CIS 2006, LNAI 4456, pp. 903–912, 2007.

But the attribute independence assumption of naïve Bayes rarely holds in real world applications. So we need to relax the assumption effectively to improve its classification performance. One possible way is to use the Bayesian network classifier which can represent the relationship between attributes effectively. Unfortunately, it has been proved that learning the optimal Bayesian network structure is NP-hard [9]. To avoid the high computation cost for learning the structure of Bayesian network, learning improved naïve Bayes has attracted much attention and researchers has proposed a lot algorithm which demonstrate improved classification accuracy on naïve Bayes, such as CL-TAN[6], HNB[7], AODE[1] , etc.

One of the most recent works on improving Naïve Bayes is Averaged One-Dependence Estimators [1], simply called AODE which achieving significantly high classification accuracy at a modest cost. In AODE, an ensemble of one-dependence classifiers are learned and the prediction is produced by averaging the probability estimates of all the qualified one-dependence classifiers. For each one-dependence classifier, a single attribute, also called super-parent attribute, is selected as the parent of all other attributes. In order to avoid unreliable probability prediction, the original work only select models where the frequency of the value for classified object of the parent attributes is larger than a limit m, such as 30, a widely used minimum number constraint on sample size for statistical inference. However subsequent work [4] shows that this constraint can result in increased error and hence the subsequent research [2][3] use m=1.

By application of the product rule it follows that for any attribute value a_i which denotes the value of attribute A_i in an instance **a**, it holds:

$$P(c,\mathrm{a}) = P(c,ai)P(\mathrm{a}|c,ai) \tag{3}$$

As this equality holds for every $a_{i,}$ it follows that it also holds for the mean over all the group of attribute values, thus:

$$P(c,\mathrm{a}) = \frac{\sum_{i:1\le i\le n \wedge F(ai)\ge m} P(c,ai)P(\mathrm{a}|c,ai)}{|\{i:1\le i\le n \wedge F(ai)\ge m\}|} \tag{4}$$

where $F(a_i)$ is the frequency of the attribute value a_i in the training instances. To this end, AODE classifies a test instance by selecting the class label c using the Eq.(5) bellow:

$$\arg\max_{c\in C}\Big(\sum_{i:1\le i\le n \wedge F(ci)\ge m} P(c,ai)\prod_{j=1}^{n} P(a_j\,|\,c,ai)\Big) \tag{5}$$

$$\propto \arg\max_{c\in C}\Big(\sum_{i:1\le i\le n \wedge F(ci)\ge m} \frac{P(c,ai)\prod_{j=1}^{n} P(a_j\,|\,c,ai)}{P(\mathrm{a})}\Big) \tag{6}$$

$$\propto \arg\max_{c\in C}\Big(\frac{\sum_{i:1\le i\le n \wedge F(ci)\ge m} P^{i}(c\,|\,\mathrm{a})}{|\{i:1\le i\le n \wedge F(ci)\ge m\}|}\Big) = \arg\max_{c\in C} \overline{P}(c\,|\,\mathrm{a}) \tag{7}$$

where $P^i(c|\mathbf{a})$ denotes the probability estimate on instance **a** for class label c of the one-dependence estimator using the i-th qualified attribute as its super-parent, and $\overline{P}(c \mid \mathrm{a})$ denotes the averaged probability estimate on instance **a** for class label c over all the qualified one-dependence estimators.

The rest of this paper is organized as follows. In Section 2, we introduce the related work on improving the performance of AODE. In Section 3, a cross-entropy based search algorithm for selective AODE is presented. In Section 4, we describe the experimental setup and results in detail. Finally, we make a conclusion and outline our main directions for further research.

2 Related Work

Since AODE demonstrates significantly good classification performance, many research works [2][3][4][8] have done to further improve its classification accuracy. The existing research on improving the performance of AODE for classification can be broadly divided into two categories: (1) model selection: selecting only helpful one-dependence estimators and uniform averaging their probability estimates; (2) model weighting: assigning a weight to each one-dependence estimators and linear combining their probability estimates.

Yang and Webb[2] proposed two algorithms CV and FSA for model selection, the basic idea for CV is that given m one-dependence estimators score each individual one-dependence estimators by its cross-validation error on the training data and generate m candidate ensembles from size 1 to m, then choose the one-dependence estimators subset with the lowest error. While FSA is a forward search algorithm which starts with an empty one-dependence estimators set, and iteratively adds a candidate one-dependence estimators whose inclusion results in the lowest error until the inclusion of the one-dependence estimators can not result in the improvement of the accuracy. Both the two algorithms are intrinsically greedy search approach. The main drawback of them is that they by nature can not cope well with optimization problem with local optima.

Zhang and Webb [3] proposed a efficient lazy attribute elimination algorithm to eliminate the highly related attribute values which can result in classification bias for AODE. And it has been identified as the best model selection method [2] because its classification accuracy is better than CV and FSA.

Cerquides[4] proposed another approach model weighting to further improve the performance of AODE. The weight vector is calculated by maximizing the supervised posterior probability on the training data and it has been identified as the best model weighting method [2] so far. But the weight vector calculation is time consuming. Jiang [8] proposed an efficient algorithm based on the mutual information between each attribute and the class to calculate the weight vector.

In this paper, we study the model selection problem for AODE and proposed a cross-entropy based method to search the optimal ensembles. The experiment results show that our algorithm achieves significantly improvement over the best model selection algorithm [3] so far and use substantially small number of one-dependence estimators than AODE which can further increases the classification speed for new instance.

3 The Cross-Entropy Method for Selective AODE

In this section we will propose a cross-entropy (CE) based search method and show that this method provides an effective and efficient way to solve the one-dependence estimator selection problem.

3.1 Cross-Entropy Method

The CE method was firstly proposed as an efficient method for the estimation of rare-event probabilities, and then it is rapidly developed into a powerful and versatile technique for combinatorial optimization with promising result and has been successfully applied to a wide range of difficult combinatorial optimization problems[10][11][12]. A tutorial introduction can be found in [12], and more information can be found at its home page [10]. It consists of two iterative steps, i.e.:

1. Generation of a sample of random data in the search space according to a specified random mechanism.
2. Updating the parameters of the random mechanism, on the basis of the data, in order to produce a "better" sample in the next iteration. This last step involves a measurement of the distance between two distributions, using the Cross-Entropy or Kullback-Leibler method; hence the name.

A difficulty with

3.2 The Cross-Entropy Method for Selective AODE

Consider an AODE for an application consist of n one-dependence estimators. Without loss of generality, we label the one-dependence estimators $1,\ldots,n$. Let V denotes all the possible candidate one-dependence estimator subsets of the whole one-dependence estimators. A candidate subset v is represented by a vector $<x_1,x_2,\ldots,x_n>$, where x_i is set 1 if the i-th one-dependence estimator is included in v and 0 otherwise, and the classification accuracy on this subset is denoted by $c(v)$. Our main purpose is to find the maximum value of $c(v)$ over V and the corresponding subset v^* at which the maximum value c^* is attained, i.e.:

$$c^* = c(v^*) = \max_{v \in V} c(v) . \tag{8}$$

To use CE method for this maximization problem, we need to (a) specify the how the random candidate subsets are generated, and (b) calculate the corresponding update formulas. The most natural and easiest way to generate the candidate subsets is let $X=<X_1,X_2,\ldots,Xn>$ be independent Bernoulli random variables vector with success probabilities vector $p=< p_1,p_2,\ldots p_n>$. Note that if $p=v^*$, which corresponds to the degenerate case of the Bernoulli distribution, we have $c(X)=c^*$, $X=v^*$, and the search algorithm yields the optimal solution with probability 1. To obtain the degenerate probability vector, the usual CE procedure proceeds by constructing a sequence of probability vectors $\{p_t, t{\geq}0\}$. The sequence of probability vectors is obtained via a two-step procedure, involving an auxiliary sequence of performance levels $\{r_t, t{\geq}0\}$ that tend to the maximum value c^* at the same time as the p_t tend to v^*. At each iteration t, for a given p_{t-1}, r_t is the 1-ρ-quantile of performances where ρ is typically chosen between 0.01 and 0.1. An estimator $\hat{r}_t$ of r_t is the corresponding 1-ρ-sample quantile. That is, generate a random sample $X_1, X_2, \ldots, X_N$ and compute the performances $r(X_i)$, $i=1,2,\ldots N$; let $\hat{r}_t = r_{(\lceil (1-\rho)N \rceil)}$, where $r_{(1)} \leq \ldots \leq r_{(N)}$ are the order statistics of the performances. The probability vector is updated via CE minimization [12] and the estimator $\hat{p}_t$ of p_t is computed using:

$$\hat{p}_{t,j} = \frac{\sum_{i=1}^{N} I\{c(Xi) \geq \hat{r}_t\} X_{ij}}{\sum_{i=1}^{N} I\{c(Xi) \geq \hat{r}_t\}} \qquad j = 1, 2, \ldots n. \tag{9}$$

To reduce the probability of the algorithm to get stuck in a local maximum, we use the following smoothed update formula (10), where the parameter β is typically chosen between 0.7 and 1. The main CESAODE algorithm for optimizing (8) is summarized in Algorithm 1.

$$\hat{p}_t = \beta \hat{p}_t + (1-\beta)\hat{p}_{t-1} \tag{10}$$

Algorithm 1. (The Main CESAODE Algorithm)

1. *Start with some* $\hat{p}_0$, *say* $\hat{p}_0 = <0.5, 0.5, \ldots, 0.5>$. *Set t=1 (iteration counter).*
2. *Draw a random sample* $X_1, X_2, \ldots, X_N$ *of Bernoulli vectors with success probability vector* $\hat{p}_{t-1}$. *Then compute the* $1-\rho$ *-sample quantile of performances* $\hat{r}_t$ *where the performance is calculated by* 10 runs of ten-fold cross-validation on the training data.
3. *Use the same sample to calculate the* $\hat{p}_t = <\hat{p}_{t1}, \hat{p}_{t2}, \ldots, \hat{p}_{tn}>$, *via Eq. (9), and smooth out* $\hat{p}_t$ *via Eq.(10).*
4. *If for some t>d, say d=5,* $\hat{r}_t = \hat{r}_{t-1} = \ldots = \hat{r}_{t-d}$ *then stop. Otherwise, set t=t+1 and reiterate from step 2.*

As an example, the detailed process of the evolution of the CE algorithm on data set labor for one-dependence estimator selection is present in Table 1 where the performance metric is the classification accuracy obtained via 10 runs of ten-fold cross-validation. From the table, we can see that the $\hat{p}_t$ and $\hat{r}_t$ converge very quickly and it uses only 9 iterations to converge to the optimal state with 97.19% classification accuracy.

Table 1. A typical evolution of the CE algorithm with N=80, ρ=0.1, β=0.8 on data set labor

t	$\hat{r}_t$	$\hat{p}_t$
0		0.50 0.50 0.50 0.50 0.50 0.50 0.50 0.50 0.50 0.50 0.50 0.50 0.50 0.50 0.50 0.50
1	0.9368	0.19 0.19 0.46 0.81 0.46 0.63 0.46 0.19 0.28 0.54 0.81 0.46 0.19 0.46 0.72 0.28
2	0.9403	0.13 0.04 0.09 0.69 0.54 0.66 0.36 0.04 0.23 0.46 0.70 0.36 0.22 0.18 0.77 0.06
3	0.9438	0.03 0.01 0.02 0.85 0.20 0.75 0.07 0.01 0.40 0.36 0.67 0.25 0.04 0.04 0.78 0.10
4	0.9509	0.01 0.00 0.00 0.79 0.13 0.42 0.01 0.09 0.70 0.52 0.58 0.32 0.01 0.01 0.42 0.02
5	0.9579	0.00 0.00 0.00 0.51 0.03 0.53 0.00 0.01 0.94 0.28 0.74 0.24 0.00 0.00 0.17 0.00
6	0.9613	0.00 0.00 0.00 0.10 0.00 0.55 0.00 0.00 0.98 0.32 0.41 0.13 0.00 0.00 0.03 0.00
7	0.9647	0.00 0.00 0.00 0.02 0.00 0.91 0.00 0.00 1.00 0.15 0.08 0.03 0.00 0.00 0.01 0.00
8	0.9719	0.00 0.00 0.00 0.00 0.00 0.98 0.00 0.00 1.00 0.03 0.01 0.00 0.00 0.00 0.00 0.00
9	0.9719	0.00 0.00 0.00 0.00 0.00 1.00 0.00 0.00 1.00 0.00 0.00 0.00 0.00 0.00 0.00 0.00

4 Experiment

Our experiments are conducted on the 36 UCI data sets [14] recommended by Weka, which are described in Table 2. All these data sets are from the UCI repository and we download these data sets in format of arff from the main page of Weka[13]. We adopted the following three preprocessing stages on each data set.

1. The missing values of each data set are replaced by using the unsupervised attribute filter of *ReplaceMissingValues* in Weka.
2. Numeric attributes are discretized by the unsupervised attribute filter of *Discretize* in Weka, so as to make all the attributes nominal.
3. The attribute useless for classification are removed. It is obvious that if the number of values of an attributes is almost equal to the number of instances in a data set, this attribute does not provide any information to classification. So we use the unsupervised attribute filter *Remove* in Weka to remove this type of attribute. In the whole 36 data sets we used, there are only three attributes of this type, namely "hospital number" in data set colic.ORIG, "instance name" in data set splice and "animal" in data set zoo.

In our experiments, we compare Selective AODE with C4.5[4], naïve Bayes, CL-TAN[6], HNB[7], AODE and LAODE[3] in accuracy of classification. We use the implementation of C4.5, naïve Bayes, CL-TAN, AODE, HNB in Weka, and implement the LAODE and CESAODE algorithm which use the proposed cross-entropy method to search over the whole possible one-dependence estimator subset. To the CE method, we use following parameters in our experiments: the sample size N is set 5 times of the attribute number of the test data set; ρis set 0.1; β is set 0.8; and d is set 5. In all experiments, the classification accuracy of each classifier on a dataset is obtained by 10 runs of ten-fold cross-validation and various classifiers are use the same random seed sequence for all ten-fold cross-validation. Finally, we calculate the mean classification accuracy and standard deviation of the 100 classification results and conduct a two-tailed t-test with 95% confidence level recommended by to compare each pair of algorithms.

Table 3 shows the detailed results on classification accuracy and standard deviation of each classifier on each data set and the averaged values are show at the bottom of

Table 2. Description of the data sets used in experiments

Datasets	Size	Attributes	Classes		Datasets	Size	Attributes	Classes
anneal	898	39	6		ionosphere	351	35	2
anneal.ORIG	898	39	6		iris	150	5	3
audiology	226	70	24		kr-vs-kp	3196	37	2
autos	205	26	7		labor	57	17	2
balance-scale	625	5	3		letter	2000	17	26
breast-cancer	286	10	2		lymph	148	19	4
breast-w	699	10	2		mushroom	8124	23	2
colic	368	23	2		primary-tumor	339	18	21
colic.ORIG	368	28	2		segment	2310	20	7
credit-a	690	16	2		sick	3772	30	2
ctedit-g	1000	21	2		sonar	208	61	2
diabetes	768	9	2		soybean	683	36	19
glass	214	10	7		splice	3190	62	3
heart-c	303	14	5		vehicle	846	19	4
heart-h	294	14	5		vote	435	17	2
heart-statlog	270	14	2		vowel	990	14	11
hepatitis	155	20	2		waveform-5000	5000	41	3
hypothyroid	3772	30	4		zoo	101	18	7

the table. Table 4 shows results of the two-tailed t-test, in which each entry w/t/l means that the algorithm in the corresponding row wins in w data sets, ties in t data sets and lost in l data sets compared to the algorithm in the corresponding column. Table 5 shows the detailed number of one-dependence estimators used by AODE and Selective AODE on each data set, and the averaged values are show at the bottom of the table.

From Table 3 and Table 4, we can see that CESAODE significantly outperform C4.5, NB, CL-TAN, HNB, AODE and LAODE. Now we briefly summarize the results as follows:

1. AODE achieves significantly improvements over C4.5, NB, CL-TAN, and little improvement over HNB.
2. CESAODE achieves significantly improvements over AODE (16 wins and 0 losses) and LAODE (15 wins and 1 losses).
3. CESAODE has better robustness and stability than all the other algorithms compared. The averaged standard deviation of CESAODE is 4.07 which is the lowest among all algorithms.
4. CESAODE using far more small number of one-dependence estimators than AODE which could make it more quickly to classify a new instance. From Table 5, we can see that the averaged number of one-dependence estimators used by Selective AODE is only about one third of AODE.
5. The standard deviation of CESAODE is lower than AODE in most data sets (only except in 3 data sets). The reason may be that using small number of one-dependence estimators lower the model complexity of Selective AODE and give Selective AODE better generalization ability than AODE.

Table 3. Experimental results on mean classification accuracy and standard deviation

Datasets	C4.5	NB	CL-TAN	HNB	AODE	LAODE	CESAODE
anneal	98.68±1.01	94.42±2.42	97.69±1.53	98.65±1.18	96.96±1.65	97.33±1.7	97.95±1.58
anneal.ORIG	90.26±2.84	88.25±3.43	91.62±2.34	91.8±2.71	89.18±3.35	89.65±3.36	91.17±2.84
audiology	77.78±7.48	71.23±6.49	62.98±6.25	73.72±5.66	71.54±6.43	76.29±6.65	72.93±5.74
autos	81.84±8.47	64.37±9.85	74.02±9.65	78.53±8.41	75.12±8.62	75.11±8.53	80.89±7.47
balance-scale	64.29±4.08	91.6±1.09	85.62±3.32	89.58±2.42	89.84±1.84	89.84±1.84	91.65±1.09
breast-cancer	75.33±5.6	72.75±6.79	67.95±6.8	70.97±6.79	73.03±6.71	72.99±6.81	74.54±6.18
breast-w	94.09±3.12	97.37±1.8	94.46±2.54	96.04±2.3	96.88±2.08	96.88±2.08	97.31±1.85
colic	84.46±4.9	78.89±6.86	79.72±6.3	81.01±6.61	80.84±6.57	80.95±6.54	82.3±5.78
colic.ORIG	70.95±5.56	74.3±6.99	70.59±7.05	72.15±6.92	76.12±6.53	76.23±6.23	78.7±5.61
credit-a	85.12±4.45	84.84±3.95	83.08±4.75	84.88±4.21	86.04±3.84	86.04±3.99	86.78±3.7
ctedit-g	72.24±4.24	75.87±3.62	74.87±4.12	76.54±3.44	76.48±3.53	76.55±3.45	77.66±3.41
diabetes	73.84±3.62	75.73±4.47	74.83±4.43	75.73±4.39	76.3±4.17	76.36±4.12	77.19±4.26
glass	58.35±9.83	58.47±8.36	59.78±9.62	59.07±9.27	62.29±8.54	62.71±8.92	64.13±8.61
heart-c	78.84±6.94	83.76±5.01	78.46±8.02	81.77±5.94	82.75±5.68	82.75±5.68	84.05±5.46
heart-h	80.02±6.91	83.69±6.5	80.89±6.7	81.51±6.29	84.23±6.51	84.37±6.54	85.15±6.49
heart-statlog	80.29±7.39	83.56±6.48	78.76±6.99	81.48±7.18	83.18±6.62	83.18±6.62	84.93±6.43
hepatitis	81.34±7.94	84.23±9.23	82.79±8.21	82.62±8.7	84.95±8.58	84.36±8.84	87.07±8.13
hypothyroid	93.24±0.45	92.82±0.75	92.99±0.69	93.34±0.6	93.57±0.69	93.61±0.69	93.76±0.41
ionosphere	87.94±4.53	90.74±4.34	92.78±3.86	92.96±3.64	91.82±4.01	91.65±3.94	93.68±3.97
iris	95.73±5.06	94.99±5.64	91.81±8.16	93.99±5.4	93.93±5.45	93.93±5.45	95.27±4.85
kr-vs-kp	99.45±0.42	87.79±1.76	93.53±1.46	92.4±1.37	91.17±1.42	92.38±1.16	94.8±1.02
labor	85.07±13.89	96.53±8.11	88.33±11.89	91.47±13.12	94.43±9.88	94.26±9.93.	97.19±7.28
letter	81.39±0.93	70.09±0.92	81.09±0.82	86.1±0.78	85.5±0.79	85.49±0.79	86.49±0.52
lymph	78.64±9.73	85.9±8.06	83.68±9.23	83.09±8.84	85.99±9.03	85.85±8.97	87.99±7.89
mushroom	100±0	95.48±0.78	99.52±0.26	99.96±0.06	99.95±0.08	99.96±0.07	99.98±0.06
primary-tumor	41.48±5.78	46.58±7.21	44.2±6.38	47.94±7.25	47.97±7.0	47.91±7.09	49.06±7.42
segment	93.47±1.31	89.03±2.06	93.88±1.62	94.69±1.36	92.96±1.44	93.09±1.47	93.98±1.21
sick	98.16±0.71	96.81±0.86	97.55±0.72	97.77±0.73	97.55±0.76	97.6±0.76	98.23±0.65
sonar	70.75±9.09	75.79±10.52	74.23±9.68	80.55±8.69	80.5±9.13	80.5±9.13	86.92±7.73
soybean	92.72±3.14	92.05±2.65	93.67±2.8	94.56±2.47	93.21±2.33	93.29±2.41	93.88±1.97
splice	94.03±1.39	95.41±1.0	95.32±1.16	95.78±1.02	96.13±1.07	97.12±0.99	97.93±0.92
vehicle	71.19±4.37	60.7±4.29	71.89±3.49	73.6±4.13	71.81±3.46	71.61±3.61	73.16±4.04
vote	96.53±2.5	90.29±4.17	93.12±3.98	94.32±3.41	94.6±3.24	94.6±3.24	95.22±3.24
vowel	75.52±4.63	65.98±4.06	92.98±2.86	93.22±2.37	90.14±2.92	90.59±3.04	92.21±2.54
waveform-5000	72.99±1.86	79.93±1.62	80.37±1.79	83.6±1.69	84.25±1.6	84.25±1.6	85.34±1.46
zoo	92.57±7.48	93.78±7.66	95.21±6.29	98.91±3.98	94.86±6.36	94.67±6.67	97.04±4.55
Mean	82.46±4.77	82.33±4.72	83.17±4.87	85.12±4.54	85.16±4.49	85.39±4.52	86.85±4.07

Table 4. Summary of experimental results with two-tailed t-test with 95% confidence level

w/t/l	C4.5	NB	CL-TAN	HNB	AODE	LAODE
NB	11/10/15					
CL-TAN	9/15/12	13/14/9				
HNB	19/10/7	18/15/3	19/16/1			
AODE	20/8/8	16/19/1	19/12/5	3/27/6		
LAODE	19/10/7	18/17/1	19/13/4	5/26/5	3/33/0	
CESAODE	25/6/5	23/13/0	28/8/0	19/15/2	16/20/0	15/20/1

Table 5. The number of one-dependence estimators used by AODE and CESAODE

Datasets	AODE	CESAODE
anneal	38	9
anneal.ORIG	38	5
audiology	69	10
autos	25	4
balance-scale	4	2
breast-cancer	9	2
breast-w	9	5
colic	22	9
colic.ORIG	26	11
credit-a	15	6
ctedit-g	20	5
diabetes	8	3
glass	9	5
heart-c	13	6
heart-h	13	5
heart-statlog	13	5
hepatitis	19	5
hypothyroid	29	16
ionosphere	34	11
iris	4	2
kr-vs-kp	36	8
labor	16	2
letter	16	10
lymph	18	6
mushroom	22	7
primary-tumor	17	7
segment	19	6
sick	29	3
sonar	60	22
soybean	35	5
splice	60	17
vehicle	18	7
vote	16	3
vowel	13	2
waveform-5000	40	11
zoo	16	3
Mean	23.56	6.81

5 Conclusions

In this paper, we study the selective AODE problem. To obtain the optimal subset of the whole one-dependence estimators, we introduce a Cross-Entropy based approach to this problem, which can deal with this problem effectively. Our experiment results show that selective AODE significantly outperforms all the other algorithms used to compare, and use far small number of one-dependence estimators and have better generalization ability compared to AODE.

Since probabilistic classification model is highly related to the ranking model measured by the area under the ROC curve, or simply AUC, a natural question is whether the method presented in this paper can also be applied to some ranking algorithms which predict the corresponding ranking location of an instance through averaging the probability estimates of a set of component estimators? This is a topic for our future research.

References

1. Webb, G.I., Boughton, J., Wang, Z.: Not so naïve bayes: Aggregating one-dependence estimators. Machine Learning 58, 5–24 (2005)
2. Yang, Y., Webb, G.I. et al.: To Select or To Weight: A Comparative Study of Model Selection and Model Weighting for SPODE Ensembles. In: Fürnkranz, J., Scheffer, T., Spiliopoulou, M. (eds.) Machine Learning: ECML 2006. LNCS (LNAI), vol. 4212, pp. 170–181. Springer, Heidelberg (2006)
3. Zhang, F., Webb, G.I.: Efficient lazy elimination for averaged one-dependence estimators. In: Proceedings of 23rd International conference on Machine Learning (ICML) (2006)

4. Cerquides, J., Mantaras, R.L.D.: Robust Bayesian linear classifier ensembles. In: Gama, J., Camacho, R., Brazdil, P.B., Jorge, A.M., Torgo, L. (eds.) Machine Learning: ECML 2005. LNCS (LNAI), vol. 3720, pp. 70–81. Springer, Heidelberg (2005)
5. Quinlan, J.: C4.5: Programs for Machine Learning. Morgan Kaufmann, San Mateo (1993)
6. Friedman, N., Geiger, D., Goldszmidt, M.: Bayesian Network Classifiers. Machine Learning 29, 131–163 (1997)
7. Zhang, H., Jiang, L.X., Su, J.: Hidden Naive Bayes. In: Proceeding of 20th National conference on Artificial Intelligence (AAAI), pp. 919–924 (2005)
8. Jiang, L.X., Zhang, H.: Weighted Averaged One-Dependence Estimators. In: Yang, Q., Webb, G. (eds.) PRICAI 2006: Trends in Artificial Intelligence. LNCS (LNAI), vol. 4099, pp. 970–974. Springer, Heidelberg (2006)
9. Chickering, D.M.: Learning Bayesian networks is NP-Complete. In: Fisher, D., Lenz, H. (eds.) Learning from Data: Artificial Intelligence and Statistics, pp. 121–130 (1996)
10. The Cross-Entropy Method, http://iew3.technion.ac.il/CE/about.php.
11. Rubinstein, R.Y, Kroese, D.P (eds.): The Cross-Entropy Method: A Unified Approach to Combinatorial Optimization, Monte-Carlo Simulation and Machine Learning. Springer, New York (2004)
12. De Boer, P-T., Kroese, D.P, Mannor, S., Rubinstein, R.Y.A: Tutorial on the Cross-Entropy Method. Annals of Operations Research. 134, 19–67 (2005)
13. Blake, C., Merz, C.J.: UCI repository of machine learning databases. In: Department of ICS, University of California, Irvine, http://www.ics.uci.edu/ mlearn/MLRepository.html.
14. Witten, I.H., Frank, E.: Data Mining: Practical Machine Learning Tools and Technology with Java Implementation. Morgan Kaufmann, San Francisco (2000)

Image-Adaptive Spread Transform Dither Modulation Using Human Visual Model

Xinshan Zhu

Institute of Computer Science & Technology of Peking University,
Beijing 100871, China
zhuxinshan@icst.pku.edu.cn

Abstract. This paper presents a new approach on image-adaptive spread-transform dither modulation (STDM). The approach is performed in the discrete cosine transform (DCT) domain, and modifies the original STDM in such a way that the spread vector is weighted by a set of just noticeable differences (JND's) derived from Watson's model before it is added to the cover work. An adaptive quantization step size is next determined according to the following two constraints: 1) the covered work is perceptually acceptable, which is measured by a global perceptual distance; 2) the covered work is within the detection region. We derive the strategy on the choice of the quantization step. Further, an effective solution is proposed to deal with the amplitude scaling attack, where the scaled quantization step is produced using an extracted signal in proportion to the amplitudes of the cover work. Experimental results demonstrate that the proposed approach achieves the improved robustness and fidelity.

1 Introduction

Digital watermarking is now one of the active research topics in the multimedia area. The goal is to conceal auxiliary information within a host digital signal. This hidden information should be detectable even if the watermarked signal is distorted (to some extent).

Over the last decade, a variety of watermarking algorithms have been proposed. In principle, these can be divided into two classes: 1) additive spread-spectrum-based methods (SS) [1] and 2) quantization-based methods. SS manifests satisfied robustness to interfering noise and lossy compression, but doesn't possess the host interference cancellation [2]. Presently, the quantization-based watermarking has received considerable attention. One of the most important methods proposed so far is quantization index modulation (QIM) [2]. An efficient implementation of QIM is called dither modulation (DM) [2], where the embedded information would modulate the dither signal of a dithered quantizer. Some recent work addresses to develop image-adaptive DM using human visual model (HVM) in DCT domain [3,4], wavelet domain [5], etc.. In these methods, the quantization steps are determined by the perceptual masks, which are derived from the adopted HVM. As a special case of DM, Spread-transform dither

Y. Wang, Y. Cheung, and H. Liu (Eds.): CIS 2006, LNAI 4456, pp. 913–923, 2007.

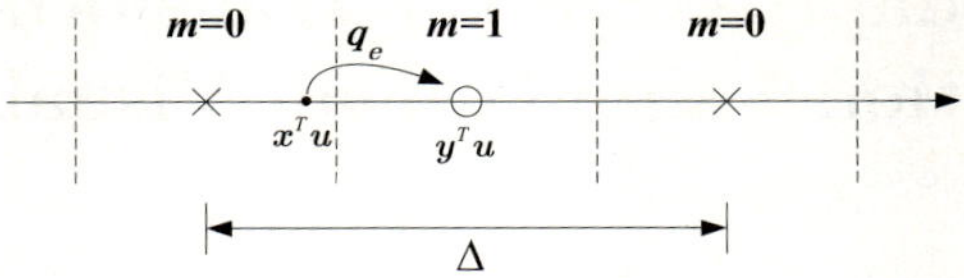

Fig. 1. STDM embedding process and decision regions. The centroids marked with ×'s and ○'s in each bin represent the hidden information 0 and 1 respectively.

modulation (STDM) [2] couples the effectiveness of QIM schemes and conventional spread-spectrum systems and performs significantly better than DM. The development of adaptive STDM watermarking is of interest in this paper.

The main weakness of quantization-based watermarking is its vulnerability against amplitude scalings attack. The solutions proposed so far in the framework of QIM watermarking, can be grouped into three main categories [6]: 1) estimating the gain factor [7]; 2) adoption of spherical codewords together with correlation decoding [6,8]; and 3) designing the value-metric scaling invariant method [3,9]. Comparing with the existing methods, a more practical and effective solution is presented in this study.

The remainder of this paper is structured as follows: Section 2 reviews the original STDM. Section 3 presents the new image-adaptive STDM and describes it in details. A practical solution is proposed to deal with amplitude scaling in Section 4. A serial of tests are done to evaluate the presented approch in section 5. Finally, Section 6 concludes.

2 Review of STDM

STDM [2] applies the dithered quantizers to modify the projection of the host signal $\boldsymbol{x} \in \mathbb{R}^L$ onto some spread vector $\boldsymbol{u} \in \mathbb{R}^L$, as shown in Fig. 1. When embedding a single bit of payload information, $m \in \{0, 1\}$, the technique can be summarized as follows. The projection $\boldsymbol{x}^T\boldsymbol{u}$ is modified as

$$\boldsymbol{y}^T\boldsymbol{u} = Q_\Delta(\boldsymbol{x}^T\boldsymbol{u} + d_m) - d_m, \tag{1}$$

where $\boldsymbol{y}$ and d_m denote the watermarked signal and the dither value respectively, and $Q_\Delta(\cdot)$ is a uniform, scalar quantizer with step size Δ. Suppose q_e is the resulting quantization error, i.e., $q_e = \boldsymbol{y}^T\boldsymbol{u} - \boldsymbol{x}^T\boldsymbol{u}$ and the embedding strength α has the form $\alpha = q_e/\|\boldsymbol{u}\|^2$, where $\|\cdot\|$ stands for Euclidean (i.e., ℓ_2) norm. Thus, the watermarked signal $\boldsymbol{y}$ is expressed as

$$\boldsymbol{y} = \boldsymbol{x} + \alpha\boldsymbol{u}. \tag{2}$$

Next, the watermarked signal $\boldsymbol{y}$ might undergo a number of distortions that are modelled as an unknown noise source, $\boldsymbol{v}$. Finally, a message $\widehat{m}$ is extracted from the received signal $\boldsymbol{r}$ using the minimal distance decoder

$$\widehat{m} = arg \min_{m \in (0,1)} |\boldsymbol{r}^T\boldsymbol{u} - (Q_\Delta(\boldsymbol{r}^T\boldsymbol{u} + \boldsymbol{d}_m) - \boldsymbol{d}_m)|. \tag{3}$$

Equation (2) demonstrates that the host signal is altered along the direction of the chosen spread vector when the quantization step is fixed. The spread vector might be generated randomly and independent of the content. However, it is well known that the ability to perceive a change depends on the content. More recently, several image-adaptive schemes based on DM [3,4] have been proposed, but they can't be straightforwardly extended to STDM due to the additional projection step. Taking into account these two factors, it is necessary to study adaptive STDM.

3 Adaptive STDM Based on Watson's Model

In this section, we will present the image-adaptive STDM using Watson's model [10] in DCT domain. The host signal $\boldsymbol{x}$ is a vector of DCT coefficients obtained by the block DCT transform (DCT is performed independently for every 8×8 image block). Watson's model is applied to calculate the JND sequence $\boldsymbol{s}$ corresponding to $\boldsymbol{x}$ and measure the perceptibility of watermarking as

$$D_p(\boldsymbol{y},\boldsymbol{x}) = (\sum_{i=1}^{N} |\frac{y_i - x_i}{s_i}|^4)^{\frac{1}{4}}, \tag{4}$$

where x_i, y_i and s_i refer to the ith elements of $\boldsymbol{x}$, $\boldsymbol{y}$ and $\boldsymbol{s}$ respectively. The value of $D_p(\boldsymbol{y},\boldsymbol{x})$ is called as the perceptual distance between $\boldsymbol{y}$ and $\boldsymbol{x}$.

Obviously, the alteration introduced to each DCT coefficient by watermark embedding should be adjusted according to its corresponding JND. Here, the strategy of weighting the alteration with the JND is used, so Equation (2) is modified to the following

$$\boldsymbol{y} = \boldsymbol{x} + \alpha' \boldsymbol{s}\cdot\boldsymbol{u}, \tag{5}$$

where $\boldsymbol{s}\cdot\boldsymbol{u}$ indicates that each dimension of $\boldsymbol{s}$ is multiplied by the corresponding dimension of $\boldsymbol{u}$: $s_i \cdot u_i$. For the sake of discussion, it is assumed that the spread vector $\boldsymbol{u}$ takes values -1, $+1$. Under the distortion constraint $D_p(\boldsymbol{y},\boldsymbol{x}) \leq D$, it is easy to derive that

$$|\alpha'| \leq D(\sum_{i=1}^{L} u_i^4)^{-\frac{1}{4}} = L^{-\frac{1}{4}} D. \tag{6}$$

Additionally, the alteration of each element of $\boldsymbol{x}$ doesn't exceed the JND value to achieve the watermark transparency, so the perceptual distance D is chosen to maintain that $|\alpha'| < 1$, which results in $D < \sqrt[4]{L}$.

With the constraint in (6), it is just guaranteed that the watermarked signal $\boldsymbol{y}$ is within the acceptable distortion region. On the other hand, the chose of α' must ensure that the projection $\boldsymbol{y}^T\boldsymbol{u}$ locates at the centroids of the detection region, as shown in Fig. 1. In this case, from (5), we derive

$$\alpha' = \frac{q_e}{\sum_{i=1}^{L} s_i}. \tag{7}$$

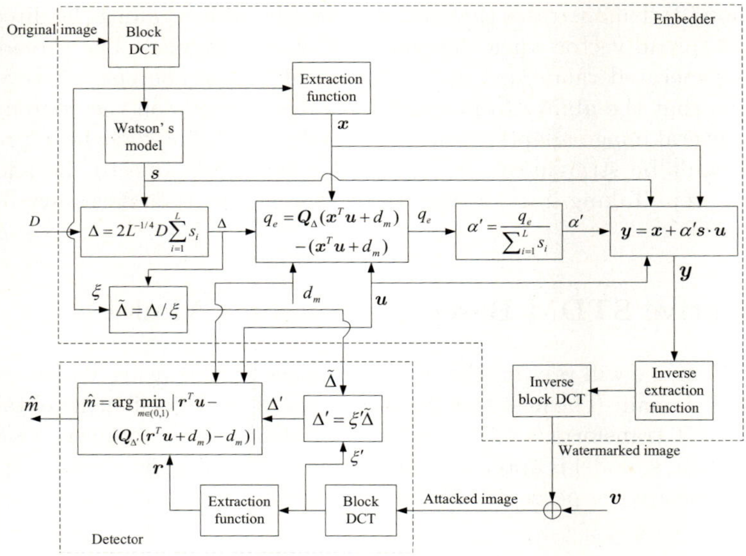

Fig. 2. Basic design of image-adaptive STDM involving the embedder and detector

Due to the fact that the quantization error q_e falls inside the interval $[-\frac{\Delta}{2}, \frac{\Delta}{2}]$, the constraint in (6) is automatically satisfied when

$$\Delta \leq 2L^{-\frac{1}{4}} D \sum_{i=1}^{L} s_i. \tag{8}$$

Inequality (8) provides a strategy to choose the quantization step Δ under the given distortion constraint. The chosen Δ is used to compute the watermark strength α' as (7) during the embedding process, and extract the hidden message as (3) at detection time.

Fig. 2 illustrates the basic procedure that one bit information is embedded. If one needs to embed n ($n > 1$) bits, a set of n length-L host signals are extracted, and each bit is inserted into a host signal using the same procedure as Fig. 2. A uniform quantization step can be derived according to the similar analysis as that described above and used for embedding all information bits.

4 The Improved Watermark Detector

The original STDM is largely vulnerable to amplitude scalings. The inherent reason is when the amplitude of the host signal is scaled by factor of β, the quantization step used for detection is not scaled accordingly. Hence, the core problem is to obtained the scaled quantization step. In what follows, we present a simple and practical solution.

(a)

(b)

Fig. 3. (a) Original image "Lena" and (b) its watermarked copy obtained by our method with $D = 4.8$ and $L = 31$

Obviously, it is difficult to straightforwardly estimate the scaling factor β, but it is possible that a signal ξ is extracted before and after amplitude scaling attack to satisfy

$$\xi'/\xi = \beta, \tag{9}$$

where ξ' denotes the modified version of ξ caused by the amplitude scaling. The following two steps can guarantee that the quantization step Δ' used for watermark detection has (approximately) the property that $\Delta' = \beta\Delta$. First, the quantization step Δ used for embedding is divided by ξ, i.e., $\widetilde{\Delta} = \Delta/\xi$ after embedding. $\widetilde{\Delta}$ is then sent to the detector. Δ' is obtained as $\Delta' = \xi'\widetilde{\Delta}$ when extracting the hidden message. The improved detector is illustrated in Fig. 2.

The issue that remains is to choose the signal ξ. Besides ξ satisfying (9), it should be also almost constant subject to other common image processing manipulations, otherwise, these manipulations will lead to a false quantization step Δ'. In DCT domain, the mean of the DC coefficients in all 8×8 blocks denoted by $C00$ is kept unchanged under a variety of image processing operations and thus, is an idea candidate, that is $\xi = C00$.

5 Experimental Results

In this section, a serial of experiments are conducted to evaluate the performance of the proposed watermarking scheme. In these tests, we used various standard images of size 512×512, for example, the "Lena" image shown in Fig. 3(a), and hence, each image consists of 4096 image blocks of 8×8 pixels. From each image block, a set of 62 DCT coefficients are extracted for embedding, i.e., the zig zag scanned coefficients 3 to 64, which results in the entire sequence of 62×4096 coefficients as the host signal vector. The vector is further decomposed in subvectors (blocks) of length L, each of which contains one bit information, so a total of $\lfloor 62 \times 4096/L \rfloor$ bits is concealed within each image. The watermark

Fig. 4. The watermarked image obtained by our method with $L = 124$ under Gaussian noise attack (the standard deviation is 6)

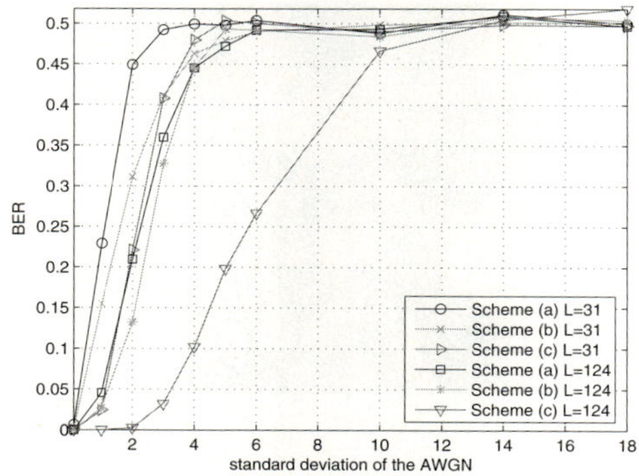

Fig. 5. Bit error rate vs. the standard deviation of Gaussian noise for different values of L, $D = 4.8$

embedding is carried out as the procedure described in Section 3. Fig. 3(b) shows the watermarked "Lena" with $L = 31$ and the given global perceptual distance $D = 4.8$. Clearly, the watermarked image looks almost the same as the original one, which shows that the embedded watermarks are invisible.

The results presented in the following permit to appreciate the robustness of image-adaptive STDM with respect to several common signal processing techniques. All the experiments were carried out on the "Lena" image which was marked with $D = 4.8$. The watermarking schemes used for comparison are marked as:

(a) The original non-adaptive STDM scheme proposed by Chen et al. [2]
(b) The adaptive QIM scheme based on Watson's model proposed by Li et al. [3]
(c) The adaptive STDM based on based on Watson's model using a uniform quantization step

First, the watermarked images undergo the additive white Gaussian noise (AWGN) attack of different strength. Fig. 4 shows one of the attacked images. The bit-error-rate (BER) of each watermarking scheme is plotted in Fig. 5 as a function of the standard deviation for $L = 31$ and $L = 124$. We observe that for $L = 31$, the scheme (a) has poorer performance than (b), but is as good as (b) for $L = 124$. That illustrates that the scheme (a) might outperform (b) as L increases in this respect. Our method (c) has superior performance in both cases.

We now put the watermarked images under the amplitude scaling attack. The gain factor β ranges from 0.5 to 1.5. Fig. 6 depicts one of the attacked images. In Fig. 7, the BER of each watermarking scheme is plotted as a function of the scaling factor for $L = 31$ and $L = 124$. As it can be seen, the original STDM is very fragile with respect to amplitude scaling. Oppositely, both (b) and (c)

Fig. 6. The watermarked image obtained by our method with $L = 124$ under the amplitude scaling attack (the scaling factor is 1.5)

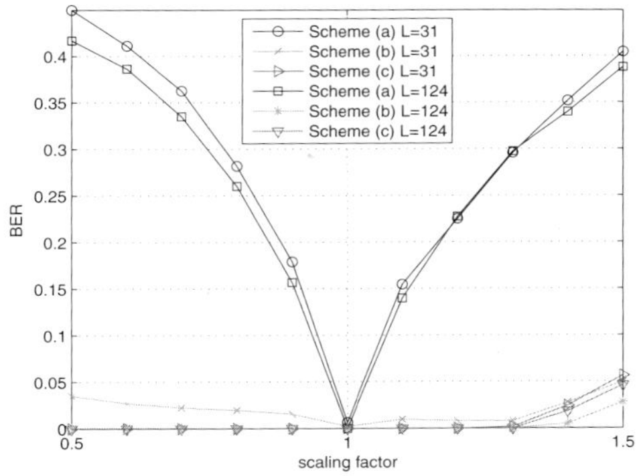

Fig. 7. Bit error rate versus the amplitude scaling for different values of L, $D = 4.8$

are very robust in the respect, which illustrates that the solution presented in Section 4 is effective. In particular, our method can achieve the BER of zero for $\beta < 1$. For $\beta > 1$, the BER of our method increases as β increases, which might be caused by the effect of clipping, but the achieved BER is still very low.

Being the most classical and ubiquitous image processing attack, JPEG compression of various quality factors is applied to the watermarked images. One of the attacked images is shown in Fig. 8. In Fig. 9, the BER of each watermarking scheme is plotted against the quality factor for $L = 31$ and $L = 124$. Although our method achieves the lowest BER among three ones under the same situations, they are not actually enough robust to resist JPEG compression. The reason for this might be that almost all DCT coefficients in each image block of 8×8 pixels are used for embedding, however, some of which are altered largely during compression. According to the analysis, the improvement can be accomplished using the low or middle frequency DCT coefficients of each block for embedding [4].

The watermarked images are next filtered by Gaussian low-pass filter with varying standard deviation (width). One of them after filtering is depicted in Fig. 10 and Fig. 11 shows the plot of BER of each scheme versus the filter width for $L = 31$ and $L = 124$. We found that all the schemes are very sensitive to filtering. The reason for this might be same as JPEG compression. However, with respect to the relative performance among them, our method is best, moreover, the advantage becomes more significant as L increases.

A number of experiments are performed to test the sensitivity of the proposed scheme to change in the DC coefficient by adding a constant intensity to the watermarked images in the spatial domain. The shift in image intensity is chosen from the range $0 - 60$. In Fig. 12, one of the attacked images is presented, while in Fig. 13, the BER of each watermarking scheme is plotted as a function of DC shift for $L = 31$ and $L = 124$. It can be observed that all schemes are robust to

Fig. 8. The watermarked image obtained by our method with $L = 124$ after JPEG compression (the quality factor is 60)

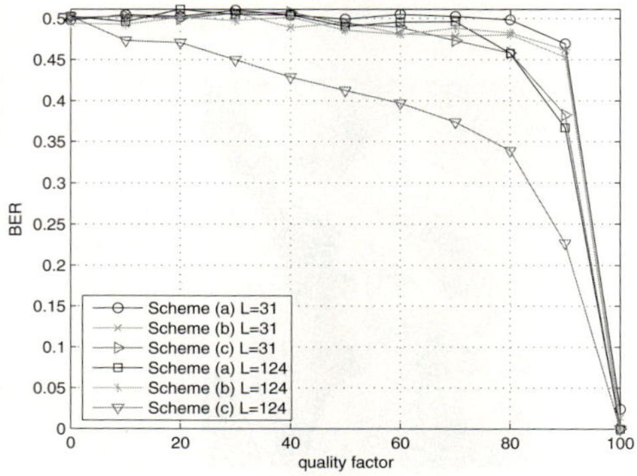

Fig. 9. Bit error rate versus the quality factor of JPEG compression for different values of L, $D = 4.8$

Fig. 10. The watermarked image obtained by our method with $L = 124$ after being filtered by Gaussian low-pass filter (the width is 0.6)

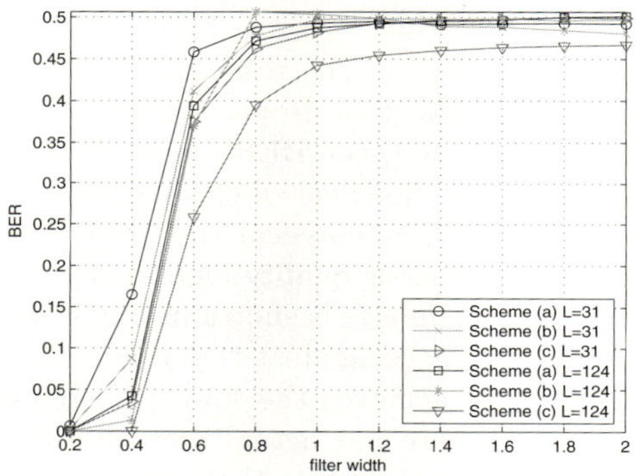

Fig. 11. Bit error rate versus the filter width of Gaussian low-pass filter for different values of L, $D = 4.8$.

DC shift. Other than the previous attacks, the original STDM manifest better performance than other ones, because the detection of (a) does not depend on the DC coefficient. The BER of our method is larger than (b), but the gap between them is not significant.

Histogram equalization is usually used for image enhancement. It modifies the dynamic range and contrast of an image so that its intensity histogram has a desired shape. The watermarked images are histogram equalized so that each of the attacked image (an example shown in Fig. 14) has a flat histogram. Table I reports the BER of each watermarking scheme in this case. Our method manifests the similar performance to scheme (b), but they are better than (a).

As to the geometric attacks, since we are only interested in the relative performance of different schemes, it is sufficient to consider the case that the attack

Fig. 12. The watermarked image obtained by our method with $L = 124$ after its DC coefficient is shifted by 60

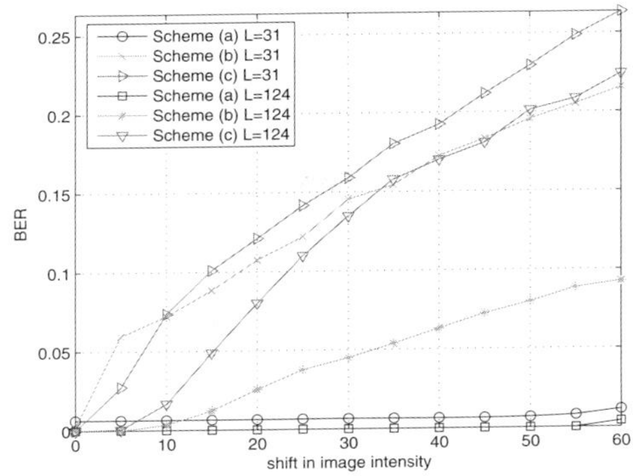

Fig. 13. Bit error rate vs. intensity shift for different values of L, $D = 4.8$

Fig. 14. The watermarked image obtained by our method with $L = 124$ after histogram equalization

Schemes	(a)		(b)		(c)	
L	31	124	31	124	31	124
BER	0.46	0.42	0.33	0.19	0.32	0.23

Table 1. Bit error rate after histogram equalization for different values of L,and $D = 4.8$

parameters are available to the detectors, so the resynchronization can be implemented by performing the inverse transforms.

We rotate the watermarked images by 0° to 45° and rotate them back before detecting. Fig. 15 shows an example of the rotated ones. The induced BER of each watermarking scheme is plotted in Fig. 16 as a function of the rotation degree for $L = 31$ and $L = 124$. We can see that the BER of them all increase rapidly as the rotation degree increases from 0° to 5°, and thereafter becomes nearly constant. Our method outperforms other ones subject to this kind of attack, and the advantage become evident for larger L.

Scaling is another kind of geometrical transformation used for test here. The watermarked images are scaled by the factor γ from 0.5 to 1.5 and then scaled back before detecting. Fig. 17 depicts one of the resulting images. Fig. 18 shows the plot of the BER of each watermarking scheme versus the scaling factor for $L = 31$ and $L = 124$. All the schemes are more robust in the case $\gamma > 1$ than

Fig. 15. The watermarked image obtained by our method with $L = 124$ after being rotated by 25°

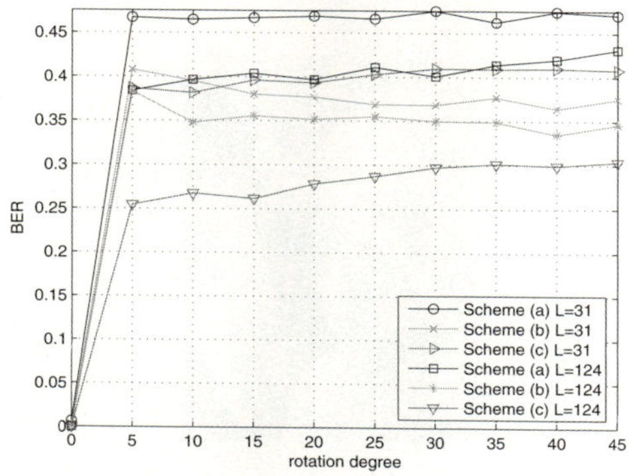

Fig. 16. Bit error rate vs. rotation degree for different values of L, $D = 4.8$

Fig. 17. The watermarked image obtained by our method with $L = 124$ after being scaled by 0.7 and then resized to the original size

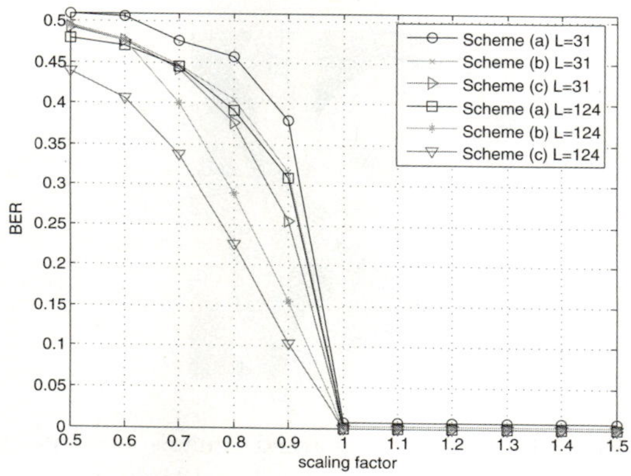

Fig. 18. Bit error rate vs. scaling factor for different values of L, $D = 4.8$

$\gamma < 1$, even scheme (b) and (c) achieve the BER of zero in the former one. The reason for this is that the scaling operation with $\gamma > 1$ results in less information loss than $\gamma < 1$. In the latter one, our method manifests superior performance.

6 Conclusion

In this paper, we proposed the image-adaptive STDM based on Watson's model. The basic idea is to weight the spread vector by the JND sequence estimated by the adopted perceptual model, and then, the obtained vector is linearly combined with the host signal to produce the watermarked signal. In this watermarking framework, we derive a strategy on the choice of quantization step under the given distortion constraint. Furthermore, the scheme need not again compute the JND of each DCT coefficient during detection, so saves the computation cost. Additionally, we presented a simple and practical solution to the amplitude scaling attack. Comparing with other relative watermarking techniques, our method yields significant improvements in invisibility and robustness.

Note that the paper only developed a basic framework of image-adaptive STDM. It is easy to extend the main idea of our method to other embedding domains and visual models. Future work should focuses on the design of extraction function and synchronization schemes against the geometric attacks.

Acknowledgments. This work was supported by China Postdoctoral Science Foundation under Grant No. 20060390009.

References

1. Cox, I.J., Kilian, J., Leighton, F.T., Shamoon, T.: Secure spread spectrum watermarking for multimedia. IEEE Transactions on Image Processing 6(12), 1673–1687 (1997)
2. Chen, B., Wornell, G.W.: Quantization index modulation: a class of provably good methods fordigital watermarking and information embedding. IEEE Transactions on Information Theory 47(4), 1423–1443 (2001)
3. Li, Q., Cox, I.J.: Using perceptual models to improve fidelity and provide invariance to valumetric scaling for quantization index modulationwatermarking. In: Proc. IEEE International Conference on Acoustics, Speech, and Signal Processing (ICASSP '05), vol. 2, pp. 1–4 (2005)
4. Saravanan, V., Bora, P., Ghosh, D.: Oblivious image-adaptive watermarking using quantization index modulation. In: Proc. The Eighth National Conf. On Communications, pp. 26–37 (2002)
5. Bao, P., Ma, X.H.: Image adaptive watermarking using wavelet domain singular value decomposition. IEEE Transactions on Circuits and Systems for Video Technology 15(1), 96–102 (2005)
6. Abrardo, A., Barni, M.: Informed watermarking by means of orthogonal and quasi-orthogonal dirty paper coding. IEEE Transactions on Signal Processing 53(2), 824–833 (2005)
7. Eggers, J.J., Bauml, R., Girod, B.: Estimation of amplitude modifications before scs watermark detection. In: Proc. SPIE Security Watermarking Multimedia Contents IV, vol. 4675, pp. 387–C398 (2002)
8. Miller, M.L., Doerr, G.J., Cox, I.J.: Applying informed coding and embedding to design a robust, high capacity, watermark. IEEE Transactions on Image Processing 13(6), 792–C807 (2004)
9. Prez-Gonzlez, F., Mosquera, C., Barni, M., Abrardo, A.: Rational dither modulation: A high-rate data-hiding method invariant to gain attacks. IEEE Transactions on Signal Processing 53(10), 3960–3975 (2005)
10. Watson, A.B.: Dct quantization matrices optimized for individual images. In: Jansen, K., Khuller, S. (eds.) Approximation Algorithms for Combinatorial Optimization. LNCS, vol. 1913, pp. 202–216. Springer, Heidelberg (2000)

Improvement of Film Scratch Inpainting Algorithm Using Sobel Based Isophote Computation over Hilbert Scan Line

Ki-Hong Ko and Seong-Whan Kim

Department of Computer Science, University of Seoul, Jeon-Nong-Dong, Seoul, Korea.
Tel.: +82-2-2210-5316; Fax: +82-2-2210-5275
jedigo@venus.uos.ac.kr, swkim7@uos.ac.kr

Abstract. Old films or photographs usually have damages from physical or chemical effects, and the damage and digitalization make stain, scratch, scribbling, noise, and digital drop out in frames. Inpainting is a well-known technique to restore damages in images. Bertalmio's inpainting scheme shows good reconstruction, but it requires much time complexity. We present a modified inpainting scheme, where we use Sobel edge operator's magnitude and angle to compute isophotes. We experimented with standard test images, and it shows that our scheme requires smaller time complexity than Bertalmio's scheme and shows comparable reconstructed image quality.

1 Introduction

Old films or photographs are injured by physical or chemical effects, and people store these films or photographs on digital media to remain unchanged forever. When these films or photographs convert into the digital media, the digitization stores films or photograph's damaged areas at the same time. These damaged areas are stain, scratch, scribbling, noise, digital drop out and so on, and the inpainting technique is to recover these damaged areas. To restore the identified damages, we can use inpainting technique. It firstly selects the damaged area, and the neighbor area's information is propagated inward from the damaged area's boundaries. The damaged areas have to be filled by the similarity of neighbors' information. The similarity of neighbors' information is well expressed by the isophote. Bertalmio's technique has the validity of mathematics and well reconstructs the damaged image, but the reconstructing time is very slow [1]. Oliveira's technique is very fast, but this method has no provisions for considering isophotes [2]. Telea's technique is used to compute directional weighting component to get the isophote, and is very fast [3].

In this paper, we propose inpainting method using Sobel operator. We use Sobel operator's magnitude and angular to represent isophotes's characters. Our proposed method is very fast and produces nearly identical results for Bertalmio's method. This paper consists of five sections. In section 2, we review the previous research works for inpainting techniques. Section 3 presents our proposed method using Sobel operator. In section 4, we experimented on our restoration scheme; finally the conclusions are drawn in section 5.

Y. Wang, Y. Cheung, and H. Liu (Eds.): CIS 2006, LNAI 4456, pp. 924–934, 2007.

2 Related Works

Image reconstructing techniques are divided into two major categories: denoising and inpainting. In the denoising, the pixels contain both information about the real data and the noise data, while in image inpainting, there is no significant information in the region to be inpainted. As above reason, image inpainting have to restore the damaged area using neighbor's area. Kokaram's technique is based on previous video frame for inpainting [4, 5, 6]. It uses adjacent frame's information using motion estimation and autoregressive models in order to restores damaged regions. It cannot be used for I-frame. For each frame, we can use still image-related inpainting techniques: (1) Bertalmio's method, (2) Oliveira's method, and (3) Telea's method. Bertalmio's method uses image Laplacian. The information of estimated image's smoothness maintains isophotes directions and propagates into damaged area. Because the information of smoothness computes iteratively, it requires much time. Also the vector to find isophotes complicates the computation [1]. Oliveira's method performs restoration by constituting 3x3 filters. Its restoration speed is fast and implementation is simple. But Oliveira's method doesn't preserve isophotes's directions. [2]. Third, Telea's method classifies information of images to level set such as BAND, KNOWN, and INSIDE. To revive isophotes, it performs restoration by constituting directional component and geometric distance component. Telea scheme is much better than Bertalmio's method in speed of performance [3].

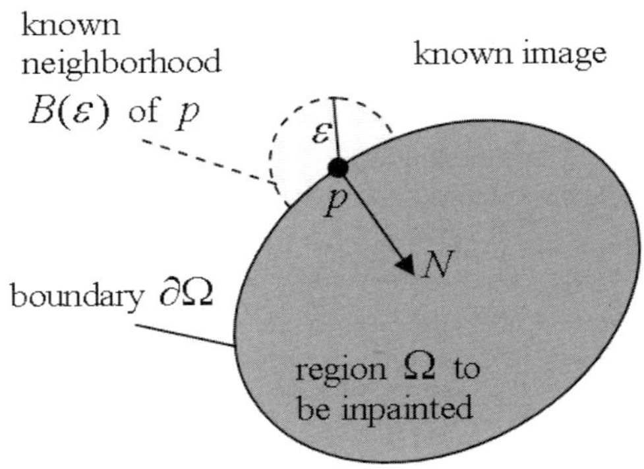

Fig. 1. Bertalmio's inpainting method

Figure 1 shows the basic idea of Bertalmio's inpainting method, in which the point p represent the pixel coordinates (i, j), Ω stand for the region to be inpainted, and $\partial\Omega$ is the boundary of Ω. Bertalmio's method will prolong the isophotes lines arriving at $\partial\Omega$, while maintaining the angle of arrival. The region Ω is filled with the structure of the area ε preserving isophote lines. In other words, the point p value on the boundary $\partial\Omega$ of the region Ω is determined by the values of the known image point q in $\boldsymbol{B}(\varepsilon)$, and the region Ω is filled with the approximated pixel value p. As in the Equation (1), we compute the improved version $\boldsymbol{I}^{n+1}(\boldsymbol{i},\boldsymbol{j})$ of $\boldsymbol{I}^{n}(\boldsymbol{i},\boldsymbol{j})$, given $I_t^n(i,j)$, where $I(i,j)$ is the intensity of the pixel coordinates (i, j), and Δt is the rate of improvement.

$$I^{n+1}(i,j) = I^n(i,j) + \Delta t I_t^n(i,j), \quad \forall (i,j) \in \Omega$$
$$I_t^n(i,j) = \overrightarrow{\delta L^n}(i,j) \cdot \overrightarrow{N^n}(i,j) \tag{1}$$

Now, Bertalmio's method has to compute $I_t^n(i,j)$ considering smoothly propagate information from outside Ω into Ω. $I_t^n(i,j)$ comes from $L^n(i,j)$ and $\overrightarrow{N}^n(i,j)$, where $L^n(i,j)$ is the propagation information, $\overrightarrow{N}^n(i,j)$ is the propagation direction, and $\overrightarrow{\delta L^n}(i,j)$ is a measure of the change in the information $L^n(i,j)$. $L^n(i,j)$ should be an image smoothness estimator, and we can use a simple discrete implementation of Laplacian as shown in Equation (2).

$$L^n(i,j) = I_{xx}^n(i,j) + I_{yy}^n(i,j)$$
$$\overrightarrow{\delta L^n}(i,j) = (L^n(i+1,j) - L^n(i-1,j),\ L^n(i,j+1) - L^n(i,j-1)) \tag{2}$$

Also we have to compute propagation direction $\overrightarrow{N}(i,j)$. Bertalmio defined $\overrightarrow{N}(i,j)$ as the normal to the signed distance to $\partial\Omega$, and decided the direction of spatial change as the discrete gradient vector $\nabla I^n(i,j)$. The normal value is stood for Equation (3), and the gradient vector value is represented by Equation (4) in which b and f denote back ward and forward difference, and m and M denote the minimum and maximum.

$$\frac{\overrightarrow{N}(i,j,n)}{\left|\overrightarrow{N}(i,j,n)\right|} := \frac{\left(-I_y^n(i,j),\ I_x^n(i,j)\right)}{\sqrt{\left(I_x^n(i,j)\right)^2 + \left(I_y^n(i,j)\right)^2}} \tag{3}$$

$$\left|\nabla I^n(i,j)\right| = \begin{cases} \sqrt{\left(I_{xbm}^n\right)^2 + \left(I_{xfM}^n\right)^2 + \left(I_{ybm}^n\right)^2 + \left(I_{yfM}^n\right)^2}, \\ \text{when } \beta^n > 0 \\ \sqrt{\left(I_{xbM}^n\right)^2 + \left(I_{xfm}^n\right)^2 + \left(I_{ybM}^n\right)^2 + \left(I_{yfm}^n\right)^2}, \\ \text{when } \beta^n < 0 \end{cases} \tag{4}$$

$$\text{where} \quad \beta^n(i,j) = \overrightarrow{\delta L^n}(i,j) \cdot \frac{\overrightarrow{N}(i,j,n)}{\left|\overrightarrow{N}(i,j,n)\right|}$$

As above results, the updated value $I_t^n(i,j)$ is represented by Equation (5).

$$I_t^n(i,j) = \left(\overrightarrow{\delta L^n}(i,j) \cdot \frac{\overrightarrow{N}(i,j,n)}{\left|\overrightarrow{N}(i,j,n)\right|} \right) \left|\nabla I^n(i,j)\right| \tag{5}$$

Now Telea's method inpaint point p as a function of all points q in known neighborhood $B_\in(p)$ by summing the estimates of all points q, weighted by a normalized weighting function $w(p,q)$ as shown in Equation (6). $\nabla I(q)$ is estimated by central differences, and $w(p,q)$ is represented by Equation (7), in which $dir(p,q)$ is directional component, $dst(p,q)$ is geometric distance component, $lev(p,q)$ is level set, and T is the distance map of the Ω to $\partial\Omega$.

$$I(p) = \frac{\sum_{q\in B_\in(p)} w(p,q)\left[I(q) + \nabla I(q)(p-q)\right]}{\sum_{q\in B_\in(p)} w(p,q)} \tag{6}$$

$$w(p,q) = dir(p,q)\cdot dst(p,q)\cdot lev(p,q),$$

$$\text{where} \begin{cases} dir(p,q) = \dfrac{p-q}{\|p-q\|}\cdot N(p) \\ dst(p,q) = \dfrac{d_0^2}{\|p-q\|^2} \\ lev(p,q) = \dfrac{T_0}{1+\left|T(p)-T(q)\right|} \end{cases} \tag{7}$$

3 Proposed Method

We propose a computationally efficient inpainting scheme, which shows comparable restoration performance as Bertalmio's. In our scheme, we use Sobel operator to compute isophote direction.

Figure 2(a) shows the isophote computation for to-be-inpainted pixel *S*. We define Q_{c1} as the set, which includes all the known neighboring pixels (ε_1 bound) of pixel *S*. For all the pixels in Q_{c1}, we apply Sobel operator as shown in Equation (8), and we get the magnitude g and angular direction θ component of each pixel's edge feature: $q_1, q_2, \ldots, q_n$ ($q_i = \{g_i, \theta_i\}$). θ. In our model, the angular direction θ corresponds to the propagation direction $\overrightarrow{N}(i,j)$. We compute the maximum value of g, and we set the pixel with maximum value g as the dominant pixel of region Q_{c1}. If the maximum value g_i is bigger than the predefined threshold (we set 30), we consider the region Q_{c1}, as directional region with direction θ_i. If the maximum is less than the predefined threshold, we consider the region Q_{c1}, as smoothly varying uniform region.

As shown in Figure 2(b), we can use θ_i to identify Qc_2, Qc_3, and Qc_4 regions, which lies in the orthogonal direction of θ_i. from Qc_1. In the same manner, we find the dominant pixels for each region: Qc_2, Qc_3, and Qc_4.

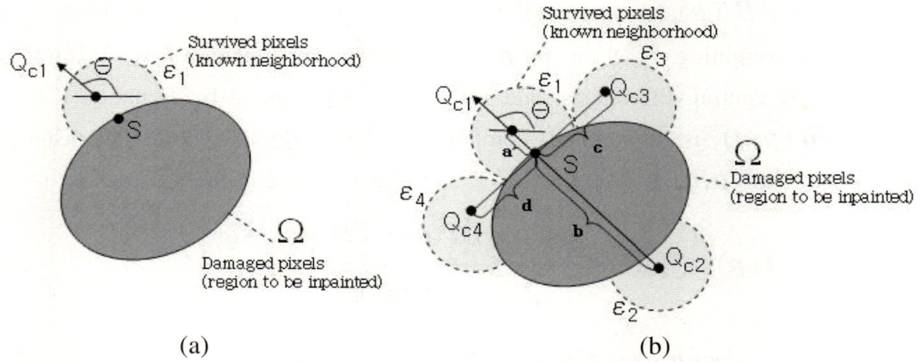

Fig. 2. Proposed inpainting scheme: (a) isophote computation for point S, (b) inpainting of point S using four dominant pixel values

$$g_x = f_{m+1,n+1} + 2f_{m,n+1} + f_{m-1,n+1} - f_{m+1,n-1} - 2f_{m,n-1} - f_{m-1,n-1} \tag{8}$$

$$g_y = f_{m+1,n+1} + 2f_{m+1,n} + f_{m+1,n-1} - f_{m-1,n+1} - 2f_{m-1,n} - f_{m-1,n-1}$$

$$g = \sqrt{g_x^2 + g_y^2}, \quad \theta = \tan^{-1}(g_y / g_x)$$

To inpaint point S, we compute the distance between S and dominant pixels. {a, b, c, d} are the distance between point S and dominant pixels { Qc_1, Qc_2, Qc_3, and Qc_4}. Equation (9) is the inpainting equation to preserve isophote at S. Also when the inpainting region Ω are wide, we can disregard the information of ε_2, ε_3, or ε_4. In this case, because the pixel for inpainting doesn't relates to far neighborhood, but relates to near neighborhood. In other word, if the distance is far away, then we ignore the pixel of Qc_i. For example, if the b is more than 10 pixels distant, we do not include Qc_2.

$$S = \frac{w_b Qc_1 + w_a Qc_2 + w_d Qc_3 + w_c Qc_4}{2} \tag{9}$$

$$where, \quad w_a = \frac{a}{a+b}, \ w_b = \frac{b}{a+b}, \ w_c = \frac{c}{c+d}, \ w_d = \frac{d}{c+d}$$

In digital images, because the pixel's coordinate is discrete, we need not consider all direction. So we consider eight directions from 0° to 180° incrementing 22.5° as shown in Figure 3. Now in this paper, we can inpaint considering isophote using Sobel operator's angular direction.

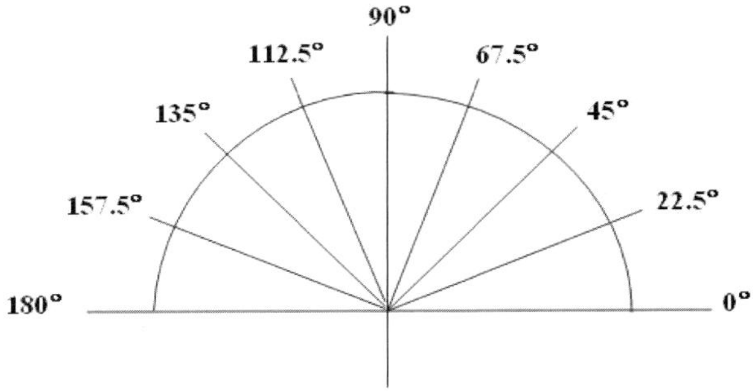

Fig. 3. The eight directions of angular direction

The following pseudo-code shows the procedure for finding dominant pixels { $\boldsymbol{d}_1$, $\boldsymbol{d}_2$. $\boldsymbol{d}_3$, $\boldsymbol{d}_4$ } in four different regions {Qc_1, Qc_2, Qc_3, Qc_4.} as directed by isophote.

```
Find_dominant_pixels // Find four dominant pixels
{
  for all pixels q_i in Qc_1
  {
    q_i's g_i = Sobel_Operator's Magnitude Component;
    q_i's θ_i [0,1,...,7] = Sobel_Operator's Angular Component;
  }
  Set d_1 to q_i with maximum g value;
  d_1's g = g_i; d_1's θ = (θ_i , i in [0,1,...7] );
  if (d_1's g > 30 ) // Region Qc_1 has Directional Component
  {
    // Find a dominant pixel in_ Qc_2 with ε_2 bound
    for all pixels q_i in Qc_2
    {
      q_i's g_i = Sobel_Operator's Magnitude Component;
      q_i's θ_i [0,1,...,7] = Sobel_Operator's Angular Component;
    }
    Set d_2 to q_i with maximum g value;
    d_2's g = g_i; d_2's θ = (θ_i , i in [0,1,...7] );
  }
  else // Region Qc_1 has Uniform Component
  {
```

```
    // Find a dominant pixel in Qc₂ with ε₂ bound
    d₂ in Qc₂ = Find the nearest pixel to S in Qc₂ with ε₂ bound
    // Find a dominant pixel in Qc₃ with ε₃ bound
    d₃ in Qc₃ = Find the nearest pixel to S in ε₃
    // Find a dominant pixel in Qc₄ with ε₄ bound
    d₄ in Qc₄ = Find the nearest pixel to S in ε₄
  }
}
```

Also we compared line-by-line scan order with Hilbert scan order. Figure 4 shows two scan order. Hilbert scan is the scheme which maximizes the inter-correlation between pixels. The line-by-line affects the inter-correlation of the only horizontal pixels because the line-by-line moves horizontal. But Hilbert scan affects the inter-correlation of the horizontal and vertical pixels because Hilbert moves right, down, left or up as shown Figure 4(b). Therefore Hilbert scan order has better restored quality than line-by-line scan order [7, 8, 9].

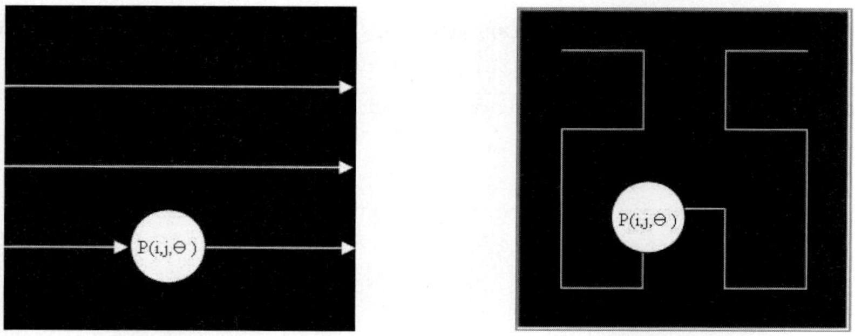

(a) (b)

Fig. 4. The order of scan: (a) line-by-line scan order and (b) Hilbert curve scan order

4 Experimental Results

We experiment our scheme with standard test images, and we used one old animation "Robot Taekwon V" (1970s in Korea). We compared our method with Bertalmio's method and Telea's method. We experimented with Pentium-4 2.5GHz and 1GB memories. Also we can acquire Bertalmio's and Telea's software in the site [10, 11]. Figure 5 shows the experimental result using "Three ladies" images. In Figure 5, proposed method's quality is better than Telea's method, and Bertalmio's method is better than proposed method, however, we can save the execution time. Also we can achieve better quality using Hilbert scan order instead of line-by-line scan order.

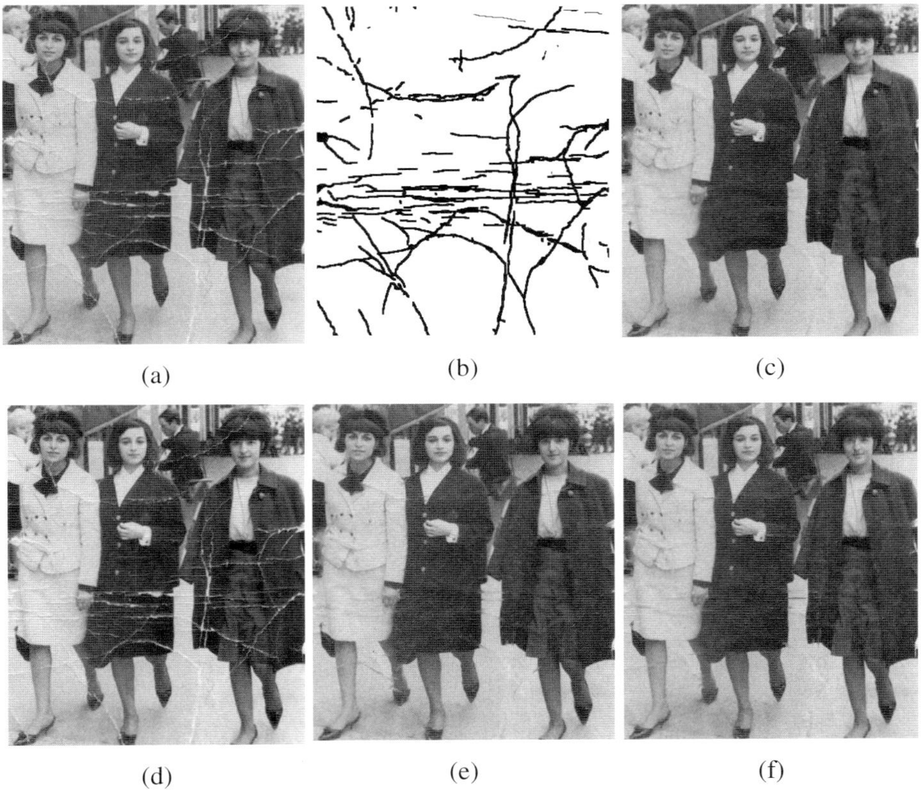

Fig. 5. Experimental Result for "Three Ladies" image: (a) Original degraded image, (b) Scratch, (c) Bertalmio's method (10 minutes), (d) Telea's method (1 second), (e) Proposed method (line by line scan, 2 seconds), (f) Proposed method (Hilbert scan, 4 seconds)

Figure 6 shows detailed view of Figure 5. Figure 6(d) shows better result than Figure 6(c), because Hilbert scan can exploit more inter-correlation between pixels than line-by-line scan.

Figure 7 shows the experimental result using "Robot Taekwon V" images. In Figure 7, proposed method's quality is better than Telea's method, and is similar to the result Bertalmio's. Also we can save the execution time. As shown in Figure 8(a), Bertalmio's method is well restored in the part of hand, but isn't well restored in the part of ear. Proposed method is well restored in the part of ear, but isn't well restored in the part of hand. We compared PSNR using human corrected image. Proposed methods have better PSNR than Bertalmio's method. For scan order, Figure 8(d) shows better quality in the hand and mustache than Figure 8(c), but Figure 8(c) is better quality in the part of ear than Figure 8(d). Hilbert scan makes 1 dB improvements line-by-line scan scheme.

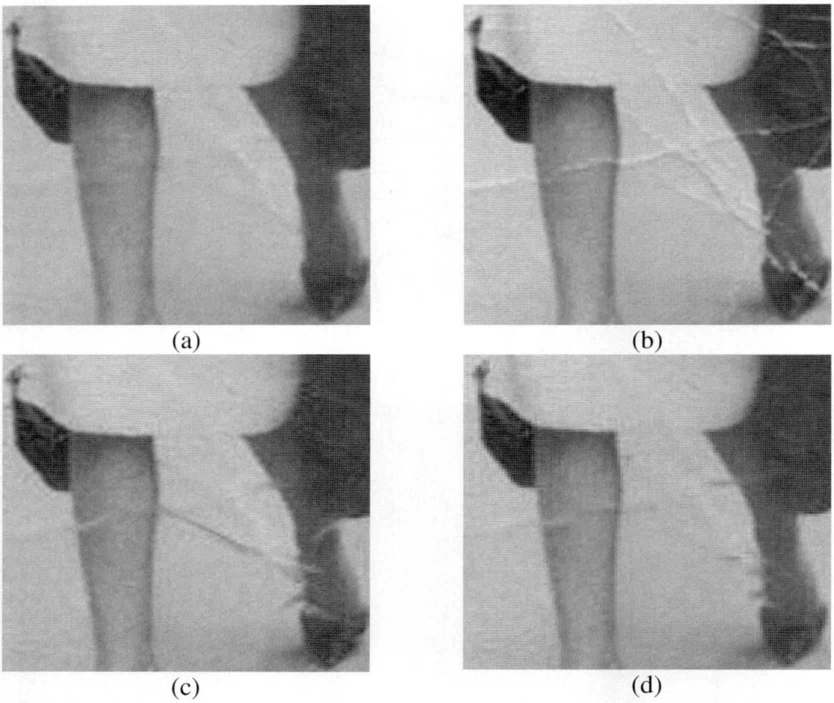

Fig. 6. Enlarged for detailed portion in Figure 5: (a) Bertalmio's method, (b) Telea's method, (c) Proposed method (line by line scan), (d) Proposed method (Hilbert scan)

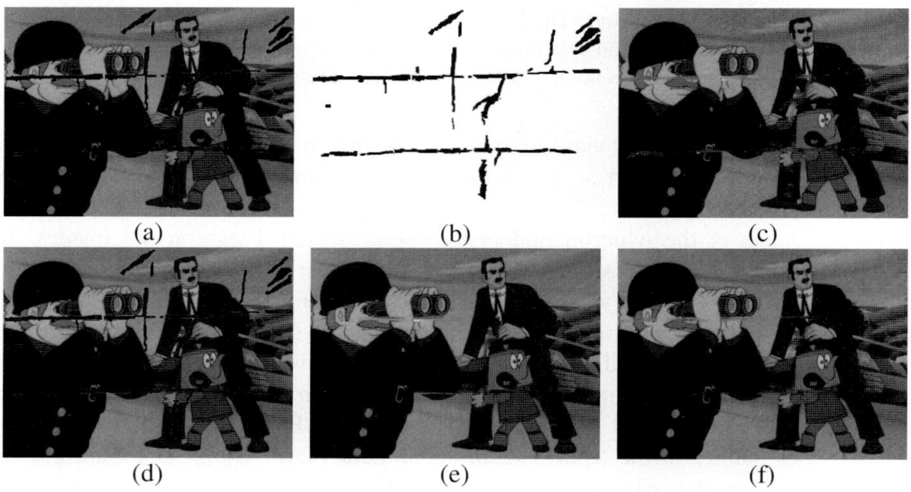

Fig. 7. Experimental Result for "Robot Taekwon V" image: (a) Original degraded image, (b) Scratch, (c) Bertalmio's method (8 minutes), (d) Telea's method (1 second), (e) Proposed method (line by line scan, 2 seconds), (f) Proposed method (Hilbert scan, 3 seconds)

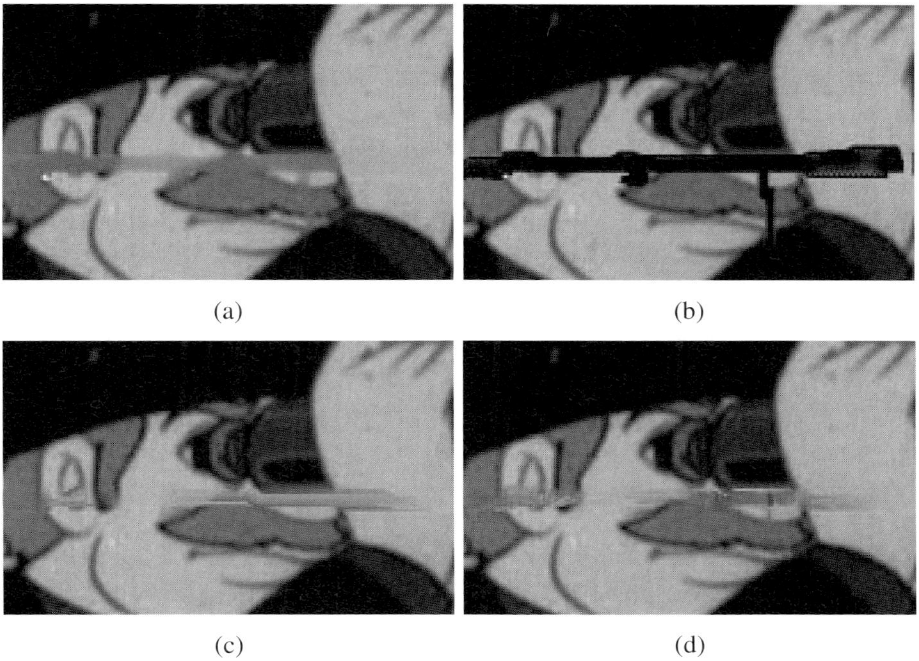

Fig. 8. Enlarged for detailed portion in Figure 7: (a) Bertalmio's method (32.98 dB) (b) Telea's method (22.85 dB), (c) Proposed method (line by line scan, 33.41 dB), (d) Proposed method (Hilbert scan, 34.43 dB)

5 Conclusions

In the image inpainting techniques, Bertalmio's technique is well known. Although Bertalmio's method has the validity of mathematics and well reconstructs the damaged image, the reconstructing time is very slow. Also Telea's technique is very fast, but doesn't well restore some specific images. Therefore this paper proposes the technique that has good restoration quality and is very fast. Proposed technique uses Sobel operator's gradient magnitude and angular directions to preserve the isophote. Also we use line-by-line scan order and Hilbert scan order to compare with inter-correlation of pixels. As a result, Hilbert scan order is better than line-by-line scan, because the object and background of the film and image is related by object's and background's neighborhood. Line-by-line scan order only considers left neighborhood, but Hilbert scan order considers up, down, left, or right neighborhood. And we can save consumed time maintaining Berlamio's quality, and we can know that the angular direction of proposed method is the same to the propagation direction $\overrightarrow{N}(i,j)$ which determines the isophote direction in Bertalmio's method.

References

1. Bertalmio, M., Sapiro, G., Caselles, V., Ballester, C.: Image Inpainting. In: Akeley, K. (ed.) Proceedings of SIGGRAPH, Computer Graphics Proceedings. ACM Press / ACM SIGGRAPH / Addison Wesley Longman, pp. 417–424 (2000)
2. Oliveira, M., Bowen, B., McKenna, R., Chan, Y.-S.: Fast Digital Image Inpainting. In: Proc. VIIP, pp. 261–266 (2001)
3. Telea, A.: An Image Inpainting Technique Based on the Fast Marching Method. Journal of Graphics Tools, A K Peters, Ltd 9, 25–36 (2004)
4. Kokaram, A.C., Morris, R.D., Fitzerald, W.J., Rayner, P.J.W.: Interpolation of missing data in image sequences. IEEE Transactions On Image Processing. 4, 1509–1519 (1995)
5. Kokaram, A.: On Missing Data Treatment for Degraded Video and Film Archives: A Survey and a New Bayesian Approach. IEEE Transactions On Image Processing 13, 397–415 (2004)
6. Kokaram, A., Bornard, R., Rares, A., Sidorov, D., Chenot, J-H., Laborelli, L., Biemond, J.: Robust and Automatic Digital Restoration Systems: Copying with Reality. International Broadcasting Convention, pp. 405–411 (2002)
7. Voorhies, D.: Space-Filling Curves and a Measure of Coherence. In: Arvo, J. (ed.) Graphics Gems II, Academic Press, pp. 26–30. Academic Press, London (1999)
8. Bially, T.: Space-Filling Curves: Their Generation and Their Application to Bandwidth Reduction. IEEE Transactions on Information Theory IT-15, 658–664 (1969)
9. The Hilbert curve available in, http://www.compuphase.com/hilbert.htm
10. Bertallmio, M., Sapiro, G., Caselles, V., Ballester, C.: Image Inpainting Software. available in, http://inpainting.alpha-sigma.net
11. Telea, A.: An Image Inpainting Technique Based on the Fast Marching Method Software. available in, http://www.acm.org/jgt/papers/Telea04

A Watershed Algorithmic Approach for Gray-Scale Skeletonization in Thermal Vein Pattern Biometrics

Lingyu Wang[1] and Graham Leedham[2]

[1] School of Computer Engineering, Nanyang Technological University, N4-#2A-32 Nanyang Avenue, Singapore 639798
wa0001yu@ntu.edu.sg
[2] University of New South Wales (Asia), 1 Kay Siang Road, Singapore 248922
G.Leedham@unswasia.edu.sg

Abstract. In vein pattern biometrics, analysis of the shape of the vein pattern is the most critical task for person identification. One of best representations of the shape of vein patterns is the skeleton of the pattern. Many traditional skeletonization algorithms are based on binary images. In this paper, we propose a novel technique that utilizes the watershed algorithm to extract the skeletons of vein patterns directly from gray-scale images. This approach eliminates the segmentation stage, and hence prevents any error occurring during this process from propagating to the skeletonization stage. Experiments are carried out on a thermal vein pattern images database. Results show that watershed algorithm is capable of extracting the skeletons of the veins effectively, and also avoids any artifacts introduced by the binarization stage.

1 Introduction

Biometrics is the science of identifying a person using physiological or behavioral features [1]. During the past few decades, various biometric features have been utilized for person verification. The most popular ones are fingerprints, faces, and iris scans as well as handwritten signatures. Each of these biometrics have their strengths and weaknesses [2]. Recently, vein pattern biometrics has attracted increasing interest from both research communities [3,4,5,6] and industries [7,8].

A Vein Pattern is the vast network of blood vessels underneath a person's skin. Anatomically, aside from surgical intervention, the shape of vascular patterns in the same part of the body is distinct from each other [9], and it is very stable over a long period of time, as a person's pattern of blood vessels is "hardwired" into the body at birth, and remains relatively unaffected by aging, except for predictable growth, as with other biometrics such as fingerprints. In addition, as the blood vessels are hidden underneath the skin and are mostly invisible to the human eye, vein patterns are much harder for intruders to copy compared to other biometric features. The properties of uniqueness, stability and strong immunity to forgery of the vein pattern make it a potentially good biometric which offers greater secure and reliable features for person identity verification.

Y. Wang, Y. Cheung, and H. Liu (Eds.): CIS 2006, LNAI 4456, pp. 935–942, 2007.

A typical vein pattern biometric system consists of five individual processing stages [3]: *Image Acquisition, Image Enhancement, Vein Pattern Segmentation, Skeletonization and Matching*, as shown in Figure 1. During the image acquisition stage, vein patterns are usually captured using infrared imaging technologies. One of the practices is using a far-infrared camera to acquire the thermal vein pattern images of the back of the hand [3,4]. After obtaining the images, the system will segment the vein pattern from the background and binarize it for skeletonization to obtain the shape of the pattern. Finally, the system recognizes the vein patterns by various pattern recognition methods such as calculating the line segment Hausdorff distances [10].

However, during the vein pattern segmentation and binarization stage of the system shown in Figure 1, errors will be unavoidably introduced. These errors will then be propagated to the skeletonization stage, and subsequently degrade the performance of all the subsequent processing stages. This paper examines the problems brought up to the skeletonization stage by the segmentation and binarization process. A new solution is then proposed, whereby skeletonization is performed directly on the gray-scale vein pattern images using the morphological watershed algorithm, which produces better skeletonization results.

This research focuses on thermal vein pattern images processing, and the paper is organized in the following manner: Section 2 investigates in detail the problems introduced by the vein pattern segmentation process. A new system model for vein pattern biometrics is then proposed. Following this, in Section 3, an in-depth discussion of our approach using the watershed algorithm to extract the skeletons of the vein patterns from gray-scale images is presented. Experiments, and their results are reported in this section with some discussion of the problems encountered using the current watershed approach. Finally, Section 4 gives concluding remarks of this paper.

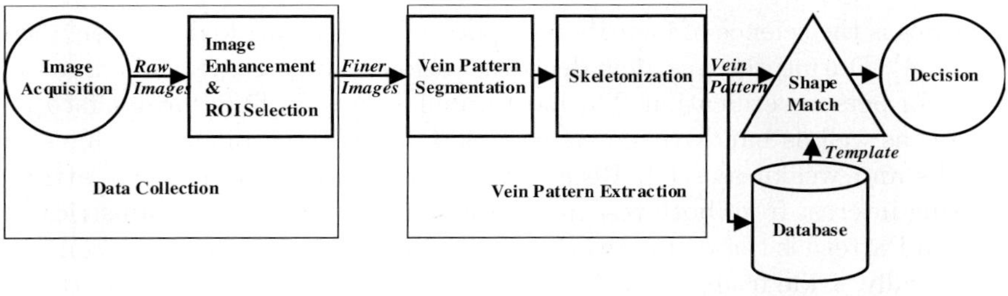

Fig. 1. A typical vein pattern verification system model

2 Traditional Binary-Based Skeletonization

2.1 Vein Pattern Segmentation

A typical thermal vein pattern image of the back of the hand is usually of low contrast and noise-prone. In addition, due to heat radiation, the tissue nearby

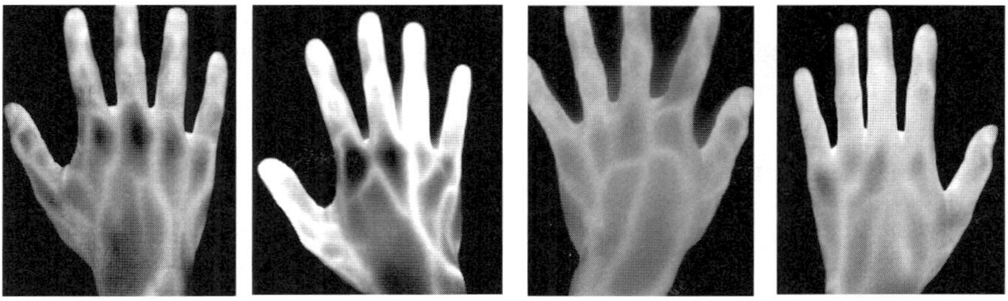

Fig. 2. Thermal vein pattern images of the back of the hands in a normal office environment

has similar temperature to the blood vessels, which results in veins being surrounded by many faint white region in the images (see Figure 2) . All these make separation of vein patterns from the background a difficult task. A popular class of segmentation methods: intensity thresholding, is usually utilized to tackle the problem, where each image pixel is classified either greater or less than or equal to a given intensity. However, due to the fact that the gray-level intensity values of the vein vary at different locations in the image, global threholding techniques do not provide satisfactory results. A more suitable method is via local adaptive thresholding, whereby the algorithm chooses different threhold values for every pixel in the image based on the analysis of its surrounding neighbors. Figure 3 shows the binary image of the vein pattern after applying our local thresholding algorithm, where for every pixel in the image, its threshold value is set as the mean value of its 13×13 neighborhood.

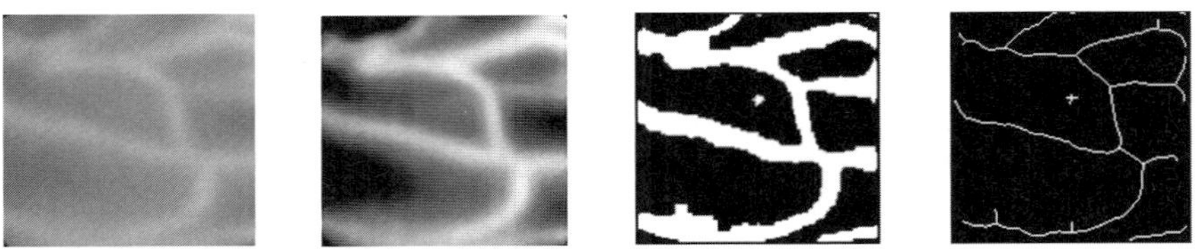

Fig. 3. From left to right: Original ROI of the vein pattern image; After image enhancement; After applying local thresholding; After skeletonization

It can been seen from Figure 3 that the shape of the vein pattern is well preserved in the binrary image after threholding. However, there are also many misclassifications of background points being the points of the vein, especially for those points near the edge of the veins. This is because the intensity thresholding method suffers from errors due to image inhomogeneities and the partial volume effect [11]. Furthermore, the choice of threshold level is subjective, and might not be optimum for all images.

The misclassification errors introduced by this binarization process will be propagated to the next stage, and may be magnified by the skeletonization algorithm, as is elaborated in the following section.

2.2 Binary Skeletonization

There are many skeletonization algorithms that can be used to thin the objects in the binary image. In this paper, we apply two different skeletonization algorithms [12,13] to the binary vein pattern images, and they give us very similar results. As can be seen in Figure 3, the misclassification points in the segmentation stage have led to numerous spur branches as well as isolated segments of skeletons. These false branches will in turn degrade the accuracy of the matching process. Whilst some pruning processes can be taken to remove some of the small artifacts, they generally have some negative impacts to the true skeletons.

2.3 Proposed New System Model

As discussed above, the binarization process of the thermal vein pattern image will result in many misclassification points, these points will create false branches during skeletonization, and hence degrade the performance of the subsequent processing stages. One solution is to improve the segmentation algorithms to reduce misclassification as much as possible. However, in this paper, we propose another solution to tackle this problem: performing skeletonization directly on the gray-scale vein pattern images. This will eliminate the segmentation stage, and hence will prevent any potential errors occurring at this stage being propagated to the subsequent stages. As a result, the system model in Figure 1 will now have 4 stages as shown in Figure 4.

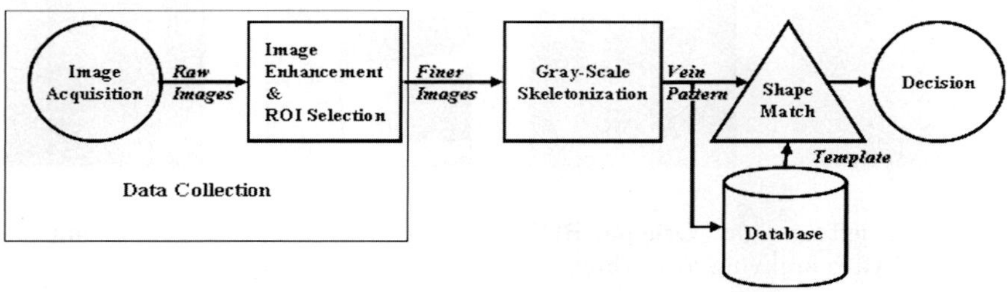

Fig. 4. The proposed new system model eliminates the segmentation stage

3 Gray-Scale Skeletonization Using the Watershed Algorithm

3.1 The Watershed Principle

The watershed concept is based on visualizing an image in three dimensions: two spatial coordinates versus gray levels, through which any grayscale image can be considered as a topographical surface. The basic idea of the watershed algorithm is a simulation of the immersion process [14,15]: At first, holes are pierced in all regional minima of the relief (connected plateaus of constant altitude from which it is impossible to reach a location of lower altitude without having to climb). Then by sinking the whole surface slowly into a lake, water springs through the holes and progressively immerses the adjacent walls. To prevent streams of water coming from different holds to intermingle, a dam is set up at the meeting locations. The flooding will eventually reach a stage when only the tops of the dams are visible above the waterline. These dam boundaries correspond to the divide lines of the watersheds.

Mathematically, this immersion process can be established by the definition of geodesic distance and geodesic influence zone [16]. The geodesic distance $d_A(x, y)$ between two pixels x and y in A is the infimum length of the paths P which join x and y and are totally included in A (Equation 1). Whilst the geodesic Influence zone is defined as: Suppose A contains a set B consisting of several connected components B_1, B_2,...,B_k. The geodesic influence zone $iz_A(B_i)$ of a connected component B_i of B in A is the locus of the points of A whose geodesic distance of B_i is smaller than their geodesic distance to any other component of B. This is expressed in Equation 2.

$$d_A(x, y) = inf\{l(P)\} \tag{1}$$

$$iz_A(B_i) = \{p \in A, \forall j \in [1, k]/\{i\}, d_A(p, B_i)\} \tag{2}$$

Hence, the watersheds can be obtained by finding the set of catchment basins of the gray-scale image I through the following recursion (Equations 3 and 4):

$$X_{h_{min}} = T_{h_{min}(I)}, \text{ where } T_h(I) = \{p \in D_I, I(p) \leq h\} \tag{3}$$

$$\forall h \in [h_{min}, h_{max} - 1], X_{h+1} = min_{h+1} \bigcup iz_{T_{h+1}(I)}(X_h) \tag{4}$$

3.2 Application of Watersheds Algorithm to Vein Pattern Skeletonization

Traditionally, the watershed algorithm is used to find the contour of the objects for segmentation purposes. Therefore, it is usually applied to the gradient images. However, when we apply the watershed algorithm directly to the gray-scale vein pattern images, it is capable of locating the skeletons of the veins. The image in the center of Figure 5 shows the result of applying the watershed algorithm to the thermal vein pattern image. It is clearly visible that the result contains too many false ridges, and this is commonly referred to as over-segmentation, which is due to noise and other local irregularities.

Many researchers have addressed the over-segmentation problem for the watershed algorithm. Markers, for example, are widely used to reduce the effect of over-segmentation. In our approach, we perform morphological opening followed by closing operations to suppress the noise and local irregularities in the image prior to the application of the watershed algorithm (Equation 5). The image

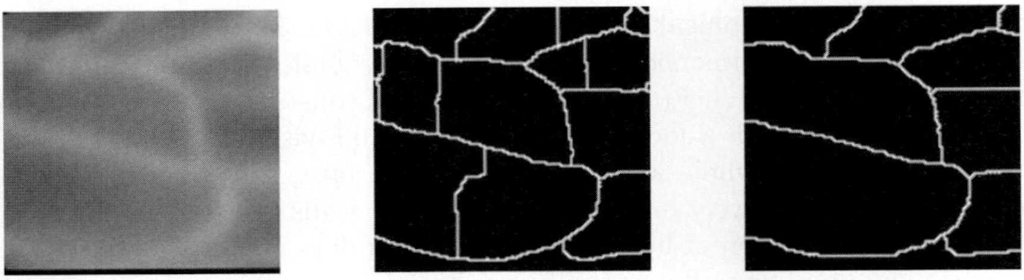

Fig. 5. From left to right: Original ROI image; Skeletons obtained by direct application of watershed algorithm, where over-segmentation is apparent; Skeletons obtained by applying morphological opening and closing first followed by the watershed algorithm

in the right side of Figure 5 shows the result with our approach, and it can be easily seen that the single pixel wide skeleton of the vein pattern is successfully extracted, and the number of false branches is significantly reduced.

$$I' = (I \circ B) \bullet B; \; \textit{where } B \textit{ is the structuring element.} \tag{5}$$

3.3 Experiments

The watershed algorithm was investigated for gray-scale skeletonization on our thermal hand vein patterns database. Most of the vein patterns can be successfully skeletonized without losing any connectivity (as shown in the examples in

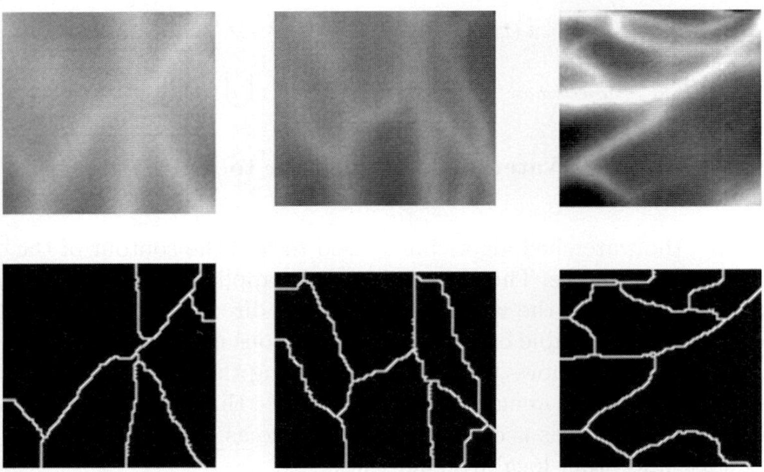

Fig. 6. Top: Original ROI images; Buttom: Skeletons obtained by applying the proposed watershed algorithm

Figure 6). However, there are some situations where the watershed algorithm fails to skeletonize the vein patterns properly:

1. when two veins are too close to each other, the watershed algorithm will tend to merge them together to become one line, as can be seen in the left image of Figure 7. This requires a better preprocessing algorithm to make the two veins more separable in gray level intensity.

2. when the vein patterns are not visually discernible, the watershed algorithm will not be able to extract any meaningful skeletons for the vein patterns . This can only be resolved by using alternative imaging devices, which is beyond the scope of this paper.

3. when the veins have floating endpoints in the image, the watershed algorithm is unable to extract this type of line, which is shown in the right image of Figure 7.

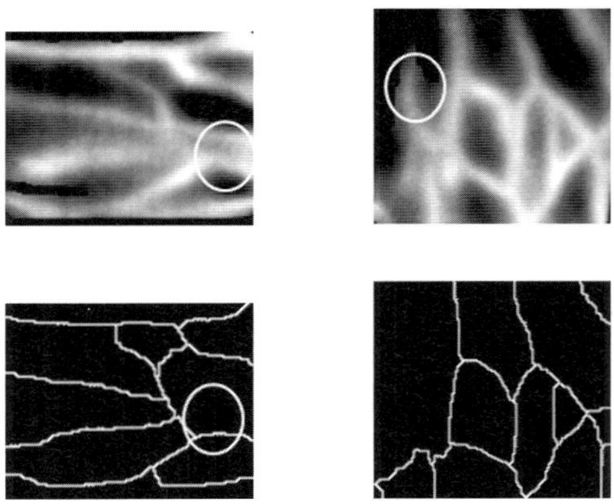

Fig. 7. Situations where watershed fails to extract the skeletons properly. Left: Two veins are too close to each other; Right: A vein has a floating endpoint in the image.

4 Conclusions

This paper presents a novel technique for extracting the skeletons of thermal vein patterns in vein pattern biometric systems. Traditional skeletonization algorithms require the object of interest to be firstly segmented from the background and binarized. However, the errors introduced during the binarization process will be propagated to the skeletonization stage, which can be magnified and degrade the system performance. The proposed watershed-based skeletonization algorithm works directly on the gray-scale vein pattern images. It eliminates the segmentation and binarization process, and hence prevents any potential errors being propagated to the subsequent stages. Experiments show that the watershed algorithm is capable of extracting the skeletons of veins from the gray-scale images. However, there are also a number of cases where the watershed algorithm fails to detect the proper skeletons, which remains an issue to be tackled in the future.

References

1. Ratha, N.K., Senior, A., Bolle, R.M.: "Tutorial on Automated Biometrics" in Proceedings of International Conference on Advances in Pattern Recognition. March, Rio de Janeiro, Brazil (2001)
2. Kim, J.O., Lee, W., Hwang, J., Baik, K.S., Chung, C.H.: Lip Print Recognition for Security Systems by Multi-resolution Architecture. Future Generation Computer Systems 20, 295–301 (2004)
3. Wang, L., Leedham, C.G.: A Thermal Hand Vein Pattern Verification System. In: proceedings of International Conference on Advances in Pattern Recognition. August, Bath, UK (2005)
4. Lin, C.-L, Fan, K.-C.: Biometric Verification Using Thermal Images Of Palm-dorsa Vein Patterns. IEEE Trans. Circuits and Systems for Video Technology 14(2), 199–213 (2004)
5. Cross, J.M., Smith, C.L.: Thermographic Imaging of Subcutaneous Vascular Network Of The Back Of The Hand For Biometric Identification. In: Proceedings of IEEE 29th International Carnahan Conference on Security Technology. October, Sanderstead, Surrey, England (1995)
6. Im, S.-K., Park, H.-M., Kim, S.-W., Chung, C.-K., Choi, H.-S.: Improved Vein Pattern Extracting Algorithm And Its Implementation. In: Digest of technical papers of International Conference on Consumer Electronics (June 2000)
7. MacGregor, P., Welford, R.: Veincheck: Imaging for security and personnel identification. Advanced Imaging 6(7), 52–56 (1991)
8. Fujitsu-Laboratories-Ltd. Fujitsu Laboratories Develops Technology For World's First Contactless Palm Vein Pattern Biometric Authentication System. [Online]. Available: (March 2003) `http://pr.fujitsu.com/en/news/2003/03/31.html`
9. Jain, A., Bolle, R.M., Pankanti, S.: Biometrics: Personal Identification In Networked Society. Kluwer Academic Publishers, Dordrecht (1999)
10. Gao, Y., Leung, M.K.H.: Line Segment Hausdorff Distance on Face Matching. Pattern Recognition 35, 361–371 (2002)
11. Yim, P.J., Choyke, P.L., Summers, R.M.: Gray-scale skeletonization of small vessels in magnetic resonance angiography. IEEE Trans. Medical Imaging 19(6), 576–586 (2000)
12. Suen, C.Y., Zhang, T.Y.: A Fast Parallel Algorithm for Thinning Digital Patterns. Communications of the ACM 27 (3) (March 1984)
13. Guo, Z., Hall, R.W.: Fast fully parallel thinning algorithms. Comput. Vision Graphics Image Process: Image Understanding 55, 317–328 (1992)
14. Bieniek, A., Moga, A.: An efficient watershed algorithm based on connected components. Journal of Pattern Recognition 33(6), 907–916 (2000)
15. Gonzalez, R.C., Woods, R.E.: Digital Image Processing. Prentice-Hall, Inc, New Jersey (2002)
16. Yu, H.G.: Morphologcail image segmentation for co-aligned multiple images using watersheds transformation. Master's thesis, The Florida State University (2004)

Estimation of Source Signals Number and Underdetermined Blind Separation Based on Sparse Representation

Ronghua Li and Beihai Tan

School of Electronic and Information Engineering, South China University of Technology 510641, China
tanpayhy@163.com

Abstract. In this paper, we propose a new two-step algorithm (PDTA) to solve the problem of underdetermined blind separation, where the number of sensors is less than that of source signals. Unlike the usual two-step algorithm, our algorithm's first step is to estimate the number of source signals and the mixture matrix instead of K-mean clustering algorithm, in which people often suppose that the number of source signals is known when they estimate the mixture matrix. After the mixture matrix is estimated by PDTA, the short path algorithm is used to recover source signals. The last simulations show the good performance of estimation the number of source signals and recovering source signals.

1 Introduction

The blind source separation (BSS) problem is currently receiving increased interests [1],[2],[3],[4],[5] in numerous engineering applications. Blind separation comes from cocktail problem [6], and it consists in restoring n unknown, statistically independent random sources from m available observations that are linear combinations of these sources, but we know little about mixture channel and source signals' distribution. In recent years, blind sources separation has been a hot topic in signal processing field and neural networks field, furthermore, it has been applied to many fields from its appearance to now, such as, wireless communication, radar, image processing, array processing and biomedicine, and so on.

Specially, the authors of paper [1] discussed separability of blind source separation in the linear mixture case. By using the information of the mixing matrix, the authors obtained the results about when the source signals can be extracted or not and how many source signals can be extracted. This paper can enrich the separability theory of blind source separation.

At the same time, in the paper [7], Xie's conjecture corrected the famous Stone's conjecture. BSS algorithms based on Xie's conjecture should be without suspicion in basic theory. From now on, researches have a reliable basis to study BSS both in theory and algorithm design.

Blind separation problem is to restore source signals in unknown mixture parameters, so the mathematics model of blind separation is

$$X(t) = AS(t) + N(t) \quad t = 1 \cdots T \tag{1}$$

Y. Wang, Y. Cheung, and H. Liu (Eds.): CIS 2006, LNAI 4456, pp. 943–952, 2007.

where $X(t)=[x_1(t),x_2(t)\cdots x_m(t)]^T$ are sensor signals, $A\in R^{m\times n}$ is the mixture matrix, and $S(t)=[s_1(t),s_2(t)\cdots s_n(t)]^T$ are source signals, and $N(t)=[n_1(t),n_2(t)\cdots n_m(t)]^T$ is noise. Blind separation aims at restoring source signals only by known sensor signals, so blind separation has two uncertainties, scales uncertainty and permutations uncertainty, but these are allowed in blind separation as a result of the information of source signals in their waveforms. Generally, we suppose noise doesn't exist.

In general, if m is more than or equal to n, just to say, the number of sensor signals is more than that of source signals, which is overdetermined blind separation. We consider m is less than n in this paper, namely, underdetermined blind separation. Although it is difficult to restore source signals, we can use some other information, such as, sparseness of source signals, to restore source signals, and if some source signals aren't sparse in time-field, we can make them sparse through some transformation, such as, fourier transformation or wavelet transformation [8],[17], so blind separation model also written as:

$$\begin{bmatrix} x_1(t) \\ x_2(t) \\ \vdots \\ x_m(t) \end{bmatrix} = \begin{bmatrix} a_{11} & a_{12} & \dots & a_{1n} \\ a_{21} & a_{22} & \dots & a_{2n} \\ \vdots & \vdots & \vdots & \vdots \\ a_{m1} & a_{m2} & \dots & a_{mn} \end{bmatrix} \begin{bmatrix} s_1(t) \\ s_2(t) \\ \vdots \\ s_n(t) \end{bmatrix} \tag{2}$$

where $m < n$, or written with vector format:

$$x(t)=a_1 s_1(t)+a_2 s_2(t)+\cdots a_n s_n(t) \quad t=1\cdots T \tag{3}$$

Up to now, the two-step algorithms are general methods for underdetermined blind separation based on sparse representation [15],[16]. The two-step algorithms include two steps, the first step is K-mean clustering algorithm for estimating mixture matrix and the second step is the short-path algorithm for restoring source signals, so we call the two-step algorithms KTA(K-mean Two-step Approach). As it mentioned above, the K-mean clustering algorithm has a key station in KTA and will have an important influence on the next work. When the mixture matrix is estimated, the source signals can be restored through linear programming. In this paper, two-step algorithms still be adopted, but it is different from KTA, and we call the new two-step algorithms PDTA(Probability Distribution Two-step Approach). In the paper, we will estimate the number of source signals first, and the mixture matrix also can be gotten accurately, finally, the work is same to KTA for restoring source signals by linear programming.

2 Sparse Representation of Underdetermined Blind Separation

To underdetermined blind separation, generally, some blind extraction algorithms are taken [9],[10] in past, but the algorithms can't realize restoring all source signals. In order to restore all source signals in underdetermined blind separation, researchers make use of some characteristics of signals, for example, sparse analysis is adopted to make signals sparse presentation, so some underdetermined blind separation are successfully. The good algorithms include in Belouchrani's [11] Maximum likelihood algorithm for discrete sources, Zibulevsky's sparse decomposition algorithm [12], Lee [13], Lewicki [14] and Li' overcomplete representation algorithms [15] and Bofill' sparse representation in frequency domain [16].

Generally, sparse signal is that whose most sample points are zero or are near to zero, and a little points are far from zero. Contrast to Gaussian signal's, sparse signal's distribution function tends to Laplace distribution, namely, there is only one kurtosis in zero point, but it doesn't tend to zero less fastly than that of Gaussian signal and represents super-gaussian, so it is less possible for two source signals have large numbers in the same time, but only one sample point has a large number in almost all time. Here, we suppose that the source signal $s_i(t)$ is nonzero and the other source signals are zero or are near to zero in the time of t. So equation (3) can be written as:

$$x(t) = a_i s_i(t) \tag{4}$$

From the above equation, we can known that a_i and $x(t)$ are collinear, so we can estimate mixture matrix $A = [a_1, a_2, \cdots a_n]$ by clustering $x(t)$ in all time. It is a very important algorithm for sparse component analysis solving underdetermined blind separation, named by K-mean clustering. The algorithm includes two steps, first, cluster centres are estimated by K-mean clustering; secondly, source signals are estimated by known mixture matrix through linear programming.

3 Model of Underdetermined Blind Separation Based on Sparse Representation

All that proposed algorithms can't separate source signals directly in underdetermined blind separation, which includes JADE algorithms, ICA algorithms and H-J algorithms and so on. But the algorithms can resolve the problem based on sparse representation, so the sparse blind separation problem comes down to solving the following optimization [16],

$$\min_{A,S} \frac{1}{2\sigma^2} \|AS - X\|^2 + \sum_{i,t} |s_i(t)| \tag{5}$$

where σ^2 is noise variance, so the equation (5) is optimization problem with multi-variables, which is difficult to resolve directly. We suppose that mixture matrix A is known in advance, then the model is also denoted concisely as,

$$\min_{s(t)} \frac{1}{2\sigma^2} \|As(t) - x(t)\|^2 + \sum_{i}^{n} |s_i(t)|, \quad t = 1,2 \cdots T \tag{6}$$

If noise doesn't taken into account, the equation (6) turns to

$$\begin{cases} \min\limits_{s(t)} \sum\limits_{i}^{n} |s_i(t)| \\ s.t.: \ As(t) = x(t), \ t = 1,2 \cdots T \end{cases} \tag{7}$$

From the equation (6) and the equation (7), we know that there is an optimization problem in every time t based on known mixture matrix A, so optimization problem (7) can be divided into T easy optimization problems.

Generally, the two-step algorithms are fast, but the estimated mixture matrix isn't rigorous as a result of unknown number of the source signals, so the effect of blind separation isn't good. In this paper, we propose a new PDTA algorithm to resolve the underdetermined blind separation problem.

For the sake of simplicity, we suppose $m = 2$, namely, the number of sensors is two, to explain the PDTA algorithms. The sensor signals can be regarded as a point in the 2-dimension plane from equation (4), and they are collinear with the columns of the mixture matrix in the 2-dimension plane. Our PDTA algorithms also include two steps, and the first step is to estimate the number of source signals and estimate the mixture matrix based on sensors signals distributions. In order to analyze the data, we initialize the sensor data first, and the method will be introduced next.

We suppose that $\hat{x}(t) = [\hat{x}_1(t), \hat{x}_2(t)]^T, t = 1,2\cdots T$ are initialized data, so

$$\hat{x}(t) = \begin{cases} \dfrac{x(t)}{\|x(t)\|}, & if \quad x_2(t) \geq 0 \\ -\dfrac{x(t)}{\|x(t)\|}, & if \quad x_2(t) < 0 \end{cases} \tag{8}$$

and we know that the data $\hat{x}(t)$ will locate in the upper half unit circle.

4 Sparse Blind Separation Algorithms of PDTA

In order to restore source signals, the mixture matrix should be estimated first, and this paper also will estimate it first.

4.1 Estimation of Number of Source Signals and Identification of the Mixture Matrix

In past KTA algorithms, because we don't know the number of source signals, so there is a lot of illegibility in the KTA algorithms and identification of number of source signals has a key effect on blind separation. From the above initialized sensor data, we know that the data points locate in the upper unit circle, so we can compute the arc distance between every point in the unit circle and the point whose coordinate is (1,0),

$$dist(t) = \begin{cases} \arctan(\dfrac{x_2(t)}{x_1(t)}), & if \quad x_1(t) > 0; \\ \arctan(\dfrac{x_2(t)}{x_1(t)}) + \pi, & if \quad x_1(t) < 0; \\ \dfrac{\pi}{2}, & if \quad x_1(t) = 0. \end{cases} \quad t = 1,2\cdots T \tag{9}$$

Because the points which are collinear in the 2-dimension plane or near in the unit circle should belong to the same cluster and the points numbers will be enough big, so we can distinguish the number of source signals from the number of columns of mixture matrix, which can be gotten from the distribution of $dist(t)$.

In order to get the distribution of $dist(t)$, we let $a = \min\{dist(t)\}, t = 1,2\cdots T$ and $b = \max\{dist(t)\}, t = 1,2\cdots T$, The interval $[a,b]$ is then divided equally into M sub-intervals which are $[a+i\delta, a+(i+1)\delta]$ $i = 0,1\cdots M-2$, and $[a+(M-1)\delta, b]$,where $\delta = \frac{b-a}{M}$,and M is a sufficiently large. By estimating the number of sample points of $dist(t)$ in each interval denoted by m_i for the i -th interval, the probability for $dist(t)$ belonging to the i -th interval can be obtained, that is,

$$P_i = \frac{m_i}{T}, i = 1,2\cdots M \tag{10}$$

To make the pdf smooth, we use the following filter,

$$\hat{P}_k = \frac{1}{16}(P_{k-2} + 4P_{k-1} + 6P_k + 4P_{k+1} + P_{k+2}) \tag{11}$$

We want to get the number of source signals, namely, to get the number of peaks in the pdf of $dist(t)$.

Definition 1. if $\hat{P}_k > \hat{P}_{k-1}$, $\hat{P}_k > \hat{P}_{k+1}$ and $\hat{P}_k > \varepsilon_j, k = 2,3,\cdots M-1$, we suppose that there is a peak in the pdf of $dist(t)$, and if $k = 1, M$,we only consider $\hat{P}_k > \varepsilon_j$ .where ε_j is a prior threshold value.

According to the definition 1, we will get the number of peaks denoted as $peaknum$, which also is the estimation of number of source signals.

Next, we will get the estimation of the mixture matrix by the method above, because we get any peak which is identified by $\hat{P}_k$, if $\hat{P}_k > \hat{P}_{k-1}$, $\hat{P}_k > \hat{P}_{k+1}$ and $\hat{P}_k > \varepsilon_j$, so we can find the every $\hat{P}_k$ which is related to a peak and also get the interval of $\hat{P}_k$, denoted as $[a+(k-1)\delta, a+k\delta]$. We let

$$\begin{aligned} length_i &= (a + (k-1)\delta + a + k\delta)/2 \\ &= a + (2k-1)\delta/2, \qquad i = 1,2,\cdots, peaknum. \end{aligned} \tag{12}$$

where $length_i$ denotes the arc distance between the center of the i th cluster of sensor data and the point whose coordinate is (1,0). Because the arc distance is radian in unit circle, and the i th cluster of sensor data is collinear with a column of mixture matrix, so

$$a_i = [\cos(length_i), \sin(length_i)]^T, \quad i = 1,2\cdots peaknum \tag{13}$$

From the above algorithm, the number of source signals and the mixture matrix are both gotten expediently, then, the second step of PDTA algorithms will be used to restore source signals by linear programming.

4.2 Restore Source Signals

From the equation (7), we know that it is a linear programming problem for restoring the source signals, and a_i denotes a column of mixture matrix in the equation (3), so $A=[a_1,a_2,\cdots a_n]$ and a_i has been normalized, namely, $\|a_i\|=1$.

The equation (3) explains that the vector $x(t)$ is composed of the normalized vectors $a_1,a_2\cdots a_n$ or $x(t)=a_1s_1(t)+a_2s_2(t)+\cdots+a_ns_n(t)$, where $s_1(t),s_2(t)\cdots s_n(t)$ are the coefficients. The geometrical graph shows that the vectors $a_1s_1(t),a_2s_2(t)\cdots a_ns_n(t)$ and $x(t)$ can form a close geometrical graph as figure 1, what's more, $\sum_i^n |s_i(t)|$ is the length sum of the vectors $a_1s_1(t),a_2s_2(t)\cdots a_ns_n(t)$ .In underdetermined blind separation, if $m<n$, the solutions of the equations (3) are not single.

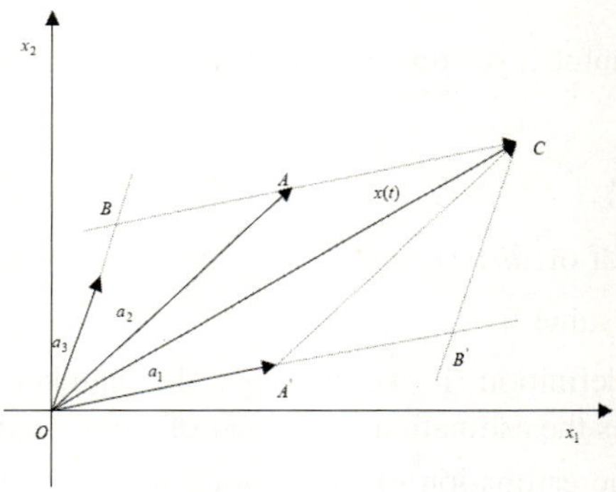

Fig. 1. The illustration of the short path

From the figure 1, we can know that the minimization of $\sum_i^n |s_i(t)|$ which satisfies the equation (7) is equal to find a shortest path from the origin (0,0) to $x(t)$. In the 2-dimension plane, the shortest path of $x(t)$ is composed of the two vectors of a_i and a_j, which are nearest to $x(t)$ respectively.

We let $A_r=[a_i,a_j]$, so $s_r(t)$ is the coefficient of $x(t)$ which is decomposed by a_i and a_j, so the solutions of $s_r(t)$ of the optimization problem (7) is

$$\begin{cases} s_r(t)=A_r^{-1}x(t) \\ s_k(t)=0, k\neq i,j \end{cases} \tag{14}$$

So only the i th source signal and the j th source signal have nonzero values gotten by equation (14) in the time of t, but zero for the other source signals in the time of t.

5 Simulation Results

In the experiment, we take $m = 2$, $n = 6$, namely there are two sensors and six source signals, and the mixture matrix is randomly taken as $A = \begin{bmatrix} 0.7660 & 0.5000 & 0.2588 & -0.1736 & -0.7071 & -0.9063 \\ 0.6428 & 0.8660 & 0.9659 & 0.9848 & 0.7071 & 0.4226 \end{bmatrix}$, and the initialized sensor data is shown in figure 2. By the method of the equation (9), we calculate the arc distances of $dist(t), t = 1,2 \cdots T$, and its probability distribution chart is shown the figure 3, which is gotten from the equation (10) and (11), sometimes, the pdf's filter should be used more times. From the definition, we can calculate the $peaknum$ is 6, and get the estimated mixture matrix $\hat{A} = \begin{bmatrix} 0.7635 & 0.5029 & 0.2672 & -0.1667 & -0.7007 & -0.9039 \\ 0.6458 & 0.8644 & 0.9636 & 0.9860 & 0.7135 & 0.4277 \end{bmatrix}$ by the (12),(13). According to the estimated mixture matrix $\hat{A}$ and the short path algorithm, the source signals are recovered in the figure 6. What's more, we calculate the correlation coefficient matrix of source signals and restored signals is

$$corrcoef = \begin{bmatrix} 0.9969 & 0.0084 & 0.0014 & -0.0021 & -0.0016 & -0.0071 \\ 0.0168 & 0.9951 & 0.0035 & 0.0009 & -0.0001 & 0.0003 \\ 0.0014 & 0.0246 & 0.9946 & 0.0162 & -0.0000 & 0.0001 \\ -0.0000 & 0.0011 & 0.0250 & 0.9950 & 0.0039 & -0.0025 \\ -0.0009 & 0.0003 & 0.0005 & 0.0202 & 0.9972 & 0.0014 \\ -0.0121 & -0.0008 & -0.0008 & 0.0014 & 0.0288 & 0.9979 \end{bmatrix},$$

which shows that PDTA algorithm is very excellent not only in estimation of the number of source signals and the mixture matrix but also in the restoration of source signals.

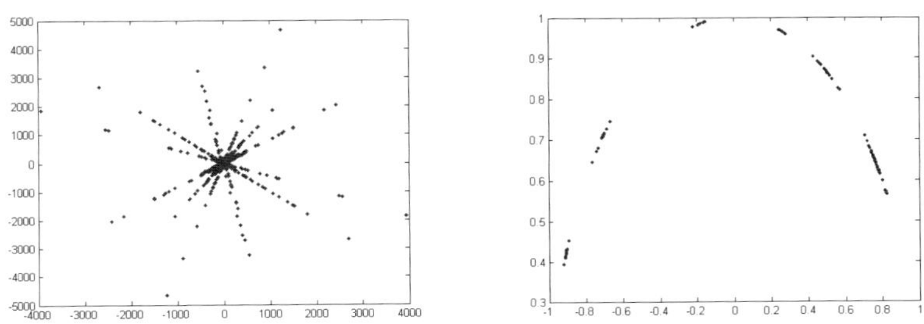

Fig. 2. The sensor signals and their initialized sensor signals

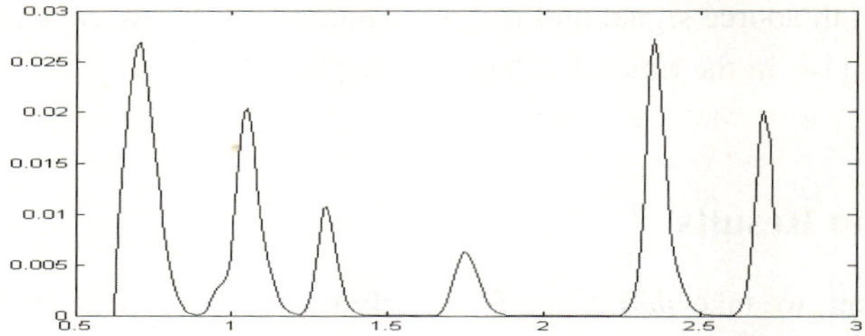

Fig. 3. The $dist(t)$ probability distribution

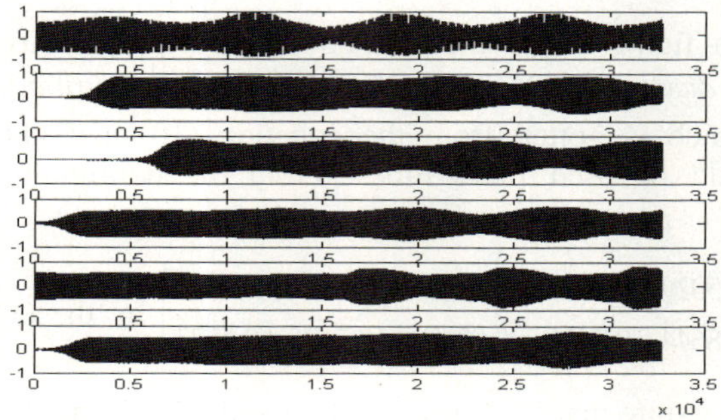

Fig. 4. Six source signals

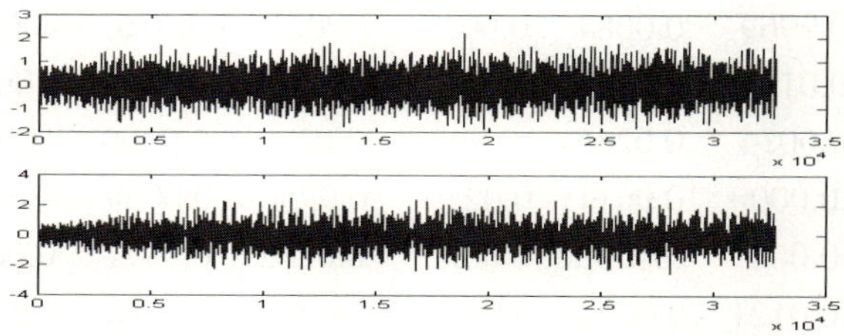

Fig. 5. Two mixture signals

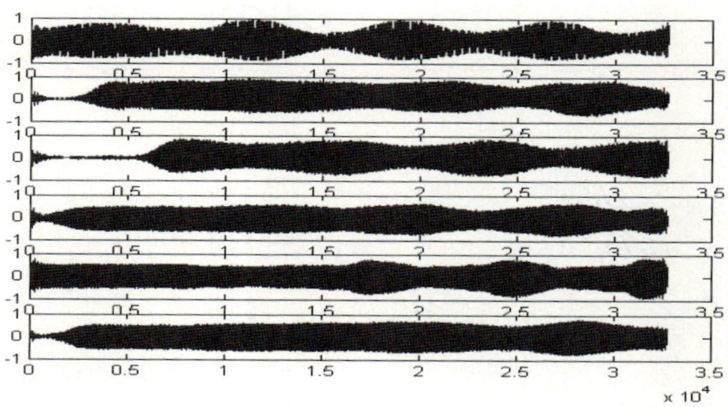

Fig. 6. Six restored source signals

6 Conclusions

In general underdetermined blind separation, source signals are recovered by the two-step algorithms KTA through the information of sparseness of source signals, but there is a big trouble for K-mean clustering algorithm in the two-step algorithms as a result of unknown number of source signals, so we give new two-step algorithms PDTA in this paper, which can estimate the number of source signals in advance by the distribution and get the mixture matrix different from the K-mean clustering algorithm, and the source signals are recovered by the short path algorithm successfully. From the simulation results and the gotten correlation coefficient matrix of source signals and restored signals, the outstanding performance of the PDTA algorithms is expressed. When the sensor number is more than two, it still will be open problem.

Acknowledgements

The work is supported by National Natural Science Foundation of China for Excellent Youth (Grant 60325310), Guangdong Province Science Foundation for Program of Research Team (Grant 04205783), Specialized Prophasic Basic Research Projects of Ministry of Science and Technology, China (Grant 2005CCA04100), Key Program of National Natural Science Foundation of China (Grant U0635001).

References

1. Zhang, J.L., Xie, S.L., He, Z.S.: Separability theory for blind signal separation. Zidonghua Xuebao/Acta Automatica Sinica 30(3), 337–344 (2004)
2. Hyvarinen, A., Oja, E.: Independent component analysis: algorithms and applications. Neural Networks 13, 411–430 (2000)
3. Yang, H.H., Amari, S., Cichocki, A.: Information-theoretic approach to blind separation of sources in nonlinear mixture. Signal Processing 64, 291–300 (1998)
4. Xie, S.L., He, Z.S., Gao, Y.: Adaptive Theory of Signal Processing. 1st ed. Chinese Science Press, Beijing, pp. 130–223 (2006)
5. Anand, K., Mathew, G., Reddy, V.U.: Blind separation of multiple co-channel BPSK signals arriving at an antenna array. IEEE Signal Process 2, 176–178 (1995)
6. Jutten, C., Herault, J.: Blind separation of sources, Part I: An adaptive algorithm based on neuromimetic. Signal Processing 24, 1–10 (1991)
7. Xie, S.L., He, Z.S., Fu, Y.L.: A note on Stone's conjecture of blind separation. Neural Computation 16, 245–319 (2004)
8. Xiao, M., Xie, S.L., Fu, Y.L.: A novel approach for underdetermined blind sources separation in frequency domain. In: Wang, J., Liao, X.-F., Yi, Z. (eds.) ISNN 2005. LNCS, vol. 3497, pp. 484–489. Springer, Heidelberg (2005)
9. Li, Y., Wang, J., Zurada, J.M.: Blind extraction of singularly mixed source signals. IEEE Trans on Neural Networks 11, 1413–1422 (2000)
10. Li, Y., Wang, J.: Sequential blind extraction of instantaneously mixed sources. IEEE Trans. Signal processing 50(5), 997–1006 (2002)
11. Belouchrani, A., Cardoso, J.F.: Maximum likelihood source separation for discrete sources. In: Proc. EUSIPCO, pp. 768–771 (1994)

12. Zibulevsky, M., Pearlmutter, B.A.: Blind source separation by sparse decomposition in a signal dictionary. Neural computation 13(4), 863–882 (2001)
13. Lee, T.W., Lewicki, M.S., Girolami, M., Sejnowski, T.J.: Blind source separation of more sources than mixtures using overcomplete representation. IEEE Signal processing letter 6, 87–90 (1999)
14. Lewicki, M.S., Sejnowski, T.J.: Learning overcomplete representations. Neural computation 12, 337–365 (2000)
15. Li, Y., Cichocki, A., Amari, S.: Analysis of Sparse Representation and Blind Source Separation. Neural Computation 16, 1193–1234 (2004)
16. Bofill, P., Zibulevsky, M.: Underdetermined source separation using sparse representation. Signal processing 81, 2353–2362 (2001)
17. He, Z.S., Xie, S.L., Fu, Y.L.: Sparse Representation and Blind Source Separation of Ill-posed Mixtures. Science in China Series F-Information Sciences 49, 639–652 (2006)

Edge Detection Based on Mathematical Morphology and Iterative Thresholding

Xiangzhi Bai and Fugen Zhou

Image Processing Center
Beihang University, 100083, Beijing, China
jackybxz163@163.com

Abstract. Edge detection is a crucial and basic tool in image segmentation. The key of edge detection in gray image is to detect more edge details, reduce the noise impact to the largest degree, and threshold the edge image automatically. According to this, a novel edge detection method based on mathematic morphology and iterative thresholding is proposed in this paper. A modified morphological transform through regrouping the priorities of several morphological transforms based on contour structuring elements is realized first, and then an edge detector is defined by using the multi-scale operation of the modified morphological transform to detect the gray-scale edge map. Finally, a new iterative thresholding algorithm is applied to obtain the binary edge image. Comparative study with other morphological methods reveals its superiority over de-noising capacity, edge details protection and un-sensitivity to the shape of the structuring elements.

1 Introduction

Edges in an image are caused by changes of some physical properties, such as illumination, geometry and reflectance of objects in the scene. For the direct relationship between edges and important features in the scene, image edge detection is a crucial and basic tool in image segmentation. The key of edge detection is to detect more edge details, reduce the noise impact to the largest degree, and meanwhile threshold the gray edge image automatically.

Mathematical morphology is based on set theoretic concepts, which is used widely in image processing, such as edge detection [1]. The main morphological edge detection methods are morphological residual edge detection, top-hat method, ASF method [2], multi-scale method [3] and multi-grade method [4]. Both of the morphological residue edge detection and the top-hat method are sensitive to the noise and the shape of the structuring elements. ASF method can not detect edge details in small and quick variations. Multi-scale and multi-grade methods perform better, but are limited by processing images with strong noise. Moreover, structuring elements selection will be a heavy work while using the multi-scale and multi-grade methods. Then, the mathematical morphology based on contour structuring elements, namely CB morphology [5] is proposed. Some operators of it are not only un-sensitive to the shape of structuring elements, but also can protect image details, which are favorable for edge detection and structuring elements selection.

Y. Wang, Y. Cheung, and H. Liu (Eds.): CIS 2006, LNAI 4456, pp. 953–962, 2007.

Accordingly, a novel edge detection method based on the multi-scale modified CB morphological operations and iterative thresholding (MMIT) is proposed in this paper. This method constructs multi-scale operations through the modified CB morphological operations first, which is based on the basic operations, and then provides an edge detector to obtain the gray-level edge map. Finally, a binary edge image is obtained by adopting a new iterative thresholding method. Experiment results showed that, this method not only detects better image edge, but also has strong de-noising capacity. Moreover, it is un-sensitive to the shape of the structuring elements.

2 Mathematical Morphology Based on Contour Structuring Elements

CB morphology which reorganizes the morphological operations through the contour of the structuring elements was proposed by Gong Wei [5].

Let f and B represent the gray-level image and a structuring element respectively, and ∂B be the contour of B. The CB dilation, CB erosion, CB opening, CB closing, $O_B(f)$ and $C_B(f)$of f by ∂B are defined by

$$CBD_B(f)=f \oplus \partial B. \tag{1}$$

$$CBE_B(f)=f \ominus \partial B. \tag{2}$$

$$CBO_B(f)=(f \ominus \partial B) \oplus B. \tag{3}$$

$$CBC_B(f)=(f \oplus \partial B) \ominus B. \tag{4}$$

$$O_B(f)=\max\{f, CBO_B(f)\}. \tag{5}$$

$$C_B(f)=\min\{f, CBC_B(f)\}. \tag{6}$$

where, $\oplus$ is dilation operator, $\ominus$ is erosion operator.

3 Edge Detector Based on CB Morphology

3.1 Modified Operators

Because the operation of ∂B, the CB opening (closing) not only realizes the abilities of classic morphological opening (closing), but also use the maximum (minimum) gray value in the region of ∂B to replace the larger (smaller) gray value pixels in the region of B. As a result, the de-noising capacity will be enhanced. Simultaneously, the classic opening (closing) function of CB opening (closing) also smoothes the details of the image, which makes it more disadvantage for edge detection. Conversely, for the operation of max (min), the operation of $O_B(f)(C_B(f))$ can only smooth the regions whose gray values are larger (smaller) than those of the pixels surrounding. Thus, the image details can be maintained, but the de-noising capacity is much depressed.

In order to improve the details protection ability and de-noising capacity, the modified operators are defined by

$$MCBO_{ij}(f) = CBO_{B_j}(O_{B_i}(CBC_{B_j}(f))) \quad (7)$$

$$MCBC_{ij}(f) = CBC_{B_j}(C_{B_i}(CBO_{B_j}(f))) \quad (8)$$

where, B_i and B_j in (7) and (8) can be the same or not.

According to the expression (7), for the $O_B(f)$ in the middle of $MCBO_{ij}(f)$, the image details smoothed by $CBC_B(f)$ are restored. And before the $CBO_B(f)$ the image details are protected by $O_B(f)$ also. But the noises are not preserved much, which indicates that the de-noising capacity is not depressed much. Consequently, $MCBO_{ij}(f)$ can both protect the edge details and filter the noise. Similarly, $MCBC_{ij}(f)$ possesses the similar ability.

3.2 Multi-scale Operation

Structuring elements of different sizes are used to extract features and filter noises at different scales, and the adaptive ability for different noise images can be enhanced. So, the multi-scale approach must be used.

Let $s=\{B_0, B_1, B_2......\}$ be a multi-scale structuring element sequence, where, $B_0=\{0\}$, $B_i=iB_1= B_1 \oplus B_1 \oplus ...... \oplus B_1$(total dilation i-1 times). That is, the structuring elements in multi-scale structuring element sequence have the same shape, and the sizes of which are increasing.

Then, the n-scale operations of s, denoted by $MO_s^n(f)$ and $MC_s^n(f)$, are defined by

$$MO_s^n(f) = \max_{1 \le i \le n}\{MCBO_{i1}(f)\}. \quad (9)$$

$$MC_s^n(f) = \min_{1 \le i \le n}\{MCBC_{i1}(f)\}. \quad (10)$$

According to (9) and (10), $MO_s^n(f)$ and $MC_s^n(f)$ use the small structuring element B_1 to protected the image details, and also use operations of max and min to obtain better edges and filter more noises.

3.3 Edge Detector Based on Multi-scale Modified Operator (MMS)

The edge detector can be defined by dilation residue based on CB morphology

$$edge(f) = CBD_{B_1}[(MO_s^n(MC_s^n(f)))^r] - (MO_s^n(MC_s^n(f)))^r. \quad (11)$$

The structuring element B_1 in the $CBD_B(f)$ operation in (11) is the smallest size of s except B_0, which can also protect the image details.

The parameters in (11) are selected as follows:

(1) The stronger noise, the larger n should be selected. In most case, n should be smaller than 5.

(2) r represents the times of operation $MO_s^n(MC_s^n(f))$. The smaller r protects the image details better. Hence, r should be smaller. Experiments show that r usually can be 1 or 2.
(3) Un-sensitivity to the shape of structuring elements is a priority of $O_B(f)$and $C_B(f)$, which makes the edge detector also not too sensitive to the shape of structuring elements. Therefore, the shape of the structuring elements can be selected more freely according to the application need. The shape of the structuring elements used in this paper is rhombus.

4 Iterative Thresholding

The residual image after MMS contains abundant low gray pixels, which is a dark background image and the histogram is usually uni-mode. Thus, the automatic thresholding method is crucial for edge binarisation. Herein, a new iterative thresholding algorithm is proposed.

4.1 Iterative Thresholding Procedure

Let R be the dark background residue image and the procedure is:

Step1: calculate the mean gray value of R as the initial value of the threshold, denoted T_h.

Step2: divide R into target and background noted T and B according to the threshold T_h.

Step3: calculate the mean gray value of T and B, noted $mean_{up}$ and $mean_{down}$ separately. The difference between the $mean_{up}$ and $mean_{down}$ is defined by

$$x = mean_{up} - mean_{down}. \tag{12}$$

Step4: calculate the new threshold of R by the following expression:

$$T_n=(1-1/f(x))\times mean_{down}+(1/f(x))\times mean_{up}. \tag{13}$$

where, $f(x)=\log_{10}(10+\alpha x)$, α is a constant coefficient according to the image and varies following different images. The smaller mean value of the image, the smaller α. Generally, α is selected from [0, 10].

Step5: check if $T_n = T_h$, then the ultimate threshold of R is noted $T_p = T_n$. Otherwise, let $T_h = T_n$ and go to step 2.

4.2 Convergence Properties

Let T_p be the ultimate threshold and T_1 be the threshold in any iterative step.

(1) If $T_1= T_p$, the x should be x_p, then the x_p, $f(x_p)$ and T_p will not change.
(2) If $T_1<T_p$, the $mean_{up}$, $mean_{down}$ and x should be $mean_{up}1$, $mean_{down}1$ and $x1$. For abundant low gray pixels image $x1<x_p$, that is $\Delta x1 = x_p - x1>0$, thus $f(x_p) > f(x1)$. After one iteration by expression (13), $1/f(x1)$ will increase, and $1-1/f(x1)$ will decrease, thus the new threshold noted T_2 will increase. At this situation, $mean_{up}$,

$mean_{down}$ and x should be $mean_{up}2$, $mean_{down}2$ and $x2$, which satisfy $mean_{up}2 > mean_{up}1$, $mean_{down}2 > mean_{down}1$, and $mean_{up}2 - mean_{up}1 > mean_{down}2 - mean_{down}1$, that is $x2 > x1$, thus $\Delta x2 = x_p - x2 < \Delta x1$. That means the difference between x and x_p noted Δx will decrease following the iterative procedure. When Δx equals 0, the corresponding threshold T can converge to the ultimate threshold T_p.

(3) If $T_l > T_p$, similarly, the threshold can also converge to the ultimate threshold T_p.

Experiment showed that, the iterative procedure would converge after less than 10 iterations. An iterative thresholding experiment on the original Lena gray edge map obtained by MMS converged after 5 iterations and the ultimate threshold was 10 (Fig.1).

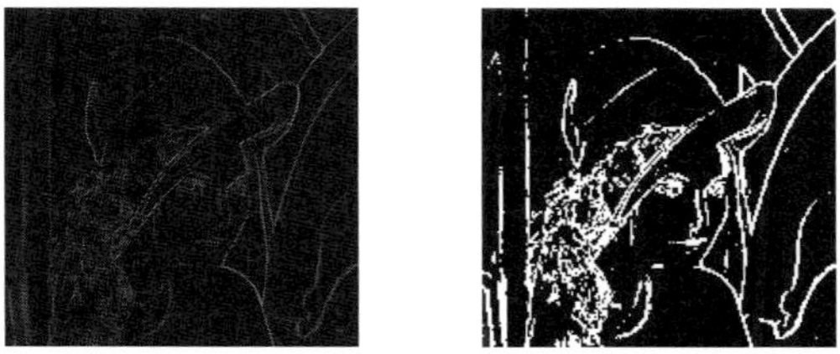

(a) Gray edge map (b) Binary edge image

Fig. 1. Iterative thresholding(α =7)

5 Edge Detection Algorithm

A new algorithm (MMIT) is presented to detect image edges. The image is first processed by MMS to generate a gray-level edge map with dark back-ground. In order to obtain binary edge image, iterative thresholding algorithm is then adopted. The whole implementation algorithm is illustrated in Fig. 2.

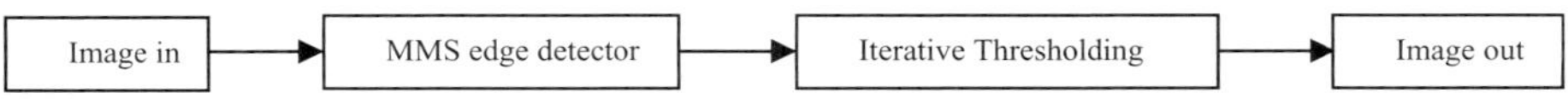

Fig. 2. Proposed edge detection algorithm

6 Experiment Results and Analysis

6.1 Properties Verify Experiment

The strong de-noising capacity and image detail protection ability of $MO_s^n(f)$ can be demonstrated through processing the image Lena (512×512) with 20% salt and pepper noise (Fig. 3 (a)) by $\max_{1\le i\le n}\{CBO_{B_j}(CBO_{B_i}(CBC_{B_j}(f))\}$, $MO_s^n(f)$ and $\max_{1\le i\le n}\{O_{B_j}(O_{B_i}(C_{B_j}(f))\}$, separately. And the result images can be denoted by f_1 (Fig. 3 (b)), f_2 (Fig. 3 (c)), f_3 (Fig. 3 (d)). As the experiment results indicated, noises of Fig. 3(b) are the smallest, but the edge details are also smoothed heavily, especially in the rumple region at the middle of the hat, which will increase the lost edges. Conversely, there are lots of noises in Fig. 3(d), which is more harmful to edge detection. Compatibly, the noises of Fig. 3(c) are very few while the edge details are protected very well, and the edge details of Fig. 3(c) are almost the same as the original image. All of these will make the detected edges more accuracy and more integrate.

Table 1. Properties comparison

f_1		f_2		f_3	
m	σ	m	σ	m	σ
1. 589	4. 237	0. 840	3. 126	1. 672	10. 971

(a) 20% salt&pepper noise

(b) f_1

(c) f_2

(d) f_3

Fig. 3. Processing result comparison of the multi-scale modified operator

Let m and σ denote the mean value and the mean variance of the absolute difference gray-value between the processed image and the original Lena image without noise denoted by f at the corresponding pixels. m and σ are defined by:

$$m = \frac{\sum_{i=1}^{W}\sum_{j=1}^{H}\left|f_k(i,j) - f(i,j)\right|}{W \times H}, \; k=1, 2, 3. \tag{14}$$

$$\sigma = \sqrt{\frac{\sum_{i=1}^{W}\sum_{j=1}^{H}\left(\left|f_k(i,j) - f(i,j)\right| - m\right)^2}{W \times H}}, \quad k=1, 2, 3. \tag{15}$$

where, W and H are the width and height of the image in pixel.

Again, as shown in table 1, m and σ of f_2 are the smallest, which indicates that f_2 is more close to f. That is, the modified operator $MO_s^n(f)$ can filter more noises and protect more image details. The similar experiments prove that $MC_s^n(f)$ also has this superior property.

6.2 Edge Detection Experiment

In order to demonstrate the performance of MMIT, some comparison experiments with morphological algorithms such as multi-scale (MS), multi-grade (MG) and MMIT (n=5,r=1, α =7) algorithms are designed. The well-known image Lena, which is doped with strong noise and without noise respectively, is used as the experiment image (Fig. 4). The edges obtained by MS are more than MG, but discontinuous in some region and too sensitive to strong noises. Also, the MG can keep edge better and have stronger de-noising capacity than MS, but some image details are neglected. As the results indicate, MMIT not only obtains better edge and have stronger de-noising capacity than MG, but also detect more edge details than MS. It can be observed that the MMIT algorithm performs better than the other two morphological detectors.

6.3 Computation Time Comparison

Because of corresponding calculation according to the structuring elements for each pixel, the computation time of the morphology-based edge detection algorithm is usually large, especially under the condition of multi-scale or large size structuring elements. Fortunately, for strong function of noise filtering, the values of n and r can be very small, which indicates that the computation time of the proposed algorithm will be short than other morphology-based algorithms. Table 2 has shown the average computation time of the three algorithms (CPU: Intel Pentium 4, 2.6Hz. memory: 512 MB). As table 2 shown, the computation time of the proposed algorithm is the shortest.

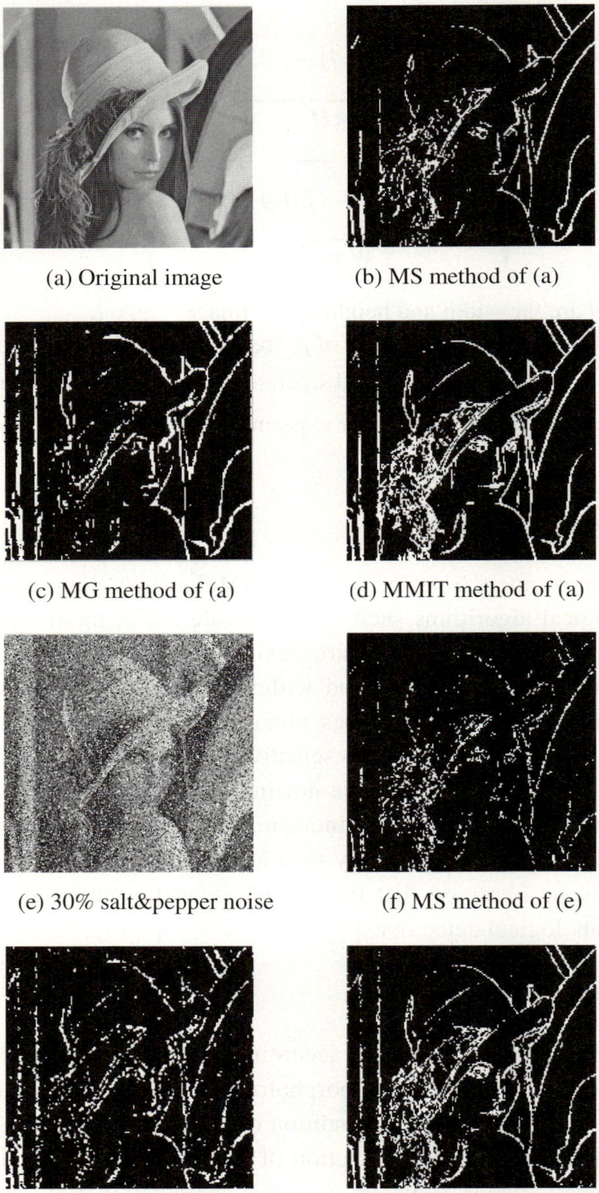

(a) Original image (b) MS method of (a)

(c) MG method of (a) (d) MMIT method of (a)

(e) 30% salt&pepper noise (f) MS method of (e)

(g) MG method of (e) (h) MMIT method of (e)

Fig. 4. Edge detection results comparison

(i) Gaussian noise (σ =0. 01)

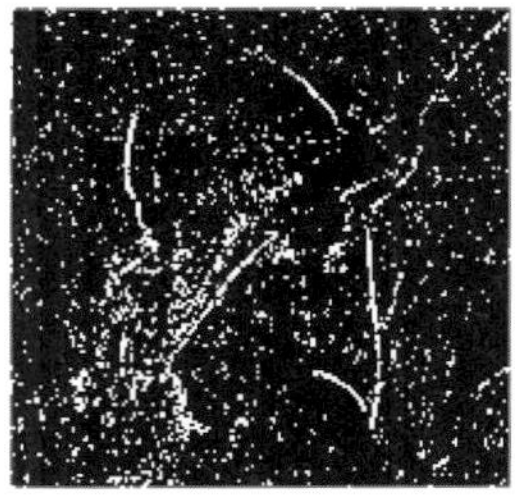

(j) MS method of (i)

(k) MG method of (i)

(l) MMIT method of (i)

Fig. 4. (*continued*)

Table 2. Computation time comparison

MS (s)	MG(s)	MMIT(s)
9. 83	15. 59	7. 39

7 Conclusion

A novel edge detection algorithm based on mathematical morphology and iterative thresholding (MMIT) has been presented. The edge detector is constructed based on the multi-scale modified CB morphological operator, which strengthens the image details protection and de-noising ability. So, a continual gray-level edge map was detected first. Then, the iterative thresholding algorithm was also proposed to threshold gray-level edge map to obtain binary edge image. Comparison experiments have been carried out on Lena image with strong noise and without noise, and the results show that MMIT out-performs other edge detection methods on both image details protection ability and de-nosing capacity. Moreover, MMIT is also lower sensitive to the shape of structuring elements and could threshold automatically. All of these made the proposed method be more suitable for edge detection of image with strong noise.

Acknowledgments. We would like to thank Dr. Li yan at Peking University, Beijing, China, and Dr. Wang Zhaozhong at Beihang University, Beijing, China, for many helpful discussions and comments.

References

1. James, S.J.L., Robert, M.H., Linda, G.S.: Morphologic Edge Detection. IEEE Journal of Robotics and Automation RA-3(2), 142–156 (1987)
2. Song, X., Neuvo, Y.: Robust Edge Detection Based on Morphological Filters. Pattern Recognition Letters 14, 889–894 (1993)
3. Chanda, B., Malay, K.K., Padmaja, Y.V.: A Multiscale Morphologic Edge Detection. Pattern Recognition 31, 1469–1478 (1998)
4. Jiang, M.Y., Yuan, D.F.: A Multi-Grade Mean Morphologic Edge Detection. In: Proceedings of the 6th International Conference on Signal Processing. Beijing, China pp. 1079–1082 (2002)
5. Gong, W., Shi, Q.Y., Cheng, M.D.: CB Morphology and Its Applications. In: Proceedings of International Conference for Yong Computer Scientists. Beijing, China, pp. 260–264 (1991)

Image Denoising Based on Wavelet Support Vector Machine

Shaoming Zhang and Ying Chen

The Research Center of Remote Sensing and Space Information Technology, Tongji University, Shanghai, 200092, China
sheva2003@gmail.com

Abstract. In this paper, a new image denoising method based on wavelet analysis and support vector machine regression (SVR) is presented. The feasibility of image denoising via support vector regression is discussed and is demonstrated by an illustrative example which denoise a 1-dimension signal with Gauss KBF SVM. The wavelet theory is discussed and applied to construct the wavelet kernel, then the wavelet support vector machine (WSVM) is proposed. The result of experiment shows that the denoising method based on WSVM can reduce noise well, the comparison between the method proposed in this paper and other ones is also given which proves this method is better than Gaussian KBF SVM and other traditional methods.

1 Introduction

The support vector machine (SVM) is a new machine learning theory based on statistic learning theory proposed by Vladimir N. Vapnik [1]. It has been widely applied to pattern recognition, function approximation and system identification because SVM is able to deal with classification (SVC) and regression (SVR) problems. In this paper, SVR is proposed to approximate an image as a 2 dimensional continuous function, Wavelet analysis is discussed in this paper and we construct the wavelet support vector machine (WSVM) to approximate image instead of traditional SVM, The ability of WSVM to reduce the noise is compared with traditional method. In section 2, the support vector regression is briefly reviewed. Section 3 discusses the feasibility of denoising based on image approximation via SVR. Section 4 introduces the wavelet theory and proposed the wavelet kernel that has better ability to approximate complex nonlinear function than traditional kernels, and then the WSVM is constructed with wavelet kernel. In section 5, some illustrative results for image denoising are given. The comparison with Gaussian KBF SVM and other method are also discussed. Section 6 comes to the conclusion.

2 Review of Support Vector Regression

Below is a brief review for SVR. There is more detailed description of SVR In [2]. Let us consider the regression in the set of functions

$$f(\mathbf{x}) = \mathbf{w}^T \varphi(\mathbf{x}) + b \tag{1}$$

Y. Wang, Y. Cheung, and H. Liu (Eds.): CIS 2006, LNAI 4456, pp. 963–971, 2007.

Given training data $\{\mathbf{x}_i, y_i, i = 1, \ldots, N\}$, where $\mathbf{w} \in \mathbf{R}^{mh}$ is the weight vector, N denote the number of training data, $\mathbf{x}_i \in \mathbf{R}^m$ are the input data, $y_i \in \mathbf{R}$ are the output data, and $\mathbf{w} \in \mathbf{R}^m$, $b \in \mathbf{R}$, $\varphi(\bullet) : \mathbf{R}^m \longrightarrow \mathbf{R}^{mh}$ mapping the input data into a higher dimensional feature space. In the support vector method one aims at minimizing the empirical risk

$$R_{emp}(\mathbf{w}, b) = \frac{1}{N}\sum_{i=1}^{N} \mid y_i - \mathbf{w}^T\varphi(\mathbf{x}_i) - b \mid_{\varepsilon} \tag{2}$$

subject to $w^T w < c_n$, The loss function employs Vapnik's $\varepsilon-$insensitive model[1]

$$\mid y_i - f(\mathbf{x}_i) \mid_{\varepsilon} = \begin{cases} 0 & \text{if } \mid y_i - f(\mathbf{x}_i) \mid < \varepsilon \\ \mid y_i - f(\mathbf{x}_i) \mid - \varepsilon & \text{otherwise} \end{cases} \tag{3}$$

and the function estimation problem is formulated then as

$$minJ(\mathbf{w}, \xi_i, \xi_i^*) = \frac{1}{2}\mathbf{w}^T\mathbf{w} + c\left\{\sum_{i=1}^{N} \xi_i^* + \sum_{i=1}^{N} \xi_i\right\} \tag{4}$$

subject to the constraints

$$\begin{cases} y_i - \mathbf{w}^T\varphi(\mathbf{x}_i) - b \leq \varepsilon + \xi_i^*, & i = 1, \ldots, N \\ \mathbf{w}^T\varphi(\mathbf{x}_i) + b - y_i \geq \varepsilon + \xi_i, & i = 1, \ldots, N \\ \xi_i^* \geq 0, & i = 1, \ldots, N \\ \xi_i \geq 0, & i = 1, \ldots, N \end{cases} \tag{5}$$

where ξ, ξ^* are the slack variables and c is a positive real constant. The solution is given by

$$\mathbf{w} = \sum_{i=1}^{N}(\alpha_i^* - \alpha_i)\varphi(\mathbf{x}_i) \tag{6}$$

where the α_i^* and α_i are the Lagrange multipliers. The function could be represented as

$$f(\mathbf{x}) = \sum_{i=1}^{N}(\alpha_i^* - \alpha_i)\varphi(\mathbf{x}_i)^T\varphi(\mathbf{x}) + b \tag{7}$$

The dimension of feature space does not have to be specified because of the application of Mercer's condition, which means that

$$K(\mathbf{x}_i, \mathbf{x}_j) = \varphi(\mathbf{x}_i)^T\varphi(\mathbf{x}_j) \tag{8}$$

can be imposed for these kernels, and $f(\mathbf{x})$can be represented as

$$f(\mathbf{x}) = \sum_{i=1}^{N}(\alpha_i^* - \alpha_i)K(\mathbf{x}_i, \mathbf{x}) + b \tag{9}$$

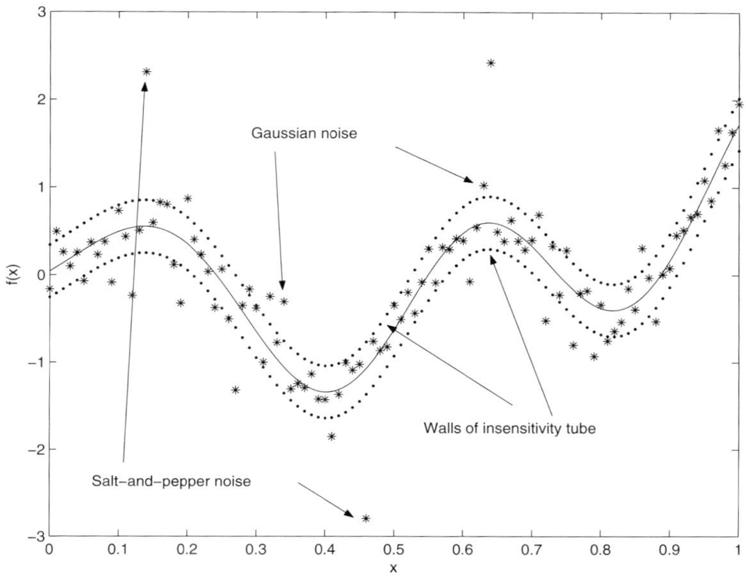

Fig. 1. One-dimension signal SVR example. *The asterisks* are sample noisy data, the noises are salt-and-pepper noise and gaussian one with mean 0 and standard deviation 0.3. *The middle solid curve* is the result of approximation via SVR. *The two dotted curves* lying above and below the blue one are the walls of the insensitivity tube.

3 Image Denoising Via SVR

Gray level image can be regarded as a two-dimensional continuous function

$$y = f_{image}(\mathbf{x}) \tag{10}$$

Where input $\mathbf{x} \in \mathbf{R}^2$ is a two-dimensional vector that indicates the position of a pixel,where output $y \in \mathbf{R}$ is a scalar value denoting the gray level of that pixel. Each pixel could be a training data. If the width of the image is M and height is N, then the number of training examples is $M \times N$. According to equation (1) and (7), the image could be represent as

$$f_{image}(\mathbf{x}) = \sum_{i=1}^{M}\sum_{j=1}^{N}(\alpha_{ij}^{*} - \alpha_{ij}\Big)K\Big(\mathbf{x}_{ij}, \mathbf{x}) + b \tag{11}$$

Image approximation via SVR could reduce two kinds of noise, salt-and-pepper noise and gaussian one. Gaussian noise can be regarded as the little distortions below or above the image gray level, and salt-and-pepper noise means the pixel's gray level has been totally destroyed. According to equation (4) and (5), we can find that the insensitivity region ε and the bound on Lagrange multipliers c are useful for us to remove the noise. ε allows training error to be within the range $\pm\varepsilon$, Therefore, random noise within this range can be smoothed by adjusting the value of ε . The value of c is used to adjust the amount of outliers. We can set c to a small value so that the salt-and-pepper noise is regarded as outlier, the image function will not approximate their value accurately and the salt-and pepper noise could be removed.

Figure 1 explains how to remove the two kinds of noises by image approximation via SVR. The example is 1-dimension signal

$$f(x) = xsin(4\pi x)\exp(x^2+1) + (2x^2)\tanh(10x)cos(2\pi x); \tag{12}$$

where x denotes scalar input. In this case , we make $\varepsilon = 0.3, c = 5$ and use Gaussian RBF [3] with $\sigma^2 = 0.8$as the SVR kernel. Gaussian RBF could be written as follow:

$$K_{RBF}(\mathbf{x}_i, \mathbf{x}_j) = \exp\left\{- \|\, \mathbf{x}_i - \mathbf{x}_j \,\|^2 / \sigma^2\right\} \tag{13}$$

According to figure1 we can find most samples are lying within the insensitivity tube, which removes the gaussian noise. On the other hand, the value of c is small enough to make the result approximate the signal accurately and remove the salt-and-pepper noise.

4 Wavelet Support Vector Machine

4.1 Conditions for Support Vector Kernel

According to equation (8), the kernel function $K(\mathbf{x}_i, \mathbf{x}_j)$ corresponds to a dot product in some feature space. The Mercer theorem [4] give the conditions that the kernel functions must satisfy. Less formally speaking this theorem means that if

$$\int\int_{X\times X} K(x,x')f(x)f(x')dxdx' \geq 0(\forall f \in L_2(X)) \tag{14}$$

holds, we can write $K(\mathbf{x}_i, \mathbf{x}_j)$ as a dot product in some feature space . Where X is the space of input data.

For translation invariant kernels $K(\mathbf{x}_i, \mathbf{x}_j) = K(\mathbf{x}_i - \mathbf{x}_j)$ derived in [5], below theorem give the necessary and sufficient condition for being an admissible support vector kernel [2][5].

Theorem 1: A translation invariant kernel $K(\mathbf{x}_i, \mathbf{x}_j) = K(\mathbf{x}_i - \mathbf{x}_j)$ is an admissible support vector kernel if and only if the Fourier transform

$$F[K(\omega)] = (2\pi)^{-d/2}\int_X \exp(-j\omega^T x)K(x)dx \tag{15}$$

is nonnegative.

4.2 Wavelet Kernel

Function $\psi(x) \in L^2(\mathbf{R})$ could be a mother wavelet if it satisfies the condition below [6]

$$c_\psi = \int_{-\infty}^{+\infty} \frac{\mid \phi(w) \mid^2}{\mid \psi \mid} dw < +\infty \tag{16}$$

Where $\phi(w)$ is Fourier transform of $\psi(x)$. The wavelet transform of a function $f(x) \in L^2(\mathbf{R})$ can be written as

$$W_f(a,b) = \langle \psi_{(a,b)} \cdot f \rangle \tag{17}$$

Where $a \neq 0$ is a dilation factor, $b \in \mathbf{R}$ is a translation factor and $\psi_{(a,b)}(x)$ is

$$\psi_{(a,b)}(x) = \frac{1}{\sqrt{\mid a \mid}} \psi\left(\frac{x-b}{a}\right) \tag{18}$$

$f(x)$can be reconstructed as follow:

$$f(x) = \frac{1}{c_\psi} \int_{-\infty}^{+\infty} \int_{-\infty}^{+\infty} W_f(a,b) \psi_{(a,b)}(x) da/a^2 db \tag{19}$$

The equation above means that a function could be express by a family of functions generated by dilation and translation of mother wavelet. If we take finite terms to approximate , then

$$f_{appr}(x) = \sum_{i=1}^{n} W_f(a_i, b_i) \psi_{(a,b)}(x) \tag{20}$$

Where $f(x)$ is approximated by $f_{appr}(x)$.
The multidimensional wavelet function could be written as [7]

$$\psi_d(\mathbf{x}) = \prod_{i=1}^{d} \psi(x_i) \tag{21}$$

Where$\mathbf{x} = (x_1, \ldots, x_d) \in \mathbf{R}^d$. Let's consider the Morlet mother wavelet as below

$$\psi(x) = \cos(1.75x) \exp(-\frac{x^2}{2}) \tag{22}$$

the multidimensional wavelet function is

$$\psi(\mathbf{x}) = \prod_{i=1}^{d} \exp\left[-(x_i - b_i)^2/2a_i^2\right] \cos\left[1.75 \frac{(x_i - b_i)}{a_i}\right] \tag{23}$$

We can construct translation invariant wavelet kernel.

$$K_w(\mathbf{x} - \mathbf{x}') = \prod_{i=1}^{d} \exp\left[-(x_i - x_i')^2/2a_i^2\right] \cos\left[1.75 \frac{(x_i - x_i')}{a_i}\right] \tag{24}$$

The result of approximation of function $f(x)$ using support vector machine (WSVM) could be written as

$$f(\mathbf{x}) = \sum_{i=1}^{N}(\alpha_i^* - \alpha_i)K_w(\mathbf{x}_i, \mathbf{x}) + b \tag{25}$$

Where N denote the number of training data.

5 Results of Experiment

In this section, we add salt-and-pepper noise and gaussian one with mean 0 and standard deviation 1 to the image with size 100×100 . We process the noisy image with the Gaussian RBF SVM, WSVM and other traditional method.

Fig. 2. Original image for denoising experiment

Fig. 3. Noisy image, The noises are salt-and-pepper noise and gaussian one with mean 0 and standard deviation 1

Figure 2 and figure 3 shows the original image and the noisy image, Figure 4 and figure 5 show the result of denoising via WSVM and gaussian RBF SVM, Figure 6, figure 7 and figure 8 shows the result of gaussian filtering, average filtering and medium filtering. We define the image signal noise ratio (SNR) as follow:

$$SNR_{image} = \sqrt{\frac{\sum_{i=1}^{M}\sum_{j=1}^{N} f(i,j)^2}{\sum_{i=1}^{M}\sum_{j=1}^{N}[f(i,j) - f_{res}(i,j)]^2}} \tag{26}$$

Fig. 4. Result of SVR by wavelet support vector machine, The dilation factor a=1

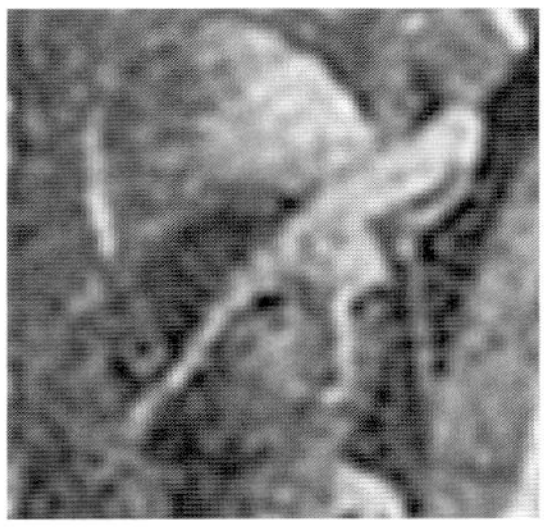

Fig. 5. Result of SVR by gaussian RBF machine, c=10,σ^2=0.05

Fig. 6. Result of filtering by mean filter, the size of filter is 3×3

Fig. 7. Result of filtering by gaussian filter, the size of filter is 3×3 and σ^2=1

Fig. 8. Result of filtering by medium filter, the size of filter is 3×3

Where $f(i, j)$ is the original image and $f_{res}(i, j)$ is the result of image denoising, M and N are the width and height of image. Table 1 lists the SNR for each method.

Table 1. SNR and parameters of the denoising method

Method	parameters	SNR
WSVM	a=1	6.2072
RBF SVM	c=10;σ=0.224	5.3094
Mean Filter		5.0564
Gaussian Filter	σ=1	4.9103
Medium Filter		5.1899

6 Conclusion and Discussion

In this paper, the function approximation via SVR is reviewed based on which we analyze the model of noise and discuss the feasibility of denoising via SVR. Wavelet theory is briefly discussed and the wavelet support vector machine (WSVM) is constructed based on wavelet kernels. At last, we process the noisy image with WSVM and other image denoising method, which indicate that the WSVM could remove the random noise and salt-and-pepper noise better than Gaussian RBF SVM and other traditional method.

References

1. Vapnik, V.N.: Statistical Learning Theory. John Wiley and Sons, New York (1998)
2. Smola, A., Scholkopf, B.: A tutorial on support vector regression. [Online]NeuroCOLT Tech. Rep. NC-TR-98-030. Royal Holloway Coll. Univ. London, UK, Available: (1998), `http://www.kernel-machines.org/`
3. Cristianini, N., Taylor, J.S.: An introduction to support vector machines and other kernel-based learning methods. Cambridge University Press, Cambridge (2000)
4. Mercer, J., Mercer, J.: Functions of positive and negative type and their connection with the theory of integral equation. Philos. Trans. R. Soc A-209, 415–446 (1909)

5. Smola, A., Scholkopf, B.: The connection between regularization operators and support vector kernels. Neural Network 11, 637–649 (1998)
6. Daubechies, I., Scholkopf, B.: The wavelet transform, time-frequency localization and signal analysis. IEEE Transaction on Information Theory 36, 961–1005 (1990)
7. Zhang, Q.H., Benveniste, A.: Wavelet networks. IEEE Transactions on Neural Networks 3, 889–898 (1992)

Variational Decomposition Model in Besov Spaces and Negative Hilbert-Sobolev Spaces

Min Li and Xiangchu Feng

School of Science, Xidian University
Xi'an 710071, China
Limin791202@163.com,
Xcfeng@mail.xidian.edu.cn

Abstract. In this paper, we propose a new variational decomposition model which splits an image into two components: a first one containing the structure and a second one the texture or noise. Our decomposition model relies on the use of two semi-norms: the Besov semi-norm for the geometrical component, the negative Hilbert-Sobolev norms for the texture or noise. And the proposed model can be understood as generalizations of Daubechies-Teschke's model and have been motivated also by Lorenz's idea. And we illustrate our study with numerical examples for image decomposition and denoising.

1 Introduction

Image decomposition is of important interest in mathematical image processing. In principle, it can be understood as an inverse problem. Consequently, it can be done by regularization techniques and minimization of related variational functionals.

One classical model of such functionals is the total variation minimizing process introduced by Rudin-Osher-Fatemi [1]. However, since ROF model will remove the texture when tuning parameter is small enough, Meyer proposes that the oscillating components (texture or noise) should be modeled using a different space of functions that is in some sense dual to BV space. So, this leads to a new image decomposition model in theory [2]. Meyer's model cannot be solved directly, due to the existence of the weaker norm. Thus, a lot of people begin to study regarding practical methods of Meyer's model. For example, Vese-Osher proposed to solve Meyer's model using three Euler-Lagrange equations based on L^p norm [3]. Osher-Sole-Vese put forward the method combing total variation minimization with the H^{-1} norm based on VO model [4]. But, it is a pity that the PDEs based these variational models is usually numerically intensive. Thus, in [5], Daubechies-Teschke suggested a special variational model for image decomposition:

$$\inf_{u,v} F(u,v) = 2\alpha |u|_{B^1_{1,1}(\Omega)} + \|f-(u+v)\|^2_{L^2(\Omega)} + \gamma \|v\|^2_{H^{-1}(\Omega)} \,. \tag{1}$$

Since function spaces of interest in problem (1) can be characterized by means of wavelet coefficients, they propose a wavelet based scheme of (1) instead of solving PDE systems. Later in [8], Linh Lieu successfully generalized Osher-Sole-Vese's

Y. Wang, Y. Cheung, and H. Liu (Eds.): CIS 2006, LNAI 4456, pp. 972–982, 2007.

model for image restoration and decomposition in a total variation minimization framework. She proposed that the oscillating component can be modeled by tempered distributions belonging to the negative Hilbert-Sobolev spaces H^{-s} ($s>0$).

Here inspired from Linh Lieu's idea, it occurred to us that the textured (or noisy) component v in (1) can be characterized via negative Hilbert-Sobolev spaces H^{-s}. In addition, since Besov spaces $B^{\beta}_{p,q}(\Omega)$ ($\beta>0$, $0<p,q\leq\infty$) cover a wide range of classical smoothness spaces and the Besov semi-norms can be expressed through equivalent norms of wavelet coefficients[6], we propose to generalize the first term $|u|_{B^1_{1,1}(\Omega)}$ to $|u|_{B^{\beta}_{p,q}(\Omega)}$ in (1). But we are only interested in the especially simple case $p=q$. Therefore, the new variational model for image decomposition is

$$\inf_{u,v} E(u,v)=2\alpha|u|_{B^{\beta}_{p,p}(\Omega)}+\|f-(u+v)\|^2_{L^2(\Omega)}+\gamma\|v\|^2_{H^{-s}(\Omega)}, \tag{2}$$

where α and γ are tuning parameters, $1\leq p\leq\infty$.

The outline of the paper is as follows. In section 2 we give minimization process of the new variational model (2). It can be understood as generalizations of [5, 6]. In section 3 we discuss some examples of the new variational problem. Section 4 shows numerical results of image decomposition and denoising examples using (2). Finally, we give the conclusions in section 5.

2 Minimization of the New Model

In this section, we consider the minimization of the new variational problem (2). Since $B^{\beta}_{2,2}(\Omega)=H^{\beta}(\Omega)$ [5], we consider only the spaces $B^{\beta}_{p,p}(\Omega)$ 、 $L^2(\Omega)=B^0_{2,2}(\Omega)$ and $H^{-s}(\Omega)=B^{-s}_{2,2}(\Omega)$ in (2).

For an orthogonal wavelet ψ, which is in $B^{s}_{2,2}(\Omega)$ ($s>\beta$), we have the following norm equivalence [5]:

$$\begin{aligned}\|f-(u+v)\|^2_{L^2(\Omega)} &\approx \sum_{\lambda\in J}|f_\lambda-(u_\lambda+v_\lambda)|^2\\ \|v\|^2_{H^{-s}(\Omega)} &\approx \sum_{\lambda\in J}2^{-2s|\lambda|}|v_\lambda|^2\\ |u|_{B^{\beta}_{p,p}(\Omega)} &\approx \left(\sum_{\lambda\in J}2^{\beta|\lambda|p}2^{|\lambda|(p-2)}|u_\lambda|^p\right)^{\frac{1}{p}}\end{aligned}, \tag{3}$$

where $J=\{\lambda=(i,j,k):k\in J_j, j\in Z, i=1,2,3\}$, $|\lambda|=j$ if $\lambda\in J_j$, f_λ , u_λ , v_λ denote the λ -th wavelet coefficients.

Replacing the norms in (2) by (3), we obtain the equivalent sequence in wavelet framework

$$W_f(u,v)=2\alpha\left(\sum_{\lambda\in J}2^{\beta|\lambda|p}2^{|\lambda|(p-2)}|u_\lambda|^p\right)^{\frac{1}{p}}+\sum_{\lambda\in J}\left(|f_\lambda-(u_\lambda+v_\lambda)|^2+\gamma 2^{-2s|\lambda|}|v_\lambda|^2\right). \tag{4}$$

Let u_λ be fixed in (4), then the derivative of $W_f(u,v)$ with respect to v_λ can be expressed by

$$D_{v_\lambda}\left(W_f(u,v)\right) = -2(f_\lambda - u_\lambda) + 2(1+\gamma 2^{-2s|\lambda|})v_\lambda .$$

Set $D_{v_\lambda}\left(W_f(u,v)\right)=0$, one has

$$v_\lambda = (1+\gamma 2^{-2s|\lambda|})^{-1}(f_\lambda - u_\lambda) . \tag{5}$$

Replacing v_λ by (5) in (4), we have

$$W_f(u,v) = 2\alpha\left(\sum_{\lambda\in J} 2^{\beta|\lambda|p}2^{|\lambda|(p-2)}\left|u_\lambda\right|^p\right)^{\frac{1}{p}} + \sum_{\lambda\in J}\frac{\gamma 2^{-2s|\lambda|}}{1+\gamma 2^{-2s|\lambda|}}(f_\lambda - u_\lambda)^2 . \tag{6}$$

Set $\mu_\lambda = \dfrac{\gamma 2^{-2s|\lambda|}}{1+\gamma 2^{-2s|\lambda|}}$ and $\phi\left((u_\lambda)\right) = \left(\sum_{\lambda\in J} 2^{\beta|\lambda|p}2^{|\lambda|(p-2)}\left|u_\lambda\right|^p\right)^{\frac{1}{p}}$ in (6), then one has

$$Q_{f_\lambda}(u_\lambda) = 2\alpha\phi\left((u_\lambda)\right) + \sum_{\lambda\in J}\mu_\lambda(f_\lambda - u_\lambda)^2 . \tag{7}$$

Note that here ϕ is positive homogeneous of degree one. Since the duality between positive homogeneous functions and convex sets holds for convex functions, we consider only the case $1\le p\le\infty$ in this paper.

In the following, we, inspired from [6, 9], minimize (7) using duality result from convex analysis.

Proposition 1. Let $\{f_\lambda\}\in \ell^2(J)$ and $1\le p\le\infty$. Then the wavelet coefficients of the minimizer of problem (7) is

$$u_\lambda = \left(Id - \Pi_{\theta_\lambda C}\right)(f_\lambda) . \tag{8}$$

where $\theta_\lambda = \alpha/\mu_\lambda$ and Π_C is the orthogonal projection onto the convex set

$$C = \left\{x\in \ell^2(J)\left|\sum_{\lambda\in J} x_\lambda y_\lambda \le \phi\left((y_\lambda)\right), \forall y\in \ell^2(J)\right.\right\}. \tag{9}$$

Proof. Since ϕ is homogeneous of degree one, it is standard [7] that the Legendre-Fenchel transform of ϕ

$$\phi^*(w_\lambda) = \sup\left(\left\langle u_\lambda, w_\lambda\right\rangle_{\ell^2(J)} - \phi(u_\lambda)\right) = \sup\left(\left(\sum_{\lambda\in J} u_\lambda w_\lambda\right) - \phi(u_\lambda)\right)$$

is the indicator function of a convex set C:

$$\phi^*(w_\lambda) = \begin{cases} 0 & if\ w_\lambda\in C \\ +\infty & otherwise\end{cases} . \tag{10}$$

Since ϕ is convex and l.s.c., $\phi^{**}=\phi$. Hence $\phi(u_\lambda) = \sup_{w_\lambda\in C}\left\langle u_\lambda, w_\lambda\right\rangle_{\ell^2(J)} = \sup_{w_\lambda\in C}\left(\left(\sum_{\lambda\in J} u_\lambda w_\lambda\right)\right)$.

If u_λ is a minimizer of (7), then necessary condition is

$$0 \in \partial Q_{f_\lambda}\left((u_\lambda)\right). \tag{11}$$

Since the subgradient of the second term of (7) with respect to u_λ is $\{-2\mu_\lambda(f_\lambda - u_\lambda)\}$, one has

$$\partial Q_{f_\lambda}(u_\lambda) = 2\alpha\partial\phi\left((u_\lambda)\right) - 2\mu_\lambda(f_\lambda - u_\lambda).$$

Hence

$$\frac{f_\lambda - u_\lambda}{\theta_\lambda} \in \partial\phi\left((u_\lambda)\right), \tag{12}$$

where $\theta_\lambda = {\alpha}/{\mu_\lambda}$. From the inversion rules for subgradients ([7] prop. 11.3), we know that (12) is equivalent to:

$$0 \in \frac{f_\lambda - u_\lambda}{\theta_\lambda} - \frac{f_\lambda}{\theta_\lambda} + \frac{1}{\theta_\lambda}\partial\phi^*\left(\frac{f_\lambda - u_\lambda}{\theta_\lambda}\right). \tag{13}$$

So $w = \frac{f_\lambda - u_\lambda}{\theta_\lambda}$ is the minimizer of $\frac{\left\| w - {f_\lambda}/{\theta_\lambda} \right\|}{2} + \frac{1}{\theta_\lambda}\phi^*(w)$.

Being ϕ^* given by (10), w is given by the orthogonal projection of $\frac{f_\lambda}{\theta_\lambda}$ on the convex set C. Indeed, from (13), one has

$$\frac{f_\lambda}{\theta_\lambda} \in \left(Id + \frac{1}{\theta_\lambda}\partial\phi^*\right)\left(\frac{f_\lambda - u_\lambda}{\theta_\lambda}\right) \Rightarrow w \in \left(Id + \frac{1}{\theta_\lambda}\partial\phi^*\right)^{-1}\left(\frac{f_\lambda}{\theta_\lambda}\right). \tag{14}$$

Set $\Pi_C\left(\frac{f_\lambda}{\theta_\lambda}\right) = \left(Id + \frac{1}{\theta_\lambda}\partial\phi^*\right)^{-1}\left(\frac{f_\lambda}{\theta_\lambda}\right)$, then $\Pi_{\theta_\lambda C}(f_\lambda) = \theta_\lambda\left(Id + \frac{1}{\theta_\lambda}\partial\phi^*\right)^{-1}(f_\lambda)$. Thus

$$\left(\frac{1}{\theta_\lambda}\right)\Pi_{\theta_\lambda C}(f_\lambda) = \Pi_C\left(\frac{f_\lambda}{\theta_\lambda}\right) = \frac{f_\lambda - u_\lambda}{\theta_\lambda} \Rightarrow u_\lambda = \left(Id - \Pi_{\theta_\lambda C}\right)(f_\lambda).$$

Here replacing u_λ by (8) in (5), one obtain the expression of v_λ. Therefore, minimizers of (2) can be expressed as:

$$v = \sum_{\lambda \in J}(1 + \gamma 2^{-2s|\lambda|})^{-1}\left(\Pi_{\theta_\lambda C}(f_\lambda)\right)\psi_\lambda, \tag{15}$$

and

$$u = \langle f, 1\rangle + \sum_{\lambda \in J}\left(\left(Id - \Pi_{\theta_\lambda C}\right)(f_\lambda)\right)\psi_\lambda, \tag{16}$$

where the scale function is equal to one and ψ is orthogonal wavelet.

3 Some Examples of the New Model

In order to illustrate concretely the minimization of the new model, we consider the three cases $p=1$, $p=2$ and $p=\infty$ separately in this section. Here what is important to us is that one can obtain the convex sets that are related to three examples. In terms of the description of section 2 and Lorenz's work [6, 9], one has

$$C=\left\{x_\lambda \in l^2(J)\left|\left(\sum_{\lambda\in J} 2^{-2|\lambda|\beta}|x_\lambda|^2\right)^{\frac{1}{2}} \le 1\right.\right\},\quad (p=2) \tag{17}$$

$$C=\left\{x_\lambda \in l^2(J)\left|\sup_{\lambda\in J} 2^{-|\lambda|(\beta-1)}|x_\lambda| \le 1\right.\right\},\quad (p=1) \tag{18}$$

and

$$C=\left\{x_\lambda \in l^2(J)\left|\sum_{\lambda\in J} 2^{-|\lambda|(\beta+1)}|x_\lambda| \le 1\right.\right\},\quad (p=\infty). \tag{19}$$

3.1 The Penalty $|\cdot|_{B^\beta_{1,1}(\Omega)}$

From (18), one obtains the convex set which is located by the projection:

$$\theta_\lambda C=\left\{x\in \ell^2(J)\left|\sup_{\lambda\in} 2^{-|\lambda|(\beta-1)}|x_\lambda| \le \theta_\lambda\right.\right\}. \tag{20}$$

Then this projection is performed by the following clipping function [6], i.e.

$$\Pi_{\theta_\lambda C}(f_\lambda)=\left(C_{2^{|\lambda|(\beta-1)}\theta_\lambda}(f_\lambda)\right)=\begin{cases} 2^{|\lambda|(\beta-1)}\theta_\lambda & f_\lambda \ge \theta_\lambda \\ f_\lambda & |f_\lambda|<\theta_\lambda \\ -2^{|\lambda|(\beta-1)}\theta_\lambda & f_\lambda \le -\theta_\lambda \end{cases}. \tag{21}$$

Clearly, (8) is a soft shrinkage function:

$$u_\lambda = S_{2^{|\lambda|(\beta-1)}\theta_\lambda}(f_\lambda). \tag{22}$$

Replacing u_λ by (22) in (5), one has

$$v_\lambda=\left(1+\gamma 2^{-2s|\lambda|}\right)^{-1} C_{2^{|\lambda|(\beta-1)}\theta_\lambda}(f_\lambda). \tag{23}$$

If set $\beta=1$ and $s=1$, (22) and (23) reduce to Daubechies-Teschke's results [5].

3.2 The Penalty $|\cdot|_{B^\beta_{2,2}(\Omega)}$

In this case, it can be seen as the example for $1<p<\infty$. From (17), we know that the projection which one must calculate is the orthogonal projection onto the convex set:

$$\theta_\lambda C=\left\{x\in \ell^2(J)\left|\sum_{\lambda\in J} 2^{-2|\lambda|\beta}|x_\lambda|^2 \le \theta_\lambda{}^2\right.\right\}. \tag{24}$$

Then this projection is characterized by the constrained minimization problem

$$\min \sum_{\lambda\in J} (x_\lambda - f_\lambda)^2 \ s.t. \sum_{\lambda\in J} 2^{-2|\lambda|\beta} |x_\lambda|^2 \le \theta_\lambda^{\ 2} . \tag{25}$$

Using Lagrange multipliers $\mu > 0$, this problem can be rewritten as

$$\min_{x_\lambda} \left\{ F(x_\lambda) = \sum_{\lambda\in J} (f_\lambda - x_\lambda)^2 + \mu 2^{-2|\lambda|\beta} |x_\lambda|^2 \right\} .$$

Set $F'(x_\lambda) = 0$, one has

$$x_\lambda = \frac{f_\lambda}{1+\mu 2^{-2|\lambda|\beta}} . \tag{26}$$

Replacing x_λ by (26) in (24) yields

$$\theta_\lambda^{\ 2} = \sum_{\lambda\in J} \frac{2^{-2|\lambda|\beta}}{\left(1+\mu 2^{-2|\lambda|\beta}\right)^2} |f_\lambda|^2 . \tag{27}$$

Here we discover that the right side of (27) is monotonically decreasing and continuous in μ. If μ increases from 0 to ∞, (27) decreases from $2^{-2|\lambda|\beta}|f_\lambda|^2$ to 0. Thus, this indicates that there is a Lagrange multipliers $\mu > 0$ such that (26) is the projection. Replacing $\prod_{\theta_\lambda C}$ by (26) in (8), one has

$$u_\lambda = \frac{1}{1+2^{2|\lambda|\beta+1}\left(\frac{1}{2\mu}\right)} f_\lambda . \tag{28}$$

This is a linear shrinkage operator which depends on the scale $|\lambda|$ and Besov smooth order β, where $\mu = \frac{1}{2\theta_\lambda}$.

Replacing u_λ by (28) in (5), we have

$$v_\lambda = \left(1+\gamma 2^{-2s|\lambda|}\right)^{-1} \frac{2^{2|\lambda|\beta}}{2^{2|\lambda|\beta}+\mu} (f_\lambda) . \tag{29}$$

3.3 The Penalty $|\cdot|_{B^\beta_{\infty,\infty}(\Omega)}$

In this section, (19) shows that the convex set which we concern is

$$\theta_\lambda C = \left\{ x \in \ell^2(J) \middle| \sum_{\lambda\in J} 2^{-|\lambda|(\beta+1)} |x_\lambda| \le \theta_\lambda \right\} . \tag{30}$$

Similar to the case $p = 2$, we have

$$x_\lambda = f_\lambda - \frac{\mu}{2} 2^{-|\lambda|(\beta+1)} \operatorname{si} gn(f_\lambda) . \tag{31}$$

From section 3.2., we know that here the projection is the soft shrinkage, i.e. $x_\lambda = S_{\frac{\mu}{2}2^{-|\lambda|(\beta+1)}}(f_\lambda)$. Therefore, replacing $\Pi_{\theta_\lambda C}$ by $S_{\frac{\mu}{2}2^{-|\lambda|(\beta+1)}}$ in (8) yields the clipping function:

$$u_\lambda = C_{\frac{\mu}{2}2^{-|\lambda|(\beta+1)}}(f_\lambda) . \tag{32}$$

Replacing u_λ by (32) in (5), one obtains

$$v_\lambda = \left(1+\gamma 2^{-2s|\lambda|}\right)^{-1} S_{\frac{\mu}{2}2^{-|\lambda|(\beta+1)}}(f_\lambda) . \tag{33}$$

Finally, replacing v_λ and u_λ separately by (23)、(29)、(33) and (22)、(28)、(32) in (15) and (16), we obtain the associated minimizers of the new model in three cases.

4 Numerical Examples

In this section we present numerical results obtained by applying our proposed new model to image decomposition and denoising in the case $p=1$, $p=2$ and $p=\infty$. In our implementation, the stationary wavelet transform is used. We will show numerical results obtained with various values of β and s. For denoising, the peak-signal-to-noise (PSNR) are used to evaluate the denoising performance.

Firstly, we try texture removal with an intercepting part of Barbara image (shown in Figure 1). The results are shown in Figure 2. We can see that the new model (2) can separates better the textured details v from non-textured image kept in u .

Secondly, we show the denoising results obtained from the proposed new model (2). We add Gaussian white noise of $\sigma=10$ to the clean Lena image (shown in Figure 3). Table 1 gives PSNR for the denosing results. In Figure 4, we show denoisng results from our proposed model using $\beta=1$, $s=1$ and $\beta=2$, $s=2$, respectively, for the $B^{\beta}_{p,q}$ semi-norm and H^{-s} norm. These show that the proposed new model (2) can denoise effectively.

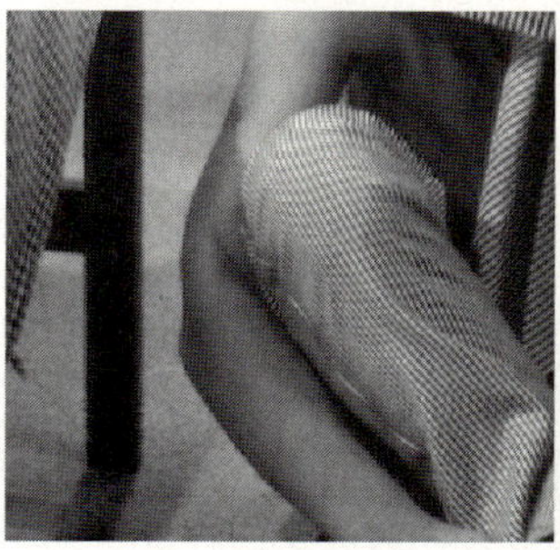

Fig. 1. Original image

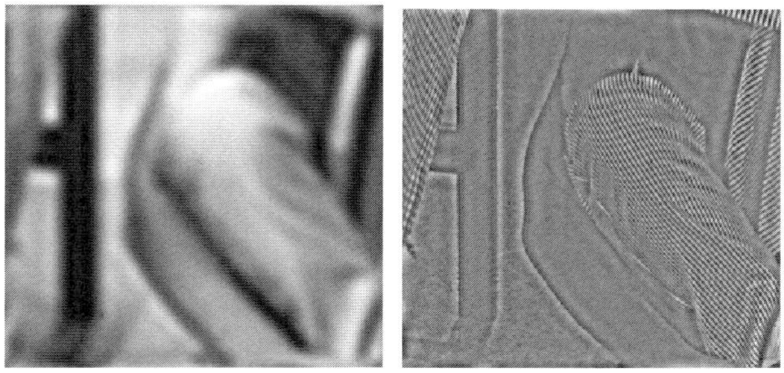

$(p, \beta, s) = (1,1,1)$ [5]

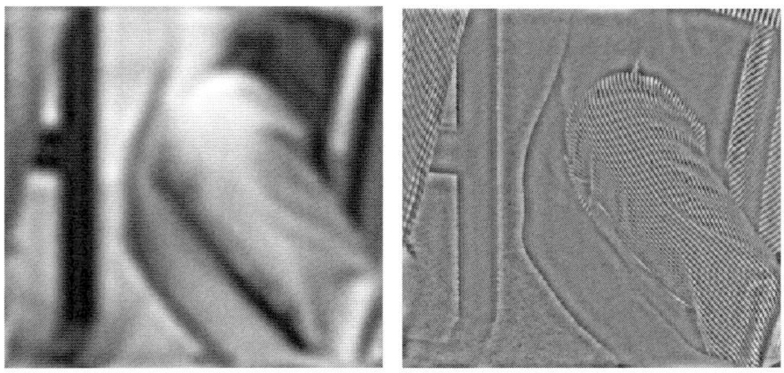

$(p, \beta, s) = (1,2,2)$

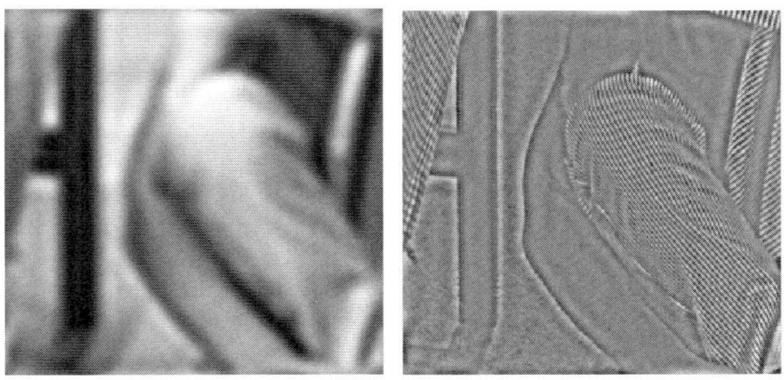

$(p, \beta, s) = (2,1,1)$

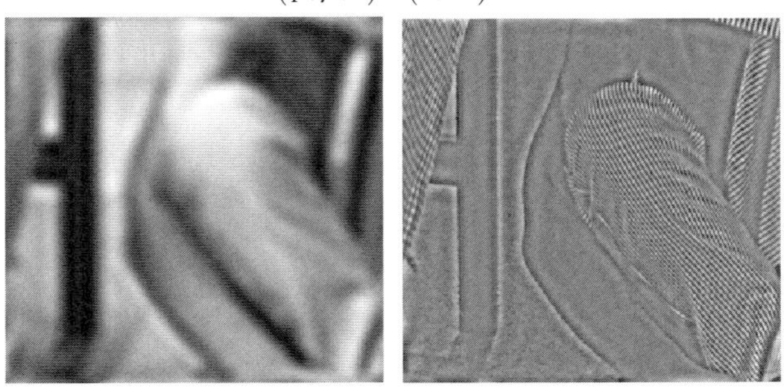

$(p, \beta, s) = (2,2,2)$

Fig. 2. Decomposition results of a natural textured image from the new model (2) based on the different parameter choice (p, β, s)

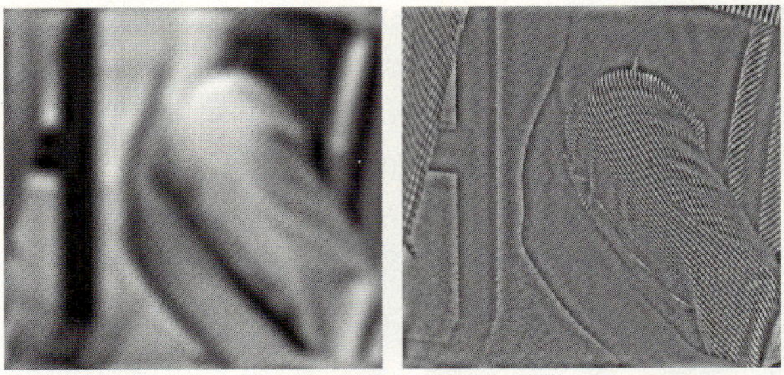

$(p,\beta,s)=(\infty,1,1)$

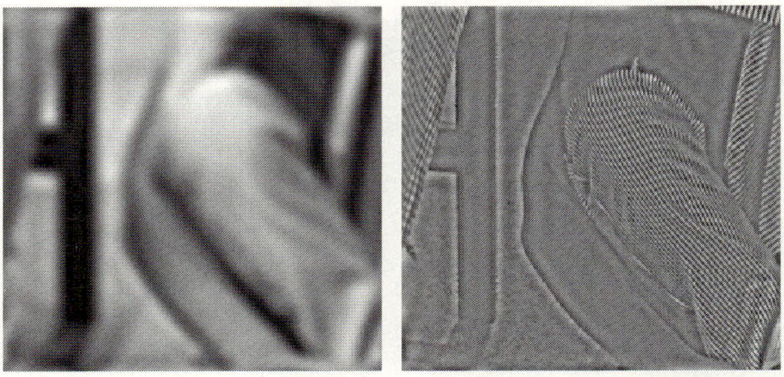

$(p,\beta,s)=(\infty,2,2)$

Fig. 2. (*continued*)

Table 1. PSNR for the denoising results

The values of p, β and s			PSNR
Noisy image			28.1058
$p=1$	$\beta=1$	$s=1$ [5]	31.0034
	$\beta=2$	$s=2$	29.5262
$p=2$	$\beta=1$	$s=1$	31.1634
	$\beta=2$	$s=2$	29.9701
$p=\infty$	$\beta=1$	$s=1$	31.3668
	$\beta=2$	$s=2$	31.3687

Fig. 3. Noisy image

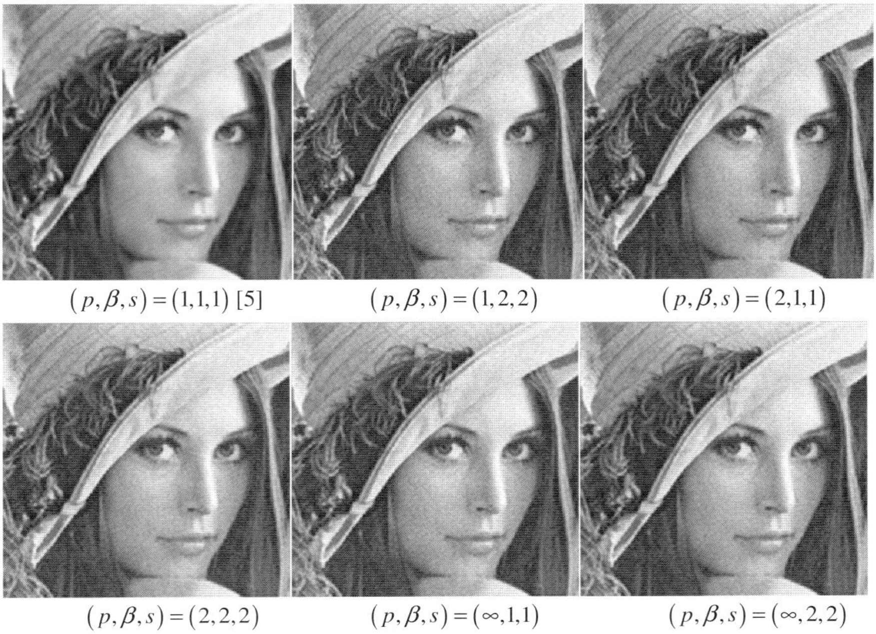

Fig. 4. Denoising results from the new model (2) for different parameter choice (p,β,s)

5 Conclusion

In this paper, we have presented a new variational model for image decomposition, which is based on Besov spaces and negative Hilbert-Sobolev spaces. And we, inspired by Lorenz, give proof for the general characterization of the solution of the proposed model based on the orthogonal projections onto the convex set, as well as some material examples. But the optimal choice of tuning parameters in new model is still a remaining problem.

References

1. Rudin, L., Osher, S., Fatemi, E.: Nolinear total variation based noise removal algorithms. Physica D 60, 259–268 (1992)
2. Meyer, Y.: Oscillating patterns in image processing and nonlinear evolution equations. Volume 22 of University Lecture Series. American Mathematical Society, Providence, RI (2001)
3. Vese, L.A., Osher, S.J.: Modeling textures with total variation minimization and oscillating patterns in image processing. UCLA CAM Report 02-19 19(1-3), 1–3 (2003)
4. Osher, S., Sole, A., Vese, L.: Image decomposition and restoration using total variation minimization and the [graphics object to be inserted manually] norm. Tech. Rep. 02-57, University of California Los Angeles CAM (2002)

5. Daubechies, G.: Teschke: Wavelet based image decomposition by variational functionals. (2004), http: // www. Math. Uni-bremen.De/zetem/ berichte.Html
6. Lorenz, D.A.: Wavelet Shrinkage in Signal and Image Processing - An Investigation of Relations and Equivalences. Ph. D thesis, University of Bremen (2005)
7. Rockafellar, R.T., Roger, J.-B.: Wets: Variational Analysis. Springer, Heidelberg (1998)
8. Lieu, L., Vese, L.: Image Restoration and Decompostion via Bounded Total Variation and Negative Hilbert-Sobolev Spaces. Tech. Rep. 05-33, University of California Los Angeles CAM (2005)
9. Lorenz, D.A.: Solving variational methods in image processing via projection-a common view on TV-denoising and wavelet shrinkage. (2004) http://www.math.uni-bremen.de/~dlorenz/docs/lorenz2004projection.pdf

Performance Analysis of Cooperative Hopfield Networks for Stereo Matching

Wenhui Zhou, Zhiyu Xiang, and Weikang Gu

Dept.Information Science and Electronic Engineering,
ZheJiang University, HangZhou, 310027, China
sunshine@hzcnc.com

Abstract. This paper proposes a dense stereo matching algorithm based on cooperative Hopfield networks. It uses two Hopfield networks with similar structure to solve energy minimization problem of stereo matching in parallel. Two strategies are applied to the performance analysis. One strategy considers each pixel as a neuron. The other is the Coarse-to-Fine strategy, which firstly divides the images into non-overlapping homogeneous regions, and each region is represented as super-pixel of the coarse images. After coarse estimation, a more refined estimation is implemented in pixel domain. Experiments indicate the method with the Coarse-to-Fine strategy has better performance and more rapid convergence speed, and less insensitive to initial conditions of the neural networks and the neuron update orders.

1 Introduction

Hopfield neural networks have been successfully applied to solve hard optimization problems over roughly the last two decades. However, how to avoid the neural networks falling into local minima, and the convergence problem always trouble the researchers in practice. Especially in stereo vision case where energy functions usually have thousands of local minima [1],[2].

To escape from local minima, many variations of Hopfield network with stochastic perturbations have been proposed, such as Boltzmann, Cauchy, and Gaussian Machines, etc. However, these methods need exponential time to approach to the global optimal solution. In fact, there is no way to ascertain the convergence time of these methods, and whether they reach the global optimum. Many Hopfield networks based stereo algorithms [3],[4],[5] also suffer these problems, and their performances are sensitive to the initial conditions and the neuron update orders.

This paper proposes a dense stereo matching algorithm based on cooperative Hopfield networks. It uses two Hopfield networks with similar structure to solve matching problem in parallel. The main dissimilarity between these two networks is the template images of matching problems are different. This paper implements the cooperation between two Hopfield networks under mutual correspondence constraint. Moreover, since the complex structure of neural network results in exponential time for convergence, we transform the optimal search problem of disparity map to iterative convergence processes of a binary-valued

Y. Wang, Y. Cheung, and H. Liu (Eds.): CIS 2006, LNAI 4456, pp. 983–990, 2007.

neural network, whose maximal number of neurons is the number of pixels or regions.

Furthermore, we analyze the performances of the cooperative networks with two different strategies. One is the general strategy in pixel domain, which considers each pixel as a neuron. The other is the Coarse-to-Fine strategy, which firstly divides the stereo images into non-overlapping homogeneous regions, and each region is regarded as super-pixel of the coarse images. After coarse estimation in the coarse images, a more refined estimation is implemented in pixel domain. Compared with the first strategy, the latter has better performance and more rapid convergence speed, and less insensitive to initial conditions of the neural networks and the neuron update orders.

2 Iterative Hopfield Neural Network for Stereo Matching

Recovering depth information from two simultaneous images, taken from two different viewpoints, is termed as the binocular stereo vision problem. The key stage of this problem is stereo matching, which is a labeling problem and can be treated as energy minimization problem. In this framework, the principle of stereo vision can be represented clearly, and many constraints can be added easily. A standard form of the energy function is:

$$E(d) = \sum_{i \in \mathcal{I}} c_i(d_i) + \lambda \cdot \sum_{\{i,j\} \in \mathcal{N}} c_{i,j}(d_i, d_j) \tag{1}$$

where $d = \{d_i | i \in \mathcal{I}\}$ is the disparity of image $\mathcal{I}$, $\mathcal{N}$ is the set of all pairs of neighboring pixels, c_i is the data penalty term for pixel i assigned with disparity d_i, $c_{i,j}$ is smoothness term which imposes punishment if neighboring pixels have different disparities, and λ is scale factor.

Since the complexity and performance of Hopfield network have relations with the size of network, we minimize an energy function with non-binary variables by repeatedly minimizing sub-problems about energy functions with binary variables [2]. The kth sub-problem can be represented as: assigning a label for each pixel of the template image from a set of labels $L \in \{-1, 1\}$. If the label of one pixel is -1 then it means the disparity of this pixel keeps unchanged. Otherwise, the disparity changes to value k. Apparently, k is within the disparity search scope.

Let $\Delta E_d^i(k)$ and $\Delta E_s^i(k)$ are variations of data term and smooth term in energy function for the disparity value of pixel i changes from d_i to k, respectively.

$$\Delta E_d^i(k) = c_i(k) - c_i(d_i) \tag{2}$$

$$\Delta E_s^i(k) = \lambda \cdot \sum_{j,\{i,j\} \in \mathcal{N}} \left[c_{i,j}\left(k, d_j^l\right) - c_{i,j}\left(d_i, d_j^l\right) \right] \tag{3}$$

where d_j^l is the disparity of pixel j assigned the label l.

The total changed value of energy of kth sub-problem is

$$\Delta E_k = \sum_{i \in \mathcal{I}} \left(\Delta E_d^i \left(k \right) + \Delta E_s^i \left(k \right) \right) \tag{4}$$

2.1 Iterative Hopfield Neural Network

We can transform the optimal search problem of disparity map to an iterative convergence process of binary-valued neural network. Each pixel of the template image will be treated as a neuron, which only connects with the nearest four neurons. Let s_i be the state of the neuron i. s_i=-1 represents the neuron is "inactive", that is the disparity $x(s_i)$ keeps unchanged. While s_i=1 represents "active" that means to update the disparity value $x(s_i)$ to a new value.

In the kth sub-problem, let w_i is the weight of the edge which connects the neuron i with itself, and w_{ij} is the weight of the edge which connects the neuron i with neighboring neuron j. According to the Eq.(2)-(4), we can obtain the following weights of neural network.

$$w_i = c_i \left(d_i \right) - c_i \left(k \right) \tag{5}$$

$$w_{i,j} = \begin{cases} \lambda \cdot \left[c_{i,j} \left(k, d_j \right) - c_{i,j} \left(d_i, d_j \right) \right], \text{ if } s_j = -1 \\ \lambda \cdot c_{i,j} \left(d_i, d_j \right), \text{ if } s_j = 1 \end{cases} \tag{6}$$

The state of the neuron i can be defined as:

$$s_i = sgn \left[\sum_{j, \{i,j\} \in \mathcal{N}} w_{i,j} s_j + w_i \right] \tag{7}$$

So, the energy function of neural network can be formulated as followed.

$$E = -\sum_i \sum_{j, \{i,j\} \in \mathcal{N}} w_{i,j} s_j s_i - \sum_i w_i s_i \tag{8}$$

Since s_i, s_j can only be 1 or -1, and $w_{i,j}$, w_i are bounded, the energy function E is also bounded. According to Eq.(7) and Eq.(8), every change in the state of neuron i results in the energy function E descending or keeping unchanged. So this network is stable and convergent.

2.2 Cooperative Hopfield Neural Network

In Hopfield network, each local minimum of the energy function is a balance state. When network arrives at these states, it will keep these states. To avoid Hopfield networks falling into local minima early, we use two cooperative Hopfield networks with similar structure to solve matching problem in parallel. The main difference between them is the template images in matching process are different, i.e. one template image is left image, and the other is right image.

After two networks running several iterations independently, we evaluate the results of them according to mutual correspondence constraint. The states of neurons whose disparities are identical with those of corresponding points are marked as "certain", and the states of them will keep unchanged in the subsequent process. The states of other neurons will be considered as "uncertain", and the disparity tabu tables of those neurons will be created according to the uniqueness constraint and order constraint, which can guide the Hopfield networks to escape from the local minima.

After two Hopfield networks approach to the stable states, it is inevitable that some pixels are still "uncertain", and all possible disparities of them are all marked in the tabu table. Apparently, these pixels usually belong to occlusion regions. The reason is the pixels in occlusion regions have no corresponding points in the other image, and we have no methods to obtain their disparities. Therefore, we estimate their disparities according to smoothness terms while ignoring data terms, i.e. we let w_i=0 in Eq.(7) and Eq.(8).

3 Two Different Strategies

In this paper, we evaluate the performance of the cooperate networks with two different strategies. One is the general strategy, the other is the Coarse-to-Fine strategy.

3.1 General Strategy

The general strategy is in pixel domain, which considers each pixel as a neuron. Directly using cooperative networks, we can estimate the disparity of each pixel in stereo images.

It is well known that local matching methods are very efficient, but they are sensitive to local ambiguous regions in images. Moreover, they perform poorly near object boundaries (i.e., depth discontinuities). The reason is local methods implicitly assume that all pixels within a fixed window have similar disparities. However, local methods can achieve good results in the rest regions. Especially the zero normalized cross correlation (ZNCC) algorithm performs even better, because it is relative insensitive to radiometric gain and bias.

Therefore, in order to avoid the selection of initial weights directly affecting the convergence of neural network, we use the disparity results of local matching algorithm to set the initial weights.

3.2 Coarse-to-Fine Strategy

In the Coarse-to-Fine strategy, the stereo image pairs are firstly divided into non-overlapping homogeneous regions, and each region is represented as a set of layers in the disparity space. Therefore, on the coarse level, the stereo matching problem becomes assigning a certain disparity to each region, which can be easily formalized as an energy minimization problem. Specifically, each region can be viewed as a super-pixel of the coarse images. The data term and smooth term of each region are the sum of the data terms and the smooth terms of pixels included in the region, respectively. Note that there are two smooth terms: non-convex smooth function with discontinuity-preserving is used on the region boundaries, and convex smooth function is used inside the regions.

On the coarse level, we apply cooperative Hopfield network method in the similar manner as that in pixel domain described in Section 2. Since the neurons are regions (super-pixels) instead of pixels, there have two advantages compared with traditional methods. One is this can lead to a simple network structure and fast convergence since the number of regions is usually much less than pixels. The other important advantage is the states of all pixels belonging to the same region will be updated simultaneously, different from the traditional Hopfield networks which only update one pixel at a time. This advantage makes our method insensitive to initial conditions of the neural networks and the neuron update orders.

Note that our method is based on the assumption that large disparity discontinuity only occurs on the boundaries of homogeneous regions, and disparity continuity or constancy is enforced inside each region. Therefore, the accuracy of estimated disparity is influenced by the performance of segmentation algorithm. Good segmentation should not only divide the image into homogeneous regions accurately, but also capture the precise region boundaries. In our method, mean shift segmentation with embedded edge confidence algorithm [6],[7] is employed.

Although the neurons of Hopfield network are regions on the coarse level, the cooperation process between two networks is in pixel domain. After cooperation process, each origin region is separated into two new regions: "certain" region and "uncertain" region, which composed of the pixels with "certain" states and "uncertain" states, respectively. The new network structure is formed by new regions in subsequent iterations, and the disparities of the "certain" regions would not be estimated.

To be clarity, the whole procedures of our method is summarized as follows:

1) The stereo image pairs are divided into non-overlapping regions.
2) Estimate and evaluate the disparity of each region using cooperative Hopfield network on the coarse level.

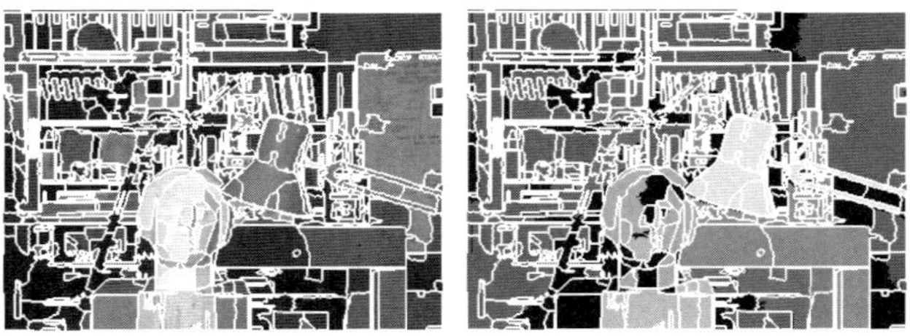

(a) (b)

Fig. 1. (a) the segmentation result by the mean shift with embedded edge confidence algorithm. (b) the "uncertain" regions in disparity map after first cooperation.

3) Estimate and evaluate the disparities of the "uncertain" pixels using cooperative Hopfield network on the fine level, i.e. in pixel domain.
4) Estimate the disparities of the rest "uncertain" pixels which can be considered belonging to occlusion areas.

Some results of the first two procedures for stereo pair "Tsukuba" are shown in Fig.1. Fig.1(a) shows the segmented regions in left image by the mean shift with

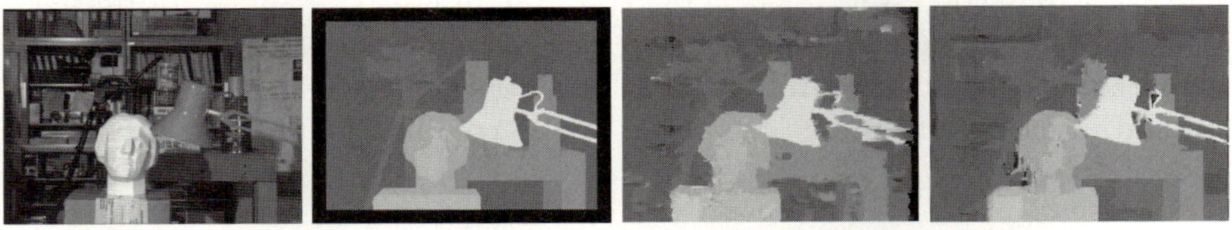

(a) Matching results of the "tsukuba" stereo image pair

(b) Matching results of the "map" stereo image pair

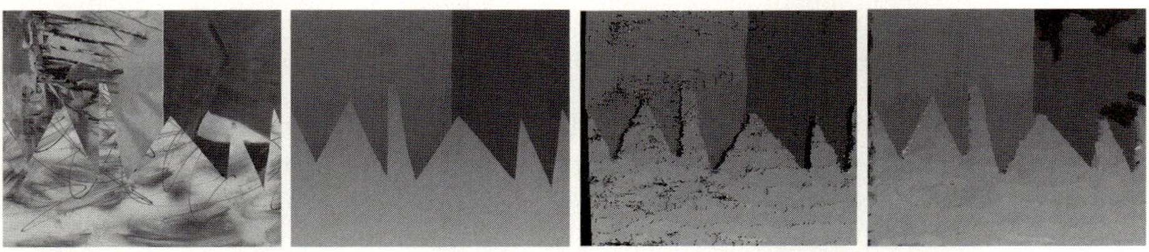

(c) Matching results of the "sawtooth" stereo image pair

(d) Matching results of the "venus" stereo image pair

Fig. 2. Results of stereo match using our methods

embedded edge confidence algorithm. After the first cooperation, the "uncertain" regions which marked black in disparity map are shown in Fig.1(b), and other regions have right disparities estimation.

4 Performance Analysis

Four pairs of standard test stereo images obtained from the Middlebury College's stereo vision research website [8] are chosen for the performance analysis. The performance results of the cooperate networks with two different strategies are shown in Fig.2. The left images of standard test stereo pairs and their ground truth are shown in the first and second columns (from left to right) of Fig.2, respectively.

In the experiments, data penalty term $c_i(d_i)$ uses the absolute difference of the luminance of corresponding pixels, and the Potts model is chosen as the smooth term $c_{i,j}(d_i, d_j)$ on the region boundaries. The scale factor λ is 2.

In general strategy, the disparity results of ZNCC are used as initial values, and the cooperation processes occur every five iterations. In the Coarse-to-Fine strategy, the initial disparities of all pixels are set to zeros, the cooperation processes occur every two iterations on the coarse level, and every three iterations on the fine level.

After 10 cooperation processes, the results of the proposed method with the general strategy are shown in the third column of Fig.2. After two cooperation processes on each level, the results of the proposed method with the Coarse-to-Fine strategy are shown in the last column of Fig.2.

Experiment results indicate that the method with the Coarse-to-Fine strategy has better performance and can escape from the local minima more quickly, and it is less insensitive to initial conditions of the neural networks and the neuron update orders.

5 Conclusions

This paper proposes a dense stereo matching algorithm using cooperative Hopfield networks. Compared with traditional Hopfield network, cooperation process according to mutual correspondence constraint can avoid our method falling into local minima early and speed the convergence of network.

Although the proposed method with general strategy is also sensitive to the selection of initial weights, the proposed Coarse-to-Fine strategy can overcome this disadvantage. Experiments indicate the latter is insensitive to initial conditions of the neural networks and the neuron update orders.

In our implementation, the disparities inside the regions are assumed to be constancy on the coarse level. Although this assumption is approximate right when the size of segmented regions are small enough, it doesn't satisfy the requirement of precise disparities estimation. Therefore, future works will focus on how to further refine the disparities of the pixels inside the regions, and study the effects of more complex cost functions, such as the functions that include occlusions model.

Acknowledgments

This paper is supported by Natural Science Foundation of China (60534070), China Postdoctoral Science Foundation (No.20060401036) and ZheJiang Postdoctoral Research Foundation (2006-bsh-28).

References

1. Boykov, Y., Kolmogorov, V.: An Experimental Comparison of Min-cut/Max-flow Algorithms for Energy Minimization in Computer Vision. IEEE Transactions on Pattern Analysis and Machine Intelligence 26(9), 1124–1137 (2004)
2. Kolmogorov, V., Zabih, R.: What Energy Functions Can Be Minimized Via Graph Cuts? IEEE Transactions on Pattern Analysis and Machine Intelligence 26(2), 147–159 (2004)
3. Ruichek, Y.: Multilevel- and Neural Network Based Stereo Matching Method for Real-Time Obstacle Detection Using Linear Cameras. IEEE Transactions on Intelligent transportation System 6(1), 54–62 (2005)
4. Binaghi, E., Gallo, I., Matino, G. et al.: Neural Adaptive Stereo Matching. Pattern Recognition Letters 25(15), 1743–1758 (2004)
5. Haifeng, H., Yingen, X.: A New Stereo Matching Approach Based on Hopfield Network. Journal of Image and Graphics 9(6), 729–736 (2004)
6. Comaniciu, D., Meer, P.: Mean Shift Analysis and Applications. The 7th IEEE International Conference on Computer Vision, Kerkyra, Greece, pp. 1197–1203 (1999)
7. Meer, P., Georgescu, B.: Edge Detection With Embedded Confidence. IEEE Transactions on Pattern Analysis and Machine Intelligence 23(12), 1351–1365 (2001)
8. `http://www.middlebury.edu/stereo`

An Improved Entropy Function and Chaos Optimization Based Scheme for Two-Dimensional Entropic Image Segmentation

Cheng Ma and Chengshun Jiang

Institute of Information Engineering
Information Engineering University, Zhengzhou, 450002, China
macheng31@gmail.com

Abstract. An improved two-dimensional entropic image segmentation method is presented in this paper. The method makes use of a new entropy function defined in a simple form, which can reduce computational amount notably. And the correctness of the new function is also proved. Then a scheme based on mutative scale chaos optimization is adopted to search for the optimal threshold. The results of simulation illustrate that efficiency of segmentation is improved significantly due to the new entropy function and searching method.

1 Introduction

The thresholding method based on maximum entropy is one of the most widely used methods in image segmentation. It uses the gray-level features of an image to choose a single or multiple thresholds by which the image pixels are classified into several regions and thus the object is extracted from the background. The one-dimensional entropic method was firstly introduced by Kapur in 1985 [1]. Abutaleb expanded it to the two-dimensional space in 1989 [2]. Compared to 1-D method, the 2-D method makes use of pixels' gray levels and average gray levels within a neighborhood, which can produce a better segmentation result. And it also shows a stronger ability of resisting noises. However, the computational amount in 2-d method increases sharply than in 1-D situation. To solve the problem, people use some optimization methods such as genetic algorithms (GA) [3,4,5], chaos optimization method [6], etc. Some researchers focused on the simplification of the mathematical expression of the entropy function and put forward some fast algorithms [7,8]. Yang proposed a segmentation method based on an optimized entropy function which reduced the computational amount efficiently, see [9]. However we find there's some irrationality in the author's work. In this paper, we analyze the function and make some modification to it. Later we will make experiment to test the new function,based on a chaos optimization scheme.We also compare the efficiency of genetic algorithm and chaos optimization method.

2 Model of 2-D Maximum Entropic Segmentation

2.1 Conventional Model

Suppose the gray level interval of a $M \times N$ sized image is $[0, L]$, so the pixels' average gray level within a neighborhood is also in $[0, L]$. Let $f(x, y)$ denote the gray level

Y. Wang, Y. Cheung, and H. Liu (Eds.): CIS 2006, LNAI 4456, pp. 991–1000, 2007.

of pixel (x, y) and $g(x, y)$ denote the average gray level of a $n \times n$ neighborhood. Then the 2-D gray level pair of pixel (x, y) is denoted by $[f(x, y), g(x, y)]$. Let $p_{ij} = r_{ij}/(MN)$represent the probability of the gray-level pair (i, j), $(i, j = 0, 1, \cdots L-1)$ where r_{ij} is the number of elements in the event $\{f(i, j) = r_{ij}\}$. Obviously we have $0 \leq r_{ij} \leq M \cdot N$ and $\sum_{i=0}^{L-1} \sum_{i=0}^{L-1} p_{ij} = 1$. For each class of pixels labeled by A and B, let

$$H_A = -\sum_{i=0}^{s-1}\sum_{j=0}^{t-1} p_{ij}^A \log_2 p_{ij}^A,$$

$$H_B = -\sum_{i=s}^{L-1}\sum_{j=t}^{L-1} p_{ij}^B \log_2 p_{ij}^B,$$

where

$$p_{ij}^A = p_{ij}/\sum_{i=0}^{s-1}\sum_{j=0}^{t-1} p_{ij}, \quad p_{ij}^B = p_{ij}/\sum_{i=s}^{L-1}\sum_{j=t}^{L-1} p_{ij}.$$

p_{ij}^A, p_{ij}^B denote the probability of the gray-level pair (i, j) in region A and B respectively. Then the sum of the two entropies

$$H_1(s,t) = H_A + H_B = -\sum_{i=0}^{s-1}\sum_{j=0}^{t-1} p_{ij}^A \log_2 p_{ij}^A - \sum_{i=s}^{L-1}\sum_{j=t}^{L-1} p_{ij}^B \log_2 p_{ij}^B \tag{1}$$

is the object function. The goal of the segmentation is to find a threshold (s^*, t^*) satisfying the following nonlinear problem:

$$F_1(s^*, t^*) = \max_{0 \leq s,t \leq L-1} H_1(s,t). \tag{2}$$

2.2 A New Entropy Function

For the purpose of reducing computational amount, researchers are focusing on proposing some fast algorithms by deducing equation (1). According to the property that an entropy function reaches its maximum in an equiprobable distribution, a new entropy function was presented by Yang in [9]:

$$H_2(s,t) = \sum_{i=0}^{s-1}\sum_{j=0}^{t-1} \left| p_{ij}^A - \frac{1}{st} \right| + \sum_{i=s}^{L-1}\sum_{j=t}^{L-1} \left| p_{ij}^B - \frac{1}{(L-s)(L-t)} \right|. \tag{3}$$

and the following problem

$$F_2(s^*,t^*) = \min_{0\le s,t\le L-1} H_2(s,t) \tag{4}$$

was proven to be equivalent to problem (2). That means all logarithmic and multiplicative operations are substituted by additions. This is an effective method in reducing computational amount.

To prove the equivalence, Yang insisted that when entropy function H_1 reached its maximum, the probability p_{ij}^A in (1) equalled to the same value $1/st$ for different (i,j) while p_{ij}^B equalled to $1/[(L-s)(L-t)]$. So the new entropy function $H_2(s,t)$ in (3) reached its minimum 0. On the contrary, when $H_2(s,t)$ equalled to 0, we had $p_{ij}^A = 1/(st)$ and $p_{ij}^B = 1/[(L-s)(L-t)]$ for each (i,j). That meant entropy H_A and H_B reached their maximums in such an equiprobable distribution. Therefore the two problems were equivalent. However, some point was ignored by Yang. If p_{ij}^A and p_{ij}^B could both reach the point $1/(st)$ or $1/[(L-s)(L-t)]$ for every (i,j), the proof was correct in theory. But we know that in a given gray-scale image, gray level pairs (i,j) are mainly distributed in regions representing object and background, and some pairs don't exist. In such a situation, whatever s and t equal to, p_{ij}^A or p_{ij}^B will equal to 0, i.e. they cannot equal to $1/(st)$ or $1/[(L-s)(L-t)]$, hence $H_1(s,t)$ and $H_2(s,t)$cannot reach their extrema. For two different functions who can reach their extrema at the same point in $[0,1]$, they may have different extremum points in a smaller interval $[a,b]$, $(0\le a\le b\le 1)$. Therefore, the proof by Yang is not totally correct.

Despite of the mistake, the work Yang has done is valuable. In this paper we make some modifications on the basis of (3) and present an improved entropy function, whose correctness will be proven in the following theorem.

Theorem. Define a new object function

$$H_3(s,t)=\sum_{i=0}^{s-1}\sum_{j=0}^{t-1}\left(p_{ij}^A-\frac{1}{st}\right)^2 + \sum_{i=s}^{L-1}\sum_{j=t}^{L-1}\left(p_{ij}^B-\frac{1}{(L-s)(L-t)}\right)^2, \tag{5}$$

where $p_{ij}^A, p_{ij}^B \in [a_{ij}, b_{ij}] \subset [0,1]$. Then the new nonlinear optimization problem

$$F_3(s^*,t^*) = \min_{0\le s,t\le L-1} H_3(s,t) \tag{6}$$

is equivalent to (2).

Proof. Denote both p_{ij}^A and p_{ij}^B by $p_{ij}(0\le i,j\le L-1)$. H_1 and H_3 can be regarded as functions of p_{ij}. For those $p_{ij}=0$ terms in H_1, we ignore them. Now let's check the existence of H_1's extremum.

Because

$$\frac{\partial(-H_1)}{\partial p_{ij}} = \log_2 p_{ij}+1, \quad \frac{\partial^2(-H_1)}{\partial p_{ij}^2} = \frac{1}{p_{ij}} > 0$$

and for any $(i', j') \neq (i, j)$, we have

$$\frac{\partial^2(-H_1)}{\partial p_{ij}\partial p_{i'j'}} = \frac{\partial}{\partial p_{i'j'}}(\log_2 p_{ij} + 1) = 0 \ .$$

So the Hessian matrix of $-H_1(p_{ij})$ is a positive definite symmetric matrix whose diagonal elements are $1/p_{ij} > 0$ while remainders are zeros. Therefore, $-H_1$ is a strictly convex function. According to the optimization theory, $-H_1$ has a unique minimum. That means H_1 has a unique maximum point. To prove the equivalence of the two optimization problems, let's firstly check a function with two variables

$$f_1 = -\sum_{i=1}^{2} p_i \log_2 p_i, \text{ where } p_1 + p_2 = 1 \ . \tag{7}$$

From (7) we have $f_1 = -p_1 \log_2 p_1 - (1 - p_1) \log_2(1 - p_1)$. This function has a unique maximum, as shown in Fig.1. If $p_1 = 1/2$, then f_1 reaches its maximum. However, if p_1 is limited within a smaller interval $[a, b]$ satisfying $1/2 \notin [a, b]$, then we know from the figure that the smaller the distance between p_1 and $1/2$, the bigger f_1 evaluates. That means f_1 is approaching its maximum as $(p_1 - 1/2)^2$ is approaching its minimum. When $(p_1 - 1/2)^2$ reaches its minimum in $[a, b]$,

$$2\left(p_1 - \frac{1}{2}\right)^2 = \left(p_1 - \frac{1}{2}\right)^2 + \left(1 - p_2 - \frac{1}{2}\right)^2$$
$$= \sum_{i=1}^{2}\left(p_i - \frac{1}{2}\right)^2$$

also reaches its minimum. So f_1 evaluating its maximum equals to $\sum_{i=1}^{2}(p_i - 1/2)^2$ evaluating its minimum.

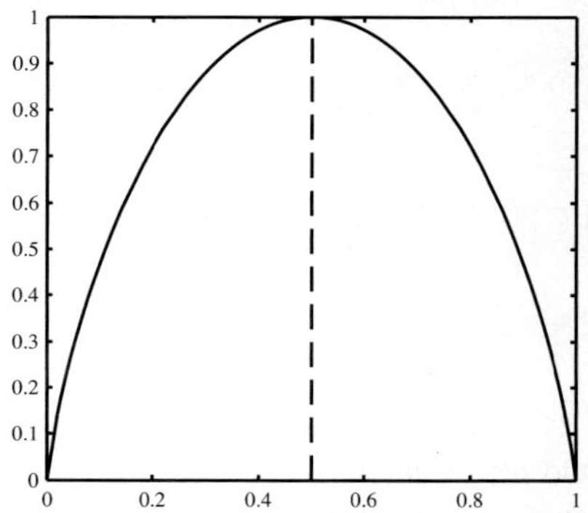

Fig. 1. Entropy function with one variable. It's a convex function with one maximum.

Let's move on to a function with three variables

$$f_2 = -\sum\nolimits_{i=1}^{3} p_i \log_2 p_i, \text{ where } p_1 + p_2 + p_3 = 1, \quad (8)$$

therefore,

$$f_2 = -\sum_{i=1}^{2} p_i \log_2 p_i - (1 - p_1 - p_2) \log_2 (1 - p_1 - p_2) . \quad (9)$$

Now let's observe its figure as shown in Fig.2.

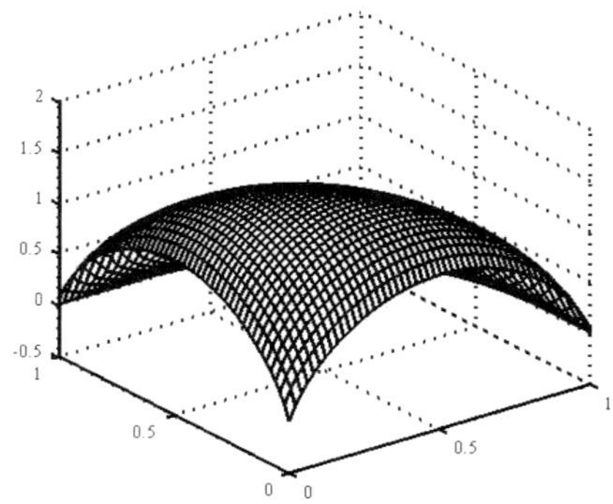

Fig. 2. Entropy function with two variables. It's a convex function with one maximum.

It is obvious that f_2 is also a convex function. We can find its maximum at point $(1/3, 1/3)$. If the domain of (p_1, p_2) doesn't include the point $(1/3, 1/3)$, as discussed above, it can be inferred similarly that the smaller the distance between (p_1, p_2) and $(1/3, 1/3)$ is, the bigger f_2 evaluates. Now we investigate p_3. Because $p_3 = 1 - p_1 - p_2$, for $\alpha \in [0, 1]$,

$$\begin{aligned} &\sum_{i=1}^{2} (p_i - 1/3)^2 + (p_3 - \alpha)^2 \\ &= \sum_{i=1}^{2} (p_i - 1/3)^2 + (1 - p_2 - p_1 - \alpha)^2 , \end{aligned} \quad (10)$$

when $\alpha = 1/3$, $f_2(p_1, p_2, p_3)$ is approaching its maximum as $\sum_{i=1}^{3} (p_i - 1/3)^2$ is approaching 0.

By analogy with above, using the convex feature of the functions and the existence of the extrema, we can conclude that for any $p_i \in [a_i, b_i] \subset [0, 1]$, $f(p_1, p_2, \cdots, p_n)$ reaches its maximum at the same point as $\sum_{i=1}^{n} (p_i - 1/n)^2$ reaches its minimum. Therefore, it can be inferred that the optimization problems (2) and (6) are equivalent.

This is the proof.

According to Shannon's information theory [10], an entropy function reaches its maximum in a equiprobable distribution. Entropy is a probabilistic measure of uncertainty. From some aspect, the equiprobable distribution $(1/n, 1/n, \cdots, 1/n)$ is the very source of the uncertainty. The closer a distribution is to the source, the bigger the value of entropy is. This is an interpretation to the theorem from the view of entropy.

3 The Mutative Scale Chaos Optimization Algorithm (MSCOA)

3.1 The Principle of Chaos Optimization

Chaos is a common phenomenon existing in nonlinear definite systems. Owing to its stochastic property, ergodicity and intrinsic regularity, global optimization methods based on chaos are widely applied in optimization problems, see [11,12,13,14,15].

The basic idea of the mutative scale chaos optimization algorithm is as follows. Firstly a sequence of chaotic variables is created by iterations. The sequence is used to check the whole solution space, which is called rough searching. Then according to the result of rough searching, a currently optimal solution is selected and the searching space is limited to a smaller one depending on the optimal solution, which is called precise searching. The MSCOA method incorporates advantages of both rough and precise searching, and achieves the goal of obtaining optimal solution quickly and effectively.

Chaos optimization is realized through chaotic variables created by chaotic mapping functions. For example, the Logistic function

$$y_{k+1} = uy_k(1 - y_k) \ , \tag{11}$$

where u is the chaotic parameter, $y_k \in (0, 1)$, $k = 0, 1, 2, \cdots$. When $u = 4$, the mapping is in totally chaotic state. Having been created, the chaotic variables need to be mapped into solution space as

$$x_k^i = a^i + (b^i - a^i) \cdot y_k^i \ , \tag{12}$$

where $i = 1, 2, \cdots n$, n is the number of function's variables. $[a^i, b^i]$ are domains of the variables. For a gray-scale image, the interval of threshold is usually $[0, 255]$.

3.2 Design of the Algorithm

The problem to be optimized is (6). According to the basic steps of the MSCOA method, we design an algorithm to search for the optimal threshold in a 2-d gray level space. The procedure is as follows:

Step 1: Initialization: $k = 0$, chaotic variables $y_0^i = y^i \in (0, 1)$, $r = 0$, $a_r^i = 0$, $b_r^i = 255$, where $i = 1, 2$, k is the chaos iteration counter and r is the iteration counter for shrinking spaces; optimal chaotic variables $(Y^1, Y^2) = (0, 0)$; initialize minimum F^* with a big value and current optimal threshold $(s^*, t^*) = (0, 0)$;
Step 2: Mapping chaotic variables (y_k^1, y_k^2) to threshold variables (s_k, t_k):

$$s_k = a_r^1 + y_k^1(b_r^1 - a_r^1), t_k = a_r^2 + y_k^2(b_r^2 - a_r^2) \ ;$$

Step 3: Calculate $F(s_k, t_k)$, if $F(s_k, t_k) < F^*$, then $(Y^1, Y^2) = (y_k^1, y_k^2)$, $(s^*, t^*) = (s_k, t_k)$, $F^* = F(s_k, t_k)$; else move on to next;
Step 4: Calculate $y_k^i = 4 \cdot y_k^i \cdot (1 - y_k^i)$, $i = 1, 2$, $k = k + 1$;
Step 5: Repeat step2-step4; if F^* remains unchanged in T_1 iterations, continue;
Step 6: Shrink the space for searching:

$$a_{r+1}^1 = s^* - \rho(b_r^1 - a_r^1), b_{r+1}^1 = s^* + \rho(b_r^1 - a_r^1),$$
$$a_{r+1}^2 = t^* - \rho(b_r^2 - a_r^2), b_{r+1}^2 = t^* + \rho(b_r^2 - a_r^2),$$

where $\rho \in (0, 0.5)$, and make sure the new space isn't beyond the original boundary:
if $a_{r+1}^i < a_r^i$, then $a_{r+1}^i = a_r^i$; if $b_{r+1}^i > b_r^i$, then $b_{r+1}^i = b_r^i$;
then make some modifications to (Y^1, Y^2),

$$Y^1 = (s^* - a_{r+1}^1)/(b_{r+1}^1 - a_{r+1}^1),$$
$$Y^2 = (t^* - a_{r+1}^2)/(b_{r+1}^2 - a_{r+1}^2).$$

Step 7: Let $y_k^i = Y^i$, repeat step2-step6; if F^* remains unchanged in T_2 iteration steps, output (s^*, t^*) and F^*.

This is the whole procedure of the algorithm, in which parametersρ, T_1, T_2 is to be adjusted to control accuracy and convergence rate for different applications.

4 Simulation Results and Analysis

To test the algorithm, we choose two 256×256 sized gray-scale images, the bacteria image and rice image. The programming tool is MATLAB v7.0, and the configuration of the computer is 1.5GHz host frequency with 512M memory.

The 2-D chaotic variables are mapped to $[l, L] \times [l, L]$, $0 \leq l < L \leq 255$, where L, l is the upper and lower boundary of gray levels. As to the selection of parameters in the algorithm, we choose $\rho = 0.4$, $T_1 = 300$, $T_2 = 3$. For comparison, the algorithm in Ref.[9] is also simulated. Segmentation results are shown in Fig.3 and Fig.4. From left to right are the original image, segmentation result by the method in Ref. [9], segmentation result by our method.

The different optimal thresholds, minimum of object functions and time cost are compared in Table.1. Due to the randomicity of chaotic algorithms, we execute the algorithm 50 times, and get the best thresholds, minimal function values and average time cost. Result I is computed by Ref. [9] and II by our paper.

Table 1. Segmentation results by two methods, compared by optimal thresholds, extrema of the entropy functions, and average time cost

		Thresholds	Minimum	Time Cost (s)
I	Rice	(126,137)	2.9075	39.87
	Bacteria	(112,116)	3.374	35.23
II	Rice	(115,123)	9.85e-3	0.98
	Bacteria	(94,106)	1.089e-2	1.21

Fig. 3. Rice image and its segmentation results by two different methods. From left to right it's the original image, result by Ref.[9], result by our paper.

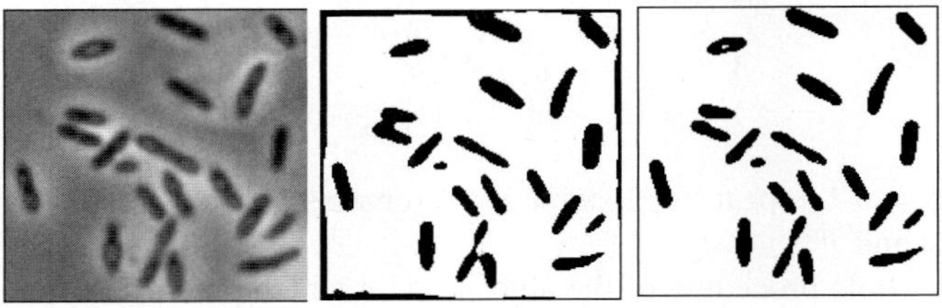

Fig. 4. Bacteria image and its segmentation results by two different methods. From left to right it's the original image, result by Ref.[9], result by our paper.

According to the segmentation results, it can be concluded that the algorithm by Ref.[9] is not likely to find the best threshold while our algorithm shows better segmentation results. It's not reasonable to judge the two algorithms by the minimums of two functions, for they are calculated in different methods. According to the time cost, algorithm in our paper shows a notable advantage over the other. As we know, the key point is how to search the 2-D threshold space. The algorithm in Ref.[9] is to search the space $(L-l)^2$ times, and $(L-l)^2$ calculations are executed for each feasible solution(s,t). So the computational complexity is $O[(L-l)^4]$. In our algorithm, according to parameters T_1 and T_2, only about 1000 iterations are executed and for every iteration $2(L-l)^2$ computations are needed. Thus the whole computational amount is $O[c\cdot(L-l)^2]$, which is much smaller than the former.

It is shown in Ref.[9] by experiment that the computational efficiency is increased by 15%-30% if function (3) is adopted comparing to function (1). However, out experimental results are not consistent with it. We test function (1) and (5) both in the MSCOA

Table 2. Two functions are both tested in the MSCOA method, compared by average iterations, the convergence rate, and average time cost

		Iterations	Convergence Rate	Time Cost (s)
I	Rice	1320	92%	4.88
	Bacteria	1171	90%	5.23
II	Rice	1294	94%	0.98
	Bacteria	1186	90%	1.21

method. The results are shown in Table.2 where I and II represents function(1) and (5) respectively.

It can be observed that the adoption of function (5) increases the computational efficiency about 4 times than function (1). The number of iterations is decided by MSCOA itself and has nothing to do with the adoption of functions. But the computational time changes noticeably, because for each iteration the time for calculating function (1) and (5) differs. Therefore, the application of the improved entropy function (5) is practical in 2-D entropic image segmentation.

By far people have been paying more attention to the genetic algorithm than chaos optimization algorithm. Theoretically both algorithms will converge to the global optimal solution, provided parameters are selected properly.Here the parameters are chosen according to Ref.[5]. There is a large body of literature focusing on the parameters for GA. Here the preferences may not be the best, but the result could illustrate something.The tool we use is Matlab v7.0, GA Toolbox.

Table 3. Comparison of GA and MSCOA in average iterations, convergence rate and time cost. I for GA and II for MSCOA. Notice that the iterations for GA is the number of generations.

		Iterations	Convergence Rate	Time Cost (s)
I	Rice	39	93.5%	2.24
	Bacteria	43	92%	2.67
II	Rice	1294	94%	0.98
	Bacteria	1186	90%	1.21

We know the GA is highly efficient for large scale optimization problems. Actually the problem here is a two dimensional case, seeming to be a little small for GA. If a segmentation method with three or more thresholds is used, GA may be a much better choice. Besides, the threshold is an integer in interval $[0, 255]$, which is very easy for binary coding and decoding. That's one of the reasons why people like to apply GA in image segmentation.

5 Conclusions

This paper presents an improved entropy function in 2-d entropic image segmentation. Compared to the original entropy function, the new one is simpler and easier for calculations. A mutative scale chaotic optimization algorithm is designed. Simulation results and comparison with other algorithms shows our algorithm is better. The MSCOA shows an excellent searching ability in our experiment, and it's easy for programming and fast in computation for such a 2-d entropic image segmentation.

Acknowledgement

The authors thank for the support of the National Natural Science Foundation of China, No.10571024.

References

1. Kapur, J.N., Sahoo, P.K., Wong, A.K.C.: A new method for gray-level picture thresholding using the entropy of the histogram. Computer Vision, Graphics, and Image Processing 29(3), 273–285 (1985)
2. Abutaleb, A.S.: Automatic thresholding of gray-level pictures using two-dimensional entropy. Computer Vision, Graphics, and Image Processing 47(1), 22–32 (1989)
3. Wang, L.S., Ou, Z.Y.: Image segmentation based on optimal histogram threshold by improved genetic algorithms. Journal of Data Acquisition and Processing 20(2), 130–134 (2005)
4. Wang, X., Wong, B.S., Tui, C.G.: X-ray image segmentation based on genetic algorithm and maximum fuzzy entropy. Robotics, Automation and Mechatronics, IEEE Proceedings 2, 991–995 (2004)
5. Lu, X.Q., Li, N., Chen, S.F., Ye, Y.K.: Two dimensional thresholding and genetic algorithms in image segmentation. Computer application and Software 18(12), 57–59 (2001)
6. Xiu, C.B., Liu, X.D., Zhang, Y.H.: Optimal entropy thresholding image segmentation based on chaos optimization. Computer Engineering and Application 27(2), 76–78 (2004)
7. Jansing, E.D., Albert, T.A., Chenoweth, D.L.: Two-dimensional entropic segmentation. Pattern Recognition Letters 20, 329–336 (1999)
8. Pal, N., Pal, S.K.: Object-background segmentation using new definitions of entropy. IEEE Proceedings 136(4), 284–295 (1989)
9. Yang, S., Gao, L.Q., Bian, L.Y.: Improvement of 2-d maximum entropy threshold algorithm based on optimal entropy function. Journal of System Simulation 17(6), 1350–1352 (2005)
10. Cover, T.M., Thomas, J.A.: Elements of Information Theory. Tsinghua University Press, Beijing (2003)
11. Fujita, T., Watanabe, T., Yasuda, K., Yokoyama, R.: Global optimization method using chaos in dissipative system. Industrial Electronics, Control, and Instrumentation, IEEE Transactions 2(2), 817–822 (1996)
12. Zhang, H.M., Yang, J.M.: Improvement and application of mutative scale chaos optimization algorithm. Control and Decision 17(6), 598–601 (2002)
13. You, Y., Wang, S.A., Sheng, W.X.: New chaos optimization algorithm with applications. Journal of Xi'an Jiaotong University 37(1), 69–72 (2003)
14. Tokuda, I., Aihara, K., Nagashima, T.: Adaptive annealing for chaotic optimization. Physical Review E 58(4), 5157–5160 (1998)
15. Chen, L.N., Aihara, K.: Global searching ability of chaotic neural networks. Circuits and Systems I: Fundamental Theory and Applications, IEEE Transactions 46(8), 974–993 (1999)

Face Pose Estimation and Synthesis by 2D Morphable Model

Li Yingchun and Su Guangda

Electronic Engineering Department, Tsinghua University, 100084, Beijing, China
liyingchun@mail.tsinghua.edu.cn, susu@tsinghua.edu.cn

Abstract. In this paper, we present face pose estimate and multi-pose synthesis technique. Through combining composite principal component analysis (CPCA) of the shape feature and texture feature respectively in eigenspace, we can get new eigenvectors to represent the human face pose. Support vector machine (SVM) has the optimal hyperplane that the expected classification error for unseen test samples is minimized. We utilize CPCA-SVM technology to get face pose discrimination. As for pose synthesis, the face shape model and the texture model are established through statistical learning. Using these two models and Delaunay triangular, we can match a face image with parameter vectors, the shape model, and the texture model. The synthesized image contains much more personal details, which improve its reality. Accurate pose discrimination and multi-pose synthesis helps to get optimal face and improve recognition rate.

Keywords: pose estimation, PCA, SVM, face recognition.

1 Introduction

Face recognition provides a direct and innocent way for person identification, which can be used in a wide range of application areas, such as video surveillance and biometrics. Though the human face remains typical features different from others, it is difficult to recognize face in an arbitrary and unconstrained environment.

Conventional algorithms can get relatively good recognition results when the face pose is in frontal view. In dynamic recognition system, most of the face images are in multi-pose view. So pose estimation and synthesis of face images are important preprocessing steps in face recognition.

Several face pose estimation methods are based on the statistical learning of images. The eigenface method has been widely applied for face recognition [1]. It is based on the Principal Components Analysis (PCA) of face images and has been proven an efficient representation method for faces. Fisherface is effective for face classification but not optimal, because it over-emphasizes the global between-class variances which may cause overlaps of neighboring classes [2]. Other approaches to pose estimation are using minimizing an error matrix based on collinearity in object space [3]. The shape-from-shading method utilized geometric technique extracted the correlation of orientation histograms for solving the image irradiation equation

Y. Wang, Y. Cheung, and H. Liu (Eds.): CIS 2006, LNAI 4456, pp. 1001–1008, 2007.

together with curvature consistency constraints [4]. Typically, these approaches rely on large sets of training data and constructing 3D face models. They can give relatively better results but at the cost of time.

As for synthesis of face, 3D faces can be generated automatically from multiple pose face [6]. It needs users to assist to face morphable modeling. A more flexible way to acquire information about how images of objects of a certain class change under pose, illumination, and other transformations, is to learn the possible pattern of variability and class-specific deformations from a representative training set of views of generic and prototypical objects of the same class.

In Section 2, we present dynamic robust face pose estimate method. We take full advantage of the characteristics of PCA representing for faces and reducing data dimension and the feature of SVM optimal classifier. The pose estimate is based on a machine learning architecture that estimates pose angles from multi-pose images through combining CPCA and SVM. In Section 3, as the large rotation view, we describe an algorithm of improved morphable model in 2D face image to synthesize the frontal face. We synthesize frontal face from single face image and at least two face images including one frontal face image respectively.

2 Face Pose Estimation

The new method combining CPCA and SVM is applied to judge the face pose angles. Through utilizing the CPCA and projecting face images to the eigenspace, eigenvalue and eigenvector to each class can be calculated. At last, we calculate and classify them with SVM. The pose angles of the face image are estimated.

2.1 Preprocess Images

First of all, we should normalize the face image including scale normalization, gray normalization and so on. Fig.1 is the result of eliminate the effect of uneven illumination.

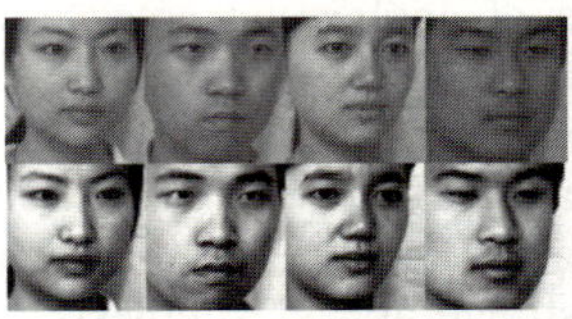

Fig. 1. Result of eliminate the effect of un-even illumination

We select 101 labeled feature points to describe face shape. Separating the shape parameters and texture parameters of face, a face shape model and the texture model were established respectively by statistical learning. With these two models we can match a face image to a parameter vector.

Our labeled training set is denoted *S*. It contains *N* shapes, each of which has *n* landmarks. Put in another way, we have *N* coordinate points for each landmark of the shape. We denote the jth landmark coordinate point of the ith shape of the training set by (x_{ij}, y_{ij}), and the vector describing the n (n=101) points of the ith shape in the training set by: $S_i = (x_{i1}, y_{i1}, x_{i2}, y_{i2}, \cdots x_{in}, y_{in})^T, i = 1, 2, \cdots N$, which N is the number of training set. We mark the profile face in face image. The shape model and labeled images are shown in Fig.2.

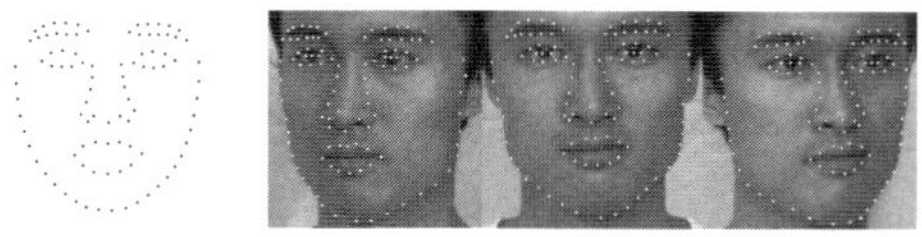

Fig. 2. The shape model and multi-pose labeled images

An appearance model can represent both the shape and texture variability seen in a training set. The training set consists of labeled images, which key landmark points are marked on each example object.

Similarly a face model requires labeled face images. Given such a set we can generate statistical models of shape and texture variation.

2.2 Composite PCA

We map the grey value to a mean face through image wrapping technology. We use PCA in shape description and texture description to acquire shape feature and texture feature of face images respectively. Afterward, we set the different weights of the two features and combine them into a new face description and get a combining PCA feature of face images.

The aligned face image is set as points in N-dimensional space representing face grey feature. Given face shape samples $S = \{S_1, S_2 \cdots, S_n\}$, which n represent the number of samples. Select randomly one of samples as mean shape model $\overline{S}$ and normalize it. We make a geometric transform to align each S_i to $\overline{S}$ .The aim is to find the shape feature which has the minimum Euclidean distance between them. Then we project the each S_i to $\overline{S}$ eigenspace. The shape feature subtracted by their mean vectors to obtain the centered sample variance μ . The texture feature ν is obtained by the same method. We set weights of two vectors p and q after two groups of features be gained. Thus the face new eigenvector is expressed as

$$\xi = p \cdot \mu + q \cdot \nu \text{, where } p + q = 1 . \tag{1}$$

By selecting the suitable coefficient of weights, we get new eigenvector ξ of each face sample. It is prepared well for the next classification. The number of eigenvectors is determined by angles selecting of the training samples.

2.3 Multi-pose Face Estimation

SVM is a learning algorithm for pattern classification. Its basic principle is to find the optimal linear hyperplane such that the expected classification error for unseen test samples is minimized. According to the structural risk minimization principle, a function that classifies the training data accurately will generalize best regardless of the dimensionality of the input space.

We shall minimize the within-class variance to construct the optimal separating hyperplane. The optimal separating decision surface in dot product space by mapping the similarity vectors to a high-dimensional space where an optimal hyperplane is constructed.

Given the labeled set of training samples $(x_1, y_1), \cdots, (x_m, y_m)$ where $x_i \in R^N$ is constructed by eigenvector ξ_i and $y_i \in \{+1, -1\}$ is class label.

Constructing an optimal hyperplane $W(\alpha)$ is equivalent to finding all the nonzero α_i. Any vector x_i that corresponds to a nonzero α_i is a supported vector of the optimal hyperplane. Finally, we get optimally classified function $f(x)$.

$$W(\alpha) = \sum_{i=1}^{n} \alpha_i - \frac{1}{2} \sum_{i,j=1}^{n} \alpha_i \alpha_j y_i y_j K(x_i, x_j) \quad (2)$$

$$f(x) = \text{sgn}\left(\sum_{\text{vector}} y_i \alpha_i^* K(x_i, x) + b^* \right) \quad (3)$$

Where $K(\cdot)$ is a kernel function. and the sign of $f(x)$ determines the membership of x. It is also a Euclidean distance among samples. b is a bias term [5].

A desirable feature of SVM is that the number of training points is usually quite small, which are retained as support vectors. Thus it provides a compact classifier. If suitably selected sets can cover all samples near optimal hyperplane, this sample set can be used as training set.

Combining the above CPCA and SVM classifier, we can draw a better classification result. The pose angle vectors were projected to eigenspace and obtained the optimal hyperplane that correctly separates data points.

2.4 Pose Estimation Results

In order to evaluate pose estimation algorithm, the off-line image test using the captured frames is done. The results of pose estimation are shown in Fig.3. It is based on the different angles training at interval less than 15º. The training sets consist of 15 frames with varying pose among 30 persons. The pose angles of the train set are {±60º, ±45º, ±30º, ±15º, 0º}. The test sets include face pose ranging from 60 ºleft to 60 ºright among 1245 persons.

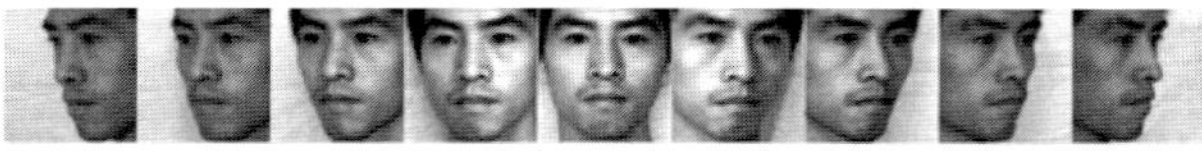

Fig. 3. The results of face pose estimation

The test accuracy rate of pose angles is near 97% and the average RMS (root mean square) is near 1.89° at a few key angles. The test samples are 245 persons at each key angle. So the method is stable and applicable. The results can be used in real-time applications.

3 Synthesize Frontal Face

It usually meets the demands of recognition system if the pose angle is between 15° and -15° . If the pose angle is over this range, it is hard to be recognized. The face image with large rotation will be synthesized to frontal view. The shape of an object can be represented as a vector and the texture represented as a vector. The appearance model of synthesis controls its shape and texture by selecting suitably parameters.

3.1 Morphable Model

The face texture is the region covered by 101 feature points linked in sequence. Since each face shape is different from others and the covered face regions is also different. We wrap face from original shape to mean shape model before we select texture feature. Delaney triangles are a serial of triangles which cover face region[6]. It's shown in Fig. 4.

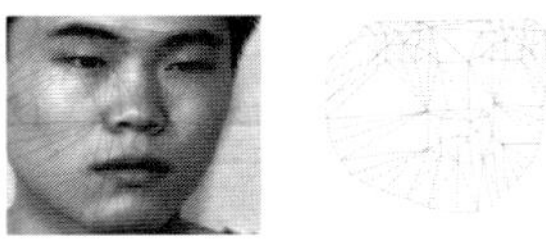

Fig. 4. Face texture information and Delaunay triangle

After Delaunay triangular mapping, face image is divided into serials of triangle without cross points. We assume that the number of valid texture values in the texture map is equal to the number of vertices. So the mapping relationship between faces can be realized by triangles. The linear relationship between two triangles:

$$\begin{bmatrix} x' \\ y' \end{bmatrix} = \begin{bmatrix} a & b \\ c & d \end{bmatrix} \begin{bmatrix} x \\ y \end{bmatrix} + \begin{bmatrix} O_x \\ O_y \end{bmatrix} \tag{4}$$

Which (x, y) is in the original shape, (x', y') is the corresponding position in the mean shape. a, b, c, d and O_x, O_y are the parameters of rotation and translation transform of original shape. Put the coordinate value of three known vertex to above formula. Then the parameters can be solved. Using Delaunay triangular mapping method, the training sets can be mapped to mean shape, and different face texture with the same dimension will be selected.

We improved the morphable model which is based on a set of 3D faces and used in 2D faces. Assume that all exemplar faces are in full correspondence. We represent the geometry of a face with a shape parameter $S=(x_1, y_1, x_2, y_2, \cdots x_n, y_n)^T \in R^{2n}$. It contains the coordinate values of the corresponding vertices. Therefore we can represent the texture of a face with texture parameters. $T=(u_1, v_1, u_2, v_2, \cdots u_n, v_n)^T \in R^{2n}$. It contains the gray values of the n corresponding vertices.

Then a morphable face model was constructed with a data set of exemplar faces, each represented by its shape parameters S_i and texture parameters T_i. Since we assume all faces in full correspondence, new shapes S and new textures T can be expressed as a linear combination of the shapes and textures of the exemplar faces:

$$S=\sum_{i=1}^{q} \eta_i S_i \tag{5}$$

$$T=\sum_{i=1}^{q} \rho_i T_i \tag{6}$$

We define the morphable model as the set of faces, parameterized by the coefficients η_i and ρ_i. Arbitrary new faces can be generated by varying the parameters η_i and ρ_i that control parameters of shape and texture.

So let S_i^r represent a sets of shape parameters of face images which possess the same rotation, which T_i^r represent a sets of texture parameters of face images with the same rotation direction. Then a new face can be expressed by shape and texture linear combination of others with the same pose angle. The precondition is that the frontal face of test image is known.

$$S^r=\sum_{i=1}^{q} \eta_i S_i^r \tag{7}$$

$$T^r=\sum_{i=1}^{q} \rho_i T_i^r \tag{8}$$

For a useful face synthesis system, it is important to be able to quantify the results in terms of their being faces. We estimated the probability distribution for the coefficients from example set of faces. This distribution enables us to control the likelihood of the coefficients and consequently regulates the likelihood of the appearance of the generated faces. When sets of faces have same pose angles, the coefficients have the same corresponding distribution.

3.2 Pose Synthesis Results

We can generate multi-pose face images from only one frontal face image. It is shown in Fig.5. We can see that the face images can generate from one frontal image to

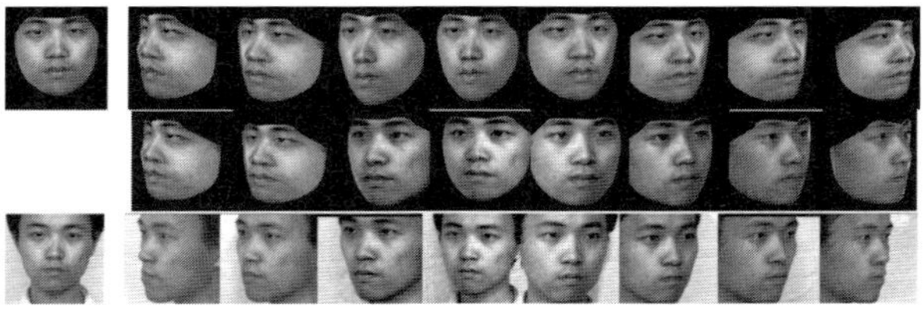

Fig. 5. Generate multi-pose image from only one frontal face image. Top: generating multi-pose images. Mid: naked face with real images. Bottom: real images.

others with various different rotation angles. They are authentic with little distortion comparing with real images. It means that each pose has one corresponding vector.

If the pose angle of a face image is known, by above algorithm, when given a test image with a known pose angle, we can get its frontal face image. It's shown in Fig.6.

(a) (b) (c) (d)

Fig. 6. Single image synthesize frontal face image. (a)real image. (b)naked face image. (c) synthesis naked face.(d) synthesis real image.

From the Delaunay triangular mapping, we can see that there is a corresponding relationship between frontal face and rotation face. So we utilize this corresponding relationship to synthesize any face with rotation to frontal face image. The synthesis results of a single face image with rotation view to frontal face image are in Fig.7.

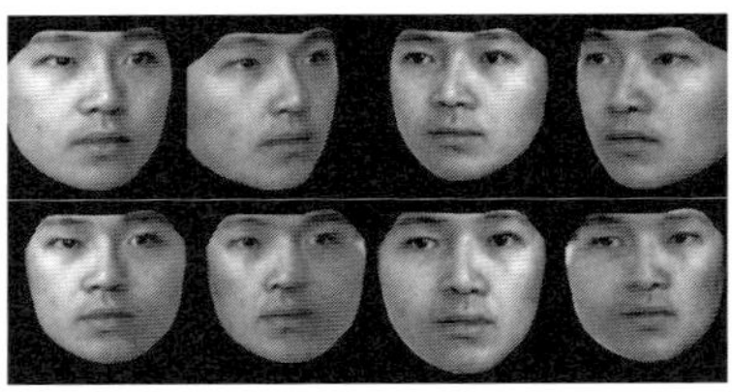

Fig. 7. Single face image synthesizes frontal face image. Top: real face images. Bottom: synthesized image.

The new method shows the wrapping is effective in 2D model. And the synthesis is to be recognized easily. The system recognition rate is improved greatly.

Actually, our method may have a lot of problems such as the poor effects to some special distributing samples. When the rotation angle is larger than 30 degree, the synthesis face will lost much personal information. There are some further researches to be done in the future.

References

1. Brunelli, R., Poggio, T.: Face Recognition: Features versus Templates. IEEE Transactions on Pattern Analysis and Machine Intelligence 15(10), 1042–1052 (1993)
2. Belhumeur, P.N., Hespanha, J.P., Kriegman, D.J.: Eigenfaces vs Fisherfaces: recognition using class specific linear projection. IEEE TPAMI 19(7), 711–720 (1997)
3. Li, S.Z., Peng, X.H., Zhang, H.J., Cheng, Q. S.: Multi-View Face Pose Estimation Based on Supervised ISA Learning. In: The 5th International Conference on Automatic Face and Gesture Recognition, pp. 20–21 (2002)
4. Tae-Kyun, K., Kittler, J.: Locally linear discriminant analysis for multimodally distributed classes for face recognition with a single model image. IEEE Transactions on Pattern Analysis and Machine Intelligence 27(3), 318–327 (2005)
5. Vapnik, V.: Statistical Learning Theory. John Wiley & Sons, New York (1998)
6. Blanz, V., Vetter, T.: A Morphable Model For The Synthesis Of 3D Faces. In: Proc. Siggraph 99, pp. 187–194. ACM Press, New York (1999)

Study of the Wavelet Basis Selections

Hua Cui and Guoxiang Song

Faculty of Science, Xidian University
Xi'an, 710071, China
cuihua7276@yahoo.com.cn, guoxiangsong@163.com

Abstract. How to choose a wavelet basis for a given signal is always important and difficult in wavelet applications. In this paper, based on the fact that the Morlet has been conventionally selected to make wavelet analysis of LFM signals, some further research on the wavelet basis selection are done. Morlet is in fact not the best choice under all application conditions related to LFM signals processing, which is proved by both the theoretical analysis and the simulation results in this paper. So we should not choose a wavelet basis randomly, but weigh it synthetically.

1 Introduction

The linear frequency modulated (LFM) signals are a very important kind of non-stationary signals and common in various areas of science and engineering (e.g., radar, television, broadcasting, sonar, communications). Extracting their instantaneous frequency has always been an important subject. There are many methods [1], [2] for that, among which Wavelet analysis method wins the favor because it can change time and frequency resolving power automatically adapted to the analyzed signal, therefore probing its characteristics more exactly and further assuring a greater accuracy in extracting its instantaneous parameters. However, wavelet analysis has many bases. As is well-known to us, different bases form different multiresolution analysis and different multiresolution analysis may result in much different analysis performance for the same signal. Which one is what we want most? Morlet wavelet has been commonly chosen in a great many of papers available [3], [4]. Is it the best choice? In this paper, we will have a probe into the problem of the optimization selection of wavelet basis functions in view of extracting the instantaneous frequency of LFM signals.

2 LFM Signals and Instantaneous Frequency

The LFM signal is given by

$$x(t) = A\exp[j2\pi(f_0 t + \frac{1}{2}at^2)]. \tag{1}$$

Y. Wang, Y. Cheung, and H. Liu (Eds.): CIS 2006, LNAI 4456, pp. 1009–1017, 2007.

The instantaneous frequency $f(t)$ is defined as

$$f(t) = \phi'(t) \tag{2}$$

$$\phi(t) = 2\pi(f_0 t + \frac{1}{2}at^2) \tag{3}$$

where A is the amplitude of the signal $x(t)$ and $\phi(t)$ its instantaneous phase, and f_0 and a are initial frequency and frequency modulation rate respectively. What we are interested in is the estimation of the parameters f_0 and a.

3 Wavelet Analysis Theory

Define 1: $L^2(R)$ is a one-dimension function space that is measurable and integrable in the sense of square. Let $\psi(x) \in L^2(R)$, satisfying

$$\int_R \psi(x)dx = 0, \tag{4}$$

then the translated and dilated functions of $\psi(x)$ is given by

$$\psi_{a,b}(x) = |a|^{-1/2}\psi(\frac{x-b}{a}) \quad , a,b \in R, a \neq 0, \tag{5}$$

which is called continuous wavelets ,where $\psi(x)$ that satisfies the admissible condition

$$\int_R |\hat{\psi}(w)|^2 |w|^{-1} dw < +\infty, \tag{6}$$

is called the mother wavelet, and a and b denote scaling factor and shift factor respectively, and $\hat{\psi}(w)$ the Fourier transform of $\psi(x)$.

Define 2: Based on Define 1, the continuous wavelet transform (or CWT) of the function $f(x)$ in $L^2(R)$ is defined as

$$\begin{aligned} Wf(a,b) &= < f, \psi_{a,b} > \\ &= |a|^{-\frac{1}{2}} \int_R f(x)\overline{\psi(\frac{x-b}{a})}dx. \end{aligned} \tag{7}$$

And its inverse continuous wavelet transform is defined as

$$f(x)=\frac{1}{C_{\psi}}\int_{-\infty}^{\infty}\int_{0}^{\infty}\frac{1}{a^{2}}Wf(a,b)\psi_{a,b}(x)dadb, \tag{8}$$

where $C_{\psi}=\int_{0}^{+\infty}\frac{|\hat{\psi}(w)|^{2}}{w}dw$.

CWT has multi-resolution performance when analyzing the signal f on a wavelet basis. However, in practice, continuous wavelet must be discretized so as to be implemented by the computer. Binary wavelet transform, achieved by binary sampling a and b, is the most popular form. Different from the discrete form of CWT, it has many advantages.

4 Main Properties of Wavelet Functions

Generally speaking, there are several properties below related to a wavelet function that affect the optimal selection of the wavelet basis:

- Vanishing moments: For $0 \le m \le M$ with $m \in Z, M \in Z$, if $\int_{R} t^{m}\psi(t)dt=0$, then the wavelet function $\psi(t)$ possesses M vanishing moments. That implies $\psi(t)$ is orthogonal to any $M-1$ polynomial. So, wavelet transform will produce small wavelet coefficients on fine scales if the analyzed signal is regular and the chosen wavelet function possesses enough numbers of vanishing moments. In usual applications, we hope the wavelet function possesses certain numbers of vanishing moments.
- Compact support: If $\Omega=\{t \mid \psi(t)\neq 0\}$, and both $\inf\Omega$ and $\sup\Omega$ are finite, then $\psi(t)$ has compact support $[\inf\Omega, \sup\Omega]$. The support performance of a wavelet function determines not only whether it can provide more practical finite filters, but also the accuracy of wavelet decomposition and reconstruction. Some wavelet functions don't possess the compact support property, but decay fast or exponentially. The compact support (or fast decay) is an important property for a wavelet function. The shorter its compact support or the faster its decay is, the better the time-frequency localization characteristic of a wavelet function will be and the more easily its algorithm will be implemented.
- Regularity: In mathematics, the upper bound of Lipschitz is usually used to describe the regularity of a wavelet function. The higher the regularity, the smoother a wavelet function and the better smoothing effect we will get while using it to process a signal, thus further reducing the quantization error. For most orthonormal wavelet bases and all biorthogonal ones, their regularity increases with the increasing numbers of their vanishing moments.

- Symmetry: If the Fourier transform $\hat{\psi}(w)$ of $\psi(t)$ satisfies $\hat{\psi}(w) = \phi(w)e^{i(aw+b)}$, let ϕ be $\pm|\hat{\psi}(w)|$ and $b = 0$,where ϕ is a real function and a, b real constants, then we will say it has a linear phase. All the symmetrical or antisymmetric real wavelet functions have linear phases. which imply the invariability of linear phase shift. Therefore, wavelet functions with symmetry can well restrain distortions such as deformation, overlapping image, and so on. Haar is the only real wavelet function that has compact support, orthonormality and symmetry properties at the same time. However it is not continuous and has only one vanishing moments, which leads to its poor applications.
- Orthonormality and biorthogonality: Let $\tilde{\psi}(t)$ and $\tilde{\varphi}(t)$ denote the duals of the wavelet function $\psi(t)$ and scaling function $\varphi(t)$ respectively, if $\psi(t)$ satisfies the biorthogonal conditions, namely

$$\langle \tilde{\varphi}(t), \varphi(t-1) \rangle = \langle \tilde{\psi}(t), \psi(t-1) \rangle = \delta(1), \tag{9}$$

$$\langle \tilde{\varphi}(t), \psi(t-1) \rangle = \langle \tilde{\psi}(t), \varphi(t-1) \rangle = 0, \tag{10}$$

- then we will say it has biorthogonality. In addition, if $\psi(t)$ is equal to $\tilde{\psi}(t)$, we will say it has orthonormality. Orthonormal wavelets have found their wide use due to their advantages of orthonormality and the least data redundance in the course of wavelet decomposition. Moreover, biorthogonality is the weak form of orthonormality, which makes it possible for a compactly supported wavelet function to be symmetrical. Therefore, in a biorthogonal setting one has more flexibility than in an orthonormal one. In fact, given a basic function, it is possible to construct infinitely many duals. This additional degree of freedom can be used to adapt the bases to the specific problem at hand.
- Time-frequency window: Let the center and radius of $\psi(t)$ be t^* and Δ_ψ respectively, with w^*, $\Delta_{\hat{\psi}}$ its corresponding center and radius in the frequency domain, then $\psi_{a,b}(t)$ has the time-frequency window

$$\begin{aligned}&[b + at^* - a\Delta_\psi , b + at^* + a\Delta_\psi]\\ &\times[\frac{w^*}{a} - \frac{1}{a}\Delta_{\hat{\psi}} , \frac{w^*}{a} + \frac{1}{a}\Delta_{\hat{\psi}}]\end{aligned} \tag{11}$$

This time-frequency window has the area of $4\Delta_\psi\Delta_{\hat{\psi}}$, only dependent on the wavelet function $\psi(t)$. The smaller its area, the better the time-frequency localization of $\psi(t)$ will be. It is the energy of the signal on these time-frequency windows that generates the wavelet coefficients. Therefore, a wavelet function with good time-frequency localization performance can efficiently avoid the signal leaking and demonstrates better orientation performance. And when the time window becomes shorter, the resolving power of the time-frequency window increases, and its central frequency $\frac{w^*}{a}$ rises, corresponding to the high-frequency parts of the signal. At the same time, the frequency window becomes wider and the frequency resolving power of the time-frequency window decreases. Therefore, we should select a wavelet basis with comparatively high central frequency for a high-frequency signal.

What is mentioned above is the main properties correlative to the performance of a wavelet basis. However, no wavelet basis has all such nice properties. For example, the length of its support is incompatible with its number of vanishing moments for an orthonormal wavelet basis. In addition, it is necessary to weigh between compact support and regularity, and a continuous orthonormal wavelet basis with compact support makes symmetry impossible.

In fact, there is a theorem proving that the length of the support for an orthonormal wavelet basis is not less than $2M-1$ if $\psi(t)$ has M vanishing moments. Therefore, we have to reduce the length of the support at the cost of depressing the number of vanishing moments. In this sense, Daubechies wavelet basis is the best because it has the shortest support $[-M+1, M]$ with M vanishing moments. That is to say, Daubechies wavelet bases (shortened for db(N)) simultaneously possesses such good performance as compact support, $\frac{N}{2}$ vanishing moments and orthonormality. Just because of that, db(N) can provide finite and practical filters, reflect the information included in the analyzed signal more precisely and reduce the computational complexity rather greatly, thus popular in many application fields such as signal processing. However, such compactly supported, real, orthonormal wavelet functions are all asymmetric except Haar wavelet basis (i.e. N=1 of db(N)), which makes their applications restricted greatly.

This asymmetry tends to cause comparatively great distortion, especially in the border. Because the symmetrical period extension method is adopted to process borders in wavelet decomposition, it is certain that comparatively great error will occur if an asymmetrical wavelet basis is selected. As a result, the compactly supported wavelet basis is required to be improved in order to get more symmetry. Daubechies had obtained Symmlet wavelets which are even more approximate to the linear phase by imposing some technique on the selection of the roots when constructing the db(N) wavelets. This kind of wavelets still have the shortest support $[-M+1, M]$, M vanishing moments and orthonormality, and are even more symmetric. There is also another improved scheme that is to abandon the orthonormality of wavelet functions to construct compactly supported biorthogonal ones that are symmetric in the strict sense. If biorthogonal wavelet functions can be designed reasonably, the length of support set, the number of vanishing moments, regularity and symmetry will be well controlled. Then a wavelet basis with best integrated performance is expected to be achieved.

5 Wavelet Basis Selection

Though all the wavelets simply satisfying Formula (6) can be used to analyze and process signals, different wavelets may bring about rather different results for the same problem. Therefore, in the practical applications, we must weigh the properties mentioned above in the Section 4 to choose the most appropriate wavelet so as to get the most satisfying processing effect. When selecting a wavelet basis, we should consider synthetically the general rules and practical applications.

Among general rules, the self-similarity rule is widely adopted, which suggests that the selected wavelet is supposed to be like the analyzed signal. In that way the energy via the wavelet transform will be very concentrated and consequently, computational complexity can be reduced greatly. Since wavelet transform is a kind operation of inner-product, moreover, correlation theory indicates that the more similar to the analyzed signal a wavelet basis, the more correlative they will be and the greater their inner-product, or the greater the wavelet coefficients and the more concentrated the energy, hence its much easier processing. In the wavelet analysis of LFM signals, it is based on the reasons above that Morlet has been popular to be chosen. In fact, one mustn't weigh a wavelet basis by a single criterion, but should consider in many ways according to the specific problem and practical conditions.

For the purpose of extracting the instantaneous frequency of LFM signals, based on their very high smoothness and according to the instantaneous frequency extraction method adopted in this paper, a kind of wavelet is expected with certain regularity, vanishing moments, symmetry and compact support. So we consider to select Symmlet and BiorNr.Nd, then compare them with Morlet that is usually selected. The fact is:

- ✧ Symmlet wavelets possess a lot of good performances: orthonormality, compact support, M vanishing moments, the shortest support $2M-1$, approximate symmetry and being able to do Discrete Wavelet Transform (DWT).
- ✧ Merits of BiorNr.Nd wavelets are: biorthogonality, compact support, $Nr-1$ vanishing moments, certain regularity, symmetry and being able to do DWT.
- ✧ Yet Morlet is virtually a rude kind of wavelet with few good performances: non-orthonormality, non-compact support, no vanishing moments and not being able to do DWT. Its advantages are having symmetry and explicit expression.

In the following, a simulation and the corresponding analysis and explanation are presented.

6 Simulation Results and Corresponding Analysis

The simulation signal is $f_0 = 20\text{MHz}$ and $a = 100\text{MHz}/\mu\text{s}$ in expressions (1), and is shown in Figure 1. Its instantaneous frequency is extracted by the method proposed in Literature [5]. The simulation results, based on the three kinds of wavelets mentioned in Section 5, are shown in Figure 2 and Table 1. The simulation indicates

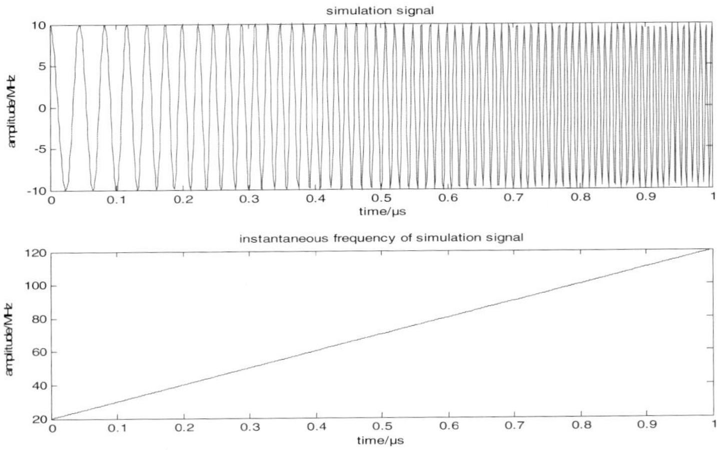

Fig. 1. Simulation signal and its its instantaneous frequency

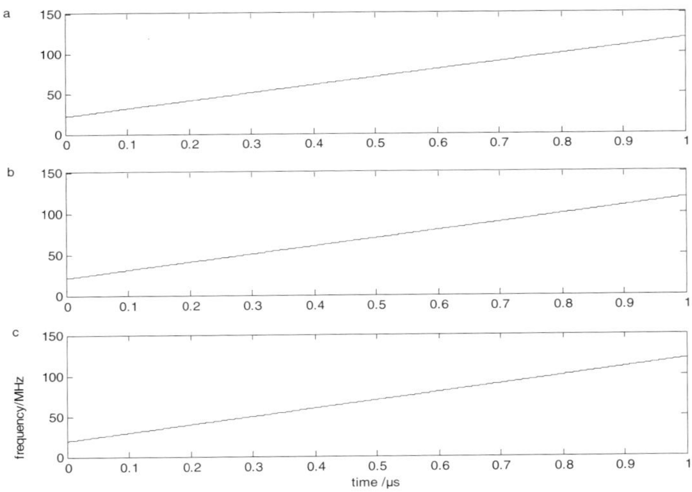

Fig. 2. Frequency extracted with three wavelets ***(a: morl; b: sym2; c: bior2.4)***

that the extraction result based on Bior2.4 is the most precision, Morlet the least and Sym2 in the middle. It lies mainly in the fact that Morlet has the widest support, which leads to a much greater truncation error in wavelet analysis, and that its central frequency is lowest, which is not suitable for the signal with relatively high frequency, thus bringing the greatest error to the extraction result. Sym2 has the shortest support, but it causes much greater error than Bior2.4 in that Bior2.4 is even more symmetric and regular than Sym2, and its central frequency is even higher than that of Sym.2. So Bior2.4 is more suitable to analyze the signal. Moreover, its support is short enough,

Table 1. Numerical results corresponding to Fig. 2

results / wavelets	frequency modulation rate	initial frequency
Morlet	96.4223	21.8304
Sym2	97.7057	20.8833
Bior2.4	**100.2819**	**19.3143**

thus it can achieve the best processing effect. On the other hand, Sym.2 and Bior2.4 can do DWT, a fast localization algorithm, by use of their very short filters, so they are able to extract the instantaneous frequency with least data and lowest complexity, which is of great importance to real-time processing of signals, especially those with small samples whose observation time is very short. Yet Morlet can't do that. In this sense, given a certain precision, Sym2 is better than Bior2.4 because of its the best orthonormality and compact support, the highest vanishing moments and smallest resulting computational quantity. But for this simulation, Bior2.4 demonstrates best. Therefore, the conclusion is arrived at that though Morlet has the best symmetry and linear phase, it is not the best wavelet basis for this specific problem, but Bior2.4 is.

7 Conclusions

How to choose a wavelet basis is always an important and difficult problem in wavelet applications. In this paper, concerning the LFM signals, some further research on the wavelet basis selection are done, based on the fact that Morlet have been conventionally selected to make wavelet analysis. Morlet is indeed the most alike with the LFM signals among all the wavelet bases in the wavelet dictionary available, and has the best symmetry. However, both Sym2 and Bior2.4 are better than it, with Bior2.4 the best selection. So we should not select a wavelet basis at will, but be cautious and make a detailed analysis based on the specific problem. Only that, can we make the most efficient analysis, therefore solving the problem with optimization.

References

1. Djuric, P.M., Kay, S.M.: Parameter Estimation of Chirp Signal. IEEE Trans on ASSP 38(12), 2118–2126 (1990)
2. Vakman, D.: On the analytic signal, the Teager-Kaiser energy algorithm, and other methods for defining amplitude and frequency. IEEE Trans on Signal Processing 44, 791–797 (1996)

3. Jing-huai, G.: Wavelet Transform and the Instantaneous Characteristics Analysis of Signals. Journal of Physical Geography 40, 821–832 (1997)
4. Scheper, R.A., Teolis, A.: Cramer-Rao Bounds for wavelet Transform-Based Instantaneous Frequency Estimates. IEEE Trans.on Signal Processing 51, 1593–1602 (2003)
5. Xiao-nan, Z.: Parameter Estimation of Single Component LFM Signals Based on Wavelet Ridge. Aerospace Electronic Warfare 21, 44–46 (2005)
6. Mallat.: A theory of Multiresolution Signal Decomposition: the Wavelet Representation. IEEE Trans on PAMI, 674–693 (1989)
7. Jian-ping, L.: Wavelet Analysis and Signal Processing. Chongqing Press, Chongqing (1997)
8. Mallat,: A Wavelet Tour of Signal Processing, 2nd edn. China Machine Press, Beijing (2002)

Feature Weighted Rival Penalized EM for Gaussian Mixture Clustering: Automatic Feature and Model Selections in a Single Paradigm*

Yiu-ming Cheung and Hong Zeng

Department of Computer Science, Hong Kong Baptist University, Hong Kong, SAR, China
ymc@comp.hkbu.edu.hk, hzeng@comp.hkbu.edu.hk

Abstract. Recently, the Rival Penalized Expectation-Maximization (RPEM) algorithm (Cheung 2004 & 2005) has demonstrated its outstanding capability to perform the model selection automatically in the context of density mixture models. Nevertheless, the RPEM is unable to exclude the irrelevant variables (also called *features*) from the clustering process, which may degrade the algorithm's performance. In this paper, we adopt the concept of feature salience (Law et al. 2004) as the feature weight to measure the relevance of features to the cluster structure in the subspace, and integrate it into the RPEM algorithm. The proposed algorithm identifies the irrelevant features and estimates the number of clusters automatically and simultaneously in a single learning paradigm. Experiments show the efficacy of the proposed algorithm on both synthetic and benchmark real data sets.

1 Introduction

Density mixture clustering has been widely applied to a variety of scientific fields such as neural networks, image processing, pattern recognition, and so forth. In such a clustering, each component of a density mixture represents the density distribution of a corresponding cluster of data, and thus clustering can be viewed as identifying the dense regions of the input densities. In general, Expectation Maximization (EM) algorithm [1] has provided a general solution for the parameter estimate in a density mixture model. However, the EM algorithm needs to pre-specify an appropriate number of components in a mixture, which, unfortunately, is difficult or even impossible from the practical viewpoint.

More recently, the *Rival Penalized Expectation-Maximization* (RPEM) algorithm has been developed from the learning framework, namely *Maximum Weighted Likelihood* [6, 7]. This algorithm makes the components in a density mixture compete with each other as given an input (also called *an obervation* interchangeably). Not only are the associated parameters of the winner (i.e. the winning mixture component) updated to adapt to the input, but also all rivals' parameters are penalized with the strength proportional to the corresponding posterior density probabilities. Compared to the EM,

* This work was fully supported by the Research Grant Council of Hong Kong SAR under Projects: HKBU 2156/04E and HKBU 210306.

Y. Wang, Y. Cheung, and H. Liu (Eds.): CIS 2006, LNAI 4456, pp. 1018–1028, 2007.

such a rival penalization mechanism enables the RPEM to gradually fade out the redundant densities in a density mixture. The experiments in [6, 7] have shown its outstanding performance on model selection, i.e., determining the number of mixture components (also called *the number of clusters* hereinafter). Nevertheless, analogous to the EM, the RPEM performs the clustering by using all variables (also called *features* interchangeably) within the whole input space without a mechanism to exclude the irrelevant variables, i.e., some variables without contribution to the cluster structure, from the clustering process. Subsequently, the performance of RPEM may deteriorate if some irrelevant variables exist.

Earlier methods for feature selection in clustering can be roughly fallen into two categories: the *feature filter* approaches and the *wrapper* approaches. The feature filter approaches, e.g. principal component analysis (PCA) [2, 3, 4], try to pick out the most influential subset of features, which reflects the characteristics of the original data set. Such an approach may significantly reduce the dimensionality, but the clustering algorithm is not involved in the feature extraction. Consequently, the extracted features may not be well suited to the follow-up clustering algorithm. In contrast, the wrapper approaches utilize a clustering algorithm to evaluate the qualities of each candidate feature subsets [3, 5] generated via a combinatorial search. The classification accuracy of such an approach may be improved in comparison to the filter approaches, but its computation is rather laborious. Essentially, these two kinds of feature selection methods are prone to find a sub-optimal solution because they perform the feature and model selections, which are closely related each other, in two separate steps. Actually, a better solution can be achieved provided that the feature and model selections are performed in a single learning paradigm. In the literature, some works have been done along this promising way. For example, Huang et al. [8] present a k-means type algorithm that weights the importance of each feature in the clustering process. The numerical results have shown that this algorithm can successfully identify noisy variables with comparatively small weights. Nevertheless, this method may be sensitive to the initial cluster centroids and the initial weights. Furthermore, its performance depends on the choice of parameter β, whose value is, however, determined by trial and error. Furthermore, Law et al. [9] adopt a definition of feature salience with respect to the independence of its distribution to a given cluster, and integrate the Minimum Message Length (MML) criterion to the log-like likelihood. Eventually, an EM-like algorithm has been developed to automatically determinate the number of clusters and the feature weights. In addition, Constantinopoulos et al. [10] utilize the same model proposed by [9], but present a variational Bayesian learning for estimating the feature weights and cluster parameters. Paper [10] has shown its superiority in the presence of sparse data by adopting the Bayesian framework other than the statistical MML criterion.

In this paper, we adopt the concept of feature salience [9] to measure the relevance of each feature to cluster structure. Subsequently, we utilize a general probability distribution model for the Gaussian mixture proposed by [9], and integrate it into the Maximum Weighted Likelihood (MWL) framework, through which we develop a variant of the RPEM, namely Feature Weighted RPEM (FW-RPEM) algorithm. Not only is this new algorithm able to make a model selection analogous to the RPEM, but also weights the features based on their relevance to the cluster structure so that the irrelevant features can be gradually excluded from the clustering process. As a result, an appropriate cluster structure in the subspace of inputs can be found. Experimental results have shown the efficacy of the proposed algorithm in comparison to the existing methods.

2 Overview of the RPEM Algorithm

Suppose an observation comes from a mixture of k^* probability density functions (pdf):

$$p(\mathbf{x}|\Theta^*) = \sum_{j=1}^{k^*} \alpha_j^* p(\mathbf{x}|\theta_j^*), \quad \sum_{j=1}^{k^*} \alpha_j^* = 1, \quad \text{and} \quad \forall 1 \leq j \leq k^*, \alpha_j^* > 0, \tag{1}$$

where the pdf $p(\mathbf{x}|\theta_j^*)$ is the jth component of the mixture, $\Theta^* = \{\alpha_j^*, \theta_j^*\}_{j=1}^{k^*}$ denotes the set of the true parameters in the mixture model, and k^* is the true number of components. The main learning purpose is to estimate the parameters Θ^* from N i.i.d. observations, denoted as $\mathbf{x}_1, \mathbf{x}_2, \ldots, \mathbf{x}_N$, where each observation $\mathbf{x}_t$ is a column vector of d features, written as $x_{1t}, x_{2t}, \ldots, x_{dt}$.

The Rival Penalized EM (RPEM) algorithm [7] has been developed from the MWL framework via maximizing the following weighted likelihood:

$$Q(\Theta; \mathbf{X}_N) = \frac{1}{N} \sum_{t=1}^{N} \mathcal{M}(\Theta; \mathbf{x}_t), \quad \mathbf{X}_N = \{\mathbf{x}_1, \mathbf{x}_2, \ldots, \mathbf{x}_N\} \tag{2}$$

with

$$\begin{aligned} \mathcal{M}(\Theta; \mathbf{x}_t) &= \sum_{j=1}^{k} g(j|\mathbf{x}_t, \Theta) \ln p(\mathbf{x}_t|\Theta) \\ &= \sum_{j=1}^{k} g(j|\mathbf{x}_t, \Theta) \ln[\alpha_j p(\mathbf{x}_t|\theta_j)] \\ &\quad - \sum_{j=1}^{k} g(j|\mathbf{x}_t, \Theta) \ln h(j|\mathbf{x}_t, \Theta), \end{aligned} \tag{3}$$

where $\Theta = \{\alpha_j, \theta_j\}_{j=1}^{k}$ and k are an estimate of Θ^* and k^*, respectively. Furthermore, we have

$$p(\mathbf{x}_t|\Theta) = \sum_{j=1}^{k} \alpha_j p(\mathbf{x}_t|\theta_j), \tag{4}$$

$$p(\mathbf{x}_t|\theta_j) = p(x_{1t}, \ldots, x_{lt}, \ldots, x_{dt}|\theta_j), \tag{5}$$

and $\forall 1 \leq j \leq k$ $(k \geq k^*)$, $\alpha_j \geq 0$, $\sum_{j=1}^{k} \alpha_j = 1$. Also,

$$h(j|\mathbf{x}_t, \Theta) = \frac{\alpha_j p(\mathbf{x}_t|\theta_j)}{p(\mathbf{x}_t|\Theta)} \tag{6}$$

is the posterior probability that $\mathbf{x}$ belongs to the jth component in the mixture. In (3), $g(j|\mathbf{x}_t, \Theta)$ is a designable weight with:

$$\sum_{j=1}^{k} g(j|\mathbf{x}_t, \Theta) = \zeta, \tag{7}$$

and

$$\forall j, \lim_{h(j|\mathbf{x}_t,\Theta)\to 0} g(j|\mathbf{x}_t, \Theta) \ln h(j|\mathbf{x}_t, \Theta) = 0, \tag{8}$$

where ζ is a positive constant. In [7], they are constructed by:

$$g(j|\mathbf{x}_t, \Theta) = (1 + \varepsilon_t)I(j|\mathbf{x}_t, \Theta) - \varepsilon_t h(j|\mathbf{x}_t, \Theta) \tag{9}$$

with

$$I(j|\mathbf{x}, \Theta) = \begin{cases} 1 \text{ if } j = c \equiv \arg\max_{1\leq i\leq k} h(i|\mathbf{x}, \Theta); \\ 0 \ j = r \neq c. \end{cases} \tag{10}$$

where the ε_t is a small positive quantity. Paper [7] learns Θ towards maximizing (2) via the following alternating steps:

- **E-step:** Given an input $\mathbf{x}_t$ and Θ^{old}, compute $h(j|\mathbf{x}_t, \Theta^{old})$ and $g(j|\mathbf{x}_t, \Theta^{old})$ through (6) and (9), respectively.
- **M-step:** Fixing $h(j|\mathbf{x}_t, \Theta^{\text{old}})$ and $g(j|\mathbf{x}_t, \Theta^{\text{old}})$, update Θ along the direction of maximizing (2) by the gradient ascent approach, i.e.

$$\Theta^{new} = \Theta^{old} + \eta \left. \frac{\partial \mathcal{M}(\Theta; \mathbf{x}_t)}{\partial \Theta} \right|_{\Theta^{old}}. \tag{11}$$

It has been shown in [7] that the RPEM can automatically select the number of components by fading out the redundant densities from a density mixture. Nevertheless, analogous to the most existing clustering algorithms, the RPEM assumes that each feature has the same importance to the intrinsic cluster structure, which, however, may not be always true from the practical viewpoint. In the next section, we therefore present the FW-RPEM algorithm that is able to identify the cluster structure by estimating the feature weights and perform the model selection simultaneously.

3 The Feature Weighted Rival Penalized EM Algorithm

Without loss of generality, we suppose that the features in each observation are independent each other, and the contribution of each dimension is invariant among all the clusters. Considering not all the features of an observation are important, we therefore adopt the measure in [9] to weight the relevancy of these features. That is, the weight is denoted as $W = [w_1, \ldots, w_d]^T$ with $0 \leq w_l \leq 1, \forall 1 \leq l \leq d$, where w_l represents the probability that the lth feature is relevant to all the clusters. The irrelevant features have little contribution to a given cluster in the subspace, thus their distributions may be common to all these clusters in this case. Then, the probability density function of a general Gaussian mixture model can be written below as in [9]:

$$p(\mathbf{x}|\Theta) = \sum_{j=1}^{k} \alpha_j \prod_{l=1}^{d} [w_l p(x_l|\theta_{lj}) + (1 - w_l) q(x_l|\lambda_l)] \tag{12}$$

where $p(x_l|\theta_{lj}) = G(m_{lj}; S_{lj}^2)$ denotes a Gaussian density function of x_l with the mean m_{lj}, and standard deviation S_{lj}. $q(x_l|\lambda_l)$ is the common density of the lth feature with the parameter λ_l if it is irrelevant. The prior knowledge about the density distribution of the irrelevant feature can be Gaussian distribution, uniform distribution, and so forth. In this paper, we let it be a Gaussian for a general purpose, i.e., $q(x_l|\lambda_l) = G(cM_l, cS_l^2)$. Subsequently, we define the full parameter set of the general Gaussian mixture model as $\Theta = \{\{\alpha_j\}_{j=1}^{k}, \Phi\}$ and $\Phi = \{\{\theta_{lj}\}_{l=1,j=1}^{d,k}, \{w_l\}_{l=1}^{d}, \{\lambda_l\}_{l=1}^{d}\}$. Note that

$$p(x_{lt}|\Phi) = w_l p(x_{lt}|\theta_{lj}) + (1 - w_l) q(x_{lt}|\lambda_l) \tag{13}$$

is a coupling form with two possible density models for each feature, where the feature weight w_l acts as a regulator to determine which distribution is more appropriate to describe the feature. By putting (13) into (3), we then obtain:

$$\begin{aligned}
\mathcal{M}(\mathbf{x}_t; \Theta) &= \sum_{j=1}^{k} g(j|\mathbf{x}_t, \Theta) \ln[\alpha_j p(\mathbf{x}_t|\Phi)] \\
&\quad - \sum_{j=1}^{k} g(j|\mathbf{x}_t, \Theta) \ln h(j|\mathbf{x}_t, \Theta) \\
&= \sum_{j=1}^{k} g(j|\mathbf{x}_t, \Theta) \ln\{\alpha_j \prod_{l=1}^{d} [w_l p(x_{lt}|\theta_{lj}) \\
&\quad + (1 - w_l) q(x_{lt}|\lambda_l)]\} \\
&\quad - \sum_{j=1}^{k} g(j|\mathbf{x}_t, \Theta) \ln h(j|\mathbf{x}_t, \Theta),
\end{aligned} \tag{14}$$

where we let the weight function $g(j|\mathbf{x}_t, \Theta)$ be:

$$g(j|\mathbf{x}_t, \Theta) = I(j|\mathbf{x}_t, \Theta) + h(j|\mathbf{x}_t, \Theta). \tag{15}$$

which satisfies the conditions in (7) and (8).

Consequently, we can estimate the parameter set Θ towards maximizing $\mathcal{M}(\mathbf{x}_t; \Theta)$ of (14) via the adaptive learning algorithm, namely Feature weighted RPEM (FW-RPEM) algorithm, whose learning mechanism is analogous to the RPEM algorithm. In the implementation of FW-RPEM, we have noticed that $\{\alpha_j\}_{j=1}^{k}$ must satisfy the constraint of $\sum_{j=1}^{k} \alpha_j = 1$. To circumvent the complicated constraint optimization, we alternatively let

$$\alpha_j = \frac{\exp(\beta_j)}{\sum_{i=1}^{k} \exp(\beta_i)}, \quad \text{for} \quad \forall 1 \leq j \leq k. \tag{16}$$

As a result, we update $\{\beta_j\}_{j=1}^{k}$s instead of $\{\alpha_j\}_{j=1}^{k}$ like the RPEM in [7].

In summary, the FW-RPEM algorithm is implemented in the following steps after initializing Θ:

- **Step 1:** Calculate $h(j|\mathbf{x}_t, \Theta^{\text{old}})$ and $g(j|\mathbf{x}_t, \Theta^{\text{old}})$:

$$h(j|\mathbf{x}_t, \Theta^{\text{old}}) = \frac{\alpha_j^{\text{old}} \prod_{l=1}^{d} [w_l^{\text{old}} p(x_{lt}|\theta_{lj}^{\text{old}}) + (1 - w_l^{\text{old}}) q(x_{lt}|\lambda_l^{\text{old}})]}{\sum_{j=1}^{k} \alpha_j^{\text{old}} \prod_{l=1}^{d} [w_l^{\text{old}} p(x_{lt}|\theta_{lj}^{\text{old}}) + (1 - w_l^{\text{old}}) q(x_{lt}|\lambda_l^{\text{old}})]} \tag{17}$$

$$g(j|\mathbf{x}_t, \Theta^{\text{old}}) = I(j|\mathbf{x}_t, \Theta^{\text{old}}) + h(j|\mathbf{x}_t, \Theta^{\text{old}}). \tag{18}$$

- **Step 2:** Update the parameter set $\{\{\theta_{lj}\}_{l=1,j=1}^{d,k}, \{\lambda_l\}_{l=1}^{d}, \{\alpha_j\}_{j=1}^{k}, \{w_l\}_{l=1}^{d}\}$ along the direction of maximizing $\mathcal{M}(\mathbf{x}_t; \Theta)$ by fixing $h(.|.)$ and $g(.|.)$ obtained in **Step 1** for each observation:

$$\begin{aligned}
\beta_j^{new} &= \beta_j^{old} + \eta_\beta \left. \frac{\partial \mathcal{M}(\mathbf{x}_t; \Theta)}{\partial \beta_j} \right|_{\Theta^{old}} \\
&= \beta_j^{old} + \eta_\beta [g(j|\mathbf{x}_t, \Theta^{\text{old}}) - \alpha_j^{old}], \\
m_{lj}^{new} &= m_{lj}^{old} + \eta \left. \frac{\partial \mathcal{M}(\mathbf{x}_t; \Theta)}{\partial m_{lj}} \right|_{\Theta^{old}} \\
&= m_{lj}^{old} + \eta g(j|\mathbf{x}_t, \Theta^{\text{old}}) h^{'}(1|x_{lt}, \Phi^{\text{old}}) \frac{x_{tl} - m_{lj}^{\text{old}}}{(S_{lj}^{\text{old}})^2}, \\
S_{lj}^{new} &= S_{lj}^{old} + \eta \left. \frac{\partial \mathcal{M}(\mathbf{x}_t; \Theta)}{\partial S_{lj}} \right|_{\Theta^{old}} \\
&= S_{lj}^{old} + \eta g(j|\mathbf{x}_t, \Theta^{\text{old}}) h^{'}(1|x_{lt}, \Phi^{\text{old}}) \frac{(x_{tl} - m_{lj}^{\text{old}})^2 - (S_{lj}^{\text{old}})^2}{(S_{lj}^{\text{old}})^3}, \\
cM_l^{new} &= cM_l^{old} + \eta \left. \frac{\partial \mathcal{M}(\mathbf{x}_t; \Theta)}{\partial cM_l} \right|_{\Theta^{old}} \\
&= cM_l^{old} + \eta \sum_{j=1}^{k} g(j|\mathbf{x}_t, \Theta^{\text{old}}) h^{'}(2|x_{lt}, \Phi^{\text{old}}) \frac{x_{lt} - cM_l^{old}}{(cS_l^{old})^2}, \\
cS_l^{new} &= cS_l^{old} + \eta \left. \frac{\partial \mathcal{M}(\mathbf{x}_t; \Theta)}{\partial cS_l} \right|_{\Theta^{old}}
\end{aligned}$$

$$= cS_l^{old} + \eta \sum_{j=1}^{k} g(j|\mathbf{x}_t, \Theta^{\text{old}})h^{'}(2|x_{lt}, \Phi^{\text{old}})\frac{(x_{lt} - cM_l^{old})^2 - (cS_l^{old})^2}{(cS_l^{old})^3},$$

$$w_l^{new} = w_l^{old} + \eta \left.\frac{\partial \mathcal{M}(\mathbf{x}_t; \Theta)}{\partial w_l}\right|_{\Theta^{old}}$$

$$= w_l^{old} + \eta \sum_{j=1}^{k} g(j|\mathbf{x}_t, \Theta^{\text{old}})\left[\frac{h^{'}(1|x_{lt}, \Phi^{\text{old}})}{w_l^{old}} - \frac{h^{'}(2|x_{lt}, \Phi^{\text{old}})}{1 - w_l^{old}}\right],$$

where

$$h^{'}(1|x_{lt}, \Phi^{\text{old}}) = \frac{w_l^{old}p(x_{lt}|\theta_{lj}^{old})}{w_l^{old}p(x_{lt}|\theta_{lj}^{old}) + (1 - w_l^{old})q(x_{lt}|\lambda_l^{old})},$$

$$h^{'}(2|x_{lt}, \Phi^{\text{old}}) = \frac{(1 - w_l^{old})q(x_{lt}|\lambda_l^{old})}{w_l^{old}p(x_{lt}|\theta_{lj}^{old}) + (1 - w_l^{old})q(x_{lt}|\lambda_l^{old})}.$$

Note that the learning rate of β_js should be chosen as $\eta_\beta < \eta$ to alleviate the sensitivity of α_js to the small fluctuation of β_js (we suggest $\eta_\beta = 0.1\eta$). Furthermore, the values of w_ls should be essentially controlled within the range of $[0, 1]$, but the update of w_ls in Step 2 may not. To avoid this awkward situation, we can use a soft-max function (e.g. see (16)) to transform w_ls to the new variables, say ϱ_ls, analogous to the case of α_js and β_js, whereby the constraints of w_ls can be automatically satisfied. Here, we alternatively adopt a simple procedure. That is, we set w_l at 0.001 when $w_l < 0.001$, and set it at 0.999 when $w_l > 0.999$ during the learning process.

Step 1 and Step 2 are repeated for each observation until Θ converges. As a result, one can identify those features that are more relevance to cluster structure than the others, and the corresponding component parameters can be picked out from $\{m_{lj}, S_{lj}\}_{l=1,j=1}^{d,k}$ with $\{w_l\}_{l=1}^{d}$ and $\{\alpha_j\}_{j=1}^{k}$ as guides.

4 Experimental Results

4.1 Experiment 1

This experiment was to investigate the performance of the FW-RPEM on identifying the cluster structure in the presence of irrelevant features. We first generated 2-dimension $1,000$ synthetic data from a mixture of 3 Gaussian components: $G\left[\mathbf{x}|\left(\begin{smallmatrix}1\\1\end{smallmatrix}\right); \left(\begin{smallmatrix}0.1 & 0.0\\0.0 & 0.1\end{smallmatrix}\right)\right]$, $G\left[\mathbf{x}|\left(\begin{smallmatrix}1\\5\end{smallmatrix}\right); \left(\begin{smallmatrix}0.1 & 0.0\\0.0 & 0.1\end{smallmatrix}\right)\right]$, $G\left[\mathbf{x}|\left(\begin{smallmatrix}5\\5\end{smallmatrix}\right); \left(\begin{smallmatrix}0.1 & 0.0\\0.0 & 0.1\end{smallmatrix}\right)\right]$,with 0.3, 0.4, 0.3 being their mixture proportions, respectively. Then we drew 2, 48 and 98 features from the Gaussian noise $G(2, 5^2)$ and appended them to the bivariate Gaussian mixture, yielding a 4-dimension (low-dimension), a 50-dimension (medium-dimension), and a 100-dimension (high-dimension) data sets, respectively. Further, we initialized k at 10, and all α_js and w_ls were set at $\frac{1}{k}$ and 0.5, respectively. The remaining parameters were initialized as following (in MATLAB form):

$$[dim, N] = size(\mathbf{x});$$
$$index = randperm(N);$$
$$\mathbf{m} = \mathbf{x}(:, index(1:k));$$
$$\mathbf{s} = repmat(sqrt(var(\mathbf{x}'))', 1, k);$$
$$\mathbf{cM} = mean(\mathbf{x}, 2);$$
$$\mathbf{cS} = sqrt(var(\mathbf{x}'))';$$

The learning rates were $\eta = 10^{-3}$, $\eta_\beta = 10^{-4}$. The algorithm was performed on these three data sets 10 times each, and the numerical results are depicted in Fig. 1-3, respectively. Fig. 1(a)-3(a) show that the three out of 10 α_js has converged to give a good estimate of the true values, meanwhile all the remaining α_js have converged towards zero. That is, the FW-RPEM has successfully identified three components in all cases we have tried so far. Furthermore, as expected, the feature weights of the first two dimensions were close to 1, while the rest dimensions were assigned close to 0 as shown in Fig. 1(b)-3(b). That is, the proposed algorithm has correctly identified a large number of noisy features in the input space.

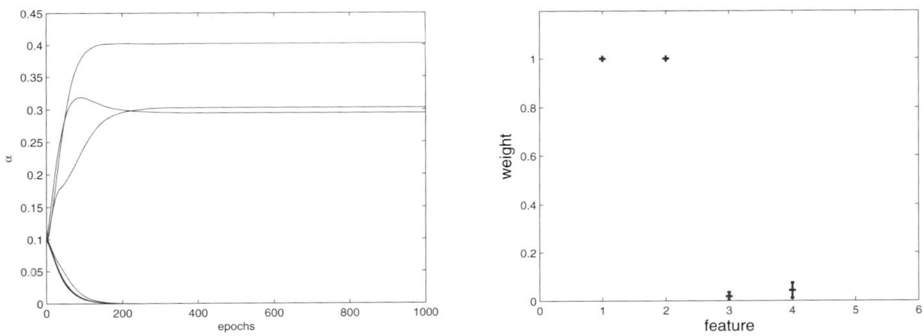

(a) (b)

Fig. 1. Results of the experiment on low-dimension data set. (a) The learning curve of α_js of a typical run. (b) The feature weights, where the average values are marked with "+", and the standard deviations over ten runs are presented by the error bars around the mean values.

4.2 Experiment 2

Besides the synthetic data, we also conducted a number of experiments on three well-known databases from UCI Machine Learning Repository [11]:

- *Wine*. There are 178 data points. The analysis is to determine the quantities of 13 constituents found in each of the three types of wines.

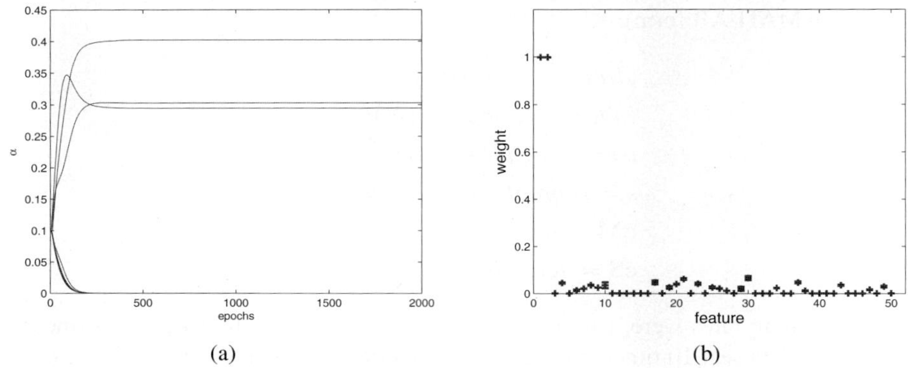

Fig. 2. The result of the experiment on medium-dimension data set. (a) The learning curve of α_js of a typical run. (b)The feature weights, where the average values are marked with "+", and the standard deviations over ten runs are presented by the error bars around the mean values.

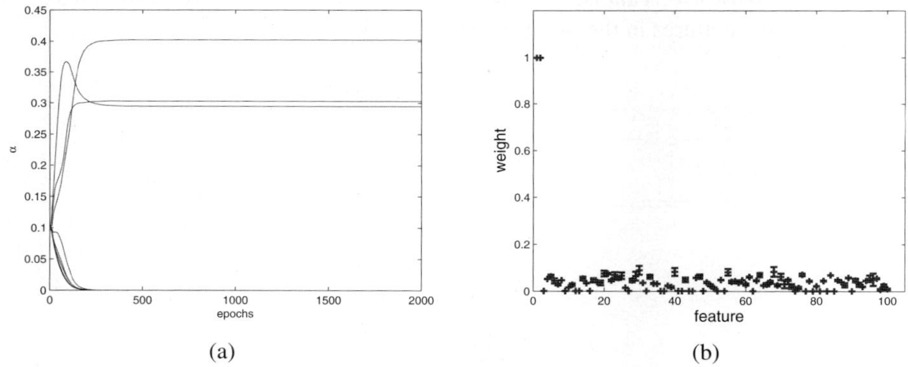

Fig. 3. Results of the experiment on high-dimension data set. (a) The learning curve of α_js of a typical run. (b) The feature weights, where the average values are marked with "+", and the standard deviations over ten runs are presented by the error bars around the mean values.

- *Australian credit card*. This data set consists of 653 credit card applications, and is classified to two classes: *approved* and *rejected* according to the first 14 features.
- *Ionosphere*. There are 351 instances and 34 attributes. The task is to classify the collections from radar into 2 classes denoting obstruction existing or not in the ionosphere.

We utilized a 50% Jackknifing procedure to separate the original data set into the training and testing sets. The training set was formed by randomly picking data from the original data set to its half size, and the remaining points were reserved for testing. The process was repeated 20 times, yielding 20 pairs of different training and testing

Table 1. Comparison on the performance for each algorithm on the real data

Data set	*FW-RPEM*		*RPEM*		*method in [9]*	
	$\%error \pm std$	$Avg.No. \pm std$	$\%error \pm std$	$Avg.No. \pm std$	$\%error \pm std$	$Avg.No. \pm std$
Wine	6.18 ± 1.04	**fixed at 3**	9.06 ± 2.61	2.5 ± 0.71	6.73 ± 2.86	3.28 ± 1.44
Australian	20.63 ± 1.68	**fixed at 2**	45.15 ± 3.37	3.2 ± 0.447	45.94 ± 12.11	3.9 ± 1.21
Ionosphere	23.15 ± 6.20	2.8 ± 0.78	44.7 ± 6.39	1.5 ± 0.527	27.44 ± 10.38	4.7 ± 0.48

sets. After abandoning the class labels in the set, the proposed algorithm was conducted 20 times on each training set. We then utilized the trained model to classify the testing data and evaluated the accuracy by comparing the obtained labels with the ground-truth class labels. For comparison, we also performed the RPEM and Law's algorithm [9] individually on the same pairs of data sets with the same initializations. Their performances over 20 runs are all reported in Table 1. Also, Table 2 lists the average weighting results of the 20 runs on the *Wine* and *Australian credit card* sets, where the feature weights for *ionosphere* are excluded because the number of their features is too large to be listed in Table 2.

Table 2. The average weighting results of *FW-RPEM* on the real data

Features	1	2	3	4	5	6	7	8	9	10	11	12	13	14
Wine	0.999	0.652	0.331	0.750	0.102	0.999	0.999	0.279	0.999	0.999	0.288	0.999	0.999	
Australian	0.001	0.001	0.455	0.999	0.208	0.001	0.001	0.999	0.999	0.001	0.001	0.999	0.001	0.001

From Table 1, we can see that the error obtained from the FW-RPEM has been significantly reduced compared to the RPEM because the FW-RPEM is able to identify the features that have unequal contribution to the cluster structure (see Table 2), whereby an appropriate cluster structure can be found in a sub-space. Furthermore, the FW-RPEM also outperforms the algorithm in [9] with the smaller error, particularly on the data of Australian credit card and Ionosphere as listed in Table 1. Further, the algorithm in [9] is prone to use more "components" for the mixture. In contrast, the proposed algorithm not only produces a lower mismatch error, but also gives a better estimation to the number of mixture components.

5 Conclusion

In this paper, we have presented the FW-RPEM algorithm, which extends the RPEM algorithm to deal with the case when some irrelevant features exist in the input space. We have adopted the concept of feature salience as the feature weight to measure the relevance of features to the cluster structure in the subspace, and integrate it into the RPEM algorithm. Consequently, the FW-RPEM can identify the irrelevant features and perform model selection automatically and simultaneously in a single learning paradigm. The promising performance of the algorithm has been shown on both the synthetic data and real benchmark data sets.

References

1. Dempster, A.P., Laird, N.M., Rubin, D.B.: Maximum Likelihood from Incomplete Data via the EM Algorithm. Journal of the Royal Statistical Society (B) 39(1), 1–38 (1977)
2. Duda, R.O., Hart, P.E.: Pattern Classification and Scene Analysis. John Wiley & Sons, Chichester (1973)
3. Dy, J.G., Brodley, C.E.: Visualization and Interactive Feature Selection for Unsupervised Data. In: Proceedings of ACM International Conference on Knowledge Discovery and Data Mining, pp. 360–364 (2000)
4. Fisher, D.H.: Knowledge Acquisition via Incremental Conceptual Clustering. Machine Learning, pp. 139–172 (1987)
5. Talavera, L.: Feature Selection and Incremental Learning of Probabilistic Concept Hierarchies. In: Proceedings of International Conference on Machine Learning, pp. 951–958 (2000)
6. Cheung, Y.M.: A Rival Penalized EM Algorithm towards Maximizing Weighted Likelihood for Density Mixture Clustering with Automatic Model Selection. In: Proceedings of the 17th International Conference on Pattern Recognition (ICPR'04), vol. 4, pp. 633–636, Cambridge, United Kingdom (2004)
7. Cheung, Y.M.: Maximum Weighted Likelihood via Rival Penalized EM for Density Mixture Clustering with Automatic Model Selection. IEEE Transactions on Knowledge and Data Engineering 17(6), 750–761 (2005)
8. Huang, J.Z., Ng, M.K., Rong, H., Li, Z.: Automated Variable Weighting in k-means Type Clustering. IEEE Transactions on Pattern Analysis and Machine Intelligence 27(5), 657–668 (2005)
9. Law, M.H.C., Figueiredo, M.A.T., Jain, A.K.: Simultaneous Feature Selection and Clustering Using Mixture Models. IEEE Transactions on Pattern Analysis and Machine Intelligence 26(9), 1154–1166 (2004)
10. Constantinopoulos, C., Titsias, M.K., Likas, A.: Bayesian Feature and Model Selection for Gaussian Mixture Models. IEEE Transactions on Pattern Analysis and Machine Intelligence 28(6), 1013–1018 (2006)
11. Blake, C.L., Merz, C.J.: UCI Repository of Machine Learning Databases (1998), `http://www.ics.uci.edu/mlearn/MLRepository.html`.

Fingerprint Matching Using Invariant Moment Features

Ju Cheng Yang, Jin Wook Shin, and Dong Sun Park

Division of Electronics & Information Engineering, Chonbuk National University, Jeonju, Jeonbuk, 561-756, Korea
yangjucheng@hotmail.com

Abstract. A method for fingerprint matching using invariant moment features is proposed. The fingerprint image is first preprocessed to enhance the original image by the Short Time Fourier Transform (STFT) analysis. Then, a set of seven invariant moment features is extracted to represent the fingerprint image from a Region of Interest (ROI) based on the reference point of the enhanced fingerprint image. The reference point is determined by the complex filters method. Finally, a Back Propagation Neural Network (BPNN) is trained with the features for matching. Experimental results show the proposed method has better performance with higher accuracy and faster speed comparing to the traditional Gabor feature-based fingerCode method.

1 Introduction

A fingerprint is a pattern of ridges and valleys on the surface of a finger. The pattern is formed by a set of ridgelines, which sometimes terminates (ridge-endings) or intersects (bifurcations). These ridge-endings and bifurcations from a set of features called minutiae. Various approaches of automatic fingerprint matching have been proposed in the literature. Finger matching techniques can be broadly classified to two main methods: minutiae-based matching methods [1-2] and texture-based matching methods [3-4].

The more popular and widely used techniques, minutiae-based matching methods, use a feature vector extracted from the fingerprints and stored as sets of points in the multi-dimensional plane. The feature vector may contain minutiae's positions, orientations or both of them, etc. It essentially consists of finding the best alignment between the template and the input minutiae sets. However, minutiae-based matching methods may not utilize the rich discriminatory information available in the fingerprints and are very time consuming [5].

The texture-based matching methods use different types of features from the fingerprint ridge patterns such as local orientation and frequency, ridge shape and texture information. The features may be extracted more reliably than minutiae. Among various texture-based matching methods, Gabor feature-based fingerCode methods are traditional and famous methods. These approaches use a fixed length representation, called as a fingerCode, to represent each fingerprint. Jain et al. [3] propose a filter-based algorithm uses a bank of Gabor filters to capture both the local and global

Y. Wang, Y. Cheung, and H. Liu (Eds.): CIS 2006, LNAI 4456, pp. 1029–1038, 2007.

details in a fingerprint as a compact fixed length fingerCode. The fingerprint matching is based on the Euclidean distance between the two corresponding fingerCodes.

An improved version of the Gabor feature-based method used for fingerprint matching is proposed by Sha et al. [4]. The authors propose a new rotation-invariant reference point location method and combine the direction features with the Average Absolute Deviation (AAD) from the mean features to form an oriented fingerCode. However, the Gabor feature-based methods suffer from the noise and the non-linear distortions. The non-linear distortions cause various regions in the sensed image to be distorted differently due to the non-uniform pressure applied by the subject. Also, the variation in position, scale and orientation angle is difficult to track when using these approaches [7].

A texture correlation matching method for fingerprint verification using Fourier-Mellin Descriptor (FMD) and Phase-Only Correlation (POC) function is proposed by Ouyang et al. [6]. It utilized FMD to construct a feature map which is used to represent, align and match fingerprints with POC function. However, to select effective and low dimensional features from obtained FMD feature vector is a difficult work for the author, so the application of this method is limited.

Jin et al. [7] propose a method based on the features extracted from the integrated wavelet and the Fourier-Mellin Transform (WFMT) framework. Wavelet transform with its energy compacted feature is used to preserve the local edges and reduce noise in the low frequency domain. The Fourier-Mellin Transform (FMT) served to produce a translation, rotation and scale invariant feature. Multiple WFMT features can be used to form a reference invariant feature through the linearity property of FMT and hence reduce the variability of the input fingerprint images. However, multiple WFMT features are acquired from different training images, which are much time consuming.

In this paper, a method for fingerprint matching using invariant moment features is proposed. A fingerprint image is preprocessed to enhance the original image by STFT analysis [8]. Then, seven invariant moment features are extracted to represent the fingerprint image from a ROI of the enhanced fingerprint image. The ROI is based on the reference point, which is determined by the complex filters method [9]. Invariant moments are one of the principal approaches used in image processing to describe the texture of a region. As one of the texture-based matching methods, the invariant moment feature-based method also takes of rich discriminatory information available in the fingerprints, so it is able to represent the fingerprint effectively. Matching the features of test fingerprint images and those of template images is realized by a BPNN, which is a supervised pattern classification method with each output unit representing a particular class or category. The BPNN has the advantage of very flexible and favorable classification ability [10].

The paper is organized as follows: The theory of invariant moments and complex filters are briefly reviewed in section 2 and 3 respectively. In section 4, the proposed matching method is explained in details and experimental results are shown in section 5. Finally, conclusion remarks are given in section 6.

2 Invariant Moments

In order to extract moment features, which may be invariant to translation, rotation and scale changes, from the ROI of the enhanced image, we used the moments defined in ref [11, 12].

For a 2-D continuous function *f(x,y)*, the moment of order (p +q) is defined as

$$m_{pq} = \int_{-\infty}^{\infty}\int_{-\infty}^{\infty} x^p y^q f(x,y)\,dxdy \qquad \text{for p, q= 0, 1, 2,...} \tag{1}$$

A uniqueness theorem states that if *f(x,y)* is piecewise continuous and has nonzero values only in a finite part of the *xy*-plane, moment of all orders exist, and the moment sequence (m_{pq}) is uniquely determined by *f(x,y)*. Conversely, (m_{pq}) is uniquely determined by *f(x,y)*.

The central moments are defined as

$$\mu_{pq} = \int_{-\infty}^{\infty}\int_{-\infty}^{\infty} (x-\bar{x})^p (y-\bar{y})^q f(x,y)\,dxdy \tag{2}$$

$$\text{Where} \qquad \bar{x} = \frac{m_{10}}{m_{00}} \qquad \textit{and} \qquad \bar{y} = \frac{m_{01}}{m_{00}}$$

If *f(x,y)* is a digital image, then Eq.(2) becomes

$$\mu_{pq} = \sum_x \sum_y (x-\bar{x})^p (y-\bar{y})^q f(x,y) \tag{3}$$

and the normalized central moments, denoted η_{pq}, are defined as

$$\eta_{pq} = \frac{\mu_{pq}}{\mu_{00}^{\gamma}}, \quad \text{where} \quad \gamma = \frac{p+q}{2} + 1 \quad \text{for p+q = 2,3,....} \tag{4}$$

A set of seven invariant moments can be derived from the second and the third moments by Hu [12]. As shown below, Hu derived the expressions from algebraic invariants applied to the moment generating function under a rotation transformation. They consist of groups of nonlinear centralized moment expressions. The result is a set of absolute orthogonal moment invariants, which can be used for scale, position, and rotation invariant pattern identification.

$$\phi_1 = \eta_{20} + \eta_{02} \tag{5}$$

$$\phi_2 = (\eta_{20} - \eta_{02})^2 + 4\eta_{11}^2 \tag{6}$$

$$\phi_3 = (\eta_{30} - 3\eta_{12})^2 + (3\eta_{21} - 3\eta_{03})^2 \tag{7}$$

$$\phi_4 = (\eta_{30} + \eta_{12})^2 + (\eta_{21} + \eta_{03})^2 \tag{8}$$

$$\phi_5 = (\eta_{30} - 3\eta_{12})(\eta_{30} + \eta_{12})[(\eta_{30} + \eta_{12})^2 - 3(\eta_{21} + \eta_{03})^2] \tag{9}$$

$$\phi_6 = (\eta_{20} - \eta_{02})(\eta_{30} + \eta_{12})[(\eta_{30} + \eta_{12})^2 - (\eta_{21} + \eta_{03})^2] + 4\eta_{11}(\eta_{30} + \eta_{12})(\eta_{21} + \eta_{03}) \tag{10}$$

$$\phi_7 = (3\eta_{21} - \eta_{03})(\eta_{30} + \eta_{12})[(\eta_{30} + \eta_{12})^2 - 3(\eta_{21} + \eta_{03})^2] + (3\eta_{12} - \eta_{30})(\eta_{21} + \eta_{03})[3(\eta_{30} + \eta_{12})^2 - (\eta_{21} + \eta_{03})^2] \quad (11)$$

3 Complex Filters

Before introduce the reference point detection method, we need to know the singular points. The singular points i.e. core and delta points are two landmarks of fingerprint. Their locations and orientations usually determine the fingerprint ridge flow patterns. Detection of the singular points is very important for fingerprint matching. Many literatures introduced all kinds of methods for locating the singular points. However, the complex filters, applied to the orientation field in multiple resolution scales, are used to detect them with high performance [9].

Complex filters, of order *k*, for the detection of patterns with radial symmetries are modeled by $\exp\{ik\varphi\}$. Let x and y denote two coordinates in image analysis, the complex filters can be computed as:

$$\exp\{ik\varphi\} = (x + iy) / \sqrt{x^2 + y^2} \quad (12)$$

$$\varphi = 1/[k \tan^{-1}(y/x)] \quad (13)$$

The local orientation patterns of φ with the second order symmetry $\exp\{\pm i2\varphi\}(k = \pm 1)$ are shown in Fig. 1, which are similar to the fingerprint orientation patterns in core and delta points.

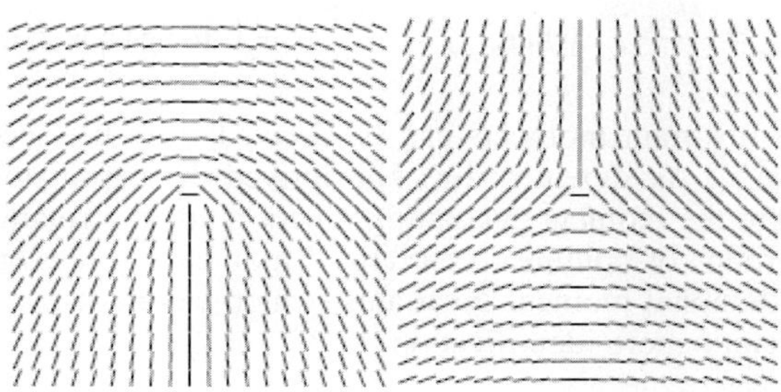

Fig. 1. The orientation patterns of φ with filter hl: $\exp\{2i\varphi\}$ (left) and filter h2: $\exp\{-2i\varphi\}$ (right)

We define the core point here as the reference point because the core point is popular than the delta point and is able to represent the oneness of the fingerprint images. Henry [5] defines the core point as "the north's most point of the inner most ridge line". This is suitable for the whole and loop conditions. For fingerprints that do not contain loop or whorl singularities (e.g. those belonging to the arch class), the core point is usually associated with the point of maximum ridge line curvature. Filter h1 satisfies both of these conditions.

Therefore, we can apply filter h1 on the fingerprint orientation field represented with the phase angle $\theta_{m,n}(1 \le m \le M, 1 \le n \le N)$ to determine the reference point. For the filtering window of size (2w+1)×(2w+1), the filter response of each block (m, n) are computed as:

$$h_{m,n} = [\sum_{x=-w}^{w}\sum_{y=-w}^{w} u_{m+x,n+y} \exp\{j2(\theta_{m+x,n+y} - \varphi_{x,y})\}]/[\sum_{x=-w}^{w}\sum_{y=-w}^{w} u_{m+x,n+y}] \tag{14}$$

Where $u_{m+x,n+y} \in \{0,1\}$ denotes the segmentation result of block (m + x, n + y), and $u_{m+x,n+y} = 1$ indicates the block is segmented as foreground valid for feature extraction. $\varphi_{x,y}$ is computed in equation (13). We can see that the filter response is complex value, the magnitude ($\in [0,1]$) represent how close the fingerprint local orientation patterns are similar to the orientation patterns of two filters, while the phase angels indicate the rotations between the local orientation patterns of the fingerprints and filters.

4 Proposed Matching Approach

The proposed matching approach contains five main steps as shown in Fig.2.

The first step is to enhance the fingerprint image using STFT analysis. The performance of a fingerprint matching algorithm depends critically upon the quality of the input fingerprint image. While the quality of a fingerprint image cannot be objectively measured, it roughly corresponds to the clarity of the ridge structure in the

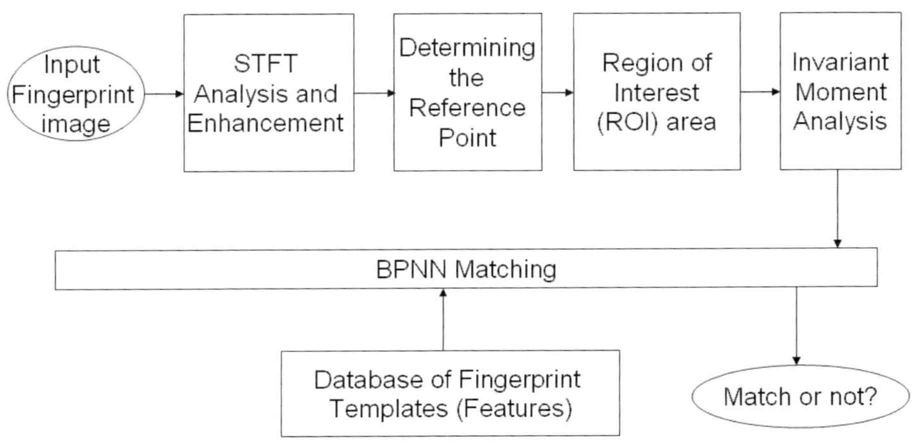

Fig. 2. The flow diagram of our matching algorithm

fingerprint image. There are many reasons that may degrade the quality of a fingerprint image. The quality of fingerprint encountered during verification varies over a wide range. It is estimated that roughly 10% of the fingerprint encountered during verification can be classified as 'poor' [5]. So it is necessary to enhance the fingerprint image before feature extraction and matching.

Since the fingerprint image may be thought of as a system of oriented texture with non-stationary properties, traditional Fourier analysis is not adequate to analyze the image completely. STFT can be used to analyze the fingerprint image both in space and in frequency. The algorithm simultaneously estimates all the intrinsic properties of the fingerprints such as the foreground region mask, local ridge orientation and local ridge frequency, and used these properties to enhance the fingerprint image [8]. The enhanced images are shown in Fig.3.

In the second step, we determine the reference point from the enhanced image. The reference point is determined by using the complex filters explained briefly in section 3.

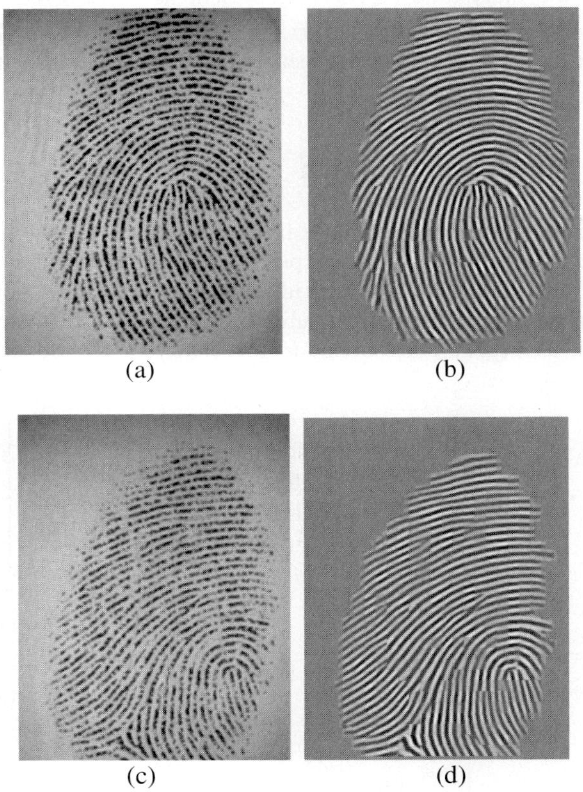

Fig. 3. (a) the original fingerprint of 101_6.tif (size 288×384) (b) the enhanced image of 101_6.tif (c) the original fingerprint of 102_8.tif (size 288×384) (d) the enhanced image of 102_8.tif

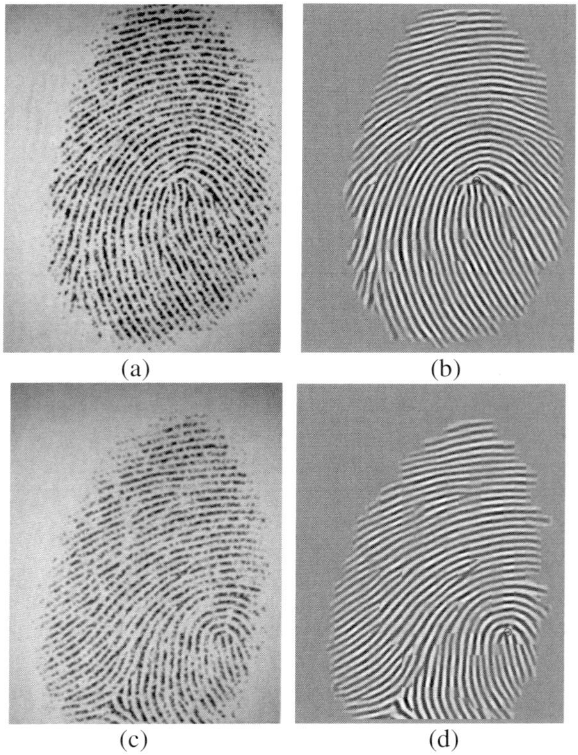

Fig. 4. (a) the original fingerprint of 101_6.tif (size 288×384) (b) the determined reference point image of 101_6.tif (c) the original fingerprint of 102_8.tif (size 288 × 384) (d) the determined reference point image of 102_8.tif

The maximum response point of the complex filter can be considered as the reference point [9]. Fig.4. show the determined reference point images.

The third step is to segment fingerprint image by cropping the image based on the reference point determined in the previous step. In order to acquire the accurate invariant moment features, we use only a certain area around the reference point (or ROI) as the input instead of using the entire fingerprint. The size of the area for cropping is experimentally determined, in this paper, a size of 64×64 ROI with a reference point at the center is used. The ROI is shown in Fig.5.

Fig. 5. (a) ROI of 101_6.tif (size 64×64)

At the fourth step, a set of seven invariant moments from the cropped image is extracted as a feature vector to represent a fingerprint. Each vector is a set of long type data which requires four bytes of storage, so the entire feature vector requires 28 bytes of storage. An example of the seven invariant moments with different fingerprint images is listed as in Table 1.

Table 1. The seven invariant moments with the different fingerprint images. (IM= Invariant Moment, DF=Different Fingerprints).

IM / DF	ϕ_1	ϕ_2	ϕ_3	ϕ_4	ϕ_5	ϕ_6	ϕ_7
1_4.tif	3.629796	1.086836	2.514599	1.045206	2.617032	3.497286	3.603378
2_7.tif	2.950884	5.423818	10.015341	10.571694	28.585308	13.183839	18.051112
3_3.tif	10.26391	19.567487	30.738309	30.713893	90.979397	40.619307	54.145245
4_5.tif	5.102269	7.961453	13.340411	13.444751	37.334768	17.706405	22.041423
5_8.tif	4.525553	4.025463	4.447207	5.479858	9.122677	8.069919	9.652528

The last step is to match the input features with features of the templates stored in the database. The matching is realized by utilizing a BPNN to distinguish between the two corresponding features of the test fingerprint image and template fingerprint image in the database into a match and non-match.

5 Experimental Results

The fingerprint image database used in this experiment is the FVC2002 fingerprint database set a [13], which contains four distinct databases: DB1_a, DB2_a, DB3_a and DB4_a. The resolution of DB1_a, DB3_a, and DB4_a is 500 dpi, and that of DB2_a is 569 dpi. Each database consists of 800 fingerprint images in 256 gray scale levels (100 persons, 8 fingerprints per person).

A BPNN with 7 input layer neurons and 2 output layer neurons was trained on 75% (600/800=75%) of patterns in each database, and tests were performed on all patterns. That is, 6 fingerprints of per person (75%) in each database were used for training, while all the 8 fingerprints of per person in the databases were used for testing. There were 7 input features and 2 output classes, so the input layer neurons and the output layer neurons were 7 and 2 respectively. The number of the hidden layer neurons was obtained empirically. Experimentally, the optimal number of hidden layer neurons was determined to 4.

The performance evaluation protocol used in FVC2002 was adopted. The Equal Error Rate (EER), revised EER (EER*), Reject Enroll (REJ_{Enroll}), Reject Match (REJ_{Match}), Average Enroll Time and Average Match Time were computed on the four databases. To compute the False Acceptance Rate (FAR) and the False Reject Rate (FRR), the genuine match and impostor match were performed. For genuine match, each impression of each finger was compared with other impressions of the same finger. The number of matches was 2800. For impostor match, the first impression of each finger was compared with the first impression of other fingers. The number of matches was 4950. A matching was labeled correct if the matched pair was from an identical fingerprint and incorrect otherwise. The test was executed on Pentium IV 1GHz machines. The performances of our proposed method with the method of Sha [4] over the four databases of FVC2002 are shown in Table 2-5. Since the EER and Average Enroll Time and Average Match Time values of our proposed method were smaller than those of the method of Sha, we considered our proposed method had better performances.

Table 2. The performances of two methods over the database of DB1_a

Algorithm	EER	EER*	REJ_{Enroll}	REJ_{Match}	Avg Enroll Time	Avg Match Time
Our proposed	3.64%	3.64%	0.00%	0.00%	1.59sec	0.15sec
Method of Sha	6.23%	6.23%	0.00%	0.00%	1.64sec	0.41sec

Table 3. The performances of two methods over the database of DB2_a

Algorithm	EER	EER*	REJ_{Enroll}	REJ_{Match}	Avg Enroll Time	Avg Match Time
Our proposed	5.38%	5.38%	0.00%	0.00%	1.15sec	0.09sec
Method of Sha	8.42%	8.42%	0.00%	0.00%	1.35sec	0.24sec

Table 4. The performances of two methods over the database of DB3_a

Algorithm	EER	EER*	REJ_{Enroll}	REJ_{Match}	Avg Enroll Time	Avg Match Time
Our proposed	4.24%	4.24%	0.00%	0.00%	1.35sec	0.24sec
Method of Sha	5.46%	5.46%	0.00%	0.00%	1.78sec	0.51sec

Table 5. The performances of two methods over the database of DB4_a

Algorithm	EER	EER*	REJ_{Enroll}	REJ_{Match}	Avg Enroll Time	Avg Match Time
Our proposed	3.07%	3.07%	0.00%	0.00%	1.68sec	0.43sec
Method of Sha	7.13%	7.13%	0.00%	0.00%	1.93sec	0.61sec

6 Conclusion

In this paper, a method for fingerprint matching using invariant moment features is proposed. STFT analysis will enhance the original fingerprint images even those with poor quality, and the location of the reference point with complex filters is reliable, so the algorithm for features extraction is effective. Besides, the feature vectors need less storage and the processing speed is fast. Experiments show that the performances of accuracy and processing speed of the proposed method are better than the traditional Garbor feature-based fingerCode method.

Similarly to most other methods, our work is based on the reference point detection. When the reference point is close to the border of the fingerprint area, the feature extraction may be incomplete or incompatible with respect to the template. Further work should be proceeded to improve the robust and the reliability of our proposed method.

Acknowledgement

This work was supported by the second stage of Brain Korea 21.

References

1. Jang, X., Yau, W.Y.: Fingerprint Minutiae Matching Based on the Local and Global Structures. In: Proc. Int. Conf. on Pattern Recognition, pp. 1024–1045 (2000)
2. Liu, J., Huang, Z., Chan, K.: Direct Minutiae Extraction from Gray-Level Fingerprint Image by Relationship Examination. In: Int. Conf. on Image Processing, pp. 427–430 (2000)
3. Jain, A.K., Prabhakar, S., Hong, L., Pankanti, S.: Filterbank-based Fingerprint Matching. IEEE Transactions on Image Processing 9, 846–859 (2000)
4. Sha, L.F., Zhao, F., Tang, X.O.: Improved Fingercode for Filterbank-based Fingerprint Matching. International Conference on Image Processing 8 (2003) II-895-8
5. Maltoni, D., Maio, D., Jain, A.K., Prabhakar, S.: Handbook of Fingerprint Recognition. Springer, Heidelberg (2003)
6. Ouyang, Z., Feng, J., Su, F., Cai, A.: Fingerprint Matching with Rotation-Descriptor Texture Features. In: The 8th International Conference on Pattern Recognition, vol. 4, pp. 417–420 (2006)
7. Jin, A.T.B., Ling, D.N.C., Song, O.T.: An Efficient Fingerprint Verification System Using Integrated Wavelet and Fourier–Mellin Invariant Transform. Image and Vision Computing 22, 503–513 (2004)
8. Sharat, C., Alexander, N.C., Venu, G.: Fingerprint Enhancement using STFT Analysis, Pattern Recognition. Corrected Proof, and Available online 22 (2006) (In Press)
9. Kenneth, N., Josef, B.: Localization of Corresponding Points in Fingerprints by Complex Filtering. Pattern Recognition Letters 24, 2135–2144 (2003)
10. Duda, R.O., Hart, P.E., Stork, D.G.: Pattern Classification, 2nd edn (2001)
11. Gonzalez, R.C., Woods, R E.: Digital Image Processing, 2nd edn. Prentice-Hall, Englewood Cliffs (2002)
12. Hu, M-K.: Visual Pattern Recognition by Moment Invariants. In: IRE Trans. on Information Theory, pp. 179–187 (1962)
13. http://bias.csr.unibo.it/fvc2002

Survey of Distance Measures for NMF-Based Face Recognition

Yun Xue[1], Chong Sze Tong[2], and Weipeng Zhang[3]

[1] School of Physics and Telecommunication Engineering,
South China Normal University,
Guangzhou Guangdong 510631, China
and Department of Mathematics, Hong Kong Baptist University,
Hong Kong, China
yxue@math.hkbu.edu.hk

[2] Department of Mathematics, Hong Kong Baptist University,
Hong Kong, China
cstong@math.hkbu.edu.hk

[3] Department of Computer Science, Hong Kong Baptist University,
Hong Kong, China
zwp@comp.hkbu.edu.hk

Abstract. Non-negative matrix factorization (NMF) is an unsupervised learning algorithm that can extract parts from visual data. The goal of this technique is to find intuitive basis such that training examples can be faithfully reconstructed using linear combination of basis images which are restricted to non-negative values. Thus NMF basis images can be understood as localized features that correspond better with intuitive notions of parts of images. However, there has not been any systematic study to identify suitable distance measure for using NMF basis images for face recognition.

In this article we evaluate the performance of 17 distance measures between feature vectors based on the result of the NMF algorithm for face recognition. Recognition experiments are performed using the MIT-CBCL database, CMU AMP Face Expression database and YaleB database.

1 Introduction

In the past three decades, face recognition has received increasing attention, and the Principal Component Analysis (PCA) algorithm has been proven to be a practical face-based approach for this task [9].

However, the traditional PCA method has some limitations. First, though it gives an accurate representation of face images, it has not a good discriminatory ability. Secondly, since there are both additive and subtractive combinations in this method, its basis images may not facilitate intuitive visual meaning. Finally, because this approach is used to find the global features in face images, it cannot achieve good performance when handling cases with occlusions.

Recently, a new method called non-negative matrix factorization (NMF) is proposed for obtaining a linear representation of data. Under the non-negativity

Y. Wang, Y. Cheung, and H. Liu (Eds.): CIS 2006, LNAI 4456, pp. 1039–1049, 2007.

constraints, this method approximately factorizes the initial data matrix into two non-negative matrix factors. Since it allows only additive, not subtractive, combinations of basis images, a part-based representation of images is consequently produced.

For face recognition, we generally project all the face images into this NMF space and extract all the relevant feature vectors. Then the comparison between faces is performed by calculating the distance between all these vectors. Usually, the Euclidean distance, the L1 distance and the Mahalanobis distance will be used at this stage.

Though the selection of distance measure is important for the performance of the face recognition system, there is only limited published research [4] which evaluates the different distance measures for NMF-based face recognition.

In this article, we compare the performance of 17 distance measures for NMF-based face recognition. Based on the experimental results, we find that a new non-negative vector similarity coefficient-based (NVSC) distance, which we are advocating for use in NMF-based recognition, is always among the best distance measures with respect to different image databases and at different settings.

This paper is organized as follows. Section 2 reviews the background theory of NMF. The detailed definition of distance measures used in this paper is described in Sect.3. In Sect.4, we give some description of the image databases used in the paper. Some experimental results of a face recognition system based on the NMF algorithm are discussed in Sect.5. Finally, we present our conclusions and discuss some future work in Sect.6.

2 Review of NMF

This section provides the background theory of NMF for face recognition, which is an unsupervised learning method. It is an algorithm to obtain a linear representation of data under non-negativity constraints. These constraints lead to a part-based representation because they allow only additive, not subtractive, combinations of the original data [6]. The basic idea is as below.

First, represent an image database as a $n \times m$ matrix V, where each column, corresponding to a initial face image, includes n non-negative elements characterizing the pixel value and m means the number of training images.

Then we can find two new non-negative matrices (W and H) to approximate the original matrix.

$$V_{ij} \simeq (WH)_{ij} = \sum_{a=1}^{r} W_{ia}H_{aj}, W \in R^{n\times r}, H \in R^{r\times m} \qquad (1)$$

where matrix W consists of r non-negative basis vectors and r is usually chosen as small as possible for dimension reduction, while column vectors of H mean the weights when approximating the corresponding column in V using the bases from W.

From the original definition, we know, in contrast to the PCA approach, no subtractions can occur in the above NMF procedure, so the non-negativity constraints are compatible with the intuitive idea of combining parts to form a whole face.

The update rule for NMF is derived as below:

First construct an objective function to characterize the similarity between V and WH:

$$F = \sum_{i=1}^{n} \sum_{j=1}^{m} [V_{ij} log \frac{V_{ij}}{(WH)_{ij}} - V_{ij} + (WH)_{ij}] \tag{2}$$

Then an iterative algorithm converging to a local maximum of this objective function is derived [6]:

$$W_{ia} \leftarrow W_{ia} \sum_{j} \frac{V_{ij}}{(WH)_{ij}} H_{aj} \tag{3}$$

$$W_{ia} \leftarrow \frac{W_{ia}}{\sum_{j} W_{ja}} \tag{4}$$

$$H_{aj} \leftarrow H_{aj} \sum_{i} W_{ia} \frac{V_{ij}}{(WH)_{ij}} \tag{5}$$

The convergence is proved in [7].

3 Distance Measures

Let X, Y be feature vectors of length n obtained by NMF method where X represents the weight of probe images, while Y means the weight of training images. And σ is the auto-covariance matrix for training images, while $\{s_i, i = 1, \cdots, n\}$ means the square root of diagonal element in σ, i.e. the standard deviation for training images. Then we can calculate distances between these feature vectors. All the definitions of distance measures used in this paper are as below [7,11,8,10,1,3].

(1) Manhattan distance (L1 metric, city block distance)

$$d(X, Y) = \sum_{i=1}^{n} |x_i - y_i| \tag{6}$$

(2) Euclidean distance (L2 metric)

$$d(X, Y) = \sqrt{\sum_{i=1}^{n} (x_i - y_i)^2} \tag{7}$$

(3) Chebychev distance (L-∞ norm)

$$d(X, Y) = \max_{1 \le i \le n} |x_i - y_i| \tag{8}$$

(4) Mahalanobis distance

$$d(X,Y) = \sqrt{(X-Y)'\sigma^{-1}(X-Y)} \tag{9}$$

(5) Lance distance

$$d(X,Y) = \sum_{i=1}^{n} \frac{|x_i - y_i|}{|x_i| + |y_i|} \tag{10}$$

(6) Statistical distance

$$d(X,Y) = \sum_{i=1}^{n} \left| \frac{x_i - y_i}{s_i} \right| \tag{11}$$

(7) Divergence

$$d(X,Y) = \sum_{i=1}^{n} (x_i \ln \frac{x_i}{y_i} - x_i + y_i) \tag{12}$$

Like the Euclidean distance, it is also lower bounded by zero, and vanishes if and only if $X = Y$. But it cannot be called a distance, because it is not symmetric in X and Y, so we will refer to it as the divergence of X from Y.

(8) Kullback-Leibler distance (Relative Entropy)

$$d(X,Y) = \sum_{i=1}^{n} x_i^{'} \log_2 \frac{x_i^{'}}{y_i^{'}}, \quad x_i^{'} = \frac{|x_i|}{\sum\limits_{i=1}^{n} |x_i|}, y_i^{'} = \frac{|y_i|}{\sum\limits_{i=1}^{n} |y_i|} \tag{13}$$

Like divergence, it also cannot be called a distance, because it is not symmetric in X and Y.

(9) Symmetrized divergence

$$\begin{aligned} d(X,Y) = &\frac{1}{2} \sum_{i=1}^{n} \left(x_i \ln \frac{x_i}{y_i} - x_i + y_i \right) + \\ &\frac{1}{2} \sum_{i=1}^{n} \left(y_i \ln \frac{y_i}{x_i} - y_i + x_i \right) \end{aligned} \tag{14}$$

(10) Symmetrized Kullback-Leibler distance

$$d(X,Y) = \frac{1}{2} \left(\sum_{i=1}^{n} x_i^{'} \log_2 \frac{x_i^{'}}{y_i^{'}} + \sum_{i=1}^{n} y_i^{'} \log_2 \frac{y_i^{'}}{x_i^{'}} \right) \tag{15}$$

here $x_i^{'} = \frac{|x_i|}{\sum_{i=1}^{n} |x_i|}, y_i^{'} = \frac{|y_i|}{\sum_{i=1}^{n} |y_i|}$.

(11) Mahalanobis angle distance

$$d(X,Y) = 1 - \frac{X^{'}\sigma^{-1}Y}{\sqrt{X^{'}\sigma^{-1}X}\sqrt{Y^{'}\sigma^{-1}Y}} \tag{16}$$

(12) Chi square distance

$$d(X,Y) = \sum_{i=1}^{n} \frac{(x_i - y_i)^2}{x_i + y_i} \tag{17}$$

(13) Exponential similarity coefficient-based distance

$$d(X,Y) = 1 - \gamma^2(X,Y), \quad \gamma(X,Y) = \frac{1}{n}\sum_{i=1}^{n} e^{-\frac{3}{4}\frac{(x_i - y_i)^2}{s_i^2}} \tag{18}$$

(14) Non-parametric similarity coefficient-based distance

$$d(X,Y) = 1 - \gamma^2(X,Y), \quad \gamma(X,Y) = \frac{n_+ - n_-}{n_+ + n_-} \tag{19}$$

here $x_i^{'} = x_i - \overline{x}_i, y_i^{'} = y_i - \overline{y}_i$, n_+ means the frequency of $\{x_i^{'}y_i^{'} \geq 0, \ i = 1, \cdots, n\}$, and n_- means the frequency of $\{x_i^{'}y_i^{'} < 0, \ i = 1, \cdots, n\}$.

(15) Cosine distance

$$d(X,Y) = 1 - \cos(X,Y) = 1 - \frac{\sum_{i=1}^{n} x_i y_i}{\sqrt{(\sum_{i=1}^{n} x_i^2)(\sum_{i=1}^{n} y_i^2)}} \tag{20}$$

(16) Correlation coefficient-based distance

$$d(X,Y) = 1 - \gamma(X,Y) \tag{21}$$

here $\gamma(X,Y) = \frac{\sum_{i=1}^{n}(x_i - \overline{x})(y_i - \overline{y})}{\sqrt{[\sum_{i=1}^{n}(x_i - \overline{x})^2][\sum_{i=1}^{n}(y_i - \overline{y})^2]}}$.

The preceding four distance measures are all similarity coefficient-based distances. We now suggest to consider a distance measure that seems not to have been used in face recognition, but which originated from the theory of multivariate clustering analysis [11]. We think it may be a suitable distance measure for NMF application because it is derived from a similarity coefficient specifically defined for non-negative vectors:
(17) Non-negative vector similarity coefficient-based (NVSC) distance

$$d(X,Y) = 1 - \gamma^2(X,Y), \quad \gamma(X,Y) = \frac{\sum_{i=1}^{n} \min(x_i, y_i)}{\sum_{i=1}^{n} \max(x_i, y_i)} \tag{22}$$

Among all the above distance functions, the Manhattan distance, Euclidean distance, and the Mahalanobis distance are the most widely-used in pattern recognition.

4 Testing Databases Used in This Paper

4.1 CBCL Database

The MIT-CBCL face recognition database contains face images of 10 subjects which is divided into two sets: high resolution pictures, and synthetic images (324/subject) rendered from 3D head models of the 10 subjects. In this paper, we used the second set which contains images that varied in illumination and pose.

4.2 CMU AMP Face Expression Database

In this database, there are 13 subjects and each one has 75 images showing different expressions. These face images are collected in the same lighting condition using CCD camera, and all of them have been well-registrated by eye locations.

4.3 YaleB Database

The Yale Face Database B (YaleB) contains 5850 source images of 10 subjects each captured under 585 viewing conditions (9 poses $\times 65$ illumination conditions). In the preprocess stage, all frontal pose images have been aligned by the centers of eyes and mouth and the other images are aligned by the center points of the faces. Then all images are normalized with the same resolution 92×112. In contrast with the other two databases, this one includes more complicated image variations and background noises, therefore the corresponding recognition result would be expected to be much poorer.

To reduce the computational complexity, we use matlab to resize all the images in the above databases to 1/16 of the original size, then apply NMF algorithm on the downsampled image sets.

5 Experiment

In this section, we build a face recognition system to provide a performance evaluation of 17 different distance measures using images from databases described in Sect.4. The system adopts traditional NMF algorithm which consists of two stages, namely, training and recognition stages. The detailed procedure is as below.

5.1 Training Stage

This stage includes 3 major steps.

First, we use a $n \times m$ matrix V_1 to represent all the training images in one database.

Secondly, the NMF algorithm is applied to V_1 and we can obtain two new matrices (W_1 and H_1) as in Sect. 2, s.t.

$$(V_1)_{ij} \simeq (W_1 H_1)_{ij} = \sum_{a=1}^{r} (W_1)_{ia} (H_1)_{aj}$$

where W_1 is the base matrix, and H_1 is the weight matrix.

Finally, we build different libraries to save the training image representations and their corresponding representational bases for all the databases.

5.2 Recognition Stage

Face recognition in the NMF linear subspace is performed as follows.

Feature Extraction. There are two ways to obtain the feature vectors of training images and test images [2,5].

1. Let $W^+ = (W^T W)^{-1} W^T$, then each training face image V_i is projected into the linear space as a feature vector $H_i^{'} = W^+ V_i$ which is then used as a prototype feature point. A test face image V_t to be classified is represented as $H_t^{'} = W^+ V_t$.
2. Using the obtained bases W_1 from the training stage, we can directly use the iterative technique in the original NMF algorithm but keeping W_1 intact [i.e. do not use the iterative update rule (3) concerning to W_1]. Then, we will get the weight matrix H_2 using a fixed set of bases (W_1) and use the matrices H_1 and H_2 as the feature vectors of training images and test images.

In this paper, we shall adopt the second approach for feature extraction.

Classification. In this step, first calculate the mean feature vector H_m of each class in training set; then all the distance measures (defined in Sect.3) between the feature vector of test image and the mean vector, $\text{dist}(H_t, H_m)$, is calculated; finally, the test image is classified into the class which the closest mean vector belongs to.

5.3 Experimental Results

A set of experiments are conducted on the above system, then we evaluate the performance of all the distance measures for NMF-based face recognition. In all the experiments, we select *tr* images per person from the database to form a training set and use the remainder as the test set.

Recognition rates for the three different databases with different experimental settings (tr=2, 10, and 20, and dimensionality of feature vectors at 40, 60, and 80) are summarized in Table 1. To facilitate comparison, we use bold fonts for the best 3 measures in each experimental setting.

From Table 1, we can see that:

The commonly used Manhattan distance (distance 1), Euclidean distance (distance 2), and Mahalanobis distance (distance 4) were not particularly effective. The Manhattan distance performed best among these three popular distance measures and was ranked in the top 3 in 3 cases. Among all the conventional distance measures (distance 1 to 16), the cosine distance (distance 15) achieved the best result and was ranked as one of the best 3 measures in 5 cases.

For the distance measures designed for non-negative vectors, the divergence (distance 7) and Kullback-Leibler distance (distance 8) were not particularly

Table 1. Recognition rate of all the distance measures

Distance measure	CBCL (tr=10)			CMU AMP (tr=2)			YaleB (tr=20)		
	p=40	p=60	p=80	p=40	p=60	p=80	p=40	p=60	p=80
distance 1	0.93949	0.93408	0.8879	0.99684	0.99579	1	0.26513	0.26549	0.28531
distance 2	0.89682	0.93057	0.89204	0.99579	0.99473	0.98736	0.23823	0.26513	0.28319
distance 3	0.67803	0.6914	0.62134	0.93888	0.9568	0.9157	0.2131	0.26319	0.25274
distance 4	0.85924	0.89459	0.84745	0.99473	0.99579	0.99473	0.34956	0.36566	0.35611
distance 5	0.77898	0.79904	0.75446	0.95258	0.95785	0.97366	0.23912	0.23115	0.2554
distance 6	0.38089	0.38917	0.43949	0.74394	0.73656	0.65753	0.16814	0.18053	0.16973
distance 7	0.87834	0.93089	0.88471	0.98103	0.97998	0.98419	0.34832	0.32991	0.36177
distance 8	0.87357	0.91783	0.86911	0.97787	0.97893	0.98419	0.34903	0.33912	0.33204
distance 9	0.91688	0.92643	0.88726	0.99789	0.99157	0.99895	0.29434	0.27097	0.30389
distance 10	0.92611	0.92771	0.91274	0.99684	0.99473	1	0.35646	0.35522	0.35009
distance 11	0.88758	0.92707	0.90382	0.99684	0.99368	0.98946	0.21788	0.25876	0.27611
distance 12	0.94427	0.95191	0.91401	1	0.99262	0.99895	0.29575	0.2931	0.32389
distance 13	0.60955	0.67134	0.64777	0.90095	0.89357	0.87144	0.18159	0.18142	0.17097
distance 14	0.1	0.1	0.1	0.076923	0.076923	0.076923	0.1	0.1	0.1
distance 15	0.93057	0.95987	0.93917	0.99579	0.99368	0.99052	0.35805	0.38655	0.38991
distance 16	0.92994	0.95064	0.92261	0.99368	0.99368	0.99262	0.36708	0.38	0.3869
distance 17	0.95924	0.96369	0.94363	1	0.99579	0.99789	0.36106	0.37982	0.37221

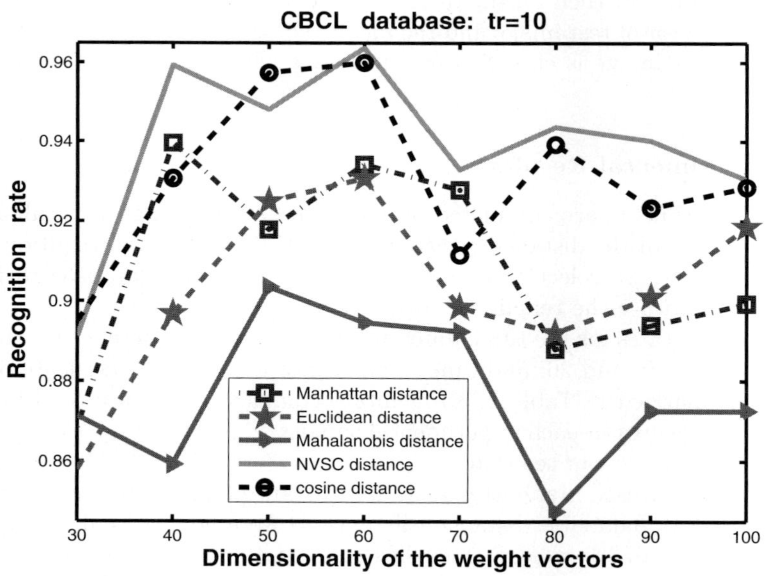

Fig. 1. Recognition rate of different distance measures

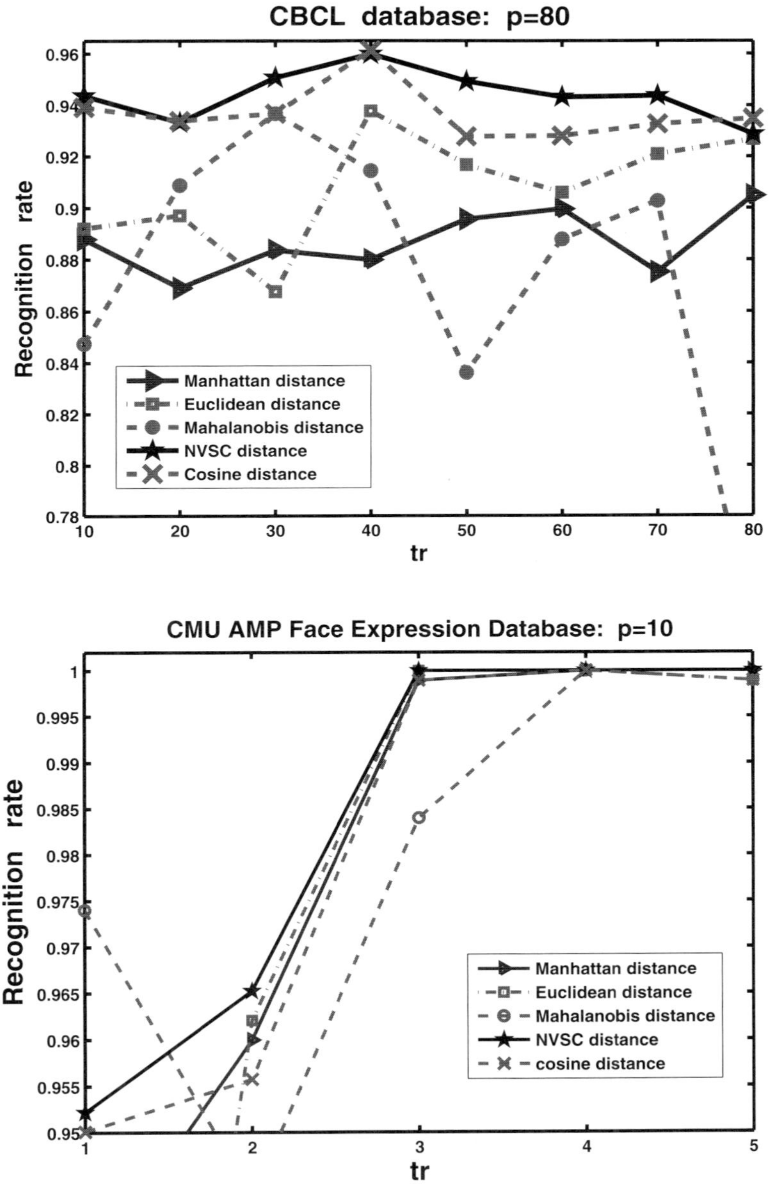

Fig. 2. Recognition rate of different distance measures when fixing the dimensionality p

effective. The symmetrized versions (distance 9, 10) performed better, but by far the best result was obtained by our NVSC distance (distance 17). The NVSC distance was ranked as one of the best 3 measures in all but one case [CMU AMP database, with dimensionality set at 80 and 2 training images]. And even then, it was in fact ranked 4th with recognition rate of 0.99789 ! In addition to being a consistently good performer, the NVSC distance was in fact ranked the top (or shared top) performer in 5 cases out of the 9 sets of experiments.

For further comprehensive comparison, we shall now concentrate on the Manhattan distance, Euclidean distance, Mahalanobis distance, cosine distance and our NVSC distance. In Fig.1, we plot the respective recognition rates vs. the dimensionality of feature vectors for the CBCL database ($tr = 10$).

From Fig.1, we see that although the cosine distance outperforms the NVSC distance at dimensionality of 50, its recognition rate curve fluctuates quite substantially and the NVSC curve is clearly the most consistent best performer across a wide range of dimensionality.

Finally, we fix the dimensionality of the feature vectors and plot the recognition rates vs. the value of tr for the CBCL and CMU AMP databases in Fig.2, where p represents the dimensionality of the feature space.

Again, the NVSC emerges as the best distance measure.

6 Conclusions and Future Work

In this paper, we compared 17 distance measures for NMF-based face recognition. Recognition experiments are performed using 3 different databases. The experiments show that our NVSC distance measure is consistently among the best measures under different experimental conditions and always performs better than the Manhattan distance, Euclidean distance, and the Mahalanobis distance which are often used in pattern recognition systems. We believe that the effectiveness of the NVSC measure stems from the fact that it is specifically designed for non-negative vectors and thus is the most appropriate for NMF-based applications. The entropy-based measures (distance 7-10) can also handle non-negative vectors, but they are primarily designed for probability distributions and are not effective in handling vectors with many zero coefficients.

References

1. Cover, T.M., Thomas, J.A.: Elements of Information Theory. Wiley, New York (1991)
2. Feng, T., Li, S.Z., Shum, H.-Y., Zhang, H.: Local non-negative matrix factorization as a visual representation. In: ICDL '02: Proceedings of the 2nd International Conference on Development and Learning, vol. 178, p. 178. IEEE Computer Society, Washington, DC, USA (2002)
3. Fraser, A., Hengartner, N., Vixie, K., Wohlberg, B.: Incorporating invariants in mahalanobis distance based classifiers: Application to face recognition. In: International Joint Conference on Neural Networks (IJCNN), Portland, OR, USA (2003)
4. Guillamet, D., Vitrià, J.: Evaluation of distance metrics for recognition based on non-negative matrix factorization. Pattern Recogn. Lett. 24(9-10), 1599–1605 (2003)

5. Guillamet, D., Vitrià, J.: Non-negative matrix factorization for face recognition. In: Escrig, M.T., Toledo, F.J., Golobardes, E. (eds.) Topics in Artificial Intelligence. LNCS (LNAI), vol. 2504, pp. 336–344. Springer, Heidelberg (2002)
6. Lee, D.D., Seung, H.S.: Learning the parts of objects by non-negative matrix factorization. Nature 401, 788–791 (1999)
7. Lee, D.D., Seung, H.S.: Algorithms for non-negative matrix factorization. Adv. Neural Info. Proc. Syst. 13, 556–562 (2001)
8. Perlibakas, V.: Distance measures for pca-based face recognition. Pattern Recogn. Lett. 25(6), 711–724 (2004)
9. Turk, M., Pentland, A.: Eigenfaces for recognition. J. Cognitive Neuroscience 3, 71–86 (1991)
10. Yu, J.: Clustering methods, applications of multivariate statistical analysis. In: Technical report, School of Electronics Engineering and Computer Science, Peking University, Beijing 100871
11. Zhang, Y., Fang, K.: An Introduction to Multivariate Analysis. Science Press, Beijing (1982)

Weighted Kernel Isomap for Data Visualization and Pattern Classification

Rui-jun Gu and Wen-bo Xu

School of Information Technology, Southern Yangtze University,
Wuxi 214122, China
grj79@hotmail.com

Abstract. Dimensionality reduction is an important task in pattern recognition and data mining. Isomap is a representative of manifold learning approaches for nonlinear dimensionality reduction. However, Isomap is an unsupervised learning algorithm and has no out-of-sample ability. Kernel Isomap (KIsomap) is an improved Isomap and has a generalization property by utilizing kernel trick. At first, considering class label, a Weighted Euclidean Distance (WED) is designed. Then, WED based kernel Isomap (WKIsomap) is proposed. As a supervised learning algorithm, WKIsomap can not only be used in data visualization, but also applied to feature extraction for pattern recognition. The experimental results show that WKIsomap is more robust than Isomap and KIsomap in data visualization. Moreover, when noise is added into data, WKIsomap based classifiers are more robust to noise than KIsomap based ones.

1 Introduction

Dimensionality reduction is an importance technique for data mining and pattern recognition. It aims at keeping only the most important dimensions, or projecting the original data into a lower dimensional space that is most expressive for the special task. For visualization, the goal of dimensionality reduction is to map a set of observations into a 2D or 3D space that preserves the intrinsic structure as well as possible. For classification, the goal is to map the input data into a feature space in which the members from different classes are clearly separated.

Principal Component Analysis (PCA) [1] and Multidimensional Scaling (MDS) [2] are classical methods of dimensionality reduction and they are efficient to find the true structure of the data in a linear subspace. In PCA, the optimal p-dimensional subspace is selected by rotating the coordinate axes to coincide with the eigenvectors of the sample covariance matrix, and keeping the p axes along which the sample has the largest variance. The MDS method maps a given set of samples into a space of desired dimension and norm. A random mapping can be served as initial embedding and a stress function is used to measure the quality of embedding. Then a gradient descent procedure is applied to improve the embedding until a local minimum of the stress function is reached. These methods are theoretically simple and easy to implement. However, an assumption has been taken in these methods: the data lies in a linear or almost linear subspace of the high-dimensional space and the embedding can

Y. Wang, Y. Cheung, and H. Liu (Eds.): CIS 2006, LNAI 4456, pp. 1050–1057, 2007.

be obtained using these linear methods. Obviously, this assumption is too restrictive as many real data cannot satisfy the linear assumption.

In recent years, a growing interest has been shown in Nonlinear Dimensionality Reduction (NLDR). Based on the notation of manifold learning, several notable recent algorithms [3] [5] [6] have been proposed. The task of manifold learning is to recover the meaningful low-dimensional structures hidden in high-dimensional data. An example [3] might be a set of images of an individual's face observed under different pose and lighting conditions: The task is to identifying the underlying variables (pose angles, direction of light, distance from camera, etc) given only the high-dimensional image data. In many cases of interest, the observed data are found to lie on an embedded sub-manifold of the high-dimensional space. The degree of freedom along this sub-manifold corresponds to the underlying variables.

Isomap [3] [4], LLE [5] and Laplacian Eigenmap [6] are representatives of manifold learning methods. They all attempt to preserve as well as possible the local neighborhood of each object while trying to obtain highly nonlinear embeddings. As an extension of MDS, Isomap uses geodesic distances instead of Euclidean distances. The geodesic distance between each pair of nodes is taken to be the length of the shortest path in the neighbor graph. These approximated geodesic distances are then used as input to classical MDS. The Locally Linear Embedding (LLE) method captures local geometric properties of complex embedding manifolds by a set of linear coefficients that best approximates each data point from its neighbors in the input space. LLE then finds a set of low dimensional points where each can be linearly approximated by its neighbors with the same set of coefficients that was computed from the high dimensional data points in the input space while minimizing reconstruction cost. Another approach is the Laplacian Eigenmap method. The goal of this method is to minimize a quadratic form over all functions mapping the manifold into the embedding space. When the continuous function is approximated by a linear operator on the neighborhood graph, the maximization problem becomes a sparse matrix eigenvalue problem and is readily solved.

Isomap is a simple and effective method for NLDR. However, it's sensitive to noise and can only run in a batch mode. So it can't be directly used in pattern classification. Based on Kernel Isomap [7] [8] (KIsomap), which is an improved Isomap and has a generalization property by utilizing kernel trick, we propose a Weighted Euclidean Distance (WED) based kernel Isomap (WKIsomap). Because class information is considered in neighbor graph construction by implementing a weight factor on the distance between any pair of points that belong to the same class. So our method is a simple and supervised kernel Isomap. WKIsomap can not only be used in data visualization, but also applied to feature extraction for pattern recognition. The experimental results show that WKIsomap is more robust than Isomap and KIsomap in data visualization. Moreover, WKIsomap based classifiers are more robust to noise than KIsomap based ones.

The rest of this paper is organized as follows. In Sec.2, we recall Isomap and KIsomap. In Sec.3, we present our method. Finally, experimental results and conclusions are given in Sec.4 and Sec.5 respectively.

2 Isomap and KIsomap

2.1 Isomap

Given N input data points $\boldsymbol{x}_1, \boldsymbol{x}_2, \ldots, \boldsymbol{x}_N \in \mathbb{R}^p$, Isomap tries to find low-dimensional output data $\boldsymbol{y}_1, \boldsymbol{y}_2, \ldots, \boldsymbol{y}_N \in \mathbb{R}^q$ $(q<<p)$ with low structure preserved as well as possible. For example, Fig.1 (a) shows that for two arbitrary points on a nonlinear manifold, their Euclidean distance in the high-dimensional input space (length of dashed line) may not accurately reflect their intrinsic similarity, as measured by geodesic distance along the low-dimensional manifold (length of solid curve). Fig.1 (b) shows an approximation of geodesic distance, which reflects the true relation between points as Fig.1 (c) indicates. The graph distance converges to the true geodesic distance asymptotically as the number of data points increases. The main steps of Isomap are listed as follows (Alg.1).

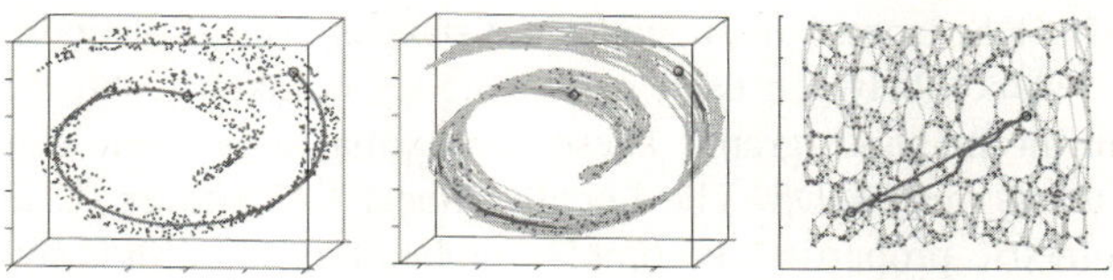

(a) (b) (c)

Fig. 1. Isomap's idea with "Swiss roll" (a) "Swiss roll" (b) Shortest path (c) Euclidian distance

(1) Compute Euclidean distance matrix $\boldsymbol{D}_e$ between any pairwise points and construct neighborhood graph G using K Nearest Neighbors (KNN);

(2) Compute the geodesic distance matrix $\boldsymbol{D}_g$ for all pairs of data points by Dijkstra's algorithm or Floyd's algorithm;

(3) Apply classical MDS to obtain low-dimensional embedding $\boldsymbol{Y}$.

2.2 KIsomap

KIsomap [7] [8] is extension of Isomap and has a generalization property. The approximate geodesic distance matrix can be interpreted as a kernel matrix. A constant-adding method is utilized to guarantee that the kernel matrix is positive definite. More important, KIsomap has a generalization property, which is very useful to pattern classification, and can project test points into feature space using kernel trick. However, general embedding methods, including Isomap, have no such a property. KIsomap algorithm for training can be briefly described as follows (Alg.2).

(1) Compute Euclidean distance matrix $\boldsymbol{D}_e$ between any pairwise points in input space, and construct neighborhood graph G;

(2) Compute the geodesic distance matrix $\boldsymbol{D}_g$ for all pairs of data points by Dijkstra's algorithm or Floyd's algorithm;

(3) Construct a matrix $\boldsymbol{K}(\boldsymbol{D}^2_g)=-\boldsymbol{H}\boldsymbol{D}^2_g\boldsymbol{H}/2$, where $\boldsymbol{H}$ is the cantering matrix given by $\boldsymbol{H}=\boldsymbol{I}-\boldsymbol{e}\boldsymbol{e}^T/N$ and $\boldsymbol{e}=[1,\ldots,1]^T\in\mathbb{R}^N$;

(4) Compute the largest eigenvalue, c^*, of the matrix $\begin{bmatrix} \boldsymbol{0} & 2\boldsymbol{K}(\boldsymbol{D}^2{}_g) \\ -\boldsymbol{I} & -4\boldsymbol{K}(\boldsymbol{D}_g) \end{bmatrix}$, and construct a Mercer kernel matrix

$$\tilde{\boldsymbol{K}} = \boldsymbol{K}(\tilde{\boldsymbol{D}}_g^2) = \boldsymbol{K}(\boldsymbol{D}^2{}_g) + 2c\boldsymbol{K}(\boldsymbol{D}_g) + c^2\boldsymbol{H}/2\,, \tag{1}$$

where $\tilde{d}_g(i,j)=d_g(i,j)+c(1-d_g(i,j))$ and $\tilde{\boldsymbol{K}}$ is guaranteed to be positive semidefinite when $c\geq c^*$;

(5) Compute the top q eigenvectors of $\tilde{\boldsymbol{K}}$, which lead to the eigenvector matrix $\boldsymbol{V}\in\mathbb{R}^{n\times q}$ and the eigenvalue matrix $\boldsymbol{\Lambda}\in\mathbb{R}^{q\times q}$;

(6) The embedding in the q-dimensional space is given by $\boldsymbol{Y}=\boldsymbol{\Lambda}^{1/2}\boldsymbol{V}^T$.

Since $\tilde{\boldsymbol{K}}$ is a Mercer kernel matrix, so its (i, j)-element can be represented by $\tilde{\boldsymbol{K}}_{ij}=k(\boldsymbol{x}_i,\boldsymbol{x}_j)=\phi^T(\boldsymbol{x}_i)\phi(\boldsymbol{x}_j)$, where $\Phi(\bullet)$ is a nonlinear mapping into a feature space. Using kernel trick, we can project a test data $\mathbf{x}_t$ in the low-dimensional space by

$$[\boldsymbol{y}_t]_i = \frac{1}{\sqrt{\lambda_i}}\sum_{j=1}^{N}[\boldsymbol{v}_i]_j k(\boldsymbol{x}_t,\boldsymbol{x}_j)\,, \tag{2}$$

where $[\bullet]_i$ represents the ith-element of a vector and $\boldsymbol{v}_i$ is the ith eigenvector of $\tilde{\boldsymbol{K}}$. The algorithm for test a new data $\boldsymbol{x}_t$ is summarized as follows (Alg.3).

(1) Compute the shortest path $d_g(t, j)$ between $\boldsymbol{x}_t$ and any data point $\boldsymbol{x}_j$ in original input space;

(2) The kernel for a test data $\boldsymbol{x}_t$ is obtained by

$$k(\boldsymbol{x}_t,\boldsymbol{x}_j)=\phi^T(\boldsymbol{x}_t)\phi(\boldsymbol{x}_j)=-\frac{1}{2}(\tilde{d}_g(t,j)-\tilde{\boldsymbol{K}}_{jj}-\frac{1}{N}\sum_{i=1}^{N}(\tilde{d}_g{}^2(t,j)-\tilde{\boldsymbol{K}}_{ii}))\,, \tag{3}$$

where $\tilde{d}_g(t,j)=d_g(t,j)+c$, $j=1,\ldots,N$;

(3) Compute the embedding $\boldsymbol{y}_t$ according to formula (2).

3 Our Method

In this section, at first, we present an improved kernel Isomap which is supervised and robust to noise. Then we apply it to data visualization and pattern classification.

In some visualization tasks, data come from multiple classes and the class labels are available. The class information can be used to guide the procedure of dimensionality or feature extraction. Since KIsomap has an out-of-sample property, it can be directly used in classification tasks. But a high error rate will be expected because class information is of no value to neighborhood graph construction i.e. all data point is treated equally. To sum up, class information, if there exists, is useful both to data visualization and pattern classification.

To utilize class information, an improved KIsomap based on Weighted Euclidean Distance (WED) is proposed. Suppose that $\boldsymbol{X}_L$ is labeled data set (for training) and $\boldsymbol{X}_U$ is unlabeled data set (for test), the WED between points $\boldsymbol{x}_i$ and $\boldsymbol{x}_j$ is defined as $d_w(i, j) = w(i, j) * d_e(i, j)$ and $w(i, j)$ is a weight function

$$w(i,j)=\begin{cases}\sqrt{1-e^{-d_e^2(i,j)/\beta}} & \boldsymbol{x}_i \in \boldsymbol{X}_L, \boldsymbol{x}_j \in \boldsymbol{X}_L, \tau_i = \tau_j \\ \sqrt{e^{d_e^2(i,j)/\beta}} & \boldsymbol{x}_i \in \boldsymbol{X}_L, \boldsymbol{x}_j \in \boldsymbol{X}_L, \tau_i \neq \tau_j \\ \frac{1}{2}\left(\sqrt{1-e^{-d_e^2(i,j)/\beta}}+\sqrt{e^{d_e^2(i,j)/\beta}}\right) & \boldsymbol{x}_i \in \boldsymbol{X}_U \ or\ \boldsymbol{x}_j \in \boldsymbol{X}_U\end{cases}, \tag{4}$$

where τ_i denotes the class label which data $\boldsymbol{x}_i$ belongs to and parameter β is a regulator, which usually is the square of the average Euclidean distance between all pairwise points. A typical plot of $w(i, j)$ versus $d_e^2(i-j)/\beta$ is shown in Fig2.

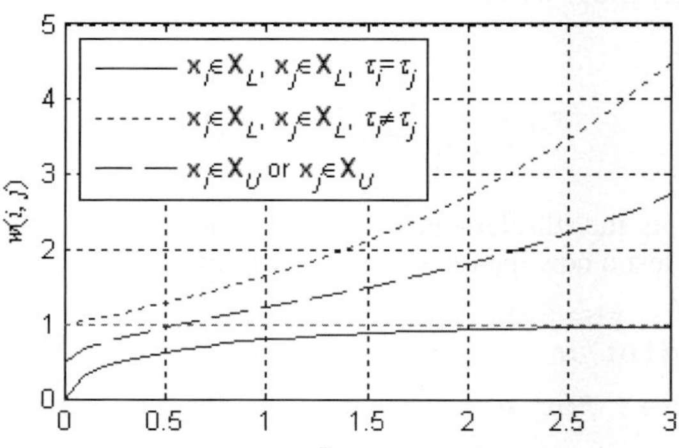

Fig. 2. A typical plot of weight function $w(i, j)$ versus $d_e^2(i-j)/\beta$

As showed in formula (4), for labeled pairwise data, if they belong to the same class, the Euclidean distance is shortened by an intra-class weight w (<1). But if they belong to different class, the Euclidean distance is lengthened by an inter-class weight w (>1). Different from [9], we make a trade-off between the weight of inter-class and intra-class as for unlabeled data, because KIsomap need to computer the distance between unlabeled data and labeled data explicitly. WED has some good properties as [9] has showed. Of them, the robustness to noise is of importance, because Isomap has a topologic instability [4].

In the context of this paper, KIsomap using weighted Eclidean distance d_w is abbreviated to WKIsomap. The algorithm of WKIsomap is almost the same as Alg.2, except that d_e is replaced with d_w as formula (4) shows.

Isomap do well in data visualization if the data lie in a uniform space and there is little noise. But, in real world, the data is often disturbed by various noises. If class information is available, supervised learning can remove noises to some extent, because noises are often some outliers and data belong to same class are usually closer to each other than those belong to different classes. Benefiting from the generation ability, WKIsomap can work in an online-like learning mode. That is, for new data out of training samples, we can use the information of samples and needn't run the whole algorithm as Isomap will do [3].

In classification tasks, the property of WED makes the data from same class more aggregative and the data from different classes more far way from each other. So it is much easier and cheaper to perform classification in such a feature space than in high-dimensional space. To summarize, the WKIsomap based classification has four steps as follows (Alg.4).

(1) Training: for labeled data set $\boldsymbol{X}_L$, replace d_e with d_w and apply Alg.2 to obtain low-dimensional embedding $\boldsymbol{Y}_L$;

(2) Test: for a test sample $\boldsymbol{x}_t$ from unlabeled data set $\boldsymbol{X}_U$, replace d_e with d_w and calculate low-dimensional coordinate $\boldsymbol{y}_t$ using Alg.3;

(3) Classification: combining $\boldsymbol{Y}_L$ and $\boldsymbol{y}_t$, predict the class label of the test data $\boldsymbol{x}_t$ using K Nearest Neighbors (KNN) or Nearest Class Center (NCC).

4 Experimental Results

In this section, several experiments were performed on artificial data and actual data. The results, compared with other classical methods, show that WKIsomap work well both in data visualization and pattern recognition

The first experiment is designed to test the robustness of WKIsomap. We also use the Swisss roll data like [3], but some Gaussian noise is added. The data is divided into 4 classes denoted by different colors as Fig.3 (a) shows. The visualization results are shown in Fig.3 (b)-(d) when Isomap, KIsomap and WKIsomap were applied to "Swiss roll" respectively.

It is clear that Isomap and KIsomap both obtained poor results because the noise make geodesic graph unstable and "short cut" occurs. But WKIsomap divided the data into 4 classes apparently as a result of the effect of weight distance, which enhances the robustness of WKIsomap.

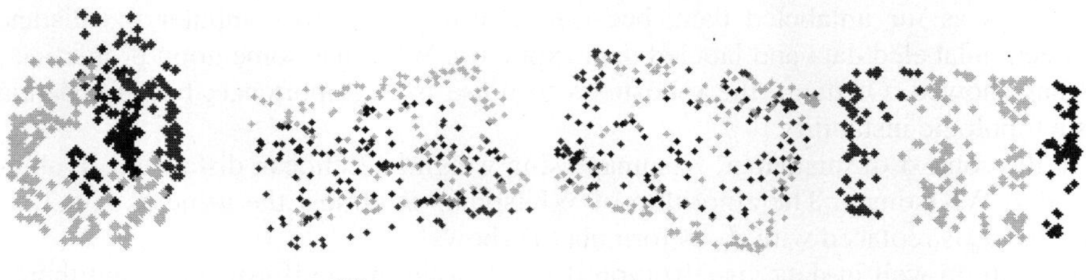

(a) (b) (c) (d)

Fig. 3. The visualization results of (a) "swiss roll" data when using (b) Isomap, (c) KIsomap and (d) WKIsomap

Then we apply WKIsomap to pattern classification using AT&T face database [10] and USPS digit database [11]. The AT&T face database contains 400 face images of 40 persons, including 36 males and 4 females. The size of every image is 112 by 92 and per pixel constrains 256 gray levels. The USPS data set contains grayscale handwritten digit images of size 16×16, with pixel values in the range -1 to 1. The original training set contains 7,291 images, and the test set contains 2,007 images.

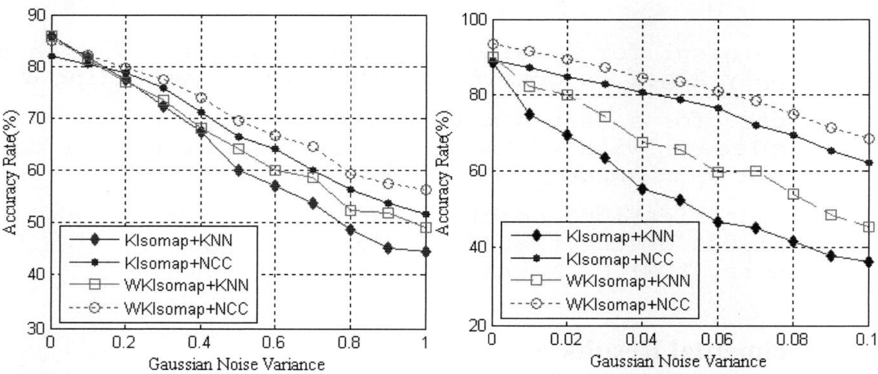

(a) (b)

Fig. 4. Recognition accuracy rate comparison when Gaussian noise is added in (a) AT&T face database and (b) USPS digit database

To reduce computational complexity, 200 face images of the former 20 persons are selected and resized to 28 by 23. For each person, 5 images are randomly selected into training data set, another 5 into testing data set. As for USPS digit database, 800 samples are selected as training data and 200 samples as test data. To test the robustness of our method, we add some Gaussian noise into the data. For each variance, the experiments were repeated 30 times and the average accuracy rates were plotted in Fig.4. The results show that WKIsomap based classifiers both outperform KIsomap based ones when noise is added. Besides this, NCC seems to work better than KNN when combined with KIsomap or WKIsomap.

5 Conclusions

In this paper, based on kernel Isomap and weighted Euclidean distance, a weighted kernel Isomap (WKIsomap) is proposed. As a supervised learning algorithm, WKIsomap can not only be used in data visualization, but also applied to feature extraction for pattern recognition. Weighted distance makes the data form the same class more closely and the data from different classes more far way. So WKIsomap is more suitable to labeled data than unsupervised KIsomap and stand Isomap both in visualization and classification as the experimental results show. Moreover, when noise is added into data, WKIsomap based classifiers are more robust to noise than KIsomap based ones. However, the error rate of WKIsomap is still high for actual application, some image preprocessing techniques may be exploited to reduce error rate in future work.

References

1. Jolliffe, I.T.: Principal Component Analysis. Springer, New York (1986)
2. Cox, T.F., Cox, M.A.A.: Multidimensional Scaling, 2nd edn. Chapman & Hall, Sydney, Australia (2000)
3. Tenenbaum, J.B., de Silva, V., Langford, J.C.: A Global Geometric Framework for Nonlinear Dimensionality Reduction. Science 290, 2319–2323 (2000)
4. Balasubramanian, M., Schwartz, E., Tenenbaum, J.B., de Silva, V., Langford, J.C.: The Isomap Algorithm and Topological Stability. Science 295:7a (January 2002)
5. Roweis, S.T., Saul, L.K.: Nonlinear Dimensionality Reduction by Locally Linear Embedding. Science 290, 2323–2326 (2000)
6. Belkin, M., Niyogi, P.: Laplacian Eigenmaps for Dimensionality Reduction and Data Representation. Neural Computation 15, 1373–1396 (2003)
7. Choi, H., Choi, S.: Kernel Isomap on Noisy Manifold. In: Proceedings of 4th IEEE International Conference on Development and Learning, pp. 208–213. IEEE Computer Society Press, Los Alamitos (2005)
8. Choi, H., Choi, S.: Robust Kernel Isomap. Pattern Recognition 40, 853–862 (2007)
9. Geng, X., Zhan, D.C., Zhou, Z.H.: Supervised Nonlinear Dimensionality Reduction for Visualization and Classification. IEEE Transactions on Systems, Man, and Cybernetics—Part B: Cybernetics 35, 1098–1107 (2005)
10. Samaria, F.S., Harter, A.C.: Parameterization of a Stochastic Model for Human Face Identification. In: Proceedings of 2nd IEEE Workshop on Applications of Computer Vision, pp. 138–142. Sarasota, FL, USA (1994)
11. Simard, P., LeCun, Y., Denker, J.: Efficient Pattern Recognition Using a New Transformation Distance. In: Proceeding of Neural Information Processing Systems, pp. 50–58. Morgan Kaufmann Publishers Inc. San Francisco, CA, USA (1992)

DT-CWT Feature Combined with ONPP for Face Recognition

Yuehui Sun and Minghui Du

School of Electronic & Information Engineering, South China University of Technology, Guangzhou, 510640, China
yuehui.sun@gmail.com,
ecmhdu@scut.edu.cn

Abstract. This paper introduces a novel face recognition method based on DT-CWT feature representation using ONPP. The Dual-Tree Complex Wavelet Transform (DT-CWT) used for representation features of face images, whose kernels are similar to Gabor wavelets, exhibit desirable characteristics of spatial locality and orientation selectivity. And DT-CWT outperforms Gabor with less redundancy and much efficient computing. Orthogonal Neighborhood Preserving Projections (ONPP) is a linear dimensionality reduction technique which attempts to preserve both the intrinsic neighborhood geometry of the data samples and the global geometry. ONPP employs an explicit linear mapping between the two. As a result, ONPP can handle new data samples straightforward, as this amount to a simple linear transformation. The experimental results have demonstrated the advantageous characteristics of ONPP in the DT-CWT feature space and achieve the better face recognition performance.

1 Introduction

Many face recognition methods have been developed over the past few decades [1]. Much more emphasis has been laid on data-driven learning-based techniques (also called appearance-based methods). Among this kind of approaches, an image is directly or indirectly represented by a vector in a multi-dimensional space called the image space or subspace respectively. A face image corresponds to a point in this space usually has very high dimension. Therefore, face recognition methodology should consider adopt good face representation in the space as well as efficient dimensionality reduction techniques issues for classification.

The Gabor wavelets are used widely in face recognition algorithms because Gabor wavelets have exhibited desirable characteristics of spatial locality and orientation selectivity [2]. However, the Dual-Tree Complex Wavelet Transform (DT-CWT) as a wavelet transform recently studied, which also provides good directional selectivity in six different fixed orientations at different scales similar to Gabor wavelets. Furthermore, it has less redundancy for images and is much faster than Gabor transform to compute. Hence, DT-CWT is a good choice to replace Gabor transform for face images representation.

Orthogonal Neighborhood Preserving Projections (ONPP) [3] is a new linear dimensionality reduction algorithm, which can be viewed as a synthesis of PCA and

Y. Wang, Y. Cheung, and H. Liu (Eds.): CIS 2006, LNAI 4456, pp. 1058–1067, 2007.

Locally Linear Embedding (LLE) [4]. ONPP is a linear method, while Isomap [5], LLE are nonlinear methods, so neither of them can deal with new test data points except training data points. ONPP seems similar to Locality Preserving Projections (LPP) [6], whereas the weights used in LPP short of consideration to the local geometric structure.

The remainder of the paper is organized as follows: In section 2 DT-CWT is briefly reviewed and derives a DT-CWT feature vector representation for face images. In section 3 ONPP is described. Experiments are presented in Section 4. Finally, conclusions are given and promising directions for future work is discussed.

2 DT-CWT Feature Analysis

As a wavelet transform proposed and studied recently, the DT-CWT [7] has been found to be particularly suitable for image decomposition and representation when the goal is the derivation of local and discriminating features like Gabor wavelet. DT-CWT provides good directional selectivity in six different fixed orientations at some scales, which is able to distinguish positive and negative frequencies. And it has a limited redundancy of four for images and is much faster than the Gabor wavelet to compute. Therefore, DT-CWT filter representation gives better performance for classifying facial actions. In this section, the basics on DT-CWT are reviewed, feature representation of images is described, and a DT-CWT feature vector for face recognition is derived.

2.1 DT-CWT

Kingsbury's complex wavelets [7], [8] have similar shapes to Gabor wavelets. DT-CWT scheme comprises two trees of real filters, which produce the real and imaginary parts of the complex coefficients.

Kingsbury summarized the properties of DT-CWT as the following properties [8]:

- Approximate shift invariance;
- Good directional selectivity in 2-dimensions (2-D) with Gabor-like filters (also true for higher dimensionality, m-D);
- Perfect reconstruction using short linear-phase filters;
- Limited redundancy, independent of the number of scales, 2 : 1 for 1-D (2m : 1 for m-D);
- Efficient order-N computation – only twice the simple DWT for 1-D (2m times for m-D).

The DT-CWT filters used are designed to give perfect reconstruction at every level. The transform has the ability to differentiate positive and negative frequencies and produces six sub-bands strongly oriented in $\pm 15^\circ, \pm 45^\circ, \pm 75^\circ$ as shown in Fig. 2.

However, these directions are fixed unlike the Gabor transform where the sub-band can be computed in any desired direction. The DT-CWT expansion of an image $f(\vec{x})$ is given by [7], [8]:

$$f(\vec{x}) = \sum_{k} W_\phi(j_o,k)\phi_{j_o,k}(\vec{x}) + \sum_{i}\sum_{j>j_o}\sum_{k} W_\psi(j,k)\psi^i_{j,k}(\vec{x}) \quad (1)$$

where $i = \pm 15^\circ, \pm 45^\circ, \pm 75^\circ$ .The scaling function $\phi_{j_o,k}$ and wavelet function $\psi^i_{j,k}$ are complex. $W_\phi(j_o,k)$ indicate the scaling coefficients and $W_\psi(j,k)$ are the wavelet coefficients of the transform. Hence six sub-bands are obtained corresponding to the directions $i = \pm 15^\circ, \pm 45^\circ, \pm 75^\circ$.

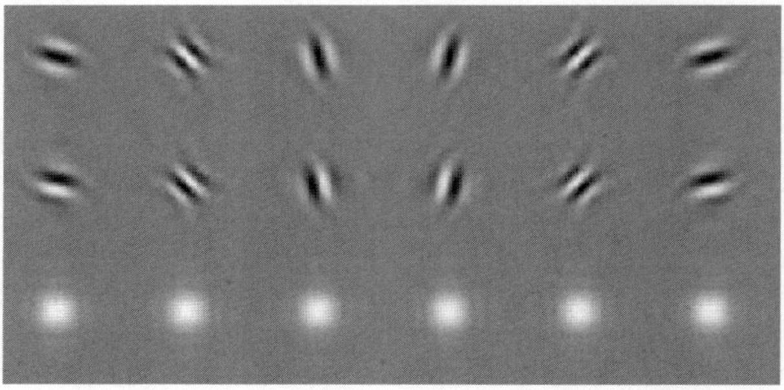

Fig. 1. Filter impulse response of DT-CWT in frequency domain. The first row is the real part of DT-CWT, the second row is the imaginary part of DT-CWT, and the third row is the magnitude of DT-CWT.

You are strongly encouraged to use LaTeX2e for the preparation of your camera-ready manuscript together with the corresponding Springer class file llncs.cls; see Sect. 3. Only if you use LaTeX2e can hyperlinks be generated in the online version of your manuscript.

If you are unable to use LaTeX, you may use MS Word together with the template sv-lncs.dot (see Sect. 4) or any other text processing system. In the latter case, please follow these instructions closely in order to make the volume look as uniform as possible.

We would like to stress that the class/style files and the template should not be manipulated and that the guidelines regarding font sizes and format should be adhered to. This is to ensure that the end product is as homogeneous as possible.

2.2 DT-CWT Feature Representation

As Fig. 2(d) shown, the magnitude response of DT-CWT for a face image is given. Considering the size of the face image shown in Figure 2(a), is 64×64, using DT-CWT with 4 levels and 6 directions, this provides twenty-four sub-bands. There are six matrices gained in the first level sub-bands, which has dimensions equal to half of original dimension of the image and the next level has half the dimensions of the previous level and so on. Hence, a DT-CWT jet corresponding to a 64×64 original image will contain six sub-bands due to different directions, and each sub-band contains four matrices, which are 32×32, 16×16, 8×8 and 4×4 wavelet coefficients respectively, as shown in Fig. 2(c), (d). Compare to the Gabor filter results, as shown in Fig. 2(b), the number of dimensions of DT-CWT features is reduced dramatically.

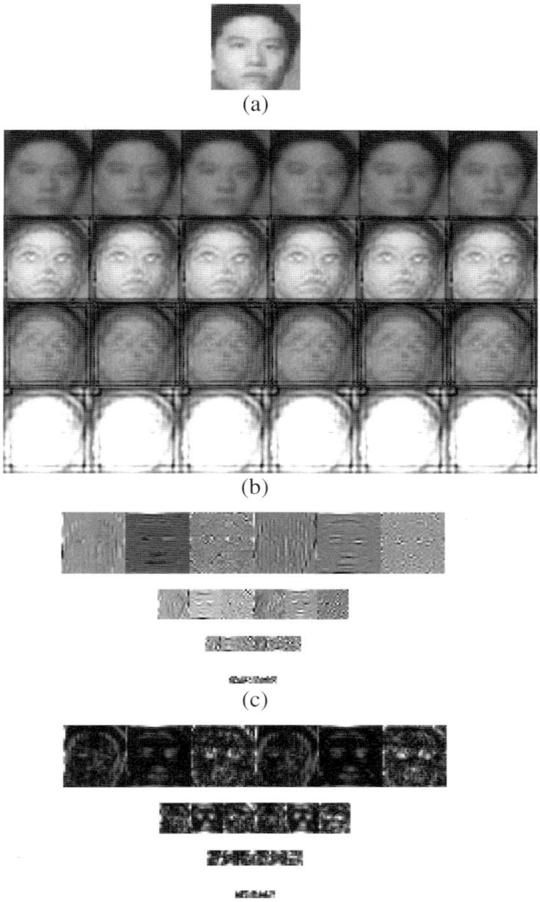

(a)

(b)

(c)

(d)

Fig. 2. (a) a face image from CMU database (b) The magnitude response using Gabor filters. (c) The real part of response using DT-CWT for levels N=1, 2, 3, 4 in the same orientations $\pm 15^\circ, \pm 45^\circ, \pm 75^\circ$. (d) The magnitude of response using DT-CWT for levels N=1, 2, 3, 4 in the same orientations $\pm 15^\circ, \pm 45^\circ, \pm 75^\circ$.

In order to derive a feature vector, the output $F_{i,j}(\vec{x})$ $(i \in \{1,...,6\}, j \in \{1,...,4\})$ which encompasses information of different spatial frequency, spatial localities and orientations are concatenated. Before the concatenation, we normalize each $F_{i,j}(\vec{x})$ to zero mean and unit variance, and then transformed to a vector $G_{i,j}(\vec{x})$ by concatenating its rows [5]. Therefore, a discriminative feature vector $G(\vec{x})$ can be derived to represent the face image by concatenating those vectors $G_{i,j}(\vec{x})$:

$$G(\vec{x}) = (G_{1,1}, G_{2,1}, \ldots G_{6,1}, G_{1,2}, \ldots G_{6,2}, \ldots, G_{1,4}, \ldots G_{6,4})^{\mathrm{T}} \tag{2}$$

where T is the transpose operator. All the outputs have been included in the feature vector as important discriminating information.

The derived feature vector $G(\vec{x})$ thus encompasses all the elements of the DT-CWT representation set $F_{i,j}(\vec{x})$ $(i \in \{1,\ldots,6\}, j \in \{1,\ldots,4\})$, as discriminating feature. However, the length of the vector is quite large. In the following section, we will introduce to use our kernel method to drive a low dimensional feature with enhanced discrimination power from the constructed DT-CWT feature vector $G(\vec{x})$

3 ONPP

Given a dataset $X = [x_1, x_2, \ldots, x_n] \in \Re^{m \times n}$ and the dimension d of the reduced space, with $d \times m$, the goal of dimensionality reduction is to produce a set Y which is an accurate representation of X, but of smaller dimension. Projection-based techniques consist of replacing the original data X by a matrix of the form:

$$Y = V^{\mathrm{T}} X \text{, where } V \in \Re^{m \times n} \tag{3}$$

The main idea of ONPP is to seek an orthogonal mapping of a given data set so as to best preserve a graph which describes the local geometry. The objective function of ONPP to minimize is as follows:

$$N(Y) = \sum_i \left\| y_i - \sum_j w_{ij} y_j \right\|_2^2 \tag{4}$$

The weights W are fixed and we need to minimize the above objective function with respect to $Y = [y_1, y_2, \ldots, y_n] \in \Re^{d \times n}$. Some constraints imposing on the y_i s in order to make optimization problem well-posed:

- $\sum_i y_i = 0$ i.e., the mapped coordinates are centered at the origin;
- $\frac{1}{n} \sum_i y_i {y_i}^{\mathrm{T}} = I$, that is the embedding vectors have unit covariance.

Note that $N(Y)$ can be written as $N(Y) = \sum_i \left\| Y(I - W^{\mathrm{T}}) \right\|_F^2$, so

$$N(Y) = \sum_i \left\| Y(I - W^{\mathrm{T}}) \right\|_F^2 = tr\left[Y(I - W^{\mathrm{T}})(I - W) Y^{\mathrm{T}} \right] \tag{5}$$

The problem will turn to computing the d eigenvalues of the matrix $M = (I - W^{\mathrm{T}})(I - W)^{\mathrm{T}}$, and the associated eigenvectors.

In ONPP an explicit linear mapping from X to Y is imposed which is in the form (3). So we have $y_i = V^{\mathrm{T}} x_i, i = 1,...,n$ for a certain matrix $V \in R^{m \times d}$ to be determined. In order to determine the matrix V , we will minimize the same objective function (5) as in the LLE approach, but now Y is restricted to being related to X by (3). When expressed in terms of the unknown matrix V , the objective function becomes

$$N(Y) = \sum_i \left\| V^{\mathrm{T}} X(I - W^{\mathrm{T}}) \right\|_F^2 = tr\left[V^{\mathrm{T}} X(I - W^{\mathrm{T}})(I - W) X^{\mathrm{T}} V \right] \tag{6}$$

If we impose the additional constraint that the columns of V are orthogonal, i.e. $VV^{\mathrm{T}} = I$, then the solution V to the above optimization problem is the basis of the eigenvectors associated with the d smallest eigenvalues of the matrix

$$\tilde{M} = X(I - W^{\mathrm{T}})(I - W) X^{\mathrm{T}} \tag{7}$$

Weight matrix W was defined using algorithm similar to LLE at the 1st part of ONPP by forming the k -NN graph.

In the case where the class labels are available, ONPP can be modified appropriately and yield a projection which carries not only geometric information but discriminating information as well. In a supervised setting we first build the data graph $Graph = (N, E)$, where the nodes N correspond to data samples and an edge $e_{i,j} = (x_i, x_j)$ exists if and only if x_i and x_j belongs to the same class. In this case it notes not need to set the parameter k , the number of nearest neighbors, and the method becomes fully automatic.

Denote by c the number of classes and n_i the number of data samples which belong to the i -th class. The data graph $Graph$ consists of c cliques, since the adjacency relationship between two nodes reflects their class relationship. This implies that with an appropriate reordering of the columns and rows, the weight matrix W will have a block diagonal form where the size of the i -th block is equal to the size n_i of the i -th class. In this case W will be of the following form, $W = diag(W_1, W_2, ..., W_c)$ .The weights W_i within each class are computed as the same as the case of unsupervised algorithm.

Consider now the case $m > n$ where the number of samples n is less than their dimension m . The matrix $\tilde{M} \in \Re^{m \times m}$ will have rank at most $n - c$. In order to ensure that the resulting matrix $\tilde{M}$ will be nonsingular, an initial PCA projection that reduces the dimensionality of the data vectors is applied to $n - c$. Define V_{PCA} the dimensionality reduction matrix of PCA. Then the ONPP algorithm is performed and the total dimensionality reduction matrix is given by $V = V_{PCA} V_{ONPP}$, where V_{ONPP} is the dimensionality reduction matrix of ONPP.

4 Experiments and Results

4.1 Data Preparation

In this section, face recognition using the method brought forward in this paper was conducted on well-known face image database AT&T/ORL dataset [9] and Yale dataset [10]. The AT&T/ORL database is used to evaluate the performance of recognition algorithm under the condition where the number of training samples is varied. The Yale database is used to examine the performance when both facial expressions and illumination are varied.

The AT&T/ORL dataset contains images from 40 individuals, each providing 10 different images. The variations of the images are across pose, size, time, and facial expression. The images are taken with a tolerance for some tilting and rotation of the face of up to 20 degrees. Moreover, there is also some variation in the scale of up to about 10 percent. All images are grayscale and normalized to a resolution of 92×112 pixels. For the purpose of computation efficiency, all images are resized to 64×64 pixels.

Fig. 3. Example ORL images with spatial resolution 92×112. Note that the images vary in pose, size, and facial expression.

The Yale face dataset which contains 165 images of 15 individuals (each person has 11 different images) under various facial expressions and lighting conditions. Each image is manually cropped and resized to 64×64 pixels in this experiment.

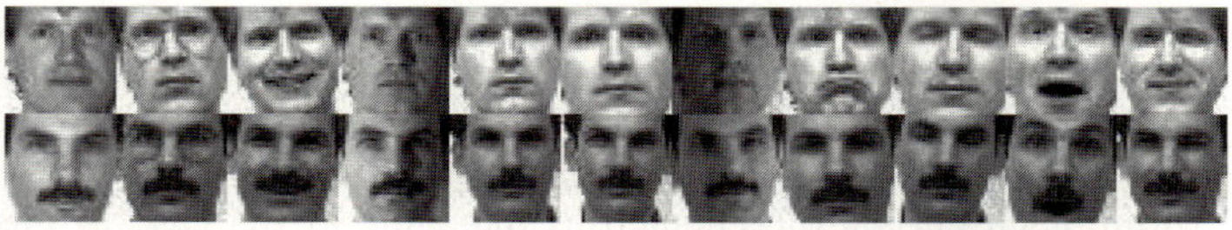

Fig. 4. Sample face images from the Yale database. Note that the illuminations vary in the images.

4.2 Similarity Measures and Classification Rule for DT-CWT Feature Based Classification

We applied the supervised ONPP on the DT-CWT Gabor feature vector derived by (2). When an image is presented to the classifier, the DT-CWT feature vector of the image is first calculated as detailed in Section 2, and the lower dimensional feature is derived using form

$$Z(\vec{x}) = V^{\mathrm{T}} G(\vec{x}) \tag{8}$$

The dimensionality of the lower dimensional feature space is determined by the supervised ONPP method, which derives the overall transformation matrix V. Let $Med(\vec{x})$ be the mean of DT-CWT feature of the training samples for class after training. Our method applies the nearest neighbor (to the mean) rule for classification using some similarity (distance) measure

$$\delta(Z(\vec{x}), Med_k(\vec{x})) = \min_j \delta(Z(\vec{x}), Med_j(\vec{x})) \rightarrow Z(\vec{x}) \in \omega_k \tag{9}$$

The image feature vector $Z(\vec{x})$ is classified as belonging to the class of the closest mean $Med_k(\vec{x})$ using the similarity measure δ.

The similarity measures used in our experiments to evaluate the efficiency of different representation and recognition methods include L_1 distance measure δ_{L_1}, L_2 distance measure δ_{L_2} and cosine similarity measure $\delta_{\cos}$ which are defined as follows:

$$\begin{aligned} \delta_{L_1}(Z,U) &= \sum_i |Z_i - U_i|; \\ \delta_{L_2}(Z,U) &= (Z-U)^{\mathrm{T}}(Z-U); \\ \delta_{\cos}(Z,U) &= \frac{-Z^{\mathrm{T}}U}{\|Z\|\|U\|} \end{aligned} \tag{10}$$

where $\sum$ is the covariance matrix, and $\|\bullet\|$ denotes the norm operator. Note that the cosine similarity measure includes a minus sign because the nearest neighbor (to the mean) rule of (9) applies minimum distance measure rather than maximum similarity measure.

4.3 Comparison Between DT-CWT and Gabor as Feature Extraction

To verify DT-CWT more efficient than Gabor filters on feature extraction of face image, we test on AT&T/ORL dataset. For simply, the same scales and orientation parameters as DT-CWT are taken when using Gabor filters convolving face images. The magnitude of Gabor filters is shown in Fig. 2 (b). And when we derive Gabor feature vector, we first down-sample each level magnitudes of Gabor $Ga(\vec{x})$ with the factor $\rho = 16$ to reduce the dimensionality of the original vector space, and then normalize each $Ga_{i,j}(\vec{x})$ $(i \in \{1,\ldots,6\}, j \in \{1,\ldots,4\})$ to zero mean and unit variance, and then transformed to a vector $H_{i,j}(\vec{x})$ by concatenating its rows. The Gabor feature vector $H(\vec{x})$ can be represented like this:

$$H(\vec{x}) = (H_{1,1}, H_{2,1}, \ldots H_{6,1}, H_{1,2}, \ldots H_{6,2}, \ldots, H_{1,4}, \ldots H_{6,4})^{\mathrm{T}} \tag{11}$$

On recognition stage, not any dimensionality reduction technique is adopted, and Euclidean distance measure and the nearest neighbor classifier are used in all of our experiments. The strategy of training set building we taken is Leave-one-out, that is, the image of one person is removed from the data set and all of the remaining images are used for training. We perform 10 times of the experiments and take the average value as result. The experimental results are shown in Tab.1.

Table 1. Experimental results based AT&T/ORL dataset for comparison of two feature extraction methods (CPU: Pentium (M) 1.4GHz, RAM: 512Mb)

Wavelet	Time cost /image/second	Time cost on training stage(s)	Best Recognition rate (%)
Gabor	0.2188	87.506	80.5
DT-CWT	0.0169	12.728	85.8

Observing Tab.1, DT-CWT uses much less time than Gabor, because DT-CWT just complete two times of DWT and the computation is only $O(N)$ while Gaber filters needs repetitive convulsions depending on the numbers of the kernel functions Gabor used. Therefore, under the condition of the same classification task, DT-CWT is more efficient than Gabor on computation. DT-CWT also performs Gabor on recognition rate. The reason is that the DT-CWT includes all the frequencies of the images which can be perfect reconstruction using short linear-phase filters, the selection of Gabor filters is dependent on the image frequency characteristics. The accurate implementation of a complete Gabor expansion would necessitate an impractical number of filters. Also the discrete versions of the Gabor function should be obtained in order to be used for image applications. So, considering the system performance, we can say that DT-CWT is a good candidate for Gabor filters on face recognition.

4.4 Algorithms Comparison Using Different Measures

We form the training set by a random subset of 5 different facial expressions/poses per subject and use the remaining 5 as a test set. For ONPP, the dimension of d = [40:10:160]. Table 2 reports the best achieved error rate and the corresponding value of d . The experimental results suggest that the orthogonality of the columns of the dimensionality reduction matrix V is very important for recognition task. This is more evident in the case of face recognition, where this particular feature turned out to be crucial for the performance.

Table 2. The best error rate achieved by all measures on the AT&T/ORL and Yale datasets respectively

measure/database	AT&T/ORL		Yale	
	d	Error (%)	d	Error (%)
L1	70	6.73	100	10.6
L2	80	10.15	120	8.32
Cos	100	15.72	140	17.22

5 Conclusion

The Orthogonal Neighborhood Preserving Projections (ONPP) introduced in this paper combined with DT-CWT image space is a novel method to face recognition, by applying algorithm, face images could be efficient represented by DT-CWT due to its good directional selectivity in six different fixed orientations at some scales capturing the local structure. The DT-CWT features use ONPP as a linear dimensionality reduction technique, which preserves not only the locality but also the local and global geometry. Experiments results showed that DT-CWT feature based classification using supervised ONPP can be very effective and the method proposed in this paper is a robust recognition technique.

Acknowledgments. The author is grateful to Dr. E. Kokiopoulou for her valuable help and insightful discussions on ONPP algorithm in the paper.

References

1. Zhao, W., Chellappa, R., Rosenfeld, A., Phillips, P.J.: Face Recognition: A Literature Survey. In: Technical Report CAR-TR-948, Univ. of Maryland, College Park (2000)
2. Liu, C., Wechsler, H.: Gabor Feature Based Classification Using the Enhanced Fisher Linear Discriminant Model for Face Recognition. IEEE Transactions on Image Processing 11(4), 467–476 (2002)
3. Kokiopoulou, E., Saad, Y.: Orthogonal Neighborhood Preserving Projections. In: IEEE Int. Conf. on Data Mining, pp. 1–8. IEEE Computer Society Press, Los Alamitos (2005)
4. Roweis, S., Saul, L.: Nonlinear Dimensionality Reduction by Locally Linear Embedding. Science 290(5500), 2323–2326 (2000)
5. Tenenbaum, J.B., de Silva, V., Langford, J.C.: A Global Geometric Framework for Nonlinear Dimensionality Reduction. Science 290(5500), 2319–2323 (2000)
6. He, X., Niyogi, P.: Locality preserving projections. In: Technical Report TR-2002-09, University of Chicago Computer Science, Chicago (2002)
7. Kingsbury, N.G.: The dual-tree complex wavelet transform: a new efficient tool for image restoration and enhancement. In: Proc. European Signal Processing Conf, pp. 319–322 (1998)
8. Kingsbury, N.G.: Shift invariant properties of the Dual-Tree Complex Wavelet Transform. In: Proc. IEEE Conf. on Acoustics, Speech and Signal Processing, vol. 3, pp. 1221–1224 (1999)
9. http://www.uk.research.att.com/facedatabase.html
10. http://cvc.yale.edu/projects/yalefaces/yalefaces.html

Precise Eye Localization with AdaBoost and Fast Radial Symmetry

Wencong Zhang[1], Hong Chen[1], Peng Yao[1], Bin Li[1,2], and Zhenquan Zhuang[1]

[1] MOE-Microsoft Key Laboratory of Multimedia Computing and Communication, University of Science and Technology of China, 230027 Hefei, China

[2] Anhui Key Laboratory of Software in Computing and Communication, University of Science and Technology of China, 230027 Hefei, China

{zwcong, alang_yao}@mail.ustc.edu.cn, binli@ustc.edu.cn

Abstract. The accuracy of face alignment affects greatly the performance of a face recognition system. Since the face alignment is usually conducted using eye positions, the algorithm for accurate eye localization is therefore essential for the accurate face recognition. In this paper, we propose a novel algorithm for eye localization. Based on the special gray distribution in the eye region, proper AdaBoost detection is adaptively trained to segment the eye region. After getting the region of eyes, a fast radial symmetry operator is used to precisely locate the center of eyes. Experimental results show that the method can accurately locate the eyes, and it is robust to the variations of face poses, expressions, illuminations and accessories.

1 Introduction

Face recognition has a variety of potential applications in public security, law enforcement and commerce. An important issue in face recognition is face alignment which involves spatially scaling and rotating a face image to match with face images in the database. It is already shown that the face alignment has a large impact on recognition accuracy. Currently face alignment is usually performed with the use of eye position. Many researchers study the recognition problem based on the assumption that the positions of the eye are manually labeled. The FERET96 test shows that the performance of partially automatic algorithms (eyes are manually labeled) is obviously better than that of fully automatic (eyes are not labeled) [1]. Therefore, getting accurate location of eyes is an important step in a face recognition system.

Like other problems of object detection under complex scene such as face detection [2], eye patterns also have large variation in appearance due to various factors, such as face pose, size, expressions, illuminations and accessories. Even having found the positions of faces grossly, robustly and precisely, locating eyes center is still a challenging task. Varieties of eye localization and tracking algorithms have been proposed in recent years. However, most of them can only deal with part of these variations or be feasible under some constraints. Zhu [3]

Y. Wang, Y. Cheung, and H. Liu (Eds.): CIS 2006, LNAI 4456, pp. 1068–1077, 2007.

and Haro [4] propose to perform real-time eye tracking based on combing its appearance, the bright pupil effect, and motion characteristics in video stream. But this technique greatly depends on the luminance conditions and size of the eyes. [5], [6] and [7] use facial structure knowledge, such as Hough transform, symmetry detector, projection analysis etc. to detect eyes.

In these methods, the physical properties of the eyes are not taken into account. The appearance-based method [8] detects eyes based on the intensity distribution of the objects. It collects a large amount of training data under different conditions, and relies on techniques from statistical analysis and machine learning to find the relevant characteristics of eyes and non-eye samples. But in the method only eye blob was considered. As a matter of fact, eyebrows or thick spectacle frames sometimes look so similar to a closed eye that the classifier often makes a wrong decision. So both the eye blob and eye neighborhood should be considered. In this paper, a novel approach for precisely locating eyes bases on AdaBoost and fast radial symmetry is devised. We apply a trained eye-region detector to segment the eye regions, which make full use of the special gray distribution in the eye region. After getting the eye region, a fast radial symmetry operator, both utilizing eye blob information and the eye neighborhood information, is used to precisely locate the center of eyes. Extensive experiments on FERET and CAS-PEAL databases show that the proposed method can accurately locate the eyes and it is robust against the variations of face poses, illuminations and so on. Furthermore, the locating speed of our algorithm is fast enough to meet the requirement of a real-time face recognition system. Fig.1 shows the flowchart of the proposed eye localization method.

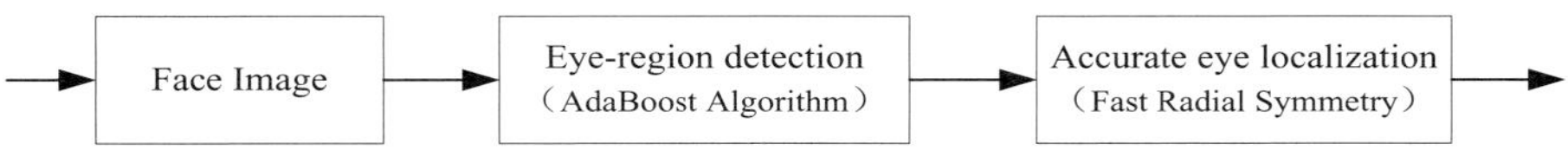

Fig. 1. Flowchart of the proposed eye localization method based on AdaBoost and fast radial symmetry operator

The remaining part of this paper is organized as follows: In section 2, we discuss the eye-region detection based on AdaBoost; Section 3 describes the fast radial symmetry-based precise eye localization method in detail; Experiment results are conducted in Section 4, followed by some discussion, conclusion and future work in Section 5.

2 Eye-Region Detection Based on AdaBoost

In this paper, a coarse-to-fine locating strategy is adopted, which firstly detects the eye region and then accurately locates the center of eyes. Eye-region detection is the base of the precise localization of pupils. Comparing the features in eye-region with other face features, we find the special gray distribution in the eye region. Considering the predominance of AdaBoost learning algorithm on fast and robust region detection, it is adopted to train the effective eye-region detector.

2.1 AdaBoost Learning Algorithm

The AdaBoost learning algorithm proposed by Freund and Schapire [10,11]is used to boost the classification performance of a simple learning algorithm, which combines a collection of weak classification functions to form a stronger classifier. AdaBoost is an aggressive mechanism for selecting a small set of good classification functions that nevertheless have significant variety, and has a high detecting efficiency. AdBoost learning algorithm has been presented as below:

– Input training example images (x_1, y_1), (x_2, y_2),...(x_n, y_n),and initialize weights $\omega_1(i) = 1/n$.
– For $t = 1, 2, ...T$:
  - For each feature t, train a weak classifier h_t which is restricted to using a single feature;
  - Calculate error rate of weak classifier ω_i, $E_t = \sum_{i=1}^{n} \omega_t(i)[h_t(x_i) \neq y_i]$, and $\alpha_t = \frac{1}{2}\ln[(1 - E_t)/E_t]$;
  - Update the weights according to error rate:
    $\omega_{t+1}(i) = \omega_t(i) * \exp(\alpha_t)$, while $h_t(x_{x_i}) \neq y_i$,
    $\omega_{t+1}(i) = \omega_t(i) * \exp(-\alpha_t)$, while $h_t(x_{x_i}) = y_i$.
– The final strong classifier is:$H(x) = sign(\sum_{t=1}^{T} \alpha_t h_t(x))$.

2.2 Training the Eyes-Region Detector

In this paper, we used standard AdaBoost training methods combined with Viola's cascade approach to build a eye-region detector [12]. The cascade structure enables the detector to rule out most of the face areas as eye with a few tests and allows computational resources to be concentrated on the more challenging parts

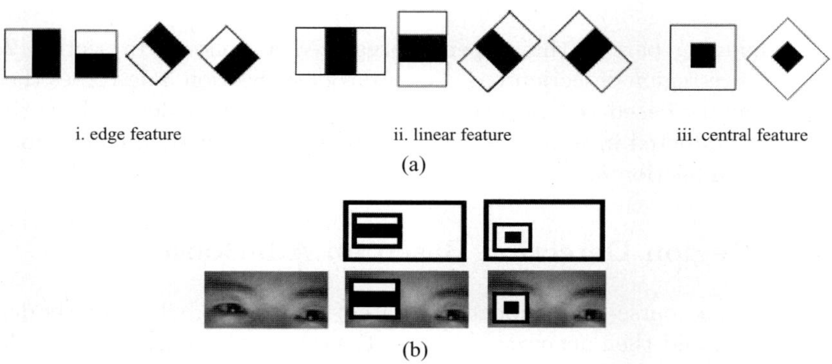

Fig. 2. Features used in AdaBoost training process. (a): the extended set of Haar-like features. (b): features of interest selected by Adboost.

of the images. The features used in AdaBoost training process are a extended set of Haar-like vectors [13] as elementary features of weak classifier, which shown in the Fig.2.(a), and choosing these extended Haar-like features is because that they indicate eye region very well as shown in Fig.2.(b). For an eye sample with size of , there are about 2,4000 features in total.

In order to detect the eye region more effectively, we chose the eye-region samples containing eyebrows because the eyebrow is an important feature that can conduce to improve the performance of eye-region detection. The negative examples are obtained by a bootstrap process [11]. All the samples are processed with gray scale normalization and size normalization to pixels, as shown in the Fig.3.

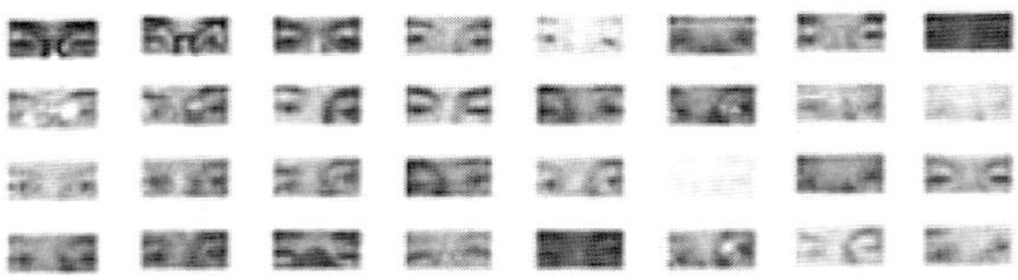

a. Positive samples after normalization

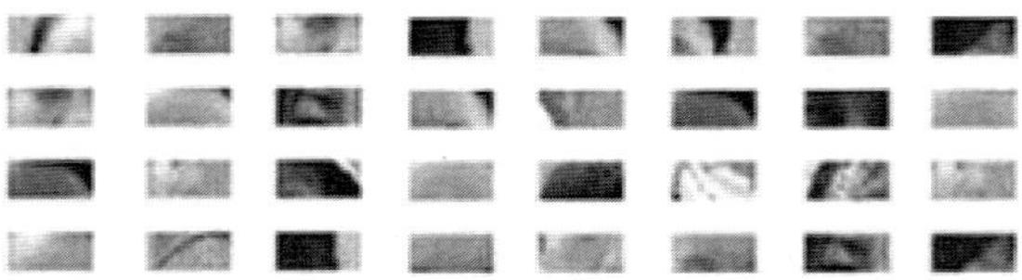

b. Negative samples after normalization

Fig. 3. The positive and negative samples used in training

3 Accurate Eye Localization with Fast Radial Symmetry

A simple approach to detect the center of pupil is to use the gray valleys. However, such an approach is too sensitive to the illumination and accessories on the face. Here, an efficient and accurate approach Fast Radial Symmetry (FRS) used in locating the center of pupil will be proposed, which is a simple and fast gradient-based interest operator detecting points of high radial symmetry. Certainly, while the detected object's shape is a circle, it is easy and fast to detect the center of the object by accumulating the effect of the pixels on circumference. An overview of the algorithm is shown in Fig.4 along with the key signals (images) involved [14].

The gradient is calculated through a 3×3 *Soble* operator which has both vertical and horizontal directions. So a gradient vector $g(p)$ for each point p will be produced. Moreover, for each point p, a positively-affected pixel $p_{+ve}(p)$ and a negatively-affected pixel $p_{-ve}(p)$ are determined. The coordinate expressions are shown as below:

$$p_{\pm}(p) = p \pm round(\frac{g(p)}{\| g(p) \|} n) . \tag{1}$$

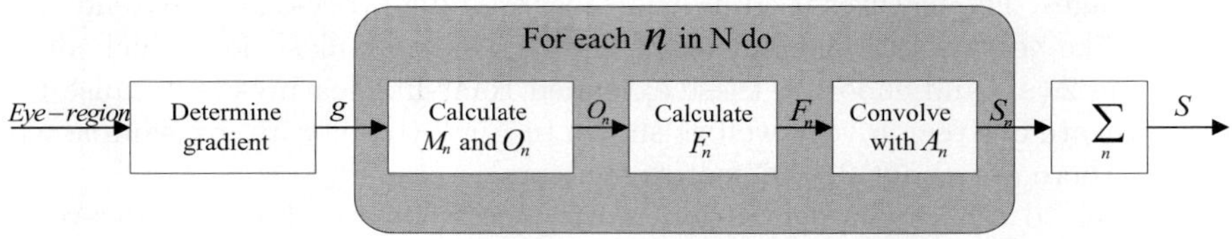

Fig. 4. Block diagram showing the steps involved in computing the transform

Where $g(p)$ is a gradient vector, *round* means rounding each vector element to the nearest integer, and n is detecting radius. For each radius n, an orientation projection image O_n and a magnitude projection image M_n are formed. The orientation and magnitude projection images are initially zero, O_n and M_n are constructed from following

$$O_n(p_{\pm ve}(p)) = O_n(p_{\pm ve}(p)) \pm 1 . \tag{2}$$

$$M_n(p_{\pm ve}(p)) = M_n(p_{\pm ve}(p)) \pm \| g(p) \| . \tag{3}$$

The radial symmetry contribution at radius n is defined as the convolution,

$$S_n = F_n * A_n . \tag{4}$$

Where

$$F_n(p) = \frac{M_n(p)}{k_n} \left(\frac{| O_n(p) |}{k_n} \right)^{\alpha} . \tag{5}$$

$$O_n(p) = \begin{cases} O_n(p), \text{ if } O_n(p) < k_n \\ k_n, \quad \text{otherwise.} \end{cases} \tag{6}$$

A_n is a two-dimension Gaussian, α is the radial strictness parameter, and k_n is a scaling factor that normalizes M_n and O_n across different radius. In our method,$k_n$is got got through statistics,

$$k_n = \begin{cases} 8, \quad \text{if } n = 1 \\ 9.9, \text{otherwise.} \end{cases} \tag{7}$$

The full transform is defined as the average of the symmetry contributions over all the radium considered.

$$SN = \frac{1}{| N |} \sum_{n \in N} S_n . \tag{8}$$

From the discussion above, all the centers of objects whose shapes are circle will be detected. Eye-region detector based on AdaBoost is to exclude the influence of some round features, such as nares and corners of mouth. The final purpose of the paper is to locate the center of pupils which are dark blobs in eye region. So FRS will be utilized, only negatively-affected pixels are considered, to accumulate the effect of the circumference points to the center of dark blobs. Moreover, to simplify computation FRS only odd numbers will be chosen as the radius. And the maximum of detecting radius is defined as below:

$$N = \begin{cases} 7 & height < 55 \\ 9 & 55 \leq height < 70 \\ 11 & 70 \leq height < 85 \\ 13 & 85 \leq height \end{cases} \tag{9}$$

where *height* is the height of eye region, and N is the maximum detecting radius. However, the selection of is different from the size of images, which is a threshold to the approach. The whole process is shown in Fig.5.

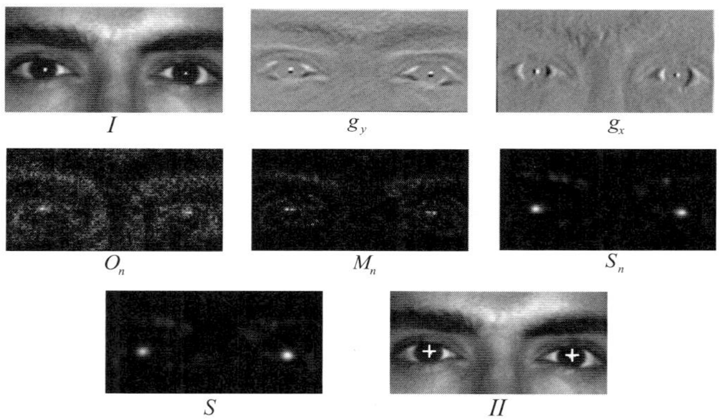

Fig. 5. The whole process of FRS

In figure 5, I is the original eye-region image, and 0_n, M_n, S_n are correspondingly the processes of the radial symmetry transform. S shows the located centers of both left and right pupils as the whitest points. And II is the result of accurate eye localization.

4 Experiment and Analysis

4.1 Database

The training set for the AdaBoost detector is selected from FERET, YALE, ORL, USTCFace database, and totally 16,000 eye-pairs are cropped and normalized. Experimental test set consists of ba, bg, bk pose subbase from FERET (200 persons, 600 images), part images from CAS-PEAL (200 persons, 4532 images) and totally 5132 faces are involved in the evaluation of localization performance.

Of the training databases, FERET, YALE, ORL, are open databases [15], and USTCFace, built by our lab, consists of 1448 face images with different poses, expressions and illumination conditions. Among the test databases, the faces in ba, bk are frontal but under different illumination conditions, and the faces in bg rotate 22.5; CAS-PEAL is also an open database [15], which is under unbalanced light condition, has different expressions, and has accessories on the faces. The characters of the three test sets are diverse, which cover eye variations in gaze angles, sizes, illumination, and accessories. Experiments based on such diverse sets are able to test the generalization performance of our eye-localization algorithm.

4.2 Evaluation Protocol

To evaluate the precision of eye localization, a scale of independent localization criterion [16]is used. This relative error measure compares the automatic locating result with the manually marked locations of each eye. Let E_l and E_r be the manually extracted left and right eye positions, $E_l^{'}$ and $E_r^{'}$ be the detected positions, d_l be the Euclidean distance between E_l and $E_l^{'}$, d_r be the Euclidean distance between E_r and $E_r^{'}$, d_{lr} be the Euclidean distance between the ground truth eye centers. Then the relative error of this detection is defined as follows:

$$err = \frac{max(d_l, d_r)}{d_{lr}}. \tag{10}$$

4.3 Comparison with Other Eye Location Methods

Three different eye-locating methods are imple-mented and evaluated on the test set.

Method 1: The proposed algorithm in this paper.

Method 2: Different from Method 1 only in the step of accurate eye localization. After grossly locating the eye region and determining the midline between left and right eye, connected components analysis and projection analysis are applied to the two regions respectively to locate the eye center position.

Method 3: Similar to the method proposed in [9]. This method is different from Method 1 mainly in the step of eye-region detection, which adopts Gabor transform to segment out the eye region.

The cumulative distribution function of localization error of three methods is shown in Fig.6. From the figure, we can see that our method achieve an excellent performance and about 98.1% when location error is below 0.20, which superior to method 2 and method 3. Because method 2 adopts the integral projection, so it is easily disturbed by the eyebrow and some accessories such as glasses frame, furthermore, this method is also sensitive to the variance of luminance. The performance of method 3 is worse than our method for the difficulty of selecting the parameters of Gabor transform and the sensitivity to the size of image. In Fig.7, we offer some examples picked out from the test sets for the visual examination.

In this paper, we utilize efficiently the special gray distribution and the radial symmetry of pupil in the eye region to realize the precise localization with the

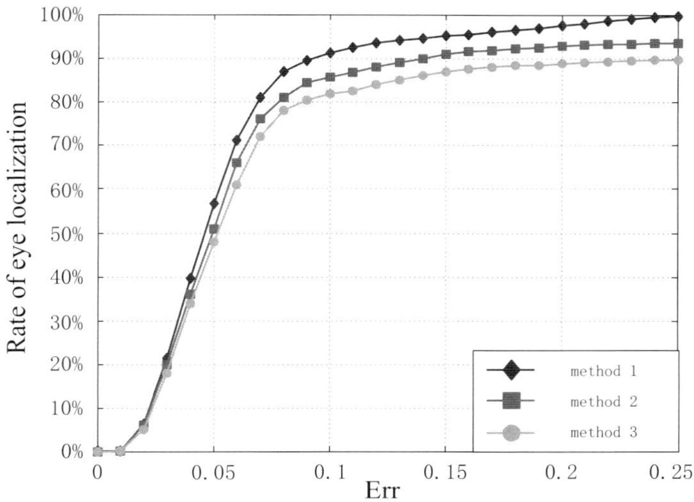

Fig. 6. Cumulative distribution of localiza- tion errors of three methods on test set

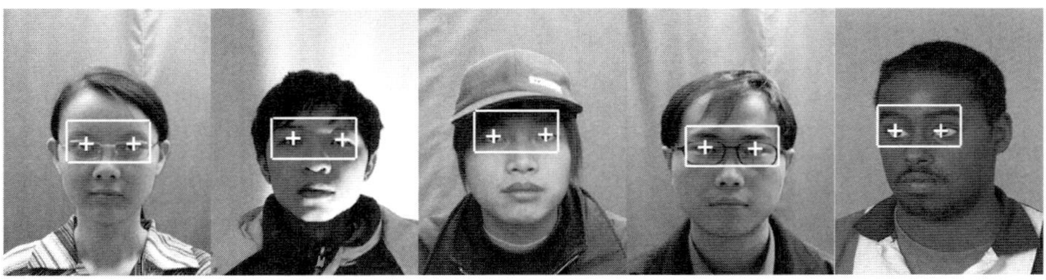

Fig. 7. Some of eye locating results from test sets

combination of AdaBoost and the radial symmetry transform. The eye-region detector based on AdaBoost can efficiently avoid the interference of other facial features like nostril and mouth corner, and moreover the detector is robust to the variations of face poses and expressions; the radial symmetry transform which accurately locates the center of pupil can avoid the interference of the accessories like eyelashes and glasses frame, moreover, it is robust to the unbalanced illumination and pose changes. The experiment also demonstrates that the locating speed of the algorithm proposed here absolutely meets the requirement of a real-time eye detection system.

5 Conclusions

In order to solve the problem of locating feature points on face image under various conditions, we present a novel eye localization method, which makes full use of the special gray distribution in the eye region and the radial symmetry of pupil. The method adopts a proper AdaBoost detector to segment out the eye region based on the special gray distribution. Based on the eye region, a fast radial symmetry operator is used to precisely locate the center of pupil. Experimental results show that the method can accurately locate the pupils, and it is robust to variations of face poses, expressions, illuminations and accessories. Furthermore, the locating speed of this algorithm is fast enough to satisfy the requirement of a real-time face recognition system.

Acknowledgement

The work is supported by the Science Research Fund of MOE-Microsoft Key Laboratory of Multi-media Computing and Communication under grant No.05071811, the talent promotion program of Anhui Province under grant No.2004Z026, the Natural Science Foundation of China and Research Grant Council of Hong Kong (NSFC-RGC) Joint Research Fund under grant No.60518002 and the open foundation from Anhui Key Laboratory of Software in Computing and Communication.

References

1. Phillips, P.J., Moon, H., Rizvi, S.A., Rauss, P.J.: The feret evaluation methodology for face-recognition algorithm. IEEE Transactions on Pattern Analysis and Machine Intelligence 22, 1094–1104 (2000)
2. Viola, P., Jones, M.: Rapid object detection using a Boosted cascade of simple features. In: Proc. of IEEE Conf. on CVPR, pp. 511–518. IEEE Computer Society Press, Los Alamitos (2001)
3. Zhu, Z., Ji, Q.: Real-time eye detection and tracking under various light conditions. ACM Press, New York (2001)
4. Haro, A., Detecting, M.F.: tracking eyes by using their physiological properties, dynamics, and appearance. In: Proc. Of IEEE Conf. on CVPR, IEEE Computer Society Press, Los Alamitos (2000)
5. Kawaguchi, T., Hikada, D., Rizon, M.: Detection of the eyes from human faces by hough transform and separability filter. In: Proc. of ICIP, pp. 49–52 (2000)
6. Reisfeld, D., Wolfson, H., Yeshurun, Y.: Context free attentional operators: the generalized symmetry transform. Journal of Computer Vision (1995)
7. Baskan, S., B., M.M., Atalay, V.: Projection based method for segmentation of human face and its evaluation. Pattern Recognition Letters 23, 1623–1629 (2002)
8. Huang, J., Shao, X.H., Wechsler, H.: Pose Discrimination and Eye Detection Using Support Vector Machines. In: Proceeding of NATO-ASI on Face Recognition: From Theory to Applications (1998)
9. Yang, P., Du, B., Shan, S., Gao, W.: A Novel Pupil Lcalization Method Based on Gaboreye Model and Radial Symmetry Operator. In: IEEE ICIP'04, vol. 1, pp. 67–70 (2004)
10. Freund, Y., Schapire, R.E.: Decision-Theoretic Generali-zation of On Line Learning and an Application to Boosting. Journal of Computer and System Science 55, 119–139 (1997)

11. Viola, J.M.: Robust real time object detection. In: Viola, J.M. (ed.) The 8th IEEE International Conference on Computer Vision, Vancouver, IEEE Computer Society Press, Los Alamitos (2001)
12. Ma, Y., Ding, X., Wang, Z., Wang, N.: Robust Precise Eye Location Under Probabilistic Framework. In: Proceedings of the Sixth IEEE International Conference on Automatic Face and Gesture Recognition (2004)
13. Lindart, R., Maydr, J.: An extended set of haar-like features for rapid object detection. In: IEEE ICIP '02, vol. 1, pp. 900–903 (2002)
14. Loy, G., Zelinsky, A.: Fast Radial Symmetry for Detecting Points of Interest. IEEE Transac-tion on Pattern Analysis and Machine Intelligence 25, 959–972 (2003)
15. Gross, R.: Face Databases. In: Li, S., Jain, A. (eds.) Handbook of Face Recognition, Springer, Heidelberg (2005)
16. Tu, Z.W., Chen, X.G., Yuille, A.L., Zhu, S.C.: Image parsing: unifying segmentation, detection, and recognition. In: Proc. of ICCV (2003)

Real-Time Expression Recognition System Using Active Appearance Model and EFM

Kyoung-Sic Cho, Yong-Guk Kim, and Yang-Bok Lee

Scholl of Computer Engineering Sejong University, Seoul, Korea
nopnse@sju.ac.kr, ykim@sejong.ac.kr, yangbok@empal.com

Abstract. We present a continuous facial expression recognition system based on Active Appearance Model (AAM) and Enhanced Fisher-Discriminant Model (EFM). AAM has been widely used in face tracking, face recognition, and object recognition tasks. In this study, we have implemented an independent AAM using Inverse Compositional Image Alignment method, which is a useful for the real-time system, because of its fast performance. The evaluation of this system carried out with the standard Cohn-Kanade facial expression database.

Keywords: Active Appearance Model(AAM.), Cohn-Kanade database, Enhanced Fisher-Discriminant Model(EFM).

1 Introduction

Facial expression recognition is one of the crucial ways to infer human emotion. Facial emotions are basically categorized into six facial expressions (surprise, fear, sadness, anger, disgust, happiness). The process flow of the present system is shown in Figure 1. Facial expression images are captured from a web camera. Active appearance model includes various shape and appearance parameters. With these images, AAM instance is generated, and its emotion is classified by EFM.

We first review the AAM in section 2. Then, the process of EFM classifier is described in Section 3. The performance of the system is evaluated using Cohn-Kanade facial expression database in Section 4. Finally, we will summarize our work in Section 5.

2 Active Appearance Model

AAM is firstly proposed in [2]. Typical applications of AAM are for modeling and recognizing the faces. And yet, AAM is also effective in modeling other object. In addition, its model can be transferred to other application. AAM created once for face recognition, for example, can be useful for facial expression recognition or tracking faces [1]. The main purpose of AAM is building a new model instance by finding the best matched parameters between input images and the model with a fitting algorithm. The fitting algorithm, which is a non-linear mode, iterates itself until the parameters of both shape and appearance satisfy some particular values. For instance, when the parameter of shape is measured, we can fit an input image on the coordinate frame of

Y. Wang, Y. Cheung, and H. Liu (Eds.): CIS 2006, LNAI 4456, pp. 1078–1084, 2007.

the model. After such match, the error between the instance of the model and pixels within the shape of input image could be acquired. This error would be applied for the fitting algorithm in order to update the parameters. Iterating this process would make optimized parameters through fitting algorithm. We adopted an Inverse Compositional Image Alignment, one of fitting algorithm used this system will be illustrated in section 2.2.

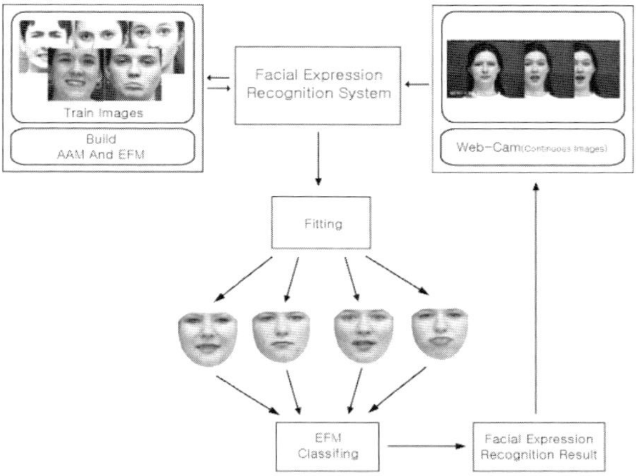

Fig. 1. Facial expression recognition system

2.1 Model Instance

Firstly, the shape of the AAM is created by combining the vectors which is made by marking on images manually.

$$\mathbf{s} = \mathbf{s}_0 + \sum_{i=1}^{n} p_i \mathbf{s}_i \tag{1}$$

In equation (1), p_i means the parameters of shape, s_0 indicates a base shape, and s_i represents shape vectors. The eigenvectors for the shape can be obtained by using Principal Component Analysis (PCA). They are the n eigenvectors corresponding to the n largest eigenvalues. Before applied PCA, AAM usually use Procrustes analysis in order to normalize Landmark points marked manually [1].

Secondly, the appearance of the AAM is defined by a pixel in a base mesh. Like the shape, appearance is also generated by the linear combination of the pixel intensity.

$$A(\mathbf{x}) = A_0(\mathbf{x}) + \sum_{i=1}^{m} \lambda_i A_i(\mathbf{x}) \tag{2}$$

λ_i indicates the appearance parameters, A_i represents the appearance vectors, and A_0 is a base appearance. After finding both the shape parameters and the appearance parameters, the AAM instance is generated by locating each pixel of appearance to the inner side of the current shape with piecewise affine warp. A model instance is indicated as equation (3).

$$M(\mathbf{W}(\mathbf{x};\mathbf{p})) = A(\mathbf{x}) \tag{3}$$

The parameters of both shape and appearance are obtained by a fitting algorithm. Figure 2 shows the process of creating the model instance.

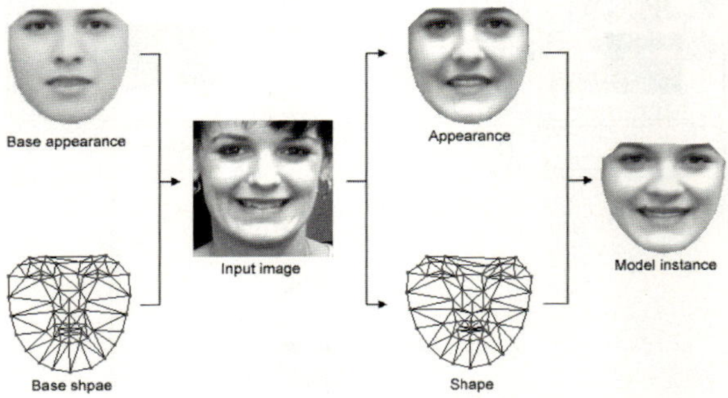

Fig. 2. Generation of an AAM instance

2.2 Inverse Compositional Image Alignment

The aim of the image alignment is to find a location of a fixed template image on an input image. Lucas and Kanade first proposed the Image Alignment Method [3]. Their algorithm is to locally align on the fixed template on an image, shown by equation (4).

$$\sum_{\mathbf{x}} \left[A_0(\mathbf{x}) - I(\mathbf{W}(\mathbf{x};\mathbf{p}))^2 \right] \tag{4}$$

The parameter p plays a role in minimizing errors between the fixed template $A_0(\mathrm{x})$ and the input image $I(\mathrm{x})$. In $\mathrm{x} = (x, y)^{\mathrm{T}}$ is the coordinator of pixel. The parameter p was linear, although $I(\mathrm{x})$ was non-linear. Thus, this formula is a non-linear optimization problem. To solve this problem linearly, Lucas-Kanade algorithm assumed that p was already known. Then, the algorithm increases the difference of p repeatedly, marked $\Delta\mathrm{p}$ in (5).

$$\sum_{\mathbf{x}} \left[A_0(\mathbf{x}) - I(\mathbf{W}(\mathbf{x};\mathbf{p}+\Delta\mathbf{p}))^2 \right] \tag{5}$$

The way of increasing p is that adding $\Delta\mathrm{p}$ to p. When changing the value of p, the performance of Lucas-Kanade algorithm is very slow because three parameters, Jacobian, gradient image, and Hessian Matrix have to be computed over and over. To improve this performance, Forwards Compositional Image Alignment method is introduced. In this algorithm, p is changed by combining the $W(x;p)$ and $W(x;\Delta p)$ as mentioned in equation (6).

$$\sum_{\mathbf{x}} \left[A_0(\mathbf{x}) - I(\mathbf{W}(\mathbf{W}(\mathbf{x};\Delta\mathbf{p});\mathbf{p}))^2 \right] \tag{6}$$

In Forwards Compositional Image Alignment method, we do not need to compute Jacobian every times, since the algorithm can compute Jacobian in $(x;0)$. In this paper, we adopt the Inverse Compositional Image Alignment method, in which we exchange the position of the input image and the template image. The ICIA can be formulated as an equation (7).

$$\sum_{\mathbf{x}} \left[I(\mathbf{W}(\mathbf{x};\mathbf{p})) - A_0(\mathbf{W}(\mathbf{x};\Delta\mathbf{p}))^2 \right] \tag{7}$$

The main advantage of this method is that the speed of updating parameters p can be very fast, since Jacobian and Gradient Image are calculated at $A_0(x)$. Once those values are acquired at the initial stage, we can use those values whenever updating a new warp parameter. Figure 3 shows three images of tracking a face using this method.

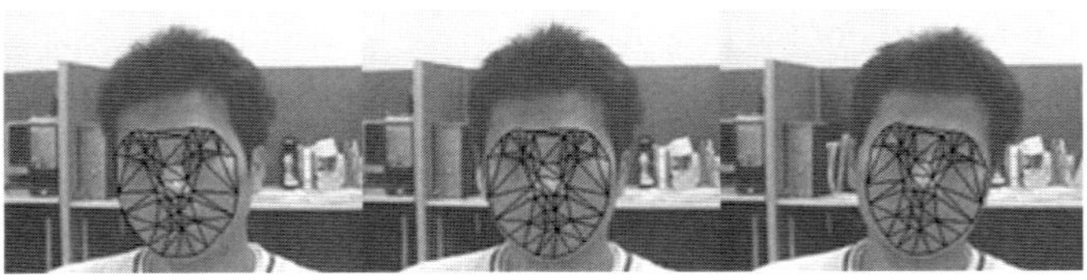

Fig. 3. Real-time face tracking using ICIA

3 EFM Algorithm

Let Y be a random vector representing the lower dimensional feature. Let $w_1, w_2, \ldots, w_L$ and $N_1, N_2, \ldots, N_L$ denote the classes and the number of images within each class, respectively. Let $M_1, M_2, \ldots, M_L$ and M be the mean of the classes and the grand mean. The within-and between-class covariance matrices Σw and Σb are defined as follows:

$$\Sigma w = \sum_{i=1}^{L} P(w_i) E\{(Y - M_i)(Y - M_i)^t \mid w_i\} \tag{8}$$

$$\Sigma b = \sum_{i=1}^{L} P(w_i)(M_i - M)(M_i - M)^t \tag{9}$$

The EFM firstly diagonalizes the within-class covariance matrix Σw.

$$\sum w\Xi = \Xi\Gamma \text{ and } \Xi'\Xi = I, \tag{10}$$

$$\Gamma^{-1/2}\Xi' \sum w\Xi\Gamma^{-1/2} = I, \tag{11}$$

where Ξ, Γ are the eigenvector and the diagonal eigenvalue matrices of $\sum w$, respectively. The EFM then proceeds to compute the between-class covariance matrix as follows:

$$\Gamma^{-1/2}\Xi' \sum b\Xi\Gamma^{-1/2} = K_b, \tag{12}$$

The EFM diagonalizes the new between-class covariance matrix K_b.

$$K_b\Theta = \Theta\Delta \text{ and } \Theta'\Theta = I, \tag{13}$$

where Θ, Δ are the eigenvector and the diagonal eigenvalue matrices of K_b, respectively. The overall transformation matrix of the EFM is finally defined as follows:

$$T = \Xi\Gamma^{-1/2}\Theta \tag{14}$$

4 Experiments and Performance

Facial expressions used, for the present study, were 4: neutral, sadness, happiness, and surprise. AAM model was established using 498 face images, and each image marked by 68 landmark points. For 54 neutral, 50 sadness, 50 happiness, and 50 surprise images, the EFM model was set up. Experiments were divided into two evaluations: one was an evaluation about how correctly each model classified images of facial expressions, and another was a test about how exactly the system analyzed sequential images including various facial expressions.

4.1 Performance Evaluation

For the performance evaluation, we employed 5 Cross Validation method, in which we took 1/5 facial expression images as a test set, and then used the rest as the EFM train set. Thus, the number of tests was five times, and each result is shown in Table 1 and 2. The result shows that the worst cases were for the neutral and sadness facial expressions. In the confusion matrix, note that the error was large between the neutral and sadness cases. It seems that it is rather difficult to distinguish between two subtle facial expressions.

Table 1. Recognition Result

	Test Image No.	Success No.	Rate(%)
Neutral	54	46	85.1
Sadness	50	41	82.0
Happiness	50	46	92.0
Surprise	50	45	90.0
Total	204	178	87.2

Table 2. Confusion Matrix

	Neutral	Sadness	Happiness	Surprise
Neutral	46	6	0	2
Sadness	8	41	0	1
Happiness	2	2	46	0
Surprise	5	0	0	45

4.2 Continuous Expression Image Analysis

Since the Cohn-Kanade database consists of sequential images of a facial expression, we are able to test our system for the continuous facial expression recognition cases using it. For instance, Figure 4 shows how the happiness expression evolves from the neutral one, in particular, between image sequence 4 and 7. Here, the horizontal axis represents the sequence number of the images, whereas the vertical axis indicates EFM distance between the facial expression ranks. After the sequence 7, the happiness expression becomes a dominant one with a large distance from the other expressions. The system can process 15 frames per second.

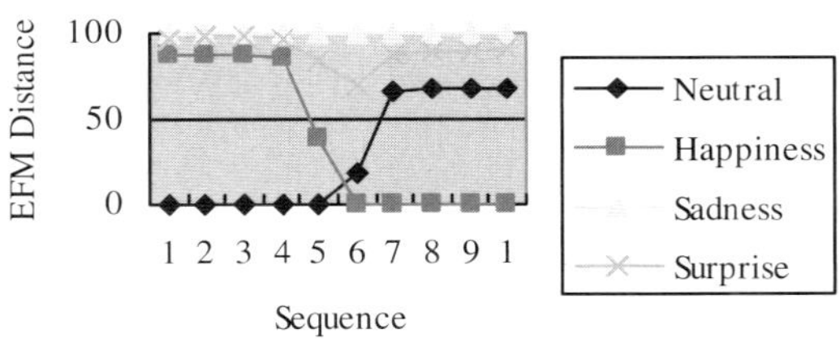

Fig. 5. Recognition of the surprise facial expression

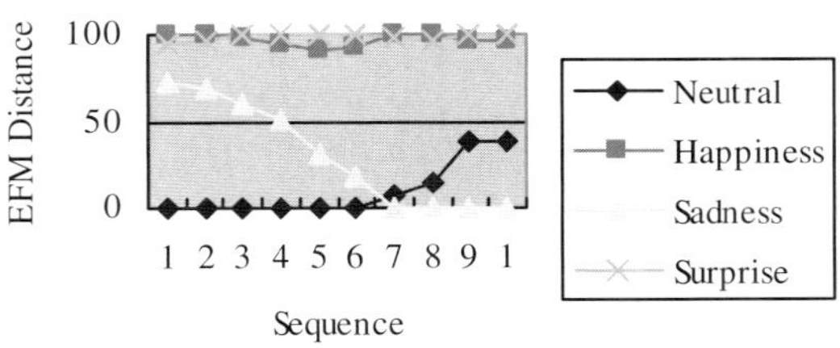

Fig. 6. Recognition of the sadness facial expression

Figure 6 shows that the sadness expression makes a distance from two expressions (happiness and surprise), as time goes by from sequence 2 to 6. And the neutral expression drifts from the bottom to upward direction. However, note that the distance between the neutral expression and the sadness one is not very far even at sequence 10, indicating that two expressions are, in a way, similar. This observation confirms the result of Table 2, in which the system appears to be confusing between two expressions.

5 Conclusions and Discussion

In this paper, we describe how real-time facial expression recognition system using AAM and EFM was implemented, and conducted two tests in order to examine the performance of the system. The result suggests that the system carried out facial expression recognition very well and it also operates in continuous facial expression recognition task. It is known that facial expression tends to accompany with head motion, we are working on a project that the head tracker is combined with the present facial expression tracker.

Acknowledgement

This work was supported by Seoul City Cluster Project.

References

1. Matthews, I., Baker, S.: Active Appearance Models revisited International Journal of Computer vision, 135–164 (2004)
2. Edwards, G.J., Taylor, C.J., Cootes, T.F.: Interpreting Face Images using Active Appearance Models. In: Proc. International Conference on Automatic Face and Gesture Recognition, pp. 300–305 (1998)
3. Lucas, B., Kanade, T.: An iterative image registration technique with an application to stereo vision. In: Proceedings of the International Joint Conference on Artificial Intelligence, pp. 674–679 (1981)

Feature Extraction Using Histogram Entropies of Euclidean Distances for Vehicle Classification

Ming Bao, Luyang Guan, Xiaodong Li, Jing Tian, and Jun Yang

Institute of Acoustics, Chinese Academy of Sciences, Beijing 100080, China
{baoming, guanluyang, lxd, tian, j_yang}@mail.ioa.ac.cn

Abstract. This paper presents a novel method for feature extraction based on the generalized entropy of the histogram formed by Euclidean distances, which is named distributive entropy of Euclidean distance (DEED in sort). DEED is a nonlinear measure for learning feature space, which provides the congregate and information measure of learning samples space. The ratio of between-class DEED to within-class DEED (J_{rd}) is used as a new nonlinear separability criterion for optimizing feature selection. Experiments on vehicle classification show that the proposed method has better performance on all the datasets than the fisher linear discriminant analysis.

1 Introduction

Feature extraction is a crucial preprocessing step for pattern recognition. It can be viewed as a process that extracts effective features from the original measurements though some functional transformations [1]. Feature extraction for classification aims to select features leading to large between-class distance and small within-class variance in the feature vector space, at the same time preserve class separability as much as possible. Various linear mapping based criteria have been proposed for evaluating the effectiveness of features [2]. Fisher linear discriminant analysis (FLDA) is a popular and powerful linear classification technique, which clusters patterns of the same class and separates patterns of different classes by maximizing the criterion function. As a measure of class separability, the Fisher criterion is defined by the ratio of the between-class variance to the within-class variance. FLDA works mostly for linearly separable classes and provides second-order statistics of data only. However, many pattern classifications are not linearly separable and features are highly nonlinear functions. Since it is difficult to capture a nonlinear relationship with a linear mapping, the basis problem is to find a proper nonlinear mapping function for the given data.

The rationale of performing a nonlinear mapping goes back to Cover's theorem on the separability of patterns, which states that a complex pattern–classification problem cast in a high-dimensional space nonlinearly is more likely to be linearly separable than in a low-dimensional space [3]. Many neural network architectures apply this idea for a linear solution obtained in the feature space [4]. Other nonlinear feature extraction approaches can be found in the Ref. [5]. In this paper, we address the feature extraction problem from an information theoretic perspective. The generalized entropies of histograms formed by Euclidean distances are employed for classification.

Y. Wang, Y. Cheung, and H. Liu (Eds.): CIS 2006, LNAI 4456, pp. 1085–1096, 2007.

The histogram entropy concept has been utilized in the image processing [6], which reflects the statistical information content of an image and hence its structure in the most general sense. A histogram of a measurement provides the basis for an empirical estimate of the probability density function. In this paper, we propose an entropy-based nonlinear mapping method for effective feature extraction. As an alternative criterion, the ratio of the between-class histogram entropy to the within-class histogram entropy is maximized to increase class separability.

The rest of this paper is organized as follows. In section 2, the distributive entropy of Euclidean distance (DEED) is defined and applied to a novel nonlinear separability criterion. Experiment results from the tracked vehicle and wheel vehicle classification problem are presented in Section 3, comparing the performance of linear and nonlinear discriminant analysis. Finally, conclusions are summarized in Section 4.

2 Distributive Entropy of Euclidean Distance

2.1 The Definition and Properties of DEED

Assume a matrix is formed by $m \times n$ dimension vectors, all vectors can be mapped to certain points in the Euclidean space. The Euclidean distances between any points can be used to compute a histogram. The Shannon entropy of this histogram is defined as distributive entropy of Euclidean distance (DEED). The value of DEED provides the uncertainty information concerning feature vectors. For a mutual classification problem, the distributive entropy of Euclidean distance between any sample and the sample mean of the same class is defined as within-class DEED (WCDEED). The distributive entropy of Euclidean distance between any sample in one class and the sample mean of other class is defined as between-class DEED (BCDEED). Theoretically, separability of features in training samples will be enhanced when the mapped points in Euclidean space are more consistently convergence to the center point. However, if the distribution of all mapped points in Euclidean space is diffusive, it should be difficult to achieve a good classification performance by using such training samples.

Shannon entropy is a strictly convex function, which reaches a maximum value when all probabilities are equal. Any approach to uniform the probability distributions will increase the entropy. Because DEED is a measure of histogram uniformity, it also shares the properties of entropy. That means the value of DEED should be large if the mapped points uniformly converge around a certain point, and the value of DEED should be small if the mapping points exhibit non-uniform convergence. Furthermore, the DEED measure can be extended to the mutual classification problem due to the additivity property of Shannon entropy. We propose DEED-based criterion function as follows:

$$J_{rd} = BCDEED / WCDEED \,. \tag{1}$$

Hence, the larger ratio of between-class DEED (BCDEED) to within class DEED (WCDEED) is, the better separability of training samples will be. Unlike FLDA, equation (1) is an efficient criterion via nonlinear mapping, because it contains high order statistical information and improves the discriminative capability. In addition, as a nonparametric method, the DEED-based algorithm provides weighting information in training procedure for further application.

2.2 DEED-Based Algorithm

Consider a matrix $W \in R^{m \times n}$ representing all the vectors in a set of $m \times n$ dimensional vectors $u_i = (x_{i,1}, x_{i,2}, \cdots x_{i,n})$, it is normalized by L_2. Let $\bar{u} = (\bar{x}_1, \bar{x}_2, \cdots \bar{x}_n)$ denote the mean of u, it is convenient to obtain the Euclidean distance between each vector and the mean vector $\bar{u}$ of W and express in terms of array δ.

$$\delta_k(u_k, \bar{u}) = (u_k - \bar{u})(u_k - \bar{u})^T, \; k = 1, 2 \cdots m. \tag{2}$$

Set $\delta_{\max} = \max(\delta)$, $\delta_{\min} = \min(\delta)$, then $\delta_k \in [\delta_{\min}, \delta_{\max}]$. Given a constant N $(N << m)$, we get:

$$\Delta\delta = (\delta_{\max} - \delta_{\min}) / N. \tag{3}$$

There are N intervals of the form Φ_i give by

$$\Phi_i = \begin{cases} [\delta_{\min} + (i-1) \times \Delta\delta, \delta_{\min} + i \times \Delta\delta] & i = 1, 2, \cdots N-1 \\ [\delta_{\min} + (N-1) \times \Delta\delta, \delta_{\max}] & i = N \end{cases}. \tag{4}$$

We have various estimates of a density function, and obtain histograms of Euclidean distances belong to each intervals of Φ_i.

If p_i is defined as the number of samples belong to interval Φ_i, the sum of p_i (i=1, 2, …, N) is m. The probability of Φ_i is derived as follows when $m \to \infty$,

$$P_i = p_i / m, \qquad i = 1, 2, \cdots, N, \tag{5}$$

and

$$\sum_{i=1}^{N} P_i = 1. \tag{6}$$

Using equations (5) and (6), we may calculate the distributive histogram of Euclidean distance, and employ it to derive the DEED,

$$E(P) = -\sum_{i=1}^{N} P_i \log_2 P_i. \tag{7}$$

Given a confidence coefficient α, we denote the maximum Euclidean distance under confidence interval as $\hat{\delta}_{\max}$, and ignore those samples out of the confidence interval. Then the modified DEED can be obtained by multiplying the $f(\hat{\delta}_{\max})$ (for simplicity, let $f(\hat{\delta}_{\max}) = \hat{\delta}_{\max}$) to the right side of equation (7),

$$\hat{E}(P) = -\hat{\delta}_{\max} \sum_{i=1}^{N} P_i \log_2 P_i \,. \tag{8}$$

The parameter $\hat{E}(P)$ contains the information of both the distribution and scatter range of mapped points in Euclidean space. We also abbreviate the name of modified distributive entropy of Euclidean distance $\hat{E}(P)$ to distributive entropy of Euclidean distance DEED for reason of convenience.

2.3 Validation in Simulation

Consider two classes of overlapping, two dimensional, Gaussian-distributed patterns labeled as 1 and 2. Let C_n denote the set of events in which a random vector X belongs to patterns labeled n. We have the conditional probability density function,

$$f_x(x/C_n) = \frac{1}{2\pi\sigma^2} \exp(-\frac{1}{2\sigma^2}\|\bar{x}-\bar{u}\|^2)\,, \tag{9}$$

where $\bar{u}$ is the mean of two dimension vectors, σ^2 is variance. In two-class problem, $n = 1,2$. Five sets of data with different separabilities can be obtained by changing the parameters $\bar{u}$ and σ^2. Assume three conditions of equal probability, the costs of correct classifications are zero, and an equal cost to all misclassifications, we determine the optimum decision boundary using the likelihood ratio test as shown in Table 1.

Table 1. Parameters of numerical simulation

	Data set 1	Data set 2	Data set 3	Data set 4	Data set 5
C_1 [1]	[(0,0); 2]	[(0,0); 1]	[(0,0); 1]	[(0,0); 1]	[(0,0); 1]
C_2 [1]	[(2,0) ; 4]	[(0,2) ; 4]	[(0,3) ; 6]	[(0,4) ; 8]	[(0,5) ; 10]
Decision boundary[2]	(-2,0); 3.68	(-0.67,0); 2.34	(-0.6,0); 2.54	(-0.57,0); 2.71	(-0.55,0); 2.86
Correct classification probability [3]	0.7428	0.8164	0.8763	0.9145	0.9385

1. The mean value and variance of Gaussian model.
2. The center and the radius of Bayesian decision boundary.
3. The average correct classification probability of 20 samples set.

The simulation results show the efficiency of J_{rd} as a separability criterion, and a large criterion value corresponds to the enhanced performance of classification.

3 Experiment Results and Discussions

In this section, we apply the separability criterion of J_{rd} to the classification of ground vehicles. The data set consists of 3250 samples of 5 types of wheeled vehicle and 4250 samples of 9 types of tracked vehicles, which is collected from four field experiments. The sampling rate is 1000 Hz, and the ground vehicles are classified by tracked and wheeled vehicles.

3.1 Various Features Extraction of Ground Vehicles

Some features of ground vehicle have been obtained by analyzing the noise signal of ground vehicles, e.g. 1) most noise energy of vehicle are spread at frequencies in the range of 0-500 Hz; 2) the tracked vehicles is distinctive from wheeled vehicle due to its stronger harmonic component; 3) there is more energy in lower frequency and the fundamental frequency varies with the status of running vehicle. These three features were adopted for the tracked and wheeled vehicle classification.

3.1.1 Non-uniform Subband Energy Feature

A filterbank with 25 bands was designed to filter the noise signal. The features were derived from energies of each band and represented by a 25-dimension vector. A second order IIR peaking filter was determined by the equation (10) [7], [8].

$$H(z) = \frac{Y(z)}{X(z)} = \frac{b_0 + b_1 \cdot z^{-1} + b_2 \cdot z^{-2}}{1 + a_1 \cdot z^{-1} + a_2 \cdot z^{-2}} \tag{10}$$

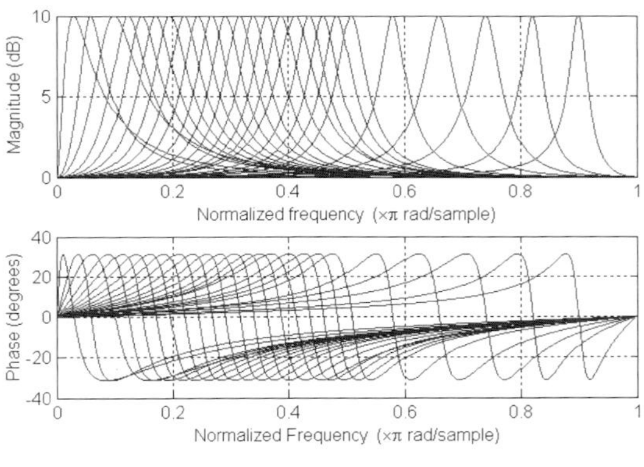

Fig. 1. Non-uniform subbands filters

The frequency and phase response of filter bank are shown in Fig. 1. Frequency bands dividing are determined by equation (11). From Fig. 1, the frequency between the 50Hz -200Hz is partitioned to 18 bands, and the frequency below 50 Hz was divided into 2 bands, while the other five bands were assigned to the frequency from 250 Hz to 500 Hz. Obviously, the frequency between 50-200 Hz was analyzed more carefully than other frequency bands.

$$\begin{cases} F_c(1) = 15 \\ F_c(2) = 30 \\ F_c(3) = 50 \\ F_c(i) = 50 + (i-2)\times 12 & 3 \le i \le 19 \\ F_c(i) = 250 + (i-19)\times 40 & 20 \le i \le 24 \end{cases} . \qquad (11)$$

3.1.2 Modified Mel Frequency Cepstral Coefficient Feature

Cepstral analysis is an effective analysis method for harmonic signal. Mel frequency cepstral coefficient (MFCC) is a feature widely used in the context of speech recognizing because it considers the hearing mechanism. The energy of recorded signal concentrate in the frequency range of 0-500 Hz, therefore we design a new nonlinear mapping function,

$$F_{smel} = 900 \times \log_{10}(1 + f_n / 300) . \qquad (12)$$

Using equation (12), we divide F_{smel} into 25 bands uniformly in the frequency range of interest. The center frequency is determined by mapping the center of each band in F_{smel} to a linear frequency. According to the center frequency in linear frequency, the triangle filter banks of modified MFCC can be designed. The relationship between F_{smel} and linear frequency are shown in Fig. 2, and the 25 triangle filters are shown in Fig. 3. The 25 dimensions features were obtained using equations (13)-(15). Similar to the hearing mechanism, the high frequency components were analyzed in a large scale and the low frequency components were analyzed in a small scale. The harmonic characteristics can be achieved by the cepstral analysis.

$$X(k) = \sum_{n=0}^{N} x(n) e^{-jwn} , \quad k = 1 : N , \qquad (13)$$

$$\hat{X}(l) = \sum_{k=0}^{N/2} | X(k) |^2 M_l(k) , \qquad (14)$$

where $M_l(k)$ corresponds to the triangle filter of the kth band.

$$c(i) = \sqrt{\frac{2}{L}} \sum_{m=1}^{i} \log_{10}(\hat{X}(l)) \cos[\frac{i\pi}{L}(m - 0.5)] , \; i = 1 \cdots L . \qquad (15)$$

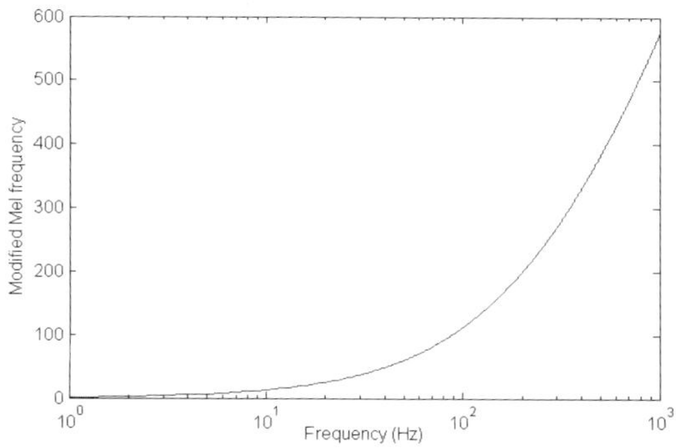

Fig. 2. Relationship of modified Mel frequency and linear frequency

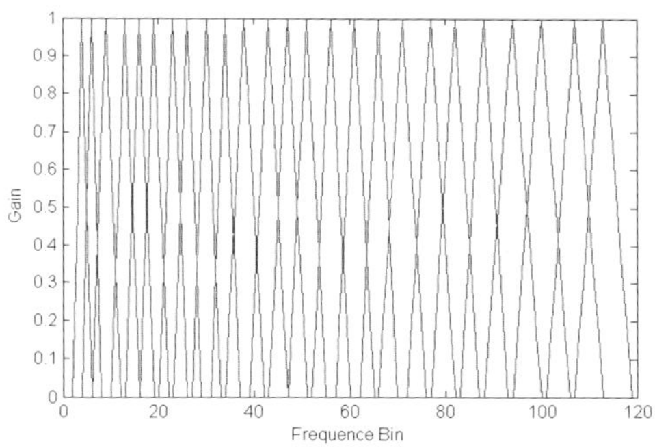

Fig. 3. Modified Mel frequency triangle filters

3.1.3 The Coefficient of Wavelet Package

The feature of wavelet package was selected by using typical wavelet kernel function 'db6'. We used 5-scale wavelet analysis of the recorded signal from vehicles and achieved 32 dimensions vector. The wavelet algorithm for features extraction is provided in the Wavelet Toolbox of Matlab.

3.2 Comparison of the Performance of Class Separability Criteria

The experiments randomly choose two third of tracked vehicle samples as training samples from database, the rest are used for test. Similarly, we obtain the training and test samples of wheeled vehicle. There are 2166 wheeled vehicle samples and 3030 tracked vehicle samples in the training set. After 20 times such selection independently, we create 20 sets of both training and test set for the classification of ground vehicles. We denote the wheel samples as 'W', and the tracked samples as 'T'.

3.2.1 Separability Estimation by the Use of Criterion J_{rd}

Distributive histogram of Euclidean distance and DEED can be calculated from the three features given in Section 3.1, and shown in Figs. 4-6 and Table 2 respectively.

The number of statistical interval is 256. From Table 2, it is seen that the best separability of feature is non-uniform subband feature, and the modified MFCC feature is inferior to the non-uniform sub-band feature. The worst feature for separating class is the wavelet package feature.

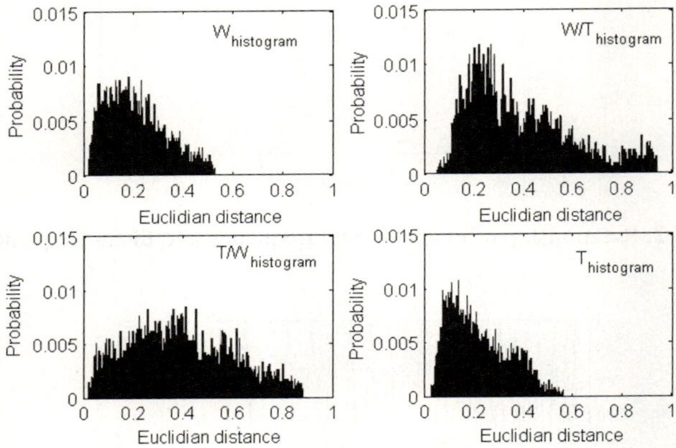

Fig. 4. Distributive histogram of Euclidean distance for the non-uniform subband filter

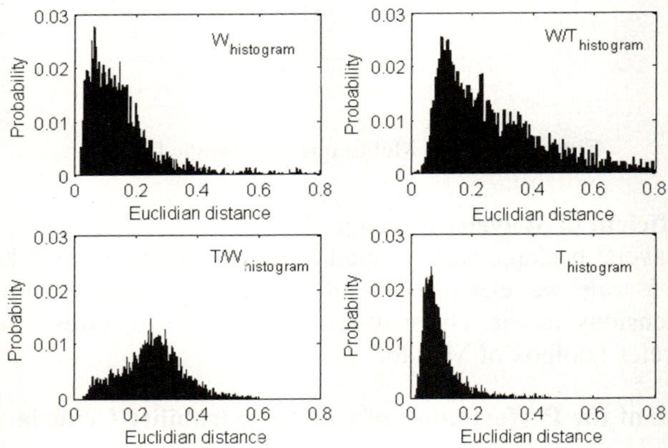

Fig. 5. Distributive histogram of Euclidean distance for the modified MFCC feature

3.2.2 Separability Estimation by the Use of Trace and Determinant Criteria

Consider the FLDA, the between-class scatter matrix S_b and within-class scatter matrix S_w are computed using the feature vectors of training samples and used in the trace criterion J_t and determinant criterion J_d defined by

$$J_t = tr(S_w^{-1} S_b)\,, \tag{16}$$

and

$$J_d = |S_w + S_b| / |S_w| \tag{17}$$

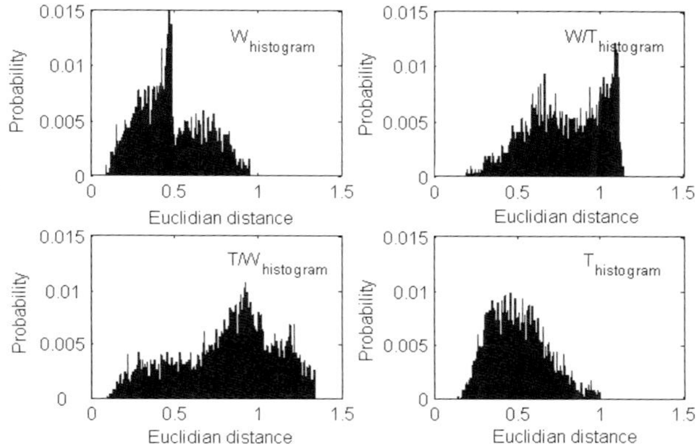

Fig. 6. Distributive histogram of Euclidean distance for the wavelet package feature

Table 2. The average DEED of three features used in experiments and criterion J_{rd}

	W	W/T	T/W	T	WT	CDEED	J_{rd}
Non-uniform subban feature	3.8082	7.3273	6.9469	3.4835	7.2917	14.2742	1.9576
Modified MFCC	4.7927	8.5399	4.1159	2.2804	7.0731	12.6558	1.7893
Wavelet package	6.2504	7.6938	9.227	6.3796	12.63	13.9442	1.1041

Note: W: WCDEED of wheeled vehicle,
T: WCDEED of tracked vehicle,
WT: sum of W and T
W/T: BCDEED by the wheeled samples to mean vector of tracked
T/W: BCDEED by the tracked samples to mean vector of wheel
CDEED: the sum of T/W and W/T

The criteria values using the three features are shown in Table 3. It is different from the observation in section 3.2.1 that modified MFCC feature is the best for the separability estimation, whereas the non-uniform subband feature is inferior one. However, the wavelet package feature is the worst one among three kinds of features. Furthermore, we employed the K-mean cluster method to analyze the separability of three features. The clustering results are also shown in Table 3. It is clear that the clustering performance using non-uniform sub-band feature is the best, modified MFCC feature is inferior while the performance using the feature of wavelet package is the worst.

Table 3. The average value of fisher criterion J_t , J_d and cluster results

	J_t	J_d	Correct clustering rate of W (%)	Correct clustering rate of T (%)	Average correct clustering rate of W and T (%)
Non-uniform sub-band feature	1.9347	2.9347	71.45	91.23	81.34
Modified MFCC	2.3569	3.5456	63.16	94.70	78.93
Wavelet package	1.7316	2.7316	70.12	87.48	78.80

3.2.3 Discussion of Three Separability Criteria

In the two-class experiments, the performances of the three separability criteria with three kinds of features are not consistent. Simulation results given in Table 3 indicate that the correct clustering rates of all tracked vehicle features are higher than those of wheeled vehicle features. It is also explained in Figs. 4-6. Take the modified MFCC feature as an example, the Euclidean distance from the feature vector of wheeled vehicle to mean vector of tracked vehicle's feature are spread in the interval of 0-0.2, which is closed to the distance distribution of tracked vehicle feature (0-0.1). That is why the misclassification rate of wheeled samples is high. In addition, the Euclidean distance from tracked vehicle feature vector to mean vector of wheeled vehicle feature are spread in the interval of 0.2-0.4, which less overlap the distance distribution of wheeled vehicle feature (0.1-0.2). It results in a good clustering performance for the tracked vehicle. We can draw a similar conclusion when considering the other two features. Hence, the distributive histogram of Euclidean distance provides a reasonable explanation for the clustering results.

3.3 Validation of the Criterion J_{rd} by the Use of Classification Algorithms

In the two-class ground vehicle classification problem, we adopted the distributive histogram of Euclidean distance and separability criterion J_{rd} . The separability estimation result shows that the non-uniform subband classification feature yields the best separability performance, the inferior one is the modified MFCC feature and the separability of wavelet is the worst. In the case of using FLDA-based J_t and J_d, the modified MFCC feature exhibits the best separability and the non-uniform subband feature is inferior to the modified MFCC feature. The wavelet package is the worst one in terms of separability. However, we have the same observation from cluster analysis as the estimation method using J_{rd}. Next, we will validate it by using three supervised classifiers.

The experiments choose 20 independent training sets for each feature. The first classifier is K nearest neighbor (KNN) classifier. Let $k = 3$ and the number of reference samples be that of training samples. The second one is a three-layer back- propagation (BP) neural network with 25 input nodes, 12 hide layers and 2 output nodes. The third one is a support vector machine (SVM) classifier. The kernel function of SVM is a radial basis function (RBF). Classification results are shown in the table 4.

It is observed from Table 4 that, in the case of using KNN classifier the classification performance of modified MFCC feature is the best, non-uniform subband feature is inferior, and the wavelet package feature is the worst one. This result is the same as the separability estimation result using FLDA-based criteria. Secondly, in the case of using SVM and BP algorithms, the non-uniform subband feature exhibits the best classification performance. The modified MFCC feature yields inferior performance and the wavelet package feature is the worst one for classification. This result is consistent with the separability estimation using the new criterion J_{rd}.

Table 4. Classification results of three kinds classifier

	Correct classification probability of wheeled vehicle (%)			Correct classification probability of tracked vehicle (%)			Average correct classification probability of wheeled and tracked vehicles (%) [1]		
	KNN	SVM	BP	KNN	SVM	BP	KNN	SVM	BP
Non-uniform subband feature	95.7	97.20	97.30	96.90	98.90	97.00	96.30	98.05	97.15
Modified MFCC	96.5	96.60	94.20	96.80	98.00	95.70	96.65	97.30	94.95
Wavelet package	93.4	95.10	96.18	92.20	96.20	88.39	92.80	96.65	92.29

[1] The classification results of KNN classifier accord well with those using J_t and J_d, whereas the classification results from BP and SVM algorithms accord well with those using J_{rd}

Experiment results show that the Fisher linear criteria J_t and J_d are suitable to use with KNN classifier as explained in Ref. [2]. The proposed criterion J_{rd} is suitable to use in the BP and SVM classification experiments. The separability criterion J_{rd} is a nonlinear parameter based on the DEED analysis, which preserves most classification information after the feature has been transformed to the high dimension space.

4 Conclusion

In this paper, we have considered the use of a new optimization criterion based on the histogram entropy of Euclidean distance for classification. A nonlinear parameter DEED is defined for pattern classification. With help of the DEEE, a criterion function J_{rd} for feature extraction can be set up. It has been shown that the larger J_{rd} (ratio of between-class DEED to within-class DEED) is, the better separability of learning samples will be. Because the entropy is an invariant for the nonlinear transform, the DEED is able to preserve most classification information.

Experiment results show that the proposed criterion can improve the classification performance of the extracted features compared to other linear Fisher criteria used in pattern recognition. The DEED-based separability estimation criterion is better than FDLA in the case of using neural network classifier. It should be noted that DEED is an information measure of distributive histogram of Euclidean distance, which provides more information for further study on dynamic learning theory. Still more research about separability criterion as well as improved methods for an optimal feature extraction are necessary.

References

1. Fukunaga, K.: Introduction to statistical pattern recognition, 2nd edn. Academic Press, Boston (1990)
2. Duda, R.O., Hart, P.E., Stork, D.G.: Pattern Classification, 2nd edn. Wiley, New York (2000)
3. Covet, T.M.: Geometrical and statistical properties of systems of linear inequalities with applications to pattern recognition. IEEE Trans. Electronic Computers 14, 326–334 (1965)
4. Haykin, S.: Neural Networks: A comprehensive foundation, 2nd edn. Prentice-Hall, Englewood Cliffs (1999)
5. Vapnik, V.N.: The Nature of Statistical Learning Theory. Springer, Berlin (1995)
6. Moore, C.J.: Medical image processing: the characterization of display changes using histogram entropy. Image Vision Computing 4, 197–202 (1986)
7. Robert, B.J.: The Equivalence of Various Methods of Computing Biquad Coefficients for Audio Parametric Equalizers. Wave Mechanics, Inc, Burlington VT, http://www.wavemechanics.com
8. White, S.A.: Design of a Digital Biquadratic Peaking or Notch Filter for Digital Audio Equalization. J. Audio Eng. Soc. 34, 479–483 (1986)

Full-Space LDA With Evolutionary Selection for Face Recognition

Xin Li, Bin Li, Hong Chen, Xianji Wang, and Zhengquan Zhuang

MOE-Microsoft Key Laboratory of Multimedia Computing and Communication, University of Science and Technology of China, 230027 HeFei, China
{simonlee, hongchen,xjw}@mail.ustc.edu.cn,
binli@ustc.edu.cn

Abstract. Linear Discriminant Analysis (LDA) is a popular feature extraction technique for face recognition. However, it often suffers from the small sample size problem when dealing with the high dimensional face data. Some approaches have been proposed to overcome this problem, but they usually utilize all eigenvectors of null or range subspaces of within-class scatter matrix(S_w). However, experimental results testified that not all the eigenvectors in the full space of are positive to the classification performance, some of which might be negative. As far as we know, there have been no effective ways to determine which eigenvectors in full space should be adopted. This paper proposes a new method EDA+Full-space LDA, which takes full advantage of the discriminative information of the null and range subspaces of by selecting an optimal subset of eignvectors. An Estimation of Distribution Algorithm (EDA) is used to pursuit a subset of eigenvectors with significant discriminative information in full space of . EDA+Full-space LDA is tested on ORL face image database. Experimental results show that our method outperforms other LDA methods.

1 Introduction

Linear Discriminant Analysis (LDA)[1] is a well-known scheme for feature extraction and dimension reduction. It has been used widely in many applications such as face recognition, image retrieval, etc. The basic idea of LDA is to find a set of projection vectors maximizing the between-class scatter matrix (S_b) while minimizing the within-class scatter matrix (S_w) in the projected feature subspace. A major drawback of LDA is that it often suffers from the small sample size (S3) problem when dealing with the high dimensional face data. When there are not enough training samples, $S_w$would be singular, and it would be difficult to compute the LDA vectors.

In recent years, direct linear discriminant analysis (DLDA)[2] and null-space linear discriminant analysis (NLDA)[3] have been proposed to overcome the S3 problem in the face recognition. DLDA discards the null space of S_b , since the rank of S_b is smaller than of S_w , that might lose some information of null space of S_w . NLDA extracts discriminant information from the null space of S_w , however, when the number of training sample is large, the null space of S_w becomes

Y. Wang, Y. Cheung, and H. Liu (Eds.): CIS 2006, LNAI 4456, pp. 1097–1105, 2007.

small, and much discriminative information outside this null space will be lost. Both DLDA and NLDA may lose some discriminative information. In order to solve the S3 problem and still preserve all discriminative information, Optimal Fisher Linear Discriminant Algorithm (OFLDA) [4] and Dual-space LDA [5] are proposed to simultaneously apply discriminant analysis in the range and null subspaces of respectively, here called Full-space LDA. A common drawback of Full-space LDA is that they use all eigenvector in the range and null subspaces of S_w . They assume that keeping all eigenvector means keeping all of the discriminative information that can improve the classification accuracy efficiently. However, from the pattern classification point of view, this assumption may not incorrect. The main reason is that not all the eigenvectors in the full space of S_w are positive to the classification performance, some of which may be passive to classification. Therefore, choosing all eigenvector of the range and null subspaces of S_w as the bases for LDA may not be optimal. As far as we known, there is no systematic way to determine which eigenvectors should be used.

Along this line, this paper focuses on the Full-space LDA as mentioned and proposes a Full-space LDA with evolutionary selection. EDA is used to pursuit a subset of eigenvectors with significant discriminative information in full subspaces of S_w . Compared with Full-Space LDA, the proposed method can effectively eliminate less discriminatory eigenvectors and improve classification accuracy. The experiments on ORL face database clearly demonstrate its efficacy.

The rest of the paper is organized as follows: Section 2 provides the background on LDA and Full-space LDA. Section 3 describes the details of EDAFull-space LDA. Experimental results are reported in Section 4. Finally, we draw the conclusion in Section 5.

2 Background of LDA and Full-Space LDA

2.1 LDA

Let the training set contains C classes and each class X_i has n_i samples, x_k is a sample belonging to class X_i , m_i is the center of class X_i , m is the center of the whole training set. and are defined as Eq. (1) and Eq. (2),

$$S_w = \sum_{i=1}^{C} \sum_{k=C_i} (x_k - m_i)(x_k - m_i)^T \tag{1}$$

$$S_b = \sum_{i=1}^{C} n_i (m_i - m)(m_i - m)^T \tag{2}$$

The total-class scatter matrix is defined as Eq. (3)

$$S_t = S_b + S_w = \sum_{i=1}^{N} (x_k - m)(x_k - m)^T \tag{3}$$

LDA method tries to find a set of projection vectors $W_{opt} = (w_1, w_2, \ldots, w_L)$ that maximizes the ratio of the absolute value of the between-class scatter matrix to the absolute value of the within-class scatter matrix (Fisher's criterion), as defined in Eq. (4).

$$J(W_{opt}) = argmax_w \left| \frac{W^T S_b W}{W^T S_w W} \right| \tag{4}$$

If S_w is not singular, $w_1, w_2, \ldots, w_L$ are the eigenvectors of $S_w^{-1} S_b$, corresponding to $L(\leq C-1)$ largest eigenvalues. However, when the small sample size problem occurs, S_w becomes singular and the inverse of S_w does not exist. To avoid the singularity of S_w , Fisherface[6] , DLDA and NLDA is usually adopted. A common problem with all these LDA approaches is that they all prone to lose some discriminative information in the high dimensional face space. Full-space LDA (OFLDA and Dual-space LDA) is proposed to simultaneously apply discriminant analysis in the range and null subspaces of S_w in order to preserve the all discriminative information, the experimental results show that full-space LDA outperforms the other LDAs[7].

2.2 Full-Space LDA

Let R^d be the original sample space, V be the range subspace of , and $V^{\perp}$ be the null subspace of S_w . That is

$$V = span\{\alpha_k | S_w \alpha_k \neq 0, k = 1, 2, \ldots, r\} \tag{5}$$

$$V^{\perp} = span\{\alpha_k | S_w \alpha_k = 0, k = r+1, \ldots, d\} \tag{6}$$

Where $r(< d)$ is the rank of S_w , is an orthonormal set, and is the set of orhtonormal eigenvectors corresponding to the nonzero eigenvalues of S_w.

From the range and null subspaces of S_w , the LDA projection vectors can be computed according to different criterions, respectively.

$$\begin{cases} J_{range}(W_{ropt}) = argmax_w \left| \frac{W_r^T S_b W_r}{W_r^T S_w W_r} \right| \\ W_r^T S_w W_r > 0 \end{cases} \tag{7}$$

$$\begin{cases} J_{null}(W_{nopt}) = argmax_w \left| \frac{W_n^T S_b W_n}{W_n^T S_w W_n} \right| \\ W_n^T S_w W_n = 0 \end{cases} \tag{8}$$

This is to say, we intend to find the discrinimant vectors of the range subspace of based on the Fisher criterion and utilize$J_{null}(W_{nopt})$ to get those of the null subspace of S_w. The two sets of discriminative features are combined for recognition.

2.3 Analysis on Full-Space LDA

Full-space LDA uses all eigenvectors in the range and null subspaces of S_w . It assumes that keeping all eigenvectors means keeping all of the discriminative information that can improve the classification accuracy efficiently. However, experimental results show that this is not definitely right. The main reason probably is that not all the eigenvectors in the full space of S_w are positive to the classification performance, some of which may be negative to classification. So simply using all the eigenvectors is not optimal from the point of view of pattern classification.

The ORL database with 40 persons (three training images/person and two test images/person) is used to perform an experiment as an example. Fig.1 plots accuracy rates with the different number of eigenvectors in full space of S_w , the eigenvectors of the null subspace of S_w are all selected. When the number of eigenvector in range subspace increases to 51, the accuracy reaches the 96.25%. However, when the eigenvectors are all selected, the rate is just 91.25%. This intuitive observation indicates that some eigenvectors might be negative to classification accuracy. Therefore, a strategy for selecting the eigenvectors with significant discriminative information in full space of within-class scatter matrix is required.

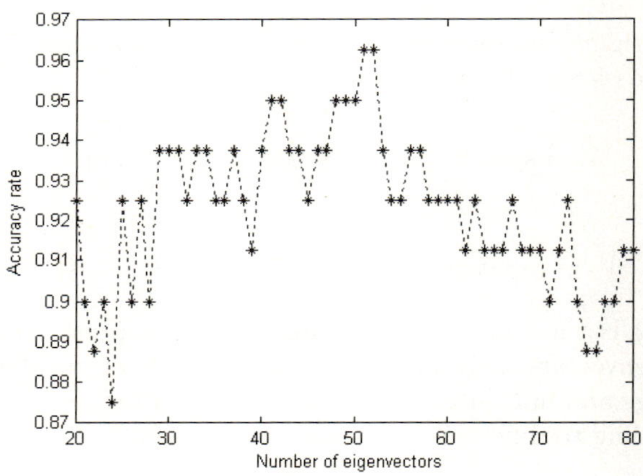

Fig. 1. Accuracy rate with the different number of eigenvectors in full space of S_w , when the eigenvectors of null subspace of S_w are all selected

3 EDA + Full-Space LDA

As discussed in the previous section, we need to find the subset of eigenvectors with significant discriminative information in full space of S_w . In this section a new algorithm is proposed, which adopts Estimation of Distribution Algorithms [8] and establishes the optimal subset of eigenvectors through evolutionary selection.

EDAs emerged as a new form of evolutionary computation during the last decade. The basic idea of EDAs is to build a probabilistic model from the parental distribution in the parameter space and to generate offspring individuals by sampling from the model. The use of EDA for selecting subset of features was reported to yield speed-up in time with respect to the traditional wrapper methods for feature selection [9]. Since eigenvectors of full space of S_w are independent to each other, we adopt here the Univariate Marginal Distribution Algorithm (UMDA, [10]) to perform feature selection, which is a simple EDA based on the assumption that all variables are independent. The main scheme of the UMDA approach is shown in Figure 2.

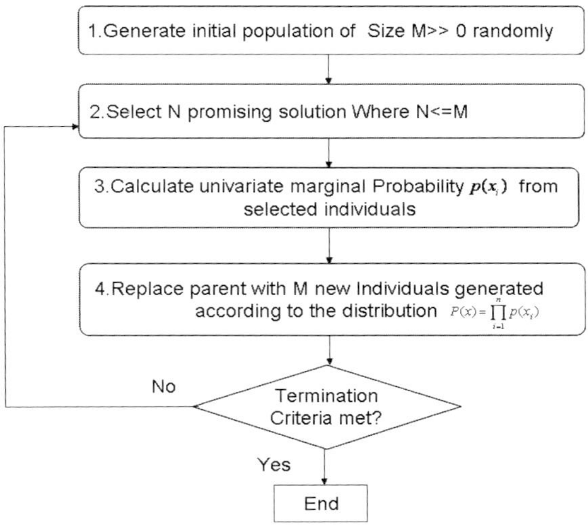

Fig. 2. Schematic overview of the UMDA algorithm

3.1 Chromosome Representation

We use binary string to represent the composition of optimal feature subset. Each bit $g_i (i = 1, 2, \ldots, l)$ is corresponding to an eigenvector, that means: if $g_i = 1$, the ith eigenvector is selected into the optimal subset, otherwise, it is not selected. The length of chromosome is set to be l according to the number of all eigenvectors in the full space of S_w . A chromosome represents a solution of feature selection problem.

3.2 Fitness Function

Fitness function plays a crucial role in choosing offspring for the next generation from the current generation. It guides the direction of the evolution. In this paper, the fitness function is defined as Eq.(9) :

$$fitness = \mu F(R) + \lambda F_{range}(G) + F_{null}(G) \tag{9}$$

Where $F(R)$ is the performance accuracy term in tuning set, $F_{range}(G)$ and $F_{null}(G)$ are the generalization terms which aim to select eigenvectors that have better generalization at the testing set. Here $F_{range}(G)$ and $F_{null}(G)$ are defined as Eq.(10) and Eq.(11),

$$F_{range}(G) = min(D_{rb})/max(D_{rw}) \tag{10}$$

$$F_{null}(G) = min(D_{nb})/max(D_{nw}) \tag{11}$$

Where D_{rb} and D_{rw} are the distance of between-class and within-class in the range subspace of S_w , respectively. D_{nb} and D_{nw} are the distance of between-class and within-class in the null subspace of S_w , respectively. μ and λ are empirically chosen to represent contribution of three terms to the fitness. By combining those two terms together(with proper weight μ and λ), EDA can evolve balanced results displaying good performance on both turning and testing set.

3.3 EDA+ Full Space LDA

The EDA+ Full-space LDA algorithm can be described as follows:

i. A m-dimensional PCA subspace is constructed first, and all samples are mapped into this subspace, calculate the within-class and between-class scatter matrices $S_w^{'}$ and $S_b^{'}$.

ii. Calculate the eigenvector matrix $P = (\alpha_1, \ldots, \alpha_q, \ldots, \alpha_m)$ of $S_w^{'}$ .Suppose the first q eigenvectors of correspond to its non-zeros eigenvalues. UMDA is performed to pursuit a subset of eigenvectors with significant discriminant information in full space of within-class scatter matrix on tuning set.

Step 1 : A projection matrix P_1 is formed by the eigenvectors selected by the UMDA in the range subspace of $S_w^{'}$. Define $\hat{S_b} = P_1^T S_b^{'} P_1$ and $\hat{S_w} = P_1^T S_w^{'} P_1$, the transformation matrix U_1 is then constructed by the eigenvectors corresponding to the largest eigenvalues of $\hat{S_w}^{-1} \hat{S_b}$. The first set of discriminant vectors are given by $W_1 = U_1 P_1$.

Step 2: A second projection matrix P_2 is formed by the eigenvectors selected by the UMDA in the null subspace of $S_w^{'}$. Define $\tilde{S_b} = P_2^T S_b^{'} P_2$, the transformation matrix U_2 is then constructed by the eigenvectors corresponding to the largest eigenvalues of $\tilde{S_b}$. The second set of discriminant vectors are given by $W_2 = U_2 P_2$.

Step 3: Fuse the two kinds of features given by W_1 and W_2 using normalized-distance for classification.

Step 4: Calculate fitness function on tuning set; select a number of individuals; estimate probability model; generate the new population by sampling the estimated model.

An iterative procedure repeating step 1,2,3 and 4 is carried out until a termination criterion is met.

iii Let $W_{opt1}^T = W_1^T W_{pca}^T$ and $W_{opt2}^T = W_2^T W_{pca}^T$. Then W_{opt1} and W_{opt2} are the optimal projections of EDA+Full-space LDA .

4 Experiment

In this section, we apply our method to face recognition and compare it with the existing variant LDA methods such as Fisherface, NLDA, DLDA and Full-space LDA approaches. The proposed method is tested on ORL face database, which contains 40 people, each person has 10 different images. The images of the same person are taken at different times, under slightly varying lighting conditions and with various facial expressions. The images in the database are grayscale and the size are rescaled to be 92×112. Figure 3 show ten images of one person in ORL.

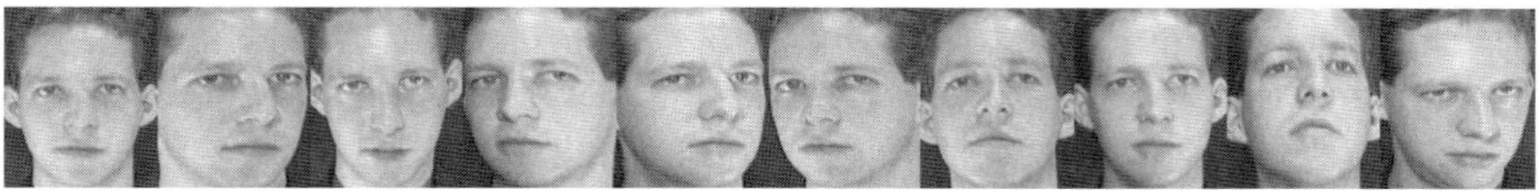

Fig. 3. Ten images of one person in ORL face database

In this experiment, the ORL face database is broken into three disjoint sets: training, tuning and testing. The tuning set is used to provide tuning feedback to the UMDA, to select a subset of eigenvectors with significant discriminant information in full space of within-class scatter matrix by UMDA, as described previously in section 3.2. Once the UMDA run was finished(the optimal subset of eigenvectors are selected), the test set was used to perform unbiased testing on the subset found by UMDA. For every person, we use the first three images for training, the 4,5 images for turning and the remaining five for testing. A 1-NN(Nearest Neighbor) classifier is adopted. The parameters of UMDA used in this experiment are set as follows: population size is 500; the maximum number of generation is 30; the number of the selected promising solution is 200.The recognition results are shown in table 1.

Table 1 shows the comparative tuning and testing performance of Fisherface, DLDA, NLDA, Full-space LDA and EDA+Full-space LDA. One can see that EDA+Full-space LDA outperforms the other LDA methods. The optimal number of eigenvectors be selected in the range and null subspace of S_w is presented in Table 2.

Table 1. Comparison of recognition result with Fisherface, DLDA, NLDA, Full-space LDA and proposed method on ORL

Method	Number of features	Recognition performance	
		Turning set	Testing set
Fisherface	39	0.875	0.815
NLDA	39	0.9	0.835
DLDA	39	0.875	0.795
Full-space LDA	78	0.9125	0.85
EDA+Full-space LDA	59	0.9875	0.955

Table 2. Comparison of number of eigenvec-tors in ranger and null subspace of S_w with Full-space LDA and proposed method

Method	Number of eigenvectors in ranger subspace	Number of eigenvector in null subspace
Full-space LDA	80	39
EDA+Full-space LDA	35	24

From Fig.4(a) , by comparing the accuracy with Full-space LDA, the effectiveness of EDA+Full-space LDA can be seen. By employing the EDA to select eigenvectors in the full subspace of , EDA+Full-space LDA can increase the accuracy rate from 85% to 95.5% at rank 1. Fig.4.(b) show Rank-1 accuracy rates with the different number of features. It can be seen that the recognition rate is close before the null subspace eigenvectors are utilized. It indicates that the recognition rate of the proposed method does not decrease even though the number of eigenvectors of S_w is less than the number of Full-space LDA. After the eigenvectors in null-space are considered, the accuracy rate of EDA+Full-space LDA increases obviously.

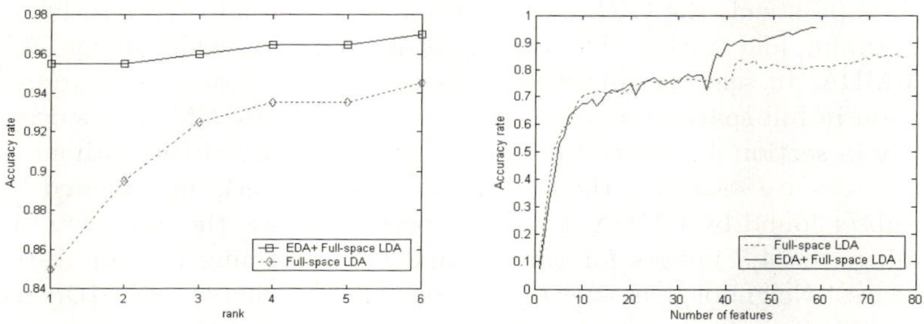

(a) (b)

Fig. 4. (a)Cumulative accuracy rates and (b)Rank-1 accuracy rates with the different number of features of Full-space LDA and EDA+Full-space LDA on ORL face database

5 Conclusions

In this paper, a EDA+full-space LDA approach for the eigenvectors selection in the full space of is proposed. EDA is used to pursuit a subset of eigenvectors with significant discriminative information. EDA+Full-space LDA is tested on ORL face image database. Experimental results demonstrate that our method is better than others LDA methods. In future research, we will investigate other more effective definition of fitness function for feature selection.

Acknowledgments

The work is partially supported by the Natural Science Foundation of China (NSFC) under grand No.60401015, the Natural Science Foundation of Anhui province under grand No. 050420201, and the Science Research Fund of MOE-Microsoft Key Laboratory of Multimedia Computing and Communication under grant No.05071811.The Natural Science Foundation of China and Research Grant Council of Hong Kong (NSFC-RGC) Joint Research Fund under grant No.60518002

References

1. Fukunaga, K.: Introduction to statistical pattern recognition, 2nd edn. Academic Press, Boston (1990)
2. Yu, H., Yang, J.: A direct lda algorithm for high-dimensional data with application to face recognition. Pattern Recognition 34(10), 2067–2070 (2001)
3. Chen, L., Liao, H., Ko, M., Lin, J., Yu, G.: A new lda-based face recognition system which can solve the samll sample size problem. Pattern Recognition 33(10), 1713–1726 (2000)
4. Yang, J., Yang, J.: Optimal FLD algorithm for facial feature extraction. SPIE Proceedings of the Intelligent Robots and Computer Vision XX: Algorithms,Techniques, and Active Vision 4572, 438–444 (2001)
5. Wang, X., Tang, X.: Dual-space Linear Discrminant Analysis for Face Recognition. In: Proceeding of Computer Vision and Pattern Recognition, vol. 2, pp. 564–569 (2004)
6. Belhumeur, P.N., Hespanha, J., Kriegman, D.J.: Eigenfaces vs. fisherfaces: Recognition using class specific linear projection. IEEE Transactions on Pattern Analysis and Machine Intelligence 19(7), 711–720 (1997)
7. Thomaz, C.E., Gillies, D.F.: A Maximum Uncertainty LDA-Based Approach for Limited Sample Size Problems - With Application to Face Recognition. In: Proceeding of Computer Graphics and Image Processing. SIBGRAPI'05, pp. 89–96. IEEE CS Press, New York (2005)
8. Larranaga, P., Lozano, J.A.: Estimation of Distribution Algorithms: A New Tool for Evolutionary Computation. Kluwer Academic Publishers, New York (2001)
9. Saeys, Y., Degroeve, S., Aeyels, D., Van de Peer, Y., Rouz, P.: Fast feature selection using a simple Estimation of Distribution Algorithm: A case study on splice site prediction. Bioinformatics 19, II179–II188 (2003)
10. Muhlenbein, H.: The equation for response to selection and its use for prediction. Evolutionary Computation 5, 303–346 (1997)

Subspace KDA Algorithm for Non-linear Feature Extraction in Face Identification

Wen-Sheng Chen[1], Pong C. Yuen[2], and Jian-Huang Lai[3]

[1] College of Mathematics and Computational Science, Shenzhen University, China, 518060
chenws@szu.edu.cn
[2] Department of Computer Science, Hong Kong Baptist University, Hong Kong, China
pcyuen@comp.hkbu.edu.hk
[3] Department of Electronics & Communication Engineering, Sun Yat-Sen University, Guangzhou, China, 510275
stsljh@mail.sysu.edu.cn

Abstract. Kernel discriminant analysis (KDA) method is a promising approach for non-linear feature extraction in face identification tasks. However, as a linear algorithm to address nonlinear problem, Fisher discriminant analysis (FDA) approach will not give a satisfactory performance. Moreover, FDA usually suffers from small sample size (S3) problem. To overcome these two shortcomings in FDA method, Shannon wavelet kernel based subspace FDA (SKDA) algorithm is developed in this paper. Two public databases such as FERET and CMU PIE databases are selected for evaluation. Comparing with the existing kernel based FDA-based methods, the proposed method gives superior results.

Keywords: Face identification, Kernel discriminant analysis, Shannon wavelet.

1 Introduction

Over the past decade, Fisher discriminant analysis [1] method has been shown to be an effective approach in face identification tasks and its superior performance has been reported in many literatures [1]-[11] . FDA is theoretically sound and its objective is to find the most discriminant feature for pattern classification. However, there are two major limitations upon FDA approach. First, it is a linear method and is hard to solve nonlinear problem, while the second is the small sample size (S3) problem, which always occurs when the sample size is smaller than the dimensionality of feature vector.

KDA is a useful approach to deal with nonlinear problem. The basic idea of KDA is to apply a nonlinear mapping $\Phi : x \in R^d \rightarrow \Phi(x) \in F$ to the input data vector x in input space R^d and then to perform the FDA on the mapped

Y. Wang, Y. Cheung, and H. Liu (Eds.): CIS 2006, LNAI 4456, pp. 1106–1114, 2007.

higher dimension feature space F. The feature space F could be considered as a linearization space. By utilizing kernel trick, the inner products $\langle \Phi(x_i), \Phi(x_j) \rangle$ in F can be replaced with a Mercer kernel function $K(x_i, x_j)$, i.e. $K(x_i, x_j) = \langle \Phi(x_i), \Phi(x_j) \rangle = \Phi(x_i)^T \cdot \Phi(x_j)$, where x_i, x_j are input pattern column vectors in input space R^d. So the nonlinear mapping Φ can be performed implicitly in input space R^d. This paper exploits Shannon wavelet kernel method [9] to address the nonlinear problems such as pose and illumination variations in face identification, while subspace FDA (SFDA) algorithm [6] will be used to solve S3 problem.

Therefore, combining Shannon wavelet kernel with subspace FDA method, we design and develop a novel Shannon wavelet kernel-based subspace FDA algorithm (SKDA) in this paper. Two public databases such as FERET and CMU PIE databases are selected for evaluation. Comparing with the existing kernel based FDA-based methods, the proposed method gives the best performance.

The rest of this paper is organized as follows. Section 2 briefly describes the Shannon wavelet based Mercer kernel function. The proposed SKDA algorithm is developed and evaluated in section 3 and section 4 respectively. Finally, Section 5 draws the conclusions.

2 Mercer Kernel Function Based on Shannon Wavelet

This section briefly reviews on Shannon wavelet based Mercer kernel function. Details can be found in paper [9].

Assume

$$\cdots \subset V_{-2} \subset V_{-1} \subset V_0 \subset V_1 \subset V_2 \subset \cdots$$

is the multiresolution analysis (MRA) [12,13] generated by the Shannon sampling function $\phi(x) = \text{sinc}(x) := \frac{\sin \pi x}{\pi x}$. Thus the scaling subspaces

$$V_j = \{f \in L^2(R) | \text{supp} \hat{f} \subset [-2^j \pi, 2^j \pi]\}$$

and the corresponding wavelet subspaces $\{W_j\}_{j \in Z}$, where $W_j \perp V_j$ and $W_j \oplus V_j = V_{j+1}$, can be generated by the Shannon wavelet:

$$\psi(x) := 2\text{sinc}(2x) - \text{sinc}(x), \tag{1}$$

whose Fourier transform is given by $\hat{\psi}(\xi) = \chi_{[-2\pi,-\pi] \cup [\pi,2\pi]}(\xi)$, where $\chi(x)$ is an indicator function. Let $H(\xi)$ and $G(\xi)$ be the 2π-periodic functions respectively as:

$$H(\xi) = \begin{cases} 1, & \xi \in [-\frac{\pi}{2}, \frac{\pi}{2}) \\ 0, & \xi \in [-\pi, -\frac{\pi}{2}) \cup [\frac{\pi}{2}, \pi) \end{cases} \text{ and } G(\xi) = H(\xi + \pi).$$

Then, we have

$$\hat{\phi}(\xi) = H(\xi/2)\hat{\phi}(\xi/2), \quad \hat{\psi}(\xi) = G(\xi/2)\hat{\phi}(\xi/2).$$

It is easy to see that $\phi(x)$ is an orthonormal scaling function and $\psi(x)$ is an orthonormal wavelet.

The necessary and sufficient condition for a translation invariant function $k(x, y) = k(x - y)$ to be a Mercer kernel is that its Fourier transform is non-negative. Under this consideration, the Shannon wavelet Mercer kernel $k(x, y)$ defined on $R^d \times R^d$ can be constructed as follows:

$$k(x, y) = \frac{1}{d}\sum_{i=1}^{d}[\psi((x_i - y_i)/\theta_i)]^p, \tag{2}$$

where $\psi(x)$ is Shannon wavelet function defined in (1), $x = (x_1, \cdots, x_d)^T, y = (y_1, \cdots, y_d)^T \in R^d$, $p \in Z^+$ and $\theta_i > 0\, (i = 1, \cdots, d)$ are kernel parameters.

3 Proposed SKDA Algorithm

This section reports Shannon wavelet kernel based subspace FDA method for face identification. Details are discussed as follows.

3.1 Some Notations

Let d and C be the dimensionality of original sample feature space and the number of sample classes respectively. The total original samples $X = \{X_1, X_2, \cdots, X_C\}$, the jth class X_j contains N_j samples, namely $X_j = \{x_1^j, x_2^j, \cdots, x_{N_j}^j\}$, $j = 1, 2, \cdots, C$. Let N be the total number of original training samples, then $N = \sum_{j=1}^{C} N_j$. If $\Phi(x)$: $x \in R^d \rightarrow \Phi(x) \in F$ is the kernel nonlinear mapping, where F is the mapped feature space, denote $df = \dim F$, the total mapped sample set and the jth mapped class are given by $\Phi(X) = \{\Phi(X_1), \Phi(X_2), \cdots, \Phi(X_C)\}$ and $\Phi(X_j) = \{\Phi(x_1^j), \Phi(x_2^j), \cdots, \Phi(x_{N_j}^j)\}$ respectively. Also, the mean of the mapped sample class $\Phi(X_j)$ and the global mean of the total mapped sample $\Phi(X)$ are given by $m_j = \frac{1}{N_j}\sum_{x\in X_j}\Phi(x)$ and $m = \frac{1}{N}\sum_{j=1}^{C}\sum_{x\in X_j}\Phi(x)$ respectively. In feature space F, the within-class scatter matrix S_w^Φ, between-class scatter matrix S_b^Φ and total scatter matrix S_t^Φ are defined respectively as:

$$S_w^\Phi = \frac{1}{N}\sum_{j=1}^{C}\sum_{x\in X_j}(\Phi(x) - m_j)(\Phi(x) - m_j)^T = \Phi_w\Phi_w^T,$$

$$S_b^\Phi = \frac{1}{N}\sum_{j=1}^{C} N_j(m_j - m)(m_j - m)^T = \Phi_b\Phi_b^T,$$

$$S_t^\Phi = \frac{1}{N}\sum_{j=1}^{C}\sum_{x\in X_j}(\Phi(x) - m)(\Phi(x) - m)^T = \Phi_t\Phi_t^T,$$

where Φ_w, $\Phi_t \in R^{d\times N}$ and $\Phi_b \in R^{d\times C}$.

The Fisher index $J_\Phi(W)$ in mapped feature space F is defined by

$$J_\Phi(W) = \det(W^T S_w^\Phi W)\,[\det(W^T S_b^\Phi W)]^{-1}, \tag{3}$$

where $W \in F^{df\times m}$. The objective of FDA is used to find a optimal projection in mapped feature space F that minimizes within-class distance and simultaneously maximizes between-class distance.

3.2 SKDA Strategy

Let $S_{wt}^{\Phi} = \Phi_w^T \Phi_t \in R^{N \times N}$. By performing singular value decomposition, there exist two orthonormal matrices $U, V \in R^{N \times N}$ and a diagonal matrix $\Lambda = \mathrm{diag}\{\sigma_1, \cdots, \sigma_r, 0, \cdots, 0\} \in R^{N \times N}$ with $\sigma_1 \geq \sigma_2 \geq \cdots \geq \sigma_r > 0$, such that $S_{wt}^{\Phi} = U\Lambda V^T$. Since $S_w^{\Phi} = \Phi_w \Phi_w^T$, we have $(\Phi_t V)^T S_w (\Phi_t V) = \mathrm{diag}\{\sigma_1^2, \cdots, \sigma_r^2, 0, \cdots, 0\} \in R^{N \times N}$. Rewrite the term $\Phi_t V$ as $\Phi_t V = [y_1, y_2, \cdots, y_r, y_{r+1}, \cdots, y_N]_{df \times N}$, where y_i is the ith column of $(\Phi_t V)_{df \times N}$. Denote $Y = [y_{r+1}, y_{r+2}, \cdots, y_N]$. It can be seen that Y is a $df \times (N-r)$ matrix and satisfies $Y^T S_w^{\Phi} Y = 0_{(N-r)\times(N-r)}$.

Having determined the null subspace of S_w^{Φ}, the projection is then determined in the subspace $\overline{N(S_b^{\Phi})}$, the complementary subspace of S_b^{Φ}. Thus, the second step is to discard the null space of S_b^{Φ} to ensure that the numerator of the Fisher index will not be zero.

To this end, we define $\hat{S}_b = Y^T S_b^{\Phi} Y$, and then $\hat{S}_b = (Y^T \Phi_b)(Y^T \Phi_b)^T$, $Y^T \Phi_b$ is a $(N-r) \times C$ matrix. By singular value decomposition, there exist two orthonormal matrices $(U_b)_{(N-r)\times(N-r)}$ and $(V_b)_{C \times C}$, such that $Y^T \Phi_b = U_b \Lambda_b V_b^T$, where $\Lambda_b = \begin{bmatrix} \Sigma_b \\ 0 \end{bmatrix} \in R^{(N-r)\times C}$ and $\Sigma_b = \mathrm{diag}\{\tau_1, \cdots, \tau_m, 0, \cdots, 0\} \in R^{C \times C}$ with $\tau_1 \geq \tau_2 \geq \cdots \geq \tau_m > 0$. Rewrite $U_b = [u_1, \cdots, u_m, u_{m+1}, \cdots, u_{N-r}] \in R^{(N-r)\times(N-r)}$ and denote $A = [u_1, \cdots, u_m]_{(N-r)\times m}$ and $D_m = \mathrm{diag}\{\tau_1, \cdots, \tau_m\}$, we have $A^T \hat{S}_b A = D_m^2$, namely, $(YA)^T S_b (YA) = D_m^2$. Let $W = (YA)_{df \times m}$, then

$$W^T S_w^{\Phi} W = 0_{m \times m}, \quad W^T S_b^{\Phi} W = D_m^2.$$

Thereby, W is the optimal SKDA projection matrix, by which the Fisher index $J(W)$ (3) reaches maximum.

3.3 SKDA Algorithm Design

Based on above analysis, the proposed SKDA algorithm is designed as follows.

Step 1: Compute the $N \times N$ matrix $S_{wt} = \Phi_w^T \Phi_t$ via the following formula:

$$\Phi_w^T \Phi_t = [N \cdot \mathbf{K} - \mathbf{K} \cdot \mathbf{1}_{NN} - N \cdot \Lambda_N \cdot \mathbf{K} + \Lambda_N \cdot \mathbf{K} \cdot \mathbf{1}_{NN}]/N^2,$$

where the kernel matrix $\mathbf{K} = \left(k(x_j^i, x_k^l)\right)_{j=1,\cdots,N_i;k=1,\cdots,N_l}^{i=1,\cdots,C;l=1,\cdots,C}$, $\mathbf{1}_{mn}$ denotes a $m \times n$ matrix with all terms equal to 1, $\Lambda_N = \mathrm{diag}[\Lambda_{N_1}, \cdots, \Lambda_{N_C}]$ is a N by N block diagonal matrix, and Λ_{N_i} is a $N_i \times N_i$ matrix with all terms equal to $1/N_i$, $i = 1, \cdots, C$.

Step 2: Perform singular value decomposition $S_{wt} \overset{svd}{=} U\Lambda V^T$, where $U, V \in R^{N \times N}$ are two orthonormal matrices, $\Lambda = \mathrm{diag}[\sigma_1, \cdots, \sigma_r, 0, \cdots, 0] \in R^{N \times N}$ with $\sigma_1 \geq \cdots \geq \sigma_r > 0$.

Step 3: Rewrite $V = [v_1, \cdots, v_r, v_{r+1}, \cdots, v_N]$ and denote $\tilde{V} = [v_r, v_{r+1}, \cdots, v_N]$ $\in R^{N \times (N-r)}$ and $Y = (\Phi_t \tilde{V})_{df \times (N-r)}$.

Step 4: Compute $Z = (Y^T \Phi_b)_{(N-r)\times C} = \tilde{V}^T \Phi_t^T \Phi_b$, it yields that

$$\Phi_t^T \Phi_b = [N \cdot \mathbf{K} \cdot D_C - \mathbf{K} \cdot \mathbf{1}_{NC} \cdot D - \mathbf{1}_{NN} \cdot \mathbf{K} \cdot D_C + \frac{1}{N} \cdot \mathbf{1}_{NN} \cdot \mathbf{K} \cdot \mathbf{1}_{NC} \cdot D]/N^2,$$

where $\mathbf{K}$ is the kernel matrix, $D_C = \text{diag}[D_{N_1}, \cdots, D_{N_C}]$ and D_{N_i} is a $N_i \times 1$ matrix with all terms equal to $1/\sqrt{N_i}$ $(i = 1, \cdots, C)$, $D = \text{diag}[\sqrt{N_1}, \cdots, \sqrt{N_C}]$.

Step 5: If the norm of one row in the matrix Z is too small (say less than $1e-6$), then discard this row in matrix Z. Accordingly, discard the corresponding column in matrix $\tilde{V}$. Denote the modified matrices Z,$\tilde{V}$and Y as Z',$\tilde{V}'$ and Y' respectively, then do singular value decomposition $Z' \stackrel{svd}{=} U_b \Lambda_b V_b^T$, where U_b and V_b all are orthonormal matrices, $\Lambda_b = (\sum_b, 0)^T \in R^{(N-r')\times C}$ and $\sum_b = \text{diag}[\tau_1, \cdots, \tau_s, 0, \cdots, 0]_{C\times C}$. Usually, $s = C - 1$.

Step 6: Rewrite $U_b = [u_1, \cdots, u_s, u_{s+1}, \cdots, u_{N-r'}]$, where u_i is the ith column of orthonormal matrix U_b. Denote $A = (u_1, \cdots, u_s)_{(N-r')\times s}$ and $W = (Y'A)_{df \times s}$, then W is the SKDA optimal projection matrix.

Step 7: For any testing sample $\Phi(x)$, we get its enhanced feature vector as

$$\begin{aligned}(W^T \Phi(x))_{s\times 1} &= (Y'A)^T \Phi(x) = A^T \tilde{V}'^T \Phi_t \cdot \Phi(x) \\ &= \frac{1}{\sqrt{N}} A^T \tilde{V}'^T [\Phi(x_j^i)^T \cdot \Phi(x) - m^T \cdot \Phi(x)]_{N\times 1}^{1\le i\le C; 1\le j\le N_i},\end{aligned}$$

where $\Phi(x_j^i)^T \cdot \Phi(x) = k(x_j^i, x)$ and $m^T \cdot \Phi(x) = \frac{1}{N} \sum_{i=1}^{C} \sum_{j=1}^{N_i} k(x_j^i, x)$.

4 Experimental Results

In this section, two popular and available human face databases, namely FERET and CMU PIE databases, are selected to evaluate the performance of our proposed SKDA algorithm. In the following experiments, Shannon wavelet kernel is with parameters $(p, \theta) = (1, 3.5)$.

4.1 Face Image Databases

For FERET database, we select 120 people, 6 images for each individual. Face image variations in FERET database include pose, illumination, facial expression and aging. Images from one individual are shown in Figure 1.

CMU PIE face database includes totally 68 people. There are 13 pose variations ranged from full right profile image to full left profile image and 43 different lighting conditions, 21 flashes with ambient light on or off. In our experiment, for each people, we select 56 images including 13 poses with neutral expression and 43 different lighting conditions in frontal view. Several images of one people are shown in Figure 2.

For all images in above two face databases, the following preprocessing steps are performed.

Fig. 1. Images of one person from FERET database

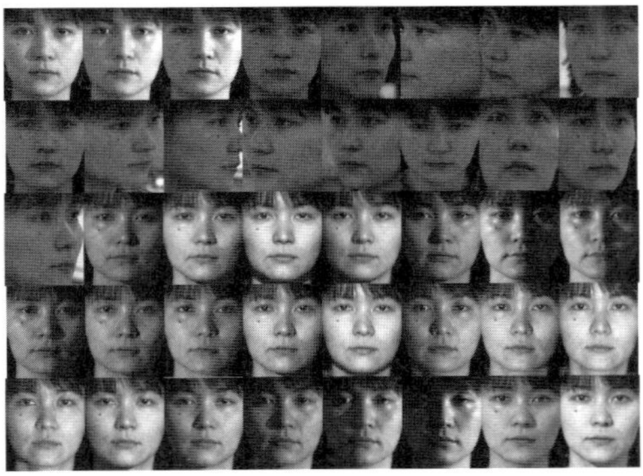

Fig. 2. Images of one person from CMU PIE face database

- All images are aligned with the centers of eyes and mouth. The orientation of face is adjusted (on-the-plane rotation) such that the line joining the centers of eyes is parallel with x-axis.
- All the original images with resolution 112x92 are reduced to wavelet feature faces with resolution 30x25 after two-level D4 wavelet decomposition [14].
- All training and testing samples in above two face databases are further normalized as follows:

$$x^* = \frac{x - mean(x)}{std(x)},$$

where x is a sample vector for training or testing, $mean(x)$ is the expectation of x and $std(x)$ is the standard deviation of x.

4.2 Results on FERET Database

This subsection reports the results of proposed SKDA method on FERET face database. We randomly select n (n=2 to 5) images from each people for training, while the rest $(6-n)$ images of each individual are selected for testing. The experiments are repeated 10 times and the average accuracies are recorded in table 1 and shown in the Figure 3. The identification rate of SKDA method increases from 75.90% with training number 2 to 93.92% with training number 5. While for RBF kernel based SFDA (RKDA), the corresponding identification accuracies increase from 71.35% with training number 2 to 92.08% with training number 5 respectively. Comparing with other kernel-based FDA methods, namely, GDA [2] with

Table 1. Comparison on different algorithms on FERET database

TN	2	3	4	5
GDA [2]	71.27%	82.31%	87.71%	92.58%
KDDA [4]	69.45%	82.69%	88.04%	93.25%
RKDA	71.35%	81.06%	87.00%	92.08%
SKDA	75.90%	84.75%	90.29%	93.92%

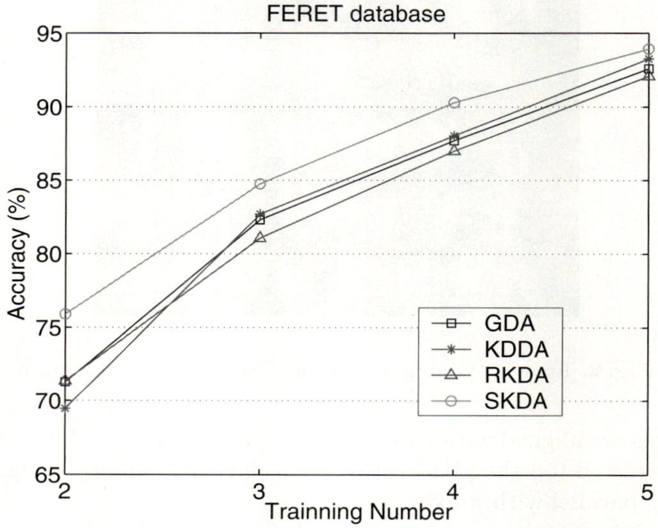

Fig. 3. Performance on FERET face database

RBF kernel and KDDA [4] with RBF kernel, the identification accuracies of GDA and KDDA methods increase from 69.45% and 71.27% with training number 2 to 93.25% and 92.58% with training number 5 respectively.

The results show our proposed SKDA methods gives the best performance for all cases on FERET database.

4.3 Results on CMU PIE Face Database

The subsection reports the results of the proposed SKDA method on CMU PIE database. We randomly select 14 images from each people for training (14×68=952 images for training), while the rest of images of each individual are selected for testing (42×68=2856 images for testing). The experiments are repeated 10 times and the average accuracies of rank 1 to rank 4 are recorded and shown in table 2 and plotted in Figure 4. The identification rate of proposed SKDA method increases from 78.31% with rank 1 to 83.31% with rank 4, while the identification accuracies of RKDA algorithm increase from 77.79% with rank 1 to 82.63% with rank 4. Comparing with other kernel-based methods, namely,

GDA [2] with RBF kernel and KDDA [4] with RBF kernel, the identification rates of GDA and KDDA methods increase from 77.86% and 77.64% with rank 1 to 83.22% and 83.07% with rank 4 respectively. The results demonstrate that our proposed SKDA method gives better performance on CMU PIE database.

Table 2. Comparison on different algorithms on CMU PIE database

Rank	1	2	3	4
GDA [2]	77.86%	80.49 %	82.10 %	83.22%
KDDA [4]	77.64%	80.39%	81.95%	83.07%
RKDA	77.79%	80.26%	81.67%	82.63%
SKDA	78.31%	80.57%	82.11%	83.31%

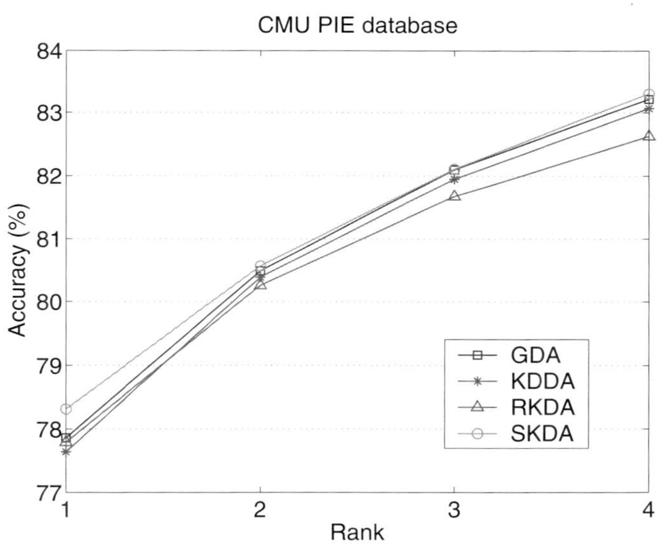

Fig. 4. Performance on CMU PIE face database

5 Conclusions

Based on Shannon wavelet kernel, this paper proposes and develops a novel subspace KDA algorithm for nonlinear feature extraction for face identification. Two human face databases, namely FERET database and CMU PIE database, are selected for evaluation. The results are encouraging on FERET and CMU PIE face databases. Experimental results show that the proposed SKDA algorithm gives better performance than existing state-of-the-art RBF kernel based FDA algorithms.

Acknowledgement

This project was supported by the Science Faculty Research grant of Hong Kong Baptist University RGC Earmarked Research Grant HKBU-211306 and NSF of China (60373082) and NSF of Guangdong province (06105776). The authors would like to thank for the US Army Research Laboratory for contribution of the FERET database and CMU for the CMU PIE database.

References

1. Belhumeur, P.N., Hespanha, J.P., Kriegman, D.J.: Eigenfaces vs. fisherfaces: Recognition using class specific linear projection. IEEE Transactions on Pattern Analysis and Machine Intelligence 19(7), 711–720 (1997)
2. Baudat, G., Anouar, F.: Generalized discriminant analysis using a kernel approach. Neural Computation 12(10), 2385–2404 (2000)
3. Martinez, A.M., Kak, A.C.: PCA versus LDA. IEEE Transactions on Pattern Analysis and Machine Intelligence 23(2), 228–233 (2001)
4. Lu, J., Plataniotis, K.N., Ventsanopoulos, A.N.: Face recognition using kernel discriminant analysis algorithms. IEEE Trans. on Neural Network 14(1), 117–126 (2003)
5. Chen, W.S., Yuen, P.C., Huang, J.: A New Regularized Linear Discriminant Analysis Methods to Solve Small Sample Size Problems. Int. J. Pattern Recognit. Artif. Intell. 19(7), 917–936 (2005)
6. Huang, J., Yuen, P.C., Chen, W.S., Lai, J.H.: Component-based subspacec linear discriminant analysis method for recognition of face images with one training sample. In: Optical Engineering, vol. 44(5) (2005)
7. Yang, J., Frangi, A.F., Yang, J.Y., Zhang, D., Jin, Z.: KPCA plus LDA: a complete kernel Fisher Discriminant framework for feature extraction and recognition. IEEE Trans. Pattern Anal. Mach. Intell. 27(2), 230–244 (2005)
8. Chen, W.S., Yuen, P.C., Huang, J., Dai, D.Q.: Kernel machine-based oneparameter regularized Fisher discriminant method for face recognition. IEEE Transactions on Systems, Man and Cybernetics, Part B 35(3), 659–669 (2005)
9. Chen, W.S., Yuen, P.C., Huang, J., Lai, J.H.: Face Classification based on Shannon Wavelet Kernel and Modified Fisher Criterion. In: Proceeding of the 7th IEEE international conference on automatic face and gesture recognition, April 10-12, 2006 pp. 467–474 (2006)
10. Huang, J., Yuen, P.C., Chen, W.S., Lai, J.H.: Choosing Parameters of Kernel Subspace-LDA for Recognition of Face Images under Pose and Illumination Variations. In: IEEE Transactions on Systems, Man and Cybernetics, Part B (2007) (Accepted to be published)
11. Xiong, H.L., Swamy, M.N.S., Ahmad, M.O.: Two-dimensional FLD for face recognition. Pattern Recognition 38(7), 1121–1124 (2005)
12. Mallat, S.: A theory for multiresolution signal decomposition: the wavelet representation. IEEE Pattern Anal. and Machine Intell 11(7), 674–693 (1989)
13. Meyer, Y.: Wavelets and operators. Cambridge Univ. Press, Cambridge (1993)
14. Daubechies, I.: Ten lectures on wavelets, CBMS-NSF conference series in applied mathematics, SIAM Ed (1992)

Author Index

Printing: Mercedes-Druck, Berlin
Binding: Stein+Lehmann, Berlin